MW01622708

Child and Adolescent Development in Your Classroom

Christi Crosby Bergin | David Allen Bergin | Barbara Ann Nilsen

CENGAGE Learning™

Australia • Brazil • Japan • Korea • Mexico • Singapore • Spain • United Kingdom • United States

Child and Adolescent Development in Your Classroom

Executive Editors:
Maureen Staudt
Michael Stranz

Senior Project Development Manager:
Linda deStefano

Marketing Specialist:
Courtney Sheldon

Senior Production/Manufacturing Manager:
Donna M. Brown

PreMedia Manager:
Joel Brennecke

Sr. Rights Acquisition Account Manager:
Todd Osborne

Cover Image:
Getty Images*

*Unless otherwise noted, all cover images used by Custom Solutions, a part of Cengage Learning, have been supplied courtesy of Getty Images with the exception of the Earthview cover image, which has been supplied by the National Aeronautics and Space Administration (NASA).

Printed in the United States of America

CHILD AND ADOLESCENT DEVELOPMENT IN YOUR CLASSROOM
Bergin | Bergin

© 2012 Cengage Learning. All rights reserved.

WEEK BY WEEK, PLANS FOR DOCUMENTING CHILDREN'S DEVELOPMENT
Nilsen

© 2010, 2007 Cengage Learning. All rights reserved.

ALL RIGHTS RESERVED. No part of this work covered by the copyright herein may be reproduced, transmitted, stored or used in any form or by any means graphic, electronic, or mechanical, including but not limited to photocopying, recording, scanning, digitizing, taping, Web distribution, information networks, or information storage and retrieval systems, except as permitted under Section 107 or 108 of the 1976 United States Copyright Act, without the prior written permission of the publisher.

For product information and technology assistance, contact us at
Cengage Learning Customer & Sales Support, 1-800-354-9706
For permission to use material from this text or product,
submit all requests online at **cengage.com/permissions**
Further permissions questions can be emailed to
permissionrequest@cengage.com

This book contains select works from existing Cengage Learning resources and was produced by Cengage Learning Custom Solutions for collegiate use. As such, those adopting and/or contributing to this work are responsible for editorial content accuracy, continuity and completeness.

Compilation © 2011 Cengage Learning

ISBN-13: 978-1-133-27269-4

ISBN-10: 1-133-27269-X

Cengage Learning
5191 Natorp Boulevard
Mason, Ohio 45040
USA
Cengage Learning is a leading provider of customized learning solutions with office locations around the globe, including Singapore, the United Kingdom, Australia, Mexico, Brazil, and Japan. Locate your local office at:
international.cengage.com/region.

Cengage Learning products are represented in Canada by Nelson Education, Ltd.
For your lifelong learning solutions, visit **www.cengage.com/custom.**
Visit our corporate website at **www.cengage.com.**

Contents

Child and Adolescent Development In Your Classroom

Week By Week
Plans for Documenting Children's Development
Fifth Edition

chapter 1

Ways of Thinking about Children

Hill Street Studios/Jupiter Images

WHAT FACTORS HAVE MADE YOU WHO YOU ARE TODAY? Does your answer emphasize genes or experiences in your family, school, or culture? Did these factors make you similar or different from others your age? In this chapter, we will discuss how research helps answer questions like these. After you read this chapter, you will understand:

- How development is studied using scientific methods.
- What science tells teachers about the influence of genes and the environment, as well as risk factors and protective factors.
- How these factors may be applied in the case of compensatory preschool.

The Science of Child Development

An 18-month-old boy is left at preschool. When his mother returns, he runs to her and wants to be picked up. She picks him up briefly and puts him down. He cries and clamors to be picked up. She turns from him. He cries strongly. She intentionally refuses to pick him up because she says she doesn't want him to be too dependent on her, "Him being a boy and all." She doesn't want him to get "funny" by having to feel secure. She says she thinks he might "go gay" if she spoils him. (adapted from Smyke, 1997)

You may be amused, outraged, or in agreement with this mother's view of what causes overdependency and homosexuality. Do you believe that feeling secure is bad for toddlers? Can you "spoil" a child by picking him up when he cries? Your belief about how a crying toddler should be handled is your personal theory about child development. Throughout this text you will learn about formal, research-based theories of child development that will help make your personal theories clearer to you and challenge the accuracy of some, so that you can provide the best possible classroom for your students.

Theories are developed from careful, systematic study as scientists seek to discover basic principles of child development. You might ask, "Are there general principles? Isn't each child unique?" To answer this question, think about weather. Scientists cannot predict the weather with perfect accuracy, but they use basic principles that apply everywhere (e.g., when a cold front meets a warm front, storms develop) to make predictions that are usually accurate. Even though London may not have the same weather as San Francisco at this moment, the same principles apply to both cities and weather can be predicted in both cities. Similarly, two children may live in different situations, but the same basic principles of child development may apply to both. What principles apply across children? The answer depends on your theory of child development.

Child Development Theories: A Brief Overview

theory an organized group of concepts or principles used to explain a particular aspect of human development.

A **theory** is simply an organized group of principles used to explain some aspect of children's development. Theories help you interpret what you observe in children, and suggest the best way to promote their development. In later chapters, you will be introduced to major theories of child development and some of their most influential proponents. To get started, we present here a brief overview of these theories.

Views of child development have changed over time. In the early 1900s, for example, many psychologists believed that children are genetically endowed with abilities that just need to unfold (Collins, 2002). Believers in this maturation perspective thought that how children change across time is genetically determined for all children, regardless of their different experiences. Arnold Gesell (1933; 1940), one of the most famous maturationists, systematically observed children to figure out what are normal motor, language, and social development "milestones," such as when babies typically begin rolling over. Gesell's milestones are still the basis of some preschool assessments today.

Unlike Gesell, some psychologists are environmentalists who emphasize the role of the environment and claim that children's development is driven by experience within the family and culture. Early environmentalists tended to see children as relatively *passive* as they received influence from their environment, like clay being molded in the hands of an artist. A new view arose that recognized that children *actively* contribute to their own development by the way they make sense of their experiences. Jean Piaget, a key figure we will discuss in Chapter 3, was a primary proponent of this view.

Table 1.1 gives a simplified overview of contemporary theories. These theories differ in their view of what drives children's development. Some theories give greater emphasis to maturation (i.e., nature) as a cause of behavior and others to the environment (i.e., nurture). These theories also differ in what aspect of child development they seek to explain and whether they see children as active or passive contributors to their own development. Spend a few minutes lightly digesting this table just to compare the theories, but do not try to memorize them. We will discuss each theory in greater detail in later chapters. Revisit the table for a review when you finish the text.

Table 1.1 Overview of major theories of child development

Theory and Major Theorist	Basic Aims	Emphasis: General Age Trends for All Children versus How Individuals Are Different	Forces That Drive Development	Emphasis: Nature or Nurture?	Domains of Development the Theory Explains Well
Bioecological Model Urie Bronfenbrenner (Chapter 1)	To highlight the multiple layers of influence on the child	Both	Heredity and environment act together to influence development. Does not specify particular processes.	Both	Any
Ethology Konrad Lorenz and Nikolaas Tinbergen (Chapter 6)	To understand the functions of behavior in different species	Focuses on species-wide age trends, but not individual differences.	Genetically based processes shaped by evolution drive development. Behavior becomes incorporated into the biology of a species because it promotes breeding success. Compares human and animal behavior. Emphasis is on innate behaviors.	Nature	Attachment Emotions Aggression Language
Behaviorism (also called Learning Theory) B. F. Skinner (Chapters 3 & 7)	To explain learned behavior	Focuses on individual differences, which are the result of different histories of reinforcement.	The child is passive; reinforcement and punishment drive development. Behaviors that are reinforced are more likely to re-occur. Emphasis is on observable behavior. Concepts of mind, cognition, and inner experiences are ignored. Useful for managing children's behavior problems.	Nurture	Any learned behavior. Does not explain innate behaviors, like smiling, or why some things are reinforcing.
Social Cognitive (or Social Learning) **Theory** Albert Bandura (Chapter 13)	To explain acquisition of behavior and cognitions such as attitudes	Greater emphasis on individual differences, especially on behavior and attitude change, not age trends.	An expansion of behaviorism/learning theory. Children learn from models or others who are reinforced. This requires children to remember and interpret things they have observed—which means cognition is involved. The child actively interprets reinforcement.	Nurture	Any learned behavior

(continued)

Table 1.1 *(continued)*

Cognitive Developmental Theory Jean Piaget (Chapter 3)	To explain the development of logical thought and moral judgment	Age trends are strongly emphasized and age-based "stages" of cognitive development are outlined.	Innate cognitive maturation (with some social interaction) drives development. Children actively "construct" their own knowledge through exploration. Abilities are similar, even with different cultural experience. Maturation limits logical reasoning ability, so children's cognitive development is stage-like.	Nature Maturation	Knowledge Logical reasoning
Sociocultural Theory Lev Vygotsky (Chapter 3)	To explain acquisition of knowledge and language ability	Age trends are not emphasized. Individual differences are a result of unique social experiences.	Development occurs through interaction with others. Cognitive growth is collaborative (not within the child). The child's thought is the result of internalizing dialogue with others. Development cannot be separated from social and cultural interaction.	Nurture	Knowledge Culturally valued skills Language
Information Processing Various theorists (Chapter 4) **Social Information Processing** Kenneth Dodge (Chapter 11)	The step-by-step processing of information.	Age trends are the result of faster and more efficient processing. Individual differences are the result of innate capacity and experience (i.e., prior knowledge).	Like a computer, the child receives sensory input, manipulates information, and then responds with output. This view focuses predominantly on what is happening inside the child's mind, but includes input from the environment. What is studied is narrow (i.e., logical flow of information). Useful for targeting interventions for specific processing problems.	Both	Problem solving Memory Decision-making Attention Aggression
Psychodynamic Sigmund Freud (Chapter 9)	Personality and neurosis.	Age trends are emphasized with age-based "stages" of psychosexual development. Individual differences in personality are the result of early parent–child interaction.	How parents gratify (vs. frustrate) biologically based drives influences personality. Children can become fixated at a particular stage. A newer version, the neo-psychoanalytic view, asserts that the goal of behavior is to regulate and maintain internal and interactional harmony with others. Early parent–child interaction is internalized and influences later experience. Emphasizes the unseen workings of the mind.	Both	Personality Attachment Emotions Morality Humor The unconscious

Theories are important to teachers because they guide decisions about classroom practices and because they guide research. Research results, in turn, are used to revise and improve theories. In the next section, we explain the research methods on which formal child development theories are based.

Research Methods

Why does a teacher need to know research methods? Federal rules and mandates require educators to use "scientifically based research" to guide decisions about how to teach. To help, the federal Department of Education maintains a *What Works*

Clearinghouse on its website. Imagine that you are Elena's preschool teacher (in case 1) and want to try a new reading program to help her learn to read, or you might be a high school teacher looking for a curriculum to help struggling teen readers. You could search the clearinghouse for either program. It would tell you if there was research on the program, the caliber of the research, and the effectiveness of the program. In this section, we will introduce you to basics of research methods so that you can learn to assess the quality of research, a professional skill that is now important for teachers. To begin, let's look at the three basic research designs—experimental, nonexperimental, and qualitative designs.

Experimental Designs

While people commonly use the term *experiment* to refer to any kind of research, for psychologists the term has a very specific meaning. In a simple experiment, you change something in the students' environment and measure the results. For example, a teacher could try a different phonics approach to see if students learn to read more easily. Such informal experiments can be useful, but cannot pinpoint the cause of an outcome like improved reading skills. To determine the cause of outcomes, scientists use controlled **experiments**.

In a controlled experiment, children are placed in an intervention group or a **control group**. The intervention group gets a special treatment, but the control group does not. Outcomes for the two groups are compared. For example, to determine whether a phonics program results in better reading skills, you could place half of your 1st-graders in a phonics program and the other half in a different program. If children in the phonics program develop better reading skills compared to the control group, you have evidence (not proof) that the phonics program might work.

experiment a controlled study comparing outcomes between people randomly assigned to a treatment group and a control group.

control group in an experiment, the group that does not receive the special treatment in order to provide a comparison group.

However, what if the children in the phonics program were "smarter" or already had better skills than the control group? For an experiment to determine cause-and-effect, the control group should be similar to the intervention group in all attributes. To increase the probability that groups are similar, researchers use **random assignment**. This means each child has an equal chance of being put in the intervention group or the control group. Even with random assignment, research is about probability, not certainty. Based on an experiment, you might conclude that a phonics program is *more likely* to produce literate children, but not that the phonics program makes *all* children literate.

random assignment each research participant has an equal chance of being assigned to the treatment or control group.

Nonexperimental Correlational Designs

Experiments cannot always be used because they may be unethical or impractical. For example, if you want to understand the effect of prenatal alcohol exposure on children, it would not be ethical to randomly assign some pregnant mothers to drink five beers a day and other mothers to drink none. In a case like this, correlational research designs are used in which researchers measure variables as they naturally occur, without intervention. (A *variable* is an attribute of the child or environment that can be measured, like number of ounces of alcohol per day.) Researchers might, for example, measure how much mothers drank during their pregnancies and compare that to their children's reading ability to determine whether the two variables are related.

correlation coefficient a statistic that measures the relationship between two variables.

A correlation is a measure of the relationship between two variables. The **correlation coefficient**, or *r*, indicates the statistical strength of the relationship. A perfect positive correlation, or $r = +1.00$, means that a plot of the variables follows a straight line (see Figure 1.1). That is, if you know a value for one variable, you can predict with perfect accuracy the corresponding value for the other variable. A *positive* correlation means that higher values on one variable go with higher values on the other. For example, *higher* levels of fathers' education predict *higher* levels of children's reading ability. If there is a perfect negative correlation, then $r = -1.00$. A *negative* correlation means that higher values on one variable go with lower values on the other. For example, *higher* levels of prenatal alcohol exposure predict *lower* levels of children's reading ability. Strong correlations can be either positive (e.g., +0.60) or negative (e.g., −0.60). If there is no association between the variables, then $r = 0$. Correlation coefficients *are not percentages*; a correlation of 0.40 does *not* mean 40% of anything.

Think About This In a study of children adopted from Romanian orphanages, the longer the time spent in the orphanage before being adopted, the lower the cognitive ability (O'Connor et al., 2000). Would this be a positive or negative *r*? How would you graph this?

Correlations between any two variables in child development research are rarely close to 1.00. In fact, very few are even as large as 0.50, and a correlation of 0.35 is considered large enough to draw attention (Hemphill, 2003). This is because important child outcomes are influenced by many variables—not just the one being measured in a study. For example, good reading ability is not the result of a single variable, like intelligence, or involved parents, or effective schools. Rather, each of these variables (and many others) combines to influence reading ability.

Figure 1.1 Correlation Coefficients.
If you covered up the "*r*" statistic, could you guess it approximately? Explain correlation to a friend, and then test him/her.

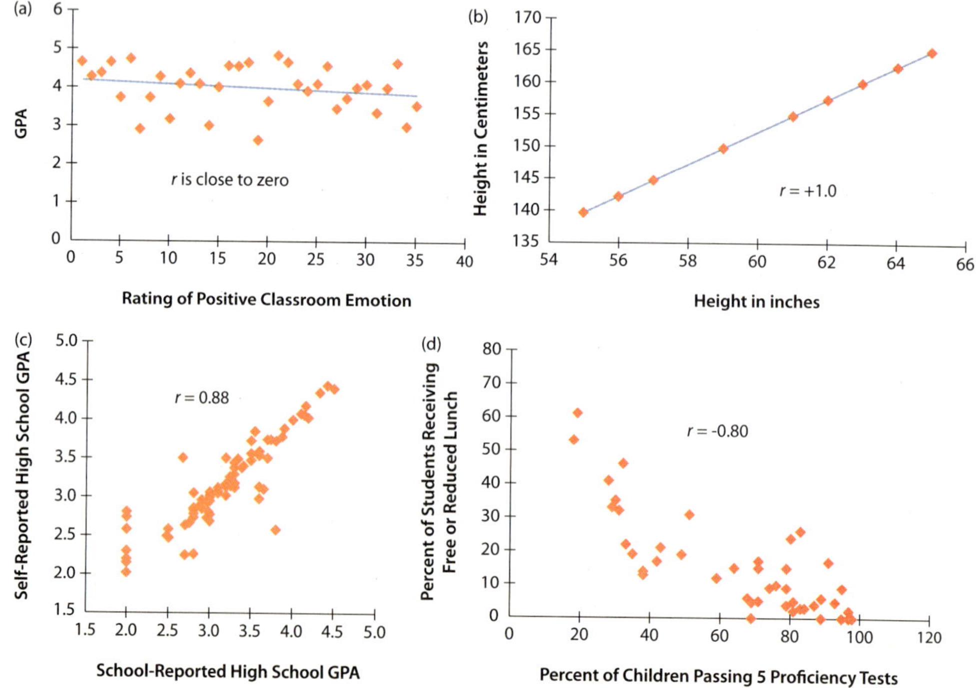

Qualitative Designs

In experiments and correlational studies, scientists apply numbers to variables, such as fathers' education and children's reading ability, and then use statistics to analyze their relationship. This is a quantitative approach. In contrast, qualitative research involves interviews, observations of natural behavior, and other forms of data that are usually reported in words rather than numbers. The researcher may spend anywhere from hours to years observing and interacting with youth in order to accurately tell their story. Qualitative researchers tend to be interested in describing how people see the world and in examining issues of social justice. Qualitative research has been used to study complex topics like experience of early child care, fear of acting White, and what makes classrooms engaging for students. For example, in one study researchers visited middle- and low-income families in their homes, followed them to lessons and sports events, interviewed teachers, and even stayed overnight (Lareau, 2003). One pattern they documented was that middle-class parents intervened at school in support of their children more frequently than low-income parents.

qualitative research nonquantitative research characterized by the researcher being the instrument of data collection (rather than a test or questionnaire). May involve observations and interviews as data.

Studies of Change over Time

Imagine you want to know how children's aggression changes with age. You could follow one group of children for twelve years, assessing the *same* children at ages 4, 10, and 16. This is a longitudinal design. What if you can't wait for twelve years? You could assess 4-, 10-, and 16-year-olds at one time, which would not really study change over time, but would suggest whether children of different ages differ in their aggression. This is a cross-sectional design. A cross-sectional design gathers data from different age groups at one point in time, and a longitudinal design gathers data from one group over several points in time.

longitudinal research design data are collected from the same or different individuals two or more times, separated by some period of time (e.g., months or years).

cross-sectional research design data are collected at one point in time from two or more age groups to investigate age trends.

Each research design has strengths and limitations. For example, longitudinal studies allow you to identify factors that might improve children's lives over time. However, they take a long time before results are available, and it is difficult to keep children involved over multiple years. Experiments can establish what causes a particular outcome; however, sometimes they are not ethical or practical, so correlational designs are used instead. Qualitative studies provide rich descriptions and deep insight into a small group of young people's lives, but may not generalize to most other youth. Because each design has limitations, a mature field of science uses multiple designs.

In addition to the design of research, there are four other key issues to understand when you read research findings: (1) causality, (2) measurement, (3) generalizability, and (4) effect size. We'll discuss these next.

Causality

Most studies of child development are correlational. Therefore, it is important to understand their critical weakness—they cannot demonstrate that one variable causes another variable. If variables A and B are correlated, A could cause B, or B could cause A, or both could cause each other, or C could cause both A and B. For

bi-directional variable A influences variable B, while B also influences A.

example: (1) hostile mothers could cause hostile children; (2) hostile children could cause hostile mothers; (3) the variables could be **bi-directional**, meaning that hostile children and hostile mothers influence each other; or (4) a third variable, like hostile fathers or a genetic predisposition to be hostile, could cause both children's and mothers' hostility.

Field Observation

Find claims about research findings on any human topic (e.g., health, academic achievement, romance, income) in a newspaper or magazine. What research design was used? If the design was correlational, does the article inappropriately assume causation?

It is common for people to mistakenly assume causality from correlational studies. For example, years ago, research found that poor readers make more erratic eye movements as they read than good readers. Interventions using special equipment and specially trained teachers attempted to teach poor readers improved eye movements (Stanovich, 1992). Later it was found that erratic eye movements do not cause poor reading, but rather poor reading causes erratic eye movements because poor readers have trouble recognizing words and understanding their meaning. Millions of dollars were wasted on special interventions. The critical lesson is that you cannot assume causation from correlational studies, although such studies can tell you the size of the relationship between two variables. The What Works Clearinghouse gives precedence to controlled experiments over correlational studies. When scientists use terms such as *predict*, *linked*, *correlated*, and *associated*, they are usually referring to correlational design. Watch for these terms throughout this text.

Measurement

Researchers measure development in many ways: direct observations of behavior, ratings by a teacher or parent, self-report, and physiological markers such as level of hormones or brain images. Each form of measurement has weaknesses and strengths. For example, self-report (when respondents tell you what they think or fill out a survey) allows you to get inside their minds, but youth can be biased, have trouble communicating, or misunderstand questions. Direct observations by researchers may be more objective, but they are costly, may not capture rare but important behaviors such as fights in school, and can change behavior because of the observer's presence. If children and youth are observed in a laboratory setting, results may not apply to real-world settings. Parent or teacher questionnaires are inexpensive and easy to administer, but they can be biased and may be different from children's and teens' self-reports. Again, a mature field of science uses multiple methods to compensate for the weaknesses of any single method.

validity the extent to which a measurement assesses what it is supposed to measure for a specific purpose.

Reliability and validity are two ways of describing how "good" a measure is. **Validity** refers to the accuracy of a test or measurement: does it really measure what it claims to measure? The validity of a measure depends on the purpose for which it is used. For example, a proficiency test might be valid for deciding whether students are mastering grade-level studies, but not for deciding which students would benefit from special education.

reliability consistency of a test or measurement.

Reliability refers to the consistency of a test or measurement. A reliable measure yields nearly the same results across time, so that you get about the same results today as next week. A reliable measure also yields the same results if administered by two different teachers under the same conditions. Short tests tend to be less reliable, so when you design a test, it is better to use twenty items than ten items. A test cannot be valid if it is not reliable.

Validity and reliability are important because many decisions are made on the basis of measures. Such decisions include who receives special education services, who gets into which colleges, and what instructional strategy you use with a particular child. You should always ask whether a test is valid and reliable. For example, are IQ tests valid for selecting gifted students? Are readiness tests valid for deciding who is ready for kindergarten? Are your classroom tests valid and reliable enough to use for assigning grades?

Generalizability

It is not possible to include all children in a study. Instead, a sample or subgroup is studied with the intent of generalizing the results to a larger group. When samples of children are carefully selected to represent larger groups, research results should apply to other children in the larger group. In the past, most research focused on White, middle-class children. It was not clear if these results could be generalized to other children. In the past few decades, researchers have been careful to sample low-income children, children of color, and children outside North America so that results are more generalizable (Hagen, 2007).

One factor that limits generalizability is the **cohort effect**. A cohort is a group of children born about the same time who experience unique political, economic, and social trends. You are a member of a cohort. A cohort effect, also called a *generation effect*, is an outcome caused by the particular era the cohort grows up in. There are cohort effects for intelligence (Chapter 5), personality (Chapter 6), and aggression (Chapter 10). That is, today's children on the average have higher intelligence, but they are more anxious, neurotic, and aggressive than past generations. Research conducted on one cohort may not always generalize to a different cohort.

cohort effect an effect upon development whose cause is specific to the particular time period in which the cohort grew up.

Effect Size

The concept of effect size has become increasingly important for teachers because of recent emphasis on raising test scores and using evidence-based curricula. **Effect size** is a measure of the strength of the relationship between two variables, or how much more effective one intervention is than another (Hedges, 2008). The What Works Clearinghouse reports the effect size of interventions to help you make decisions about your classroom practices. For example, you could compare the effect size of different curricula designed to help Elena, or struggling teens, learn to read.

effect size a measure of the strength of the relationship between two variables, or the size of the difference between the treatment and control group

Effect size is reported in decimal numbers. Effect sizes of 0.10 to 0.20 are commonly considered small, 0.25 to 0.40 medium, 0.50 to 0.80 or greater as large, and anything over 1.0 is quite large, but this is only a fuzzy standard. What effect size is meaningful? Hattie (2009) has pointed out that you should look for an effect size of at least 0.40 if you are comparing programs or interventions. An effect size of 0.40 or bigger is likely to result in noticeable learning in real classrooms. However, a smaller effect size of 0.30 is important because it means that the 50th-ranked student in a group of 100 would move to 39th place if only he or she experienced the intervention (Cooper, 2008). Table 1.2 shows effect sizes of interventions in different fields.

Whether an effect size is meaningful depends on the situation. Even a small effect can be important if the stakes are high. For example, the effect size of taking aspirin to prevent heart attacks is only 0.07, or a 3 to 4% difference between those who get

Table 1.2 Effect sizes of interventions in different fields

Intervention	Effect size
Medical treatments (life-threatening illness)	0.08–0.47
Medical treatments (non-life-threatening illness)	0.24–0.80
Counseling interventions (social skills training, drug use prevention, career education, in-school prevention programs)	0.27–1.20
Study skills and strategies	0.59–0.69
Teacher training/teacher education	0.47–1.31
Spaced practice rather than massed practice (cramming)	0.71
Direct instruction	0.59
Inquiry-based teaching	0.31
Cooperative learning	0.41
Retention (holding students back a grade)	−0.16 (outcomes are worse)

Adapted from Hattie (2009) and Lipsey & Wilson (1993).

heart attacks after using aspirin compared to those that do not, yet many physicians recommend aspirin therapy to save lives (Lipsey & Wilson, 1993). Similarly, although maternal sensitivity has a modest effect on attachment, you might consider it important if *your* child's emotional well-being is at stake. As a teacher, you may want to change classroom practices that have a small effect if the outcomes are important, the changes are cheap or easy to make, and you do not have more effective alternatives (Duncan & Magnuson, 2007). Thus, interpreting the importance of effect sizes requires judgment.

One major topic of research in child development is the relative contribution of, or effect size for, genes and the environment. This is the nature-versus-nurture question. *Nature* refers to the influence of a child's genes on development. *Nurture* refers to the influence of a child's physical and social environment on development. It is important that you understand the influences of nature and nurture on a child's development, because this understanding will help you create an optimal environment for your students. In the next section, we take an in-depth look at the nature-and-nurture balance.

Nature and Nurture

Crystal and Garth are twins in the same kindergarten class. Garth likes to point out his superiority in sports and school. He says, "I scored two goals in our last game, and Crystal didn't score any." He says, "My teacher always tells me I am a good reader, but she has to help Crystal all the time." Garth does not get praised for doing well in school, but his sister does; in fact, she got a bracelet for improving her reading. When their mother picks them up from school, she always asks to see Garth's schoolwork, but just tells Crystal that she looks cute. Garth does better in all academic subjects. He can read and write his name. Crystal does not read, and writes her name poorly. Their puzzled teacher asks about these differences. Mother explains that Crystal has always liked to dress up and was never interested in books. She says that Crystal was "just born that way," implying the twins' differences are genetic. She does not seem to notice that she treats her children differently.

Could Crystal and Garth's differences be due to genetics (nature) or to the way their mother treats them (nurture), or both? The bioecological model (see Box 1.1) helps frame an answer to this question. In this model, *nature* refers to the innermost biological circle of influence, which includes genes. *Nurture* refers to all circles beyond the child, which can include parent–child relationships, peer interaction, school experiences, and culture. In this section we will discuss how both genes and culture—the two extremes in the bioecological model—influence child development.

Theories and Theorists **Box 1.1**

The Bioecological Model

The bioecological model shows how biology and environment interact to influence children's development. It was developed by Urie Bronfenbrenner (1917–2005), a Russian-born psychologist who pointed out that children are influenced by social, economic, and political forces as well as their family. The model is portrayed with concentric circles (see Figure 1.2) that represent nested systems. Each system is an ecological level, with the biological child at the core, hence the name *bioecological.* The child is at the core because the effects of any other factor in the model are modified by the child's traits (Bronfenbrenner & Morris, 2006). The child's traits can be biological (e.g., low birth weight or physical attractiveness) or psychological (e.g., temperament or intelligence).

The next level is the *microsystem.* This includes the interactions, activities, and relationships of the child in settings that physically contain the child, such as the family, school, neighborhood, and peer group. The *mesosystem* is a system of two or more microsystems, such as home and school. The *exosystem* refers to the linkages between two settings, one of which does not physically contain the child but influences the child indirectly, such as the parent's workplace.

The *macrosystem* refers to culture, which contains specific patterns of micro-, meso-, and exosystems. Culture determines what is acceptable and possible in the other levels. Public policy may be thought of as macrosystem. For example, welfare policy does not affect children directly, but affects them by changing the child care environment (Yoshikawa & Hsueh, 2001). The *chronosystem* adds the dimension of time. It refers to change and consistency across the life course of a particular child, as well as cohort effects over historical time.

These ecological levels form a hierarchy of influence on children's development from proximal (near) to distal (far) factors. Proximal processes exist in the immediate environment, such as parent–child interaction; *they are the most powerful processes* (Bronfenbrenner & Morris, 1998). A key proposition of the model is that both the child and the environment influence these proximal processes.

In later chapters you will see how each of these levels influences child outcomes. For the time being, consider the case of drug use. *The child:* Children's traits like decision-making skills, cultural pride, and attitude toward drug use are associated with drug use. *The microsystem:* Children's drug use is higher in families where parents use and the family environment is dysfunctional. Children's drug use is lower in schools that are caring and where they feel bonded. *The mesosystem:* Children are more vulnerable to attending an uncaring school if they also come from a dysfunctional family (Ennett et al., 2008). *The exosystem:* Children's drug use is higher in communities that approve of use among adults (Coate & Grossman, 1985). One implication of this model is that interventions will be most effective if they target multiple levels of the child's environment. Thus, an effective intervention for drug use would alter children's attitudes about drugs, change parents' drug use, create more caring schools, and change community acceptance of use.

Figure 1.2 Bioecological Model. According to the bioecological model, the child is embedded within a series of increasingly distal sets of influences. *Based on Bronfenbrenner & Morris, 2006.*

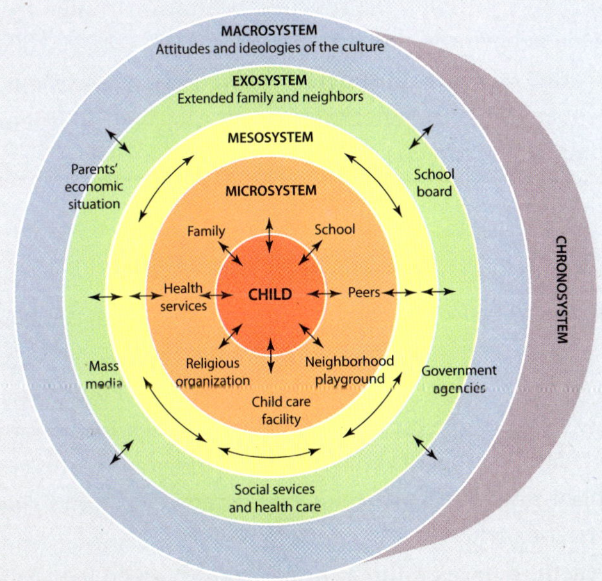

Nature: The Role of Genes in Individual Diversity

behavioral genetics the study of how genes and the environment contribute to individual differences in behavior.

Behavioral genetics is the study of how genes and the environment contribute to differences among children. According to behavioral genetics, differences in any trait are due to three sources (Pike, 2002): (1) genes, (2) shared environment, and (3) nonshared environment.

Genes and Heritability

Heritability is a statistical estimate of the amount of variation of a trait in a population that is due to genes. Thus, if intelligence has a heritability of 0.50 among White, middle-class adolescents, then 50% of the variation in intelligence within that population is due to genes and the remaining variation is due to shared or nonshared environment.

How do scientists make such estimates? They compare children with different genetic relatedness, such as twin, adopted, and half siblings. A common approach is to compare identical twins with fraternal twins. Identical twins share 100% of their genes, and fraternal twins share about 50% of their genes, as do nontwin full siblings. Half siblings share about 25% of their genes. Adopted and stepsiblings are genetically unrelated.

Rosemarie Gearhart/iStockphoto

Heritable traits should be more similar for identical twins than for non-twin siblings.

If genes affect a trait, then siblings who share more genes should be more similar in that trait. This means that identical twins should be more similar than fraternal twins, and biological siblings should be more similar than adopted siblings (see Figure 1.3). Some recent studies of heritability have found that shyness is about 40 to 50% heritable, intelligence is about 40 to 80% heritable, mental illnesses (e.g., schizophrenia, depression, alcoholism) range from 20 to 80% heritable, and antisocial behavior is about 40% heritable (Bouchard, 2004). However, other studies conclude that even the most heritable traits are rarely as much as 50% heritable (Pike, 2002). Thus, estimates of heritability can vary widely depending on the trait and the group being studied.

Shared (SE) and Nonshared Environment (NSE)

shared environment (SE) factors that make individuals residing in the same family similar to each other.

nonshared environment (NSE) factors that make individuals in the same family different from each other.

Environmental influences can be shared or nonshared among family members. Shared environment (SE) refers to any factors that make siblings residing in the same family similar. SE effects are small for mental illness and personality traits. However, SE effects are large for delinquency, alcohol use, and college attendance (Pike, 2002).

Nonshared environment (NSE) refers to factors that make siblings in the same family different from each other. A child's peers are a powerful part of NSE. Imagine that Garth, as he enters high school, has friends who enjoy music and coax him to join a jazz band. Crystal may have friends who coax her to join the school soccer team. These peer influences will lead them to develop different talents and social networks, making them even more different. NSE effects are often larger than SE effects (Pike,

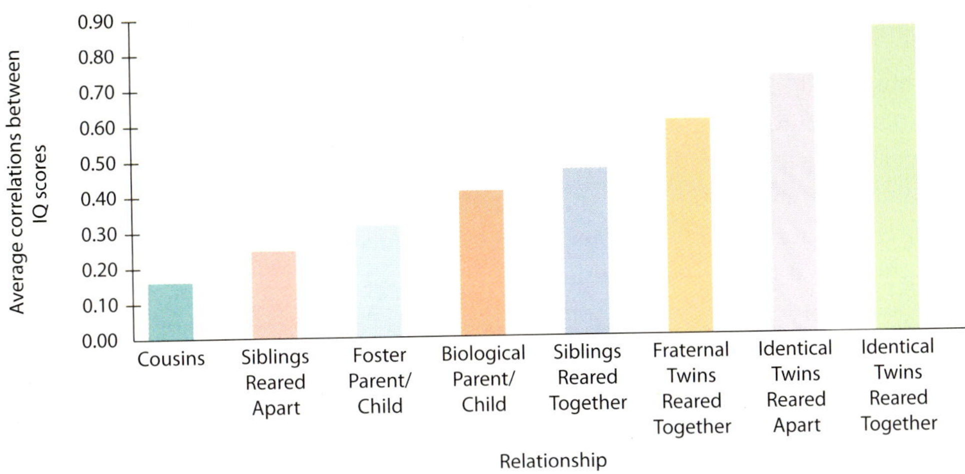

Figure 1.3 Relationship between IQ Scores and Relatedness.
The graph depicts data from a series of studies. The data show that correlations for IQ are stronger between people who share genetics and environment. Thus, identical twins—who share all their genetic material—have more-similar IQs if they were reared together than if they were reared apart; even if they were reared apart, their IQs are more similar than fraternal twins who were reared together. *Based on data in Bouchard, Lykken, McGue, Segal, & Tellegen, 1990.*

2002; Turkheimer, 2000). Does this seem counterintuitive to you? It should if you assume that siblings share the same family environment. But do they?

Is the Family a Shared or Nonshared Environment?

Family is mostly a nonshared environment. There are at least two reasons for this. First, families do not influence all children in the same way. For example, in a family with an alcoholic mother, children could react differently—one could become the family caretaker and another could become a drug user. This would be a *nonshared* environment factor, because the outcome is sibling differences. Notice that NSE is *defined by outcome,* not by whether or not you think the environments are the same.

Second, families change. The firstborn may live in poverty and go to low-cost child care as her parents struggle to get a family business going, and she may experience her mother's postpartum depression when a second child is born. The third child may be born ten years later, after the family business is thriving, the father has completed a college degree, the mother has become much warmer in her parenting style, and the family has moved to a high-income neighborhood with good schools. If there is a divorce, one child may spend fourteen years in a two-parent household, whereas another may spend only four years. These children are *not* growing up in identical families, even though they are siblings.

> ***Think About This*** Who are more accurate observers, researchers or parents? Keep in mind that observers typically watch children for a limited time in a specific environment. Parents watch children for years across many environments. Does this make them better observers? How might they compare to teachers?

Problems with Estimating Heritability

There are several problems with estimating heritability, SE, and NSE effects. One problem is that they depend on variation of a trait in a population. If there is no variation in a trait—like having two eyes—then the **heritability estimate** would be zero because identical twins are no more similar than strangers. Yet, this trait is under

heritability estimate the amount of variation in a trait in a population (not individuals) that is attributable to genetic influences. Notated as h^2.

strong genetic control (Sternberg, Grigorenko, & Kidd, 2005). Heritability can only tell you how much *variation of an attribute within a population* is linked to genes—not how much that trait is actually under genetic control.

Another problem is that estimates of heritability, SE, and NSE depend on who does the measuring and how it is done.[1] Data gathered through researchers' observations tend to overestimate SE. Parent ratings, on the other hand, *tend to underestimate SE* and overestimate heritability, perhaps because parents exaggerate differences between their children. It takes very large samples to make accurate heritability estimates, but large-sample studies usually rely on parent surveys because they are relatively cheap (Goldsmith, Lemery, Buss, & Campos, 1999).

Finally, another problem in behavioral genetics is the assumption that genes and environment affect children separately. This is false, because genes and environment are correlated (Price & Jaffee, 2008; Reiss, 2005). For example, intelligent parents may have intelligent children because they pass on intelligent genes *and* because they provide an intellectually stimulating home. When parents provide an environment that matches the genes they provide to their children, this is a *passive* **gene–environment correlation**. Further, intelligent children may seek out books or watch educational TV, which increases their intelligence. When children seek out (whether consciously or not) environments that match their genetic dispositions, this is an *active* gene–environment correlation. Finally, parents may react to intelligent children by teaching them advanced concepts. When children evoke responses from the environment that match their genetic dispositions, this is an evocative gene-environment correlation. Because genes and the environment are correlated in these ways, it is difficult to tell which accounts for differences in final intelligence—genes or the environment.

gene–environment correlation both genes and social contexts interact to contribute to children's development.

At best, heritability, SE, and NSE estimates should be considered ballpark rather than precise figures to describe how much genes and environment contribute to child outcomes. Keep this in mind as you read about heritability in later chapters. Let's turn next to a discussion of how genes might influence behavior.

How Can Genes Influence Behavior?

genotype the set of genes that is directly inherited and transmitted to descendents.

phenotype observable characteristics of a person.

Your **genotype** is the set of genes in every cell that is directly inherited by you and transmitted to your descendants. Your **phenotype** is your observable characteristics. You might consider the genotype as the hidden starting point and the phenotype as the observable end point of development (Geary & Bjorklund, 2000). Is everything in your genes expressed in who you have become? Whether a genotype becomes a phenotype depends on the environment. For example, individuals who have genes for depression may only become depressed if they also have rejecting mothers or major life stress (Haeffel et al., 2008; Monroe & Reid, 2008). Both genotype and environment set limits on phenotype. The limits set by genes are probably very broad. You'll learn more about gene–environment interaction in Chapter 6.

Genes do not determine or cause behavior (except in the case of rare diseases), but they do influence probability. For example, genes do not dictate reading ability in Crystal or Garth. Instead, genes dictate things like the building of proteins. A gene is a region of DNA on a chromosome. The gene is activated when the environment

---

[1]There are many studies that support this conclusion, just a few of which are listed here (Deater-Deckard, 2000; Pike, 2002; Roisman & Fraley, 2006; Towers et al., 2000).

(at the cellular level) asks for information. This is typically done by chemicals (e.g., hormones). Chemical levels, in turn, are affected by your biological and psychological environment. No *behavior* is directly inherited; what is inherited is the potential structure of specific proteins that can regulate the nervous system, hormones, and other body processes. For example, the *DRD4* gene that is linked to behavior problems might dampen the effect of chemicals in the brain, which might make children less responsive to the threat of discipline, but it does not directly cause misbehavior (Bakermans-Kranenburg, Van IJzendoorn, Pijlman, Mesman, & Juffer, 2008).

The human genome contains 20,000 to 25,000 protein-coding genes (International Human Genome Sequencing Consortium, 2004). You share all but about 2% of your DNA material with apes. The vast majority of human DNA is shared by everyone; you share about 99.9% of your genes with every other human on the planet. That leaves only 0.1% of genes to create human diversity (Quartz & Sejnowski, 2002). The genes that are free to vary are called **segregating genes**. When we said full siblings share an average 50% of their genes, we meant 50% of their segregating genes; full siblings actually differ only 0.05% genetically.

segregating genes genes that are free to vary and that dictate individual differences.

What does this mean? There is little room for genetically based individual differences (Bjorklund & Pellegrini, 2000). Natural selection preserves any successful phenotypes that result from these genetic differences. Any attribute that contributes to survival would quickly spread through the species. Thus, attributes important for survival will have less genetic variation than attributes that are not important for survival.

With so small a genome, how is it possible that humans are radically more adaptable and intelligent than apes and so different from one another? Part of the answer is that your DNA dictates the construction of a brain that is *designed to adapt to your environment*. Natural selection favors organisms that can adapt. If personality, behavior, and language were minutely prescribed by DNA, you would be less adaptable and would need substantially more DNA. Instead, your nervous system adapts and *changes biologically* as a result of experience (see Chapter 2). Gross brain structure is genetically programmed, but experience can change the fine structure and chemistry of your brain permanently. Because humans are designed for adaptability, you should expect differences between siblings like Crystal and Garth to result from NSE or unique environmental experiences (e.g., illness, quality of parenting, schooling). This is what behavioral geneticists generally find.

Nurture: The Role of Culture in Group Diversity

You are a product not only of your genes, but also of the culture in which you live. According to the bioecological model, both genes and culture work together to create variation among people. Genes operate at the level of the cell, at the innermost circle of the model. Culture, on the other hand, operates at the level of large groups, at the outermost circle of the model.

> ***Think About This*** What cultures and subcultures have influenced your own experiences, beliefs, and values? Do your classmates share your culture? Can you identify ways your subcultures are different and the same?

What Is Culture?

Culture is the pattern of values, beliefs, institutions, and behaviors shared by a group of people and communicated from one generation to the next (Cohen, 2009). Culture dictates physical contexts, social contexts, customs for childrearing, and beliefs about the nature of children (Kennedy, 2000). Culture influences how much time children spend with their mothers versus fathers versus peers. Culture influences beliefs about whether children's fate is written when they are born or whether it is the parents' role to shape children (Harkness, 2002). You may be surprised to know that whether you believe that small or large classes are better for children is largely a matter of your culture. Small classes are valued in cultures where children are expected to develop independence, such as the United States, but large classes are valued in cultures where children are expected to develop interdependence and learn to function as part of a large group, such as Japan.

There can be considerable overlap among cultures, as well as variation within a culture, and there are many subcultures. For example, the United States and China have different cultures. Yet, within each country there are varied subcultures based on ethnicity, class, region, and religion. Thus, culture can refer to large groups such as whole countries or to smaller subgroups within a country.

Ethnicity

ALANA an acronym that stands for the most populous non-White ethnic groups in the United States: African, Latin, Asian, and Native American.

Ethnic group refers to a group that shares a cultural heritage and/or a common ancestry. The United States is comprised of many different ethnic groups. Collectively, non-White groups are sometimes referred to as ALANA (African, Latin, Asian, and Native American). The U.S. Census Bureau (2008) estimated ethnic group populations as follows: 66% White, non-Hispanic; 12% Black; 15% Latino; 4% Asian; 1% American Indian, Alaska Native, Native Hawaiian, and Other Pacific Islander; and 2% two or more races. By 2020, government estimates project that nearly one in four children in the United States will be of Hispanic or Latin origin. Each of these major ethnic groups has distinct subgroups. For example, among Latinos, there is cultural variation among Puerto Rican, Salvadoran, and Mexican Americans. Among Asian Americans there is variation among Chinese, Filipino, and Southeast Asians. Among African Americans, there is variation among those who have been in the United States for centuries and those who have recently emigrated from Africa.

Ethnicity is linked to success in school (see Chapter 5). For example, Figure 1.4 displays group differences in scores on the National Assessment of Educational Progress (NAEP), which is often called the Nation's Report Card. Hispanic and African American students have lower average achievement than White and Asian American students throughout K–12 schooling (García & Jensen, 2009; Planty et al., 2009). Multiracial youth tend to have achievement similar to the group with which they identify. Thus, White-Black youth who think of themselves as Black tend to have lower achievement than White-Black students who think of themselves as White (Herman, 2009).

Why do children from some ethnic groups have lower achievement? We will discuss three explanations next: cultural capital, cultural mismatch, and involuntary minority status. In Chapter 5, we will discuss other explanations.

Cultural Capital

cultural capital knowledge and social relationships that allow people to reap benefits within their culture.

Financial capital refers to possessions like money and property that can be invested to gain wealth. Cultural capital refers to knowledge and relationships[2] that can be "invested" to

[2]Some researchers use the term *social* capital to refer to relationships that foster benefits (Horvat, Weininger, & Lareau, 2003; Ream & Palardy, 2008), but for simplicity we will use the term *cultural* capital to include relationships.

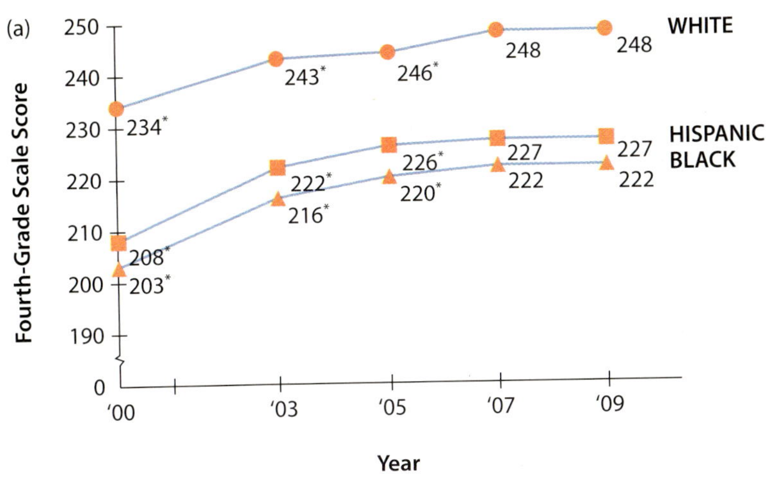

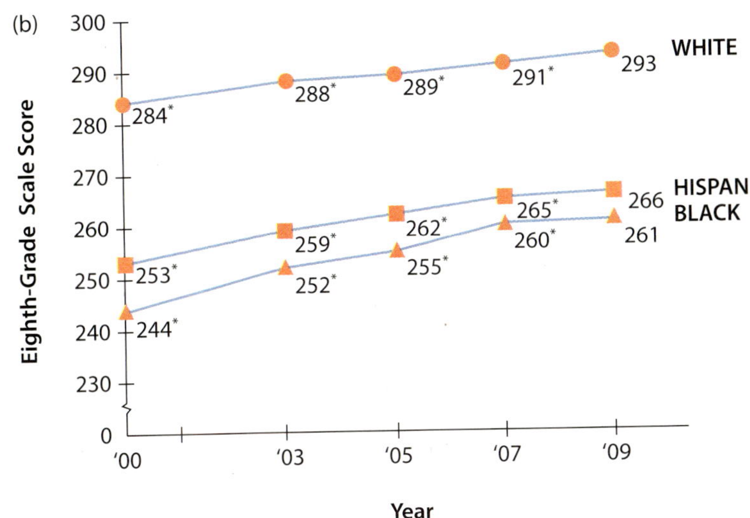

Figure 1.4 Average Mathematics Scores by Ethnic Group for 4th and 8th Grades, Based on the National Assessment of Educational Progress. Graphs depict the achievement gap between White students and Black and Hispanic students. *From Mathematics 2009, National Center for Educational Statistics website.*

gain benefits (Lareau & Horvat, 1999). In school settings, cultural capital includes *knowledge* about school policies, what language usage is acceptable, how to learn class content, how to take tests, who can intervene to help a child (e.g., teacher, principal, or classroom aide), how to find mentors, what credentials are necessary for specific jobs, how to use the Internet, and so forth. Students who have school-relevant knowledge, or who have parents who do, have cultural capital in school settings.

Cultural capital also includes *relationships*. One study found that upper-middle-class parents tended to know teachers, resource specialists, principals, counselors, and special educators because they were friends, relatives, and neighbors. In contrast, working-class parents tended to know gas station attendants, construction workers, convenience store cashiers, janitors, and factory workers (Lareau, 1989). Thus, upper-middle-class families had more school-relevant social connections. Students have cultural capital for schooling when they have relationships with people who help them access opportunities (like special education or gifted programs) or institutions (like elite universities), advocate for them, serve as models of success, and give sound advice. In case 1, one purpose of Elena's home visitor was to provide some cultural capital.

Field Observation

Ask people of varying levels of education and income the following questions. *(1) Do you own the most current cell phone? most current large-screen television? (2) What jobs do your neighbors and close relatives have? Do you personally know a judge? doctor? principal? (3) How long is law school? What does it take to get in? (4) What do you do on family vacations?* How might their answers be related to cultural capital and their children's achievement?

In the United States, cultural capital is linked to both class and ethnicity (Ream & Palardy, 2008). For example, a large national study found that Black students come from families with lower incomes and fewer household resources; are less likely to visit museums; and are less likely to experience out-of-school art, music, or dance classes than White students (Eitle & Eitle, 2002). These differences in cultural capital may lead to differences in academic achievement. Even when their income is the same, middle-class families of color often have less wealth than White families because they are less likely to have inheritances or income-producing assets.

Cultural Mismatch

cultural mismatch a pattern of incompatibilities between home and school.

Some ethnic groups experience cultural mismatch at school. **Cultural mismatch** refers to a pattern of incompatibilities between home and school. Cultural mismatch can be subtle, like how close you stand when talking with other people, or more obvious, like attention to punctuality. It also includes language and narrative style.

Language

A child may speak a different language than the one used in school, like Elena in case 1. A child may also use language in a different way from teachers, textbooks, or tests. An example is African American Vernacular English, which involves different pronunciation and syntax from the school's language. We will discuss this vernacular in Chapter 12.

Narrative structure

Within U.S. school culture, stories follow a traditional format of telling who was involved, what happened, and when. Typical stories build a series of events up to a climax and problem solution. Think of fairy tales like Cinderella. However, not all cultures share this conception of story. For example, Japanese children's stories may resemble Haiku—a succinct, short, and restrained form of poetry. African American children's stories may weave multiple events into a long, out-of-order account in a way that has been compared to jazz (Bliss & McCabe, 2008). The alternative story formats are not wrong within their cultures, but may be unexpected and considered wrong by some teachers.

Involuntary Minority

involuntary minorities nonimmigrant peoples who have been conquered, colonized, or enslaved.

voluntary minorities people of minority status who immigrated voluntarily.

Ethnic groups can have histories in a country as either **involuntary** (nonimmigrant) or **voluntary** (immigrant) **minorities**. Involuntary minorities "are people who have been conquered, colonized, or enslaved... to be a part of the U.S. society permanently against their will" (Ogbu & Simons, 1998, p. 165). Many African Americans are descended from Africans who were enslaved and brought to the United States against their will. Many Latinos are descended from Mexicans who were colonized when the United States took the Southwest from Mexico. Voluntary immigrants of color from Mexico, Africa, the Caribbean, and other places often become assimilated into involuntary minority groups and come to have the attributes of involuntary immigrants.

Involuntary minorities have suffered a long history of oppression and discrimination. For example, even after slavery ended in the United States, African Americans were hindered by laws that gave them less access to property, less wage protection in jobs, and less access to high-quality schools. Such discrimination causes people to band together, forming a group identity or *fictive kinship* with other members of their group. This group identity sometimes includes a united rejection of things associated with their historical oppressors. They may shun *acting White.* For example, some African American youth may underachieve because when they study hard to get good grades they are accused of acting White. However, the research on fear of acting White is mixed. While some students of color may resist White dominance and the school power structure by *avoiding* academic achievement, others are motivated to prove they can excel (Bergin & Cooks, 2002; Stinson, 2008; Walker, 2006). They *seek* academic achievement in order to achieve better lives *and* to resist White dominance.

Classroom Implications of Culture

Sonia is a Mexican American. Her mother wants her to do well in school but does not know how to help. Sonia's friends reject academic achievement; they skip classes and get in trouble together. At school no one ever talks with her about her future or speaks positively about Mexican culture. In fact, teachers and non-Mexican peers are negative about her ethnicity. Not surprisingly, although she had good grades until 8th grade, her grades in high school are terrible. (adapted from Phelan, Davidson, & Cao, 1991)

Sonia is experiencing cultural mismatch; she sees school as having no connection to her home world. Cultural mismatch is stressful. It can lead to poor adjustment to school and placement in special education. It can also lead to emotional disturbance (Gibbs, Huang, & Associates, 2003). Children who lack cultural capital and who experience cultural mismatch at school may need support. There are several things you can do to help your students:

- Become aware of your students' cultural capital and how it affects their achievement. For example, when given an assignment to develop a travel brochure for France in a social studies class, some students had home access to computers, high-speed Internet, color printers, and relatives who had traveled to France and spoke French. Their brochures made them look "smarter" than other students who were equally adept at writing, using the library, and asking questions, but had fewer resources. You will need to provide ways for students with little cultural capital or material resources to be successful in your classroom.
- Be careful as you think about cultural capital, because it can lead to a deficit view that highlights what students lack. Think about the strengths of your students and their cultural backgrounds. For example, Latino students may have a particularly strong sense of family connection and be more likely than European American children to help around the house by cooking, cleaning, and babysitting (Telzer & Fuligni, 2009).
- Become knowledgeable about and accept the language and dialect of your students, but at the same time teach standard English. This is discussed in Chapter 12. When directly asked, "Do you understand?" students with limited English want to appear competent in front of their peers, so they may say yes even when they do not understand. Some students report that they guess because they don't want to ask for help (Monzó & Rueda, 2009). Thus, you will need to be perceptive.

- Become aware of your students' narrative style. Do not assume that different styles do not "make sense," but also teach school narrative style so that your students will be successful in school.
- Build bridges between home and school. For example, in the play section of an early childhood classroom, the kitchen area should include items familiar in your students' home cultures, like tortillas or pita, not just hamburgers and pancakes.

Stock Connection/SuperStock

Learn about your students' home cultures in order to build bridges between school and home.

You may not know the different cultural values and practices of all your students, but genuinely trying to understand different perspectives will help you overcome mismatches in your classroom.

While addressing cultural and ethnic differences is important, you should be careful that you do not stereotype your students or lower your expectations based on the fact that certain groups have lower average test scores than others. Learn about your students through your experiences with each of them, not based on generalizations about their ethnic group.

Reconciling the Role of Genes and Culture

Behavioral geneticists generally find that most variation in the traits children possess is due to genes and nonshared environment (NSE), with relatively less contribution of shared environment (SE). If culture is SE, does this mean culture is not important in predicting child outcomes? Not really. Behavioral geneticists study *individual differences within a culture.* Factors that predict differences within cultures may not predict differences across cultures. For example, in China and the United States, level of parent education predicts academic achievement *within each country* to a similar degree (Stevenson et al., 1990). Chinese children outperform U.S. children in math, yet Chinese mothers have lower educational attainment than U.S. mothers. Parent education does not account for *across-country differences*, but cultural differences in values and expectations may (Lytton, 2000).

Recall from the bioecological model that multiple levels of influence, such as genes and culture, act together to predict child outcomes. "Underlying the bioecological model is a cardinal theoretical principle... that genetic material does not produce finished traits but rather interacts with environmental experience in determining developmental outcomes" (Bronfenbrenner & Ceci, 1994, p. 571). Culture (the macrosystem or outer circle) determines what genes will be manifest by the opportunities that are available in the culture. For example, alcohol use is partially heritable, but heritability is lower in religious households and in communities that spend less money on alcohol (Dick & Rose, 2002). Heritability of a trait may depend on culture-based opportunities for the trait to be manifest.

Some environments place children at risk for poor outcomes regardless of their genotype, whereas others are protective of children, fostering optimal outcomes. We will turn to a discussion of risk and protective factors next. Two risk factors will be used as examples: *socioeconomic status* is a part of culture that affects large groups of children, whereas *maternal depression* affects proximal processes and differences among individual children. Other risk and protective factors will be discussed in later chapters.

Risk and Resilience

Kathleen is a lively, smiling toddler with five older siblings who dote on her. Suddenly, her father leaves the family for a teenage girlfriend. Her mother begins drinking heavily, but denies that she is an alcoholic. Kathleen's siblings take care of her, until one by one they graduate from high school and leave home. As a teenager, Kathleen becomes her mother's caretaker when the mom is "sick." One of her brothers returns to live at home when he is not in jail. Kathleen manages to always be tidy, but not stylish, in appearance. She attends a low-achieving inner-city high school. She pays attention during class, turns in homework on time, and earns good grades. Teachers like her. She is a member of the school choir and her church's youth group. Kathleen feels depressed and anxious about her mother and her own future, but she keeps these feelings to herself. Through hard work, she later receives a scholarship to nursing school. By her late twenties Kathleen is married, has two children, and is a practicing nurse.

Why do some children, like Kathleen, seem to fare well even when they have adverse lives? This is the question of risk and resilience. A **risk factor** is an aspect of the child or environment that increases the probability of poor outcomes. Risk factors can be *biological,* such as low birth weight; *cognitive*, such as low intelligence; *social or emotional,* such as aggression or depression; *part of the family*, such as an alcoholic parent; or *part of the community*, such as neighborhood violence. In the bioecological model, risk factors in the microsystem (e.g., parenting quality) have a stronger impact than risk factors in the macrosystem (e.g., neighborhood violence), but risk factors at any level can undermine children's development. Common risk factors for children include the following:[3]

risk factor a variable associated with negative child outcomes.

Little positive mother–child interaction
Low maternal affection
Negative parental attitude toward child
Physical or hostile discipline
Rigid beliefs about child rearing
Low maternal education
Unstimulating home environment
Low family income—receive welfare
Unskilled head of household
Maternal anxiety or depression
Antisocial parent
Low birth weight
Low intelligence
Abuse
Parental drug use
Mother works long hours
Low parental monitoring
Single parent
Change in parent's marital status
Conflict or separation between parents
Parent has multiple sexual partners
Long hours in child care
Overcrowding or large family
Frequent moves
Foster care or living with another family
Negative, stressful life events
Involuntary minority status

[3]This list is derived from many studies, a few of which are listed here (Ackerman, Izard, Schoff, Youngstrom, & Kogos, 1999; Blair, 2001; Brennan, Hall, Bor, Najman, & Williams, 2003; Scher & Mayseless, 2000).

Rob Crandall/PhotoLibrary

Poverty is a powerful risk factor.

resilience positive development despite adversity or risk.

protective factor a factor that decreases the likelihood of poor outcomes in children at risk.

You probably know resilient children, like Kathleen, who succeeded in school in spite of risk factors. **Resilience** refers to the ability to adapt and flourish in the face of adversity. It includes the ability to recover from trauma (Luthar, 2006).

Protective Factors

Resilient children usually have one or more protective factors in their lives. **Protective factors** decrease the likelihood of poor outcomes in children at risk. Protective factors include good reading ability, participation in extracurricular activities like 4-H, special talents, a surrogate parent like a favorite teacher or relative, and a supportive spouse (Werner, 1994). Additional protective factors include the following:

1. High-quality parenting—especially a warm, nurturing mother (Burchinal, Roberts, Zeisel, & Rowley, 2008; Kim-Cohen, Moffitt, Caspi, & Taylor, 2004).
2. High intelligence (Luthar, 2006).
3. A strong relationship with a father figure (Grant et al., 2000).
4. Social competence, outgoing personality, and peer acceptance (Criss, Pettit, Bates, Dodge, & Lapp, 2002; Kim-Cohen et al., 2004).
5. Religious involvement (Grant et al., 2000; Pearce, Jones, Schwab-Stone, & Ruchkin, 2003).

Can educators be protective factors for children? Listen to the story of Olly Neal, who grew up African American in Arkansas during the segregated 1950s.

During his senior year in high school, Olly cut class one day and was hanging around in the library when he noticed a book with a provocative woman on the cover. He wanted to read the book, but was afraid to check it out because his friends might find out that he was reading. He said he wanted to be known for fighting and cussing, not reading, so he stole the book. Weeks later when he returned the book to its place on the shelf, he noticed another book by the same author. He stole that one too, and ended up reading four books by Frank Yerby, an African American author. Olly Neal became a reader, went to law school, and became an appellate judge in the Arkansas Court of Appeals. He learned a hidden part of his own story for the first time at his thirteenth high school reunion. The librarian had noticed him stealing the first book, realized why he was stealing, drove to Memphis to buy another Yerby book, and placed the new book on the shelf where he would find it. She made three trips to Memphis. (adapted from Taing, 2009)

This school librarian served as a protective factor for Judge Neal. Many teachers serve as similar protective factors when they promote their students' success at school.

Even resilient children may experience depression and anxiety or stress-related health problems. That is, something that protects children from one negative outcome does not necessarily protect them from all problems. High-risk children are more likely to be resilient in academic achievement than in social or emotional well-being. For example, Kathleen did well in school, but still struggled with depression through adolescence and into adulthood.

Provided courtesy of StoryCorps, a national nonprofit dedicated to recording and collecting stories of everyday people www.storycorps.org

Judge Olly Neal

Throughout this text you will learn how specific risk and protective factors influence children. You may personally know exceptions to the research. This is because research tells us what *probably* happens for most children, not what definitely happens for each child. For example, children's risk status when they enter school predicts school problems with about 75% accuracy (Pianta, Nimetz, & Bennett, 1997). While this accuracy is substantial, there is clearly room for exceptions.

Typically, a single risk factor has only a small effect size because a particular child's development is a complex array of risk and protective factors. The more risk factors a child experiences, the greater the likelihood that one or more problems will emerge. The *combined number of risk factors* better predicts child outcomes than a single risk factor.

Accumulation of Risk

Risk factors tend to go together—they are correlated. For example, in a study of African American 4th-, 5th-, and 6th-graders, several risk factors—single mother, low maternal education, poverty, many siblings, maternal depression, many poor classmates—were highly correlated in the 0.79–0.97 range (Burchinal et al., 2008). This means that a child who had one of these risk factors was likely to have some of the other risk factors as well.

When risk factors accumulate, they have a stronger effect. For example, the Rochester Longitudinal Study followed children from before birth through adolescence. Ten risk factors were measured. Each risk factor reduced IQ by only about four points, but children with eight or nine risk factors averaged IQ scores thirty points lower than children with zero risk factors (Sameroff, Seifer, Baldwin, & Baldwin, 1993). Another study found that no 1st graders with 0–1 risk factors had severe behavior problems, but 56% with five or more risk factors had severe behavior problems (Ackerman et al., 1999). Other studies have found similar effects for aggression, school absence, in-class behavior, GPA, and math, reading, and social studies test scores (Brennan et al., 2003; Burchinal et al., 2008; Gutman, Sameroff, & Eccles, 2002; Scher & Mayseless, 2000; Yumoto, Jacobson, & Jacobson, 2008). See Figure 1.5.

Some risk factors are more potent than others. Risk factors can reside within a child biologically or within the social environment. Biological risks include low birth weight, neurological problems, prenatal drug exposure, not being breastfed, and so forth. Social risks include poor-quality parenting, mother's depression, or parental divorce. Among typical children, *biological risk factors are generally not as powerful*

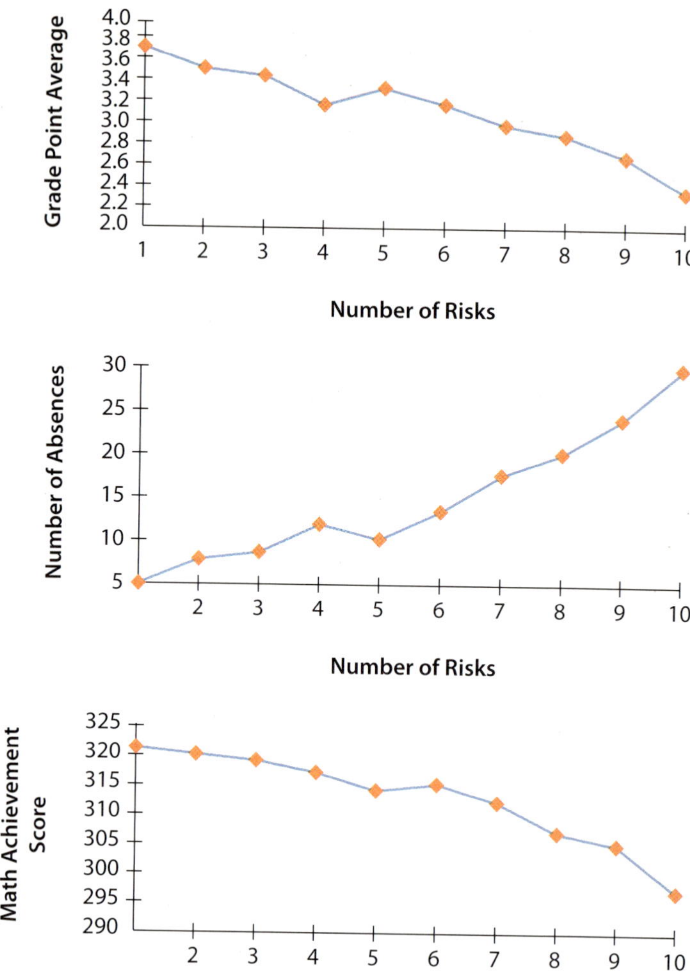

Figure 1.5 Relationship between Number of Risk Factors and School Outcomes.
Risk factors included low maternal education (high school diploma or less), maternal depression, unmarried mother, three or more children in the household, unskilled work, living in high-poverty neighborhoods, and stressful events like victim of a crime or lost a job. *Gutman, Sameroff, & Eccles (2002).*

in predicting outcomes as social risk factors (Sameroff, 1998; Werner, 1994), though an exception is severe biological problems that delay development. Children with *both* biological and social risk are most likely to develop problem behavior, like serious aggression (Belsky, Bakermans-Kranenburg, & Van IJzendoorn, 2007; Brennan et al., 2003). There are three key points for teachers: (1) when risk accumulates, there is a steep increase in the odds of poor outcome, (2) children may fare well if only one or two risk factors operate in their lives, and (3) quality of the social environment is critically important. Keep these key points in mind as you read about risk and protective factors throughout this text.

Stability in Development

Does risk or resilience in early childhood have effects into adulthood? The answer varies for different areas of child development, but overall there is continuity in development because there tends to be stability in environment.

Stability of Risk across Childhood

In the Rochester Longitudinal Study, when 4-year-olds were followed to adulthood, their risk factors remained the same. Only two risk factors were likely to change: some mothers obtained a high school diploma or equivalent (decreased risk), and some mothers became single (increased risk). Only one child in the study moved from high to low risk, and only one moved from low to high risk over the course of childhood. What this suggests is that risk status is stable.

Revisiting Case 1

Identify the risk factors Elena had, based on what you know about her. What protective factors does she have? Are her risk and protective factors likely to be stable across time? According to research, what outcomes might you expect for Elena?

In spite of the general stability of risk factors, some children's life circumstances do change. Major family turning points such as marriage, a new job, a move to a different community, and religious conversion change a child's life course. A child may be developing poorly but make a dramatic recovery when circumstances improve dramatically. Another child may be doing fine, but experience a major life blow, such as the death of a parent, from which the child may not recover. More mundane changes can also alter a child's risk, such as moving, entry and exit of parents' partners, parents' drug use, and decrease in income (Ackerman, Brown, & Izard, 2004a). Intermittent risk that comes and goes, such as moving in and out of poverty, can be as toxic as stable, persistent risk (Ackerman, Brown, & Izard, 2004b).

canalization genetically based restriction or channeling of development to a limited range of outcomes despite differences in environment.

Canalization protects children from early risk factors for a short time. Canalization refers to the tendency of genes to restrict development to a limited range of outcomes, despite quite different environments. For example, children learn to walk at about 13 months whether parents help their infants practice walking or not. Canalization often leads children to "self-right" in spite of early deprivation. For example, one of our sons developed a medical problem when he was 2 weeks old. His stomach was not functioning properly, so he began to starve. After the condition was corrected surgically, he quickly "self-righted" to a normal weight.

Canalization is stronger for physical development than for social, emotional, or cognitive development. For example, severely deprived Romanian orphans were more likely to catch up in physical growth than in social behavior, language, or cognitive ability after adoption (see Chapter 14).

The Importance of Early Experience

A child's early experiences are important because these experiences influence later opportunities and color how the child interprets later experiences (Turkheimer, 2000). For example, imagine that Ahmad bumps 15-year-old Duane in the hallway. If Duane experienced hostile, angry parenting as a toddler, he is likely to assume that Ahmad bumped him on purpose. He will slug Ahmad. His aggression will make other children avoid him, which will prevent him from developing better social skills. In contrast, if Duane experienced soothing, compassionate parenting as a toddler, he is likely to assume it was an accident, behave kindly toward Ahmad, and be sought out by other children, which will provide him with the opportunity to develop even better social skills. Duane could take widely different developmental paths depending on his early experiences.

In spite of the power of early experience to influence later experience, children are potentially flexible and adjust to the quality of their environment at any age. In some instances, children can remain scarred from severe early deprivation, but improvement is always possible, although it may be small. Thus, at any age both the child's historical and current profile of risk and protective factors are important. We next turn to a discussion of the effects of two of the most powerful risk factors—maternal depression and poverty.

Maternal Depression as a Risk Factor

When a mother is clinically depressed, she may experience sadness, loss of interest in daily activities, fatigue, and inability to think clearly. This may affect her children. Research shows that maternal depression is associated with children's *biological* and *cognitive* problems, such as failure to thrive, behavior problems, poor sleep, limited play, poor language ability, high heart rate, and abnormal brain functioning. Maternal depression is also associated with children's *social* and *emotional* problems, such as irritability, depression, wariness, unresponsiveness to others, ADHD (attention-deficit/hyperactivity disorder), suicidal thoughts, aggression, and social withdrawal.[4] Interestingly, some children with depressed mothers take on the caretaking of their depressed mothers to an extreme degree—as Kathleen did (Field, 1998). Some of these effects appear as early as 2 months of age. They have been found in diverse families, from children of low-income teenage mothers to middle-class adult mothers (Dawson et al., 1999). Effects depend on the severity and longevity of the mother's depression. However, early effects can be long-lasting. Effects of maternal depression in the first few years of life are still evident in adolescence, even if the mother has recovered by then (Karevold, Røysamb, Ystrom, & Mathiesen, 2009).

Catchlight Visual Services/Alamy

Maternal depression can interfere with quality of parenting.

How does maternal depression influence such a wide array of outcomes? Perhaps through other risk factors such as divorce, marital conflict, and low education that are linked to maternal depression. Perhaps children "catch" emotional negativity by imitating their depressed mothers (Field, Healy, Goldstein, & Guthertz, 1988). Depressed parents model and reinforce depressed behavior in their children (Webster-Stratton & Herman, 2008). Perhaps depression compromises the mother–child relationship. Depressed mothers tend to be more intrusive, more critical, and less responsive to their children (Dix & Meunier, 2009; Milan, Snow, & Belay, 2009). These parent–child interactions are among the most powerful processes discussed in the bioecological model.

At least two factors protect children from maternal depression: affluence and good fathers. Depressed but high-income mothers are more likely to be sensitive to their children despite their depression, and their children have fewer problems (NICHD

[4]There are many studies that support these conclusions, just a few of which are listed here (Dawson & Ashman, 2000; Dawson et al., 2003; Field, 1998; Lesesne, Visser, & White, 2003; Shaw, Gilliom, Ingoldsby, & Nagin, 2003; Wachs, Black, & Engle, 2009; Weinberg & Tronick, 1998).

Early Child Care Research Network, 1999; Petterson & Albers, 2001). Children of depressed mothers have fewer problems if they have a mentally healthy, nondepressed father in the home (Field, Hossain, & Malphurs, 1999; Radke-Yarrow, Cummings, Kuczynski, & Chapman, 1985).

Most research on maternal depression is nonexperimental, making it hard to determine what causes what. Does maternal depression cause problems in children, or do problems in children cause their mothers to be depressed? Experimental studies can help answer this question. It turns out that interventions that help depressed mothers improve their parenting skills result in better outcomes in their children. This suggests that maternal depression causes child problems (Baydar, Reid, & Webster-Stratton, 2003; Field, 1998).

Poverty as a Risk Factor

Poverty is another powerful and all-too-common risk factor for children. According to the 2000 U.S. census, almost one in five children lives in poverty, which is twice the rate of elderly people (Hernandez, Denton, & Macartney, 2008). About 34% of children will experience poverty at some time during their childhood, with most experiencing it in early childhood rather than adolescence. The remaining children, who are above poverty, are distributed among low (21%), medium (34%) and high (30%) income (Rank & Hirschl, 1999). In 2008, the federal government defined poverty as an annual income below $11,000 for a family of two parents and two related children; low income was $21,000 to $43,000; medium was $44,000 to $87,000; high was more than $87,000; and very high was more than $131,000.

The term *poverty* is often used broadly to refer to very low socioeconomic status, rather than strictly adhering to the federal definition. Socioeconomic status (SES) refers to a combination of parental education, occupation, and income. Families are designated as low, middle, or high in SES. You may think income is the key component of SES, but as you will learn in later chapters, parent education more strongly predicts child outcomes.

socioeconomic status (SES) categorization based on parental education, income, and occupational status; often simplified as low, middle, and upper class.

Low SES is a risk factor for many child problems. For example, low SES is linked to *health* problems like drug exposure, respiratory illness, cavities, obesity, and complications following injuries or infections. Low SES is also linked to *socioemotional* problems like depression, delinquency, and psychiatric problems. Low SES is strongly linked with aggression. Low SES is also linked to *cognitive* problems like low verbal ability, low intelligence, and low achievement. Table 1.3 gives the probabilities of poor children experiencing negative outcomes compared to nonpoor children. For example, poor children are two times more likely to be retained a grade than nonpoor children.

Poor children tend to have low-average performance on cognitive tests in early childhood, with gradual declines into middle childhood, so that the gap between affluent children and poor children gets larger with age. For example, in one study, poor children were on average only one month delayed at 2 1/2 years, but were eight months delayed by 5 years of age (Carta et al., 2001). In a study with older children, poor children scored one-third of a grade lower in 1st grade but 5.8 grade levels lower in 8th grade than affluent children (Greenwood et al., 1992). This means that if you

Table 1.3 Risk for poor children relative to nonpoor children

	Risk
Emotional or behavioral problems	1.3
Learning disability	1.4
Low birth weight	1.7
Mortality (death)	1.7
Hospitalization	2.0
Grade repetition	2.0
Dropping out of high school	2.0
Experiencing violent crime	2.2
Teenage, out-of-wedlock birth	3.1
Lead poisoning	3.5
Child abuse or neglect	6.8

Adapted from Duncan & Brooks-Gunn (2000).

Think About This Stanford University has a "housing project" for graduate students with children. Many children live there for years, with stressed parents and incomes well below the poverty level. How do you predict the children fare? Weigh risk and protective factors.

teach in secondary grades, you are likely to see the effects of poverty more than if you teach preschool.

However, if you teach in an elite private school, you will see that the top rungs of the ladder are not ideal either; wealth poses risk for children. High-SES youth have higher levels of stress, pressure to achieve, anxiety, depression, and drug use than inner-city youth (Luthar & Latendresse, 2008). Children may fare best in middle-income, *but not wealthy*, neighborhoods (Caspi, Taylor, Moffitt, & Plomin, 2000). This is right where you are likely to be with a teacher's salary!

How Does Poverty Have These Effects?

Two major models have been proposed to explain the many effects of poverty on children.

Family investment model

According to the family investment model, poverty is associated with less access to cultural or financial capital that the family can "invest" in children, which leads to poorer health and a low-quality learning environment in the home (Duncan & Brooks-Gunn, 2000). Home-learning environment refers to time spent reading, preschool experience, language stimulation, number of puzzles and books, outings to museums or theaters, and family meal routines. The quality of the home-learning environment, in turn, predicts achievement and behavior problems among Latino, African American, and White children (Bradley, Corwyn, Burchinal, McAdoo, & Garcia Coll, 2001; Linver, Brooks-Gunn, & Kohen, 2002).

Family stress model

According to the family stress model, poverty is associated with conditions that stress parents, such as lack of food, single parenthood, divorce, frequent moves, and job loss. This leads to depression, marital conflict, and other problems. These, in turn, lead to *diminished quality of parenting* (Bradley & Corwyn, 2002). Home or job stress tends to result in parents' emotional and physical withdrawal from children (Repetti, Wang, & Saxbe, 2009). The family stress model has been supported for Latino, African American, and White families (Lugo-Gil & Tamis-LeMonda, 2008; Raver, Gershoff, & Aber, 2007). Both of these models may be true—the family stress model may explain behavior problems better, while the family investment model may explain academic problems better (Gershoff, Aber, Raver, & Lennon, 2007).

Field Observation

After school, drive through low-, medium-, and high-income neighborhoods. Walk through grocery stores or carry outs. What differences do you observe (e.g., home size, police presence, play activities, adults, children)? How might the things you observe affect children? What might be hidden from view?

In addition to the family investment and stress models, the effects of poverty could result from a simple accumulation of risk factors. Poor children are exposed to more risk factors—such as family violence and instability, low-quality parenting, heavy TV watching, pollution, lead, parental smoking, and a variety of other risk factors (Dilworth-Bart & Moore, 2006; Evans, 2004). One major risk factor for impoverished children is frequent moving (Adam, 2004). Another is household chaos—noise, crowding, and few household routines. In fact, when chaos levels are statistically accounted for, the effect of poverty on children almost disappears, suggesting that chaos may be a key path through which poverty affects children (Evans, Gonnella, Marcynyszyn, Gentile, & Salpekar, 2005).

Another major risk factor is living in a poor neighborhood. Neighborhood effects are modest in size but noticeable (Leventhal & Brooks-Gunn, 2003). Crime, noise, dilapidated housing, and lack of money cause stress for residents. Children who live in such neighborhoods are more likely to exhibit antisocial behavior and have lower academic achievement, from preschool to high school age (Cutrona, Wallace, & Wesner, 2006; Hart, Atkins, & Matsuba, 2008; Odgers et al., 2009). A protective factor for children in high-risk neighborhoods is *collective efficacy*, meaning that neighbors look out for each other (Odgers et al., 2009).

Ethnicity and Poverty

In most countries, poverty and ethnicity go hand in hand. In the United States, the majority of poor children are White, but children of color are disproportionately poor. For example, 69% of Black children compared to 26% of White children will experience poverty in their lifetime. Three risk factors linked to poverty are having a single mother, having a mother who did not finish high school, and being African American. Children with all three risk factors have a staggering 99% chance of being poor at some point in childhood, whereas children with none of these risk factors have a 15% chance (Rank & Hirschl, 1999).

Classroom Implications of Poverty

Poor children are more likely than wealthier children to develop problems that undermine their achievement in school. However, keep in mind that this is only a probability, not destiny. Many poor children will do well in school. Let's listen to an adult who grew up poor.

> *Poverty is like a gravity that pulls you down to earth (p. 3)....*
> *There's no way to jump high enough to overcome gravity by "hard work." Effort alone won't make you fly (p. 3).... I was aware that people judged my mother negatively because she did not have a job (p. 33).... I was torn between wanting to side with those who judged my mother as lazy and irresponsible—and*

> *wanting to protect her from those judgments because I loved her and saw all the good things she did do and the intelligence inside her, the beautiful bright interesting person she is. (pp. 33–34) (Summer, 2003)*

This was written by a girl who was so poor she was homeless in childhood but later attended Harvard. How did she come to be successful in school (and write so well)? She may have had protective factors that offset her poverty. Protective factors for poor children include full-time educational child care beginning in infancy.

Family protective factors include a married mother, a mother with high intelligence, stimulating care at home, income adequate to meet basic needs, a family that provides structure, and social support. Personal protective factors include optimism, sense of humor, emotional competence, and intelligence (Bradley & Corwyn, 2002; Dearing, McCartney, & Taylor, 2001). How can you be a protective factor to your students?

- Amplify their protective factors and highlight their strengths. Children like Kathleen have remarkable skills. Recognize them. Recognize that many low-SES children are taking care of parents or raising younger siblings.
- Teach a rigorous, engaging curriculum. Low-SES children tend to get less exposure to academic content. For example, one study found that they spent 5% less time on academic subjects per school day than high-SES students, particularly in reading and science. This may have been partly due to low-SES students being pulled out of class for special services (Greenwood, 1991).

Each chapter throughout this text will provide you with additional tools to help you be a protective factor for your students. High-quality school experiences can compensate for lower school readiness among poor students. Indeed, this is the aim of compensatory preschool.

Classroom Implications: The Case of School Readiness and Preschool

What is compensatory preschool? It is preschool designed to promote better-than-expected school readiness for high-risk children, or in other words, to be a *protective factor.* (The term *compensatory* is somewhat negative because it implies deficits in the child's environment, but there is no consensus yet on a replacement term.) Because risks accumulate, interventions targeting a single factor are not very successful (Masten & Reed, 2002). Thus, compensatory preschools often include services that go beyond traditional preschools, like parent education and job training. Compensatory preschools typically target children based on either low income or low birth weight (see Chapter 2). Head Start is a prime example.

It is important to place children on a positive developmental path as early as possible. It was a common, but mistaken, belief during the years when Head Start was begun that much of a child's crucial brain development was over by age 6, or even age 3. In fact, intervention can help children throughout the lifespan. However, change is more rapid in younger children. The use of compensatory preschool to foster school readiness in poor children touches upon each of the major topics of this chapter—the science of child development, the nature–nurture balance, and risk and resilience—so we will use it as a case to illustrate how ways of thinking about children influence educational practices.

School Readiness

School readiness refers to skills that prepare children for formal instruction, such as being able to follow directions; having self-control; and knowing the alphabet, basic numbers, and colors. While only 10% of teachers say that children should know their alphabet and be able to count to 20 to be ready for kindergarten, 60% say they need to have self-control, that is, be able to follow directions and not be disruptive (Blair, 2002). Nevertheless, several large studies across several countries show that math skills, like knowing numbers, predict later academic success with an effect size of 0.34 (Duncan et al., 2007). Knowing the alphabet and having attention skills had smaller effects (0.17 and 0.10, respectively). This does not mean that social and emotional skills are not important to how children get along later in school—indeed, you will learn in subsequent chapters that these are important skills—but rather that preschool math knowledge is a particularly important predictor of later achievement.

Preschoolers vary in school readiness. Some children entering kindergarten read at a 5th-grade level, but others have no reading skills (Christian, Morrison, & Bryant, 1998). Some children (16%) have serious problems adjusting to kindergarten, another 32% have some problems, and the rest do fine according to more than 3,500 kindergarten teachers. The most common problems are inability to follow directions, work independently, and communicate. Low SES is a risk factor for entering school unprepared. Both minority and nonminority teachers in districts with many poor and minority students report that more than half their students have problems adjusting to school (Rimm-Kaufman, Pianta, & Cox, 2000).

Measuring School Readiness

Some states require tests of kindergarten readiness. Some readiness tests measure beginning academic skills, like knowledge of letters, numbers, or shapes. But others, like the commonly used Gesell School Readiness Test, are more like intelligence tests in that they measure global functioning. Many readiness tests (e.g., the Gesell) do not meet standards for validity or reliability, yet are still used by schools (La Paro & Pianta, 2000). Some experts object to their use as gatekeepers to school because children with low scores have the greatest need to be in school and because they encourage advantaged parents to hold back their children so they will be at the top of their class. This inflates teachers' concepts of what a typical kindergartener is capable of, which pushes excessively academic curricula onto younger children (Shepard, 1997).

Many districts use age as a gatekeeper to school. Should parents place their September-birthday son in kindergarten where he will be the youngest, or wait until next year when he will be the oldest? Research shows that "underage" kindergarteners perform well in high school (Vecchiotti, 2003). The youngest 1st-graders may be a little behind the oldest 1st-graders in reading and math, but this effect washes out by the middle of elementary school (Morrison, Griffith, & Alberts, 1997). Furthermore, when children who are placed in school young are later tested in 1st grade, they are more advanced than their same-age peers who are in kindergarten. School makes kids smarter. Some parents have their children start kindergarten a year late, assuming that this will give them an academic advantage; evidence suggests it does not, and it may even create disadvantage (Martin, 2009). Thus, entrance age is not a good predictor of academic success.

What Should Be Done for Children Who Are Not Ready for School?

The answer to this question depends on your theory of children's development. A *maturationist* assumes that school readiness depends on abilities driven by a genetic timetable. Thus, waiting for the child to mature biologically is the logical answer. The practice of holding back children in kindergarten is evidence that this view is common in schools. In contrast, an *environmentalist* would assume that school readiness is driven by having the right experiences. Thus, providing compensatory preschool experiences would be the logical answer. The difference in these views is the nature–nurture contrast.

> ***Think About This*** If the quality of the environment affects children's school readiness, should children who perform poorly on readiness tests be kept out of school? Describe how another year in their home environment might affect the school readiness of children from different backgrounds.

What does the research say about this contrast? The maturationist view is undermined by two lines of research. First, kindergarten retention does not have an academic payoff; children learn more if they are promoted (Hong & Yu, 2008b). Second, quality of the home environment affects school readiness. A major twin study shows that shared environment makes a substantial contribution to school readiness—even bigger than genes or nonshared environment (Forget-Dubois et al., 2009; Lemelin et al., 2007). Aspects of the environment that affect school readiness include mothers' education, preschool experience, and books at home (Christian et al., 1998). The logical conclusion from this evidence is that school readiness could be promoted in high-risk children by providing enriched preschool experiences.

What Does the Research on Compensatory Preschools Say?

One approach to helping poor children become ready for formal schooling is to provide publicly funded preschool, like Head Start and pre-kindergarten.

Head Start

The most famous compensatory preschool program is Head Start. Eligibility for Head Start is based on family income. The largest single federal program exclusively for poor children, Head Start provides health, education, and social services. Most programs are half day and operate on a school-year calendar. Most children enrolled in Head Start are 3 or 4 years old. Roughly one-third of Head Start children are African American, another one-third are Latino, another one-third are White, and a small number are other ethnicities (Administration for Children & Families, 2007).

How effective is Head Start? Evidence from the 1990s and before suggests Head Start was associated with short-term cognitive gains that diminished over time (Lamb, 1998). Head Start children also behaved worse in school than children in no preschool or other preschools, but the effect was small (Lee, Brooks-Gunn, Schnur, &

Liaw, 1990). Because these effects of Head Start were modest at best, some programs were extended up to 3rd grade and down to toddlers, like Early Head Start, in order to increase impact.

Did these innovations help? Scientists used randomized experiments to answer this question. One experiment found no difference between the control and Head Start children on social-emotional or cognitive skills (Goodson, Layzer, St.Pierre, Bernstein, & Lopez, 2000). Recent national studies of Early Head Start found slight positive results (Love et al., 2005). For example, the average cognitive test score for Early Head Start children was 91 compared to 90 for control children. The national norm is 100. Another national experiment mandated by Congress found that Head Start increased some of children's preliteracy skills but not all, and not math. There was a decrease in problem behavior, but no effect for other social skills. The positive effects were modest (effect size of 0.1 to 0.3). The children remained below the national norm, but the gap was smaller for Head Start children (Puma, Bell, Cook, Heid, & Lopez, 2005).

Pre-Kindergarten

Elementary schools serving large numbers of poor children often have compensatory pre-kindergarten programs at the school site. Some are funded by Title I (also called Chapter 1), a federal program for schools with high rates of poverty. They tend to have more-educated teachers than other preschools, including Head Start (Lee, Loeb, & Lubeck, 1998). Some pre-K programs result in better readiness skills at school entry, but few results last beyond 1st grade (e.g., Gormley, Gayer, Phillips, & Dawson, 2005). A review of pre-K programs found that of eleven outcomes, the only robust long-term effect was less grade retention (Gilliam & Zigler, 2000). For example, in Maryland, 44% of pre-K attenders, but 64% of nonattenders, had been retained at some point by 10th grade. Yet, some studies find positive long-term effects on delinquent behavior and educational achievement. For example, in Chicago, children in pre-K were more likely to finish high school (56 versus 47%) and not be arrested for crimes (13 versus 22%) by age 20 than nonattendees (Reynolds, Ou, & Topitzes, 2004). Some programs also find an effect on math and reading achievement beyond 3rd grade, but the effect is very small (Gilliam & Zigler, 2000). There is little effect on behavior problems, parent involvement, self-esteem, or health.

To summarize, the research suggests that Head Start and pre-K programs have small, short-term benefits. However, university-run model programs generally have stronger effects, with effect sizes of 0.15 to 0.43 (Lipsey & Wilson, 1993; Magnuson, Meyers, Ruhm, & Waldfogel, 2004; Reynolds et al., 2004). They also tend to have more extensive components. One of the most successful is the *Abecedarian Project*, which provided educational child care of exceptional quality eight hours daily for five years and home visits from a resource teacher for the first three years of school. Researchers have followed children in this project, and a control group, into adulthood. The project resulted in better cognitive and academic ability, less depression, increased college attendance, and reduced marijuana use (Campbell et al., 2008; McLaughlin, Campbell, Pungello, & Skinner, 2007). See Figure 1.6.

Compensatory preschool effects are short term in that once intervention children enter school, their test scores drop and often the control group children's rise (Barnett,

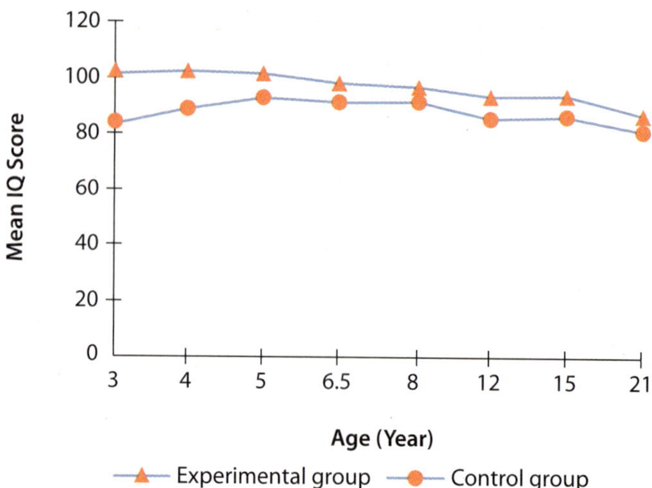

Figure 1.6 Cognitive Growth in Children in the Abecedarian Project and the Control Group over Time. Children were randomly assigned to the Abecedarian Project or to a control group when infants. Both groups were followed longitudinally and administered IQ tests. Results suggest that the intervention had a consistent but modest long-term impact. Data are from Campbell, Pungello, Miller-Johnson, Burchinal, & Ramey (2001).

1995; Magnuson et al., 2004). Similar effects are found for full- versus half-day kindergarten; small gains in achievement for full-day kindergarten wash out by 3rd grade (Votruba-Drzal, Li-Grining, & Maldonado-Carreno, 2008). Children who fare best over the long run are those who continue to have enrichment into the elementary years—either by continuing in an intervention program or by entering high-quality elementary schools (Reynolds et al., 2004). This suggests that pre-K programs need to be carefully aligned with high-quality elementary programs (Bogard & Takanishi, 2005).

In conclusion, compensatory preschool can enhance the development of high-risk children if it is of high quality and extensive. Some programs are more effective than others, but even among successful programs, effects on achievement diminish over time and cannot fully compensate for disparities between poor and advantaged children. Given that risk factors are stable, the results are encouraging but not magical (Brooks-Gunn, 2003). Although the effects are small, they have important benefits for individuals and society and, over the long run, may outweigh costs if they result in less special education placement, lower crime rates, and better adult employment (Duncan & Magnuson, 2007; Ludwig & Phillips, 2007). The fact that children's outcomes can be modestly improved by preschool suggests a role for nurture beyond the family (Rutter, 2000). You can enhance the development of your high-risk students by providing optimal education environments.

Reflections on Practice: Checklist for Teachers

It is important for teachers to understand the science of child development as they apply research findings to their classrooms. They also need to understand the multiple factors, from genes to culture, that influence children. The ways teachers think about children will influence whether they promote positive outcomes and resilience in their students. Ask yourself the following questions about the ways you think about children:

1. What do my classroom practices and image of an ideal classroom reveal about my personal theories of child development?
2. What are my assumptions about the heritability of a student's academic achievement, athletic prowess, or social competence? What is my role as teacher in fostering ability in these domains?
3. Am I a careful consumer of information about supposedly effective interventions? Do I check to see if the information is research based and whether the research was carefully conducted? Do I consider whether causality can be determined, if results should generalize to my students, and whether effect size is adequate?
4. When I use information from tests, am I careful to consider their reliability and the validity for their use?
5. What factors are operating on my students in each ring of the bioecological model? What personal and cultural strengths does each child bring to the classroom?
6. What is the cultural capital of my students? What can I do to provide cultural capital? Do my assignments favor students who have cultural capital?
7. Am I careful not to make assumptions about students based on ethnicity, income, or language (e.g., accent or use of Black English)?
8. Am I sensitive to how voluntary and involuntary minority students may have different perceptions of academic achievement and of the topics we discuss in class?
9. Are my students comfortable at school? Is there a cultural mismatch between my students and my classroom? Do I genuinely celebrate the strengths of different cultures?
10. What is the profile of risk and protective factors for each of my students? Do I facilitate resilience by enhancing their protective factors?
11. Do the at-risk, low-income children in my classroom spend as much academic time-on-task as their more-affluent peers? Do I have appropriately high expectations for them?
12. What is my school's vision of school readiness (maturationist or environmentalist)? Do we use age or readiness tests to keep children out even though they need school experience? What are my district and school doing to improve readiness in preschoolers?

Chapter Summary

The Science of Child Development

- There are many different theories of child development. Theories vary in the emphasis given to biological processes (i.e., maturationist) or the environment (i.e., environmentalist).
- Research designs include experiments, correlational studies, and qualitative studies. Experiments use random assignment and control groups to make strong claims about causality that correlational studies cannot. Longitudinal designs document change across time, and cross-sectional studies simulate change across time.
- Use of reliable and valid measures is fundamental to research and education.
- Research should be crafted to generalize to a variety of children. Research in recent decades has included more diverse populations than in the past.
- Effect size refers to the size of difference between groups, or correlation between variables, and helps you judge how important a research finding may be.

Nature and Nurture

- The bioecological model suggests that nested systems influence the child, with proximal processes like the family being the most powerful.
- Behavioral geneticists attribute variation in any trait to heritability, shared environment, or nonshared environment. Estimates of their relative contribution are based on indirect methods, such as comparing twins or adopted siblings.
- Genes make a contribution to many aspects of development, but environment typically makes a greater contribution.
- Families can be a nonshared environment, because children react differently to the family environment and because families change over time.
- Whether a genotype becomes a phenotype depends on the environment. Genes do not minutely program behavior or the brain, which makes adaptation possible.
- Genes and environment interact. Gene–environment interaction means that the heritability of a trait varies depending on context, including culture.
- Within the United States, Asian children tend to have the highest achievement, followed by White, African American, and then Latino children. However, within ethnic groups there are large differences in achievement. Plausible explanations include cultural capital, cultural mismatch (language and narrative style), and involuntary minority status.

Risk and Resilience

- Risk factors predict poor outcomes for children. Social risk factors are usually more powerful than biological risk factors. A single risk factor is not likely to strongly predict poor outcomes. Risk factors tend to accumulate, greatly increasing the likelihood of a poor outcome. Protective factors reduce the likelihood of poor outcomes among high-risk children, leading to resilience.

- Development is generally stable because early development influences later development and because risk factors tend to be stable across childhood. In spite of early risk, canalization leads children to "self-right" to a species-typical trajectory. Canalization is strongest in the first two years, and for physical development.
- Maternal depression and poverty are major risk factors that have pervasive effects on child outcomes. Both may affect children by compromising the quality of mother–child interaction. Poverty may also affect children through parents' limited ability to invest in the children, and through neighborhood influences.

School Readiness and Compensatory Preschools

- School readiness refers to social and emotional skills as well as basic knowledge that help children experience success in school. Many children are not ready for school, but keeping children out of school based upon readiness tests or age does not promote their development.
- Large-scale, community-based compensatory preschools (e.g., Head Start and pre-K programs) generally have positive short-term cognitive effects, but slight or no long-term effects, although participants are less likely to be retained in grade. Most studies find little or no improvement in parenting. In contrast, intensive, high-quality programs can produce modest, long-term benefits; but participants do not continue to make gains after they enter school, and they still perform below grade level.

Accompanying Education CourseMate Website Resources

Visit the **Education CourseMate** website at **CengageBrain.com** to find resources and study aids for this chapter, including self-tests, additional print and website resources, glossary flashcards. The following news-clip videos portray issues from this chapter and demonstrate how teachers can make a difference in their student's development:

- A Positive School Climate Reduces the Achievement Gap
- Freedom Writers: Teachers Can Inspire Students to Learn and Achieve

Physical Development and Health

Dennis MacDonald/Alamy

SHOULD YOU BE CONCERNED ABOUT YOUR STUDENTS' PHYSICAL WELL-BEING, SUCH AS NUTRITION, PHYSICAL ACTIVITY, DRUG USE, AND SLEEP? We think you will answer with a resounding yes at the end of this chapter. We will discuss three aspects of physical development—the brain, growth and motor development, and contemporary health challenges. After you read this chapter, you will understand:

- How the brain develops in infants, children, and adolescents; typical patterns of growth; and some of the health challenges today's children face.
- How physical well-being contributes to students' success in your classroom.
- How you can foster optimal physical well-being among your students.

The Brain

All of Mrs. Z's kindergarten students receive a free breakfast, which they eat at 8:45 in the morning. Their assigned lunchtime is 12:40. Even if you assume they actually ate their breakfast, four hours is a long time without food or drink. Mrs. Z decided to provide a 10:30 snack. She reports, "I have seen a big difference in the children's ability to stay on task, greater desire to complete their work to the best of their abilities, and there seems to be less conflict in the centers or during free time just before lunch. I cannot believe the difference it has made."

Your students are biological beings. This may seem obvious, but it is easy for teachers to overlook physical needs, as Mrs. Z initially did. Abraham Maslow, a psychologist, argued that children cannot attend to classroom tasks unless their basic physical needs are met first (see Box 2.1). Meeting the needs of one part of the body—the brain—is especially important because the brain regulates learning, behavior, and other physical functions.

Interest in the brain has surged recently thanks to new technology that allows neuroscientists to view the brain in action. Neuroscience is the study of how the brain is involved in perception, memory, and emotions. Among the most important discoveries of neuroscience is that *the brain is constructed by experience.* This means that as a teacher, the way that you interact with children will contribute to their brain development. Before we discuss how this happens, let's begin with a quick lesson on how the brain works.

Structure and Function of the Brain

The basic unit of the brain is the nerve cell, or neuron. There are about 100 billion neurons in the brain (Beatty, 2001). A neuron has three parts: the cell body (with a nucleus much like other cells in the body), the dendrites (receiving units that bring information from other cells), and the axons (sending units that carry information away to other neurons or to muscle cells). See Figure 2.2.

Neurons communicate with each other through electrical signals. These signals are affected by **myelin**, a fatty substance that forms an insulating sheath around axons. This myelin sheath makes the electrical signals more efficient, increasing their speed. Some diseases damage the myelin sheath, such as Multiple Sclerosis (known as MS), which may result in muscle weakness or problems with thinking.

myelin a fatty substance that forms an insulating coating, called a myelin sheath, around axons that allows them to function efficiently.

Neurons also communicate with each other chemically at synapses. A **synapse** has three parts: the sending end of one neuron, the receiving end of another, and the space between them. At synapses, neurons release a chemical, called a **neurotransmitter**, when an electrical signal arrives, which is then received by another neuron. Some neurotransmitters you will commonly hear of are dopamine, serotonin, noradrenaline, and norephinephrine. A single neuron may receive input from tens of thousands of synapses. There are more than 100 trillion synapses in the brain (Beatty, 2001). The synapse is where many drugs operate, including drugs that are abused (such as heroin), as well as psychiatric drugs. For example, Ritalin, used to treat ADHD, inhibits the activity of dopamine and norepinephrine.

synapse a junction where neurons communicate with each other, or with other kinds of cells.

neurotransmitter a chemical that allows neurons to communicate across synapses.

Theories and Theorists: Box 2.1

Maslow's Hierarchy of Needs

Abraham Maslow (1908–1970) was the oldest of seven children of uneducated Russian Jewish immigrants to the United States. He was encouraged by his parents to excel in school. He did not; his grades were mediocre. Yet he read voraciously, which may explain why he got into the University of Wisconsin to study psychology. He became a professor at Brooklyn College in his home state of New York in 1937.

Maslow was a leader of humanistic psychology, which was quite different from two prevailing theories of his time: Freudian psychology and behaviorism. Humanistic psychology emphasizes growth and fulfillment. Maslow wanted to know what makes people mentally healthy, rather than mentally ill. He studied exceptional people, such as Abraham Lincoln, Jane Addams, and Albert Einstein. His studies led him to develop the concept of a hierarchy of needs.

Maslow's hierarchy of needs is usually portrayed like a pyramid (see Figure 2.1). The most basic human needs are at the bottom of the pyramid. These are physical needs like air, water, food, sleep. At the next level are safety needs. These include psychological safety (e.g., stability, security, and order) as well as physical safety. Then come social needs, such as love and acceptance. At the next level are esteem needs, such as admiration from others and self-respect. The highest level is self-actualization.

Figure 2.1 Maslow's Hierarchy of Needs.
Can you identify where you currently are in this pyramid? Which of your needs are mostly met, and which are pressing issues for you now? Do the same for a child in your class.
Based on Maslow (1970).

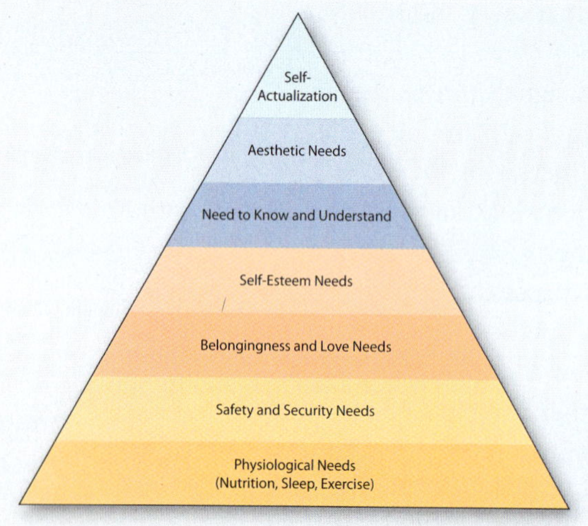

Self-actualization is the process of fulfilling one's potential. This is not a self-centered state. Rather, self-actualizing people are concerned with issues that affect humanity. Self-actualizing people are unpretentious, ethical, compassionate, and creative. However, they are not perfect, nor do they display these attributes at all times. Most people do not become self-actualized; perhaps less than 5% of people truly achieve it. Self-actualization is a very long process. Maslow believed college students are too young to reach this level (Maslow, 1970, p. 150).

According to Maslow, your students' first concern is to fulfill the lowest level of unsatisfied need. When a need is met, it becomes unimportant, and the next level of need becomes pressing. After physiological needs are met, then safety needs become pressing. When these needs are met, belonging becomes pressing, and so on. In contrast, when basic needs are not met, children will not go on to higher steps. Needs are not "all or nothing," but rather emerge gradually. That is, a child does not have to have 100% of each lower need met before the next level of need becomes relevant. Motivation to satisfy needs produces growth as the child comes to pursue higher needs.

According to Maslow, unmet needs are the root of misbehavior and most mental illnesses. For example, hungry students may become distractible, selfish, and aggressive, as Mrs. Z's students did. Older youth with unmet belongingness needs may join violent gangs.

There are many criticisms of Maslow's work. It was not scientific, because he decided who were self-actualizers and studied their life stories in retrospect. In addition, people behave as self-actualizers even when lower needs are not met. For example, there were individuals in World War II concentration camps who were deprived of food but were still creative, compassionate, and ethical.

Despite these criticisms, Maslow's hierarchy of needs is useful for teachers. In Maslow's view children are inherently good, tending toward self-actualization. If a student misbehaves in your classroom, it may mean that the student's needs are not being met. In Maslow's view, you do not need to control negative impulses as much as to help satisfy basic needs so that your students are free to become all that they can be. Children must be fed, well rested, and feel cared for if they are to achieve in school. This is why understanding children's physical and socioemotional needs will help you become a more effective teacher.

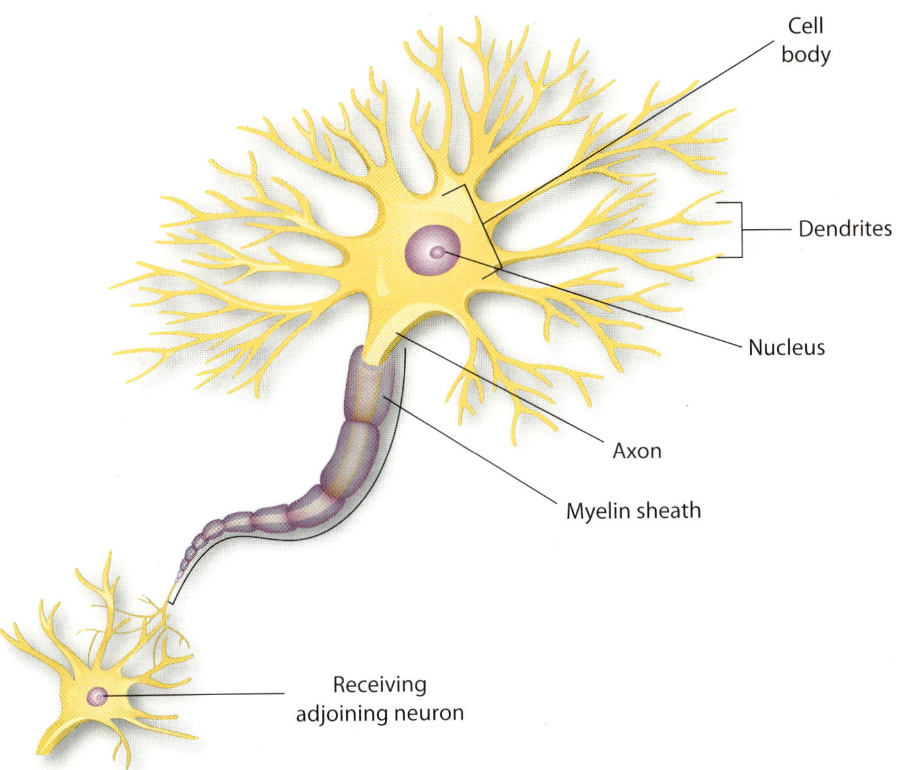

Figure 2.2 Anatomy of a Neuron.
Notice the myelin sheath; this is an important component of the neuron. The neuron is floating in a chemical soup that includes transmitters.

self-actualization the process of fulfilling one's potential in a way that shows concern for society.

You can think of the brain as a mass of these neurons. This mass has two sides, or hemispheres. The left hemisphere is biased toward language, analytical, and sequential processing. The right hemisphere is biased toward spatial, holistic, and integrative processing (Hopkins & Cantalupo, 2008). Within each hemisphere there are specialized regions. However, there is no such thing as a single place where complex functions, like vision or language, occur. Most tasks use both hemispheres (Byrnes & Fox, 1998). The brain is a collection of systems that are interconnected. The particular function of a region in the brain depends on which systems it belongs to and where it is in the system. We will briefly describe some key regions next:

1. The *brainstem* (midbrain and hindbrain) is part of the lower brain, which is believed to be an evolutionarily old region that regulates body functions like the sleep–wake cycle (Joseph, 2000). It develops around six weeks after conception. The *hypothalamus* is located in the midbrain. It regulates internal organs, hormones, body temperature, hunger, emotion, and many other activities. See Figure 2.3.
2. The *limbic system* is also part of the "old" brain. It sits like a donut on the brainstem. Three of its important structures are the *cingulate gyrus*, the *hippocampus*, and the *amygdala*. The limbic system is involved in emotion, attention, and motivation. The hippocampus is essential to memory. The cingulate gyrus is involved in problem solving.

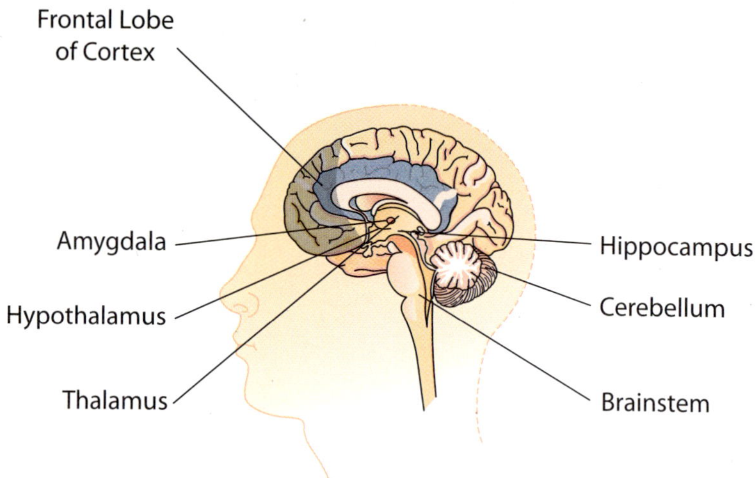

Figure 2.3 The Brain.
Notice that the prefrontal cortex sits just behind your forehead. This is the last area of your brain to reach maturity.

3. The *cerebellum* is a latticework of neurons at the back of the brain. It is involved in movement, muscle tone, concentration, and learning from errors. It works with the cortex in producing finely coordinated movements, like speech.
4. The *cerebral cortex*, or *neocortex*, is like a cap covering the other regions of the brain. It takes many years to develop fully. Complex functions like language and abstract thinking are coordinated in the cortex. The cerebral cortex has four lobes, or areas: frontal, parietal, temporal, and occipital. The frontal lobe is especially important for teachers to know about.
5. The *frontal lobe* is the largest part of the cortex and is disproportionately large in humans compared with other species. It is involved in organizing information in your mind as you read this text, resisting distraction, and inhibiting impulses. A portion of the frontal lobe, the *prefrontal cortex*, is particularly important in working memory and emotions, which you will read about in later chapters. The prefrontal cortex comprises about one-third of the entire cortex. It directs activity in other parts of the brain, like the conductor of a symphony (Huey, Krueger, & Grafman, 2006).

When a task activates the prefrontal cortex, it also activates the cerebellum. This is why cognitive and motor problems often go together. For example, poor balance or poor handwriting (i.e., motor problems) are found in more than half of students with ADHD. Motor problems are also found in students with dyslexia and autism. Thus, many, but not all, children in your classroom who have cognitive problems may also have motor problems (e.g., Roebers & Kauer, 2009).

Age does not bring changes in the overall structure of the brain, but it does bring changes in the brain's fine architecture and functioning. Let's look at age trends next.

Age Trends in Brain Development

The brain develops in an orderly way. The first areas to mature are involved in motor skills and basic senses, like vision. Next come language areas. Last to mature is the prefrontal cortex. Areas mature by increasing myelination, specializing, building connections, and pruning synapses (M. H. Johnson, Grossmann, & Kadosh, 2009). The brain also grows in volume across childhood; the cerebral cortex peaks in size by age 11 in girls and 15 in boys; the cerebellum peaks a couple of years later (Giedd et al., 2009).

Early Childhood (Prenatal to 5 Years)

The *prenatal* period, before birth, is critically important in brain development. Most of the neurons in the adult brain are produced before birth. Neurons proliferate, migrate to different areas, and develop specialized functions beginning just a few weeks after conception (Nowakowski & Hayes, 2002). Errors in this process can be caused by infection, malnutrition, or mother's alcohol use. **Myelination** begins during the last three months of pregnancy. Myelination increases the connections between key areas of the brain. Over the next five years, some areas of the prefrontal cortex will become more interconnected, which is linked to young children's increasing ability to follow rules, sit still, and raise their hands during group time (Bunge & Zelazo, 2006). However, the brain is capable of learning even before birth, such as infants learning to recognize their mothers' voice (Joseph, 2000).

myelination the development of myelin.

Glucose fuels the brain. At birth, glucose consumption rate is about two-thirds that of adults, but it increases steadily. The consumption of glucose indicates energy use in the brain. By 4 years of age, both **glucose rate** and blood flow to the cortex are *twice that of adults* (Chugani, 1998). This is a dramatic increase in energy demand in the cortex. In contrast, the brainstem remains fairly stable in glucose use across childhood.

glucose rate the rate of consumption of glucose, an indicator of energy use in the brain.

Another dramatic increase is the explosive growth of synapses. **Synaptogenesis** is an extreme overproduction of synapses that occurs from about three months before birth until about age 2 (see Figure 2.4). The number of brain cells does not increase substantially after birth, but there are many more neuron branches and synaptic connections between cells when children enter kindergarten than when they were born, and more than you have now. Preschoolers have more synapses than adults.

synaptogenesis a spurt in synaptic connections of the brain that occurs from the third trimester of gestation until about 2 years of age.

Why would young children have more synapses than you? Your neurons have been "pruned" of their branches. Pruning is not random. It is based on experience. When enough electrical signals are sent to a synapse, and the chemical environment of the synapse is favorable, the synapse gets stronger. If neurons are repeatedly activated together, they form stable circuits; *those that are not used are pruned.* A cliché you may hear is, "Neurons that fire together wire together." When you interact with your students in ways that cause specific neurons to fire together often, you influence which brain cells remain connected; you contribute to the final architecture of your students' brains.

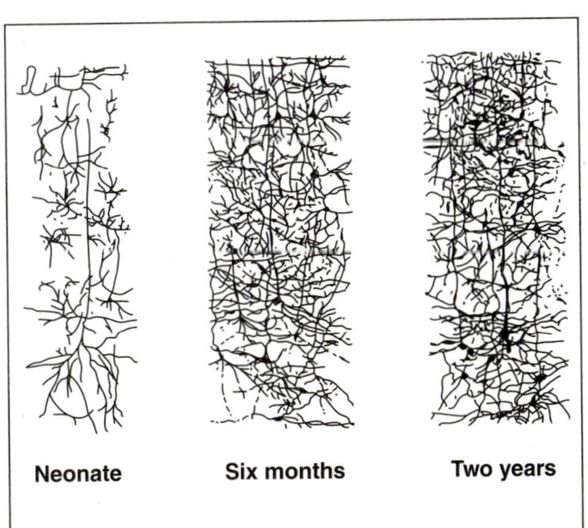

Figure 2.4 Synaptogenesis. The remarkable increase in neuron connections across the synapses in the first 2 years allow the brain to be shaped by experience.

Middle Childhood (6 to 12 Years)

Glucose rate in the brain tends to plateau at twice the rate of adults until 9 to 10 years of age. After this, it gradually *declines.* Synaptic proliferation also plateaus during middle childhood. These changes suggest the brain is becoming

sensitive period a biologically determined time period, typically early in life, in which a child readily develops specific abilities. Change is less likely before or after the sensitive period.

more efficient. Some neuroscientists believe the first ten years may be a **sensitive period** in brain development (see Chapter 6), because the child's brain is twice as active as an adult's (American Academy of Pediatrics, 1999).

Adolescence (13 to 19 Years)

The brain becomes even more efficient in adolescence. Glucose rate slows to adult levels at 16–18 years, indicating less energy use. There are three key changes that make the brain more efficient: (1) Different areas of the brain become more interconnected. (2) Pruning continues—synapses in the frontal cortex diminish to adult levels. (3) Myelination of the prefrontal cortex increases. Axons gradually get thicker from ages 4 to 17, particularly in speech and motor-skill areas. Both myelination and thick axons make information flow more quickly and precisely (Giedd et al., 2009; Paus, 2005). By mid-adolescence, your students have adult-like memory and information processing ability.

There is also a chemical shift in the adolescent brain. Some neurotransmitters are reduced, but dopamine increases (Spear, 2000). Dopamine affects motivation by changing how rewarding something feels, like driving fast or listening to loud music. Adolescents in many species, including humans, increase in social interaction, sensation seeking, and risk taking, perhaps due to this chemical shift. These increases may help with leaving the home nest, but in excess can be a problem. Dopamine is also linked to psychopathology, such as depression (see Chapter 8), and many mental illnesses emerge in adolescence. The combination of risk taking and mental illness has led some people to perpetuate negative stereotypes of teens by blaming the adolescent brain. Some psychologists counterargue that teens who use drugs, are promiscuous, or commit crimes are just imitating adult models (Bessant, 2008; Males, 2009).

Nevertheless, adolescent brain development does present a challenge. Dopamine increases in *early* adolescence (before about age 16), but the prefrontal cortex does not fully mature until *late* adolescence or the mid-20s. The prefrontal cortex controls other thinking processes. It is involved in reasoning, impulse control, motor coordination, controlling emotions, weighing risks with rewards, and long-term planning. Can you see the potential problem? Young teens may see risky behaviors as overly rewarding before they have adult-like self-control (Steinberg, 2009). For example, when a group of boys are discussing racing their bikes down the stadium bleachers, younger teen brains are more likely to register "Great FUN! Let's do it!" whereas older teen brains are likely to register "maybe a little bit fun, but not enough to risk breaking my neck."

> ***Think About This*** The tendency for young teens to view risky behavior as overly rewarding before they have fully developed self-control has implications for many social policies. Discuss how this might affect age-based policies like when youth can get a driver's license, buy alcohol, vote, enter the military, or be tried as an adult for crimes.

Are adult brains, like yours, done developing? Animal research shows that adult brains continue to develop; they can grow synapses, dendrites, and supportive tissue like blood vessels as a result of learning (Kolb & Whishaw, 1998). However, early life experience may have disproportionate influence on brain architecture because it literally dictates the basic framework.

Individual Diversity in Brain Development

We have discussed brain structure and age trends as though all brains develop similarly. There is *general* similarity in size, shape, and location of specific brain structures from one child to another. However, there are individual differences in synaptic pruning, myelination, and other factors.

What Do Individual Differences in the Brain Predict?

Brain differences may explain intelligence. That is, more intelligent people have faster neural response and do not have to consume as much glucose to solve a problem (Sternberg & Kaufman, 1998). Brain differences may also explain social and emotional abilities. To help you understand this, let's look at stress reactivity and behavioral inhibition, because they are the basis of abilities you will learn about in later chapters.

Stress reactivity

When a student feels stress, the hypothalamus secretes a hormone that causes the body to produce **cortisol**. Cortisol, in turn, alters energy level, emotions, learning, and immune functioning. Children differ in how easily this stress response is activated based on density of neurons and amount of chemicals in their brains. Children who have an *underreactive* stress response—perhaps because their brains have adapted to chronic stress within their families—tend to be aggressive, impulsive, delinquent, and have ADHD (Blair, Granger, & Razza, 2005; van Goozen, Fairchild, & Harold, 2008). They do not feel stress as readily as other children and so are not as deterred by the negative consequences of their misbehavior. Children who have an *overreactive* stress response tend to have depression, anxiety, or anorexia (Susman, Dorn, Inoff-Germain, Nottelman, & Chrousos, 1997). They have higher levels of cortisol after mildly stressful events, such as a six-minute discussion with their parents about getting homework done (Granger, Weisz, McCracken, & Ikeda, 1996). Balance is ideal; a little cortisol helps you focus attention and control thought and emotion.

cortisol a hormone that the body generates as a response to stress.

Behavioral inhibition

Children with an overreactive stress response may have behavioral inhibition, or a tendency to avoid new people, events, or objects. In social situations, behavioral inhibition is commonly called shyness. Inhibited children's hearts speed up, pupils dilate, muscles tense, and cortisol starts flowing during mild stress more than other children's do (Schmidt & Fox, 2002). When you see shy students hang back in your classroom, it is likely that their hearts are racing.

Behavioral inhibition is linked to brain differences. Inhibited children have more electrical activity in the right hemisphere and less in the left as early as 4 months of age (Hane, Fox, Henderson, & Marshall, 2008). Children with more *right* hemisphere activity tend to become inhibited toddlers who cry at separation from their mother, or shy older students whose hearts pound when they have to make a class presentation (Davidson, 2000). On the other hand, children with more *left* activity tend to be outgoing. The left frontal lobe is involved in positive emotions and approaching novel things.

In summary, individual differences in brain function are linked to intelligence, coping with stress, and greeting strangers, as well as many other outcomes. Let's discuss next where these brain differences may come from.

What Predicts Individual Differences in Brain Development?

Brain differences occur in infancy and have a biological base, so you might assume they are caused by genes. This is not necessarily true. They may be caused by differences in experience. The brain adapts to experience, so that experience becomes biology. Both nature and nurture shape the brain.

Genetics

In coming chapters you will learn that most traits have some heritability. Heritability presumably works through genetically caused brain differences. The size of some areas of the brain may be 60 to 80% heritable (Giedd et al., 2009). However, as you learned in Chapter 1, there are not enough genes to specify the precise architecture of the quadrillions of synapses in the brain. Instead genes tell the brain to overproduce synapses and then prune them. *The purpose of synaptogenesis is to capture experience and incorporate it into brain architecture.* This is genetically efficient—it requires fewer genes than if all important connections had to be precisely coded in the genes (Thompson & Nelson, 2001).

Experience

brain plasticity the brain's ability to change structure and function as a result of experience.

The brain's ability to change as a result of experience is known as **brain plasticity**. Brain plasticity has been studied more in animals than in humans. For example, in monkeys each finger is served by a different area in the cortex. If a monkey loses a finger, the cortex reorganizes itself so the neurons in the area that once served the missing finger now respond to the adjacent fingers instead (Beatty, 2001). Also, when monkeys are trained to pick up a small object from a cup, the cortex area for that finger increases. Human brains also respond to experience—jugglers and musicians develop greater density in areas of the brain related to those skills (Paus, 2005). Similarly, in blind people the area of the brain that processes vision adapts to process other things instead (Amedi, Merabet, Bermpohl, & Pascual-Leone, 2005). Much of the cortex is *not* dedicated to a specific function and can adapt to other functions.

Is there an age when the brain no longer responds to experience? There is a subtle, gradual diminishing in the brain's plasticity. Learning is not equally easy over time (Thomas & Johnson, 2008). This is why early deprivation can have long-lasting effects in spite of later intervention. Plasticity begins to be lost at about 10 years of age. For example, if there is damage to the language areas of the brain before age 10, there is better recovery of language skills than if damage occurs after age 10. The ability to acquire language is not completely lost after age 10, but the potential is diminished. The plasticity of children's brains may help them learn subjects like algebra or second languages more efficiently than adults (Luna, 2004). However, keep in mind that the brain remains plastic across the life span to some extent, or you could not be learning about child development right now.

Experiences that shape the brain can include *biological* factors. We will discuss the role of exercise, nutrition, sleep, and drug exposure later in the chapter. Experiences can also include *social* factors. We will focus on three social factors next—attachment, stress, and stimulating environments—that are relevant to you as a teacher.

First, attachment powerfully affects the developing brain. *Attachment* is an enduring relationship between children and caregivers. Insecure attachment, and the chronic anxiety that goes with it, can alter brain chemistry. It may also lead to a poorly developed, inefficient right cortex (Schore, 2000). This area regulates emotions. Thus, the kind of relationship you have with children as a parent or teacher may shape children's brains. You will learn more about how to have healthy attachments in Chapter 6.

Field Observation

Interview two bilingual people who acquired a second language by living in a different country. Choose one individual who acquired the second language after age 10 and one who acquired it in toddlerhood. Is there a difference in how difficult the language was to acquire? Is there a difference in current fluency or accent?

Second, stress also powerfully affects the developing brain (Gunnar, 2000). In animals, stress early in life alters neurotransmitters in the brain, which leads to strange social behavior and poor memory. We do not know all the effects stress has on humans because experiments are not ethical, but it is linked to smaller head size in children and faster aging of the brain when stressed children become adults (Gunnar, 1996; Nelson, 1999).

Third, stimulating environments promote brain development. In a classic experiment, Hebb and his students showed that when baby rats were raised in laboratory cages, they could not solve problems as adults as well as rats raised in more stimulating environments. The "more stimulating environment" was free range of his house with the enthusiastic help of his 7- and 5-year-old daughters (Forgays & Forgays, 1952; Hebb, 1949). Other researchers later found similar results in monkeys, chicks, mice, squirrels, and cats, although they used elaborate cages with toys rather than letting animals roam their houses. The brains of animals in stimulating cages have more chemical activity, a thicker cortex, larger synapses, more cells, more blood vessels, and more dendrites compared with the brains of isolated animals in barren cages (Kolb & Whishaw, 1998).

Enriched environments may also stimulate human brains. For example, people with a college education have more dendrites in the language area of the cortex than other people (Kolb & Whishaw, 1998). In addition, musicians who play string instruments have a larger fine-motor area than nonmusicians (Nelson, 1999). In contrast, in Chapter 14 you will learn that children in unstimulating orphanages have less brain activity than other children. This might be due to overpruning of the synapses (Nelson, 2007).

The key lesson is that brains are built over time by both genes and experience. Genes determine the basic architecture of the brain, but experience fine-tunes how circuits are formed.

Classroom Implications of Brain Development

"Brain-based education" has been a popular movement, with some claiming that neuroscience is revolutionizing education. Ironically, this movement has led to approaches that actually have no basis in science, such as teaching to the different "sides" of the brain or to brain-specific learning styles. Be cautious about claims for brain-based education. Some claims may be genuine, but experiments show that people are too ready to accept inadequate explanations when they are accompanied by statements like "brain scans indicate . . ." (Weisberg, Keil, Goodstein, Rawson, & Gray, 2008). The prestige of neuroscience is seductive, making information seem more legitimate or useful than it sometimes is (Steinberg, 2009).

Nevertheless, neuroscience has shown that some aspects of brain functioning are linked to school success. For example, mathematically gifted 8th- and 9th-graders have greater connection between the two hemispheres of their brains, relaying signals across hemispheres, than average students (Singh & O'Boyle, 2004). The problem is that neuroscientists do not know what causes this brain capacity, how to create this capacity in other children, or what it means for classroom instruction. That is, neuroscientists currently do not know enough about brain functioning to help you with specific educational practices in your classroom (Ansari & Coch, 2006; Varma,

McCandliss, & Schwartz, 2008). However, some broad implications for your role as a teacher are:

- Provide optimal experiences for your students, because experience alters the brain. Unfortunately, neuroscience cannot tell you precisely what classroom experiences are optimal (Thompson & Nelson, 2001). The "stimulating" environment of rats with well-developed brains simply mimicked their natural environment. This could mean that a merely "adequate" environment is ideal for children. In fact, children may be overstimulated by a "too-rich" environment filled with many distractions.
- Keep the brain well nourished. Throughout the day your students need plenty of oxygen (stretching, movement) and glucose to fuel the brain. In the opening vignette, Mrs. Z found that providing a snack improved her students' ability to stay on task. Teachers at the secondary level may need to give special emphasis to keeping their students nourished, because teens often skip lunch.
- Reduce stress at school by creating nurturing and predictable environments. Early, frequent stress interferes with learning and may lead to aggression and negative emotions. Children with chronically high levels of cortisol have more cognitive, motor, and social delays than other children (American Academy of Pediatrics, 1999).
- Give children repetitive practice of important skills in order to strengthen synaptic connections.
- Capitalize on young teens' hyper-response to rewards by emphasizing the rewards of learning and appropriate behavior. Capitalize on older teens' reasoning and planning abilities by emphasizing the implications of learning and appropriate behavior for their futures.
- Advocate for early childhood education. The first ten years of life are a sensitive period in brain development. By the time children enter elementary schools, half of that period is over. This period when children are avid learners could be more fully exploited for many children whose first five years are spent in unstimulating environments. Preschoolers are capable of learning skills in language, mathematics, music, and art when taught in developmentally appropriate ways.

The importance of early childhood for brain development is not a myth, but it is sometimes exaggerated. Early childhood education has rightfully benefited from media attention on early brain development and the push to provide quality programs for young children. However, remediation is possible, and quality programs are needed for struggling students at older ages as well (Thompson & Nelson, 2001).

In summary, the new view from neuroscience is that actions, thoughts, and experiences alter the brain, rather than genes strictly dictating brain development (Stiles, 2009). In Chapter 1 you learned that genes and environment interact to affect development. In Chapter 6 you will learn the latest remarkable research showing that experience can change genes, so stay tuned. The key message is that what happens in your classroom can alter your students' brain development. Let's turn now to other aspects of physical development that also have implications for your classroom.

Growth and Motor Development

At age 4 Benji said to his mother: "I'm all growed up now." A little surprised, his mother asked how he knew this. He replied, "Cuz I can cross the street all by myself; I can turn on the light all by myself; and I have hair on my arm just like Daddy—so I'm growed up."

Ben is now 16. He is 100 pounds heavier and four feet taller. Not only can he reach the light switch, he now has the coordination to wire an electric circuit. Not only can he cross the street, he now drives a car on it. Yet, he is still not quite "growed up" because he has not reached the final stage of puberty. The next two years will bring a few more inches of height and more muscle mass. In this section we discuss normal growth and motor development.

Growth refers to changes in height, weight, and body composition. *Motor development* refers to changes in control and proficiency in movement. At first, infants have very little motor control, but will develop *fine* motor skills. These involve small muscle movements, like picking up a bean. They will also develop *gross* motor skills. These involve large muscle movements, like walking or throwing.

Age Trends in Growth and Motor Development

Rate of growth changes with age. The U.S. Centers for Disease Control and Prevention (CDC) publishes growth charts indicating what height and weight are average at each age. Figure 2.5 illustrates this growth. Quality of movement also increases with age.

Early Childhood (Prenatal to 5 Years)

The last three months of pregnancy are primarily a period of rapid growth, because most major body structures already function. Normal birth size can range from 5.5 to 10 pounds, but birth size does not predict adult size. For example, one of our sons was born very large, weighing 9.3 pounds, but he grew to be about average in height. However, size at age 4 strongly correlates ($r = 0.80$) with adult size (Tanner, 1985); that is, tall 4-year-olds will likely become tall adults.

Growth is dramatic in early childhood. After birth, infants gain more than a pound a month so that birth weight is doubled by 5 months of age. Infants grow about ten inches in the first year, five inches in the second year, and have doubled their birth height by age 3 to 4 years (Rogol, Roemmich, & Clark, 2002). Then, rate of growth slows to about three inches in height and four pounds per year. See Figure 2.6.

Motor development during early childhood is as dramatic as growth (see Table 2.1). Newborns cannot grasp a toy you hold in front of them, but four years later they can throw a ball or stack cubes. The toddler's "drunken sailor" walk becomes a stable, smooth movement by 4 years of age, similar to the quality of adults' walk.

Middle Childhood (6 to 12 Years)

Growth in middle childhood is less dramatic than in infancy, but keeps to an average of two to three inches and five to six pounds per year for both boys and girls until

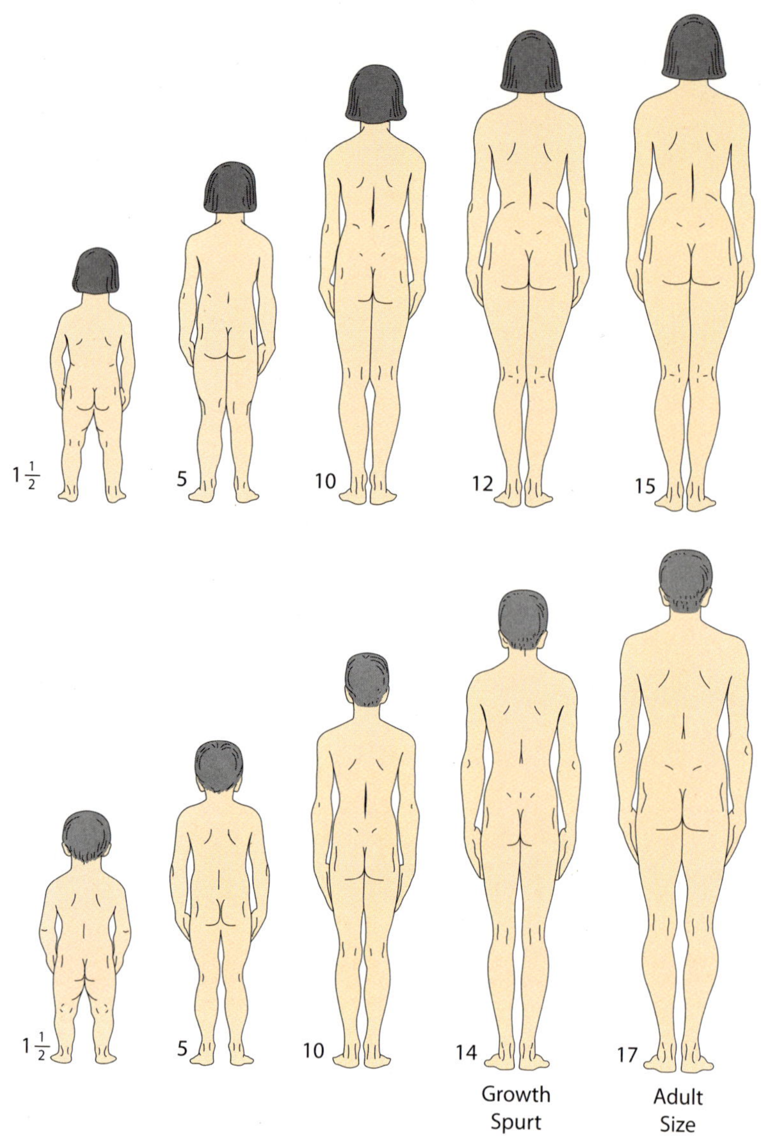

Figure 2.5 Growth in Boys and Girls from 1 to 17 Years.
What do you notice about change in proportion and shape, as well as size? *Tanner (1973).*

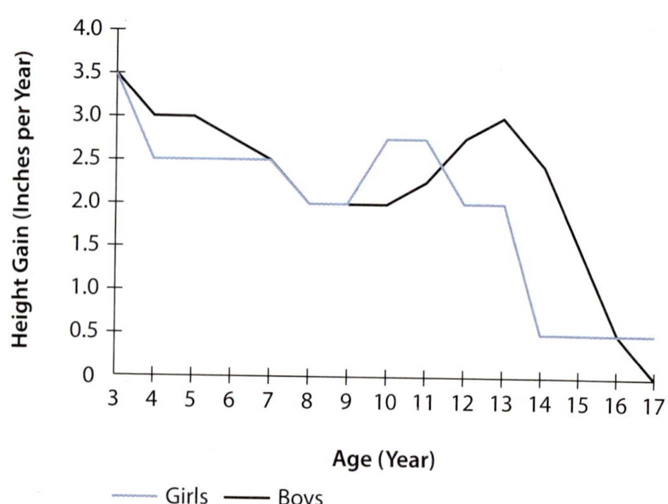

Figure 2.6 Rate of Growth for Boys and Girls by Age.
What conclusions would you draw about how the rate of growth changes across childhood? At what age do girls and boys diverge in growth patterns? At what age do girls and boys have their adolescent growth spurt? *National Center for Health Statistics (2000).*

Table 2.1 Motor milestones from infancy to 10 years

Age	Fine Motor Skill	Gross Motor Skill
2–3 months	Sweeping or batting motions with the arm	Hold head up Roll from stomach to side
4–6 months	Hold objects in the palms with all fingers	Sit without support Reach for feet to play with them
6–10 months	Use thumb and index finger to pick up small objects—known as "pincer grasp" Bang objects together across chest Poke with index finger	Crawl or creep Sit up without help Roll from back to stomach Stand while holding onto objects, then pull to standing
10–14 months	Drink from cup Turn pages of book Stack two cubes	Walk with support, then walk independently
15–24 months	Use spoon or fork Scribble Stack three cubes Hold pencil with all four fingers, forming a fist around it. Movement of the pencil comes from the shoulder.	Squat to pick up objects Walk up stairs Run, but stiff legged Climb up on furniture Kick ball Throw ball with overhead motion
2–4 years	Unscrew lids Put puzzle pieces together Roll clay into shapes Grasp toward the tip of the pencil Print recognizable letters. Letters are large, uppercase, uneven, and get larger toward the end of a word. Draw "tadpole" people	Squat in play Walk down stairs Run forward Jump with both feet Walk on tiptoe Begin to stand on one foot Ride tricycle Begin to catch a bouncing ball
5–7 years	Zip zippers and lace shoes Able to learn to play piano or violin Control pencil with the finger and thumb. Movement comes from the elbow. Write and draw with more control, but writing looks choppy and uneven. Letters are getting smaller. Uppercase letters are somewhat mastered, but lowercase letters continue to be challenging through 3rd grade, especially letters with slants or curves.	Hop Skip on alternating feet Jump rope Walk on a balance beam Throwing, catching, and kicking become smoother Begin to participate in organized games (e.g., hopscotch) and sports (e.g., soccer or baseball) Skate, ski, bike, and other specialized skills with training
10 years	Pencils are controlled by rotating the forearm and bending the index finger less when writing. Properly spacing letters is mastered around 4th grade.	Fully participates in sports; can do same activities as adults but has less strength and somewhat less coordination

Note: These are approximate age trends. Do not use this table for diagnosis of delays. The online Additional Resources lists websites that give more information about motor delays if there is a child you are concerned about.

Adapted from Payne & Issacs (1994) and Johnson & Blasco (1997).

puberty (Rogol et al., 2002). Growth is not consistent across the year; children grow more in the spring. In addition, rate of growth slows just before puberty.

Quality of fine motor skills increases dramatically in middle childhood. This is why the writing of a 1st-grader is clearly distinguishable from an adult's (see Figure 2.7). There is also improvement, although less dramatic, in speed, agility, and control of gross motor skills like jumping, throwing, balancing, and hanging (Malina, Bouchard, & Bar-Or, 2004). One of the amusing aspects of teaching 1st-graders is how often they

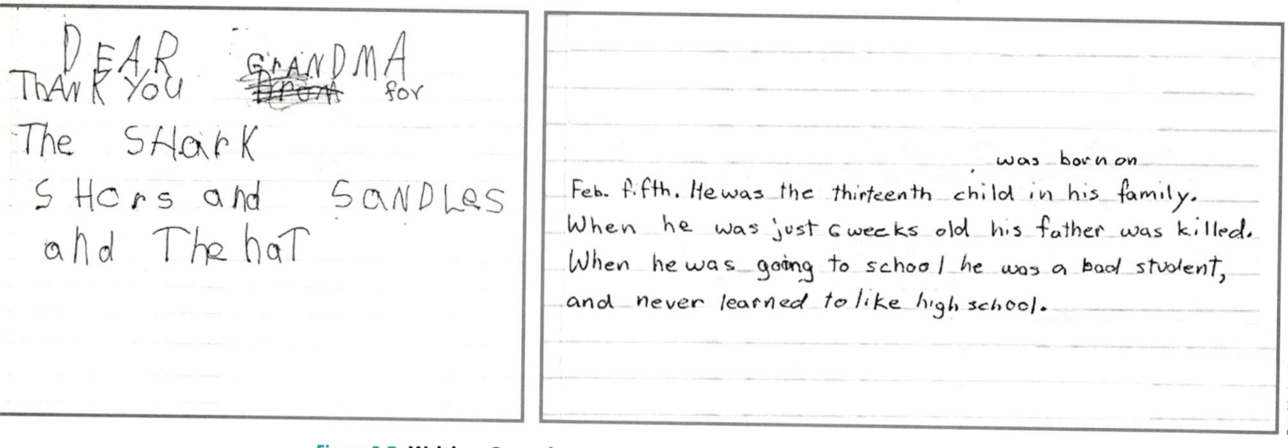

Figure 2.7 Writing Samples.
These writing samples are from the same boy, at ages 6 and 10. The first note says, "Dear Grandma thank you for the shark shorts and sandals and the hat." What attributes in his writing have changed over the four years?

fall out of their seats. They have trouble raising their hand while maintaining balance in their seat. During middle childhood they will become better at coordinating movement with perception so they can maintain balance, catch a ball, or write their name (Thelen, 1995). They will also become coordinated enough to play sports like baseball and games-with-rules like hopscotch and tag.

Many people believe preschoolers are the most active of any age. Actually, physical activity peaks in middle childhood. Motion recorders (actometers) strapped to arms and legs have been used to record round-the-clock movement in people from toddler age to young adults. Results indicate that movement increases from infancy, peaks at ages 7 to 9 years, and then decreases (see Figure 2.8).

Figure 2.8 Activity Level by Age.
Dots represent children, showing wide individual differences. The line represents the average for each age. What age is the most active on average? *Eaton, McKeen, & Campbell (2001).*

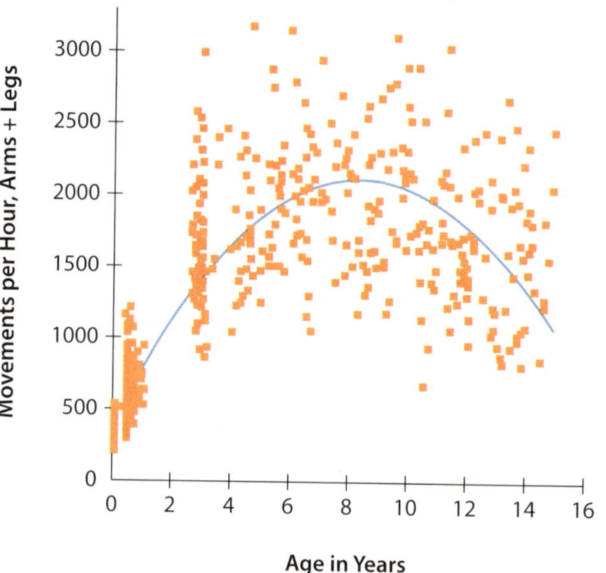

Adolescence (13 to 19 Years)

Adolescents experience a dramatic spurt or acceleration in growth (refer back to Figure 2.6). The timing and speed of the adolescent growth spurt varies. Variation in this spurt does not correlate with final adult height. That is, teens who spurt early do not necessarily become taller adults.

Does this growth spurt make adolescents clumsy? Not for most. However, 20 to 25% of teens may decline in athletic performance and balance during the spurt, particularly boys, but it is temporary (Beunen & Malina, 1988). You may have heard the adage "trip over their own feet" to describe adolescent clumsiness. For example, during his adolescent growth spurt one of our sons tripped three times just walking across the kitchen. He'd jump up, with a sheepish grin, and say, "I meant to do that!" At the same time, he was a varsity athlete, the clumsiness only lasted a few months, and bleeding was minimal, so we weren't too concerned!

Think About This Children's movement peaks at the same age when there is a peak in diagnosis of ADHD—around 7 to 9 years. What might this mean for whether you view hyperactivity as normal or pathological? What might this imply for the structure of school at this age?

Puberty

The adolescent growth spurt is part of **puberty**, which refers to physical changes that occur as children move into adulthood. The changes include:

puberty physical changes that occur as children move into adulthood, including development of primary and secondary sex characteristics and capacity for reproduction.

1. The growth spurt.
2. Changes in proportion of muscle and fat. Girls develop more fat in the thighs, and boys develop more fat in the upper body.
3. Development of primary sex characteristics, such as testes in males and ovaries in females.
4. Sexual maturation, such as menarche, or first menstruation, for girls and spermarche, or first ejaculation, for boys.
5. Development of secondary sex characteristics (Shirtcliff, Dahl, & Pollak, 2009). Girls follow this sequence: acne, breast development, height increase, pubic hair, weight increase, and finally menarche. Boys follow this sequence: testicular growth, height increase, pubic hair, strength spurt, spermarche, voice change, and finally facial hair. For boys, puberty also brings hormone changes and increased cardiovascular capacity that enhance athletic skills.

Puberty is a *gradual process* over several years. Puberty is not sudden, as though a switch were turned on. It is also not just menarche for girls or spermarche for boys, but begins much earlier. Newborns have elevated sex hormones that drop off after a few months and stay low for several years. Then at 6 to 11 years of age—or around 4th grade—*adrenarche* begins, which is the maturation of the adrenal glands. These glands secrete androgens. During adrenaarche children develop body odor, oily skin, and pubic hair; have mini growth spurts; and have some external genitalia change. The hormones then plateau until *gonadarche* triggers another rise in hormones to the adult level. Gonadarche brings the final maturation of the testes or ovaries, which secrete the hormones estrogen (girls) or androgen (boys).

While height spurts can occur rapidly, and menarche or spermarche occur suddenly, other developments like breast or testicle growth tend to take three to five years (Archibald, Graber, & Brooks-Gunn, 2003). On average, menarche occurs for girls at ages 12 to 13 and spermarche for boys at ages 14 to 15 (Chumlea et al., 2003; Rogol et al., 2002). Thus, you can think of puberty as hormonally starting about 6 to 8 years of age and finishing about 15 to 22 years of age. Youth of the same age can vary radically in their phase of puberty.

Individual Diversity in Growth and Motor Skills

The age trends just described in growth and motor development are averages, but there are large differences among children. For example, most children learn to walk around 12 months of age, but anywhere between 9 and 17 months is normal. Our first child began walking at 8 months. Our second child began walking at 14 months—a difference of six months!

What Do Individual Differences in Growth and Motor Skills Predict?

You might assume that early walkers are more intelligent. This is not true. *Within normal ranges*, early motor development does not reflect intelligence. However, when children fail to develop within the normal age range, or develop unusual patterns of movement, they may have cognitive problems as well.

Motor, cognitive, and social problems may occur together because they share an underlying neurological problem, such as the link between ADHD and motor skills you learned about earlier. In addition, serious motor delays can cause other delays because children learn about the world through movement. For example, an infant crawls with gusto toward a toy to see it better, touch it, grab it, bang it, and put it in the mouth. Motor skills make it possible for children to connect with other people. Motor skills also make possible other abilities—like talking, reading, and writing—that are critical for school success. That is why pediatricians routinely note motor milestones at checkups.

Pediatricians also routinely measure children. This is because when children fail to grow within normal ranges, there may be problems. One type of growth problem is being born very small, which is linked to later school problems. This is discussed in Box 2.2. Another type of problem is going through puberty unusually early or late.

Girls who mature earlier than their peers are more likely to have behavior problems, experience depression, use drugs, and view themselves as less attractive than later-maturing girls (Ge & Natsuaki, 2009). Even within families, girls who mature early may be more likely to use drugs than their twin sisters (Dick, Rose, Viken, & Kaprio, 2000). Early maturing may lead to associating with older boys, dating, and promiscuous sexual activity. However, girls who mature early are not any different in academic achievement than on-time peers. To be late in puberty is not ideal either. Late-maturing girls experience more depression than on-time peers.

Early and late maturing can also be a challenge for boys, but effects are inconsistent and short-lived. For example, body image is poor for late-maturing boys, but it improves by late adolescence. Still, early- and late-maturing boys are more likely to be depressed and use drugs than on-time peers (Ge et al., 2003).

Early maturing has negative outcomes, primarily for children who already have other problems. That is, early maturing alone may not cause negative outcomes, but it can magnify difficulties for children who have risk factors like harsh parents, a poor parent–child relationship, a poor neighborhood, or a move to a new school (Ge, Brody, Conger, Simons, & Murry, 2002).

Challenges in Development Box 2.2

Low Birth Weight

Low birth weight (LBW) is defined as less than 5.5 pounds (2,500 grams). About 8% of infants are LBW—14% of Black infants, but 6–8% of other ethnic groups.* The most common cause of low birth weight is being born before thirty-seven weeks of gestation, or preterm. However, infants can also be small for their gestational age (SGA), regardless of whether they are preterm or not. Infants who are *both* preterm and SGA are at greater risk than infants who are preterm but of normal size. LBW, SGA, and prematurity are each risk factors, and they often occur together.

Another common cause of LBW is mothers' drug use during pregnancy. LBW is also linked to being a twin, having a teenage mother, and having a stressed mother during pregnancy, which reduces blood to the fetus (DiPietro, 2004; FIFCFS, 2009). However, some infants are born preterm and/or SGA for unknown reasons, despite mothers' careful prenatal care.

Why Does It Matter if Infants Are Born Small? LBW, SGA, and prematurity are associated with many developmental problems, including:†

- Somewhat smaller size, including head size, into adolescence.
- Delayed motor development. There may be catch-up for some children, but motor delays are often evident at school age.
- Socioemotional problems such as difficulty controlling emotions and behavior, low self-esteem, and peer rejection, particularly for boys.
- Cognitive problems such as low IQ, poor memory, slow processing speed, and attention deficits.
- School problems such as low math and reading test scores, learning disabilities (particularly math), grade retention, and special education placement.

These problems are detectable in infancy through adolescence, although some problems may become more pronounced in early adolescence (S. Rose & Feldman, 2000; Taylor, Klein, & Hack, 2000).

*For updated statistics see the Center for Disease Control's "Child Trends DataBase" website, or the FIFCFS' "Childstats" website.
†There are many studies that support these conclusions, just a few of which are listed here (Aarnoudse-Moens, Weisglas-Kuperus, van Goudoever, & Oosterlaan, 2009; Blair, 2001; Clark, Woodward, Horwood, & Moor, 2008; Goosby & Cheadle, 2009; Li-Grining, 2007).

The lower the birth weight, the greater the likelihood of these problems (Aarnoudse-Moens, Weisglas-Kuperus, van Goudoever, & Oosterlaan, 2009). That is, infants weighing 1.5 pounds tend to achieve less in school than infants weighing 3.5 pounds. They are also more likely to have serious medical problems such as bleeding in the head or lung disease, and immature myelination and brain development (e.g., Clark, Woodward, Horwood, & Moor, 2008).

Not all LBW, SGA, or preterm infants will develop problems. Thanks to improvement in neonatal medicine, even very LBW children may now fare well (Rickards, Kelly, Doyle, & Callanan, 2001). In one study, 32% of infants weighing 1.5 pounds or less did not develop obvious problems (Taylor, Klein, Minich, & Hack, 2000). LBW children fare worse if they have both medical problems and insensitive parents (Landry, Smith, Miller-Loncar, & Swank, 1997).

Think About This Across countries, the effect size for very LBW infants doing more poorly than other children in math, reading, spelling, and controlling attention was 0.43 to 0.76 (Aarnoudse-Moens et al., 2009). What does this mean? Should you assume that your students who were born very small will have problems in your classroom? Defend your answer using what you learned about research and effect sizes in Chapter 1.

What Can Be Done to Help LBW Children? A good home environment can do much to compensate for LBW (Goosby & Cheadle, 2009). LBW children may develop well if they have responsive, sensitive caregivers and a stimulating home. Thus, one way to help LBW children is to improve quality of parenting. This needs to occur early, because the gap in academic achievement is already in place at school entry.

Improving quality of parenting is difficult. The government funded a large, national study—the Infant Health and Development Program—to improve development of LBW preterm infants. The intervention was intense: two to four home visits per month, daily high-quality child care, and parenting classes for parents of 1- to 3-year-olds. Preschool effects looked promising, but by 8 years of age, effects were very small. Still, at 18 years, some intervention children had higher math test scores (but not reading or IQ) than the control group (McCormick et al., 2006).

A few simpler programs have shown promise. One of these is called "Kangaroo Care." The tiny infants are positioned

(continued)

Challenges in Development *(continued)*

on the mother's chest with direct skin-to-skin contact, like a kangaroo, rather than in incubators to regulate their temperature (Feldman, Weller, Sirota, & Eidelman, 2002). Another approach is to massage infants (T. M. Field, Hernandez-Reif, & Freedman, 2004). Breastfeeding is another simple, yet particularly important intervention for preterm infants.

Implications for Teachers. Some LBW students may have difficulties in understanding arithmetic, grasping new concepts, and thinking flexibly. These difficulties occur as early as kindergarten and continue or grow worse as schoolwork gets more abstract in high school (Aarnoudse-Moens et al., 2009; Goosby & Cheadle, 2009). The students may need more time processing classroom tasks and help with organizing work. However, not all LBW students will have these difficulties. Other risk factors, such as a single mother with a low education level, have a stronger effect than birth weight (Breslau, Johnson, & Lucia, 2001; Goosby & Cheadle, 2009). Many more students are in special education due to environmental risk than to LBW.

As a teacher you can help children avoid the pitfalls of early puberty by conveying that being "different" is only temporary—their peers will catch up to them. You may also need to help girls deal with sexual harassment. Most importantly, you can treat them as the children that they are; do not expect adult abilities even if they look like adults. An 11-year-old who is "fully developed" is still only an 11-year-old.

What Predicts Individual Differences in Growth and Motor Skills?

There are many factors that influence growth and motor development. We will discuss four here—genes, exercise, nutrition, and quality of parent–child relationships.

Genes

In 1925 Arnold Gesell identified an orderly sequence of normal growth and motor development in young children. This is the foundation for "motor milestones" still used by pediatricians today. Gesell was a *maturationist*, meaning that he believed motor development was so strongly genetically programmed that the environment was not able to speed it up or slow it down.

There is some support for this maturationist view. For example, restricting infant's movements by strapping them to a cradle board, as Hopis once did, does not delay normal motor skills (Thelen, 1995). In addition, you learned in Chapter 1 that growth is strongly canalized. When a child is ill or undernourished to a degree that slows growth, growth may accelerate to catch up once the problem is resolved. Yet an extreme maturationist view is not entirely correct. While genes may dictate the basic sequence of physical development, children are susceptible to their environment. For example, a poor diet over several years will permanently retard growth. Thus, the environment contributes to physical development, as you will see next.

Exercise

Ardent maturationists, like Gesell, believe that there is no point in training children until they are developmentally ready to learn a skill. In 1935, Myrtle McGraw tested this belief in a famous study of twins named Johnny and Jimmy. The twins were children #6 and #7 in an American Irish-Catholic family that lived in five "dark, poorly ventilated rooms" heated by a single coal stove in the kitchen, as was typical of middle-class urban tenements then (McGraw, 1935, p. 35). The children played in the street, and the family was described as happy and intelligent. McGraw took the twins to her lab five days a week, from 1 to 26 months of age. They went home evenings and weekends. At the lab, Jimmy was kept in a crib, but Johnny was given special training in motor skills. Johnny learned these skills—reaching, swimming, climbing up a slide, and roller skating—at a younger age than Jimmy. However, Jimmy learned some skills at roughly the same age—walking, sitting up, and riding a tricycle. In addition, Jimmy learned some skills (e.g., roller skating) *more quickly* than Johnny when given a chance at an older age than Johnny.

The conclusion of this experiment was that you can speed children's motor development with exercise, but only to a limited extent. Older children will acquire motor skills at a faster rate, and some skills will not be mastered until there is biologically based maturation regardless of training. Ben, from our opening story, could not do a single pull-up when he was 14, although he tried hard. A year later, after puberty improved muscle mass, he could do seven pull-ups. Thus, there is a role for both exercise and maturation.

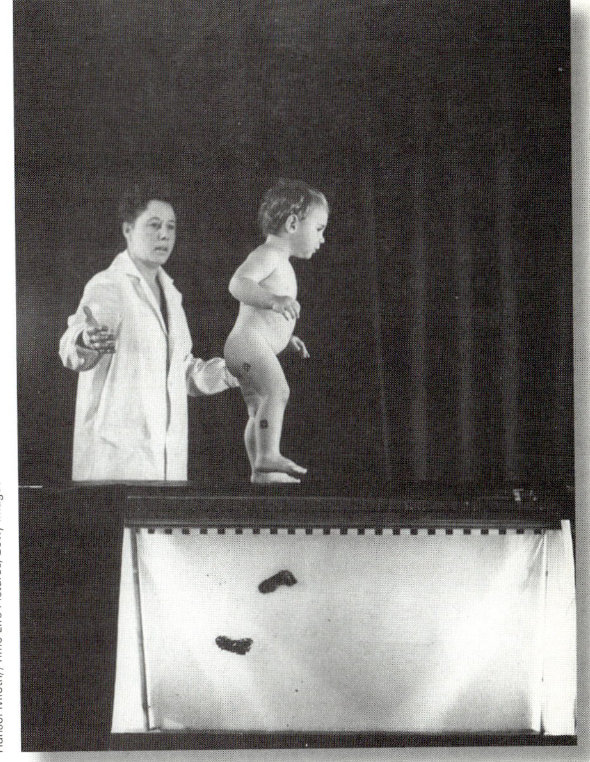
Hansel Mieth//Time Life Pictures/Getty Images

Myrtle McGraw observing one of the twins exercising.

Exercise does more than promote motor skills. It promotes brain functioning. Studies find that active, physically fit children control their attention better and have higher test scores than non-fit children, beyond the effects of IQ and SES (Castelli, Hillman, Buck, & Erwin, 2007; Hillman, Buck, Themanson, Pontifex, & Castelli, 2009). These studies are correlational, but randomized experiments (see Chapter 1) with adults also show that exercise causes better brain functioning. Perhaps this is because exercise promotes growth of brain cells (Woodlee & Schallert, 2006).

Exercise also improves strength and endurance, builds healthy bones and muscles, increases positive emotions, and reduces anxiety and stress. It can promote socializing with other children, as well as self-esteem and attractiveness (Malina, 1996). However, it is possible to overdo exercise. The intense training of elite, national-caliber child athletes can be stressful and disrupt peer relationships. It might also stunt growth, at least temporarily, but this effect is not always found (Rogol et al., 2002).

Unfortunately, many children do not exercise enough. The U.S. Surgeon General has called physical inactivity a major epidemic (Morrow, Jackson, & Payne, 1999). Many babies are deprived of exercise as they are increasingly "packaged," meaning that they spend much of their time in baby seats, strollers, and other equipment that keep them from moving. Preschoolers may be remarkably sedentary at school (W. H. Brown et al., 2009). Roughly 30% of adolescents do not get sufficient exercise (Grunbaum et al., 2002). Sufficient exercise is enough to make you sweat or breathe hard for more than twenty minutes, three times per week. On the other hand, 55% of adolescents participate in a team sport and do get plenty of exercise.

Nutrition

Undernutrition is the single most common cause of stunted growth in the world. Undernutrition delays puberty, while obesity accelerates it. Undernutrition is also associated with low intelligence, poor academic achievement, irritability, and apathy (Wachs, 2000). Undernutrition affects brain cell growth, neurotransmitters, and myelination.

The two most common nutritional deficiencies affecting the brain are iron and protein deficiencies. In the United States, toddlers and teenage girls are most at risk for iron deficiency; about 9% of them are iron deficient. Iron-deficient infants score about ten to twelve points lower on intelligence tests than other infants (Rao & Georgieff, 2000). Effects can be permanent if the deficiency occurs in pregnancy or early infancy, but if the deficiency occurs in later childhood, iron supplements can help. This is one of many reasons breastfeeding is important.

Breast milk has a unique profile of nutrients that meet an infant's needs. Substitutes, like formula, are adequate for growth, and babies do not need to be breastfed to develop a strong mother–child bond, but infants who are breastfed have some advantages, such as:[1]

- Fewer illnesses in infancy (e.g., diarrhea, earaches, asthma) as well as later in life (e.g., allergies, digestive problems).
- Lower rates of obesity later in childhood.
- Better problem-solving skills in infancy, and slightly higher intelligence test scores through young adulthood.
- Lower rates of depression in adolescence.

Health benefits to mother from breastfeeding include delayed menses, faster shedding of pregnancy pounds, lower risk of cancer, and healthier bones, as well as financial savings.

Scientists have tried to imitate breast milk, but have not been entirely successful. Specific fatty acids needed for brain growth are present in breast milk (Soliday, 2007). Formula-fed infants have less of these fatty acids in their brain. Experiments in which these fatty acids are added to formula have found that infants may develop better memory, attention, and problem solving, but the effects have not always been found; and there may be negative side effects, like increased infection (Drover et al., 2009).

Both the World Health Organization and the U.S. government are trying to increase breastfeeding. The U.S. goal is that infants exclusively get breast milk the first six months, and then breast milk plus additional foods with iron supplements until twelve months. This goal is not yet being met. There are many reasons mothers or infants cannot breastfeed. In addition, mothers who have specific illnesses like AIDS or who are drug-users should not breastfeed, because toxins can pass through the milk to the infant (American Academy of Pediatrics, 2001).

What should older children eat to be healthy? In 2005, the U.S. government released *MyPyramid* and *Dietary Guidelines for Americans*. The basic message is that children should eat well-balanced meals, augmented with healthy snacks such as fruits, vegetables, whole grains, and low-fat dairy products. (Sorry, but French fries,

---

[1]There are many studies that support these conclusions, just a few of which are listed here (Drover, Hoffman, Castañeda, Morale, & Birch, 2009; Jansen, de Weerth, & Riksen-Walraven, 2008; Kramer & Kakuma, 2004; Mortensen, Michaelsen, Sanders, & Reinisch, 2002; Soliday, 2007). See also the American Academy of Pediatrics (AAP), official policy statement of February 1, 2005, and the AAP website home page.

ketchup, and chips do not count as vegetables.) Ideally, less than 30% of calories would come from fat.

Based on these guidelines, most U.S. children eat too much fat and sugar and not enough fruits and vegetables. As children get older, their diet quality gets worse. About 27% of 2- to 5-year-olds, and less than 10% of 6- to 9-year-olds, have a good diet (Federal Interagency Forum on Child and Family Statistics [FIFCFS], 2009). Adolescent girls are less likely than boys to get sufficient milk, fruits, and vegetables, which can cause them to have inadequate calcium for their bones, which are still developing (Grunbaum et al., 2002). Carbonated soft drinks make matters worse. Teenage girls who drink such beverages have a higher risk of bone fracture than other girls, and greater risk for adult osteoporosis (Wyshak, 2000).

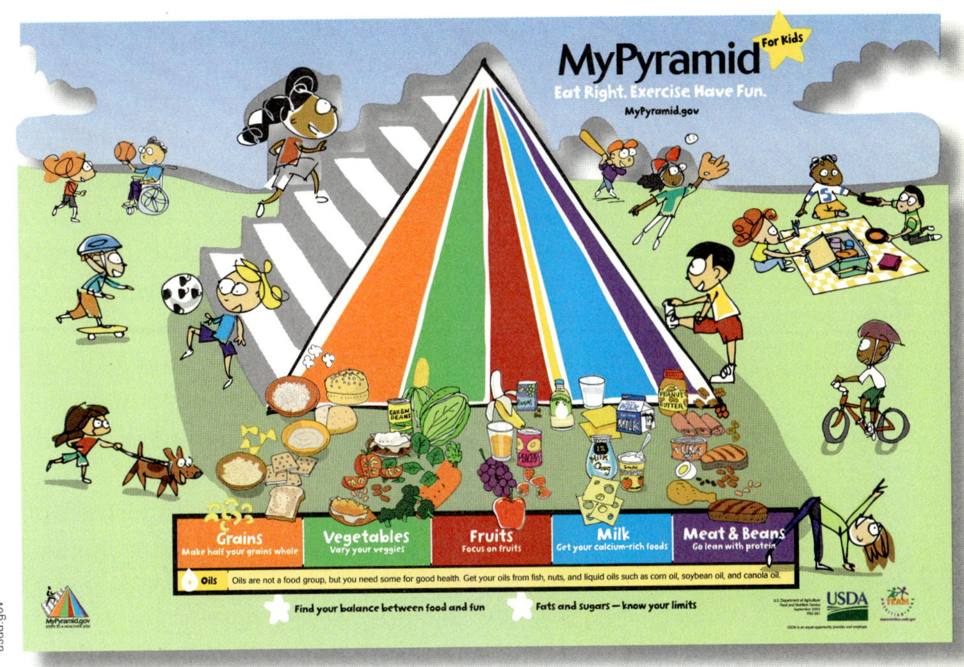

The U.S. Department of Agriculture's food pyramid. USDA's website: http://www.mypyramid.gov/Kids.

It is a common myth that sugar makes children "hyper." Research shows that sugary treats do not affect the behavior of typical children (Sciutto, Terjesen, & Bender Frank, 2000). This is an opportunity for a lesson on research. Early *correlational* studies found a link between sugar and overly active behavior. However, later research using well-controlled *experiments*, where the control group received a placebo instead of sugar, found no connection. The simplest explanation is that when children act wild during a class party, it is more likely due to having a party than due to sugar. However, some children may react to other chemicals in a sugary treat, such as caffeine or dyes.

Field Observation

Ask a few children to provide you with a diet "diary" of the past three days. How many servings of fruits did they eat daily (a serving is about half a cup)? What beverages did they choose? What did they know about nutrition? Try the same for your own diet.

Parent–child relationship

The effects of genes, exercise, and nutrition on physical development should not surprise you. However, you may be surprised to learn that parent–child relationships also affect physical development. A few decades ago physicians at Johns Hopkins Medical School had thirteen children between 3 and 11 years referred for growth failure. Their height was 30 to 66% of normal, which is a huge deficit. They had delayed speech and delayed walking. They had protruding stomachs. Yet, they were not malnourished. The children almost all stole food, gorged themselves (like eating a whole loaf of bread), and ate from garbage cans. The physicians suspected pituitary problems at first, but later realized the problem was the parents (Powell, Brasel, & Blizzard, 1967). Most of the children's parents abused alcohol, were promiscuous, and quarreled.

When the children were placed in a convalescent hospital, they grew rapidly. Their average growth in the hospital was 0.65 inch per month; the typical rate is 0.20

(see Figure 2.9). They also quit stealing food, their speech developed, and they appeared happier and less withdrawn. When the children were returned to their homes, growth slowed again. Similar growth failure occurs for children in bleak orphanages. Many children surge in growth when caregivers develop warmer relationships with children or when the children are adopted out of the orphanage (St. Petersburg–USA Orphanage Research Team, 2008).

Growth failure can also occur in less-extreme environments, such as those of children who are raised by their mother but have an insecure attachment to her (Valenzuela, 1990). Low-quality parenting is a key cause of **nonorganic failure to thrive**. This is a medical label for children who fail to grow adequately without any apparent medical reason. Children who have this condition may catch up to peers mentally once they begin school, but usually remain physically small (Boddy, Skuse, & Andrews, 2000).

nonorganic failure to thrive failure to grow adequately without any apparent medical reason.

Although poor parent–child relationships are linked to *delayed* growth, they are also linked to *accelerated* puberty. Girls experience puberty earlier in cold, harsh families, and in father-absent families where the mother is single, depressed, has conflict with her romantic partner, or exposes her daughter to a boyfriend (Archibald et al., 2003; Belsky, Steinberg, Houts, & Halpern-Felsher, 2010). In contrast, when fathers and mothers are affectionate and supportive, their daughters are likely to experience later puberty (Ellis & Essex, 2007).

Figure 2.9 Growth of a Boy from a Negative Home.
This boy was delayed in growth when brought to a medical center. At age 7 he looked like a substantially younger child. He grew dramatically after he was removed from his negative home.
Powell et al., (1967).

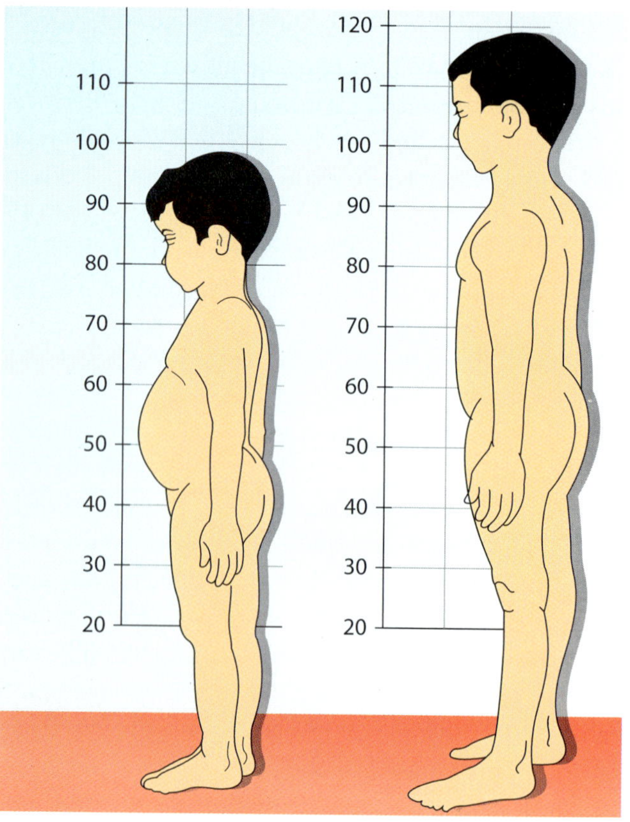

Group Diversity in Growth and Motor Development

There are strong gender differences in growth and motor development, particularly after puberty. There are fewer, but some, SES and ethnic differences in physical development. Let's look at these next.

Gender

There are greater gender differences in physical development than in any other domain discussed in this text. Gender differences in growth begin before birth. At birth girls' skeletons are four to six weeks more mature than boys'. Boys and girls then grow at similar rates until puberty. Boys experience some aspects of puberty about two years later than girls.

Boys may exercise and participate in team sports more than girls (Grunbaum et al., 2002). Is this because boys need an outlet for their higher activity level? Perhaps. In the studies using actometers discussed earlier, no gender differences in activity level were found, but some studies do find that boys are somewhat more active than girls (Saudino & Zapfe, 2008). Is this because boys are better athletes? Not initially. Girls are as strong as boys of similar body size until puberty, except that in middle childhood boys throw farther, but girls are more flexible. Both boys and girls steadily increase in strength and athletic skill from ages 4 to 14. However, gender differences emerge with puberty.

Boys' strength accelerates rapidly with puberty. Girls have no comparable spurt in strength; their strength typically plateaus around age 14. After puberty, boys have larger hearts, lungs, and muscles (particularly in the upper body), as well as greater oxygen-carrying capacity than girls (Malina et al., 2004). They have 1.5 times the lean body and bone mass, and half the body fat of girls, whereas prior to puberty they have similar amounts (Archibald et al., 2003).

When Ben, in the opening vignette, was suddenly able to do several pull-ups, thanks to puberty, he wore sleeveless T-shirts to show off his new muscles. When our 9-year-old daughter saw his bulging biceps, she said, "Mommy, that boy is really strong!" Mom replied with a twinkle, "That's exactly what he wants you to think." Not surprisingly, studies find that boys feel positive about their gains in strength and growth. In contrast, girls tend to dislike their normal puberty-caused weight gain (Archibald et al., 2003).

Socioeconomic Status

There is no relationship between motor development and SES in school-aged children in the United States (Malina et al., 2004). However, there is a relationship between nutrition and SES. Low-SES children eat more high-fat, high-sugar foods. This may be due to living in neighborhoods with convenience carryout stores instead of supermarkets, making healthy food less accessible (Morland, Wing, Diez Roux, & Poole, 2002).

As many as one-third of children in developing countries are undernourished, making it one of the most common risks of childhood worldwide. However, in the United States, children go hungry in less than 1% of households. What is more common is food insecurity, or periodic lack of adequate-quality food, which occurs in 17% of households with children (FIFCFS, 2008).

What happens when children lack food security? They are more likely to be anxious, aggressive, friendless, suspended from school, and quarrelsome than well-fed

Field Observation

Food insecurity in children is assessed by questions such as: Did you ever go to bed hungry? Did you ever skip a meal, or cut back on portions, or eat the same thing repeatedly because there wasn't enough money for food? Ask yourself or friends these questions. What is your experience of food insecurity?

low-income children. They are also more likely to be in special education, have low math scores, and be retained a grade. They have more colds, stomachaches, and headaches, but are not absent from school more often (Alaimo, Olson, Frongillo, & Briefel, 2001). Hunger may cause these problems, or both the problems and the food insecurity may be the result of some other underlying problem, such as a mentally ill parent.

Ethnicity

Within the United States there are some ethnic differences in growth. African American infants are smaller at birth and are less likely to be breastfed than White or Latino children (Ruowei, Zhao, Mikdad, Barker, & Grummer-Strawn, 2003). However, African American infants grow more quickly during the first few years of life and tend to be more advanced in skeletal development (Rogol et al., 2002). They are slightly larger in childhood, but not in adulthood.

There are also ethnic differences in puberty. African American children have their adolescent growth spurt and puberty earlier than other children (Archibald et al., 2003; Malina et al., 2004). At age 8, 48% of African American and 15% of White girls have begun pubertal development. Smaller differences occur for menarche. Average age of menarche is 12.1, 12.3, and 12.7 for African American, Latina, and White girls, respectively (Chumlea et al., 2003).

There are also some ethnic differences in motor development. For example, Black children have more advanced motor development up to 2 years of age than White children; thus, Black children walk earlier. Black school-age children, especially boys, tend to run faster and jump farther than White children, but there are no differences in other motor skills like throwing, balance, or sit-ups. There are not much data comparing motor development of other ethnic groups within the United States (Malina et al., 2004).

African American and Latino children, particularly girls, get less exercise than White and Asian children and participate less in school sports (Grunbaum et al., 2002). Thus, Elena in case 1 is not likely to be involved in sports. However, one of her Latina cousins is the junior high soccer star. There are many such exceptions to these group trends. In fact, ethnic differences are small compared to SES differences (Malina et al., 2004). Some ethnic differences may be the result of SES. Children in high-crime neighborhoods are less likely to exercise vigorously (Gordon-Larsen, McMurray, & Popkin, 2000). In contrast, children with highly educated mothers are more likely to get vigorous exercise, regardless of ethnicity.

Classroom Implications of Growth and Motor Development

There are several ways you can help your students be physically healthy. One is to *prevent the school climate from becoming stressful to children.* A famous experiment occurred after World War II in Germany when food was rationed. British researchers gave children in orphanage A additional bread and juice for six months. Children in orphanage B were not given supplements, yet the children in orphanage B grew larger (Widdowson, 1951). Why these surprising results? At the time of the experiment, orphanage A just happened to get a new headmistress, Frauline Schwarz, who was mean and used mealtime to berate children. The children's growth slowed. Yet, she had eight favorite children in the orphanage who escaped her wrath and grew robustly. The moral of the story is to keep Frauline Schwarz out of your school. We will discuss school climate in more depth in Chapter 6.

Two other ways to help your students be physically healthy are to promote (1) good nutrition and (2) physical activity. You should also become aware of the role of motor development in your classroom. Let's discuss these next.

In-School Nutrition

Since 1946 the U.S. Department of Agriculture (USDA) has provided cash subsidies to schools and child care centers to feed low-income children. In 2008 the National School Lunch program provided free breakfast to 7 million and lunch to 15 million children. Does in-school nutrition affect learning for low-income children? Research suggests it does. In Massachusetts, just three months after starting a school breakfast program, low-SES Latino 3rd- through 6th-graders were tardy less often and scored higher on achievement tests (Meyers, Sampson, Weitzman, Rogers, & Kayne, 1989). In New York City, after schools improved the quality of meals they served, children's achievement test scores went from the 39th to the 55th percentile (Schoenthaler, Dorax, & Wakefield, 1987). You may help your students by following these guidelines:

- Advocate for better nutrition in the breakfasts and lunches served to your students.
- In secondary schools where snack foods and beverages are sold, advocate for healthier options than candy, sport drinks, or soda pop. About two-thirds of principals report improved snacks in the last few years, but more improvement is needed (Centers for Disease Control and Prevention, 2009a).
- If needed, allow children to bring a healthy snack, as Mrs. Z did in the opening vignette. At class parties, have healthy treats like apple slices instead of cupcakes.
- Be a good nutrition role model yourself and directly teach principles of good nutrition in class.

Physical Activity at School

A goal of the government's *Healthy People 2010* was daily physical education (PE) at school, in which at least 50% of children's time is spent in vigorous exercise. Was this goal met? Not yet. In preschools, children tend to be sedentary (sitting, lying down, or standing); even outdoors they may be vigorously active only a small percentage of the time (W. H. Brown et al., 2009). Older children don't fare much better. A study of hundreds of 3rd-graders across the country found that they averaged only two PE classes per week; in those classes they spent only five minutes in vigorous exercise and twelve minutes in moderate exercise. Most of the time, they did things like wait for a turn or listen to instructions (NICHD Early Child Care Research Network, 2003b).

PE and recess have been reduced in many schools for at least two reasons:

1. Need for more time on academics. This is misguided. In Chapter 11 you will learn that physical play and recess *enhance* learning from preschool through high school. When schools double or triple PE time, test scores do not go down,

and often rise (Robert Wood Johnson Foundation, 2009). Physically fit children have higher test scores, better attendance, and fewer discipline problems.

2. Budget crunches reduce money for PE teachers, facilities, and playground supervisors. In our local high school of 1,700 students, there is one gym and one weight room that was converted from a storage closet. Students can only take one semester of PE in their high school career because there simply is not enough room for more PE classes.

What can you do to help children get active? Try the following:[2]

- In preschools, give children balls and plenty of space for vigorous physical activity. Children tend to be more active in games they have initiated, but if they are not active you may need to initiate games that involve running, jumping, or climbing (W. H. Brown et al., 2009).
- In schools, advocate for *daily* physical education, even for high school students. The percentage of high school students in daily PE dropped from 42% in 1991 to 30% in 2007.[3] Students who are involved in extracurricular sports could be exempted. For younger students, provide school time for unstructured physical activity, like jumping rope at recess.
- Offer PE classes that emphasize enjoyable activities that are done throughout life, not just competitive sports. Some high schools offer "Fitness for Life" classes that include jogging, bicycling, and other activities that students can do after they leave school.
- Make sure that during PE classes each child is active for most of the class period.
- Discourage withholding of physical activity as a punishment. Withholding recess from an overactive child is not only unkind, it is counterproductive.
- Provide diverse extracurricular activities appropriate for different abilities that involve physical activity. For example, a junior high Earth Club could take hikes through parks to study nature.
- Build physical activity into classroom lessons when appropriate. Even adding ten minutes during the day may help (Ahamed et al., 2007). For example, one teacher had her 2nd-graders gather at a start line. She would call out a vocabulary word. The children had to briskly walk to their seat to spell the word, then return to the start line for the next word.

Your school may be interested in a model program developed by the National Institutes of Health, called CATCH (Child and Adolescent Trial for Cardiovascular Health), to improve the health of students. In the program, fat, sodium, and calories in school meals are reduced and nutrients are increased. Physical activity during PE is increased and students are taught activities to try after school. Classroom lessons focus on how to choose nutritious foods, be physically active, and abstain from drug use. Parents are involved through homework and family fun nights. The health of students in CATCH schools improves compared with a control group (Perry et al., 1997).

---

[2] See also the CDC's website on school programs.

[3] You can see updated state data for different grades at http:apps.nccd.cdc.gov/YRBSS/. Data come from the Centers for Disease Control and Prevention, "Youth Risk Behavior Surveillance System."

Motor Skills in the Classroom

Motor skills are foundational to success in school. About 30 to 60% of children's school-day activities require motor skills. These are mostly fine motor skills using paper and pencil, but also some less obvious skills like posture control (McHale & Cermak, 1992). Furthermore, most classroom learning is measured with motor output, such as writing, playing an instrument, making an art project, or using a keyboard (Pape & Ryba, 2004). Imagine how difficult school would be if you struggled with these skills.

Young children do struggle with these skills. Before age 6, they have difficulty moving their eyes deliberately across lines of small print and controlling hand movements, which makes reading and writing challenging. Even among older children, some have motor problems. They may have difficulty writing letters, fastening clothing, using scissors, folding papers, opening containers at lunch, or finding a folder in a messy desk. They may appear clumsy and disorganized and may be the last ones chosen for a team. When writing, they cannot stay on a line and may mush words together. Tasks that require them to listen and write at the same time (such as taking notes) are especially difficult. Motor problems can lead to further language and social problems.

You are likely to have children with motor problems in your classroom. Under the Individuals with Disabilities Education Act (or PL 101-476), children with physical difficulties are to be educated in the *least restrictive environment.* This is often interpreted to mean a regular classroom. Your school district likely will have an occupational or physical therapist whose job is to help children who have motor problems adapt to your classroom. The occupational therapist will help you make classroom accommodations, as well as provide exercises to help increase motor skills in targeted children.

Contemporary Health Challenges

Several common children's health issues that affect classroom performance will be discussed in other chapters: child abuse (Chapter 7), ADHD (Chapter 4), depression (Chapter 8), and sexually transmitted diseases (Chapter 11). In this chapter we focus on sleep deprivation, obesity, and drug use. These threats to children's health are preventable, and schools can help.

Sleep Deprivation

During the summer, 10th-grader Jay routinely stayed up until 3 a.m. and woke up at noon. In the fall, when school began, he tried to go to bed at 10 p.m., but couldn't fall asleep until 3 a.m. He was anxious about school beginning, which made it harder to sleep. He got up at 6 a.m. for school the first week, but was exhausted. When the weekend came, he stayed up late and slept until 3 p.m. on Saturday to "catch up." He continued this pattern for several weeks. Sometimes he would oversleep and miss class, or fall asleep during class. This made his teachers and parents angry. He became irritable, had difficulty paying attention, and began failing his classes. This increased his anxiety, which made it harder to sleep, creating a vicious cycle. Eventually he was diagnosed with ADHD and depression; sleep deprivation symptoms mirror these psychiatric disorders. (adapted from Dahl & Lewin, 2002)

Adolescents may need more sleep than adults.

In addition to masquerading as depression and ADHD, sleep deprivation can trigger mental illness. Sleep deprivation and emotional disorders, like depression or anxiety, are bi-directional, meaning each can cause the other. Children with unhealthy sleep habits, like sleeping less than six hours a night or having more than a two-hour difference between school-night and weekend bedtimes, tend to be more depressed than other children (Dahl & Lewin, 2002).

Sleep deprivation decreases motivation, ability to concentrate or reason, speed and accuracy of information processing, memory, motor control, and emotion regulation (which makes children sillier, angrier, or sadder). It increases restlessness, irritability, illness, injuries, impulsivity, mistakes, drug use (such as caffeine or nicotine) to stay awake, daytime sleepiness (such as dozing off during class), and tardiness in morning classes. Some of these effects occur even if people are not aware of feeling sleepy, because they have adapted to sleep deprivation (Horowitz, Cade, Wolfe, & Czeisler, 2003).

Age Trends in Sleep Patterns

Newborns sleep more than they are awake. By school age, children no longer need daytime sleep; sleepy children may need to go to bed earlier rather than nap. As they grow older, youth gradually need less sleep until they reach adult levels. One way to remember students' sleep needs is "10 for 10," or ten hours for 10-year-olds—younger students need more, older students need less. An important exception is that adolescents need more sleep during growth spurts; if they continue to sleep the same amount, they feel sleepier. There may be a cohort effect for sleep in that children may be sleeping less now than a few decades ago (Iglowstein, Jenni, Molinari, & Largo, 2003).

Table 2.2 Sleep needs by age

Average Number of Hours of Sleep Needed Daily		
Age	**Nighttime**	**Daytime**
1 month (full term)	8–12	4–9
6 months	8–10	4–6 (about two naps per day)
1–3 years	11	1–2 (one mid-day nap)
6 years	11–12	None
9 years	9–10	None
12 years	8–9	None
Adolescence	8–10	None
Adults	7–9	None

Adapted from Carskadon & Dement (2000); Iglowstein et al. (2003); Minde (2002); and Ollendick & Schroeder (2003).

Many U.S. children do not get enough sleep, particularly adolescents like Jay. From ages 3 to 17 children tend to get up at the same time. However, as they enter adolescence, they stay up two and a half hours later, on average (Snell, Adam, & Duncan, 2007). They work more—in sports, homework, and employment—which keeps them up too late. They also wake more easily during the night than younger children (Carskadon & Dement, 2000). As a result about 85% of adolescents are mildly sleep deprived, 10 to 40% significantly so (Dahl & Lewin, 2002). Adolescents often go to bed later on weekends than school nights, creating a jet-lag effect each week. Keeping consistent bed and wake times eliminates this effect. To make up for sleep loss, adolescents may sleep excessively on weekends so that their total sleep time is similar to that of younger children (Ohayon, Carskadon, Guilleminault, & Vitiello, 2004). Still, many high school students function at a level of sleep deprivation characteristic of people with sleep disorders.

Sleep Disorders

Children with sleep disorders can go to bed at a reasonable hour, yet still not be refreshed, because their sleep is of poor quality or they wake frequently. Occasional nighttime waking is normal, but excessive waking is not. Nightmares are the most common sleep disturbance in preschoolers (Minde, 2002). Sleep talking (22 to 60% of children) and sleepwalking (15 to 75%) are common in middle childhood. A delayed sleep–wake cycle (i.e., the night owl) is the most common (7%) sleep disorder in adolescence. Overall, studies in Sweden, the United States, and Belgium have found that about 20 to 40% of children have some sleep problem (e.g., Luginbuehl, Bradley-Klug, Ferron, Anderson, & Benbadis, 2008).

Sleep **apneas**, or repeated periods without breathing during sleep, are another common sleep disturbance. Apnea is characterized by snoring, restlessness or gasping for breath during sleep, sleeping with the mouth open, morning headaches, crankiness, and daytime sleepiness. Brief apneas are common in healthy people, but not periods long enough to disturb sleep. In children, apneas are typically caused by enlarged tonsils or adenoids, or obesity.

apnea a sleep disturbance that consists of repeated periods without breathing, and snoring or gasping for breath.

Sleep apnea may be linked to **sudden infant death syndrome (SIDS)** or crib death. SIDS refers to the sudden death of an infant for whom a cause of death cannot be determined. SIDS typically occurs at night, but 20% of cases may occur in child care settings (Moon, Patel, & McDermott Shaefer, 2000). It is a leading cause of infant death. It is most common for boys; preterm, low-SES, and African American and Latino infants; and infants with young mothers who smoke or have little prenatal care. However, the cause of SIDS is still unknown. The probability of SIDS can be reduced if infants sleep on firm surfaces without pillows and on their backs (Hauck et al., 2003).

sudden infant death syndrome (SIDS) the sudden death of an infant for whom a cause of death cannot be determined.

Classroom Implications of Sleep Deprivation

Sleep affects students' classroom performance. Well-rested children do better mentally and socially—they have better memory; longer attention spans; higher self-esteem; and less aggression, hyperactivity, and depression (Bates, Viken, Alexander, Beyers, & Stockton, 2002; Fredriksen, Rhodes, Reddy, & Way, 2004). Students with healthy sleep habits earn higher grades and test scores, beyond the effect of earlier test scores (Buckhalt, El-Sheikh, Keller, & Kelly, 2009). Sleep deprivation may be especially detrimental to low-SES and African American children, yet these children are also less likely to have consistent bedtime routines (Buckhalt, El-Sheikh, & Keller, 2007; Hale, Berger, LeBourgeois, & Brooks-Gunn, 2009).

Most sleep research is correlational, so direction of causation is not clear. Perhaps positive outcomes linked to more sleep actually result from healthy family routines. To test this possibility, Israeli researchers asked parents to put their 4th-, 5th-, and 6th-graders to bed thirty to forty minutes earlier, or later, than usual for three nights in a row (Sadeh, Gruber, & Raviv, 2003). The children who slept more improved in memory, motor speed, and attention. The size of effect was equivalent to two years' development.

Further evidence comes from a study of 1st-graders who were doing poorly in school. A whopping 18% of these low achievers had sleep apneas. (Apnea only occurs in 1 to 2% of children in general.) Children whose apneas were surgically corrected improved in school performance in 2nd grade compared to the children who were not treated (Gozal, 1998). Thus, low achievement in some of your students may be caused by sleep deprivation.

Sleep is not idle time. Learning depends on sleep; you remember information and solve problems better when you have had a chance to "sleep on it" (Strickgold & Walker, 2004). Sleep helps you remember information because memories are consolidated during sleep (Rasch & Born, 2008). What can you do about your student's sleep deprivation?

- Watch for signs of sleepiness. In one 8th-grade science class, five students were sleeping at 10:15 in the morning! They were not high achievers.
- If a student is performing poorly, inform parents and ask about sleep loss. Teach parents about age-specific sleep needs from Table 2.1 presented earlier. Watch for students who have been diagnosed with ADHD, learning disability, or depression who may actually suffer from sleep deprivation (Luginbuehl et al., 2008).
- Avoid contributing to sleep deprivation. End school-sponsored activities, like open houses or play practices, early enough that children can be in bed on time. Give homework assignments that do not require staying up late.
- Avoid early start times for secondary schools (Hansen, Janssen, Schiff, Zee, & Dubocovich, 2005). Typically, when adolescents transition from middle schools to high schools that have an earlier start time, they do not go to bed earlier. Thus, after starting high school they may sleep an hour less each night, becoming significantly sleep deprived. In districts that change their start time, say from 7:30 to 8:30 a.m., teens get substantially more sleep each week because they continue to go to bed at the same time as before (Danner & Phillips, 2008; Wahlstrom, Davison, Choi, & Ross, 2001).

Improving Sleep

Sleep *needs* may not be under voluntary control, but sleep *amount* and *schedule* are. If a child, like Jay, has an unhealthy sleep cycle, it can be gradually changed by changing bedtime in increments of fifteen to thirty minutes over several weeks (Ollendick & Schroeder, 2003). If parents seek your advice about how to help their child sleep better, suggest the child (1) have the same bedtime and wake time seven days a week; (2) have a bedtime routine that is calming, with dimmed lights; (3) wake up without the use of an alarm; and, (4) if school-age, keep daytime naps to a maximum of thirty minutes. They will also need to eliminate conditions that disturb sleep. These include noise, light, stress, anxiety, overtiredness, lack of exposure to daylight, and some medicines. These also include eating a large meal, exercising, watching TV or using the computer, and consuming caffeine or alcohol within an hour of bedtime. Caffeine disrupts sleep even in the small amounts found in soft drinks, chocolate, and over-the-counter drugs (Roehrs & Roth, 2008). The more children watch TV, especially just before bedtime, the more likely they are to sleep less and have difficulty going to bed or falling asleep (Owens et al., 1999).

Field Observation

Ask a few children who are at the age you wish to teach or their parents to keep a sleep diary for seven consecutive days. If they do not get adequate sleep, ask them to improve the quality and quantity of their sleep for another seven days using the suggestions here. Report on changes in behavior and well-being. Try the experiment yourself.

Obesity and Other Eating Disorders

The Donovan family has four children. Both parents are obese. Their refrigerator is stocked with soda pop and hotdogs. The oldest child, Jacob, is tall and fit. He is on the football and basketball teams in high school. His dream is a college athletic scholarship. His 8th- and 5th-grade siblings are both obese and not involved in sports. His 1st-grade brother is very thin—nicknamed "skinny boy." If the children are good all week, they are rewarded on Friday night with a trip to a fast-food restaurant and a double-feature video at home. The real motive for the reward is that the parents are too tired to cook after they get home from work.

Families with weight problems, like the Donovans, are becoming common. The World Health Organization has declared obesity one of the top health problems in developed nations. In the United States, the number of overweight children has tripled since 1970.

Obesity or *overweight* is defined by body mass index (BMI). *BMI* is weight in kilograms divided by the square of height in meters (kg/m^2). For adults, overweight is BMI $\geq$ 25, and obesity is BMI $\geq$ 30. For an adult this means being at least thirty pounds over ideal weight (Grunbaum et al., 2002). In children, the BMI indicators of obesity are similar, but vary by gender and age. (They can be found on the CDC's growth charts.)

Age Trends in Obesity

Fat level, or adiposity, naturally changes across the lifespan. There is an increase in adiposity from birth to about 1 year of age, then a decrease. A rebound in adiposity sets in between 4 and 8 years of age, then decreases again. The body peaks in leanness around age 25; afterward adiposity increases again. While obesity can develop at any age, the primary grades are a risk period because of the adiposity rebound. The Donovans are typical. "Skinny boy" is not likely to deserve his nickname once the adipose rebound sets in, just as it did for his older, inactive siblings.

What Does Obesity Predict?

Obesity can cause serious health problems in both children and adults. In children, being overweight may cause type 2 (non-insulin-dependent) diabetes. There has been a dramatic increase in diabetes, which puts children at risk for hardening of the arteries, kidney problems, eye disease, and death. Obesity is also linked to early onset of puberty in girls, sleep apnea, asthma, and problems with joints or bones (Davison, Susman, & Birch, 2003; Krishnamoorthy, Hart, & Jelalian, 2006).

Obesity can also cause social and emotional problems. Obese children are more lonely, depressed, anxious, and lacking in self-control in the classroom (Gable, Krull, & Chang, 2009). They are seen as less likeable by their peers, even as young as age 3 (Bell & Morgan, 2000). Perhaps because of this, obesity is linked to lower self-esteem in school-age children (but not in preschoolers), particularly if peers tease and parents criticize the child's weight (BeLue, Francis, & Colaco, 2009). By early adolescence not all obese teens have low self-esteem, but those that do are at risk for other problems such as smoking and drinking (Strauss, 2000). Obese adolescents are less likely to attend college (Crosnoe, 2007). The link between obesity and these problems is stronger for girls than boys, and stronger for Latino and White children than for African American children.

What Predicts Obesity?

Factors linked to the obesity epidemic over the last few decades include:

1. *Exercise.* BMI is a direct function of calorie intake (diet) relative to calorie output (exercise)—known as the *energy equation.* It only takes a small imbalance in the equation to become overweight. You learned earlier that many children today do not get enough exercise.
2. *Diet.* More families, like the Donovans, eat out and eat too much. In the United States, portion sizes have increased, particularly for soft drinks and salty snacks like crackers and chips (Nielsen & Popkin, 2003). Portion sizes are especially large at fast-food restaurants. Coke was originally served in six-ounce glasses in the early 1900s; now it is served in forty-eight-ounce cups. One additional serving of sugary drinks per day can increase obesity by 60% in 6th- and 7th-graders (Ludwig, Peterson, & Gortmaker, 2001).
3. *Sleep deprivation.* Children who sleep fewer hours and go to bed later tend to have higher BMI than other children (Snell et al., 2007). Less than ten hours of sleep per night is linked to obesity in children across countries, such as the United States, China, Tunisia, and Brazil (Cappuccio et al., 2008).
4. *Television viewing.* Television viewing reduces activity level and promotes calorie intake. Many children watch TV during meals, which is linked to eating fewer fruits and vegetables and more pizza, salty snacks, and soda pop (Coon, Goldberg, Rogers, & Tucker, 2001). Children who watch more than two hours daily tend to be more obese than their peers (Kaiser Family Foundation, 2004).
5. *Parent behavior.* Parents who are highly controlling about their child's eating (e.g., "No soda at any time") may have children who overeat the wrong foods when the controls are lifted (Drucker, Hammer, Agras, & Bryson, 1999). Parents who use food as a reward may distort their children's food preferences (Birch, 1999). Saying "eat your peas if you want ice cream," will increase pea eating in the short run, but not in the long run. Parents who do not cook meals at home tend to purchase less-nutritious, higher-calorie food for their children (Krishnamoorthy et al., 2006). Parents who are obese may have children who are obese. In fact, *mothers' obesity* may be the strongest predictor of child obesity (Strauss & Knight, 1999), because parents and children share eating habits.

Group Diversity in Obesity

Obesity rates vary by ethnicity and SES in the United States. Ethnic differences in BMI are small, with the exception that Black girls are more overweight than other groups (Ogden et al., 2006). In most countries, higher-SES children are taller and heavier than low-SES children. However, in developed countries, low-SES children with single parents, or a mother who did not finish high school, are more likely to be obese (Strauss & Knight, 1999). Mrs. Donovan did not finish high school.

It may seem ironic that low-SES children who are more likely to have food insecurity would be obese, but in the United States, high-calorie food is plentiful and cheap. For example, a box of cookies provides more calories per dollar than fresh fruit. Children living in poverty are more likely than high-SES children to eat cookies rather than fruit, although most (71%) nonpoor children do not have stellar diets either (FIFCFS, 2008).

Tim Boyle/Getty Images

Can you think of more than one reason why mothers' obesity is a powerful predictor of children's obesity?

Classroom Implications of Obesity

What can you do to help your students if they are overweight?

- Help your students reduce calorie intake and get more exercise, as discussed earlier. For example, where appropriate, suggest walking and biking instead of busing students to school.
- Teach students about appropriate quantities and types of food. Unfortunately, schools may offer unhealthy foods through vending machines, snacks, and fundraising sales.
- Advocate for longer lunch periods in a socially pleasant environment where students are presented with choices among healthy foods. Nutritional foods take longer to eat.
- Focus attention on becoming healthy, not on dieting or losing weight. Communicate to overweight students that they are valued regardless of their weight.

Three federal agencies (USDA, CDC, Department of Health and Human Services [DHHS]) have combined to identify success stories from schools that have become healthier.[4] These schools make healthy foods more accessible. Some offer healthy rewards such as a walk with the principal instead of a pizza party. Some adopt a "fruits and veggies only" policy for snacks. Some have removed all soda and candy from vending machines, replacing them with yogurt, string cheese, fruit, or beef jerky. Contrary to many people's beliefs, schools can make money selling healthy options.

Should you encourage overweight students to diet? Generally, no. Food restriction can negatively affect later eating habits. If too stringent, diets can create a failure experience that further diminishes self-esteem. Diets can create nutritional

[4]At the home page of the CDC website, visit the "School Nutrition Success Stories, Making It Happen!" page.

deficiencies in growing bodies (Rogol et al., 2002). Instead, interventions should focus on teaching parents to use rewards other than food, developing healthy eating behavior, and reducing TV viewing. Some students may need behavior therapy with a psychologist, especially family-based therapy, rather than dieting (Kitzman, Dalton, & Buscemi, 2008).

Although youth should not diet, many do. In a national study, a whopping 62% of high school girls and 28% of boys reported trying to lose weight in the past month. Generally they do this by exercising more or by eating fewer calories, but 14% went without food for more than twenty four hours, 9% tried diet pills, and 5% used vomiting or laxatives (Grunbaum et al., 2002). Sometimes this attempt to lose weight can develop into an eating disorder (Rome et al., 2003).

Other Eating Disorders

Obesity is the most prevalent eating disorder. Less common eating disorders involve the extreme pursuit of thinness. Two of the most well known are *anorexia nervosa* and *bulimia nervosa*, which affect 1 to 4% of the U.S. population. Anorexia is self-starvation and can be fatal. Anorexics refuse to maintain minimal body weight, have distorted perception of their size (think that they are fat when they are not), and base self-value on weight. Bulimia has similar psychological factors, but the person is *not underweight.* Bulimia is binge eating, followed by vomiting, use of laxatives, fasting, or excessive exercise. It is diagnosed when binge-purge episodes occur at least twice a week for three months (Smolak & Thompson, 2009). Bulimia is less apparent than anorexia because there is no emaciation, so it may go undiagnosed.

These eating disorders generally emerge in adolescence and are 10 to 15 times more prevalent in girls than boys (Grunbaum et al., 2002). Boys and girls do not differ in weight concerns at age 9, but by age 14 girls are more likely to try to lose weight (A. Field et al., 1999). Eating disorders emerge with puberty as girls' dissatisfaction with their increased fat level grows. Dissatisfaction with body weight is so common that it has become normal among American girls. However, not all girls who are dissatisfied with their bodies develop eating disorders.

Besides body dissatisfaction, other risk factors for eating disorders include pressure to be thin, fat phobia, dieting, depression, low self-esteem, feelings of inadequacy, impulsiveness, drug use, and lack of social support. Families of youth with anorexia and bulimia may go to excessive lengths to avoid conflicts; they may be excessively enmeshed and overprotective; or they may be detached, hostile, disorganized, and conflict ridden. The eating disorder may arise from adolescents' attempts to have some control over their own lives or from perfectionist strivings to please critical parents (Polivy, Herman, Mills, & Wheller, 2003). Daughters may learn distorted body perceptions from their mothers. In addition, there may be a genetic susceptibility to eating disorders (Striegel-Moore & Bulik, 2007). No single risk factor produces eating disorders, but an unfortunate combination of multiple risk factors may.

Eating disorders respond to some of the same treatments that are used for depression, anxiety, and panic disorders, such as medication and psychotherapy, because the conditions may share the same underlying causes (Rome et al., 2003; Stice & Shaw, 2004). Treatment may also involve hospitalization to foster weight gain.

Drug Use

Elaine's mother frequently got into physical fights with her boyfriend. Whenever he stormed from the house, Elaine's mother would smoke a blunt (cigar-sized marijuana) to help her calm down. One day she generously (in her view) invited 13-year-old Elaine to join her. That was Elaine's first drug use. When we met her, Elaine was a 35-year-old cocaine addict. Five of her seven children were cocaine-exposed during pregnancy.

Drug use is one of society's most challenging problems. The term *drug use* refers to the use of alcohol and tobacco (which are legal), to the use of illegal drugs, and to the misuse of prescription medicine. Collectively they are known by the acronym ATOD (alcohol, tobacco, and other drugs).

U.S. government-sponsored national surveys of high school students[5] find that the number of youth using ATOD has decreased since 2002. Among youth who use drugs, *alcohol is the most common drug.* Roughly 70% of adolescents try alcohol at some time. However, most are not consistent users; about 25% report drinking in any given month. This means that *most youth abstain* in any given month, but some adolescents are heavy drinkers.

Tobacco is the next most commonly used drug. About 11% of teens use tobacco, and by their senior year, 45% have tried cigarettes. Marijuana is the third most commonly used drug. About 7% of teens use marijuana, and by their senior year 45% have tried it. Additionally, 3% of 8th-graders and 16% of 12th-graders reported using any illegal drugs in the previous month, including ecstasy, steroids, heroin, inhalants, cocaine, or marijuana. Youth who use these illegal drugs are likely to use more than one drug. That is, most youth who use marijuana or cocaine also smoke or drink alcohol (Jeynes, 2002). Thus, some youth are polydrug users. Again, *most youth are not regular users of any drug.*

Age Trends in Drug Use

You might think drug use is a teen problem. This is both true and false. *Moderate* users typically begin drug use in adolescence. However, *heavy* users typically begin drug use in elementary school (Grunbaum et al., 2002). In addition, the factors that lead to heavy use begin in early childhood (Dodge et al., 2009). We will discuss these factors later in this section.

You might also think that adolescents use drugs—and engage in other risky behavior (such as driving fast)—because they are irrational and do not understand the risk involved. Actually, their logical reasoning may be as good as that of adults. Instead, they engage in risky behavior because it feels more rewarding, especially in the presence of peers, and because they are imitating adults. Thus, merely "informing" teens about the risks is not likely to deter drug use.

What Does Drug Use Predict?

Drug use is common in most countries, yet it is condemned by most. This is because drug use has negative outcomes that range from mild to severe, depending on whether

[5]The numbers are updated annually. For the latest statistics and to find out about your state specifically, see SAMSHA's website http//.oas.samsha.gov/p0000016.htm.

it is short-lived experimentation or chronic, heavy use. At the severe end, drugs can cause death. Smoking was the single leading cause of death in the United States in 2000, including deaths attributable to secondhand smoke and infant death due to mothers' smoking. Moderate drug use can also cause physical illness and injury (Mokdad, Marks, Stroup, & Gerberding, 2004; Windle & Windle, 2003). Drug use leads to motor vehicle accidents, a leading cause of death among adolescents. More than 30% of high school students, particularly boys, report having ridden in a car with a driver who had been drinking (Grunbaum et al., 2002).

Drug use is also linked to social problems. Youth who use drugs are more likely to have risky sex and commit crimes than other youth (Fisher et al., 2000). Early involvement, before age 15, with *any* drug is a risk factor for later adult problems like crime, sexually transmitted diseases, dropping out of school, marital fights, and poor job performance (Odgers et al., 2008; Windle & Windle, 2003). The heavier the early drug use, the greater the risk of these problems.

What Predicts Drug Use?

One of the most powerful risk factors for drug use is parents' use (Ennett et al., 2008; Windle & Windle, 2003). Some children, like Elaine, use drugs with their parents as a time to bond with parents (Lopez, Katsulis, & Robillard, 2009). Other children merely observe their parents' use and get their drugs from parents' stash at home. Cigarettes and alcohol are readily available in about 30% of homes. Some parents who want to be "cool" provide alcohol for their children's parties, even though it is a crime. Most teens who drink do so in their own or a friend's home (SAMHSA, 2008a). *Thus, many drug users are introduced to drug use by their parents.*

Think About This Children with a specific gene (called *5-HTTLPR*) are more likely to use drugs. However, even if they have this gene, they usually do not use drugs if they have a good home. Children with *both* the gene and family problems are twice as likely to use drugs as children without the gene or without family problems (Brody, Beach, Philibert, Chen, & Murry, 2009). Which concepts from the "Nature and Nurture" and "Risk and Resiliency" sections of Chapter 1 does this support or refute? (You can fast-forward to Box 6.3 in Chapter 6 for more insights.)

Another strong risk factor is whether the child's friends use drugs. This does not mean the child was introduced to drugs by the friends. Youth who use ATOD *select* friends who also use ATOD. Schools with large numbers of drug-using students make this selection easy. This is not to say that peers never cause drug use. If a child has a close friend who uses drugs, there is a small chance that the child will come to use drugs also, beyond the selection effect (e.g., Jaccard, Blanton, & Dodge, 2005). Once drug-using cliques are formed, youth influence one another to continue use.

Another strong risk factor is mental health problems. Many youth who abuse ATOD also suffer from depression, ADHD, and conduct disorder (see Chapters 8, 7, 10), particularly those who start using early. Perhaps this is because drug use is linked to family risk factors like domestic violence, harsh discipline, marital conflict, single parents, and mentally ill parents (Dodge et al., 2009). Additional risk factors include life stress, low school grades, early puberty, appearing older than peers, working at least twenty hours per week, low religiosity, and low self-esteem. Children with multiple risk factors are more likely to become drug users.

On the other hand, parents really can be the "anti-drug" (Lac & Crano, 2009). Parents protect their children from drug use by monitoring them, being home, sharing activities with them, being authoritative (see Chapter 7), disapproving of drug use, setting rules against drug use, and having a secure attachment with their children (see Chapter 6). These parenting factors may be especially powerful in protecting African American youth in high-risk neighborhoods (Cleveland, Gibbons,

Gerrard, Pomery, & Brody, 2005). Several personal characteristics also protect children from drug use. These include having a valued skill, high IQ, success, and strong school bonds (Wills & Yaeger, 2003; Windle & Windle, 2003). These personal protective factors—which you can influence as a teacher—are about as powerful as parenting factors.

Many people believe school sports protect children from drug use. This is not necessarily true. Sport participation is associated with an *increase* in smokeless tobacco and performance-enhancing drugs; a *decrease* in cigarette use; and *no difference* in alcohol, marijuana, or barbiturates (Melnick, Miller, Sabo, Farrell, & Barnes, 2001; Naylor, Gardner, & Zaichkowsky, 2001). In one study, 38% of high school students reported violating the athletic association's rules against drug use (Naylor et al., 2001). Most were not caught, but among those that were, many were not sanctioned. Drug use is part of the culture of some sports. Professional athletes model ATOD use to youth. When we discussed avoiding drug use with a high school cross-country team, they responded with "look at Prefontaine!" Steve Prefontaine was an Olympic runner known to use alcohol.

Group Diversity in Drug Use

There are *gender differences* in drug use. Boys are more likely to drink heavily and use illicit drugs than girls, but boys and girls have similar rates of smoking (SAMHSA, 2008b). There are also *ethnic differences* in drug use. White youth smoke and drink the most, Black and Asian youth the least. Latino youth are inbetween (SAMHSA, 2008b). There are also *socioeconomic differences* in drug use. High-SES youth more frequently use drugs than middle-SES youth (Blum et al., 2000). High-SES youth's drug use is linked to depression and anxiety, which suggests they are self-medicating for unhappiness. This may be due to overemphasis on achievement, so they can attend elite universities, or isolation from parents in large, empty homes (Luthar & Latendresse, 2008). These ethnic, SES, and gender differences have a small effect on drug use, personal and parenting factors are more powerful

Classroom Implications of Drug Use

Students' drug use is linked to lower grades and test scores, absences and dropping out, and misbehavior that interferes with learning (Jeynes, 2002). This may be due to compromised brain functioning. ATOD use affects the frontal cortex and the limbic system. For example, marijuana use diminishes motivation, short-term memory, and motor coordination (Schonberg, 1997). Alcohol use hampers memory, attention, and information processing (S. Brown, Tapert, Granholm, & Delis, 2000). In fact, youth may be more susceptible to brain damage from drug use than are adults (Lubman, Yucei, & Hall, 2007). Remember that myelination and synapses continue to develop through adolescence.

Nationally, 29% of youth report having been sold, offered, or given illegal drugs at school sometime during a year (Grunbaum et al., 2002). As many as 13% report coming to school under the influence (Jeynes, 2002). However, there is huge variation in this rate across schools (R. Rose et al., 2003). Some schools have greater need for ATOD interventions than others do. What can you do about ATOD use at your school?

Think About This Two sisters, ages 8 and 10, helped their mother carry several packs of beer from the grocery store to their car. The oldest girl asked, "Mommy, are these for the party or just for you?" What are the girls learning from their mother? As a teacher, what is your role in ATOD prevention with these girls? What type of school-based program is likely to prevent their ATOD use?

- Avoid modeling acceptance of drug use by joking about it or using drugs yourself. Students know which teachers smoke, drink alcohol, or are addicted to caffeine, even when teachers try to hide it.
- Convey that abstaining from drugs, including alcohol, is *normal.* Research shows *most youth do not use drugs.* Youth who believe that everyone else is doing it are more likely to use drugs.
- Promote school bonding. In Chapter 6 you will learn how to do this. Children who feel cared for at school are less likely to abuse alcohol (Ennett et al., 2008). Among 7th- to 12th-graders, school bonding accounts for as much of the variance in ATOD use as family and personal factors (Resnick et al., 1997).
- Advocate for effective drug-use prevention programs. We will discuss these next.

Since enactment of the Drug Free Schools and Communities Act in 1986, almost all schools have some type of ATOD prevention program. Most are aimed at resisting "peer pressure" to use drugs. The most common program was Drug Abuse Resistance Education (DARE), which was used in almost 75% of elementary schools. Dozens of studies indicated that DARE does not curb ATOD use, although newer versions of the program might be a little more effective (Perry et al., 2003). Even the best peer pressure resistance programs have modest effects for only some children (Windle & Windle, 2003).

Fortunately, there are school-based programs that are effective in reducing drug use. The most effective interventions address multiple levels of the bioecological model: individual, family, peers, school, and community (see Chapter 1). They teach the children social skills and coping strategies (see Chapter 8). They encourage parents to set anti-drug policies at home and strengthen families. They emphasize school bonding. They also change community norms for ATOD use. The U.S. government maintains websites that list research-based programs to help you select a program for your school (see Additional Resources on the textbook's Education CourseMate website).

Prenatal Drug Exposure—Behavioral Teratogens

One of the most serious consequences of children's drug use is that some continue drug use into their 20s, which are the prime childbearing years. Drugs are teratogens. A **teratogen** is an agent that harms the developing fetus. Teratogens include many things besides drugs, such as stress, pollutants, or illnesses (Hubbs-Tait, Nation, Krebs, & Bellinger, 2006).

teratogen an agent that harms the developing fetus.

Some teratogens have effects that are obvious at birth because they cause physical abnormalities, such as deformed limbs. However, other teratogens have effects that are not obvious at birth. For example, alcohol severely disrupts synaptogenesis (Ikonomidou et al., 2000). You cannot see this, but it will affect thought and behavior later in childhood. Such teratogens are called *behavioral teratogens.* They may affect infants by depriving them of oxygen or altering neurotransmitters in their brain in the womb and by making children more reactive to stress later (Eiden, Yvette, & Granger, 2009; Mayes, 2002).

Alcohol is one of the most powerful and common behavioral teratogens. Prenatal exposure to alcohol is the leading preventable cause of mental retardation. It can result in fetal alcohol syndrome (FAS). Symptoms of FAS are small head size, facial abnormalities such as a flat nose and wide eyes, attention and behavior problems, and low intelligence (Boyle, 2002). Children with less severe symptoms may have fetal alcohol spectrum disorders. FASD symptoms are low birth weight (see Box 2.2), slow thinking, poor memory, difficulty focusing attention, and impulsive behavior, such as talking constantly in class (Richardson,

Ryan, Willford, Day, & Goldschmidt, 2002). Alcohol-exposed children may also have poor motor development, particularly poor fine motor skills, making handwriting difficult.

Alcohol is linked to these problems even at common social levels of drinking and when the child is *not* diagnosed with FASDs (Jacobson, Chiodo, Sokol, & Jacobson, 2002). For example, in one study 14-year-olds' scores on a reasoning test were correlated with the number of drinks their mothers had at the beginning of pregnancy—before the mothers knew they were pregnant (Hunt, Streissguth, Kerr, & Olson, 1995). The more alcohol exposure, the faster, more impulsive, but inaccurate the child's responses fourteen years later.

Tobacco is another common teratogen. Like alcohol, prenatal tobacco exposure is associated with low birth weight and with slightly smaller stature beyond birth as well. Tobacco exposure is robustly linked to low self-control, ADHD, aggression, and the child's own drug use in adolescence. It has also been linked to SIDS, poor language development, poor memory, slower learning, and lower IQ (Lewis et al., 2004; Wakschlag, Leventhal, Pine, Pickett, & Carter, 2006; Wiebe et al., 2009).

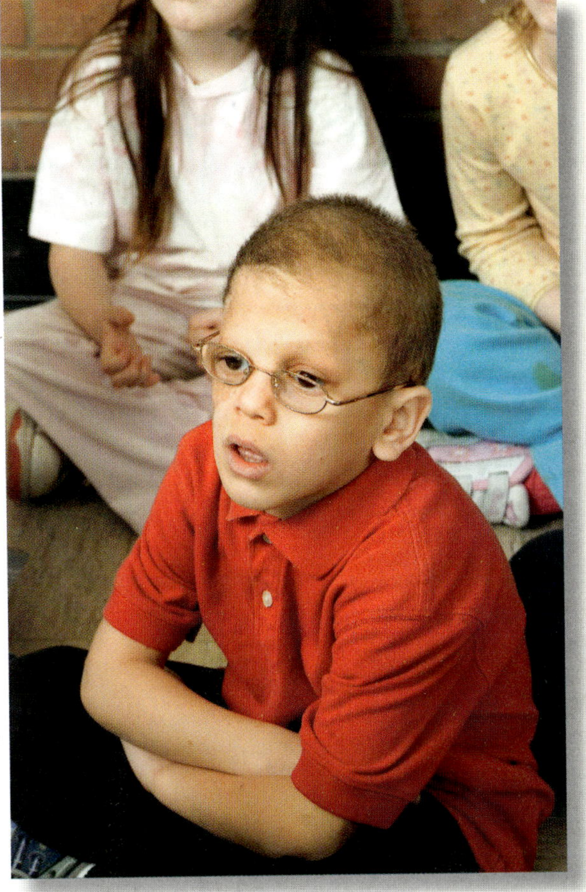
Ellen B. Senisi/The Image Works

Do you recognize the symptoms of Fetal Alcohol Syndrome in this child?

These effects of prenatal ATOD exposure last beyond infancy into adolescence and adulthood. Generally, the effects are subtle. That is, *most exposed children tend to function within "normal" ranges, but at the low end of the range.* The degree of problems depends on the amount of exposure and whether exposure occurred early in pregnancy, when the brain is developing rapidly. There are no known safe periods of the pregnancy or safe quantities.

We have focused on how mothers' *prenatal* use of drugs affects children. However, *postnatal* (after birth) drug use can affect children also. For example, when parents smoke, their children are more likely to have respiratory illnesses like bronchitis and asthma. Furthermore, ATOD use can diminish the quality of care parents give their children. For example, cocaine can cause parents to "crash" or be unwakeable for several hours at a time, during which time no one is talking to, feeding, or comforting the child. Let's look at the classroom behavior of 4-year-old Jenny, whose mother uses alcohol daily:

Jenny chases imaginary children. She talks to objects. One day she sees a pumpkin in the room, stops to pat it, and asks how it is doing. She says, "You are a beautiful pumpkin—so big and fat!" One child says, "Nobody likes her; she's weird." Jenny plays alone unless someone feels bad for her and lets her into their group, usually at teacher urging. The other children say they don't play with her because they are afraid of hurting her. She looks fragile; she is very small for her age, awkward, and has a surgically corrected cleft palate. Unlike other children, she is not excited to go home after school and see her mother.

Are Jenny's problems due to prenatal drug exposure, or the ongoing drug use of her mother? Probably both (Bergin & McCullough, 2009; Yumoto, Jacobson, & Jacobson, 2008).

The implications for you as a teachers are: (1) a key reason for preventing or reducing drug use in your students is to deflect them from becoming drug-using parents; (2) prenatal drug exposure can have long-term repercussions for some students in your classroom; and (3) parents' current drug use can interfere with your students' success at school. If your district implements drug prevention programs, try to get parents included in the programs.

At the conclusion of this chapter, it should be clear that physical well-being affects children's behavior and achievement at school. As a teacher, you have a vested interest in promoting the health of children. Many districts acknowledge this by having a school nurse on staff. There is a movement in the United States to go a step further and create school-based health centers. (Other countries already have such centers.) The idea is to bring medical care to children, where they are usually found—at school. This reduces costs and promotes better outcomes for ill children (Lear, 2003). For example, children with asthma had fewer costly hospitalizations and missed school less if their school had a health center (Webber et al., 2003). Asthma is the leading medical cause of school absence. Even in schools without health centers, you can promote the physical development of your students through the suggestions discussed in this chapter.

Reflections on Practice: Checklist for Teachers

Brain architecture is influenced by the environment, including quality of education. In addition, other aspects of children's physical development both influence and are influenced by experiences at school. To ensure you are promoting your students' physical well-being, periodically ask yourself:

1. Do I understand that brains change as a result of experience—such as the way I instruct or interact with each student? Do I provide a stimulating environment that will foster brain development and learning, without being overstimulating?
2. Do I provide a relatively low-stress environment by being accepting and predictable? (See Chapter 8.) For example, do I provide a list of assignments and due dates well in advance? Do I avoid yelling, criticizing, or punishing publicly?
3. Do I observe my students closely to verify that they are reaching appropriate physical milestones? Is my school screening the health, vision, and hearing of children?
4. Do I provide emotional support to children who are overweight, or unusually early or late in puberty?
5. Are my students getting enough exercise? Do I encourage exercise, perhaps by providing physical activity in the classroom or by taking my class out to play? Does my school offer a safe approach for students who are walking or biking?
6. Do I model eating healthy food and encourage students to do so also? Does my school offer healthy food? Do students have adequate time for lunch in a pleasant space? Do I encourage students, especially toddlers and teen girls, to get adequate iron and avoid soda? Should I allow healthy snacks in class?
7. Are my low-income students receiving free or reduced-price breakfast and lunch? If not, what can I do to help?
8. Are my students sleepy? Do I encourage them to get enough sleep? Does my school schedule events to end early enough?
9. Do I avoid inappropriately modeling or discussing smoking, drinking, or drug use with students? Do I convey the message that abstaining from drug use is normal (instead of talking as though all teens drink and will be doing so on the coming weekend)?

Summary of Age Trends in Physical Development

	Brain Development	Growth and Motor Development	Health Challenges
Early Childhood (Prenatal–5 Years)	Brain development begins early in gestation. Before birth to 2 years, synaptogenesis occurs. At birth, glucose rates are about 2/3 of adult rates. Metabolic activity in the cortex is low, but in sensory, motor, and emotion areas it is high. At 4 years, glucose rates and blood flow are twice those of adults. Increased activity begins in the cerebral cortex.	Normal birth size can range from 5.5 to 10 pounds. After birth, infants gain more than a pound a month. Birth weight doubles by 5 months and height doubles by 3–4 years. By preschool age, rate of growth is about 3 inches in height and 4 pounds per year. The development of fine and gross motor skills follows a sequence.	Newborns sleep more than they are awake. Their sleep need gradually diminishes to about 11 hours for preschoolers. Children need daytime naps until ages 3–5. SIDS is most likely to occur in children under 1 year old. Infants increase in fat level until about 1 year, and then decrease. Prenatal drug exposure, including alcohol and nicotine, is linked to low birth weight.
Middle Childhood (6–12 Years)	Glucose rate plateaus until ages 9–10, then gradually declines. Synaptic proliferation also plateaus. Pruning occurs in the frontal cortex until about 11 years of age. There may be a decline in brain plasticity after age 10.	Children grow about 2.5 inches and gain 5–6 pounds per year until puberty. Coordination of movement with perception allows children to maintain balance, catch a ball, or write their name. Amount of physical movement peaks around 7–9 years. Hormones that trigger puberty begin about 6–8 years.	At age 6, children need about 11–12 hours of sleep. Fat increases at 4–8 years. Girls who are overweight at 5–7 tend to enter puberty early. Heavy drug users usually begin use in elementary school.
Adolescence (13–19 Years)	Glucose rate declines to adult levels at about 16–18 years—less energy is required. Synaptic pruning continues well into adolescence. Synaptic densities in the frontal cortex stabilize at adult levels in mid- to late adolescence. Myelination of the prefrontal cortex becomes adult-like. The cerebellum reaches full maturity. A chemical shift in some neurotransmitters alters motivation and psychopathology. Adult brains continue to grow synapses, dendrites, and supportive tissue due to learning.	Puberty culminates during adolescence. This includes a growth spurt, changes in ratio of muscle and fat, and a spurt in strength for boys. It includes development of primary sex characteristics, like testes in males and ovaries in females, and secondary sex characteristics, like pubic, facial, and body hair and breasts in women. On average, menarche occurs for girls at ages 12–13 and spermarche for boys at ages 14–15.	Adolescents need about 8–10 hours of sleep, with the higher amount applying to rapidly growing or physically active teens. About 85% of teens get inadequate sleep. About 7% of teens have delayed sleep, which is a sleep disorder. Girls become more dissatisfied with their bodies, which is linked to anorexia nervosa and bulimia. Most adolescents try ATOD but are not consistent users.

Chapter Summary

The Brain

- The brain has billions of nerve cells. Neurons communicate with each other through electrical impulses and neurotransmitters at synapses. Nerve cells have axons with a coating called a myelin sheath, which increases the speed of impulses.
- During infancy, synaptogenesis results in overproduction of synapses. During childhood, some connections are strengthened and others are pruned. Neurons that are repeatedly activated form stable circuits and brain structures.
- The brain has two sides, or hemispheres, and several major structures such as the brainstem, the limbic system, the cerebellum, and four lobes of the cortex. The prefrontal cortex carries on functions that make us uniquely human, like problem solving.
- Genes do not specify the precise architecture of the brain. Instead, synaptogenesis allows the brain to capture experience, which shapes brain architecture. An enriched environment promotes brain development. Stress and insecure attachment can have negative effects.
- There is a gradual loss of brain plasticity for some functions, but remediation is usually possible when early disadvantage occurs.

Growth and Motor Development

- Children develop gross and fine motor skills in a predictable sequence.
- Puberty is a long, gradual process that includes development of primary and secondary sex characteristics, as well as growth spurts and changes in body composition.
- Youth who mature early, especially girls, are at risk for behavior problems, substance use, and sexual activity.
- Genes and the environment combine to drive physical development. You can speed motor development, but only to a limited extent.
- Undernutrition causes stunted growth, delays puberty, and undermines brain development. Breast milk is the best nutrition for infants and is related to improved health and higher intelligence.
- Harsh or unresponsive caregiving can undermine physical growth and well-being.
- Most U.S. children consume too much fat and sugar and not enough fruits and vegetables. Nor do they get adequate exercise. Good nutrition and exercise are linked to success in school. Teachers can influence nutrition, exercise, and motor skills.

Contemporary Health Challenges

- Well-rested children behave better at school and have higher academic achievement. Unfortunately, many children, particularly adolescents, are sleep deprived.
- Many American children are overweight, particularly low-SES children. Childhood obesity predicts type 2 diabetes, social and emotional problems, early onset of female puberty, and adult obesity.
- Obesity is linked to low activity level, excessive television viewing, poor diet, and parent behaviors such as attempting to control children's eating.
- Anorexia nervosa and bulimia are severe eating disorders that afflict girls more commonly than boys.
- Use of ATOD is predicted by parents' and friends' use. A sizable minority of adolescents are users, but at any given time most adolescents are abstainers. Among drug-using students, alcohol is the most common drug, followed by tobacco and then marijuana. Heavy drug users typically begin use in elementary school.
- White youth smoke and drink the most and Black youth the least. Boys use illegal drugs more than girls and drink alcohol more; they have similar rates of smoking. High-SES children use more than middle- or low-SES children.
- Prenatal drug exposure undermines infant development and predicts negative outcomes through adolescence.

Accompanying Education CourseMate Website Resources

Visit the **Education CourseMate** website at **CengageBrain.com** to find resources and study aids for this chapter, including self-tests, additional print and website resources, and glossary flashcards. The following videos illustrate concepts discussed in the chapter:

0–2 Years	**Fine Motor Development for Infants and Toddlers**
0–2 Years	**Gross Motor Development for Infants and Toddlers**
2–5 Years	**Fine Motor Development for Early Childhood**
2–5 Years	**Gross Motor Development for Early Childhood**
5–11 Years	**Fine Motor Development for Middle Childhood**
5–11 Years	**Gross Motor Development for Middle Childhood**
12–18 Years	**Physical Development in Adolescence, Puberty**

section 2 The Cognitive Child

How do children learn, and what are their cognitive capabilities? In this section, we discuss four major theories that address these questions. Chapter 3 introduces you to behaviorism, Piaget's theory of cognitive development, and Vygotsky's sociocultural theory. Chapter 4 introduces you to information processing theory. When you teach, you will apply at least one, and probably all four, of these theories in your classroom. We end this section with Chapter 5, which discusses differences in cognitive ability among children. Let's begin our study of learning by eavesdropping on Mrs. Harl's 3rd-grade class.

Case 2 **Monica Learns Three-Digit Addition**

Monica Learns Three-Digit Addition

H&S Produktion/Flirt Collection/PhotoLibrary

Mrs. Harl is preparing to teach her 3rd-graders a new math concept. She projects an addition problem on the whiteboard:

$$\begin{array}{r} 203 \\ +\ 518 \end{array}$$

Seeing the three-digit problem, the children erupt with comments. One child says: "Whoa! That's a hard problem!" Mrs. Harl responds, "Shhh. I know you guys have trouble with these kinds of problems, so that is why we are working on them right now." Mrs. Harl points out which columns are the ones, tens, and hundreds. She adds the ones column and finds that they add to more than ten. She explains that she will have to carry one to the tens column to arrive at the answer of 721.

Mrs. Harl then writes several similar problems on the board. She asks for volunteers to go to the board to solve each problem. Not a single hand goes up. With no volunteers, Mrs. Harl selects Monica, who slowly walks to the board and then whines, "This is hard. I don't know how to do this." Mrs. Harl helps her split the numbers into three columns and says, "See, you know how to do this." Monica smiles and begins to solve the problem on her own.

$$\begin{array}{r} 319 \\ +\ 248 \end{array}$$

Monica adds the ones column and gets 17. She then places the 7 under the ones column, and places a 5 under the tens column. Mrs. Harl points out that she forgot to add 1 to the tens column. Monica fixes her mistake and continues solving the problem. Mrs. Harl narrates for the rest of the class each step Monica takes, including her mistake. "See? Monica almost forgot about carrying the 1, and I bet a lot of you make this mistake too. You need to make sure you don't forget about carrying your ones."

After Monica sits down, Mrs. Harl asks a few more students to solve problems on the board. Having seen Monica work through the math problem, her classmates feel more confident. They add correctly, with no errors. Mrs. Harl then writes another problem on the board.

$$\begin{array}{r} 199 \\ +\ 204 \end{array}$$

She says, "This is how I would do the problem. I would take 1 from the 204 and add it to 199 to make an even 200. Then I would add 203 + 200, which is a much easier problem." Sam yells out, "Yeah. That's easy. The answer is 403." Mrs. Harl says, "Very good Sam! Does anyone have a different way to solve this problem?" Lisa raises her hand, "I added each column separately and still got the right answer."

Mrs. Harl says, "If you want to do it another way, then that is fine, as long as you are getting the right answers." She makes it clear to her students that there are different ways to solve the problems, and tells the children to use the way they feel most comfortable.

Which theory of cognitive development is Mrs. Harl applying as she teaches Monica and her classmates? Is this an appropriate way to teach this cognitive skill? Should she have let the children discover their own way to add three-digit numbers, rather than directly teaching them an algorithm for doing it? Will she confuse her students by giving them multiple strategies for solving the problems? After reading this section, you should be able to answer these questions and have a better understanding of how to foster learning and cognitive development in your students.

Classic Theories of Learning and Cognition

Bob Ebbesen/Alamy

HOW HAVE THE CONSEQUENCES OF YOUR BEHAVIOR SHAPED THE KIND OF STUDENT YOU ARE? Do you learn best by figuring out answers, or by being told the answers? In this chapter, we will discuss several theories of how students learn that address these, and other, questions. After you read this chapter, you will understand:

- Major theories of learning and cognition.
- What research suggests about the theories.
- How to apply the theories in your classroom.

Behaviorism

In a 2nd-grade classroom, Naomi finishes her assignment and begins reading a book about Sacajawea. The class is supposed to be reading biographies in their free time, so the teacher announces to the whole class how happy she is to see that Naomi is reading. Her teacher then rewards Naomi with a ticket that she can use at the end of the week to buy candy, stickers, and small stuffed animals at the school store. Tickets are given out each time a child does something positive in class. The next day Naomi reads her biography during free time again—and so do several other children.

Naomi's teacher is using a behaviorist approach when she rewards Naomi for reading. When she gives Naomi a ticket, she influences Naomi to repeat the behavior and other students to follow Naomi's example. We will discuss behaviorism next. Two other influential theories that we will discuss in this chapter are cognitive developmental theory and sociocultural theory. The primary difference among these three classic theories is their perspective on what causes children to learn and reason better with age.

Behaviorism is the scientific study of observable behavior. According to behaviorists, control of behavior is located outside the child, in the environment. John Watson (1878–1958), a leader of behaviorism, made the following assertion:

behaviorism the scientific study of overt, observable behavior.

> *Give me a dozen healthy infants, well-formed, and my own specified world to bring them up in and I'll guarantee to take any one at random and train him to become any type of specialist I might select—doctor, lawyer, artist, merchant-chief and yes, even beggar-man and thief, regardless of his talents, penchants, tendencies, abilities, vocations, and race of his ancestors (Watson, 1924, p. 82).*

Do you agree with this statement? Watson is exaggerating the point that both the credit and the blame for what children become rest squarely on their environment. Behaviorists believe that children come to behave in their own unique way because each has a unique learning history.

According to behaviorists, behavior is learned. In fact, **learning** is defined as a relatively permanent change in *behavior* that occurs as a result of experience. In Mrs. Harl's math class, you would know that Monica has learned to solve math problems if she is able to *do* three-digit addition days or months after the lesson. You would know she had not learned if she were not able to add three-digit numbers. According to behaviorists, the same principles of learning apply to a 9-month-old as to a 19-year-old. Thus, whether you teach preschool or high school, the following discussion applies.

learning according to behaviorists, a relatively permanent change in observable behavior that is the result of experience, not maturation or some other cause.

Behaviorists use the term **conditioning** to refer to creating situations that result in learning. Conditioned behavior is the same as learned behavior. In the vignette, Naomi and her classmates learned to read biographies as a result of their teacher's conditioning. We will discuss two forms of conditioning that are relevant to classrooms—classical conditioning and operant conditioning.

conditioning learning, or creating conditions conducive to learning.

Classical Conditioning

classical conditioning a form of conditioning in which a neutral stimulus is paired with a stimulus that causes an involuntary response until the neutral stimulus becomes a conditioned stimulus and also causes the response.

Classical conditioning is often called Pavlovian conditioning after Ivan Pavlov, a Russian physiologist who won the Nobel Prize in 1904. Classical conditioning starts with a stimulus that causes an *involuntary* response, without learning. In his most famous study, Pavlov placed meat powder in dogs' mouths, which caused them to salivate. The meat powder was an *unconditioned stimulus.* The salivation was an *unconditioned response*, meaning it was involuntary, not learned, and not under the dogs' control. At the same time, he presented a sound—for example, a bell. This was a *neutral stimulus* because it did not have anything to do with salivation. After repeatedly pairing the food and the sound, the dogs began salivating at the sound alone, so the sound changed from neutral stimulus to *conditioned stimulus.* Salivation at the sound of the bell, without the food, became the *conditioned response.* The dogs had learned (changed their behavior) to salivate at the sound. Pavlov's studies are so famous that they even appear in cartoons (see Figure 3.1).

extinction (classical conditioning) the conditioned stimulus and unconditioned stimulus are repeatedly not paired until the conditioned stimulus no longer elicits the conditioned response.

Learned behavior can be unlearned. **Extinction** within the realm of classical conditioning refers to repeatedly providing the conditioned stimulus (bell) *without* the unconditioned stimulus (food) until the conditioned stimulus (bell) no longer elicits the conditioned response (salivation); that is, if conditioned dogs hear the bell repeatedly but do not receive food, after a while salivation will stop.

Classical conditioning occurs in humans as well as dogs. It explains some emotional responses, particularly fear and anxiety, such as math anxiety. The sight of math problems should not cause anxiety, but if you are repeatedly humiliated for doing poorly on math problems, you might be conditioned to associate math with humiliation and learn to feel anxious at the sight of math problems.

Classical conditioning can explain why some children dislike school and drop out or graduate early. Children who have negative experiences at school, like shame and embarrassment, have an unconditioned negative emotional response, which becomes paired with school. If this happens often, the mere sight, smell, and sounds of the school come to elicit sweaty palms, anxiety, shame, or anger. After conditioning, the negative emotional response to the school is automatic, not under the child's control.

Figure 3.1 Pavlov's Cat.
Pavlov's research on salivating dogs is so well known that it even permeates cartoon culture. It appears that cats are not as predictable as dogs.

These feelings can apply to new situations, like other schools. Such children may grow up to become parents who will not attend back-to-school night because of the negative emotions school evokes. In contrast, students who experience academic success and close friendships at school may be conditioned to feel happiness in school buildings. After reading this text, you will have the tools to condition your students to enjoy school.

Operant Conditioning

While classical conditioning focuses on automatic or involuntary behavior, operant conditioning focuses on *voluntary* behavior like doing homework or getting in fights. **Operant conditioning** refers to learning voluntary behavior through consequences, which are either reinforcing or punishing.

operant conditioning voluntary behavior is conditioned through its consequences.

Reinforcement and Punishment

A **reinforcer** is a consequence that increases the probability of a behavior. There are two types of reinforcers: positive and negative. Positive refers to *presenting something* and negative refers to *removing something*. Thus, a **positive reinforcer** increases the probability that a behavior will occur again by *presenting* a consequence. A teacher may present students with praise, treats, increased recess time, and good grades as positive reinforcers (Kodak, Northrup, & Kelley, 2007; Penrod, Wallace, & Dyer, 2008). If children work hard on a class project, receive good grades, and then work hard on another project, they have been positively reinforced for hard work. If children on the playground punch other children in order to get a basketball, find that it works, and use punching in the future to get what they want, they have been positively reinforced for punching.

reinforcer a consequence that increases the probability of a response.

positive reinforcement the provision or introduction of a consequence that increases the probability of a response.

Think About This When people train dogs to roll over by giving them dog biscuits, or when they train dolphins to jump through hoops by giving them fish, are they using classical conditioning or operant conditioning? Explain.

Negative reinforcement also *increases* the probability that a behavior will occur again but by *removing* a negative or aversive stimulus. Seat-belt buzzers are an example of negative reinforcement. Drivers are reinforced to fasten the seat belt because something negative (the buzzer) is removed when they fasten their seat belt, which increases the probability of the target behavior (fastening the seat belt). When people learn to escape aversive environments, they are being negatively reinforced (e.g., Gardner, Wacker, & Boelter, 2009). For example, when students harass a teacher about too much homework, the teacher might reduce the homework in order to terminate the harassment, and the teacher is negatively reinforced. Children who hate sports may report feeling ill and have to go to the nurse during PE class. They are negatively reinforced, because they escape from a situation that is aversive for them. This is why negative reinforcement is sometimes referred to as *escape conditioning*.

negative reinforcement removal of an aversive stimulus. This increases the probability of a response. This is *not* punishment.

Notice that *negative reinforcement is not the same as punishment*, even though many people confuse them. **Punishment** refers to consequences that *reduce* the probability of a behavior. It does not necessarily refer to physical punishment, but can include scolding or having to sit in a less preferred seat. Punishment functions through *presenting* something or *removing* something. For example, presenting a student with a demerit could function as punishment. Removing recess from a student could function as punishment. These consequences would only qualify as punishment if they actually change the student's behavior, regardless of the teacher's intention.

punishment consequences that reduce the probability of a response.

Is it wise to punish children? B. F. Skinner (1972), one of the most famous proponents of operant conditioning, was staunchly opposed to punishment (see Box 3.1). Skinner argued that behavior resulting from punishment was not as predictable as behavior resulting from reinforcement. It is better to reinforce appropriate behavior than to punish misbehavior. Nevertheless, punishment can be effective in stopping misbehavior. We will discuss the role of operant conditioning as a form of discipline in Chapter 7.

Theories and Theorists **Box 3.1**

B. F. Skinner

B. F. Skinner (1904–1990) was one of the most influential psychologists in history. Skinner studied rats in specially designed cages, which became known as *Skinner boxes.* A rat was put in a cage with a lever. If the rat pressed the lever, a pellet of food was released into the cage. No one told this to the rat beforehand, so it often made many movements before randomly pressing the lever. After being reinforced, the rat would press the lever again and again, until it was no longer hungry. If the lever only operated when a light was on, then the rat quickly learned to press the lever as soon as the light came on, and not at any other time. (Skinner also invented a teaching machine that reinforced human students, but it did not involve rat-food pellets!) From these kinds of experiments, Skinner demonstrated the effects of reinforcement.

Nina Leen/Time Life Pictures/Getty Images

B.F. Skinner

Skinner believed that the purpose of science is to predict and control behavior. Behavior is lawful. If you understand all the contingencies operating on a student, you will understand the student's behavior. The environment, not internal events like thought or feeling, is the primary cause of behavior. Skinner argued that internal events in the mind are not a complete cause of behavior, because you still have to understand where they come from, and ultimately the answer would be the environment. So why invoke the concept of internal events at all? In his last talk at the American Psychological Association, eight days before he died, he ardently exclaimed that there was no need to invoke the concept of mind to explain behavior.

Skinner applied behaviorism in schools and any other situation where reinforcement was possible. He even began training pigeons to guide missiles. This led to animals being used in early space flight to determine if being in space would alter behavior. He believed that advances in physical and medical science would never solve the world's problems. Only behavior change would. To convey this view he wrote a utopian novel called *Walden Two* (1948). The book evoked many strong, and often angry, responses. People compared it with Orwell's totalitarians in *Nineteen Eighty-Four,* Hitler's Nazism, and Stalin's Communist regime because Skinner advocated controlling behavior. It was threatening to people who want to view themselves as masters of their own destiny rather than as robots controlled by their environments.

Skinner addressed his critics in another book, *Beyond Freedom and Dignity* (1971), in which he argued that lack of awareness of the forces controlling your behavior could make you feel free, but the feeling is illusory. It is dangerous to be controlled by forces you are not aware of. Skinner believed it was better to make control systematic rather than haphazard. To his credit, his methods have been applied to produce freedom for drug addicts, delinquents, and others who, without behavior therapy, relinquish their freedom to prisons or mental hospitals. His books advocate that society eliminate punitive forms of control and use only positive reinforcement to change behavior.

It is easy to misapply reinforcement and punishment in the classroom. Two common mistakes are (1) ignoring behavior that deserves reinforcement and (2) confusing punishment and reinforcement. For example, praise, intended as reinforcement, can actually be punishment for children who do not want praise. A teacher may intend reinforcement when she says, "Wallace, I am so glad to see that you did your homework today! And your score on the quiz was very good!" However, Wallace may be embarrassed and choose to do less homework. On the other hand, scolding, intended as punishment, can actually be reinforcement for children who seek attention. Positive attention is preferred, but for some children even negative attention can reinforce.

How do you know whether you are correctly applying reinforcement and punishment in your classroom? If the consequence reduces the probability of a behavior, it is functioning as punishment. If the consequence increases the behavior, it is functioning as reinforcement. Let's see how this works in a 3rd-grade classroom:

Othman dislikes math work. Anytime Mr. Samms, his teacher, passes out difficult math work, Othman makes inappropriate noises and comments, flicks materials across the room, throws books, and instigates a rumpus. Mr. Samms puts Othman in time-out for his misbehavior. Othman begins to act out every day in math, so that he will get sent to time-out.

Although Mr. Samms intends to punish Othman, the misbehavior continues or even increases, which means that *the intended punishment is functioning as reinforcement.* Othman was allowed to leave the aversive math lesson, so Mr. Samms is negatively reinforcing Othman, thus increasing misbehavior.

Shaping

As a teacher, one of your responsibilities is to get students to enact specific behaviors. Yet, if a student never displays a target behavior, like completing homework neatly, you cannot reinforce it. What can you do? Behaviorists use a technique called **shaping**, which means that you reinforce behaviors that are in the *direction* of the target behavior. Behaviorists call this *reinforcing successive approximations* to the target behavior. For example, 10-year-old Doug has illegible handwriting. He does not close the letters *d* or *a*, so they look like *cl* and *u*. His teacher describes how she uses shaping to help him:

shaping reinforcement of successive approximations to a target behavior.

Whenever I saw an "a" or a "d" on Doug's papers that was closer to the standard, I circled it and wrote "better" beside it. One time I asked Doug to look over one of his own papers and tell me which "a" he thought was best and which "d" best. I did not comment on the poorly written letters. . . . After three weeks his handwriting had improved markedly. I retrieved one of the papers he had written a month earlier, and we compared it with his current handwriting. He was impressed . . . and could see how much he had improved. (Krumboltz & Krumboltz, 1972, p. 42)

Be aware that you can inadvertently shape student behavior in undesirable ways. If you ignore children's requests for attention until they shout loudly, you are training them to shout; you will have extinguished quiet hand-raising by ignoring it, and shaped a new behavior.

Stability and Extinction

Behavior tends to be stable as long as the system of reinforcement remains stable. If what is reinforced changes, new behaviors will appear. Thus, if Naomi in the opening vignette is reinforced for writing in her journal during free time, rather than silently reading, then she is likely to begin writing more and reading less in class.

extinction (operant conditioning) the elimination or decline in response caused by stopping reinforcement.

Sometimes you will be interested in stopping a behavior in your students. **Extinction** (in relation to operant conditioning) refers to eliminating or reducing a behavior by stopping reinforcement. In order to extinguish a classroom behavior, you need to figure out what is reinforcing the behavior and then eliminate the reinforcer. For example, if Mr. Samms had ignored Othman's misbehavior, the misbehavior might have extinguished. However, when you attempt extinction, the misbehavior may *increase initially*, as the student seeks the attention that he or she has come to expect. Thus, Othman probably would have intensified his misbehavior temporarily, when Mr. Samms first started to ignore it, but over time might have quit misbehaving during math.

continuous reinforcement reinforcement occurs after every correct response.

intermittent reinforcement reinforcement occurs after some, but not all, responses.

If you want to teach a new behavior, it is best to use **continuous reinforcement**—that is, reinforce every correct response, and reinforce it immediately. However, if you want to maintain an existing behavior and make it less susceptible to extinction, it is best to use **intermittent reinforcement**—that is, reinforce some but not all appropriate responses. For example, gambling is reinforced on an intermittent schedule, and is highly resistant to extinction. Gamblers go for long periods without winning but continue to gamble. Thus, if you want your students to maintain a behavior over the long term, like bringing their books to class daily, reinforce them occasionally but not every time, after the behavior is reasonably stable.

> ***Think About This*** Teachers sometimes place misbehaving students in time-out, like sitting on a solitary chair. Is extinction the goal of time-out? What other principles of conditioning might be at work in time-out? Is the intent to increase or decrease the target behavior? What do you think students of different ages are thinking about during time-out? Use a concrete example to make your case.

Classroom Implications of Behaviorism

When applied well, behaviorism is a powerful tool for promoting learning and positive behavior in students. We will discuss general guidelines for applying operant conditioning in your classroom, and then discuss a specific approach to instruction that evolved from behaviorism, called direct instruction.

Operant Conditioning

Operant conditioning has been effectively used to improve paying attention in class, completing assignments, and studying (Greenwood et al., 1992). To apply behaviorism successfully in your classroom, follow these guidelines:

- Figure out what your students find reinforcing. Your attention may be reinforcing for many, though not all, students (Austin & Soeda, 2008). Pride in new knowledge and problem solving may be reinforcing. Different students may find different things reinforcing. One study found that when seventeen items such as stickers, toy dinosaurs, and candy bars were ranked by teachers and early elementary students, the items ranked highest by the teachers were never ranked higher than fourth by the children (Resetar & Noell, 2008). This suggests you may have to put effort into figuring out what is truly reinforcing to your students.

- Be aware of how grades function for each of your students. Grades are one of the key consequences that teachers control in classrooms from 3rd through 12th grade. Grades can serve as reinforcement, punishment, or neither. One child may be thrilled to get a C, another child may be disappointed, and still another may not care. If good grades result in children studying and trying hard, they function as reinforcement.
- Intentionally condition positive behavior in students. Be careful not to mistakenly reinforce misbehavior, as Mr. Samms did with Othman, or extinguish good behavior by ignoring it.
- Focus on reinforcement, not punishment. Be clear about what you want to reinforce, such as solving problems or continuing to try after failure.
- Shape student behavior when teaching complex skills; that is, reinforce successive approximations to the target behavior. Earlier, we showed how this was done with handwriting. Shaping can also be applied to teaching preschoolers to count and to coaching adolescents in sports. For example, novices were taught to golf by first hitting short putts. Then they progressed to longer putts, then to chip shots with irons, then to long drives with drivers. Compared with students who started with long drives, students whose skills were carefully shaped were more likely to win a playoff (Martin & Pear, 2003).
- Use material rewards with care. While material rewards, like the tickets Naomi's teacher used, can be quite effective in classrooms, there are several drawbacks to their use. One is that managing them can become a burden for the teacher. Another is that students come to expect them: "If I do my homework, can I get a prize from the treasure box?" Another especially important drawback is that *material rewards do little to foster intrinsic motivation for the task.* This will be discussed more in Chapter 7.

If you follow these general guidelines from behaviorism in your classroom, student learning should improve. However, you may not be able to apply operant conditioning in all situations, because you cannot always control the consequences of behavior. You are likely to have more control of consequences in preschool, elementary school, or special education self-contained classrooms than in typical secondary classrooms, because adolescents can acquire their own reinforcers like food and money. Schools try to control teens' behavior using demerits, grades, exclusion from sports, or special honors, but many teens are not reinforced or punished by these consequences. Nevertheless, one powerful reinforcer that you control, and that most students respond to, is caring from you. We will discuss this more in Chapter 6.

When teachers deliberately apply operant conditioning to children, it is called **behavior modification** or **applied behavior analysis**. One of us (CB) taught reading in a program that used behavior modification with children up to age 12 who had failed to learn to read in their regular classroom. Teachers sat at a table with six children. When a child correctly paired a sound with a letter, the teacher would place

behavior modification operant conditioning used to change human behavior, frequently applied in psychotherapy and special education classrooms. Token economies may be used for reinforcement.

applied behavior analysis controlled application of behaviorist principles to experimentally alter behavior. Overlaps with behavior modification.

a chip in front of the child. After children mastered this basic skill, they were given a chip for a slightly more advanced skill, like blending sounds. When this was mastered, they were given a chip for sounding out simple words, and so on. Thus, their behavior was gradually *shaped* toward reading. Twice a day children turned in their chips for a prize. Because these children had experienced serious failure in school, they came to the program angry and frequently kicked the teachers under the table. The teachers wore shin guards so that they could ignore *all* disruptive behavior (*extinction*) and respond only to positive behavior (*reinforcement*). The approach was highly successful in that most students were soon reading at grade level. When behavior modification uses tokens like chips that children earn and use to pay for objects or privileges, it is called a *token economy.* In the opening vignette, Naomi's teacher was using a token economy.

Applied behavior analysis is especially common in the treatment of children who experience autism, ADHD, and mental retardation (e.g., Eikeseth, 2009). It has also been used to change a variety of behaviors in typically developing preschoolers to adolescents, such as not to touch hand guns, to use seat belts, and to stay on-task in the classroom (Austin & Soeda, 2008; Clayton & Helms, 2009; Jostad, Miltenberger, Kelso, & Knudson, 2008).

Direct Instruction

direct instruction a didactic form of instruction largely based on operant conditioning.

In addition to these general guidelines for applying behaviorism in your classroom, there is a particular approach to instruction, known as *direct instruction*, that has its origin in behaviorism. There are two types of **direct instruction**. In the first type, a teacher follows this general format (Rosenshine, 1987):

- Begin a lesson with a short statement of goals.
- Begin with a short review of previous, prerequisite learning.
- Present new material in small steps, with student practice after each step.
- Give clear and detailed instructions and explanations.
- Ask a large number of questions to check for student understanding.
- Provide systematic feedback and corrections.
- Obtain a student success rate of 80% or higher during initial practice.

Mrs. Harl used this approach when teaching Monica three-digit addition.

The second type of direct instruction uses commercially prepared scripts. Some well-known direct instruction curricula include DISTAR, *Connecting Mathematics Concepts*, and *Reading Mastery*. In scripted direct instruction, teachers are provided with the *exact wording* to use when teaching. Both forms of direct instruction provide frequent and immediate feedback to every student. Reinforcement should occur immediately after correct responses.

Direct instruction does not rely on discovery; everything that children are expected to know is explicitly taught. No assumptions are made about what students already know from their home life. The creed is: *if the student has not learned, the teacher has not taught* (Adams & Engelmann, 1996). Thus, low income, poor motivation, or lack of family support cannot be used to explain low student achievement; the teacher keeps instructing until the student has learned.

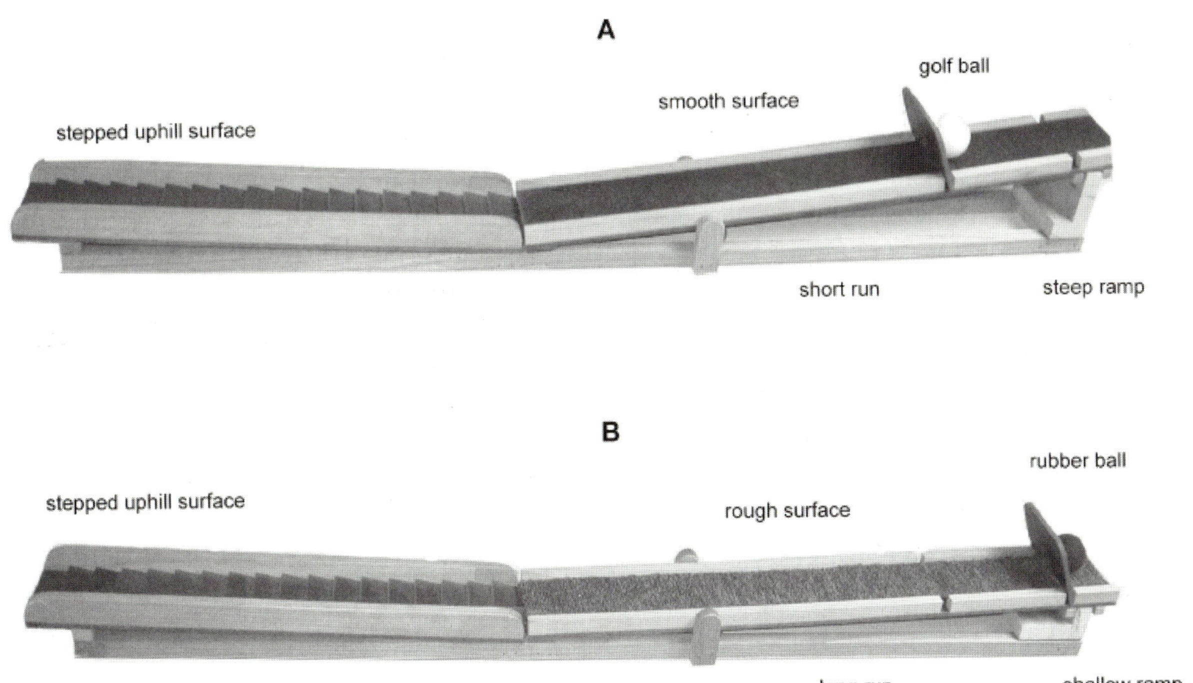

Figure 3.2 Inclined Ramps Used During a Direct Instruction Experiment.
This apparatus was used to test 3rd- and 4th-graders' ability to conduct a controlled experiment on the effect of four different variables by isolating a single variable at a time. *Klahr & Nigam, 2004 and Sage Publications.*

There is clear evidence that direct instruction is effective, particularly for teaching *skills* like decoding words, reading comprehension, arithmetic, and basic science or social studies *facts*, although not all researchers agree (Adams & Engelmann, 1996; Dean & Kuhn, 2006; Rittle-Johnson, 2007). Direct instruction is also effective for teaching *concepts*. For example, in one study 3rd- and 4th-graders experimented with a ball rolling down an incline (Klahr & Nigam, 2004). See Figure 3.2. Children could alter four variables: type of ball, steepness, surface, and length of the run. They were asked to determine how each variable affected the distance the ball would roll. They could only do this if they used a controlled experiment, where they altered just one variable at a time. The children were randomly assigned to direct instruction or unguided discovery learning.

More children (77%) in the direct instruction group learned the concept of controlled experimentation than in the discovery group (23%). When asked to transfer their newfound knowledge to a different and more challenging task—evaluating science-fair posters—the children who learned the concept were equally successful whether they learned through discovery or instruction. However, in a critique of this study, researchers found that if they gave students more time to *discover* the concept of controlled experimentation on their own, they later outperformed students who received direct instruction (Dean & Kuhn, 2006).

Some educators argue that direct instruction is effective for disadvantaged children who are unfairly burdened when left to discover academic knowledge on their own. For example, Delpit (1988), an African American educator, points out that students of color and poor students who lack background knowledge about the sounds that go with specific letters or about how to speak and write Standard English should not have to discover the rules of literacy; they need to be *taught* the rules so that they too can experience the power that goes with knowledge. Yet, direct instruction, especially the scripted form, has critics. Some feel it is too heavy handed, unresponsive to student differences, and developmentally inappropriate. Let's turn to Piaget's theory next, which presents a different concept of how children learn and grow cognitively that leads to quite different approaches to instruction.

Piaget's Theory of Cognitive Development

We asked him why a boat floats on the water whilst a little stone, which is lighter, sinks immediately. Vern reflected and then said: "The boat is more intelligent than the stone.—What does 'to be intelligent' mean?—It doesn't do things it ought not to do." (Piaget, 1929/1963, p. 223)

cognition mental processes like thinking, planning, reasoning, and remembering.

This is an interview between Swiss researcher Jean Piaget (1896–1980) and a 6-year-old boy. Piaget used interviews such as this one to develop a theory of children's cognitive development. The term **cognition** refers to mental processes like thinking, problem solving, categorizing, and remembering. *Cognitive development* means the orderly change across age in these mental processes. Piaget believed that to understand children's cognitive development, you must not only observe their behavior (as behaviorists do), but also consider *why* the child behaved that way. In particular, Piaget focused on why children give incorrect answers to questions, like why stones sink but boats do not. Because of children's consistent errors in reasoning, Piaget concluded that the logical structures of children's thought are different from adults'.

constructivist one who believes that knowledge acquisition is a process of construction rather than duplication (creating a mental copy of what is observed).

assimilation the process by which children incorporate experience into existing mental structures or schemes, according to Piaget.

scheme a cognitive structure or piece of understanding constructed through experience.

Before Piaget developed his theory of cognitive development, a prominent view was that knowledge is simply a recording of something perceived in the environment; that is, the mind makes a copy of the perception and stores it. Piaget rejected this view. He said that knowledge is not just a copy of the world, but that knowledge is an invention or construction in the mind of each person. He wrote, "In order to know objects, the [child] must act upon them, and therefore transform them: he must displace, connect, combine, take apart, and reassemble them" (Piaget, 1970, p. 704). This emphasis on each child constructing his or her own knowledge makes Piaget a **constructivist**.

Piaget also believed that learning involves assimilation. **Assimilation** refers to a child incorporating a new perception into existing schemes. A **scheme** is a cognitive structure, such as an image, perception, or thought. For example, in a 4th-grade class the teacher was reading aloud from a book about pioneers in early Ohio. She read about a peddler coming to an isolated farm in the wilderness. She stopped to clarify her students' understanding:

Teacher:	*Who knows what "isolated" means? (Several hands wave.) Jorge?*
Jorge:	*There's a lot of ice there?*
Teacher:	*No. Lacey?*
Lacey:	*It is really, really, really cold there.*

Through making the students' thinking public, the teacher has discovered that the children had constructed their own understanding of the word *isolated* based on their previous knowledge of the word *ice*. The children were mistakenly assimilating a new word, *isolated*, into their preexisting scheme of *ice*.

The counterpart to assimilation is accommodation. **Accommodation** refers to a child revising a scheme so that a new experience makes sense. In the 4th-grade class, the teacher helped the children accommodate their scheme of *isolated*:

accommodation the process by which children modify existing mental structures or schemes in order to adapt to new experience, according to Piaget.

> *Teacher:* *Scott, will you go stand in the corner by the sink for a minute? OK. Now Scott is isolated from the rest of us. What does "isolated" mean? (All hands go up.) Trevor?*
> *Trevor:* *Away from others?*
> *Teacher:* *Right. The author means they don't have any neighbors. No one lives within miles of them.*

According to Piaget, every act of learning includes both assimilation and accommodation, though the amount of each may vary. Some experiences may involve more assimilation, and some more accommodation. For example,

> *Manny, a toddler who has a pet cat, sees a new cat. He assimilates the new experience into his existing scheme for* kitty. *At the same time, the new cat is not identical with his own, so his scheme of* kitty *expands to other small, four-legged furry animals. One day Manny cries, "Kitty, kitty!" as he runs toward a skunk. His mother cries, "No. It's a skunk!" and whisks Manny away.*

His mother's reaction then causes Manny to accommodate and modify the existing kitty scheme into separate *skunk* and *kitty* schemes. Two children with the same experience may construct different knowledge because they had different preexisting schemes.

The tug-of-war between assimilation and accommodation is the result of the need for **equilibrium**, a state of cognitive balance and comfort. Piaget suggested that as you experience the world, you become perplexed and wish to resolve your cognitive disequilibrium. You assimilate and accommodate as you seek a state of equilibrium, which results in cognitive development.

equilibrium a state of cognitive balance or cognitive comfort.

Age Trends in Piaget's Cognitive Developmental Theory

According to Piaget, cognitive development happens in stages. He described four major stages: sensorimotor, preoperations, concrete operations, and formal operations. While Piaget gave approximate ages for each stage, he did not claim that specific ages go with each stage. Piaget believed that some children may reach a stage at a slightly younger or older age than average. The only way to infer a child's stage is by observing the child, not by merely knowing his or her age.

The four stages are linked with *qualitative*, as opposed to *quantitative*, differences in children's logic; that is, older children reason and solve problems in a different way than younger children. For example, a toddler who thinks that when her mother breaks a cookie in two she has more cookie, could be said to be reasoning in a different way than a teenager would. Piaget believed that a key difference between teens' and toddlers' cognitive ability is that teens can think accurately about abstract concepts, but younger children cannot. As children's experience with concrete objects accumulates, abstract concepts and higher-level knowledge develop. Let's examine each stage.

The Sensorimotor Stage (Birth to 2 Years)

When infants are born, they immediately begin to observe the world and attempt to make sense of it. Through rooting, sucking, grasping, and looking, they lay a foundation for cognitive growth. At this stage, thought and action are indistinguishable. The infant's first cognitions are sensory and motor oriented. A child learns about a new toy by grasping and chewing on it.

symbolic thought the cognitive ability to have one thing stand for, or represent, another.

sensorimotor stage children rely on senses and behavioral schemes to acquire knowledge. Roughly birth to 2 years.

deferred imitation ability to mentally represent and then imitate an action that was observed in the past.

object permanence the knowledge that objects that are out of view continue to exist.

Later in this stage, children become capable of **symbolic thought**—that is, the ability to have one thing stand for another. Language is a key marker for symbolic thought because to use language, children must understand that words like *mama* and *juice* stand for objects. As they grow older, children engage in symbolic thought as they use rocks as dishes or colored blocks as cars. This makes symbolic, make-believe play possible. During the **sensorimotor stage**, children become capable of **deferred imitation**; that is, they can mentally represent, remember, and then imitate an action they observed in the past. This ability is also related to make-believe play, which requires that children remember and reproduce what they have observed, such as putting the baby doll to sleep, or leaping like Superman into the air.

Sensorimotor infants develop **object permanence**, or the knowledge that objects that are out of view continue to exist. Infants who lack object permanence behave as though an object that has gone out of view has ceased to exist. Object permanence follows a predictable sequence. Newborns may show interest in an object, say, an attractive toy, but do not visually search for the toy if it is removed from view, suggesting no mental representation of the toy. At 4 to 8 months, infants will visually track the toy and reach for it if it is partially hidden beneath a blanket, but not if it is fully hidden. At 8 to 12 months, infants will search for the toy if it is hidden before their eyes. But they make an interesting mistake consistently: they will search for the object at point A even if the object is moved to point B in full view. For example, Piaget twice hid his 10-month-old daughter's toy parrot under her mattress at point A while she watched. Both times Jacqueline retrieved the parrot. Then, Piaget hid the toy parrot under the mattress in a different place, at point B, while she watched. Jacqueline searched for the parrot at point A instead of point B (Piaget, 1954). This is called the **A-not-B error** (see Figure 3.3). Piaget believed this occurred because older infants still have an incomplete understanding of object permanence.

Field Observation

Play with infants of different ages. Try hiding an attractive toy, and watch what each infant does. Did they follow this developmental sequence for object permanence? Test for the A-not-B error as well.

A-not-B error children observe an object being moved from hiding place A to hiding place B, but they search in hiding place A. Typical of the sensorimotor stage.

operation according to Piaget, mental actions or manipulations that follow rules.

The Preoperational Stage (About Ages 2 through 7)

Operations are mental actions that follow rules. You could think of an operation as an act of logic. The term *preoperational* refers to Piaget's view that children in this stage are not yet capable of thinking logically. He believed they have other limitations as well, like inability to think about how an object might look from different points of view, which requires mental manipulation. He believed they do not fully understand

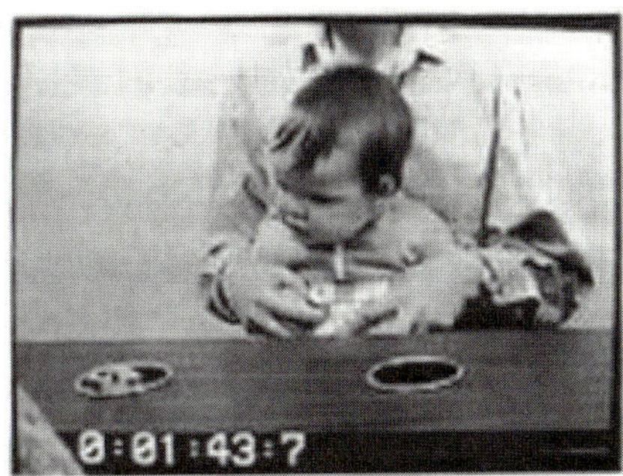

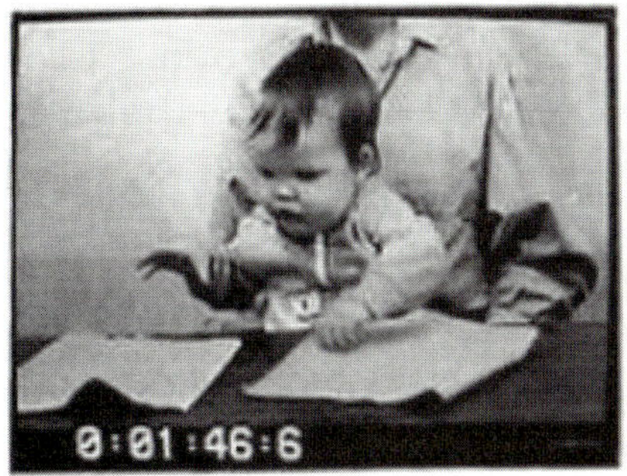

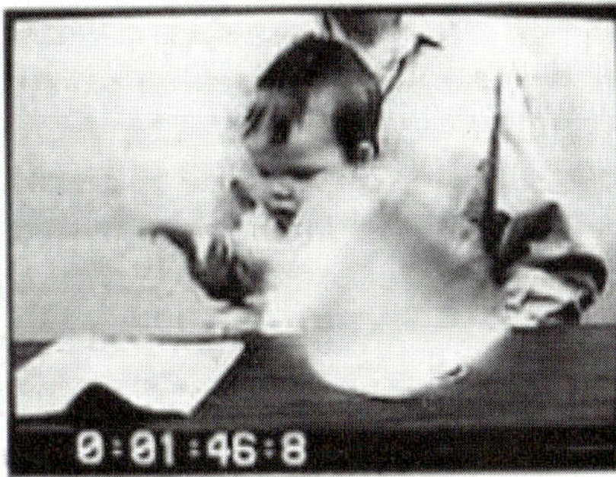

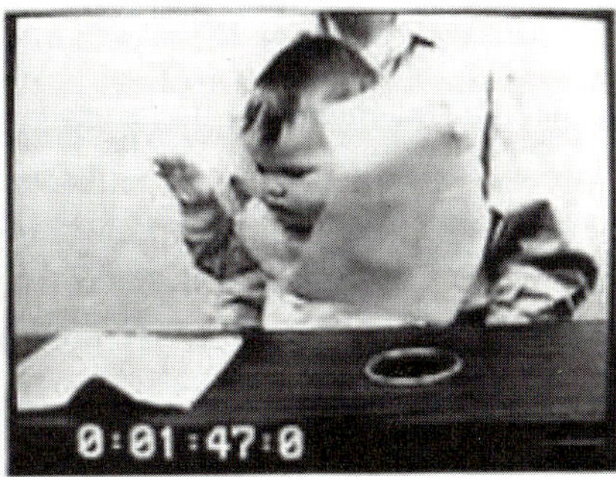

Figure 3.3 A-Not-B Error.
While the child was watching, a toy was placed in the opening to your right (location A, see top photo); then the toy was placed in the opening to your left (location B in top photo). In the next three photos, you can see the child reach for location A while looking intently at location B. The looking behavior suggests object permanence, but the reaching behavior suggests an inability to inhibit behavior. *Adapted from Inhelder & Piaget (1958) and Adele Diamond.*

cause-and-effect sequences (Desrochers, 2008). Other cognitive deficits according to Piaget include the following:

Animism

animism attribution of lifelike qualities, like intention, to nonliving, inanimate objects.

Animism is the belief that nonliving, inanimate objects have lifelike qualities. For example, children may think that boats are intelligent, that the sun or the moon is following them, that a single flower might get lonely, and that things that move, such as a flickering flame, are alive. They believe that objects or natural phenomena (rain, wind, snow) have intention, including intent to harm. For example, they might cry because they think that a leaf blowing toward them is chasing them.

Hierarchical classification

hierarchical classification the ability to classify or place objects into superordinate and subordinate categories.

Hierarchical classification means that things can be members of multiple levels of categories at the same time. For example, a collie is a dog and a mammal at the same time. Preoperational children have trouble classifying objects in a hierarchy. They have trouble understanding that all collies are dogs, but not all dogs are collies. We heard a young child correct someone by saying, "That's no woman—that's my mommy!" indicating trouble with hierarchical classification.

How did Piaget study children's trouble with hierarchical classification? He used *class inclusion* tests (Piaget & Inhelder, 1964). For example, he presented children with two colors of beads—ten red and five blue. He asked, "Are there more red beads or more beads?" Preoperational children tend to answer more red beads even though there are clearly more beads. Piaget argued that this is because the child cannot at the same time think of the whole class of beads and the parts (red and blue) that compose it, which is part of a general deficiency in mental flexibility.

Egocentrism

egocentric the tendency to see the world from your own point of view while failing to see other people's point of view.

Young children are **egocentric**, which is the tendency to see the world from their own point of view and to assume that other people do too (Piaget, 1926/1959, p. 9). Have you seen young children on the phone silently nod their head to say yes, when the person on the other end of the line cannot see the nod? Have you seen them close their eyes in order to hide from you? Preschoolers also show their egocentrism when they hold **collective monologues** in which they speak with another child and even take turns talking so they appear to be conversing, but neither is listening to the other.

collective monologues children appear to be conversing with each other, but are really not addressing thoughts or adapting speech to their conversation partners.

One way that Piaget demonstrated children's egocentrism was with the "three-mountain task" (see Figure 3.4). A child is presented with a three-dimensional model of three mountains that are distinctive because they have different objects at each peak: snow, a cross, or a house. The child is given ten pictures of different views of the three mountains. A doll is placed at various points around the model, and the child is asked to pick the picture that shows what the *doll* sees. Children in the **preoperational stage** tend to choose the picture that depicts *what the child sees*, not what the doll sees.

preoperational stage children are able to use symbolic thought, but unable to think logically, particularly to conserve or decenter. Roughly ages 2 to 7.

Conservation

conservation understanding that the properties of objects like mass, volume, and number do not change just because the objects' appearance changes.

center (or centration) the child focuses on one aspect of a task to the exclusion of other aspects.

Conservation refers to the fact that the properties of objects such as mass, volume, and number do not change just because the objects' appearance changes. For example, if you have a ball of clay, the amount of clay in the ball does not change if you smash it down it into a pancake shape, though the appearance changes (see Figure 3.5). Preoperational children might say that the smashed lump of clay has more mass than the ball. This is because they **center** on the superficial attributes of

Figure 3.4 Piaget's Three-Mountain Task. When preoperational children are asked to choose photos depicting the doll's view, they tend to choose photos of their own view.

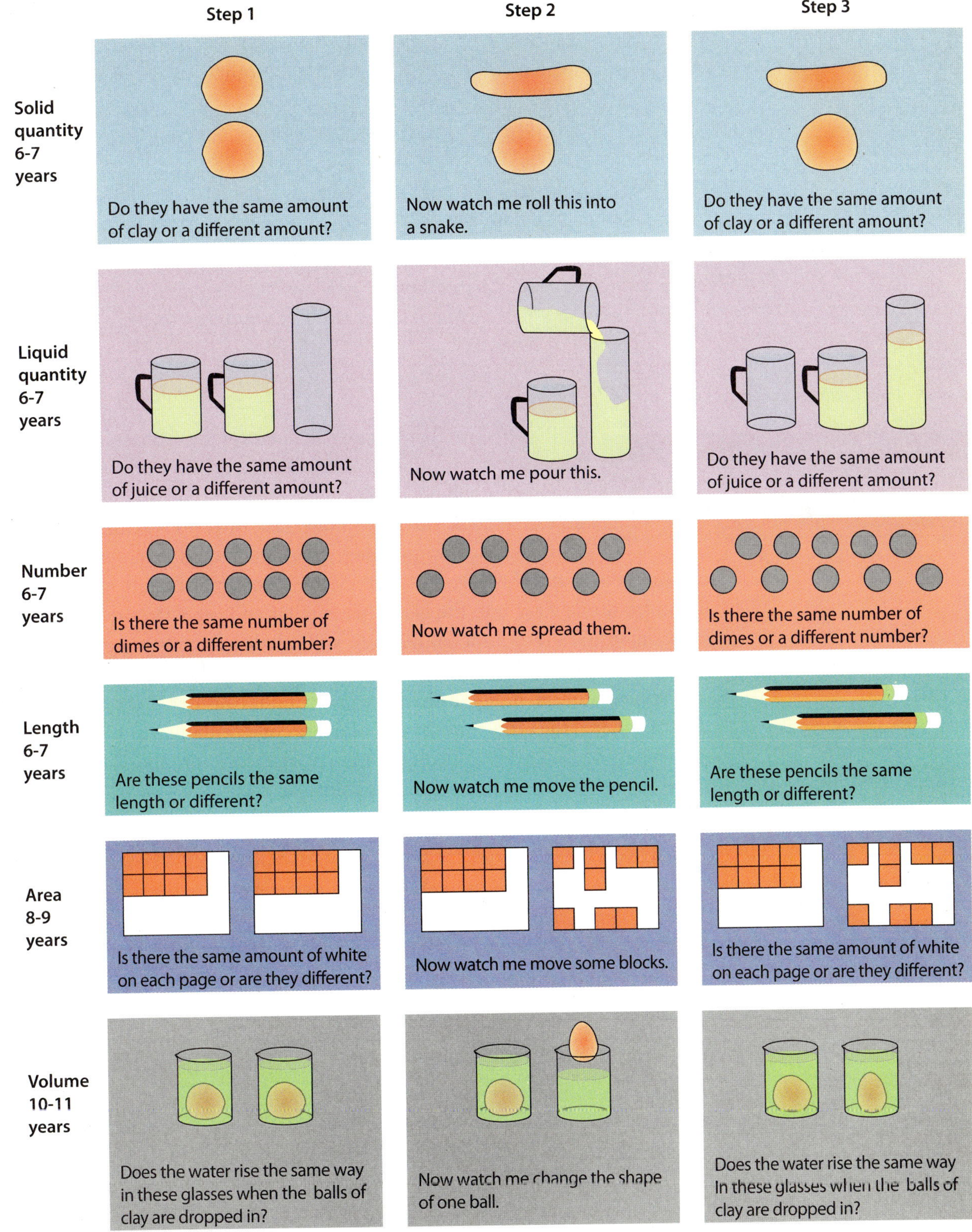

Figure 3.5 **Piagetian Conservation Tasks.**
Examples of different types of conservation tasks. Notice that children master different types at different ages.

decenter (or decentration) ability to think about multiple aspects of a task simultaneously.

objects. They are unable to decenter and simultaneously consider that the smashed clay covers more surface area but is thinner than it was. You can see this when you cut an apple in half for one child, but not the other. Listen to this conversation between two brothers:

5-year-old:	*Ha, ha, I got more than you!*
11-year-old:	*You did not. They are the same.*
5-year-old:	*Nut-uh. I got two and you only got one.*
11-year-old:	*It doesn't matter. They are still the same size.*
5-year-old:	*They are not! I have two, so that is bigger!*
11-year-old:	*Look, if you put your two pieces together, they are the same size as mine.*
5-year-old:	*Oh, I see. But I still have more!*

Field Observation

Do two of the tasks described in Figure 3.5 with a young child (age 3 to 5) and an older child (age 9 to 10). How do their responses compare?

Piaget is probably most famous for his conservation tasks, even though they constituted a small part of his work. They are popular because they illustrate the apparent illogic of young children and are fun to replicate. The best-known task involves two identical glasses and a third taller, skinnier glass. You pour liquid carefully into the identical glasses until the child agrees that they have the same amount. You then pour the liquid from one glass into the glass that is taller and ask, "Do they still contain the same amount?" Preoperational children will say that there is more liquid in the tall skinny glass, even though no liquid has been added or subtracted. The child centers on the height of the liquid in the glass and cannot consider the height and width of the container at the same time. In addition, the child cannot reverse operations—that is, mentally consider that if the liquid were poured back into the glass from whence it came, the height would be the same as before.

reverse operations ability to mentally reverse or negate an operation.

The Concrete Operational Stage (About Ages 7 through 11)

concrete operational stage children are able to decenter and think logically about concrete objects and experience. Roughly ages 7 to 11.

Once children reach the concrete operational stage, they think more logically. Now they can decenter, reverse operations, classify, and conserve successfully. You may notice children at this age collecting, sorting, and classifying—for example, collecting stamps and sorting them by country, and within country by theme (e.g., flowers, political figures, historical events). Children at this age may also use the full address to Grandma: Grandma Collins, 400 Orchard Street, Oradell, NJ 07649, The United States, North America, The Western Hemisphere, The Earth. This reflects hierarchical classification ability.

Toward the middle of the concrete operational stage (about age 9), children can successfully complete the bottle and mountain drawing tasks (Piaget & Inhelder, 1956). In the bottle drawing task, the child is presented with a picture of a bottle with liquid at the bottom and three other bottles that are tilted or inverted. The child is asked to draw where the water would be in the next three bottles. In the mountain drawing task, children draw a mountain with trees or people or houses. Figures 3.6 and 3.7 compare children's responses in the preoperational and concrete operational stages. Although children at this stage are now better at logical reasoning, they still are not skilled at abstract thinking, which comes with the next stage.

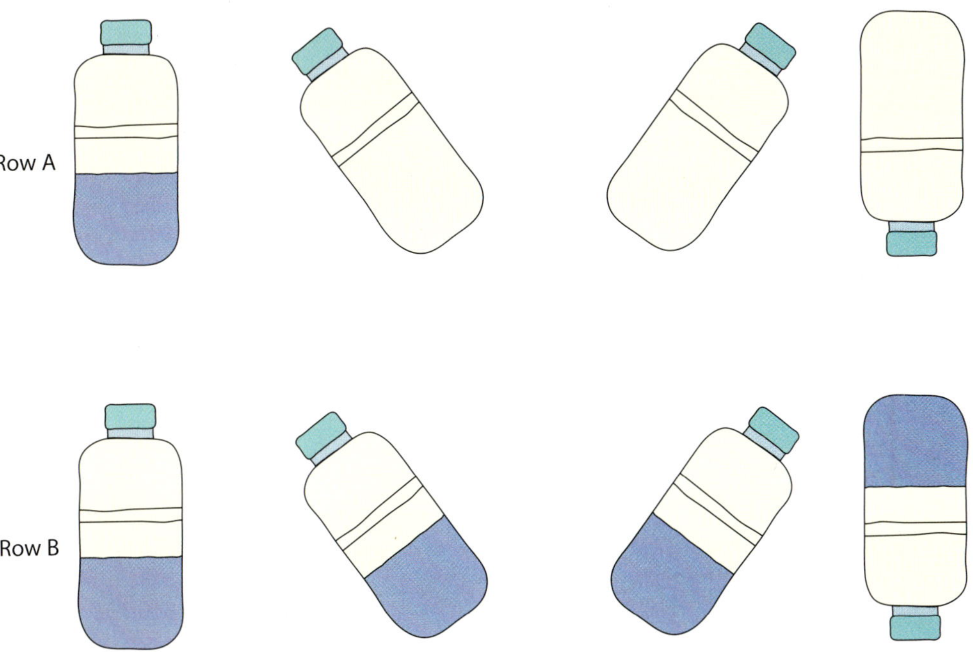

Figure 3.6 **Bottle Drawing Task.**
A child is presented with row A and asked, "Look at the water in the first bottle. Draw where the water would go in the next three bottles." Row B depicts drawing by a preoperational child.

Figure 3.7 **Drawings of a House and Mountain.**
When preoperational children draw a house or mountain, they tend to place the chimney and trees perpendicular to the surface instead of vertical. You may notice this in their art.

The Formal Operational Stage (about Age 12 and Older)

In the formal operational stage, children can think in the abstract; that is, they can think about possibilities that may not physically exist. They can follow clear logic and reason in a hypothetical-deductive manner, even if the premises are not true. For example, if all New Yorks are Chicagos, and all Chicagos are Seattles, is it true that all New Yorks are Seattles? Young, concrete thinkers cannot see this as a pure logic problem: if all As are Bs, and all Bs are Cs, is it true that all As are Cs? In contrast, formal thinkers can reason that As must be Cs, and all New Yorks are Seattles.

formal operational stage children are able to think abstractly about hypothetical events and systematically test hypotheses; roughly age 12 to adulthood.

Children at the formal operational stage can systematically test possible solutions to problems. They can isolate variables, form multiple hypotheses about which variable is relevant, vary one factor at a time to test each one, and assess each in light of evidence. Piaget believed that children younger than age 12 are rarely able to do this. How did Piaget know? In one task, he asked children to test what factor causes the rate of oscillation, or swinging, of a pendulum (see Figure 3.8). Possible variables are the length of string, the weight of the object at the end of the string, the height from

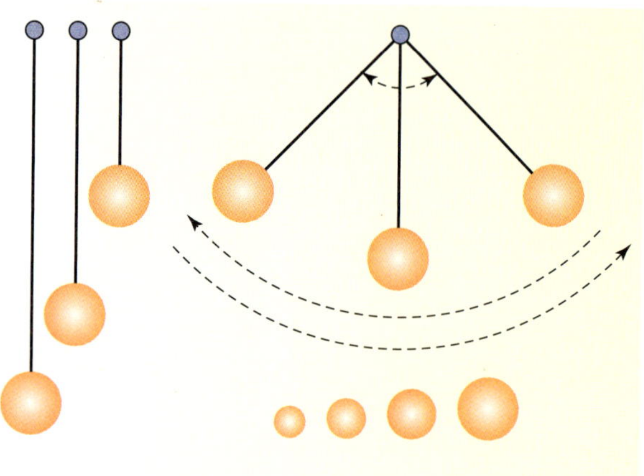

Figure 3.8 **Piaget's Pendulum Problem.**
What determines how fast the pendulum swings? Length of the string? Weight of the object? Height from which the weight is dropped? Force of the push? Formal operational children are able to vary one variable at a time, systematically, to determine what causes the rate of oscillation. *Adapted from Inhelder & Piaget (1958).*

Field Observation

The following two tasks measure formal operations (Gray, 1976). Try them out on a child who should be, and a child who should not yet be, in formal operations. Compare their responses.

Task 1.

All of the following sentences are true. What determines whether or not the mice will fight with each other?

1. *The mice are not brown; the mice are not old; the mice have food; the mice do not fight.*
2. *The mice fight; the mice do not have food; the mice are old; the mice are brown.*
3. *The mice are not old; the mice do not fight; the mice are brown; the mice do not have food.*
4. *The mice have food; the mice are not brown; the mice fight; the mice are old.*

Task 2.

Teresa (T), Carol (C), Peggy (P), and Sharon (S) are going to form teams for a contest. Teams can have one, two, three, or four members. Write all of the possible teams that can be formed. Use the first letter of each girl's name in the answer.

which the weight is dropped, and the force of the push used to begin swinging. If you are a formal operational thinker, you might try different lengths of string while keeping all the other variables the same. Then, you would hold length of string and the other variables constant while varying only one other variable, such as weight. After such systematic testing, you would discover that only length of string affects oscillation rate. This sort of controlled experimentation is important in everyday life. For example, if a car won't start and the mechanic replaces both the starter motor and the battery at the same time, the car may start, but the owner may have paid for an unneeded repair.

Try the two formal operations tasks in the margin. To successfully solve the mice problem, you have to suppress knowledge of how mice really act, and you must reason only from the facts given in the task. Children who are not yet formal thinkers use personal experience rather than abstract logic to solve the problem. They tend to say that mice who do not have food will fight, which is wrong given the third proposition. To be scored in the formal operational stage on the second task, the response must provide 14 or 15 teams (the correct answer is 15 teams) and the response must be *systematic*. One example of a systematic response is

T	TC	TCP	TCPS
C	TP	TCS	
P	TS	TPS	
S	CP	CPS	
	CS		
	PS		

Formal operational thought is important for understanding science, mathematics, history, literary analysis, and other school subjects. To understand the scientific process, students must be able to see the logic of controlled experimentation. To successfully solve mathematical problems, students must be able to think in the abstract. For example, in algebra the variable x is used to represent many different numbers, which is an abstract notion.

Evidence That Contradicts Piaget's Stages

Today, Piaget's stages are not widely accepted among researchers. Some researchers also challenge his notion that knowledge begins with experience through the five senses, which is then stored as concrete knowledge and later becomes the basis for abstract concepts (Uttal, Liu, & DeLoache, 2006). Children often acquire abstract concepts before the concrete examples of them. For example, young children apply abstract grammar rules to language when they say *foots* instead of feet, even though they have never heard adults say *foots*.

Underestimation and Overestimation of Abilities

Recent research suggests Piaget *underestimated the cognitive abilities of young children.* In Chapter 5 you will learn that infants know many surprising things about their world—scientists call this *core knowledge.* In your interactions with toddlers, you will see evidence of nonegocentrism, or an ability to anticipate others' perspectives. For example, an 18-month-old hid under the kitchen table while stuffing herself with cookies from the cookie jar. Why hide if you cannot anticipate that your dad will scold you? Similarly, young children often show good reasoning ability, such as this 3-year-old who wants crackers:

Mother: *They're all gone.*
Boy: *No they aren't. I want some!*
Mother: *Yes they are. What makes you think they aren't?*
Boy: *'Cause if they was all gone, I seed them [the empty package] in the garbage. Look, nothing in the garbage!*

Or this conversation between two 7-year-old boys eating lunch in the school cafeteria, after one had been pondering an abstract concept:

Boy 1: *Everyone is related to each other.*
Boy 2: *Huh? Show me your logic.*
Boy 1: *Well, I have cousins. And they have cousins, who have cousins, who have cousins, who have cousins, who have cousins . . .*
Boy 2: *Stop! I get it.*

Piaget also *overestimated the ability of adolescents.* Adolescents can be remarkably egocentric, as in this conversation between two 14-year-olds after swim team practice at the high school:

Boy: *What a bear of a practice. I'm wiped out.*
Girl: *My hair smells good. I got this new shampoo. It smells like coconuts.*
Boy: *If we keep working out like that, we ought to all be able to improve our times. If we're not wasted!*
Girl: *Kendra's got this cool shampoo too. I like hers better.*

> Boy: *I could qualify for state if I could take two more seconds off my freestyle.*
> Girl: *Kendra's dad sells it. They won a trip to Hawaii for selling the most, or something like that. Her mom and dad, I mean.*

This example has the turn-taking quality of a dialogue, but it is really a collective monologue with neither youth attending to the other, which Piaget said was characteristic of preoperational children.

In the 1970s researchers began to demonstrate that with modest changes in the tasks used by Piaget, young children could reverse, decenter, use logic, and classify hierarchically (Donaldson, 1978; Gelman & Baillargeon, 1983). For example, the "Sleeping Cows Task" is a modified test of class inclusion. In this task, some black and white toy cows are placed on their sides as though they are sleeping. The standard Piagetian approach would be to ask the child, "Are there more black cows or more cows?" When asked in this way, only 25% of 6-year-olds respond correctly. If one word is added—"Are there more black cows or more *sleeping* cows?"—then 48% of 6-year-olds respond correctly. Only one word is changed, but responses are substantially different. Another example is the "Police Task," which tests egocentrism. A child is asked to hide a child doll from police dolls. Partitions are set up so that the child must consider two different points of view simultaneously (see Figure 3.9). Most (90%) 3-year-olds can do this task correctly, whereas few can do the three-mountain task, even though both tasks require the child to consider what another person would see.

Thus, current evidence suggests that there is less difference between the logic of children and adults and that young children are not as egocentric or illogical as

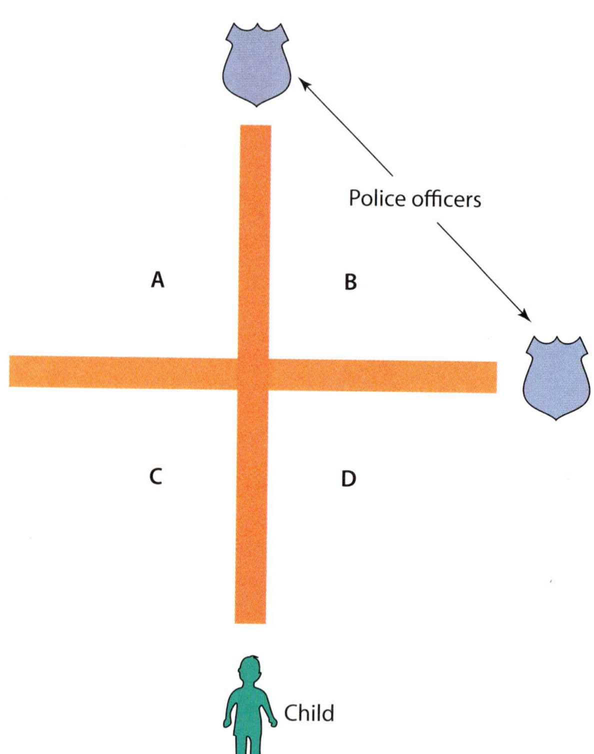

Figure 3.9 Hide-from-Police-Officer Task.
A child is given a doll and asked to hide it so that neither police officer can see it. About 90% of 3- to 5-year-olds get the task correct, even though results of the three-mountain task would predict a much lower proportion. *Donaldson, 1978.*

Piaget believed, though there continues to be some controversy about it (Kagan, 2008). However, it is also true that if you carry out Piagetian tasks in the same way that Piaget did, you will tend to get the same responses. This suggests that young children do have cognitive limitations. Their abilities are fragile. Their knowledge is often implicit, meaning the child cannot reflect on and discuss the knowledge. In addition, young children do not give primacy to language, which may cause them to fail at Piagetian tasks.

Primacy of Language

When children begin to learn language, they pay more attention to context than to words. In fact, they often learn words through clues from the context. The child first makes sense of the context and then uses that to make sense of what is said. For example, a 2-year-old is taking a bath "by herself" with instruction from her mother:

> *Mom: Take the wash cloth and wash your mouth.*
> *(Child does.)*
> *Mom: Good! Now wash your eyes.*
> *(Child does.)*
> *Mom: Good! Now wash your ears (while unconsciously scratching her nose).*
> *(The child washes her nose.)*

When there was conflict between what her mother *said* and what she *did*, the child gave primacy to the mother's action. The language-learning child gradually moves from understanding words in conjunction with action to understanding words in isolation. Children must have a great deal of experience with language before they can give primacy to language—that is, more weight to the meaning of words than to the meaning of the context. Children are not able to give primacy to language until they are confident about their understanding of language and have sufficient experience to know when to give primacy to language and when not to.

> ***Think About This*** Do any of the Piagetian tasks seem like trick questions to you? Might they to a child? Explain.

Many Piagetian tasks require children to give primacy to language and require responses that conflict with contextual clues. For example, the class inclusion task "Are there more beads or more red beads?" is likely interpreted by the child as "Are there more *blue* beads or more red beads?" because that is what the context suggests, even though that is not literally what is asked.

You will know that your students have primacy of language when they correct *your* language inaccuracies, as was the case in this 8th-grade classroom:

> *Teacher:* *Below what temperature does water freeze?*
> *Devin:* *33 degrees.*
> *Teacher:* *No. It's 32 degrees.*
> *Devin:* *No it isn't! You asked* ***below*** *what temperature does water freeze. It freezes* ***at*** *32 degrees. So it freezes* ***below*** *33 degrees.*

Imagine what Devin's answer will be after he takes physics!

Diversity in Cognitive Developmental Theory

Piaget believed that stages of cognitive development occur in a predictable sequence from child to child because each stage is necessary for the formation of the next stage. He was interested in universal patterns in how children think, so he paid little attention to individual differences. He did not investigate whether some children achieved a stage earlier than other children. Yet, listen as Lisa reacts to the conservation-of-liquid task in her 2nd-grade class:

Lisa: *The tall glass has more water. It is bigger. The other one is short.*
Teacher: *Does everyone agree with Lisa? (Some students nod yes, but others shake their heads no.) Aaron, you do not agree?*
Aaron: *The glasses are not the same shape. The tall one is really skinny and the short one is really fat. I think they might be the same, or the short one might hold more.*
Teacher: *How many of you thought about how big around the glasses are, and not just how tall they are? (Some hands shoot up, but it is clear that many 2nd-graders were just beginning to think about the possibility.)*

Piaget's theory does not explain the differences in performance between Lisa and Aaron, or other children in your classroom.

Think About This Discuss parallels between the poor performance on concrete operations tasks for adults who are not familiar with the researcher's language or materials, and a young child's poor performance.

Piaget also believed the stages of cognitive development are the same across cultures. Members of some cultures may be faster or slower in their rate of development, but he believed that the sequence would be the same. He believed that nearly all people in all cultures would achieve concrete operations; that is, their thinking would become logical. However, early research *using Piaget's interview method* found that in some cultures many adults do *not* achieve concrete operations. This finding was met with skepticism. For example, Cole (1975) asked how a people who experience water shortages could function if they thought water in tall thin cans was more than the same amount in short wide cans. Later research indicated that when people are interviewed in their native language, with familiar materials, they do achieve concrete operations across cultures and ethnic groups (Laboratory of Comparative Human Cognition, 1998). Thus, supposed cultural differences in logic may be a result of the research methods used, but not of real differences in cognitive ability.

The formal operations stage is a different story. In most cultures, many people never attain this stage when tested with standard Piagetian tasks. For example, even Americans who are in their teens or 20s have trouble with formal operational tasks (like the mice-fighting task), with only 30 to 40% being successful (Dimant & Bearison, 1991; Moshman, 1998). This raises the possibility that formal operations is not a stage, but a type of cognitive specialization linked to formal schooling. Some scientists dismiss Piaget's notion of formal operations altogether because evidence suggests that there are different types of reasoning—analogical, legal, logical, and scientific—that develop during adolescence and adulthood depending on one's area of specialized education (Moshman, 1998). Advanced schooling may be necessary, but not sufficient, to develop formal operations.

If Piaget is wrong about some things, why study him? For two reasons:

1. His theory is a good starting point because it caused scientists to try to understand why children respond so oddly to Piaget's tasks. Science evolves through our quest for understanding. As a result of newer research that tests Piaget's theory, we now understand more about children's cognitive development, which you will learn about in the next two chapters.
2. Piaget's theory continues to be widely applied in education. Sometimes this is misguided, but not always. Let's look at these applications next.

Classroom Implications of Cognitive Developmental Theory

There are several school-based legacies from Piaget's theory. One legacy is the notion of school readiness (see Chapter 1). Piaget believed little can be done to accelerate development because each child has a biologically based rate of transition from one stage to the next. In fact, Piaget was annoyed with teachers who wanted to speed up cognitive development. In contrast to Piaget's view, current research does not support stage-based readiness for school, nor does it support the notion that some concepts should not be taught to young children because they are not yet at the appropriate stage. Some researchers believe that a strong readiness stance can deprive children of valuable experiences. Unfortunately, Piaget's theory is sometimes mistakenly used as a rationale for not teaching children valued content, like history, because the children are supposedly not ready to learn it (Hinde & Perry, 2007).

Developmentally Appropriate Practice

Another concept that was influenced by Piaget's theory is *developmentally appropriate practice* (DAP), which is an approach to educating children from birth to age 8 that emphasizes the child as an active participant in learning, not just a passive receiver of knowledge. The teacher's role is to create an environment in which the child can construct meaning from interactions with people and objects. Young children learn through active exploration and play. A DAP position statement has been published by the National Association for the Education of Young Children (NAEYC, 2009).

Is DAP actually beneficial to children? Little research has directly addressed this question. One study of more than 3,000 1st-, 2nd-, and 3rd-graders found that classrooms that were more developmentally appropriate did not foster greater academic achievement in diverse, low-income students than traditional classrooms (Van Horn & Ramey, 2003). Although children may not do better academically in DAP classrooms, children may feel less stress and anxiety, which is important (Van Horn, Karlin, Ramey, Aldridge, & Snyder, 2005).

Constructivist Teaching

A third legacy from Piaget's theory is constructivist teaching. Piaget asserted that children construct their own knowledge and should be encouraged to do so. He stated that "each time one prematurely teaches a child something he could have discovered for himself, that child is kept from inventing it and consequently from understanding it completely" (Piaget, 1970, p. 715). Piaget is attacking the notion that learning is the transfer of knowledge from one person to another, where the teacher pours knowledge into children's minds. Instead, Piaget asserts that when children act on their own, they form permanent mental models; when they are told the facts, they may just memorize them in a superficial way. Every mind must construct its own understanding. Learning is a constructive process that depends on the prior experience and knowledge of the learner.

constructivist teaching an approach to instruction in which teachers provide students with experiences that facilitate their personal construction of knowledge.

In **constructivist teaching**, teachers minimize (but do not eliminate) adult authority. Instead of simply lecturing on facts, constructivist teachers provide experiences, ask questions, provoke discourse, and encourage experimentation and deep thought. This facilitates students' personal construction of understanding. As constructivist math educators put it, "Piaget showed that children acquire logico-mathematical knowledge not by *internalizing* rules from the outside but by *constructing* (making or creating) relationships from within, in interaction with the environment. We, therefore, give problems to children and ask them to do their own thinking to solve them in their own ways" (Kamii, Pritchett, & Nelson, 1997, p. 5, emphasis in original).

Mrs. Harl taught Monica to do three-digit addition using an algorithm—add the ones column first, then carry over to the tens. An algorithm is a procedure that, if followed, guarantees a correct answer. Some constructivists oppose teaching children algorithms because children can just memorize the procedure, without really understanding the underlying concept. For example, if they follow an algorithm for doing three-digit addition with carrying, they do not have to keep an understanding of place value foremost in their minds.

There are many variations on constructivism that you may hear about, such as project-based instruction, whole language, discovery learning, inquiry approach, transformational approach, teaching for understanding, and minds-on instruction. Common attributes of various versions of constructivism include the following (adapted from Kamii et al., 1997; Krajcik, Czerniak, & Berger, 1999; Palincsar, 1998):

- Using hands-on materials when appropriate, particularly for novices.
- Encouraging students to connect new material to familiar objects and events.
- Allowing students to choose some of their learning activities when possible.
- Following the children's lead. Following up on their questions. Talking less and listening more.
- Asking more questions than giving answers. Asking open-ended questions that foster deep thinking rather than questions that ask for a single-word answer.
- Presenting students with puzzling or unexpected information that causes them to revise their schemas, such as asking, "Is coral a plant or animal?" in a biology class.
- Allowing long wait time (at least five seconds) after asking questions, in order to promote thinking. Intelligent responses require thinking time.
- Requiring students to justify their answers regardless of whether their answers are correct or not. Ask "What is your evidence?" or "Why do you think that?"
- Not stating that answers or reasons are correct or incorrect. Instead, ask more questions, or provide experiences that allow students to correct their own errors. Encourage the children to discuss among themselves and to come to conclusions themselves.

- Making student thinking public. Encourage students to explain their thinking process and how they came up with particular answers.

Making student thinking public is important because your students' misconceptions will remain hidden unless you attempt to understand their thinking process. In traditional instruction, teachers ask students questions in a recitation format or in tests, which makes students' *answers* public, but not their *thinking*. For example, Ms. Wilson was teaching 3rd-graders about state government. As she questioned them, she found that some students thought that being governor bestowed ownership of the whole state. She tried to use an analogy to correct them:

> *"Who is the leader of this school?" I asked, hopefully.*
> *"Dr. Tough," they replied in unison.*
> *"And what does that mean?" I probed.*
> *"That she owns the school. That's why she gets to tell everyone what to do. . . . "*
> *I felt like I was being sucked into a . . . veritable whirlpool of misconceptions.*
> (Ball & Wilson, 1996, pp. 160–161)

If Ms. Wilson had not asked for student thinking, she would not have discovered students' misunderstandings.

It is not always easy to get students to reveal their misconceptions. Think about a time when you have been unwilling to answer a question in class. Were you trying to avoid showing your ignorance? If you give students responsibility for their learning, as constructivists would recommend, but ask them to demonstrate their understanding before they actually understand, you may end up with students who avoid making their thinking public and avoid seeking help.

Two additional guidelines for instruction have roots in Piaget's research:

- Conduct error analysis—that is, when children respond incorrectly, ask why they responded the way they did. This will give you insight into what they do and do not know. For example, a 4-year-old was being tested for school readiness. The examiner asked her which shape among a triangle, square, circle, and rectangle was different from the others. The correct answer was the circle, because it does not have any straight lines or angles. The child responded, "the triangle." Fortunately, the examiner did not simply mark her answer wrong, but asked her why. The child said, "The others would be easier to divide into fourths." That ended the test. The examiner stated the child was ready for kindergarten (if not junior high).
- Keep learning embedded in a context that makes sense and supports the child's use of language. This is especially important for children who are young, immigrant, or have poor verbal ability, and for children from subcultures that rarely use abstract language. Schools use a lot of abstract language that does not fit these children's experience. Learning may need to be grounded in a supportive context for an extended period of time for children who do not yet give primacy to language. This is why beginning reader books have pictures (context) to support the written word.

Piaget's theory was too lean in three ways. (1) He was vague about how children transition from one stage to another. In Chapter 4 you'll learn what current research tells us about how children come to reason better with age. (2) He was silent on the issue of individual differences in cognitive abilities. You'll learn about individual differences in Chapter 5. (3) He commented on the importance of sociocultural influences on learning, but this was not his focus. Sociocultural influences are the focus of Vygotsky, who was also a constructivist.

Vygotsky's Sociocultural Theory

One morning, a 5th-grade class is working on long division. Most of the students grasp the concept, but not all. A new worksheet is passed out. Darius begins the first problem, but quickly becomes frustrated and gives up, saying, "I just don't know how to do these!" His teacher works through the first problem with him and realizes that Darius has all the component skills—how to multiply, divide, and subtract. But he cannot remember the complex steps in sequence. His teacher prompts him about when to apply each component (e.g., subtract or carry down) but lets Darius do the calculations himself. Darius can complete problems as long as the teacher guides him in this way. After a few problems, his teacher provides guidance only when Darius clearly needs it. By the time they reach the twentieth problem, Darius remembers the steps himself.

Darius began the class without the cognitive ability to do long division, but he developed the ability, although still fragile, by the end of the class period. This newfound ability was a result of interaction with his teacher. Vygotsky believed that social interaction with others is the primary force driving cognitive development.

Lev Semenovich Vygotsky (1896–1934) was born in Belorussia in eastern Europe, lived through the Bolshevik revolution of 1917, and later became a major intellectual in Russia. He died of tuberculosis at age 37. For political reasons, his works were largely banned after his death, but in the 1960s and 1970s, some of his works began to appear in English. Since that time, his views on children's cognitive development have had a substantial impact on education.

sociocultural theory a theory of how children learn, largely based on Vygotsky's writings, that emphasizes social interaction, historical context, and culture.

Vygotsky's theory of cognitive development has been labeled **sociocultural** or *cultural-historical* because of his focus on how social relationships, social interaction, historical context, and culture interact to promote cognitive development (Rogoff, Mosier, Mistry, & Göncü, 1993). Like Piaget, he believed that knowledge cannot be directly communicated from the teacher's head to the student's head; such attempts result in "meaningless acquisition of words," not understanding (Gredler, 2009, p. 16). The most basic premise of his view is that cognitive growth results from interaction with parents, teachers, and peers within cultural contexts.

The Role of Social Interaction

According to Vygotsky, children grow into the intellectual life of those around them. Vygotsky wrote, "Every function in the child's cultural development appears twice: first, on the social level, and later, on the individual level; first between people (interpsychological), and then inside the child (intrapsychological)" (Vygotsky, 1978, p. 57). That is, social interaction with a more competent person in a shared activity drives cognitive growth. The more competent person and the child first *co-construct* skills and understanding out of their interaction, which then is internalized by the child.

Whether a toddler is learning to count or an adolescent is learning to solve liquid dynamics problems, the child may initially merely observe the expert. Next, the expert does most of the work, both cognitive and physical, while guiding the child through the task. The child may have the appearance of doing the task, but could make no progress without the expert's aid. As the child gains increased competence, the expert gives more and more of the responsibility to the child, who grows in expertise. The expert's support is reduced. The expert may still need to give hints and reminders for a time, until at last the child can perform the task independently.

Darius's teacher was gradually placing more of the responsibility for solving the long division problems on him, as he was increasingly able to work independently. Similarly, Mrs. Harl first did the three-digit addition for Monica and her classmates. Then, she gradually placed more of the responsibility for solving the problems on her students. These are one-lesson examples. Some skills take substantially longer to develop. A child learning to read, or to solve calculus problems, requires several months or years of working with more-competent others before developing proficiency. Whether you are teaching a skill within a single class period, or across several years, the same mechanism is at work; a more competent individual scaffolds students' performance within their zone of proximal development.

Zone of Proximal Development

The **zone of proximal development (ZPD)** is the level of competence between what a child can do alone and what he or she can do with assistance. Darius's learning of long division occurred in his zone of proximal development. Without his teacher's scaffolding, he experienced failure. Yet, with a little help, he was successful. In case 2, Monica was functioning in her ZPD. Without Mrs. Harl's help, she experienced failure and felt overwhelmed. With just a little scaffolding from Mrs. Harl, she was successful at adding three-digit numbers.

zone of proximal development (ZPD) the distance between what students can do independently and what they can do with the assistance of a competent other.

The zone of proximal development emphasizes the social dimension of cognition. Alone, through trial-and-error, children may eventually learn; Darius may have eventually learned long division. But with the assistance of a more competent teacher, Darius and Monica learned much more quickly, primarily through scaffolding. With their teachers' assistance, the students' performance reveals a level of development to come. In these day-to-day interactions are the roots of higher mental functions.

> ***Think About This*** If a child is easily attaining straight A's in class, is he or she operating in the zone of proximal development? Explain your answer.

Scaffolding

Scaffolding is support for learning and problem solving that comes from outside the learner (Wood, Bruner, & Ross, 1976); it usually includes social interaction with a more competent other, but could also include textbooks or prompting from a computer. Scaffolding occurs when an expert helps a novice master new skills by breaking the skill into small units and guiding performance to a higher level. Scaffolding can occur in the emotional, physical, social, or cognitive realm. Darius's teacher is

scaffolding a more competent person helps a child master new skills by breaking the tasks or subskills into small units and guiding performance to a higher level.

Field Observation

Ask a child to perform a task that he or she cannot do alone (e.g., use a jump rope, understand difficult text, solve an algebra problem). Model the task for the child. Then ask the child to imitate you. If the child is successful, try it with another child who you believe has less capability. If the child is not successful, try it with another child who you believe has greater capability. Can you tell where these children's zones of proximal development are for this task?

providing scaffolding when she prompts him about when to apply basic skills he already has. So is the parent who holds the back of the bicycle while a child learns to ride. So is the coach who reminds the angry athlete to count to 10 before talking to the referee. From Vygotsky's perspective, a teacher's primary role is to scaffold children in their zone of proximal development. You will do this largely through language.

Language and Private Speech

Language is one of the most important tools of any culture because it provides an extremely efficient means of learning. For example, in Chapter 8 you will learn that when adults talk about emotions with children, the children become better at perceiving others' emotions. In Chapter 4 you will also learn that when adults talk about an event, the children remember the event better. That is, perceptions, memory, and reasoning are enhanced by talk.

According to Vygotsky, language first arises as a social/cultural tool that a child uses to communicate with others. Subsequently, as language is converted to private speech, it becomes a tool for controlling one's own thoughts and behavior (Vygotsky, 1978). **Private speech** refers to talking to oneself out loud, partially out loud like mouthing words or whispering, or silently in one's mind. Private speech can be relevant to a task at hand (such as a child mouthing instructions to herself about the steps in a science class experiment) or irrelevant (such as a child yawning and saying, "I'm tired" to himself).

private speech talking to oneself out loud, partially out loud, or silently in one's mind to help regulate one's own behavior or solve problems.

While all children use private speech, research shows they are more likely to use it when (1) engaged in goal-directed activities, like academic work rather than play; (2) their task is challenging as opposed to easy; (3) an adult is aiding, as opposed to controlling, their problem solving; and (4) they are alone rather than with someone (Winsler, Carlton, & Barry, 2000). Let's see if children and adolescents differ in their use of private speech.

Age Trends in Sociocultural Theory

Vygotsky's sociocultural theory is not as stage oriented as Piaget's theory. One aspect of Vygotsky's theory that does show age trends is private speech. Children progress from task-irrelevant out-loud talk, to relevant and self-regulatory out-loud talk, and then to partially silent inner speech, such as whispers and quiet muttering (Winsler, Diaz, Atencio, McCarthy, & Chabay, 2000). The out-loud talk increases during the preschool period, peaks around 4 to 6 years of age, and then becomes replaced by increasingly silent talk. Thus, private speech becomes more internal as children progress from preschool through the school years (Patrick & Abravanel, 2000).

However, adolescents, and even adults, revert to out-loud private speech as they attempt to solve problems or do difficult tasks. For example, let's peek at 12th-grader Zaheen in biology class:

The task is complicated, and the room is overcrowded and noisy. Zaheen is working alone, but talking out loud. He reads the directions aloud to himself: "Obtain nine test tubes and place them in the rack. Fill each tube with five milliliters of the substance indicated on the label." He then mouths the directions to himself again as he touches each object referred to. Finally, he actually enacts the instructions.

Zaheen was clearly using private speech to regulate his own thought and behavior. Similarly, you probably mouth some phrases in this text as you try to master details (and you may learn more if you do), particularly if you are studying in a noisy place.

Diversity in Sociocultural Theory

According to Vygotsky, *what* a child learns is determined by the culture in which the child lives. That is, children learn what is valued in their culture. Furthermore, *how* a child learns and the scaffolding the child receives is also influenced by culture. For example, one study found that mothers in Salt Lake City scaffold toddlers differently than Mayan mothers in Guatemala. While doing a task, such as a puzzle, Salt Lake mothers tended to propose a division of labor with each working on separate parts, and they directly instructed their children (Chavajay & Rogoff, 2002). They also tended to focus on one thing at a time, to impose their own agenda, and to interrupt their children. In contrast, Mayan mothers tended to focus on multiple activities simultaneously, with no division of labor and no direct instruction. Mother behavior was related to formal schooling. Mayan mothers with substantial schooling (twelve-plus years) behaved more like Salt Lake mothers than like less-educated Mayans. This is relevant to teachers who work with immigrant children whose parents may have had very little schooling. Such children may be used to a more collaborative, whole-group approach to work than children of more-educated immigrants or of U.S.-born parents.

The tools children have available for thinking are also determined by the culture. *Cultural tools* can be concrete objects such as rulers, books, or computers. They can also be tools of the mind that are symbolic, such as written language or counting systems. Children's competence depends on the cultural tools available to them. For example, multiply 578 times 264. Is it difficult? If the equation were written in a vertical format with 578 below 264, you would probably have an easier time as you first multiply 8 times 4, then 8 times 6, and so forth. You would be benefiting from a cultural tool, an algorithm for multiplication, that was developed by others and made available to you through the culture of schooling.

cultural tools concrete objects and symbolic tools that allow members of a culture to think, build, record, problem solve, and communicate.

Writing is a key cultural tool. It allows individuals to record and remember with more accuracy and less effort than was possible before its invention. Genres or types of writing are also cultural tools. For example, a story is a narrative that usually follows chronological order and often uses suspense, while a science report focuses on analysis of processes and seldom has elements of suspense. Young children lack these cultural tools of genre writing and often produce a story when asked to write a science report (Kamberelis & Bovino, 1999). They must be taught how to do it.

Written language is a school-learned cultural tool that transfers widely across many different contexts because it is seen in many contexts, not just school. Writing is used in stores, restaurants, street signs, and magazines. However, students tend to see most cultural tools embedded in a single place and tend not to transfer those tools elsewhere. For example, our young daughter was baking cookies and asked, "Do two quarters make a half? I know they do in math class, but do they in cooking?" In another example, a high school chemistry teacher found that her students only used the study strategies that she taught when she was present; they would not even use them with the student teacher in the same classroom (Moje, 1996). If you want your students to transfer the use of a cultural tool from one context to another, you will need to help them see how the tool is used in other settings.

In summary, culture influences what children learn, how they are taught, what tools they acquire, and where those tools are applied. One lesson for you as a teacher is to be careful not to jump to conclusions about a child's capability based on a single cultural context. Students may appear unskilled in some classroom contexts, but be quite skilled in other contexts.

Classroom Implications of Sociocultural Theory

There are at least four general implications of Vygotsky's perspective on cognitive development for your role as a teacher:

- Use language as a tool to help students organize their thoughts and to consolidate memories. Private speech should be tolerated and encouraged, particularly for young children or during difficult problem solving in older students.
- Teach students in their zone of proximal development, using appropriate scaffolding. It is not easy to determine each student's ZPD, and it is a moving target, always changing. It takes attention and insight on the part of the teacher to continually adjust to each student's abilities.
- Help students actively observe and participate in activities with adults and peers through **apprenticeship** and **guided participation** (Rogoff, 1990). In an apprenticeship, a novice develops competence through interaction with a more expert person who guides or scaffolds participation in the developing activity. Children are apprentices in school as they learn how to be a student and learner. The apprenticeship is directed by you, the teacher, as you plan specific learning experiences and help the learners understand the experiences.
- Work with students together as a *community of learners* in which everyone contributes to the learning process. In a community of learners, the teacher is not the only person who has knowledge, but rather expertise is distributed among the members of the classroom. A community of learners experiences *distributed cognition* in which thinking and knowledge exist not only in the minds of individuals, but also in their social interaction and the artifacts that they use and create, like books and computers (Salomon, 1993). Students can become experts in certain areas and know more than even the teacher in those areas; other students and the teacher may look to them for help.

apprenticeship a learner actively observes and participates with an expert in order to improve competence.

guided participation a novice learns through an expert's scaffolding.

Think About This How might attachment to teachers and bonding to school affect cognitive development from a sociocultural perspective?

These broad implications for classrooms stem from sociocultural theory. In addition, you may want to apply a specific style of teaching that stems from this theory—social constructivism.

Social Constructivism

Social constructivism shares with Piagetian constructivism the assertion that knowledge is not poured into children's brains, but rather knowledge must be constructed. It uses the term *social* because it emphasizes social interaction as the source of knowledge construction. Social constructivist teaching includes scaffolding, classroom discussion, and reciprocal teaching.

social constructivism the view that knowledge is not poured into learners' brains, but that knowledge is constructed through social interaction.

Scaffolding in the classroom

Recall that scaffolding involves a more competent individual (like a teacher) helping novices master new skills. You've already seen how Darius's and Monica's teachers scaffolded their math skills. Scaffolding is important at other ages as well. Imagine that you want to teach preschoolers how to play number-oriented board games, like *Chutes and Ladders.* (In Chapter 4 you will learn that number-oriented board games foster children's understanding of numbers.) Initially you might model how to count and move the pieces, pointing to each square in turn. After several episodes of scaffolded play, children may be able to play with each other with no support from you.

Imagine you want to teach high school students how to write a research paper. You could tell the students what to do, and then turn them loose to apply what they've learned. Such a technique tends to lead to poor writing and weak papers from novice writers. A better technique is to use scaffolding to help the students construct, through interaction with others, a shared understanding of high-quality writing. One scaffolding technique is to break the tasks into small units. Thus, you might require students to choose a topic, then to read and write notes about references, then to write a research question or thesis statement for the paper, then to outline the major sections of the paper, and so forth. At each stage of the paper, you review the students' work and provide feedback. Social constructivism also involves interaction among peers, so you would have students provide feedback on each others' draft manuscripts. Students at all ages, from preschool to graduate school, can benefit from scaffolding.

Scaffolding can be indirect or direct. One study found that when students revealed their lack of understanding and asked for help, successful teachers carefully scaffolded the students through a solution process, sometimes by having other students help with the instruction (Turner et al., 2002). Teachers did not tell students how to do the problem, but asked questions and gave hints until the students understood what was being taught. However, the following is an example of a music teacher taking a more directive style while scaffolding 10-year-old Lauren in piano lessons:

> *Lauren is learning a complicated piano sonata that has a difficult rhythm and many chords, including some that require her to stretch her small hand across six keys. Looking at the piece, Lauren felt overwhelmed, and she quickly became frustrated trying to read the notes. She pounded the piano and her posture collapsed, communicating "I give up!" The teacher pointed her to a single measure with four chords in the left hand. The teacher modeled the first chord and had Lauren play just that chord. The teacher repeated this with each chord. Then she had Lauren play the four chords in succession, modeling when necessary. After Lauren mastered these four chords, the teacher asked Lauren to play them with her eyes closed several times. When Lauren was finished, the teacher enthusiastically congratulated Lauren and explained to her that anything is easy if you break it down into little steps. Lauren grinned with pride.*

In this example, the teacher had Lauren focus on only one hand, and one measure of music, at a time. The scaffolding took less than five minutes, yet it changed Lauren's whole perspective of her ability to master the sonata.

Classroom discussion

Through classroom discussion, children can co-construct understanding in their zones of proximal development and achieve greater skill. When students explain their thinking aloud, they may notice their errors and correct them (Gredler, 2009). Deep discussion requires that students agree, disagree, and critique each other's reasoning—hence the social dimension of social constructivism. In constructivist classrooms, there should be a great deal of student-to-student commentary, rather than just teacher-to-student commentary.

In a constructivist 2nd-grade classroom, the teacher poses an arithmetic question: 19 + 13. One child gives her answer—26—and the classroom erupts into a loud cacophony of *"Agree!"* and *"Disagree!"* This sort of discussion is usually extolled as a virtue of social constructivist instruction. But how do students feel about it? Some like it, but some do not. According to a 5th-grader: "[I]t can get sort of embarrassing at times, because like . . . you say something and everybody will raise their hand and want to say something different or they all disagree with you. And it makes you sort of feel like you want to crawl into a hole and die" (Lampert, Rittenhouse, & Crumbaugh, 1996, p. 742).

Students will not engage in the kind of classroom discussion that makes social constructivist instruction work if they feel vulnerable to ridicule, teasing, or appearing stupid. Teachers must work hard to provide a supportive environment and keep the discourse civil without squelching it. This means maintaining a neutral stance, using a warm tone, and providing supportive comments. It also means training the students to be able to discuss respectfully.

In constructivist classrooms, children are given the opportunity to work together so that they will be confronted with different views. Students of differing levels of ability are placed together so the more advanced students will clarify their knowledge by having to explain to others, and the less advanced will be challenged to understand thinking a bit above their own. However, you cannot assume that just because students are discussing classroom content they are learning; even if they are on-task, their conversations may not lead to understanding. In Chapter 11 you will learn how to implement group work in an effective way.

reciprocal teaching students take turns in the teacher role. A student-teacher summarizes, asks questions, clarifies, and predicts the content of a passage of text in a small group of other students.

Michael Newman/PhotoEdit

Students engaged in reciprocal teaching.

Reciprocal teaching

One of the best-known applications of the principles of Vygotsky's social constructivism is **reciprocal teaching**, which research suggests is effective (Palincsar & Brown, 1984; Spörer, Brunstein, & Kieschke, 2009). Reciprocal teaching puts the student in the teacher role. It is applied most often to reading comprehension. Students read a text in a group of two to six students with the teacher's expert scaffolding. The teacher introduces the reading by asking students to state what they already know about the topic and to predict what the passage is about based on the title. Then a student is assigned to be the student-teacher for a passage. After the group reads the passage, the student-teacher asks a *question* about the main point, *summarizes* the passage, and then makes a *prediction* about what might come next. The teacher scaffolds the student-teacher's responses and provides feedback. Eventually the teacher can leave the reading groups alone to scaffold each other.

The following are two examples of reciprocal teaching by a 7th-grade student, Charles, as he gradually becomes a competent reader (from Palincsar & Brown, 1984, pp. 138–139).

Day 1.

TEXT: *The water moccasin, somewhat longer than the copperhead, is found in the southeastern states. It lives in swampy regions. It belongs, as do also the copperhead and the rattlesnakes, to a group of poisonous snakes called pit vipers. They have pits between their eyes and their nostrils which, because they are sensitive to heat, help the snakes tell when they are near a warm-blooded animal. Another name for the water moccasin is "cottonmouth." This name comes from the white lining of the snake's mouth.*

Charles: *What is found in the southeastern snakes—also the copperhead, rattlesnakes, vipers—they have . . . I'm not doing this right.*

Teacher: *All right. Do you want to know about the pit vipers? What would be a good question about the pit vipers that starts with the word "why"?*

Charles: *(No response)*

Teacher: *How about, "Why are the snakes called pit vipers?"*

Charles: *Why do they want to know that they are called pit vipers?*

Teacher: *Try it again.*

Charles: *Why do they, pit vipers in a pit?*

Teacher: *How about, "Why do they call the snakes pit vipers?"*

Charles: *Why do they call the snakes pit vipers?*

Teacher: *There you go! Good for you.*

Day 11:

TEXT: *One of the most interesting of the insect-eating plants is the Venus's flytrap. This plant lives in only one small area of the world—the coastal marshes of North and South Carolina. The Venus's flytrap doesn't look unusual. Its habits, however, make it truly a plant wonder.*

Charles: *What is the most interesting of the insect eating plants, and where do the plants live at?*

Teacher: *Two excellent questions! They are both clear and important questions. Ask us one at a time now.*

This example makes clear why reciprocal teaching is beneficial to reading comprehension. Most students, like Charles, are often unaware that they do not comprehend a reading passage. Even among our hundreds of university students, only a few have ever come to class asking for clarification of an obscure passage, although all textbooks (except this one) contain obscure passages.

You can apply reciprocal teaching to content areas besides reading. For example, students studying history can take on the student-teacher role to *summarize*, *question*, *clarify*, and *predict* as they read historical texts.

A Note of Caution About Constructivist Teaching

Both Piaget and Vygotsky present a theory of constructivist *learning*. This does not necessarily translate to a case for constructivist *teaching* as it is typically construed. Many teachers assume constructivist teaching must involve hands-on activities, group discussion, interactive games, and other behaviorally active forms of instruction. They view lectures, books, worksheets, and online presentations as too passive. They also assume constructivist teaching must be based on discovery learning. Neither is necessarily true. A constructivist teacher helps students make sense of incoming information, organize it coherently, and integrate it with previous knowledge. Passive methods (such as lecture) can foster these processes, and active methods (such as hands-on experiments) can fail to foster these processes. It is *cognitive* activity rather than *behavioral* activity that matters. Children learn by thinking.

Some teachers are concerned about implementing a constructivist curriculum because they view it as incompatible with the proficiency exams and college entrance exams for which they need to prepare students. However, research shows that curricula that are based on constructivist methods do provide students with the skills to do well on standardized tests (McCaffrey et al., 2001; National Mathematics Advisory Panel, 2008).

Comparing Theories of Learning and Cognition

Although John Watson (a behaviorist), Jean Piaget, and Lev Vygotsky were contemporaries, each advocated a different theory of how children learn and develop cognitively. Some aspects of their theories are simply unrelated because they address different issues. For example, both behaviorism and sociocultural theory say little about age trends in cognitive development. Instead, these theories focus on processes of learning such as reinforcement and scaffolding. In sharp contrast, Piaget had little to say about processes of learning—or *how* children move from stage to stage—yet he focused extensively on age trends in cognitive development. In addition, Piaget sought to understand how the *nature of logic* develops similarly across cultures. On the other hand, socioculturalists seek to understand how *specific cognitive abilities* are different across cultures.

Some aspects of the three theories are similar, and others directly contradict one another. One example of similarity is that both Piaget's and Vygotsky's theories are considered constructivist because they view children as active participants in constructing or co-constructing their own knowledge. Behaviorists have a more passive view of the child's role. Piaget's constructivism is sometimes called *cognitive constructivism* or *individual constructivism* to distinguish it from Vygotsky's *social constructivism*. However, many educators meld Piaget's cognitive constructivism with Vygotsky's social constructivism, so while researchers make distinctions among the various brands of constructivism, many educators do not.

Piaget's cognitive-developmental theory differs from the other two theories in two ways. First, both behaviorists and socioculturalists stress direct teaching by adults, but Piagetians stress children's self-directed learning through exploration. Second, Piagetians give greater emphasis to maturation (i.e., nature). In other words, Piaget believed mental maturation is a *prerequisite* for learning, not a result of learning. By contrast, Vygotsky believed learning and education *cause* mental maturation.

Vygotsky believed that instruction that is oriented toward a level of cognitive development (or stage) that has already been reached is ineffective. *Good instruction pushes development* (Vygotsky, 1978). As you read in Chapter 1 regarding school readiness, research supports Vygotsky's view on this issue.

Behaviorism is one of the most commonly applied theories in classrooms. All classrooms use reinforcement and punishment, whether intentional or not. Behaviorism is powerful in promoting learning and altering behavior. However, children can learn without being directly reinforced. They can learn from watching other children being reinforced, as in the opening vignette when Naomi was rewarded for getting out a book to read during free time and several other children imitated her. Children learn rapidly from observing others, even as young as 6 months of age. Recognition of this has led to a revision of behaviorism, now called

Theories and Theorists Box 3.2

Social Cognitive Theory

In the opening vignette, Naomi's teacher wanted the children to read biographies in their free time, so she announced to the whole class how happy she was to see Naomi reading and gave Naomi a reward. The next day several other children read biographies during free time. This event highlights two key points: (1) Children can learn from watching others be reinforced without being directly reinforced themselves. (2) Children can learn without immediate behavior change; the learning might not be apparent until a day later, or years later. For example, when Elena's mother was 6, she watched her grandmother make tamales in Mexico, but was not allowed to help. At age 15 she made tamales herself. She had learned through observation despite nine years of no behavior change. These points may seem obvious to you, but they present a challenge for behaviorism. Recall that behaviorists define learning as a change in behavior. Along with others, Bandura questioned this.

Albert Bandura was born in 1925 in tiny Mundare, Alberta, Canada. He became a psychologist when behaviorism was dominant. Bandura began to study how children learn through observation. Perhaps his most famous studies were the Bobo-doll experiments. Bobo was an inflatable clown doll that was weighted in the bottom and bounced back up if you punched it down. See Figure 3.10. Children watched an adult act aggressively toward the Bobo doll (Bandura, 1965; Bandura, Ross, & Ross, 1961, 1963). The adult yelled, punched, kicked, and hit it with a mallet. The children were then invited to play alone with the Bobo doll. Children who had observed the aggressive adult were more aggressive toward the Bobo doll than children in a control group. In fact, they were aggressive in the very same ways as the adult. The children had clearly learned to be aggressive from a model.

(continued)

Albert Bandura/Dept. of Psychology, Stanford University

Figure 3.10 Bandura's Bobo-Doll Experiments.
Children watched a film of an adult being aggressive. They later imitated the same aggressive behaviors during free-play.

Theories and Theorists (continued)

Bandura's Bobo-doll experiments made him famous. In fact, he told of checking into a hotel where the desk clerk asked: "Aren't you the psychologist who did the Bobo-doll experiment?" Bandura replied, "I'm afraid that's going to be my legacy." The clerk replied, "That deserves an upgrade!" (Bandura, 2007). So there are some perks to being a psychologist.

Bandura developed a theory about how children learn from observation. He initially called it *social learning theory* because it added a social dimension to classic learning theory. Social learning theory claimed that in addition to direct reinforcement, behavior can also be changed when the child observes someone else being reinforced, termed *vicarious reinforcement*. In Chapters 8 and 9 you will learn that neuroscience shows that from birth children's brains are designed for imitating others.

As Bandura's research developed, his theory became more *cognitive* as well as more *social*. His research showed that children's beliefs and expectations about their behavior strongly influence their behavior. Thus, Bandura, like Piaget, came to view children as actively influencing their own development through mental processes—they attend to, interpret, and select which behaviors to imitate. Today Bandura's theory is called social cognitive theory.

A key mental process in social cognitive theory is self-efficacy. **Self-efficacy** refers to your belief that you can accomplish some behavior. It is a judgment about your competence. Self-efficacy powerfully influences behavior in both the social and academic domains. A boy who believes aggression works, and who has high self-efficacy for aggression (i.e., believes he is good at it), will tend to behave more aggressively. A boy who has self-efficacy for mathematics (i.e., believes he is good at it) will tend to work harder at difficult math problems, and earn higher grades.

Jon Brenneis/Life Magazine/Time & Life Pictures/Getty Images

Albert Bandura

Self-efficacy and vicarious reinforcement are linked. Students come to feel greater self-efficacy if they watch a model they feel is *similar to themselves* being reinforced for success. For example, in case 2, Monica's classmates felt more self-efficacy for three-digit addition after she gave it a try, but not after their teacher worked an example. Similarly, high school students learn physics from watching a peer successfully complete a problem better than if they just watch an expert work an example during a tutoring session (Craig, Chi, & VanLehn, 2009). Thus, one way that you can improve students' self-efficacy in your classroom is to provide a successful model who is similar to themselves. In Chapter 13 we will discuss how you can enhance students' self-efficacy in order to improve their motivation in your classroom.

social cognitive theory. This theory is discussed in Box 3.2 and will be further discussed in Chapter 13.

self-efficacy belief that you have the capability to perform a specific task.

Social cognitive theory moves behaviorism closer toward Piaget in that children are now viewed as actively influencing their own development through mental processes—they attend to, interpret, and select which behaviors to imitate depending on attributes of the models and their own feelings of confidence. The revised theory is also more similar to Vygotsky in that the social nature of learning is emphasized. Although all three theories may have moved closer toward one another as new research provides insight into how children develop, there currently is no single grand theory that adequately unifies them.

Although these theories differ in their view of what drives development—reinforcement, maturation, or social interaction—each is "true" in some ways and incomplete by itself. Reinforcement does lead to learning, as behaviorists posit. Children are innately motivated to explore the world and they do construct their own knowledge, as Piaget posited. Children do learn through social interaction and dialogue with others, as socioculturalists posit.

Nevertheless, constructivism and behaviorism can lead to two very different approaches to instruction—direct instruction and discovery learning. Which is most effective according to research? If only one approach is used and test scores are the outcome measure, there is some evidence that direct instruction tends to be more effective, particularly for weak learners and for basic skills (Kirschner, Sweller, & Clark, 2006), but the topic is controversial. A combined approach that draws on powerful elements of constructivism, such as cooperative learning and having students explain their thinking out loud, may be ideal. We will compare these approaches in more detail for math instruction in Chapter 4 and literacy instruction in Chapter 12, so that you can judge how to apply each in your classroom in appropriate situations.

Reflections on Practice: Checklist for Teachers

Behaviorism, cognitive developmental theory, and sociocultural theory each include important implications for the classroom. To determine if you are promoting student learning in your classroom according to these three theories, periodically ask yourself:

1. Am I aware of the full array of reinforcers operating in my classroom? Are they facilitating learning? Do I mistakenly reinforce inappropriate behaviors?
2. Do I avoid using punishment? If I do use punishment, does it actually stop the misbehavior? (If it does not, it may actually be reinforcing.)
3. Do I use direct instruction? Would my students benefit?
4. Do I model how to think about problems? Am I aware of which models my students imitate?
5. Do I help children construct their own understanding by guiding experiences, encouraging experiments, asking questions, and provoking discourse? Do I wait at least five seconds after asking a question in order to promote thinking? Do I ask open-ended questions? Could I talk less and listen more?
6. Do I conduct error analysis? When children make mistakes, do I try to understand why rather than just correcting them?
7. Do I keep learning embedded in a context that makes sense to children? Do I use context to support learning so that children do not have to rely on language alone? (This is particularly important for young children and for older children with poor language skills.)
8. Do I connect new material to familiar objects and events? Do I use hands-on materials when appropriate, particularly for novices?
9. Do I make student thinking (not just answers) public? Do I encourage students to justify their answers regardless of whether they are correct?

(continued)

Reflections on Practice: Checklist for Teachers *(continued)*

10. Do I allow children to choose some of their learning activities when possible? Do I follow the children's lead? Do I follow up on their questions?
11. Do I know what each child's zone of proximal development is for a particular task? Am I helping each child operate in his or her zone of proximal development?
12. Do I encourage private speech when children are solving difficult problems?
13. Do I scaffold classroom tasks by helping children master subskills so that each child can achieve success?
14. Am I taking advantage of opportunities to use reciprocal teaching in my classroom?

Summary of Age Trends in Cognition

	Behaviorism	Piaget's View	Vygotsky's View of Private Speech
Early Childhood (Birth–5 Years)	Behaviorists have little to say about age trends in cognitive development. Both classical and operant conditioning principles apply to this age, as well as other ages. Even newborn infants can be conditioned. Language acquisition provides additional avenues for conditioning.	The sensorimotor stage is roughly birth–24 months. In this stage thoughts and actions are not distinguishable. Mental schemes are based on sensory or motor input. Children develop symbolic thought. At 4–8 months they develop object permanence. At 8–12 months they make the A-not-B error in searching. They begin pretend play using symbols. At the end of this stage, they are capable of deferred imitation. The preoperational stage corresponds to roughly 2–7 years of age. In this stage children are capable of symbolic thought, but not of logic or mental manipulations. They do not understand cause-and-effect or hierarchical classification. They engage in animism, egocentrism, and centration. They cannot reverse operations.	The principles of Vygotsky's theory, such as scaffolding in the ZPD, apply to all age groups. However, private speech changes with age. During infancy, adult speech regulates children's behavior. Toddlers begin to use private speech to regulate their own behavior. Out-loud private speech peaks at about 4–6 years.
Middle Childhood (6–12 Years)	Both classical and operant conditioning principles apply to this age, as well as other ages. Increases in self-control allow reinforcement to be more effective even after delay in older children.	The concrete operational stage corresponds to roughly 7–11 years of age. Children are able to conserve and have mastered some of the limitations of preoperational thought. They reason about objects in everyday life, but are still not skilled at abstract thinking.	Private speech continues to become more internal and silent, and more task-relevant.
Adolescence (13–19 Years)	Both classical and operant conditioning principles apply to this age, as well as other ages. Adolescents have access to their own sources of reinforcement (e.g., food and money) which limits adults' control over their behavior.	The formal operational stage corresponds to roughly 12 years of age through adulthood. Some adolescents, but not all, are now capable of formal abstract logic. They can follow clear logic, and they reason in a hypothetical-deductive manner even if the premises are not true. They can systematically generate possible solutions to problems. They can isolate variables to test hypotheses.	Private speech is typically "underground" or silent. However, adolescents and adults will talk out loud to themselves if the task is very difficult.

Chapter Summary

Behaviorism

- Behaviorism is the science of observable behavior. Control of behavior is located in the environment. For behaviorists, learning (also called conditioning) is synonymous with behavior change.
- Classical conditioning involves involuntary behavior. An unconditioned stimulus that evokes an unconditioned (involuntary) response is paired with a neutral stimulus until the neutral stimulus evokes the same response. This conditioning can be extinguished by ceasing to pair the unconditioned and conditioned stimuli.
- Operant conditioning involves voluntary behavior. Reinforcement increases the probability of a behavior occurring, and punishment decreases its probability. Negative reinforcement refers to increasing the probability of a behavior by removing an aversive stimulus.
- Shaping is used to train behavior that does not spontaneously occur, by reinforcing behaviors that come closer and closer to the target behavior.
- Continuous reinforcement is best for training new behavior. Intermittent reinforcement is best for maintaining existing behavior. Extinction results when reinforcement ceases.
- Teaching is viewed as the arrangement of reinforcers. One application of operant conditioning is direct instruction. It is effective for teaching basic skills and concepts, particularly to high-risk students.
- B. F. Skinner is one of the most famous behaviorists. He wanted to use science to make society better by carefully controlling behavior.

Piaget's Cognitive Developmental Theory

- A key point in Piaget's theory is that children actively construct knowledge rather than passively copying what they perceive. Children construct knowledge as they assimilate new information to existing mental structures or accommodate those mental structures to fit new information. These processes result in cognitive balance or equilibrium.
- Piaget believed children progress in logical reasoning ability through qualitatively distinct, universal stages that follow an invariant sequence. Piaget believed that maturation combined with experience drives cognitive development.
- Research suggests Piaget underestimated the cognitive abilities of young children and overestimated those of adolescents and adults. Young children may fail to conserve on standard Piagetian tasks for reasons other than inability to think logically, such as inability to give primacy to language.
- Formal schooling, which varies by culture, is associated with differences in formal operational thinking.

- Constructivist teaching is an outgrowth of Piaget's theory. This includes providing hands-on experiences, provoking discourse, asking questions, following students' lead, guiding discovery learning, and making student thinking public.

Sociocultural Theory

- Vygotsky emphasized social and cultural influences on cognitive development. Cognitive growth is a function of social interaction with others. The child's abilities are first *inter*personal and then become *intra*personal. Culture determines what students learn, how it is taught, and what tools are available for learning.
- Private speech is typically out loud in younger children and then becomes internal and silent, but even teens will use audible self-talk to solve difficult problems.
- A more competent person scaffolds the student's performance by guiding performance to a higher level. The more competent person provides less and less support as the student becomes more expert.
- The zone of proximal development (ZPD) is the difference between what a student can achieve alone and what the student can achieve with the help of a more competent person. Vygotsky believed that instruction in the ZPD drives cognitive development.
- Instruction may emphasize reciprocal teaching and scaffolding in the student's zone of proximal development. Implementation of Vygotsky's views in the classroom are referred to as social constructivism, and Piaget's are referred to as cognitive constructivism. There is overlap between these two approaches, particularly the emphasis given to classroom discussion.
- Social cognitive theory combines some elements from other theories with behaviorism. It emphasizes the roles of vicarious reinforcement and self-efficacy beliefs in learning.

Accompanying Education CourseMate Website Resources

Visit the **Education CourseMate** website at **CengageBrain.com** to find resources and study aids for this chapter, including self-tests, additional print and website resources, and glossary flashcards. In addition to the TeachSourceVideo Cases, the following videos illustrate concepts discussed in the chapter:

- 2–5 Years: Piaget's Preoperational Stage
- 5–11 Years: Piaget's Concrete Operational Stage
- 12–18 Years: Piaget's Formal Operational Stage, Abstraction and Hypothetical Propositions

TEACHSOURCE VIDEO CASES

Watch the video cases *Constructivist Teaching in Action: A High School Classroom Debate* and/or *Middle School Science Instruction: Inquiry Learning*. As you view the videos and artifacts, think about the following:

1. **Which of the classroom implications of constructivism is the teacher implementing?**
2. **In what way does the teacher scaffold the students' performance in their zone of proximal development?**
3. **Describe a role for direct instruction in this classroom.**

Information Processing, Memory, and Problem Solving

John Archer/istockphoto.com

HAVE YOU MET PEOPLE WHO SEEM EXCEPTIONALLY GOOD AT REMEMBERING INFORMATION OR SOLVING PROBLEMS? You may have wondered whether you can help your students develop these abilities to their fullest potential. In this chapter we will discuss the general information processing model, and then discuss two specific types of processing—remembering and problem solving—at length. We will conclude the chapter by applying this model and the theories from Chapter 3 to mathematics. After you read this chapter, you will understand:

- How students process information, remember, and solve problems.
- How these abilities affect student success in your classroom and what you can do to promote them.
- How the major theories of learning and cognition apply to teaching mathematics.

Information Processing

In a high school class, students are told they will silently read a passage from The Crucible, *after which they will write answers to five questions about themes, symbols, and moral behavior of each character. Their teacher briefly quizzes them to make sure they understand the instructions; then they begin reading. Nick is a struggling reader. The teacher gives him occasional help on difficult words. After he finishes laboring through the passage, he asks, "What were we supposed to write again?"*

information processing model a model of cognition that focuses on how children acquire, store, and use knowledge.

Why did Nick forget the instructions? One possibility is limited working memory. Nick had to remember what he was supposed to write about while also doing a difficult task—decoding words and comprehending text—which overloaded Nick's working memory. Working memory is a key component of the **information processing model**.

This model describes how students receive, reason with, and remember information. It clarifies the process by which children grow cognitively, which is not clear in the three classic theories—behaviorism, cognitive development, and sociocultural theory—you read about in Chapter 3. For example, behaviorism ignores thinking. Piaget is vague about how a child moves from one cognitive stage to the next. Vygotsky's sociocultural theory does not specify how growth occurs in the zone of proximal development. In contrast, the information processing model outlines how students become better at processing information.

Components of the Information Processing Model

There are different versions of the information processing model, the most common of which is the *multistore model*. This model has three storage areas—sensory register, working memory, and long-term memory. The key components of the model are illustrated in Figure 4.1 and described next.[1]

Sensory Register

sensory register the component of the information processing model where initial stimuli from the environment are briefly held.

When you encounter information through seeing, hearing, feeling, tasting, and smelling, this information enters your **sensory register**. The sensory register takes in a great deal of information, but stores it for a very short period of time (perhaps one to three seconds). As you are reading this text, your sensory register is taking in patterns of colors on the page, the feeling of your clothes, food you may be chewing, your thoughts, noises in the room, and so forth. The fact that you cannot remember much of this information shows how briefly it is stored.

Attention

Most of the information you take in through your sensory register is forgotten because you do not pay attention to it. Attention acts as a gatekeeper of what information gets into

[1]There is not yet consensus among scientists about the one best model, so we provide a common, simplified version that will help you understand classroom learning.

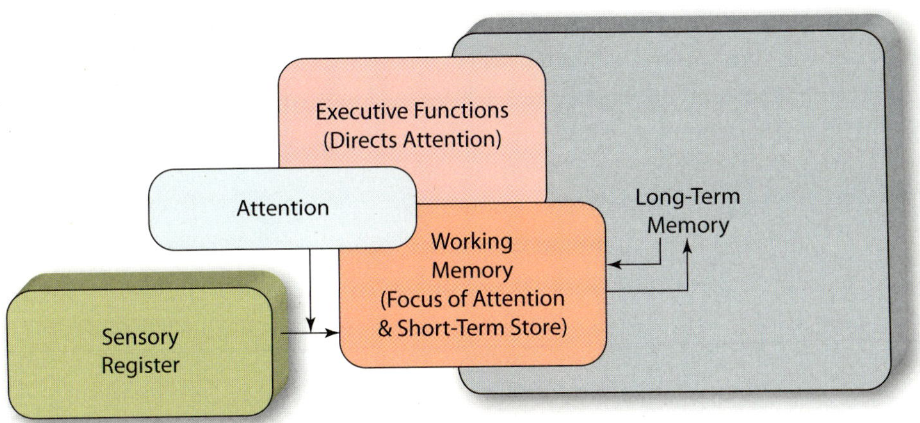

Figure 4.1 **Multistore Model of Information Processing.**
Attention can focus on sensory input or on information drawn from long-term memory.

working memory from the sensory register. Only information that receives some form of attention is remembered. You pay attention to information for at least three reasons:

1. It is new.
2. It is relevant to something you are actively processing.
3. It has emotional importance. (Downing, 2000; Raymond, Fenskey, & Tavassoli, 2003)

For example, if you express anger at a student in your classroom, you will immediately grab the attention of the class.

Working Memory

working memory the component of the information processing model where items of information are temporarily held for encoding or processing.

Information in the sensory register that is given attention may enter **working memory**. Working memory contains small amounts of information that you are processing at a given moment. This information comes through your senses from what you are experiencing at that moment (e.g., watching a video about the Battle of the Bulge), or can be retrieved from your long-term memory (e.g., remembering what you know about the Battle of the Bulge), or information could come from both. Working memory allows you to maintain some information during the processing of other information. For example, you might compare what you are watching with what you know about the Battle of the Bulge. Thus, working memory is where thinking occurs.

The capacity of working memory is relatively small and of short duration. Early research suggested that your working memory capacity is about seven items, plus or minus two (Miller, 1956). That is, an adult can keep about five to nine items active in working memory by repeating the items or by using them in some way. For example, a phone number consists of seven digits. Most adults can remember a new phone number long enough to dial it, but only if nothing interrupts them. Recent research is more pessimistic, suggesting that adult working memory capacity is about one to four chunks of information that can only be retained a few seconds, and for young children it is even less (Alvarez & Cavanagh, 2004).

You can more easily remember a phone number if you reduce memory load by *chunking* the seven digits into fewer items. Imagine you want to remember 882–2006. If 882 is a common prefix in your town, and if you graduated from high school in 2006,

Field Observation

Create lists of two to ten digits (e.g., 5, 7, 3, 2, 5, 8, and 9). Read a two-item list, one item per second, to a preschooler. Ask the child to repeat it back in order. Then try a three-item list, and so on. How many digits or words can the child remember? Try it with an older child and an adolescent. Did you observe age trends in working memory?

the phone number may effectively consist of only two chunks for you—882 and 2006. It is much easier to hold two chunks in working memory than seven individual items. Chunking helps you remember other types of information as well. For example, memorizing a list of vocabulary words is easier if you place them in a sentence that makes sense.

How do researchers know the capacity of working memory? One approach uses **memory span** tasks. Memory span refers to the number of items, usually presented rapidly, that you can recall in exact order. When digits are used (e.g., 5, 1, 3) as the thing to remember, the measure is called *digit span*. Some tests use nonsense words like "woog," "spleg," "symo." Visual-spatial working memory is tested by tasks like recalling a route through a pictured maze. A complex task for 3- to 6-year-olds requires them to remember a list of one-syllable words (e.g., nest, fire, hole, hand) in backwards order (Noël, 2009). The most complex tasks, known as *storage-and-processing* tasks, ask you to remember numbers or words, while also processing other information such as counting to 100 by fives. The classroom task in the opening vignette is equivalent to a storage-and-processing task for Nick.

memory span a common measure of working memory that tests the number of items, usually presented rapidly, that a person can recall in exact order.

Executive Functions

executive functions the brain's control of its own information processing.

Executive functions refer to the brain's control of its own information processing (Banich, 2009). The brain must control attention and focus on a task, hold information during reasoning, retrieve information from long-term storage, monitor sequences of behavior, detect errors and make corrections, and shift ongoing functions to more urgent functions. These executive functions are also called *executive control* or the *central executive.* Executive functions are essential for self-control and for higher-order cognition, that is, any activity that requires effortful, complex thought.

Two important executive functions are:

1. *Shifting* from one task to another. In the opening vignette, Nick could not remember the worksheet instructions because he did not occasionally shift from the reading task to reactivate his fading memory of the instructions.
2. **Inhibitory control**. This is the ability to keep from processing irrelevant information, or to suppress a response. One way scientists measure this ability is by showing children cards that are either black with a moon and stars, or white with a yellow sun. Children must say *night* when shown a sun card and *day* when shown a moon card.

inhibitory control the ability to inhibit processing irrelevant information or to suppress a response.

Attention, working memory, and executive functions are intertwined. Indeed, some models portray them as all one component. Preschoolers who are particularly good at controlling their attention can hold more in working memory and are likely to become teenagers who are fast and accurate at inhibitory control tests (Eigsti et al., 2006). In Figure 4.1 we overlapped these components to convey the current uncertainty about whether or not attention, working memory, and executive functions are separate components.

Metacognition

You are not always conscious of your executive functions; however, sometimes you *think about your thinking*, which is called **metacognition**. Metacognition refers to your knowledge of your own learning processes and how to regulate them. It takes

metacognition cognition that reflects on, monitors, or regulates other cognition.

metacognition to choose a strategy to apply to a problem. It takes metacognition to answer the question "What do you know, and how do you know it?" When you finish reading a page of this textbook and suddenly realize that you have not processed a single word, that is metacognition at work. Planning and using effective learning strategies is part of metacognition.

Two types of metacognition are important for learning. *Metacomprehension* refers to judging when you have understood something. Even college students have difficulty with this. You can improve metacomprehension by practicing summarizing what you have read (Dunlosky & Lipko, 2007). *Metamemory* refers to what you know about your own memory and how to store or retrieve information from it. Students have metamemory when they know that learning precise facts takes more effort than learning the gist of history or that stories are easier to remember than lists. Students with better metamemory are better at recall and use better memory strategies (Pierce & Lange, 2000).

Long-Term Memory

Long-term memory refers to the relatively permanent storage of information, also known as knowledge. Information in working memory might become stored in long-term memory—but not always. Much is lost. Later we will discuss strategies for increasing the odds that you will remember information over the long-term. Scientists do not know if long-term memory has limits. It may not be possible to know too much, although you may have felt cognitive overload in some classes.

long-term memory the relatively permanent storage of information. Duration is long and capacity is very large, perhaps unlimited.

Age Trends in Information Processing

Information processing is linked to brain development. As the brain continues to mature across childhood—through synaptic pruning and myelination—processing speed, working memory capacity, attention control, executive functions, and knowledge all steadily improve. Some of these abilities reach adult levels by 6th grade, others in adolescence, and still others continue to improve in adulthood (Bayliss, Jarrold, Baddeley, Gunn, & Leigh, 2005; Luna, Garver, Urban, Lazar, & Sweeney, 2004).

Early Childhood (Birth to 5 Years)

Processing speed is slower in young children because myelination, knowledge, and language are limited. Each of these factors influences processing speed. Language affects processing speed because it organizes the storage and retrieval of information. Processing speed, in turn, limits working memory. During early childhood there is improvement in each of these components, and as a result, *working memory* capacity increases (Nelson et al., 2000).

Executive functions develop dramatically in the preschool years. In fact, you can measure improvement within a year's time (McClelland et al., 2007). You can measure executive functions with cards depicting two shapes (e.g., flowers and cars) that are drawn in two colors (e.g., red and blue). Ask children to first sort by one dimension (e.g., color). After sorting several cards, ask children to *switch tasks* and sort by a different dimension (e.g., shapes). You will find that 3-year-olds across the world will usually continue sorting by the old rule (color), even though they can tell you they should be sorting by the new rule (shape). Why is this task so difficult? Executive functions draw upon working memory and

Field Observation

You can easily test inhibitory control in young children using the "Head-to-Toes" game. Ask 3- to 6-year-olds to "touch your head" or "touch your toes" several times. Then ask them to switch—touch their head when they are told to touch their toes. Do you see a developmental difference?

attention control, which have limits. To do this task, young children must pay attention to instruction, keep the new rule in working memory, and inhibit their original response (Zelazo, Müller, Frye, & Marcovitch, 2003). Most children become successful at this task by age 5.

Middle Childhood (6 to 12 Years)

In middle childhood, *processing speed* continues to improve, although the rate of change eventually slows down (Kail & Ferrer, 2007). Figure 4.2 shows how processing speed increases from 5 to 18 years of age. (If you immediately thought, "Ah! That is a quadratic equation," you were right. Negotiate for extra credit.)

Working memory improves substantially (Nelson et al., 2000). The number of items that can be processed increases steadily from 3 to 15 years, when adult capacity is reached. Memory span grows in roughly two-year steps such that an average 3-year-old can remember one number or word, a 5-year-old two items, a 7-year-old three items, a 9-year-old four items, an 11-year-old five items, a 13-year-old six items, and a 15-year-old seven numbers or words (Kemps, De Rammelaere, & Desmet, 2000).

The improvement in working memory is partly due to better *control of attention*. Figure 4.3 shows that children's working memory capacity gets larger, and control

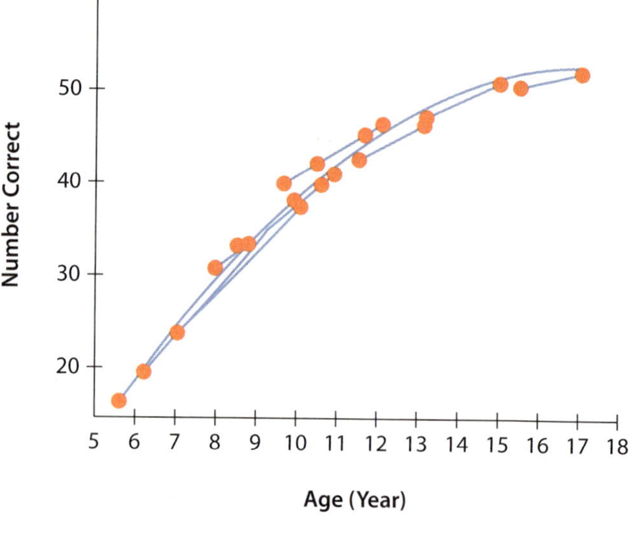

Figure 4.2 Processing Speed by Age. Children were given rows of six numbers, like 8,9,5,3,9,7, and asked to circle the identical numbers. The number of rows they can do in a three-minute period is a measure of processing speed. Can you describe how processing speed develops with age in this graph? Graphs of working memory tend to have the same shape (e.g., Dempster, 1981). Try this with children of different ages to see if you get a similar age trend. Be prepared with about sixty rows if you are testing intelligent adolescents! *Source: Kail & Ferrer (2007).*

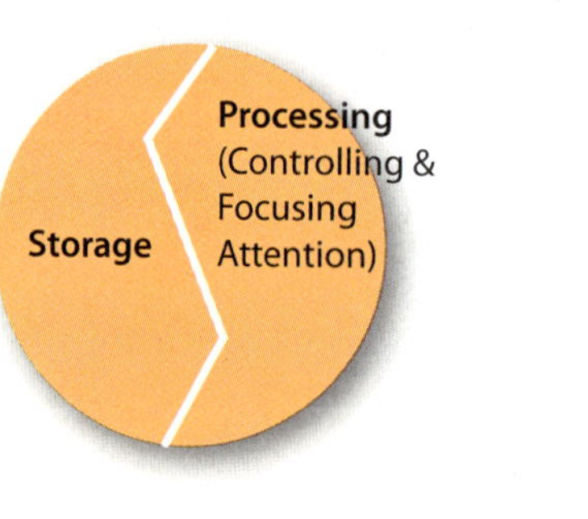

Figure 4.3 Working Memory Capacity. Working memory capacity increases with age, as indicated by a larger circle. At the same time, the proportion of that capacity that is needed for processing diminishes.

of attention becomes more efficient, freeing memory capacity as they get older. The improvement in working memory is also partly due to faster processing speed and better executive functions. The difficulty that Nick, in the opening vignette, had with shifting between the reading task and remembering the instructions is more typical of primary-grade children. Indeed, 2nd-graders are just on the cusp of this ability (Barrouillet, Gavens, Vergauwe, Gaillard, & Camos, 2009). Older children should have less difficulty with it.

Adolescence (13 to 19 Years)

We are sorry to tell you that *processing speed* appears to peak around age 15, levels off, then begins to get slower after age 18 (Kail & Ferrer, 2007). Thus, if you teach high school, you are likely to have students who are faster than you are. This improvement supports formal operational thinking, better athletic performance, and greater impulse control compared to younger children.

Executive functions increase in adolescence (Kuhn, 2006). Adolescents are better at controlling their thinking. They are faster and more accurate on tests of inhibitory control, which peaks in the late teens. Task switching, like sorting cards by a new rule, is easy for typical adolescents. However, they will sort cards at a slower rate using the new rule compared to the old rule (Diamond & Kirkham, 2005). A harder test of executive functions used with adolescents is the Stroop test (see Figure 4.4).

Peak levels of performance on complex *working memory* tasks that require strategy use, incorporating new information, and monitoring progress are also reached around ages 14 to 16 (Luciana, Conklin, Hooper, & Yarger, 2005; Steinberg, 2009). However, on simple working memory tasks, like recognizing a face you've seen before, adult levels of performance are reached as early as ages 9 to 10.

These abilities are linked to brain development. The impressive improvement in working memory and executive functions in adolescence is thought to result from maturation of the prefrontal cortex and the cingulate gyrus in the brain. In Chapter 2 you learned that these brain areas are slow to develop, coming to maturity in adolescence or young adulthood.

Word Set #1

Red Purple Grey
Yellow Orange Black
Red Green Pink
Yellow Brown Purple
Black Blue White
Blue Orange Green
Pink

Word Set #2

Red Purple Grey
Yellow Orange Black
Red Green Pink
Yellow Brown Purple
Black Blue White Blue
Orange Green Pink

Figure 4.4 **The Stroop Test.**
In set 1 read the words and time yourself. In set 2 you must say the *color* the word is printed in, while inhibiting the automatic tendency of skilled readers to *read* the word. Time yourself again. The difference in time between the sets is your "inhibitory control" score. Get friends and children of different ages to try it. Try it online. There are various Stroop test sites.

Individual Diversity in Information Processing

The same components of the information processing model that increase with age also vary from student to student. That is, some students process information faster, have larger working memory, and control their thinking better than other students who are the same age. In the opening vignette, Nick had difficulty with executive control compared to other classmates.

Individual differences in information processing are apparent as early as 9 months of age (Bauer, Wiebe, Carver, Waters, & Nelson, 2003). However, individual differences are far larger in adolescence than in early childhood. Cognitive development may be canalized in early childhood, with development being closely linked to age. By adolescence, two children the same age can be quite dissimilar. Some 12-year-olds perform like the average adult on cognitive tasks. Some adults are no better than the average 12-year-old (Kuhn, 2006).

Each of the information processing components—faster processing speed, better attention and executive functions, and larger working memory capacity—has been linked to academic success. For example, students who have better information processing abilities are better at solving math problems and comprehending what they read, and get higher standardized test scores (e.g., Alloway, Gathercole, Kirkwood, & Elliott, 2009a; Swanson, 2008; Valiente, Lemery-Chalfant, Swanson, & Reiser, 2008). Students with poor working memory, like Nick, may struggle more as they progress through school because school tasks will increasingly demand working memory.

Information processing abilities are also linked to emotional and social skills at school. Students with poor attention control and poor executive functions tend to have more problems like anxiety, depression, impulsiveness, aggression, and acting out in the classroom (e.g., Eisenberg et al., 2004; Zhou et al., 2007).

selective attention attending to task-relevant input while suppressing irrelevant input.

In classrooms, students must ignore distractions when given a task that requires concentration; they must suppress irrelevant information. This is known as **selective attention**. Two-year-old Akiva is skilled at selective attention:

> *In the toddler class, the teacher is presenting a brief lesson on fall leaves, with pictures and sample leaves to capture the toddlers' attention. Two children are pushing chairs around the room, taking off their shoes, and jumping about. These two children capture the attention of the other toddlers, but not Akiva. She listens to the teacher with unwavering attention, softly imitating occasional words like* pretty, golden, fall down, *as though nothing else were happening in the room.*

In contrast to Akiva, children with poor inhibitory control are described by their teachers as "inattentive, easily distracted, can't concentrate, daydreams." Inhibitory control tends to be stable. For example, one study found that 1st-graders who have trouble controlling their attention continue to have trouble in 8th grade (N. P. Friedman et al., 2007). Inability to control attention is a defining feature of **attention-deficit/hyperactivity disorder (ADHD)** (see Box 4.1). Many scientists believe that poor inhibitory control is the core problem underlying ADHD, but the evidence is not definitive (Castellanos, Sonuga-Barke, Milham, & Tannock, 2006).

attention-deficit/hyperactivity disorder a neurobehavioral disorder characterized by hyperactivity, low impulse control, and inattention.

Challenges in Development **Box 4.1**

ADHD

In an 8th-grade history class, Clayton is supposed to be completing a worksheet. While looking at the paper, he constantly taps his pencil and drums the desk with his thumb. He gets out of his seat to throw away a piece of paper. He wanders the room and taps another student on the shoulder. He sits down, but in a few minutes gets up to read the classroom rules posted by the door. He sits down again, but soon walks over to talk to his friend. The teacher tells him to return to his seat. Clayton only works on the worksheet for two minutes without interruption when the teacher stands next to him.

Clayton has attention-deficit/hyperactivity disorder (ADHD). You will have students like Clayton in your classroom. ADHD is the most common neurobehavioral disorder in childhood. Roughly 6 to 9% of school-age children have ADHD, with boys having three to four times the rate of girls (Loe et al., 2008).

The primary symptoms of ADHD are impulsivity and lack of self-control. ADHD usually becomes apparent during the first few years of elementary school. Symptoms may last into adulthood, but they usually diminish across childhood.

What might lead to ADHD? ADHD is highly heritable (heritability is about 0.77) and runs in families. It is commonly assumed that this is due to brain abnormalities; however, neuroscience evidence is not yet definitive (Biederman, 2005).

Experience also makes a contribution. ADHD is linked to the mother feeling stress during pregnancy, low birth weight, birth problems, and the mother's use of tobacco or alcohol during pregnancy (M. Schneider & Moore, 2000). It is also linked to quality of parenting. Children with a mother who has chronic depression, anxiety, or other emotional disturbance are four times more likely to have ADHD. There is also higher prevalence among children in step, adoptive, foster, or single-parent households; households that move frequently; and negative, conflict-ridden households (Lesesne, Visser, & White, 2003). Children with insecure attachment to their parents are more likely to have ADHD symptoms (see Chapter 6).

ADHD is substantially more likely in children who have *both* a genetic predisposition and environmental risk factors (Pennington et al., 2009). For example, children whose mother smoked during pregnancy and who have genetic propensity are particularly likely to be distractible (Wiebe et al., 2009). If you recognize this as a gene-environment interaction, you have been paying attention!

Why does it matter if children have ADHD? Children with ADHD may have cognitive and behavior problems as early as age 3 (Loe et al., 2008). They are more likely to be injured, such as in bicycle accidents (DiScala, Lescohier, Barthel, & Li, 1998). They are also more likely to be involved in theft, assault, and use of a weapon as teenagers. In school they are likely to underachieve, as they struggle to comply with classroom demands (Molina et al., 2009). Although symptoms of ADHD diminish with age, academic problems tend to persist and may increase (Barkley, 2006).

What can be done about ADHD? Treatment for ADHD usually includes behavior therapy and/or medication. Behavior therapy typically involves behavior modification (see Chapter 3) as well as therapy aimed at altering the child's thoughts (e.g., "I need to pause before acting"). Medication reduces children's fidgety and impulsive behavior, but a large randomized experiment showed it may not reduce academic or other behavior problems (Molina et al., 2009). The American Medical Association recommends combined medication and behavioral treatment for parent and child (Goldman, Genel, Bexman, & Slanetz, 1998).

Drug treatment for ADHD is controversial because all drugs have side effects. These may include growth deficits, muscle tics, sleep problems, lack of emotion, and possibly an increase in suicide (National Institute of Mental Health, 2008). The U.S. Food and Drug Administration now requires warnings to be placed on ADHD drugs. In spite of these concerns, drug treatment is common and increasing, even among preschoolers.

Implications for teachers. You may need to provide extra monitoring to prevent injuries for a student with ADHD. You may be involved in a behavior modification plan that includes parents and the school counselor. It may help to (1) seat the child away from objects or classmates that are distracting, (2) check frequently that the child understands directions, (3) give instructions in short bouts rather than lengthy lists, and (4) praise good behavior and classroom

(continued)

Challenges in Development *(continued)*

success. Follow the guidelines on classroom implications for information processing in this chapter. Chapter 7 provides other suggestions to help children control their impulses.

In addition, you may be called upon to provide evidence as part of a diagnosis. * Teachers' assessments of ADHD may be more valid than parents' assessments (Mannuzza, Klein, & Moulton, 2002). Recognizing this, the American Academy of Pediatrics (2000) stated, "*The assessment of ADHD requires evidence directly obtained from the classroom teacher … regarding the core symptoms of ADHD, the duration of symptoms, the degree of functional impairment, and coexisting conditions*" (p. 1165).

*A teacher and parent checklist used in the process of diagnosing ADHD can be found at http://www.adhd.net/SWAN_SCALE.pdf. It is called the SNAP after its authors: Swanson, Nolan, and Pelham.

What might predict differences in information processing? One factor is genes, which may influence how efficiently the brain functions. Another factor is the quality of a child's home environment. Mothers who are sensitive and provide activities that stimulate their children's cognitive and language development tend to have children who have better memory and control over their attention. Akiva's mother is a former teacher who creates a stable and stimulating home. In contrast, children who are placed in multiple foster homes tend to have poor executive functions compared to children with similar risk but who were fortunate enough to be adopted before having been in multiple foster homes (Lewis, Dozier, Ackerman, & Sepulveda-Kozakowski, 2007). In Box 4.1, you learned that ADHD is associated with several aspects of the home environment. How might this work? The home environment influences development of the brain, where information processing takes place (see Chapter 2 and 6). Let's discuss the school environment next.

Classroom Implications of Information Processing

Information processing ability affects students' academic and social success in your classroom. Academic tasks—such as correctly spelling words while keeping in mind the point of the essay you are writing—require working memory and executive functions. If you have students like Nick who have difficulty shifting between tasks, forget lengthy instructions, forget letters in words or words in sentences, are easily distracted or poorly organized, cannot complete a multistep task, or raise their hand but forget the response when called upon, they may have limited information processing ability (Alloway, Gathercole, Kirkwood, & Elliott, 2009b). There are a few things you can do as a teacher to help such students be successful.

Reduce Working Memory and Executive Load

Your students cannot learn new things when their working memory capacity is overloaded. To reduce the load on working memory:

- Present information at a speed that allows students to fully process the information.
- Reduce distractions in your classroom so that there is less demand on children's executive functions.
- Increase your students' expertise. The more automatic their processing, the more space is freed in working memory. If reading is automatic for you, you

would not have been overwhelmed by the task in the opening vignette, but it would be overwhelming to young beginning readers and to struggling older readers, like Nick.

- Provide external storage. Do this by teaching students to take notes. Better yet, you can provide partial notes (i.e., a rough outline of your lesson, but not details), which frees students' working memory to attend to the information. You can write instructions on the board so students like Nick do not have to store the instructions while processing the task. For example, a 2nd-grade teacher might write on the board: "Read for 20 minutes. Write summary of what you read. Look at the sample on the wall, if you need to."
- Carve problems into smaller subtasks that can be performed sequentially—such as the algorithm Mrs. Harl taught Monica for solving three-digit problems in case 2. In math and science this includes providing formulas.

Imagine that you teach physics to 11th-graders, who have adult-like working memory capacity and speed. You ask your students, "What would be the acceleration of an object if the object travels the same distance again in half the time?" Solving complex problems that require processing three or four variables at once taxes their working memory. However, if your students know that velocity equals distance divided by time ($V = d/t$), they can determine what the new velocity is. They can then apply velocity as a single variable to compute acceleration, which is the difference between velocity at time 1 and time 2 ($A = V_1 - V_2$). These formulas take care of whole chunks of the problem. *Part of educating children toward expertise is to give them the tools to chunk problems into a manageable size that fits their processing capacity* (Halford, Baker, McGredden, & Bain, 2005).

Focus Attention

To be an effective teacher, you need to attract student attention and maintain it on important information, particularly if you teach students who have difficulty controlling their attention. Students can be so focused on one thing that they miss something else going on at the same time, which is **inattentional blindness**. They may miss critical observations during an experiment, or a change in instructions, or key pieces of a lesson, because they are focused on something else.

inattentional blindness the tendency of children to not perceive obvious objects or events if they are concentrating on something else.

Strengthen Executive Functions

You can strengthen your student's executive functions in the short run by promoting healthy habits and in the long run by promoting exercise of executive functions. Exercising executive functions makes them stronger, just like muscles. Follow these guidelines:

- Promote adequate sleep and good nutrition among your students (see Chapter 2). Executive functions require a large amount of glucose (the brain's fuel, as you undoubtedly remember from Chapter 2). Part of why you don't think clearly when you are tired or hungry is because your brain is depleted of fuel. The brain's store of glucose is replenished during sleep (Gailliot, 2008).
- Reduce stress in your classroom. Coping with stress consumes mental energy and depletes the brain's fuel (Gailliot, 2008).

- Help students practice using their executive functions through mundane, daily activities like requiring them to sit up straight, persist in rigorous physical exercise even when they want to stop, or participate in other activities that require self-control (Gailliot, 2008). Some researchers developed the *Tools of the Mind* curriculum to help teachers do this with preschoolers. It incorporates Vygotskyan concepts with information processing. For example, children are taught to control themselves by talking out loud using private speech. A randomized controlled experiment shows that it is effective (Diamond, Barnett, Thomas, & Munro, 2007).

Scientists are experimenting with whether carefully designed computer games can improve information processing ability. The games ask children to remember where an object is on a 4 × 4 grid, or find matching figures among many figures. After several weeks of playing such games for perhaps forty minutes per day, children have better working memory and executive functions. Effects have been found for preschoolers and school-age children with ADHD (Klingberg et al., 2005; Thorell, Lindqvist, Nutley, Bohlin, & Klingberg, 2009). Thus, research suggests information processing may be improved through training. Scientists don't know yet if this kind of training would improve classroom performance, or whether it lasts over the long run, but it seems hopeful.

Think About This A study of Swedish children with ADHD found that after playing a specially designed computer game for forty minutes per day for five weeks, executive functions increased (Klingberg et al., 2005). The effect size was 0.93. The effect size for ADHD medication is 0.4 to 1.2. What does this mean? Which intervention would you use and why?

From an information processing point of view, cognitive growth is the result of greater *knowledge* as well as greater processing speed, attention control, working memory, and executive functions. Greater knowledge enhances these other components of information processing because knowledge that is overlearned and automatic frees resources and is processed more quickly. (So even if your high school students are faster than you, hopefully you have the advantage of knowing more.) Greater knowledge is the focus of the next section.

Memory

Mr. Glazer helps his 6th-grade students learn new vocabulary words by reciting the definitions out loud several times across the week. They also do a worksheet matching definitions and words. At the end of the week, Mr. Glazer has the children write their own sentences using the vocabulary words.

Mr. Glazer is helping his students secure vocabulary words in their long-term memory. Information in long-term memory can be stored unintentionally, like a conversation with a friend, or intentionally, like studying for a test. Deliberately attempting to remember is called *memorizing*. Schooling often requires memorizing, like these 6th-graders are doing. While education is not only about memorization, memorization is necessary for many types of problem solving and conceptual understanding.

Remember? Maybe, Maybe Not

In this section we will discuss limits in remembering and then strategies students can use to overcome those limits and memorize important information.

Memory Errors

Memory is not an exact replica of an object, event, or experience. There are two types of memories: verbatim traces, which are detailed accurate memories, and **fuzzy traces**, which are general, vague memories, or the gist of an experience. Can you remember a lecture word-for-word from last week? Probably not, but you might remember the gist of it. Most of your remembering involves fuzzy, not verbatim, traces. This may not seem ideal, but in fact fuzzy traces are adequate for most endeavors.

fuzzy traces a distilled gist of an experience rather than an exact memory.

You may have worked hard to teach students something—a piece of music, sight words, anatomy terms—which they appear to learn at one time, but later forget. Verbatim memories are forgotten more readily than gist memories. For example, if you have a verbatim trace of the algebra test scores for two students in your class (e.g., 97% and 84%), this would soon deteriorate such that you could not remember the exact scores but you could remember which student did better. Like you, students remember details only if they use them frequently.

There are at least three reasons students forget things:

1. Decay. The memory decays over time.
2. Retrieval failure. Students may know something but then go blank during a test. They cannot retrieve the information when they need it.
3. **Interference**. New knowledge can make retrieval of old knowledge difficult and vice versa (Wixted, 2005). For example, Kevin is an English speaker who knows the word *embarrassed* (old knowledge). In Spanish class, he learns that *embarazada* means *pregnant* (new knowledge) but has trouble remembering the new definition because of interference from the word *embarrassed.* When he does something embarrassing, he says, "*Estoy embarazado*," which unfortunately means "I am a pregnant boy" (adding to his embarrassment).

interference existing information in long-term memory prevents accurate retrieval of new information, or information learned recently prevents accurate retrieval of older information.

Another type of memory error, besides forgetting things that you once knew, is remembering things that never happened, or *false memories.* Our youngest daughter remembered family vacations that occurred before she was born. Apparently, she was a precocious child. (Actually, she saw photos and then created a "memory" of the vacation.) Other children do this, too. A sneaky researcher intentionally told another adult at a preschool—in front of some of the children—that an escaped rabbit was eating carrots in another classroom. Later 55% of the *classmates* of those children, not the children who overheard the story, reported having actually seen the rabbit, which did not exist (Principe, Kanaya, Ceci, & Singh, 2006)—that is, rumor mongering caused false memories.

False memories can be planted in adolescents and adults as well (Bernstein & Loftus, 2009). For example, researchers doctored family photographs into a picture of a hot air balloon ride, and family members remembered taking the ride, which never occurred (Garry & Gerrie, 2005). Just imagining an event can create false memories, making you believe the imagined event actually happened.

Why do we have false memories? Memory always contains pieces of reality mixed with creation. False memories are intelligent errors—that is, the mind makes sense of a situation and recalls details that were not there but logically fit our expectations. The memory students construct is influenced by their previous experience, so different students construct different memories of the same event. Just because students express a memory with confidence, detail, and emotion does not necessarily mean it is factual.

source monitoring memory of the source or origin of information.

One type of false memory you'll need to help students with is the **source monitoring** error, or a false memory of the source of their information. For example, children may think they learned history facts in school when they actually learned them from not-quite-accurate cartoons (Roberts & Blades, 2000). Source monitoring is crucial for critical thinking about the meaning and accuracy of information. A supposed "fact" is evaluated differently based on whether it came from a supermarket tabloid, a research journal, or Internet advertisement.

Another kind of false memory occurs in mental maps. It is easier to remember a straight boundary than to remember every twist and turn. Thus, mental maps tend to over-regularize space by straightening curved lines. For example, U.S. students tend to believe that the western coast of North America is due north of the western coast of South America, so much so that when given an accurate and inaccurate map, many prefer the inaccurate map (Tversky, 2000). In fact, Miami is further west than every major city in South America. Thus, if you teach geography, it is important to teach how each region is situated compared to other regions.

Context and Memory

Memory can be influenced by aspects of the physical context. Noise, for example, can affect students' memory. Background noise tends to disrupt memory if the noise is meaningful, such as people talking (Knez & Hygge, 2002). This causes divided attention because the student is attending to two things at once. Background noise that is not meaningful can also disrupt memory. When an airport was moved, the elementary children who lived nearby improved in long-term memory, short-term memory, and reading performance (Hygge, Evans, & Bullinger, 2002). Unfortunately, children living near the new location of the airport decreased in these same abilities.

encoding specificity aspects of the context are encoded with the target information so that retrieval is enhanced when retrieval context is similar to the original context.

In addition, when information is encoded in memory, the context in which the information was stored is stored along with it. This is known as **encoding specificity**. When students learn about certain subjects in one class, they are more likely to recall those subjects in that same class than in a different class. A student is more likely to recall something if the physical setting, language, and mood are the same as the context in which the learning occurred (Brown & Craik, 2000; Neisser & Marian, 2000).

Memory Strategies

encoding the process of forming mental representations of information for storage.

rehearsal mentally repeating information over and over in working memory.

Although memory has plenty of errors, it works reasonably well if you are not too concerned about precision. However, in some situations precise, accurate details must be consciously memorized. The process of putting information into long-term memory is called **encoding**. There are three types of effective strategies for encoding.

1. *Rehearsal.* Repeating items over and over again keeps them active in working memory and facilitates encoding into long-term memory. **Rehearsal** is commonly used by students of all ages, and is more effective than a one-shot exposure to material such as reading through a chapter once, but it is less effective than the next two strategies.
2. *Organization.* Organizing or clustering related items into groups facilitates memory. For example, a student who is trying to remember the attributes of two civilizations in social studies class might create a Venn diagram that

includes two overlapping circles to organize attributes that the civilizations share and attributes that are different.

3. *Elaboration.* **Elaboration** involves creating visual or verbal links between items. You can help students elaborate by asking them to put things into their own words, generate examples, or apply information. Mr. Glazer, in the vignette, did this when he had his 6th-graders use new vocabulary words in sentences. Help students see meaningful relations among the items, or make up relations solely for the purpose of remembering. For example, to remember that latitude lines are horizontal on a globe, students might think LATitude sounds like LADder, and visualize ladderlike lines. Children who use elaboration strategies tend to remember more (W. Schneider & Bjorklund, 1998).

elaboration a method of enhancing memory that involves creating visual or verbal links or representations to associate two or more items.

How do you know if a strategy has been successful? An important next step in memorizing is self-testing. Have you ever been sure you were ready for a test because you had the content down cold, yet when you actually took the test, you didn't do so well? Such misjudgments of memory are common. Self-testing helps students more accurately judge what they know—if they diligently check their answers without cheating (Dunlosky & Lipko, 2007). Self-testing improves both memory and metamemory. Thus, after reading this chapter, come back later and test yourself without the answers in front of you.

Age Trends in Memory

Children know more and become better at remembering and memorizing with age. They come to use memory strategies more effectively. Let's look at these age trends in greater detail.

Early Childhood (Prenatal to 5 Years)

Can you remember anything from when you were a toddler (1 to 2 years)? The average age of the first memory that U.S. adults can recall is around 3 or 4 years, sometimes as early as 2 for dramatic events. Any early memories you have are likely to involve strong emotions, such as very frightening events. Early memories are also likely to be sparse—like a snapshot without context. Most people have only a few memories before 6 to 8 years of age (Bauer, 2002).

The inability to remember things that occurred to you from infancy to your first memories is called **childhood** (or *infantile*) **amnesia**. There is currently no single explanation for childhood amnesia. One possibility is that it is due to absence of language. Language helps children encode memories so that they can tell you about events later (Richardson & Hayne, 2007). Another possibility is that it is due to a lack of sense of self in young children (Howe, 2003). Children cannot have personal memories if they have no sense of themselves as a person who is separate from others. Yet another possibility is that it is due to an immature brain, although key brain structures that support long-term memory become functional before 1 year of age (Bauer et al., 2003; Lloyd, Doydum, & Newcombe, 2009).

childhood amnesia the inability to recall things that occurred during infancy, typically from birth to about 3.5 years of age. Also called "infantile amnesia."

Infants do have some long-term memory. During the last month of pregnancy, fetuses may remember experiences for a few weeks, like specific sounds or vibrations (Dirix, Nijhuis, Jongsma, & Hornstra, 2009). In Chapter 5 you will read about habituation studies that show that 3-month-olds can remember simple things for up to three months. Deferred imitation studies show that older infants also have long-term memory for complex information. In deferred imitation studies, the experimenter demonstrates actions that are unfamiliar to the infant—such as placing a toy car into a tunnel and then pushing it with a rod so it rolls to the end and turns on a light. The infant is given the opportunity to reproduce the same actions weeks later. If the infant forgets either step, the light does not turn on (Bauer et al., 2003). Older infants learn faster, retain memories longer, and need less training than younger infants. Long-term memory increases steadily through infancy.

Preschoolers often display good long-term memory, but they may need adult support. For example, scientists asked children who were 3 and 4 years old when they visited Disneyworld to recount their trips several months later (Hamond & Fivush, 1991). The children remembered a great deal of accurate information about their trip. However, the 3-year-olds needed cues to help them remember, such as "What rides did you go on?" "What did you eat?" The 4-year-olds recalled more spontaneously, without cues, and they provided more details.

Young children often fail to use memory strategies. They may use rehearsal, but are not likely to use organizational strategies before age 5 or 6. You can teach kindergarteners memory strategies, but they are unlikely to apply them to situations outside the training context, may not see the value of using the strategies, and will need more time to learn the strategies than older children (Kuhn, 2000; W. Schneider, 2000).

Middle Childhood (6 to 12 Years)

Elementary-age children's memory improves in at least five ways. First, they know more; they have greater long-term memory. Second, they get better at metamemory. For example, they understand that they are more likely to forget details than gist and that they can remember details better if they are linked to easy-to-remember events (W. Friedman, 2007; Jaswal & Dodson, 2009). For example, they can remember when they went to the zoo if that detail is linked to their summer visit to Grandma's house. Third, they get better at remembering to do something in the future, like return a permission slip or library book (R. E. Smith, Bayen, & Martin, 2010).

Fourth, they get better at generating effective memory strategies. When presented with a task like remembering vocabulary words, younger children will use no strategy or they will use simple rehearsal. By about 3rd grade, children will use organization (Lehmann & Hasselhorn, 2007). They are not likely to generate elaboration spontaneously, but it becomes easier to get them to use it (Waters, 2000).

Field Observation

Play *Concentration* separately with two children of different ages. Can you tell what strategies they used by watching (e.g., moving lips)? Can the children articulate their strategies? Let them use notes. Did it help? Are there age differences?

One of the most effective memory strategies is to write something down. This is why you take notes during class. Do children use written notes, and do they actually help? Researchers asked 1st- through 7th-graders to play the game *Concentration*, in which they memorize the location of cards with identical pictures (Eskritt & Lee, 2002). They were given paper and told they could write anything that would help them remember where each card was. Only 50% of the children, regardless of age, chose to use notes. Of the children who did use notes, many used notes that were not helpful. Those whose notes were helpful were mostly 5th-, 6th-, and 7th-graders. Thus, older children were not more likely to use notes, but if they did use notes they used them more effectively.

Children do not gradually transition from nonuse of memory strategies to full use, as you might expect. Instead, they inconsistently use strategies. Some children discover a strategy at one age, lose it at a later age, and then rediscover it still later. A child may use old and new strategies at the same period in time.

Fifth, they may have fewer false memories. For example, in one study, children were asked to recall events from a birthday party. About half of 5-year-olds reported an event that did not occur, but only 20% of 7- to 12-year-olds did (Odegard, Cooper, Lampinen, Reyna, & Brainerd, 2009).

Adolescence (13 to 19 Years)

Two aspects of memory increase through adolescence. First, quality improves. As children move into adolescence they shift from vague-to-vivid recall. That is, 9th-graders are better able to recall specific, vivid details than 2nd-graders. This occurs for word lists, narratives, pictures, and numbers (Brainerd, Holliday, & Reyna, 2004).

Second, memory strategies improve. With age, children are more likely to use elaboration. Elaboration strategies develop later than rehearsal and organizational strategies, and seldom before adolescence. However, many adolescents, and even college students, may not use elaboration spontaneously or effectively.

Individual Diversity in Memory

The age trends in memory just discussed are generalizations. Two children of the same age can differ in their ability to remember and deliberately memorize. Let's look next at what these differences mean.

What Do Individual Differences in Memory Predict?

Earlier you learned that students with greater *working memory* capacity have higher achievement. Students who have greater *long-term memory*—or know more—also have higher achievement. This is obvious because achievement tests measure how much children know. Less obvious is that knowing more also makes children better problem solvers because memorized knowledge can be applied to the problem at hand, like solving math problems or writing a persuasive essay. Students with better *metamemory* also have higher achievement. That is, they know how and when to apply memory strategies to their advantage.

What Predicts Individual Differences in Memory?

Individual differences in long-term memory are the result of differences in exposure to information, resistance to memory error, and effective use of memory strategies. Some of these factors are linked to information processing ability. For example, children with better working memory use memory strategies more effectively, which helps them come to know more (Lehmann & Hasselhorn, 2007). Two additional factors that predict remembering, that teachers can influence, are prior knowledge and conversation.

Prior knowledge

Children who have prior knowledge about a topic learn new material about that same topic more easily—whether the topic is ant behavior, lowest common denominators, or *The Crucible*. For example, when a group of children were tested on newly learned vocabulary, children who knew a lot about baseball and those who did not had about the same memory capacity for new nonbaseball terms (Gaultney, Bjorklund, & Schneider, 1992). However, children with high baseball knowledge had better memory for new baseball terms, and they were more likely to use a better strategy (categorizing) to remember. This effect is so powerful that *low-ability students with prior knowledge about a topic may learn more effectively than high-ability students without prior knowledge.* In Chapter 5 you will learn that expertise in an area can compensate for low intelligence.

Prior knowledge has a powerful influence on memory because knowledge is organized in long-term memory as webs or networks of related information. The more connections between individual items of knowledge, the better. When items of knowledge are encoded with many connections, they are easier to retrieve because more things can activate them. For example, if you learn that the Mexican author Mariano Azuela wrote *The Underdogs*, you are not likely to remember it if you have no other connections to it. Someone with a richer network might trigger *The Underdogs* from the Mexican Revolution, Francisco Madero, Pancho Villa, and the novel *Maria Luisa*.

schema an organized network of information.

script a schema for how to do something or for an event.

These networks of knowledge are called **schemas**. (They are sometimes called *schemata* and are similar to Piaget's schemes.) Much of education is an attempt to build accurate schemas for specific topics like British romantic poets in high school or animal camouflage in preschool. One type of schema is a **script**. Scripts focus on *how to do something*. Much of education is also an attempt to develop automatic scripts for behavior like counting, reading books, or solving algebra problems.

Conversation

> ***Think About This*** The fact that talking aids memory suggests that memory is a social event. How does this fit with Vygotsky's sociocultural theory?

Language is a powerful tool in helping students store information and create schemas. If you talk about novel objects with students as they are handling them, students are more likely to remember the objects (Haden, Ornstein, Eckerman, & Didow, 2001). If you talk about an event, like a visit to a museum, as it is happening or shortly afterward, students recall the event better.

How you converse matters. If you ask questions and add additional details as students recall events, students remember more (Fivush & Nelson, 2004). Ideally you should ask open-ended questions (e.g., who, what, where) and follow the student's lead by talking about things the student brings up (Reese & Newcombe, 2007). For example, in one study toddlers whose mothers elaborated, not merely repeated, what they talked about could remember things from early childhood at ages 12 to 13 better than could other teens (Jack, MacDonald, Reese, & Hayne, 2009).

Talking about things helps your students retain a memory longer. Talking about things also helps them understand the information better or focus their attention on important features. Thus, to help your students remember, talk with them about what you want remembered.

Classroom Implications of Memory

You may be able to raise your student's academic achievement by enhancing their memory. How can you do this? Earlier you learned that conversation enhances memory. In addition, combining verbal and visual information enhances memory (Roediger, 2008). A picture may not actually be worth a 1,000 words (perhaps only

789 words?), but it helps. There are at least five more ways you may help your students remember: (1) help them connect knowledge, (2) teach memory strategies, (3) increase exposure to content, (4) provide spaced practice, and (5) test them. Let's discuss each next.

Connect Knowledge

Earlier you learned that prior knowledge promotes remembering new information. This is because rich networks of connections between new and old knowledge helps students store and retrieve information. To help students connect knowledge, use these guidelines:

- *Help students develop a broad knowledge base.*
- *Help your students activate relevant prior knowledge* to show them what they already know about a new topic. One approach is known as KWL, which stands for what do you *know*, what do you *want* to know, and what have you *learned* (Carr & Ogle, 1987). The *know* and *want* questions are asked before instruction, and the *learned* question comes after instruction. For example, if you were teaching about animal camouflage, ask students what they already know about it. They might talk about owls the color of snow or camouflage clothing for hunting. Then ask them what they want to know about animal camouflage, such as why zebras have stripes. This helps students connect prior and new knowledge. There are other more complex versions of the technique, such as adding an *H* (KWHL) for *how* can you find out.
- *Refer to content from other classes or from different units within your own class.* For example, in history class, students may learn about World War II in the context of Pearl Harbor and connect the war with the end of the Depression. Across

Bonnie Kamin/PhotoEdit

An example of the KWL approach

> classes, they could connect World War II with literature published during the war, like Steinbeck's *The Moon is Down* and Faulkner's *Go Down, Moses.*

In the past, secondary schools tended to compartmentalize content rather than build connections. For example, students might never discuss literature or popular culture in connection with World War II. Today, more schools actively try to connect content, such as combining social studies and English classes.

Facilitate Memory Strategies

Students must sometimes memorize details like dates in history, formulas in geometry, or vocabulary in foreign languages. Many students do not know how to memorize, particularly young children. Research shows that effective teachers deliberately teach their students memorization strategies (Coffman, Ornstein, McCall, & Curran, 2008). To do this, use these guidelines:

- Create a network of fuzzy traces and stories that help bind together important information to connect the verbatim traces, or details.
- Let your students know which details must be memorized and why. Use phrases like "remember" and "don't forget."
- Frequently demand remembering. For example, "Yesterday we talked about states of matter. What are the three forms that water can take?" In many cultures educators require young children to memorize poems, religious texts, or music.
- Ask your students to think about their memory strategies. For example, "How did you remember…?" This exercises their metamemory skills.
- Directly teach memory strategies. Unfortunately, observations of elementary classes have found that teachers in only 1 to 10% of the observations do this (Coffman et al., 2008; Moely et al., 1992).

There are a variety of ways to teach memory strategies to your students. Teach them to use flashcards, a type of *rehearsal,* to memorize things like multiplication facts. Teach them to *organize* items to be remembered. For example, memorizing anatomy terms is easier if they are organized by body regions. Teach them to use *elaboration.* For example, remembering when the California gold rush occurred is easier if it is paired with the San Francisco Forty-Niners football team, which is named after the 1849 gold-rush miners.

mnemonics techniques for improving memory

You can also teach your students to use **mnemonics** to memorize material that is not yet meaningful to them. Mnemonics are commonly used to memorize information such as the state capitals, vocabulary words, and ordered lists like the presidents of the United States or artists and their major works. Two types of mnemonics are acronyms and the keyword method.

acronym a mnemonic technique that takes the first letters of words to be remembered and combines them into a word or phrase.

An **acronym** takes the first letters of words to be remembered and combines them into a word or phrase. For example, *HOMES* is used to remember the Great Lakes, which are Huron, Ontario, Michigan, Erie, Superior. Similarly, *sentence mnemonics* (sometimes called *acrostics*) use the first letter of each item to create a sentence that is more easily remembered. For example, *Please excuse my dear Aunt Sally* is used to remember the order of operations in algebra (parentheses, exponents, multiplication, division, addition and subtraction).

The **keyword method** is a two-stage mnemonic. First, the student chooses a keyword that has a *sound* similar to the target word. Second, the student creates an *image* that links the keyword with the target word. For example, Mrs. Patel used a keyword to help sophomores in her chemistry class remember whether cations or anions are positive.

keyword method a mnemonic in which a keyword that *sounds* like the target word is chosen and then an *image* is linked with it.

Mrs. Patel draws a picture of a cat with a bib on the whiteboard. Then she draws a large plus sign on the bib. A student looked at the picture with a puzzled expression, then suddenly smiled, saying "Oh! I thought it was kay-shun, not cat-ion. And I guess it is an-ion, not an-yun—well, duh—they're ions! Well, that makes more sense!"

Not only did this picture help the student remember cations are positive, it also resolved her confusion over reading about "kayshuns" in a chapter that was supposed to be about ions.

Mnemonic strategies can be complex. Young children, and low-ability older students, may need your scaffolding to use them, and you may need to convince them that the effort is worth the payoff. Over time they will be able to apply these strategies without support. Once students become expert in a domain, they no longer need mnemonics because the information is encoded in so many ways and so deeply.

Increase Exposure to Material to Be Learned

Children need multiple high-quality exposures to material in order to remember it effectively. For example, Mr. Glazer exposed his 6th-graders in the vignette to vocabulary words in three different ways. A study of middle school students learning about Antarctica found that in order to remember material over an eight-month period, students had to have at least three activities in which they had full exposure to the material (Nuthall, 2000). (Do not assume that three is a magical number or that children will remember anything they come across three times.) If the exposure was partial, indirect, or not explicit, more exposure was necessary. A caution is that you should monitor student understanding so that *misconceptions* do not have multiple exposures and become entrenched.

Space Practice

Exposure to material and practice with it needs to be spaced out over time. For example, Mr. Glazer had his students practice vocabulary words over a week's time, but he could have done all the learning activities back-to-back. Which is best? **Spaced practice** (also called *distributed practice*) is more effective than massed practice. Whether you space or mass practice can influence how well you remember information several years later. Massed practice creates an illusion of learning, but the material is quickly forgotten; it creates false confidence rather than true competence. The *spacing effect* applies to memorizing facts and to learning concepts (Kornell & Bjork, 2008).

spaced practice multiple periods of practicing, or studying, over a period of time rather than in a single massed episode. Also referred to as distributed practice.

The longer you want to remember something, the longer the spacing needs to be. Table 4.1 gives approximate lengths of spaced practice for optimal remembering based on research; these are suggestions, not sure-fire recipes. If Mr. Glazer wants his students to remember their vocabulary words permanently, he will need to do some of the same activities months later. In addition, he could test them—our next suggestion.

Table 4.1 Approximate interval of practice needed to remember for long periods

Length of Time to Remember	Interval to Space Practice or Review Content
1 week	1 day apart
1 month	1 week apart
1 year	3–4 weeks apart
Several years	Several months apart

Sources: Adapted from Cepeda, Vul, Rohrer, Wixted, & Pashler (2008); and Rohrer & Pashler (2007).

Test Students

Finally, a fifth way to help your students remember is to test them. This may surprise you, but *testing can be more effective at helping students learn than reviewing the content* (Johnson & Mayer, 2009; Karpicke & Roediger, 2008). Students remember content better that they have been tested on. Perhaps this is because students have to put effort into recalling the content. Perhaps this is also because tests provide an immediate purpose for remembering, and having a purpose for remembering aids memory. Research suggests tests will help your students learn if you use these guidelines:

- Test frequently. This tends to discourage cramming, to foster spaced practice, and to lower test anxiety because each test counts less. Cramming can result in good short-term, but not long-term, test scores.
- Use recall rather than recognition tests, such as short-answer rather than multiple-choice. However, multiple-choice tests are better than no tests for enhancing memory.
- Use cumulative tests. Students are more likely to integrate new material with old if they know that tests will cover material that goes beyond the time period since the last test.
- Provide feedback immediately after the test. You can provide an answer key to multiple-choice tests immediately following the test. For essays and other constructed responses, provide models of an ideal response, or ask students to share their responses with each other so that they learn from other models.

In this section, you have learned several ways to improve the memory of your students. Helping children remember important information is a key goal of education. Let's turn now to another key goal of education: helping children learn to reason and problem-solve.

Reasoning and Problem Solving

A 3rd-grade teacher, committed to helping her students connect their mathematics problem-solving skills to real-world experiences, brings in grocery coupons clipped from the newspaper. Today the coupons are for brownie mixes from two companies: Martha White's 10-oz for $0.99 and Pillsbury's 15-oz for 2/$3. She asks the students: "Which is a better deal?" An 8-year-old boy responds with great certainty—as though this were an easy task—"Martha White. Because it's 2 for 2 dollars. This other one is 2 for 3 dollars."

> *A 5th-grade teacher in the same school borrowed the coupons. She also asks her students: "Which is a better deal?" An 11-year-old boy responds with less confidence, "They're the same. Thirty ounces would be 3 dollars for the Martha White, and 30 ounces would be 3 dollars for the Pillsbury. Am I right?"*

The older boy is right; the younger boy does not take into account that the cheaper package is also smaller. Why do these boys use different problem-solving strategies to arrive at their answers? How can teachers help students reason accurately? To address questions like these, researchers analyze how children reason and solve problems.

Reasoning is a type of critical thinking. Increasing children's critical thinking skills is a key outcome of education. Reasoning is goal-directed. The goal might be to simply understand something, like why wood floats, or be highly specific, like how to answer question 17 on the quiz. Reasoning often involves inference. You make an inference any time you go beyond the information you have to reach a new conclusion, generalize to a new situation, or find a solution to a problem. Thus, inference is one way to generate new knowledge; it is a source of learning.

Problem solving is a type of reasoning. Problem solving is a goal-directed, higher-order thinking skill involved in solving a problem and achieving a goal. After solving the problem, you then evaluate whether the solution was a success.

Problem solving in school is often artificial because the teacher or textbook sets up a series of problems in a constrained way that helps students arrive at correct answers but does little to train them to solve real problems. Typically, textbooks introduce a strategy for approaching one type of problem, such as three-digit addition or physics velocity problems. The students are then given practice problems that require the same strategy for solution. These *well-structured* problems might be useful during early phases of learning, but *ill-structured* problems that are more like real-world problems and that require students to draw upon all their knowledge, not only the strategy they just learned, should also be used. One teacher said of her lesson:

> *It was set up too much for success ... I made the lesson safe for the kids—no fail—which was my goal at the time. I now think I need to let them go through the frustration that goes with problem solving. The lesson probably wouldn't have looked as smooth, but I think it would have stretched the kids more.*
> *(M. S. Smith, 2000, p. 362)*

Students have a repertoire of strategies that can be used to solve a problem. Development occurs when students gradually give up less-effective strategies and increase their use of more-effective, advanced strategies. For example, in one study children learning to multiply used two strategies: (1) retrieval from memory ($2 \times 5 = 10$; more advanced) and (2) adding one digit the number of times dictated by the other digit ($2 \times 5 = 2 + 2 + 2 + 2 + 2 = 10$; less advanced). Most children used both strategies across the school year, but the more-advanced strategy was used more frequently as the children grew older (Siegler, 2000).

The advanced strategy was also used more for easier problems and the less advanced for more difficult problems. This is typical. Children select faster, less effortful strategies on easier tasks and slower, more effortful ones on difficult tasks. In case 2

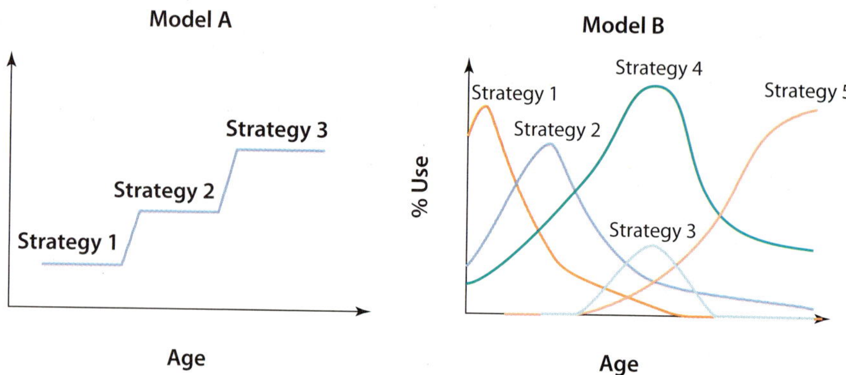

Figure 4.5 Models of Problem-Solving Strategies.
Model A is a stage-based model. According to this model, as children acquire a new, better strategy, they no longer use old, less-adequate strategies. Model B is an overlapping wave model. According to this model, children may use multiple strategies at any given time, but over time increasingly use more-adequate strategies. Research indicates model B more accurately describes children's strategy use. *Source: Siegler (1995).*

(three-digit addition), Mrs. Harl used the faster regrouping strategy to add 199 + 204 (change it to 200 + 203). However, she used the slower algorithm—split the number into columns and carry from the ones column to the tens column—to add 203 + 518 because the problem was more difficult.

Your students' development of problem-solving strategies may resemble overlapping waves. That is, some strategies are used initially and then used less frequently, others become more frequent, others rise from infrequent to frequent and back to infrequent, and still others are seldom ever used. The overlapping wave model is depicted in Figure 4.5. The essence of the model is that children know and use multiple strategies. Earlier, you learned that the same is true for the use of memory strategies. This model contrasts with a Piagetian view of problem-solving development, that children have stagelike improvements in strategy use with age.

Age Trends in Reasoning and Problem Solving

Problem-solving ability improves with age. This is the result of improved strategies, knowledge, working memory capacity, and ability to manage the process using executive functions and metacognition.

Early Childhood (Birth to 5 Years)

induction a form of reasoning in which a child detects generalizations, rules, or regularities, often, but not always, through comparison and contrast.

In the first months of life, infants use simple forms of reasoning such as trial-and-error, where they try all possible strategies until one works. By 13 months, toddlers clearly use **induction**, or a form of reasoning in which they generalize information beyond what is known to new situations. For example, when shown a toy that rattles, which they are told is a *flum*, they will try to rattle a different-looking toy that is also called a flum (Graham, Kilbreath, & Welder, 2004). This means the toddlers took information about an object and used it to make inductive inferences about a new object.

By 2.5 years, toddlers *use induction to generate a simple abstract rule.* For example, show a child two objects, a cup and a cone, with a raisin under the cone. Then give the child another set of objects, say a cup and an inverted box. The child will look for the raisin under the inverted box (Deloache, Miller, & Pierroutsakos, 1998). The child has logically induced the rule "choose the object different from the cup."

Young children also show *deductive reasoning* in their everyday behavior. Deduction is a form of reasoning where a conclusion follows logically from a set of premises. An example was given in Chapter 3 of the 3-year-old who deduced that there must still be crackers based on two premises: (1) when crackers are gone, Mom throws the box away, and (2) there is no box in the garbage.

Young children are also able to *reason by analogy.* For example, in one study children were told to move balls from one bowl on a table to another out-of-reach bowl. On the table were many objects, including an aluminum cane. The children were told a story about a genie who moved his jewels from one bottle to another using a magic staff to pull one bottle closer. Even 4-year-olds used the analogy to solve their own problem by pulling the bowl closer with the cane (Deloache et al., 1998).

Although this evidence shows that young children are capable of reasoning in a variety of ways, two important improvements occur. First, preschoolers come to understand that *inference is a source of knowledge.* For example, imagine an adult and child both see a jar full of only blue balls. Then the adult leaves, and one ball is removed and hidden. Upon returning, the adult is asked the color of the hidden ball. By 5 to 6 years, children know that the adult can infer that the ball is blue without guessing, but younger children do not (Pillow, Hill, Boyce, & Stein, 2000).

Second, preschoolers come to understand *when evidence is sufficient for drawing conclusions.* For example, imagine you draw a flower on white paper with a purple marker. Then you show a child three boxes with lids. Ask the child which box contains the marker used to draw the flower, without opening them. After the child guesses, ask: "Do you know for sure, or do you have to guess?" Then open the boxes, one at a time, revealing a green, then purple, then red marker, repeating the question. Only when all three boxes are open can the child "know for sure" which box contains the marker used to draw the flower. A more complex version uses four boxes. The fourth box will contain another purple marker. Even when all four boxes are open, the child cannot determine which box contains the marker used to draw the flower. Most preschoolers can do the three-box task, and about 70% can do the four-box task (Klahr & Chen, 2003).

Preschoolers' logic is not flawless, however. When two boxes are open, and one reveals the purple marker, preschoolers often say that purple marker must be the one—even though the third, still-closed box may also contain a purple marker. The single positive instance captures the children's attention and blinds them to the fact that the third box might render the problem unsolvable. Even adults have this bias to some extent, which is why advanced scientific reasoning requires extensive education.

Reasoning can be improved through direct instruction. When children are told *why* their response is correct or not, they improve in reasoning on the purple-marker task (Klahr & Chen, 2003). Five-year-olds, but not younger 4-year-olds, will improve with simple experience, even without feedback. They also learn faster from feedback, improve more dramatically, and transfer their improved ability to other similar tasks more than 4-year-olds. This is probably the result of better working memory and executive functions.

In summary, young children can reason and problem-solve. They become gradually more reliable, systematic, and efficient in their reasoning with age, but there is not a stagelike shift (Deloache et al., 1998). Young children are substantially more logical than Piaget believed them to be. Young children possess some reasoning abilities long before they reach the formal operations stage.

Middle Childhood (6 to 12 Years)

Although children are capable of reasoning in early childhood, as they mature, their abilities improve. In middle childhood, children become better at distinguishing reasoning from guessing or acting on a hunch (Amsterlaw, 2006). Their private speech becomes more internal (see Chapter 3), although children may still talk out loud to themselves when they try to solve difficult problems. They also become capable of "if-then" inference. For example, when told, "If something is a car, then it has a motor," they can answer questions like:

Suppose that something does not have a motor. Is it a car?

Suppose that something has a motor. Is it a car?

Suppose that something is not a car. Does it have a motor?

Such reasoning requires the child to retrieve relevant counterexamples from memory. For example, given the preceding statement, "If something is a car, then it has a motor," children in middle childhood can recognize that something that has a motor does not have to be a car, because they know that boats have motors. They also recognize that the statement *if car then motor* is not the same as *if motor then car* or *only cars have motors.* Children's increased knowledge, speed in retrieving counterexamples, and increased size of working memory help them reason in tasks like these (Markovits, Fleury, Quinn, & Venet, 1998).

Older children also become better at problem solving because they try new strategies after initial strategies fail, while younger children may continue to use the same inadequate strategy. For example, researchers asked 5-, 7-, and 9-year-olds to use wooden blocks to build a bridge over an imaginary river (Thornton, 1999). No block was long enough to span the river; the children had to use a counterweight approach, a very difficult task for these ages. All children started out with ineffective strategies. After only a few collapsed bridges, most 7- and 9-year-olds changed their approach, but 5-year-olds persisted in their unsuccessful approaches. Eventually all 9-year-olds, 80% of 7-year-olds, and only 20% of 5-year-olds were able to build a bridge.

Adolescence (13 to 19 Years)

Basic scientific reasoning, in which a student must vary only one factor at a time in order to draw conclusions from an experiment, develops in adolescence. A key component of Piaget's formal operations stage is the ability to reason about causal relations like what causes a pendulum to swing faster (see Chapter 3). Not until adolescence can most students design and correctly interpret a simple experiment or explore hypotheses on their own. For example, in one study 6th- and 9th-graders were shown foods eaten by healthy and sick children (Deloache et al., 1998). They were asked if a particular food made the children sick. If both sick and healthy children ate tomato soup, then a logical response was, "Tomato soup doesn't make you sick." Illogical responses were irrelevant or contrary to the evidence, like "I get sick when I eat...." Ninth-graders were more logical than 6th-graders. Almost one-third of the 6th-graders provided no logical or evidence-based responses.

Field Observation

Observe a group of children conducting a science experiment or solving a math problem in class. (Use a game of *Tic-Tac-Toe* if you do not have access to a classroom.) Listen to their discussion, observe their strategies, and ask them about their approach. Are they using logic and effective strategies? Is their approach age-typical? Are there individual differences in problem solving?

This research has implications for inquiry-based lessons. In some inquiry learning, students design a study, collect and analyze data, and draw conclusions. This approach assumes students have the ability to effectively carry out such activities. However, young adolescents often do not. For example, in one study 6th-, 7th-, and 8th-graders were asked to determine what factors affect flooding—water pollution, temperature, soil, and elevation. A computer simulation program allowed them to alter each variable and see what happened to flooding. If they changed only one variable at a time, holding all others constant, they could figure out that temperature and soil affect flooding. Even after experience, not all the students could use logical strategies to find the solution (Kuhn, Black, Keselman, & Kaplan, 2000). However, some students did come to use effective strategies more frequently, suggesting that practice can cause strategy change. Recall the discussion in Chapter 3 about the difficulty that students have learning to isolate variables, whether they learn via direct instruction or discovery.

Individual Diversity in Reasoning and Problem Solving

Students of the same age can vary substantially in their reasoning ability. In the study cited earlier, 70% of 6th-graders could make a logical argument connecting food and sickness, but 30% could not. In another study, 23% of 3rd- and 4th-graders discovered how to reason scientifically during a science experiment, but most needed direct instruction, and still others never got it. A precocious 7% were able to do it before the study began (Klahr & Nigam, 2004).

What Do Individual Differences in Reasoning Predict?

Differences in reasoning ability influence all aspects of behavior. For example, reasoning ability influences how successful you are at parenting, as a citizen in a democracy, and in your career as a teacher—teachers must figure out how to teach, test, and discipline students. Reasoning ability also influences academic achievement and is a key part of intelligence.

Reasoning ability is also linked to antisocial behavior. For example, 12-year-old Steven may be frustrated on the school bus by Allen's loud talking. If he is poor at problem solving, he might solve the problem by slugging Allen. Antisocial children tend to come from families with meager problem-solving abilities (Spotts, Neiderhiser, Hetherington, & Reiss, 2001). You will learn more about this in Chapter 10.

image100/Jupiter images

Teachers promote learning when they model or provide feedback to students.

What Predicts Individual Differences in Reasoning?

Students with better processing speed and working memory capacity have advanced reasoning ability. Other factors that predict reasoning ability that are under greater teacher control are feedback, modeling, and prior knowledge.

Feedback

Students learn to use more-efficient problem-solving strategies through feedback about whether the strategy was successful

(Hattie & Timperley, 2007). If feedback is negative, some (but not all) children revise their strategy. Students will improve strategy use following success as well as failure. Students who adjust their problem-solving strategies as a result of feedback are more likely to have used multiple strategies to begin with. They are able to choose among the strategies to find one that works best (Siegler, 2000).

Modeling

Students often watch others model problem-solving strategies, but the models do not explain their strategy. Students must figure out the strategy themselves. Can young children do this? In one study children watched a *Tic-Tac-Toe* game in which a child model used a more sophisticated strategy than the children themselves used. The strategy was to find two separate winning paths, or a fork, so that even if your opponent blocks one, you can win with the other path. Second-graders were more likely to learn the fork strategy than kindergarteners, although some kindergarteners learned it as well. They were able to use the strategy whether the model directly explained the strategy or they had inferred the explanation themselves. Thus, the children learned from direct instruction as well as through discovery (Rittle-Johnson, 2007).

Prior knowledge

Can you solve the following analogy? Beat is to 45 degrees as Reach is to _____.

The answer is "90 degrees." *Beat* and *reach* are sailing terms. If you are not familiar with sailing, you could not logically derive an answer. Such analogy-based reasoning is heavily dependent on your prior knowledge. Indeed problem-solving ability in any area is dependent on level of knowledge in that area. This is one reason members of groups with less school-relevant knowledge have difficulty with problem solving on school tasks. (Do you recognize this as part of cultural capital from Chapter 1?) Let's look at other reasons for group differences in problem solving next.

Classroom Implications of Reasoning and Problem Solving

One of your primary responsibilities as a teacher is to help your students become more skilled at reasoning. You can promote their reasoning ability in six ways: (1) identify what strategy they are using, (2) teach them more-effective strategies, (3) help them understand the problem, (4) foster argument, (5) use inquiry-based experiments, and (6) directly train induction. Let's look at how to do this in more detail.

Identify Students' Strategies

Talk to students about their strategies. Frequently ask "How did you know?" or "Why?" as they solve problems. Often children cannot articulate what strategy they are using, particularly when they are just transitioning to using new strategies. You can sometimes determine this yourself. Use these guidelines:

- Notice their gestures and speed to infer what strategies are being used. For example, it is faster to answer multiplication problems from memory than to add all the operands, so faster children are probably using the better strategy (Siegler, 2000).
- Slightly alter the task to reveal their strategies. For example, give addition problems that do and do not require carrying to reveal their competence with carrying.

Teach Effective Strategies

You may help your students use more-effective strategies if you follow these guidelines:

- Use feedback and modeling. You can help children learn to use better strategies either by telling them through direct instruction or by allowing them to infer for themselves from modeling. For example, when a 10th-grader was struggling with literary analysis of *To Kill a Mockingbird*, her teacher modeled how he would extract themes and symbols and think about characterization. In Chapter 3 you learned that students can also learn by observing another student successfully solve physics problems, and that this was more effective than just watching an expert work an example (Craig, Chi, & VanLehn, 2009). Ask students to explain their own reasoning, or ask them to explain *your* (or another model's) reasoning. They should tell why the model is solving the problem in a particular way. *This may be the most important way to improve your students' problem solving.* When students must explain strategy use, their understanding of strategies grows (Rittle-Johnson, 2007).
- Ask students to share and compare strategies. For example, 7th- and 8th-graders might be asked to compare two different strategies to solve algebra problems like $5(y + 1) = 3(y + 1) + 8$. Expert math teachers ask students (1) "to describe how their strategies are different" and (2) "Which is the most efficient strategy?" This helps students learn procedures as well as abstract concepts. However, there are two important caveats. First, such comparison is most effective when combined with direct instruction afterwards (Rittle-Johnson & Star, 2009). Second, for students who have no prior knowledge, it may be ideal to practice just one strategy for a while so their working memory is not overloaded by making comparisons (Rittle-Johnson, Star, & Durkin, 2009).

Don't expect that students will use a new strategy effectively right away. Sometimes when they try a new, better strategy they don't have better performance. However, if they keep using the strategy it eventually leads to better performance (Schwenck, Bjorklund, & Schneider, 2007).

Knowing how to use a strategy to solve a problem does not guarantee that a student will choose to use it. For example, a strategy for ensuring you get the right answer in a physics problem is to write out the units as well as the numbers (e.g., 10 m/s × 15 s = 150 m), and make sure the units on both sides of the equal sign cancel out. Students resist using this strategy because it is effortful. As a teacher, you can convince them of the effectiveness of this strategy by providing examples from their own work showing incorrect responses because they did not use the strategy.

Revisiting the Case

Which of these guidelines did Mrs. Harl follow in case 2? Were there guidelines she did not follow? How would you improve her lesson?

Help Students Understand the Problem

Students sometimes need help understanding the meaning of a problem. For example, try solving this problem: "There are 125 sheep and 5 dogs in a flock. How old is the shepherd?" This problem is unsolvable, but many 1st- and 2nd-graders may come up with a solution anyway (Schoenfeld, 1991). One student tried addition (130) and subtraction (120) and reasonably concluded that 120 and 130 were too old for a shepherd's age; he then tried division and gave the answer as 25! Even students with many more years of formal schooling will make similar errors because they do not pay attention to the meaning of problems, and just plug numbers into memorized formulas. You can help your students understand the problem when you:

- Ask students to reflect on and think about the problem. For example, in one study, 8th-graders were trained to ask themselves questions about math problems such as "What strategy could be used to solve this problem?" or "How is this problem similar to the previous problem?" Those who received this metacognitive-strategy training developed better reasoning ability (Kramarski & Mevarech, 2003).
- Provide students with ill-structured problems or problems with a variety of structures. For example, if 3rd-, 4th-, and 5th-graders are given an equation like $7 + 4 + 5 = 7 + ?$, they typically will respond with 23 instead of 9. They make this mistake because they have had extensive practice in school with problems of the "$x + y + z =$ answer" structure. From their well-structured problems, they infer false rules like "all equations have the form 'operations = answer'" and "the equal sign means 'the total.'" They forget the correct concept that the equal sign means that the two expressions on either side must be equivalent (McNeil & Alibali, 2005). Experience with varied equations would help them understand the problem better.

Foster Argument

Both Piaget and Vygotsky believed that argument promotes reasoning ability. It also promotes metacognition. To foster rational argument in your class:

- Respectfully require students to defend their claims during class discussion. Ask students to elaborate on their reasons, support them with evidence, and evaluate them.
- Require students to respectfully identify and address weaknesses in the opponent's argument or the counterargument. This may be even more effective than having them explain their own position (Kuhn & Udell, 2003).

This will give your students experience thinking and reasoning in a cognitively rich classroom environment.

Use Inquiry-Based Experiments

Some educators argue that education should focus more on reasoning abilities rather than focusing on content knowledge. However, as you learned earlier, knowledge is critical to reasoning, so a balance may be ideal. You may help your students become better problem-solvers when you:

- Involve students in experiments that use the scientific method of problem solving—that is, experiments that emphasize controlling variables, with multiple replications, peer review, and using the data rather than preexisting beliefs to guide conclusions.

- Explicitly guide children through these carefully chosen experiments so that they understand the power of scientific problem solving.

Explicit guidance can be critically important. For example, teachers in an urban 5th grade in New York had their students plant seeds in multiple cups that contained three different types of soil (Hogan & Corey, 2001). They wanted their students to investigate which soil was best for growth by applying the scientific method—such as treating all the plants identically so the only thing that varies is the soil or replicating—because if one plant died in soil A it could have been a bad seed, but if many died it might be poor soil. Many of the students never did understand these concepts. Some thought that the purpose of replication was to give everyone a turn, some focused only on the data from their own plants rather than from the whole class, some said that they already knew which soil was best and did not need an experiment, and some saw the experiment as a sort of race to see who would "win." This study, along with the experiment on flooding discussed earlier, suggests that unguided inquiry learning does not always result in better problem solving.

Directly Train Reasoning

When you foster argument in your classroom, ask challenging questions, and use inquiry-based experiments, you are giving students practice reasoning. For example, when you read a book about animals to toddlers you might point to one animal and say, "This one has a wing. Does one of these other animals have a wing?" Children have to use reason through induction to figure out what a wing is (Gentner, Loewenstein, & Hung, 2007). Some media, like *Sesame Street* and *Highlights* magazine, have tasks designed to train reasoning in preschoolers, like those in Figure 4.6. Practice with such tasks improves reasoning if children are taught to ask questions like, "What do I have to look at? What should I do to find the solution? How should I check my solution?" After just ten 45-minute practice sessions, children score better on intelligence tests compared to control groups. (Induction tasks are part of many intelligence tests because induction is a critical component of intelligence and part of school readiness tests.) After such training, children learn more during later academic lessons across

Figure 4.6 Tasks for Training Problem-Solving Ability.
Inductive reasoning involves comparison. Children make sense of the world by searching for similarities and differences in objects or the relationships between them. Tasks like these help children practice reasoning. Task A requires children to generalize attributes and classify. Tasks B and C require children to recognize relationships.

Task A: Which three objects belong together?

0, 1, 1, 2, 3, 5, 8, 13, 21, 34, ?

Task B: What number comes next?

Task C: What object belongs in the empty square?

subjects like biology, geography, grammar, and foreign languages. The effect size is impressive (0.50 to 0.70) and long lasting (Klauer & Phye, 2008).

In Chapter 3 and this chapter you have learned about four theories of learning and cognitive development that can be generally applied to your classroom. Let's finish our discussion of these theories by comparing how they might apply to learning mathematics, since increasing math achievement is currently a national priority. In Chapter 12 we will focus on how they might apply to learning reading and writing. If you do not teach math or literacy, you can use your reasoning ability to extrapolate to other content areas.

Putting the Theories to Work: The Case of Mathematics

A 5-month-old sits before a large box (see Figure 4.7). He sees a hand holding one mouse doll enter the box from a hole in the side and place the doll in the box. The hand retreats empty. A screen rotates up to hide the doll. The infant sees the hand enter from the side with a doll again. It presumably adds another doll behind the screen because it also retreats empty. The screen then rotates down to reveal only one doll. (A doll was removed through a trap door.) The infant looks longer at this impossible event than he did in preceding trials when two dolls were revealed.

Figure 4.7 Infant Number Sense.
Infants see a toy mouse placed on a table, then covered with a screen. The hand presumably places a second mouse behind the screen because it retreats empty. The screen then drops to reveal either two mice (a possible event) or only one mouse (an impossible event). Infants look longer at the impossible event, suggesting rudimentary number sense. *Source: Wynn (1992).*

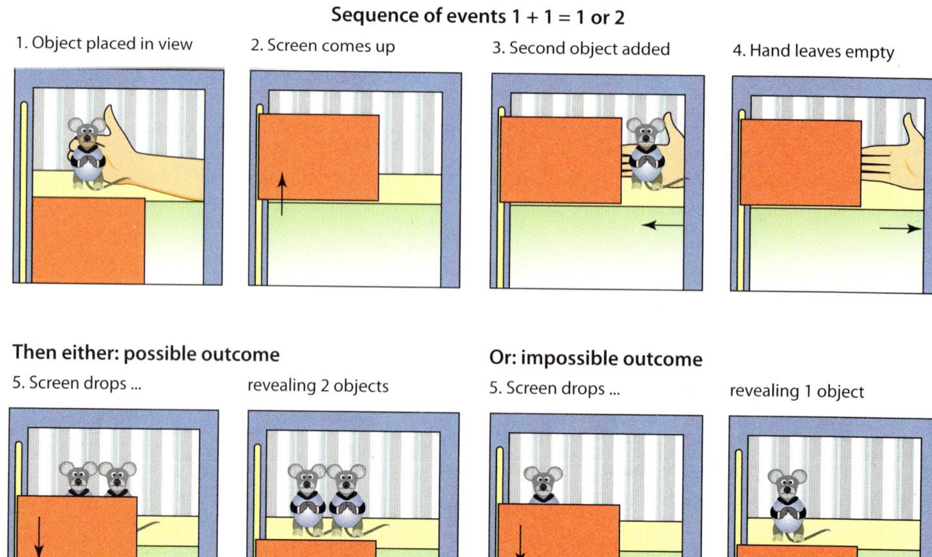

We suspect the infant looks longer at the impossible event because he is surprised that there are not two dolls in the box. Monkeys have similar reactions (Beran & Beran, 2004). Does this mean that infants and monkeys can count? Can they add? At age 3 our daughter enthusiastically announced a revelation: "6! There are 6 people in our family: 3 girls and 3 boys!" If infants, 3-year-olds, and monkeys can do basic math, why do children have so much difficulty learning math in school? In the following section, we briefly apply what you have learned in this and the previous chapter to the domain of mathematics. You will also be introduced to some concepts from Chapter 5. Key concepts are italicized. First, we will begin with an overview of math development.

Catchlight Visual Services/Alamy

Age Trends in Mathematics

Infants are able to detect changes in quantity. For example, when liquid is added to a container, infants expect to see a change in amount (Gao, Levine, & Huttenlocher, 2000). Because infants have quantity and number sense as soon as they are old enough to be testable, some researchers believe this is a biologically determined, innate ability—or a *core domain*. That is, number sense does not depend on learning (Barth, Beckmann, & Spelke, 2008). However, infants can only succeed in these types of tasks with small quantities—say, under four items (Desrochers, 2008). Furthermore, infants' innate number sense stands in stark contrast to other math concepts like propositions, percentages, and algebra that are acquired later with considerable effort and varied success. Number sense may be innate, but fully mature mathematical competence is not innate; it requires learning.

Informal Math

Preschoolers' understanding of basic math concepts is referred to as "informal math" because it is acquired without formal schooling. What kinds of math abilities do preschoolers have? They understand that adding to a set produces more and taking away produces less. They can tell which quantities are larger. For example, they know a row of twelve has more than a row of eight objects, even before they can count. Typical children begin counting around 2 years. For example, 22-month-old Connor counted his blocks by pointing to each one in turn and saying, "nine, nine, nine, nine." He had the concept of assigning a number to each object, but he did not yet know the number names except nine. Learning number names begins at 2 to 3 years. At 4 to 5 years, most children can count up to 20 or even 100, and may use a combination of finger and verbal counting. Typical children can evenly divide treats by 3 to 4 years. They can also solve simple arithmetic problems: "If you had 4 candies and someone gave you 3 more, how many candies would you have?" (Ginsburg, Klein, & Starkey, 1998; Huntley-Fenner & Cannon, 2000).

Although most children will acquire these informal math skills before entering school, low-SES preschoolers may not (Jordan, Kaplan, Olah, & Locuniak, 2006). This is a concern because, as you learned in Chapter 1, the strongest predictor of academic achievement—even stronger than reading ability—was math skills at entry to kindergarten (Duncan et al., 2007; Jordan, Kaplan, Ramineni, & Locuniak, 2009). Given that other preschoolers are developmentally ready to learn and reason about math, low-SES preschoolers' meager math skills may be due to less opportunity to learn these concepts.

What can you do to help? First, use math talk with preschoolers, like "Count how many cups we need for snack." This helps low-SES preschoolers develop better number sense (Klibanoff, Levine, Huttenlocher, Vasilyeva, & Hedges, 2006). Second, play number-oriented board games. After just one to three hours of playing games that involve counting pieces along a number line (but not a circle), like *Chutes and Ladders* or simple homemade games, preschoolers develop better math skills (Siegler & Ramani, 2009). Finally, directly teach math. There are several playlike math curricula such as *Big Math for Little Kids*, *Building Blocks*, *Number Worlds*, and *Rightstart* that are designed for 3- to 5-year-olds based on developmental science (Clements & Sarama, 2008; Ginsburg, Lee, & Boyd, 2008). The *Building Blocks* curriculum involves *asking children to explain their strategies* (e.g., "How did you know?"), and *spacing practice* over time. Some preschool teachers resist using math curricula, preferring that children learn through teachable moments that exploit naturally emerging play situations. Unfortunately, many such moments are overlooked and may not provide enough opportunity to learn for low-SES children (Ginsburg et al., 2008).

Think About This Middle-SES preschoolers are twice as likely to play board games like *Chutes and Ladders* and card games like *Uno*, whereas low-SES preschoolers are twice as likely to play video games (Ramani & Siegler, 2008). How might this partially explain lower academic achievement of low-SES children? Most cultures have children's games that promote such basic skills. Why might low-SES children not engage in them? Defend your argument using the Family Investment and Family Stress models and cultural capital from Chapter 1.

School-Age Math

As children enter kindergarten, they commonly progress through the following strategies when solving a simple problem like 2 + 7: counting-all (1,2,3,4,5,6,7,8,9), to counting-on-from-the-first-number (2,3,4,5,6,7,8,9), to counting-on-from-the-largest-number (7,8,9). Thus, children are *using more-sophisticated strategies* and becoming faster and more accurate at addition.

To master fractions and other mathematical concepts, children must transition from additive to multiplicative reasoning. Children can be taught multiplication/division as young as age 4, like: "If 4 dogs want 3 treats each, how many treats do you need?" Typical children develop these concepts without instruction by age 6 for small numbers, perhaps because they have experience with division each time they share with peers. However, understanding the concept does not mean they will do computations correctly or use efficient strategies. This takes instruction and practice. In U.S. schools, relevant instruction usually begins in 2nd grade. Children who are going to have serious difficulties with math are usually identified by about 3rd grade.

Children's counting strategies are eventually replaced by *memorizing* facts like 2 + 3 = 5 and 3 × 4 = 12. Doubles (5 + 5 and 6 × 6) are memorized especially rapidly. These facts are stored in long-term memory as the result of frequent *spaced practice*. **Retrieval** is an efficient *problem-solving strategy* as it becomes more rapid and automatic. Children then progress to using known facts to *reason* about unknown facts (9 + 9 = 18, so 9 + 8 must be 17). Some general rules are learned easily, like to get 10*n* just put a 0 on the right side of *n*, or 1*n* is always *n*. Knowing such general rules frees the child from having to memorize multiples of 10 or 1. Thus, memorized facts facilitate reasoning (De Brauwer & Fias, 2009; Sophian & Madrid, 2003).

retrieval finding items in long-term memory and placing them into working memory.

Estimation is another important skill that develops in school-age children. Estimation is used often in daily life, like estimating how much each team member will have to contribute to buy the coach a $50 gift, and is foundational to math ability. One way estimation is measured is by giving children a number line with only 0 and 100 indicated at each end. The child is asked where a number, like 29, would be on the line. Preschoolers and kindergarteners typically can place numbers accurately on a 0 to 10 number line; 2nd-graders on a 0 to 100 number line; 6th-graders on a 0 to 1,000 number line. Thus, the ability to estimate improves with age. However, there are individual differences within each grade. Children who are better at number line estimation have higher math test scores (M. Schneider, Grabner, & Paetsch, 2009; Siegler & Booth, 2004). Number line estimation is important because it helps children understand the meaning of numbers and facilitates learning math in school.

Implications for Teachers from Different Theories

This brief review raises three questions: (1) *What causes these age trends in math?* (2) *What causes individual differences in math?* With schooling some children will master calculus, but others will fail to develop basic math competence. (3) *How should math be taught?* Apparently some number sense (e.g., adding 1 + 2) is a core domain and does not need to be taught. However, more advanced mathematics (e.g., adding $\frac{1}{5} + \frac{1}{6}$) is not a core domain. There is still much to be learned that requires formal schooling. The answer to these three questions varies with each of the four major theories you have learned about.

Behaviorism and Math

From a behaviorist perspective, learning (or conditioning) begins with simple stimulus–response connections and then progresses to the complex level of abstract reasoning. Students cannot solve advanced problems if they do not have the prerequisite low-level skills mastered. Understanding whole numbers is essential to mastering fractions, which is essential for success in algebra, which is essential for success in higher mathematics and science. *Behavioral objectives*, that is, statements of specific behaviors student must manifest to show that they have learned, are used to structure lessons and are organized hierarchically, with basic skills mastered before attempting advanced skills.

Behaviorists tend to emphasize *direct instruction* with drill and *practice* to create strong basic connections. Some behaviorist teachers use the "mad minute," where students do as many math problems as possible in sixty seconds, several times a week, until the skill becomes automatic.

According to a behaviorist perspective, some aspects of learning should not be substantially more difficult than others, yet they are. For example, young children understand that every number has a number after it, so that the concept of infinity does not have to be taught. However, fractions have to be taught, and most children struggle to understand them. The fact that a fraction like $\frac{1}{2}$ is larger than $\frac{1}{4}$ does not readily map onto what children know about numbers—4 is bigger than 2, so $\frac{1}{4}$ should be bigger than $\frac{1}{2}$. Existing knowledge structures can *interfere* with new learning. The cognitive developmental model explains this better than behaviorism.

Piaget's Theory of Cognitive Development and Math

According to Piaget's cognitive developmental theory, children construct knowledge. This means children reinvent number concepts on their own, based on experience. They *assimilate* what they are taught with what they already know, creating strategies that teachers may not have intended. This was evident in the case discussed earlier, where children assume the answer to 7 + 4 + 5 = 7 + ? is 23. From a constructivist perspective, errors are intelligent and a natural part of knowledge construction. Errors give you a window into the child's thinking process. A constructivist teacher would ask if the child is doing something mathematically reasonable. What principle is the child using?

Constructivism is probably the most popular approach in mathematics education and is clearly reflected in the National Council of Teachers of Mathematics (NCTM) standards. A constructivist teacher emphasizes hands-on tools to illuminate concepts. This involves direct manipulation of materials relevant to math whenever possible and emphasis on student-initiated problem-solving activities. Algorithms are deemphasized, such as in popular constructivist curricula like *Everyday Mathematics.*

What does the research say? Research suggests that accurate pictures, like diagrams or graphs, may promote math more than manipulatives, even in young children. For example, in one study 1st-graders were either given accurate pictures of addition problems on a number line or they were asked to generate their picture, like 29 + 17 in Figure 4.8. Children who were given the accurate picture learned addition better than those who generated their own (Booth & Siegler, 2008).

When direct instruction and invention are compared, students tend to perform better following direct instruction. In another study, a researcher gave 3rd- and 5th-graders a lesson on equivalency (e.g., 4 + 9 + 6 = 4 + ?). Some were directly instructed to "add 4, 9, and 6 together, then subtract the 4 that's over here, and that amount goes in the blank." Other students were left to invent their own strategy, with feedback about whether the answer was correct. Instructed students got more problems correct and were more likely to transfer the skill to new, different problems. More than a fourth of the children in the invention method never developed a correct procedure (Rittle-Johnson, 2007).

An important lesson from this, and other studies, is that *asking children to explain their strategy is important.* Explainers learned more regardless of instructional approach (Rittle-Johnson, 2007). This suggests the instructional approach may not

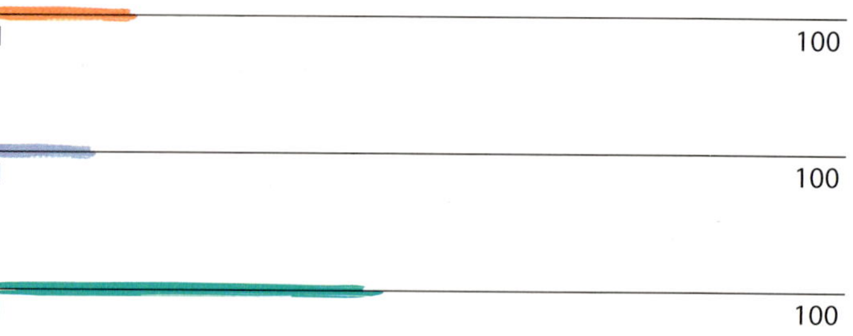

Figure 4.8 Estimation on a Number Line. A 1st-grader was asked to first show where 29 would be on a number line in red ink. Then he was asked to show where 17 would be in blue ink. He was then asked where 29 + 17 would be in turquoise ink. His response was fairly accurate. Based on the research, is this boy likely to have high achievement in school? Try this with younger and older children, and 0 to 10 or 0 to 1,000 number lines.

matter as much as getting children to actively process the strategy. Ironically, explainers were more likely to invent a second way to solve the problem following direct instruction. Thus, *direct instruction does not preclude invention, but helps prevent invention of incorrect strategies.* Research suggests that while exemplary teachers may use hands-on activities effectively, they seldom ask students to provide explanations (Silver, Mesa, Morris, Star, & Benken, 2009).

Piaget was right that children can reinvent math to a limited extent. Children do develop logic and number sense on their own. Thinking is a source of knowledge. However, children cannot by themselves reinvent the mathematical notation system, which is a cultural tool they need for math achievement.

Vygotsky's Sociocultural Theory and Math

According to sociocultural theory, social interaction and cultural transmission are also important sources of knowledge. A child could draw a fishbowl with eight fish in it and cross out three (they died) to indicate five are left. Or, a child could write 8 – 3 = 5. The latter is more efficient, and it is transferable to a wide array of other situations. The math symbol system used in writing 8 – 3 = 5 is a cultural tool. Cultural tools transform thinking. Children must be taught these tools. School-based instruction, a cultural creation, accelerates mathematical development.

This is illustrated by child street vendors in Brazil who can perform simple arithmetic with 98% accuracy when buying and selling, without schooling. However, if those same children are given problems in writing (e.g., 200 – 35 = ?), they drop to 37% accuracy (Schliemann & Carraher, 2002). They understand arithmetic but have trouble with mathematical notation. Unschooled child street vendors and 2nd- and 3rd-graders who had learned multiplication in school were asked to solve two problems:

1. *A boy wants to buy 3 chocolates that cost 50 cruzeiros each. How much money does he need?*
2. *Another boy wants to buy 50 chocolates that cost 3 cruzeiros each. How much money does he need?*

Schooled children solved the first problem with multiplication and were able to solve the second problem without doing any computation because they understood that 3 × 50 = 50 × 3. In contrast, the street vendors used addition to solve both problems. Adding 3 cruzeiros 50 times was slow and resulted in errors.

The sociocultural view is that full development of mathematical ability requires social interaction—opportunities to use and observe strategies, and receive *scaffolding* from experts. In school, children should *talk* about how they solved a problem because they learn by reasoning about a problem and explaining to others why it is right. *Cooperative learning* in the classroom—which we will discuss in Chapter 11—is linked to greater math achievement (Slavin & Lake, 2008).

The Information Processing Model and Math

The information processing model focuses on how children remember and reason. It is complementary to the other theories, with the exception of some aspects of Piaget's theory. Information processing theorists accept Piaget's idea that children construct their own understanding, but they tend to a more direct instructional approach akin

Revisiting the Case

Which of these theoretical approaches to teaching math do you think that Mrs. Harl exemplified as she taught her students three-digit addition?

to behaviorism and socioculturalism. In addition, rather than portraying children as thinking differently than adults, as Piaget does, they portray children as knowing less and having slower processing and more-limited working memory.

All aspects of information processing are involved in math. To solve the problem 2 + 3 = 4 + ? a child must access *long-term memory* to get 2 + 3 = 5, then maintain this in *working memory* while again accessing long-term memory to get 5 − 4 = ? *Long-term memory* of addition facts helps them *reason* about the problem. *Working memory* allows children to compare previously solved problems with the current problem. *Executive functions* keep them moving through the steps of problem solving. *Metacognition* acts on feedback about whether the strategy was useful or not.

Research shows that both age-related growth in math ability and individual differences in math ability are linked to each component of the information processing model. For example, preschoolers to adolescents who have better *working memory* are faster and more accurate at addition, multiplication, algebra, and solving word problems (Lee, Ng, & Ng, 2009; Noël, 2009; Swanson, Jerman, & Zheng, 2008). In contrast, children with slow processing speed and limited working memory are likely to have math disability. Knowledge also makes a contribution. Preschoolers who know their numbers, youth who can readily retrieve math facts from long-term memory, and children with good *executive functions* have higher math achievement (Blair & Razza, 2007; Geary, Hoard, Byrd-Craven, Nugent, & Numtee, 2007; Noël, 2009).

This suggests that your role as a teacher is to help children acquire more knowledge. You can help children *memorize* math facts and procedures through *spaced practice* and *frequent tests.* Instead of practicing one type of problem in a massed block and then moving on to the next type, space practice of each type across time. Having more knowledge will help your students with problem solving, because one of the most efficient problem-solving strategies is simple retrieval of the answer from memory. You can teach other strategies through *direct instruction* and *modeling.* The *overlapping wave model* suggests that children will gradually shift toward more efficient strategies. You can facilitate this shift by providing *feedback* to students. You can also make children aware of their strategies by having them *explain the strategy*, which facilitates metacognition.

In summary, some number sense is innate. However, children still have much to learn about math. While Piaget underestimated young children's mathematical reasoning ability, he was correct that children construct their own understandings of math. Contrary to Piaget, children do not follow an orderly progression in moving from less-advanced to more-advanced strategies for solving problems, but rather follow an overlapping wave model. They also do not reinvent the numerical notation system, but as Vygotsky pointed out, learn this cultural tool in informal interactions as well as in formal school settings. Behaviorists tend to focus on very specific behavioral objectives in math learning, with emphasis on skill-and-drill. Behaviorists and constructivists are often at odds with one another—educators tend to avoid one and support the other. The information processing model, on the other hand, is complementary to either perspective. Information processing researchers have demonstrated that children learn by direct instruction, skill-and-drill practice or rehearsal, modeling from more-skilled others, and constructing their own knowledge through insight and metacognition as they receive feedback about the success of their strategies.

How to teach math has been a polarizing issue, particularly when traditional methods (often based on behaviorism) are compared with reform methods (often based on constructivism). Yet, when implemented well, both methods may be effective. Researchers find small effect sizes on student achievement when they compare one curriculum with another (0.10 at elementary, 0.03 at secondary school), probably because most curricula are well designed. Other aspects of teaching, such as using cooperative learning, promoting time-on-task, and motivating students, have larger effect sizes (Harwell et al., 2009; Slavin, Cheung, Groff, & Lake, 2008; Slavin & Lake, 2008). You'll learn about these topics in later chapters, so stay tuned ....

Reflections on Practice: Checklist for Teachers

Efficient information processing forms the basis of good memory and problem solving, which are important for success at school. You can influence each of these abilities in your students. Ask yourself the following questions as you think about your classroom practices:

1. Do I help students focus attention on critical information? Am I sensitive to inattentional blindness, understanding that students may concentrate so much on one thing that they miss other things they need to learn?
2. Do I keep working memory load to a level that is appropriate for my students (e.g., by repeating key points, speaking slowly when covering new ideas, providing partial notes)?
3. Do I exercise students' executive functions through the kinds of activities I plan for them? Do I keep stress levels to a minimum and make sure children have food and exercise so that their executive functioning is optimal?
4. Do I recognize that most memory exists as fuzzy traces and plan instruction accordingly? When students need verbatim traces, do I help them memorize? Do I teach and use memory strategies like organization, elaboration, and mnemonics?
5. Do I teach in a way that shows connections between different topics and helps students construct a rich mental web of information? Do I give students multiple exposures to key concepts over time (i.e., spaced practice)?
6. Do I teach reasoning and problem solving in my classroom, in addition to content? Do I provide my students with both well-structured and ill-structured problems? Do I provide opportunities to practice problem solving, such as during storybook reading or games?
7. Do I require students to explain or justify their (or others') strategy use? Do I provide feedback that will improve problem-solving ability rather than just indicate if students are correct? Do I foster informed debate in the classroom whenever possible?

Summary of Age Trends in Information Processing

	Information Processing	Memory	Reasoning and Problem Solving
Early Childhood (Prenatal–5 Years)	Executive functions improve dramatically from 3–5 years—children become able to do the card rule-switching task. Speed of processing increases.	Fetuses can remember simple things for a few weeks, and 3-month-olds can remember up to three months. Deferred imitation studies suggest that infants' memory increases steadily. Yet, early events are seldom verbally recalled due to childhood amnesia. Long-term memory improves from infancy to 5 years, but may need to be supported by cues. Children make source monitoring errors. Children are poor at using memory strategies.	Infants can do rudimentary problem solving. Toddlers can induce a simple abstract rule and can reason by analogy. Between 3 and 5 years, children learn more-effective problem-solving strategies through experience or instruction, and understand that inference is a source of knowledge. Preschoolers can, in simple tasks, deduce when evidence is sufficient to draw conclusions. That is, preschoolers are logical.
Middle Childhood (6–12 Years)	Speed of processing continues to increase, but the rate of increase slows. Working memory improves substantially and reaches adult-levels for simple tasks. Metamemory becomes apparent. Attention control increases.	Children have greater long-term memory than do preschoolers. They are better at metamemory. They become better at remembering to do something in the future. Children become better at deliberate use of memory strategies. They typically store information through rehearsal. They use organization strategies effectively. They can use elaboration, but need scaffolding. They learn to take notes. They have fewer false memories.	Children become better at distinguishing guessing from inferences. Private speech becomes more covert during problem solving. Children become skilled at formal "if-then" reasoning. Greater prior knowledge helps them generate counterexamples. Children become more likely to try new strategies if old ones don't work.
Adolescence (13–19 Years)	Processing speed, working memory capacity (for complex tasks), attention control, and executive functions peak. Executive functions show dramatic improvement. Metacognition (and metamemory) and knowledge continue increasing into adulthood.	Adolescents continue to use rehearsal and organization strategies, but also become effective at using elaboration on their own. Verbatim memory increases. Social and emotionally laden experiences are particularly memorable for years to come.	Adolescents can reason about abstract hypothetical propositions that may be counter to the real world. They can distinguish logical from nonlogical statements given a set of premises. Some adolescents develop scientific reasoning—varying only one factor at a time in order to draw conclusions—but not all youth (or even adults) do so.

Chapter Summary

Information Processing

- The information processing framework explains how students acquire, store, and use information. The multistore model includes the sensory register (large capacity, brief duration), working memory (limited capacity, brief duration), and long-term memory (unlimited capacity, long duration). Attention is required for information to be encoded (stored) into memory. Executive functions monitor flow of information and metacognition.
- There are individual differences in each component of the model, which are linked to academic and social skills.
- Teachers should avoid overloading working memory and help students focus their attention on important details. Teachers can also help students exercise executive functions.
- Attention-deficit/hyperactivity disorder, the most common neurobehavioral disorder among children, is believed to result from poor executive functions. ADHD is linked to poorer academic achievement, behavior problems, and injury proneness.

Memory

- There are a few common errors in memory. Source monitoring error refers to forgetting the source of information. Memory for geographical spaces tends to be more regular than reality. False memories are intelligent constructions of things that did not happen.
- Most memory is a fuzzy trace rather than a verbatim trace. To remember details, children must use memory strategies.
- Memory strategies include rehearsal, organization, elaboration, and mnemonics. Mnemonics are particularly appropriate for material that is not yet meaningful to the student. Teachers should teach memory strategies.
- Prior knowledge facilitates remembering new knowledge and can compensate for low intelligence. Schemas and scripts, which are interconnected networks of information, facilitate learning.
- Teachers should help students connect pieces of knowledge, provide multiple exposures to the material, space practice, and test frequently. Teachers should converse with students about things to be remembered.

Reasoning and Problem Solving

- *Reasoning* usually involves some kind of inference. *Problem solving* is a type of reasoning. School-based problems tend to be artificial and well-structured, while real-world problems are ill-structured.

- The overlapping wave model represents the way that students improve in the strategies that they use to solve problems and to memorize.
- Antecedents of individual differences in reasoning include information processing ability, feedback, modeling, and prior knowledge. Poor reasoning ability can affect functioning in all domains of life, including academic and social domains.
- Teachers can teach reasoning by identifying students' strategies, teaching more-effective strategies, altering students' belief in the effectiveness of a strategy, fostering classroom argument, modeling, providing feedback, giving direct training, and guiding inquiry-based experiments.
- Modeling and feedback are more effective if students are required to explain the strategy.

The Case of Math

- Number sense may be a core domain; it is present in infants. Rudimentary concepts are acquired informally by preschoolers. However, schooling is necessary for more-advanced math.
- The behaviorist view is that math learning is hierarchical, with basic skills learned first through skill-and-drill. The Piagetian constructivist view is that students construct their own arithmetic. The sociocultural view is that mathematics is a cultural tool acquired in interaction with others. The information processing view is complementary to each perspective, emphasizing processes involved in solving math problems. From the information processing view, individual differences in math ability are due to processing speed, working memory capacity, prior knowledge, and executive functions.

Accompanying Education CourseMate Website Resources

Visit the **Education CourseMate** website at **CengageBrain.com** to find resources and study aids for this chapter, including self-tests, additional print and website resources, and glossary flashcards. In addition to the TeachSource Video Case, the following video illustrates concepts discussed in the chapter:

- **5–11 Years: Memory in Middle Childhood, Rehearsal Strategies**

TEACHSOURCE VIDEO CASE

Watch the Video Case *Metacognition: Helping Students Become Strategic Learners*. As you view the video clips and artifacts, think about the following:

1. **Can you identify examples in which the students or teacher use metacognition?**
2. **This case shows students solving the problem of how to comprehend difficult text. In what ways does the teacher teach problem-solving strategies or help the students understand the problem? (Hint: See Classroom Implications of Reasoning and Problem Solving section).**

Cognitive Ability: Intelligence, Talent, and Achievement

AP Photo/Tim Roske

ARE SOME CHILDREN ACADEMICALLY TALENTED BECAUSE THEY ARE INTELLIGENT, OR BECAUSE THEY PRACTICE MORE, OR FOR SOME OTHER REASON? In this chapter, we will discuss what intelligence and talent are and how they relate to achievement. After you read this chapter, you will understand:

- What intelligence is and what it predicts.
- How talent and expertise develop in children.
- What you can do to improve your students' achievement.

Intelligence

Alex and Chuck are two 12-year-old boys in the same suburban school, but in different 6th-grade classes. Alex's teacher presents a twenty-minute group lesson on homonyms. He then passes out two worksheets to give students practice with homonyms. The homonym worksheets include items like: "I took (there, their, they're) book." *and* "He began to play the (bass, base)." *Alex takes twenty-five minutes to complete the first worksheet. Then he notices that the rest of the class has already finished and has started other tasks. He quickly completes the second worksheet in five minutes. The first worksheet has three errors and the second has six errors.*

To provide you with a clear contrast in student performance, Chuck is given the same two worksheets to complete during lunch in the cafeteria. Chuck completes both worksheets in four minutes while also joking and talking with friends. He completes the items he is sure about first, and then goes back to those he is less sure about. Chuck says the worksheets are "too easy" for 6th grade. He cannot remember having had a lesson on homonyms.

What might account for the difference between how Alex and Chuck perform on this task? Neither seems to have a problem focusing attention on the task. Is it because Chuck reads more fluently, which results in greater prior knowledge of words, better memory for homonyms, and faster information processing? Why might Chuck have greater reading expertise? Perhaps these boys have different levels of **intelligence**.

intelligence a general mental capability including the ability to reason, plan, solve problems, think abstractly, comprehend complex ideas, adapt, and learn quickly.

None of the three classic theories that you read about in Chapter 3—behaviorism, cognitive developmental theory, or sociocultural theory—emphasizes individual differences in cognitive ability. Jean Piaget, founder of cognitive developmental theory, was not very interested in individual differences but focused on age trends instead. While he noticed individual differences in the rate at which children move from stage to stage, he described patterns of how *most* children develop rather than how they *differ*. Therefore, it is difficult to explain the difference in Alex and Chuck's performance from a Piagetian perspective. Teachers, however, are keenly interested in such differences because it is a significant challenge to teach children with widely different levels of intelligence in the same classroom.

What is intelligence? The following definition appeared in a statement that was signed by fifty-two experts in intelligence:

> *Intelligence is a very general mental capability that, among other things, involves the ability to reason, plan, solve problems, think abstractly, comprehend complex ideas, learn quickly and learn from experience. It is not merely book learning, a narrow academic skill, or test-taking smarts. Rather, it reflects a broader and deeper capability for comprehending our surroundings—"catching on," "making sense" of things, or "figuring out" what to do.* (Gottfredson, 1997, p. 13)

Intelligence also refers to the ability to adapt to different situations, to think about one's thinking processes (i.e., metacognition), and to be competent in one's culture (Sternberg & Berg, 1986).

These attributes of intelligence should feel familiar to you from Chapter 4. The basis of intelligence is fast, accurate information processing. In particular, working memory and executive functions may be the core of intelligence because they form the capacity to control attention and the capacity to zoom in and zoom out from the big picture to the small pieces of a task without losing track of the goal (Swanson, 2008). For example, 1st- through 5th-graders who were in a gifted program due to high IQ scores had faster processing speed, larger working memory capacity, and better executive functions, including attention control, than their peers in regular classrooms (Johnson, Im-Bolter, & Pascual-Leone, 2003). They tended to perform information processing tasks comparable to average children one to two years older. Some researchers believe that intelligence and working memory are practically the same thing, though not all experts agree (Ackerman, Beier, & Boyle, 2005).

Field Observation

In a backwards digit span test, you state random numbers between 1 and 10, and the person being tested repeats them, from last to first. Try giving a backward digits test to a few children, stating one digit per second. Try about three digits for 6-year-olds and more for older students. Did your "smart" participants perform well? If you feel brave, have a friend test you.

Intelligence as *g*

Children who score highly on one cognitive test tend to score highly on other tests as well. This means that test scores correlate with each other across a wide range of cognitive abilities, such as intelligence tests, college entrance tests (e.g., the SAT and ACT), vocabulary tests, analogy tests, proficiency tests, and so forth. For example, the SAT correlates a whopping 0.82 with the military's IQ test (Frey & Detterman, 2004). You may know individuals who seem to be exceptions, such as someone who received a high score on the SAT math section but a low score on the SAT verbal section. However, individual exceptions do not invalidate the general finding that high scores tend to go with high scores.

Some researchers interpret the correlation among different tests as evidence that there is a *general cognitive ability* that underlies specific cognitive abilities. This general cognitive ability is called **g** or general intelligence. General intelligence can be thought of as a cognitive capability that cannot be directly observed, but that accounts for all sorts of intelligent behavior and learning. It is sometimes called "Spearman's *g*" after Charles Spearman, who was a major proponent of the *g* view (Spearman, 1904).

g general intelligence.

While is it widely accepted that there is a general intelligence factor that influences performance in a variety of tasks, most experts would agree that intelligence can also be domain specific. For example, mathematics, literacy, and social competence are domains. Through experience and practice, children can have high levels of expertise in some domains without having high *g*. Also, *expertise in a domain can compensate for low* g *in that domain.* Through effortful study, one can develop expertise in a domain without high *g*. Thus, when you have students who are particularly intelligent in a subject area, it may be the result of either high *g* or domain-specific ability that developed through experience and practice (Larivee, Normandau, & Parent, 2000).

Experts also agree that intelligence has distinguishable components. Two theories involving different components of intelligence that apply to your classroom are discussed next.

Theory of Successful Intelligence

Think About This Have you heard parents refer to a child with learning difficulties as smart? Is it possible for a child to have trouble with school learning yet be "bright" in other ways? If intelligence means to learn complex material quickly and easily, how is this possible?

Robert Sternberg expands the common notion of intelligence. He points out that intelligence tests predict academic achievement because that is what they were designed to do, but it would be more useful to predict successful adaptation to life. He defines *successful intelligence* as "the use of an integrated set of abilities needed to attain success in life, however an individual defines it, within his or her sociocultural context" (Sternberg, Grigorenko, & Zhang, 2008, p. 487). Success may be different if you are a Yup'ik Eskimo child in Alaska concerned with fishing, a Brazilian street child concerned with selling goods on the street, or a middle-class suburban American concerned with admission to an elite university. Success depends on taking advantage of one's strengths and compensating for one's weaknesses, and possibly changing weaknesses to fit one's strengths.

According to Sternberg there are three components to successful intelligence: (1) analytic, (2) practical, and (3) creative. The *analytic* component includes the ability to recognize and define a problem, generate a solution, and evaluate progress toward a solution. It is measured on typical intelligence tests. The *practical* component of intelligence includes putting ideas into practice in the real world, being street smart, selecting activities and settings that match one's abilities, and changing settings as much as possible to match one's abilities. For example, the following 6th-grade girl shows practical intelligence:

Just before band practice, students hurriedly take their instruments out of their cases and leave the cases in the hallway just outside class, which not only creates a safety hazard but also a cluttered mess. However, if students put their cases in their lockers, it takes so long to unlock their lockers that they are late to their next class. As a solution to this problem, a 6th-grade girl suggests that students put their cases in the lockers, but not lock them. The band teachers are so pleased with this suggestion that they make the girl "queen for the day" for solving a problem that had eluded them (even though in hindsight the solution seemed obvious).

The *creative* component of intelligence involves generating new or different ideas—creating, inventing, discovering, or hypothesizing. Sternberg tells the true story of an executive in the automobile industry who was fed up with his boss. The executive hired a headhunting firm to find him a new job. His wife helped him redefine the problem; he asked the headhunter to find a job for the *boss,* which he did. The executive ended up much happier, and with the boss's job (Sternberg, 1996, pp. 208–209). According to Sternberg, all three components can operate simultaneously. Thus, the executive who finds a job for his boss is showing analytic skills and practical street smarts while thinking creatively.

Sternberg believes that understanding the three components of intelligence can help teachers identify children's strengths and weaknesses and potentially improve intelligence. When intelligence is considered a single factor that cannot be broken into component parts, like a *g* factor, there is little that you can do to improve intelligence. Another view that seeks to expand notions of intelligence beyond *g* is the multiple intelligences model.

Multiple Intelligences

Howard Gardner asserts that there are **multiple intelligences** that explain human abilities (Gardner, 2006). According to Gardner there are eight intelligences as depicted in Table 5.1. These multiple intelligences are fairly independent, meaning that a child could be strong in some intelligences and weak in others. Gardner's model arose partly from his dissatisfaction with the notion that the ultimate in intelligence is the ability to reason like a scientist—logically, precisely, mathematically. That is the sort of reasoning that is assessed in most intelligence tests.

Mariya Bibikova/iStockphoto.com

Students may have different types of intelligence.

Sternberg's and Gardner's theories of intelligence are complementary. That is, Sternberg's three components of intelligence can be applied within each of Gardner's intelligences (Williams et al., 2002). For example, while using Gardner's notion of linguistic intelligence, a student could use analytic intelligence to analyze anti-Semitism in the novel *Ivanhoe*, or creative intelligence to write a new story, or practical intelligence to compose the story in a way that will impress the teacher.

multiple intelligences Gardner's theory of intelligence that proposes that there are various independent intelligences rather than just a dominant *g* factor.

Gardner's theory has influenced schools to expand their curriculum focus from reading, writing, and arithmetic to emphasize the arts, athletics, and social skills as well. Reaction to Gardner's theory of multiple intelligences is mixed, with many

Table 5.1 Description of multiple intelligences

Intelligence	Attributes	Examples of types of people who tend to manifest the intelligence
Linguistic	Capacity to use language to express oneself and to understand others	Poet, writer, speaker, lawyer, journalist
Logical/ mathematical	Capacity to understand underlying principles of cause-and-effect, logic, number manipulation	Scientist, mathematician, engineer, computer scientist
Spatial	Capacity to represent the spatial world in one's mind, to mentally transform spatial relationships, to recreate visual images	Sailor, pilot, sculptor, architect, physician, navigator, painter, chess players
Musical	Capacity to think in music, hear, recognize, and perhaps manipulate aural patterns	Musician
Bodily/kinesthetic	Capacity to use whole body or parts of body to solve a problem, make something, or portray something	Athlete, actor, dancer, rock climber, surgeon, mechanic
Naturalist	Capacity to discriminate among living things like plants and animals, to notice natural features like geological features, to recognize patterns	Botanist, chef, farmer, biologist, naturalist
Interpersonal	Capacity to understand other people	Teacher, therapist, salesperson, politician
Intrapersonal	Capacity to understand oneself: knowing what you can do, what you desire, what you should avoid, what you should engage	Relevant to many careers or activities

Source: Adapted from Checkley & Gardner (1997); Gardner (1999); and Torff & Gardner (1999).

intelligence experts finding his list of intelligences arbitrary and his claims about independence unsupported (Brody, 1992; Sternberg, 1988).

These two theories of intelligence are helpful because they emphasize that there are many kinds of abilities, not just general intelligence. However, *g* remains important because it is associated with academic success, which is valued by society and linked to socioeconomic advancement. We will discuss how these different views of intelligence might apply to your classroom later.

While Sternberg's theory of successful intelligence and Gardner's theory of multiple intelligences have both been influential in thinking about intelligence and classroom curriculum, neither plays a part in how intelligence is typically measured at school.

Measurement of Intelligence

Modern intelligence testing began in France, with Alfred Binet, who in 1904 was one of a group asked to generate a method for distinguishing children who would benefit from normal schooling from those who would need an alternative form of education (Bergin & Cizek, 2001). He and Theophile Simon generated the Binet-Simon scale, which was the forerunner of today's Stanford-Binet intelligence test. Intelligence tests are still used to screen whether children might qualify for special educational services, making these tests high stakes for children.

Individual intelligence tests are administered by a trained psychologist to one child at a time. They are expensive to administer because they require several hours of a trained professional's time. *Group intelligence tests* are paper-and-pencil tests that can be administered to large groups. They are also referred to as *school ability tests* or as *academic aptitude tests*. They are cheap to administer and are objectively scored. That is, each item has a single correct answer. Group tests can be used with children as young as kindergartners, but only if you make sure each child understands the directions. As a teacher, you should be more cautious about accepting low scores on a group test than on an individual test, because in group-test settings, children may know the answer but write it down incorrectly, get discouraged, or not care about the test.

The most commonly used intelligence tests are the *Wechsler scales* (Kaufman, 2000). In 1917 during World War I, David Wechsler was a 21-year-old soldier who administered intelligence tests to other soldiers. Wechsler, who died in 1981, went on to develop individual tests that were precursors to today's Wechsler tests for preschoolers, children, and adults. Additional commonly used individual intelligence tests are the Stanford-Binet, Woodcock-Johnson, Kaufman, and Das-Naglieri. Common group tests of intelligence include the Lorge-Thorndike, Otis-Lennon, and Cognitive Abilities Tests (CogAT).

While these tests are widely used to measure children's intelligence, some experts argue that they do not actually measure some of the key components of intelligence, such as ability to learn quickly or adapt, but rather measure *past learning* (Sternberg, Grigorenko, & Kidd, 2005). This is an important distinction because it implies that intelligence as measured by tests is the result of past opportunity to learn, not just innate processing capacity.

IQ intelligence quotient. An index of general cognitive ability that is no longer used, but the term is still common.

The intelligence quotient, or **IQ**, is an old-fashioned way to represent scores on intelligence tests. The term *IQ* is still commonly used, but testing experts use standard scores, rather than quotients. Standard scores are reported with a mean and standard deviation. Most intelligence tests are created so that the mean score is 100 and the standard deviation is 15. *Standard deviation* is a number that describes the spread in scores. Most children's intelligence scores (about 68%) are between plus or minus one standard deviation from the mean, or between 85 and 115. Children and adults vary in their measured intelligence, which brings up the next topic: individual differences.

Individual Diversity in Intelligence

Children vary in their ability to solve problems, think abstractly, comprehend complex ideas, and learn quickly. Are these differences stable? **Stability** refers to whether a child's rank on a trait remains the same over time. In the case of intelligence, do young children who score higher on intelligence tests than their peers remain more intelligent at a later age?

stability a term child psychologists use to refer to whether children's rank-ordering on a trait remains the same across time.

Stability of Intelligence

Generally, intelligence scores are among the most stable psychological attributes across the lifespan (Neisser et al., 1996). One classic study of stability of intelligence took advantage of the fact that all 11-year-old Scottish children attending school on June 1, 1932, were given intelligence tests. When individuals were found and retested 69 years later with the same test, scores from age 11 to age 80 correlated 0.66, which indicates substantial stability from middle childhood to late adulthood (Deary, Whiteman, Starr, Whalley, & Fox, 2004). However, intelligence test scores are not as stable before age 11 as afterward. Between one-third and two-thirds of children may change scores by as much as ten to fifteen points from early childhood to middle childhood (Sternberg, Grigorenko, & Bundy, 2001).

Traditional intelligence tests do not attempt to measure intelligence before about age 3. While traditional intelligence test scores for young children may not predict later intelligence, infant habituation tasks do predict later intelligence (see Box 5.1). Some infants may only need about ten seconds and others may need forty seconds to explore a novel picture thoroughly before they turn away, or some infants may remember a picture better than others do. Infants who habituate faster or have better recognition memory have higher intelligence scores up to twenty years later, suggesting a high level of stability (Bornstein et al., 2006; Fagan, Holland, & Wheeler, 2007; Sigman, Cohen, & Beckwith, 1997). Habituation probably predicts later intelligence because it reflects stability in general information processing abilities like memory and executive functioning.

Can intelligence be changed? Yes and no. Removing children from seriously deprived environments, such as bleak orphanages, and placing them into more-enriched environments results in increased intelligence (T. O'Connor et al., 2000). On the other hand, programs aimed at trying to enhance cognitive ability, such as compensatory preschool programs (see Chapter 1) or programs aimed at older children, generally have little long-term effect on measured intelligence (Sternberg et al., 2001). Thus, intelligence can be increased to some degree with intensive intervention, but improvements tend to decay over time if the environment does not improve. However, expertise and achievement can be substantially increased. We will discuss these topics later.

Theories & Theorists **Box 5.1**

Habituation and Core Knowledge

Have you ever wondered what babies know? Infants only a few months old cannot be tested through interviews or questionnaires, so scientists use habituation to test their knowledge. Infants look longer at new things than at familiar things. Habituation is a reduction in attention to a repeatedly presented or continuously available stimulus (the familiar stimulus), which could be a picture of a face or a checkerboard pattern. When infants' attention declines to 50% of the amount of time they first looked at the stimulus, we say they have habituated to the familiar stimulus. Then a new stimulus is presented, like a different face or a checkerboard with a slightly different pattern. Usually infants increase their looking time when the stimulus is changed. This is known as dishabituation. We know several things about infants' cognitive abilities from habituation and other memory studies:

- Infants have a sense of number, size, and amount. Infants habituate to repeated displays of the same number of objects, then dishabituate when a different number of objects is shown (Gelman & Williams, 1998).
- Infants form categories to organize objects and events. For example, 3-month-olds will look longer at pictures of furniture after habituating to pictures of animals (Haith & Benson, 1998).
- Infants perceive causal sequences (Saxe, Tenenbaum, & Carey, 2005). For example, infants habituate to seeing a toy car bump another toy car into moving. Then, when they see the first toy car bump into the second, but the second car does not move for a few seconds (a delayed launch), the infant dishabituates to this novel event and pays increased attention (Cohen, Rundell, Spellman, & Cashon, 1999).
- Infants know physical objects are continuous and solid. That is, they understand that objects cannot spontaneously appear or disappear, nor can they occupy the same space as other objects (Baillargeon, 2008). Infants respond with interest to "impossible events" such as balls that fall through solid objects or a ball on a table that does not fall when the table is removed. Infants understand object permanence much earlier than Piaget believed, perhaps by about 3 months. (See Figure 5.1.)
- Five-month-olds can distinguish liquids from solids (Hespos, Ferry, & Rips, 2009).

Infants do not reason correctly about everything. For example, under some conditions they are not surprised by objects suspended in midair (Baillargeon, Kotovsky, & Needham, 1995). Nevertheless, it is clear that infants know a surprising amount about the world, and *they know it without handling physical objects*, within the first months of life, suggesting the presence of core knowledge.

What is core knowledge?

Core knowledge refers to innate ideas, or concepts and principles that are genetically preprogrammed in the human brain. Core knowledge is present early, is universal in normal children, and is triggered by a normal environment. It does not appear to depend on feedback or imitation. Core knowledge seems to be acquired effortlessly, presumably because the conceptual structures are already in the mind, which helps children learn new content in that domain. Innate ideas are not easily explained by behaviorist or Piagetian views of cognitive development (Baillargeon, 2008; Gelman, 2006).

habituation a reduction in attention to a continuously available or repeated stimulus.

dishabituation attention that has become habituated is renewed after a change in the stimulus.

What Do Individual Differences in Intelligence Predict?

A comedian once bragged about how intelligent she was. Although she was only 42 years old, she could read at a 45-year-old level! Her joke underscores the emphasis people give to intelligence. Parents want to believe their children have high IQ. Why this obsession with intelligence? Does intelligence really influence how well a child's life is lived? Somewhat. Intelligence does affect academic achievement, as well as other life outcomes. However, as you read this section, keep in mind that social and emotional well-being, and motivation (discussed in later chapters), may have an even greater effect on life outcomes.

Think About This In Chapter 1 you learned that correlation does not prove causation. Thus, it is not clear whether (1) high intelligence causes achievement, or (2) achievement causes high intelligence, or (3) something else causes both. Drawing on this chapter and Chapter 4, make a case for option 1, 2, or 3.

Academic achievement

Academic achievement is measured by achievement tests and classroom grades. Achievement tests are standardized tests that measure what children have learned in school. They include tests such as the Iowa Test of Basic Skills (ITBS), Comprehensive Test of Basic Skills (CTBS), Metropolitan

Theories & Theorists (continued)

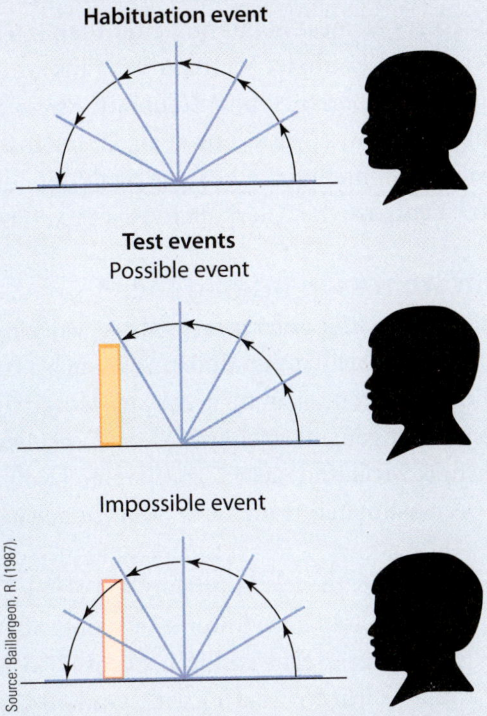

Habituation event

Test events

Possible event

Impossible event

Source: Baillargeon, R. (1987).

Figure 5.1 Object Permanence May Exist before 4 Months of Age.
Renée Baillargeon (1987) used this technique to test whether infants understood object permanence. First the infant observed a screen flip back and forth like a book cover as in the first drawing. This process demonstrated that nothing was behind the screen and was continued until the infant showed habituation. Then a box was placed behind the screen, which stopped when it reached the box, as in the middle drawing. Then the researcher secretly removed the box, and the screen was moved all the way down, which would be impossible from the infant's perspective. The infants looked longer at the impossible event depicted in the last drawing.

Nativists believe that the only role environment plays in core knowledge is to provide some minimal experience to trigger innate ideas (Newcombe, 2002). However, most psychologists adhere to an *interactionist* view that there is a role for both nature and nurture. Core knowledge may be like a muscle that has a genetic basis, but is modified by experience (Gelman & Williams, 1998).

There are few core domains. They appear to include *number sense*, like understanding quantity, or what is more and what is less, and basic arithmetic as you learned in Chapter 4. They also include understanding the *physical movement of objects*, understanding *other people's thoughts* (see Chapter 9), and *language* (see Chapter 12). Noncore domains, which are most domains, do not have innate structures and are acquired through experience. These include the ability to read, use computer software, or play chess. All normal children should acquire knowledge in the core domains, but there is great variation in noncore domains.

Achievement Test (MAT), Stanford Achievement Test (SAT or SAT10, not to be confused with the SAT college entrance exam), and state proficiency tests.

Intelligence tests generally predict achievement test scores with high correlations of about 0.70 to 0.90, and they predict grades with moderate correlations of about 0.50 to 0.60, but different studies range from a poor prediction of 0.11 to a very high 0.93 (Kubiszyn & Borich, 2003; Sternberg et al., 2001). Still, on average, children who score higher on intelligence tests learn more in school and tend to attain more years of schooling. Among your most intelligent students who go on to earn graduate degrees, those with higher intelligence are likely to secure more patents and publish more scientific articles (Park, Lubinski, & Benbow, 2008).

core knowledge innate, skeletal conceptual structures that develop early and easily, without instruction, and are universal, but may require experience to fine-tune.

nativists those who believe that competence in core domains is largely innate and little influenced by the environment.

Life outcomes

Think about your relatives and friends. Are the intelligent ones more successful in life? That may depend on how you define success. Children with high intelligence are more likely to become adults with higher SES and better job performance (Neisser et al.,

1996; Sternberg et al., 2001). A review of more than 50 longitudinal studies (Strenze, 2007) found that intelligence predicted three measures of success: amount of education (correlation = 0.56), status of occupation (0.45), and income (0.23). Grades and parents' SES also predicted these measures of success, but no better than intelligence. Intelligence is also linked to resiliency. For example, Vietnam veterans with higher intelligence test scores were less likely to experience post-traumatic stress disorder (PTSD) than those with lower intelligence scores (Vasterling et al., 2002). Intelligence is also linked to health. Children with high intelligence become healthier adults and live longer (Der, Batty, & Deary, 2009; Leon, Lawlor, Clark, Batty, & Macintyre, 2009).

What Predicts Individual Differences in Intelligence?

Higher *g* could be due to information processing differences, such as working memory and executive functions, which could be due to brain differences, such as dendrite branching and myelination. These brain differences, in turn, may be caused by genes. A preponderance of evidence suggests that general intelligence, or *g*, is substantially heritable (Plomin, DeFries, McClearn, & McGuffin, 2001). In Chapter 1 you learned that heritability of intelligence has been estimated from 40 to 80% (Bouchard, 2004; Pike, 2002).

While genes influence intelligence, so does the environment. You also learned in Chapter 1 that children with multiple risk factors have lower intelligence than those with few risk factors. You learned in Chapter 2 that children exposed to prenatal teratogens have lower intelligence. You also learned that rats in standard cages had less-developed brains and worse problem-solving ability than rats in elaborate cages. In fact, back in 1958 researchers bred rats that were bright and dull at finding their way through mazes. They assumed that the differences were genetic, due to breeding. However, when they placed juvenile dull rats in enriched environments, and bright rats in impoverished environments, the differences disappeared (Champagne, 2009). This suggests that genetic effects depend on the environment—which you'll learn more about in Chapter 6. In addition, some researchers believe the effect of genes is overestimated, while the effect of shared environment is underestimated. Evidence to support this view is that brothers who are close in age, so that they probably had greater shared environment in the family, are more similar in intelligence than brothers who are far apart in age (Sundet, Eriksen, & Tambs, 2008). This suggests the importance of the home environment.

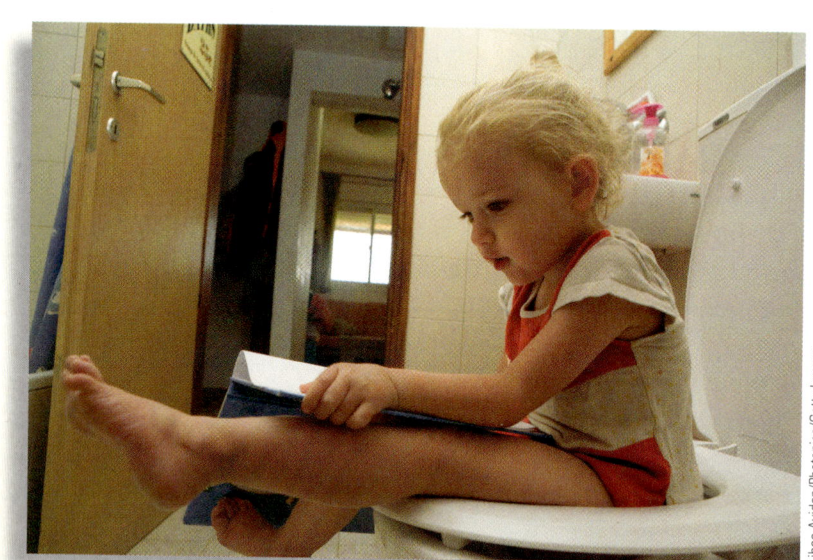

Lihee Avidan/Photonica/Getty Images

Children with access to books at home—apparently at any moment of the day—tend to have higher intelligence

Home environment

The quality of a child's home environment predicts later intelligence (Espy, Molfese, & DiLalla, 2001). Home attributes linked to intelligence include learning materials in the home and parent–child conversations. For example, a study of infants found that the amount that mothers talked to their babies predicted intelligence at 18 years (Sigman et al., 1997). Parental sensitivity and affection also predict children's later cognitive ability (Stams, Juffer, & van IJzendoorn, 2002). Such nurturance promotes feelings of security and self-regulation in children, which affects ability to cope with novelty and learn.

Schooling

School attendance also affects intelligence. Students who drop out of school early, are chronically absent, and delay starting kindergarten have lower intelligence than comparable peers (Ceci, 1991, 2003). The effect of schooling on cognitive ability is one reason many experts object to readiness tests being used to exclude children from starting school. Children who are judged as not ready to begin school most need to be in school (see Chapter 1).

Nonacademic schooling, like music lessons, may improve intelligence (Rauscher & Hinton, 2006; Southgate & Roscigno, 2009). For example, in one study children in Toronto were randomly assigned to have music lessons, drama lessons, or no lessons. Children who had music lessons showed greater increases in intelligence than drama and no-lesson children (Schellenberg, 2004). Taking music lessons for longer periods appears to be linked to higher intelligence and academic achievement. In one study, six years of lessons was linked to a 7.5-point-higher IQ (Schellenberg, 2006).

Think About This Given what you have learned about intelligence, is higher intelligence likely to be the cause of taking music lessons, or the result? What other factors might be involved? (SES was controlled statistically.) Can you explain the correlation between music lessons and IQ from a gene – environment correlation perspective?

Group Diversity in Intelligence

Are there differences in intelligence based on gender, SES, or culture? The following sections deal with group differences in intelligence, and also test bias and the rising trend in IQ scores.

Gender

Gender differences are seldom observed in *general* intelligence scores (Colom, Juan-Espinosa, Abad, & Garcia, 2000). However, boys score nearly a full standard deviation higher than girls on tests of *spatial* ability, particularly mental rotation (Halpern et al., 2007). Mental rotation is measured by tasks like the one depicted in Figure 5.2. In fact, there is evidence that as early as 5 months of age, baby boys are better than baby girls at mental rotation (Moore & Johnson, 2008). Spatial ability is important because it can influence science and math ability and choice of

Source: Adapted from Halpern (1992).

Figure 5.2 Example of Mental Rotation.
Mental rotation task. Children are asked if the figure on the left and the one on the right are the same. This requires them to rotate the figures in their minds. Can you do it?

college majors like engineering. In the past, boys on average were higher in *mathematical* ability and girls were higher in *verbal* ability, but these differences have diminished.

Keep in mind that all these differences are averages of many males and females and do not say anything about individuals. In addition, it is important to understand that aside from spatial ability, gender differences are small; there is much more variation in ability among boys and among girls than between boys and girls. Furthermore, spatial ability in girls can be trained (Spence, Yu, Feng, & Marshman, 2009). In one study, college students were asked to play shoot-'em-up action video games for ten hours. Afterward, girls' performance was nearly as good as boys, on spatial tasks (Feng, Spence, & Pratt, 2007).

Socioeconomic Status

Middle- and high-SES children tend to score significantly higher on intelligence tests than low-SES children (Bradley et al., 1989; Englund, Luckner, Whaley, & Egeland, 2004). How might SES influence intelligence? In Chapter 1 you learned about the family investment and family stress models. The family investment model suggests that a child's lack of access to material or social resources can lead to a low-quality learning environment in the home (e.g., fewer books, less conversation, less stimulation, more punishment), which in turn predicts lower intelligence. The family stress model suggests that low SES can result in diminished quality of parenting, which also predicts lower intelligence. In addition, low-SES children tend to experience high numbers of risk factors that can affect intelligence.

Risk factors linked to poverty can be so powerful that they overwhelm positive genetic effects on intelligence. For example, one study found that genes accounted for almost no variance in IQ, but shared environment accounted for 60% among impoverished 7-year-olds (Turkheimer, Haley, Waldron, D'Onofrio, & Gottesman, 2003). The opposite pattern was found for advantaged children. That is, intelligence was less heritable for low-SES children and more heritable for higher-SES children.

Ethnicity

Children of different ethnicities differ in average intelligence test scores. In the United States, the average intelligence score of European Americans and Asians is about 100 to 102. For African Americans it is about 87 to 90; Latinos score between Whites and African Americans. Keep in mind that these are average scores and say nothing about individuals. In fact, there may be ten times the variation within groups than there is between groups (Rosenberg et al., 2002).

What might account for these differences in intelligence test scores across ethnic groups? There is no single clear explanation (Hunt & Carlson, 2007). Perhaps they are due to test bias, which is discussed later. Perhaps they are due to socioeconomic status, because African American and Latino children tend to be of lower SES than Asian or European American children. Perhaps they are due to differences in the opportunity to learn; when groups have equal opportunity to learn, ethnic differences may disappear (Fagan & Holland, 2002). Perhaps they are due to stereotype threat, which refers to a tendency to perform poorly due to fear that one's performance will confirm a negative stereotype. This will be discussed in Chapter 13.

Think About This Think of the most intelligent person you know. Describe that person's attributes or behavior that led you to believe he or she is intelligent. What does this say about your personal view of what constitutes intelligence?

Cross-National Comparisons

Lihee Avidan/The Image Bank/Getty Images

Different cultures may value different forms of intelligence and require different measures of intelligence.

Different countries vary in what components of intelligence they value. Some national cultures view speed of thought as part of intelligence, while others view slow, deliberate thought as part of intelligence (Sternberg et al., 2001). Some island cultures value the ability to navigate the high seas without electronic equipment, while most people in the United States would find this ability useless. Thus, intelligence is embedded within a cultural setting.

These cultural differences affect measurement of intelligence. Simply translating a test to another language does not necessarily make it a valid test in another culture. Intelligence tests pose questions and tasks. One's success is influenced by whether one understands the question, already has strategies for dealing with the task, or already knows the answer. Tasks might include navigation on the high seas in one culture and comprehending text in another. The influence of cultural background on intelligence tests can be reduced, but not eliminated.

Culture-reduced tests, such as the Universal Nonverbal Intelligence Test or the Ravens Matrices (see Figure 5.3), reduce reliance on language. For example, the Ravens Matrices display patterns with a piece missing. Children are given several possible choices for the missing piece. They circle the one that best completes the pattern. Notice that we do not call it a culture-free test. Even this test requires a mindset of recognizing patterns that move from left to right and top to bottom. Children who have this mindset and are used to viewing two-dimensional patterns have an advantage over children from cultures without this experience (Greenfield, 1998). There may not be such a thing as a culture-free test.

Test Bias

Intelligence tests have been accused of being biased because some groups on average score lower than other groups. **Test bias** exists when a test unfairly penalizes a group of test takers because of their gender, SES, cultural background, or other characteristic that is not relevant to the purpose of the test. Tests can be biased if they have culture-specific content. Cultures may vary in their knowledge of sports such as basketball

test bias a test has less validity for one group than another group. Predictive bias means members of two groups who have the same score are not predicted to have the same outcome.

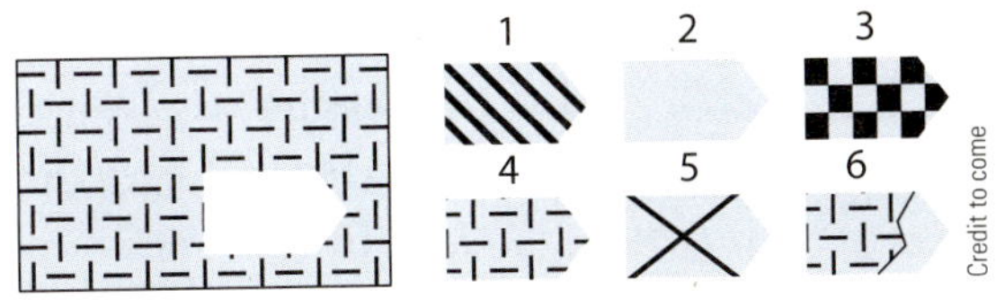

Figure 5.3 Example of Raven Test Item.
Select the segment on the right that best fits into the larger pattern on the left. Try this item. Does it seem culture-reduced to you? *Source: Bukatko, D. (2008).*

versus rugby, music such as opera versus hip hop, and leisure pursuits such as playing bridge versus playing poker. When tests refer to culture-specific content, they could disadvantage certain groups. Most standardized tests today do not have items that are obviously biased, because panels of experts from different cultures examine each test item. This does not guarantee that tests are not biased, but reduces the likelihood.

An important type of test bias is *predictive bias*, which refers to whether members of two groups who have the same score on a test are predicted to have the same outcome, like grades or probability of attending college. Diverse experts agree that intelligence tests do not have predictive bias. One group of experts stated, “Intelligence tests are not culturally biased against American Blacks or other native-born, English-speaking peoples in the U.S. Rather, intelligence scores predict equally accurately for all such Americans, regardless of race and social class” (Gottfredson, 1997, p. 14). In fact, on some intelligence tests, for Blacks and Whites who have the same score, Blacks are predicted to have better outcomes (Sackett, Borneman, & Connelly, 2008).

Note that the technical definition of *test bias* is not the same as *unfairness*. If one group consistently scores higher than another group, it does not necessarily demonstrate unfairness in the *test*. Instead, it may demonstrate unfairness in *opportunity to learn* and quality of schools, which historically have been worse for African American and Latino children. Helms (2006) points out that race is merely a category and does not directly cause anything in children; their experiences *due* to their race cause differences in learning that are reflected in test scores. That is, the children might experience an unfair environment rather than an unfair test. But can tests be fair if they affect some groups in a negative way? That is a question that educators, as well as lawyers, judges, and legislators, struggle with.

Rising Intelligence

Flynn effect the worldwide pattern of rising intelligence scores.

You may be surprised to learn that today’s youth have higher intelligence scores on the average than their grandparents. Researcher James Flynn documented the worldwide pattern of rising intelligence scores, which is now termed the **Flynn effect**. For example, U.S. data show IQ scores improving about eighteen points between 1947 and 2002. This is a huge gain of more than a standard deviation. Flynn (2007) describes similarly strong data for many countries, both so-called developed and undeveloped nations, including the United States. The effect even pertains to infants and toddlers who are now scoring higher than in previous decades on tests of infant mental development (Black & Matula, 2000). The Flynn effect applies to all groups, but Black children have increased IQ at a faster rate than White children, so that the IQ gap has narrowed by about five points over the last few decades (Dickens & Flynn, 2006).

Image copyright Lisa F. Young. Used under license from Shutterstock.com

Youth today have higher intelligence scores than older generations. This is called the Flynn effect.

However, as Flynn (2007) points out, if real intelligence had increased substantially over thirty years—essentially a single generation—the current generation should be massively outperforming the previous generation, and grandparents should be unable to keep up with their grandchildren in conversation or intellectual activities. No such massive advantage for the young has occurred. He points out that the rising IQ scores are much stronger for tests of abstract reasoning—such as "what do dogs and rabbits have in common?"—than for other types of IQ items. The correct answer is that they are both mammals. This sort of categorical thinking—mammal is a category that contains both dogs and rabbits—is the basis for much scientific reasoning and is much more common today than in the past. Flynn suggests that in 1900, the most common answer would have been that you use dogs to hunt rabbits.

No one knows just what has caused the Flynn effect, but Flynn's analysis suggests that a key factor is the fact that schooling and the broader culture emphasize the categories of science and abstract problem solving more than in the past. Additional plausible hypotheses include changes in the environment such as improved nutrition; less childhood disease; increased complexity of modern life; urbanization; increased socioeconomic status; reduced family size; increased formal education; more parental attention to children; increased testing, which leads to improved test-taking skills; and movie viewing or videogame playing, which are linked to spatial ability (Colom, Lluis-Font, & Andres-Pueyo, 2005; Dickens & Flynn, 2001; Gauvain & Monroe, 2009).

Think About This How was your childhood different from that of your grandparents? Which of these differences do you think might account for the Flynn effect?

Classroom Implications of Intelligence

You may find Sternberg's theory of successful intelligence useful in your classroom because it may help you think about teaching and testing in different ways. Sternberg's theory was applied in a summer psychology course for gifted high school students (Sternberg & Grigorenko, 2004). First, students were tested to determine if their strongest intelligence was analytic, creative, practical, or balanced among all three types. Then, students were taught in different classes that all used the same text and had an identical morning lecture, but the afternoon instruction emphasized either analysis (compare and contrast, evaluate, critique), creativity (create, invent, imagine, design, suppose that), or practical applications (apply, use, or implement). The students were given final tests that emphasized analytic (e.g., compare and contrast two theories of depression), creative (e.g., create your own theory of depression), or practical (e.g., How can this help people who are suffering from depression?) processing. Students performed better if both the instruction and mode of assessment matched, rather than mismatched, their type of intelligence. However, students with either analytic or balanced intelligence performed best overall.

As a teacher, you will not be able to always customize your curriculum based on each student's level of analytic, creative, or practical intelligence. However, you can devise tasks that draw upon each component of intelligence. Many students may have greater creative or practical intelligence than analytic intelligence; yet if tasks only draw upon analytic intelligence, their strengths will be hidden (Stemler, Grigorenko, Jarvin, & Sternberg, 2006). You will need to explicitly consider how a task engages analytic, practical, and creative intelligence.

Multiple Intelligences in the Classroom

You may also find Gardner's model of multiple intelligences useful in your classroom. Here are two suggestions that stem from Gardner's model:

- Become aware of children's different profiles of intelligences. Help individual students succeed by drawing on their strengths, and promoting growth in weak areas.

    For example, in a classroom of 2-year-olds, Wyatt has high bodily/kinesthetic intelligence. Wyatt can kick a ball across the room, well-aimed and standing on only one foot. His classmate, Jana, cannot do this, but has high logical/mathematical intelligence. She can already count to 20 accurately. Their teachers' instructional goal is to help each child learn to count better. They have Wyatt throw puff balls into a bucket as he counts from 1 to 10. They then encourage Jana to continue counting to 25 as she throws more puff balls into the bucket. This expands both children's abilities, while drawing on their strengths.

- Plan lessons that engage multiple intelligences based on your instructional goals. For example, imagine your instructional goal is for students to understand World War I. You could ask students to write analyses of how population trends and the number of victims of the flu epidemic of 1918 influenced the end of the war, which would use verbal/linguistic and logical/mathematical intelligences. Or, students could sculpt relief maps that trace the progress of the war, which would use visual/spatial and bodily/kinesthetic intelligences. Or, students could review popular music of the era and write a new piece of music that reflects differing national goals, which would use musical intelligence. You cannot engage every intelligence in every lesson, but you can engage a variety across several assignments—as long as they result in achieving instructional goals.

Here are two common misapplications of his theory that Gardner cautions you to avoid:

- Avoid confusing an intelligence with a domain. Biology is a domain, but there is not a biological intelligence. Intelligences relevant to mastering biology could include verbal, logical/mathematical, spatial, and naturalist. Every domain can draw upon multiple intelligences. In addition, a specific intelligence like spatial intelligence can be relevant to multiple domains, such as sports, sewing, or car mechanics.
- Avoid confusing an intelligence with a learning style. A learning style is a way of approaching learning, while an intelligence is an ability. For example, children who have bodily/kinesthetic intelligence, like Wyatt, do not necessarily learn best through movement. They are competent at moving in complex ways, but that does not mean they could best learn about the history of the United States or anything else through movement.

Gardner's model is valuable because it expands the ideal curriculum. Traditional curriculum emphasizes reading, writing, and computing using two types of intelligence: linguistic and logical/mathematical. Schools emphasize writing, computing, analyzing, comparing, showing cause-and-effect, and understanding equations. They do not emphasize skilled movement, creating or appreciating music, or understanding other people, nor are these part of state proficiency tests. A curriculum that seriously engages multiple intelligences will support diverse intelligences. For example, there will be more than one roving art teacher with one art cart per elementary school.

You may have students with different intelligences who seek to do assignments in ways that draw on their strengths. For example, in a high school chemistry class some students ask if they can use graphs or diagrams to answer essay questions. Their teacher lets them, but then asks them to *tell* her what the graph says. Then she says, "OK, write that down." This usually results in a better essay for students whose strengths are not linguistic. Any time her students ask to do an assignment in a different way, she asks them what they think the purpose of the assignment is and whether their alternate approach will fulfill that purpose. If it will, she lets them try it.

Intelligence Tests and the Classroom

Two major classroom purposes of intelligence testing are to diagnose students for special education services—both gifted programs and remedial programs—and to diagnose learning disabilities (see Box 5.2). While intelligence tests are useful as one piece of evidence that could help place a student, you should not rely solely upon one test. Stories abound of children who were clearly struggling with the regular curriculum but were denied remedial services because their intelligence scores were too high; or of children who were exceptionally able, as demonstrated in projects, but who were denied gifted education because their intelligence scores were too low. Multiple pieces of evidence, such as ability manifest in classroom discussions or assignments and standardized achievement tests, should be used in addition to intelligence tests for placement decisions.

Talent and Expertise

The Mission Viejo Nadadores swim team has long been a training place for Olympic hopefuls. Coaches come from all over the world to discover Coach Schubert's "secret."

> *After one visitor had been at Mission [for a week] . . . watching all the time, Schubert came over to him and asked, "Well, got us figured out yet?" The visitor said no, that it would take more than a week, maybe more than six months. Schubert chuckled and walked on. Schubert knew . . . that there is no "big secret." There is only the will to swim for miles and miles, all the turns done correctly, all the strokes done legally, all the practices attended, all the weights lifted, and all the sprints pushed to the point of simple exhaustion, day after day for years.* (Chambliss, 1988, p. 55)

A central goal of education is to improve students' expertise. But how is that done? Research shows that *time spent in practice* is critical, just as Coach Shubert will tell

Challenges in Development — Box 5.2

Learning Disabilities

The legal definition of **learning disability** (LD) varies by state, but in the past, the most common definition focused on an intelligence-achievement discrepancy, that is, achievement that is lower than what you would expect based on a child's measured intelligence (Reschly & Hosp, 2004). This definition is based on the assumption that students with a learning disability are cognitively different from students who experience low achievement *and* low intelligence. It is also based on the assumption that they are cognitively different from students who merely experience low achievement due to poor instruction or lack of motivation. However, it is not clear exactly what these cognitive differences are. Most research shows that mere low achievers are *not* different from students diagnosed with a learning disability. Furthermore, intelligence-achievement discrepancy has not turned out to be an accurate way of thinking about learning disabilities (Fletcher et al., 1994; Stanovich & Siegel, 1994).

These problems with diagnosing a learning disability have led to the *response to intervention* (RTI) model (Fletcher & Vaughn, 2009). Under this model students are diagnosed with a learning disability if they do not learn from the instruction that most students learn from. Thus, poor instruction does not explain their low achievement, so a disability may be responsible, and specialized intervention may be needed. RTI models are mostly implemented in elementary schools and require frequent screening of all students so that learning problems can be caught before students fall behind and experience failure. RTI models also require powerful interventions that have been demonstrated to be effective.

RTI models are tiered. In tier 1, good instruction for all students is combined with assessment of all students. In tier 2, in-class interventions are used to improve achievement for targeted low-achieving students. In tier 3, more intensive, smaller group services are provided for students who do not respond to tier 2 interventions. A large study in Florida showed that RTI was linked to reductions in the number of students identified as learning disabled and improvements in reading scores (Torgesen, 2009). However, critics of the RTI model argue that it is unproven and does not detect all the students who may benefit from services; they claim that some students with mental retardation or emotional disorders can be mistakenly identified as learning disabled (Reynolds & Shaywitz, 2009).

The prevalence of diagnosed LD varies from a high of 9% of students ages 6 to 17 in Rhode Island to a low of 3% in Kentucky (Reschly & Hosp, 2004). Diagnosis of learning disabilities has increased over the past thirty years, and boys are more likely to be diagnosed with a learning disability than girls (Oswald, Best, Coutinho, & Nagle, 2003). Low-SES children are more likely to be diagnosed with a learning disability, particularly if their mother has little education. The rate of LD diagnosis between Blacks and Whites is about the same, although in some states like Georgia, African American students are *under*represented in LD programs (Colarusso, Keel, & Dangel, 2001).

learning disability defined as a discrepancy between a student's achievement and intelligence or as lack of response to instruction that is effective for most other students.

you. Expertise requires practicing correctly over and over. For a swimmer, it might mean making every turn correctly. For a toddler, it might mean talking constantly during pretend play. For a college student, it might mean pondering the assigned text before coming to class every day. For a teacher, it might mean being well prepared for every lesson.

Some people believe expertise is more about genetics than practice. After all, aren't some children just born talented? Don't they find it easy to become expert? The answer depends on what you mean by *expertise* and *talent*.

Expertise refers to having a high level of skill or knowledge. *Talent* also refers to having a high level of skill, but it is often used to refer to natural or innate ability. Some scientists have rejected this notion of talent because it is a thoughtless explanation of expertise. So-called talent is not just an innate attribute; it is a product of intense practice. This does not mean there are no innate differences among children, but rather that innate differences are not the only explanation for expertise.

Age Trends in Talent and Expertise

Talent is defined as having more skill at some activity than do others of the same age, so there are no age trends. In some domains, it takes at least ten years of intensive practice to attain an international or eminent level of expertise (Ericsson & Ward, 2007). This seems to hold true for chess players, musicians, composers, writers, and scientists. For this reason, eminence is not likely to be reached before the teens, and may not be reached until middle age or beyond.

Some talents or areas of expertise are age-related in the sense that a late start may prevent the development of world-class expertise. For example, some skating coaches agree that age 8 is the latest one could begin skating and hope to become an expert skater (Starkes, Deakin, Allard, Hodges, & Hayes, 1996). So ten years of practice starting at age 18 could result in a highly competent skater, but not a world-class skater. On the other hand, great surgeons do not begin practicing surgery at age 8. A late start is not a handicap, but a necessity, in some domains.

Individual Diversity in Talent and Expertise

By definition, talent is an individual difference. That is, some children are more talented than others in a given domain. Let's look at what talent and expertise mean for children, and where talent may come from.

What Do Individual Differences in Expertise Predict?

There are obvious outcomes of expertise. Youth who have greater expertise than their classmates perform at higher levels. Their skills can result in new creations in music or technology or winning competitions like science fairs, sports, or quiz bowls. Children who show unusual verbal or math ability, by high scores on the SAT, are more likely to have publications or patents for inventions by middle age (Park, Lubinski, & Benbow, 2007). Another outcome is enjoyment, because expertise can be inherently rewarding. An advanced calculus student may thoroughly enjoy differential equations. A sculptor may delight in producing statues.

Jim Commentucci/Syracuse Newspapers/The Image Works

Children develop expertise through practice.

A less obvious outcome of expertise is improved thinking and memory in the area of expertise. For example, child chess experts have better memory than adult novices for chess boards. Researchers presented chess boards to child and adult chess experts and novices, removed the boards, and asked the participants to reproduce the pattern of chess pieces (Schneider, Gruber, Gold, & Opwis, 1993). The child chess experts remembered arrangements of chess pieces better than did the adult novices, and as well as the adult experts, *if* the pieces were in the pattern of a real game. The researchers repeated the study with nonchess pieces and with chess pieces in a random pattern. These were remembered equally poorly by child and adult experts and novices. So the chess experts' advantage was only for meaningful chess patterns; they did not have superior memory for random patterns or for nonchess items.

Research shows that background knowledge affects memory to a significant degree. Thus, if you teach U.S. history you might expect that students who have read about the Civil War or visited Civil War battlefields would have better memory of your instruction on the Civil War than would other students.

Research on chess experts has also revealed differences in what experts and novices see and how long it takes them to see it (Reingold, Charness, Pomplun, & Stampe, 2001). Expert chess players are able to see and understand larger areas of the chessboard in a single glance than are novices, and with fewer eye movements, but only if the chess pieces are arrayed as though in a real game. Similarly, expert psychologists recognize attachment disorders from brief parent–child interactions, expert pediatricians recognize children's medical problems that perplex novice pediatricians, and master teachers perceive and solve problems in classrooms better than novice teachers.

What Predicts Individual Differences in Expertise?

Researchers who study talent as the *development of expertise* tend to view ability as caused by practice. In contrast, researchers who study talent as an aspect of *giftedness* tend to view ability as innate. What is your perspective? Among your most talented friends, did they learn their particular talent or were they just born with the talent? Research suggests that talent is a result of long years of deliberate practice.

Deliberate practice

deliberate practice activities specifically designed to increase competence that are effortful, use specialized facilities or materials, and require expert feedback.

Deliberate practice is critical to the development of expertise. Deliberate practice refers to activities that are specifically designed to increase competence and that (1) are goal directed; (2) require effort and concentration; (3) require teachers who structure the practice, analyze performance, and provide feedback; (4) involve repetition with refinement; and (5) are not inherently motivating. The fact that deliberate practice is not inherently motivating means that while children in training may enjoy the training, it is different from play.

In one study, scientists selected violin students at the Music Academy of West Berlin, including remarkable violinists who would likely go on to play in the best orchestras in Germany (Ericsson, Krampe, & Tesch-Römer, 1993). All had started playing at about the same time and all had spent at least ten years practicing the violin, yet there were big differences in their expertise, their success at music competitions, and how much music they knew.

Were the best students more talented? Yes, if you define talent as level of expertise. However, if you define talent as innate ability, it is not clear that they were more talented. It was clear that the groups differed in deliberate practice (not just playing, but *deliberate* practice). The best students were practicing the most. The same pattern was seen in their history of practice up to age 18. The best students reported having practiced an average of 7,410 hours, while the lesser accomplished students practiced about 3,420 hours. It is not helpful to say the best students were "more talented." It is more accurate to say that the best students practiced substantially more. Other studies have found that pianists and chess masters may practice more than 11,000 hours, or as much as four hours per day (Gobet & Campitelli, 2007; Jabusch, Alpers, Kopiez, Vauth, & Altenmüller, 2009). A long period of practice is required for high levels of expertise. Imagine if your students studied a single topic four hours per day!

Practice plays a role in developing skill in all domains. Let's consider reading for example. While reading practice may not have all the attributes of deliberate practice, it affects later expertise. Some children enter kindergarten with more than 1,000 hours of practice in joint storybook reading with their parents. Other children may have only 10 to 20 hours (Adams, 1990). These children enter school with different levels of expertise in pre-reading skills. Differences in amount of reading practice occur through the school years as well. Although the average 5th-grader reads about 1,000,000 words of text per year, there are great individual differences. Some would rather clean their room than read. Youth who read more become more skilled readers. This difference in reading practice may account for the difference between Alex's and Chuck's performance on the homonym worksheets in the opening vignette.

Use of time

A study of teens who were talented in art, athletics, music, math, and science found that they were well disciplined in using time (Csikszentmihalyi, Rathunde, & Whalen, 1993). For example, they engaged in more productive activities and spent less time than other teens hanging out with friends. They were less likely to engage in sexual activity. They wasted less time and understood that messing around with friends does not lead to skill development.

Innate ability

Some chess experts need more practice time to reach mastery than others, and some children who practice will not become chess masters (Gobet & Campitelli, 2007). Perhaps practice is necessary, but not sufficient for expertise. The significant role of practice and time use in developing expertise does not rule out the possibility of inherited innate ability. Heritability is difficult to document for complex skills that may require the simultaneous inheritance of several traits, all of which must be present for talent to be manifest. Nevertheless, as discussed earlier in this chapter and in Chapter 1, heritability has been documented for intelligence and efficient information processing, which facilitate other talents.

Field Observation

Interview an older child or teen who is especially talented. What kinds of experiences led to the child's ability? How much did the child practice? How did the parents influence the child's amount of practice? Is the child especially talented in many domains, or just one?

If intellectual giftedness has some genetic basis, then other forms of giftedness may as well. Researchers disagree about the role of innate talent. Some view the concept of innate talent as a destructive myth because it discourages people from investing the effort needed to become expert. Others believe that talented performers were born with an advantage in their domain (Winner, 1996). Or, giftedness may be the result of high levels of motivation.

Motivation

Motivation is a key ingredient in the development of expertise. Children who become expert may have a higher level of drive to improve and greater willingness to practice. While it is hard to get some children to practice, it may be hard to get talented children to quit practicing. We knew a mathematically gifted 4th-grade boy who got algebra books from the public library. His mother struggled to get him to go to bed on time because he would beg to do "just one more" problem. However, researchers have not been able to determine exactly where such motivation comes from. It is possible that inherited talent and practice may be linked. That is, children who work the hardest and earliest may do so because they have more ability.

Remember 2-year-olds Wyatt and Jana? Wyatt has athletic parents and three older siblings who are avid soccer players. He has attended soccer games since birth. Is his remarkable kicking due to practice, or does he have inherited bodily/kinesthetic intelligence? Similarly, Jana's parents are both math teachers. Is her remarkable counting ability due to a math-rich environment that provides her with lots of opportunity to practice, or inherited logical/mathematical intelligence? It is probably an interaction of practice, genes, and motivation (review Chapter 1 for active, passive, and evocative gene interactions).

Group Diversity in Talent and Expertise

Cultures vary in how much they value specific talents. This is reflected in which talents are developed, how expertise is taught, and at what age children begin practicing. For example, Chinese children are taught from early childhood how to produce traditional Chinese paintings. They copy scenes of bamboo, goldfish, roosters, and so on, and ordinary Chinese children become very competent at this sort of art (Winner, 1996). Chinese children would appear gifted to Americans because their culture emphasizes art in a way that American culture does not (see Figure 5.4). Similarly, chess players in Moscow join chess clubs at younger ages than players in Berlin or Toronto, and become better players, which reflects the value of chess in Russia (Charness, Krampe, & Mayr, 1996). Japanese children trained in Suzuki violin appear gifted compared to other young violin players. Talents that are valued in a culture are often introduced at younger ages, and children spend more time practicing them.

Another example of how cultures influence talent is found in sports among African American youth. Historically, African Americans were very interested in baseball, and by the early 1970s, African American ballplayers held 25% of the slots in Major League Baseball. By 2001, the percentage was down to 13%. Contrast that

Figure 5.4 Art by Chinese 6-Year-Old Child.
This is an example of a brush-and-ink painting by a typical, nongifted Chinese 6-year-old. Traditional painting is a skill that is valued in the culture, and directly taught to children at young ages.
Source: Winner (1996).

Courtesy of Ellen Winner

with the National Basketball Association, which is currently about 80% Black. Today, African American youth are more likely to develop their talents in basketball than in baseball because basketball is more highly valued within their current culture (Ogden & Hilt, 2003).

Classroom Implications of Talent and Expertise

In schools, talent and giftedness are often equated. *Giftedness* is typically defined as extraordinarily high intelligence, yet this is only one form of giftedness. Giftedness can include high ability in any area. Children can have expertise in some domains without having high general intelligence.

There is disagreement about how academically talented children should be educated, although some evidence suggests they benefit from ability grouping (Winner, 2000). That is, they benefit from being in classrooms with other academically talented children. Whether schools directly support ability grouping or not, it happens indirectly at the high school level through advanced classes such as calculus, Advanced Placement (AP) classes, and honors classes. AP classes allow academically talented students to take advanced classes for college credit while still in high school. About 60% of high schools offer such classes, and about one-third of college-bound seniors take at least one (Bleske-Rechek, Lubinski, & Benbow, 2004).

AP classes are linked to greater school enjoyment for academically talented students. Students who take AP classes report that the lack of challenge in non-AP classes is distressing and that AP classes are their favorites. They are more satisfied with the intellectual climate of their school and attain more education over the next fifteen years compared with talented peers who do not take AP classes (Bleske-Rechek et al., 2004). Thus, AP classes are one large-scale way to provide curriculum that is commensurate with academically talented youth's ability.

Whether children are gifted or not, or in advanced classes or not, you can help all your students develop expertise when you:

- *Provide time to practice.* If students do not put in the time, they will not gain the skill. However, mere time is not sufficient.
- *Make sure practice is deliberate.* Assign challenging and complex tasks that require effort and mindfulness. Provide feedback so students accurately understand what it takes to be successful. Make sure adequate materials and facilities are available.
- *Help students feel motivated to engage in deliberate practice.* Motivation is discussed in Chapter 13.
- *Explain to students the importance of deliberate practice.* Provide students with models who practiced. This can be done through literature or personal examples. One teacher used the example of a Korean-born student who, when in Korea during elementary school, was determined to learn English. She had studied English seven hours per day and developed considerable English skill!

You can apply principles of deliberate practice to your own teaching skill. Deliberate practice for you might include participating in (not

Revisiting Case 2

How might Mrs. Harl help Monica and her other students become expert at three-column addition? Or, how might Alex's teacher, in the opening vignette, help Alex become expert at using homonyms correctly in his writing?

just attending) workshops, observing other teachers' classrooms, revising lesson plans based on reflection, and practicing delivery of lessons. Feedback is critical to deliberate practice. Because teaching tends to be private, you will need to make a concerted effort to get feedback from observers. This requires avoiding defensiveness because feedback is not as useful if it is all positive and uncritical. Be courageous.

Achievement

One morning in November, during a student Geography Bee, I listened as teenagers from privileged families identified Jamaica as an island in the Pacific . . . then to their teachers defend that ignorance by arguing, "We don't waste time on simple memorization. We'd rather spend it on 'higher orders' of thinking." But the next afternoon, I watched . . . Calculus students perform mathematical feats that were dazzling . . . later, I was horrified to read students' papers and realize that even the best hadn't mastered basic grammar, punctuation or spelling—or to hear scores of students blithely inform me, perhaps even boast to me, that they had never read a complete book. (Burkett, 2001, p. 310)

This is an account from journalist Elinor Burkett (2001), who spent a year observing a typical suburban high school in the Minneapolis area. The fact that journalists are focusing on high schools reflects increased interest by both educators and the public in how to explain both appalling and impressive academic achievement.

academic achievement a measure of knowledge based on grades or standardized tests.

Academic achievement is usually measured in one of two ways: (1) Teacher-assigned grades or grade point average (GPA). Grades are subjective and can vary by teacher, school, and district. That is, an A might be much easier to earn from one teacher or in one school than another. (2) Standardized test scores. Tests are *standardized* when everyone has the same testing materials, time, instructions, and scoring standards. Standardized tests allow comparison of students' knowledge across teachers, schools, and districts. The achievement tests listed earlier in the chapter are standardized tests, as are college entrance exams like the ACT and SAT. Achievement tests are different from intelligence tests; *they are designed to measure what children already know, rather than capacity to learn*, although this is difficult to separate and, as you learned earlier, they are highly correlated.

Think About This What is the difference between grades and standardized test scores, which are modestly correlated? Do they measure the same thing? How might intelligence affect the correlation?

Age Trends in Achievement

Standardized tests are typically customized for each grade, so they are not designed to reveal age trends. However, *grades* tend to decline from 6th to 12th grade. The decline is particularly noticeable at major transitions, like the transition from elementary school to junior high, or from junior high to senior high (Eccles et al., 1993; Ryan, 2001). This may be partly due to students' perceptions that the teachers in their new school do not care about them in comparison to teachers at the previous school, especially among minority students (Lee, 1999; Roderick & Camburn, 1999). The decline may also be partly due to increasing demands on personal responsibility and organization—things like do your homework on your own, show up for class, keep track of when homework is due, and complete assignments on time (Gregory, 1995).

Individual Diversity in Achievement

Students vary in their academic achievement. This variation is relatively stable and predicts later outcomes like dropping out of school.

Stability of Individual Differences in Achievement

Can you remember who were the highest or lowest achievers in your 1st-grade class? If you stayed in the same school district, you probably saw these same peers maintain their status through high school. Achievement rank tends to be fairly stable across childhood, whether measured by standardized tests or by GPA (Ladd & Dinella, 2009; Marsh, Hau, & Kong, 2002). That is, children who are high achievers at one age tend to be high achievers at another age. Early achievement may be particularly important because competence in kindergarten and 1st grade predicts achievement in 10th, 11th, and 12th grades (Stipek, 2001). However, this does not mean that children never change. Even though achievement is quite stable, it does change for some students (Phillips, Norris, Osmond, & Maynard, 2002).

What Do Individual Differences in Achievement Predict?

To the extent that grades and test scores reflect meaningful knowledge, high academic achievement is its own reward. Greater knowledge helps children be more informed citizens and better problem-solvers. High achievement also opens doors of opportunity for a college education, which becomes an avenue for high-status employment that requires advanced training. One study found that youth with high SAT college admission scores are more likely to have career success and high income, although they may have average levels of life satisfaction (Lubinski, Benbow, Webb, & Bleske-Rechek, 2006).

You may be interested to know that achievement in *college* also predicts career success. College grades have a small to moderate relationship with adult salary, promotions, job performance, and success in graduate school, with grades in one's major having the greatest predictive power (Roth, BeVier, Switzer, & Schippmann, 1996).

In contrast, *low achievement*, as early as elementary school, is associated with dropping out of school, particularly when low achievement is combined with other factors such as low classroom engagement and low parental expectations. Retention in grade is one of the consequences of low achievement. Retention is also associated with later dropping out, even when it occurs in 1st grade (Stearns, Moller, Blau, & Potochnick, 2007). Dropping out, in turn, is associated with lower wages, higher rates of welfare dependency, and criminality (Alexander, Entwisle, & Kabbani, 2001).

A special form of low achievement, known as **underachievement**, is also linked to negative outcomes. Underachievement refers to receiving grades that are substantially below those of other students *with similar cognitive ability*. Research suggests that underachievers participate less in extracurricular activities, date more, and tend to have either extremely close or extremely distant relationships with their parents. After high school they hold lower-income first jobs, complete fewer years of college, are not promoted in their jobs as fast, change jobs more frequently, and are more likely to divorce than normal achievers and overachievers (McCall, Evahn, & Kratzer, 1992). However, some underachievers catch up to their same-ability peers after high school. Those who catch up may have higher educational aspirations, better-educated

underachievement earning grades that are substantially below those of other students with similar cognitive ability as measured by standardized tests.

parents, and less-serious underachievement in high school. They may be exceptions. For most students, underachievement may be chronic.

What Predicts Individual Differences in Achievement?

A variety of factors contribute to children's achievement in school—the child, family, culture, and school. You've read about several factors in earlier chapters and will read about more in each of the subsequent chapters. For example, child factors that contribute to higher achievement include emotional and social competence, which will be discussed in Chapters 6 through 11. In addition, children who are able to assess their own competence have higher achievement, while low achievers tend not to recognize their incompetence. For example, one study found that students who did quite badly on an exam estimated that they had done just fine (Dunning, Johnson, Ehrlinger, & Kruger, 2003). In contrast, high achievers tended to be more accurate about, or even underestimate, their performance. This means that your lower-achieving students are more likely than high achievers to be surprised by exam results.

Several family characteristics are associated with academic achievement. You have already seen that maternal depression, parental substance use, family stress, and family investment are linked to children's achievement. In Chapter 6 you will learn that secure attachment between parent and child is linked to higher achievement. In Chapter 7 you will learn that parenting style and discipline are linked to achievement. Other factors that affect academic achievement, such as divorce, social skills, and motivation, will also be discussed in later chapters. Thus, you will keep revisiting the issue of child and family characteristics linked to achievement throughout this text.

Group Diversity in Achievement

There are popular books that claim that schools short-change boys and others that claim the same for girls. Just how do boys and girls differ in achievement?

Gender

Girls tend to earn higher grades than boys at all grade levels, including in math and science. However, there are only a few differences between boys and girls in standardized test scores:

- Girls have an edge in language arts. They have higher reading and writing scores in elementary school (Kurdek & Sinclair, 2001). By high school, gender differences in reading scores are very small. However, writing differences are robust and get larger in high school (Halpern et al., 2007).
- Girls tend to take more foreign-language Advanced Placement exams like French and Spanish and also earn slightly higher scores than boys (Stumpf & Stanley, 1996).
- Boys tend to take more physics, chemistry, and computer science Advanced Placement exams and earn slightly higher scores than girls (Hyde, Lindberg, Linn, Ellis, & Williams, 2008).
- The math gender gap favoring boys has now shrunk to almost nothing (Hyde et al., 2008), with the exception of SAT scores.

- Boys have higher math scores on the SAT, but there are no gender differences on verbal SAT scores (Benbow, Lubinski, Shea, & Eftekhari-Sanjani, 2000). Math differences are small. The SAT is taken by a select group of college-bound youth and may not reflect average differences in the total population. Boys tend to stack at both the highest and lowest ends of math tests, indicating more variability among boys than girls (Hyde et al., 2008). Boys at the highest end may be "carrying" the male advantage in math. More girls take the test, so the sample of boys is more highly selected. Also, the SAT underpredicts the performance of girls—they go on to earn higher grades in college math classes than their SAT scores would predict (Spelke, 2005).

Thus, in most of your classes boys and girls will be similar in achievement, with the exception that girls may write better, and the most advanced math and science classes in high school may be disproportionately male. Gender differences are small, whereas SES differences can be large.

Socioeconomic Status

Hundreds of studies have shown that on the average, low-SES children tend to have lower academic achievement than higher-SES children (Sirin, 2005). In Chapter 1 you learned that the effects of SES emerge in the preschool years and get larger with age. For example, in one study, 75% of the children in an upper-middle-income school already had informal arithmetic knowledge before entering school (see Chapter 4), whereas only 7% of children in a lower-income school had this knowledge (Case, Griffin, & Kelly, 2001). By the time they enter school, impoverished children have lower math and reading abilities, and do not catch up to nonpoor children (Pianta, Belsky, Vandergrift, Houts, & Morrison, 2008; Votruba-Drzal, Li-Grining, & Maldonado-Carreno, 2008).

The SES achievement gap occurs across countries (Akiba, LeTendre, & Scribner, 2007). The Program for International Student Assessment (PISA) monitors achievement in many countries throughout the world. They find that the achievement gap in the United States is moderate; some countries have larger and some have smaller achievement gaps. Parental education, rather than income, is particularly powerful in predicting children's academic achievement.

How does SES affect academic achievement? In Chapter 1 you learned that two plausible explanations are the family stress and family investment models. These models suggest that SES influences children through quality of parenting and opportunities that parental income and education make possible, such as owning books, visiting museums, or travel. However, some high-SES parents do *not* provide such experiences, and some low-SES parents do. Achievement-promoting family activities include things like reading to the child, high-quality discussions, church attendance, help with homework, going to the library, and encouraging achievement. Both high- and low-income families do these things, so some of your low-SES students will do well in school and some high-SES students will be underachievers.

While low achievement among poor children may be partially explained by family factors, it is also explained by less *opportunity to learn* (OTL) at school. A key part of OTL is having high-quality teachers (O'Connor & Fernandez, 2006). Poor children are less likely to have high-quality teachers. There are many components to teacher quality, but those that are easily measured are a college degree in the subject you teach, a master's degree, high scores on certification exams, more than three years' experience teaching, and knowledge of child development and pedagogy. These teacher qualities predict student achievement (Darling-Hammond, 2007). The higher the percentage of qualified teachers in a school, the higher the achievement test scores of students. Tuerk (2005) estimates that in a school of 400 8th-graders, for every percentage point gain in qualified teachers, ten to twenty more children would pass their proficiency tests.

Unfortunately, as the percentage of poor children in a school rises, so does the percentage of classes taught by teachers who are not certified in the area in which they teach (Tuerk, 2005). Thus, inequality of education exacerbates differences in family resources between high- and low-SES children. The achievement gap is lower in countries that assign the best teachers to the poorest students (Akiba et al., 2007).

Ethnicity

Some children in all ethnic groups do well in school. However, in Chapter 1 you learned that there are large average differences in achievement among ethnic groups in America. From kindergarten to high school, students of Asian descent tend to have high achievement, and African American and Latino students tend to have relatively low achievement, on average (Palacios, Guttmannova, & Chase-Lansdale, 2008; Raudenbush, 2009). White students are in between. The average 17-year-old African American or Hispanic student can do math and read as well as an average White 13-year-old (Rampey, Dion, & Donahue, 2009). Nationwide, the graduation rate is about 50% for African American students, 53% for Hispanic students, and 75% for White students (Orfield, Losen, Wald, & Swanson, 2004).

The National Assessment of Educational Progress (NAEP) has been tracking student achievement in the United States at 4th, 8th, and 12th grade for more than thirty-five years. The Trends in International Mathematics and Science Study (TIMSS) is a large, international study that has been tracking math and science achievement across forty-five countries for more than ten years. Both studies have found that Black and Latino children's achievement has risen since the late 1990s, slightly narrowing the achievement gap in the United States.

Why is there an achievement gap? Researchers have tried to answer this question for decades, teachers have tried to close the gap, and the federal government has outlawed the gap. Yet the gap remains. This suggests there is no single large cause, but probably many subtle causes working together. One cause is that SES and ethnicity are linked. In Georgia, Illinois, New York, and Virginia, the correlation between number of poor students in schools and number of African American students is 0.63 to 0.69. In Arizona and California, the correlation between number of poor students and number of Latino students is 0.65 to 0.66 (Kim & Sunderman, 2005). Thus, the same factors explaining the SES achievement gap may largely, but not completely, explain the ethnicity gap.

Schools tend to be somewhat racially segregated; 35 to 45% of White, Black, and Latino students attend schools where 90% of the students match their own ethnicity. In contrast, Asian, American Indian, and other ethnic groups are more dispersed across schools. Schools with predominantly ALANA (African, Latin, Asian, and Native American) students tend to be overcrowded, lack textbooks, and have fewer qualified teachers (Darling-Hammond, 2007). Minority students may also experience overly harsh discipline and low expectations from teachers (O'Connor & Fernandez, 2006; Stinson, 2006; Wiggan, 2007). For example, in one study Black and Latino students who perceived that their teachers played favorites and held lower expectations for minority students achieved substantially less than same-ability White or Asian students (McKown & Weinstein, 2008). The children responded to the low expectations of their teachers.

Other plausible causes were discussed in Chapter 1. To review, one explanation is differences in school-related *cultural capital*, which refers to knowledge and relationships that foster opportunity to learn and ability to move through the system. For example, ALANA students tend to be tracked out of honors or AP classes, regardless of standardized test scores, partly due to lack of mentors or knowledge about how the system works (Darling-Hammond, 2007). Another explanation is *cultural mismatch*, or a pattern of incompatibilities between home and school in language and narrative style. Students who experience more compatibility between home and school are at an advantage for school achievement.

Despite cultural mismatch and discrimination, many immigrants manage to achieve in school. Students whose parents were foreign-born, or themselves foreign-born, tend to have higher achievement than students whose parents were born in the United States. It may surprise you, but this is true even in English class (Urdan, 2004). This fits with the theory that *voluntary* immigrants who move seeking a better life tend to do well in school.

Teachers who succeed with low-SES and ALANA students tend to be highly engaging and very demanding. For example, Garfield High School, a primarily Latino school in East Los Angeles, became extraordinarily successful at preparing students to pass the AP Calculus exam. Jaime Escalante, a teacher whose story was made into the film *Stand and Deliver*, was instrumental in this success. At his school students performed better than at any non-magnet inner-city high school in the country. "Garfield produced 27% of all Mexican Americans in the country who scored 3 or higher in Calculus AB [typical exam], and 22% of Mexican Americans who scored at that level on the BC [more advanced exam]" (Mathews, 1988, p. 301). The AP test is scored from 1 to 5, with 3 being a passing grade that receives credit at most colleges and universities. You can personally help narrow the achievement gap by developing expertise as a teacher—which this text is designed to help you do.

Warner Bros./Everett Collection

Actor Edward James Olmos and Jaime Escalante on location at Garfield High School in East Los Angeles in 1988.

Cross-National Comparisons

There are significant differences in the academic achievement of children in the United States compared with children in other countries. Cross-national studies provide some insight into these differences and how education might be improved within cultures. There are two sets of standardized assessments conducted in countries across the world. The TIMSS (Trends in International Mathematics and Science Study) is conducted every four years with 4th- and 8th-graders. The PISA (Program for International Students Assessment) is conducted every three years with 15-year-olds in fifty-seven countries.

According to the 2007 TIMSS, 4th- and 8th-graders in the United States are above average in math and science compared with students in other countries. However, Asian and some European countries score better. Table 5.2 ranks twelve countries from a TIMSS and PISA comparison. In math, 8th-grade U.S. students are roughly two years behind the top countries, such as Singapore and Japan, and one year behind in science. Achievement is not related to spending; the United States spends more per pupil than many higher-achieving countries.

These national differences appear early. Chinese children may have better math skills than U.S. children as early as preschool (Siegler & Mu, 2008). What might cause these Asian students to perform so well? Perhaps the following home and school factors (Stevenson et al., 1990):

- Asian parents provide a desk for each child despite crowded homes.
- Asian parents give greater emphasis to the role of effort, rather than innate ability, in achievement (see Chapter 13).
- Math ability is more highly valued in Asia than in the United States, and Asian children spend more time practicing math.
- Asian children spend more time in school and they spend more time-on-task during class.
- Asian children have more breaks during the day and twice as much recess time.
- Asian elementary schools average two to five times the size of American schools, and have larger classes, often forty to fifty students.
- Asian teachers remain with the same students for two to three years.

Table 5.2 Ranking for mathematics among twelve industrialized countries

Country (alphabetical)	Rank		
	TIMSS Grade 4	TIMSS Grade 8	PISA Age 15
Austria	10	8	5
Belgium	3	3	4
Hong Kong	1	1	1
Hungary	7	5	8
Italy	9	11	12
Japan	2	2	3
Latvia	5	6	9
Netherlands	4	4	2
New Zealand	11	10	6
Norway	12	12	7
Russian Federation	6	6	11
United States	8	9	9

Source: From Ginsburg, Cooke, Leinwand, Noell & Pollock (2005, p. 8).

Another reason for high Asian achievement is the high quality of teaching. One study compared 5th-grade math lessons in the United States and in Asia (Stevenson & Stigler, 1992). In one Asian class, the teacher entered with containers of different sizes and asked the class which container would hold the most water. The children disagreed with each other, so she asked them how to solve the problem. They suggested putting water in the containers and measuring it. They divided into small groups to do this, and then graphed the results on the board together. The teacher reviewed what they had done, introduced the concept of graphing, and posed the original question again before the class ended. In a comparable U.S. class, the teacher sent some children out of the room for band or other activities before beginning the math lesson with the remaining children. He went over a problem assigned for homework the previous day, and then had the children silently go over a new assignment in their books. He walked about the room quieting children. These differences were typical of the two cultures. Many (47%) of the U.S. 5th-grade classrooms were interrupted by irrelevant activities (e.g., presenting lunch choices) whereas only 0 to 10% of Asian classrooms were.

Eightfish/The Image Bank/Getty Images

Asian classes tend to be large, but achievement is high.

Asian teachers only teach three to four hours, or 50 to 60% of the school day. The rest of the day is spent doing other tasks and polishing the next day's lessons. Asian master teachers are given leave from the classroom to coach novice teachers. Teachers work with colleagues to perfect lesson plans. In contrast, U.S. teachers have little discretionary time to plan lessons and spend too much time in the classroom. U.S. curriculum is also "an inch deep and a mile wide," meaning too many topics are covered, and hence are covered superficially (Stedman, 1997).

Classroom Implications of Research on Achievement

We can learn from the research on cross-national achievement. For example, U.S. schools could improve by providing children with more recess time and keeping teachers and children together for multiple years, as schools in some other countries do. However, U.S. schools should not necessarily imitate other countries in all ways. U.S. children already dislike school more than do Asian children. If the United States instituted longer school days, without increasing recesses, the children would probably dislike school even more.

We can also learn from the research on SES and ethnic differences within the United States. Teachers need to be tuned in to the cultural capital of their students and find ways to help those with few resources succeed. Sometimes providing cultural capital can be as simple as reminding students when they must sign up for classes for the next year and recommending what classes to take. It can be explaining to students what is required to become a firefighter, teacher, or lawyer. It can be providing school resources like access to computers, or crayons, so that students can be successful at school tasks.

High-achieving children of color have reported receiving cultural capital through mentoring by a caring person outside the family. For example, one child reported that a counselor had taken notice of him and let him work in her office for a school year. Another was dragged by a friend to a religious retreat that he said turned him around, and another was nurtured by her boyfriend's mother (Cordeiro & Carspecken, 1993; Stanton-Salazar & Spina, 2003). Teachers and counselors can fill the role of a caring mentor.

Research has identified many school factors that affect achievement. Earlier in this chapter, you learned that deliberate practice and feedback are critical to developing expertise. Eight additional school factors that are linked to achievement will be discussed next: study skills, achievement press, time-on-task, homework, time spent in school, retention in grade, class size, and high-stakes tests.

Study Skills

Many students never develop good study skills. You can teach study skills to your students, which can improve their achievement. Study skills training works best when situated within a specific subject matter (e.g., biology, math, reading) rather than when taught in the abstract as general skills. Three study skills discussed in Chapters 3 and 4 that you might teach in your class are reciprocal teaching, mnemonics for memorizing, and spaced practice. In addition, in Chapter 4 you learned that testing helps students learn more because they remember content better that they have been tested on. Teach your students to test themselves. Self-testing helps students determine whether they have understood and will remember what they studied, and it may result in deeper conceptual learning than rereading. For example, in one study physics students were asked to periodically stop reading their text and rate how well they thought they had understood the passage. Then they took a quick quiz on what they had read to see if their assessment was accurate. Later they performed better on a test than students who did not try self-testing (Dunning, Heath, & Subs, 2004). The old-fashioned 3R (read–recite–review) approach builds on these ideas. It involves reading text, then self-testing by reciting out loud all that you can remember, and then rereading (McDaniel, Howard, & Einstein, 2009). Delayed self-testing is best. Teach your students to wait a little while rather than self-testing right after studying.

Achievement Press

Achievement press refers to *teachers'* perceptions that the school is focused on improving student learning and to *students'* perceptions that teachers challenge students to reach high levels of performance. Achievement press exists when students think their teachers expect them to do their best all the time, to work hard, to complete homework daily, and to take the most advanced classes they can. A national study found that growth in mathematics from 7th to 12th grade was related to teacher achievement press (Wilkins & Ma, 2002). Achievement press is also linked to better behavior in high-poverty schools (Balfanz, Herzog, & MacIver, 2007). Achievement press is most effective for youth who have support from teachers, parents, peers, and the community. Students who lack support may not benefit from press, and students who lack both press and support achieve the least (Lee & Smith, 1999).

Time-on-Task

Time-on-task, or *academic learning time*, is the amount of time spent learning at school after subtracting time for taking attendance, messing around, lunch, recess, daydreaming, and so forth. Thus, time-on-task is much less than *allocated learning time*, which is the time that is set aside for a particular topic. Time-on-task is linked to the amount of academic growth children experience, after controlling for prior achievement (Pianta et al., 2008). Time-on-task tends to be low in U.S. schools, and varies greatly from class to class.

A study of science learning found that when 8th-graders were given less time to study the same material as other students, their performance on multiple-choice items was about the same, but performance on written questions that assessed conceptual understanding was much lower for the less-time students (Clark & Linn, 2003). Off-task time can be due to child characteristics such as their ability to control attention. It can also be the result of student sabotage, such as when students get the teacher talking about his dating life, in order to avoid discussing the course topic (Burkett, 2001). It is important to establish relationships with students, but not in ways that detract from learning time.

Off-task time can also be the result of poor teaching. In a junior high we observed a teacher spend forty minutes of a fifty-minute class going over instructions for an assignment, like breaking down how many points each component was worth, how to turn it in if it was late, and so on. No content was taught. In contrast, another teacher put children to work solving a geometry problem at their desks as soon as they entered the room. When most had finished, she had three students solve the same problem on the board. As a class, they compared different approaches and discussed better ways to solve it. The teacher modeled how to solve one problem, and students modeled how to solve others. Only five minutes of fifty were spent discussing the next assignment. Thus, a key classroom variable that you, the teacher, will directly influence is time-on-task.

Homework

Does homework facilitate achievement? Not as robustly as you might think. The relationship between achievement and homework is complex because diligent, but low-ability, students might do lots of homework yet earn low grades. Some high-ability students with good grades boast about doing almost no homework; they finish their schoolwork on the bus or during easy, boring classes. Still others take several AP classes and have a crushing load of homework. Overall, research shows almost no relationship between elementary school students' homework and achievement, a weak relationship for junior high students, and a moderate relationship for high school students (Cooper & Valentine, 2001; Pezdek, Berry, & Renno, 2002).

The National PTA (a parent–teacher organization), the NEA (national teachers' union), and researchers recommend that appropriate homework would be about ten to twenty minutes per day in grades K–2, and about thirty to sixty minutes per day in grades 3–6 (Cooper & Valentine, 2001). They did not make a specific recommendation for junior or senior high school. While parents and youth sometimes complain about an increasing homework load, the proportion of students doing large amounts of homework—two or more hours per day—has not changed much over five decades (Gill & Schlossman, 2003).

Time Spent in School

Achievement increases when children spend time in school. Three lines of evidence support this. First, the cognitive growth of a national sample of kindergartners and 1st-graders was compared from October to April (six months of school) and April to October (months that include summer vacation). Cognitive ability grew over the more-school period relative to the less-school period (Huttenlocher, Levine, & Vevea,

1998). Second, the achievement of children whose birthdays fall just before or just after the kindergarten cutoff (so that they are almost the same age but some begin school and others do not) shows that reading and mathematics skills are greater for children allowed to enter school (Morrison, Griffith, & Alberts, 1997). Third, low-SES students' achievement is higher with a longer school year or a shorter summer vacation (Frazier & Morrison, 1998).

Time spent in school is especially beneficial to low SES children. High-SES students' achievement may increase over the summer, whereas low-SES and African American students tend to lose ground or stay even over the summer (Burkam, Ready, Lee, & LoGerfo, 2004; Downey, von Hippel, & Broh, 2004). This is known as *summer setback*, and could be related to what children do during the summer—watch TV versus read, travel, and pursue hobbies.

This is not necessarily an argument for year-round schools. Year-round schools redistribute summer vacation into several shorter breaks throughout the year so that children might attend school for forty-five days and then have fifteen days off. (This is not the same as extended-year schools with more than 180 days.) Year-round schooling may prevent summer setback and provide struggling students with opportunity to be tutored during the breaks. However, what little research exists on year-round schools suggests that there is not much effect on overall achievement (McMillen, 2001).

Retention in Grade

One way that schools attempt to increase time spent in school for low-achieving students is by having them repeat a grade. Some believe retention is a "gift of time" for late-developing children to catch up to their peers. Others believe it harms children because it is viewed as punishment and makes children feel inferior. What does the research say? Generally, retention is neutral to bad for students, and they hate it (Jimerson & Ferguson, 2007; Stearns et al., 2007).

Retention in *1st grade or beyond* clearly has harmful effects that may last several years after retention (Hong & Yu, 2008a). Retention predicts later dropping out (Alexander et al., 2001). It also predicts worsening achievement, greater anxiety, increased disruptive behavior, and increased inattentiveness across elementary school, beyond preexisting problems. Students who are retained are more likely to be male and to have other risk factors such as low SES, low birth weight, and poor social skills (Pagani, Tremblay, Vitaro, Boulerice, & McDuff, 2001). Minority students are more likely than White students to be retained, and subsequently to drop out.

Some have claimed that *early retention, in kindergarten or 1st grade*, is helpful, but with little support. A national study found that children retained in *kindergarten* felt more competent, more interest in school, less sadness, less loneliness, and less low self-esteem. This small effect suggested retention was not harmful to kindergarteners' socioemotional well-being. However, their math and reading scores were lower than comparable children who were promoted. This negative effect washed out by 5th grade (Hong & Yu, 2008b). A study of students retained in 1st grade found that over the next four years, they showed some improvement in achievement, but also erosion of their improvement, suggesting an unhealthy pattern of failure, success, and failure (Wu, West, & Hughes, 2008). Staying in kindergarten an extra year means that the student will likely be 19 at graduation, not 18, and being older is a risk factor for not graduating at all.

Thus, retention is an expensive intervention (about $10,000 per student for an extra year of school) with neutral or negative effects. The fact that retention contributes to students' risk does not mean that mindless social promotion is acceptable either. Instead, students who are candidates for retention may need other interventions, like tutoring or summer school.

Class Size

Some studies find that small classes of about twelve to seventeen are linked to achievement gains in the primary grades. The longer students are in small classes, the greater the effect. However, some studies find the effects only occur up to 1st grade, and primarily for high-achieving students.[1] Furthermore, not all studies find a positive effect, and when positive effects are found, they are quite small. The effects may be small because teachers do not change their teaching approach much when they move from large to small classes (Ehrenberg et al., 2001; Stasz & Stecher, 2000). The small positive findings may not generalize to districts that cannot hire additional *qualified* teachers (due to a shortage) and that lack additional classrooms. Districts with these limitations may reduce "class size" by adding teachers to a classroom, so that instead of a 15:1 student–teacher ratio, it is 30:2. In these situations teachers may simply trade off teaching 30 students at a time—one does clerical work while the other teaches—without altering their teaching approach (Graue, Hatch, Rao, & Oen, 2007). This approach seems *not* to improve achievement (Finn et al., 2001).

High-Stakes Tests

To raise the achievement of all students and to close the achievement gap between SES and ethnic groups, the federal government requires schools to test all students to determine if the gap is closing and to ensure that all students have grade-level proficiency in core content. These are **high-stakes tests**, designed to create strong incentives to improve achievement. Based on test scores, schools are designated as *in need of improvement* or as making *annual yearly progress.* When a school is designated as needing improvement for a few years or more, drastic measures can be taken such as replacing teachers, giving students the option to transfer to another school, or even the takeover of the school by the state or other group. This is an example of *standards-based reform*, which refers to attempts to improve achievement by setting standards and holding educators accountable for achieving those standards.

high-stakes tests tests used to make decisions that have educational or financial impact.

In some states, these mandated tests are not high stakes for students because nothing happens to individual students who get low scores. There is little reason for students to try hard on the tests. However, other states make the tests high stakes for students because they cannot graduate or be promoted if they do not achieve a specific score.

Is this approach working? The data so far suggest that there is a small increase in math and reading scores on the NAEP, but it is not closing the achievement gap (Lee, 2008). It is more effective for math than reading, and for elementary than secondary students. Some have suggested that children who are just at the border of proficiency are nudging up, but there is no change for higher and lower achievers (Porter & Polikoff,

[1]Many studies have documented this, just a few of which are listed here (Ehrenberg, Brewer, Gamoran, & Willms, 2001; Finn, Gerber, Achilles, & Boyd-Zaharias, 2001; Hanushek, 1999; Konstantopoulos, 2008; Nye, Hedges, & Konstantopoulos, 2001).

You can teach your students test-taking skills.

2007). States that respond to accountability testing by raising teacher certification standards, improving professional development, and increasing school resources are more successful (Lee, 2008). Schools designated as needing improvement tend to have a majority of poor or ALANA students enrolled.

You can prepare your students for high-stakes tests by teaching test-taking skills such as the following (adapted from Kubiszyn & Borich, 2003, pp. 38–42):

- Follow directions carefully.
- Read test items, passages, and related information carefully; this may require highlighting, rereading, and double-checking.
- Manage test-taking time. You can provide practice with timed assignments.
- Attempt easier items first. Some students quit when they come to a difficult item, assuming they will not be able to get further items correct. You can provide practice on classroom tests so that students get used to tests *not* being ordered from easy to difficult.
- Eliminate obviously incorrect options before choosing an answer.
- Check answers if there is time.
- Take advantage of preparation materials that are available. For example, many states provide practice tests.

However, avoid overemphasizing proficiency tests. You can undermine your students' motivation if you hold the test up as the primary reason for learning. If students do not care how they perform on the test, then students see no point in the learning. Listen to one 7th-grade girl:

> *All the teachers care about is the proficiency test. They don't care if we learn anything. They're always saying stuff like, "Now, you'd better restate the question, because if you don't, you'll lose points on the proficiency test." Who cares? In life, do you have to restate the question?*

In summary, school factors associated with academic achievement include teaching better study skills, holding high expectations for students' hard work, and fostering more time-on-task. Sometimes assigning homework is useful. More time in school is also associated with achievement, but primarily for low-achieving students. Retaining low-achieving students in grade is associated with worsening achievement. Small class size is sometimes found to be associated with higher achievement in the early grades. High-stakes testing has not yet demonstrated strong positive effects on achievement, although that is the intent. In the next chapters you will see how emotional well-being contributes to achievement and other child outcomes.

Reflections on Practice: Checklist for Teachers

Children differ in cognitive abilities such as intelligence, talent, and achievement. While intelligence may have some basis in genes, all cognitive development is influenced by the environment, including the quality of education a child receives. As a teacher you can improve each student's cognitive ability by asking yourself the following:

1. How do I define intelligence? Do I view it as changeable?
2. What does it mean to be intelligent within the culture of my students? Do differences between my view and my students' view place them at a disadvantage?
3. Do my instruction and assessments include analysis, creativity, and practical applications? Do I value all types of "intelligence" in my students? Which types of intelligence best fit my mode of instruction and assessment? How can I better accommodate all my students?
4. What do I view as the cause of talent? What talents do I value? Do my students value the same talents? Does my school recognize forms of giftedness besides high intelligence? Does my school use multiple pieces of evidence to place students in gifted or remedial programs?
5. How am I helping to develop talent in my students? Do I provide opportunities for deliberate practice to my students? Do I maximize time-on-task in my classroom?
6. How can I apply principles of deliberate practice to improve my teaching? Have I sought feedback from others about my teaching? Do I frequently reflect on the quality of my teaching? Could I improve my training in both content area and in teaching methods?
7. Am I careful to be tuned in to underachievers? Is my school doing all it can to prevent retention in grade for low-achieving students?
8. Do I teach students effective study skills within the content I teach?
9. Which practices of Asian schools might I adopt to enhance student achievement—such as emphasizing effort rather than ability, spending more time-on-task, giving children more recess, staying with the same children for multiple years, collaborating with colleagues to polish lessons, or eliminating interruptions?
10. Do I communicate high expectations for my students' achievement?
11. Do my students suffer from summer setback? Should my school consider lengthening the school year? Would my students benefit from smaller class size?

Summary of Age Trends in Cognitive Ability

	Intelligence	Talent	Achievement
Early Childhood (Birth–5 Years)	Individual differences in speed of habituation predict intelligence years later. Habituation and recognition memory studies demonstrate that 3- to 5-month-olds have many cognitive abilities like object permanence, a sense of time and quantity, understanding of causation, reasoning, and categorization.	There is no age trend in talent because talent refers to having greater competence than age-mates. Talents valued by a culture are often introduced in early childhood, and children are given more practice in those talents.	Asian superiority in math achievement appears in preschool. The achievement gap emerges in preschool. Standardized achievement tests are usually not administered, nor are grades given, in early childhood.
Middle Childhood (6–12 Years)	There are no age trends in intelligence test scores because intelligence tests are designed for comparison to same-age peers. Intelligence scores have risen across the world over the past several decades. Intelligence scores are least stable before age 12.	Children who are experts in a domain have better memory for new experiences in that domain than do adult novices. Middle childhood may be the latest one can start in some, but not all, domains in order to develop world-class expertise.	Small class size may promote a slight increase in achievement when implemented in the primary grades. National and international trends in achievement begin to be tracked in 4th grade. Homework has little effect on elementary school achievement.
Adolescence (13–19 Years)	Intelligence scores are largely stable after age 12.	Expertise is the result of practicing hundreds of hours, for several years, so it is often not manifest before the teens.	The achievement gap is largest in high school. Grades tend to get worse from late elementary through high school. Homework is weakly related to achievement in junior high and somewhat stronger in high school. The relationship is complex because weaker students might do more homework but earn lower grades.

Chapter Summary

Intelligence

- Intelligence is a general mental capability that includes the ability to reason, solve problems, think and learn quickly, and deal with abstraction and complexity.
- Tests of cognitive abilities and academic achievement tend to correlate with each other, suggesting a *g* factor.
- According to Sternberg's Theory of Successful Intelligence, there are three components to intelligence: (1) analytic, (2) practical, and (3) creative. Each should be addressed in instruction and assessment.
- According to Gardner there are multiple intelligences—linguistic, logical/mathematical, spatial, musical, kinesthetic, natural, interpersonal, and intrapersonal. His theory has been criticized and has little research support. However, the theory helps teachers reconsider their perceptions of what ability is, and their decisions about what to teach and how to teach it.
- Intelligence is measured with individual or group tests. Intelligence test scores typically have a mean of 100 and a standard deviation of 15.
- Nativists believe innate knowledge in core domains, such as number and language, may be hard-wired into the brain. However, mature competence in core domains requires learning, suggesting an interactionist view.
- Through habituation and recognition memory studies, we know that infants only a few months old have greater cognitive abilities than previously believed.
- Intelligence scores are quite stable after age 12. Before age 12, intelligence scores do not necessarily predict later intelligence, but infant habituation does.
- Genetics accounts for some (but not all) of the differences in intelligence. The genetic contribution to intelligence is greater for high-SES children.
- Higher intelligence is associated with higher school achievement, higher SES, and better job performance in adulthood. Intelligence protects children from life stresses and poor health.
- Low-SES children have lower average intelligence test scores than high-SES children.
- There are few gender differences in *general* intelligence. However, on average, males score higher on tests of spatial ability.
- Differences in intelligence test scores across ethnic groups may be a function of socioeconomic status, differences in opportunity to learn, and cultural differences in abilities that are valued. Generally, tests are equally good predictors of future performance across ethnic groups.
- The "Flynn effect" is a worldwide cohort effect of rising intelligence scores.
- Intelligence tests are commonly used to diagnose students for remedial or gifted education. They should not be used as the sole basis for program admission.

Talent and Expertise

- Talent and expertise both refer to having great skill compared to peers. Deliberate practice, good instruction, and feedback are critical for developing talent.
- In some domains, world-class performance typically requires at least ten years of intensive practice, and a late start may prevent its development.
- Talented students use their time more productively than do their peers and have greater motivation to practice.
- Experts have better memory and pattern recognition for their domain of expertise than do nonexperts.
- Cultures vary in how much they value specific talents and how they introduce young children to talent development.
- Schools tend to take a narrow view of giftedness, equating it with high intelligence. However, students can be talented in some domains without having high *g*.
- Teachers can apply principles of deliberate practice to improve their students' expertise and their own teaching.

Achievement

- Achievement is measured by grades or standardized tests. Achievement tends to be fairly stable across time, though some students do change their achievement levels.
- High achievement is linked to career success. Low achievement predicts retention and dropping out, and later, erratic employment.
- School factors associated with higher achievement include teaching study skills, providing greater achievement press, and providing more time-on-task and more time in school. Small class size is sometimes found to be associated with higher achievement.
- Cross-national studies indicate that U.S. students are low-average in science and math. Asian students are higher achieving. These differences begin in elementary school and may be due to more time-on-task, more emphasis given to effort, and more teacher time spent polishing lessons.

Accompanying Education CourseMate Website Resources

Visit the **Education CourseMate** website at **CengageBrain.com** to find resources and study aids for this chapter, including self-tests, additional print and website resources, and glossary flashcards. In addition to the Video Case, the following videos illustrate concepts discussed in the chapter:

- 0–2 Years: Early Learning in Infants and Toddlers
- Learning Disabilities
- Intelligence: What Do Intelligence Tests Measure? Clip from ABC News

TEACHSOURCE VIDEO CASE

Watch the video case *Preparing Students for Standardized Testing: Strategies for Success.* As you view the videos and artifacts think about the following:

1. What do the teachers do to improve students' test scores?
2. In what ways would that also improve the students' thinking and reasoning?

section 3 The Emotional Child

If you ask your friends what makes students successful in school, they will probably answer "being smart." Many people do not realize that students' emotional well-being is also important for school success. In this section, you will learn about students' emotions and their link to the classroom. In Chapter 6, you will learn how relationships with teachers and students affect students' personality and achievement. In Chapter 7, you will learn how to promote self-control in your students and use discipline effectively. In Chapter 8, you will learn how to help your students regulate their emotions. This information is critically important for your success as a teacher. Teachers who do not learn how to promote the emotional and social well-being of their students tend to have poorly behaved students, become cynical about teaching, and burn out (Jennings & Greenberg, 2009). The next three chapters of this text will help you be a more effective and happy teacher. Let's begin our study of the emotional child by watching Le'Raun interact with two different teachers.

Le'Raun's Changing Personality

Case 3 Le'Raun's Changing Personality

Richard Shock/Stone/Getty Images

Le'Raun's 6th-grade class switches teachers and rooms three times a day. In each class, Le'Raun is quiet. He does well on his assignments, so his teachers assume he has normal intelligence, but he seldom participates in class and has to be reminded to do his assignments. Le'Raun's teachers deal with him in very different ways.

Le'Raun's science teacher, Miss Loeb, excitedly greets students as they enter the classroom. "Hello Guys! Are we ready to play 'stump the teacher'?" Several children gleefully shout: "Yes!" The students have been asked to read a chapter on ecosystems and come up with questions to test Miss Loeb. If she answers correctly, she gets a point. If she answers incorrectly, the students get a point. "Who wants to ask the first question?" Miss Loeb asks. Almost all hands go up, with children wiggling in their seats so they'll be noticed. Molly asks the first question: "What is the average temperature on the grasslands?" Miss Loeb scores a point for "65 °F in the summer." After several more questions, the children are still exuberant. As the class period comes to an end, however, Le'Raun has not raised his hand yet. He is smiling and paying attention though. When Miss Loeb asks him if he wants to pose a question, he looks down at his desk and does not answer.

Case 3 (continued)

After the game, while the other children take out their homework assignments, Miss Loeb goes to Le'Raun and asks if he would like to pose a question in private. Le'Raun asks: "What famous song was written about the Grasslands region?" After Miss Loeb correctly answers "Home on the Range," Le'Raun asks her to sing the song. Miss Loeb sings a few lines, laughs, and affectionately pats his shoulder. Le'Raun smiles.

The class moves on to a homework review. Knowing that he didn't do the assignment, Le'Raun frantically tries to complete it in class. Noticing his distress, Miss Loeb tells Le'Raun to go to the quiet reading area of the classroom to finish it. Miss Loeb often gives Le'Raun extra time for homework because his home is not supportive. As Le'Raun finishes the homework assignment correctly, it is clear that he understands the content.

The entire class then goes to Mrs. Richardson's math room. The children enter the room somberly and pull out their books from under their desks. There is no enthusiasm and very little talking. Mrs. Richardson begins the lesson and then notices that Le'Raun has not taken out his book. She marches to Le'Raun's desk, leans into his face and sternly whispers, "Take out your book!" Le'Raun shows no emotion at all. Mrs. Richardson then goes back to the front of the room and resumes the lesson. Le'Raun continues to sit still for a few seconds. Then he covers his face with his hands.

A few minutes later, Mr. Rohm, the school principal, comes to observe the class. Noticing that Le'Raun does not have his book out, he goes over and puts his hand on Le'Raun's shoulder, smiles, and whispers: "Hey, Le'Raun. Do you want me to get your book for you?" Le'Raun nods. While Mr. Rohm picks up the book, Le'Raun gets his homework out of the desk and begins searching for the problem the class is working on. Mrs. Richardson looks at the principal and angrily says, "I've been down that road already today!" Some of the students look down at their books in embarrassment; others look at Le'Raun in sympathy. Mr. Rohm smiles, says something kind to Le'Raun, and leaves the room. Le'Raun appears more relaxed and engaged now. He continues to follow along with the lesson. He does not look at Mrs. Richardson or ask her any questions at all, but Le'Raun does ask his desk partner questions and turns in the day's work.

How might the teaching styles of Mrs. Richardson and Miss Loeb affect Le'Raun's personality and self-control? Did Mrs. Richardson or Miss Loeb help Le'Raun become emotionally competent? How do emotions like anxiety or happiness affect students' achievement? This section on the emotional child will address these questions and help you understand how to promote emotional well-being in your students.

Attachment and Personality

Big Cheese Photo/Jupiter Images

DOES THE ATTACHMENT RELATIONSHIP STUDENTS HAVE WITH THEIR PARENTS INFLUENCE THE RELATIONSHIPS THEY HAVE WITH TEACHERS OR THE GRADES THEY EARN IN SCHOOL? In this chapter, we will discuss attachment at length, because it sets the stage for children's academic and social success from preschool through high school. Then we will discuss temperament, which combines with attachment to form children's personalities. After you read this chapter, you will understand:

- Different types of attachment and what they can mean for children's well-being.
- What temperament and personality are and how they influence students' success at school.
- How to promote secure attachment and school bonding and provide a good fit for the personalities in your classroom.
- Additional concepts from topics you encountered in earlier chapters—nature/nurture and ethology.

Attachment

Audrey is a 10th-grader who drops in on the counselor frequently for long visits that typically involve tears as she describes things her parents have done that hurt her feelings. Audrey was recently diagnosed with ADHD. Her school counselor identified the ADHD, not her parents. The counselor is also concerned about anorexia. Audrey is very thin. She proudly says she is "not fat like my mom." Yet Audrey also tells the counselor that her parents are "awesome" and that she wants to be "just like them." Her homeroom teacher says Audrey does not seem to have close friendships with other girls but has a new boyfriend every couple months. She does her work in class, yet her test scores are surprisingly low.

attachment a deep and enduring affectionate bond that connects one person to another across time and space.

Why does Audrey criticize and then lionize her parents? Why does she seem distant from girlfriends? Audrey's puzzling behavior could be explained by her attachment history. **Attachment** is a deep, enduring emotional bond between people (Ainsworth, 1973). Typically, the most powerful attachments children have are with their parents. Parent–child attachment forms the foundation for children's personality and emotional well-being in the classroom.

Psychologists began to understand the importance of attachment in the early 1900s. At that time, orphanages had high death rates—in some orphanages an astounding 70 to 100% of infants died (Spitz, 1945). With improved conditions death rates decreased, but many surviving infants failed to grow normally (see Chapter 2) and became mentally retarded or delinquent as adolescents. Psychologists puzzled over why these children fared so poorly. Orphanage caregivers were purposely rotated so that children would not get overly attached to them and experience the trauma of separation. Suspecting that these rotations might be the problem, Renee Spitz compared two institutions. One was a nursery for infants of incarcerated mothers who were typically young and mentally ill or delinquent. The infants had full access to their mothers in jail, and they developed normally. The other institution was a foundling home for infants of mothers too poor to keep them. Many children became retarded because, according to Spitz, they would do nothing but lie on their backs for months, wearing a hollow into their mattresses so deep that they could not even roll over (p. 63). Social interaction was rare. By the time infants were a year old, they would silently huddle and rock themselves. They had bizarre reactions to strangers—either extreme friendliness or blood-curdling screams. Spitz's films of these children are sad to watch and helped convince people that attachment is a basic need in children. So did the work of John Bowlby and Mary Ainsworth, discussed in Box 6.1.

attachment hierarchy the vertical organization of primary and secondary attachment figures for a specific child, with a preferred attachment figure at the top.

secure base an attachment figure who engenders a child's confidence and security, because of willingness to be available when needed, while the child explores novel environments.

Most children are attached to more than one person, but they are highly selective. They typically attach to just a few people. Together these attachments form an **attachment hierarchy**, with a preferred person at the top. That preferred person is commonly the mother. Attachments can include nonfamily members, such as a teacher or babysitter. We will refer to a target of the child's attachment as an *attachment figure*.

Children show preference for attachment figures. Children go to them when upset, protest separation from them, and use them as a **secure base** from which to explore

Theories & Theorists **Box 6.1**

John Bowlby and Mary Ainsworth

John Bowlby (1907–1990) treated 150 children at the famous Tavistock clinic in London. The children were aggressive, destructive, and thieving and had night terrors that he believed were the result of separation from their mothers (Bowlby, 1940). At that time, scholars in different countries from Scotland to Africa were reporting the effects of mother–child separation due to World War II, incarceration, hospitalization, and employment. Bowlby wrote a synthesis of these other scientists' reports for the World Health Organization, concluding that children who are separated from their mothers suffer physical and mental illness. His report led to changes in the care of children in hospitals and orphanages. He wrote:

The mother-love which a young child needs is so easily provided within the family, and is so very very difficult to provide outside it . . . In no other relationship do human beings place themselves so unreservedly and so continuously at the disposal of others. This holds true even of bad parents—a fact too easily forgotten. . . . Children thrive better in bad homes than in good institutions. (Bowlby, 1952, pp. 67–78)

Before Bowlby, psychologists believed that children could be too attached, such as when they were clingy and cried at separation. The negative term *dependent* was commonly used to refer to attachment. Instead, Bowlby argued that attachment was not just a phase of dependency to be outgrown. He wrote: "*dependence is maximum at birth and diminishes more or less steadily until maturity is reached, attachment is altogether absent at birth and is not strongly in evidence until after an infant is past six months*" (1969, p. 228). Secure attachment *liberates* children and should *not* be considered dependency. Bowlby shaped the current view that attachment (1) is a characteristic of the relationship, not the child; (2) is normal; (3) is innate with biological underpinnings; and (4) is essential to mental health. It was Mary Ainsworth who focused psychologist's attention on differences in attachment security.

Ainsworth (1913–1999) was hired by Bowlby to work at the Tavistock clinic with school-aged children who had lengthy separations from their parents for tuberculosis treatment. She noticed that the separation affected their personalities. In the 1950s, Ainsworth went to Uganda, where she observed babies in their village homes. She was struck by how much infants *actively* initiate attachment relationships—seeking proximity to, smiling toward, and responding preferentially to their mothers. Several years later she replicated the Uganda study in Baltimore (Ainsworth, 1973). She saw the same array of attachment behaviors in the U.S. infants as those in Uganda, although they were from very different cultures.

Ainsworth's great insight was that children who display intense attachment behaviors are not more attached. The happy, secure child may *seem* to take mother for granted, while the anxious child may *seem* to be more strongly attached, but the anxious child who will not get off mother's lap to explore is actually insecurely attached.

Ainsworth was among the first to connect quality of mothering with differences in security of attachment and to point out that it is exploration and reunion behavior—not separation distress—that distinguishes secure from insecure children. Her contributions included the design of the Strange Situation Procedure, which allowed attachment to be measured in a reliable way, placing it within the realm of science. This fostered thousands of studies on how early attachment relates to later development.

the world. Toddlers protest separation from their primary attachment figure more than from other attachment figures and prefer that person when hungry, tired, or ill. However, a child might prefer a different attachment figure, such as a sibling or father, when ready to play (Bowlby, 1969). Having a strong preference for an attachment figure is normal. In fact, children who show attachment behaviors toward almost anyone with no clear, strong preference may develop psychological problems.

Why is attachment important for children? Ethology (see Box 6.2) helps answer this question. Ethology seeks to describe the *function* of behavior from an evolutionary perspective. Attachment serves two important functions:

1. It provides a *safe haven* from danger by keeping children close to an adult protector.
2. It provides a *secure base* for moving outward to explore the world.

Theories & Theorists **Box 6.2**

Ethology and Critical Periods

Attachment behavior is innate and universal, suggesting it is biologically programmed into children. Adults do not have to teach attachment behaviors; they simply have to respond to children. All children seek to be attached. In fact, seeking an attachment figure when frightened is such a strong innate response that children will even seek an abusive parent.

Ethology, the subdiscipline of biology concerned with the study of animal behavior, helps explain attachment. From an evolutionary perspective, the ultimate purpose of animal (including human) behavior is to pass on genes. This means that species develop attributes that help closely related kin survive to pass on their shared genes. Attachment behavior, like staying close to the mother, protects the young, ensuring their survival and ability to pass on genes (Geary & Bjorklund, 2000).

Ethology often provides insight into child development (Hofer, 2006). However, behavior in animals is not always relevant to behavior in humans. For example, critical periods may apply to attachment in animals, but not humans.

Are There Critical Periods in Attachment? Konrad Lorenz (1903–1989) found that young geese follow their mother soon after hatching. If raised in an incubator, they follow the first creature they see, which is called *imprinting*. Once this imprinting takes place, they cannot be made to attach to another goose, even their own parents. Lorenz believed that imprinting takes place within minutes of hatching and is irreversible. Thus, there is a *critical period* for imprinting (see Chapter 2). Attachment is considered a type of imprinting by ethologists. Human children become attached regardless of the quality of care, implying it is simply the presence of the caregiver that matters. (It is not attachment, but the *security* of attachment, that is affected by quality of care.) For their research, Lorenz and two other ethologists won the Nobel Prize in 1973.

Bowlby was struck by Lorenz's early studies of imprinting. Bowlby believed that the first years of life are a critical period for human attachment and that later good mothering could not make up for bad or absent mothering in infancy. He was only partly right. Research has confirmed that attachment in infancy does indeed predict later development; however, parenting matters throughout childhood. Change in attachment security is possible. Thus, a critical period for attachment probably does not exist in a strong form for humans. Nevertheless, there appears to be a *sensitive period* for attachment in the first 18 to 24 months. A "sensitive period" means the effect of experience is strongest during a relatively brief period in the lifespan.

De Agostini/World Illustrated/Photoshot

Konrad Lorenz followed by birds who have imprinted on him. Does he look like their mother?

ethology a subdiscipline of biology that seeks to understand the cause and function of animal (including human) behavior.

Do these seem like conflicting functions? Children want to feel secure. If this were their only goal, they would never leave their parents' side. Fortunately, they are also curious and want to explore. Yet, exploration puts them in potential danger, making them feel wary. Children balance wariness and curiosity by using the attachment figure as a secure base when there is no threat and as a safe haven when they feel threatened. Let's take a look at how these functions operate at different ages.

Age Trends in Attachment

Children's attachment behaviors change dramatically with age, but the function of attachment—feeling secure—continues across the lifespan.

Early Childhood (Birth to 5 Years)

Infants show attachment as they cling to caregivers when frightened or greet caregivers with delight, like kicking excitedly when Daddy smiles at them. As infants begin to crawl or walk and seek their parents, the *parents'* attachment to the infant deepens. It is gratifying to parents to be preferred and sought out. Most toddlers cry and cling when their attachment figure tries to leave. This *separation distress* peaks between 1 and 2 years of age. Typically, between 3 and 4 years children outgrow separation distress.

Most toddlers will explore new environments if their attachment figure is nearby, occasionally looking at or touching the attachment figure. After age 3 most children are comfortable in strange places with secondary attachment figures, like a sibling or a teacher. Thus, attachment *behaviors*, such as clinging to the attachment figure, are not as frequent or intense, but the attachment *relationship* continues.

Infants become wary of strangers at around 8 to 9 months of age (Sroufe, 1996). This surprises some parents because when younger, their baby seldom protested when held by strangers. However, *stranger wariness* is part of normal attachment development. It occurs across widely diverse cultures at the same age. Stranger wariness typically lasts a few months, peaking at about 12 months, and then gradually decreasing.

If strangers simply approach toddlers and pick them up, most will cry (Waters, Matas, & Sroufe, 1975). How can you approach a toddler who is wary of you? First, give the child time to gradually become familiar with you. Play a familiar game, like peek-a-boo, or offer something familiar, like a favorite blanket. Second, give the child control over the interaction (Sroufe, 1996). If the child backs away, you back away. If the child offers you a toy, take it and then offer it back. Third, recruit the parent's help. If the parent looks happy to see you, rather than worried, the child is more likely to react positively to you. This effect, known as *social referencing*, will be discussed in Chapter 9.

Middle Childhood (6 to 12 Years)

Compared with toddlers, elementary-age children tolerate greater separation from attachment figures. They need less physical contact; nonphysical contact, like a phone call, can make them feel secure. By 5th or 6th grade, children who frequently seek physical contact with their attachment figure may be overly anxious (Crittenden, 1992). Children still want to be close, but their behavior is subtle and might simply involve drifting toward the attachment figure while engrossed in another activity. For example, while Dad cooks dinner, a toddler may be right under his feet banging pans, while her older sister absent-mindedly moves into the kitchen and sits at the table to draw. The attachment figure's availability—physical presence, willingness to talk, and awareness of the child's needs—remains very important.

Field Observation

Choose a family with children of varied ages whom you believe are securely attached. Ask the mother to go to a room in the house alone, when the family is home and relaxing. She should *not* invite anyone to join her, but rather should do something on her own (e.g., reading). Have her time how long it takes each child to either enter or settle in the room she occupies. Describe how children of different ages respond. Compare your results with classmates' results.

Adolescence (13 to 19 Years)

Adolescents sometimes avoid their parents. They often withhold information about school activities because they don't want their parents to show up at school, so savvy teachers can communicate directly with parents. When our 14-year-old daughter was rollerblading with friends in the neighborhood and saw that we were strolling in their direction, she turned around and skated away. This active avoidance of parents in the presence of peers typically lasts for a year or two. (Wise parents and teachers do not take it personally.)

Does such avoidance mean that adolescents are not attached to their parents? Quite the opposite. Adolescents' age-appropriate independence may be the *result of feeling secure attachment.* That is, teens become independent because they know that their parents will be available to them despite their behavior. This knowledge is the bedrock of healthy personality in adolescence. The infant's experience of being comforted by daddy becomes the adolescent's belief that "Dad is always there for me" (Bretherton & Munholland, 1999). Teenagers "touch base" by gravitating toward where their parents are. Even when our daughter avoided us at the park, at home she would drift into the kitchen, help us make dinner for a few minutes, and then disappear again. Attachment even persists into adulthood. When you experience a crisis, you probably seek out your attachment figures.

Do teens shift their primary attachments to peers rather than parents? Most do not. Mothers are usually the primary attachment figure through adolescence for teens with secure attachments. But not all teens have secure attachments. A best friend or boyfriend/girlfriend may be the primary attachment figure for adolescents who feel unsupported by their parents (Freeman & Brown, 2001). Next we consider how healthy attachment develops.

Individual Diversity in Attachment

Strange Situation Procedure a twenty-two-minute laboratory task designed to test quality of attachment in which children under age 6 are stressed by maternal separation and stranger presence.

All children have attachment relationships; however, the *quality* of attachment varies. Scientists assess quality of attachment with the **Strange Situation Procedure (SSP)**. The SSP begins with a child and parent entering an unfamiliar room full of new toys (Ainsworth, Blehar, Waters, & Wall, 1978). The child plays with the toys while the parent sits in a chair. After three minutes, a stranger enters the room, chats with the parent, and then plays with the child. Every three minutes thereafter, one of the adults leaves or returns in this order: the parent leaves, the parent returns and the stranger leaves, the parent leaves the child all alone, the stranger returns, and finally the parent returns. The entire SSP takes only twenty-two minutes, but it provides a remarkably good snapshot of attachment. It reveals whether the child prefers the parent to the stranger and whether the child's distress is soothed by the parent's return. Quality of attachment is determined primarily by what happens during the two reunion episodes, not the separation episodes. We will describe typical child reactions later.

Adult Attachment Interview a lengthy interview designed to determine adolescents' or adults' "state of mind" regarding the quality of attachment to each parent.

The SSP is the most common way to assess attachment in toddlers; it has been used with children up to age 6 by increasing separation time to more than an hour (Stevenson-Hinde & Verschueren, 2002). Yet, how would you assess attachment in adolescents who do not fall apart when their parent leaves the room for an hour? Scientists use the **Adult Attachment Interview (AAI)**. They ask questions about early attachment memories. For example, they ask adolescents to list five adjectives that describe their relationship with each parent and tell about specific experiences that support each adjective. They determine quality of attachment by how coherently the adolescents talk about the relationship. A different method involves asking a parent and teen to discuss an emotionally charged topic, like curfew time, and watching how they interact.

Using the SSP, AAI, and other assessments, children's attachments can be classified as either secure or insecure using one type of secure and three types of insecure attachment. These four types do not capture all the variation in attachment relationships, but they will help you understand attachment (Fraley & Spieker, 2003).

Secure Attachment

During the SSP, toddlers with secure attachment freely explore the new toys while their parent is present. They may or may not cry when separated, but play less when their parent is gone. When reunited, they show delight and readily go to their parent and are quickly soothed (Ainsworth, 1979). They clearly prefer their parent over a stranger.

secure (balanced, autonomous) attachment a form of attachment characterized by feelings of security, open communication, and mutual delight.

Elementary-age secure children are referred to as *balanced*. They openly negotiate about their parent's availability, like asking "how long will you be gone?" After separation, they greet their parent with genuine pleasure, converse pleasantly, invite the parent to join in their play, and move closer (Behrens, Hesse, & Main, 2007). They clearly communicate positive, *as well as negative*, feelings toward the parent. Anger and distress are readily resolved or soothed.

avoidant (defended, dismissing) attachment a form of insecure attachment characterized by anxiety, emotional distancing, rejection, and anger.

Secure adolescents are referred to as *autonomous*. During the AAI, they coherently discuss their parents' positive and negative influence. During disagreements with their parents over hot topics like money, grades, or curfews, they are civil and come to mutual solutions (Beijersbergen, Bakermans-Kranenburg, Van IJzendoorn, & Juffer, 2008). They value relationships.

Insecure Avoidant Attachment

During the SSP, toddlers with avoidant attachment explore the room while ignoring their parent. They do not seem to care when their parent leaves, nor do they clearly prefer their parent over a stranger. When their parent returns, they *ignore or turn away*, appearing to avoid their parent. Ironically, at home these same children are quite distressed if their parent simply moves to another room (Ainsworth, 1979).

Elementary-age avoidant children are referred to as *defended* because they hide emotions, like anger, from their parent. This defends them from rejection by their parent. After an hour's separation they may stiffen when the parent returns and subtly try to exclude the parent from their activities (Behrens et al., 2007). They might avoid their parent by appearing engrossed with a toy, or by using it as an excuse to move away. Avoidant children may be prematurely friendly with strangers rather than wary.

OJO Images/Jupiter Images

Young children feel distress when separated from their attachment figure.

Avoidant adolescents are referred to as *dismissive*. In the AAI, they dismiss the importance of relationships. They idealize their parents in global ways, like "My parents are the best!" that are contradicted by memories of specific events, like "They locked me out of the house." When they describe events of rejection they say, "it was no big deal." They might not stop what they are doing to greet their mother after a week's absence (Hodges, Finnegan, & Perry, 1999). They avoid discussions of emotionally hot topics with their parents, but their rare discussions are quite angry (Allen & Land, 1999).

Insecure-Resistant Attachment

resistant (coercive, preoccupied) attachment a form of insecure attachment characterized by exaggerated emotions, clinginess, and intense attachment behaviors.

During the SSP, toddlers with **resistant attachment** hover near their parent, exploring very little. They are distressed by separation, and difficult to soothe after the parent returns. They seem *ambivalent* because when their parent returns, they go to their parent but act angry and sulky. They might ask to be picked up, but then arch away, or hit the parent.

Elementary-age resistant children are referred to as *coercive*. They coerce their parents with tantrums, helplessness, pouting, whining, or coy babyishness (Stevenson-Hinde & Verschueren, 2002). They seek contact with their parent, but are not comforted by it. They may show subtle signs of hostility, such as sitting on their parent's lap but wriggling to make their parent uncomfortable. After an hour's separation, they might hug mother but then swat her (Behrens et al., 2007). They appear immature, hyperactive, and unsettled in play, as they move from object to object.

Think About This Think about Audrey in the opening vignette. Which type of attachment is her behavior congruent with? Defend your conclusion through logic supported by your readings.

Resistant adolescents are referred to as *preoccupied*. They have excessive concern over their parent's whereabouts, express a strong need for their parent in stressful situations, and have trouble separating and recovering from distress. For example, after losing mother at the mall and finding her again, such teens take a long time to calm down and continue to worry about losing her again (Hodges et al., 1999). Their responses on the AAI are incoherent, with rambling and excessive, irrelevant detail. They convey anger, as well as preoccupation with trying to please the parent (Hesse, 1999).

Disorganized Attachment

disorganized (controlling, unresolved) attachment a form of insecure attachment characterized by no coherent pattern of response to the parent.

Toddlers with **disorganized attachment** are strongly conflicted by a desire to be with their parents and to avoid them at the same time. When their parent returns in the SSP, their stress intensifies and they behave bizarrely. For example, they may approach the parent, then suddenly run away, or freeze in a trancelike state. Some children rock back and forth, or walk sideways toward their parent. Sometimes this behavior is subtle, and not easily identified by novices.

Elementary-age disorganized children are referred to as *controlling* because they take control in an overly cheerful way or by punishing the parent (Behrens et al., 2007). For example, when their parent returns they may jump and clap in extreme cheerfulness, or they might say, "Don't bother me!" Because they take control they appear confident, but are actually brittle and anxious (Stevenson-Hinde & Verschueren, 2002). They make up stories filled with catastrophic events, like the mother being killed when she went shopping and left the child at home. Their play involves themes of unusual violence and helplessness.

Disorganized adolescents are referred to as *unresolved*. During the AAI, they may report past traumas involving loss. Their reasoning may break down or become incoherent. For example, they might suddenly become silent in the middle of a sentence

Table 6.1 Types of attachment by age group

Early childhood	Middle childhood	Adolescence and adulthood
Secure	Secure/balanced	Autonomous
Avoidant	Defended	Dismissing
Resistant	Coercive	Preoccupied
Disorganized	Controlling	Unresolved

or discuss a parent who is dead in the present tense. They may be strongly hostile in talking about a parent, or frequently say they feel fearful (Bernier & Meins, 2008). Table 6.1 summarizes the four attachment types and helps you think about how each type evolves across childhood.

How Stable Is Attachment?

Attachment is fairly stable. This means you probably have the same type of attachment now as you had when you were a toddler. About 75% of toddlers will stay secure, or stay insecure, throughout childhood. However, *secure children can become insecure* due to negative events like divorce. Even common stresses, like changing from ten to twenty hours per week of child care, have sometimes been linked to becoming insecure (Lewis, Feiring, & Rosenthal, 2000; NICHD Early Child Care Research Network, 2001b; Weinfield, Sroufe, & Egeland, 2000). Children with multiple risk factors are most likely to become insecure. It is also possible, but not as common, for children to become *more secure* over time, if family functioning improves. Thus, attachment is typically stable, but if situations in a child's life change substantially, attachment can change, for better or worse.

Attachment in Adult Romantic Relationships

Attachment to parents in childhood can affect adult attachments. You may have seen different types of attachment in the romantic relationships of your friends. *Ambivalent* adults tend to be jealous, worry about abandonment, and lack trust in their partners, yet are eager to be in relationships. They share personal information too early in a relationship, fall in love quickly, and frequently break up and reunite. *Avoidant* adults tend to be uncomfortable with closeness or sharing personal information, and disinclined to be in long-term relationships. *Unresolved* adults, particularly those unresolved due to abuse, tend to be aggressive early in their marriages (Cooper, Shaver, & Collins, 1998; Crowell, Treboux, & Waters, 2002).

Secure adults tend to form stable, long-term romantic relationships. They tend to be satisfied in relationships, which are trusting, committed, and interdependent. They are a secure base for their partners to openly express worries and receive reassurance when distressed. Secure couples have fewer arguments, feel greater intimacy, and are less likely to threaten to leave than insecure couples.

Which of your friends is likely to have a secure romantic relationship? Those who had a secure attachment in childhood. However, both one's *history* of attachment to parents and one's *current* attachment to a spouse influence the quality of a relationship. A secure attachment to a spouse can help compensate for insecure parent–child attachment. Still, people who are securely attached both to their parents and to their spouse tend to have the most satisfying relationships (Treboux, Crowell, & Waters, 2004). Let's turn next to other outcomes predicted by childhood attachment.

What Do Individual Differences in Attachment Predict?

You might be wondering why attachment is in this section on the "emotional" child. Doesn't it really belong in the section on the social child, because it is a relationship? It is here because attachment is the foundation of personality, self-control, and emotional well-being. Attachment predicts many other outcomes as well. For now let's focus on two that are important in the classroom—academic achievement and social competence.

Academic achievement

Secure children are likely to be curious, have good verbal ability and academic skills, and earn high grades (e.g., Aviezer, Sagi, Resnick, & Gini, 2002; Granot & Mayseless, 2001). In contrast, *insecure* preschoolers are more likely to have poor prereading skills and negative attitudes toward reading. Insecure school-age youth are more likely to have lower math and reading test scores and lower grades (e.g., Bus & Van IJzendoorn, 1997; Diener, Isabella, Behunin, & Wong, 2007; Weinfield, Sroufe, Egeland, & Carlson, 1999). Insecure students are anxious, which interferes with learning (see Chapter 8), and they have difficulty getting along with teachers and classmates.

Social competence

Secure students are more likely than insecure students to have harmonious friendships, empathy for others, and resistance to negative peer pressure. Peers and teachers are more likely to view them as socially competent from preschool through high school (e.g, Allen, Porter, McFarland, McElhaney, & Marsh, 2007; DeMulder, Denham, Schmidt, & Mitchell, 2000; McElwain, Booth-LaForce, Lansford, Wu, & Dyer, 2008). Even in college, secure freshmen may feel more cared for and have a better social support network than insecure students (Grabill & Kerns, 2000).

Insecure students are more likely to have poor relationships with peers. In one study, some insecure 10-year-olds reported having many friends but were unable to name one (Grossmann & Grossmann, 1991). Peers and teachers tend to view insecure students as angry, mean, dishonest, disruptive, withdrawn, or anxious. *Avoidant* and *disorganized* students may be the most at risk for serious aggression and behavior problems in preschool through elementary school (e.g., Granot & Mayseless, 2001; NICHD Early Child Care Research Network, 2006b).

Other outcomes

Besides social competence and academic achievement, attachment quality predicts other outcomes:

- Growth. Insecure attachment is linked to poor physical growth (e.g., St. Petersburg-USA Orphanage Research Team, 2008; Valenzuela, 1990).
- Compliance. Secure students are more compliant with adults. This doesn't mean they are meekly submissive; they may challenge adult directives, but ultimately are more cooperative with reasonable demands (Laible, Panfile, & Makariev, 2008).

- Independence. Secure students are more likely to work independently and make their own decisions than insecure students, from preschool through high school (Sroufe, Fox, & Pancake, 1983; Weinfield et al., 1999).
- Emotional openness. Secure students can express anger or say "I hate you" without fear that they will be rejected or abandoned. In contrast, avoidant students tend to have trouble discussing emotions (Laible & Thompson, 2000).
- Emotion regulation. Secure students tend to have good emotion regulation, as early as 4 months of age. As they get older, they tend to discuss hot topics without anger, take on difficult challenges, and not fall apart when distressed (Braungart-Reiker, Garwood, Powers, & Wang, 2001; Sroufe, 1996).
- Stress. Insecure students tend to have overactive stress responses, are easily aroused, and often feel anxiety (Perry, 1997). This may explain why insecurity is linked to health problems (Maunder & Hunter, 2001).
- ADHD. Insecure students are more likely to show ADHD symptoms whether they are formally diagnosed or not. Secure students tend to have longer attention spans and greater cognitive ability (Clarke, Ungerer, Chahoud, Johnson, & Stiefel, 2002; Goldwyn, Stanley, Smith, & Green, 2000; Moss & St-Laurent, 2001).
- Psychopathology and delinquency. Insecure adolescents are more likely to have suicidal thoughts, depression, conduct disorders, substance abuse, eating disorders, and anxiety.[1]

Clearly, secure attachment is an important asset for youth, and insecure attachment is a risk factor. However, as you learned in Chapter 1, risk factors are about probability, not certainty. For example, although insecure youth are *more likely* to have eating disorders than secure youth, most insecure youth do not develop this problem. The development of children and teens depends on the full array of risk and protective factors they experience.

What Predicts Individual Differences in Attachment?

Ideally all children would be securely attached. In reality about half (50 to 60%) are secure, another quarter (20 to 23%) are avoidant, and the rest are resistant (8 to 10%) or disorganized (10 to 24%) (O'Connor & McCartney, 2007). How do children come to be secure?

> ***Think About This*** Some people advise new mothers not to pick up their babies when they cry because they will become dependent and clingy. Based on what you know about sensitive responsiveness, is this good advice? Is it possible to be overly responsive? Does responsiveness create a dependent, clingy child? What does?

Sensitive responsiveness

Sensitive, responsive parents are more likely to have secure children (Koren-Karie, Oppenheim, Dolev, Sher, & Etzion-Carasso, 2002; Nievar & Becker, 2007). Such parents provide encouragement, assistance, and reassurance *when the child indicates need*, not according to the parents' agenda. They attend to and accurately interpret a child's signals, respond promptly, and understand the child's feelings. For example, if a baby grunts in frustration while trying to grasp an out-of-reach toy, the parent attends to the grunt, realizes the baby wants the toy, and promptly moves it within reach. An *insensitive* parent might not notice the grunt, or not realize what the baby wants.

[1]There are many studies that support this conclusion, just a few of which are listed here (e.g., Allen & Land, 1999; Branstetter, Furman, & Cottrell, 2009; Hesse, 1999; Lewis et al., 2000; Weinfield et al., 1999).

An *unresponsive* parent might notice, but not respond to the baby. For another example, if a teenager begins acting overly irritable, a sensitive, responsive parent notices the change in behavior, realizes the child is anxious about an upcoming performance, and helps the child prepare for the performance.

Parents of *avoidant* children tend to be unresponsive and intrusive, meaning they frequently interrupt the child's activities with their own activities (Ainsworth, 1979). For example, a father might wave a toy in front of his baby's face when the baby is engrossed with a different toy. Parents of *resistant* children tend to respond inconsistently or only to strong signals from the child (Stevenson-Hinde & Verschueren, 2002). For example, a 5-year-old could show many signs of exhaustion that the mother does not notice until the child has a tantrum.

Other parent behaviors

Although parent sensitivity is considered key to secure attachment, other behaviors are also important. Parents of *secure* children tend to communicate openly and directly with, and show interest and enjoyment in, their children. In contrast, parents of insecure children are often negative, depressed, anxious, and dissatisfied with family life. Parents of *avoidant* children may be angry and reject their children. They may also withdraw when their child needs help with difficult tasks. Parents of *resistant* children may be relatively accepting, but vacillate between irritation and empathy with their child and may inappropriately need their child's approval (Scher & Mayseless, 2000; Stevenson-Hinde & Verschueren, 2002).

Parents of *disorganized* children may be the least sensitive. They are more likely to be single parents, intrusive, psychologically unavailable, or neglectful. However, most importantly, they may be *frightening* (Bernier & Meins, 2008; Stevenson-Hinde & Verschueren, 2002). How does this happen? Parents frighten children through fearful facial expressions, trancelike behavior, approaching the child in an aggressive way, and handling the child like a bag of groceries. They also frighten children through abuse. The child's need for nurturing and protection is constant, whereas incidents of abuse are typically brief, so the child turns to the parent for safety but is frightened by the parent. This terrible paradox results in the bizarre behavior characteristic of disorganized attachment. Parents may behave in frightening ways due to drug use, depression, their own history of experiencing abuse, or loss through death or divorce.

Jan Tyler/iStockphoto.com

Parents of secure children communicate clearly with them and express interest and delight in them.

Improving attachment

Can we help parents create secure attachments? Yes, according to studies using randomized experiments (see Chapter 1). Interventions that improve mothers' sensitivity also improve children's security, suggesting that maternal sensitivity *causes* child attachment. Successful interventions include making home visits to the mother, educating the mother about child development, and keeping the mother and child in physical contact

(Bakermans-Kranenburg, van IJzendoorn, & Juffer, 2003). For example, in one study, Latina and African American mothers were given soft baby carriers that kept infant and mother in a chest-to-chest position (Anisfeld, Casper, Nozyce, & Cunningham, 1990). Several months later, 83% of the children were securely attached, while only 38% of those who used plastic infant seats were secure. Kangaroo Care, where the infant is positioned on the mother's chest with direct skin-to-skin contact, has similar effects (Tessier et al., 1998).

> ***Think About This*** *Sue arrived at the library with her three children, ages 3 to 7 years. Sue went to the children's section and sat down to read her own book. The children wandered about looking at books. One child asked Sue, "Wanna read me dis one?" Sue said, "Momma's gonna sit here and read her book." Looking over the child's book, she continued, "That's a scary one. Why don't you put that back and get another one?" Her oldest boy several times brought a book to show Sue. She would look at it briefly, chuckle or comment, and return to her own reading. When the children were out of sight, Sue would look up from her book, quietly call out their names until they answered, and then return to reading.*
> How would you rate Sue on these four dimensions: sensitive or insensitive? accessible or neglecting? cooperative or interfering? accepting or rejecting? How might you judge the attachment behaviors of her children?

Attachment to Father

Most research has been on *mother*–child rather than *father*–child attachment. Nevertheless, fathers are usually part of children's attachment hierarchy. Infants may protest separation from fathers, explore less when separated, and feel comforted when father returns. Just over half of children are securely attached to their fathers. Children can be securely attached to father but insecurely attached to mother, or vice versa, but they tend to have similar attachment to both. Children who have secure attachment to both mother and father have the most optimal outcomes, while children who have two insecure attachments have the worst outcomes (e.g., Diener et al., 2007).

How Does Attachment Have Such Far-Reaching Consequences?

Scores of studies show that attachment is linked to many important outcomes—aggression, GPA, depression, growth, ADHD, and so forth. Why might this be? One explanation is internal working models.

Internal working models (IWMs) are memories and expectations—based upon thousands of daily interactions with attachment figures—that children carry into new situations. They are models of both the self and others. A secure child's internal working model is that the *self* is valuable, socially successful, and worthy of love and that *others* are trustworthy, responsive, and caring. In contrast, an insecure child's internal working model is that the self is unworthy and others are hostile, rejecting, or inconsistent. Let's see how a secure model works in a kindergarten:

> **internal working models** memories and expectations of the self and others that influence whether children approach or avoid others, with either positive or hostile emotions.

> *The children are sitting on the floor in a circle. Janie gets up to get a tissue. When she returns, she says to Lilly, "Thank you for saving my seat." Janie assumes Lilly has saved her seat, but actually Lilly has not noticed she was gone.*

Because Janie has a secure internal working model, she expects caring from others, and treats them accordingly. Children show evidence of their internal working models every day at school.

Internal working models may be apparent by infancy, although they are still developing (Johnson, Dweck, & Chen, 2007). By age 3, they are fairly stable. Although change is possible, internal working models are resistant to change because they are not conscious. They are also resistant to change because children behave in ways that confirm their models. In contrast to Janie, insecure children tend to alienate others, preventing the very social experiences that might help them change their internal working models.

> ***Think About This*** Can you explain attachment types from a behaviorist perspective? A behaviorist would argue to an ethologist that any behavior that promotes survival has consequences and therefore can be conditioned. Based on what you learned in Chapter 3, discuss how resistant attachment might result from an intermittently responsive parent, or avoidant attachment from a punishing parent.

Children's views of other people become self-fulfilling prophecies that become more validated as they grow older.

Another explanation for why attachment is linked to so many child outcomes is that sensitive parents who promote secure attachment in infancy continue to be sensitive throughout the child's life. This ongoing good parenting promotes the child's competence, not just secure attachment. Research suggests that both earlier and current parenting are important. That is, early secure attachment has long-term effects that are supported by current parenting (NICHD Early Child Care Research Network, 2004).

Group Diversity in Attachment

There are few gender differences in attachment. The same factors—parents' sensitivity, warmth, and open communication—predict secure attachment in both girls and boys. In addition, the same outcomes are associated with attachment in both girls and boys. However, there are differences in attachment across socioeconomic status and across countries.

Socioeconomic Status

Low-SES children are more likely to be insecurely attached than other children. They are almost twice as likely as middle-SES children to have disorganized attachment. Perhaps this is due to the accumulation of risk factors linked to low SES (see Chapter 1) that may lead to insensitive parenting, such as drug use, little education, and father absence (Tarabulsy et al., 2005). However, *secure attachment occurs in spite of poverty when parenting quality is good.* In a study of families on public assistance, 4- to 5-year-olds were secure if their mother was warm and accepting, not intrusive, and did not use physical punishment (Barnett, Kidwell, & Leung, 1998).

At the other end of the spectrum, both Bowlby and Ainsworth felt that high-SES parents who try to produce super-achieving children place their children at risk for insecure attachment by being intrusive. These parents may not understand that **sensitive responsiveness** *does not mean devoting complete attention to children.* For example, in a classic study, mothers of highly competent children interacted with them only ten to thirty seconds at a time, briefly responding to the child but seldom spending even five minutes "teaching" something (White & Watts, 1973). After a question had been answered, help rendered, or applause given, both the parent and child returned to their tasks. If it was inconvenient to attend to the child at a particular moment, the mother said so, but she was available at other times. Thus, these mothers were consistently available and sensitively responding to the child, with limits, but were not intrusively imposing their own agenda onto the child.

sensitive responsiveness a style of interaction in which an adult responds promptly and appropriately to a child's signals, with accurate understanding of the child's perspective.

Cross-National Comparisons

Attachment behavior is remarkably similar across varied countries like Sweden, Chile, Japan, and Mali. In addition, parents' views of what behaviors are healthy are similar across countries. However, security of attachment differs if national cultures dictate differences in caregiving, like how sensitive parents are or how much time they spend with their children (Waters & Cummings, 2000). Research finds higher rates of secure attachment in cultures where mothers are always with their infants, like in Mali in West

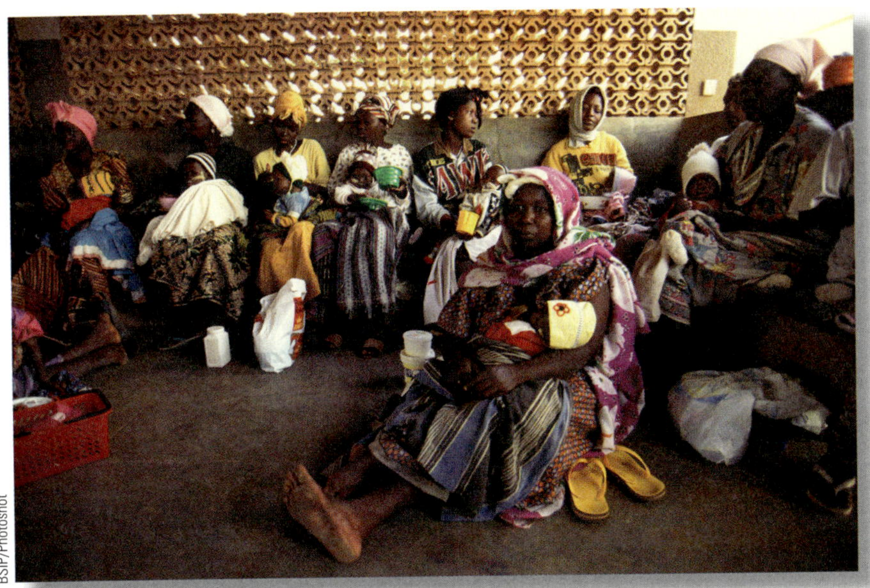
BSIP/Photoshot

Cultures where mothers spend more time with and are in physical contact with their infants may have more secure children.

Africa, than in cultures where they spend less time together (True, Pisani, & Oumar, 2001). However, in most countries, the majority of infants are securely attached.

Taken together, the research on group diversity in attachment suggests that whether boys and girls grow up in a low-SES or high-SES household, or whether they grow up in West Africa or North America, is not as important as the quality of parenting they receive. If parents are sensitive, responsive, and positive, their children are likely to be securely attached regardless of group membership.

Classroom Implications of Attachment

You learned earlier that achievement and social competence in the classroom are linked to parent–child attachment. They are also linked to teacher–child attachment and school bonding. Teachers are not simply dispassionate deliverers of information; good teachers develop positive relationships with students (Beishuizen, Hof, van Putten, Bouwmeester, & Asscher, 2001).

Teacher–Student Relationships

There are differences in the quality of relationships between students and teachers, just as there are with parents. Students do not always attach to teachers, because the structure of some schools provides too little opportunity for a relationship to develop. When relationships are possible, students who feel *secure* with their teachers accept comfort from their teachers when upset, communicate affection, readily share activities, and seem genuinely happy to see the teacher. In *avoidant* relationships students may act as if they do not hear or notice the teacher, quickly leave after being requested to come to the teacher, and move away if the teacher tries to comfort them. In *resistant* relationships students may frequently act frustrated, cry over every little irritation, and demand teacher attention, yet resist classroom routines like cleanup. They may constantly seek help or reassurance and be possessive, clingy, and overly reliant on the teacher (Howes & Ritchie, 1999; Pianta, Nimetz, & Bennett, 1997).

Do secure relationships help students? Your students are likely to have greater academic and social competence if you develop close, positive relationships with them. Secure, positive teacher–student relationships may protect students from social problems like aggression, misbehavior, drug use, violence, and early sexual activity.[2] They may also promote academic motivation, reduce retention or special education referrals, and improve GPA and test scores.[3] For example, in one study low-SES students who had a positive teacher–student relationship in 1st grade were more engaged and effortful in 2nd grade and had higher test scores in 3rd grade (Hughes, Luo, Kwok, & Loyd, 2008). Positive relationships with teachers provide students with a secure base to explore and master difficult school tasks.

The effect size (see Chapter 1) of teacher–student relationships for school-age children is quite large, suggesting it may be more significant than which curriculum or instructional approach you use (Cornelius-White, 2007). For preschoolers, the effect of teacher–child interaction on academic, language, and social skills is larger than teacher–child ratio, curriculum, class size, space and furnishings, and so forth (Mashburn et al., 2008). At any age, teaching quality centers on positive teacher–student relationships.

How do you develop secure relationships with students? One of the most powerful predictors of teacher–student relationships is attachment at home. Children with insecure parent–child attachment are likely to have insecure teacher–student relationships (DeMulder et al., 2000). This is because insecure children draw negativity from teachers. Teachers tend to be angry and rejecting with *avoidant* children, viewing them as defiant. Teachers tend to be more tolerant and nurturing toward *resistant* children, viewing them as immature and needy. In contrast, teachers tend to be sensitive and warm toward *secure* children and expect good behavior from them (Pianta, 1999). Thus, you may find it more difficult to develop a positive relationship with your insecure students, like Audrey in the opening vignette. Nevertheless, it is possible; in one study of thousands of children, about one-third of insecure children developed secure teacher–student relationships (Howes & Ritchie, 1999). How might this happen?

Revisiting Case 3

What kind of attachments did Mrs. Richardson and Miss Loeb have with Le'Raun? Apply what you have learned about antecedents of attachment to defend your conclusion.

The *teacher's behavior* contributes to the teacher–student relationship. If teachers are depressed, or feel ineffective, they tend to develop conflict-ridden relationships with challenging students (Hamre, Pianta, Downer, & Mashburn, 2007). In contrast, if caring teachers disconfirm insecure children's internal working model that adults are hostile, rejecting, or unresponsive, then secure teacher–student relationships can develop. If you can develop a secure relationship with students who are insecure with their parents, like Audrey, those students are likely to do better socially and emotionally and have higher achievement in your classroom (O'Connor & McCartney, 2007). To promote a secure relationship with your students follow these guidelines (adapted from Bergin & Bergin, 2009):

---

[2]There are many studies that support this conclusion, just a few of which are listed here (e.g, Howes & Ritchie, 1999; NICHD Early Child Care Research Network, 2002; Pianta et al., 1997; Stipek & Miles, 2008).

[3]There are many studies that support this conclusion, from kindergarten to secondary school, just a few of which are listed here (e.g., Curby, Rimm-Kaufman, & Ponitz, 2009; Hamre & Pianta, 2001; Jia et al., 2009; Ladd & Burgess, 2001; O'Connor & McCartney, 2007).

- Be sensitive and have frequent positive interactions. Sensitive teachers accurately detect and interpret students' cues, respond to students' distress, and are warm.
- Study this textbook carefully. Teachers with greater knowledge of child development are more sensitive toward students.
- Be well prepared for class and hold high expectations for students. This shows you care about their achievement.
- Be responsive to students' agendas by providing choice whenever possible. Students feel greater rapport with teachers who give them some control over what they do. When you cannot provide choice, give a reason.
- Use noncoercive discipline. Coercive discipline involves threats and control of resources, like taking away recess for misbehavior. Good discipline builds positive relationships so the student is motivated to obey. You will learn how to do this in Chapter 7.
- Try interventions designed to repair poor teacher–student relationships when you feel challenged by a particular student. In one such intervention, called banking time, you "save up" positive experiences in relationship "capital" that can later be "drawn upon" (Pianta, 1999). For example, five to fifteen minutes each day the teacher gives the student undivided attention and follows the student's lead in an activity the student chooses. (This can be done during gym, free time, lunch, recess, or small-group instruction). The teacher conveys acceptance of and interest in the student. This is easiest in preschool or elementary school, but a junior high teacher did his own form of banking time. He spent half an hour every day after school phoning a portion of his students and their parents to tell them what he liked about having them in his class. Another high school teacher phoned ill students from his classroom so that he and the rest of the class could tell the absent students they were missed.

In schools where many students are at risk for insecure attachment because of abuse, neglect, parent drug use, or other problems, schoolwide interventions can be implemented. These interventions involve all teachers in the school being consistently positive in order to disconfirm students' internal working models of adults as inconsistent, neglectful, or harsh. Students bond to school as well as to parents and teachers.

School Bonding

School bonding refers to a student's attachment to school. School bonding includes liking school and engaging in school activities, which tend to go together (Hallinan, 2008). School bonding stems from feeling cared for by teachers and peers. In contrast, students who are not bonded to school feel uncared for. They may say that they have no friends and that no one talks to them at school, they do not know the principal, and their teachers do not notice their absences or care about their learning (Mouton, Hawkins, McPherson, & Copley, 1996). In one study, about 25% of elementary students felt their school was an uncaring place (Watson, Battistich, & Solomon, 1997).

school bonding a sense of belonging at school and having a network of relationships with peers and teachers.

Although school bonding is important at any school, it is most important in schools with high rates of poverty and other risk factors (Osterman, 2000). School bonding may be particularly important, but less likely, in secondary schools. Transitions from elementary to junior high or middle school, and then again to high school, are linked to lower grades, less school interest, and less extracurricular involvement (Juvonen, 2007; Skinner, Furrer, Marchand, & Kindermann, 2008). This is particularly true for students experiencing other changes such as a divorce and students with multiple risk factors (Burchinal, Roberts, Zeisel, & Rowley, 2008; Zanobini & Usai, 2002).

Students in K–8 systems, who do not have to transition to middle/junior high school, fare better. Why? Just when students are seeking greater freedom and autonomy, middle/junior high schools emphasize teacher control and deemphasize student choice. Ironically, students tend to have greater autonomy at the end of elementary school than in middle/junior high school. In addition, teacher–student relationships are less personal and positive. Some students see teachers as less friendly, and some teachers see students as less trustworthy. People enjoy blaming "raging hormones" for adolescent negativity at school, but the real problem may be school factors. Adolescents in other countries do not necessarily decrease in school bonding. In the United States, 11- to 15-year-olds feel markedly less bonded and dislike school more than in other countries (Juvonen, 2007). What can you do to promote school bonding?

- Develop secure teacher–student relationships. The primary ingredient of school bonding is close relationships. Students like school better when they think their teachers care about them and praise them for hard work. This may be especially important for students at risk for school disengagement, like those who move a lot or immigrant youth (Green, Rhodes, Hirsch, Suarez-Orozco, & Camic, 2008; Gruman, Harachi, Abbott, Catalano, & Fleming, 2008).
- Promote other adult–student relationships, such as with coaches or counselors. Audrey's teacher, in the opening vignette, could support Audrey's relationship with the counselor. Some schools with many at-risk youth have child development specialists on staff whose sole job is to establish relationships with students. They help increase school bonding, as well as achievement and social skills (Malti, Schwartz, Liu, & Noam, 2008).
- Advocate keeping peers and teachers together long enough to form relationships, which can take several months to a few years. Classroom management problems may decrease, and motivation and achievement may increase, when a teacher stays with the same students for multiple years (Pianta, 1999).
- Advocate keeping schools small or implementing learning communities. The optimal size for bonding in high school is 300 students, although the optimal size for providing strong academic programs may be 600 to 1,200 (McNeely, Nonnemaker, & Blum, 2002). Some secondary schools partially mimic the positive effects of smaller schools by creating small learning communities, which may also be called teams, pods, or schools-within-schools (Felner, Seitsinger, Brand, Burns, & Bolton, 2007).
- Eliminate overly harsh discipline, like expelling students for relatively minor infractions. Students like school better when they perceive teachers as fair.
- Provide extracurricular activities. Youth who participate in a variety of activities (e.g., debate club, jazz band, sports) tend to be less depressed and get into less trouble (Simpkins, Eccles, & Becnel, 2008). Students report feeling

happier and more motivated during extracurricular activities than during classes (Mahoney, Harris, & Eccles, 2006).

- Help students be kind, helpful, and accepting of one another. How to do this will be discussed in Chapter 10.

These factors may be especially important for students who are in the ethnic minority at your school. Adolescents are less likely to feel school bonding when most of the other students at school do not share their ethnic background (Johnson, Crosnoe, & Elder, 2001). Does this mean segregated schools are ideal? No. Segregated schools present a different array of problems. It does mean that in multiethnic schools you will need to work to make sure all students feel attached to school.

In summary, students vary in the security of their attachment, which influences their school success. Parents, teachers, and schools can influence security of attachment. Attachment is also important because it is foundational to healthy personality in children. Let's turn next to temperament, another foundation of personality.

Temperament

Eric is a very shy toddler. He is late to talk and walk, but when he does begin talking it is in full sentences. In preschool, he will not join group time. Instead he presses his back to the furthest wall and intently, but silently, watches the group while twirling a strand of hair. He cries and puts himself in time-out when he breaks a household rule, even before his mother knows he has misbehaved.

Eric never speaks to his kindergarten teacher. During 1st grade, a baby sister is born whom he adores. Each morning he heads straight to his teacher's desk to tell her about the cute things his baby has done, then goes to his seat and does not say another word the rest of the day. When other teachers greet him, he looks down and does not respond. His 1st-grade teacher says, "He certainly isn't like his older sister!" who is buoyant and extraverted and often has to be told not to talk during class. Eric's teacher suspects he is not quite as bright as his older sister, although his vocabulary is exceptional.

Several years later, Eric's 6th-grade teacher asks him to be a buddy to a new student because Eric is the most popular child in the class, and he is compassionate. He is a leader at recess, organizing large groups of boys in fantasy play (as Jedi knights). He is at the top of his class academically and exudes self-confidence.

In high school Eric ranks in the top 1% for achievement nationally. He has a network of good friends who particularly enjoy his witty sense of humor. However, he remains relatively quiet and seems as content to play solitary games as to be with his friends. He goes to the homecoming dance because a very popular, outgoing girl invites him. However, he generally does not go to dances or other large social gatherings where there might be people he does not know.

As a toddler Eric has **behavioral inhibition,** which refers to strong, negative reactions to *new* people, events, or objects. Was he born with this temperament trait? Did he outgrow it? It is important that you understand temperament, because it can affect classroom success.

behavioral inhibition the tendency to be wary and restrict one's approach to new people, events, or objects.

temperament an individual characteristic pertaining to differences in the intensity and pattern of emotions and arousal.

Temperament refers to individual differences children have in the intensity and pattern of their emotions and tendency to react to their environment. Temperament is typically thought of as a collection of psychological traits (such as shyness) and physiological traits (such as energy level) that have a genetic basis, are present early in life, remain stable over time, and predict later personality. This is only partly correct. Most temperament traits are not highly heritable, nor stable. Yet they are present early in life and do predict later personality.

Psychologists do not fully agree on which traits are part of temperament, but four traits appear in most definitions of temperament (Rothbart, 2007):

1. *Activity*, which refers to how much children move.
2. *Effortful control*, which refers to controlling attention and behavior, such as inhibiting impulses, concentrating, following instructions, and resisting distractions. This trait requires good executive functions (see Chapter 4).
3. *Negative emotionality*, which refers to how easily children become irritated, angry, or scared; how intense the emotions are; and how well they control the emotions. Children who are emotionally negative also tend to have problems with effortful control (Zhou, Lengua, & Wang, 2009).
4. *Behavioral inhibition.* Inhibited children, like Eric, react strongly to potential threats, so they are wary of novel things, whereas bold, uninhibited children embrace novelty.

Early temperament researchers Alexander Thomas and Stella Chess believed that temperament *traits* can be organized into three temperament *types*:

Michael Newman/PhotoEdit

Children with behavioral inhibition are cautious about new objects, events, and people.

1. *Difficult* infants (about 10%) cry a lot, are demanding, are irregular in eating and sleeping, withdraw from novelty, are difficult to soothe, and are slow to adapt. They have negative emotionality.
2. *Easy* infants (40%) are biologically regular, like novelty, adapt quickly, have low-intensity emotions, and are cheerful.
3. *Slow-to-warm-up* infants (15%) are less active, dislike novelty, are slow to adapt, have low-intensity emotions, and have moderately negative moods. (Thomas, Chess, & Korn, 1982)

Although more than one-third of the babies they studied could not be classified into one of these three types, the types are still a common way to think about temperament. Some research on temperament focuses on individual traits, and some focuses on these three types.

Individual Diversity in Temperament

Thomas and Chess wondered why some children from dysfunctional families developed problems but others fared well. They concluded that child temperament explained why cold, demanding parents made one child submissive but another defiant. They also believed temperament has a large effect on children's long-term adjustment. We will look at whether research confirms this, but first let's examine whether temperament remains the same across childhood.

How Stable Is Temperament?

In a famous study, Thomas and Chess observed 141 children from eighty-five families beginning in 1956 when the children were 2 to 3 months old (Thomas, Chess, & Birch, 1970). After following the children for fourteen years, they concluded that some, but not all, temperament traits tend to persist over time. Later research suggests that *negative emotionality* is modestly stable; negative preschoolers tend to be negative adolescents. *Activity* is more stable, and *inhibition* is less stable (Wachs, 2006). For example, one longitudinal study found that two-thirds of infants who were highly reactive to new noises, smells, or sights—they cried, arched, moved their arms and legs—were no longer inhibited at age 15 (Kagan, Snidman, Kahn, & Towsley, 2007). Roughly 15% of children at the extreme stay inhibited over time. Nonextreme children, who include most inhibited children, often overcome their inhibition in school settings by 4th grade, particularly intelligent children with social skills, like Eric. Other children are likely to become more inhibited over time if their parents act anxious rather than encouraging in new situations (Murray et al., 2008).

Whether temperament appears stable depends on whether the same person reports the child's temperament. Two people can view the same child very differently. For example, teacher and parent reports of preschoolers' temperament do not closely agree, nor do mothers' and fathers' (Bishop, Spence, & McDonald, 2003; Wachs, 2006). Parents' perceptions of their child's temperament reflect their own internal working models. Secure mothers tend to perceive their babies as easy, and avoidant mothers tend to perceive their babies as difficult (Priel & Besser, 2000). Parents may have an overly negative view of their child's temperament when they are depressed, unhappily married, or have little social support (Harrison & Ungerer, 2002). Thus, when a parent describes one of your students as difficult, this could mean that the parent has poor coping skills rather than that the child really is difficult.

Whether temperament is stable also depends on the environment (Wachs, 2006). For example, infants who are not inhibited may become inhibited later due to conflict among parents, abuse, or excessive criticism. In contrast, positive events could help some children improve. Thomas and Chess tell about a difficult child with behavior problems. A religious conversion at age 16 changed her, and by age 22 she was well adjusted (Thomas et al., 1970). Thus, temperament may remain the same for some children who have extreme traits or whose environment sustains their traits, but many children's temperament changes across childhood.

What Does Temperament Predict?

Children with any temperament could develop behavior problems, but *negative emotionality* is a risk factor. For example, Thomas and Chess found that 70% of difficult, but only 18% of easy, babies developed behavior problems across a fifteen-year span (Thomas et al., 1970). More-recent research has found that children with negative emotionality are more likely to experience drug use, depression, anxiety, aggressiveness, peer rejection, and low achievement (Rothbart & Bates, 1998; Sanson, Hemphill, & Smart, 2004; Schmitz et al., 1999).

Behavioral inhibition, on the other hand, is a protective factor for some of the same problems. Inhibited, cautious children are less prone to aggression and injuries than uninhibited, sensation-seeking children (Schwebel & Plummert, 1999). However, behavioral inhibition can also be a risk factor for social problems, but only for nonsociable children. This is a key distinction—inhibited children can be sociable or nonsociable. Remember that inhibition has to do with novelty. Inhibited, nonsociable children avoid social settings. Inhibited, sociable children avoid social settings with strangers, but enjoy social settings with people they know; they only appear shy with strangers. One of our children is a shy-sociable child. When we moved, she was silent in her new 5th-grade class and did not speak to any of her new peers at lunch for three months. She was miserable. However, some months later she was leading noisy "choo-choo trains" of children while waiting to board the school bus; they had become familiar peers. This distinction is important because nonsociable children are likely to be lonely and rejected by peers, while shy-sociable children have social skills and friends (Schmidt & Fox, 2002; Shiner, 1998).

Behavioral inhibition can also be a risk factor if the child remains quite shy until 9 to 10 years of age. Shyness in younger children is generally not a cause for concern. Some inhibited young children continue being mildly uncomfortable around new people into adolescence, like Eric, but not to the point of poor social skills. However, about half of children who continue to be extremely shy *are* more likely to develop anxiety disorders (Prior, Smart, Sanson, & Oberklaid, 2000). Thus, inhibition is a protective factor for aggression and injury, and only extreme shyness toward familiar others that persists through middle childhood is a risk factor for problems (Coplan & Armer, 2007; Sanson et al., 2004).

We have used the example of two traits, negative emotionality and behavioral inhibition, to show that temperament may affect child outcomes like aggression or academic achievement. However, child outcomes depend on the match, or **goodness of fit**, between temperament and the social environment, not temperament alone.

goodness of fit the degree of match between temperament and environmental demands, values, or expectations.

Goodness of Fit

A *good fit* exists when children's temperament matches the demands of their environment. Even if children have a genetic propensity toward a negative temperament trait, a good fit may result in children not manifesting the trait or manifesting it to a small degree, whereas a poor fit may magnify the trait. For example, one common poor fit is punitive parents of a child with a difficult temperament; this combination is linked to emotional and behavior problems in the child (De Clercq, Van Leeuwen, De Fruyt, Van Hiel, & Mervielde, 2008).

To illustrate the concept of goodness of fit, Thomas and Chess (1984) give the example of two difficult little girls. One had a warm, but firm father. She developed positively until her father died when she was 13. Her mother felt overwhelmed and could not set limits for her four children. The girl developed severe behavior problems in her teens as the fit went from good to bad. The second difficult girl had a rigid, critical, and punitive father; she became intense and explosive. Around age 10, she developed musical talent that her father admired. He became more positive toward her as he changed from thinking she was "rotten" to thinking she had an "artistic" temperament. She improved through adolescence and was well-adjusted by age 22 as the fit went from bad to good.

One aspect of goodness of fit is agreement between the child's "real" temperament and the parents' view of the "ideal" temperament. Imagine asking parents what child behaviors they find most annoying and then to rate their own child on those annoying behaviors. Parents who see their child as having few annoying behaviors have a good fit. You can do the same exercise. Ask yourself what child behaviors you find most annoying and which children in your classroom display those behaviors. You can help your students in two ways: become more accepting of the annoying behaviors if they are not harmful and kindly help them reduce the annoying behaviors.

Children fare best when parents and teachers adapt to them. Let's look at Eric again. Eric's parents seldom disciplined him because he was overly harsh on himself. His parents gently drew him into activities after modeling how to do things that Eric hesitated to do. At preschool he clung to his mother, so she stayed with him each day until he said that he was ready for her to leave—giving him control over the separation. The preschool teachers disapproved of this. They tried coercing Eric into participating in group time by giving him stickers, fearing that he was not learning anything. His mother did not worry, because at home Eric repeated everything that was said during group time, verbatim. Because of the good fit between parenting and child temperament, Eric developed strong academic and social skills and self-confidence. However, Eric did not become a dramatically outgoing adolescent. A good fit may result in optimal development of children, but not in movement to the opposite extreme of temperament traits.

What Predicts Temperament?

By the time babies are 4 months old, their temperament is apparent (Kagan et al., 2007). Does this mean temperament is genetic? Not necessarily. Even at this early age, temperament traits could be a result of social experience. Let's examine relevant factors.

Physiology and genetics

One temperament trait, behavioral inhibition, is known to have a physiological basis. In Chapter 2, you learned that compared to average children, inhibited children have faster heart rates, increased pupil dilation, more muscle tension, and higher levels of cortisol (a stress hormone) when they encounter a new situation.

Where do such physiological responses come from? They may be inherited. There is moderate-to-strong heritability ($h^2 = 0.30$ to 0.77) for inhibition, negative emotionality, and activity level. In contrast, other temperament traits, like soothability, positive emotionality, and effortful control, appear to have little heritability (Bokhorst et al., 2003; Ganiban, Saudino, Ulbricht, Neiderhiser, & Reiss, 2008).

However, heritability estimates are probably inflated because of **sibling-contrast bias**. That is, most studies of temperament use mothers' reports, and mothers tend to exaggerate differences among their children. When mothers' reports are used, temperament traits seem to have more heritability and less shared-environment contribution. But when observers' reports or objective measures (like activity meters) are used, the shared-environment contribution is substantial (Ganiban et al., 2008; Saudino & Zapfe, 2008).

sibling-contrast bias the tendency of family members to report greater difference among siblings than actually exists by evaluating them relative to each other.

What might cause such bias? Parents may have two children who are *less active than average*, but they view one child as highly active and the other as very calm

epigenetic a process where phenotype, or gene expression, is altered through social experience, or other mechanisms, rather than change in DNA.

allele a version of a gene that contributes to a specific type of attribute. For example, a gene that influences dopamine in the brain may have different alleles, one that leads to high levels of dopamine and another that leads to low levels.

because their frame of reference is their own children, rather than all possible children. Such comparison between siblings is a powerful component of the nonshared family environment (see Chapter 1).

Even if temperament has a physiological base, this does not mean it is entirely under genetic control. Physiological systems, including the brain, change with experience. For example, infants whose mothers are insensitive and intrusive develop a brain pattern characteristic of behavioral inhibition—an overly active right frontal lobe—by 9 months of age, regardless of how their brain started developing earlier in life (Hanes & Fox, 2006). Thus, even if some traits are partly heritable, there still is room for substantial contribution from parents and teachers. See Box 6.3 for remarkable research on how parenting and genes may interact.

Parenting and attachment

Parenting and attachment predict temperament. For example, children with parents who are negative or restrictive, and children with insecure attachment, tend to have low *effortful control* and be *emotionally negative* (Paulussen-Hoogeboom, Stams, Hermanns, & Peetsma, 2007; Valiente, Lemery-Chalfant, & Reiser, 2007). For another example, ambivalent children tend to be *nonsociably shy.* Perhaps this is because their parents are overly critical, or overly shielding, even during playtime when it is not called for (Burgess, Rubin, Cheah, & Nelson, 2005).

> ***Think About This*** How do the concepts of "genotype" and "phenotype" and "gene-environment interaction" from Chapter 1 pertain to the concept of goodness of align? How does the concept of differential susceptibility align with the concept of goodness of fit?

These data are correlational (see Chapter 1). This means you could argue that the child's temperament causes parent behavior, or vice versa. Perhaps parents have difficulty securely attaching to children who are fearful, irritable, or highly active. Yet, research supports Ainsworth's view that secure attachment is primarily driven by parent behavior, and the child's temperament makes only a small or no contribution. Many difficult infants become securely attached and less difficult over time with sensitive parenting (Bokhorst et al., 2003; Pauli-Pott, Haverkock, Pott, & Beckmann, 2007). Figure 6.1 presents a model for how parenting and temperament may combine to influence a child's emotional and social well-being.

differential susceptibility children differ in the extent to which they are susceptible to a good or bad environment based on their genotype.

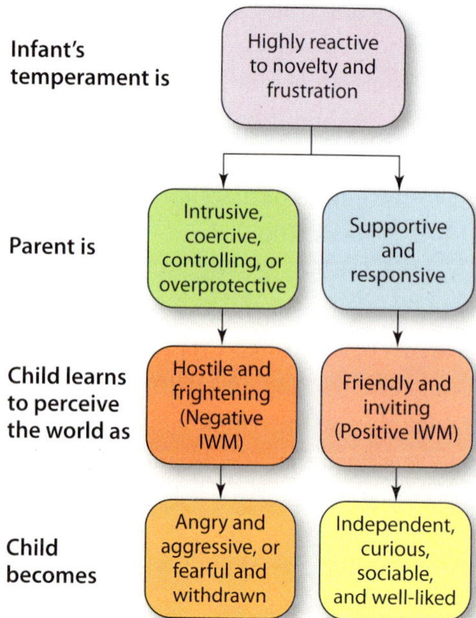

Figure 6.1 The Relationship Among Temperament, Parenting, and Child Outcomes. Which side of the model do Eric's experiences and development follow? Describe a child you have known who may have developed according to the other side of the model (IWM = internal working model).

Theories & Theorists **Box 6.3**

Revisiting Nature and Nurture

In Chapter 1 you were introduced to the interplay of nature (genes) and nurture (environment). This interplay applies to temperament and attachment, as well as many other child outcomes. Three principles of this interplay build on what you learned in Chapter 1.

1. *The environment may influence whether genes are expressed or not.* Genes are seldom destiny. In fact, many genes are never expressed. Genes are like a library filled with books that have the potential to influence you, but they have to be read to have their effect (Champagne & Mashoodh, 2009). Social experience can determine whether a gene is read or not. How might this work? One possibility is called *methylation*. Ongoing stressful experiences, such as having a hostile parent, can cause a methyl group to bind to some genes, which blocks the gene from being read. (A pat on the back if you remember methyl groups from chemistry class!) Methylation of genes can alter neurotransmitters in the brain, which can alter behavior. Through methylation social experience becomes biologically embedded in genes across generations (Champagne & Curley, 2009). This is how early childhood experiences can influence you in adulthood—and perhaps even your grandchildren. This process is called **epigenetic**, which means "beyond genetics."
2. *Genes may only influence child outcomes when acting together with environmental factors.* Genes alone seldom explain complex child behavior. For example, children have a gene called *DRD4*. One version of this gene—or **allele**—predisposes a child to be insecurely attached and to be highly reactive (e.g., their heart rate speeds up) to arousing events, like being separated from their mother. Whether children with this allele actually become insecure or highly reactive depends on their mothers' sensitivity (Propper et al., 2008). If their mothers are sensitive, they tend not to be any more reactive than children without the allele, and they tend to be secure. However, if children have the risk allele *and* poor parenting, they are nineteen times more likely to become insecure than children without the allele (Bernier & Meins, 2008). Other studies have found that children may only develop problems if they have a combination of both high-risk genes and a poor environment (e.g., Kim-Cohen & Gold, 2009; Wiebe et al., 2009).
3. *Genes may make some children more susceptible to their environment—for good or ill.* Children with high-risk genes may have below-average outcomes in negative environments, but above-average outcomes in positive environments because they process experiences more strongly than other children. This concept is known as **differential susceptibility**. For example, children with the high-risk *DRD4* allele tend to have more behavior problems and lower achievement than other children if they have insensitive parents. However, they tend to have higher achievement and behave exceptionally well if their parents are sensitive, emotionally positive, and use positive discipline (Bakermans-Kranenburg, Van IJzendoorn, Pijlman, Mesman, & Juffer, 2008). In other words, *some children are more susceptible to both good and bad parenting.* Perhaps this is why two children in the same family turn out differently—one is more susceptible to the family environment than the other.

Some psychologists borrow Swedish expressions: *orkidebarn* meaning "orchid child" to describe children who are more sensitive to their environment and *maskrosbarn* meaning "dandelion child" to describe children who thrive in whatever environment they are in—poor soil and too much or too little sun or rain (Ellis & Boyce, 2008). Eric, in the vignette, may be an orchid child. His life story fits research showing that temperamentally challenging children fare not just average, but exceptionally well when their environmental fit is good.

Image copyright Worakit Sirijinda. Used under license from Shutterstock.Com

Indars Grasbergs/iStockphoto.com

Orchids are exquisite, but only thrive in the right environment. Resilient dandelions thrive in many environments.

Figure 6.2 illustrates these last two principles. Children with high-risk genes often have harsh or insensitive parents, perhaps because of a passive gene–environment correlation (Propper et al., 2008). Notice the red arrow, which indicates that even when children have both a negative environment and genetic risk, some may develop well. What might lead to such resiliency? Two possibilities are (1) interventions to help the child and (2) a supportive relationship with an adult (Kim-Cohen & Gold, 2009). Thus, your students' social environment—including how you interact with them—powerfully shapes their development and may even modify their genes.

(continued)

Theories & Theorists (continued)

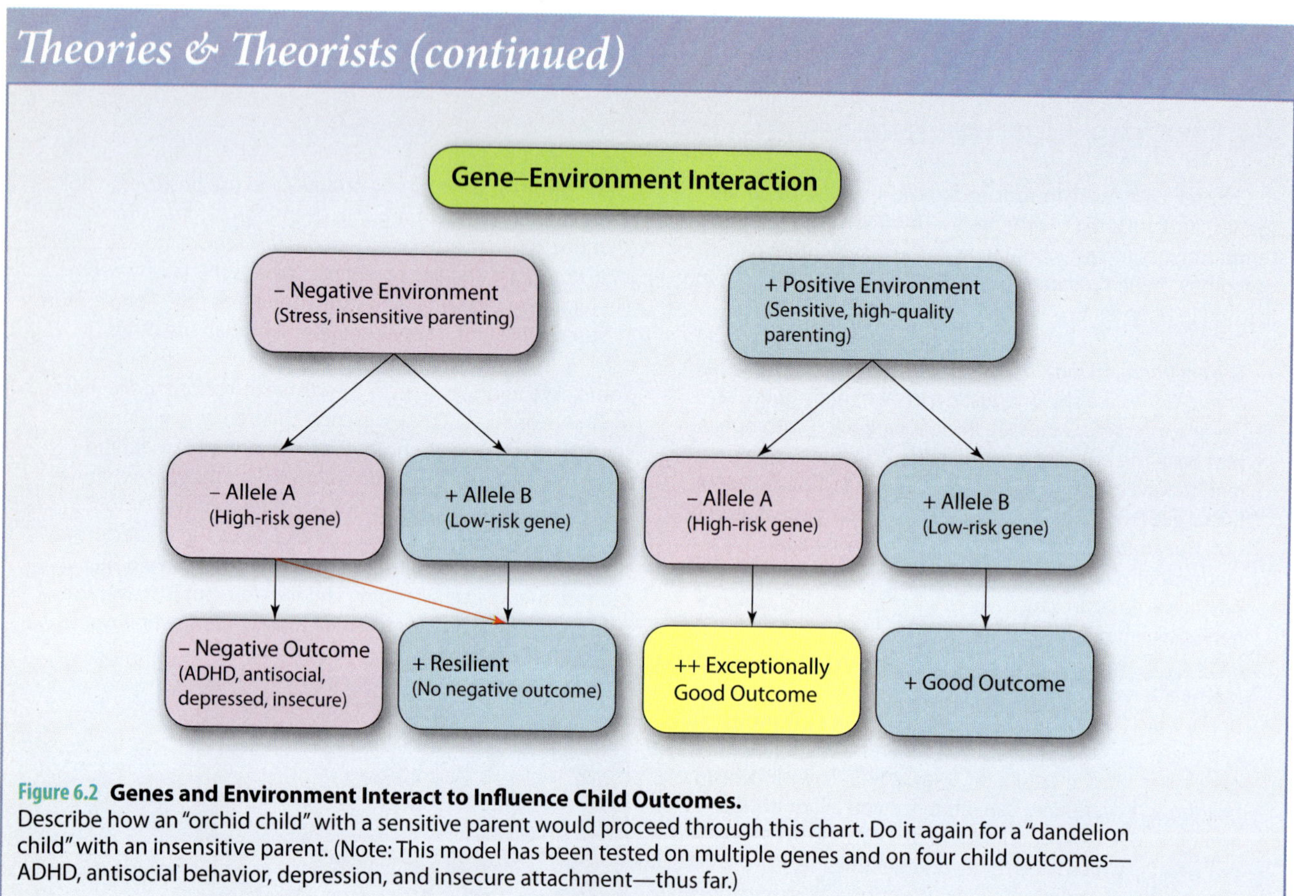

Figure 6.2 Genes and Environment Interact to Influence Child Outcomes.
Describe how an "orchid child" with a sensitive parent would proceed through this chart. Do it again for a "dandelion child" with an insensitive parent. (Note: This model has been tested on multiple genes and on four child outcomes—ADHD, antisocial behavior, depression, and insecure attachment—thus far.)

Group Diversity in Temperament

Have you heard others claim that there are stereotyped gender and national differences in temperament, like boys are more active than girls? Let's see if research confirms this.

Gender differences in temperament are small to nonexistent, with one clear exception: girls tend to be higher in effortful control, meaning they are less distractible or impulsive. This may help explain boys' higher rate of ADHD. In addition, parents report that school-age boys are more active than girls; however, motion detectors do not always confirm this. Adolescent girls report themselves as being more shy than boys; however, observers do not confirm this (Rubin, Burgess, & Coplan, 2002). Generally, no gender differences are found in negative emotionality or inhibition (Else-Quest, Hyde, Goldsmith, & Van Hulle, 2006). Thus, it is possible that small gender differences in both inhibition and activity actually exist, or that they are the result of biased perceptions.

Similar temperament traits are readily recognized across countries, and often have the same consequences. For example, in both China and the United States, children with negative emotionality and low effortful control have behavior problems at school. However, countries can vary in which temperament traits are valued, which influences goodness of fit. For example, there is a good fit for shyness, but not joviality, in Chinese culture. Chinese teachers view happy, boisterous children as behavior problems, and shy children as more socially competent. U.S. teachers tend to hold the opposite views (Chen & Tse, 2008; Zhou et al., 2009). In China inhibited toddlers are more likely to become well-liked, cooperative, and successful later in school compared with bold children (Chen, Chen, Li, & Wang, 2009). Interestingly, in the United States, shy children tend to have overcontrolling parents. In China, shy children tend to have accepting, encouraging parents who are not overcontrolling (Burgess et al., 2005). That is, *in both countries ideal parenting predicts valued traits.*

National differences in shyness may be changing as China is becoming a market economy. Recent research on children in urban Shanghai has found that shy behavior is less valued, while assertive, competitive behavior is becoming more valued (Chen, Gen, Li, & He, 2005). This is an example of the chronosystem in the bioecological model (see Chapter 1), which suggests that children will change as their culture changes over time.

This research on group diversity suggests that in your classroom you may not observe gender differences in temperament, except that girls, on average, may be better able to control their attention and behavior than boys. Cross-national differences may be larger than gender differences. Students in your classroom may have different temperament traits depending on what their home culture values. What are other implications for your classroom?

Classroom Implications of Temperament

Temperament affects classroom success. Children whose temperament fits their teacher's expectations earn better grades, have better relationships with the teacher and classmates, and have higher self-esteem than students with poor fit. Most teachers prefer students with (1) low activity and (2) high control (Lerner, Lerner, & Zabski, 1985). Children with these traits have a good fit in most classrooms. One exception is that *highly active* children may have higher test scores despite this trait *not* being valued by teachers (Lerner, 1983). Let's look at how the concept of goodness of fit applies to Kevin.

Kevin is in a team-taught 7th-grade class with two teachers. He is a good student, but never takes his seat at the beginning of class. Instead, he goes to the bookshelf to flip through an atlas, look through a kaleidoscope, and talk to classmates for a few minutes. This annoys one of his teachers, who scolds him and, as a result, the two are constantly irritated with each other. His other teacher, in contrast, appreciates Kevin's curiosity and high energy level. She allows him the few minutes at the beginning of class to "cruise" the room while she puts other students to work. They have an agreement that in return for this privilege, he will not get out of his seat during the lesson.

Kevin's temperament is a poor fit with his first teacher's expectations, whereas it is a good fit with his second teacher who values, or at least accommodates, high activity in her classroom.

> ***Think About This*** *David was a shy-sociable, cautious child. His younger brother, Raul, was a sociable, highly active, boisterous, risk-taking child. David earned primarily A's in high school, and scored at the 94th percentile on the SAT. Raul earned primarily C's in the same classes, and scored at the 95th percentile on the SAT.*
>
> What do you suspect about the goodness of fit at school for these brothers? Do their different achievements fit the research?

Two key lessons about temperament may help you be a more effective teacher. First, you may need to occasionally change how you think about specific children who are challenging for you. To do this:

- Recognize that temperament traits that are a good fit in some settings may not be a good fit in the classroom. For example, high activity level is not a problem during a soccer game, but it is a problem when a child is asked to sit still for forty-five minutes during a lesson. Appreciate the positive side of temperament traits, like Kevin's second teacher did, rather than getting annoyed by them.
- Avoid mistakenly assuming children who cannot sit still do not want to learn or are intentionally disobeying you. They may simply find the sit-still demands of the classroom too difficult.
- Avoid confusing shyness with poor social skills. Shy-nonsociable children, who are shy even with known peers, *are* likely to have social problems, but not shy-sociable children.
- Avoid confusing shyness with low self-esteem or low ability as Eric's 1st-grade teacher mistakenly did. Anxiety in novel situations is not the same as being anxious about one's personal worth. Although shy children may not show off their intellect in your class, this does not mean they know less than uninhibited children.

The second key lesson is that as the teacher you are responsible for creating a good fit between the child and the classroom whenever possible. Children's temperament can influence the quality of relationship you develop. One study found that teachers developed conflicted relationships with children low in effortful control and distant relationships with shy children (Rudasill & Rimm-Kaufman, 2009). You will have to problem-solve to adapt the classroom to individual students you find challenging. Here are a few suggestions to get you started:

- Ensure that highly active children have an outlet for their energy, like adequate recess or freedom to move about the room, as Kevin's second teacher did.
- If available, use more computer-directed instruction with distractible, active children. They may spend more time-on-task with computer-directed instruction because it is gamelike, provides immediate feedback, and requires one-on-one attention toward the computer.
- Give shy children control whenever possible. Allow them to pace their approach to new situations. For example, Miss Loeb allowed Le'Raun to decide whether he wanted to play "stump the teacher," and let him do it privately. Do not be overzealous, intrusive, or push shy children. Shyness is a way of coping with strong physiological reactions, like a racing heart. Intrusive teachers interfere with the child's coping mechanism of gradual comfort and cause the child to feel greater stress (Nachmias, Gunnar, Mangelsdorf, Parritz, & Buss, 1996).
- Reduce shy children's stress by giving them repeated exposure to a new task or situation and by keeping them with their friends when making group assignments.

Some temperament traits will challenge even the most adaptive teachers, particularly negative emotionality. We will discuss how to handle negative emotions and aggression in Chapters 8 and 10.

In summary, the major lessons on temperament for teachers are that (1) many aspects of temperament are not heritable, and even those that are heritable are influenced by the environment; (2) while temperament may stay the same over time, it is not very stable in most children; (3) negative emotionality and poor control are associated with behavior problems, but inhibition and high activity level are not in the United States; and (4) even children with difficult temperament can develop secure attachment, social competence, and high academic achievement when there is good fit with classroom demands. Thus, temperament does not *determine* life outcomes. We turn our attention now to personality, the result of temperament, attachment, and other childhood experiences.

Personality

As 4th-graders crowd around their teacher's desk to retrieve corrected homework, Adam hangs back, sitting quietly at his desk. After the crowd clears, Adam timidly approaches and asks the teacher a question. Adam rarely speaks in class or raises his hand, yet he stays focused. On writing assignments, he carefully reads through sentences and corrects them before going on to the next. At recess, he stands by himself and watches some boys play basketball in the courtyard.

That same morning Cory goes to the front of the room and yells, "Something stinks over here! Who cut the cheese?" The other students laugh. Cory is always smiling. Occasionally, he makes funny faces at classmates until they smile back. He usually answers questions correctly, but when he answers incorrectly, he just laughs at himself. He stays focused on assignments and pays attention when the teacher speaks. At recess, he plays jump rope with a group and invites others to join in.

That same morning Brian runs into the classroom late. He stumbles and drops his papers on the floor. He throws his wrinkled folder on his desk and bends down to pick up the papers, but realizes his shoes are untied. He forgets the papers and ties his shoes. His teacher gives extensive instructions about a test, but when handed the test, Brian scowls and asks the girl next to him, "What's this?" During the test he scratches his head, picks his fingernails, and whispers "this sucks!" every few seconds. Brian writes an answer, erases it, and writes another, then erases some more. The test is illegible. At recess, he chases other kids around, falling down or running into others. He hurts his leg.

These three boys have obvious personality differences. **Personality** refers to enduring behavior and temperament traits. Do you recognize the temperament traits of behavioral inhibition in Adam or negative emotionality in Brian? Temperament is the activity and emotion core of personality. Personality, however, includes much

personality a constellation of traits that distinguishes one person from another.

Field Observation

Rate yourself on a 5-point scale (1 = low; 5 = high) on the five traits. Do the same for a child you know well. What traits do each of you have? What personality type do you fall into?

more. Personality can be thought of as a hierarchy (see Figure 6.3). Temperament and attachment form the foundation for specific personality traits, which are organized into a few personality types.

personality traits the tendency to behave, think, and feel in certain consistent ways. Five traits that account for much of the variation in personality are openness, conscientiousness, extraversion, agreeableness, and neuroticism (OCEAN).

openness to experience a personality trait that includes curiosity, exploration, imaginative dreaming, creativeness, good self-expression, and being smart.

conscientiousness a personality trait contrasted with lack of direction. It includes getting things done, not giving up easily, being dependable, planning ahead, and orderliness.

extraversion a personality trait contrasted with social inhibition. It includes high energy; talkativeness; emotional expressiveness; and being fast-paced, reactive, and full of life.

agreeableness a personality trait contrasted with antagonism. It includes thoughtfulness, warmth, kindness, cooperation, and getting along with and pleasing others.

neuroticism a personality trait contrasted with emotional stability. It includes nervousness, worry, perseverating or falling apart under stress, insecurity, and needing reassurance.

Personality traits refer to "individual differences in the tendency to behave, think, and feel in certain consistent ways" (Caspi, 1998, p. 312). There are thousands of words you might use to describe yourself—outgoing, kind, patient, explosive, talkative, creative. Psychologists have identified five broad traits that account for most of the words people use to describe adults and children. They are known as the five-factor model (FFM) or the *Big Five.*

1. **Openness to experience**. Open people are smart (but may not necessarily get good grades), creative, and curious. They enjoy exploring new situations, express themselves well, and get lost in thought and wrapped up in projects.
2. **Conscientiousness**. Conscientious people are neat, orderly, and reliable. They get things done, do not give up easily, set high standards for themselves, and think before acting.
3. **Extraversion**. Extraverts are energetic, talkative, sensation seeking, and full of life. They react quickly and show emotions openly.
4. **Agreeableness**. Agreeable people are thoughtful of others, warm, kind, helpful, and cooperative. They are liked by others.
5. **Neuroticism** (versus emotional stability). Neurotic people are anxious and insecure. They worry excessively, go to pieces or get sick under stress, and feel hurt easily.

(You can remember these five traits with the mnemonic "OCEAN.") You have probably noticed links between temperament traits and the Big Five personality traits:

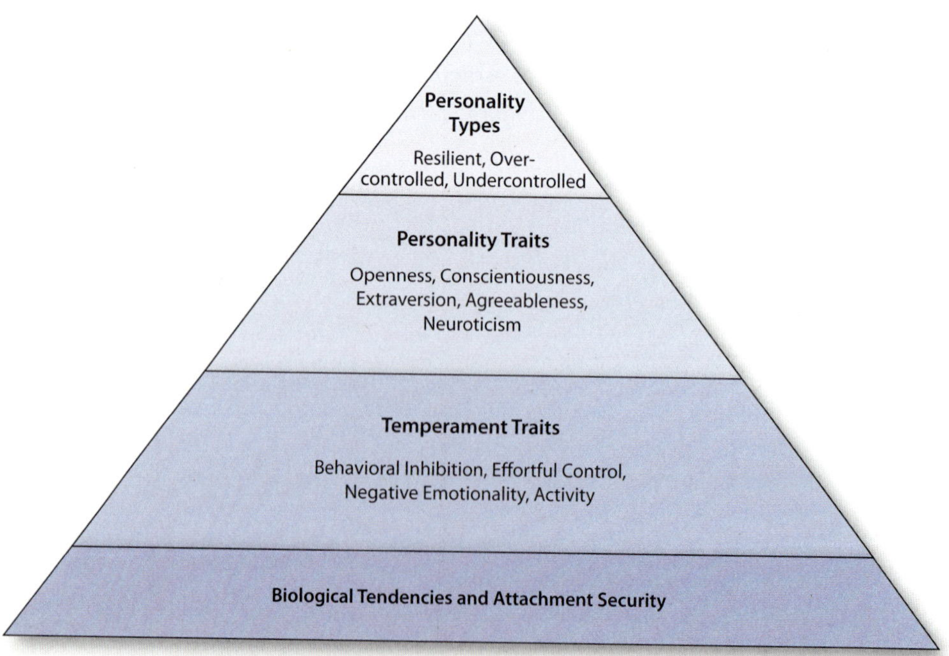

Figure 6.3 **Hierarchical Organization of Personality.**
Can you describe your own personality as you begin at the bottom and progress up the pyramid?

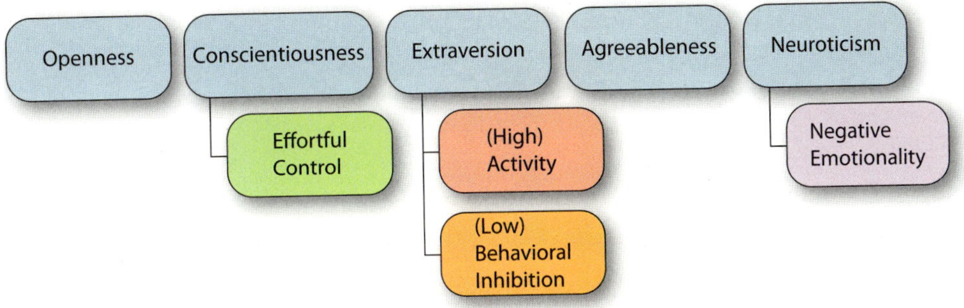

Figure 6.4 **The "Big Five" Personality Traits and Their Core Temperament Traits.** Read the descriptions of each of the Big Five traits. Can you see why each core temperament trait might lead to a specific personality trait?

negative emotionality is the core of neuroticism; activity and lack of inhibition are the core of extraversion; control is the core of conscientiousness (Rothbart, 2007). (See Figure 6.4.)

These five traits do not include all personality dimensions, but they are inclusive enough to predict important outcomes (Kline, 2001). These traits are somewhat independent. That is, a particular child may score high in one trait but low in another. However, the five *traits* tend to cluster together to form three personality *types*.

Research has identified three distinct personality types in children—resilient, overcontrolled, and undercontrolled. This doesn't mean that there are only three types, but rather that these three are easily identifiable. More than 75% of children—across ages, ethnicities, and countries—readily fit into one of these personality types, with most having the resilient type. Table 6.2 shows the traits that comprise each personality type.

personality types clusters of personality traits that tend to occur together. The most commonly identified in children are resilient, overcontrolled, and undercontrolled types.

resilient a personality type characterized by very high levels of openness and conscientiousness, above average levels of extraversion and agreeableness, and very low levels of neuroticism.

overcontrolled a nonresilient personality type characterized by high agreeableness and neuroticism, and particularly low extraversion.

undercontrolled a nonresilient personality type characterized by particularly low agreeableness and conscientiousness, but also low-average neuroticism and openness.

Individual Diversity in Personality

Adam's and Cory's personalities may fit the classroom better than Brian's. What does personality mean for children in the classroom and beyond? Before developing this idea, let's see if children have the same personality across time and across situations.

How Stable Is Personality across Time?

Temperament and attachment are considered the foundation of personality. Given that both temperament and attachment can change across childhood, but generally do not, you might expect the same for personality. Research confirms that personality traits and types sometimes change, but not frequently. For example, in one study, the personality of 8-year-olds predicted their personality at age 36 in two out of three cases (Laursen, Pulkkinen, & Adams, 2002).

Positive traits and types tend to be more stable than negative. For example, agreeable children tend to become agreeable adults. Resilient children tend to remain resilient, whereas under- or overcontrolled children are more likely to change. Change depends on the environment. If the environment is stable, personality tends to remain stable. However, personality can change, even into old age (Dweck, 2008; Roberts & Mroczek, 2008). Indeed, that is one of the goals of psychotherapy.

Table 6.2 Personality types by personality traits

Personality type	Resilient	Overcontrolled	Undercontrolled
Percentage of children	50–70%	10–30%	20–30%
Big Five traits	High openness High conscientiousness Low neuroticism	Low extraversion High agreeableness High neuroticism	High extraversion Low agreeableness Low conscientiousness
Other traits	Confident, competent, verbally fluent, concentrates well, reasonable, compliant, and helpful. Not fearful or anxious.	Helpful, obedient, well-liked, quiet, inhibited, compliant, and indecisive. Not aggressive, assertive, or competitive.	Energetic, restless, antisocial, impulsive, active, cheerful, indecisive, assertive, and unable to concentrate.

The percentage of children in each type comes from studies in the United States and Europe.

Sources: Asendorpf & Van Aken, 1999; Hart, Atkins, & Fegley, 2003; Robins, John, Caspi, Moffitt, & Stouthamer-Loeber, 1996; van Lieshout, 2000.

How Stable Is Personality across Situations?

Would you be surprised to find that Adam is bossy at home with his siblings, even though he is timid at school? An individual's personality can change from situation to situation. A famous 1971 study, known as the Stanford University Prison Experiment, showed that situations can powerfully affect behavior. For two weeks, twenty male Stanford students were randomly assigned to be either inmates or guards at a pretend prison in the basement of the psychology building. All the students were chosen for their stable, healthy personalities, yet the experiment had to be cut short after just a few days because the "guards" changed from being agreeable to being cruel to the "inmates." This experiment shows how personality can change based on the situation. Both personality traits and the situation contribute to how a child will behave at any given moment.

Your intuition at this moment is probably telling you this is not true; personality cannot be situation-dependent because you like specific friends due to traits, such as extraversion, that they seem to have all the time. The conflict between such intuitive beliefs and the research indicating personality changes across situations is called the *personality paradox*. To help resolve this paradox, scientists observed children in five different situations: (1) being teased or threatened by a peer, (2) receiving a warning from an adult, (3) being punished by an adult, (4) being praised by an adult, and (5) being approached socially by a peer (Mischel, Shoda, & Mendoza-Denton, 2002). The scientists found consistency in the children's personalities *within similar situations*, but not across the five different situations. For example, they found that one child was less aggressive than average when approached by a peer, but more aggressive than average when warned by an adult. A second child had the opposite pattern.

Revisiting Case 3

What were Le'Raun's "if . . . then" patterns?

This means that personality is not a simple collection of traits (e.g., "he is aggressive"), but rather a series of "if . . . then" scenarios. For example, if a child is threatened by an adult, then he is aggressive, but if he is approached by a peer who wants to play, then he is not aggressive. Two children may have the same average level of aggression, but their "if . . . then" pattern could be different. Personality is more consistent across different situations when we know the "if . . . then" patterns for each child. The situation dictates the "if" conditions, and the personality dictates the "then" responses.

What Does Personality Predict?

Your students' Big Five traits predict important outcomes, often *better than IQ* or *SES* (Meyer et al., 2001). Personality traits in childhood have been linked to physical and mental health, length of life, happiness in marriage, and career success in adulthood. In particular, high conscientiousness and low neuroticism are linked to better outcomes (Hampson, 2008; Lahey, 2009). Personality is also linked to academic achievement and social competence in students.

Academic achievement

Personality *traits* predict achievement, regardless of intelligence (Noftle & Robins, 2007; Zsolnai, 2002). Highly conscientious, agreeable, and open students tend to have higher GPAs. One exception is that at the high school level, high-open students tend to have higher SAT scores, but not necessarily good grades. *The effect of conscientiousness is about as large as intelligence* (Poropat, 2009). The other two personality traits—extraversion and neuroticism—are not consistently linked to achievement. Extraverted or neurotic children may be either good or poor students.

Personality *types* also predict achievement. Resilient and overcontrolled students tend to have higher achievement than undercontrolled students. For example, in one study the achievement of undercontrolled students declined steadily across elementary school; the decline was equivalent to missing a full year of school (Hart et al., 2003). (See Figure 6.5.) You can understand how personality types might affect achievement if you compare Adam and Cory with Brian in the vignette. Brian, who is undercontrolled, misses out on much of what happens in his classroom, whereas Adam and Cory are fully engaged.

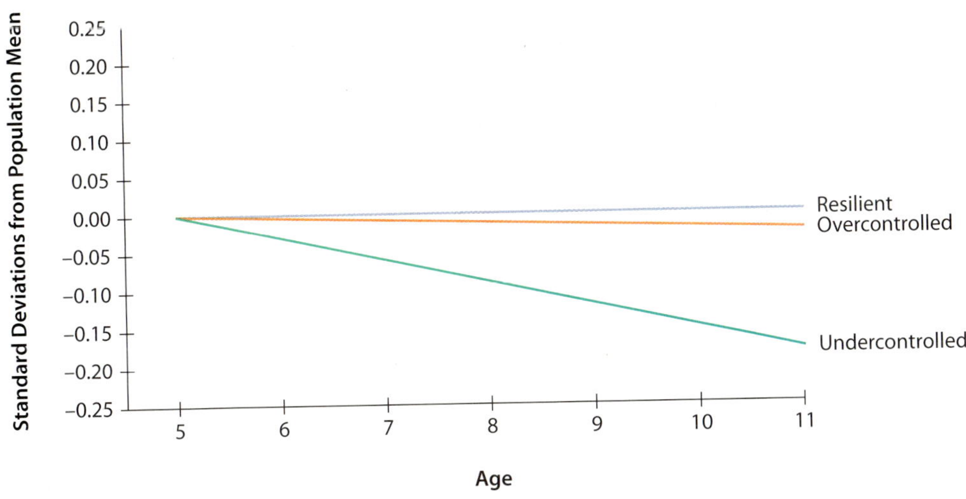

Figure 6.5 Personality Type and Achievement over Time.
In this graph, 0 is the average of all children (also called the "population mean"). Positive numbers indicate achievement that is above average, and negative numbers indicate achievement that is below average. When children are followed from ages 5 to 11, those with resilient and overcontrolled personality types remain near average. What happens over time for children with undercontrolled personalities? *Hart et al. (2003).*

Social competence

Personality *traits* predict students' social competence. Highly conscientious, agreeable students tend to have fewer behavior problems at school (Caspi, 1998; Laursen et al., 2002). In contrast, adolescent boys low in conscientiousness and agreeableness but high in *extraversion* are more likely than other youth to be seriously delinquent, like selling drugs, breaking and entering, and joy riding (John, Caspi, Robins, Moffitt, & Stouthamer-Loeber, 1994). Personality *types* are also related to social competence. Overcontrolled boys tend to be socially withdrawn, while undercontrolled boys tend to be aggressive (Asendorpf & Van Aken, 1999; Hart, Hofmann, Edelstein, & Keller, 1997).

What Predicts Personality?

Where do Adam's, Cory's and Brian's personalities come from? According to attachment theory, their personalities are primarily the result of their temperament and attachment history. Parent–child attachment may become part of the child's personality through the child's internal working models (Hagekull & Bohlin, 2003). Research confirms that attachment security is related to many personality traits such as curiosity, persistence, enthusiasm, cheerfulness, sociability, impulsiveness, anger, and anxiety.

Personality may also be the result of genes. Research suggests that 20 to 60% of the Big Five personality traits may be heritable, but it varies by trait. Agreeableness, which is strongly influenced by the family environment, may be the least heritable and most stable trait (Laursen et al., 2002). In contrast, openness has the strongest genetic component, presumably because it overlaps so much with definitions of intelligence. In fact, there is debate about whether openness is a personality factor or a cognitive ability (Kline, 2001; Noftle & Robins, 2007). As you learned in Chapter 5, intelligence is one of the most heritable traits among nonimpoverished students.

Extraversion also has a strong genetic component. This is probably because activity level and behavioral inhibition, which form the basis of extraversion, are among the most heritable temperament traits. However, these temperament traits do change when the environment changes. Thus, even among the two most heritable traits, openness and extraversion, there is substantial room for environmental contributions, such as family relationships and school experiences.

Group Diversity in Personality

Socioeconomic status is linked to personality types. Students with low SES are more likely to change from resilient to undercontrolled over time, presumably because risk factors make it difficult to remain resilient. Yet, low-SES students who are resilient are likely to do well because personality type can be as powerful a predictor of academic achievement as SES (Hart et al., 2003). Thus, helping low-SES students develop resilient personalities is important.

Cohort Effect

Have you ever heard veteran teachers say, "Kids today just aren't like they used to be?" Children do vary in personality depending on when they were born. Society-wide changes can result in personality differences in birth cohorts, or children born at one time compared with children born at another time. For example, anxiety/neuroticism increased steadily in the United States from the 1950s to the 1980s among

9- to 17-year-olds (Twenge, 2000). The increase was large; the *average* scores in the 1980s were equivalent to scores for children with psychiatric problems in the 1950s. This increase in anxiety/neuroticism may be related to social changes—like more divorces, fewer siblings, less trust in others, and more crime.

Cross-National Comparisons

National culture contributes to differences in personality. Cultures dictate what attributes are valued and emphasized in childrearing. For example, we have already discussed how shyness is valued more in China than in the United States. Thus, it is not surprising that U.S. adolescents whose parents emigrated from China are less extraverted than European American adolescents (Huntsinger & Jose, 2006).

Does this mean that people from different countries have different personalities? Research comparing dozens of countries, using careful translations, indicates that the Big Five personality traits are readily identified across countries and that there are national differences (Heine & Buchtel, 2009). For example, when nations are grouped together, Europeans, on average, are more extraverted than Asians and Africans (McCrae, Terracciano, & 79 Members of the Personality Profiles of Cultures Project, 2005; Oakland, Mogaji, & Dempsey, 2006).

Does this mean that common stereotypes of national personalities are true—like Germans are industrious, English are reserved, Australians are extraverted, and so forth? Studies in more than thirty countries have found that the personalities of most people do *not* match international stereotypes. For example, the English and Australians are similarly outgoing, despite opposite stereotypes (McCrae & Terracciano, 2006). Nevertheless, there is some evidence in support of national personalities (Heine, Buchtel, & Norenzayan, 2008). Let's look at how cultural influences on personality affected Janea in an American high school.

Classroom Implications of Personality

Janea's (pronounced "j ahn ae") parents are well-educated war refugees from a central African culture that values soft voices and reticence. At Open House, they wait at the door of the classroom until invited to step in by the teacher. They find the loud voices and assertiveness of Janea's classmates distasteful. Her teacher initially thought Janea was not very bright or self-confident because she was hesitant to answer questions in class, but over time it became clear that Janea was a gifted student. Janea became more extraverted and louder as she interacted with American classmates over time, but when she talked to her parents her voice dropped dramatically to a quiet, gentle tone.

Janea, like many immigrant children, is developing a dual personality. This is stressful, particularly when traits from the heritage culture are not valued by the new culture. However, Janea is resilient, partly because her teacher genuinely admires Janea and is a sensitive teacher. You, too, can help your students be resilient.

There are two key lessons for teachers from the research on personality. First, the personality traits and types of your students can have as large an effect on their

Think About This A well-known saying in personality psychology is "every child is like all other children, like some other children, and like no other children" (we've liberally paraphrased). Can you apply attachment, temperament, and personality to this phrase? In what way is every child alike or different?

success in your classroom as intelligence or SES. Second, personality can change across childhood and across situations, as it did for Janea. If a child has traits that lead to social or academic problems, you may try to modify the child's personality. No one is completely bound by their personality traits. Think about Le'Raun in case 3. In Miss Loeb's room he was open, agreeable, and conscientious, but not in Mrs. Richardson's room. Le'Raun illustrates the situation-specific nature of personality; different teachers evoked different personality traits in him. Thus, how you interact with your students can influence which personality attributes they develop.

How can you bring out the best personality traits in your students? Follow the guidelines for creating secure attachment and providing a good fit for your students' temperament, discussed above. Two additional guidelines are:

- Learn the "if" triggers for behavior in specific children. If you can reduce each child's triggers for misbehavior, and increase triggers for good behavior, the best of each child's personality will come through.
- Be aware of culturally based differences in personality. For example, some students may come from cultures that value extraversion, but others do not, like Janea. Respect cultural differences in personality among your students. Try to make what families value fit with your expectations in class. This requires getting to know each student's culture and examining your own values. However, also remain appropriately skeptical about personality stereotypes, and do not assume a child has a particular trait based on the child's culture, such as assuming all Chinese American students are shy. Remember that, as with most group differences, variation within cultures can be greater than the variation between cultures.

Now that we are at the conclusion of this chapter, you should have a deeper understanding of the importance of attachment relationships in forming a student's personality and behavior. You can serve as an attachment figure to students, and influence their personalities. Personality is partly dependent on the classroom situation. You can do much to create a good fit for children with varied temperament and personality in your classroom. However, you will find that some students will make this challenging because of their misbehavior. Managing misbehavior is the focus of the next chapter.

Reflections on Practice: Checklist for Teachers

To consider whether you are promoting secure attachment and positive personality traits in your students, periodically reflect on your classroom practices. Ask yourself the following:

1. What is my attachment to my own parents? How does it affect my expectations of my students and my sensitivity toward them?
2. Do I have a sense of the kind of relationship students have with their parents and its effect on the relationship they have with me? Can I recognize insecure or secure attachment in my students? What attachment behaviors are age-appropriate for my students?
3. What sort of relationship do I have with each student? Could it be considered secure?
4. Am I sensitive and responsive with each student? Is it clear that I care for each student? What kind of internal working model might my students develop about relationships based on their interaction with me?
5. What am I doing to promote school bonding? Are most students likely to report that they feel cared for at my school?
6. Am I aware of the temperament of each child in my class? Is there a good fit with my teaching approach? (You can test this by listing the traits you expect in your classroom. Then rate each child on those traits.)
7. Am I giving very shy or inhibited children control and allowing them to warm up slowly to novel situations?
8. Which of the Big Five personality traits do I observe in each of my students? Can I respond appropriately to students who fit into the three personality types (resilient, overcontrolled, and undercontrolled)?
9. Am I aware of the "if . . . then" triggers for good and bad behavior among my students?
10. Am I aware of how students' cultural backgrounds might affect their behavior? At the same time, do I avoid stereotyping?

Summary of Age Trends in Attachment and Personality

	Attachment Behaviors	Consequences of Secure Attachment	Temperament	Personality
Early Childhood (Birth–5 Years)	Infants' attachment becomes apparent between 6 and 12 months by their smiling and orienting toward the attachment figure (AF). Stranger wariness is typically apparent about 8–9 months, and wanes after 12 months. Internal working models (IWMs) are in place by 12 months. After age 3, IWMs tend to be stable. Children's attachment to their teacher and others is likely to reflect the quality of their primary attachment. Secure base behaviors are activated less easily and are less intense after age 3. By 3–4 years, extreme separation distress has waned. Children can feel secure in a strange place with subordinate AFs.	Secure attachment fosters the following: good emotion-regulation ability, frustration tolerance, persistence, flexibility, compliance, enthusiasm, and cheerfulness. Longer attention span, and less hyperactivity. More inclination to stay on mother's lap and be attentive to the book while reading. Better prereading skills and attitudes toward reading. Social competence. More liked by teachers and peers. More harmonious and intimate friendships. Less anger and aggression. Less likely to start fights and victimize others or be victims.	Temperamental traits are reliably observed by 4 months. Early childhood shyness does not predict later outcomes, but early negativity does predict later antisocial behavior.	Temperament may be synonymous with personality in infancy. The "Big Five" personality factors have been identified in 3-year-olds. The three personality types—resilient, undercontrolled, and overcontrolled—have also been identified in preschoolers.
Middle Childhood (6–12 Years)	Children still enjoy proximity to their AF but need less physical contact, explore more widely, and tolerate greater separation. Attachment behaviors are more subtle, and a larger range of conditions can make children feel secure. The AF's availability remains very important.	Secure attachment fosters the following: Social competence. More friends. Less anger, aggression, dishonesty, argumentativeness, disruptiveness, withdrawal, and anxiety. Less likely to be ridiculed or excluded by peers. Less likely to start fights, be victims, or victimize others. Less likely to be either clingy or defiant with teachers. Less likely to have ADHD symptoms and academic problems.	Extreme behavioral inhibition that persists through middle childhood predicts social anxiety in adolescence.	Conscientiousness, agreeableness, and openness all predict achievement. Each personality type has been associated with a specific pattern of school achievement and social competence.
Adolescence (13–19 Years)	"Touching base" behaviors are less frequent and more subtle. Self-reliance and independence result from feeling secure. Mother, rather than peers, remains at the top of the hierarchy for most. Teens who were securely attached as infants are likely to be securely attached in adolescence, unless negative events occur. Secondary schools are less likely to meet children's needs for attachment and bonding than elementary schools. Participation in extracurricular activities becomes important. Security of attachment is associated with quality of romantic relationships.	Secure attachment fosters the following: Social competence and independence. Less anger and aggression. Less likely to start fights and be victims or victimize others. Less likely to experience depression, suicidal thoughts, substance use, conduct disorders, eating disorders, or social withdrawal. More likely to have higher math scores, better reading comprehension, and higher GPAs.	Difficult infants are more likely to have behavior problems in adolescence. Temperament is only modestly stable, except at the extremes. Behavioral inhibition in toddlerhood generally does not predict inhibition in adolescence.	Conscientiousness and agreeableness predict achievement.

Chapter Summary

Attachment

- Attachment keeps the parent and young child in proximity to each other, and the older child feeling secure. Ethologists believe attachment promotes survival and exploration of new environments. John Bowlby pointed out that attachment is normal, innate, and necessary for healthy development. Mary Ainsworth pointed out that clingy or avoidant behavior indicates insecure attachment and that quality of care predicts security of attachment.
- Attachment varies in quality. Children with secure attachment are readily soothed, emotionally open, and able to use their attachment figure as a secure base to explore. There are three types of insecure attachment. Resistant children have exaggerated emotions and are not able to use their attachment figure as a secure base. Avoidant children appear emotionally indifferent to their attachment figure. Disorganized children have no coherent response to their attachment figure. Quality of attachment is fairly stable across childhood but can change if risk factors change.
- Secure children have sensitive, responsive parents. Resistant children have confusing, inconsistent parents. Avoidant children have intrusive, rejecting parents. Disorganized children are frightened by their parents. Across SES groups, there are differences in the rate of secure attachment, which are related to differences in quality of caregiving.
- Security of attachment predicts social competence, academic achievement, and many other factors. Attachment is thought to have such wide effects through internal working models that become a part of the child's personality by age 3.
- Children can securely attach to teachers who are sensitive and positive. Attachment to teachers and bonding with school affect social and academic success in school.

Temperament

- Temperament traits are observed early in infancy, but are only moderately stable—unless children have extreme traits, and their environments sustain the traits.
- Some, but not all, aspects of temperament are partially heritable. What is inherited may be differences in physiological arousal, which are also influenced by attachment.
- Some temperament traits have long-term consequences for children. Emotional negativity is a risk factor for antisocial behavior, while inhibition is a protective factor. Inhibition is linked to social or emotional problems, but only for nonsociable children who are extremely shy past early childhood.
- Genes and the environment interact to determine a child's temperament and attachment in three ways: (1) The environment may influence whether genes are expressed. (2) Genes may only influence child outcomes when acting together

with environmental factors. (3) High-risk genes may make some children more susceptible to both a good and bad environment.

- Development depends on the goodness of fit between the child's temperament and the environment. Children whose temperamental traits match the teacher's expectations may have greater social and academic success at school.

Personality

- Five traits have been identified that account for much of the variation in personality: openness, conscientiousness, extraversion, agreeableness, and neuroticism (OCEAN). The Big Five traits tend to cluster together into three personality types: resilient, overcontrolled, and undercontrolled.
- Temperament and attachment are the basis of personality. They are both moderately stable, but modifiable, so personality is only moderately stable. Culture also influences personality.
- Personality can be inconsistent across situations. Personality may be thought of as a series of "if . . . then" combinations. If the situation is similar, then behavior is consistent.
- Personality traits and types are linked to social and academic competence. Agreeable and conscientious traits and resilient types are linked to school success.
- Teachers can help children with different personalities fare well in their classrooms by learning if-then triggers for each child, providing a good fit, and respecting cultural differences.

Accompanying Education CourseMate Website Resources

Visit the **Education CourseMate** website at **CengageBrain.com** to find resources and study aids for this chapter, including self-tests, additional print and website resources, and glossary flashcards. In addition, you can watch the following video, which illustrates the development of attachment in infancy:

- 0–2 Years: Attachment in Infants and Toddlers

chapter 7

Self-Control and Discipline

Dave & Les Jacobs/Blend Images/Jupiter Images

HOW CAN YOU HELP A STUDENT WHO DISRUPTS YOUR CLASS DEVELOP MORE SELF-CONTROL? What is the best way to handle discipline so that learning is not derailed? These are questions teachers face daily. In this chapter we will discuss self-control, effective discipline, and teaching styles. After you read this chapter, you will understand:

- How students develop self-control and why it matters.
- How to discipline effectively and manage your classroom to maximize learning.
- How styles of parenting and teaching influence students' self-control.

Self-Control

Clint, who is in 8th grade, talks with his classmates before class starts. He is not being loud or obnoxious. His teacher, Mrs. Reinhardt, asks him to be quiet, but says nothing to the others. Later in the class, Clint joins a conversation of students sitting behind him. Mrs. Reinhardt tells him he should know the rules and stop acting up. He asks, "Why do you pick on me when everyone else is talking?" Mrs. Reinhardt gives him a red card, as a warning for misbehavior, and tells him that if he misbehaves again, she will send him to the principal's office. In irritation Clint snarls, "This sucks!" He is sent to the office.

When Clint arrives at the principal's office, he is too angry to speak coherently. The principal tells him to sit in the hallway until he calms down. Instead, Clint walks away. The principal catches Clint. They discuss what happened and the principal tells Clint to apologize to Mrs. Reinhardt, which he does.

Clint has difficulty resisting impulses or anticipating the consequences of his behavior. He has low self-control. Will Mrs. Reinhardt's approach to discipline improve Clint's self-control? This chapter will help you answer this question and clarify how your use of discipline influences your students' self-control. First let's discuss what self-control is and how it develops.

self-control the ability to control one's own behavior and emotions, obey rules, inhibit inappropriate action, and focus attention.

delay of gratification an aspect of self-control in which children delay what they desire right now in order to get something more desirable later.

Self-control is the ability to inhibit impulses, obey rules, ignore distractions, be patient, and stay focused on a task. Children with self-control are also able to regulate their emotions. Instead of snarling at the teacher, like Clint, they would cope with their anger in a more acceptable way. You will learn more about emotion regulation in Chapter 8. In this chapter we will focus on inhibiting impulses and delaying gratification. A **delay of gratification** means delaying what you desire in the moment in order to get something more desirable in the long term.

Age Trends in Self-Control

Students are asked to inhibit impulses and delay gratification many times every day at school. Toddlers are asked to inhibit the impulse to stand on their chairs during snack time. Adolescents are asked to inhibit the impulse to talk during class. Impulsivity decreases as self-control increases dramatically with age.

Early Childhood (Birth to 5 Years)

Infants' behavior is impulsive. For example, when they are hungry they want to be fed *immediately.* As they become toddlers, we expect them to wait a short time to be fed. Scientists measure young children's ability to wait and delay gratification by placing a tempting item—a marshmallow, a toy, or a present—in front of them and telling them to wait before touching the item. Older toddlers can wait longer than younger toddlers (Li-Grining, 2007). Preschoolers can wait even longer. However, even though preschoolers have more self-control than toddlers, their capacity to wait is fairly short-lived, lasting a matter of *seconds* in a delay-of-gratification test. This is why young children need your help to wait for a snack or for their turn to use a toy.

Middle Childhood (6 to 12 Years)

David Young-Wolff/PhotoEdit

Young children need help controlling their impulses.

Children in elementary school are able to delay gratification longer than preschoolers. Their delay-of-gratification tests last several minutes rather than seconds. For example, when children were told to wait before eating candies that were placed before them, 8-year-olds waited an average of about seven minutes compared to about five minutes for 6-year-olds (Toner, Moore, & Emmons, 1980). In elementary school, children also become better at staying focused on tasks in spite of distractions. One study had 4-, 6-, and 8-year-olds work on tasks while a clown box periodically distracted them by talking, flashing lights, and playing music (Holtz & Lehman, 1995). The 4-year olds had the most trouble, while the 8-year-olds had the least trouble staying focused. Distractions occur all the time in elementary classrooms—announcements come over the loud speaker, parents enter the classroom to deliver forgotten lunches, and conflicts erupt—and on average, older children are better at controlling impulses than younger children (Vazsonyi & Huang, 2010).

Adolescence (13 to 19 Years)

A national study showed that youth continue to become less impulsive from age 10 to age 30 (see Figure 7.1). Self-control requires executive functions. In Chapter 4 you learned that executive functions increase into adolescence. This is probably because, as you learned in Chapter 2, the prefrontal cortex matures in late adolescence or early adulthood. The prefrontal cortex is activated during tests of self-control (Shamosh et al., 2008).

Adolescents are so skilled at delay of gratification that the tests used with young children are simply too easy for testing adolescents. They are given more challenging tests, like choosing between having $200 now or $1,000 a month from now (Steinberg et al., 2009). An unintended experiment occurred at a high school carnival. Students were given a choice of prizes for winning at games—a dollar bill or a piece of penny

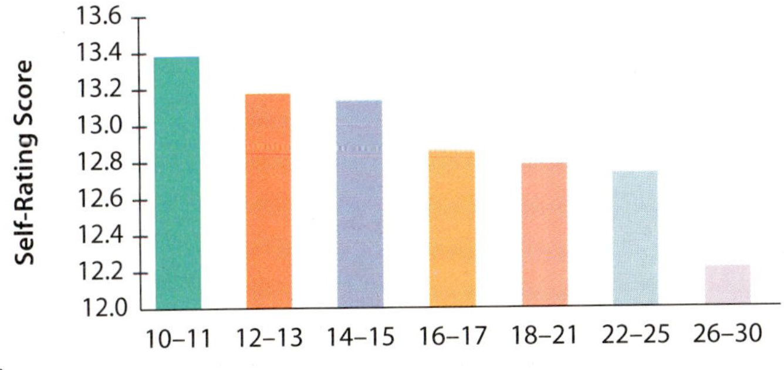

To come

Figure 7.1 Age Differences in Self-Reported Impulsivity. Where are you on this graph? *Steinberg et al. (2008).*

candy. Which do you think a typical teenager would choose? Most chose the candy; it has immediate payoff whereas the dollar has delayed payoff. Yet, in their daily lives adolescents are capable of remarkable delay of gratification. For example, they can delay hanging out with friends in order to study for a test that will help them get into college in order to become an engineer, which is years away. Not all adolescents are capable of such self-control. Let's look at individual differences next.

Individual Diversity in Self-Control

Although toddlers clearly have less self-control than a 6- or 16-year-old, you will find large individual differences in self-control among same-age children. Are these differences stable? Is Clint likely to have had self-control problems in preschool and elementary school?

Stability across Childhood

Young children who have high self-control tend to be the same children who have high self-control when older (Vazsonyi & Huang, 2010). For example, in one study 4-year-olds who chose not to eat one marshmallow so that they would get two later were more self-controlled and less distractible in their late teens (Eigsti et al., 2006). In contrast, preschoolers who could not delay gratification continued to have less self-control as adolescents. Remarkably, the number of seconds of delay in a simple preschool task predicts self-control with a fair degree of accuracy more than 10 years later! This means that your students with less self-control than their classmates are not likely to simply outgrow the problem and may need your help developing self-control.

Stability across Situations

Self-control varies depending on the situation. It is easier for children to inhibit their impulses if their attention is diverted from temptations. For example, your students may be able to refrain from touching a forbidden object, like a colorful piñata, if other interesting activities are occurring. Children may be able to wait longer to eat a treat if they think about something other than the treat, like playing with a favorite toy. Preschoolers who are particularly good at delay-of-gratification tests generate their own diversions, like singing songs to themselves (Mischel, 1996).

Removing temptations from sight increases self-control. In delay-of-gratification tests, if treats are removed from view and the children have to request them, they can wait much longer than if the treats are in view (see Figure 7.2). Some parents and teachers mistakenly believe that giving students a small taste of a treat, or telling them to keep the treat in mind, will help them delay gratification. This actually undermines their self-control. However, for students with low self-control, whether treats are in view or not may not matter. Some students have low self-control regardless of the situation.

Labeling students as patient also increases self-control. For example, in one study, children who were told "you are patient" waited twice as long to claim their candy as a control group (Toner et al., 1980). Communicating positive expectations to students is a simple but powerful way to improve their behavior in your classroom. For example, you might say, "You are so patient. I know I can count on you to wait quietly."

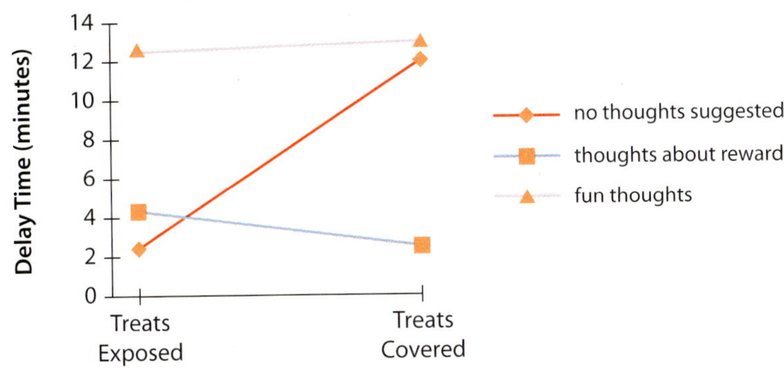

Figure 7.2 Number of Minutes Preschoolers Delayed Gratification.
Children who think about pleasant things, other than the reward, are able to delay the longest. Can you describe what effect having the treats exposed or not has? *Source: Adapted from Mischel, Shoda, & Rodriguez (1989).*

What Do Individual Differences in Self-Control Predict?

Self-control helps students benefit more from classroom instruction. Imagine if students acted on every impulse. They might text-message their friends or chat with classmates instead of participating in a learning activity. Thus, it is not surprising that self-control is linked to academic achievement and social competence.

Academic achievement

Students with high self-control tend to have higher academic achievement, probably because they have less trouble paying attention, staying on task, and ignoring distractions (Ponitz, McClelland, Matthews, & Morrison, 2009). In fact, some research shows that self-control *predicts GPA better than intelligence* does (Duckworth & Seligman, 2005). This pattern may be stable across time: 4-year-olds who were better at delay-of-gratification tasks not only had higher self-control at 15 to 16 years of age, but they were also more attentive, better able to concentrate, and had higher SAT scores. At age 20 they had more total years of education, were less likely to use drugs, and felt a greater sense of well-being (Ayduk et al., 2000).

Social competence

Students with high self-control may also have higher achievement because they participate more in class, are more cooperative, and have better relationships with teachers and classmates. They tend to be less aggressive and less prone to behavior problems at school than students with low self-control (Eisenberg et al., 2003; Valiente, Lemery-Chalfant, Swanson, & Reiser, 2008). For example, in a study where preschoolers were told not to peek while an experimenter noisily wrapped their present, those who had more self-control and did not peek also had fewer behavior problems at preschool (Kerr, Lopez, Olson, & Sameroff, 2004).

> **Field Observation**
> Watch two students in a classroom—one you think has high self-control and one with low self-control. Describe their behavior. How does their self-control affect peer acceptance? What do they do that might affect academic achievement?

Youth with low self-control are more likely to use drugs and alcohol. The connection between delinquency and low self-control is strong, especially for boys (Wills & Stoolmiller, 2002; Wulfert, Block, Santa Ana, Rodriguez, & Colsman, 2002). For example, in one study kindergarteners who had low self-control and trouble with attention were more likely to have used alcohol or other drugs by age 12 (Kaplow, Curran, Dodge, & Conduct Problems Prevention Research Group, 2002). Because such important outcomes are linked to self-control, it is important to understand what factors might lead to high self-control.

What Predicts Individual Differences in Self-Control?

One of the most powerful ways to promote self-control in your students is to use effective discipline, which we will discuss later in this chapter. Here, you will learn about five other factors linked to self-control: cognitive abilities, practice, attachment, religiosity, and parental monitoring.

Cognitive abilities—intelligence and inhibitory control

Students with high IQ are more likely to wait for larger, delayed rewards than to choose smaller, immediate rewards (Shamosh et al., 2008; Steinberg et al., 2009). Why might this be? Recall from Chapters 4 and 5 that working memory and executive functions are key parts of intelligence and that inhibitory control is part of executive functions. Inhibitory control refers to the ability to suppress inappropriate behavior or irrelevant thoughts. So inhibitory control and intelligence share the same underlying executive functions and brain circuits (Eigsti et al., 2006; Li-Grining, 2007). Such brain functions can result from experience (see Chapter 2). The next four factors show that experience is linked to differences in self-control.

Practice and fatigue

Every student's self-control has limits, just as yours does. You know this if you have tried to stick to a diet or keep a resolution to study harder. In fact, self-control may be like a muscle in that you can only exert so much self-control, just as you can only lift so much weight (Baumeister, Vohs, & Tice, 2007). Like muscles, self-control can be fatigued by resisting temptation. For example, if students are asked to sit still and pay attention in class for a long time, their self-control may become fatigued. The more self-control is exercised without rest, the more likely it will fail. The part of the brain responsible for self-control is less capable just after it has been exercised (Inzlicht & Gutsell, 2007). Even students who have age-appropriate self-control may need a break, such as free time to move about or be noisy.

Over time, the more self-control is exercised, the more it grows, just like exercising a muscle causes it to become stronger. For example, one teacher describes how her preschool students get "stronger" as they "exercise" their self-control:

> *The children eagerly line up when I tell them it's time for PE, but once in the gym, they cannot wait in line for more than a few minutes without trying to play with the tempting equipment. They can't wait for balls to be passed out. They get better as the school year progresses, however. For example, one little girl would push and poke to get a ball or jump rope. She would cry if she did not get one right away. Months later, she is able to wait her turn.*

This little girl is growing in self-control partly by exercising it. Thus, in your classroom you may want to avoid demanding more self-control than students can maintain without a break, but you may also want to stretch them just a little.

Attachment

In Chapter 6 you learned that secure attachment predicts social competence, academic achievement, and other positive outcomes in children like compliance with adults. This may be due to attachment's link with self-control. Children who have secure attachment and who have mothers who are sensitive and positive are more likely to develop high self-control than insecure children (e.g., Gilliom, Shaw, Beck, Schonberg, & Lukon, 2002; Laible & Thompson, 2000).

Religiosity

Research shows that religiosity is linked to less drinking, smoking, gambling, and depression. It is linked to more seat-belt wearing, greater well-being, longer wait before first intercourse, longer lifespan, and higher academic achievement. Notice that each of these outcomes has a self-control component. A recent review of dozens of studies found that youth who are religious, on the average, exhibit more self-control than those who are not (McCullough & Willoughby, 2009). Religiosity may affect self-control through its emphasis on self-mastery.

Parental monitoring

How closely parents monitor their children also plays a role in self-control. For young children, parental monitoring includes things like influencing with whom the child plays and restricting television viewing. For adolescents, parental monitoring includes knowing what homework the child has been assigned, how the child spends money, where the child is, and what the child does away from home. Notice that a key aspect of monitoring is *parental knowledge* (Stattin & Kerr, 2000).

Parents monitor their children to different degrees. Parents whose teens are securely attached are more likely to know what their teenage children are doing (Branstetter, Furman, & Cottrell, 2009). Parents with their own risk factors as less likely to monitor their children. For example, parents who are single, low SES, high school dropouts, and who have a history of substance abuse, depression, or other mental illness are less likely to monitor their children (Evans, 2004).

Lack of parental monitoring is linked to low self-control, as well as aggression, depression, dislike of school, drug use, risky sexual behavior, and delinquency.[1] Parental monitoring is even linked to driving. Teens whose parents do not monitor their driving are more likely to have a traffic violation or crash (Hartos, Eitel, Haynie, & Simons-Morton, 2000). The importance of parental monitoring may depend on the neighborhood. Lack of monitoring may be especially detrimental in impoverished, unsafe neighborhoods where youth hang out after school, unsupervised by adults (Pettit, Laird, Bates, & Dodge, 1997). However, wealthy suburbs can be detrimental as well, if there are no adults home after school to monitor the children (Luthar, 2003).

The research on parental monitoring is correlational. As with all correlational data, you can ask which comes first; does parental monitoring *cause* self-control in children, or do well-behaved children *cause* their parents to be better monitors? Research suggests that parents' knowledge of teens' activities is largely due to children freely telling their parents about their activities, but also to parents carefully observing and listening to their children (Crouter, Bumpus, Davis, & McHale, 2005; Stattin & Kerr, 2000). When parents have

> ***Think About This*** Some psychologists use the term *parental knowledge* rather than *parental monitoring*, to highlight that children contribute information, instead of the process being driven only by parents. What was your experience? How did your parents know what you were doing throughout your youth, or did they know? How did their monitoring or lack of monitoring affect your behavior?

[1]Many studies support this finding, just a few of which are listed here (e.g., Branstetter et al., 2009; Coley, Votruba-Drzal, & Schindler, 2009; Lac & Crano, 2009; Laird, Pettit, Bates, & Dodge, 2003; Pettit, Laird, Dodge, Bates, & Criss, 2001).

to question their children, or rely on others for information (e.g., siblings, neighbors, teachers, friends' parents), the children are likely to become more delinquent over time. In fact, children who feel overly scrutinized by their parents tend to have low self-esteem, depression, and expectations of failure. Thus, skillful monitoring may need to be subtle and may be motivated by the child as well as the parent. Now that we have discussed individual differences in self-control, let's turn our attention to differences across groups.

Group Diversity in Self-Control

There are both gender and SES differences in self-control. As early as preschool, girls tend to have more self-control than boys (Kerr et al., 2004; Li-Grining, 2007). In addition, children who come from middle- or high-SES backgrounds, on average, have more self-control than low-SES children, and this difference in self-control predicts school grades and cognitive development (Evans & Rosenbaum, 2008).

There are also cultural differences in self-control, depending on what aspects of self-control are valued. One aspect of self-control is conformity to authority and rules. Some cultures value conformity over independent decision making. For example, Figure 7.3 displays data from California showing that conformity is valued more among immigrant parents from Cambodia, Mexico, the Philippines, and Vietnam than among U.S.-born White and Mexican American parents. Even when youth are not immigrants, if they have a cultural heritage from these other countries, they report greater respect for parental authority and less expectation for making their own decisions than European American youth (Hardway & Fuligni, 2006). Cross-national studies similarly find that Asian cultures value conformity more than European and North American cultures, and Asians tend to be more self-controlled (Weisz, Rothbaum, & Blackburn, 1984). This may be due to a greater emphasis on collectivism among Asian cultures (see Box 7.1).

In your classroom, you may find that your students vary in conformity to rules depending on the value of these behaviors in their heritage cultures. Understanding these group differences may provide insight into your students, but you will also need to be careful not to stereotype based on gender, SES, or ethnicity.

Think About This Imagine that you have a student in your classroom who regularly misbehaves. Would your response be "How can I help this student have greater self-control?" This response is typical for North American or European teachers. They place blame for misbehavior within the student. Japanese teachers are more likely to place blame for misbehavior within the classroom. Their response might be "How can we create a greater sense of community so that this student wants to cooperate in class more?" (Hoffman, 2009). Would the strategies you use to eliminate the misbehavior be different depending on which response you had? Explain.

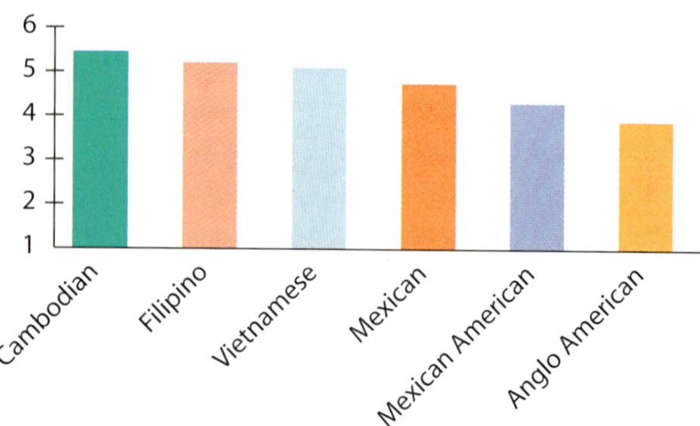

Figure 7.3 Parents' Ratings of Importance of Conformity. This graph depicts parents' ratings of how important conformity in their children is to them (6 = extremely important, 1 = not at all important). What can you say about the pattern of results from this graph? *Source: Adapted from Okagaki & Sternberg (1993).*

Theories & Theorists — Box 7.1

Collectivism and Individualism

How do cultures differ in ways that influence children's development? One difference is collectivism versus individualism. In *collectivist* cultures, the needs of the group are more important than individual needs. Interdependence among people and harmonious relationships are emphasized (Kennedy, 2000). Identity stems from the group, and life satisfaction stems from meeting group obligations. In contrast, *individualist* cultures emphasize independence, self-reliance, personal freedom, rights, and liberty above duties. Identity stems from personal accomplishments. One's obligation to one's family is freely chosen (Giles-Sims & Lockhart, 2005). The following examples give you a flavor of cultural differences:

- The American acceptance of a "lively discussion" in which people argue their points does not exist in Japan because it could disrupt group harmony (Nisbett, 2003, p. 73).
- Some Asians find it odd that Americans frequently thank family members for fulfilling their obligations, like setting the table (p. 49).
- A Turkish psychologist was shocked that her American colleagues considered charging their 21-year-old son rent to live at home (Kagitcibasi, 1996).
- Hispanics value *familism*, giving priority to family interdependence, support, and obligations. Thus, Hispanic youth are more likely to prefer living at home during college than White or Black youth (Desmond & Turley, 2009).

Some psychologists assert that northern European and American nations are individualistic while Asian nations such as China, Korea, Japan, Pakistan, and India, and also African and Latin nations, are collectivistic (e.g., Rudy & Grusec, 2006). However, this may be an oversimplification. Most cultures are a mixture, and cross-national differences tend to be small (Giles-Sims & Lockhart, 2005). For example, many Americans would disapprove of charging young adult children rent to live at home. Researchers are increasingly critical of assertions that groups are either collectivist or individualist. Groups may value individual autonomy, and also value close relationships, the welfare of the group, and cooperation (Tamis-LeMonda et al., 2008).

Ethnicity in North America. Some psychologists assert that European Americans are less collectivistic than other ethnic groups within North America. Collectivism has been used to explain why Asian American children have relatively *high* achievement on average, which is that they are obligated to their family to work hard in school. Paradoxically, collectivism has also been used to explain why Latino children have relatively *low* achievement on average, which is that obligations to the family divert them from school work (Desmond & Turley, 2009; Vázquez García, García Coll, Erkut, Alarcón, & Tropp, 1999). Collectivism has been used to explain why authoritarian parenting does not have as negative consequences among other ethnic groups as it does for European American children; that is, authoritarian parenting is thought to be less detrimental because deference to authority is emphasized in collectivist cultures (Rudy & Grusec, 2006).

In Chapter 1 you learned that some children experience mismatch between their heritage culture and the culture of the school. One cause of mismatch can be differences in collectivism and individualism. For example, in one study Asian American children learned more and preferred learning situations where important others made decisions for them such as what task to do or what level of difficulty to attempt, while European American children learned more and preferred learning situations where they made their own decisions (Iyengar & Lepper, 1999). To be an effective multicultural teacher, you will need to become aware of your students' cultures, as well as your own culture and teaching style.

Classroom Implications of Self-Control

In one study children were told not to peek at an answer to a test question while the adult was out of the room. Most 1st-graders (78%), 43% of 3rd-graders, and 31% of 5th-graders peeked (Talwar, Gordon, & Lee, 2007). This study highlights both age trends and individual differences in school-relevant self-control. The situation was too taxing for most 1st-graders. However, among 5th-graders only one-third had low self-control in the situation. Students with low self-control are likely to misbehave and have low achievement in your classroom. You may promote their self-control by following these guidelines:

- Reduce distractions and interruptions. For example: encourage the central office not to use the public address system during the day; have orderly procedures to address common disruptions like late arrivals; do not give instructions and then constantly interrupt the class to clarify; keep tempting objects out of sight, such as glass beakers in science class, until they are needed (Mauro & Harris, 2000).

- Give students' self-control regular exercise, like a muscle, but without fatiguing it. If a student with low self-control manages to behave well for a while, give the student a short rest from self-control. Try to keep students out of situations that overtax their self-control. For example, one boy was always touching other students—hitting, kicking, punching, and pushing. His teacher put him at the front of every line to limit temptations to touch. She had him put his hands in his pockets while in the hallway or cafeteria. These simple tactics helped substantially.
- Feed students healthy foods. Self-control uses up glucose, the brain's fuel. Children have more self-control when they have adequate glucose supplies in their bodies (Baumeister et al., 2007).
- Plan to do the classroom activities that require the most self-control earlier in the day. Self-control tends to be highest early in the day and lowest in the evening (Gailliot, 2008). (Your wise parents probably knew this, which is why they insisted on an early curfew!)
- Use statements like "You are patient" to communicate positive expectations of students.
- Refer students with serious self-control problems to the school counselor for intervention.

In summary, research suggests that self-control increases steadily with age, so secondary teachers can expect more self-control from their students than can preschool teachers. Even among students of the same age, there are large individual differences in self-control. These differences in self-control are linked to information processing ability, opportunity to practice self-control, and parenting practices. They are also linked to the gender, SES, and home culture of your students. One of the most powerful things you can do to promote your students' self-control is to use *effective* discipline. Use of effective discipline is a key part of an authoritative style of teaching. Let's discuss effective discipline, and then examine why you may want to be an authoritative teacher.

Effective Discipline

In a preschool classroom, 4-year-old Sammy has scattered the blocks across the room. He leaves them there as he moves on to do a puzzle. Mrs. Sanchez asks him to clean up, but he refuses at first.

Mrs. Sanchez:	*Sammy, please pick up the blocks before you start your puzzle.*
Sammy:	*No.*
Mrs. Sanchez:	*We have to clean up one mess before we start a new activity.*
Sammy:	*[Shakes his head "no."] Not gonna clean up. Don't wanna.*

Mrs. Sanchez: *These blocks are dangerous. Someone could trip and fall on them. Pick them up.*
Sammy: *[Shakes his head "no."]*
Mrs. Sanchez: *[Still speaking kindly, but firmly] Sammy, you know that you should clean up the blocks. Let's do it now.*

Sammy ignores her. Mrs. Sanchez tries again, as she places two blocks in the container.

Mrs. Sanchez: *Come on. Would you like me to help you with the first blocks? Come on. Let's get this picked up.*

Sammy watches her, and then silently begins to pick up blocks.

Mrs. Sanchez: Thank you, Sammy. You are a helpful boy.

Was this effective discipline? Is Sammy likely to develop greater self-control as a result of this discipline episode? As a teacher, you will face these important questions every day because misbehavior is common in classrooms. *Discipline* refers to attempts to correct misbehavior; it is a subset of classroom management, which includes discipline and also attempts to structure the classroom in a way that avoids the necessity of disciplining. We discuss discipline next, and then classroom management.

Most children do not obey every rule all the time—you probably did not when you were a child. Your students are more likely to misbehave than you did because American children have become less obedient over the last few decades (Achenbach, Dumenci, & Rescorla, 2002; Coie & Dodge, 1998). Thus, you will probably need to discipline children on a daily basis. Even though classroom discipline is a constant issue for teachers, it is not as well researched as you might expect; for example, over a ten-year period, less than 1% of articles in education journals addressed discipline (Hardman & Smith, 2003). We will discuss different approaches you can use, but first let's be clear about the goal of discipline.

Robert Dant/iStockphoto

The long-term goal of effective discipline is to promote self-control.

The Goal of Discipline

The short-term goal of discipline is to influence children to behave appropriately right now, but the more important long-term goal of discipline is to instill values and promote self-control. If children are to become responsible adults who contribute to society, they must learn the values of their culture. A child's value system is learned in everyday discipline encounters. Discipline teaches children the boundaries of socially acceptable behavior. How adults discipline influences whether children learn to become compassionate and self-controlled.

The goal of discipline should not merely be compliance, but rather *internalization* of positive values (Bergin & Bergin, 1999; Freiberg, 1999). **Internalization** means that children personally adopt the values and rules of society, believing that they are important and worth using as guides for behavior. Their compliance is **committed** if they endorse and accept the authority figure's agenda as their own, even when they are not being supervised. Children who have *not* internalized values may behave well when they are being watched, but break the rules when authority figures are out of sight. In this case, children's compliance is **situational**, which means that they lack sincere commitment to the rule. For example, if a student kicks classmates whenever the teacher is not looking, he has not internalized the value of not hurting others. *Self*-control emerges out of committed compliance, not situational compliance.

internalization the child adopts the adult's values and rules as his or her own guide for behavior. The child complies or behaves appropriately without being monitored.

committed compliance children accept the authority figure's agenda as their own.

situational compliance children comply with demands, but lack sincere commitment and require sustained control by the authority figure.

Is compliance always an appropriate goal? This depends on your understanding of what compliance is. Compliance is obedience to a specific request or rule, or long-term adherence to a set of general rules. Besides compliance, there are three ways a child can respond to adult directives: (1) direct *defiance* or refusal; (2) *passive noncompliance*, which means the child ignores the directive; and (3) *negotiation*, which means the child asserts his or her own agenda and negotiates a compromise. Direct defiance is a marker of behavior problems in older children, but not in 1- to 2-year-olds. Well-adjusted toddlers can occasionally be quite defiant, although they are generally positive (Dix, Stewart, Gershoff, & Day, 2007). Between ages 2 and 5, direct defiance and passive noncompliance decline, but negotiation increases as children develop social skills (Kuczynski & Kochanska, 1990). Is 4-year-old Sammy's defiance age-appropriate? Not if he consistently defies adults. However, there is no need for concern if he is usually compliant and has good social skills.

You might think that compliance is always the ideal response, but negotiation may be better in many situations. For example, when a child is told to clean up, she might say, "I'll clean up after I finish this puzzle." Negotiation, rather than unquestioning compliance, marks the child's emerging ability to balance autonomy with social responsibility. Toddlers who say no to their parents and then engage in negotiation are likely to be securely attached and developmentally advanced (Crockenberg & Litman, 1990). They are more likely to become socially competent several years later (Kuczynski & Kochanska, 1990). Successful negotiation requires sophisticated social skills on the child's part. Thus, adults who are open to negotiation during discipline may provide opportunity for children to develop social skills. In addition, the *type* of discipline that adults use can promote children's social skills and emotional well-being.

Types of Discipline

We will discuss three types of discipline: induction, love withdrawal, and power assertion. Both love withdrawal and power assertion are linked to negative child outcomes. Induction is more likely to result in internalization, so let's begin with induction.

Induction

induction a form of discipline in which the adult gives the child a reason for why behavior must change or a rule must be complied with.

Induction is a type of discipline in which an adult explains the reason for rules and points out the consequences of breaking rules. Discipline is more effective when accompanied by a good rationale (Maccoby, 1992). Giving students reasons for doing the right thing helps them understand why a rule is important. For example, when you say, "If everyone wrote in the library books, the pictures would not look nice and other people might be disappointed," you help the student understand your reasons and share in your goals. A particularly important form of induction is *victim-centered induction*, in which the adult points out how the student's behavior has made someone else feel. For example, you might say, "You really hurt Juanita's feelings when you didn't let her join you."

Andersen Ross/Photodisc/Jupiter Images

Induction is the most effective form of discipline for promoting self-control.

Induction is linked to self-control and social competence. Students who are disciplined with induction rather than other types of discipline are more likely to internalize values and obey rules even when adults are not present. They are more likely to negotiate about rather than defy directives. They also are more likely to be empathic, be kind to others, and have fewer behavior problems (Kerr et al., 2004; Krevans & Gibbs, 1996; Paulussen-Hoogeboom, Stams, Hermanns, & Peetsma, 2007).

Induction may be the most effective form of discipline *regardless of age of the child.* It makes sense that induction would be effective with teenagers, but what about 1-year-olds? If a toddler approaches the parking lot, shouldn't you just firmly say "No!" rather than "Don't go there; you'll get run over!"? Apparently not. Much of the research on the positive effects of induction has been conducted with toddlers, indicating that even toddlers learn from induction. While the first part of the communication—Don't go there—may be the most important for preventing disaster, the second part—you'll get run over—is also important for training future behavior.

Simply saying, "No!" or "Stop that!" in response to misbehavior is the opposite of induction, and may be effective at stopping a behavior (or not), but it does not guide the student with reasons. One mother was concerned about her toddler's strange behavior; he would freeze when he approached walls. It turned out that his mother slapped his hand or yelled "Stop!" whenever he got near an electrical outlet. He did not understand the reason for the punishment and developed a generalized fear of walls!

Unlike induction, which appeals to children's reason, love-withdrawal appeals to children's need for approval and affection. Although some disapproval of the child is communicated in any discipline, it is minimal in induction. In contrast, disapproval of the child is the central focus of the love-withdrawal approach.

love-withdrawal a form of discipline in which the adult manipulates the love relationship with the child. This can include withdrawing affection or attention, isolating the child, and expressing disapproval of the child.

Love-Withdrawal

Love-withdrawal is a type of discipline in which an adult expresses anger and disapproval toward a child by withdrawing love and affection. Love-withdrawal includes a broad array of behaviors such as ignoring the child, stating dislike for the child, or asking the child to go away. For example, a coach might say, "Get out of here. I don't want to see you when you behave like that." It also includes frequent criticism or trying to make children feel excessive guilt. For example, a teacher might say, "Are you trying to bring this whole class down?" Children who are disciplined with love-withdrawal tend to have more depression and misbehavior and less self-confidence (Aunola & Nurmi, 2005).

Field Observation

Go to a mall, playground, or somewhere that many different families are interacting and likely to be using discipline. Observe different families. Do you see examples of each of the different discipline approaches? What are the children's responses to the different approaches?

Power Assertion

power assertion a coercive form of discipline in which the adult controls the child's behavior by virtue of greater power or resources. It often includes an "or else" clause.

Power assertion is a form of discipline in which the adult relies on power or resources to control a child's behavior, as Mrs. Reinhardt did with Clint in the opening vignette. Power assertion can take four forms: (1) physical punishment, like spanking; (2) deprivation of material objects or privileges, like taking the car keys away from a teenager; (3) direct application of power, like carrying the child away from a conflict; or (4) threats to use forms 1, 2, or 3. Power assertion is common in schools, particularly removal of privileges. An easy way to recognize power assertion is the presence of an "or else" clause, either explicit or implied, in the command. For example, a teacher might say, "Quit talking or else I'll move your desk."

Think About This What type of discipline is "time-out?"? Is it an effective form of discipline? Base your answers on what you have learned about discipline in this chapter.

Costs of power assertion

There are five serious costs to using power-assertive discipline.

1. Children become less compliant. Adults using power-assertive discipline often achieve *immediate* compliance, which reinforces the adults' use of power assertion in the future. However, it results in less compliance over the long run (Erath, El-Sheikh, & Cummings, 2009; Gershoff, 2002).
2. Children do not internalize values (Kochanska, Aksan, & Joy, 2007). Even if misbehavior improves, the emotions and thoughts that are influencing that behavior do not necessarily change. Situational compliance may be achieved, but not committed compliance.
3. Children resent the disciplinarian. Power assertion jeopardizes the caring relationship between adult and child. How do you feel toward someone who threatens you if you don't do what they want? Children often have similar negative feelings toward those who wield power over them, just as Clint did.
4. Children need more and more coercion. When children are constantly threatened until they comply, they begin to ignore mild threats and comply only for stronger threats. They come to *expect* overt power assertion and threats *before* they will comply (Patterson & Bank, 1989).
5. Children learn aggression from power-assertive adult models. Children who experience power-assertive discipline are more likely to be aggressive and delinquent later (Bender et al., 2007). This is especially a problem with corporal punishment, a subset of power-assertive discipline.

Research, both correlational and experimental, robustly shows that heavy-handed, power-assertive discipline leads to angry, resentful children who are likely to become aggressive. This effect occurs for children of all ages, toddlers to teens. Secure attachment is a protective factor. This means that even when parents are power assertive, if they have a secure attachment with the child, the child is less likely to become aggressive (Kochanska, Barry, Stellern, & O'Bleness, 2009).

Corporal punishment

corporal punishment power-assertive discipline that involves bodily harm to the child, ranging in severity from light spanking to abuse.

Corporal punishment, a form of power assertion, is physical punishment such as hitting or spanking. Spanking is common, about twice per week for 35 to 45% of parents of children ages 1 through 9, though many parents choose not to spank (Berlin et al., 2009; Straus, Sugarman, & Giles-Sims, 1997). People hold strong, opposite opinions on whether spanking and other forms of corporal punishment are appropriate. What does the research say?

Like other forms of power assertion, corporal punishment is associated with *less* obedience in the long term (Gershoff, 2002; Lansford et al., 2009). In addition, children who are spanked become aggressive and antisocial over time, even if they were not prone to misbehavior to begin with. Severe corporal punishment that goes beyond spanking, including punishment that could be considered abuse, is linked to later violence against dating partners in young adults, like shoving, slapping, and beating up the partner (Swinford, DeMaris, Cernkovich, & Giordano, 2000). Parents who were physically abused as children may be more likely to spank their own children, including 1-year-olds (Chung et al., 2009).

Revisiting Case 3

Which discipline approaches did Mrs. Richardson and Miss Loeb use? How do you think Le'Raun felt about Mrs. Richardson compared with Miss Loeb? Which teacher was more likely to help Le'Raun develop self-control? Which approach elicited the most compliance from Le'Raun?

The research is clear that frequent and severe spanking leads to antisocial behavior in children, yet is all corporal punishment bad? You probably have friends who were spanked as children (perhaps you were as well) but did not become aggressive. There are degrees of corporal punishment, ranging from mild spanking to abuse (see Box 7.2). Spanking may not be harmful under the following conditions: (1) it is mild, not abusive; (2) it is used infrequently and in conjunction with induction; (3) it is used by parents who generally have a positive relationship with the child; (4) it is used by parents who communicate a teaching goal rather than anger; and (5) it is used with children between 2 and 6 years of age, but not younger or older (Dodge, McLoyd, & Lansford, 2005; Lynch et al., 2006).

How can you decide which is the best disciplinary approach? There are three principles of effective discipline that can guide your decision.

Principles of Effective Discipline

The first principle of effective discipline is that *you must achieve compliance.* If you can get a student to obey you today, that student is more likely to obey you tomorrow, and so are observing classmates. Conversely, if you do not achieve compliance in one encounter, it will be even harder to achieve compliance in the next encounter. You can never completely ensure compliance. No matter how much power you have, you cannot force students to do what you want. Without taping his mouth shut, you cannot force Clint or any other student to stop talking. You cannot force Sammy to pick up the blocks. Students must choose to obey you. However, there are ways to increase the likelihood of compliance.

One way to increase the likelihood of compliance is to use *high-probability requests*, or requests that you know the student will comply with, before working up to requests that are low-probability (Lee, 2005). For example,

> *Five-year-old Jesse's teacher told him he could not go outside to play without his coat on because it was too cold. Jesse refused to put his coat on. For several cold days, the conflict over the coat grew. The teacher decided to try using high-probability requests. Jesse loved to clap his hands when asked. The teacher said, "Jesse, clap your hands!" He did, and she clapped hers. She asked again. He did again. She asked a third time. He did it again. She said, "Jesse, put your coat on!" He did.*

Challenges in Development — Box 7.2

Child Abuse

Child abuse is related to discipline because many incidents of physical abuse are the result of corporal punishment from an adult who has lost self-control. Child abuse takes four forms: physical, emotional, and sexual abuse, and criminal neglect. *Physical* abuse refers to harming children physically, like hitting them with an object, or burning them with cigarette butts. *Emotional* abuse refers to nonphysical harm such as excessive criticism, blaming, or telling them they are not loved or wanted. *Sexual* abuse refers to any type of sexual violation against a child including fondling, exhibition, or exposure to pornography. *Criminal neglect* refers to ignoring children or depriving them of food, shelter, and adequate hygiene.

Prevalence. In the United States, about 800,000 children may be abused or neglected and about 1,700 may die of that abuse or neglect each year. As distressing as these numbers are, they are probably underestimates. Much abuse is never reported. Among reported cases, neglect is most common, followed by physical abuse (see Figure 7.4). Notice in Figure 7.4 that multiple maltreatments are more common than physical abuse alone and can include physical abuse.

Physical and emotional abuse and neglect begin anywhere from infancy to adolescence. Sexual abuse occurs most often at about ages 4 to 5 and 14 to 15 (Snyder, 2000). Some children experience a single incident of abuse, whereas others experience many years of abuse. Neglect is the most likely to begin early and last a long time (Bolger & Patterson, 2001). Girls are more likely to be reported as sexually abused than boys (Dong, Anda, Dube, Giles, & Felitti, 2003). Boys and girls are about equally likely to be victims of other kinds of abuse.

Who abuses? Most children know the person who abuses them. About 80% of abuse and neglect perpetrators are parents or step-parents. The exception is that *sexual* abusers are more likely to be friends and neighbors, followed by relatives, and then child care providers (U.S. Department of Health and Human Services, 2009). Men are more likely than women to murder children, and killers are most likely to be the father or the mother's boyfriend (Fujiwara, Barber, Schaechter, & Hemenway, 2009).

What factors predict child abuse? Most families in which a child is abused (90%) report significant financial hardship (Bolger & Patterson, 2001). Families are likely to be poor, live in subsidized housing, and have an unemployed father. Mothers who suffer from depression or who feel they have little control as parents and who think power assertion is the best way to discipline are more likely to abuse (Bugental & Happaney, 2004). Children resulting from unwanted pregnancy are more likely to be abused. Children with vulnerabilities, such as low birth weight, poor health, and developmental delays are more likely to be abused, although this does not mean that children invite their own abuse (Sidebotham, Heron, & The ALSPAC Study Team, 2003).

What are the long-term consequences of child abuse? Abuse is linked to lower academic achievement. Physically abused students are more likely to be distractible and inattentive than nonabused classmates because they are

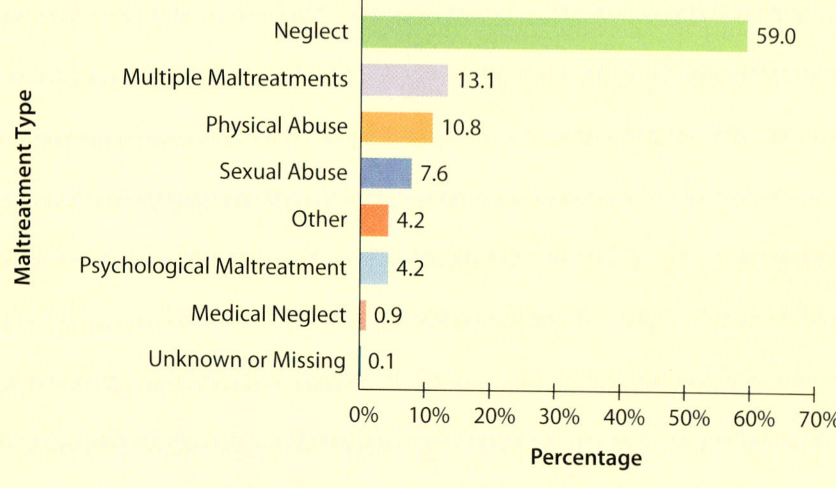

Figure 7.4 **Rates of Child Abuse 2007.** This graph depicts child abuse in the United States in 2007. Of all types of maltreatment, what is the single most common? The second most common? *U.S. Department of Health and Human Services (2009, p. 26).*

Challenges in Development *(continued)*

always on the look-out for others' aggression. Abused students are more likely to be in special education, to have low achievement test scores, to fail a grade, and to have poor work habits at school (Shonk & Cicchetti, 2001).

Abuse is also linked to emotional problems. Abused students may have less empathy, lack warmth toward others, and not read others' emotions as well as nonabused students. They may experience poor emotion regulation, such as being depressed or falling to pieces under stress (Kim & Cicchetti, 2006; Teisl & Cicchetti, 2008). There is increasing evidence that abuse causes changes in brain development that create problems in regulation of stress or negative emotions (Pollak, 2008).

Abuse is also linked to social behavior. Most students who are maltreated have disorganized attachment, and may become aggressive, or overly compliant and too eager to please adults (Cullerton-Sen et al., 2009). A common finding is that students who were *physically* abused tend to be aggressive and perceived negatively by their peers. Mothers who were abused as children show lower levels of responsiveness and empathy toward their infants (Bert, Guner, & Lanzi, 2009).

However, some students survive abuse reasonably well. The degree of negative outcomes depends on the risk and protective factors operating in their lives. Outcomes depend on how severe, frequent, and early the abuse and how much shame, depression, and stress the student feels.

Implications for teachers. Teachers are **mandated reporters.** Mandatory reporting laws, which vary by state, require professionals who work with children to report evidence of child abuse. School personnel are the largest single source of abuse reports, responsible for 17% of reports (U.S. Department of Health and Human Services, 2009). The most obvious signs of *physical* abuse you may see are bruises, broken bones, and burn marks that are unlikely to have happened through normal accidents. The main evidence that a student has been sexually abused is when a child tells someone of the abuse (Goodman, Emery, & Haugaard, 1998). Emotional abuse and neglect are difficult to detect. Can children accurately report their own abuse? They can, although memories are subject to distortion (Bruck, Ceci, & Principe, 2006; Goodman & Quas, 2008).

Some schools have implemented child sexual abuse prevention programs that attempt to teach students how to recognize abuse, appropriate touching, and good versus bad secrets. Such programs may have some positive effects, but the evidence is sparse (Topping & Barron, 2009).

Maltreated students are particularly prone to want a close relationship with their teachers, even though insecure students are more challenging to like (see Chapter 6). Attachment to teachers may foster resiliency in abused students.

Students' compliance with high-probability requests creates a cooperative mindset in the student that increases the likelihood of complying with low-probability requests (Williams & Forehand, 1984). Another way to increase the likelihood of compliance is to ask nicely, in the context of a warm teacher–student relationship, which brings us to the next principle.

mandated reporters people who must by law report suspicion of child abuse and neglect. Laws vary by state, but in most states, teachers are mandated reporters.

The second principle of effective discipline is to *keep the emotional tone positive during the discipline encounter.* Commands are more effective when adults give them accompanied by positive acts, such as smiling or complimenting the student. Students in a positive mood are more likely to comply with requests (Feldman & Klein, 2003). Students in a warm, secure relationship are more likely to respond with committed compliance (Kochanska, Aksan, & Carlson, 2005). Keeping the tone positive is particularly important for difficult, anger-prone students.

One way to keep discipline emotionally positive and to promote compliance is to cooperate with your students. Whenever it is reasonable, cooperate with students' agendas, allowing them control of activities, rather than always imposing your agenda on them. (Recall from Chapter 6 that this is one way to promote secure relationships with students.) One concrete strategy to help you become more cooperative with students is to say no less often. Instead of saying, "No, you can't read your book now," you could say "OK. As soon as you finish your spelling words you can read your book." The message is the same—you must practice spelling before doing free reading—but the second approach acknowledges the student's agenda, is cooperative, and is more likely to elicit compliance. The more you say no, the more often you will hear it come back to you.

The third principle of effective discipline is to *use the least amount of power that is sufficient to achieve compliance.* All discipline involves some form of power. Yet, when power is minimal in discipline encounters, students are more likely to believe that they complied due to choice (Gershoff, 2002; Lepper, 1983). The student may think, "I'm doing this because it's the right thing to do and I chose it." On the other hand, when power is blatant and excessive, students will likely believe they complied because of the teacher's show of power. The student may think, "I'm doing this because if I don't, I will be punished. I don't want to do it, but I will to avoid punishment." In this case, the student's compliance is situational. The student will probably feel free to change behavior when the teacher is out of sight.

This helps explain why power assertion tends not to foster internalization. You can promote internalization by influencing your students' thinking in a way that emphasizes their motives for good behavior. For example, you might say, "You feel bad because you hurt Teresa's feelings" rather than saying, "You feel bad because I caught you."

One way to minimize the power you exert in a discipline encounter is to use subtle rather than obvious forms of control. For example, you can whisper so a noisy class must be quiet to hear you instead of threatening them with a late lunch if they don't quiet down. Similarly, if Clint is being noisy and distracting nearby students, you could simply stand near Clint and gently tap his shoulder rather than scolding from the front of the room. In each case, both behaviors are likely to get students to quiet down, but one draws students' attention to your power and the other minimizes students' awareness of your power.

In summary, effective discipline leads to internalization and self-control, whereas ineffective discipline leads to defiance and undermines long-term self-control. *Even if you achieve compliance for the moment, if you have not moved the student toward internalization, your discipline encounter has not been fully effective.* Of course, you are not interested solely in promoting self-control in the classroom; you must also teach academic content. You cannot allow some students to detract from the learning of other students because of misbehavior. Effective discipline will achieve both purposes.

What can you do if you prefer to use induction but feel trapped into power assertion because some students in your classroom are already angry and defiant, come from families that emphasize power assertion, and have already adapted to high levels of coercion? You need a form of discipline that is powerful enough to encourage compliance but subtle enough to allow students to believe they obeyed due to personal choice. The discipline should also foster a positive relationship between you and students. One approach you could use is to persuade students, in a persistent way, until they obey. Let's look at how this works.

Applying the Principles of Effective Discipline: Persistent Persuasion

When a student in your classroom is not complying, you can continually restate the command until the student complies, but without increasing the level of power assertion (Bergin & Bergin, 1999). You don't need to use threats or increasingly hostile tones. Instead, present commands in a reasonable or friendly tone of voice. You don't need to use an "or else" clause (either implicitly or explicitly) as in "you better do this or else…" Avoiding threats helps lower the student's expectation for coercion. You can reframe the command, or give additional rationales for compliance with each repetition. You should respond to the student's negotiation and remain in control until compliance is achieved. Afterward, you can attribute the compliance to the student's good intentions. For example, you might say, "You are such a helpful boy; I knew you wanted to do what is right!"

The critical aspects of this **persistent persuasion** approach are: (1) you *do not quit* making the request *until compliance is achieved*, and (2) you *do not escalate* demands by getting louder or by making threats. Thus, you achieve compliance without encouraging the student to expect coercion and threats. Mrs. Sanchez used it with Sammy. Does it work with older, defiant students? Let's look at an example in a residential facility for difficult teens.

persistent persuasion an approach to discipline that uses induction repeatedly until the child complies, but without escalating the power level.

Counselor:	*Michelle, you need turn off the TV.*
Michelle:	*No, b---.*
Counselor:	*Michelle, you need to turn off the television so you can do your chores. (Michelle ignores the counselor.) Michelle, the other girls are doing their chores. (Other girls are standing holding brooms and cleaning supplies, watching the television.) Well . . . they are supposed to be. The TV is distracting.*
Michelle:	*So?*
Counselor:	*I can help you get started.*
Michelle:	*No! (Slumps down in sofa and glares at television.)*
Counselor:	*C'mon. You know the rules. No television during chore time.*
Michelle:	*(Gets up slowly, swaggers over to the television, and turns it off.)*

You can follow up persistent persuasion by *reminding the student of previous compliance* when the same or similar rules are broken later. "Do you remember yesterday, when I asked you to turn off the TV, and you did it?" Students are more likely to obey in the next encounter with *less effort* on the part of the adult. Recall that with power assertion the opposite is true.

You may have noticed that induction takes patience, effort, and time. Yet it can take less time away from instruction than other, less effective, forms of discipline. Consider a 5th-grade classroom, where Peter has a history of aggression.

Ms. Schwab tells the students to get out their books. Peter picks up Marcus's book and tosses it on the floor, laughing. Marcus pushes Peter. Ms. Schwab shouts, "Boys, that is enough. Out in the hallway now!" (Neither boy moves.) "I said out in the hallway, and when I say now, you better move. Now!" (Neither boy moves.)

Peter:	*"I don't have to!"*
Ms. Schwab:	*(Shouting louder) "Get out there now."*
Peter:	*"No."*

Ms. Schwab: *(Still shouting) "Get out in the hallway now!" (Peter sits in his seat, ignoring the teacher. Marcus goes to the hallway.) Ms. Schwab stands over Peter's seat, lowers her voice to a hard edge, and says, "I said get out in the hallway."*

Peter finally goes to the hallway. Ms. Schwab follows. The boys begin to laugh. Ms. Schwab says they better do what she says. They look down and giggle. In frustration, she tells them to get back in the classroom and get out their books. They do.

Ms. Schwab eventually achieved compliance, but her approach cost instructional time, damaged her relationship with Peter and Marcus, and damaged her relationship with the rest of the class who were watching. Neither Peter nor Marcus is likely to internalize appropriate values from this encounter. Had Ms. Schwab used persistent persuasion, she would have achieved compliance, with similar or less time and effort, and still maintained her authority in the classroom.

Why Persistent Persuasion Should Work

Some teachers might disapprove of Sammy's teacher and Michelle's counselor because they appeared to ignore student disobedience. However, remember that effective discipline has two goals. The first is to obtain compliance. The second, more important goal is to teach *self*-control, or help students internalize positive values. The persistent persuasion used by Mrs. Sanchez incorporates all three principles of effective discipline that lead to internalization:

1. *The discipline does not rely upon obvious power.* While teachers do have more power than students, in persistent persuasion the display of power is weak, unclear, and not enough to account for students' compliance. This allows students to interpret their compliance as the result of choice, rather than force. Students are not obeying just to avoid a threat of punishment because there is no clear threat.
2. *The interaction is not negative.* Too often disciplinary encounters become struggles for control between an angry teacher and an angry student, like Ms. Schwab and Peter, or Mrs. Reinhardt and Clint. Contrast their experiences with that of Mrs. Sanchez and Sammy; neither was angry. Persistent persuasion helps teachers maintain a positive feeling in the classroom. One teacher said that she had not realized how negative her classroom had become until she tried persistent persuasion. She said that the classroom became more pleasant, she liked the students more, and she was less exhausted at the end of the day.
3. *The child can negotiate.* Some teachers believe that negotiation with students shows weakness, and students should obey simply because they are students. However, allowing students to negotiate with you during discipline has three positive effects: it (a) creates a more reciprocal relationship between you, (b) increases the likelihood of committed compliance, and (c) provides you with opportunity to develop increased empathy for students as you learn to listen to them. The process of negotiation can also reveal to you when your requests are inappropriate. One teacher found that when he tried to give a

Field Observation

Try using persistent persuasion the next time you are involved in a discipline encounter. Did you have enough self-control to succeed? What was the outcome?

reason why the student had to comply with his command, he could not think of one. He abandoned the command.

Persistent persuasion is a form of induction that has a sound theoretical basis derived from research. You may find other discipline approaches that you are comfortable with. Whatever approach you adopt, evaluate it to be sure it improves compliance, internalization, and emotions in your classroom.

Group Diversity in Discipline

What kind of discipline did you receive when you were growing up? Your answer may be influenced by your SES and cultural background.

Socioeconomic Status

Research consistently shows that low-SES students are more likely than high-SES students to experience and approve of power assertive or harsh discipline at home, including corporal punishment (e.g., Evans, 2004; Kochanska et al., 2007). This is true across cultures and countries (Douglas, 2006; Erkman & Rohner, 2006; Tang, 2006). One reason for this may be that low-SES families are more likely to live in unsafe neighborhoods and use power-assertive discipline in order to protect their children. However, as you learned earlier, in the long term power assertion typically has the opposite of its intended effect, increasing disobedience. Induction, in which consequences of breaking rules are explained to children, tends to be more effective in promoting long-term obedience.

Ethnicity

Rules about how children should behave during discipline encounters may vary by ethnicity. For example, in some ethnic communities children are taught to look a parent in the eye when they are being disciplined to show that they are paying attention. In other ethnic communities, looking an authority figure in the eye is a sign of disrespect. For another example, in some (but not all) East Asian cultures, students may smile or even giggle while being disciplined. American teachers may think the child is laughing at them, and become angry, if they do not realize that smiles in this situation can mean that the students admit guilt (Weinstein, Tomlinson-Clarke, & Curran, 2004). If there is a mismatch between the school culture and their home culture, students can be misunderstood during discipline encounters.

Corporal punishment may also vary by ethnicity. Spanking is used more by Black than White parents in the United States and less by Latino parents (Berlin et al., 2009; Lansford et al., 2009; Wissow, 2001). You learned earlier that spanking is linked to behavior problems in children. This linkage has been found for children from 3 to 13 years of age across three major ethnic groups—Latino, African American, and White—in a large, national study (Bradley, Corwyn, Burchinal, McAdoo, & Garcia Coll, 2001). However, this linkage tends to be weaker in Black families than in other ethnic groups (Lansford, 2004; Polaha, Larzelere, Shapiro, & Pettit, 2004), although some studies find equally negative effects for Black and White children (e.g., Mulvaney & Mebert, 2007).

Why might corporal punishment have different effects in different ethnic groups? One possibility is that corporal punishment has different *meanings* for different groups.

For example, spanking can be a viewed as either a legitimate use of parental authority or as an act of aggression. African American youth may be more likely to see spanking as a legitimate use of parental authority than do White youth (Deater-Deckard, Lansford, Dodge, Pettit, & Bates, 2003). Spanking may not have negative effects if it is considered normal and if it is mild, used in the context of a positive relationship, and used as a teaching tool. However, there is an increasing attitude in the United States to reject corporal punishment, including among African Americans. If spanking becomes less acceptable, it could have more negative effects for all groups.

Cross-National Comparisons

Use and approval of corporal punishment also varies by country and even by region of the United States. In one study, mothers from six countries were asked how often they spank, slap, grab, shake, and beat their child (Lansford et al., 2005). Responses varied from almost never to about once a month. In order from lowest to highest use of physical punishment were Thailand, China, Philippines, Italy, India, and Kenya.

In countries where physical discipline is accepted, the link between physical discipline and negative child outcomes is not as strong as in countries where physical discipline is frowned upon. However, regardless of how accepted corporal punishment is in different countries, it is associated with high rates of aggression in children (Lansford et al., 2005). For example, harsh power assertion is linked to negative child outcomes, like aggression, in China as well as Western countries. Love withdrawal is also linked to negative child outcomes across nations (Nelson, Hart, Yang, Olsen, & Jin, 2006; Wang, Pomerantz, & Chen, 2007).

Understanding diversity in discipline is important because you might have students from backgrounds quite different from your own. Your students may misunderstand your attempts to discipline if you are not aware of the differences. You will need to find a discipline approach that both you and your students are comfortable with, but that still involves principles of effective discipline and promotes self-control in your students. This is not likely to be corporal punishment, according to research across cultures. Let's turn next to a discussion of how you can apply research on discipline to your classroom.

Classroom Implications of Discipline

Discipline is one of the primary tasks of teachers. Learning to use effective discipline is important. You may eliminate about 75% of the misbehavior in your classroom if you use effective discipline, even if you teach in a school with difficult-to-manage students (Balfanz, Herzog, & MacIver, 2007). You may eliminate another 15 to 20% of misbehavior through efforts beyond just effective discipline—such as a close teacher–student relationship, with daily monitoring of behavior. Eliminating the remaining 5 to 10% of misbehavior might require a counselor's intervention.

How do you know if your discipline is effective? Ask yourself: "What did I teach the student?" If the answer is good values and self-control, you are on the right track. Think of discipline encounters as teaching moments. You will hear about many approaches to classroom discipline—Behavior Intervention Support Team (BIST), Assertive Discipline, Discipline with Dignity, Positive Discipline, School-Wide Positive Behavior Support, Teacher Effectiveness Training, to name just a few. Before you select an approach, confirm whether it has been evaluated using good science (see Chapter 1). You will be an effective disciplinarian if you follow these guidelines suggested by research:

- When deciding how and when to use discipline in your classroom, keep in mind that effective discipline (1) results in compliance, (2) is positive in tone, and (3) uses the least amount of power possible.
- Use induction as your primary approach to discipline because it promotes self-control. However, power assertion may be appropriate when students are physically hurting each other and you need to forcibly separate them quickly.

If you choose to use power assertion, there are more- and less-effective ways to use it. In Chapter 3 you learned about behavior modification. Behavior modification is power assertion in that it operates by virtue of the teacher wielding power, or control of resources, that the child does not have. However, power-assertive discipline tends to be negative and punishment oriented, whereas behavior modification tends to be positive, emphasizing reinforcement rather than punishment. You have seen two negative examples of power assertion in this chapter. Mrs. Reinhardt used it with Clint, in the opening vignette, when she gave him a red card for talking in class, and then sent him to the principal. Ms. Schwab used it with Peter and Marcus when she made them go out in the hallway for misbehaving. These two discipline encounters were not successful, but when used effectively, behavior modification can be quite successful. Let's discuss how you can use behavior modification in your classroom.

Think About This See Figure 7.5.
A 13-year-old girl was told to write "This is a quiet study hall" fifty times as punishment for talking during study hall. Is this effective discipline? Explain your response. What would you do if students talked during study hall?

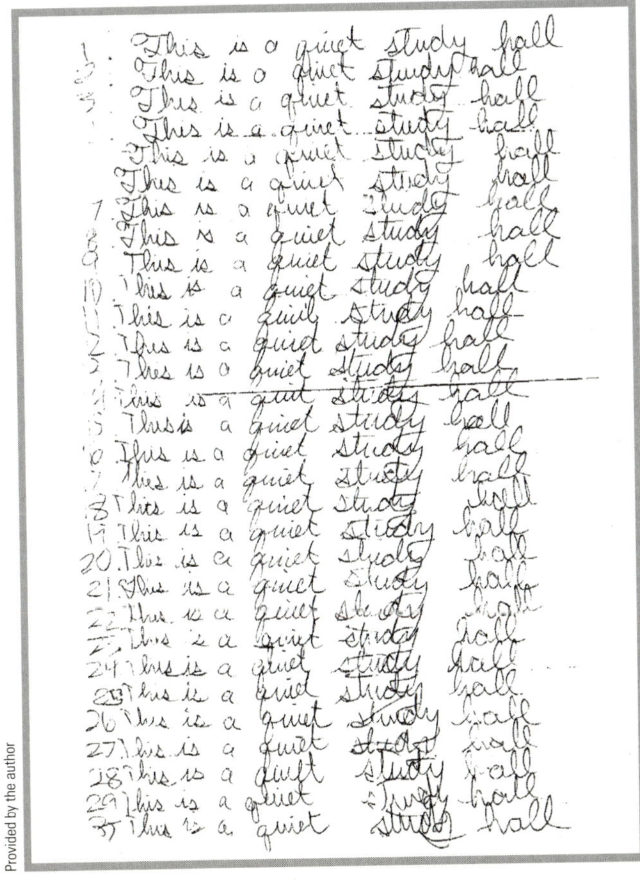
1. This is a quiet study hall
2. This is a quiet study hall
3. This is a quiet study hall
This is a quiet study hall
This is a quiet study hall
This is a quiet study hall
7. This is a quiet study hall
8. This is a quiet study hall
9. This is a quiet study hall
10. This is a quiet study hall
11. This is a quiet study hall
12. This is a quiet study hall
13. This is a quiet study hall
14. This is a quiet study hall
15. This is a quiet study hall
16. This is a quiet study hall
17. This is a quiet study hall
18. This is a quiet study hall
19. This is a quiet study hall
20. This is a quiet study hall
21. This is a quiet study hall
22. This is a quiet study hall
23. This is a quiet study hall
24. This is a quiet study hall
25. This is a quiet study hall
26. This is a quiet study hall
27. This is a quiet study hall
28. This is a quiet study hall
29. This is a quiet study hall
30. This is a quiet study hall

Provided by the author

Figure 7.5 Punishment?
This is a 13-year-old girl's punishment for talking during study hall. Was this effective discipline? Think about the principles of effective discipline and the goal of discipline as you answer this question.

Revisiting Behavior Modification

[My school] had an unusually large number of hyperactive, uncooperative 3rd grade children one year. The principal took all the unmanageable kids and formed one class. I was assigned to teach these eighteen children, many of whom were on medication for hyperactivity . . . the next five months can be described only as a nightmare. Each day's class was filled with fights, yelling, throwing chairs, and comments like "Try and make me do that!" Many mornings I cried as I anticipated going to school. I often called in sick. . . . In January I told the principal I was quitting because I could not take it any more. He talked me into staying.

I . . . went to [a psychologist] for help. He . . . told me how to implement tactics which would re-direct their aggressive, anti-social hyperactivity into achievement-oriented, socially-acceptable activities. . . . Within three weeks . . . my students . . . were doing their schoolwork. In class they studied vocabulary words, read books, and helped each other learn. Many even asked to take schoolwork home . . . The principal, the other teachers, and I could not believe our eyes . . . (Robinson, Newby, & Hill, 1981, pp. vii–viii)

Steve/Mary Skjold/PhotoLibrary

Effective classroom discipline reduces misbehavior and increases time-on-task.

What did the psychologist help this 3rd-grade teacher do? Implement behavior modification in her classroom. Behavior modification is largely based on operant conditioning. That is, as behavior becomes associated with certain consequences, behavior will increase or decrease. Reinforcement refers to a consequence that *increases* the probability of a specific behavior. Punishment refers to a consequence that *reduces* the probability of a specific behavior.

School psychologists and special education teachers often use behavior modification because it is a powerful method for quickly changing behavior even among quite challenging students. You can also use it successfully with typical students. Behavior modification is most successful when used in a deliberate, analytical way. In fact, it is also called *applied behavior analysis* because you must analyze the child's behavior to develop a solution. To effectively use behavior modification in your classroom, follow these guidelines:

- Before you begin an intervention, document a base rate for behaviors. Count the misbehaviors. Note the events that occur before the behavior (antecedents), and the consequences that follow the behavior and may be reinforcing it. Then, systematically alter the antecedents and consequences and observe what happens. Figure out what combination of antecedents and consequences best changes the target behavior (Epstein, Atkins, Cullinan, Kutash, & Weaver, 2008).
- Apply the principles of effective behavior modification deliberately:

- Provide positive consequences for positive behavior.
- Change the child's behavior in small steps (i.e., shaping).
- Give immediate feedback.
- Be consistent.
- Set explicit goals.
- Allow adequate practice or rehearsal.

- Reinforce good behavior, rather than punishing misbehavior. Most advocates of behavior modification are critical of using punishment because it can elicit aggression, fear, or resentment; it does not teach anything new; and it provides a negative model that students may imitate.
- If you feel you must use punishment, tell your students exactly what behavior will result in punishment and exactly what the punishment is. Administer the punishment as soon as possible after the infraction. Do this in the context of a warm, caring environment. Combine the punishment with induction; that is, give reasons for why the behavior is prohibited

Punishment is quite challenging to use effectively in classrooms. Let's take a look at Paul, a 10th-grader, who was punished for tossing a condom onto a girl's desk. He and his friends thought it was funny. His group of friends often plays inappropriate practical jokes, so they are often sent to in-school suspension (ISS). Today he enters his social studies class following three days of ISS:

His teacher says, "Nice to see you are finally out of ISS." Paul smiles and says, "Yeah, but it won't be long until I am back there—it's only Thursday." Paul says ISS is not a punishment, but rather, "like a time-out except my friends are in there and I don't have to see teachers that I don't like. The teacher never pays attention to what we are doing. We can do anything we want as long as we are quiet."

Paul's experience illustrates important pitfalls you want to avoid in your classroom:

- Avoid punishing students in ways that remove them from opportunities to learn. Paul is missing substantial instructional time.
- Make sure that intended punishment is not reinforcing. Because Paul and his friends enjoy each others' company immensely, the supposed punishment is actually reinforcing. With preschoolers, if time-out is intended to punish by removing the child from sources of reinforcement, verify that the child is not being removed from an aversive situation or reinforced with attention.
- Make sure that intended rewards are actually reinforcing. For example, is praise a reinforcer? Only if it *increases the probability of a behavior.* Some students would rather disappear than be praised in front of peers by a teacher. Praise for them would function as a punishment, or decrease the probability of a behavior, even though the teacher intended to reward the student.
- Avoid punishments that send a negative message about doing productive things. For example, don't use homework as punishment or homework exemptions as rewards.

If you apply behavior modification principles effectively in your classroom, you are likely to see improvement in student behavior.

Are there limits to behavior modification? A strict behaviorist, like Skinner, would argue that all behavior is controlled by consequences, whether you are aware of it or not, so you might as well control it consciously. Other psychologists argue that, despite its effectiveness at changing behavior, there are limitations to behavior modification. One is that behavior change may be short-lived and not generalize to other situations. Another limitation is that controlling consequences may undermine students' feelings of autonomy in a way that makes a student want to rebel. Finally, while behavior modification changes behavior, attitude change and internalization of values may not accompany behavior change.

This last problem—lack of internalization—is particularly linked to use of material reinforcement. Some teachers reward good behavior with objects like a sticker or candy. Although this may seem positive, there can be subtle, unintended negative effects on internalization. In a famous experiment, preschoolers who liked to draw were randomly assigned to a control group or to a group that was rewarded for their drawing (Lepper, Greene, & Nisbett, 1973). Later, the children who received the reward showed *less* interest in drawing. The reward appeared to *undermine intrinsic interest* in the task. This effect has been replicated many times with children, teens, and adults doing many different tasks (Lepper, Keavney, & Drake, 1996; Ryan & Deci, 1996). This suggests that rewarding students for good behavior can undermine their intrinsic motivation for the behavior, possibly short circuiting their development of self-control.

However, the undermining effect of rewards generally applies only to activities that students already like. It is difficult to undermine intrinsic motivation if there is none to begin with. Rewards can be useful to get students to do things they do not like. In addition, subtle reinforcers are less likely to undermine motivation than material rewards. That is, a pat on the back or word of praise is less likely to undermine motivation than candy or stickers.

Another problem with using rewards is that it is remarkably difficult to distribute them fairly in real classrooms. Not all deserving students may get recognized. At award time, one student smiles while others frown. For example, in one elementary school students are rewarded for positive traits such as caring, respect, or responsibility. Their names are placed in a drawing for a prize. One well-behaved boy had his name placed in the drawing many times, but never won in six years. He told his mother he didn't know why he even tried. At another school, an astute, well-behaved 5th-grader told us, "They only give the prizes to the bad kids so that they'll behave better. I'll never get one."

How do you balance the pros and cons of behavior modification? One approach is to use explicit behavior modification only in situations where students' classroom behavior is substantially out of control. Use it for the short term until behavior is back to reasonable levels, and then discontinue it, or use it intermittently over time, while gradually increasing use of induction. You may have to problem solve to see what discipline approach works best in your classroom, but keep in mind that short-term compliance is not the only goal of effective discipline; you want to help students internalize good behavior and develop self-control.

Including Parents in Classroom Discipline

When students misbehave in class, should their parents be involved in their discipline? This depends on the skills of the parents. Parents with poor child management skills may respond by harshly punishing the child in ways that undermine the child's self-control. Some parents are even abusive. The student may resent you for causing their parent's harsh punishment. Thus, while it is reasonable to expect parental support in some cases, in other cases it can lead to greater problems.

In one case, enlisting the parent's help for a child's misbehavior was highly effective. Marta, a Latina 1st-grader, was a behavior problem in the classroom and did her schoolwork carelessly (Goldenberg, 1992). Marta's teacher went to much effort to talk with Marta's mother, despite the mother's long work hours and discomfort communicating in English. After talking with the teacher, Marta's mother started reminding Marta to behave in school, and she helped Marta learn how to blend consonants and vowels to read syllables and words. Marta turned around academically and behaviorally, becoming a better student. Her story illustrates a successful teacher intervention through a parent.

Effective classroom management is a key to avoiding disciplinary confrontations. If you manage your classroom well, there should be less need for discipline. That is the next topic.

Think About This The president of the National Association for the Education of Young Children visited a school in China, where she witnessed forty 3-year-olds sit still at their desks for forty minutes watching a peer performance. In India, she saw sixty 1st-grade boys sit on the floor (only the teacher had a desk) in rapt attention during a lesson. There was no misbehavior in either class. Both countries have high achievement (Katz, 1999). What might explain these children's self-control? Base your response on what you know about the development of self-control, cultural differences, and classroom management.

Classroom Management

Before the class bell rings, Ms. Callahan stands at the door to her 11th-grade English class. As students enter her room, she greets each by name with a smile. Objectives for the day's lesson are written on the board, with instructions for students to begin an activity as soon as they sit down. Ms. Callahan remains at the door until the bell rings, but occasionally calls to students who have already sat down and begun their assignment. She says, "Lin, I'm glad to see that you have begun writing," and "Graciela, would you please show Kayla where to start?" Within minutes after the bell rings, every student is engaged in writing, and they are smiling.

Ms. Callahan is a skilled classroom manager. The casual observer cannot see her skill because it looks like the students are naturally obedient. In fact, Ms. Callahan carefully organized appealing classroom procedures that would prevent misbehavior and foster achievement. Discipline is a part of classroom management, but classroom management goes beyond discipline. **Classroom management** refers to all aspects of managing the classroom, from setting clear rules, to scheduling daily events, to the emotional relationship between teacher and students. Skillful classroom management can reduce the need for discipline by preventing misbehavior before it happens. Students in classrooms that are well managed tend to have better self-control, engagement, and achievement (Freiberg, Huzinec, & Templeton, 2009; Rimm-Kaufman, Curby, Grimm, Nathanson, & Brock, 2009). Here are some guidelines for managing your classroom effectively:

classroom management all aspects of managing the classroom, including but not limited to, discipline.

- Establish procedures or routines for common classroom activities like arriving in the morning, handing in homework, dividing into groups, and passing out materials, as Ms. Callahan did (Emmer, Evertson, & Worsham, 2000).
- Provide an interesting curriculum. (In Chapter 13 we will discuss interest in the classroom.) Boredom fosters distraction and misbehavior.

- Avoid competitive activities that make some students feel that no matter how hard they try, they won't be successful. Activities to avoid include giving prizes for reading the most books, displaying only the best papers, and rewarding the fastest math problem solvers.
- Have a *few* clear rules that everyone knows, such as "respect other persons and their property" and "listen quietly while others are speaking." You can have the students help develop the rules.
- Create a physical environment that fosters appropriate behavior. This can include removing distracting objects, placing desks in patterns that foster attention and collaboration, and seating students with nondistracting peers (Epstein et al., 2008).

These practices can be implemented in all grades, from preschool to high school. Let's listen to a veteran teacher in elementary school:

We begin class with sustained silent reading (SSR). My students come into the room, put homework on my desk for me to check, and find a place to read. While they read, I check their homework and record attendance and lunch money. The children want to read their books, so they get right to work. I also end the school day with reading, but I read aloud to them. The children dawdle less so that they have more time for the read-aloud. I can tell how much the children like the book by how fast they quiet down. I wish I had started this years sooner.

This teacher and Ms. Callahan both work with challenging students, yet manage their classrooms in ways that help their students experience success at school.

Teachers who are good classroom managers spend time at the beginning of the school year explaining rules and procedures. Teachers who are less effective classroom managers set rules but do not clearly explain or enforce them. When teachers give vague rules, or do not teach students how they should behave, students use their own impulses to guide their behavior. Students may want to please the teacher but do not know exactly what they should be doing.

Classroom management is important because when teachers effectively manage classrooms, student achievement tends to rise. This is probably because students spend more time on-task and there is less disruptive behavior in well-managed classrooms.

Culturally Responsive Classroom Management

Cultural mismatch can occur in classroom management when teachers and students have different ideas about appropriate behavior. The same students can be a behavior problem in one classroom but not another, depending on fit (Gregory & Weinstein, 2008). Students who are most likely to be disciplined or suspended from school are African American, male, low SES, low achieving, and in special education. This suggests a possible cultural mismatch for these students in some classrooms. These guidelines may help you make your classroom a better cultural fit for more students (Weinstein et al., 2004):

- Recognize your own cultural biases. You have expectations about language use, profanity, obedience, punctuality, appropriate levels of freedom, strictness, and so forth that are based on your background experience.

- Use management strategies that fit your students' cultural backgrounds. Cultures differ in their preference to be singled out for achievement versus not being singled out, for independence versus dependence on adult authority, for unsupervised play versus play supervised by adults, for group versus solitary work, and so forth. You can learn your students' culture through reading books, close observation, talking with parents, and visiting neighborhoods. At the same time, you may need to shape students' behavior so they can function effectively in the culture of the school.
- Recognize patterns of institutional bias, like penalizing an African American male for wearing pants that sag while allowing White students to wear pants with holes in the thighs (Nieto, 2000). Another example is defining "good" students as those who have high test scores, are outgoing, participate in sports, and have stable families—even though these attributes may apply to some groups of students more than others (Meador, 2005).
- Help all students feel cared for. Students of color are less likely to feel cared for than European American students, and this undermines their achievement and attitude toward school. In one study, Black high school students who were suspended from one teacher's classroom were cooperative and engaged in the classrooms of teachers who focused on building positive relationships with students. Thus, building relationships may narrow the distance between teachers and students who have different social class and ethnicity (Gregory & Ripski, 2008). "Students want to know how much you care before they consider how much you know" (Freiberg et al., 2009, p. 66).

David Grossman/Alamy

In some schools, students of color are less likely to feel cared for than White students.

Your approach to discipline and classroom management is the foundation of your teaching "style." You can learn from the research on parenting styles about how different teaching styles may affect self-control in your students.

Teaching Self-Control: What Parenting Styles Tell Us

Mr. Dunlop, a 7th-grade science teacher, enforces rules strictly. One rule is that he does not accept late homework. When Anita hands in homework a day late, Mr. Dunlop says, "Keep it. You know I do not accept late homework." Anita pleads, "I was sick yesterday." Mr. Dunlop responds, "Sick does not count as an excuse. You knew two weeks ago this would be due." When Anita protests, Mr. Dunlop talks over her until she turns and walks back to her desk in disgust.

As the class begins, she looks annoyed and is not paying attention. During the science lesson, Owen calls out an answer without raising his hand. Mr. Dunlop writes Owen's name on the board. When Owen breaks his pencil in a show of anger, Mr. Dunlop places a check mark next to his name. Mr. Dunlop gives advice to a new teacher: "You've got to rule them, or they'll rule you!"

What do you think of Mr. Dunlop's style of controlling his classroom? Teachers who rigidly enforce rules in power-assertive ways are unlikely to promote self-control in students. At the same time, teachers who are lax with rules are also unlikely to promote self-control. So what teaching style is the best for promoting self-control in students? Research on parenting style suggests some answers.

Four Styles of Parenting

Parenting style is defined primarily by two dimensions: (1) the degree to which parents are *warm*, *accepting*, and *responsive* toward their children and (2) the degree to which parents are *controlling* and *demand mature behavior* of their children (Maccoby & Martin, 1983). You might mistakenly think "controlling" is always negative, such as when parents are intrusive or domineering. However, it also refers to positive control such as guidance, firmness, and structure (Grolnick & Pomerantz, 2009). Many decades of research have found that both parenting dimensions—warmth and control—are critical to children's well-being. Four parenting styles have been identified based on whether parents are high or low on the two dimensions (see Table 7.1.) We describe each style and the child outcomes associated with them next.

Indifferent Style

indifferent parenting style parents are low on both control and acceptance. They are not affectionate or responsive and have few rules. They are self- rather than child-centered. Also called neglectful or uninvolved.

Indifferent parents are *low on both control and acceptance.* They do not set rules for their children, nor do they show much affection, support, or responsiveness. In a child's everyday life, indifferent parents show little interest in events at the child's school, seldom converse with the child, do not consider the child's opinion, and often do not know where their child is or who their child is with. Parents are self-centered rather than child-centered (Maccoby & Martin, 1983). Indifferent parents may use a lot of harsh discipline, but also yield to their children's demands (Fletcher, Walls, Cook, Madison, & Bridges, 2008). At the extreme, they are considered *neglectful.* Severe depression or drug use may cause some parents to be neglectful.

Children with indifferent parents tend to have the lowest self-control and poorest academic performance of the four groups. They are the most likely to engage in delinquent behavior, including smoking, drug use, violence against dating partners, and sexual activity (Baumrind, 1991; Steinberg, Blatt-Eisengart, & Cauffman, 2006;

Table 7.1 Parenting styles based on control and acceptance

		Control and Demandingness	
		Low	**High**
Acceptance and Responsiveness	Low	Indifferent style	Authoritarian style
	High	Indulgent style	Authoritative style

Straus & Savage, 2005). One study found that the less responsive and demanding the parents, the more likely their adolescents had hit or beat up a peer, carried a weapon to school, or threatened a peer with a weapon (Jackson & Foshee, 1998).

Indulgent Style

indulgent parenting style parents are low on control, but high on acceptance. They have few rules and avoid controlling their children. Also called permissive.

Indulgent, or permissive, parents are *high on acceptance and responsiveness*, but *low on control* of their children. They have few rules governing their children's schedules, like regular mealtime or bedtime. They seldom discipline and avoid asserting authority or imposing restrictions on their child. For example, they may not require their children to follow through on assignments. But they are warm and supportive toward their children.

Children of indulgent parents have relatively low self-control and poor academic performance. They are more likely to engage in delinquent behavior, such as smoking, drug use, and sexual activity, than are children of authoritative and authoritarian parents. At the same time, they may feel self-confident and be socially skilled. They tend to be peer oriented and involved in activities valued by adolescents but not adults, like partying (Durbin, Darling, Steinberg, & Brown, 1993; Steinberg & Silk, 2002).

Authoritarian Style

authoritarian parenting style parents are high on control but low on acceptance. They discourage verbal give-and-take, value their authority, and tend to be power assertive.

Authoritarian parents are *high on control* of their children, but *low on acceptance and responsiveness* to the child's agenda. In authoritarian households, rules are not discussed or negotiated; in fact, negotiation with children is often viewed as a threat to the parent's authority. Authoritarian parents do not welcome input from their children or give reasons why something should be done. Phrases like "Because I say so" may be commonly used. Authoritarian parents tend to be more punitive than other parents, and use power-assertive discipline (Maccoby & Martin, 1983).

Children of authoritarian parents are somewhat obedient and often conform to rules set for them. They have been pressured into obedience and may misbehave when the pressure is absent. They perform adequately in school, but they tend to lack self-confidence (Steinberg & Silk, 2002).

Authoritative Style

authoritative parenting style parents are high on control, acceptance, and autonomy support. They maintain authority and enforce rules, but are responsive to their children.

Authoritative parents are *high on both acceptance* and *control* of their children. A key attribute of authoritative parents is that they *support autonomy* in their children (Steinberg & Silk, 2002). How can parents be highly controlling and still support their children's independence and self-direction? They do so by having clear standards and high expectations for mature, polite behavior, but without taking away choice (Grolnick, 2003). They firmly enforce rules, using commands and sanctions when necessary, but give reasons for their decisions. They provide household structure, like set bedtimes. However, there is also open communication between parents and children, with encouragement of verbal give-and-take. Authoritative parents are interested in what their children have to say. While children are required to be responsive to parental demands, parents are as responsive as possible to their children's reasonable demands and points of view (Maccoby & Martin, 1983).

> ***Think About This*** Think back to two classes you had in school—one that was managed very well and one that was not. What attributes of the classes were different? Did they result in different amounts of learning or elicit different behavior from you? Could you categorize the teachers as indifferent, indulgent, authoritarian, or authoritative? Explain your response.

A 3rd-grade girl provided an example that will help you understand how parents can be both highly controlling and responsive. She told her teacher she had a bedtime of 8:10 p.m. Why such an odd time? She said that if she had to be in bed by 8:00, she would have to start brushing her teeth at 7:50 in order to be in bed on time, and she would always miss the end of her favorite television show. By setting the bedtime at 8:10, the parents maintained control by enforcing a strict bedtime but were responsive to their daughter's desire to watch the program.

Children of authoritative parents tend to have the highest self-control of the four groups. They tend to be securely attached (Karavasilis, Doyle, & Markiewicz, 2003). They also tend to be highest in self-esteem, social competence, and academic achievement (Fletcher, et al., 2008; Spera, 2005; Steinberg et al., 2006). Children's decision-making autonomy, which is provided by authoritative parents, is especially important as they grow into adolescence because it is related to improved emotional functioning (Qin, Pomerantz, & Wang, 2009).

There are four possible reasons for these positive child outcomes:

1. Authoritative parents tend to use inductive discipline, which promotes self-control. Furthermore, parents who use induction typically remain in control of themselves when disciplining their children, which serves as a model for the child.
2. Authoritative parents' warmth and respect for their children's views makes the children more willing to adopt their parents' views.
3. Authoritative parents are very clear about rules or standards for behavior, so children know how to behave in a variety of situations.
4. Authoritative parents permit negotiation and compromise, when appropriate, which fosters their children's development of these important social skills, even in very young children. (Kuczynski & Kochanska, 1990).

In adolescence, when parents jointly make decisions with them, teens have better self-control than when parents either impose decisions or leave the decision to their children (Fletcher, Darling, Steinberg, & Dornbusch, 1995).

How common is each parenting style? Large studies involving hundreds or thousands of adolescents tend to find about one-third of parents are indifferent, one-third are authoritative, one-sixth are authoritarian, and one-sixth are indulgent (Lamborn, Mounts, Steinberg, & Dornbusch, 1991; Rosen, Cheever, & Carrier, 2008). Another study of younger children found that as few as 5% were indulgent, so this may be the least common type of parenting (Baumrind, 1991).

Parents do not always fit clearly into a single parenting style, and parents may change across time (Holden & Miller, 1999). For example, parents may be authoritarian with their older children but become indulgent with the youngest. In addition, there can be considerable variation within each of the four parenting styles. For example, some authoritarian parents may be consistently harsh while others are occasionally warm toward their children. Furthermore, parents may have a somewhat different style with different children; some children may draw more control or more warmth from their parents.

The Adolescent Challenge

Across cultures adolescents develop a greater desire for autonomy. Regardless of parenting style, from age 11 to 17 children view their parents' authority as less legitimate and feel less obligated to obey parents compared to younger children. It is normal for teens to moderately resist parental authority, particularly in early adolescence. Yet, *authoritative* parents are more likely to be viewed by adolescents as legitimate authorities —and deserving of obedience (Darling, Cumsille, & Martinez, 2008).

In contrast, *authoritarian* parenting becomes a problem during adolescence. The power imbalance between children and their authoritarian parents diminishes, and authoritarian parents lose control over adolescents. For example, when children are able to hold their own jobs, have friends who drive, and can run fast, parents can no longer control their children by withholding money, hiding car keys, or chasing them down. As children enter adolescence, both parents and children become increasingly frustrated as authoritarian parents continue to try to assert their dwindling control. As we will see next, this frustration is more common in some groups.

Group Diversity in Parenting Style

Religion, socioeconomic status, family structure, and ethnicity are associated with parenting style. Authoritative parents are more likely to be religious, at least among Protestants, Mormons, Catholics, and Jews (Gunnoe, Hetherington, & Reiss, 1999). This may not be true for other religious groups. Authoritative parents are also more likely to be middle class than working class or impoverished and more likely to be part of an intact family than of a single-parent family or stepfamily (Carlson, Uppal, & Prosser, 2000; Deater-Deckard, 2000). Parents who lack a stable relationship, adequate income, and social support may find it more difficult to be authoritative. In addition, parents who fear the future, because they think the world is unsafe or that they cannot make a decent living, are more likely to be highly controlling with their children (Gurland & Grolnick, 2005). Thus, parenting style is not just a reflection of parents' personality, but also the context in which they live.

Indifferent parents are most likely to be at the two SES extremes—low and high. In some high-SES neighborhoods, there are no adults home after school to monitor the children. One teacher, at an expensive private school, tells the story of Kent.

> *Kent has high test scores, but he never completes his homework on time. He is barely passing his classes. When I call his parents, they tell me they are getting a tutor and he will be doing his homework, but nothing changes. Kent's parents work long hours so that sometimes he does not see them for days. I have never met the parents because they do not attend school events. Kent has started smoking, and other students say he uses drugs.*

Kent's parents are wealthy with demanding jobs, and they have an indifferent parenting style. Indifferent parenting is linked to drug use in children among high- and low-SES families (Luthar, 2003).

Ethnicity

Authoritarian parenting is linked to more behavior problems and lower achievement, compared to authoritative parenting, for all children, but the effects are weaker for Black or Asian children than for White and Latino children (Hill, Bush, & Roosa, 2003; Ho, Bluestein, & Jenkins, 2008; Pittman & Chase-Lansdale, 2001). African American parents tend to be more authoritarian and make more decisions for their adolescents than do European American parents (Gutman & Eccles, 2007). In addition, although authoritarian parenting is linked to lower academic achievement among

Golden Pixels LLC, 2009/Used under license from Shutterstock.com

Authoritative parents set limits but are warm and listen to their children.

Latino children, it is also linked to respect for elders and family cohesion, which are highly valued outcomes within the culture (Halgunseth, Ispa, & Rudy, 2006).

What might explain ethnic differences in outcomes of authoritarian parenting? Perhaps quality of neighborhood. Parents who raise children in difficult settings, such as unsafe neighborhoods, or in societies that are racist or foreign to them, may be more restrictive in an attempt to protect their children (Supple & Small, 2006). African American children living in high-crime neighborhoods are not as negatively affected by restrictive parenting as children of other ethnicities or in other neighborhoods. However, even in this subgroup, by the time children finish elementary school, restrictive parenting becomes linked to depression and lower academic achievement (Dearing, 2004).

Another explanation is that the meaning of parenting may vary by culture. As mentioned earlier in this chapter, punitive control may be interpreted in some communities as a sign of parental caring, rather than rejection (Grusec & Goodnow, 1994). The effect of parenting depends on how it is interpreted. For example, Chinese American mothers tend to value "training" their children (Chao, 1994). For them, training means teaching, educating, or inculcating in a positive way. In contrast, for European American mothers, training means being militaristic or overly strict. Because of their different views of the meaning and value of training children, an authoritarian parenting style may be less detrimental for Chinese American children. Thus, the effects of parenting style may depend on how it is interpreted in a particular culture.

Cross-National Comparisons

Results of research across nations on the topic of parenting tend to mirror that of North America. That is, authoritative parenting is linked to optimal child outcomes. For example, children's behavior that is valued in both China and the United States—academic achievement, emotional well-being, self-regulation, minimal anger and frustration, ability to concentrate, and social acceptance—is linked to authoritative parenting in both countries (Zhou, Eisenberg, Wang, & Reiser, 2004). Interestingly, in China *authoritative* parenting is related to shyness, which is a valued attribute (Chen, Dong, & Zhou, 1997). In contrast, in the United States *authoritarian* parenting is related to shyness, which is not valued. Thus, in both countries authoritative parenting style is linked to valued traits. Furthermore, low-SES Chinese parents are less likely to be authoritative, just as in the United States.

Some studies have found that Asian and Latino parents in North America tend to be quite strict. They tend to be controlling, power assertive, and intolerant of give-and-take from their children, yet their children tend to feel that they are not overly controlling. This is because strict Asian and Latino parents are often more indulgent and warm than strict

European American parents (Chao, 1994; Halgunseth et al., 2006; Steinberg, 1999). This hybrid style is primarily authoritative, but with some authoritarian components.

In summary, authoritative parenting predicts culturally valued child behavior across ethnic subcultures in North America, and across nations. In addition warm, involved parenting is protective, while hostile, rejecting parenting is a risk factor across cultures. However, in cultures where restrictive, undemocratic parenting is prevalent and accepted, *if combined with warmth*, children may not develop the behavior problems associated with authoritarian parenting. Therefore, how your students respond to their parents' style depends on nuances in that style and the values of the community in which they live.

Classroom Implications of Parenting Style

A critical lesson from this discussion on parenting styles is that *the effect of discipline depends on whether it takes place within the context of a warm adult–child relationship.* The same lesson applies to teaching. Teachers have patterns of control and warmth that parallel parenting styles. The following are descriptions of real teachers. Can you identify their styles?

1. Mr. Graham has no classroom rules and low expectations for his students. He has said to other teachers, "Rules will be broken by these monsters, so why set them?" He does not assign homework and is consistently late to class, while his students roam the halls disturbing other classes. Students leave during class; he does not know or care where they go. He allows students to threaten each other during class—fights have broken out in his class. He never attends extracurricular activities. In his class, students are slackers who do not care about their grades; most were not like that before Mr. Graham's class.
2. Mrs. Sinclair is always kind-hearted. She wants people to like her. She will do anything parents demand of her. Her kids run the class. She begs them to behave, but they ignore her. She struggles to get papers graded and exams written on time. Her students are slackers who do not care about their grades and do as they please, but they are kind to each other.
3. Mr. Dunlop you have already met (in the section-opening vignette). He has high standards for his students. They learn what they are supposed to learn. His students do not step out of line for fear of punishment. His room is neat and orderly. He spends a lot of after-school time in his classroom. Most parents approve of his style, but when a parent does not, there is a major power struggle.
4. Miss Loeb is one of Le'Raun's teachers (in case 3). She has high standards for her students. She also has a good personal relationship with most. Students feel she cares for them and is fair to all in both her grading and her discipline. She has total control over her classroom, but in a way that students don't even notice. She is well organized. Papers are graded in a timely way.

Which teaching style do you think is most effective? What style characterizes you at this time? Teachers who are warm, but lax, are not likely to help their students develop self-control or learn much, although the students may like them and be happy in class. Teachers who are harsh and overly controlling are also not likely to help their students develop self-control, or enjoy school, although the students may learn. Teachers who are indifferent to their students and exert no classroom control may be the least effective. Effective teachers behave like authoritative parents. They are demanding, have high expectations, and are perceived as fair and caring by their students (Wentzel, 2002).

Authoritative teaching may be beneficial for all children, but particularly for African American students, who receive a disproportionate number of suspensions and discipline. This is a grave problem because suspension is linked to less opportunity to learn and school bonding. How can this trend be reversed? Students are less disobedient toward authoritative teachers, whom they view as having more legitimate authority. Recall from Chapter 6 that personality can be situation specific. In one study, African American students who were quite defiant with some teachers behaved better in authoritative teachers' classes. They felt these teachers cared for them and expected more of them, and felt obligated to cooperate with the teacher. They were more engaged, paid attention, and skipped class less for authoritative teachers. Listen to what three 11th- and 12th-graders said about their teachers:

- *. . . she nice, but she strict . . . nobody, like, try to go against her judgment.*
- *Well, actually, it is not that he enforces his rules cause he don't have to because all the students respect him . . . if he ask the class, you know, be quiet so that we could get our class discussion started, they automatically be quiet.*
- *. . . when she talk to you with seriousness, she mean it, but then she also have a smile like "I'm on your side." I mean, "I feel where you're coming from but I'm still your teacher." (Gregory & Weinstein, 2008, pp. 469–470)*

The authoritative, respected teachers were equally likely to be male or female, and White, Black, Asian, or Latino (and so were the teachers who drew defiance).

A veteran high school teacher shared the story of her movement toward a more authoritative style (Armstrong, 1999). For years she had either played the role of judge, evaluating the merits of each sob story for late papers, or taken the dictator stance. She decided to opt out of both roles. After twenty-nine years of teaching, she decided to give students more choice about homework deadlines, as long as students were reasonable and met her clear standards. She now gives students a recommended due date. If they fall behind, all they have to do is write her a note explaining when she can expect their papers. One student wrote: "*I'm really sorry I haven't finished those essay questions yet. . . . For the past two weeks I've had to work until 9 each night. I want to hand in my best work . . . but I don't want to inconvenience you too much. Could you please accept them on Monday?*" (p. 50). Her students are low SES with after-school jobs, some are parents, and most are sleep deprived because of hectic schedules. The result of responding to student needs has not been chaos, but better teacher–student relationships, and more conscientious students who accept responsibility for their own achievement.

This approach may not work in every classroom; however, the research presented throughout this chapter suggests that in most situations students do not need a power-assertive "or else" threat in order to behave responsibly. In fact, consistent use of power assertion may undermine students' self-control in the long run. Reasoning with students and respecting their agendas, while holding them to high standards, may be a better teaching style. You foster high achievement, as well as self-control, in your students by being appropriately demanding and controlling, but also displaying substantial warmth, acceptance, and respect.

At the conclusion of this chapter you should have a clear understanding that, as a teacher, you may promote or undermine students' self-control through the way you discipline them and through your interaction style in the classroom. One aspect of self-control that affects students' classroom functioning is their ability to control their emotions. This is the topic of the next chapter, the final chapter in this section on the emotional child.

Reflections on Practice: Checklist for Teachers

Are you using effective discipline with your students and promoting their self-control? Periodically ask yourself the following questions to gauge your mastery of these skills:

1. How was I disciplined in my family of origin? How is this linked to my culture and my own disciplinary style?
2. What was the goal of my last disciplinary action? What values did I teach the child?
3. Am I open to negotiating and compromising with my students during discipline encounters? Or, do I expect instant obedience? Do I demand compliance even when it does not matter?
4. Have I used love-withdrawal techniques like isolating a child? Have I used negative language—such as "I am not happy with you today"—and then ignored a child?
5. Do I regularly use an "or else" clause that threatens consequences such as red cards, keeping children in from recess, or calling the office?
6. Do I avoid using extrinsic rewards that students expect?
7. Do I explain the rules and consequences of misbehavior to my students? Do I give children reasons for obeying? Do I avoid saying "no" without explanation?
8. When seeking compliance, do I continually restate a command until the child complies, but without increasing the level of power or using threats (persistent persuasion)?
9. Do my students have committed compliance or situational compliance? Do they break class rules or misbehave when I am not present?
10. Do I maintain a positive emotional tone even during discipline? Do I have a warm relationship with students?
11. Do I recognize that some situations could make anyone lack self-control, and therefore create a classroom that avoids such situations? For example, do I keep temptations out of sight if they are likely to distract?
12. Am I appropriately controlling or lax? Am I warm, accepting, and responsive toward my students or cold and distant?

Summary of Age Trends in Self-Control and Discipline

	Self-Control	Compliance	Discipline and Parenting Style
Early Childhood (Birth–5 Years)	Infants have little self-control. Toddlers have some self-control. Delay of gratification steadily increases through toddlerhood, but is measured in seconds. Their fledgling ability to control impulses may disappear if a desired object is in sight. Preschoolers have more self-control but easily lose focus when distracted.	Infants have little ability to perceive or comply with demands. This ability emerges in toddlerhood. Among preschoolers, direct defiance and passive noncompliance, which are less skilled strategies, decline but negotiation, which is a more skilled strategy, increases.	The principles of effective discipline pertain to all ages. Induction is more effective than power assertion or love-withdrawal at any age, including toddlerhood. It may seem counter-intuitive to reason with preverbal children, yet induction is associated with more compliance and prosocial behavior in toddlers.
Middle Childhood (6–12 Years)	Delay of gratification is measured in minutes, suggesting greater ability than preschoolers to control impulses. Children are able to generate their own strategies of self-distraction to increase delay of gratification. Children increase ability to control attention in the face of distractions.	Children are generally capable of compliance, but may have trouble controlling impulses and may choose not to comply.	Induction continues to be a more effective form of discipline in the long term than love-withdrawal or power assertion.
Adolescence (13–19 Years)	Adolescents have increased ability to control their impulses. Youth have increased ability to consider the consequences of their immediate actions in the near future by early adolescence. By late adolescence, they can consider the consequences of their actions far into the future, but this is still not fully developed.	Adolescents are generally capable of compliance, but may choose not to comply.	For all age groups, authoritative parenting is most beneficial. Power-oriented parents lose their control over adolescents who develop their own sources of power.

Chapter Summary

Self-Control

- Self-control is the ability to inhibit impulses, control one's behavior, and follow rules. It includes the ability to delay gratification.
- There are large individual differences in self-control, even in preschoolers. These differences tend to be stable over the course of childhood and predict later outcomes, including academic achievement and social competence.
- The antecedents of self-control include (1) effective discipline, (2) practice (without taxing the self-control "muscle"), (3) secure attachment, (4) parental monitoring, and (5) authoritative parenting style. In addition, the structure of the situation can affect self-control.
- There are cultural differences in emphasis on conformity to rules and self-control. U.S.-born Americans tend to place less emphasis on conformity than do immigrants. Asian parents tend to emphasize self-control to fulfill group obligations.

Effective Discipline

- There are different kinds of compliance and noncompliance. The goal of effective discipline is committed, not just situational, compliance. Committed compliance is also known as "internalization."
- Induction is a form of discipline in which the adult gives the child a reason for changing misbehavior. Induction seems to be the most effective form of discipline for promoting social skills and self-control.
- Love-withdrawal is a type of psychological discipline in which the adult withdraws love or attention from the child for misbehavior and makes critical statements. It is linked to low self-esteem and high anxiety in children, which interfere with learning.
- Power assertion is a type of discipline in which the adult directly controls the child physically or by withholding resources. Power assertion is a common form of discipline, but it has serious drawbacks: it increases angry defiance, reduces internalization, damages relationships, models aggression, and raises children's expectation for more coercion. Corporal punishment, a form of power assertion, is associated with increased antisocial behavior.
- Physical abuse often begins as corporal punishment. Other forms of abuse include emotional abuse, sexual abuse, and neglect. Abuse is distressingly common and often perpetrated by family or acquaintances. Effects of abuse depend on its severity but can include emotional, social, and academic problems.
- The three principles of effective discipline are to (1) achieve compliance because present compliance predicts future compliance, (2) use the minimum power needed to obtain compliance so that children attribute their compliance to internal motives, and (3) keep the emotional tone of the interaction positive and cooperate

with the child whenever possible. Persistent persuasion is a type of discipline that uses all three principles. It involves calmly restating the command, giving reasons for compliance, and not escalating the level of coercion, until the child complies.

- Behavior modification is commonly used in classrooms to control behavior. It can be effective for controlling behavior, but there are two cautions: (1) rewards can be detrimental to children's intrinsic motivation and self-control, and (2) punishment should be avoided because it has negative side effects.
- Classroom management includes discipline, classroom structure, and routines. In well-managed classrooms, there is less need for overt discipline. Students spend more time on-task and experience higher achievement.

Parenting Style

- Adults vary in how controlling or lax they are with children. The effect of control depends on how warm, accepting, and responsive the adult is. These two dimensions combine to form four distinct parenting styles.
- Indifferent parents are low on both control and acceptance. Their children fare the worst and tend to be low in self-control and academic achievement and high in delinquent behavior.
- Authoritarian parents are high on control but low on acceptance. They are more likely to use power-assertive discipline. Their children tend to be externally controlled, average in achievement, and low in self-confidence. There are cultural and ethnic differences in whether authoritarian parenting has negative effects.
- Indulgent parents are low on control, but high on acceptance. Their children tend to have low self-control, low academic achievement, minor delinquency, and relatively strong self-confidence.
- Authoritative parents are high on both control and acceptance. Their children fare the best. They tend to be high in academic achievement, self-confidence, social competence, and self-control. Teachers who adopt this style may have students who behave better in class and learn more.

Accompanying Education CourseMate Website Resources

Visit the **Education CourseMate** website at **CengageBrain.com** to find resources and study aids for this chapter, including self-tests, additional print and website resources, and glossary flashcards.

TEACHSOURCE VIDEO CASE

Watch the video case *Classroom Management: Handling a Student with Behavior Problems*, which is about elementary school, and *Managing an Inclusive Classroom: High School Math Instruction*. As you view the videos and artifacts think about the following:

1. Which principles of effective discipline and good classroom management are manifest in the video cases?
2. Do the techniques suggested in the video cases foster self-control and internalization?

chapter 8

Emotional Development

Westend61/Jupiter Images

DO YOU KNOW A STUDENT WHO IS ALMOST ALWAYS HAPPY AND SENSITIVE TO OTHERS' FEELINGS? Do you know a student who is easily upset or often angry? Which student is more successful in school? In this chapter we will discuss why emotions are important at school. After you read this chapter, you will understand:

- How students learn to regulate their own emotions.
- How students come to understand others' emotions.
- What these skills mean for students' success in your classroom and how you can help your students develop emotional competence.
- How emotions influence thought.

Emotions

As Hailey's 5th-grade class begins a math worksheet, she cannot find her pencil. Her classmate Evan has a pencil on his desk, so Hailey snatches it. Evan grabs it back. Hailey is consumed with anger. She slugs Evan and shoves his friend, Roshni, out of his chair. As Roshni gets up, other children join the mêlée shouting at Hailey, "He had it first!" Hailey turns red, screams at Evan, and then begins sobbing and hiccupping.

The teacher, Mrs. Ng (pronounced like "ing"), quickly walks to Hailey's side. Although she is angry with Hailey, she says in a soothing but firm tone: "OK. Let's all calm down now. Roshni, are you all right?" Roshni nods yes as he glares at Hailey. Mrs. Ng then tells Hailey: "Why don't you go wash your face in the bathroom and get a drink of water. That will help you feel better." As Hailey leaves the room, Mrs. Ng tells the students, "Everything is all right. Take a deep breath and relax. Turn around and finish your work." With the class focused on the assignment, Mrs. Ng goes to the door to catch Hailey returning. She quietly asks Hailey how she made Evan and Roshni feel and how she might have behaved differently. Hailey begins to relax and adopt Mrs. Ng's calm demeanor as they talk. When Mrs. Ng sees that Hailey has her emotions under control, she pats Hailey on the back, smiles, and says, "I know you'll behave better next time. Now get a pencil from my desk, and get to work."

emotional competence the ability to regulate your own emotions, and read others' emotions, so that you emerge from an emotional event having accomplished your goals.

Hailey is frequently unable to control her anger and has little empathy for others' feelings. She lacks **emotional competence**—the ability to regulate one's own emotions and to understand others' emotions. Mrs. Ng is helping Hailey develop emotional competence through the way she manages Hailey's outbursts. Effective teachers, like Ms. Ng, promote children's emotional competence as well as their academic skills. Emotional competence is a powerful factor in school success from preschool to high school because emotion is foundational to classroom behavior and thought.

emotion a subjective reaction to an important event, involving physiological or observable behavioral change.

An **emotion** is a subjective reaction to an important event and involves physiological change, readiness to act, and appraisal of the event (Saarni, Mumme, & Campos, 1998). Notice that there are four components to this definition. First, the event must be *important.* If you do not have strongly held values or goals in an event, then you are unlikely to feel emotion about it. Second, emotions involve *physiological changes* in heart rate, glucose in the brain, hormone levels, and temperature—which are linked to outward signs of emotions, like flushed cheeks or sweaty hands. Third, emotion involves *readiness for action.* Fourth, emotions depend on how you *appraise,* or interpret, an event (Izard, 2007). For example, imagine Hailey is in your classroom. Another teacher tells you, "I had that trouble-maker last year. She is just plain mean!" You might feel angry toward Hailey. But if the other teacher tells you: "I had her last year. Her father left the family, and the poor child is so distraught that she lashes out at others," you might feel compassion instead of anger. Changes in your **appraisal** of an event lead to different emotions.

appraisal the meaning given to an event.

Different emotions have unique patterns of these four components. For example, you feel anger when you appraise an event to be demeaning, such as a student cursing at you. Physiologically, your face flushes, eyebrows furrow, and heart races. You feel a desire to counterattack. In contrast, you feel shame when you appraise an event as your failure, such as when your term paper gets a low grade. Physiologically, your cheeks flush, posture collapses, eyes lower, heart slows, and you smile weakly. You feel a desire to withdraw or hide.

Field Observation

Explain to a child what "emotion" is. Was it difficult? Try defining a particular emotion, such as anger.

Why Do Children Have Emotions?

Emotions serve important functions. Emotions focus our attention, motivate us, enable us to take action, and help us communicate. For example, a student who feels fear *focuses* attention on the frightening object. The student is *motivated* to change behavior, like run away. The student's heart rate and blood flow will increase, helping the student run fast. In Hailey's example, her anger toward Evan focused her attention on him, motivated her to attack him, and physiologically prepared her for the exertion of slugging him. In contrast, positive emotions like interest and joy motivate students to continue, not change, their behavior.

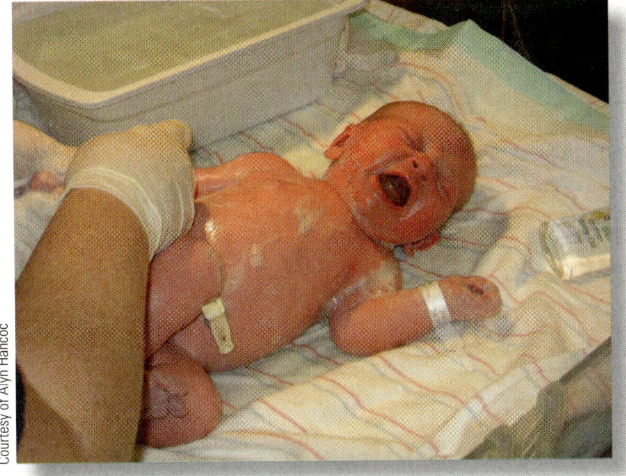

Courtesy of Alyn Hancoc

Less than an hour old, this infant communicates through emotion. Which does he feel about his first bath–anger, joy, sadness, or interest?

Children use emotion to communicate as soon as they are born. Infants cannot talk, but their emotions signal their needs. As children get older and enter adulthood, they continue to use emotions to communicate. Hailey was clearly *communicating* to Evan that she did not want him to take back his pencil.

What Emotions Do Children Have?

More than a century ago, Charles Darwin (see Box 8.1) noted that some facial expressions are recognized by people across the world. Carroll Izard (2007) took Darwin's work a step farther and identified six **basic emotions** that he claims are innate to the human species:

basic emotions universal, innate emotions appearing in the first months of life (joy, sadness, anger, interest, disgust, and fear).

1. Interest.
2. Joy/happiness.
3. Sadness.
4. Anger.
5. Disgust.
6. Fear.

There is controversy over how many different emotions actually exist in humans. Some scientists would expand Izard's list to include love, pride, hope, gratitude, compassion, jealousy, and anxiety (e.g., Fontaine, Scherer, Roesch, & Ellsworth, 2007). Others would narrow the list to just a few emotion dimensions, like pleasant versus unpleasant and high activation versus deactivation. If you feel unpleasant, but activated, you are angry. If you feel unpleasant, but deactivated, you are bored (Barrett, 2006). Part of the controversy stems from differences in basic and complex emotions.

Theories & Theorists — Box 8.1

Charles Darwin

Charles Darwin (1809–1882) is among the most famous scientists in history. In 1872, thirteen years after his famous book *The Origin of Species* was published, he published a book about emotion expression. He took an ethological perspective. Recall from Chapter 6 that *ethology* is a science concerned with explaining animal behavior. In his book, Darwin asked thought-provoking questions such as the following: Do we have to learn which expressions to make when sad, frightened, or happy? Do all people, regardless of geography or culture, express the same emotion in the same way? After painstaking documentation of animals and humans in widely different cultures, he concluded that emotion expression is not learned, but innate and universal. Humans even share many expressions with cats, dogs, horses, and monkeys. For example, primates' expressions of fear, anger, sadness, and happiness are similar to those of humans. Like humans, gorillas laugh in response to tickling. Darwin believed that we communicate within and *between* species through emotional expression.

Darwin sought to explain facial expressions. For example, he pondered why the brows contract when we concentrate:

Now, when anyone with no covering on his head (as must have been aboriginally the case with mankind) strives to the utmost to distinguish in broad daylight, and especially if the sky is bright, a distant object, he almost invariably contracts his brows to prevent the entrance of too much light;... There is, indeed, much analogy, as far as the state of the mind is concerned, between intently scrutinizing a distant object, and following out an obscure train of thought. (Darwin, 1965/1872, pp. 222–224)

Darwin thus suggested that furrowed brows have become an innate part of our response to concentration.

In the 1960s, Paul Ekman set out to prove that Darwin was wrong about universal emotional expressions by studying an isolated, primitive people in Papua, New Guinea (Ekman, 1973). To his surprise, his work and that of later scientists largely confirmed Darwin's views, though not entirely (Barrett, 2006; Hess & Thibault, 2009). There are some subtle differences in facial expressions of emotion across cultures. In addition, culture influences aspects of emotion besides expression, such as how we regulate emotions. Thus, both nature and nurture influence children's emotional lives.

Contemporaries admired Darwin as a scholar because he expressed gratitude for thoughtful criticism of his work. Darwin spent the last forty-two years of his life confined to his home by illness. T. H. Huxley said that Darwin's condition would have made nine out of ten men aimless invalids. Rather than languish, Darwin wrote books that would foster debate into a second century.

Early Basic Emotions

Basic emotions occur rapidly and automatically; they may be built into the human species because they promote the survival of infants (Izard, 2009). For example, fear protects the infant from dangers like crawling down a steep flight of stairs. The joy infants feel when seeing their father motivates them to stay near.

Infants display Izard's six basic emotions within the first months of life. Four of these emotions—interest, joy, sadness, anger—comprise about 95% of infant emotional expressions (Izard & Harris, 1995). However, other scientists believe there are only two basic emotions: negative and positive. For example, during infancy, distress, anger, sadness, and disgust would all fall under the umbrella of negative emotion. They believe that as children grow cognitively and gain experience, specific emotions emerge out of the basic negative or positive emotions.

Scientists disagree about early emotions because it is difficult to tell when an infant feels a particular emotion. To shed light on this, scientists videotaped infants' faces during emotional events like getting a shot, tasting something sour, or seeing their mother smile. They developed a system to measure infants' emotions from facial expression. Test your ability to recognize infant emotions by covering the answers in Figure 8.1 while you decide which emotion the infant expresses.

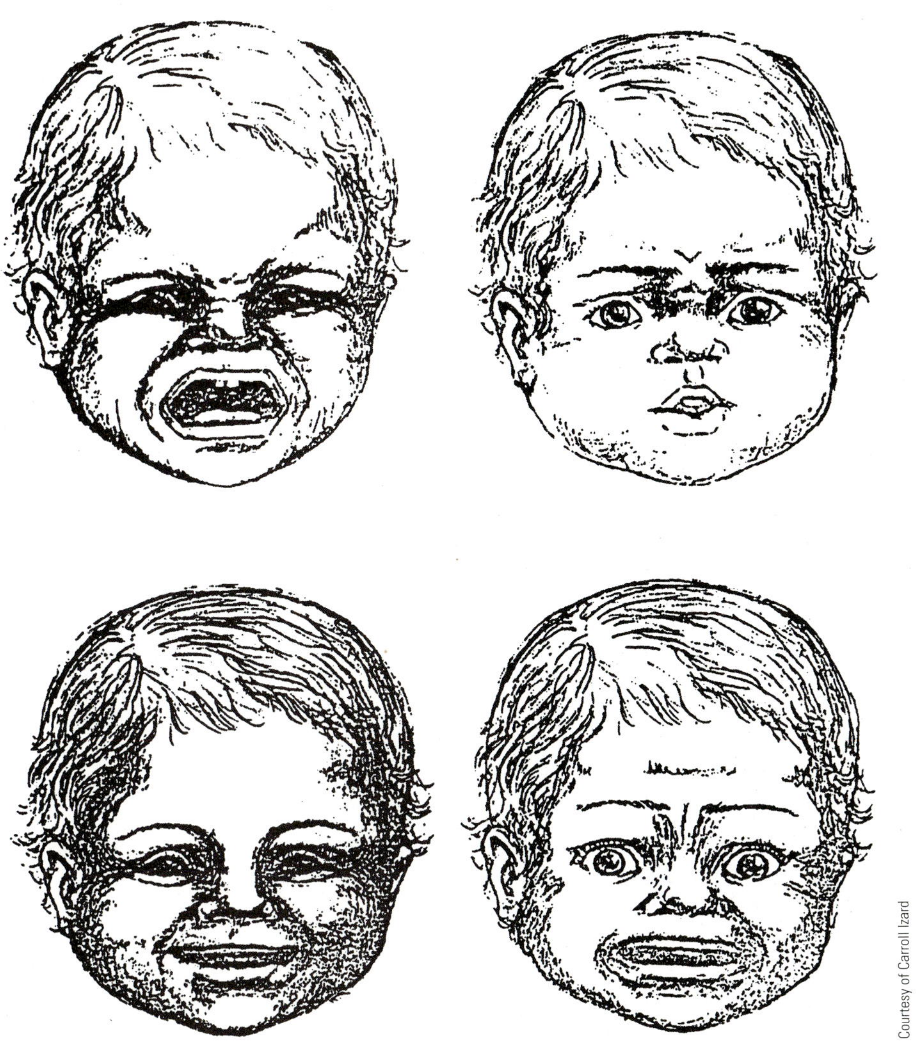

Courtesy of Carroll Izard

Figure 8.1 Infant Emotion Expression.
These photos depict infants expressing emotions according to Izard's categories. Can you tell what emotion each infant is expressing? They are anger, distress, joy and fear.

Complex Social Emotions

social emotions complex emotions that emerge later than basic emotions (shame, embarrassment, guilt, pride, and envy). Also called "self-conscious" or "moral" emotions.

Social emotions emerge during the toddler years. These include envy, embarrassment, shame, guilt, and pride (see Figure 8.2). Envy and embarrassment emerge between 15 and 24 months. Shame, guilt, and pride emerge at about 30 to 36 months. Social emotions are more complex and emerge later than basic emotions because they require at least four cognitive abilities in children: (1) awareness that they are a separate self from their attachment figures, (2) awareness that rules exist, (3) ability to evaluate their self against those rules, and (4) ability to judge whether they caused something. If children do not believe they caused something, they are unlikely to feel guilt, shame, or pride about it. For example, 3-year-olds may feel guilt if they snatch a toy from an infant and it cries, but not if the infant cries because of hunger.

Toddlers may feel social emotions, but they are not always accurate in their judgments about whether they caused something. This inaccuracy may lead them to feel guilty for events that are not their fault. For example, some 2- to 3-year-olds try to

	Positive Emotions	Negative Emotions	
Birth	Interest Pleasure	Disgust Distress	Basic Emotions
3–7 Months	Surprise Joy	Sadness Anger Fear	Basic Emotions
Self-Awareness Develops			Social Emotions
15–24 Months		Embarrassment Envy	Social Emotions
Awareness of Rules & Responsibility Develops			Social Emotions
30–36 Months	Pride	Guilt Shame	Social Emotions

Figure 8.2 **Emergence of Basic and Complex Social Emotions.**
Have you seen infants or toddlers you know express each of these emotions? Do they fit these research-based age trends?

Field Observation

Tell a 4-year-old and a 10-year-old the following story (adapted from Piaget):

"Mary was helping her mother get ready for dinner. She was carrying some dishes, and they were so heavy she dropped them. Mary broke eight dishes. John was upset because he did not want to eat his peas for dinner, so he threw his dish on the floor and broke it."

Then ask:

"Who was naughtier, Mary or John? Why? Who should be punished more? Why?"

Compare their responses. Do they agree with Piaget's research?

make up for their mothers' depression or their parents' divorce by apologizing (Cummings, Zahn-Waxler, & Radke-Yarrow, 1981; Zahn-Waxler & Robinson, 1995).

Piaget devised an interesting way to test whether preschoolers correctly judge guilt. He told them stories of Mary and John. Mary was trying to help by carrying dishes. She dropped and broke eight dishes by accident. John did not want to eat his peas, so he threw his dish and broke it. Who was naughtier? Most preschoolers believe Mary was naughtier than John because she broke more dishes. To preschoolers, greater damage often means more guilt; they may not consider Mary's and John's intentions.

Children get better at judging intention and guilt with age. Most 2nd-graders can accurately judge simple situations, like the contrast between Mary and John. However, most cannot accurately judge between shame and guilt until 5th grade. Guilt results from morally wrong behavior that you have control over. Shame results from a social blunder that you may or may not have control over (Tangney, Stuewig, & Mashek, 2007). Fifth-graders, but not 2nd-graders, know they are likely to feel shame after clumsily falling in the hallway but feel guilt after telling a lie.

To summarize, preschoolers may not accurately judge guilt, but children in the primary grades usually can, and by the end of elementary school they may understand the difference between guilt and shame. The important lesson for teachers is that because young children do not fully understand guilt, they may be *vulnerable to unrealistic expectations or misplaced blame.*

The social emotions motivate important behaviors among your students. Guilt motivates repairing harm to others and inhibits aggression. Pride motivates achievement. Shame motivates conformity to class rules. For example, during a museum tour a teacher scolded an 8th-grader for talking with friends and interrupting the docent. The student's shame kept her from talking for the rest of the field trip. Children who experience too much shame are not emotionally healthy; they are likely to become aggressive and feel worthless. Any emotion can be a problem if it is out of control, like Hailey's explosive anger. Let's turn to children's control of their emotions next.

Regulating One's Own Emotions

Shonese, a 2nd-grader, calmly gets off the school bus and walks toward her house. When she sees her mother waiting at the door, she bursts into tears. Between sobs Shonese tells her mother that some mean kids on the bus ridiculed her name. Shonese's mother lovingly rubs her back and says, "Calm down. The best way to handle kids like that is to ignore them. Pretend you didn't hear a thing. They'll quit eventually, because it won't be fun." The next day, when the ridicule starts again, Shonese follows her mother's advice and ignores them. Seeing that they are not getting a reaction, the kids leave Shonese alone.

Shonese is able to control her emotions until she is safely home, where she bursts into tears. Contrast Shonese's behavior with Hailey's. Although Shonese is only a 2nd-grader, she is better at regulating her emotions than Hailey, a 5th-grader.

Emotion regulation is the ability to control one's emotions. Children with good emotion regulation can alter the *intensity* and *duration* of their emotions so that goals are met. Shonese dampens her distress to meet her goal of stopping the ridicule. Mrs. Ng dampens her anger to preserve a good relationship with Hailey. Emotion regulation does not always involve dampening emotions; it can also involve maintaining or increasing emotions (Cole, Martin, & Dennis, 2004). For example, Roshni may need to increase anger in order to stand up to Hailey's aggression.

emotion regulation the capacity to control the intensity and duration of emotions.

Strategies Children Use to Regulate Emotion

Her mother helps Shonese develop emotion regulation by suggesting strategies for coping with distress. Mrs. Ng helps Hailey develop emotion regulation by suggesting strategies for coping with anger—leave the room, wash her face, think about how others feel, relax, and then solve the problem of where to get a pencil. **Coping strategies** are deliberate attempts to change thoughts or behavior when you are overwhelmed by emotion. Coping strategies can be either *problem focused* or *emotion focused*. **Problem-focused coping strategies** are action oriented and involve *trying to change the situation*. For example, if you feel shame over a bad grade, you decide to study the textbook better. **Emotion-focused coping strategies** involve *trying to change emotions*, such as changing one's thoughts about the situation or seeking comfort from others. For example, if you feel shame over a bad grade, you may tell yourself the grade isn't that important or talk with friends about how the teacher is unfair. *Which strategy is best depends on the situation.* In situations that are controllable, problem-focused strategies may be more helpful. For example, academic achievement is controllable—if you work harder you achieve more. In situations that are not controllable, emotion-focused strategies may be more helpful.

coping strategies deliberate attempts to change thoughts or behavior to try to manage strong emotions. They are usually divided into problem-focused or emotion-focused strategies.

problem-focused coping strategies action-oriented strategies that involve trying to change the situation.

emotion-focused coping strategies strategies that involve trying to change emotions, such as changing one's thoughts about the situation or seeking comfort from others.

Scientists have identified several strategies that children use to cope with daily emotions in situations like getting a bad grade, being ridiculed, or arguing with

Table 8.1 Coping strategies commonly used by children

Less Constructive	1. Do nothing 2. Aggress—to resolve the problem (e.g., grab a pencil away) 3. Aggress—to release pent-up feelings (e.g., kick the chair) 4. Use alcohol or drugs to escape the emotions 5. Cry—to release pent-up feelings 6. Cry—to elicit help from others
More Constructive	7. Avoid the situation or leave; just walk away 8. Talk to friends, teachers, parents, or pray 9. Distract yourself or try not to think about the problem 10. Seek help from friends, teachers, or parents 11. Take constructive action to improve the situation (e.g., study harder when anxious about a test) 12. Reappraise—try to think about the situation in a positive way, or change your goal (e.g., it's better that I wasn't elected to student council because I'll have more free time now) 13. Exercise (for low-arousal emotions like sadness) 14. Relax (for high-arousal emotions like anger or anxiety)

Source: Compiled from Eisenberg et al. (1997); Seiffge-Krenke, Aunola & Nurmi (2009); and Zimmer-Gembeck & Skinner (2008).

friends. You will find these in Table 8.1. Both scientists and children view the first six strategies as less constructive ways of coping than the last eight for most situations. For example, in one study, 6- to 12-year-olds thought the best strategy to cope with sadness was talking to parents and the best strategy to cope with taunting was to walk away (Saarni, 1997). Students agreed the worst strategy in general was aggression. Thus, if students need your help getting their emotions under control, coach them in the best choice among the last eight strategies, as Mrs. Ng and Shonese's mother both did. Your students will fare better if they have several strategies they can draw upon.

Emotional Dissemblance—Faking It

emotional dissemblance altering the expression of felt emotion by expressing no emotion or expressing a different emotion.

Shonese practiced emotional dissemblance when she did not respond to the children teasing her. **Emotional dissemblance** refers to expressing no emotion or expressing an emotion that is different (but more acceptable) from what you actually feel. Emotional dissemblance helps children fit into their culture because cultures have rules about expressing emotions. For example, it may be acceptable to show anger toward a classmate at recess but not toward the teacher in class. To be a successful member of any culture, children must know the rules for emotional display, anticipate how others will react to their emotions, and control their emotional display. Although this is a sophisticated ability, even young children dissemble. For example:

In preschool, 4-year-old Jason builds a car from Duplo blocks and gives it to his friend Daniel. Daniel acts excited about getting the car, but when he is beyond hearing distance, Daniel tells his teacher that he does not really like the car.

Emotional dissemblance can be positive or negative. Daniel's was positive because he was protecting Jason's feelings. It is negative when children give false impressions for dishonest reasons, such as looking innocent so they will not get into trouble for misbehavior.

Dissemblance goes hand-in-hand with emotion regulation. Darwin argued that hiding emotions dampens them and expressing emotions intensifies them (Darwin, 1965/1872). Research generally confirms Darwin's view. When you express an emotion, your facial muscles provide feedback to the brain, which then alters your experience of the emotion (Matsumoto, 1987). For example, if you are having a sad day, but you pretend to smile and show happiness to your students, you will come to feel a little happier (e.g., Bonanno, Papa, Lalande, Westphal, & Coifman, 2004). This is contrary to a popular volcano myth that if you do not let your negative emotions out, they will explode.

Revisiting Case 3

Le'Raun showed no emotion when Mrs. Richardson sternly scolded him directly in his face. He sat quietly and then hid his face. Was this emotional dissemblance good or bad for Le'Raun? Would you say Le'Raun had age-appropriate emotion regulation?

Age Trends in Emotion Regulation

There is dramatic improvement in emotion regulation across childhood. Infants have minimal coping ability, but by age 10, good coping ability is in place for most children (Brenner & Salovey, 1997).

Early Childhood (Birth to 5 Years)

Infants cannot yet voluntarily control their emotions, but they do have a few basic coping strategies for overwhelming situations. For example, when newborns are passed from relative to relative at a noisy family gathering, they cope by sucking on their cheeks or a pacifier. They also cope by *appearing to sleep*; their eyes are closed and their brows furrowed. They also cope by looking away, called *gaze aversion*. When you play with infants, they may become overstimulated. When this happens, infants look away while they get their emotions back to a comfortable level, at which point they turn back toward you.

Toddlers have more control of their emotions than do infants. This is due to brain maturation that allows them to delay emotional responses and to shift between emotions (Thompson, 1994). Toddlers who were born prematurely may lag in emotional development in the first two years of life until their brain development catches up (Malatesta, Culver, Tesman, & Shepard, 1989).

Toddlers can sometimes dissemble. For example, some 2-year-olds can hold back tears—although their lips may tremble—when left with a babysitter. While this shows some self-regulation ability, toddlers often need your help to regulate their emotions. They need hugging, rocking, or other forms of soothing to calm down when they are upset. Because such emotion regulation involves a partnership between caregiver and toddler, it is referred to as *guided self-regulation*.

Preschoolers are increasingly able to control their emotions without adult help. They become more capable of emotional dissemblance, but their ability is still limited. For example, they are better at exaggerating than squelching an emotion, such as howling as though in great pain over a trivial hurt. They may choose to cry after an injury only if a caregiver is watching but not if they are alone.

Catchlight Visual Services / Alamy

Adults guide toddlers' emotion regulation until they are able to regulate their own.

Preschoolers occasionally have breakdowns in emotion regulation, particularly if they are tired, stressed, or hungry, but by age 3, episodes of intense crying and tantrums typically diminish (Saarni, 1999).[1]

Preschoolers develop regulation ability when they "try on" different emotions during play. A girl who pretends to be an angry mother spanking her doll, and then comforts the crying doll, is practicing feeling and controlling anger. Preschoolers also develop emotion regulation as they use their increased language abilities to talk about emotion.

Middle Childhood (6 to 12 Years)

By 1st grade, children can regulate their emotions in settings away from a caregiver, as Shonese did on the school bus, and they continue to improve across the elementary years (Blandon, Calkins, Keane, & O'Brien, 2008). They become better at coping in four ways:

1. They use social support less, like talking less to others about their distress. Social support shifts somewhat from parents to peers, but even 12-year-olds are likely to turn to parents for help with emotions.
2. They have more coping strategies.
3. They are able to select the best strategy to use because they are better judges of how much control they have over a situation. Remember that emotion-focused strategies are better in situations where a child has no control.
4. They come to rely more on emotion-focused strategies, but they continue to use problem-focused strategies as well (Brenner & Salovey, 1997). For example, when feeling distress over a bad test score, 14-year-olds are more likely than 10-year-olds to try to calm down (emotion-focused coping), but both age groups will do more homework (problem-focused coping).

Although she is just 8 years old, Shonese is skilled at emotional dissemblance. This ability grows during elementary school so that adult-like ability is reached by about 5th grade. Scientists study emotion regulation using a disappointing gift like a baby toy. When 6-year-olds unwrap their gift, they tend to show negative emotions. Older 8- to 9-year-olds may show neither positive nor negative emotions and may appear anxious about what to express; they may bite their lip, touch their face, and glance at the experimenter. Still older 10- to 11-year-olds may completely hide their disappointment and show positive emotions toward the experimenter (Cole, 1986). Thus, kindergarteners' emotions are largely transparent, but most 5th-graders can readily conceal their emotions.

Adolescence (13 to 19 Years)

Adolescents report feeling a lot of daily stress, usually about relationships with friends, sweethearts, or parents, and pressure to do well in school (Gutman & Eccles, 2007; Seiffge-Krenke et al., 2009). This might explain a common stereotype that adolescents are moody and negative, implying poor emotion regulation. Is this stereotype true? To answer this question, scientists compared the emotions of adults, adolescents, and elementary students (Larson & Richards, 1994). They were all given beepers and told to report their

[1] Extreme tantrums that are long, involve aggression, and are followed by intense shame or guilt may suggest emotional disorders in preschoolers (Cole, Luby, & Sullivan, 2008) and may merit professional help.

feelings when the beeper sounded at random times for a week. Adolescents reported more frequently feeling bored, tired, and sleepy (see Chapter 2). They also reported more frequently feeling social discomfort, like awkwardness and loneliness, than their parents. They reported less frequently feeling extremely happy than elementary students. However, *most of the adolescents reported being fairly happy most of the time.*

Although most adolescents are not moody, some are frequently angry, anxious, or sad. In the beeper studies, only adolescents who had a pileup of transitions—a family move, a new school, or parents' divorce—were moody. Moodiness was *not* associated with puberty or the "raging hormones" that are often blamed for negativity in adolescents. An important lesson for secondary teachers is that *you should not simply dismiss emotional negativity as a normal phase, but should address the needs of teenagers who are chronically unhappy or moody.*

Individual Diversity in Emotion Regulation

Shonese has good emotion-regulation ability for her age, but Hailey does not. In an emotionally charged situation, these girls would differ in emotional response, intensity of their emotions, and recovery time. Children with poor emotion regulation either experience too little emotion or too much emotion; that is, they can be overregulated or underregulated. Underregulated children, like Hailey, experience chronic negative emotions, or rapidly change from one extreme emotion to another.

Negative emotionality is a temperament trait (see Chapter 6). Individual differences in this trait appear in the first months of life and remain somewhat stable. This means that children who are irritable are not likely to simply outgrow negativity at a later age, unless their environment improves substantially. This is a problem because poor emotion regulation is a risk factor, whereas good emotion regulation is a protective factor, as we will discuss next (Bonanno et al., 2004).

What Does Emotion Regulation Predict?

Good emotion regulation predicts better *language* skills in early childhood (Robinson & Acevedo, 2001). Perhaps controlling negative emotions allows toddlers to pay attention and learn more, or perhaps sensitive parenting facilitates both emotion regulation and language ability. Good emotion regulation also predicts fewer *emotional disorders* and greater *social competence.*

Emotional disorders

Students with chronic negative emotions approach new situations with a negative bias and use destructive coping strategies (Terwogt & Olthof, 1989; Tronick, 1989). For example, Hailey's negative bias led her to view Evan's reasonable behavior, taking his pencil back, as an attack. She was so overwhelmed by anger that she physically attacked two of her classmates. Such overwhelming negative emotions can lead to emotional disorders.

Emotional disorders are classified as either externalizing or internalizing. **Externalizing disorders** involve aggression and anger. Students with externalizing disorders "act out." We will discuss these problems in Chapter 10. **Internalizing disorders** involve withdrawal or sadness. The two most common internalizing disorders in youth—depression and anxiety—are discussed later in this chapter. Youth with poor emotion regulation can have *both* internalizing and externalizing disorders, such

externalizing disorders emotional disorders based on anger, characterized by aggression and other antisocial behaviors.

internalizing disorders emotional disorders based on sadness or anxiety, characterized by withdrawal.

as being both depressed and aggressive (Silk, Steinberg, & Morris, 2003). Internalizing disorders may get less attention from teachers because they do not usually disrupt schooling for anyone but the student, yet they need intervention.

Emotional disorders are prevalent. As many as 25% of students from kindergarten through high school have a disorder, such as depression, anxiety, or behavior problems. Yet most (about 75%) of these students do *not* receive the treatment needed to develop better emotion regulation (Leadbeater & Hoglund, 2009; Weissberg, 2000). Beginning treatment early increases its success. Thus, early childhood teachers should address possible emotional disorders as early as possible. Even children who do not have diagnosable disorders, but have poor emotion regulation, may need intervention.

Mark Lewis/Photodisc/Jupiter Images

Students with good emotion regulation are happier and have more friends.

Social competence

Students with good emotion regulation are liked better by both teachers and peers (McDowell, O'Neil, & Parke, 2000; Rydell, Berlin, & Bohlin, 2003). This is because they may use their ability to protect others' feelings, such as Daniel pretending to like Jason's car. This is also because they *typically express more positive than negative emotions*, which leads to less aggression and more positive behavior (Bartlett & DeSteno, 2006; Denham et al., 2003). When students are happy, they greet others warmly, engage in class activities enthusiastically, and make activities fun for others. This attracts classmates and keeps interactions running smoothly, which leads to friendship.

In contrast, students with poor emotion regulation are often angry. They are at risk for being disliked by peers and teachers because anger makes peers uneasy and because chronically angry students cope by being aggressive (Eisenberg et al., 1997). Classmates prefer peers who use problem-focused coping strategies rather than aggression.

Teachers, on the other hand, prefer students who use avoidant coping strategies, such as backing out of anger-filled situations (Kliewer, 1991). Teachers prefer such students because they are not likely to act out at school, which makes them easier to handle. However, avoidant strategies are not always best because students do not learn to stand up for themselves or problem-solve. Given the importance of these outcomes, our next concern is how to help students develop good emotion regulation.

What Predicts Emotion Regulation?

Students who have better executive functions (see Chapter 4) also have better emotion regulation. How quickly you can accurately do the Stroop test predicts your ability to cope with stress! Perhaps this is because emotion regulation and executive functions use the same brain systems (Compton et al., 2008). Genes may influence emotion regulation through differences in executive functions, or through the temperament trait of negative emotionality (see Chapter 6), but the way parents interact with children may have a larger influence (Calkins, 1994). Let's discuss seven parenting factors next.

Attachment

Your students learned emotion regulation from attachment figures during routine activities like feeding, bathing, and playing in infancy. To help you understand, imagine two infants are playing peek-a-boo with their mothers. The first infant is giggling, but turns his face away from his mother when the game gets too intense. His mother does not wait for him to return to the game. Instead, she looms over him making noises, trying to get him to come back to the game. This overstimulation causes the infant to begin fussing and makes him turn even further away as he struggles to get his emotions under control. The mother ignores emotional signals from her infant; she is being insensitive and intrusive. This infant may develop an angry emotional core and poor regulation if his mother continues to be intrusive over time.

Think About This A mother was preparing to leave her 4-year-old with a babysitter. The child pleaded with his mother not to leave, but she silently continued putting her coat on. Finally he shouted, "I hate you!" She sighed, rolled her eyes, and said, "You can't hate me. I'm your mother" and left. What type of attachment is this child likely to have? How might this affect his emotion regulation? What about his behavior with peers? Defend your conclusions using this chapter and Chapter 6.

The second mother stops the game when her infant turns away and waits until he turns to face her again. Then she smiles and says, "Oh, now you're back!" and they resume playing. When adults stimulate young children to an almost, but not quite, overwhelming level and then back off, as this mother did, children learn to control intense emotion (Sroufe, 1996). Many repeated experiences like this alter networks in the brain, which results in a brain that regulates emotions well. This may be why infants with sensitive mothers later become children who are good at emotion regulation (Blair et al., 2008). Research suggests this kind of parenting may be particularly important for infants with difficult temperament (Leerkes, Blankson, & O'Brien, 2009).

Securely attached children, whose parents are sensitive, tend to have good emotion regulation (Morris, Silk, Steinberg, Myers, & Robinson, 2007). They learn that others are readily available to soothe their emotions. They are more likely to have constructive coping strategies that help them express their emotions, receive others' emotions, take on emotionally charged situations, and talk about hot topics without anger. As adolescents they are less likely to become depressed (Allen, Porter, McFarland, McElhaney, & Marsh, 2007).

By comparison, *resistant* children are more likely to underregulate their emotions. They learn that others will not soothe them until their emotions reach overwhelming levels. For example, the parent may ignore subtle signs of distress and wait until children are sobbing loudly before attempting to soothe them. This trains children to have a rapid rise of intense emotions in order to attract attention. They become increasingly difficult to soothe and frequently feel frustrated and anxious (Thompson, 1991).

Avoidant children are more likely to overregulate their emotions. They learn that others are unresponsive, emotionally unavailable, or hostile. For example, parents may ignore intense distress in children. To cope, children may suppress emotions and not seek help, which prevents their learning better coping strategies (Cassidy, 1994). They may particularly suppress emotions that make them feel vulnerable and avoid emotional closeness to others, appearing hostile or detached.

Response to children's emotions

Accepting and responding appropriately to children's negative emotions may help them be more positive (Davidov & Grusec, 2006). For example, if a teenager is in tears over a bad grade, an appropriate response might be, "I can see you're upset. Let's talk about what you can do about it." Inappropriate responses include dismissing the child's emotions ("It's nothing to get upset about"), mocking or belittling the child ("Don't be a crybaby"), placating the child ("You can have ice cream if you'll stop crying"), eye rolling, or yelling. Parents who routinely use inappropriate responses tend to have children who have poor emotion regulation, are angry, and behave badly at school (e.g., Lunkenheimer, Shields, & Cortina, 2007).

Responding appropriately to children's exuberant positive emotions is important also. Imagine a child is playing happily with friends in a boisterous way on the front porch. Some parents would invalidate the child's emotions by reprimanding the child or acting embarrassed. Other parents would be comfortable allowing the child to have fun. In one study, children whose parents invalidated their positive emotions tended to have poor emotion regulation and depression (Yap, Allen, & Ladouceur, 2008).

Expression of emotions

Parents' emotions influence their children's emotion regulation. Parents who are often cheerful have children who control their own negative emotions and have more coping strategies. Parents who are often negative and model poor emotion regulation—such as frequently yelling or acting depressed—have children with poor emotion regulation. Their children tend to have fewer, primarily aggressive, coping strategies and feel depressed or anxious (Blandon et al., 2008; Stocker, Richmond, Rhoades, & Kuang, 2007).

Parents should not completely avoid expressing negative emotions; rather, they should express substantially more positive than negative emotions. In fact, parents who are more emotionally expressive, with both positive and negative emotions, have children who are well liked (Cassidy, Parke, Butovsky, & Braungart, 1992). As a teacher, you may want to also express a wide range of emotions, but be primarily positive.

Talk about emotions

Parents who talk with their children about their own and others' emotions tend to have children who are more positive than negative (Denham, Mitchell-Copeland, Strandberg, Auerbach, & Blair, 1997). For example, during a conflict the parent might say, "Ahmad hit you because he was *angry* that you and Bill were playing without him, and he *felt* left out." Language is a tool for managing emotions (Izard, 2009). The more children can talk about emotion, the more they know about emotion, and the better they can regulate their emotions.

There are several reasons that talking about emotions is helpful. First, parents are responding calmly, which helps children get their emotions under control. Second, conversations provide children with information about why people behave in certain ways, like why Ahmad hit. Third, conversations teach coping strategies, like reappraising whether Ahmad meant to hurt them. Fourth, conversations raise children's awareness of emotions and ability to label emotions. Fifth, when adults converse with children, they feel valued and worthy of attention, which leads to positive emotions. You will have opportunities to talk with your students about emotions. If you take these opportunities, you may help them learn to regulate their emotions.

Coaching

Parents can directly coach children in how to cope with emotions. For example, when a 10-year-old was afraid to go to theater class, she told her mother, "I'm kinda afraid because of the time I was in dance and I forgot my routine in front of the judges." Her mother helped her reappraise the situation: "You're older now. Everybody forgets their lines sometimes. Give it a chance." The girl did—and enjoyed her class. Similarly, following divorce parents may coach their children to seek support, distract themselves, or think about the situation in a new way (Brenner & Salovey, 1997). Parents who coach their children tend to have children with better emotion regulation, health, impulse control, attention, and social competence (Lunkenheimer et al., 2007; Morris et al., 2007). You can coach your students by suggesting coping strategies, as Mrs. Ng did with Hailey.

> ***Think About This*** What might be the implication for youth whose parents are not home or available to coach the child in regulating emotions when the youth is exposed to violent, sexually explicit, or emotionally intense movies or video games?

Effective discipline

Discipline influences children's emotion regulation. When an adult overreacts to a child's misbehavior, the child can be overwhelmed by emotion. For example, imagine a 1-year-old is gleefully rolling grapefruit down the basement stairs. He has some sense that he is misbehaving because when he sees his mother, he says "ut oh." His mother can use induction, as she frowns and firmly says, "No. You'll bruise them. Let's get a ball instead." Or, she can use power assertion as she grabs the child, spanks him, and says, "bad boy!" while he cries. In the first case, the child learns that he can cope with disapproval and repair mistakes. In the second case, the child learns that disapproval leads to overwhelming emotions. Adults who are often angry during power-assertive discipline are teaching poor emotion regulation to children.

Abuse

Abuse influences children's emotion regulation. Some abused children are underregulated; they have substantial anger, fear, and shame. They may rapidly shift from positive to negative emotions (Shipman et al., 2007). However, other abused children are overregulated; they are emotionally unresponsive and difficult to engage. They may have blank or sober expressions.

Suppressing emotions, or refusing to "feel," helps abused children cope when they cannot get help or avoid the abuser. However, this suppression prevents them from learning good coping strategies for typical emotions, like frustration at school, so that when their tight emotion control fails, they are explosive. This was characteristic of a teenager who was hospitalized for aggression (Cole, Michel, & Teti, 1994). After many weeks of good behavior, he earned a weekend visit home. He eagerly awaited his mother, but she never came to get him. When he phoned her, she lightheartedly told him she was too busy to come. He showed no emotions when he hung up the phone. He acted like his mother's rejection did not hurt. Shortly afterward, he was caught hurting another child as he vented despair and anger. In therapy, he learned strategies for coping with his grief that his mother would never care for him.

In summary, when adults are sensitive and secure attachment figures, express mostly positive emotions, respond well to children's emotions, talk with children about emotions, directly coach them in coping strategies, and use effective discipline, they provide children with the tools to develop good emotion regulation. In contrast, when adults are negative, harsh, rejecting, or abusive, children are likely to develop poor emotion regulation. One of the most common emotion-regulation problems is depression.

Depression: Emotion Regulation Gone Awry

Shelly, a 4th-grader, is described by her teacher as "quiet, spacey, and overly sensitive to others' feelings." Shelly often says she does not feel well, but the school nurse finds nothing physically wrong. Shelly comes from a middle-class, intact family. Shelly's mother helps at school, yet her own childhood history of abuse leads to bouts of depression and interferes with her emotional availability to Shelly. Shelly occasionally says she wishes she were dead. Shelly has behaved this way since preschool, but no teacher has referred her for help.

depression a common internalizing disorder in which feelings of sadness are severe for at least two weeks, or milder but chronic.

Kristy-Anne Glubish/Design Pics Inc/Photolibrary

Depression is one of the most common psychological disorders in students, particularly among teenage girls.

Shelly has classic symptoms of **depression**: social withdrawal, poor concentration, lack of interest in school, and feeling worthless. Other symptoms of depression that you might see in students include changes in appetite, self-criticism, irritability, poor hygiene, can't-sit-still behavior, frequent crying, and sleep problems (American Psychiatric Association, 2000). These symptoms occur across ages; however, in teens depression usually involves too much sleep, and in young children too little sleep. Any student might have these symptoms occasionally, but if symptoms are severe for at least two weeks, or less severe but last for a year or more, students may have clinical depression, like Shelly.

Depression is a disorder of emotion regulation. Other disorders often accompany depression, such as anxiety, ADHD, learning disorders and, mostly in teens, eating disorders (American Psychiatric Association, 2000). Depressed students, particularly boys, may also be angry and act out.

Prevalence of Depression

Depression occurs in infants, but it is rare. Children as young as 6 can accurately report their own depression (Ialongo, Edelsohn, & Kellam, 2001). As children enter school and grow into the teens, depression rates increase. They may peak around 15 to 17 years, and then decrease (Gutman & Eccles, 2007). Thus, teachers in secondary schools are more likely to observe depression in their students than teachers in elementary or preschools.

In one year, an astounding 8% of 12- to 17-year-olds may have a major depressive episode (FIFCFS, 2009). More students, perhaps 10 to 25%, may have milder forms of depression or be undiagnosed. Depression and anxiety are among the most common forms of psychological disorders in students, followed by substance use and behavior problems. Schools commit substantial resources to substance use and ADHD, yet very little to the more prevalent depression and anxiety.

Antecedents and Consequences of Depression

Children who have trouble up-regulating positive emotions and down-regulating negative emotions may become depressed (Feng et al., 2009). They feel less happy and more sadness or anger than other children. The same factors that predict poor emotion regulation (discussed earlier) are risk factors for depression—parents who are negative, do not accept children's emotions, and do not coach children on how to cope with their emotions (Katz & Hunter, 2007; Stocker et al., 2007). Other risk factors for depression include:[2]

- Chronic stress, particularly stress within relationships in the family or rejection by peers.
- Family problems such as conflict, lack of closeness, criticism, harsh discipline, disregard for the child's view, and insecure attachment.
- Maternal depression, which affects children through emotion contagion and lower-quality parenting. Having a depressed parent doubles or quadruples the risk of a child's becoming depressed.
- Negative life events such as death or divorce in the family.
- Feeling helpless to do anything about negative events.
- Using poor coping strategies such as thinking over and over again about negative events.
- Pessimistic explanation style, such as "I got lucky" rather than "I am smart" to explain a good grade.

The first factor, chronic stress in relationships, may be the most common cause of depression, but even so, most youth with this risk factor will not become depressed (Hammen, 2009). Youth who have multiple risk factors are more likely to become depressed than youth with a single risk factor. In addition, genes may make some children more vulnerable to the effects of negative parenting or life stress, but *genes alone probably do not cause depression* (Haeffel et al., 2008; Monroe & Reid, 2008).

Depression itself is a serious consequence. However, depression is linked to other consequences, like low academic achievement, inability to pay attention, slow mental processing, unpopularity as a play or work partner, loneliness, drug abuse, eating disorders, truancy, crime, and car accidents.[3] Not all depressed children will have these problems; many recover before these problems develop. Those who use good coping strategies, like exercise or going to a movie with friends, rather than dangerous escapist strategies, like alcohol abuse, are more likely to recover. However, intervention may be needed. School-based interventions will be discussed later.

---

[2] Each of these factors is well-documented in research. Just a few studies are listed here (e.g., Allen et al., 2007; Clements, Aber, & Seidman, 2008; Cole et al., 2008; Feng et al., 2009; Hammen, 2009; Milan, Snow, & Belay, 2009; Webster-Stratton & Herman, 2008).

[3] Many studies have demonstrated these effects, just a few of which are listed here (e.g., Cole, Martin, Peeke, Seroczynski, & Fier, 1999; Foersterling & Binser, 2002; Ialongo et al., 2001; Lewinsohn, Hops, Roberts, Seeley, & Andrews, 1993; Pomerantz & Rudolph, 2003).

Group Diversity in Emotion Regulation

Research suggests there are gender and SES differences in emotion regulation. In addition, there are both differences and similarities in emotion regulation among children from different cultures. Let's look at gender differences first.

Gender

As early as infancy, girls are more skilled at regulating emotions. In one study, 6-month-old boys showed anger, cried, or turned away more than girls when their mothers were unresponsive to them (Weinberg, Tronick, Cohn, & Olson, 1999). In the primary grades, girls are better at emotional dissemblance—appearing happy when they are not. Girls also smile more than boys, which helps regulate emotions and keep interactions pleasant (Saarni, 1999).

Paradoxically, despite better emotion regulation, girls are twice as likely to be depressed than boys (Hammen, 2009). This gender difference is not apparent in early childhood, but emerges by 7th grade and becomes dramatic by mid-adolescence. Why might girls be more depressed than boys? Research supports two possibilities: (1) they have more relationship stress, and (2) they cope in ways that result in depression (Zimmer-Gembeck & Skinner, 2008). In one study, 8th- and 10th-graders reported the worst thing that had happened that day. Girls reported more bad events. Their bad events were interpersonal, like a fight with a friend, whereas boys' were school-related, like an F on a quiz or losing a football game (Hanish & Guerra, 2000). Adolescent girls are more likely to have negative family interactions (Gutman & Eccles, 2007). These daily stresses are linked to greater depression in girls.

Girls are more likely to cope by ruminating, or thinking about the situation and their feelings over and over (Nolen-Hoeksema, Wisco, & Lyubomirsky, 2008). Ruminating can lead to depression. Girls are also more likely to use *emotion-focused strategies*, like talking to a sibling (Seiffge-Krenke et al., 2009). This is a problem in some situations where *problem-focused strategies* are more helpful, like studying more after getting a bad grade.

Socioeconomic Status

Low-SES students tend to be less able to regulate their emotions than middle-SES children, although the differences are small. Students living in poverty have more distress to cope with, often have new stressors emerge before they've had time to cope with existing ones, and have fewer supportive people to help them cope (Zimmer-Gembeck & Skinner, 2008). Among low-SES children, those whose parents provide the positive experiences discussed earlier—secure attachment, positive emotions in the home, discussions about emotions, coaching, appropriate responses to emotion, and effective discipline—develop good regulation despite their economic disadvantage (Raver, 2004).

Ethnicity

Studies of ethnic differences in depression find inconsistent patterns (Brown, Meadows, & Elder, 2007; Choi, Meininger, & Roberts, 2006; Gerard & Buehler, 2004). Although it is currently not clear if some ethnic groups have more depression than others, immigration status is clearly linked to depression. Immigrant youth have higher rates of depression and anxiety than native-born youth, though most immigrant youth *do not become depressed.* Two factors are linked to whether immigrants become depressed: family and acculturation. Like other youth, immigrants' primary source of stress is within the family. If immigrant youth have dysfunctional families, they are at higher risk of depression (Flook & Fuligni, 2008). Immigrant youth have additional sources of stress: severed relationships from their heritage country, the struggle to speak English at school, and hearing derogatory ethnic jokes (Romero & Roberts, 2003).

Field Observation

The following two scenarios (adapted from Saarni, 1997) are used to assess students' emotion regulation:

1. *A student bought a special pair of shoes after saving for a long time. The student told a friend about them over the phone. At school the next day the friend made fun of the shoes and got the other kids to join in.*
2. *In a hurry to get to school, a student accidentally left the bird cage open after feeding the pet bird. When the student and a friend got home after school, the bird was gone.*

Ask students of different cultures how they would cope with these two situations. Are there cultural similarities or differences in their responses?

acculturation the long-term process of adapting to a new culture.

Acculturation refers to adaptation to a new culture. Children can adapt in different ways; they can maintain their heritage culture while adopting the new culture (bi-culturalism), or they can reject one or both cultures. Immigrant youth are less likely to be depressed if they become bi-cultural. Bi-cultural youth tend to be more extraverted and open to new experiences (Ryder, Alden, & Paulhus, 2000). In Chapter 12 you'll learn that children who maintain their heritage language *and* learn English fare well. Thus, helping your immigrant students maintain their heritage culture may foster their well-being if they are also open to their new culture.

Cross-National Comparisons

Basic emotions may be universal, but cultures dictate which emotions are valued. For example, European Americans tend to value high-arousal emotions like enthusiasm, excitement, and elation, whereas Asian Americans tend to value low-arousal emotions like serenity, peace, and relaxation (Tsai, 2007). European American adults are more inclined to stimulate children when Asian adults would soothe and quiet children. In Chapter 6 you learned that Chinese teachers view happy, exuberant students as behavior problems, whereas American teachers do not. These values affect whether a classroom is a good fit for different students. If you often say to students, "Great!" or "Let's have some fun today!" you may value high-arousal emotions.

Cross-national studies in China, Japan, India, the United States, Britain, and Italy have found that children in some countries express less emotion. For example, Japanese children are less expressive than American children (Zahn-Waxler, Friedman, Cole, Mizuta, & Hiruma, 1996). However, this does not mean they *feel* less emotion (Lewis, Ramsay, & Kawakami, 1993). Children learn to conform to their cultures' rules for expressing emotions.

Despite cultural differences in emotion expression, children's coping strategies are quite similar across cultures. Across widely diverse cultures, including China and the United States, aggression and avoidance are considered worse coping strategies than problem-focused strategies. In addition, causes of emotions and facial expressions of emotions are similar across cultures (see Box 8.1).

These cultural similarities suggest that most of the time you will understand your students' emotional expressions and you may help them develop valued coping strategies, even if they are from different cultures. However, cultural differences could sometimes result in miscommunication. For example, you may think a student is not happy in your classroom because he does not seem enthusiastic. Yet, he could feel happy, but come from a culture that does not value public displays. For another example, a student may begin giggling when you scold her. Is this a sign of disrespect or a sign of shame? The answer may depend on the child's culture. To correctly interpret emotional expressions in your students from other cultures, you will have to learn about those cultures. Let's turn to other implications for your classroom next.

Classroom Implications of Emotion Regulation

Emotion regulation skills influence students' success in your classroom. Students who are able to regulate their emotions will tend to be happier, better liked, and better able to pay attention and learn. Perhaps this is why schools that are effective in promoting learning also promote emotional well-being in children (Mortimore, Sammons, Stoll, Lewis, & Ecob, 1988). There are three ways you can help your students develop good emotion regulation in your classroom: (1) *be sensitive to children's emotions*, (2) *directly teach emotion regulation*, and (3) *create a positive classroom*.

Be Sensitive to Children's Emotions

You can tell whether your students have good emotion regulation or not as you become more sensitive to their emotions. Use these guidelines:

- Notice whether each student is emotionally positive or negative most of the time. Well-regulated students should be predominantly positive, and only occasionally negative. Chronic negativity or exaggerated moodiness is not normal, even among 2-year-olds and teenagers.
- Notice whether each of your students has age-appropriate emotion regulation (review the Age Trends section). Hailey does not have age-appropriate abilities, but Shonese does.
- Seize opportunities to talk about emotions. Help students label, describe, and understand the emotions they experience. Mrs. Ng talked with Hailey about how Evan was *surprised* and *angry* with her, and that Hailey should feel *guilt*.
- Be aware of emotional disorders, especially internalizing disorders like depression and anxiety. Although they are more common in girls, do not overlook them in boys. Notify a counselor if you suspect a student has an emotional disorder. The sooner they are detected the better, because treatment is more successful with young children.
- Be aware of dissemblance, or emotions that students may be hiding.

Dissemblance can be positive if done out of kindness, as in the story of Daniel. However, it can also lead to misunderstanding your students. For example, when you discipline youth, some youth who do *not* show regret or embarrassment may actually feel these emotions, and some youth who *do* show these emotions may actually be faking to appease you. For another example, students may pretend they understand something they really do not or pretend to be baffled by a task they find easy (DePaulo, 1991). They may pretend they are not distressed by something that they actually find quite distressing. Dissemblance ability is well-developed by 4th or 5th grade, but even younger children can hide distress from you. Let's look in a preschool:

A girl was bullied by a boy and bit him in self-defense. She had never hurt another child before and was deeply distressed. However, she did not let her teacher see how upset she was. The teacher phoned her mother and said, "she's dealing with it just fine." However, a few hours later when her mother entered the classroom at the end of the school day to take her home, she burst into tears.

This traumatized little child had been holding back tears for two hours. Students are more likely to dissemble with an authority figure, like a teacher (Saarni, 1999). However, parents are not always aware of children's emotions either. It is common for divorcing parents to think their children are coping well because they are not acting out and are relatively compliant. In reality, the children may feel depressed or blame themselves for the divorce, but may feel too vulnerable to show these feelings.

Directly Teach Emotion Regulation

You can help your students develop emotion regulation by teaching coping strategies and by responding appropriately to children's emotions. Draw upon the more constructive strategies in Table 8.1. Remember how Mrs. Ng taught Hailey effective ways of coping with anger—distract yourself with a walk to the bathroom and get a drink. Mrs. Ng also taught Hailey that anger must be contained and not allowed to disrupt other activity in the classroom. Imagine if, instead, Mrs. Ng had scolded, "I'm giving you a demerit!" or sent her to the office. By taking this action, Mrs. Ng would have modeled escalation in angry encounters. She would not have taught Hailey effective ways of coping with anger.

Similarly, in an 8th-grade English class, a teacher helped Raj cope with anxiety about giving a book report in front of his classmates. She told Raj to take slow, deep breaths:

During his report Raj pushed and pulled at his shirt sleeves, dragged his hand through his hair, rocked back and forth, and averted his gaze. At one point he tried to control his anxiety by taking slow deep breaths and closing his eyes until he regained his composure and could carry on.

In this case Raj, who is older than Hailey, was generating his own coping strategies, like rocking and closing his eyes. However, he still needed a little help from his teacher. Her advice to take slow, deep breaths helped him. Help your students identify their coping strategies, and then encourage them to adopt more constructive strategies if needed.

Image copyright Monkey Business Images. Used under license from Shutterstock.com

Students have higher achievement in positive classroooms.

Create a Positive Atmosphere

Your students' emotions at home affect their emotions at school, and vice versa. Youth who have a stressful experience at home—like being punished—feel more distress at school for the next few days. Likewise, students who have a stressful experience at school—like not understanding class work—feel more stress at home for the next few days.

(If you recognized this spillover effect as part of the mesosystem in the bioecological model, negotiate for extra credit!) The more students feel such daily stressors, at school or home, the lower their GPA becomes over the years (Flook & Fuligni, 2008).

You cannot control the emotional climate of your students' homes, but you can create a positive climate in your classroom. A positive classroom atmosphere helps students feel safe communicating their real feelings. It can also promote achievement. For example, in one study 5th-graders who felt emotional support in the classroom had higher math achievement (Pianta, Belsky, Vandergrift, Houts, & Morrison, 2008). Positive emotions also help reenergize self-control when students' self-control is spent (Baumeister, Vohs, & Tice, 2007). To create a positive climate, use these guidelines:

- Establish secure teacher–student relationships. In Chapter 6 you learned how to do this by sensitively responding to students. Classroom climate is affected by teacher–student relationships and how much a teacher enjoys students.
- Use effective, positive discipline. In Chapter 7 you learned that ineffective discipline harms relationships and makes students angry.
- Express positive emotions. Students need to see adults express a wide range of emotions, but positive emotions more often than negative. Wise teachers sometimes act happy even if they don't feel happy, and often their dissemblance improves their mood. Listen to one 1st-grade teacher:

During recess Tim complains that Kurt won't let him have a ball. I see that Kurt is carrying two balls. He is not playing with them, but keeping them from other children. My spirits sink. I know from past experience that Kurt will defy my authority. As I head for the showdown, I decide to force myself to feel happy. I smile at Kurt (as genuinely as I can) and ask him to give one of the balls to Tim. Kurt begins to resist, but I keep smiling. Surprisingly, I do not feel angry. Kurt hands Tim a ball. I smile more broadly and say, "That was a nice thing to do!" Amazingly, Kurt smiles back.

We have discussed what you can do to promote emotion regulation in typical students. Next let's focus on how you might help students with depression.

Interventions for Depression

Depressed students tend to have lower achievement than you would expect based on their intelligence. You can help your depressed students develop good emotion regulation and coping strategies just as you would any student, using the approaches discussed in the previous section. You may also minimize depression in students when you:

- Help students feel more capable. Teach skills and provide realistic goals. Striving for unrealistic goals makes students feel less capable.
- Help students reappraise situations. Challenge their pessimistic thoughts and suggest more optimistic thoughts; help them see the silver lining. Attribute

their failure and success to effort, not innate ability, like "You got that B because you worked hard" rather than "because you are smart." Students who can explain, and control, their successes feel less depressed.

- Help students find an activity to lift the depressed mood, like an activity the student is good at or enjoys. Also consider pleasant music, a funny book, or exercise.

Teachers are not therapists; you should rely on school counselors for help with students who are at high risk for depression. The counselor may implement special school-based preventions. These are programs designed to teach coping strategies and optimistic thinking. Some depressed students may need professional interventions. Medication is a possibility, but has serious side effects; some medication has been linked to risk of suicide. For this reason, experts recommend trying other interventions first, and medication only as a last resort, with very careful monitoring (Hollon, Thase, & Markowitz, 2002).

In summary, you have learned that emotions are present from birth and serve important functions for students. Yet, emotions must be regulated. Students who are better at regulation tend to be liked by others and academically successful; students who are poor at regulation sometimes develop emotional disorders that interfere with classroom learning. However, regulating their own emotions is half of students' emotional competence. They must also learn to read others' emotions.

Understanding Others' Emotions

Shaunt'a (pronounced "Shawn-tae") has recently moved to a new high school. She is quiet and has few friends. In French class, a boy makes fun of her clothes. Shaunt'a acts as though she doesn't hear. However, another classmate, Dirk, knows she hears. Dirk says that he likes Shaunt'a's clothes, which silences the other student. Dirk then tries to make Shaunt'a more comfortable by talking with her about whether she is going to try out for show choir.

Dirk understood how Shaunt'a felt. The ability to accurately perceive another person's emotions is called **affective perspective-taking**. Affective perspective-taking is an important part of emotional competence because it influences success in social settings, including school. However, as with any ability, it can be put to good or bad use. The con artist may read others' emotions well but does not share their feelings. When affective perspective-taking includes sharing others' feelings, we call it **empathy**.

When children have empathy for another child, they may respond with either sympathy or personal distress. **Sympathy** is feeling concern for the *other's* feelings. **Personal distress** is a negative emotional reaction to someone else's distress where children focus on *their own* feelings. While Dirk felt sympathy for Shaunt'a, other students felt so uncomfortable in the situation that they focused on their own distress and moved away from Shaunt'a.

affective perspective-taking perceiving the emotions of another person.

empathy an emotional state similar to what another person is feeling that results from perceiving the other's emotions.

sympathy an emotional response that consists of feeling concern for a distressed other.

personal distress a self-focused, aversive emotional reaction to someone else's negative emotion.

The distinction between sympathy and personal distress is important because they have different results. Sympathy often leads to helping the person in distress, as Dirk did. In contrast, personal distress leads to a desire to relieve one's own distress. Children might help a distressed person in order to alleviate their own distress, but they are more likely to try to avoid the distressed person, as other students in the class did with Shaunt'a (Losoya & Eisenberg, 2000).

emotion contagion the emotions of one person, through facial, vocal, or gestural cues, generate a similar emotion in another person.

Affective perspective-taking is related to two other important concepts: emotion contagion and social referencing. **Emotion contagion** occurs when the emotion of one person causes a similar emotion in another person. For example, a teenage girl laughed heartily over a joke that her friends thought was lame, but they began laughing too because her mirth was contagious. This mimicking of others' emotions is unintentional and actually changes the emotion you feel. This happens because brain cells, known as *mirror neurons*, respond the same way whether you feel an emotion or you see someone else express an emotion, such as when you are laughing or you are watching someone else laugh (Iacoboni, 2009).

social referencing children read another's emotional expression to determine how they should respond in an ambiguous situation.

Social referencing refers to reading another person's emotional expression to decide how you should respond. For example, a 4-year-old boy looked at his teacher's face before approaching a dog. The teacher smiled, so the child petted the dog. If the teacher had looked worried, the child would have backed away. *Social referencing is especially influential in ambiguous situations* where the child is not sure what to do or feel. Social referencing provides children with information about a situation, including what emotions are appropriate in the situation.

An interesting apparatus often used to study social referencing in infants is the visual cliff (see Figure 8.3), which is a platform with an abrupt drop-off. Crawling infants are placed on the platform, but typically refuse to cross the cliff because they think they might fall. (Plexiglas covers the deep end, so that infants cannot actually fall off.) The cliff can be raised so there is only a short drop-off, making it ambiguous to infants whether it is safe to cross or not. In one study, mothers were asked to stand at the far end of the cliff and express joy or fear. If mothers expressed joy, most (75%) infants crossed the cliff. If mothers expressed fear, none of the infants crossed the cliff. This experiment demonstrates social referencing because the infants were directly influenced by their mothers' emotion expressions (Sorce, Emde, Campos, & Klinnert, 1985).

Age Trends in Understanding Others' Emotions

Empathy, emotion contagion, and social referencing are present in children at all ages, but change over childhood. Let's look at this development next.

Early Childhood (Birth to 5 Years)

Emotion contagion is present at birth. Infants' brains respond to emotion expressions in ways similar to adult brains (Leppanen, Moulson, Vogel-Farley, & Nelson, 2007). Infants pay particular attention to expressions in the eye region. Within the first days of life, infants can imitate the facial expression of others. Within the first months of life, infants can distinguish different emotions, like happiness or sadness, and respond differently to them (Soken & Pick, 1999). For example, infants may look away or move their mouths (forms of self-soothing) if their parent looks

Figure 8.3 The Visual Cliff.
This is a "visual" cliff. The baby is hesitating about crawling over the drop-off and is reading the emotional signal from a parent about whether it is OK to continue. Have you seen children exhibit social referencing in other situations?

sad, or open their eyes wide and kick excitedly if their parent looks happy (see Figure 8.4).

Clearly, infants react to others' emotions, but do they understand what emotions mean, or are they just responding with mindless mimicking? Social referencing suggests they do understand the meaning of emotions (Repacholi & Meltzoff, 2007). Social referencing emerges between 6 and 10 months of age. It increases over the next year, so that by 18 to 20 months old, toddlers are not likely to approach a stranger or a scary toy, like a smoking robot, until *after* they have a reassuring look from a parent, and they will not approach if the parent expresses fear. Older preschoolers also read others' emotional cues to see if a joke is funny, or if their behavior is acceptable. However, preschoolers can deliberately ignore adults' emotional information if they convey disapproval for misbehavior that the child is enjoying.

As children begin to talk they become better at understanding others' emotions because they can label and discuss emotions. By age 2,

Field Observation

Smile at a baby. What does the baby do in response? After a pause, frown at the baby. What does the baby do in response? Try surprise and fear as well. Does the baby's response match the research? What effect do you think this would have on attachment?

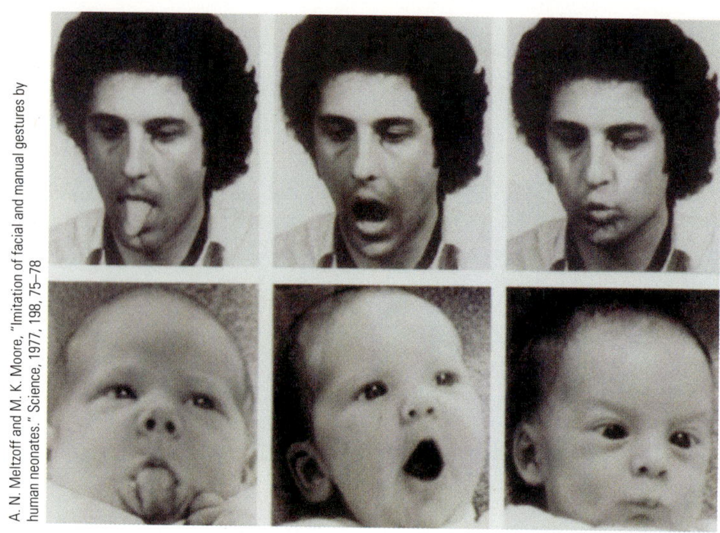

A. N. Meltzoff and M. K. Moore, "Imitation of facial and manual gestures by human neonates." Science, 1977, 198, 75–78

Figure 8.4 Emotion Imitation.
Within the first days of life, infants can imitate the facial expressions of others.

most children understand the words *happy* and *sad*. By age 3, most children talk about consequences and causes of emotions. For example, when one of our sons was almost 3, he said, "Mommy, if you tells peoples you love them, them happy!"

As children get older they talk more about emotions, use more emotion labels, and read emotions more accurately. In one study, children were asked how people in several photographs were feeling. The photos clearly conveyed six different emotions, yet the 3-year-olds used only two emotion labels. The 5-year-olds used four labels on average, but seldom used all six (Widen & Russell, 2003). In general, children first use the label *happy*, then later use *angry* or *sad*, still later use *scared* and *surprised*, and lastly use labels for less common emotions, like *disgust*.

Middle Childhood (6 to 12 Years)

By the age of 6, many children comprehend complex emotion labels like nervous, embarrassed, jealous, and miserable. However, during middle childhood they add variety, accuracy, and complexity to their talk about emotions. For example, a classmate teased 6th-grader Hector for getting a perfect score on his math test. Hector said, "I was *surprised* to find myself *embarrassed* about being a good student, but I knew he was just *jealous*." Hector's 6-year-old sister may know what these words mean, but she is not likely to use them with such skill. The ability to talk about emotions helps older children understand others' emotions better. (See Figure 8.5 for an essay on feelings by an elementary student.)

Social referencing continues in middle childhood but occurs less often at this age because children use social referencing primarily in ambiguous events, and fewer events are ambiguous for older children (Saarni, 1999). Sixth-graders do not carefully watch their teachers' faces for emotional reactions as much as 1st-graders do, because they know more about which classroom events make their teachers happy or angry.

Twelve-year-olds are substantially better than 6-year-olds at taking into account *multiple, even competing, emotions*. For example, most 12-year-olds can understand

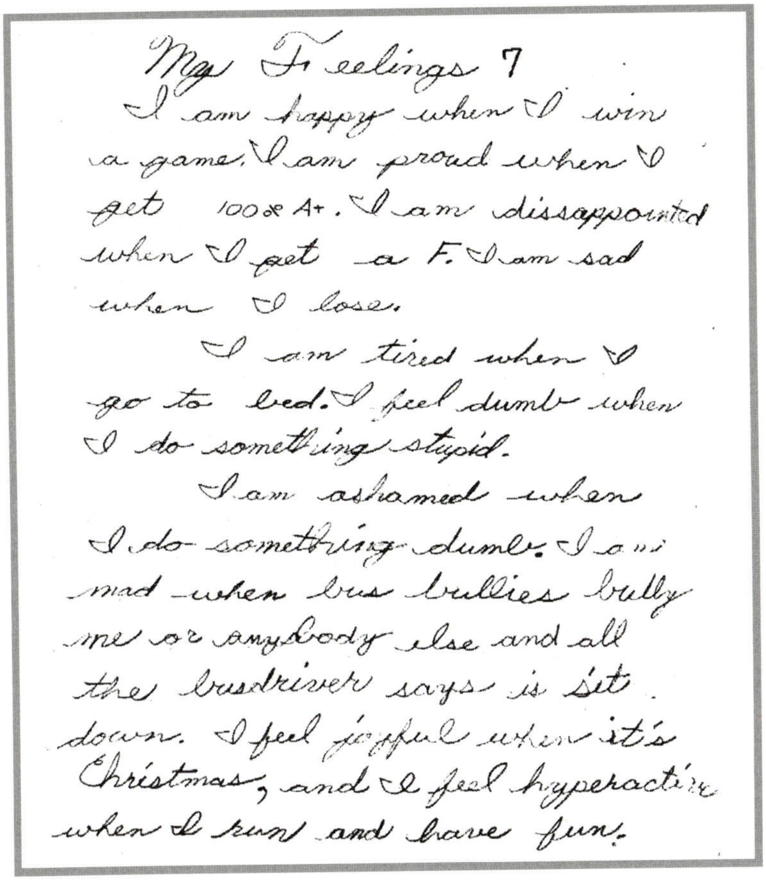

My Feelings 7
I am happy when I win a game. I am proud when I get 100 & A+. I am dissappointed when I get a F. I am sad when I lose.
I am tired when I go to bed. I feel dumb when I do something stupid.
I am ashamed when I do something dumb. I am mad when bus bullies bully me or anybody else and all the busdriver says is sit down. I feel joyful when it's Christmas, and I feel hyperactive when I run and have fun.

Provided by the author

Figure 8.5 Essay on feelings.
This is from the classroom journal of a 6th-grade boy. He is able to label a wide variety of emotions and readily link them to experiences. Would it surprise you to know that he is a well-liked student?

feeling both good and bad emotions after misspelling a familiar word during a spelling contest, but still winning a ribbon, while few 6-year-olds can (Larsen, To, & Fireman, 2007).

Adolescence (13 to 19 Years)

Both social referencing and emotion contagion continue in adolescence. Social referencing occurred on the day after Halloween when Mr. Murray barked at a student in his biology class, "Empty your bulging pockets and hand over the candy immediately!" The other students quickly looked at Mr. Murray. They noticed his eyes were twinkling and he was trying to repress a smile. They began smiling, and sharing their favorite candy with Mr. Murray.

You might expect adolescents and elementary-age children to be substantially more empathic than preschoolers because of their greater ability to read others' emotions. However, research does *not* clearly show they feel more strongly for someone in distress, and some studies even find a decrease in empathy with age (Hastings, Zahn-Waxler, Robinson, Usher, & Bridges, 2000; Zahn-Waxler, Kochanska, Krupnick, & McKnew, 1990). Perhaps this is because empathy competes with older children's growing self-protection. Take a peek in a 1st-grade classroom:

Think About This What are the implications of emotion contagion for teens who listen to hostile, angry music? Should such media be allowed at school functions? What about soothing, or upbeat energizing music? Defend your conclusions drawing on research discussed in this chapter.

A boy is sent to the bathroom after wetting his pants in class. When he returns to the classroom, a girl loudly says, "That happened to me once." Several other children affirm that it has happened to them. The boy visibly relaxes at this empathic outpouring.

Would 5th- or 10th-graders do the same when empathy competes with possible embarrassment? In Chapter 9 you will learn that adolescents can be self-centered in their moral judgments, and in Chapter 10 you will learn that adolescents can choose not to help others because they understand the cost of helping better than do younger children.

However, when adolescents choose to behave empathically, their greater knowledge helps them respond in more genuinely helpful ways than younger children. If they see a peer in distress, they can help solve the problem or help the peer cope by reappraising the situation. For example, a girl was distraught that she didn't get selected for the school play. A friend helped her see the advantages of not spending hours and hours in rehearsals with the cranky director. Adolescents' greater knowledge also helps them to empathize with the plight of unfortunate people in distant countries. They are able to intentionally imagine the feelings of others they cannot see. This is why some adolescents become zealous about compassionate causes, such as raising money for faraway victims of natural disasters.

Individual Diversity in Understanding Others' Emotions

Individual differences in the ability to read others' emotions remain fairly stable over time. That is, children who are especially good at reading emotions and being empathic at one age tend to be better than their peers at a later age (Losoya & Eisenberg, 2000). Dirk is likely to have been more empathic than average since he was a preschooler. This ability has important consequences for students like Dirk.

What Does Understanding Others' Emotions Predict?

Students who are good at labeling and reading others' emotions have higher academic achievement, have greater self-control, and are more cooperative (Izard et al., 2001). They are also sought out by peers (Fabes, Eisenberg, Hanish, & Spinrad, 2001). This is because they accurately interpret others' perspectives and easily establish rapport, as Dirk did with Shaunt'a. Dirk is well liked by both boys and girls, as well as teachers.

In contrast, children who are poor at reading emotional cues are less liked by peers. They tend to be aggressive and have behavior problems in the classroom (Arsenio, Cooperman, & Lover, 2000; Coie & Dodge, 1998). They may confuse sad and angry expressions or not notice when others are irritated with them. For example, a group of 6th-grade boys avoided a classmate who kept telling the same joke over and over. The classmate could not tell that the other boys were irritated by his repetition. His inability to read emotion cues led to social rejection.

What Predicts Understanding Others' Emotions?

Just as with emotion regulation, empathy may have a small genetic basis. Identical twins tend to have more-similar empathic responses than fraternal twins (Emde, 1998). In addition, children's emotion regulation makes a strong contribution to understanding others' emotions, as do the same parent factors that are linked to emotion regulation. Let's discuss these next.

Emotion regulation

Students understand more about others' emotions and are more sympathetic if they can regulate their own emotions (Denham et al., 2003; Eisenberg et al., 1997). When students witness someone else's distress, they will feel *sympathy* if they can keep their own emotions at a moderate level, but they will feel *personal distress* if their own emotions are overly intense.

Attachment

Students with secure attachment tend to be better able to read others' emotions and more empathic than insecure students, who tend to respond to others' distress with personal distress rather than sympathy (Mikulineer & Shaver, 2005). Secure attachment may contribute to empathy because attachment promotes emotion-regulation ability.

Response to children's emotions

Parents who respond compassionately to their children's negative outbursts serve as role models of empathy (Denham et al., 1997). However, parents should not accept children's negativity when it hurts someone else. In one study, parents who allowed their children to express anger when frustrated, but not if it might hurt another's feelings, had more sympathetic children (Eisenberg, Fabes, Schaller, Carlo, & Miller, 1991). Parents who prohibited all displays of anger had children who had personal distress rather than sympathy.

Expression of emotions

Empathy is linked to emotions expressed in the family. Preschoolers whose mothers communicate warmly and are seldom negative toward them are more likely to become adolescents who are sympathetic toward others (Michalik et al., 2007). In contrast, children raised in families with mostly negative emotions may have low levels of sympathy.

> ***Think About This*** Think about a child you know well. How would you respond if the child:
> 1. Looked annoyed at receiving an undesirable gift.
> 2. Looked shaky while waiting to get a shot.
> 3. Won a race and jumped around boasting about it.
> 4. Were very angry, muttered threats, and slammed doors.
>
> How should you respond in order to promote the child's emotional competence? Defend your choices. (Adapted from Saarni, 1999)

Talk about emotions

Talking about emotions helps children understand others' emotions (Denham, Zoller, & Couchoud, 1994). Some families talk a lot about emotions and some almost never do (Dunn, Brown, & Beardsall, 1991). Conflict between siblings provides a rich opportunity to talk about emotions. Conversations about negative emotions are especially helpful because they focus more on the causes of emotions and involve more extensive vocabulary than conversations about positive emotions (Lagattuta & Wellman, 2002). It may seem ironic that sibling conflict contributes to children's emotional competence, but keep in mind these are normal family conflicts, not intense conflicts. The emotions may be negative, but they are contained enough to allow (mostly) civil conversation.

Abuse

Abused youth are less likely to read others' emotions as accurately as nonabused youth. At the same time, they can be overly sensitive to negative emotions. For example, neglected youth have a bias toward perceiving sadness in others, perhaps because their mothers tend to be depressed. Physically abused youth have a bias toward perceiving anger and are more sensitive to subtle anger cues than other youth (Pollak & Sinha, 2002).

Abused children may not be as empathic as nonabused children. They are more likely to respond to peers' distress with either personal distress or attack. They might laugh, hit, or withdraw when they see another child in distress. These inappropriate responses occur even after spending considerable time with nonabusive caregivers and peers in child care. Nonabused children, by comparison, are more likely to watch, help, or comfort the other (Klimes-Dougan & Kistner, 1990).

Abused adolescents may not want to talk about emotions, particularly negative emotions (Pollak, Cicchetti, Hornung, & Reed, 2000). Some teens with a history of abuse claim they are not affected by the abuse, but they act out through substance use, abusive relationships with peers, and other problem behaviors. Such teens are unable to acknowledge or discuss their emotions. One purpose of therapy is to help traumatized youth communicate emotions. This can help them recover from abuse and develop emotional competence.

Group Diversity in Understanding Others' Emotions

Robust differences in affective perspective-taking have not been found across groups. However, small gender and cultural differences may exist. Let's look at these next.

Gender

Are girls more empathic than boys? Some studies have found that girls show more concern for others and are better at reading distress in others, but other studies find no gender differences (Hastings et al., 2000; Saarni, 1999). Studies that use self-report rather than physiological measures like heart rate are more likely to find that girls are more empathic. This means that girls may think they should be more empathic and therefore report that they are, or girls may actually be more empathic than boys. The best summary of research to date is that gender differences in empathy are not consistently found, but when differences are found, girls are more empathic.

Culture

As you learned earlier, Darwin argued more than a century ago that facial expressions are universal. Recent research confirms that people can read emotions across cultures through facial expressions, tone of voice, and body language (Ekman, 2009; Elfenbein & Ambady, 2003). People express emotion in basically the same way across cultures, but some subtle cultural differences exist, much like different dialects of the same language. As a result you are a little more accurate at reading emotions expressed by members of your own culture.

These subtle differences can sometimes lead to misunderstanding. For example, a 10-year-old girl from Mexico tried to get her European American teacher's attention by holding her notebook in front of the teacher's face while the teacher talked with another student (Whiting & Edwards, 1988). Then the girl leaned against the teacher's body, steadfastly looking at the teacher's face. The teacher did not acknowledge her, so the girl walked slowly back to her seat. In the girl's culture, children often communicate visually and through touch without speaking. The teacher viewed the child as annoying, while the child viewed the teacher as unresponsive. Each misunderstood the others' emotional signals. This suggests that you may need to work at creating emotion understanding when you or your students must cross cultural boundaries.

Classroom Implications of Understanding Others' Emotions

Skill at reading others' emotions influences success in the classroom. Students with this skill tend to be less aggressive, higher achievers, and more popular among teachers and classmates. Other students need help developing these skills. There are several strategies you can use to help your students develop sensitivity to others' emotions:

- Use victim-centered discipline. Victim-centered discipline is a type of induction (see Chapter 7) that involves pointing out to children during the discipline encounter how their misbehavior made someone else feel. This trains empathy in children.
- Use emotion contagion and social referencing to your students' advantage. If you vividly convey enjoyment of your students and the content you teach, your students might imitate you. Students are more likely to catch the emotions of those they like, such as a favorite teacher. Students are also more likely to accurately read and catch the emotions of those who clearly and strongly express their emotions (Zaki, Bolger, & Ochsner, 2008).
- Help students improve emotion regulation. Factors that predict emotion regulation also predict affective perspective-taking skills. This means you can help students both control their own emotions and understand others' emotions better by following the suggestions given in the previous section.

Mrs. Ng did each of these things with Hailey. She established a warm relationship with Hailey and maintained a positive classroom climate. She accepted Hailey's rage, but did not tolerate her behavior. She sent Hailey to the bathroom to wash her face and calm down, teaching Hailey a coping strategy. Then she used the opportunity to talk with Hailey about emotions. She used inductive, victim-centered discipline by pointing out how Hailey's behavior affected others. As a result, Hailey may become better at both controlling her own anger and understanding the feelings of others.

In addition to the strategies just discussed, there are dozens of curriculum programs designed to help children understand others' emotions. One example is Promoting Alternative Thinking Strategies (PATHS) for preschools and elementary schools. This program includes sixty lessons on how feelings are acceptable, how feelings provide information, how to recognize feelings, and how one's behavior can affect others' feelings. As part of the program, children create a "feelings box" that holds pictures of faces expressing specific emotions. The children can place one of these faces on their desk to indicate what they are feeling at that time. The intent of this program is to raise children's awareness of their own and others' emotions. Among preschoolers, PATHS has resulted in less negative emotion, less aggression, greater social skills, and more classroom involvement. Among elementary students, PATHS has resulted in greater ability to talk about emotions and less aggression or behavior problems. The greatest gains were made by children who initially had behavior problems (Greenberg & Kusche, 2006).

Figure 8.6 provides a visual summary of the ways you can affect children's ability to regulate their own emotions and understand others' emotions. It also shows the child outcomes linked to emotional competence. Use this figure as a quick guide to help you think about ways you can help your students, like Hailey, become more emotionally competent.

Throughout this chapter you have seen how *thought influences emotion.* For example, emotions are triggered by how children think about an event. Children can cope with emotions by trying to think about something else or reappraising the situation. In addition, as children develop greater knowledge about emotions, they

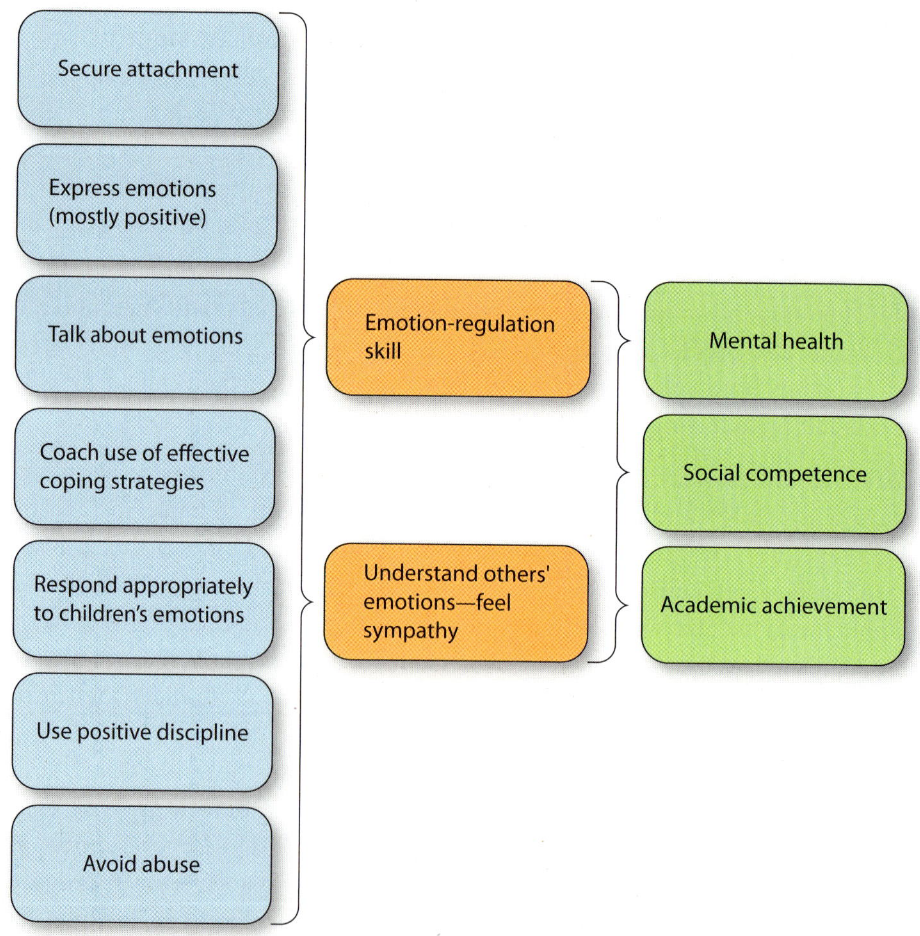

Figure 8.6 Model of Emotional Competence.
This model summarizes the seven teacher and parent behaviors (in blue) that predict children's emotional competence (in orange) and the outcomes linked to emotional competence (in green). Use this model to think about your own behavior and your students' emotional competence.

become more sensitive to others' emotions. Now we turn attention to how *emotion influences thought.*

Emotions and Thought

In a 9th-grade class, the teacher says, "Sangita, you were talking! I'm taking a point off your assignment." Actually, Sangita was not talking; she is wrongfully accused. Sangita becomes angry. She does not defend herself because her heritage culture dictates that children do not argue with teachers. However, she silently smolders with thoughts of how unfair it is, how the teacher doesn't like her, how she will tell her friends about it at lunch, and so on. Sangita does not hear the rest of the lesson.

Sangita's anger hijacked her thoughts and affected her learning. Although emotions may not be as intense as Sangita's, emotions are ever present and constantly influencing thought. Some students are able to use emotions to make thinking more intelligent and to think intelligently about emotions. Psychologists call this ability **emotional intelligence** (Mayer, Roberts, & Barsade, 2008; Mayer & Salovey, 1997, p. 5). However, the term may be used in the media to refer to the same abilities that comprise *emotional competence*—to accurately perceive, understand, express, and regulate emotions. In this text, we will use the term *emotional competence* to refer to this broader array of abilities. Emotions influence thought in many ways:

emotional intelligence the ability to think intelligently about emotions and use emotions to make thinking more intelligent. Sometimes defined more broadly to mean emotional competence.

- Emotions focus attention; students pay more attention to things with emotional significance (Mather, 2007). For example, students learning about civil rights will pay rapt attention to a debate on the emotionally charged Rodney King beating in Los Angeles. However, too much emotion can swamp attention. Perhaps this is because emotions and attention draw upon the same areas of the brain (Fenske & Raymond, 2006).
- Emotions organize recall and memory. Students remember more when the mood they are currently in matches the mood they were in when they encoded the memory. Students also tend to remember details of emotionally strong experiences (Kensinger, 2007). For example, they might remember disgust over dissecting a frog more than other lessons in the same class.
- Emotions determine whether students approach or avoid a learning task, and how much effort they put into learning. For example, a student who enjoys the topic will expend more effort writing a research paper.
- Emotions interfere with information processing if cognitive resources needed for working memory are instead being used to try to suppress intense emotions

Revisiting Case 3

How did emotions affect learning for Le'Raun? Contrast his emotions in Miss Loeb's and Mrs. Richardson's classes. In which class were his thoughts focused on trying to contain his distress versus learning? What happened to his learning ability after the principal's visit?

(Bonanno et al., 2004). For example, while Sangita was trying to contain her anger, she had less working memory space available to process the lesson.

Emotions can have different effects on learning and thought, depending on what emotion is experienced. Let's compare positive and negative emotions.

Positive Emotions

Positive emotions—like interest, happiness, or excitement—promote learning and creativity. Happy students are more productive, perform better on projects and tasks, and solve problems more creatively than students in a negative mood (Ashby, Isen, & Turken, 1999). Are positive emotions always beneficial? *Intensely* positive emotions can result in worse performance on tasks that require detailed analytic processing, like some physics problems. However, when a task is important to the individual, positive emotions do not impair performance (Hirt, Melton, McDonald, & Harackiewicz, 1996). In other tasks, neutral or *mildly* positive emotions, like interest, may be ideal for focused attention and fast information processing (Rose, Futterweit, & Jankowski, 1999). Thus, whether your students perform better in a highly versus a mildly positive mood may depend on the task at hand.

Why does positive emotion enhance productivity and creativity? Positive emotions broaden thought (Fredrickson, 2001; Izard, 2007). When you feel joy, you are motivated to learn, to be open to new information, to generate more ideas, and to participate in activities. When you feel interest, you are motivated to focus attention on pursuing a goal (Gable & Harmon-Jones, 2008). Positive emotions may have these effects by altering neurotransmitters in the brain. Positive emotions are linked to small increases of dopamine in the part of the brain responsible for working memory and creativity (Ashby et al., 1999). A different set of outcomes is linked to negative emotions.

Negative Emotions

Negative emotions—like anger, sadness, and boredom—impair learning. When students feel negative emotions, they have difficulty attending to classroom tasks, as Sangita did. Students who frequently experience anger tend to be easily distracted and are often off-task (Eisenberg et al., 1993). Students who are bored or sad tend to be less creative. Students who are depressed tend to underachieve. However, *brief sadness* may not have these negative effects. While people are briefly sad, they may process information in systematic, detailed ways that can be helpful in some tasks, such as doing a karyotype in biology class (Bodenhausen, Gabriel, & Lineberger, 2000). Thus, your students are likely to learn less if they are chronically negative, but occasional sadness is not a problem for some tasks.

Optimal Arousal

One way to make sense of research showing that a little sadness and a little joy are sometimes helpful, but that high levels may not be, is to think of optimal levels of arousal. **Arousal** refers to the physiological component of emotion that prepares students for action. When arousal is too high, students are overwhelmed. When arousal

arousal a person's physiological readiness for action.

is too low, they are not engaged. Both extremes may result in less learning than at an optimal level. This notion of optimal arousal may only apply to complex tasks that require concentration, like reading a difficult passage, and tasks that require careful fine-motor skill, like playing golf or drawing. In contrast, for simple tasks that require perseverance, the more arousal the better.

What is the optimal level of arousal in your classroom? Unfortunately, there is no quick formula. The answer depends on the task, on students' capacity for arousal, and on how much arousal they already feel. This is something you have to judge in each situation.

Anxiety

anxiety disorder a common internalizing disorder in which the child feels worried about future threats, or threats to the sense of self.

test anxiety a dispositional proneness toward anxiety in test situations that interferes with performance.

Anxiety is a negative emotion that impairs learning. We will take a close look at anxiety because anxiety disorders are among the most common childhood disorders. Do not confuse anxiety with fear. Fear is a response to present threats, whereas anxiety is a feeling of helplessness focused on future threats or threats to the sense of self. You can recognize anxiety in your students through behaviors such as foot kicking, hair twirling, mouth touching, lip licking, lip twisting, crying, chewing on objects, and nail biting. Both the frequency and intensity of these behaviors may indicate the child's degree of anxiety. These symptoms are found across all age groups and for ethnically diverse students (Ialongo, Edelsohn, Werthamer-Larsson, Crockett, & Kellam, 1994).

Depression and anxiety tend to occur together in the same student. As with depression, girls are more likely to be anxious (Silk et al., 2003). Anxiety emerges at younger ages than depression, so early childhood educators need to watch for signs of anxiety.

A little anxiety can be optimal, such as when it motivates students to study for a test. However, when anxiety becomes intense, it impairs learning by undermining their ability to pay attention (Ialongo et al., 1994). Instead of attending to the task at hand, anxious students worry about irrelevant things or attend to potential threats, such as "my dad will go ballistic if I fail this assignment." Anxiety can make students appear less intelligent because they are so consumed by anxious thoughts that they may not remember, learn, or make good decisions. Chronic anxiety is also linked to illness (Maier & Watkins, 2000). Thus, anxious students may often be absent from school, which will further interfere with learning.

Any child can occasionally feel anxiety strong enough to interfere with learning. However, some children have chronic intense anxiety that results in an anxiety disorder. One type of anxiety disorder is test anxiety (see Box 8.2). Chronic anxiety can result from (1) social referencing if children live with an overly anxious parent, (2) inherited tendencies toward negative emotions, (3) mother's anxiety during pregnancy, (4) parents' overreactions to the child's failures, and (5) feeling helpless to control the environment (Murray et al., 2008; van den Bergh & Marcoen, 2004). What might lead a child to feel helpless? Intrusive, overcontrolling, emotionally overinvolved parents foster helplessness in children; so can unresponsive teachers and coaches and negative events like parental divorce or academic failure. Anxious parents may be overprotective toward anxious children; so right now you are thinking, "Ah ha! A classic, evocative gene–environment correlation" (Narusyte et al., 2008). Good thinking!

Challenges in Development — Box 8.2

Test Anxiety

Stefanie, a 10th-grader, has been a self-described worrywart since preschool. She is chronically anxious about a lot of things, but especially about doing well in school. She gets so nervous before a test, worrying that she will fail it, that she gets physically sick. She has poor test scores, but earns adequate grades because she does her homework and extra assignments.

Test anxiety is a trait toward anxiety in test situations. It is rare in the primary grades, rises from 3rd to 5th grade, stabilizes through adolescence, and drops in college (Hembree, 1988). Some psychologists believe this age trend indicates it is learned, rather than innate.

Why Does It Matter if Children Are Test-Anxious? Test anxiety is linked to reduced test scores as early as 3rd grade, and the linkage becomes stronger with age (Ferrando, Varea, & Lorenzo, 1998). Anyone might feel anxiety during a test, but test-anxious students like Stefanie engage in so much worry that it consumes much of their working memory, leaving less space for processing test items (Beilock & Carr, 2005). This "choking under pressure" probably results from cortisol, the stress hormone. A little cortisol enhances executive functioning and working memory (see Chapter 4), but too much reduces capacity (Blair, Granger, & Razza, 2005).

Test anxiety is not a lack of ability, but difficulty in trying to show ability. This is important to understand because teachers form expectations about students' abilities based on test scores, and teacher expectations can affect student performance. It is clear that for some students, test anxiety is not merely a lack of ability because when test anxiety is reduced through intervention, performance increases.

What Can Be Done about Test Anxiety? Students tend to have test anxiety when either parents' or teachers' expectations are unrealistically high or when tests are overly difficult (Zeidner, 1998). You help your test-anxious students when you have reasonable expectations and reasonable tests and do the following:

1. Help students experience academic success. Anxiety is linked to repeated failure in exams.
2. Improve the testing situation. Test-anxious students will perform better if you give low-stress instructions, give cues to trigger recall, have minimal distractions, and have more-frequent tests.
3. Provide training for test-taking skills.
4. Avoid drawing attention to poor performance, and deemphasize grades. Anxiety is linked to emphasis on competition or social comparison, and standards that are based on how other students perform (grading on the "curve").
5. Avoid attributing success or failure to the child's innate ability.
6. Avoid time limits during testing. Timed tests promote anxiety.

The school counselor may suggest additional interventions. One common therapy helps children change worrisome thoughts. For example, a student might be worried about failing an exam, and thereby failing school, and never being able to find a job. The counselor might counter this by asking the student, "What is the *worst* possible thing that might happen if you fail this exam?" The student might have to take the class over again—which does not doom anyone to a life of unemployment. This approach has a large effect, when combined with teaching study or test-taking skills (Tuncay, 2003). There are other less powerful but still effective treatments, like relaxation and hypnosis.

How did Stefanie survive her test anxiety? Her concerned teachers sent her to talk to the school counselor, who asked her "What is the *worst* possible . . . ?" She realized that failing an exam would not ruin her life. She learned to cope with her anxiety, and is now a teacher who is very sensitive about her own students' test anxiety. She never gives surprise tests and makes sure students know the material well. Instead of the "test" word, she tells her students, "show me what you know."

Classroom Implications of Emotions and Thought

The research on emotions and thought suggests that positive emotions promote creative problem solving and, for some tasks, analytic thought. Thus, if you induce positive emotions in your students you may help raise their achievement. Let's look at how Mr. Pugh did this in his 6th-grade science class on electricity:

The students were out of their seats, excitedly using the Van de Graaf machine and balloons to make their hair stand on end. When one boy began jumping up and down, begging to be next to perform the experiment, Mr. Pugh said he was already too "charged" up. The boy and his classmates laughed. The classroom climate was fun and engrossing. The children were also learning—when asked why their hair was standing up, they could explain static electricity.

Even if you teach a content area that is not as inherently fun as static electricity, positive emotions strong enough to affect thinking are remarkably easy to induce. In research, positive emotions are induced by giving participants an unexpected reward, helping them succeed at a task, having them watch a funny film, or asking them to recall a pleasant memory for a minute. These brief interventions result in faster learning during laboratory experiments. Applying this to the classroom, you may induce positive emotions when you:

- Create a positive classroom climate, using the suggestions given in the previous sections. These include developing strong teacher–student relationships, expressing positive emotions, and using positive rather than harsh discipline.
- Celebrate students achieving a goal or succeeding on a difficult task. Unexpectedly reward students for good effort. However, keep in mind that when rewards are routine or expected, they no longer induce positive emotions.
- Share happy stories or jokes with students, as Mr. Pugh did.
- Occasionally have activities that require students to think fast. Have you ever played a game that requires you to think fast? It is fun and energizing. Thinking fast is linked to better moods (Pronin & Jacobs, 2008). This may be why fast, upbeat music sometimes has positive effects.

Tony Freeman/PhotoEdit

"Charging" students up with positive emotions may help them think better.

Upbeat music can induce positive emotions in students. One fad in education circles is the Mozart effect, which refers to the notion that children are smarter after listening to Mozart's music. Georgia's former governor, Zell Miller, even pushed his state to provide a classical recording for every infant born in the state, and an industry of recordings for creating genius infants has sprung up. Is there any substance to this claim? In one study, students listening to a pleasant, happy Mozart piece performed better on an IQ test than students listening to a slow Albinoni piece (Thompson, Schellenberg, & Husain, 2001). The Mozart effect has been replicated with different music, such as upbeat children's songs, and with listening to a story rather than music, but the effect is not always found (e.g., Schellenberg, 2005). The Mozart effect is believed to result from positive emotions. That is, the music puts you in a better mood. Thus, playing upbeat music may sometimes help your students learn and perform well on tests, but so should other approaches to inducing positive emotions.

Intense or chronic negative emotions can interfere with students' learning in your classroom, although a little sadness or anxiety may not be a problem. You reduce negative emotions in students when you:

- Foster better emotion regulation, using methods discussed earlier.
- Minimize daily hassles at school. These are small stressors—such as hearing teachers yell at other students, getting low grades for trivial errors, or having to sit still for too long. Daily hassles can also be time related, such as not having enough time to eat lunch, get from class to class, or play at recess. A group of honors students said their single biggest concern about starting high school was getting to class on time. This may seem trivial to you, but it caused anxiety in these 14-year-olds because the school was large and they had only five minutes between classes.
- Reduce anxiety by providing a predictable classroom and giving students as much control over activities as possible. The most important part of a predictable classroom is a teacher who is consistent and responsive to students. When teachers are responsive, rather than critical or detached, students are more positive and less anxious (Hestenes, Kontos, & Bryan, 1993).

Students who are prone to emotional negativity can still be successful in school, if they are able to control their attention. However, if you have students who are unusually negative or anxious despite your attempts to maintain positive emotions in your classroom, the school counselor may help with intervention. Specific suggestions for helping students cope with test anxiety are given in Box 8.2.

We close this chapter, and this section on the emotional child, by reiterating the importance of emotional competence for students' school success. Promoting students' emotional competence is central—not merely an add-on—to the teacher's role. Compared with students who struggle with their emotions, emotionally competent students like school, have higher achievement, and are liked better by peers and teachers.

Reflections on Practice: Checklist for Teachers

A positive teacher and school climate promotes emotional competence in students and might compensate for, or at least not worsen, challenges faced by students in negative homes. Two powerful factors associated with both greater emotion regulation and empathy have been discussed in previous chapters:

- Develop a secure teacher–student relationship. How to do this is described in Chapter 6.
- Use victim-centered inductive discipline. How to do this is described in Chapter 7.

In addition, to promote the emotional competence of students, periodically ask the following:

1. Is there a positive emotional climate in my classroom and the school? This will be evident if students in your classroom are predominantly in a positive or neutral, but not negative, mood.
2. Do I express emotions of moderate intensity and wide range, although primarily positive? Do I model good regulation and coping when I am emotional?
3. Are there simple interventions I can use to create positive moods, like helping students succeed at a task, asking them to think about happy things, or playing upbeat music?
4. Am I aware of the coping strategies used by each of my students, particularly those with poor regulation? Do I teach appropriate coping strategies? Do I help students reinterpret emotional situations in a positive light and challenge their pessimistic explanations?
5. Do I respond promptly when students are overly aroused, before they lose control? Do I validate their negative emotions (but not accept hurtful behavior)?
6. Do I converse with students about their own and others' emotions? Do I use students' emotions, conflicts, or stories as opportunities to talk about emotions?
7. Do I watch for internalizing disorders like anxiety or depression? Am I learning to read students' emotions, particularly those from cultures different from my own?
8. Are there cultural mismatches between myself and my students in coping strategies? If so, how can I resolve the mismatches in a way that is respectful to my students?

Summary of Age Trends in Emotional Competence

	Emotions Experienced	Emotion Regulation	Understanding Others' Emotions
Early Childhood (Birth–5 Years)	Basic emotions such as distress, interest, and disgust are exhibited by newborns. Social smiles emerge at about 5 weeks. Complex emotions such as envy and embarrassment emerge at about 15–18 months. Social emotions that involve moral judgment—pride, shame, guilt—emerge soon afterward. Preschoolers are vulnerable to guilt even when not responsible for events. Gender differences in anxiety emerge (girls are more anxious).	Newborns cope by appearing to sleep. Gaze aversion and self-comforting strategies emerge before 6 months. Stable individual differences in emotionality may be present as early as 2 months. Toddlers begin to take on responsibility for emotion regulation. They are able to delay emotional expression. In pretend play, they try on different emotions. By age 3, brain maturation allows greater control of emotions. Intense crying and tantrums diminish. Preschoolers can dissemble to protect others' feelings. They are better at exaggerating than at squelching an emotion. Older preschoolers are able to regulate their own emotions under normal conditions.	Emotion contagion is present at birth. Newborns mimic others' facial expressions. They can tell one emotion from another and respond uniquely to different emotions. Social referencing appears at about 8 months and peaks around 22 months. Toddlers' empathy and understanding the cause of others' emotions are indicated by their comforting distressed others and teasing. Stable individual differences in empathy may be present at 2–3 years of age. Toddlers understand a few basic emotion words. Positive emotion words are learned before negative. By age 6, children understand complex emotion words.
Middle Childhood (6–12 Years)	Children become able to accurately judge responsibility, and therefore guilt. Test anxiety rises until 5th grade, then stabilizes. Depression may emerge. Average onset of mild depression is age 11.	Adult-like coping ability should be in place by age 10. Children are now able to generate more coping alternatives and begin to use peers to cope, but still primarily use parents. Ability to judge controllability of the situation allows them to select the best coping strategy. They are better able to use emotion-focused strategies, but prefer problem-focused strategies. Ability to dissemble grows dramatically. Children are able to fake liking something by 4th grade.	Use of social referencing diminishes, but is still present. Children are able to consider others' beliefs and attitudes when judging the cause of emotions. Understanding of multiple and competing emotions in the same situation is manifest by 8–10 years. The ability to accurately discuss and label emotions continues to grow.
Adolescence (13–19 Years)	Rate of depression rises in adolescence. Gender differences in depression emerge (girls are more depressed).	Most teens are not moody. They feel positive most of the time, although less happy than 10-year-olds. They report more boredom, drowsiness, and social discomfort than their parents do.	Emotion contagion and social referencing are reduced but still present. Teens can respond to emotion signals in others that are so subtle they are not aware of them. Teens are not more empathic than younger children.

Chapter Summary

Emotions

- Emotions involve physiological arousal, tendency to act, and appraisal (or thought). The functions of emotion are to focus attention, motivate behavior, prepare for action, and communicate.
- Charles Darwin argued that emotional expression is innate and universal. Basic emotions are present in early infancy, but complex social emotions do not appear until toddlerhood.

Emotion Regulation

- Emotion regulation is the ability to control emotions. Children do this by using coping strategies, some of which are more adaptive than others. Children also do this through emotional dissemblance. Negative emotions fade when you do not express them.
- Children who are good at emotion regulation are better liked by teachers and classmates. They have better language skills, better academic achievement, and fewer emotional disorders.
- Antecedents of good emotion regulation include parents who foster secure attachment, express mostly positive emotions, avoid harsh discipline, directly coach coping strategies, and respond appropriately to and talk with children about their emotions.
- Two prevalent emotional disorders are depression and anxiety. They often occur together. Depressed children are at additional risk for ADHD, substance use, poor school performance, dropping out, and loneliness. Children are likely to be depressed if they have stressful relationships, family conflict, a depressed mother, poor coping strategies, and negative life events they feel helpless about.
- Girls may be somewhat better at emotion regulation and dissemblance than boys, yet girls experience more depression by adolescence.
- Cultures dictate differences in appraisal, emotion regulation, and rules for emotional dissemblance. However, many aspects of emotional experience and expression are similar across cultures.
- Teachers can promote students' emotion regulation by developing secure relationships, directly coaching students in coping strategies, responding appropriately to their emotions, minimizing daily hassles for students, and improving school climate.

Understanding Others' Emotions

- Affective perspective-taking is the ability to read other's emotions and is linked with empathy. This ability is present in infancy, as indicated by emotion contagion in newborns and infants' use of social referencing.

- Students may respond to another's distress with sympathy or with personal distress. Students who are sympathetic and skilled at understanding others' emotions are liked better by peers and less aggressive.
- Antecedents of affective perspective-taking skill include good emotion regulation and secure attachment. Skilled children have parents who accept their emotional displays without overreacting, express positive emotions at home, talk about emotions during sibling conflict, and are not abusive. Teachers can apply the same behaviors to promote emotional competence in the classroom.

Emotions and Thought

- Emotions influence memory and thought processes. Positive emotions promote creativity, problem solving, attention, and fast information processing. Neutral or mild negative emotions promote detailed, analytic thought, but strong negative emotions interfere with thought.
- Teachers can minimize negative emotions by reducing daily hassles and making classrooms predictable. Positive emotions can be induced through simple events, like an unexpected reward or upbeat story.
- Anxiety is linked to insecure attachment, loss of control, and negative life events. Girls tend to have more anxiety than boys, even in early childhood.
- Test anxiety results in an attention deficit during testing. Teachers can minimize test anxiety by helping students experience academic success, changing the test situation, avoiding timed tests, training students in test-taking strategies, attributing failures to effort rather than ability, and avoiding comparison between students.

Accompanying Education CourseMate Website Resources

Visit the **Education CourseMate** website at **CengageBrain.com** to find resources and study aids for this chapter, including self-tests, additional print and website resources, and glossary flashcards.

section 4 The Social Child

THE TERM *SOCIAL* REFERS TO INTERACTIONS WITH OTHER PEOPLE. In this section you will learn how children develop social competence. In Chapter 9 you will learn how children apply cognition to social situations. In Chapter 10 you will learn how prosocial and antisocial behavior and conflict resolution skills develop. In Chapter 11 you will learn that peer interaction and play are critically important to children of all ages. Let's begin our study of social development by watching Preston interact with peers in science lab.

Preston's Behavior in Science Lab

Ellen Senisi

In a 9th-grade science class, four students are sitting at a lab table watching a beaker of rapidly boiling water. An adult visitor asks the group, "What's in your beaker?" Preston says, "I don't know. Why don't you stick your hand in there and find out?" He laughs at his joke, but no one else does. Two girls roll their eyes, and the third, Tessa, politely remains quiet. Tessa breaks the awkward silence by telling the others that the dipstick in her car is broken. Preston retorts, "You broke your dipstick? How stupid can you be? . . . That's why dumb girls like you shouldn't be driving in the first place." The others turn a cold shoulder to Preston.

The group continues their lab project. They are instructed to drop a large metal rod into the beaker of boiling water for five minutes and then transfer the rod to a cup of water at room temperature for five minutes. Preston prepares to drop the rod from six inches above the beaker. "Don't! That's how you broke the beaker last time," says one of his lab partners. "And the time before that," adds Tessa sarcastically. "Give me the tongs. You always screw it up. Just let me do it." Preston shoves the tongs to her, rolls his eyes and says, "Whatever."

Tessa says, "Time it, Preston." He replies, "Sure, whatever." A few minutes later, one of the girls asks how much time they have left. Preston says, "I don't know. Ask someone else." She responds, "You were supposed to time how long it has been in the beaker for our group." Preston, grinning widely, says, "Oh well. I didn't. You should have said that before." Tessa's eyes fill with tears. "Now we have to start all over again. The bell is going to ring before we finish." Another student says, "We'll all do bad because you messed up," pointing at Preston. Preston says, "Whatever," as his lab partners begin the experiment again. Preston turns his attention to the visitor, asking, "Where did you get your shoes?... Because they are ugly." Tessa tells the visitor, "Ignore everything he says. We do."

Does Preston use antisocial humor because he lacks social skills and cannot see that he is hurting others' feelings? Or, does he not care if he hurts others? How will his aggression affect his academic achievement and his social standing with his peers? What can his teacher do to help him? At the end of this section, you will be able to answer these questions. You will have a stronger understanding of how to help your students develop social competence.

chapter 9

Social Cognition

Image Source/Jupiter Images

DO YOU KNOW INDIVIDUALS WHOM EVERYONE SEEMS TO ENJOY BEING AROUND BECAUSE THEY HAVE EXCEPTIONAL SOCIAL SKILLS? Chances are that they are skilled at "reading" other people and have a good sense of humor. If they are respected, they probably also abide by widely held moral rules. All three of these key aspects of social cognition will be discussed in this chapter. After you read this chapter, you will understand:

- The development of students' ability to read other people.
- Why humor matters in the classroom.
- How morality develops.
- What you can do to foster these aspects of social cognition in your classroom.

Theory of Mind

Wally:	*Mrs. Crites said I wasn't doing my math today, just because I was looking out the window.*
Counselor:	*She probably thought you were daydreaming.*
Wally:	*Yeah, but I wasn't. I was thinking about the problem I didn't know how to do. But I fooled her! In social studies I had my book open on my desk, and I looked like I was reading, but I wasn't! I was dreamin'.*

social cognition thought processes applied to the social domain.

Although only 9 years old, Wally is pretty smart about people; he has good social cognition. You learned in Chapter 3 that cognition refers to thought processes like reasoning and problem solving. **Social cognition** refers to cognition applied to social situations. A goal of schools is to help children think clearly and solve problems. In what domain is clear thinking and problem solving more important than the social domain? In this chapter, you will learn how to foster three aspects of your students' social cognition: theory of mind, humor, and moral judgment (including academic dishonesty).

Wally knew that Mrs. Crites would assume he was learning from his textbook if he looked like he was reading. He cleverly led her to a *false belief* by acting as though he were in one mental state (reading), while actually being in another mental state (daydreaming). He deliberately manipulated Mrs. Crites's mind. Wally has developed a landmark ability of childhood called *theory of mind.*

theory of mind the ability to infer mental states in others, such as beliefs, desires, knowledge, and intentions. It is sometimes called people reading.

Theory of mind (ToM) refers to students' understanding that other people have mental states—beliefs, desires, knowledge, and intentions—that are different from their own and to the ability to infer or figure out others' mental states. Thus, a simple definition of ToM is "people reading." This ability helps students explain and predict others' behavior.

Field Observation

In the presence of a 2- to 3-year-old and a 6- to 8-year-old, have another person place a candy bar out of sight (e.g., in a drawer). Ask the person to leave the room. While that person is gone, move the candy bar, allowing the two children to see where you move it. Then ask the youngest child where the other person will look for it when he/she returns. Repeat this with the older child. What do their responses suggest about their ToM? Try measuring their ToM in other ways.

ToM is usually studied using two types of false-belief tests. In one test, George leaves an object, like a candy bar, in one location. While George is gone, someone else moves the object to a new location. Children are asked where George will first look for the object upon return. In the second test, children are shown a box, like a crayon box, and asked what they believe will be inside (e.g., crayons). Children are shown that something unexpected is inside (e.g., buttons). Children are then asked what George would think is inside the box. In each test George has a reasonable but *false belief* about where the candy bar is or what is inside the crayon box.

ToM is also assessed with "appearance versus reality" tests. Children are shown a deceptive object, such as a sponge that looks like a rock. After playing with the object, children are asked what the object looks like (e.g., a rock) and what the object really is (e.g., a sponge). Then children are asked what George would think it is.

Typically, young children fail these tests. They claim that George would look in the new location for the candy bar, would know that there were buttons in the crayon box, and would think that the object is really a sponge (Lewis & Carpendale, 2002). Success on these tests requires ToM because children must separate their own knowledge of the true condition from George's belief in the false condition. This ability develops with age. Failure to develop age-appropriate ToM is a key feature of autism (see Box 9.1).

Challenges in Development

Box 9.1

Autism

James was a bubbly 2-year-old who loved "mashed totatoes" and playing with swords. But he soon became a nearly silent, unhappy child who "pulled cowboy boots on and off until his feet were raw." His father described the change as "falling out of the world." James forgot his name. After intensive one-on-one treatment (at home, at preschool, and with a speech therapist), James began to talk again. By kindergarten, he was able to enroll in a regular classroom but also went to a resource room and had an in-class aide. By 3rd grade, he was told that he had autism. He raged, cried, and denied it—and then began to come to terms with it. James continues to adjust to school, with the help of parents and teachers—and best of all, a friend. His friend has provided a giant step toward helping James develop social skills. (Adapted from O'Neil, 2004)

Autism. This is a disorder characterized by abnormal social cognition. Children with autism may also have poor verbal ability (Morgan, Maybery, & Durkin, 2003). They may have trouble comprehending emotions in others and have poor emotion regulation, like giggling for no reason. They may have repetitive movements like flapping the hands or putting on and removing cowboy boots, preoccupation with a narrow interest like maps or light switches, and self-injury like head banging. They may have temper tantrums and have difficulty controlling their movements. Some (8 to 25%) may have seizures (American Psychiatric Association, 2000; Yeargin-Allsopp et al., 2003).

There is a wide spectrum of functioning among children with autism, so the disorder is referred to as autism spectrum disorder (ASD).

Children with ASD tend to have poor general cognitive ability. About 41% have low cognitive ability—that is, an IQ below 70 (CDC, 2009). They also tend to have poor executive functions (Pellicano, 2007). However, low scores on IQ and executive function tests may be due to language problems. On IQ tests like the Raven's Matrices (see Chapter 5), which do not require much verbal ability, children with autism may score in the average to high range (Dawson, Soulières, Gernsbacher, & Mottron, 2007). Furthermore, children with autism may have a strong ability that stands out, like reading at a very young age. They may have excellent long-term memory for facts. Some have exceptional ability to focus attention, resist distractions, and pick out objects in a field of other objects, like in Figure 9.1 (Gernsbacher, Stevenson, Khandakar, & Goldsmith, 2008; Yeargin-Allsopp et al., 2003).

Autism and Theory of Mind. Children with autism, regardless of cognitive ability, have ToM deficits (Yirmiya, Erel, Shaked, & Solomonica-Levi, 1998). Some can pass simple ToM tasks such as, "Jane saw her pencils on the shelf earlier this morning. Where will she look for them?" With limited ToM, children are not motivated to communicate with others, which could explain why children with autism

Figure 9.1 **Visual Search Tasks that Distinguish Children With and Without Autism.**
If asked to find the striped ball in the left panel, most children experience a sense of "pop out." They do not need to examine each object to locate the striped ball. But if asked to find the orange cube in the right panel, children without autism typically examine each item until they find the target. In contrast, children with autism easily search the field and are little thwarted by the distracters. Children with autism are nearly twice as fast as other children at these sorts of tasks.

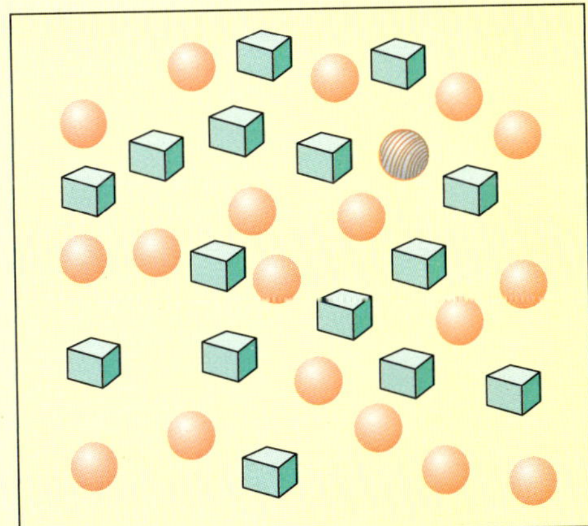

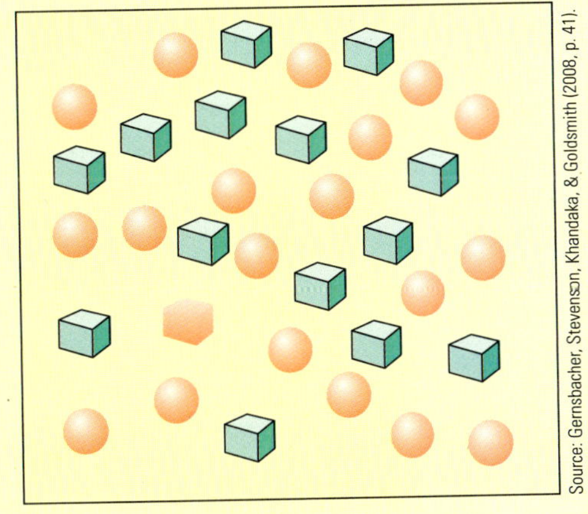

Source: Gernsbacher, Stevenson, Khandaka, & Goldsmith (2008, p. 41).

(continued)

Challenges in Development *(continued)*

have language delays. They are less likely than other children to look at faces and follow another person's gaze, which prevents them from sharing attention and experience with other people.

Asperger's disorder. This occurs at the high-functioning end of the autism spectrum disorder. Children are diagnosed with Asperger's if they *do* have impairment in social interaction and have restricted, repetitive patterns of behavior and interests but *do not* have delays in language, cognitive abilities, self-help skills, or curiosity about the environment (American Psychiatric Association, 2000).

Prevalence and Development of Autism Spectrum Disorder. Diagnosis of autism has increased in recent years (see Figure 9.2). The Centers for Disease Control and Prevention (2009) estimates that 1 in 110 children in the United States has some form of ASD. The increase in ASD may be due to better diagnosis, rather than real increases in ASD. Boys are four to five times more likely to have ASD than girls, but girls with ASD are more likely to have severe mental retardation (American Psychiatric Association, 2000). Severe autism is clearly recognizable by 3 years of age, but may be diagnosed younger. Asperger's is diagnosed much later, typically not until school age.

You may be asked to help with the diagnosis, because teachers are accurate reporters of autistic symptoms (Constantino et al., 2007).

Children with severe autism are not likely to be able to live and work independently as adults. However, adults with milder forms of ASD can lead independent lives and have successful careers, although they may have social oddities and problems with empathy. Youth with autism who are capable of insight can become depressed when they realize their limitations, and may need support from you.

What Can be Done about Autism? The cause of autism is not yet clear, so currently there are no preventive measures. Intervention can help many children with autism improve in behavior, social interaction, and language ability (e.g., Yang, Huang, Schaller, Wang, & Tsai, 2003). The younger the intervention begins, the more successful it is, preferably beginning by age 4. Behavior modification (see Chapter 3) is one common approach to reducing problem behaviors and teaching new skills (Corsello, 2005; Simpson, 2004). This was the approach used with James. Some children with autism can be taught social skills such as how to converse, make eye contact, or read emotional cues in others (Bauminger, 2002).

Figure 9.2 Increase in Diagnosis of Autism.
Percent change in children ages 3 to 21 served in federally supported programs for disabled children over time. *Data from Table 50, Digest of Education Statistics 2008, published by National Center for Educational Statistics, U.S. Department of Education.*

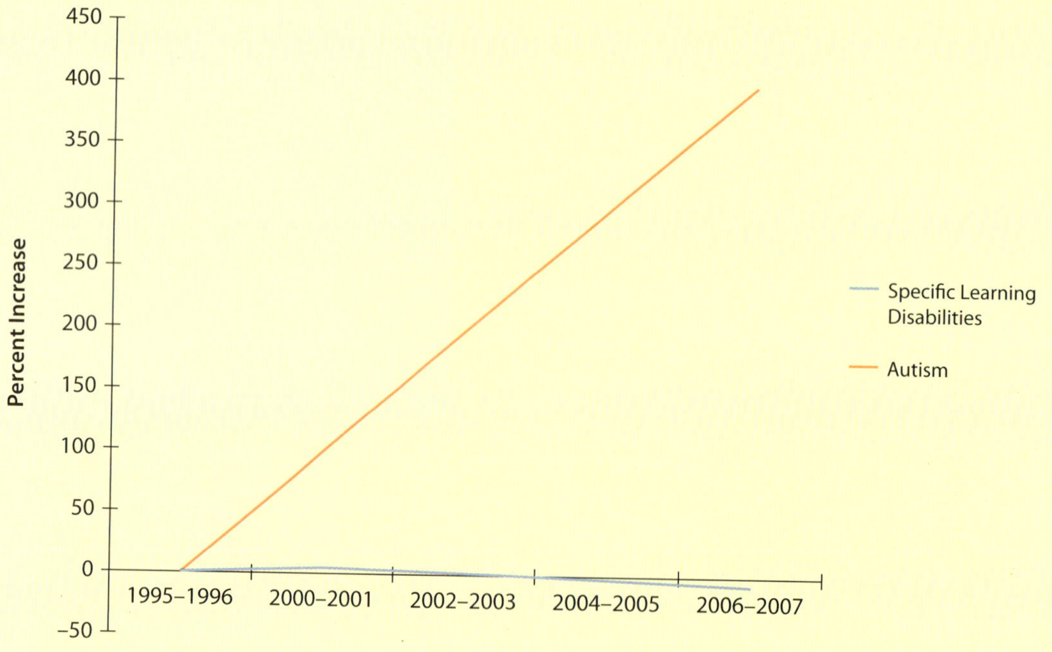

(continued)

Challenges in Development *(continued)*

You can help children with autism function in your classroom by keeping the physical environment stable (e.g., don't move chairs around); providing lecture notes and extra time for writing; and capitalizing on the good rote memory and intense, obsessive interests (e.g., dinosaurs, astronomy, maps) of some children with autism (Brownell & Walther-Thomas, 2001). You can also help promote their ToM by talking to them about others' emotions, thoughts, and desires, which will help your other students as well (Slaughter, Peterson, & Mackintosh, 2007).

Where Does Theory of Mind Come From?

There are different views of where theory of mind comes from. One view is that it is the result of a specialized mental structure that is innate and part of the human genetic endowment. This makes ToM a type of core knowledge that you will read about in Chapter 5. The fact that ToM develops early, is universal in normal children, and seems to be acquired effortlessly supports this notion (Scholl & Leslie, 2001).

A contrasting view is that children slowly build a theory of others' minds as they grow in reasoning ability and have more social experience. Children build naïve theories about many topics, not just others' minds, to explain their world. Children's cognition develops as they generate, test, and improve their theories—much like adults do in science. This view is known as **theory theory** because it is a theory about how children develop their own theories of the world. Children's theories may be simpler and less accurate than adults' theories because children have less experience.

A third view is that ToM is just part of a general increase in information processing ability. As children develop better executive functions, they are more likely to succeed at ToM tests (Pellicano, 2007). One executive function important in ToM is inhibitory control. Recall from Chapter 4 that inhibitory control is measured with tests like asking children to say "night" when shown a white card with a yellow sun. Can you see how false-belief tests would require inhibitory control? The child must hold information in mind (e.g., George will think there are crayons in the box) in the presence of conflicting information (e.g., there are actually buttons in the box). Children tend to be biased by their own knowledge that there are buttons in the box when deciding what George believes. Even adults have this "curse of knowledge." Young children find this curse of knowledge more difficult to inhibit than do adults (Birch & Bloom, 2007). When children fail ToM tests, it may be due to poor inhibitory control, rather than a lack of understanding of others' beliefs.

autism a disorder characterized by markedly abnormal social interaction; poor language ability; restricted, repetitive behavior patterns; and poor emotional perspective-taking. It commonly occurs with mental retardation.

Asperger's disorder a disorder characterized by impaired social interaction and restricted, repetitive behavior patterns, similar to autism, but with normal language and cognitive abilities.

theory theory a theory that asserts that children form naïve theories to explain and predict their world. These theories are tested and changed based on experience.

Age Trends in Theory of Mind

There are dramatic increases in ToM in early childhood, but only modest increases in older children. Let's look at age trends next.

Early Childhood (Birth to 5 Years)

Children rarely pass false-belief tests before age 4. However, even infants have some rudimentary people-reading ability. Infants as young as 1 hour old are predisposed to look toward faces rather than other objects (Mondloch et al., 1999). Infants distinguish their mother's voice from others' voices, and they can match a happy voice with a happy face (Flavell, 1999). Infants imitate others' emotional expressions (see Chapter 8). They will

Andrea Gingerich/iStockphoto

Joint attention. Even infants are capable of understanding that when they look at the same thing as another person, they share something in the other person's mind.

call to people who disappear but not objects that disappear. If they see an adult look with interest at an object, they express surprise if the adult picks up a different object (Wellman, Lopez-Duran, LaBounty, & Hamilton, 2008). This suggests they understand that others have intentions.

Infants are attracted to eyes and will follow others' gazes and look with interest at objects that others are looking at (Moore, 2008). Gaze following makes joint attention possible. **Joint attention** occurs when child and caregiver look together at an object and talk about it. Joint attention is a rudimentary form of the infant's sharing something in the caregiver's mind. Toddlers (1 to 2 years) are better at gaze following than infants, but are not yet fully skilled. A study of 2-year-olds found that most (67 to 75%) could not successfully answer the question "Which one is Sam looking at?" in a drawing like Figure 9.3, but most 3-year-olds could (McGuigan & Doherty, 2002).

Toddlers' behavior suggests they can read people. They tease siblings. They comfort a crying baby by bringing a blanket. They feign injury to get sympathy (Newton, Vasudevi, & Bull, 2000). One toddler told her mother she was sick and faked coughing so that she would get a sweet-tasting cough drop. Such deception requires understanding others' mental states. So why do toddlers fail false-belief tests? The tests may overwhelm their language and information-processing abilities. Recall from Chapter 4 that executive functions, especially inhibitory control, develop dramatically during the preschool years as the prefrontal cortex of the brain matures. By 5 to 6 years of age, children perform similarly to adults on false-belief tests (Wellman & Liu, 2004).

joint attention both the child and another person visually explore an object together.

Middle Childhood (6 to 12 Years)

By middle childhood most children have fully mastered false-belief tests, but their ToM continues to improve. Children become able to distinguish intentional from unintentional acts. This ability is critical for moral judgment, discussed later in this chapter. Children also become better able to use others' beliefs to make persuasive arguments. For example, 3rd- and 6th-graders are more likely to use belief-oriented arguments to convince their mother to buy a bird, such as "tell her I'll keep the cage clean," whereas preschoolers and 1st-graders are likely to use belief-irrelevant arguments, such as "tell her I want one" (Bartsch & London, 2000).

Think About This ToM research is an indirect product of Piaget's research—that is, modern scientists were testing whether his view of young children's egocentrism was true. Review egocentrism in Chapter 3. Does the research on ToM support Piaget's view? Which of the possible causes of ToM discussed earlier best fits the research on ToM abilities in early childhood? Does this support Piaget's theory? Explain.

In elementary school, children begin to understand that they know more about their inner thoughts and feelings than do other people. Five-year-olds mistakenly believe parents and teachers know what they are thinking better than they themselves do, but 10-year-olds realize that they are the best judge of what they are thinking (Burton & Mitchell, 2003). Wally clearly realized this, and used it to his advantage with Mrs. Crites.

Adolescence (13 to 19 Years)

Although elementary children, like Wally, are quite skilled at ToM, even adolescents sometimes make mistakes in people reading, so there is still room for improvement.

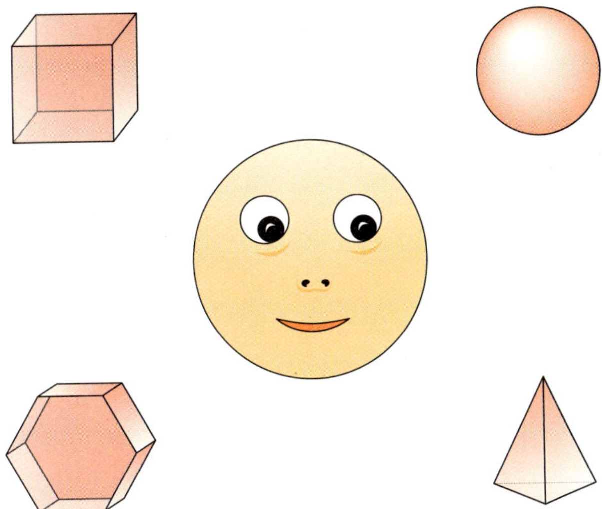

Figure 9.3 **What Is Sam Looking At?**
Children are asked to point to the shape that "Sam" is looking at. *Based on McGuigan and Doherty (2002).*

Two inaccuracies common to adolescents are: (1) the *spotlight effect*, which means they think that they are the center of others' attention, and mistakenly assume people will remember what they are wearing or their "bad hair" day; and (2) *the illusion of transparency*, which means they think others can easily read them, like perceiving that they are nervous when making a presentation. These same errors are sometimes made by adults (Gilovich & Savitsky, 1999).

It is not clear when or if ToM ability stops developing (Apperly, Samson, & Humphreys, 2009). However, a study comparing college students with 60- to 80-year-olds found that the older adults had significantly better ToM ability (Happe, Winner, & Brownell, 1998). Perhaps ToM should be thought of as "still under construction" in adolescence and young adulthood.

Individual Diversity in Theory of Mind

All typical children will eventually pass false-belief tests. However, some children are more skilled than age-mates at people reading. Are these differences important?

What Do Individual Differences in Theory of Mind Predict?

Theory of mind ability predicts *social competence* (Bosacki & Astington, 1999). It helps children take another person's perspective when trying to resolve conflict, consider what kind of help someone needs, decide how to tell a joke, and so on. To function socially, a child must take into account the mental state of others. This explains why young children with better ToM skills tend to have high-quality play with friends; they are better at joint planning, such as "pretend you are squirting me again," and role assignment, such as "let's be fire fighters now" (Jenkins & Astington, 2000).

ToM ability also predicts *deception*, or intentionally giving someone a false belief. Deception is among the earliest indicators of ToM. Even children too young to pass standard false-belief tests are capable of deception, like putting a label on a box to make you think a toy is in it when the box is empty (Carlson, Moses, & Hix, 1998). Young children are quite willing, even eager, to play games of deception. Deception is a positive skill when it is used to make others feel good, such as telling a joke.

When deception involves controlling emotions it is called *emotional dissemblance*, which you learned about in Chapter 8.

ToM ability also predicts *language development*. By 4 months, infants use another person's gaze to know what to look at as they learn. Imagine a toddler is looking at a novel object. His father speaks a new word while looking at a different object (Baldwin, 2000). What keeps the child from applying the label to the wrong object? The toddler follows the father's gaze. This is why joint attention is foundational to language learning.

What Predicts Individual Differences in Theory of Mind?

Genes may play a small role in ToM ability, probably through their influence on information processing and verbal ability. We will examine these abilities next, and then three influences from the social environment.

Information processing

Children who have better executive functions, especially inhibitory control and greater working memory capacity, have better ToM.[1] Executive functions make it possible for children to reflect on their thoughts, to distance themselves from the immediate situation, and to ignore false information (e.g., what the crayon box appears to hold but does not), which all contribute to ToM. Greater working memory capacity helps children keep all this relevant information in mind at once. Wally had to keep in mind what behavior his teacher expected and monitor whether he looked like he was reading, while his mind was busy daydreaming.

Think About This In Chapter 1 you learned that a correlation means that two variables go together, but not necessarily that one causes the other. Discuss how this might apply to the link between verbal ability and ToM.

Verbal ability

Verbal ability is strongly related to whether children pass false-belief tests (Milligan, Astington, & Dack, 2007). The relationship is bi-directional (see Chapter 1). This means that good verbal ability predicts children's ToM ability and that ToM ability predicts children's verbal ability.

Why is verbal ability correlated with ToM? One possibility is that conversation with others exposes children to different points of view, helping them learn about others' mental states while also helping them become verbally fluent (Ensor & Hughes, 2008). This may be why deaf children who have people fluent in sign language to converse with have normal ToM development, but deaf children who are unable to converse are significantly delayed in ToM (Schick, de Villers, de Villers, & Hoffmeister, 2007). Lack of opportunity to converse with others may slow development of ToM.

Parent's mind-mindedness and attachment

Parents sometimes say "you want . . ." or "you know . . ." in pseudo-conversation with their infants. These parents are making mind-related comments about their infants' desires and thoughts. This may seem like a silly way to talk to an infant, but parents who do this tend to have children with better ToM and verbal ability (Meins et al., 2003). Psychologists call this *mind-mindedness* (with the same pedantic sense of humor as "theory theory").

Parents' mind-mindedness may foster ToM because it helps them perceive their children's experience, respond sensitively, and form secure attachment. ToM requires an understanding of emotional states in others, which grows from the attachment

[1] Many studies support this conclusion, just a few of which are listed here (Apperly et al., 2009; Carlson & Moses, 2001; Hughes & Ensor, 2007; Sabbagh, Xu, Carlson, Moses, & Lee, 2006).

relationship (De Rosnay & Harris, 2002). Parents' mind-mindedness may also foster ToM just because they talk more about others.

Talking about others

Children whose parents frequently talk about others' mental states have greater ToM (Ensor & Hughes, 2008). With 1-year-olds, parents may just talk about desires that are highly relevant to the child, like "You *want* juice?" As children's ability to understand their own desires grows, and they start to use *I* and *me*, sensitive parents get more challenging—talking about others rather than the child, and talking about thoughts as well as desires (Taumoepeau & Ruffman, 2008). "She doesn't realize . . ." "They are really pretending . . ." "He remembers . . ."—these are all ways that families talk about others' mental states with older children. (If you recognize this as scaffolding in the child's zone of proximal development, which moves as the child's competence increases, you go to the head of the class!)

Families vary considerably in how much they use words like *think, know, believe, wonder,* and *understand.* Let's consider two different mothers showing their preschoolers a picture book with no words in which a dog named Carl babysits a toddler:

> *Mother 1:* *"[Carl the dog is] all happy because the baby's in bed, nice and clean, and he's cleaned up and Mom doesn't know that they had fun in the house."*
>
> *Mother 2:* *Oh, here she comes! And there's Carl waiting for her. Look at that! She's home. And the baby's still safe in bed." (Slaughter et al., 2007, p. 846).*

The first mother talks about the mental states of Carl and mother, but the second does not. This may seem subtle, but over time the first mother may use thousands more mental-state words with her child than the second mother. Better-educated mothers talk more about others' mental states, which may explain why their children have greater ToM ability (Jenkins, Turrell, Kogushi, Lollis, & Ross, 2003). Researchers have been able to improve 3-year-olds' ToM after just two training sessions in which they discussed a puppet's beliefs about deceptive objects, like a pen that looks like a flower (Lohmann & Tomasello, 2003). They were careful to use words like *think* and *know* in the discussions.

Seeing others' reactions may contribute to ToM. Blind children tend to be delayed in ToM, passing false-belief tests much later, at about 12 years of age (Peterson, Peterson, & Webb, 2000). Their inability to use social referencing, joint attention, or emotional displays as they hear talk about others may delay their people-reading abilities.

Alexandra Day/CORBIS

Children develop ToM ability when their parents talk about others' mental states during storybook reading.

Peers and siblings

Younger children in large families develop ToM earlier than do other children (Hughes & Leekam, 2004). Preschoolers with older siblings are exposed to more talk about mental states than only or eldest children (Jenkins et al., 2003). Siblings and peers provide children with the opportunity to talk about others during humor, conflict, and play. Thus, interacting with minds that are different from their own may promote children's ToM (Cassidy, Fineberg, Brown, & Perkins, 2005). However, the beneficial effect of siblings occurs mostly in families with positive sibling relationships and in middle-class (not low-SES) homes (Lewis & Carpendale, 2002; Recchia & Howe, 2009). Let's look at other group differences next.

Group Diversity in Theory of Mind

Gender and SES are linked to ToM. From preschool through secondary school, girls perform better than boys on ToM tests (Bosacki & Astington, 1999; Cutting & Dunn, 1999). This may help to explain why girls generally have higher ratings of social competence than boys. In addition, children whose parents have higher-status jobs and higher education levels perform better on ToM tests. This has been found across countries (Shatz, Diesendruck, Martinez-Beck, & Akar, 2003).

Do children in some countries have better ToM abilities? Children in different countries tend to acquire ToM abilities and begin talking about others' minds in a similar sequence (Liu, Wellman, Tardif, & Sabbagh, 2008). Although they may follow the same *sequence*, development may occur at different *rates*. If results in the United States and England—where most studies have been conducted—are used as a baseline, then children in Korea develop similarly; children in Australia, Canada, and Africa (hunter-gatherer Bakas) develop faster; and children in Austria, Hong Kong, Japan, and Peru (indigenous Quechua-speaking) develop more slowly (Wellman, Cross, & Watson, 2001). Few children in any country pass false-belief tests at age 3, but almost all in every country pass by age 6 (Callaghan et al., 2005). See Figure 9.4.

Classroom Implications of Theory of Mind

The ability to understand others' mental states is one of the crowning achievements of childhood. Theory of mind helps children navigate their social worlds, including school. Yet, students (and teachers) sometimes misinterpret the mental states of others, particularly when different cultures come together. For example, in a midwestern high school, misunderstandings about others' intentions led to strong racial tension between Black and Asian students (Lei, 2003). Black girls were viewed as loud. Some onlookers assumed their loudness was intended to be obnoxious and to convey an aggressive attitude. The girls, however, said they only intended to have fun

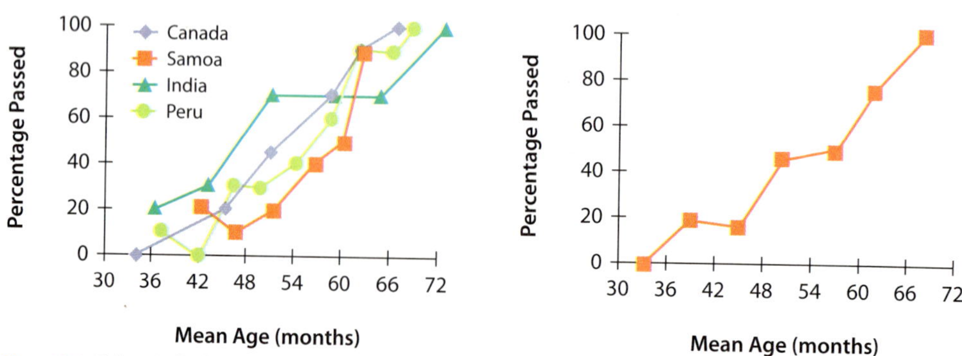

Figure 9.4 False Belief Comparisons for Four Countries
Percentage of children passing false-belief tests by age across four countries. Left panel shows countries separately, and right panel show average across all four countries.
Callaghan et al. (2005).

or express themselves. In contrast, Asian males were viewed as overly quiet. Some assumed their quietness was intended to convey a rejection of U.S. culture. The boys, however, said they were quiet to avoid being teased about their limited English. Teachers did not discuss these behavioral differences for fear of being accused of racism, yet an open discussion might have helped different groups understand each other's mental state. That is, greater ToM across ethnic groups could improve school atmosphere.

Greater ToM could also improve individual children's well-being. Students in your classroom who have better ToM are likely to get along well with peers and teachers. There are four things you can do to promote each student's ToM skills:

> ### *Revisiting Case 4*
>
> **For the sake of argument, assume that Preston does not have age-appropriate ToM skills. What consequences might this have for Preston? Does his behavior actually fit with your conclusions? What would you do as a teacher to help Preston? Explain your response.**

- Help students develop good verbal ability. You'll learn how to do this in Chapter 12.
- Converse with students about others' mental states. Use words like *think, know, believe, wonder, remember, forget, guess, expect, pretend,* and *understand.* This can be done when discussing content in class, such as "*Do you think John Adams believed the French foreign minister?*" or "*Is Joel guessing, or does he know 317 + 42 = 359?*" This can also be done when students have conflict, during social interactions in class, or when reading to students, like the first mother in the earlier vignette who commented on a false belief while reading the book about Carl the dog.
- Provide students with the opportunity to interact with peers who might have different perspectives. For example, you can encourage social interaction during noninstructional time, such as lunch, or you can organize cooperative learning during instruction, as discussed in Chapter 11.
- Establish a secure, positive relationship with students. You learned how to do this in Chapter 6. Secure attachment is linked to greater ToM ability.

ToM ability also promotes humor, or the ability to make others laugh, which is one of the most pleasurable aspects of classroom social interaction.

Humor

In a 7th-grade honors algebra class, the teacher wrote a problem on the SMART board. She asked the students to use their calculators to find the solution. After a few minutes she called out, "Joseph, what does your calculator say?" Joseph promptly replied with a deadpan face, "Battery low. Suggest replacement." Both the teacher and students laughed.

This class is in the oldest school building in the city. It is overcrowded and insufferably hot on the third floor. Yet, the ambiance is pleasant. The children often use humor, but not in destructive ways. For example, they know the teacher wants them to show all the steps of their problem solving. They resist because "showing your work" takes effort. They prefer shortcuts. Kyle is called to the board to solve a problem where he takes an "extra" step. In friendly teasing, a classmate says, "Kyle's such a hard worker!" Everyone smiles.

Many teachers believe humor enhances classroom climate, improves student motivation, and increases learning. On the other hand, some teachers view children's clowning around as disruptive. Which view is correct? Let's see what the research suggests, but first we will clarify some basic concepts about humor.

What exactly is humor? It is a kind of social-cognitive play that produces smiling or laughing and feelings of amusement. Humor can be intentional or accidental. It can be verbal like a joke, pun, or witticism, or nonverbal like a funny face.

Not all smiles or laughs are caused by humor. In fact, most laughter occurs during day-to-day social interaction, such as "I'll see you guys later," which is not humorous but is often accompanied by a small laugh (Provine, 2000). People also giggle when they are socially uncomfortable. Only about 15% of laughter occurs in response to humor or a joke. Thus, laughter helps create positive feelings between people, in addition to being a response to humor.

Causes and Functions of Humor

In the parking lot of a hospital, one of our preschool-aged children asked what a sign said. Mom replied, "Patient Parking." Our child promptly asked, "Then where do the daddies and impatient people park?"

Adults find this question funny, but our child did not. (Dad did, sort of.) One cause of humor is processing information with one interpretation (e.g., patients park in one place and medical staff in another), encountering incongruent information (e.g., the meaning of patience), and then rapidly reinterpreting it (Wyer & Collins, 1992). Our preschooler's question is humorous if you can interpret the contrast between "patients" and "patience." Young children with limited language and information processing ability would not find this humorous. Good ToM ability helps you further comprehend that our child believed daddies have less patience than mommies, which adds to the humor. That is, cognitive insight triggers humor.

Humor has many social functions: to entertain, to make others feel good, to save face, to give information, to communicate liking or disliking, to smooth awkward situations, and to put others in their place. Freud said that humor channels hostility in less harmful ways (see Box 9.2). However, humor can be quite harmful. Antisocial humor involves dirty or gross jokes and jokes that are disparaging to other people. In case 4, Preston's "joke," inviting the visitor to put her hand in boiling water, was antisocial.

Playful Teasing

Teasing is commentary that is playful, intentional, and provocative (Keltner, Capps, Kring, Young, & Heerey, 2001). It often involves humorous taunts or mock insults, threats, or challenges, but it can also be nonverbal. Teasing is generally humorous and for fun, like Kyle's classmate teasing him for taking an extra step to solve the math problem. Much like rough-and-tumble play (see Chapter 11), you distinguish teasing from aggression by its playful qualities, like good-natured facial expressions. However, teasing can go too far. It can be used in a hostile way, like to belittle someone. If a child is teased repeatedly in a hostile way, that would constitute bullying. Ridicule and sexual teasing that border on harassment also constitute bullying (see Chapter 10), and are different from playful teasing.

Playful teasing is pervasive in social interactions. It serves the same functions as other forms of humor: it strengthens social bonds, communicates information,

Theories & Theorists — Box 9.2

Sigmund Freud

Sigmund Freud.

Sigmund Freud (1856–1939) is among the most famous theorists in history, like both Darwin (Chapter 8) and Skinner (Chapter 3), with whom his life overlapped. He was born in the Austro-Hungarian Empire to a Jewish family (Isbister, 1985). The family moved to Vienna when he was a young child, where he lived until just before his death. (Hitler also lived in Vienna when Freud was in his 40s.) In the 1930s the Nazis burned his books and sent his sisters to death camps. In 1938 he fled to London, where he died as World War II was beginning. He was an obsessive smoker who suffered from mouth cancer, which was linked to his death.

Freud came to believe that unconscious memories of trauma often have an energy that remains dammed up because the memories cannot be expressed in a socially acceptable way, so they are converted to physical symptoms. The symptoms are relieved when the repressed memories are made conscious. Freud did this through *free association,* in which patients lay on a couch and said whatever passed through their minds. He called his approach *psychoanalysis.*

Freud made some revolutionary contributions to psychology and coined many terms you may have heard, such as *sibling rivalry.* One of his greatest contributions is the concept of the *unconscious.* He asserted that the unconscious often holds destructive or sexual impulses that are repressed, but occasionally leak out, such as a *Freudian slip* that occurs when you say something that is symbolic of an unconscious attitude that you have repressed. For example, the groom asks what time the funeral is, when he means the wedding.

A second great contribution is his assertion that dreams have meaning. To Freud, dreams represented fulfillment of wishes that are hidden from consciousness. Even in dreams, wishes

and helps resolve conflicts in a nonconfrontational way. In a study of teasing in a school lunchroom, 10- to 14-year-old girls used teasing to draw positive attention to a friend who had a new haircut. They also used it to communicate disapproval without hostility when a friend violated a group norm, like girls wrestling (Eder, 1991). Among elementary children, teasing often occurs when a child talks to someone of the opposite sex (Voss, 1997). Thus, teasing is used to strengthen gender boundaries (see Chapter 11). Generally, children are more likely to tease those to whom they feel close. Popular high-status children are more likely to tease than low-status children (Keltner et al., 2001).

Age Trends in Humor

What children think is funny changes with age. As cognitive ability increases, children can detect more subtle attempts at humor. You can think of children's humor as a window to their cognitive development. For example, the shift from the 3-month-old who smiles in response to Daddy talking, to the toddler's smile of satisfaction after successfully solving a puzzle, to the 10-year-old's smile at a play on words is a reflection of cognitive development.

Theories & Theorists (continued)

may be hidden by symbols of real wishes, known as *Freudian symbols*. Sometimes they have to do with a child's jealousy of the father and love of the mother, which Freud called the *Oedipus complex*, named after the Greek character Oedipus who kills his father and marries his mother.

The Id, Ego, and Super-Ego. Freud devised a model of the psyche with three components: the Id, Ego, and Super-ego. The *Id* is present at birth and consists of drives that seek pleasure. The *Ego* seeks to control the Id. He said the Id was like a horse, and the Ego like the rider. The horse supplies the locomotive energy but the rider decides on the goal and guides the animal. The Ego produces anxiety and repression, which keep impulses out of consciousness (Freud, 1905/1960). The *Super-ego* is the conscience that castigates the Ego for failing to control the Id. Moral behavior is the result of a strong Super-ego. The Super-ego is a *"substitute for a longing for the father . . . As a child grows up, the role of father is carried on by teachers and others in authority; their injunctions and prohibitions remain powerful . . . and continue, in the form of conscience, to exercise the moral censorship"* (Freud, 1923/1961, p. 37). Thus, in Freud's view, you have a dual nature—amoral gratification of instincts and the moral Super-ego.

Humor. Freud believed that jokes, like dreams, can have hidden meaning. The purpose can be simply to make others happy and laugh, or it can be to snub them, show aggression, or defend oneself. *"By making our enemy . . . comic, we achieve in a roundabout way the enjoyment of overcoming him"* (Freud, 1905/1960, pp. 102–103). Through jokes you can say things that are forbidden, or displace anger with laughter. Jokes allow the sneaky Id to evade control by the Ego.

Morality. Freud believed that morality comes from emotions experienced within the family. Children identify with their parents as a result of love and attachment. Children transfer emotions that they feel toward parents to other authority figures such as teachers. Emotions, particularly guilt, regulate behavior because children behave morally in order to control emotions (Tangney, Stuewig, & Mashek, 2007). Research supports Freud's view that emotions and attachment are foundational to moral development. Notice that Freud's view is different from that of Piaget, who viewed morality as constructed by the child through cognitive development, or that of Skinner, who viewed moral behavior as learned through reinforcement.

Freud died when Skinner was 35. They are often portrayed as polar opposites. Freud focused on the mind and the meaning of behavior, while Skinner ignored mind and focused on environmental consequences that shape behavior mechanically. Despite their differences, they both believed that child development is controlled by the environment. They also both believed that people suffer when they are not aware of the forces that control behavior, and both applied their theories to improve society. In fact, Skinner often cited Freud's work and tried to get psychoanalyzed himself (Overskeid, 2007).

While Freud had some far-fetched ideas, like the universal fear of castration in little boys, other aspects of his theory have provided insight into human nature. In addition, psychoanalysis can be productive for healing emotional problems. Freud suggested that teachers should be analyzed, and trained in psychoanalysis, in order to appropriately help children control their Id (Freud, 1933/1964). Do you want to give it a try?

Children produce and appreciate humor that is neither too easy nor too difficult for them to understand. When they have just mastered a concept, they enjoy jokes about it.

Early Childhood (Birth to 5 Years)

Infants' smiling and laughing emerges with their ability to interact socially. Laughter in response to physical stimulation, like blowing on the tummy, emerges at about 4 months of age. Laughter in response to tickling emerges at about 6 months and almost disappears in adult middle age (Provine, 2000). By 12 months, laughter results more from the child observing unusual behaviors, like putting a dishcloth on your head, than from physical stimulation.

By 2 to 3 years, as they begin to talk, children find word distortions amusing, like calling Daddy "doodoo." Pretend play may be a type of joking, such as when a toddler pretends to fix soup for you, and you loudly slurp it, saying, "very good!" The toddler will laugh and rush to make more. By 3 to 5 years, children find incongruities in appearances and distortion of the physical world humorous, like a cow brushing its teeth. They are more likely to laugh at their own spontaneous distortions than others' distortions (Bariaud, 1989).

Middle Childhood (6 to 12 Years)

What children find funny shifts in middle childhood (Bariaud, 1989). They still find exaggerated movements and facial expressions funny. However, they move from word distortion, which preschoolers find funny, to interpretation of word meaning as they begin to understand puns and wordplays. For example, 1st-graders are enthusiastic about jokes like *Knock knock. Who's there? Orange. Orange who? Orange you glad I knocked*? Such jokes require phonetic awareness, which 1st-graders are busy learning. Younger children do not understand such jokes, and older children do not find them funny anymore. Many 3rd- to 7th-graders enjoy the incongruity of a verbal joke like "*Order! Order in the Court!*" "*Ham and cheese on rye, please, Your Honor*" that most 1st-graders do not yet "get." This explains why books of riddles are popular reading material among elementary-age children.

There is a movement toward antisocial jokes around 4th grade, whereas such jokes are seldom heard in younger children (Socha & Kelly, 1994). At this age, children also begin to understand sarcasm. An observer who watches a driver run into a mailbox might say, "You're a great driver!" Five-year-olds are likely to take the sarcastic remark as truthful—he really is a good driver. Slightly older children may realize the speaker means the opposite, but not find it funny. Ten-year-olds would likely find it funny.

Children's understanding of teasing shifts in middle childhood. Because they do not always understand when a peer is kidding, 1st-graders are more likely to react negatively to teasing than 3rd-graders. By 3rd grade, children are reasonably good at recognizing teasing, irony, and sarcasm, but cannot articulate how they recognize it until about 5th or 6th grade (Keltner et al., 2001). Children also get better at communicating playfulness, so that they less often have to say, "I was just kidding." Perhaps for this reason, 6th-graders view teasing more positively than do younger children. With age, children change the issues that they tease about. For example, there is more teasing about the opposite sex among late elementary than early elementary children.

Adolescence (13 to 19 Years)

In the teens, particularly among boys, put-downs become popular across cultures. In addition, adolescents' humor includes broader social topics than the humor of younger children. For example, many teens find the *Darwin Awards* amusing (Northcutt, 2000). The awards are given to people who die as a result of their own foolishness and "improve the gene pool by removing themselves from it." Younger children do not understand such satirical humor. Adolescents are capable of understanding puns and double entendres, like the song title "If I Said You Had a Beautiful Body, Would You Hold It against Me?" and other witticisms. This is what draws some teachers to work in secondary schools—adolescents' humor is imaginative, clever, and fun from an adult's perspective.

Individual Diversity in Humor

Humor is so widely valued in many cultures that it is an insult to accuse someone of having no sense of humor. However, you probably know people with a great sense of humor and others with a paltry sense of humor. Let's look at a 2-year-old with an unusually good sense of humor:

Akiva hands her teacher a toy phone. The teacher puts the phone to her ear and says, "Hello? Uh huh, Uh huh, Uh huh, Uh huh, Uh huh, Uh huh. Goodbye!" Akiva giggles at this absurd conversation with such enthusiasm that some of her classmates begin laughing too.

Akiva consistently laughs more than most of her classmates. Her good sense of humor may affect her health, social acceptance, and learning. Let's look at this next.

What Do Individual Differences in Humor Predict?

You may have heard the biblical proverb "A merry heart doeth good like a medicine." Research confirms that having a good sense of humor and exposure to humor, like listening to a Bill Cosby recording, are both linked to better immune functioning and tolerance of pain (Martin, 2002). Humor may have this effect by reducing stress or strengthening social support. However, there is not yet consistent evidence that a sense of humor lowers blood pressure, promotes longevity, or reduces illness symptoms.

Humor helps people cope with difficult situations by taking a lighthearted view of stressful events (Lefcourt, 2002). Imagine two children are getting acquainted, and one tells the other that he is repeating 3rd grade. The second child responds, "You must be pretty dumb." In one study, most 8- to 12-year-olds agreed that the best response to this stressful situation is to use humor, like, "You have an interesting way of making friends." Unfortunately, the children were not very good at generating humorous responses for themselves; the only coping strategy most could think of was to ignore the remark (Lightner, Bollmer, Harris, Milich, & Scambler, 2000). Thus, children sometimes need help to use humor as a coping strategy.

Humor also predicts social acceptance. Children with a good sense of humor are liked better by both teachers and peers. In a study of more than 5,000 2nd- through 12th-graders, children who were popular leaders were described as having a sense of humor (Zeller, Vannatta, Schafer, & Noll, 2003). Adolescents who are humorous are less likely to be socially withdrawn, but they are also more likely to occasionally misbehave in class (Sletta, Sobstad, & Valas, 1995). Humor used effectively, and at the right time, in social interaction is a key part of social competence. However, antisocial, derisive humor can undermine social acceptance, as it did for Preston in case 4. Thus, playful humor contributes to social acceptance, but antisocial humor does not.

Humor may also facilitate learning (Bryant & Zillmann, 1989; Powell & Andresen, 1985). In one study, scientists embedded slapstick routines and one-liners into short educational videos for kindergarteners and 1st-graders (Zillmann, Williams, Bryant, Boynton, & Wolf, 1980). Although the humor was unrelated to the educational content, children who watched the humorous videos learned more than did a control group. Humor may grab the attention of inattentive students long enough to facilitate learning things that otherwise would have been missed.

What Predicts Individual Differences in Humor?

At least two factors might lead some children to have a better sense of humor: information processing ability and creativity. Appreciation of verbal humor is related to working memory, verbal ability, and cognitive flexibility (Shammi & Stuss, 1999). ToM ability is required for jokes involving others' mind states. Knowledge of one's culture is required for puns, jokes with hidden meanings, and incongruities. For example, children must understand how doorstep dialogue is supposed to occur in order to find "knock knock" jokes funny. Thus, it takes both knowledge and rapid information processing to "get" jokes.

Humor is often delayed in children with delayed cognitive abilities (Short, Basili, & Schatschneider, 1993). In contrast, cognitively advanced children tend to have advanced humor, like 2-year-old Akiva. For example, in a 9th-grade English class, the teacher was explaining when to use "good" or "well." One boy raised his hand and said, *"I just use whichever sounds well."* The teacher chuckled with this bright boy, but many of the other students missed the joke. Medications for ADHD that alter information processing may reduce sense of humor or readiness to laugh in children (Panksepp, 2000).

Humor is also linked to creativity. This is because humor is triggered by incongruity, like seeing an idea or object out of its normal place or seeing something familiar with new eyes. Generating this incongruity is a creative activity, a type of mental gymnastics. In one study, 10th- and 11th-graders who were nominated by their peers as being unusually humorous were also more creative (Ziv, 1989). In Chapter 8 you learned that positive emotions may promote creativity. Thus, creativity may be both a cause and a consequence of humor.

Group Diversity in Humor

There are some gender and ethnic differences in humor. Boys and girls tease about the same amount, but girls are more likely to back off if the target reacts negatively, by saying, "I was just joking," or by cajoling the target to laugh. Boys, on the other hand, may escalate the teasing to a higher level when the target reacts negatively, laughing and enjoying it more, while they duck as the target swings at them (Eder, 1991). In a study of 3rd-graders, boys were more likely to cross the line from teasing to ridicule, particularly when the target was a girl (Voss, 1997). Thus, boys may go too far with teasing more often than girls.

Ethnic groups differ in their styles of teasing. Research has focused on two ethnic groups—African Americans and American Indians. One type of teasing among African American children is known as *signifyin'*. It is verbal teasing that uses double meaning and irony, with clever twists and surprises (Smitherman, 2000). For example a pregnant woman told her sister, "Yes, I guess I am putting on a little weight." In response, the sister signified on her: "Now look here, girl, we both standing here soaking wet and you still trying to tell me it ain't raining" (Gates, 1988, p. 83). Other terms for signifyin' include *woofing, talking smart, putting down, sounding, shucking, jiving, rapping*, and *sweet-talking*. Another form of African American verbal teasing is *playing the dozens*, which refers to a verbal game of insulting a male's mother by making exaggerated, humorous comments about the mother. For example, "Yo momma so dumb she thought a quarterback was a refund" (Smitherman, 2000, p. 116). Like other forms of verbal humor, the aim might be to put others down, show verbal virtuosity, display cleverness, expose truth indirectly, or just have fun.

Marmaduke St. John/Alamy

Humor in the classroom can enhance attention and make learning enjoyable.

One type of teasing among some American Indians is called *razzing*. A common topic of the razz is eating dog meat. For example, a woman razzed a man saying, "Hey . . . quit picking up our dogs. I know you're taking them down south to use for your feasts . . . ," to which the man replied, "It's not me. It's those Kiowas" (Pratt, 1998, p. 67). Razzing often includes tribal insults and is usually directed at persons of equal status, but not elders. Razzing someone about his or her family is usually not acceptable and can lead to a fight. Thus, the cultural rules for razzing are different from those of playing the dozens. Clearly, culture influences what is considered acceptable and funny.

Classroom Implications of Humor

Some teachers advocate use of humor in the classroom because they believe it enhances attention, creates a more pleasant environment, reduces test anxiety, makes learning enjoyable and effective, and creates more positive relationships (Fitzsimmons & McKenzie, 2003). There is not much research on the effects of humor on learning, but the little that exists supports this view (Martin, Preiss, Gayle, & Allen, 2006). You can promote humor in your classroom by initiating your own humor, and by accepting children's humor.

Be Humorous Yourself

Being humorous may be more challenging for secondary teachers, who tend to use less humor than elementary teachers. One review of several studies found that humor occurs on average about six times per hour in upper elementary school, but three times per hour in junior high (Bryant & Zillmann, 1989). Use these guidelines to incorporate more humor in your classroom:

- Keep humor positive. For example, a study that compared two 6th-grade math teachers found that one teacher used positive humor while the other used negative humor, like referring to the class as "brain dead." The positive teacher's students had better achievement-related behaviors and more positive emotions (Turner, Meyer, Midgley, & Patrick, 2003). Sarcastic, anti-social humor can damage teacher–student relationships. Humor based on gross-out comments, sex, bodily functions, or obscenity has no place in the classroom.
- Plan humor, especially if it does not come naturally to you. Build humor into lessons. Practice being humorous, field-test material, and memorize jokes. Use props like food and toys. Use cartoons and TV clips to illustrate concepts or dramatize material. For example, when you teach new material, you could use theme music or clothing from familiar television shows (Berk, 2002).

Accept Children's Humor (When Appropriate)

You do not need to be the primary source of humor in your classroom. Your students will generate humor if you encourage it. Just as with teacher-initiated humor, child-initiated humor may be more common in elementary than secondary school. In one study, smiling and laughter occurred two to three times more in a 3rd-grade versus an 11th-grade classroom (Fabrizi & Pollio, 1987). If you want to increase children's humor in your classroom, use these guidelines:

- Respond positively to children's humor. Elementary teachers tend to respond more positively than secondary teachers. In addition, teachers tend to respond more positively to the humorous remarks or behavior of children with whom they have a better relationship (Fabrizi & Pollio, 1987). Thus, you may have to try harder to appreciate the humor of students with whom you have a difficult relationship.
- Be aware of the culture-based humor of your students if they are from a different ethnic group than you.
- Invite children to share humor. One of our children's favorite elementary teachers enthusiastically encouraged children to share jokes with her at the beginning of each school day. This set a positive tone for the class, and also kept humor within teacher-set bounds.
- Clearly distinguish between playful teasing and antisocial humor. One adult recalled how distressing it was to be called "banana nose" because of his large nose: "I was very insecure and it killed me. I would go home or in the bathroom at school and cry and cry. It was miserable" (Kowalski, 2000, p. 234). This kind of teasing is antisocial. In Chapter 10 you will learn how to decrease antisocial behavior among students.

Child-initiated humor can sometimes disrupt class and may need limits. In middle school, humorous children are likely to call out, be out of their seats, not do their schoolwork, and interact with other students. That is, they are highly active, social children. By high school, humorous children are more skillful at abiding by classroom rules while still being humorous (Fabrizi & Pollio, 1987). Most child-initiated humor is only mildly disruptive to class. For example, Joseph's response—"*battery low*"—in the opening story briefly disrupted the algebra lesson. It also added zest to class. Joseph was a good class clown—a delightful, upbeat child who made teaching fun. He was also a good person in the moral sense, which is our next topic.

Moral Judgment

I was standing in the classroom, looking out the window, and I saw Ruby coming down the street, with the federal marshals on both sides of her. The crowd was there, shouting, as usual. A woman spat at Ruby but missed; Ruby smiled at her. A man shook his fist at her; Ruby smiled at him. Then she walked up the stairs, and she stopped and turned and smiled one more time! You know what she told one of the marshals? She told him she prays for those people, the ones in that mob, every night before she goes to sleep! (Coles, 1986, pp. 22–23)

AP Photo

Ruby Bridges was a moral exemplar at age 6.

This is the account of a teacher watching 6-year-old Ruby Bridges, the African American child who initiated school desegregation in New Orleans in 1960. Ruby was the only student in the entire school for a while because the other students' parents kept them home. She even received death threats.

How does a 6-year-old come to know what is morally right, and act on it in spite of threats, including from authority figures? There are different views on what motivates moral behavior. The ethologist view is that humans have an inborn tendency to care for others because it promotes their survival (Krebs, 2008). The behaviorist view is that children acquire values through imitation and reinforcement (see Chapter 3). Freud's view was that children identify with and internalize their parents' values (see Box 9.2, presented earlier). Yet another view is that rather than learning morality from external sources, children internally construct principles of right and wrong as they develop cognitively. The last view emphasizes moral judgment, which we discuss next.

Different Views of Moral Judgment

moral judgment reasoning about moral dilemmas that involve justice in a context where rules, laws, formal obligations, and authority are emphasized.

Moral judgment refers to how children *reason* about moral issues and laws. Notice that this is not the same as moral *behavior* because it focuses on *thinking*, not *behaving*. Cognitive developmental theorists believe that with age, children develop increasingly advanced reasoning about justice, which leads to increased morality. That is, children are not morally mature until they are cognitively mature. Piaget was a leader of this view.

Piaget's View

Piaget believed that children do not simply copy the moral standards of their culture, but rather that conflict during interaction with peers leads children to *construct* their own notions of right and wrong. Piaget viewed *justice* as the essence of morality. To study children's concepts of justice, Piaget told them stories of misbehavior, like playing with a ball in the house and breaking a lamp. Then he asked children what would be fair and unfair punishment. Based on their responses, Piaget concluded that children have two kinds of moral reasoning:

heteronymous morality an authority-oriented morality in which rules are rigidly followed in order to avoid punishment, but not for internal reasons.

autonomous morality a reciprocity-oriented morality in which cooperation is internally motivated.

1. **Heteronymous morality** is authority oriented. Rules are viewed as fixed and unalterable, and should be rigidly followed. Heteronymous children behave well in order to avoid punishment and because of the pressure of external authority.
2. **Autonomous morality** is based on reciprocity, mutual respect, and cooperation, rather than external pressure. (Piaget, 1965, p. 196)

Kohlberg's View

Lawrence Kohlberg developed a stage-based model of moral development that followed Piaget's ideas. He gave children hypothetical dilemmas and asked them to make a judgment about the morality of an act. The most famous is the *Heinz dilemma*, which involves stealing:

> *In Europe, a woman was near death from a special kind of cancer. There was one drug that the doctors thought might save her . . . but the druggist was charging 10 times what the drug cost him to make. He . . . charged $2,000 for a small dose of the drug. The sick woman's husband, Heinz, went to everyone he knew to borrow the money, but he could only get together about $1,000 . . . He told the druggist that his wife was dying and asked him to sell it cheaper or let him pay later. But the druggist said, "No, I discovered the drug and I'm going to make money from it." So Heinz gets desperate and considers breaking into the man's store to steal the drug for his wife.*
> (Colby, Kohlberg, Gibbs, & Lieberman, 1983, p. 77)

Children would then be asked a series of questions such as "Is it morally wrong to steal the drug?" Kohlberg outlined six stages in the development of moral judgment following the pattern of Piaget's stages you learned in Chapter 3, although Piaget did not emphasize stages of morality (Piaget, 1965). Kohlberg believed the stages occur in the same sequence across cultures, as follows (Colby et al., 1983):

Level I: Preconventional Morality: Punishment and Obedience to Authority

Stage 1: "Right" is being obedient, not breaking laws, and not damaging others or property. The reason for doing right is to avoid punishment.

Stage 2: "Right" is fairness, or following rules when it is to your advantage. The reason for doing right is to serve your own interests.

Level II: Conventional Morality: Laws Are Supreme

Stage 3: "Right" is living up to what is expected of you, being loyal, trustworthy, and supporting your family or friends. The reason for doing right is to be viewed as a "good" person, caring for others, or living the Golden Rule.

Stage 4: "Right" is fulfilling duties you've agreed to, contributing to society, and upholding laws (except in extreme cases). This is the "law-and-order" stage. The reason for doing right is to keep society functioning.

Level III: Postconventional Morality: Abstract Principles of Justice and Rights

Stage 5: "Right" is acknowledging that values and rules are relative, but should be upheld to support society. Some absolute values exist (e.g., life, liberty). The reason for doing right is protection of rights, doing the "greatest good for the greatest number," and commitment to contracts.

Stage 6: "Right" is following self-chosen ethical principles. If principles and laws conflict, follow the principles. The reason for doing right is a commitment to universal moral principles of justice, equality, and dignity.

The stages are hierarchical. That is, higher stages represent higher moral reasoning, because justifications are more philosophically sound (Carpendale, 2000).

There are many criticisms of Kohlberg's model, one of which is his restricted view of morality. Stages 1, 2, and 3 are intuitively recognized by people as hierarchical. That is, most people would agree that stage 1 reasoning is of lower quality than stage 3 reasoning. However, there is disagreement with Kohlberg's ranking of supposedly higher stages. In addition, it is not clear where some values, such as obligation to one's elders

Think About This Do you agree with the sequence of stages Kohlberg proposed? Do you see any biases that Kohlberg may have had in what he considered "higher" levels of morality? Ask a few friends to describe the attributes of the most moral person they know. Do the attributes fit with Kohlberg's, or your own, notion of morality?

or religious faith, fit in the model. When educated North American adults are asked to describe moral exemplars, they list attributes like law abiding, loyal, faithful to spouse, honest, caring, and helpful (Walker & Pitts, 1998). These aspects of morality go beyond Kohlberg's limited emphasis on justice.

In Kohlberg's model, caring is in stage 3, which is lower than the law-and-order stage 4. Is upholding laws morally higher than caring? The tension between justice and caring has been a key philosophical and religious issue throughout history. A treatment of this tension is beyond the scope of this text, but clearly Kohlberg's view of morality is limited, although most would agree that justice is an important part of morality. This issue is related to gender differences that we will discuss later.

Prosocial Reasoning

prosocial reasoning reasoning about moral dilemmas in which one person's needs or desires conflict with another's, but in a context where laws, rules, or formal obligations are minimal.

Prosocial reasoning is reasoning about dilemmas in which caring about others is pitted against self-interest, rather than dilemmas about justice and laws (Eisenberg, Carlo, Murphy, & Van Court, 1995). Many real-world dilemmas involve prosocial reasoning, rather than moral judgment. To study prosocial reasoning, psychologists give children hypothetical dilemmas, such as keeping food versus sharing with others, playing with friends versus helping a classmate study for a test, or standing up for a peer being teased. One commonly used dilemma involves a birthday party:

> *On the way to a party, Emmalee saw a girl who had fallen down and hurt her leg. The girl asked Emmalee to go get her parents. But if Emmalee did run and get the girl's parents, Emmalee would be late to the party and miss the fun with her friends.* (adapted from Carlo, Koller, Eisenberg, Da Silva, & Frohlich, 1996, p. 233)

Children are asked what they should do, and why. In addition, researchers sometimes observe children's natural moral behaviors and then ask them why they behaved that way. Five different types of reasoning have been identified:

1. Hedonistic. The focus is on self-oriented consequences, such as "I like her," or "She'll do the same for me."
2. Needs-oriented. The focus is on the other's need, such as "She needs my help."
3. Approval. The focus is on others' approval, such as "Her parents will thank me."
4. Stereotyped. The focus is on what "good" people do and a desire to be considered "good," such as "People will think I'm a good person if I help."
5. Internalized. The focus is on how being good makes one feel, such as "I would feel better if I help."

Field Observation

Try out the story of the birthday party, and one or two other dilemmas you make up, on children of widely different ages. Try it with children who are especially kind and children who are not. Compare their responses. Are there age trends, or individual differences, that conform with the research?

These types of reasoning are hierarchical in that the fifth is considered a higher form of prosocial reasoning than the first. This sequence is subject to criticism, as with Kohlberg's stages, because focusing on how Emmalee would feel if she did not help (level 5) may not be morally higher than focusing on the other girl's needs (level 2).

Lying

Lies are intentionally false statements. False statements that are not intentional, like mistakes, are not lies. Lying is a moral issue that is especially important today because, according to parent report, lying and cheating have increased among U.S. children (Achenbach & Howell, 1993). Academic dishonesty has also become more prevalent (see Box 9.3).

Challenges in Development **Box 9.3**

Academic Dishonesty

In a high school biology class, some students got copies of the final exam just before the test. At least one student bragged about it to another student, Todd, who mentioned test items to his mother. Misunderstanding, Todd's mother called the teacher to find out why her son had not been given a practice test like other students. The teacher figured out what had happened, but was never able to determine who had cheated. Students knew, based on the glares they gave to the cheaters, but no one confessed. The teacher gave the entire class an alternative, more difficult, exam at the beginning of the next semester. This left bad feelings all around. Students who legitimately had high scores were suspected. Some honest students' grades were worse after the time lag. One of the cheaters actually did better on the retest.

Did these students cheat because they did not understand that other students want a level playing field? If so, they lack theory of mind. Or, did they fully appreciate the fact that cheating hurts others, and simply not care? If so, they lack moral principle.

You may have heard a teacher tell students, "When you cheat, you only hurt yourself." This is not true. Cheating is an assault on students who behave honestly. It is an immoral act because it is uncaring toward others. Cheating undermines fairness, equity, and trust. It also undermines the validity and purpose of tests. Cheating hurts the whole community.

This example is not the only form of cheating. Cheating in school, or academic dishonesty, can take many forms. These include copying answers for a test, lying about why homework was not turned in, and plagiarism, which is presenting someone else's intellectual work (or words) as your own.

How can you tell if a child is cheating or lying? You probably cannot. Most adults are not skilled at detecting lying (Ekman, O'Sullivan, & Frank, 1999). Similarly, detecting cheating on tests is very difficult (Cizek, 1999). Todd's teacher would not have known students had cheated if Todd's mother had not accidentally let the teacher know. Most cheating is not detected.

So how do you know how prevalent cheating is? It is not clear how common cheating really is. Most studies use self-report to determine cheating, which may underestimate the real prevalence. In one study, 20 to 25% of 7th- to 11th-graders reported cheating on a science-fair entry—they made up data, copied someone else's work, or received inappropriate help (Syer & Shore, 2001). In another study, 39% of 6th-, 7th-, and 8th-graders reported sometimes cheating in their science class, while 61% reported never cheating (Anderman, Griesinger, & Westerfield, 1998). In still another study, 89% of high school students had copied off someone else's homework within the past year (Jensen, Arnett, Feldman, & Cauffman, 2002). Thus, cheating is common and may vary by task, such as homework versus projects.

The frequency of cheating may be increasing (Jensen et al., 2002). Surveys of high school students found a steady increase in cheating from 1969 to 1989 and an increase in pessimism about others' honesty (Schab, 1991). For example, 68% of students reported having used a cheat sheet in 1989, but only 34% in 1969. Students also became more lenient toward cheating. In 1989 they felt a cheater should simply get a reduced grade, but in 1969 they felt a cheater should fail the test, fail the course, and parents should be called in.

What might cause dishonesty in children? Most adolescents perceive cheating as unacceptable, yet many do it. Why? The most common reasons include a fear of failure, being too lazy to study, and parental pressure to get good grades (Schab, 1991). Here are three students' views of cheating.

Student 1: *"If ... cheating is going to get you the grade, then that's the way to do it."*

Student 2: *"People cheat. It doesn't make you ... worse of a person. There are times when you just are in need of a little help.*

Student 3: *"I guess the first time you do it, you feel really bad, but then you get used to it. You keep telling yourself you're not doing anything wrong ... Maybe you might know in your heart that it's wrong, but it gets easier after a while to handle it."*

These quotes are from three college-bound high school students (McCabe, 1999, pp. 682–683). The first two are remarkably tolerant of dishonesty. The third is less tolerant of dishonesty, but finds a way to appease her conscience.

There are individual differences in tendency to cheat. Students who are tolerant of cheating, who believe "everyone else is doing it," and believe there is little disapproval for it are more likely to cheat (Jensen et al., 2002). Students who have low confidence in their

(continued)

Challenges in Development *(continued)*

academic ability, focus on how they compare with other students, have low GPA or low IQ, and have low self-control are more likely to cheat than other students (Jensen et al., 2002; Murdock, Hale, & Weber, 2001; Schlievert, 2001). There are also group differences in cheating. Some studies find that boys are more likely to cheat than girls and are more accepting of cheating (Jensen et al., 2002; Schlievert, 2001), but not all studies find gender differences (Murdock et al., 2001).

How can you reduce cheating? The nature of the situation may influence cheating more than these individual and group differences. In a classic study (Hartshorne & May, 1928), some classrooms had virtually no cheating and others had almost universal cheating. There are several things that you can do to make cheating less likely in your classroom:

1. Challenge the belief that "everybody does it." Define cheating and make it clear that cheating is not acceptable.
2. Be a role model of honesty. Make the fact that you value honesty very clear. In one study, 63% of preservice teacher education students reported that they were dishonest (Schlievert, 2001). There have been allegations of teachers giving students answers to proficiency tests in order to raise test scores in low-achieving schools. Such negative modeling is likely to increase students' dishonesty.
3. Develop a warm, mutually respectful relationship with students. Students who view the teacher as disrespectful of students and who do not respect the teacher are more likely to cheat (McCabe, 1999; Murdock et al., 2001).
4. Care about student learning. When students believe the teacher cares about teaching them the subject, students are less likely to cheat (Murdock et al., 2001; Schab, 1991).
5. Avoid negative competition. Cheating is less likely when there is an emphasis on improvement and learning, rather than on extrinsic rewards like grades or athletic eligibility (Anderman et al., 1998; Schab, 1991).
6. Enforce serious consequences for dishonesty. Most cheating that is detected is not punished, and high school students are blasé about cheating if they know they will not be punished and if they think the teacher does not care (Cizek, 1999; McCabe, 1999).
7. Be fair. Students cheat more in classes that they see as unfair. Give assignments well ahead of deadlines so there is time to honestly study or write. Give fair tests that do not test material that was not taught.
8. Make cheating more difficult. Remove temptations. Carefully proctor exams, but without making students feel like prisoners.

If you follow each of these guidelines, you should be able to greatly reduce dishonesty in your classroom and help your students become morally principled.

Most children and adults believe that trivial lies that benefit others or are humorous are not immoral, such as "We're glad the principal is visiting our classroom today" (Bussey, 1999). These are known as *white lies*, *altruistic lies*, and *trick lies*. Even as young as 5, children judge white lies less harshly than lies intended to harm others (Strayer & Roberts, 1997).

Age Trends in Moral Judgment

Piaget (1932) studied how children understand and evaluate lying. Not surprisingly he found age trends in understanding lies that parallel age trends in moral judgment and prosocial reasoning. Let's discuss these age trends next.

Early Childhood (Birth to 5 Years)

When do children know right from wrong? By age 3, they tend not to violate parents' prohibitions, they are distressed if they do, and they confess wrongdoing (Emde, Biringen, Clyman, & Oppenheim, 1991). They view lying to cover up a misdeed as morally wrong (Talwar & Lee, 2008). They judge actions that result in harm to others as morally wrong (Helwig & Turiel, 2002). Thus, the rudiments of morality may emerge in toddlerhood.

Mel Yates/Getty images

Rudimentary morality is present by age 3.

By age 4 or 5, children distinguish between social convention and morality. **Social conventions** are standards of behavior dictated by culture. Preschoolers know that a breach of social convention, like calling a teacher by her first name, is wrong only if there is a rule against it, and the rule can be changed. They also know that it is wrong to hit someone in order to get a swing even if the school has a rule saying it is all right (Helwig & Turiel, 2002). They believe that a **moral transgression** is wrong regardless of rules, and its wrongness is unchangeable. They also view moral transgressions, like stealing, as deserving more punishment than do social-convention transgressions, like eating with your hands (Stern & Peterson, 1999).

social conventions standards of behavior dictated by culture.

moral transgression behavior that is inherently wrong, independent of culture and regardless of rules.

Young children do not fully understand what a lie is. They equate exaggeration, "naughty" words, incorrect statements, and mistaken guesses with lies. Despite this overly generous view of what a lie is, they are quite willing to lie. Children lie as soon as they are able to talk. Two-year-olds intentionally deceive others, such as erasing footprints leading to a hiding place (Chandler, Fritz, & Hala, 1989), and they are capable of emotional dissemblance (see Chapter 8). About half of 3-year-olds and even more 4-year-olds will lie about their misbehavior to avoid punishment (Talwar & Lee, 2008). In one study, 3-year-olds were as likely as 7-year-olds to tell an experimenter that he "looked OK" when he actually had a smudge on his nose, and they were remarkably adept at it (Talwar & Lee, 2002).

Still, because their ToM ability and executive functions are fledgling, preschoolers are not always successful at lying. Scientists have a sneaky way of testing this. They put a secret toy behind young children and say, "Do not turn around and peek at the toy. I'll be back in a minute" and leave the room. Hidden cameras reveal that about 80% of young children peek at the toy. Among the peekers, approximately 30 to 65% lie, saying they did not peek (Talwar & Lee, 2008). Follow-up conversations with preschoolers often go something like this:

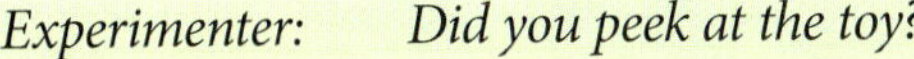

Experimenter: *Did you peek at the toy?*
Child: *No.*
Experimenter: *What do you think the toy is?*
Child: *A Barney doll because it was purple.*

The truth often leaks out because preschoolers do not have sufficient ToM or executive functions to maintain the lie.

Preschoolers begin to use their fledgling ToM abilities to make moral judgments based on intention. For example, 4-year-olds are as likely as 11-year-olds to consider white lies less bad than antisocial lies, because the intent behind a white lie is benevolent (Bussey, 1999). For another example, they forgive a teacher who gives more snack to girls than to boys if the teacher believes girls need more food, but not if the teacher believes it is all right to be nicer to girls (Chandler, Sokol, & Wainryb, 2000). Yet, preschoolers still struggle with judging behavior based on intent. Recall from Chapter 8 that preschoolers justify punishment for misbehavior *based on degree of damage rather than intention*; they believe Mary should be punished more for breaking eight dishes accidentally than John should be punished for breaking one dish on purpose. This has been confirmed in later research as well (Helwig, Zelazo, & Wilson, 2001).

In summary, children behave as though they have some moral sense by 3 years of age. They sometimes take intention into account in their moral judgments, and they are able to distinguish social conventions from moral issues. They are prolific, but not very successful, liars, even though they believe lying is wrong.

Middle Childhood (6 to 12 Years)

Elementary children are able to reason about morality and do not rigidly adhere to laws as Kohlberg suggested. For example, 6- to 10-year-olds can reason about whether it would be all right to violate harmful laws (Helwig & Jasiobedzka, 2001). In addition, they believe lies are morally wrong because they interfere with trust and social justice, not simply because authority figures prohibit them (Carpendale, 2000). However, most 9-year-olds (85%) and many 11-year-olds (28%) still give punishment as the reason for not telling lies (Peterson, Peterson, & Seeto, 1983).

By 1st or 2nd grade, children have the ToM and executive functions to maintain a lie, so that the truth doesn't leak out. By 5th or 6th grade, they come to understand what a lie is—any statement that is intentionally false is a lie, and exaggeration, sarcasm, or irony are not lies (Talwar & Lee, 2008). The less plausible the lie, the more naughty it is for preschoolers, but the less naughty it is for older children (Carpendale, 2000). For example, older children would view telling Dad that you saw a dog as big as a cow as less naughty than lying to Dad that you got a good grade on a test, because dad probably will not believe the dog story. Older children, unlike preschoolers, do not equate wrong guesses and exaggerations as lies, like a dog as big as a cow.

In middle childhood, children are better at taking intention into account when judging others' behavior. For example, both kindergarteners and 3rd-graders judge Sariah as only "a little bit bad" if she lies to Peter that she is too sick to play with him because she wants to shop secretly to buy a present for him. They judge Sariah as "very bad" if she lies because she wants to shop for herself (Stein & Trabasso, 1989). By 10 years of age, children can weigh guilt, taking into account degree of harm, intention, and degree of control in the situation. In other words, at this age children begin to think the same way a judge would in determining a criminal's sentence (Ferguson, Stegge, & Damhuis, 1991).

Adolescence (13 to 19 Years)

Kohlberg's view was that in adolescence youth may reach stage 3. Stage 4 is typically reached by college students. Stages 5 and 6 are only reached by some adults. Thus, according to Kohlberg, adolescents and most adults are unlikely to be reasoning at the highest levels of morality.

Piaget's view is a little rosier. He believed adolescents have autonomous morality. He also believed that, around 11 years old, children develop notions of relative equality. That is, they can see that some people

Think About This If children become better at moral judgment with age, as cognitive developmental theorists would assert, how can you explain adults who spit on 6-year-olds, as some did to Ruby? What factors might lead to such behavior?

should get more resources because their need is greater (Piaget, 1965). Research confirms that adolescents are better than younger children at judging complex issues of justice (Wainryb, Brehl, & Matwin, 2005). Yet, recent research shows that sometimes children as young as 3rd grade distribute resources based on deservingness (e.g., who worked hardest) and special needs (Gummerum, Keller, Takezawa, & Mata, 2008).

In contrast to moral judgment, prosocial reasoning does not improve much in adolescence. In fact, many adolescents regress in prosocial reasoning. When teens are involved in conflict between self-interest and others' needs, they may be *more hedonistic*, and no more other-oriented than younger children (Carlo et al., 1996; Janssens & Dekovic, 1997). Thus, with age children may become more logical when discussing laws and justice, but they are not necessarily more selfless. Children vary in these abilities. Let's discuss this variation next.

Individual Diversity in Moral Judgment

A famous study was conducted by Hartshorne and May (1928) during the 1920s to address the question of how religious education affected cheating, stealing, and lying. More than 11,000 1st- through 12th-graders from diverse communities were tested in ordinary classrooms using twenty-nine different tasks that challenged children's moral behavior. For example, the researchers would give children the answer key and tell them to score their own tests (after a copy of the original answers had secretly been made). They gave the children athletic tests, like pull-ups, and told them to record their own results. They planted a dime in a puzzle box to see if children returned the dime.

Two major conclusions came from this famous study. One was that religious instruction did not keep children from behaving immorally in the face of temptation, which was very disappointing to their Sunday school teachers. The second was that moral behavior is quite situation specific, and some situations can tempt almost any child into dishonesty. For example, 92% of children cheated at least once on timed arithmetic tests. However, there were also large individual differences in cheating; some children seldom cheated, and others cheated at every opportunity.

These results are still relevant today. Research indicates that honesty is influenced by the situation and that individual differences in honesty appear by early childhood. For example, in studies of toy peeking, more than one-third of guilty 3-year-olds confess and tell the truth, but the rest do not (Talwar & Lee, 2008). In a study of elementary children, half peeked at a test and half did not. Of those that peeked, 93% lied about it (Talwar, Gordon, & Lee, 2007). Are such differences in moral *behavior* the result of differences in moral *judgment*? That is, are children who discuss moral dilemmas at a more sophisticated level than their peers also more honest, just, and compassionate? Let's see what the research says.

Sean Locke/iStockphoto

The classic Hartshorme and May study found that there were large individual differences in moral behavior, but some situations could tempt almost any child.

What Do Individual Differences in Moral Judgment Predict?

Teachers are generally more interested in moral behavior than in moral judgment. There is no clear relationship between *moral judgment* and moral behavior. Children with *above-average* moral judgment and understanding of lying are not consistently more honest, fair, generous, or compassionate than average children, although *below-average* moral judgment is linked to aggression and delinquency (Gummerum et al., 2008; Talwar & Lee, 2008). In addition, compassion emerges in the first years of life (see Chapter 10), but sophisticated moral judgment does not appear before adolescence. Furthermore, some adolescents engage in antisocial activities, like shoplifting, even though they have greater moral judgment than younger children who do not engage in antisocial activities (Kuther & Higgins-D'Alessandro, 2000).

Fifteen-year-old Heather exemplifies this disconnect. She is old enough to reason about moral issues, but she cheats in school, and feels bad about it, but she feels pressure to get good grades. She also lies to her parents when she thinks they are being overly protective. She says that she believes in right and wrong, but her views of morality are based on not getting caught. She recalls drinking alcohol: "The first time I did it, I was a wreck, like paranoid [about getting caught], but other times when I think I won't get caught it's taken a lot of pressure off, so a lot depends on if I think I'm gonna get caught." Heather cannot explain what makes things right and wrong beyond the consequences. She says, "I don't really think about this stuff too much! . . . I don't really know where morality comes from" (adapted from Smith & Denton, 2005, p. 198).

There is also no clear relationship between *prosocial reasoning* and moral behavior among older children. However, among children below a 3rd-grade level, *hedonistic* reasoning is related to less-kind behavior, and higher-level *needs-oriented* and *internalized* reasoning are related to more kind behavior (Carlo et al., 1996; Janssens & Dekovic, 1997).

Why is there no strong relationship between moral judgment or prosocial reasoning and moral behavior? There are other components to moral behavior besides reasoning (Thoma, 2000). When faced with a moral issue, a student must (1) see the situation as being moral in nature; (2) judge which action is morally right (this is what Kohlberg emphasizes); (3) give priority to moral values; and (4) have the integrity, courage, and skill to act on the values. For example, if adolescents view drug use or sexual activity as issues of personal choice, rather than moral issues, there will be no link between moral judgment and these behaviors (Kuther & Higgins-D'Alessandro, 2000). Even if a student sees a situation as moral in nature (component 1) and knows what is right (component 2), he or she may not care (component 3), or may succumb to self-interest (component 4). Moral principles are supposed to keep people from acting in their own self-interest over the interests of others. Yet self-interest is a powerful motive, even for adults. In experiments, most adults (75%) assign themselves the more pleasant of two tasks and another person the least pleasant, rather than opting for a fair coin toss to assign tasks (Batson & Thompson, 2001).

What Predicts Individual Differences in Moral Judgment and Behavior?

In the 1920s study, children with higher SES and higher intelligence cheated less. In contrast, children with poor manners, like not tipping their hats at women they passed, cheated more. No single variable distinguished cheaters, but cheaters had a greater number of risk factors. Similar factors are still associated with differences in morality today—such as abilities of the child (e.g., theory of mind), characteristics of the family (e.g., authoritative parenting), and the child's education (secular and religious). We discuss these next.

Theory of mind

Theory of mind is foundational to moral judgment (Leslie, Knobe, & Cohen, 2006). Whether or not you blame someone for misbehavior (moral judgment) depends on whether you view the misbehavior as intentional (ToM judgment). Humans are unique in their ability to assess *intentional* states that allow moral judgment (Killen & de Waal, 2000). Children with better ToM are more likely to have mature moral reasoning.

Children with better ToM may also be better liars because lying is the deliberate attempt to instill false beliefs in someone else. Children have been found to lie and deceive before they are able to pass false-belief tasks, meaning full-blown ToM is not necessary for dishonesty. However, individual children with better ToM are better liars in that they do not let the truth leak out as much as other children; they can maintain their lies despite questioning by an adult (Talwar & Lee, 2008).

In young children, moral behavior is also related to inhibitory control. Preschoolers with good inhibitory control are more likely to obey the rule to clean up their mess or not cheat in a game when unsupervised. They also give less-selfish responses to prosocial dilemmas, like Emmalee helping an injured child and missing the birthday party, than children with less inhibitory control. Both inhibitory control and prosocial reasoning are linked to authoritative parenting.

Authoritative parenting

Children whose parents are authoritative have higher levels of moral reasoning than other children (M. Pratt, Arnold, Pratt, & Diessner, 1999). In Chapter 7 you learned about two characteristics of authoritative parents that would explain this. First, authoritative parents are warm. Parent–child relationships that are warm motivate the child to be receptive to parents' influence and to embrace their values (Kochanska, 2002). Having older siblings who are warm and affectionate is also linked to moral maturity in children (Dunn, Brown, & Maguire, 1995).

Second, authoritative parents are likely to use induction rather than power assertion. Induction is a form of discipline in which the adult explains the need for a rule and points out the consequences for others of the child's misbehavior. Induction leads to internalization, or conscience, which refers to doing the right thing because it is right, not to avoid punishment (Kochanska, 2002). Induction promotes guilt, a moral emotion that inhibits immoral behavior (Tangney et al., 2007). Children whose parents use induction are more likely to feel bad if they cheat at a game, grab a toy, or do not help someone (Dunn et al., 1995).

Education

Scores on Kohlberg's moral-judgment interview are correlated with education level. Learning-disabled children perform poorly (Derr, 1986). Typically, only college graduates score at stage 4 or 5. This is not surprising because scores are based on ability to make a logically coherent argument about abstract concepts and competing perspectives. This is a problem for Kohlberg's model because common sense tells you that morality and education are not synonymous. As Ruby Bridges "uneducated" mother said, there are some folk who "just put their lives on the line for what's right, and they may not be the ones who talk a lot . . . they just do a lot!" (Coles, 1986). Ruby could not read or write when she started school, and may not have made it past Kohlberg's stage 2 during an interview, but she had moral integrity. Piaget pointed out that "intelligence alone might suffice to sharpen the child's evaluation of conduct without necessarily inclining him to do good actions . . . an intelligent scamp would perhaps give better answers than a slow-witted but really good-hearted little boy" (1965, p. 116).

Religiosity

Kohlberg stated that "religion is not a necessary or highly important condition for the development of moral judgment and conduct" (1981, p. 304). He distinguished morality from religiosity. He argued that because children in all religions proceed through the same invariant sequence of stages in moral judgment, religion cannot be a source of moral development. In Kohlberg's model, people who justify moral behavior based on conformity to God or their religion score at lower levels than those who use more justice-oriented reasoning.

Many adults and youth do not share this view. They believe that religious faith motivates moral behavior and forms the basis for judging whether a behavior is moral or not (Smith & Denton, 2005; Walker & Pitts, 1998). Ruby Bridges said that every Sunday she went to church, where she said people were admonished "to pray for everyone, even the bad people, and so I do" (Coles, 1986, p. 23).

Research robustly links both parents' and children's religiosity with moral behavior.[2] Parents' religiosity predicts their children's moral behavior and the children's own religiosity. Youth who frequently participate in religious activities are less likely to be depressed, delinquent, violent, cut classes, drop out, lie and cheat, watch TV or play videogames excessively, view pornography, use drugs, or be sexually active at a young age. They are more likely to feel cared for, spend time with adults, get higher grades, get along with parents and siblings, attend college, feel guilt for transgression, behave kindly, help others, perform community service, and express concern about racism and poverty—actually giving more of their own money to causes. Religious participation may especially contribute to the resilience of inner-city youth.

On the other hand, there is also evidence that some religious people are not more honest and may be more discriminatory toward people who threaten their values (Goldfried & Miner, 2002; Saroglou, Pichon, Trompette, Verschueren, & Dernelle, 2005). Some people commit acts of violence motivated by their religion. Thus, in general religiosity is linked to greater moral behavior, but the beneficial effects of religiosity do not apply to all situations.

Group Diversity in Moral Judgment

Gender, SES, and culture are linked to moral judgment. Can you guess whether boys or girls have "higher" levels of moral judgment? Let's see what the research says.

---

[2] Many studies support this conclusion, a few of which are listed here (King & Furrow, 2004; Loury, 2004; Petts, 2009; Rostosky, Wilcox, Wright, & Randall, 2004; Smith & Denton, 2005).

Gender

There are no gender differences in the attributes that people ascribe to morally exemplary women or men, like honesty, loyalty, or religiosity (Walker & Pitts, 1998). However, there may be some gender differences in moral reasoning. Early research showed that females scored lower than males in Kohlberg's model. Gilligan criticized Kohlberg's theory as a male version of morality and, based on interviews with women, suggested that women have a different moral voice. They focus more on *care reasoning*—giving priority to maintaining relationships and meeting others' needs—and men focus more on *justice reasoning* (Gilligan, 1982). More-recent research shows the effect size for girls favoring care reasoning is 0.28, and for boys favoring justice reasoning is 0.19. This means that while there are small gender differences in moral orientation, most boys and girls use *both* care and justice reasoning (Jaffee & Hyde, 2000). Girls' judgments of morality may be more influenced by relationships than boys' judgments (Eisenberg, Zhou, & Koller, 2001). For example, adolescent girls are more likely than boys to say it is all right to let a friend copy one's homework, but not a nonfriend (Singer, 1999). Boys' judgments are the same for friends and nonfriends. Ironically, despite the focus on justice, more boys than girls are frequent liars (Gervais, Tremblay, Desmarais-Gervais, & Vitaro, 2000) and boys tend to cheat more at school (see Box 9.3, presented earlier).

Socioeconomic Status

Scores on Kohlberg's moral-judgment interview are correlated with SES. This is not surprising because education is a component of SES, and education affects moral judgment scores. This is true for prosocial reasoning as well. Most research linking SES and prosocial reasoning has been conducted in the United States, but the same pattern was found in Brazil, where 7th- and 10th-graders with highly educated, prosperous parents scored higher in prosocial reasoning (Eisenberg et al., 2001).

Cross-National Comparisons

Across cultures, children value equity, justice, and fairness. However, culture influences other values that children hold. A study that compared Chinese and U.S. reading textbooks found that the Chinese texts emphasized respectfulness, modesty, preservation of traditions, and cooperation, while the American texts emphasized enjoyment and creativity (Zheng & Horgan, 2001). These cultural differences in values can alter children's moral judgments. For example, in one study both Chinese and Canadian 7- to 11-year-olds thought lying about doing a misdeed was wrong (Lee, Cameron, Xu, Fu, & Board, 1997). However, Chinese children thought denying having done a good deed was more acceptable than did Canadian children, perhaps because the Chinese value modesty more.

Cultures can also influence the line between moral laws and social convention. Across countries—including Indonesia, Nigeria, Korea, Zambia, Brazil, and India—children share the belief that to cause others harm is a moral transgression, not merely a social transgression. However, cultures vary in what is considered harmful. For example, some people in India believe a son eating chicken the day after his father's death is a moral issue because it could prevent the father from receiving salvation. Most Americans do not see this as a moral issue because most do not believe it would harm the father (Helwig & Turiel, 2002). Even within a country there can be disagreement about whether something is a moral issue. For example, while Americans generally agree that is it wrong to kill, there is heated disagreement over whether abortion is killing. Both culture and moral judgment combine to influence how an individual thinks about a moral issue.

Classroom Implications of Moral Judgment

Moral education goes on in every classroom—indeed in every social group. It is unavoidable; you teach values to your students through the rules you choose to enforce and the way you behave. You make moral decisions when you decide what text to read, whom to hold up as an example, and so forth. In U.S. schools today, moral education is typically haphazard, rather than deliberate; it is a part of the hidden curriculum. In the past people believed education should be deliberately moral. For example, the McGuffey readers—a widely used text series in the 1800s—used moral stories to teach reading and arithmetic. However, deliberate moral education was avoided in U.S. schools during the latter half of the twentieth century. Recently there has been a resurgence of interest, partly fueled by concerns about declining civility and rising aggression.

Many teachers are not comfortable with deliberate moral education. Yet, educator-philosopher Nel Noddings (1992) argues that, "Teachers should not be allowed to avoid their responsibilities as moral educators by claiming that they are not prepared for this work. All decent adults are, or should be, prepared for this work. It is a human responsibility—one that belongs to all of us" (p. 69).

So how should you approach moral education? Piaget and Kohlberg believe children's morality is *constructed* out of social interaction and principled reasoning. Behaviorists and Freud hold a different view; morality is *handed down* from elders to children. The term *moral education* is often used to refer to programs based on the first view, and the term *character education* is often used to refer to programs based on the second view (Berkowitz & Grych, 2000). However, both terms are sometimes applied to any education aimed at promoting morality. Let's take a look at what a moral teacher might do from each approach.

Moral Education (Constructing Morality)

Kohlberg believed the purpose of moral education is to stimulate development of moral judgment, but not to inculcate values. He did not approve of indoctrination. Instead, children should be encouraged to examine the pros and cons of their behavior. He argued that moral education should promote autonomy. For example, to force children to agree that cheating is dishonest when they do not really believe it will only teach them to comply when it is expedient. Kohlberg later decided it was all right for teachers to advocate a particular moral view as long as they respected the child as an autonomous moral agent and did not appeal to their authority over the child. Justice is the main moral value that teachers should try to stimulate (Kohlberg, 1981).

Kohlberg advocated creating "just community" schools at the secondary level. A just school emphasizes discussion of moral issues and joint decision making. His approach adheres to the principles of constructivist education that you learned about in Chapter 3. To promote moral judgment from this perspective, use these guidelines:

Hill Street Studios/Blend Images/Jupiterimages

Active discussion of moral issues can promote moral judgment from preschool to high school.

- Be democratic, be cooperative, and share power with students. Create an atmosphere of mutual respect in adult–student relationships. Allow students to help make classroom rules and have a voice in decision making. Kohlberg advocated that just community schools hold weekly small-group meetings, of 10 to 12 students, to discuss issues and form bonds, as well as weekly all-school meetings to discuss and vote on school policies, such as how to deal with stealing.
- Encourage classroom discussion about moral issues. An *active* discussion style, in which students request clarification, justification, and feedback, is associated with greater moral reasoning than is a passive discussion style, simple disagreement, or an opinionated lecture. Small-group debate promotes moral reasoning in students from kindergarten to high school (Damon & Killen, 1982; Walker, Hennig, & Krettenauer, 2000).

This approach can even be used in preschool when reading stories. For example, a teacher fostered moral discussion while reading a well-known book to preschoolers called *Heckedy Peg,* wherein a witch has abducted children and their mother is trying to get them back. The witch tells the mother she cannot come into her house because the mother's feet are dirty, so the mother pretends to cut off her feet, but really just hides her legs (DeVries, Hildebrandt, & Betty, 2000). Here's how the dialogue went:

Teacher:	*Do you think that what the mother is saying is OK?*
Edward:	*Uh-uh, it's—she's lying.*
Teacher:	*Is it OK to lie in this case?*
Children:	*No!*
Teacher:	*No? Why? Can you tell me why it's not OK?*
John:	*It's bad, and she will look at her and say, "You have feet," and she'll say, "Yes I do." That's a lie, right?*
Amanda:	*I think that she's just trying to trick the witch. I think that she's just trying to get her children back.*
Teacher:	*OK, Edward has a disagreement. Tell us what you think. Do you think . . . it's OK to lie to save your children?*
Edward:	*Uh-uh, it's not.*
Teacher:	*Well, we have a difference of opinion.* (adapted from pp. 26–28)

In this constructivist approach adults are not supposed to impose their values on children, yet critics point out that in constructivist practice adults typically do impose their values by indicating which response is acceptable (Goodman, 2000). If adults remain truly neutral, then what values should children internalize? Critics would further argue that a traditional approach in which the teacher clearly states a rule ("Telling lies is wrong—except to a witch who has stolen your children") is more honest.

Character Education (Handing Down Morality)

In contrast to Kohlberg, proponents of character education believe that character is a collection of virtues like honesty, kindness, courage, politeness, and obedience. These virtues are not innate, but are inculcated in the child. To promote moral behavior in your students from this perspective, use these guidelines (Benninga & Wynne, 1998):

- Identify the virtues that you hope students will learn, and make them an explicit goal for students and teachers. Some teachers even post their goals on the wall.
- Provide opportunities for students to practice the virtues. Some advocate volunteerism or service learning as one approach, but there are plenty of opportunities for students to be kind, helpful, and honest in routine classroom activities. Students need to practice and develop well-worn scripts for moral behavior.
- Praise students who behave in accord with the virtues. This can be done privately or publicly in school ceremonies. However, keep in mind that extrinsic rewards for virtuous behavior can be coercive and may not produce moral students, although rewards might elicit temporary compliance with school rules (see Chapter 7).
- Prohibit undesirable behaviors and punish misbehavior, like cheating. However, keep in mind the costs of punishment that you read about in Chapter 7. If you must use punishment, combine it with other-oriented induction.
- Discuss honesty with students and inculcate the value of honesty as a virtue. Asking students to promise to tell you the truth results in more-truthful students (Lyon, Malloy, Quas, & Talwar, 2008).
- Highlight virtuous role models. Use literature with moral heroes and virtuous deeds. However, be aware that elementary-age students, even as old as 5th grade, may not understand the theme of a moral story unless you make it explicit (Narvaez, 2002), or they may take a different message from the story than you intended, such as identifying with the bad character.

Critics of the character-education approach argue that behavior without principled reflection is not moral—indeed, that this may be the goal of totalitarian regimes. Rote obedience should not be the aim of moral education, because principled objection to oppressive rules is also moral. Proponents would counter that while self-determination based on moral principles is important, moral judgment is meaningless without habits of moral behavior.

Does Moral or Character Education Work?

Effective moral education should foster all four components of morality discussed earlier: (1) awareness that morals are involved in a situation, (2) ability to judge which action is morally right, (3) desire to do what is morally right, and (4) strength of character to act. However, few programs focus on all the components. The constructivist approaches focus on components 1 or 2, and traditional character-education programs focus on 3 or 4.

Currently there is not enough research to know which methods are most effective for any of these components, except perhaps component 2 (moral judgment). That is, studies find that moral education improves moral *judgment*, particularly for older students (Schlaefli, Rest, & Thomas, 1985). The two types of programs that are most effective, although they have small effects, are (1) intense self-reflection after engaging in activities that serve others, such as cross-age tutoring, and (2) peer discussion of moral dilemmas, such as in high school civics classes. After just a few months of discussing moral issues and being exposed to the next higher stage of reasoning, approximately one-third of students will move up a stage in moral judgment. Without such experience, it typically takes several years to move up a stage. Academic courses in the humanities, literature, or social studies (like the Great Books program) that highlight moral issues generally do *not* have an effect on moral judgment.

Does moral education affect moral *behavior*? Research on just community high schools finds that students reason at a higher level than at comparison schools, but there is no difference in their delinquency (Kuther & Higgins-D'Alessandro, 2000). Many companies have produced character-education curricula that schools purchase, but there is remarkably little evidence that they improve moral behavior. However, you can make a difference through everyday interactions with students.

> ***Think About This*** Imagine that your school implemented a moral-education program. What would you measure in order to decide whether the program was a success or not? What kind of evidence would you want to see before deciding to adopt it? (Review Chapter 1.)

Teach Morality through Everyday Interactions

The way you interact with your students may be more important in producing moral students than a moral education program. Among the most important parenting factors associated with moral development are *modeling*, *authoritative* parenting, a *democratic* family structure where parents show respect for children, and *induction* (Berkowitz & Grych, 2000). The same factors can be applied to your classroom. They overlap with guidelines we have already discussed:

1. Authoritative teachers are democratic and allow verbal give-and-take with students, including discussing moral issues. They are demanding and set high standards for moral behavior, but are also warm and caring.
2. Moral teachers model moral behavior.

Let's focus next on two factors we have not yet discussed in this section:

- Use inductive discipline and be careful about what you discipline students for. As you learned in Chapter 7, inductive discipline results in internalization, or students who obey even when no one is looking. Recall that discipline is a teaching act. It is during discipline that students learn adults' core values. Students are able to infer that the issues you are most demanding about, like hitting someone, are core values and nonnegotiable. The issues that you are flexible about are not core values and choices are acceptable, like whether to raise your hand before answering. Teachers tend to present students with choices about personal issues but state rules and give commands about moral issues (Killen & Smetana, 1999).

- Care for students. You learned how to foster teacher–student attachment and school bonding in Chapter 6. In the Hartshorne and May study, there were remarkably large differences in the amount of cheating in different schools and classrooms. For example, at one school only five dimes were taken from the puzzle box out of 260 possibilities. Other schools had almost universal cheating. Cheating was low in classes with positive teacher–student relationships and where the atmosphere of the class was cordial and cooperative.

Noddings (1992) asserts that the first job of schools is not to enhance academic ability, but to care for students because morality comes from the memory of being cared for. Every student should feel cared for by you and by classmates. Effective ways you can encourage kind, helpful behaviors, inhibit aggression, and resolve conflicts peacefully among your students will be discussed in the next chapter. Stay tuned.

Reflections on Practice: Checklist for Teachers

The way that you interact with students can influence their people-reading skills, sense of humor, and morality. Several factors that promote social cognition have been discussed in previous chapters; you should review the "Reflections on Practice" sections from these other chapters. They include:

- Developing secure attachment with students, which is associated with ToM and morality. This is described in Chapter 6.
- Creating a positive classroom atmosphere, which is associated with less cheating. This is described in Chapter 8.
- Promoting students' information processing ability, which is associated with ToM and humor. This is described in Chapter 4.
- Being authoritative and warm, encouraging give-and-take, and using induction, which are associated with morality. This is described in Chapter 7.

In addition, to make sure you are promoting your students' social cognition, periodically ask yourself the following:

1. Do I talk with students about others' perspectives, thoughts, and beliefs? Do I use words like *think* and *know* in these conversations? Do I provide students with opportunity to interact and talk with peers who have different perspectives?
2. Do I initiate jokes and humor in the classroom to promote creativity, problem solving, and positive emotions?
3. Do my students initiate humor in my classroom? Do I respond positively? Am I able to respond positively to the humor of students with whom I have a difficult relationship?
4. Do I promote small-group debate of moral issues among peers, making sure the discussion style is "active" (i.e., participants request clarification, elaboration, justification, and feedback) rather than passive?
5. Do I discuss moral issues when the opportunity arises, such as in literature, history, or when conflict erupts? Do I expose students to higher levels of moral reasoning? Do I help students recognize moral issues?
6. Do I share power with students when it is feasible? Do students help set classroom rules?
7. Do I recognize virtuous or moral behavior? Do I inadvertently reinforce immoral behavior?
8. Do I make it clear that I value honesty? Am I a model of honesty? Are there serious consequences for cheating in my class?
9. Am I aware of the virtues I would like to inculcate in students? Do I provide opportunity for students to practice virtues? Do I highlight virtuous role models for students, making their virtues explicit?
10. Do I give students the opportunity to care for others in my classroom? If so, do I provide time for self-reflection about it?
11. Do I give respect to students, and earn their respect? Are my tests, assignments, and other aspects of the classroom fair?
12. What is the culture of morality in my classroom? What rules do I actually enforce? Are they the same as the ones that I claim to enforce? Which rule violations really upset me? What does this communicate to students about my core values?

Summary of Age Trends in Social Cognition

	Theory of Mind	Humor	Moral Judgment and Prosocial Reasoning
Early Childhood (Birth–5 Years)	Infants are innately predisposed to look at human faces, distinguish facial expressions, and follow others' gazes. Toddlers understand that others have feelings, intentions, and desires. Before age 3, children typically fail false-belief tasks and appearance-reality tasks. By 5–6 years, they perform at adult levels on these tasks. However, they still believe that wishing can make things happen, like magic. Autism is typically diagnosed by 3 years of age.	Social smiling emerges at about 1 month of age. Laughter emerges at about 4–6 months. Toddlers laugh at word distortions, unusual behaviors, and pretend play. Preschoolers laugh at unusual appearances and distortions of the physical world. Causes of laughter become more subtle and varied with age. Children find concepts they have just mastered most amusing (e.g., word distortions are funny to toddlers who have just acquired language abilities.)	Toddlers feel guilt and try to repair their transgressions. Children are "moral" beings by age 3. Both Piaget and Kohlberg underestimated young children's moral development. Children this young are not even tested in Kohlberg's model. Preschoolers often use more-advanced needs-oriented, rather than just punishment-oriented, prosocial reasoning. They are able to distinguish social convention from moral rules. They have difficulty judging intent and assign punishment based on degree of damage rather than intent. They mistake exaggerations and mistakes for lies. The more exaggerated the lie, the naughtier it is. They can distinguish "white" lies from antisocial lies, and view white lies as less naughty by 4–5 years. Children are adept at lying by 2–3 years. Individual differences in honesty are manifest by age 3.
Middle Childhood (6–12 Years)	Children become better able to use ToM to generate persuasive arguments. They understand that they know more about their own inner thoughts and feelings than others do. They become better at distinguishing intentional from unintentional acts. Asperger's disorder is typically diagnosed in middle childhood.	Complex verbal jokes become funny. Children enjoy puns, wordplays, and knock knock jokes. Joke and riddle books become popular for 3rd- to 5th-graders. They become better at reading others' intent so that they understand when someone is joking or serious, teasing or not. They enjoy teasing more. They tease about different subjects—in upper elementary grades they tease about boyfriends or girlfriends. They are able to see the benefit of using humor to cope with stress, but need help doing so. By age 10, children understand sarcasm. Children and teachers initiate more humor in elementary classrooms than in secondary. Humorous children are likely to act out somewhat in class because they are highly active, social children.	Children are typically in Kohlberg's stage 1 or 2. According to Piaget, at about 8 years children value equality above obedience to authority, and by 11 years stress relative equality. They may be slightly more likely to use "internalized" and less likely to use "approval" prosocial reasoning, but they are still likely to use hedonistic reasoning. They are able to coherently discuss whether laws are good or bad and whether a white lie is acceptable or not. They are able to judge in a deliberate way how bad an act is based on both intent and degree of damage. They develop a clearer concept of what constitutes a lie. The more believable a lie, the naughtier it is (in contrast to preschoolers).

Summary of Age Trends in Social Cognition (*continued*)

Adolescence (13–19 years)	Adolescents have better ToM ability than do younger children, but they still tend to believe that others know what they know. They overestimate whether people will notice and remember something about them (*spotlight effect*). They overestimate how easily others can read them (the *transparency illusion*). ToM continues to develop—older adults have better ToM ability than do young adults.	Adolescents find humor in the wider world and enjoy puns, double entendres, and witticisms that younger children would not understand. Put-downs become popular, especially among boys. Both teacher-initiated and child-initiated humor is less common in high school than elementary school. Humorous students are no longer as disruptive in class because they have learned to use their humor appropriately.	Adolescents have reached Piaget's autonomous morality. They may be in Kohlberg's stage 3. Only well-educated adults score a 5 or 6. Young adolescents may increase in stereotyped prosocial reasoning. They may slightly increase in hedonistic reasoning. Needs-oriented reasoning may decline slightly, indicating moral regression. Cheating is more prevalent in secondary school than elementary school.

Chapter Summary

Theory of Mind

- Social cognition refers to cognition applied to the social domain.
- Theory of mind (ToM) is the ability to read other people's mental states. It is commonly tested with false-belief or appearance-reality tests.
- Poor ToM is a hallmark of autism and Asperger's disorder. Autism (but not Asperger's) often occurs with other cognitive and language delays.
- There are different views of how ToM develops. One is that children are born with an innate ToM capacity. Another is that ToM is a function of a general increase in information processing abilities, particularly executive functions. A third is that children generate a theory of others' minds through reasoning and social experience, much like a scientist generates a theory.
- Children who have better ToM ability tend to be more socially competent, better at deception, and have advanced language ability.
- Factors that predict good ToM ability include genetics, verbal ability, conversations about others' thoughts, interaction with peers, parents who acknowledge their children's thoughts, secure attachment, and information processing ability.
- Girls and high-SES children tend to have better ToM than boys or low-SES children. ToM develops more slowly in some countries than in others.

Humor

- Humor is social-cognitive playfulness. It can be caused by physical play, or by encountering information that is puzzling and then suddenly resolved by insight. Humor can serve several functions, such as insulting others or creating social bonds.
- Teasing is playful and provocative commentary on others. It can be physical, and it can be positive or antisocial.
- Children with a good sense of humor are better liked by others. Individuals with better information processing abilities often have a better sense of humor than their peers.
- Positive (nonsarcastic) humor in the classroom promotes positive teacher–student relationships and enhances creativity, positive emotions, and learning. Humor is less frequent in secondary than in elementary schools.
- Freud emphasized the power of unconscious feelings, and that dreams have meaning. He developed a form of therapy, psychoanalysis, which is widely used today. He believed jokes, like dreams, have hidden meanings and allow people to express forbidden feelings. He believed emotions and attachment are the basis of morality.

Moral Judgment

- Piaget believed that children construct their own sense of justice, rather than adopting others' moral standards, through social-cognitive conflict with others. He believed that children progress from heteronymous to autonomous morality.
- Kohlberg believed that children's moral judgment develops in an invariant, universal sequence of stages. The lowest level is authority-punishment oriented, and the highest level is justice oriented. Not everyone agrees that justice is a higher form of morality compared with other values, such as caring.
- Prosocial reasoning refers to reasoning about dilemmas where needs conflict but no laws are involved. Hedonistic reasoning is considered lower than internalized reasoning.
- Academic dishonesty is prevalent and increasing in frequency. Students who view cheating as no big deal, who have low ability, and who do not respect the teacher are more likely to cheat. Teachers can diminish cheating by being fair, respectful, and caring toward students and by conveying that dishonesty is not acceptable.
- Scores on Kohlberg's stages are not strongly related to moral *behavior.* Prosocial reasoning is related to moral behavior in younger, but not older, children.
- Children who have inhibitory control, authoritative parents, religious affiliation, and better ToM tend to have higher levels of moral judgment and behavior.
- High-SES children, and boys, tend to score higher on moral judgment. Girls have a slight tendency to be more caring oriented in their moral judgment, whereas boys are more likely to be justice oriented. However, boys do not behave with greater honesty.
- Culture affects the values that children adopt and whether an issue is considered moral or not.
- Moral education, based on Piaget's and Kohlberg's views, emphasizes peer discussion of moral dilemmas and a democratic school. Character education emphasizes indoctrination of virtues and providing practice, rewards, and models of virtue. There are critics and proponents of each approach.
- Teachers' use of induction, care for students, and creation of a positive classroom atmosphere foster moral behavior.

Accompanying Education CourseMate Website Resources

Visit the **Education CourseMate** website at **CengageBrain.com** to find resources and study aids for this chapter, including self-tests, a glossary, and additional print and website resources. The following videos illustrate concepts from this chapter:

- 5–11 Years: Moral Development in Middle Childhood
- 12–18 Years: Moral Development in Adolescence
- Rebecca and Ben: Creating Structured Educational Programs for Students with Autism
- Tyler: Augmentative Communication Techniques for a Kindergarten Student with Autism and Language Issues
- Autism in Girls

10 chapter

Social Behavior

daaronj/iStockphoto

WHY ARE SOME STUDENTS KIND AND HELPFUL, BUT OTHERS ARE AGGRESSIVE? How should you handle aggressive students who defy authority?In this chapter we will discuss three aspects of social behavior—prosocial behavior, antisocial behavior (which includes bullying), and conflict resolution. After you read this chapter, you will understand:

- What social behavior is typical for different ages and groups of students.
- How social behavior contributes to students' success in your classroom.
- How individual differences in kindness and aggression develop, and how you can foster optimal social behavior among your students.

Prosocial Behavior

In a 3rd-grade class, Patrick felt frustrated and pled for Ted's help on an assignment: "I don't know what to do. Can you please help me?" Ted said, "No! Leave me alone; I got to get my own done." Lizzie overheard them. She said to Patrick, "I don't know how to do it either, but maybe Lauren can help us. She always knows what to do." She asked Lauren for help, and the two got their assignment done.

Classrooms present plenty of opportunity for children to be kind and helpful, like Lizzie. Some children not only decline to be nice, like Ted, but they are actively aggressive toward classmates, like Preston in case 4. Lizzie is more likely to be a good student than either Ted or Preston because *success in the classroom depends on social competence as well as academic ability.* In this chapter, you will learn about three aspects of social competence: prosocial behavior, antisocial behavior, and conflict resolution. *Prosocial* refers to positive interactions, and *antisocial* refers to negative interactions with others. You might mistakenly assume that antisocial means "asocial," but it does not. Nor does prosocial mean "outgoing." Rather, these terms refer to the *quality*, not the *amount*, of interaction.

The term *prosocial* was coined to reflect the opposite of antisocial behavior (Wispe, 1972). **Prosocial behavior** is voluntary behavior that benefits others or promotes harmonious relations with others. Sometimes it is confused with altruism. **Altruism** refers to behavior that benefits someone else *at the expense of the self.* Prosocial behavior can include altruism, but it can also include behaviors with little cost to the self. Lizzie was prosocial, and more socially competent than Ted, because she found a way to benefit Patrick as well as herself.

prosocial behavior voluntary behavior that benefits others or promotes harmonious relations with others.

altruism behavior that benefits others at the expense of the self. It is a subset of prosocial behavior.

What types of prosocial behavior do children engage in? In one study, 6th-graders with different ethnic and SES backgrounds said their prosocial classmates do the following (Bergin, Talley, & Hamer, 2003):

- Comfort distressed peers.
- Help others with sports, schoolwork, or social difficulties.
- Make others smile or laugh with their humor.
- Share things like food, CDs, or jewelry.
- Compliment and encourage others.
- Invite others to join in the group and are friendly.
- Confront those who have done wrong, and stand up for those who have been wronged.
- Admit mistakes and apologize.
- Use good manners and behave politely.
- Break up fights, give in to avoid fights, and broker peace among peers.
- Are honest.
- Avoid hurting others' feelings, and avoid bragging.

Other studies have found similar kinds of prosocial behaviors in 2- to 18-year-olds (Bergin, Bergin, & French, 1995; Caldarella & Merrell, 1997; Greener & Crick, 1999). As you can see, prosocial behavior encompasses a variety of positive social behaviors that include social convention, such as saying "thank you," and morality, such as being honest. It requires a blend of self-assertion, such as standing up for victims, and conceding to others, such as giving in to avoid fights.

Age Trends in Prosocial Behavior

Do children become more prosocial as they get older? The *frequency* of prosocial behavior does not appear to increase with age, but children's *competence* at enacting prosocial behavior does improve with age.

Early Childhood (Birth to 5 Years)

Infants have a universal tendency to help and share that is apparent by 8 months of age (Eisenberg, Fabes, & Spinrad, 2006). By 12 months, sharing and cooperating with parents is so common that the absence of these behaviors indicates developmental disorders, like autism. By 18 months, children try to help their parents with chores without being asked.

On the other hand, as children leave infancy and enter toddlerhood, they share less and their motives for prosocial behavior shift toward self-interest. Sharing begins to be used as a tool. Two-year-olds are more likely to use sharing to resolve a dispute with a peer compared with 1-year-olds. Two-year-olds are also more likely to share with a friend than with a mere acquaintance and less likely to share just because a peer has asked. They are more likely to share a treat they do not especially like. Thus, *self-interest begins to inhibit the impulse to share* by 2 years of age (Hay, Castle, Davies, Demetriou, & Stimson, 1999).

An impulse to respond kindly toward victims is also present very early in life. Toddlers express sympathy as soon as they are able to talk. They also try to comfort

altrendo images/Getty Images

Very young children have a universal impulse to be kind and helpful.

others who are sad or upset. You will even see them rehearse compassion in their pretend play. In one study, 18-month-olds gave a stranger a balloon to cheer her up after an actor had been mean to her by tearing her picture (Vaish, Carpenter, & Tomasello, 2009). The mistreated stranger did not express any emotion, so the toddlers were using their theory of mind (see Chapter 9) to infer that she needed comforting, which shows a remarkable level of sensitivity to others. Over time, preschoolers become more genuinely helpful when others are distressed—a toddler might simply cry when another child cries, but a 4-year-old might fetch the child's comfort blankie. Thus, by age 4 children have a range of helping behaviors that they can draw upon.

Middle Childhood (6 to 12 Years)

In middle childhood, children become more skilled at comforting others who are upset. For example, 6th-graders are more likely to reassure them, whereas kindergarteners are more likely to want to give them a toy. They become more competent than preschoolers at expressing positive emotions toward sad peers in order to cheer them up (Saarni, 1999). This increase in skill partly explains why many societies assign children to care for younger siblings starting at about 6 to 8 years of age (Whiting, 1983).

Elementary children can be organized and charming in their prosocial behavior. A teacher reported that one day she saw "*a little battered automobile festooned with flowers in the school parking lot. Red, pink, orange, yellow, purple flowers were stuck in every crevice of that car, into keyholes and cracks around the doors, the windows, the hood, the gas cap . . . The car belonged to one of the Puerto Rican teachers. Many of her fourth-grade students had recently come from the island. They had sneaked out at lunchtime to decorate the car of their* maestra" (Kidder, 1989, pp. 61–62).

Adolescence (13 to 19 Years)

Adolescents become even more skilled at prosocial behavior. For example, 2-year-olds comfort others by bringing their own favorite blanket to them, whereas adolescents comfort others by trying to solve the problem or helping them control their emotions. Similarly, helpful 5-year-olds might push other children on a swing, but helpful adolescents are able to do much more for their peers, such as help with schoolwork, sports, or disagreements (Bergin et al., 2003).

Despite this greater skill, the *frequency* of prosocial behavior does not increase from toddlerhood to adolescence in natural settings, and may even decrease (Eisenberg et al., 2006). (However, in artificial laboratory studies that involve strangers—such as having children donate prize winnings to an anonymous charity—older youth tend to behave more prosocially than younger children.) How is this possible, given the effort adults put into teaching children to be kind and polite?

There are at least four reasons children may not become more prosocial with age:

1. Adults sometimes train children to inhibit their natural prosocial impulses, such as telling them it is the teacher's job to take care of distressed classmates, not theirs.
2. Children have many antisocial models, both live and in the media, that may counter their prosocial tendencies.
3. Children become better able to regulate their own emotional response, so that they do not impulsively respond to others' distress.

4. Children become more aware of the costs of prosocial behavior and learn to protect their self-interests better. After all, if you give away your cookie, you won't have one.

You learned in Chapter 9 that hedonistic prosocial reasoning, which focuses on "what's in it for me?" may *increase* for some adolescents. As prosocial behavior shifts from being a universal impulse of toddlers to a more controlled choice for older youth, individual differences in prosocial behavior become apparent. Let's look at this next.

Individual Diversity in Prosocial Behavior

Prosocial behavior is almost universal in the first year of life, but by 2 to 3 years of age, there are clear individual differences that remain fairly stable (Vaish et al., 2009). That is, toddlers who are more prosocial than their peers will likely be the most prosocial adolescents. Lizzie is more likely to be prosocial than Ted across childhood. One study even found that sharing in preschool predicted prosocial behavior nineteen years later (Eisenberg et al., 1999). These individual differences have important consequences for children.

What Do Individual Differences in Prosocial Behavior Predict?

Prosocial behavior is linked to academic achievement. Students who are prosocial tend to have higher grades and test scores than less prosocial students, from 1st grade to high school (Miles & Stipek, 2006; Wentzel, 1993).

Prosocial behavior is linked to happiness. For example, adolescents who help their parents at work, or with cleaning and cooking, or tending younger siblings are happier (Telzer & Fuligni, 2009). They may be happier because they feel that they are a better son/daughter and brother/sister. Prosocial students may also be happier because they are better liked by others.

Prosocial behavior is also linked to popularity with peers and teachers. For example, in one study 3- and 4-year-olds were asked to place pictures of their classmates into one of three boxes: liked a lot, kinda liked, and did not like (Denham, McKinley, Couchoud, & Holt, 1990). The best predictor of whether a child was "liked a lot" was prosocial behavior. This is true for older youth as well. Prosocial students may be better liked by peers, less depressed, and have fewer behavior problems in elementary and secondary schools (Bandura, Barbaranelli, Caprara, & Pastorelli, 1996).

Is it possible for students to be overly prosocial? Yes, when students must take on a parenting role because parents are substance users, depressed, or emotionally dependent on their children. For example, preschoolers with severely depressed mothers may be substantially more prosocial than other children (Radke-Yarrow, Zahn-Waxler, Richardson, Susman, & Martinez, 1994). Similarly, elementary children who worry excessively about family members (e.g., hurrying home from school to check on their mother) are also substantially more prosocial than other children (Hay & Pawlby, 2003). Students who feel excessive, chronic, misguided guilt for the distress of others, which in fact is not their fault, might be overly prosocial. Some students who are abused or abandoned may also become too eager to please (Klimes-Dougan & Kistner, 1990). Thus, exceptionally high levels of prosocial behavior in your students may result from difficult home situations; however, as you will see next, in most families prosocial behavior is the result of positive parenting.

What Predicts Individual Differences in Prosocial Behavior?

Are some children just born nicer than others? There is a modest genetic component to prosocial behavior (Gregory, Light-Häusermann, Rijsdijk, & Eley, 2009). However, as you have learned in Chapters 1 and 6, genes interact with experience. Specific experiences that contribute to prosocial behavior are discussed next.

Emotional competence and empathy

In Chapter 8 you learned that emotional competence involves both the ability to control one's own emotions and the ability to read others' emotions. Both abilities are linked to prosocial behavior. Students who can control their own emotions, and fake their emotions in order to protect other's feelings, are more prosocial than other students (Fabes et al., 1999). Students who are more accurate in reading other's emotions are also more prosocial (Denham, Mason, & Couchoud, 1995; Wentzel, Filisetti, & Looney, 2007). These abilities work together because good emotion regulation allows students to respond to others' distress with sympathy, rather than with personal distress. Recall from Chapter 8 that when students feel empathy for someone in distress, they can react with either sympathy or personal distress. In the opening vignette, Lizzie was able to perceive Patrick's distress and felt enough sympathy to come to his aid. In contrast, Ted seemed to feel personal distress.

You might expect that sympathy leads to prosocial behavior. Some studies confirm this, but sympathy is not strongly or consistently linked to more prosocial behavior (Michalik et al., 2007; Vaish et al., 2009). In contrast, personal distress is clearly linked to *less* prosocial behavior. Does it seem puzzling to you that sympathy is not a strong motivating force for prosocial behavior? Consider that in Chapter 9 you learned that moral reasoning also is not always linked to moral behavior. There are forces, such as self-interest, that compete with sympathy and reasoning to prevent a student from behaving prosocially. However, when both the mind and heart work together, students are more likely to be prosocial. Students who have *both* high levels of moral reasoning and sympathy may be the most prosocial (Malti, Gummerum, Keller, & Buchmann, 2009).

Parental responsiveness and attachment

You learned in Chapter 8 that parents' responsiveness to children's emotions is linked to their emotion regulation. It won't surprise you then that responsive parents have more prosocial children (Davidov & Grusec, 2006). When parents meet children's emotional needs, their children become able to meet others' needs. You also learned in Chapter 6 that parents' responsiveness is linked to children's attachment. Secure attachment, in turn, is linked to prosocial behavior. Securely attached children are more affectionate and helpful toward parents and more prosocial toward peers (Bohlin, Hagekull, & Rydell, 2000; Eberly & Montemayor, 1998).

Parents' values

Parents who value prosocial behavior tend to have prosocial children (Eisenberg, Wolchik, Goldberg, & Engle, 1992). For example, 5th-graders are more likely to stand up for others and be careful not to hurt other's feelings if both their mother and father rank prosocial behavior as highly important to them (Hoffman, 1975). Warmth enhances the effects of parents' values. Parents who are warm *and* who hold prosocial values have children who are more prosocial than others (Bergin, 1987). How do children learn their parents' values? One way is during discipline.

Discipline

Children's prosocial behavior is influenced both by what they are disciplined for and the type of discipline. In Chapters 7 and 9 you learned that parents communicate core values to children during discipline encounters based on what they become upset about. If they become upset about unkind behavior, they communicate that kindness is important.

victim-centered induction a form of inductive discipline in which the adult points out how the child's behavior made the victim feel.

Parents who use **victim-centered induction** when children misbehave tend to have more prosocial children (Krevans & Gibbs, 1996). During victim-centered induction, the parent (1) points out how the child's misbehavior affects others, (2) asks the child to imagine being in the others' place, and (3) suggests concrete acts of reparation. Thus, during victim-centered discipline children learn to focus on *others'* well-being. In contrast, power assertion and love-withdrawal turn the child's attention to the *self* because they arouse resentment and anxiety.

Tim Laman / National Geographic/Getty Images

Children become more prosocial when adults accept their offers of help or assign them chores that benefit others.

Reinforcement

Recall from Chapter 3 that behaviorism asserts that reinforcement increases behavior. However, recall from Chapter 7 that tangible rewards can sometimes undermine intrinsic motivation. Does this apply to prosocial behavior? Research confirms that tangible rewards may *decrease* prosocial behavior in the long term (Warneken & Tomasello, 2008). In contrast, praise is linked to increased prosocial behavior, particularly if the praise comes from a respected adult (Mussen & Eisenberg, 2001). In addition, praise may be more powerful if it is directed at the child rather than the act, such as "*You are a good boy*" rather than "*That was a good thing to do*" (Mills & Grusec, 1989).

Practice

Many situations that call for prosocial behavior do not require sophisticated moral reasoning but simply require well-rehearsed habits. Students who are given opportunities to practice prosocial behavior become more prosocial (Mussen & Eisenberg, 2001). Even as young as age 2, if parents let their toddlers help with tasks, like folding clothes, the children become more prosocial than their peers (Bergin, 1987). Similarly, 9- to 14-year-olds become more prosocial if they are assigned household tasks that benefit others rather than just themselves, like preparing dinner or caring for a pet rather than cleaning their own room (Grusec, Goodnow, & Cohen, 1997). However, in conflict-ridden homes with poor parent–child relationships, chores may lead to increased conflict rather than prosocial behavior (Call, Mortimer, & Shanahan, 1995).

You may think that adults always encourage children to practice prosocial behavior. However, if you watch carefully, you will notice that some adults reject children's offers of help because it is faster and easier to do it themselves. They may reject children's offers to wash dishes, bag groceries, and hold the baby. Fortunately, other adults graciously accept such offers.

All of the parenting factors discussed tend to go together. Parents who are warm, hold prosocial values, use induction discipline, and praise their children also tend to provide them with opportunities to practice prosocial behavior.

Gender Diversity in Prosocial Behavior

Girls are more likely than boys to be nominated when researchers ask students or teachers, "Who is nice to others?" Are girls really more prosocial than boys? Most, but not all studies, find clear gender differences favoring girls, from preschool through adolescence (e.g., Caprara, Barbaranelli, & Pastorelli, 2001; Davidov & Grusec, 2006; Pagani, Tremblay, Vitaro, Boulerice, & McDuff, 2001).

Girls and boys may engage in different kinds of prosocial behaviors, and for different reasons. In many societies, for example, nurturing children is the province of women, whereas rescuing people from fires is the province of men. Prosocial behaviors such as providing physical assistance and sharing may be more salient for boys, whereas providing emotional support, keeping confidences, and including everyone may be more salient for girls (Bergin et al., 2003; Hay, 1994).

Classroom Implications of Prosocial Behavior

Prosocial behavior is worth cultivating in the classroom for its own sake. You and your students will be happier in a classroom filled with kind, polite, and cooperative students. Prosocial behavior is also worth cultivating because it is linked to achievement. Prosocial students are more likely to show interest in schoolwork, work independently, take turns, listen, and stay on-task (McClelland & Morrison, 2003).

In addition, students fare better *if their classmates are prosocial.* In Chapter 6 you learned that students with caring teachers have higher GPAs. So do students with caring, prosocial classmates (Jia et al., 2009). Indeed, having prosocial classmates is a protective factor for students who are poor. For example, a study found that 1st-graders from impoverished, unstable homes did not develop more problems if they were in highly prosocial classrooms (Hoglund & Leadbeater, 2004). This is noteworthy because generally students in poverty develop more behavior and emotional problems across the school year.

How can you promote prosocial behavior in your classroom? You have learned part of the answer in previous chapters:

- *Reinforce prosocial behavior* (see Chapters 3 and 7). However, avoid tangible rewards because they can undermine motivation. For example, in one study tangible rewards undermined 3rd-graders' later willingness to tutor 1st-graders and made their tutoring more tense and hostile (Szynal-Brown & Morgan, 1983). Instead, praise students when they are prosocial.

- *Use victim-centered induction.* You learned how to do this in Chapter 7. During discipline, suggest to students how to make reparation. This reduces guilt and teaches students to value others' well-being. It also provides practice of prosocial behavior. In one study, after preschool teachers were trained to use induction, prosocial behavior increased dramatically (Ramaswamy & Bergin, 2009). In cases where one child hurts another, discipline may not be necessary if the transgressor appears to feel guilty and tries to make reparation.
- *Increase students' emotional competence.* You learned how to do this in Chapter 8. Focus on creating an emotionally positive classroom (Jennings & Greenberg, 2009). Help students feel and express gratitude in your classroom. Gratitude is linked to increased prosocial behavior toward others, whether they were the cause of the gratitude or not (Bartlett & DeSteno, 2006; McCullough, Kimeldorf, & Cohen, 2008).
- *Increase students' moral reasoning.* You learned how to do this in Chapter 9. While reasoning alone is a poor predictor of moral behavior, when combined with sympathy it is linked to prosocial behavior.
- *Establish a warm, secure relationship* with students. You learned how to do this in Chapter 6. Secure attachment to the teacher is associated with greater prosocial behavior (Howes & Ritchie, 1999; Mitchell-Copeland, Denham, & DeMulder, 1997). In a classic experiment in a nursery school, a teacher varied how warm she was and how much prosocial behavior she modeled (Yarrow, Scott, & Waxler, 1973). Only under conditions of *both* warmth and modeling did the children increase their prosocial behavior. Warmth from an adult makes imitation of the adult more likely.
- *Espouse prosocial values.* Talk about your values and model prosocial behavior. Students feel cared for by teachers who behave prosocially. Table 10.1 provides students' descriptions of caring and noncaring teachers.

Table 10.1 Student Descriptions of Caring and Noncaring Teachers

Caring Teacher Behavior	Noncaring Teacher Behavior
Helps each student academically. Asks if I need help, calls on me, makes sure I understand.	Doesn't explain things or answer questions, doesn't try to help.
Makes special effort, teaches in a special way, makes class interesting.	Gets off-task, teaches while students aren't paying attention, boring.
Talks to me, pays attention, listens, asks questions.	Screams, yells, ignores, interrupts.
Asks what's wrong, talks to me about my problems, acts as a friend.	Forgets my name, doesn't ask why I'm sad, doesn't care if I do something wrong.
Compliments and encourages, checks work, tells me when I do a good job, praises me.	Sends me to the office, gives bad grades, doesn't correct work.
Trusts me, tells the truth, keeps promises, respects students, avoids hurting students' feelings.	Embarrasses, insults, or picks on students.

Adapted from Wentzel (1997).

Let's next discuss two additional ways you can promote prosocial behavior in your students: help them feel responsible for others and provide opportunities to practice prosocial behavior. Then, we will take a look at a school-based intervention to enhance prosocial behavior.

Help Students Feel Responsible for Others

Students do not help if they believe it is someone else's responsibility. In preschools, teachers respond so swiftly to distress that preschoolers can rarely do anything other than watch a distressed peer (Hay, 1994). School-age children may not go to the aid of another unless given permission to do so, because they would get in trouble if they did. For example, let's look at Mrs. Hessy's elementary classroom:

> *Anna accidentally spilled her colored pencils on the floor. Students around her scurried to help her pick them up. Mrs. Hessy said, "Please get back in your seats. Anna can do it." Later, when another student needed help with an assignment, Blake asked, "Can I help him?" Mrs. Hessy said, "No. I will help him."*

Mrs. Hessy posted a list of classroom rules on the wall that included "Help Others." Yet, she rejected students' overtures of help, making them feel it was not their responsibility. Students learn these subtle lessons early. When asked why they do not help, students indicate that they are not supposed to do anything when adults are available (Caplan & Hay, 1989). You can reverse this lesson by telling students they are responsible for what happens to others in your classroom and accepting their offers to help, even if it is a little inconvenient.

Provide Opportunities to Practice Prosocial Behavior

Practice builds students' prosocial habits. Students should be given opportunities to care for each other (Noddings, 1992). These can include just day-to-day events, as in Mrs. Hessy's classroom, or can be part of a formal school program, such as tutoring other students. Such opportunities can also include community-based service, like food drives. Roughly half of adolescents do volunteer service in their community (Hart, Donnelly, Youniss, & Atkins, 2007). Students who volunteer in the community are more prosocial in the classroom. They are also more likely to have high GPAs; be idealistic, sociable, and religious (much volunteerism is through church); and have prosocial parents.

Is volunteerism good for students? Youth volunteerism predicts many positive outcomes such as self-esteem, responsibility, acceptance of diverse groups, commitment to the community, school bonding, less delinquency, life goals of civic involvement, and advanced moral reasoning (Hart et al., 2007; Stukas, Clary, & Snyder, 1999). Because of these benefits, many high schools and organizations, like the National Honor Society, require community service from students. But do the benefits of volunteerism extend to *mandatory* service? Is it logical to coerce students to behave prosocially? Perhaps. Some studies find mandatory service is linked to greater disengagement from school and less intention to volunteer in the future, but others find it is beneficial (Hart et al.,

> ***Think About This*** Does forcing children to do any activity result in intrinsic motivation for that activity? Could mandatory service promote moral development under any conditions? Draw on what you learned in Chapters 7 and 9 to defend your answer.

2007). Students benefit from mandatory service when it is a high-quality experience. The same is true for voluntary service.

What constitutes a high-quality experience? Service is most beneficial when students meet real needs, interact with recipients (versus anonymous service), serve regularly, have challenging responsibilities, have choice, have a good relationship with those at the service site, work in a group (versus alone), and have opportunity to reflect on the experience such as during class discussion (Youniss, McLellan, Su, & Yates, 1999).

Jim West/PHOTOLIBRARY

Students benefit from voluntary or mandatory service when it is a high-quality experience.

Schoolwide Intervention: The Caring School Community

Schoolwide interventions have been designed to promote prosocial behavior. One evidence-based intervention is the Caring School Community (CSC). The CSC has two components: (1) building a strong sense of community in the school through activities like cross-grade buddy relationships and schoolwide activities for the whole family; (2) developing caring classrooms. Teachers are encouraged to be warm and supportive, use inductive discipline, read "values-rich" literature, encourage cooperation among students, and use an authoritative teaching style. You learned how to do these things in Chapters 6 through 9.

The effects of the CSC program have been measured with diverse students in diverse schools (large/small, rural/urban, poor/wealthy) across the United States. Results indicate that 4th-, 5th-, and 6th-graders who see their classroom as more caring become more cooperative, supportive, and friendly. In addition to these prosocial behaviors, they have higher self-esteem, reading comprehension, academic motivation, and school bonding (Solomon, Battistich, Watson, Schaps, & Lewis, 2000). Effects are strongest in high-poverty schools. In highly caring schools, the poorest students have as positive attitudes toward school as the most affluent students. The U.S. Department of Health and Human Services has recognized the CSC as an exemplary program.

In summary, there are several things you can do to help your students become more prosocial, which in turn may help them be better liked and academically successful. You should recognize substantial overlap with moral and character education from Chapter 9. This is because prosocial behavior *encompasses* morality but goes *beyond* morality. Moral behavior refers to abiding by obligatory, universal laws in order to do what is right. For example, honesty is both moral and prosocial. However, complimenting another child is not moral behavior, nor does it involve moral judgment, but it is prosocial. Such kind behavior is vitally important because it enhances relationships and happiness in others. Next we turn to behavior that has the opposite effect.

Antisocial Behavior and Aggression

As Caleb and his mother enter the office at his high school, his mother loudly swears at him. She threatens Caleb: "Your behavior had better stop! If this principal tells me you've done something else that you haven't told me about, I'm gonna let you have it! Is that clear?" Caleb, humiliated, says in an undertone laced with profanity, "Would you shut up? I heard you. They just don't like me at this school." His mother then begins swearing profusely at the principal and threatening him because he had suspended Caleb. Before her visit is over, other school personnel and a police officer join the confrontation.

Caleb is often in trouble at school and has repeated a grade. Caleb is an antisocial child. If the thought of having students like Caleb in your classroom makes you want to switch careers fast, keep reading. In this section, you will come to understand and learn how to help antisocial students. Caleb needs you, because he is not going to learn social skills from his mother.

Behavior is antisocial if it is aversive, annoying, or harmful to others. In case 4, you were introduced to another antisocial 9th-grader, Preston. Preston is a constant irritant in the classroom, but he has never been suspended. In contrast, Caleb has demonstrated more serious antisocial behavior, has often been suspended, and may not graduate. **Antisocial behavior** includes delinquency (breaking the law, truancy, running away from home, vandalism), substance abuse, and inappropriate sexual activity. It is called *antisocial* because it disrupts the functioning of society. Aggression is a subset of antisocial behavior.

antisocial behavior behavior that disrupts the functioning of society, such as aggression and delinquency.

Aggression and other antisocial behaviors are co-morbid, meaning they often go together. That is, the same youth tend to be violent, sexually promiscuous, and drug using. However, this pattern is not true of all antisocial youth; some are mildly delinquent for a limited time during adolescence and are not aggressive (Burt & Neiderhiser, 2009). Aggression and ADHD are also co-morbid; one- to two-thirds of aggressive students are hyperactive (Offord, Boyle, & Racine, 1991). Aggression, hyperactivity, inattention, and impulsivity together form a cluster called *externalizing* disorders (see Chapter 8). This may surprise you, but aggressive students also tend to have *internalizing* disorders, such as depression and anxiety (Whitbeck, Hoyt, & Wa-Ning, 2000). Seriously antisocial students may be diagnosed with **oppositional defiant disorder** (ODD) and **conduct disorder** (CD). See Box 10.1.

oppositional defiant disorder a clinical diagnosis given to children under age 8 who are excessively antisocial for at least six months.

conduct disorder a clinical diagnosis given to older children, who are excessively delinquent or aggressive for at least six months.

In Chapter 6, we asked you if you had ever heard veteran teachers say, "Kids today just aren't like they used to be." We discussed how neuroticism has increased. Antisocial behavior in the United States has also risen since the 1950s. Children have become more argumentative, disobedient, anxious, depressed, delinquent, aggressive, and tired. More 7- to 16-year-olds had clinical levels of behavior problems in 1999 than in 1976 (Achenbach, Dumenci, & Rescorla, 2003). Antisocial behavior among youth peaked in the 1990s but has stabilized or declined since then; today's youth are less likely to commit violent crime, to use drugs, and have sex than in 1995 (FIFCFS, 2008). The increase in antisocial behavior since the 1950s occurred across gender, ethnicity, and SES and in rural and suburban areas. Still, most students are not antisocial, and those who are can be helped. Because substance use is discussed in

aggression behavior that harms others, or is intended to dominate others. It is a subset of antisocial behavior.

Challenges in Development **Box 10.1**

Conduct Disorder

Adara is a 10th-grade bully. In the classroom, she gives nicknames to classmates based on physical flaws, like "Zit Face." In the hallways, she punches other students or deliberately bumps into them. She criticizes her teacher's appearance and personality, like "That's an ugly sweater." She breaks class rules, is often tardy, and annoys other students by writing in their notebooks.

Adara has conduct disorder. Conduct disorder (CD) is a clinical diagnosis given to students who consistently violate social norms and the rights of others. Students with CD have hostile attribution bias and little guilt or empathy. CD can range from mild (lying, truancy, staying out after curfew) to severe (rape, physical cruelty, breaking and entering). CD is diagnosed in middle childhood or adolescence.

Oppositional defiant disorder (ODD) is a clinical diagnosis given to students under age 8 who are defiant, are hostile toward authority figures, do not accept blame for misbehavior, deliberately annoy others, and are verbally aggressive. Many students with CD, like Adara, had symptoms of ODD earlier. ODD is less severe than conduct disorder. For both ODD and CD diagnoses, antisocial behavior must last for six months and be severe enough to disrupt social or academic functioning (American Psychiatric Association, 2000). That is, brief or typical levels of antisocial behavior do not qualify.

You are likely to have students with ODD or CD in some of your classes. Conduct disorder is one of the most prevalent psychiatric diagnoses of children, occurring in 2 to 16% of children. Both ODD and CD have increased over the past few decades (Achenbach et al., 2003; Farrington, 2009). Boys are two to three times more likely to have CD than girls.

What Does CD Predict? Students with CD, compared to peers, are four times more likely to be friendless and have achievement below what you might expect for their IQ. They are often reckless and prone to injuries. ODD and CD are strongly co-morbid with ADHD, meaning they often occur in the same child (e.g., Trzesniewski et al., 2006). How these students fare in adulthood depends on the severity of their CD and what other problems they have. Boys who have *both* CD and depression or ADHD are two to three times as likely to commit crimes or develop mental illness in adulthood compared with typical boys (Sourander et al., 2007).

What Predicts CD? The most powerful risk factor for ODD and CD is family dysfunction, combined with genetic predisposition (Dodge, 2009). Family dysfunction refers to parental rejection; harsh discipline; abuse; frequent change of caregivers; marital discord; and antisocial, alcoholic, or depressed parents. Adara missed several months of school because her mother and aunt were fighting over custody.

Therapy for CD typically focuses on training parents to reinforce prosocial behavior and to enforce clear and consistent limits on misbehavior without escalating conflict (Dishion & Kavanagh, 2002). That is, parents are taught to behave in accordance with the principles you learned in this chapter and in Chapter 7. Adara's teacher decided to implement these principles, in addition to using humor with Adara. As a result, Adara quit skipping class and became less disruptive. She even became kind and thoughtful toward her teacher; one snowy day Adara offered her coat to her teacher who was headed out the door for bus duty.

Chapter 2 and sexual behavior in Chapter 11, we will focus primarily on aggression next.

Revisiting Case 4

Based on the symptoms of CD and what you know of Preston's behaviors, do you think Preston may have CD? Compare his behavior with that of Caleb. Might Caleb have CD? Justify your answer.

Types of Aggression

Aggression is behavior intended to harm another person. You could also consider forceful attempts to dominate someone else as aggression, even if no obvious harm is done. There are different forms (physical, verbal, social) and different motives (proactive and reactive) for aggression. Understanding these differences is important because they predict different outcomes for students.

Physical, Verbal, and Social Aggression

Physical aggression is hitting, pushing, or fighting. **Verbal aggression** is threatening or name calling. Preston was a master of verbal aggression with comments like "dumb girls like you shouldn't be driving" or "your shoes are ugly." Both physical and verbal aggression are sometimes called *direct* or *overt* because they are easily observed. **Social aggression** involves undermining someone else's relationships or social status (Archer & Coyne, 2005). This might include spreading rumors, refusing to talk to the victim, and excluding the victim from a clique. Social aggression can be conveyed through body language, like rolling the eyes. Social aggression is sometimes called *indirect*, *covert*, or *relational* aggression. Teachers are better at detecting overt than social aggression, although you may sometimes be aware of your students' social aggression.

physical aggression behavior that harms others through physical means such as hitting, pushing, or kicking.

verbal aggression behavior that harms others through verbal means such as threatening or name calling.

social aggression behavior that harms others through manipulating their relationships or peer-group status, such as spreading rumors or excluding the victim from a social clique. It is sometimes called relational aggression.

Physical, verbal, and social aggression are highly correlated (Meehan, Hughes, & Cavell, 2003; Murray-Close, Crick, & Galotti, 2006). This means that most students who use one type of aggression use the others as well. However, the correlations are not perfect, so a student can be high in one but low in other types of aggression. For example, Caleb used all forms of aggression. On the other hand, Preston used both verbal and social aggression, but rarely physical aggression.

Reactive Aggression and Bullying

Aggression can be either reactive or proactive. **Reactive aggression** is provoked retaliation, accompanied by anger or frustration. **Proactive aggression** is a means to achieve personal goals. There are two types of proactive aggression: instrumental and bullying. **Instrumental aggression** is the use of threat or force to obtain something. It is usually goal-oriented rather than person-oriented. For example, in a school lunchroom, Andrew was making an irritating noise by blowing across a straw. Another child threw a small plastic container and hit Andrew's head. Andrew stopped making the noise. The primary goal was not to hurt Andrew, but to stop the noise.

reactive aggression aggression that is aimed at retaliation for a provocation, usually involving anger or frustration.

proactive aggression aggression that is directed at achieving personal objectives, but that was not clearly provoked.

instrumental aggression a type of proactive aggression in which the primary aim is to obtain an object, territory, or privilege, but not to hurt the victim.

Bullying is proactive aggression that is repeated and in which the bully has greater power in some way than the victim (Swearer, Espelage, Vaillancourt, & Hymel, 2010). Both reactive aggression and bullying are considered **hostile aggression** because the *intent is to harm the other.* You might think of reactive aggression as "hot-headed" and bullying as "cold-hearted." In contrast, instrumental aggression is not hostile. Sometimes it is hard to distinguish between these types of aggression, and certainly an act of aggression can have multiple motives. Figure 10.1 helps you understand the types of aggression.

bullying a type of proactive aggression in which the goal is intimidation or dominance over another person that occurs repeatedly over time and involves someone of greater power victimizing someone of lower status or power.

hostile aggression a type of reactive or proactive aggression in which the primary aim is to harm another person.

Not all aggression is bullying. Aggression is bullying when it is repeated; when there is an imbalance of power; and when the aggressor intends to harm, seeks power, and is not remorseful. If two students of similar size have a one-time fight, this is not bullying. If a large student who has a gang of deviant friends standing behind him repeatedly threatens a smaller child, this is bullying. Bullying can be psychological rather than physical, such as when a high-status student shames or ostracizes a low-status student. The most common forms of bullying are making fun of others and spreading rumors (Dinkes, Kemp, & Baum, 2009). Box 10.2 discusses the effects of bullying on victims.

Revisiting Case 4

Does Preston use reactive or proactive aggression? Is it instrumental or hostile? What leads you to this conclusion?

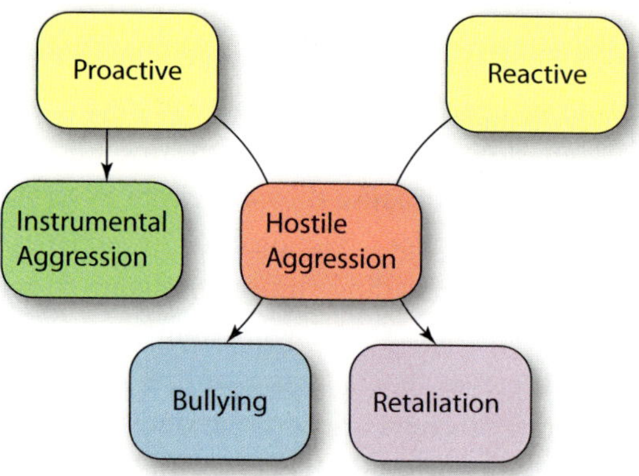

Figure 10.1 Types of Aggression. Proactive and reactive aggression are defined by whether they are in response to a provocation or not. Either can be hostile. Bullying is hostile, proactive aggression. Retaliation is hostile, reactive aggression, or a "hot-headed" response to provocation. Instrumental aggression is nonhostile and proactive. Try to generate an example of each to test your understanding.

One form of bullying that occurs in schools is sexual harassment. For example, the following incident occurred in a rural middle school:

> *A boy hung out in the restroom. When other boys entered he would say, "I'm your husband," slap their bottoms, or tell them they had nice bodies, and that he wanted to "get some of that." Several boys complained to teachers about this harassment. Nothing changed, so a victim decided to "take care of the problem" himself. Fortunately, a teacher stopped him before anyone was hurt.*

Teachers have a legal and moral obligation to stop sexual harassment. The Supreme Court (*Davis v. Monroe County Board of Education*, 119 S.Ct. 1661) ruled that a school's "deliberate indifference" to known harassment is prohibited by Title IX because it undermines victims' education, effectively denying equal access to education. In the legal case, a 5th-grade girl told her teacher that a male classmate was repeatedly touching her, rubbing against her, and speaking to her lewdly. The principal was aware of the problem. The girl was not moved away from the bully for three months. The bully was not disciplined, and his offensive behavior escalated until the case went to court. The court indicated that an isolated instance of name-calling does not constitute victimization, but continued harassment does, and should not be tolerated in schools.

cyberbullying bullying that occurs through interactive technologies.

Bullying primarily takes place on the playground or during recess for younger students, in the corridors and classroom for secondary students, and to a lesser extent on the way to and from school (Rigby, 2002; Whitney & Smith, 1993). Today cyberbullying also takes place on the Internet through aggressive text messages, derogatory websites, and display of compromising pictures (Raskauskas & Stoltz, 2007). For example, youth have taken cell phone photos of peers undressed in the locker room and posted them on websites.

Age Trends in Antisocial Behavior

The type and frequency of aggression changes with age. What is normal for 2-year-olds may not be for 14-year-olds. Let's look at age trends next.

Challenges in Development — Box 10.2

Victims

First-grader Lauren is very small for her age and young for her grade. She appears an easy victim. During the first week of school, a large and older boy in Lauren's class bullies her at recess. He pushes her around the playground. Lauren tells him to stop, she tries to avoid him, she tells the playground supervisors, but still he bullies her. Finally, she bites him, hard. The bullying ends. Apparently Lauren is not an easy victim.

The boy continued to bully other students, but Lauren was not bullied again. Being a victim is a common experience. In elementary, middle, and high schools, roughly one-third of the students may experience some type of victimization each year, like being called names or having items stolen from a locker (Dinkes et al., 2009; Frey et al., 2005; Nylund, Bellmore, Nishina, & Graham, 2007).

Victimization is most often short-lived, particularly for young children, as for Lauren. However, as many as 5 to 20% of students are regularly victimized in a given school year (Dinkes et al., 2009; Haynie et al., 2001). Victims and bullies are often in classes together for years, so students can be chronically victimized. When students transfer from primary to secondary school, so that they become the youngest and smallest students at school, there is a brief surge in victimization even among students who are typically not victims (Nylund et al., 2007). Despite the media hype, cyberbullying is rare; only about 4% of adolescents report being the victims of cyberbullies (Dinkes et al., 2009). Thus, most students are never victimized, some are occasionally, and a smaller number are chronically victimized.

Who Is Victimized? Most chronic victims are submissive. *Submissive victims* tend to be physically weak, insecure, and friendless; they may cry easily and worry excessively (Leadbeater & Hoglund, 2009; Stevens, Van Oost, & de Bourdeaudhuij, 2000). A minority of victims are aggressive. *Aggressive victims* tend to have poor emotion regulation and be hot-headed. They provoke bullies because they irritate. The more aggressive they are, the more victimized they may become over time (Leadbeater & Hoglund, 2009). Some of these aggressive-victims are themselves bullies.

What Might Lead to Victimization? Victims tend to be friendless. Bullies need fear no retaliation from friends of the victim, and the victim is often alone, making victimization easy. Quality of parenting also predicts victimization. Victims tend to have insecure attachment (Smith & Myron-Wilson, 1998). *Submissive victims* tend to have either hostile mothers or overly protective, intensely close mothers, or fathers who are negative and distant. *Aggressive victims* tend to have hostile, aggressive parents, and a history of abuse or father absence (Ladd & Pettit, 2002).

What Are the Consequences of Victimization? The same factors may be both cause and consequence of victimization—depression, low self-esteem, anxiety, friendlessness, and peer rejection. Being a victim increases risk for each of these problems, as well as suicide (Putallaz et al., 2007; Swearer et al., 2010). Victims feel humiliated, anxious, and angry while at school (Nishina & Juvonen, 2005). In Chapter 8 you learned that *these emotions interfere with learning.* Victims also feel less academically competent (Thijs & Verkuyten, 2008). Cyberbullying may be especially traumatic because it can be anonymous and make children feel vulnerable even in their homes (Raskauskas & Stoltz, 2007). *Aggressive bully-victims* fare worse than other victims because they have all the negative outcomes of both bullies and victims (Nansel et al., 2001; Veenstra et al., 2005). When these victims can no longer tolerate the bullying, they may perpetrate serious violence at school.

Should a Victim Seek Your Help? Seeking help can be good or bad. Not seeking help when they need it can put students in danger. Yet seeking help when students should be able to handle the situation themselves may lead other students to see the victim as weak or a tattletale. Ideally, students should seek help *only when it is necessary* (Newman, 2008). Notice that Lauren only sought help after she had tried to stop the bully herself. She did not get help, so she solved the problem as most young children would—with counteraggression.

What Can You Do to Help Victims? The first step is to perceive victimization. Less than half of victims tell teachers they are being bullied, so you have to watch for it (Berger, 2007; Dinkes et al., 2009). When you identify a victim, teach the student to cope using social support or avoidant (rather than anger-venting) coping strategies (see Chapter 8). Help the student establish friendships at school (see Chapter 11). Recruit your school counselor to help address any other problems that may have led to victimization.

Stop the culture of bullying. Teach students to stand up together when they see a peer being bullied, then tell you (you must be willing to do something about it), and then befriend the victim. When victimization stops, the victim's psychological well-being does not necessarily improve (Kochenderfer-Ladd & Wardrop, 2001). This means some victims need help to regain feelings of belonging at school. See Chapter 6 for how to do this.

Early Childhood (Birth to 5 Years)

Infants are not yet capable of aggression, but they are capable of anger as young as 4 months (Sullivan & Lewis, 2003). Try taking away food or restraining an infant's arms and you are likely to see anger. Aggression toward peers, such as fighting over toys, begins around 12 months (Alink et al., 2006). Toddlers primarily engage in *instrumental* aggression that is short-lived. Let's take a peek at 2-year-olds in a preschool classroom:

> *The students are happily catching and throwing balloons, until Payton decides the yellow balloon is his alone. As Luke catches the yellow balloon, Payton yells, "Mine!" He shoves Luke in the chest and snatches the balloon away. Payton smiles, but Luke begins to cry. Payton looks at Luke in surprise, baffled at what is wrong with him. Payton brings Luke his sippy cup to cheer him up.*

Payton did not intend to hurt Luke. He simply wanted the balloon. In toddlers, such instrumental aggression toward a peer is normal in that it does not portend later conduct disorder (Hay, Castle, & Davies, 2000). In addition, young children like Payton are often "happy victimizers," meaning they feel happy after successfully aggressing (Ramos-Marcuse & Arsenio, 2001). Among older school-age children, only antisocial children are happy victimizers.

Physical aggression grows from age 1 to 2, peaks around age 2, and then decreases by age 4. Between 2 and 3 years, as children learn to talk, their physical aggression is replaced with verbal aggression, but they also become less aggressive overall. Language reduces the need for instrumental aggression because children are able to achieve their goals without snatching or hitting. For example, while 2-year-old Payton may shove Luke to get the balloon, by age 4 he can ask for it. Preschoolers may also become less aggressive as they develop self-control, emotional perspective-taking, and theory of mind (see Chapters 7, 8, and 9). However, approximately 13% of 3-year-olds still physically fight with peers (Underwood, 2002) and, on average, 2- to 4-year-olds are the most aggressive of any age group.

Middle Childhood (6 to 12 Years)

Physical aggression diminishes even more in middle childhood and becomes rare when adults are present (Underwood, 2002). Behaviors that may be considered normal in 2-year-olds—temper tantrums, defiance, argumentativeness, irritability—are indicative of serious behavior problems if they are still present at age 8. A diagnosis of conduct disorder is given to children who continue to show frequent physical aggression into middle childhood.

Social aggression may become more apparent in middle childhood. Some researchers believe physical, verbal, and social aggression represent a developmental continuum. Physical aggression is the most immature form, and social aggression is the most mature, not developing until children understand they can harm others through manipulating social status (Bjorkqvist, 2001). Thus, 1st-graders may use less social aggression than 4th-graders, who may use less than 7th-graders (Xie, Farmer, & Cairns, 2003). The opposite pattern is found for physical aggression, as it is replaced by the more subtle verbal and social aggression.

While children are generally less aggressive during middle childhood than during the preschool years, when they are aggressive it is more likely to be *hostile rather than instrumental.* This is because the major cause of aggression is no longer dispute over toys but threat to self-esteem (Hartup, 1974).

Bullying emerges at school entry, and then declines between 7 years of age and adolescence (Rigby, 2002). However, there may be a temporary resurgence in bullying when children first transition to middle/junior high school (Nansel et al., 2001). In elementary school, bullies are not liked, but in middle school some may attain a type of status. For example, some jocks are bullies with status. In addition, some girls who are cool because they act and dress older than their age are bullies. Their social status allows them to get away with bullying.

Adolescence (13 to 19 Years)

Aggression steadily decreases from early childhood through adolescence—other than the temporary spike at the middle school transition (Grunbaum et al., 2002; Nansel et al., 2001). Despite the decrease in aggression, most adolescents are mildly aggressive occasionally, like bickering with siblings or calling someone a name. In contrast, delinquency tends to increase in early adolescence, peaking around ages 14 to 15, and then decreases from 15 to 19 years (Gutman & Eccles, 2007).

A few adolescents continue to be highly aggressive. In a national study of high school students, 6% had carried a weapon to school in the past 30 days and 12% were in a physical fight on school property in the past year (Dinkes et al., 2009).

The aggressive acts of these youth may be criminal. Behaviors that are somewhat tolerated in very young children, like hitting someone, can result in the arrest of an 18-year-old. Crimes are most commonly perpetrated in the late teens and young adulthood (Tremblay, 2000). Half of criminals commit their first offense between ages 14 and 17. Serious violent offense (e.g., rape, robbery, and aggravated assault using a weapon) begins to rise at about age 12, peaks at age 17, and falls off by young adulthood. While most youth stop their antisocial behavior as they enter adulthood, *particularly if they are employed and married*, those who commit crimes as children are more likely to remain career criminals through age 40 (Elliott, 1994).

Individual Diversity in Antisocial Behavior

Some students are more aggressive, and more victimized, than others. Studies in several countries (Norway, Sweden, England, the United States) have found that among school-age youth, between 4 and 27% are bullies and 2 to 10% are both bullies and victims on a regular basis (Berger, 2007).

An individual child's level of aggression is stable; students who are more or less aggressive than their peers tend to stay that way over time (Schaeffer, Petras, Ialongo, Poduska, & Kellam, 2003). In fact, *aggression may be one of the most stable personal traits*; its stability is as great or greater than the stability of IQ. This is the case across ethnic groups in the United States and across countries.[1]

[1]Many studies support this conclusion, a few of which are listed here (Broidy et al., 2003; Guerra, Huesmann, & Spindler, 2003; Ladd & Burgess, 2001; Rigby, 2002; Rubin, Burgess, Dwyer, & Hastings, 2003).

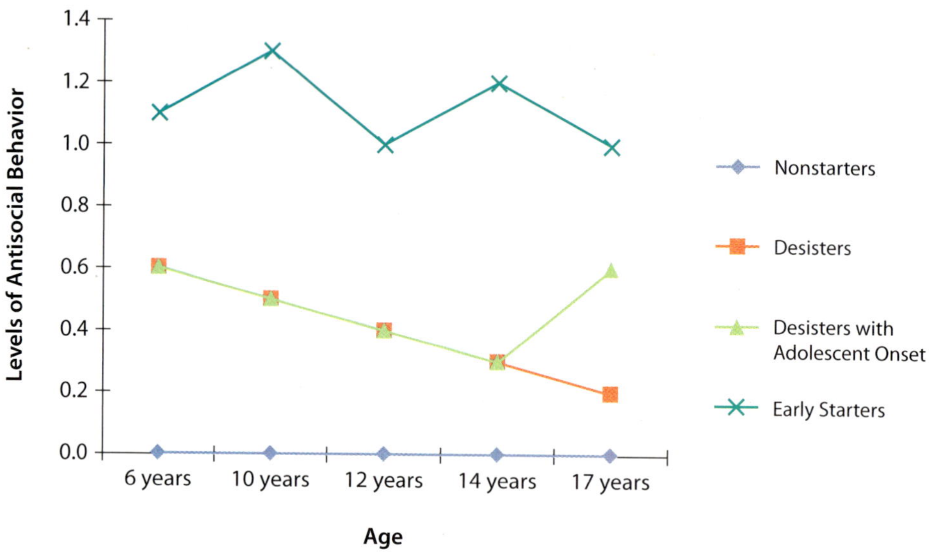

Figure 10.2 Trajectories of Children with Different Levels of Antisocial Behavior. *Nonstarters* are children who seldom show aggression throughout childhood. *Desisters* are children who are aggressive early in childhood, but taper off with age. Some desisters may become temporarily delinquent in adolescence; they have a *late-onset adolescent-limited* pattern. *Early starters* begin early with aggression and antisocial behavior that persists throughout childhood. Can you think of someone you know, or a literary or movie character, who followed each pattern? *Adapted from Broidy et al. (2003) and Piehler & Dishion (2007).*

What Do Individual Differences in Antisocial Behavior Predict?

Most children (about 70 to 80%) are consistently low in aggression throughout childhood or are moderately aggressive in early childhood (about 15%) and taper off to almost no aggression later (Broidy et al., 2003; Pepler, Jiang, Craig, & Connolly, 2008; Shaw, Gilliom, Ingoldsby, & Nagin, 2003). However, some children (about 5 to 15%) begin early with behavior problems that persist throughout childhood (see Figure 10.2). This pattern is called *early-onset persistent.* Thus, an aggressive teen, like Caleb, was probably an aggressive preschooler. Some nonaggressive children engage in a *brief* episode of antisocial behavior in the teens. This pattern is called *late-onset adolescent-limited.* This pattern tends to occur when there is a significant increase in life stress during adolescence (Aguilar, Sroufe, Egeland, & Carlson, 2000; Brennan, Hall, Bor, Najman, & Williams, 2003). These patterns have academic and social consequences for children.

Academic achievement

Antisocial behavior is both a cause and a consequence of low academic achievement. That is, low achievement leads children to act out at school, and acting out leads to low achievement. It is a *bi-directional* effect that has been found across ethnicities. Toddlers with substantial behavior problems are likely to have lower achievement when they are in elementary school (Bub, McCartney, & Willett, 2007). From kindergarten through high school, aggressive students are likely to have attention problems, reading and learning difficulties, lower GPAs, and lower test scores (French & Conrad, 2001; Malecki & Elliot, 2002; Trzesniewski, Moffit, Caspi, Taylor, & Maughan, 2006). However, aggression is more strongly linked to low achievement in high school than in primary grades.

How might antisocial behavior affect academic achievement? Teachers are likely to develop negative relationships with antisocial students (see Chapter 6). The students may then do less homework, disengage from classroom tasks, put less effort into class work, and develop poor academic skills (Kiefer & Ryan, 2008; Stipek & Miles, 2008). In case 4, notice that Preston is not participating in the learning activities. Antisocial students tend to have low achievement even when other risk factors, such as low IQ or family problems, are statistically controlled (Masten et al., 2005).

Social competence

Antisocial behavior is also a cause and a consequence of social rejection. A child who is aggressive may not be rejected immediately in the classroom. However, over time peers become less able to tolerate the aggression. Some aggressive children, particularly girls, feel lonely, but other aggressive children are not lonely and actually feel overly optimistic about their ability to attract friends (Nansel et al., 2001). Preston is likely to believe that he has plenty of friends in class—which is not true.

One of the problems with social rejection is that antisocial children are precluded from opportunities to develop social skills with normal peers. One of Preston's classmates told the visitor to "just ignore him; we always do." Antisocial behavior may follow the pathway depicted in Figure 10.3. First, the child has models of aggression at home in parents and siblings, and is treated harshly. The child becomes aggressive, entering school with poor academic skills and behavior problems. As a result, the child has low achievement and is rejected by normal peers. Parents withdraw from monitoring the child. Then the child, as early as 10 years of age, begins to associate predominantly with other antisocial peers, who promote delinquency. Minor delinquency is followed by alcohol and marijuana use, then hard drug use and serious violent offenses. This progression is partly fostered by schools, which tend to group students together based on academic performance, sometimes creating a pool of antisocial peers.

Aggressive children tend to grow into adults with many problems such as criminality, substance use, drunk driving, low job status, periods of unemployment, spouse abuse, divorce, and harsh parenting of their own children (e.g., Kokko & Pulkkinen, 2000; Nansel et al., 2001; Serbin & Karp, 2003). Fortunately, children can drop off this pathway; not all delinquent teens become antisocial adults. They are more likely to become antisocial adults if they have the early-onset pattern and are *proactive* rather than reactive aggressors. Let's take another look at Caleb, who is on the pathway to adult criminality.

Caleb is hot-headed. Some classmates call him "fatso" to get a rise out of him. He reacts by fighting them every time, so he is often in trouble. His mother can barely tolerate him. She says he is "stupid" and "good for nothing." His father left after abuse charges; he punched Caleb for complaining about his dinner. Caleb is an angry boy who hates school. He only feels accepted among his friends. Together, they smoke marijuana and steal things. One of Caleb's teachers, Mrs. Wentz, decides to form a secure relationship with him. At the same time, Caleb begins to attend church, where he adopts the youth minister as a father figure. Today, as a young adult, Caleb is a skilled tradesman, an involved father of two, and physically fit. He is also divorced—the aggression has not stopped altogether.

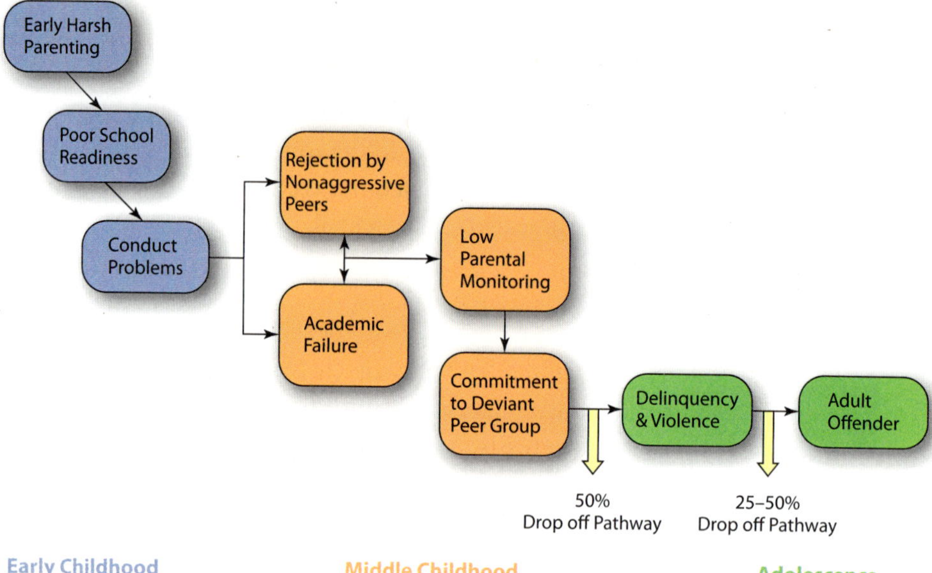

Figure 10.3 Developmental Path of Antisocial Behavior from Preschool through High School. Notice the two points at which children may drop out of this negative pathway. About 50% of children in deviant peer groups as they leave childhood will not become delinquent as teens, and 25 to 50% of delinquent teens will not become adult criminals. *Adapted from Patterson et al. (1989) and Dodge et al. (2008).*

Caleb's story has a happier (although not perfect) ending than prison. How did Caleb get off the trajectory to criminality? Antisocial children are less likely to become antisocial adults if they have at least some prosocial behaviors, develop an admired skill, or become part of a healthy social network (Pulkkinen, 2001). In Caleb's case, his teacher and church became his social network. As a teacher, you can help some children get off the criminal trajectory if you help them develop prosocial behavior and talents or find better social support networks. Later, you will see how Mrs. Wentz helped Caleb.

What Predicts Individual Differences in Antisocial Behavior?

Let's examine four major risk factors for antisocial behavior: (1) genetic and biological factors, (2) parenting practices, (3) self-esteem, and (4) social cognition.

Genetic and biological factors

Delinquency has a strong shared environment component (Burt & Neiderhiser, 2009; Roisman & Fraley, 2006). This means siblings, regardless of their genetic relatedness, have similar levels of vandalism, truancy, and lawbreaking. However, *aggression* has a moderate to strong genetic component; it is about 50% heritable. This finding is supported by twin and adoptive studies in multiple countries.[2]

Four other biological factors are also linked to aggression:

1. *Neurotransmitters.* Low serotonin and norepinephrine levels are linked to impulsiveness, aggression, and attention deficits (Quay, 1993).

[2]Heritability is larger if self-report or parent report is used and smaller if behavior is observed (Brendgen et al., 2008; DiLalla, 2000; Dionne, Boivin, Tremblay, Laplante, & Perusse, 2003; Hudziak, Rudiger, Neale, Heath, & Todd, 2000; Trzesniewski et al., 2006).

2. *Hormones.* Despite stereotypes, a consistent link between normal levels of testosterone and aggression has *not* been found (Archer, 2006). However, extreme levels of testosterone that result from steroid use are linked to aggression, sometimes called "'roid rage." In addition, as you learned in Chapter 2, children with low cortisol levels tend to have behavior problems because they lack normal responses to fear or danger and may have strong anger responses (van Goozen, Fairchild, & Harold, 2008).
3. *Temperament—emotional negativity.* Children with high levels of anger, distress, and irritability are more likely to have behavior problems (Eisenberg et al., 2009; Morrell & Murray, 2003).
4. *Cognitive abilities that have strong genetic components.* Children with low IQ, poor working memory, and less ability to control their attention are more likely to be antisocial (Eisenberg et al., 2009).

Are each of these factors—neurotransmitters, hormones, temperament, and cognitive ability—genetically influenced? They could be. However, whether a child with a genetic tendency for aggression actually becomes aggressive depends on the social environment, such as whether parents are nurturing or harsh. Furthermore, genes cannot explain the rise in children's aggression across the last few decades because there has not been time for genes to evolve.

Think About This How do the concepts of "genotype" and "phenotype" and "gene-environment interaction" from Chapter 1 pertain to antisocial behavior? Scientists have found that adopted children with antisocial biological parents evoke harsher parenting from their adopted parents than do other adoptees (Moffitt, 2005). What type of gene-environment correlation does this support?

Parenting factors

In previous chapters, you learned about several parenting factors that are associated with antisocial behavior in children. Table 10.2 shows which are protective and which are risk factors. Remember that risk factors are not certainties. For example, while abused children have a heightened tendency to become antisocial, many do not.

Table 10.2 Protective and risk factors for antisocial behavior

Protective Factors	Risk Factors
1. *Parental involvement*, such as monitoring, taking interest in, and spending time with children (unless the parent is antisocial). 2. *Parental warmth.* Infants with sensitive, positive parents are likely to be less aggressive into young adulthood. 3. *Firm control.* For example, parents who do not let children stay up late, or do not let 7th-graders decide whether they can date, have children who are less likely to be antisocial. 4. *Religiosity.* This is also linked to children forgiving aggressors rather than retaliating.	1. *Insecure attachment*—at all ages. The effect is weaker for children from two-parent families because stable families are a protective factor. 2. *Power assertive discipline, spanking, and authoritarian parenting.* These factors undermine self-control and create angry, defiant children, even as early as age 4. Secure attachment may protect children from power assertion. 3. *Maternal depression.* This is particularly a risk factor for early-onset antisocial behavior. 4. *Parental smoking.* 5. *Abuse and domestic violence.*

Barber, Stolz, & Olsen (2005); Blatt-Eisengart, Drabick, Monahan, & Steinberg (2009); Bowes et al. (2009); Degnan, Calkins, Keane, & Hill-Soderlund (2008); Fincham (2000); Galambos, Barker, & Almeida (2003); Goldstein, Davis-Kean, & Eccles (2005); Hay et al. (2003); Joussemet et al. (2008); Kochanska, Barry, Stellern, & O'Bleness (2009); Lorber & Egeland (2009); Michiels et al. (2008); Pearce, Jones, Schwab-Stone, & Ruchkin (2003); Shaw et al. (2003); Snyder, Cramer, Afrank, & Patterson (2005); Stevenson-Hinde & Verschueren (2002); Wakschlag et al. (2006).

Unfortunately, many of these risk factors go together. An accumulation of risk factors (see Chapter 1), rather than a single factor alone, more strongly predicts antisocial behavior (Pettit, 2005).

coercive family cycle a cycle of negative reinforcement in hostile families in which negative parenting leads to child aggression, which leads to more parental hostility, which leads to more child aggression, and so on.

Coercive families are particularly problematic. A **coercive family cycle** is created when negative parenting leads to aggression in a child, which causes parents to respond with hostility, which causes the child to retaliate more aggressively, and so on. For example, a parent (or sibling) may yell at Caleb, modeling aggression and anger. Caleb may retaliate with yelling. The exchange escalates with the parent threatening and hitting. Caleb fearfully quits misbehaving, which *negatively reinforces* the parent to use aggression in the future (see Chapter 3). In coercive families, parents often reinforce aggression, but seldom reinforce prosocial behaviors (Snyder & Patterson, 1995). Siblings can also contribute to the cycle because they train each other in aggression and delinquency (Natsuaki, Ge, Reiss, & Neiderhiser, 2009).

Think About This How would an attachment theorist (Chapter 6) explain how parenting causes aggression in children? How would a social learning theorist (Chapter 13) explain how parenting causes aggression in children? Defend your assertions.

Parents can learn to be more positive with their children through intervention, which in turn leads to improvement in the child's behavior (Connell, Dishion, Yasui, & Kavanagh, 2007; Dishion et al., 2008). This means the cycle can be broken; the earlier the better so that children do not develop early-onset aggression.

Self-esteem

You might assume that low self-esteem causes children to behave aggressively. This may be partially true for some children. There is a small correlation between low self-esteem and antisocial behavior (Donnellan, Trzeniewski, Robins, Moffitt, & Caspi, 2005). However, bullies may have *unrealistically high self-esteem*. They may feel superior, more deserving than others, and more likeable than others see them (Salmivalli, Ojanen, Haanpaa, & Peets, 2005). They may rationalize their aggression by derogating, blaming, or belittling their victims (Madhavi et al., 2007). It makes sense that bullies would have high self-esteem because it takes confidence to attack someone. Bullies' self-esteem is based on power.

However, aggression can also result from *threatened self-esteem*. Children with high self-esteem, but whose self-image is fragile, may act aggressively to protect their self-image if someone threatens to make them look bad (Baumeister, Bushman, & Campbell, 2000). These children's self-image is grandiose and vulnerable at the same time. Gaining respect becomes all-important. An important lesson for teachers is that *programs to enhance self-esteem that simply make aggressive students feel more entitled could lead to more aggression*. Programs that help aggressive students learn skills and feel cared for will be more productive.

Social cognition—hostile attribution bias

Antisocial behavior often occurs because of misguided social cognition—that is, faulty thinking about others. In Chapter 9 you learned that low levels of moral judgment are linked to aggression. Another type of social cognition that is linked to aggression is **hostile attribution bias**, where students assume hostile intent on the part of others when it is not clear if there is hostile intent or not. It is akin to a "chip on the shoulder." For example, 1st-grader Allen was not paying attention to where he was going and accidentally bumped into Evan. Evan immediately tackled Allen to the floor and tried to punch him. Evan assumed that Allen ran into him on purpose. A less aggressive child would have assumed it was an accident.

hostile attribution bias the tendency to assume hostile intent on the part of others in situations where it is not clear if there is hostile intent or not.

Children with hostile attribution bias, like Evan, have many negative peer interactions. As a result, they develop a bad reputation, so that their *own* ambiguous behavior is interpreted by *others* as hostile. For example, a 5th-grade girl explained why there was a fight at school one day:

> *Jenny threw a basketball at Cassie in gym. She was supposed to be throwing it to her, but instead it hit the wall behind Cassie and hit her in the face. Cassie told Jenny to apologize and she wouldn't. So Cassie and her friends threatened to beat Jenny up. At least Jenny says they did—I don't really believe it. Besides, it wasn't an accident. Well, it* could *be an accident, but Jenny is mean. I mean, like if it was me, nobody would think I did it on purpose. But* everyone *knows Jenny did it on purpose.*

Jenny is an aggressive child who attracts bias against her—"Jenny is mean." Thus, hostile attribution bias becomes a self-fulfilling prophecy. Aggressive students overreact, then meet with aggression from others, which confirms their belief that others are hostile, which leads to more aggression on their part.

Hostile attribution bias is a type of faulty thinking in social situations. What causes such bias? One possibility is insecure attachment. Notice the similarity between this bias and internal working models from Chapter 6? When parents are hostile and rejecting, their children may develop negative working models of others, so that they expect peers at school to be hostile (McElwain, Booth-LaForce, Lansford, Wu, & Dyer, 2008; Michiels et al., 2008). The social information processing (SIP) model reveals additional thought processes that occur in a child's mind that determine whether the child will behave aggressively (see Box 10.3).

Field Observation

Choose an aggressive and a prosocial child. Separately, tell them the following story:

"Imagine that you get your lunch at school and then walk over to a table where you want to sit. Several other kids are already seated there and there is one empty seat. As you begin to sit down, one of the kids says, 'You can't sit there. It's taken.' A couple of other kids laugh."

Then ask the child, "Why do you think this happened? What would you do or say if this happened to you?" Analyze each child's thinking about the situation and their emotional reaction (from Burks, Laird, Dodge, Petit, & Bates, 1999). Is there evidence of hostile attribution bias?

In summary, there are many risk factors for antisocial behavior. In Figure 10.3, we gave you a fairly simple model of how risk factors cascade over time. It begins with harsh parenting and ends with an antisocial youth. Reality is a little more complicated. Imagine combining Figure 10.3 with the bioecological model. According to the bioecological model, at each point in time the child's aggression is influenced by (1) biology; (2) thoughts about others and the self; (3) social experiences besides parenting, like low-quality child care; and (4) cultural factors, like violent media. Harsh parenting has a larger effect than biological risk factors in predicting serious aggression (Brennan et al., 2003). However, in later chapters you will learn that peers, media, child care, and divorce also play a role in predicting antisocial behavior.

Group Diversity in Antisocial Behavior

Both gender and poverty are linked to antisocial behavior. Let's take a look at group differences in aggression next.

Gender

Perhaps the single most robust gender difference in child development is that boys are more aggressive than girls. This difference holds across SES groups and across

Theories & Theorists **Box 10.3**

The Social Information Processing Model

Dozens of students are eating lunch in the high school's outdoor courtyard. Rob and Marshall are horsing around. Rob throws his apple core at Marshall. Marshall ducks, so the core hits Katie instead. Katie immediately picks up her drink and throws it at Rob, splattering it all over his clothes.

Why did Katie retaliate? Partly because she assumed Rob did it on purpose. Other student witnesses said they assumed it was an accident, and that Katie was "a jerk." Students' behavior is influenced by their interpretation of the situation, or by their *processing of social information.* Figure 10.4 shows one model of social information processing (SIP) (Crick & Dodge, 1994; Lemerise & Arsenio, 2000). The figure makes it appear that each step happens sequentially, but in reality the steps are rapid, occurring at the same time, with each step looping back to inform the previous step. Most processing is probably not conscious. Table 10.3 explains the steps of the model.

Figure 10.4 Social Information Processing Model. Step 2 is where hostile attribution bias and theory of mind take effect. Step 5 is where empathy and moral judgment take effect. Use one of the vignettes in the chapter and follow the child's thinking through this model. *Adapted from Lemerise & Arsenio (2000).*

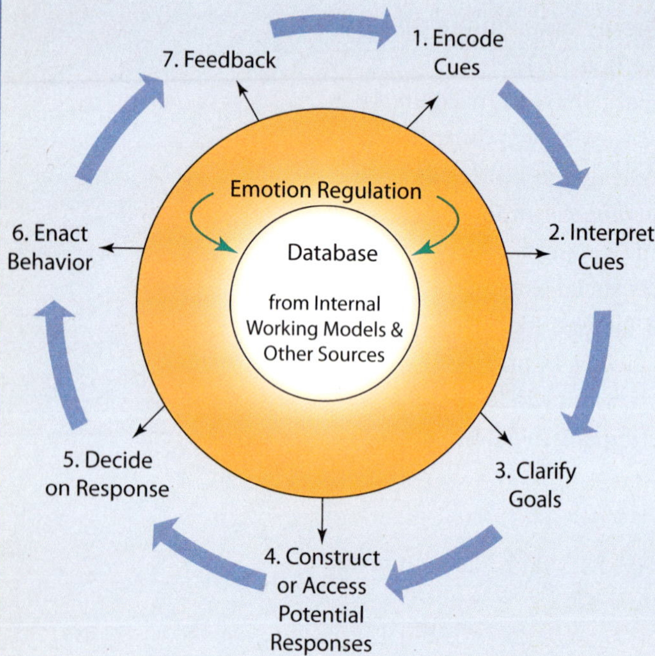

Hostile attribution bias occurs at step 2, when students attribute intent to others' behavior. Attributing intent is easy to do when the cues are clear. However, in many social situations, intent is not clear and has to be inferred. Students then fill in missing information from their database of memories from past social experience. Usually this database is helpful because students do not have to decide what to do in every new encounter. However, this database is a problem if it is hostile. In the example at the beginning of this box, the apple thrower's intent was not clear, but Katie assumed hostile intent. The more ambiguous the situation, the more students have to rely on their database, distortions and all.

What Difference Does Social Information Processing Make? Appropriate processing leads to social competence, but distorted processing or bias can lead to aggression. Aggressive students have biases at several steps. They pay more attention to aggressive cues and attribute hostile intent to others. They generate fewer possible responses, and the responses they generate are more likely to be aggressive. Bullies are more likely to view aggression as morally acceptable, such as "it is OK to beat someone up who deserves it" (Paciello, Fida, Tramontano, Lupinetti, & Caprara, 2008). They believe the benefits of aggression outweigh possible punishment. If aggression is successful, the student is likely to become even more aggressive. These information processing biases have been found from preschool to adolescence (Arsenio, Adams, & Gold, 2009; Fontaine, Yang, Dodge, Pettit, & Bates, 2009).

On the positive side, *prosocial* students have the opposite pattern of biases. Prosocial students are more likely to assume kind intent in ambiguous situations. They are also more likely to think that aggressive solutions are morally bad and that prosocial solutions are best. They hold goals of maintaining relationships, even with a provoking peer. For example, when another child takes their seat at lunch, they are more motivated to maintain good relationships than to get their seat back.

(continued)

Theories & Theorists (continued) Box 10.3

Table 10.3 Components of the social information processing model

Step	Description	Example
1. Encode cues	Students read others' emotions and the situation. In any social situation, there are more cues than can be processed, so each student must select which to attend to.	A student is waiting for another student to pass his test back to him. The other student drops the test on the floor.
2. Interpret cues	Students use their *theory of mind* and *internal working models* to infer the other's intention, and generate emotions.	He did it on purpose. I feel anger.
3. Clarify goals	Goals come from emotions, instruction, modeling (What would my dad do?), cultural norms, the media (What would Harry Potter do?), and so forth. Students can have multiple, competing goals.	Do I want to maintain my relationship with him? Get even? Stay out of trouble?
4. Construct or access potential responses	Students can access responses from memory, or a new behavior may be generated.	Glare at him and roll my eyes. Or, act like I don't care. Or, tell the teacher. Or, slug him.
5. Decide on response	Students evaluate the selected response. *Moral judgment* may be activated. Students have expectations about the outcomes of each response, and their ability to pull it off. This can be conscious, but is more likely based on well-worn scripts. Impulsive students may not consider options, but simply act on the first response that comes to mind.	It is morally OK to slug him if he deserves it. I don't have good enough emotion regulation ability to act like I don't care. My teacher won't help; she doesn't like me. I'm good at slugging.
6. Enact behavior	Students' behavior can be simply a display of emotion (e.g., a glare) or more active.	Slug him.
7. Feedback	Students evaluate the outcome. If it wasn't successful, they may repeat the effort, select a different strategy, or abandon the goal.	I feel successful. I showed him not to mess with me.
8. Encode cue	The cycle begins again.	Here comes the teacher!

nations, from Britain to Ethiopia to Mexico. This difference occurs early and persists through adulthood (Joussemet et al., 2008). Even before age 2, boys grab, push, shove, and hit more than girls (Alink et al., 2006; Baillargeon et al., 2007). Gender differences get larger with age. Boys continue to be more aggressive, dishonest, disruptive, and delinquent than girls from elementary through high school (Gutman & Eccles, 2007; Ho, Bluestein, & Jenkins, 2008).

Some people believe that while boys are more physically aggressive than girls, girls are more socially aggressive, like gossiping or excluding peers. This "mean girls" view may be just a stereotype (Underwood, Galen, & Paquette, 2001). Where might this stereotype come from? Although girls are *less often aggressive*, by 4th grade *when girls are aggressive*, they are more likely to use social aggression than physical aggression, especially gossip (Putallaz et al., 2007; Xie et al., 2003). However, dozens of studies across countries have found that boys are socially aggressive as often, if not more often, as girls (Card, Stucky, Sawalani, & Little, 2008). This makes sense because physical, verbal, and social aggression are highly correlated.

Bj rn Andr ©n/Nordic Photos/Photolibrary

Boys are more aggressive than girls. This is the most robust gender difference in behavior.

Socioeconomic Status

On average, children from low-SES homes are more likely to be antisocial than high-SES children (Bradley & Corwyn, 2002). Recall from Chapter 2 that one exception is that high-SES children tend to use more alcohol and other drugs. Low-SES children have higher rates of aggression when they begin school and increase in antisocial behavior across the school years (Aber, Brown, & Jones, 2003). The link between SES and antisocial behavior has been found in many countries like the United States, England, Scotland, and the Netherlands, but not in Sweden, Spain, or Portugal (Rigby, 2002).

Why is there a link between SES and antisocial behavior? One reason may be exposure. Low-SES students tend to use more-violent media, live in more-violent neighborhoods, and experience harsher parenting than middle- or high-SES students (Dodge, Pettit, Bates, & Valente, 1995; Evans, 2004). For example, in one study low-SES parents were hostile toward their kindergarteners on average every two minutes while playing and reading together. The more hostile the parent, the more aggressive the child was on the school playground (Snyder et al., 2005). Parents who feel financial stress when they are not able to pay the bills tend to treat their children with more hostility (Williams, Conger, & Blozis, 2007). This fits the family stress model from Chapter 1. Children who have hostile parents are likely to develop hostile attribution bias. They tend to have stronger physiological reactions, like a rapidly beating heart, in ambiguous situations (Chen, Langer, Raphaelson, & Matthews, 2005).

Many low-SES children are not aggressive. Those who are *not* aggressive have less-harsh parents with less substance use than low-SES children who are aggressive (Ackerman, Brown, & Izard, 2003). Children's aggression may change when risk factors change, such as a mother's boyfriend moving in or out or parental drug use increasing or decreasing.

Ethnicity

In many countries, belonging to an ethnic minority is associated with aggression. Adults of minority status tend to be victims of discrimination, have low income, and have less education. Minority children are more likely than majority children to have harsh or single parents and other risk factors. Minority children tend to aggress toward other minority children (Rigby, 2002).

In the United States, large studies of thousands of youth have found that African American and Hispanic youth are more likely than White youth to be both physically and socially aggressive (Blum et al., 2000; Putallaz et al., 2007). However, differences in the percentage of African American (36%) and European American (25%) 17-year-old males who have been violent are not as large as differences in arrest rates, which are five times higher for African American males. This means that White youth are less likely to be arrested for the same offenses for which Black youth are arrested (Elliott, 1994). In addition, extreme violence at school, like school shootings, are most likely to be perpetrated by White, rural boys (Brown, Osterman, & Barnes, 2009).

Classroom Implications of Antisocial Behavior

Three girls are working at a table. Gretchen (the victim) joins them. As she approaches the table, Kay (the bully) says, "I can't wait until recess, because I hate you, and I am going to beat you up." Gretchen threatens to tell the teacher. Kay responds, "Tell her. I don't care," and then chases Gretchen away. A classmate warns Kay: "You better not. You'll get in all the trouble." Gretchen comes back to the table. Kay tries to hit her across the table. A classmate says, "Leave her alone." Gretchen tells the teacher. The teacher says, "Don't worry because if Kay hurts you, she will get in trouble." (Adapted from Atlas & Pepler, 1998, p. 99)

This bullying is occurring in an elementary classroom. As many as two aggressive incidents per hour may occur in elementary classrooms, and even more often in the lunchroom and playground (Grossman et al., 1997; Pellegrini & Bartini, 2000). Due to age trends in aggression, preschool classrooms are likely to have more incidents of aggression, like Payton shoving Luke for the balloon. In contrast, secondary classrooms are likely to have fewer incidents. One exception to the downward trend in aggression is that there is a temporary spike in bullying at the transition to middle school (Nylund et al., 2007).

Often peers do not intervene to help victims of aggression. They may feel it is not their business, or fear they may become the target, or don't care, or simply don't know what to do (Stevens et al., 2000). Courageous students who defend victims tend to have better emotion regulation, secure attachment, empathy, prosocial orientation, and high self-esteem compared to passive bystanders (Nickerson, Mele, & Princiotta, 2008). Teachers often do not intervene to stop aggression; for example, the teacher did nothing to stop Kay's aggression (Xie et al., 2003). Thus, *aggressors often get away with misbehavior at school.*

Levels of aggression vary widely by school and by classroom. In some classrooms as few as 1% of the interactions are aggressive, but in other classrooms as many as 20% are (Cairns & Cairns, 1994; Kuppens, Grietens, Onghena, Michiels, & Subramanian, 2008). Schools that are large, overcrowded, and have more low-SES students tend to have more bullying (Bowes et al., 2009). However, some schools are oases of peace despite being in poor, violent communities, because of caring relationships among staff and students (Astor, Benbenishty, & Estrada, 2009).

Reducing Bullying and Aggression

How can you stop bullying, reduce aggression, and create such an oasis of peace? Once again, you have learned part of the answer in previous chapters—that is, by addressing the larger issue of promoting your students' emotional and academic competence, as well as their prosocial behavior. This includes:

- *Eliminate hunger and tiredness* (see Chapter 2). Hunger and tiredness foster aggression (Anderson, 2001). For example, allow a snack if students must wait too long for lunch. Let parents know when students are overtired in your class.
- *Avoid using retention* (see Chapter 1). Some teachers assume that if given an extra year to mature, aggressive students will behave better. However, retention is associated with *increased* aggression at school (Pagani et al., 2001).

- *Promote school bonding through warm teacher–student relationships and participation in extracurricular activities.* You learned how to do this in Chapter 6. Attachment in school is linked to greater classroom participation, positive behavior, and liking of school regardless of how aggressive students are to begin with (Ladd & Burgess, 2001; Meehan et al., 2003).
- *Avoid power-assertive discipline* (see Chapter 7). Power assertion causes resentment and models aggressive interaction styles. In particular, avoid using suspension because it undermines students' academic skills.
- *Be thoughtful about what behavior you reinforce* (see Chapter 3). Aggressive students are reinforced when they get what they want through aggression. Peers can inadvertently reinforce bullies by becoming an audience for them.
- *Build academic skills* (see Chapter 5). Interventions that improve students' academic skills result in less antisocial behavior, which suggests that low achievement causes aggression (McEvoy & Welker, 2000). In fact, interventions that specifically target aggressive behavior may not be any more effective for reducing aggression than those that target academic skills (Wilson, Lipsey, & Derzon, 2003).

These six factors should be familiar to you by now. They are powerful classroom factors that influence many child outcomes. Four more guidelines apply more narrowly to stopping bullying and other forms of aggression:

- *Involve all students in learning.* It is natural to want to interact more with prosocial students than with aggressive students. However, when teachers do not attend to their difficult students, call on them, or provide information to them, the students become even less engaged in the classroom (Stipek, 2001).
- *Create a school climate that does not accept bullying.* Make school rules against bullying explicit, and enforce them. Don't gloss over aggression, like letting star athletes or teachers' pets get away with bullying. Teach student bystanders to stand up for victims or report bullying, but not to passively watch or reward bullies with attention (Olweus, 1994; Swearer et al., 2010).
- *Provide supervision.* Most aggression in class takes place when students work on solitary or small-group tasks, like Gretchen and Kay were doing, but seldom during teacher-led activities. There is more aggression in the lunchroom and playground when there is less adult supervision (Mooij, 1999). However, we do not want to leave the impression that whenever teachers are absent aggression reigns. Even on unsupervised bus rides, students tend to be more prosocial than aggressive toward each other (Galliger, Tisak, & Tisak, 2008).
- *Screen for behavior problems early.* Aggression becomes stable at an early age and is difficult to change. Students who are at high risk for conduct problems can be identified as early as 3 years of age because they are impulsive, irritable, and noncompliant. Primary-grade teachers should be especially concerned about students who have a high ratio of negative to positive behaviors. Such students should receive intervention, preferably before age 8 (Patterson, DeBaryshe, & Ramsey, 1989). However, even adolescents can benefit from intervention.

These guidelines will help you reduce aggression in your students, even in bullies like Kay. Let's see how Caleb's biology teacher, Mrs. Wentz, applied some of these guidelines:

When Caleb returned from a three-day suspension, a student made a derogatory remark about having Caleb back. Mrs. Wentz stopped the class and held an impromtu discussion about how such remarks would make Caleb feel. She said their role was not to hold mistakes over each other, but rather to model better behavior and help each other.

Mrs. Wentz began talking with Caleb about things that interested him. He began hanging out in her classroom, sometimes straightening chairs and feeding the pets. Mrs. Wentz said he "soaked up positive attention," yet he would suddenly test her by misbehaving, as though he wanted her to yell at him. Mrs. Wentz refused to give in; she used induction instead. Caleb was the most difficult child Mrs. Wentz had in twenty-five years of teaching. However, she knew she had made a difference on the day he came to her to help him resolve a conflict with a classmate, rather than fighting his way through it.

The majority of students are not aggressive like Caleb; a small number of students enact most of the aggression at school. For example, a study of low-SES schools in the Los Angeles area found that only about 15% of students accounted for 87% of the office referrals (Hudley & Graham, 1993). These highly aggressive students may need to see a counselor.

School-Based Counseling Interventions

Counselor-led interventions typically focus on promoting more positive parent–child interaction, reducing students' hostile attribution bias, or improving conflict resolution skills (Connell et al., 2007; Dodge, Dishion, & Lansford, 2006; Hudley, Graham, & Taylor, 2007). In schools with high levels of bullying, counselors may lead a schoolwide anti-bullying program. A famous program was implemented nationwide in Norway. It resulted in a 50% reduction in antisocial behaviors (Olweus, 1994). How did they reduce bullying? By implementing the same guidelines discussed earlier.

Programs similar to Norway's have been adopted in Canada, England, the United States, and the Netherlands. However, most anti-bullying programs are not as successful as Norway's (Swearer et al., 2010). One review of research found that 33% of programs had small effects, and 67% had negligible or *negative* effects (Smith, Schneider, Smith, & Ananiadou, 2004). Negative effects? Interventions that are implemented in a halfhearted way, or that *group deviant youth together* (who then promote each others' problems) can actually be harmful (Dodge et al., 2006). Effective interventions may reduce aggression, but they usually do not eliminate it completely.

© Cindy Charles/PhotoEdit

You can teach your students to have better conflict resolution skills.

Despite this cautionary note, some school-based interventions are successful. Expert-led programs can translate into about half as many fights at school, and a 25 to 33% reduction in disruptive behavior (Wilson & Lipsey, 2007). In one simple intervention, aggressive 12- to 15-year-olds with fragile self-esteem were asked to write about the skills or attributes they value most in themselves (e.g., artistic, athletic, sense of humor). They were less aggressive over the next several weeks, according to their classmates (Thomaes, Bushman, Orobio de Castro, Cohen, & Denissen, 2009). The website accompanying this text summarizes effective interventions that have been evaluated with rigorous scientific methods. This resource may help you select a program appropriate for your school. Research suggests that it is important to choose a program that is a good fit for you and your school (S. J. Wilson & Lipsey, 2007). Let's turn next to how to resolve one cause of aggression: conflict.

Conflict Resolution

Two Latina high school students were talking in Spanish. An African American girl asked them not to use Spanish, and they agreed. However, two other African American students defended the rights of Latinos to speak Spanish, and a fight nearly erupted before a teacher intervened. The teacher talked with each student individually in the hall to quell the conflict. (adapted from Lustig, 1997, p. 583)

conflict the behavior of one person interferes with the goals of another person who resists or protests the behavior. It is not the same as aggression.

These girls experienced conflict. **Conflict** occurs when the behavior of one person interferes with the goals of another person, who then resists or protests. Conflict is inherent in all social relationships. Conflict can be as harmless as two children disagreeing on what to play, or it can involve serious aggression. *Conflict and aggression are not the same* because aggression involves intent to harm, but conflict does not. However, conflict can be the result or cause of aggression, as it almost was for these girls, and as it was for 2-year-old Payton who wanted his balloon back.

Do you think of conflict as bad? Actually, nonaggressive, day-to-day conflict—such as disagreeing whether to play soccer or dodgeball during recess—can be good for students because it helps them learn to negotiate and problem-solve. It helps them understand justice, fairness, and equality. It helps them refine social skills and emotion regulation. Nonaggressive conflict does not interrupt relationships or even activity much; students go back to playing together following conflict episodes. However, conflict can be disruptive if it is not resolved well.

How Should Conflict Be Resolved?

There are three main types of conflict resolution: (1) *compromise*, which means to negotiate, share, or take turns, as each side concedes something; (2) *disengagement*, which means to walk away, stop the discussion, and change the activity or topic; and (3) *coercion*, which means to command or aggress so that one side submits (Laursen, Finkelstein, & Betts, 2001).

There are two goals in most conflict situations: to (1) achieve your own aims and (2) maintain the relationship. The optimal way to resolve a conflict depends on the importance of each goal. A *constructive* conflict resolution occurs when each child is satisfied with the outcome, the relationship between the children is improved, and their ability to resolve future conflicts is enhanced.

Age Trends in Conflict Resolution

The amount of conflict children have, its source, and how they resolve it changes with age.

Early Childhood (Birth to 5 Years)

Conflict is present early in life. By 8 months, infants protest others' behavior. Between ages 1 and 7, children may have conflict every three to twelve minutes, depending on the age and setting (Chen, Fein, Killen, & Tam, 2001; Miller, Danaher, & Forbes, 1986). Thus, if you think young children are often in conflict, you are right. However, most of their conflicts are brief, lasting less than a minute.

The sources of conflict change with age (Chen et al., 2001). Toddlers mainly have conflict over objects, like Payton's balloon, while older preschoolers argue over social control, like who has to be the "baby" during play. Preschoolers also often have conflict over who can join the group. When children try to enter an ongoing playgroup, the group resists about half of the time (Shantz, 1987).

Ability to solve conflicts improves with age. Two-year-olds resolve disputes with words and use more prosocial solutions than 1-year-olds, like offering one toy in exchange for another (Caplan, Vespo, Pederson, & Hay, 1991). Four-year-olds are even more skilled. About half of 4-year-olds, but only a quarter of 2-year-olds, can resolve their own conflicts, and 4-year-olds use more-sophisticated strategies such as saying, *"How about we share it?"* rather than just saying, *"No! Mine!"*

Middle Childhood and Adolescence (6 to 19 Years)

Ability to resolve conflicts continues to improve throughout childhood (Laursen et al., 2001). Coercion is used less often, and disengagement is used more often than among preschoolers. Even adolescents most often resolve conflicts with disengagement rather than compromise or coercion. Not until young adulthood are conflicts more often resolved with compromise.

In summary, from preschool to young adulthood, there is a decrease in coercion that is first replaced with disengagement and then finally with compromise. At all ages, students say they prefer compromise in hypothetical situations, but in actual conflict they may resort to coercion. Thus, preference for compromise does not translate into actual behavior until young adulthood.

Individual Diversity in Conflict Resolution

Some children master compromise at young ages, while some adults still rely on coercion. In this section we will address what these individual differences mean and how they might come about.

What Do Conflict Resolution Skills Predict?

Students with good conflict resolution skills achieve their personal goals while also maintaining healthy relationships. Not surprisingly, such students are liked by peers more than are students with poor skills. From preschool on, well-liked students use more compromise, while rejected students use more coercion in peer conflict (McElwain, Olson, & Volling, 2002).

Students who can resolve conflict without "giving in" tend to be the most socially competent. For example, in one study when a conflict involved a peer taking something the child had, well-liked 4th- and 5th-graders were most likely to endorse verbal—but not physical—assertiveness. They said they would not share, but they would politely request the object back (Asher & Hopmeyer, 1997). Good conflict resolution does not involve caving in to another, but it also does not involve escalating conflict.

BananaStock/Jupiter Images

When parents teach their children to resolve conflict through compromise, sibling conflict becomes a training ground for good social skills.

What Predicts Conflict Resolution Skills?

Home is a training ground for conflict resolution. Some of the parenting factors that have been discussed in Chapters 6 through 9 are related to conflict resolution skills. Specifically, *authoritative parents* model negotiation and compromise. In addition, parents of *securely attached* children have high-quality conflict; they are more likely to compromise and justify their side of an argument without aggravation (Laible, Panfile, & Makariev, 2008). Furthermore, parenting that promotes *empathy*, *emotion regulation*, *theory of mind*, and *moral judgment* also promotes conflict resolution skills, because each of these abilities is needed to constructively resolve conflict. In Chapter 8 you learned that siblings provide opportunity to learn emotional competence. They also provide opportunity to learn conflict resolution skills.

sibling rivalry conflict between siblings due to jealousy over parental love and attention. The concept was emphasized by Freud.

Sibling conflict tends to be more frequent and intense than conflict in other relationships. What is the primary cause of sibling conflict? Freud thought it was rivalry for parental love. Freud made the term **sibling rivalry** popular. He argued that when a sibling is born

> *what the child grudges the unwanted intruder and rival is not only the suckling but all the other signs of maternal care. It feels that it has been dethroned . . . ; it casts a jealous hatred upon the new baby and develops a grievance against the faithless mother . . . It becomes "naughty" . . . and disobedient and goes back on the advances it has made towards controlling its excretions.* (Freud, 1933/1964, pp. 152–153)

Freud claimed that such sibling rivalry and regression of the older child when a baby is born are self-evident. However, the exuberant delight of a young child with a newborn sibling is also self-evident. Despite Freud's concern, rivalry is reported by only about 9% of children. Sibling rivalry may be limited to families where parents mishandle sibling conflict or play favorites. Most sibling conflict is more mundane—it is most often about sharing personal possessions, like one child using another's bike. The next most common sources of conflict are physical aggression and general annoyance with the sibling (McGuire, Manke, Eftekhari, & Dunn, 2000). Concern about who is being treated better by parents is the least common source of conflict, even though siblings are exquisitely aware of and willing to remind parents of any unfairness.

What happens when siblings squabble? *Both* older and younger siblings say that the *other* sibling usually initiates the conflict, but that the older sibling most often wins (McGuire et al., 2000). Compromise, rather than coercion, is more likely when siblings have a good relationship (Recchia & Howe, 2009). Yet, sibling conflicts rarely involve spontaneous compromise, and about half the time end with parent intervention (Ross, Ross, Stein, & Trabasso, 2006). Following parent intervention, children are more likely to compromise. Thus, skilled parents scaffold conflict resolution skills during sibling conflict. However, parents who have limited resolution skills themselves cannot do this. When unskilled parents are trained to mediate their children's conflicts, children develop theory of mind, read others' emotions better, and solve conflict more constructively (Smith & Ross, 2007).

Group Diversity in Conflict Resolution

Approaches to conflict resolution, and a teacher's role in student conflict, varies by gender and culture. Let's look at these differences next.

Gender

Boys may engage in somewhat more conflict than girls. For example, in one study 5- and 7-year-old boys averaged fifty-six conflicts during seven hours of group play, while girls averaged forty (Miller et al., 1986). This suggests there is plenty of conflict in both girls' and boys' play. In another study, as girls played hopscotch they carefully watched for opponents to step on a line, shouted out infractions, and negotiated rules (Goodwin, 1998). This conflict and its resolution were part of the fun.

Once involved in a conflict, boys may use coercion more, and girls may use disengagement more. Elementary-aged girls are more likely to seek teachers' help to resolve conflict than are boys. Girls are particularly likely to seek help when the aggressor is a boy (Newman, Murray, & Lussier, 2001).

Ethnicity

Ethnic groups may vary in their approach to conflict resolution. For example, in the study of hopscotch just mentioned, African American and Latina girls were more forceful than White girls when enforcing or resisting rules ("You hit the line." "I AIN'T HIT NO LINE!"). In contrast, the White girls often showed uncertainty or said that it was OK if someone accidentally jumped on the line (Goodwin, 1998). In another study, White girls found "the teasing, oppositional style of Latina and African-American girls to be threatening, bossy, and mean, while African-American and Latina girls saw the mitigated and polite style of middle-class White girls as patronizing" (Corsaro, 1997, p. 181). This difference in conflict style is a type of cultural mismatch discussed in Chapter 1.

Cross-National Comparisons

Cultures influence which conflict resolution tactics are most appropriate. For example, collectivist cultures may emphasize resolutions that maintain relationships while individualist cultures may emphasize resolutions that protect individual choices.

Cultures also dictate whether teachers should intervene in conflict. For example, Japanese teachers try to avoid intervening. If Japanese preschoolers ask for teacher intervention, they are told, "*Work it out with each other*" (Killen & Sueyoski, 1995). If a child is actually harming another, teachers may use induction. They believe that if you explain to children how their behavior affects others, children will stop misbehaving. When U.S. teachers watch a video of a Japanese preschool in which a boy punches and kicks another boy, they tend to be appalled that the teacher does not intervene (Tobin, 1989). Yet, Japanese teachers approve when the teacher simply tells the victim to *"Go tell him you do not like to be hit."* U.S. teachers do not expect preschoolers to solve their own peer conflict; they intervene frequently.

Classroom Implications of Conflict Resolution

Major and minor conflicts occur frequently at school. If your students learn to resolve conflict quickly and effectively, there will be both social and academic payoffs. Students with good resolution skills are liked better, spend more time on classroom tasks, and have higher achievement. How can you help your students develop good resolution skills?

Promoting Conflict Resolution Skills

Some methods of helping students develop conflict resolution skills were discussed in previous chapters:

- *Be authoritative* (see Chapter 7). Authoritative teachers model negotiation, give-and-take, fairness, and respect for others' views.
- *Promote emotional competence in your students* (see Chapter 8). Students who can regulate their own emotions, not respond in hot-headed ways, and read others' emotions will resolve conflicts more constructively.
- *Promote social cognition in your students* (see Chapter 9). Students with better people-reading skills, sense of humor, and moral judgment will resolve conflicts more constructively.

In addition, you may need to directly address conflict resolution skills. Many teachers do not feel confident about handling student conflict and may opt for quick, short-term fixes to achieve peace rather than focusing on building long-term skills in students (Jenkins, Ritblatt, & McDonald, 2008). In the earlier vignette that involved interethnic conflict between Latina and African American girls, the teacher was able to maintain order, but he did not help the students grapple in a respectful way with issues of ethnicity, language, and feeling excluded, nor did he help them develop better conflict resolution skills. He promoted disengagement, but his students would have benefited more had he promoted compromise. You may be more effective if you follow these guidelines:

- Carefully observe your students' conflict resolution abilities. Students may not tell you about their conflicts. Older students are less likely to seek teacher help for peer conflict than are younger students (Newman et al., 2001). Typically, students try to resolve conflict with coercion before going to the teacher, using the teacher only as a fall-back strategy. They are more likely to go to the teacher if their goal is to achieve justice, or if the aggressor is bigger than themselves.
- Do not intervene in conflicts unless it is necessary or someone is victimized. Give students the opportunity to develop resolution skills.
- Scaffold compromise and negotiation, rather than disengagement, when intervention appears necessary.

You may also want to adopt a specific program designed to enhance conflict resolution skills across your school.

Conflict Resolution Education

Conflict resolution education in schools can be part of the curriculum and be designed to train skills that prevent conflict, or it can involve peer mediation and be designed to help students deal with existing conflict. Such programs might target the entire student body, or only a subset of students.

Conflict resolution education can be an alternative to punishment. One supposed punishment—suspension—seldom works, as evidenced by the fact that most students who are suspended are repeat offenders. Suspension puts students at further risk of low achievement and dropping out, as it did for Caleb. Students do not learn skills from such punishment. In one Chicago-area high school, students were given the option of a reduced suspension in return for joining a conflict resolution program. Those who chose to join the program were less likely to get a repeat suspension for fighting later, compared to a control group (Breunlin, Bryant-Edwards, Hetherington, & Cimmarusti, 2002). The program involved four 90-minute sessions on negotiation, listening, anger management, and problem solving.

Other programs have similar results. Reviews of research have concluded that conflict resolution education helps students use more-constructive strategies and reduces office referrals and suspensions. Conflict resolution education is also linked to higher achievement and improved school climate. In addition, high-risk students (and their teachers!) feel less depression, less anxiety, and higher self-esteem after improving conflict resolution skills at school. Effects may be largest for adolescents, but children can benefit from such programs as early as preschool (Garrard & Lipsey, 2007; Johnson & Johnson, 2006). One example of an effective program is the "I Can Problem Solve" program.

The I Can Problem Solve (ICPS) program

This program is designed to help students from preschool through middle school solve everyday social problems. It focuses on (1) thinking of different *alternative solutions* and (2) *thinking about the consequences* of those solutions. In daily twenty-minute lessons, the teacher discusses hypothetical conflicts, such as a child being excluded from play by others. The teacher asks the class to explain the problem and how the child feels and to brainstorm alternative solutions. The teacher asks what might happen if the child used each solution. The same procedure is used when real students misbehave in the classroom.

This is akin to the inductive discipline you learned about in Chapter 7. However, ICPS dialogues go beyond induction (Shure, 2001). There are four levels (from bad to best) of discipline quality. Only the fourth constitutes an ICPS dialogue, but the third would constitute induction:

1. Demand, command, belittle, punish (e.g., *Do you want a referral?*)
2. Offer suggestion without explanation (e.g., *Why don't you ask him for it?*)
3. Explain and reason (e.g., *He will feel angry if you grab.*)
4. Problem-solving dialogue (e.g., *What's the problem? How do you think she felt when . . . ? Can you think of a different way to solve this problem?*)

When students think through conflicts by talking with an adult as the problem is occurring, they learn to problem-solve better. Let's eavesdrop on a 1st-grade classroom:

Allen complains, "Max kept trying to take our ball. When I told him to stop it, he kicked me." Mrs. Wang asks Max his side of the story. Max says, "I wanted to play with them, but they ignored me." Mrs. Wang asks, "How would you feel if Allen took your ball and kicked you?" Max admits, "I guess I'd be mad." Mrs. Wang asks the class for suggestions of how to solve the boys' problem. Three suggestions are given: (1) Allen should kick him back; (2) Max should tell Allen how he feels; and (3) Max should walk away when he feels like kicking. Mrs. Wang turns to Max, "OK, which of these suggestions will you use next time?" Max decides to try walking away.

In one study, after just three months in the ICPS program, low-SES kindergarteners were less impulsive, more cooperative, and shared more than control-group students. Gains were sustained for one to two years follow-up, but the effects were small (Shure, 2001). In another study, 6th-graders had half as many violence incidents and five times fewer in-school suspensions than a control group (Farrell, Meyer, & White, 2001). Older students who participate in ICPS also have improved reading skills and standardized test scores, but it takes longer to get effects in older students. Parents can also be trained to use ICPS dialogues with their children. Students have more long-term gains if they participate in the program for two school years and if their parents participate (Shure, 2001).

Think About This In the vignette with Max, which of the solutions provided by the other children are coercion, disengagement, or compromise? Is Max's preference typical for his age? Is he likely to actually use it? Explain.

Similar skills can be taught at the high school level. Typically, conflict resolution curricula are used during advisory periods, or in literature and social studies classes. For example, reading *A Midsummer Night's Dream* could be used as an opportunity to discuss different ways to resolve conflict. The website accompanying this text provides a list of programs that address aggression and bullying. Many of the programs also address conflict resolution skills. Use this resource to help you select a program appropriate for your school. Another approach to conflict resolution is peer mediation.

Peer mediation

mediation a neutral, impartial third person facilitates negotiation between two children in conflict.

Mediation occurs when a neutral third party facilitates compromise. Mediation involves four steps:

1. Set ground rules, like escalation of hostility is not allowed.
2. Identify the issues and define the problem.
3. Make each child's beliefs, views, or emotions clear.
4. Find a solution that satisfies both students.

You will recognize these as similar to the components of ICPS. In peer mediation at school, either a small cadre of students is trained to be the mediators for peers or the whole student body is trained. Proponents like peer mediation because it replaces punishment; punishment may stop misbehavior but does not teach students positive social skills.

Peer mediation is successful in that most problems brought to peer mediators are resolved constructively. Students trained as mediators become better able to generate positive conflict resolutions. Disciplinary referrals and suspensions sometimes decline after peer mediation programs are implemented in schools. In addition, instructional time may increase because teachers do not have to spend as much time disciplining. (Garrard & Lipsey, 2007; Smith, Daunic, Miller, & Robinson, 2002). However, programs must be well implemented and mediators must be well trained or they come to be viewed as negative police.

In this chapter you have learned how to help your students become more prosocial, control their aggression, and resolve conflicts constructively. You have heard the stories of both Caleb and Adara, who were quite difficult students, yet both learned to be less aggressive and more prosocial at school. They each developed a positive relationship with a teacher because that teacher deliberately practiced the guidelines in this chapter. Students who develop more positive social behavior have better relationships, which is the topic of the next chapter.

Richard Hutchings/Digital Light Source/PhotoLibrary

Peer mediation programs can reduce conflict and increase instructional time.

Reflections on Practice: Checklist for Teachers

There are many things that you can do to increase prosocial behavior, decrease antisocial behavior, and promote conflict resolution skills in your students. Several of these have been discussed in previous chapters; review the "Reflections on Practice" sections from these other chapters. They include:

- Developing a secure teacher–student attachment (see Chapter 6).
- Being authoritative (see Chapter 7).
- Using inductive discipline, especially victim-centered induction (see Chapter 7).
- Promoting students' emotional competence (see Chapter 8).
- Promoting students' social cognition (see Chapter 9).

In addition, periodically ask yourself the following questions:

1. Are my students prosocial toward each other? Do I make students feel responsible for others' well-being?
2. Do I provide opportunities for my students to practice being prosocial? Do I accept offers of help even when it is inconvenient? When service opportunities are provided to students, are they meaningful and is there time for group reflection?
3. Do I clearly communicate prosocial values? Do I model kind and polite behavior? (Teachers who combine warmth with valuing and modeling prosocial behavior are most effective.) Would my students characterize me as a caring teacher?
4. Do I refrain from using extrinsic rewards for prosocial behavior (e.g., stickers) but use praise instead? Do I emphasize praising prosocial behavior rather than punishing antisocial behavior?
5. Am I aware of aggression and bullying among my students? (This is especially important for early childhood teachers because early intervention is important.) Am I aware of which students are being victimized?
6. Is my school anti-bullying? Do high-status students get away with bullying? Do I teach students how to stand up for and befriend victims? Are all areas of the school, and my own classroom, well supervised?
7. Am I helping aggressive students increase their academic skills by including all students in classroom learning?
8. Do I intervene in conflicts only when necessary? When I do intervene, do I promote compromise, rather than just suggest disengagement (e.g., leave the area)?
9. Does our school offer conflict resolution skills training as an alternative to suspension for unruly students? Would our school benefit from a peer mediation program?

Summary of Age Trends in Social Behavior

	Prosocial Behavior	Aggression	Conflict Resolution
Early Childhood (Birth–5 Years)	A universal tendency to share is apparent by 8 months. At 12 months, an absence of sharing indicates serious developmental delay. Prosocial behavior is an impulse. There is a decline in sharing from infancy to toddlerhood as self-interest becomes manifest. By age 2, children use prosocial behavior as a tool in social interactions. Individual differences in prosocial behavior are apparent and stable by 2–3 years of age. A variety of prosocial behaviors are exhibited by 2-year-olds, such as comforting, helping, and sharing. By age 4, children have extensive prosocial repertoires. Gender differences in prosocial behavior emerge.	By 4 months, infants are capable of anger. Aggression toward peers is observed by 12 months. Toddlers exhibit other antisocial behaviors like defiance and tantrums. Coercive family cycles can begin in toddlerhood. *Physical* aggression peaks at age 2, and then decreases (but does not disappear) as *verbal* aggression increases. Young children tend to express happiness when they are victimizing others. Preschoolers are the most aggressive of any age. Aggression is primarily instrumental among preschoolers. Children with severe behavior problems may be diagnosed with oppositional defiant disorder.	Infants protest others' behavior by 8 months. Toddlers' conflicts are brief. Two-year-olds resolve disputes with words and use more prosocial solutions than do 1-year-olds. Toddlers' conflict is about objects. Older preschoolers tend to argue over group play activity. More 4-year-olds than 2-year-olds are able to resolve their own conflicts, and use better strategies.
Middle Childhood (6–12 Years)	Children become better at soothing others' distress and cheering them up. They are able to do this verbally, rather than physically. They are often given caretaking responsibilities of younger children by age 6–8. They develop a better sense of what prosocial behaviors are expected of them, and make donations to anonymous charities in laboratory studies.	Physical aggression continues to diminish. If it persists beyond age 8, children may be diagnosed with conduct disorder. Children with CD have early-onset antisocial behavior. Aggression is more likely to be hostile than instrumental. Social aggression becomes apparent. Bullying emerges, and then declines.	Ability to resolve conflict improves. Coercion is used less and compromise and disengagement are used more compared with early childhood, although they still are not common. Children are able to serve as peer mediators in elementary school. As they grow older, they are less likely to seek teachers' help in resolving conflict.
Adolescence (13–19 Years)	Adolescents are more competent at helping. They are less affectionate and helpful in the family, but helpfulness rises again in late adolescence. Adolescents who provide needed help to their family tend to be happier. Adolescents are not prosocial more frequently than younger children, perhaps because they are better at suppressing impulses to help others, are motivated by self-interest, learn from antisocial models, and have been trained not to help. Prosocial behavior is more a controlled choice than an impulse.	Rate of aggression declines in adolescence, although most young adolescents do engage in aggression occasionally. Bullying may briefly spike in middle school. Bullies are not liked in elementary school, but may have some status in middle school. A minority of adolescents may have a temporary surge in antisocial behavior, known as adolescent-onset. This typically includes delinquency more than aggression. Aggression becomes more dangerous in adolescence. Criminals begin their career in, or before, adolescence. Crime peaks at about age 17.	Adolescents have less conflict than preschoolers. The most conflicted relationship is with siblings. Adolescents engage in less coercion than do younger children, typically using disengagement. Young adults typically use more compromise than do adolescents, including with siblings.

Chapter Summary

Prosocial Behavior

- Prosocial behavior is a behavior that benefits others. Altruism is prosocial behavior that involves personal cost.
- Individual differences in prosocial behavior appear in toddlerhood and are stable. Across cultures, prosocial children are liked better by teachers and peers and have higher achievement. Yet, excessive prosocial behavior can indicate problems.
- Girls tend to be more prosocial than boys.
- Parents promote children's prosocial behavior by espousing prosocial values, using victim-centered inductive discipline, being warm, being authoritative, and having secure attachment. Tangible rewards can undermine long-term prosocial behavior, but praise promotes it. Opportunity to practice promotes prosocial behavior.
- Teachers can do the same things parents do to promote prosocial behavior. In addition, teachers can promote prosocial behavior by making students feel responsible for others' well-being and providing high-quality opportunities to serve. The Caring School Community project increased prosocial behavior and academic achievement by making the school a more caring place.

Antisocial Behavior and Aggression

- Antisocial behavior is behavior that disrupts social functioning. It is co-morbid with ADHD and internalizing disorders. Aggression is a subset of antisocial behavior that involves harming others.
- Aggression can be physical, verbal, or social. Students who use one type are likely to use the other types. Aggression can be proactive or reactive. Bullying is a type of proactive aggression.
- Students' misbehavior has increased over the last few decades, including clinical levels of behavior problems.
- Individual differences in aggression are stable over time. Students with early-onset aggression have the most negative outcomes, including adult criminality. Students with severe behavior problems are diagnosed with conduct disorder or oppositional defiance disorder.
- Individual differences in aggression may have a genetic component that may operate through hormones, neurotransmitters, temperament, and cognitive ability. Aggressive children also have distorted social cognition, such as hostile attribution bias, as explained by the social information processing model.
- There are several parenting factors that are associated with aggression. When negative parenting factors co-occur, families form coercive cycles of interaction.
- Antisocial behavior is linked to both low academic achievement and social rejection, but not necessarily low self-esteem.

- Occasional victimization is common, but some children are chronic victims. Chronic victims may or may not be aggressive themselves. They are likely to have either overprotective parents, or hostile, intrusive parents. They are also likely to be friendless.
- Boys are more aggressive than girls. Gender differences are greater for physical than social aggression. Boys are more likely than girls to have conduct disorder and to be victims of aggression. Across countries, low-SES and minority children are more likely to exhibit antisocial behaviors.
- Teachers may reduce aggression when they build warm teacher–student relationships, avoid using power-assertive discipline, promote academic skills, supervise activities, avoid retention, and avoid reinforcing aggression.

Conflict Resolution

- Conflict occurs when one student's behavior interferes with another student's goals. Conflict can be resolved through compromise, disengagement, or coercion.
- Students who have good conflict resolution skills are more likely to have authoritative parents who promote emotional competence and social cognition in their children.
- Sibling relationships are the most conflicted. Conflict is mostly over possessions but seldom over parental love. Sibling conflict is typically resolved with coercion, unless parents intervene and scaffold compromise.
- Students who have good conflict resolution skills are better liked by peers.
- Boys engage in more conflict than do girls. Boys more often resolve conflict with coercion, and girls more often recruit the teacher's help.
- In some cultures (e.g., Japan) children are given responsibility for resolving conflict, while in other cultures (e.g., the United States) teachers intervene in peer conflict.
- Students do not often seek a teacher's help to resolve conflict and are less likely to do so with age. If teachers intervene in conflict, they should scaffold compromise.
- Effective conflict resolution programs result in increased academic achievement and better school climate. Such programs can be an effective alternative to suspension.

Accompanying Education CourseMate Website Resources

Visit the **Education CourseMate** website at **CengageBrain.com** to find resources and study aids for this chapter, including self-tests, additional print and website resources, and glossary flashcards. You will also find a table listing evidence-based interventions to reduce aggression and increase conflict resolution skills that may be used in your school or classroom.

chapter 11

Peers, Friends, and Play

PIX PIX/Digital Light Source/Photolibrary

SHOULD YOU BE WORRIED ABOUT A STUDENT WHO DOES NOT APPEAR TO HAVE ANY FRIENDS IN YOUR CLASSROOM? What about a student who does not play? Is play important beyond the preschool years? In this chapter we answer these questions as we discuss three aspects of social behavior—peer status, friendships, and play. After you read this chapter, you will understand:

- How students differ in their popularity with peers and in the number and quality of their friends.
- What differences in popularity mean for student success in your classroom, and how you can help friendless, disliked students.
- The role of play in your classroom.

Peer Status

In a 3rd-grade classroom, Paul pushes other students, breaks their pencils, steps on their homework, and calls them stupid. When he sits at a table, children move to avoid sitting by him. One day Paul says, "I am having a birthday party and everyone wants to come because I am the most popular boy in this class." A girl sitting nearby says, "Paul, no one likes you. You say nasty things. And you hit." Paul replies, "You're just jealous." His inflated self-esteem seems genuine.

In contrast, his classmate Nadya is well liked. When the teachers are busy, students go to Nadya for help. She always stops what she is doing to help. She is remarkably patient. Several of the children in the class consider Nadya their "best friend." She is consistently cheerful and happy.

Two other classmates, Lydia and Eleanor, are best friends. A new girl asks Lydia a question. Lydia says, "We don't talk to newbies," and turns her back. She whispers to Eleanor and they begin giggling. Nadya tells the new girl, "Don't be sad. They're not nice to anyone." Lydia and Eleanor control a part of the classroom where others can only come with their permission. Some girls follow them everywhere and imitate what Eleanor says. Yet, these girls do not actually interact with Lydia and Eleanor. Eleanor says that she and Lydia are popular. A girl later says, "Lots of girls want to be their friends, but lots of girls don't like them either. Some kids are scared of them. I don't know why anyone would want to be their friend. They are rude."

These four children are in the same 3rd-grade classroom, yet are having very different peer experiences. Why are some students popular while others are rejected in the classroom, and what effect will this have on them? In this chapter you will see that peers make a substantial contribution to students' well-being. First, we will focus on students' place in the peer group (i.e., peer status) and their friendships. Then we will discuss play, a primary activity of friends.

Paul, Nadya, Lydia, and Eleanor have different peer status. **Peer status** refers to how students are received by the social group. One way scientists assess this is to ask students which classmates they like, or prefer to play or work with, and which they dislike. This is known as a *sociometric* method. This method is used with children from preschool to high school. It results in five categories of peer status as indicated in Figure 11.1.

peer status a measure of how accepted children are in a peer group.

1. *Popular* children (about 15%) are liked by many peers and disliked by few.
2. *Rejected* children (about 15%) are disliked by many and liked by few.
3. *Neglected* children (about 10%) receive few liked or disliked votes; they go unnoticed by most children.
4. *Controversial* children (about 6%) receive many liked and disliked votes.
5. *Average* children (40 to 60%) are moderately liked and disliked.

Notice that rejection involves active dislike, avoidance, and exclusion by peers, not mere neglect. Most children are average, and the fewest are controversial (e.g., DeRosier & Thomas, 2003).

Think About This Based on the opening vignette, which category of peer status best fits Paul, Nadya, Lydia, and Eleanor? Justify your conclusion.

Scientists use the term "popular" to mean "well liked." But when teachers or children are asked who is popular, they nominate some children who are *not* well liked, like Lydia and Eleanor. These children may be *controversial* (especially girls) or

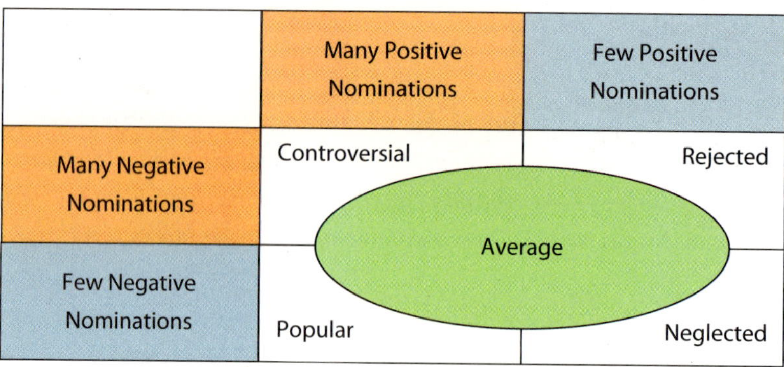

Figure 11.1 Types of Peer Status.
Most students are average, and the fewest are controversial. Think about a classroom you are familiar with. Do you know specific children who fit each type?

rejected (especially boys). Psychologists call these children "bully-leaders" or "tough/popular." Although they are more disliked than popular or average children, they manage to have high status. They are readily identified by 5th grade, and sometimes even as early as 2nd grade.

Peer status is also measured with sociograms or social maps of the classroom. Figure 11.2 is an example of a social map of a 3rd-grade classroom. Observers map which students interact or hang around together. About 2 to 10% of students are isolated from the social networks in their classroom (Cairns & Cairns, 1994). Can you find isolates in Figure 11.2?

Individual Diversity in Peer Status

For many children, peer status is stable. Roughly 40% of elementary students maintain their status over a year and 25% over four years. Controversial and neglected children

controversial children children who are liked by many and also disliked by many peers. They have high social impact.

neglected children children who are neither liked nor disliked by many peers. They have low social impact.

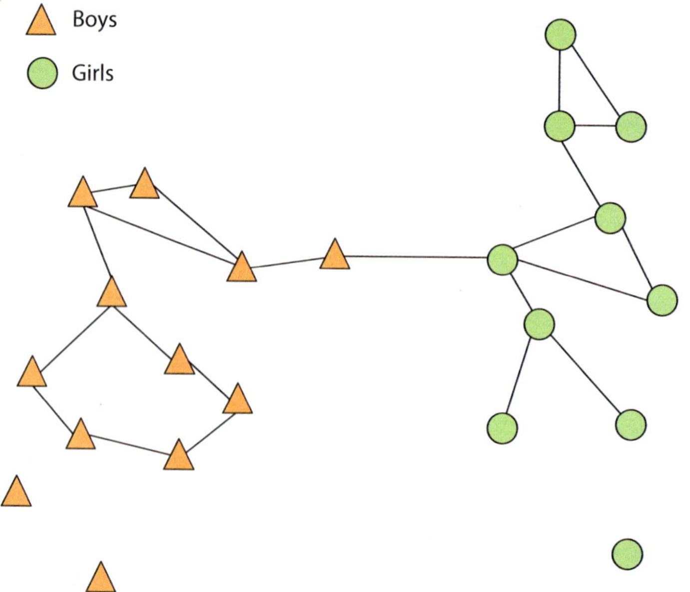

Figure 11.2 Sociogram of a 3rd-Grade Classroom.
Lines represent regular interaction between children. Notice that only one girl has interaction with boys. Which children are the most connected with others?

are most likely to change status, and rejected children are least likely. Thus, popular children are likely to stay popular, and rejected children are likely to stay rejected across time between kindergarten and high school (Cillessen & Mayeux, 2004; Gazelle & Ladd, 2003; Hymel, Vaillancourt, McDougall, & Renshaw, 2002).

However, it is possible for some rejected children to become more accepted over time, if they become less aggressive. Such improvement gets less likely as children grow older. Preston, in case 4, was rejected as a 10th-grader; his classmate said, "We ignore everything he says." He is likely to have been rejected for several years. Later, we will discuss how you can help children like Preston. Because rejection has negative consequences, it is fortunate that most children are never rejected.

Field Observation

Ask four children with varying peer status (based on your best judgment), "Do you ever feel sad and alone in school?" Analyze whether their responses match their peer status.

What Does Peer Rejection Predict?

Temporary peer rejection does not portend long-term problems. However, when children are rejected for a school year or more, there can be serious consequences such as psychological distress, aggression, and low academic achievement.

Psychological distress

Rejected children tend to experience more victimization, loneliness, low self-esteem, and depression than average children (Burt, Obradovic, Long, & Masten, 2008; Ladd, 2006; Putallaz et al., 2007). However, not all rejected children have these problems. There are different kinds of rejected children. **Rejected-aggressive children** account for about 40 to 50%, and **rejected-withdrawn children** account for about 10 to 20% of rejected children (Hymel et al., 2002). Rejected-*withdrawn* children see themselves as socially incompetent, which matches their peer status, but rejected-*aggressive* children think they are more popular than they are. In the opening vignette, Paul mistakenly believed he was the most popular boy in the class. In contrast, average and popular children tend to underestimate their social competence (Cillessen & Bellmore, 2002). Not surprisingly, rejected-withdrawn children may feel greater loneliness than rejected-aggressive children; they may anticipate rejection even from friends, and feel helpless and stressed by mild rejection (Asher & Paquette, 2003; Gazelle & Druhen, 2009).

rejected-aggressive children children who are actively disliked by many peers and are highly aggressive; about 40 to 50% of rejected children.

rejected-withdrawn children children who are actively disliked by many peers, are not aggressive, but tend to avoid social interaction; about 10 to 20% of rejected children.

Popular children may fare best. However, even if children are not popular, they fare well as long as they feel confident and comfortable among their peers (McElhaney, Antonishak, & Allen, 2008). That is, students' *feelings* about their peer status matter in addition to their actual status.

Aggression

Rejection may cause students to become aggressive, disruptive in class, hyperactive-distractible, and delinquent. Rejected students often watch closely for any sign of others' hostility (hostile attribution bias). They may expect and quickly overreact to perceived rejection, whether it is real or not. They may respond with aggression, which leads to more rejection. Thus, they create a self-fulfilling prophecy of rejection (see Figure 11.3).

Rejection for just one year in the primary grades can predict antisocial behavior five years later (Dodge et al., 2003). Children rejected for two to three years by 2nd grade have a 50% chance of having serious behavior problems before adolescence, compared with only a 9% chance for nonrejected children. The degree of rejection matters.

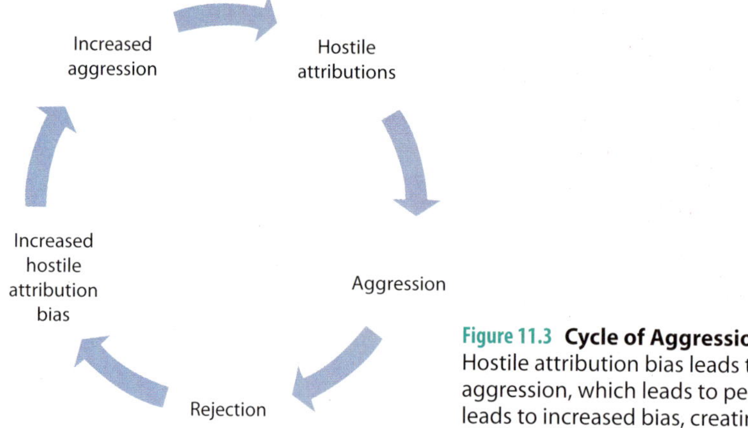

Figure 11.3 Cycle of Aggression. Hostile attribution bias leads to increased aggression, which leads to peer rejection, which leads to increased bias, creating a negative cycle.

Highly rejected and highly controversial children tend to develop more problem behavior than mildly rejected children (DeRosier & Thomas, 2003).

Low academic achievement

Rejected students tend to have lower GPA, IQ, and test scores than accepted students (Buhs & Ladd, 2001; Zettergren, 2003). How might this happen? One possibility is that teachers give preferential treatment to better-liked students, boosting their academic ability (Czeschlik & Rost, 1995). Another possibility is that rejected students' low self-esteem leads them to give up on challenging school assignments (Flook, Repetti, & Ullman, 2005). Another possibility is that their feelings of anxiety and depression and their behavior problems interfere with learning. Still another possibility is that rejection from peers causes them to disengage from classroom activity.

Students who are rejected by their peers, even if they have brought the rejection upon themselves through misbehavior, tend to dislike and avoid school, and some eventually drop out. Would you want to go every day to a place where you are disliked? Rejected-*aggressive* children are particularly at risk, with as many as 50% dropping out (French & Conrad, 2001; Hymel et al., 2002).

What Predicts Peer Status?

Students are accepted or rejected for a reason—usually their social competence. Let's first discuss four aspects of social competence: prosocial behavior, aggression, social withdrawal, and social skills. Then we will discuss parenting factors that contribute to both social competence and peer status.

Prosocial behavior

Prosocial students are liked by nearly everyone, have many friends, make new friends easily, are listened to, and are leaders. For example, a study of White and Latino 3rd-, 4th-, and 5th-graders found that popular children were more prosocial, whereas rejected children were less prosocial than other children (Greener, 2000). Prosocial behavior predicts popularity from preschool through high school.

Aggression

Earlier you learned that rejection may cause students to behave aggressively at school, but the reverse is also true; aggression causes rejection. Aggressive students tend to

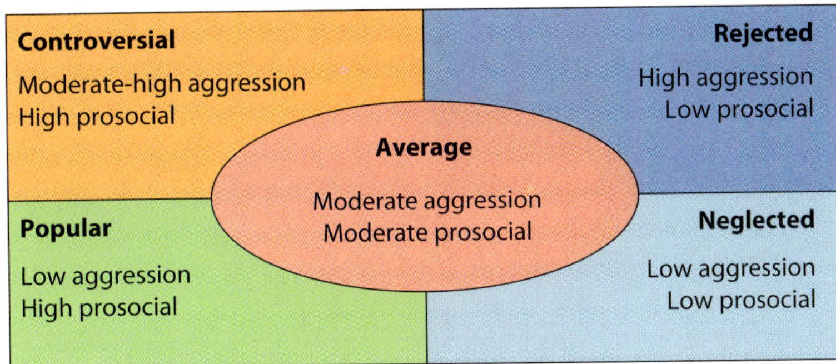

Figure 11.4 Relations between Peer Status and Social Behavior.
How are aggression and prosocial behavior related to peer status?

be rejected by their peers from preschool through high school (French & Conrad, 2001; Pedersen, Vitaro, Barker, & Borge, 2007). Students do not like peers who hit them, snatch their belongings, or insult them. The greater the aggression, the greater the rejection. Rejected and controversial students are more aggressive than average students, who are more aggressive than popular students (Putallaz et al., 2007). Preston, in case 4, is rejected because he is verbally aggressive and sabotages the science experiment. Figure 11.4 shows the relationship among prososcial behavior, aggression, and peer status.

While most aggressive students are rejected, there is a subset of aggressive students who have high social status but are not well liked by peers. These bully-leaders, or tough/popular students, may have attributes that compensate for their aggression, such as attractiveness, cool clothes, athletic prowess (especially for boys), and involvement in extracurricular activities (Farmer, Estell, Bishop, O'Neal, & Cairns, 2003; LaFontana & Cillessen, 2002). Tough/popular students have less-irritating behavior—less argumentativeness, disruption, hyperactivity, and inattention—and are more covert in their aggression than rejected students. They may use social aggression, such as pointedly excluding some students in order to maintain their social status, rather than overt, physical aggression. Lydia did this when she turned her back on the new student. Tough/popular students may be disliked by their victims, but not by those they have not harmed. Thus, some peers like them, but others do not. This makes them controversial.

Social withdrawal

Some rejected students are not aggressive, which means that there are other routes to rejection (French & Conrad, 2001). Rejected-withdrawn students withdraw from social interaction, like extremely shy, nonsocial students who are shy even *in the context of familiar peers* (see Chapter 6). Rejected-withdrawn students may be sad, play alone, watch peers play, seldom talk, have easily hurt feelings, and have trouble making friends. For example, Tara has just moved to a new kindergarten class because she is now in foster care following abuse. Her behavior leads her to be rejected:

Tara seldom speaks, does not know the alphabet, and clings to adults. The other children are caretaking of her, at first. They treat her like a toddler. For example, one girl said, "Hi Tara! Can you find a T for Tara? Let's see if we can find one in your book." Tara does not respond to these overtures; she says nothing and makes no eye contact. Over time, her peers' response to her is quite different. They reject her instead of babying her. During a class project, some children hide her paper and scissors. Tara slowly states, "That's not funny!" so they mimic her poor speech. She leaves the work area. When the teacher tries to get her to return, she kicks the teacher and folds herself into a ball.

Children reject withdrawn peers as early as preschool if their timid, nervous behavior is extreme, like Tara's. Young children are fairly tolerant toward more moderately withdrawn peers. However, by 3rd grade on through high school, withdrawn students tend to be rejected by classmates (Rubin, Coplan, & Bowker, 2009).

Social skills

A final route to peer rejection is through odd behavior or poor social skills. For example, Angie tries to enter a group of 4th-grade girls who are already talking, so that she can tell them a story.

"I want to tell you something!" The girls ignore her and continue talking. Angie does not try to figure out what the conversation is about. Instead, she says, "I have something to say!" but the girls continue to ignore her. She gets louder: "Stop talking! Listen to me!" Some girls glance at her, but continue talking. Hands on her hips, she shouts, "Listen to me!" The other girls ignore her, so she stamps her foot and leaves.

Entering the ongoing activity of a group requires social skill, and many entry bids are rebuffed. Students' skill in group entry affects their peer acceptance. Popular students listen to the group, figure out what they are doing, and make comments relevant to ongoing activities as they enter the group. Unpopular students call attention to themselves, try to take control, or appeal to adult authority. Like Angie, they are disruptive and self-centered during group entry (Putallaz & Wasserman, 1990). Sadly, Angie has few friends.

Students may be rejected for other reasons as well, such as physical unattractiveness or hyperactivity (Hymel et al., 2002; Stormshak et al., 1999). They may behave oddly, like making strange noises, talking to themselves, or making odd faces.

Parenting influences

Parenting factors that influence children's prosocial or antisocial behavior, discussed in Chapter 10, also influence peer status. Parental risk factors for rejection include (1) marital conflict and divorce; (2) harsh and power-assertive discipline; (3) father's negativity—such as anger, frustration, or irritability—while playing with his children; and (4) maltreatment and abuse. Parental protective factors for rejection include authoritative parenting and secure attachment.

Parents also influence their children's peer status by the way they *select their child's peer world.* Parents choose—within limits—neighborhood, school, child care, lessons, and community activities for their children. Safe neighborhoods with sidewalks, playgrounds, and closely spaced houses provide more opportunity for peer interaction than do wealthy neighborhoods where each house is its own castle, rural settings without recognizable neighborhoods, or dangerous urban neighborhoods where people are afraid to go out.

Parents can also *directly coach* their children's social skills. Popular children have parents who direct their toddler's peer play, but by preschool age they direct play *only when needed*, in contrast to parents who are overly involved and intrusive. Their coaching might involve stopping their child's aggression; showing how to take turns; suggesting strategies for entering a play group; framing conflict in a positive way, such as "he didn't mean to knock your tower down"; and encouraging resilience, such as "you can build another one" (Colwell, Mize, Petit, & Laird, 2002). By middle childhood or adolescence, parents of popular children mostly monitor their children's peer interactions, rather than directly intervening.

Group Diversity in Peer Status

Up to this point you have learned that, in general, prosocial students are popular and aggressive or withdrawn students are rejected. However, students are rejected by peers only if they are more aggressive or withdrawn than is *normal for their group*. That is, aggressive students may not be as rejected in aggression-filled classrooms as they are in other classrooms (Hymel et al., 2002). Withdrawn students may not be as rejected in classrooms with lots of solitary play and little social interaction. The more a child fits the group norm, the less rejected the child will be. One exception is that prosocial behavior is linked to popularity regardless of the classroom norms, because it is valued in almost all cultures and groups (Chang, 2004).

Gender

There may be small gender differences in peer status. Usually students are accepted or rejected by both boys and girls in the classroom, although students are slightly more likely to favor same-sex peers (Hymel et al., 2002). Some studies find that boys are more often rejected (e.g., Bost, Vaughn, Washington, Cielinski, & Bradbard, 1998). However, these gender differences are not consistently found, even though boys are consistently more aggressive than girls. Perhaps this is because boy groups tolerate more aggression than girl groups.

Socioeconomic Status

On the average, low-SES students are less popular than middle-SES students. This may be due to low-SES students tending to have more risk factors that are linked to peer rejection. In one study of hundreds of elementary students, only 8% of children without risk factors were rejected, but a whopping 75% were rejected if they had several risk factors, such as an absent mother, unemployed father, divorced parents, low income, or recent move to a new school (Patterson, Vaden, & Kupersmidt, 1991). Still, 25% of children with several risk factors were *not* rejected.

Ethnicity

Most studies find that ethnicity does not predict peer status. For example, in two studies of hundreds of 2nd- through 7th-graders, being a member of one ethnic group did not predict peer status any more than being a member of a different ethnic group

(Patterson et al., 1991; Wentzel, 1991). Characteristics that predict peer status are similar across ethnic groups—students prefer peers who are more prosocial and less aggressive. However, young African Americans may be more accepting of aggressive peers than White students (Jones, Parker, Joyner, & Ulku-Steiner, 1999).

Cross-National Comparisons

Patterns of peer status are similar across several countries. For example, studies of elementary students in Germany found similar proportions of popular, neglected, rejected, controversial, and average students as are found in North America (e.g., Brendgen, Little, & Krappman, 2000). In addition, peer rejection is linked to low academic achievement in both the United States and China (Chen, Rubin, & Li, 1997). Furthermore, aggression predicts rejection, and prosocial behavior predicts popularity, in the United States, China, Italy, Costa Rica, Russia, Finland, and the Netherlands (e.g., Chen, Chang, & He, 2003; Hart et al., 2000; Ojanen, Gronroos, & Salmivallie, 2005). One cultural difference is that whether withdrawn behavior predicts rejection depends on whether or not the culture values shy behavior, as discussed in Chapter 6.

Classroom Implications of Peer Status

Peer status influences your students' school success. You might assume popular students are ideal in a classroom, but actually neglected students are often *preferred* by teachers because they are easiest to manage. For example, in a study of 6th- and 7th-graders, teachers viewed neglected students as compliant, and teachers liked having them in class (Wentzel & Asher, 1995). Students who are neglected by their peers, but who are liked by teachers, may do fine academically.

In contrast, as you learned earlier, *rejected* students tend to have low test scores, be aggressive, participate less in class activities, and avoid school—all of which make them harder to manage. Their sadness and anxiety about being rejected may interfere with motivation and ability to pay attention in class. Even students who are temporarily rejected participate less in class during the period in which they are rejected. When the rejection stops, their classroom participation increases (Ladd, Herald-Brown, & Reiser, 2008).

How can you help an isolated student in your classroom? First, you must determine whether the student is neglected or rejected, because neglected students do not necessarily lack social skills or need intervention. Rejected students are actively disliked and do need intervention. You can help rejected-withdrawn (shy nonsocial) students by creating a positive emotional climate (see Chapter 8), using good classroom management, and refraining from being overly controlling (see Chapter 7). Such students are not as likely to be rejected or victimized in a positive classroom (Gazelle, 2006). Three other ways you can improve students' peer status are: (1) improve their behavior, (2) influence their reputation, and (3) provide more peer interaction, such as through cooperative learning.

Improve Students' Behavior

You may think that moving a rejected student to a new peer group will help the student. Unfortunately, unless the student's behavior improves, the student will soon be rejected in the new group. For example, in a classic study 1st- and 3rd-grade African

American boys who did not know each other played together for forty-five-minute sessions (Dodge, Coie, Pettit, & Price, 1990). Within one session rejected boys were disliked, and within three sessions they were as rejected in the new playgroup as they were in their regular classroom. Instead of moving them, help rejected students by following these guidelines:

- *Help the student reduce aggression and increase prosocial behavior.* See Chapter 10 for how to do this.
- *Help the student develop better emotion regulation abilities.* See Chapter 8 for how to do this.
- *Promote the student's academic skills.* Students who are more academically successful in the classroom are less aggressive and better liked. See Chapter 5 for how to do this.
- *Capitalize on the student's strengths.* An admired skill or talent promotes a student's acceptance. For example, 2nd-grader Rudy seldom plays with other students and is behind in reading skills. He would be a rejected-withdrawn student, except that he has good drawing ability. One classmate said, "Rudy's drawings are so good! He can draw anything. And he makes it look real. He even drew a velociraptor!"
- *Pair the student up with a buddy.* Ask a prosocial, popular, same-sex student in the classroom to befriend and include the rejected student. You should plan to support the process as needed.
- *Arrange for the student to work or play with younger students* (Furman, Rahe, & Hartup, 1979). One-on-one activity with younger students is different from classroom interaction with age mates because it prompts withdrawn students to speak up and direct the activity, which promotes their social skills.

Special education teachers designed an intervention for 2nd-grader Marcel, who was aggressive and working below grade level. He was disciplined frequently, but the discipline was clearly not working. He wore dirty clothes and had recurring infections. Children's protective services had been involved in his home life. What was the intervention and its results?

Marcel was given a star each time he completed academic tasks in his classroom. When he earned enough stars, he could go to the kindergarten room to be a helper. The beginning was rocky because Marcel intimidated the kindergarteners with his aggressive behavior. With a little guidance, Marcel learned to actually help the kindergarteners. He read to a few children from picture books that he practiced each morning. His reading skills improved. Marcel's teacher praised him for being helpful. She phoned Marcel's mother to tell her how well he was doing. After this, his mother attended an Individualized Education Program (IEP) meeting for the first time. Marcel began to do his homework, and his aggression dropped noticeably. His classmates began to view him as a valuable person, and he began to enjoy his own classroom.

This intervention combined some of the factors discussed earlier with behavior modification. It also altered Marcel's reputation with his peers, which is the next topic.

Myrleen Pearson/Alamy

You enhance students' reputation by pointing out their prosocial behaviors to their peers

Influence Students' Reputation

Students are keenly aware of one another's status in the classroom. For example, Figure 11.5 shows the "social grades" a 4th-grade girl and her friends gave to classmates. Students' attitudes toward peers are affected by your attitudes; peers like a student better if the student has a good relationship with the teacher (Jennings & Greenberg, 2009; Osterman, 2000). Students judge a peer based on whether adults say the student is mean or nice, and when a supposedly mean student behaves nicely, peers skeptically judge the behavior as less nice (Stein & Trabasso, 1989). Students' judgment of a peer depends on teachers' public praise and discipline of the peer (White & Jones, 2000). This means you can harm a students' status by focusing peers' attention on misbehavior, like saying *"Marcel, you are always causing trouble!"* You can also enhance a student's status by focusing on positive behavior, like saying *"Marcel, thanks for helping the kindergarteners."*

Provide Opportunity for Peer Interaction at School—Cooperative Learning

Another way you can promote students' peer status is to provide opportunity to learn social skills. It may surprise you, but students have relatively few opportunities in the

Samantha A+ pretty
Gabe A+ oo-la-la ♡
Rick C+
Brice B-
[illegible] F-- BRAT!!!!
Katrina A+ nice
Domanique B+
Keafer ? never realy met him
Karisa A+
Kent A+ oola-la
Katie A
Derak A+ nice
Aabrie A+
Mike C. A+ adventeras huh?
Mike V. C- likes me ew grose sick
Me A

Provided by the author

Figure 11.5 "Grading" Classmates.
Sociometric ratings are clearly not only for psychologists. What grade does this self-confident 4th-grader give herself? What attributes earn classmates an A, C, or F?

school day to socialize. For example, in one suburban high school students averaged 1.5 interactions with a peer per fifty minutes for mid-level classes and 1.8 for advanced-level classes (Osterman, 2000). One way you can provide opportunity for peer interaction is through cooperative learning.

cooperative learning collaboration among students in small groups, where the group has a shared learning goal, and interdependence is required to achieve the goal.

Cooperative learning (CL) refers to collaboration among students in small groups, where the group has a shared learning goal, and students must work together to achieve the goal. The main impetus behind CL is that it promotes academic achievement. Cooperative learning is effective for students of different SES, ethnicity, and ability levels. The overall effect size is 0.29 to 0.55 for achievement (Roseth, Johnson, & Johnson, 2008; Slavin & Lake, 2008). Some people worry that high achievers are held back by working with lower achievers, but high achievers often actually gain more from CL because they do more explaining. In addition to promoting academic achievement, an important side effect is that CL also promotes social interaction, good peer relationships, and motivation (Roseth et al., 2008). Students report that CL is more fun than traditional classroom learning, and they like one another better during CL (Gillies, 2003).

While many teachers report using CL, it is not implemented equally well across classrooms. Some teachers casually state, "*You can work together if you like,*" for one class period, while others organize formal groups that work together on a project for several days or weeks, such as building a mechanical model for a roller coaster or presenting a book report. Simply putting students in groups is not CL; you must structure the lesson so that students learn cooperatively. For effective CL lessons follow these guidelines:

- *Hold both individuals and groups accountable.* For example, each student might be required to turn in work or take a quiz, and the group is evaluated on the achievement of each individual, such as giving the group a grade based on the average test score of *each* team member. This makes high achievers less likely to do everything while low achievers loaf (Slavin, 1996).
- *Make evaluation criteria clear to students.* Students need to know what constitutes a successful product.
- *Actively monitor groups and provide feedback.* Move among the groups, listen to their interaction, and question or prompt groups (Emmer & Gerwels, 2002).
- *Use small groups of two to five students.* Pairs result in more collaboration among students, but small groups produce more discussion (Fuchs et al., 2000). Larger groups, of about fourteen, may be ideal for electronic discussion boards.
- *Use tasks that are open-ended or ill-structured,* meaning students do not simply follow a step-by-step sequence to get the one right answer. Such tasks require group discussion.
- *Make sure each student has a role.* Convince students that each student brings valuable and different abilities to the task. Point out what each student has to contribute (Cohen, Lotan, Scarloss, & Arellano, 1999). Without this help, rejected students and low achievers may be ignored or barely participate.
- *Train students to explain.* Students who are instructed to explain the answer, not just state the correct answer, are more successful in CL.

This last suggestion may be particularly important with your students who have such poor social skills that they do not seem to benefit from cooperative learning.

For example, in one study boys ages 9 to 13 who had difficulty working cooperatively—because they had ADHD, were domineering, and irritated peers—benefited from CL if they had the right partners. Who were the right partners? High-achieving, prosocial girls who had been trained to reflect on, validate, and elaborate on the boys' comments (rather than just saying "no"); to give positive feedback; and to think aloud during their own problem solving. The boys actively listened and cooperated more with these trained partners (Watkins & Wentzel, 2008).

In summary, there are several things that you can do to foster peer acceptance even for difficult students in your classroom. If a student's rejection is severe, and the student does not respond to any of these in-class interventions, you may need to seek the help of the school counselor. Let's turn next to the issue of friendship and peer networks.

Friendship and Peer Networks

Three elementary boys responded to questions about what a friend is. Mark said, "A friend is someone who thinks you are cool and laughs at the 1st graders with you. You show off with them."

Joey said, "A friend is someone who talks to you and does things with you. I don't have many friends."

Nick said, "A friend is someone who is nice. I am nice and my friends are nice. We have fun together and don't fight."

Field Observation

Make a social map of children in a classroom or some other group. Ask children, *"Which kids in the group hang around together a lot?"* Also ask which is their group. Use short lines to indicate children with lots of interaction. Use long lines to indicate less frequent interaction. No lines should connect children who seldom interact. Identify cliques, loose groups, isolated friendships, and isolates. Are the percentages similar to those in the research?

Can you predict each student's peer status based on their understanding of what a friend is? Their answers reveal their social competence. Nick is popular, Joey is neglected, and Mark is rejected. Yet, *peer status* and *friendship* are not the same thing. Typically, popular and average students are most likely to have friends, but a rejected student may have a friend. Having a friend can buffer rejected students from some of the negative effects of rejection (Laursen, Bukowski, Aunola, & Nurmi, 2007). Unfortunately, rejected students sometimes have friends who are mean to them. This raises the question of just what is a friend.

reciprocated friendship both children nominate each other as a friend.

unilateral friendships one child nominates another as a friend, but the other does not.

Friends are peers with whom students most like to play or spend time, and can be readily identified even in preschoolers. A **reciprocated friendship** exists when both children nominate each other as a friend. Children can also have one-sided, or **unilateral friendships**, where only one child nominates the other as a friend. While you might think reciprocated friendships are the only real friendships, many friendships are not reciprocal. In one study of 7th-graders, only about half their friendships were reciprocated (Ryan, 2001).

clique a tightly knit group of about two to ten friends, usually of the same sex and same age.

A tightly knit group of about two to ten friends, usually of the same sex and age, is called a **clique**. Most students (70 to 85%) belong to a clique, 5 to 15% are part of an isolated friendship, and 10% may be isolates without friends (Espelage, Holt, & Henkel, 2003; Ryan, 2001). Even rejected students belong to cliques, often low-status cliques (Bagwell, Coie, Terry, & Lochman, 2000). Can you tell which category 16-year-old George falls in?

George is sitting alone at lunch. He has just finished in-school suspension for skipping school. He says he has no friends at school. He claims to have older friends who like to make fun of the "populars" and "jocks." George says, "Outsiders like me, we laugh at the nerds together."

George is an isolate, but he is keenly aware of cliques at school, and even has names for them. He avoids school and is at high risk for dropping out because school is not a friendly place for him.

Birds of a Feather Flock Together

This is an old adage meaning similar people tend to associate with each other. Psychologists call similarity within a peer group **homophily**. Friends tend to be similar in many ways: ethnicity, religiosity, peer status, physical maturation, athleticism, attractiveness, academic achievement, prosocial behavior, delinquency, and dropping out of school. Similarities among friends in attractiveness and academic achievement are stronger for teens than for younger children. For example, high school students are more likely to take hard math classes if their friends do so (Crosnoe, Riegle-Crumb, Field, Frank, & Muller, 2008). One of the strongest group similarities is aggressiveness, meaning aggressive students form cliques. Another strong similarity is gender.

homophily the tendency to prefer and bond with similar others.

Gender segregation refers to the fact that boys affiliate with other boys, and girls with other girls. Gender segregation appears early, by 30 to 36 months of age. Gender segregation is found in cultures across the world. It is driven by children, not adults, and occurs more strongly when adults are *not* in control. This suggests it may be innate. Gender segregation occurs because children prefer same-sex peers for playmates (Bigler, Brown, & Markell, 2001).

gender segregation when given a choice, boys affiliate with other boys and girls with other girls.

Peer Pressure: Is It Good or Bad?

Friends are similar because they *select* others like themselves. For example, among identical twins, the one who is more antisocial at age 14 will tend to select more deviant friends at age 17 than will the co-twin (Burt, McGue, & Iacono, 2009). In contrast, prosocial students tend to select prosocial friends. Friends then become more similar over time because they *socialize* each other to conform to the clique's norms. They do this through reinforcement, modeling, teasing/joking, and gossip within the clique (Ryan, 2001). This socialization process is what people mean by the term **peer pressure**. Let's look at the peer pressure 8th-grader Justin experiences:

peer pressure friends exert pressure on each other to conform to group norms. It is typically positive, but can be negative.

In algebra class, when exams are returned, students cluster around the high achievers. Several students praise Justin for getting 99%. Later in Spanish class, a substitute teacher says, "Get out your homework." Some students try to trick the sub, saying they did not have homework. Justin says that they did. A girl scolds, "Justin! Let's be smart."

Peer pressure is usually considered negative. This is misguided. It can be positive or negative, as it was for Justin. Peer pressure is *more likely to be positive*, but that depends on the peer network. For example, in Chapter 2 you learned that while most peers encourage their friends not to use drugs, students in drug-using cliques promote each other's use. Similarly, most peers encourage their friends to avoid risky sex, but about 5% are a negative influence (Henry, Schoeny, Deptula, & Slavick, 2007). Most peers encourage achievement, as Justin's classmates did, but some students underachieve for fear of being called a nerd, braniac, or teacher's pet (Boehnke, 2008).

Some youth are more powerful at exerting peer pressure, and some are more vulnerable to it. Youth who are high-status, and cliques that are highly visible, are particularly powerful in influencing average peers (Cohen & Prinstein, 2006; Ellis & Zarbatany, 2007). Youth who are most likely to succumb to *negative* peer pressure tend to (1) be insecurely attached to their parents; (2) be rejected by the larger peer group, but have delinquent friends; (3) dabble in delinquency, but are not yet fully committed to it; or (4) believe that minor delinquency is common, like "everyone" tries alcohol or sneaks into movies without paying (Allen, Porter, McFarland, McElhaney, & Marsh, 2007; Dodge, 2008). Popular youth who do *not* believe everyone is delinquent experience more positive peer pressure. Let's turn next to how friendships and peer pressure change with age.

Age Trends in Friendship and Peer Networks

Students' friends, number of friends, and time spent with friends all change with age.

Early Childhood (Birth to 5 Years)

An elderly neighbor used to slowly shuffle by our house on his daily walk. Our 3-year-old son would run to join him, skipping alongside and jabbering nonstop. The neighbor was deaf and never responded. This did not bother our son. He would race back home and exclaim, *"Him my friend!"* At 3 to 4 years of age children use the word *friend*, but may not really understand what is a friend (Hartup & Abecassis, 2002). They typically call anyone they have opportunity to play with their friend, like the next-door neighbor or children of their parents' friends. The opportunity to be together, or proximity, is the foundation of friendship at all ages, but more so for young children.

When they have a choice of playmates, children prefer same-sex peers beginning as young as 2½ years of age. In early childhood, socially competent children tend to be friends with both boys and girls, but later, having mixed-gender friendships is associated with social incompetence. Typically preschoolers' best friend is same-sex, and secondary friends are boys and girls (Vaughn, Colvin, Azria, Caya, & Krzysik, 2001).

Field Observation

Interview four children about their friendships. Ask: *What is a friend? How do you become friends? Describe your friends. Do you have a friend who is a [opposite sex]? How old are your friends? How many friends do kids your age usually have?* Choose children of different ages and peer status. Did you find an age or status trend? Discuss your results.

Roughly 30% of 3- to 7-year-olds may have *imaginary friends* (Taylor, Carlson, Maring, Gerow, & Charley, 2004). Imaginary friends can either be invisible people or objects that have been personified, like our daughter's toy lamb, named "Lambykins." Firstborn and only children are more likely to create invisible people friends, perhaps because of less opportunity for social interaction at home (Gleason, Sebanc, & Hartup, 2000). Children with imaginary friends tend to be more imaginative, happy, and cooperative at preschool and tell higher-quality stories (Trionfi & Reese, 2009). Thus, imaginary friends are not a cause for concern in early childhood.

Middle Childhood (6 to 12 Years)

Most preschoolers (75%) have friends, but even more school-age children do (85%). School-age children average three to eight friends. These friends form networks, or cliques, that average about five to thirteen children (Farmer et al., 2003; Hartup & Abecassis, 2002; Ryan, 2001). As children get older they spend substantially more of their after-school time with child companions than with adult companions (see Figure 11.6).

Homophily is stronger in middle childhood than in early childhood (Hartup & Abecassis, 2002). In particular, aggressive children select each other as friends (Bukowski, Sippola, & Newcomb, 2000; Poulin & Boivin, 2000). In Chapter 10 you learned that some children are genetically predisposed to aggression, but such children tend to become aggressive only if they also have aggressive friends (Brendgen et al., 2008). Aggressive children are usually part of a peer network that supports aggression.

Peer networks are highly gender segregated during middle childhood. Friends become increasingly same-sex from preschool through early adolescence. At age 4, children play three times more with same-sex peers than with opposite-sex peers. At age 6, they play ten times more with same-sex peers. By 4th grade, 95% of preferred friends are same-sex. In middle school, 90 to 95% of the cliques are same-sex (Espelage et al., 2003; Ryan, 2001). At home children play with whomever is available, including opposite-sex peers, because they have limited playmates in the neighborhood. However, at school, where more playmates are available, same-sex preference is strong.

Children not only prefer same-sex peers, but they actively avoid opposite-sex peers. A study of 9- to 11-year-olds at a day camp found that not a single child associated

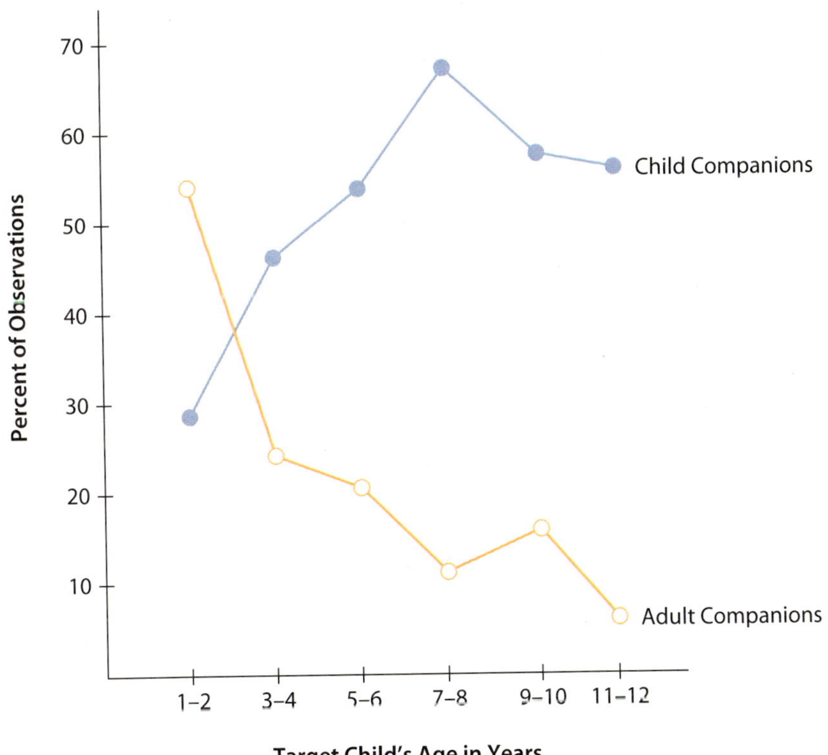

Figure 11.6 Children's Time with Companions by Age.
Percent of observations of children on summer afternoons in a neighborhood in Salt Lake City, both when only children were present and when adults were present. This is just one study, so it doesn't reflect all children at all times, but is suggestive of age trends in child versus adult companions.
Source: Ellis, Rogoff, & Cromer (1981, p. 403).

primarily with children of the opposite sex, but they did have contact on occasion (Sroufe, Bennett, Englund, Urban, & Shulman, 1993). They seemed to adhere to the rules for contact listed in Table 11.1. Violation of these rules is associated with having fewer friends and low peer status. Some teachers mistakenly believe that children who cross gender boundaries, such as flirting at a young age, are socially mature. Instead, maintenance of clear gender boundaries in preadolescence is characteristic of socially competent children, whereas early interest in the opposite sex and early dating may forecast problems.

Adolescence (13 to 19 Years)

Allison, a 16-year-old, sits at a crowded lunch table. Other students are trying to find room to squeeze in at her table. Allison says that none of her friends has a boyfriend, but they have lots of male friends with whom they "watch movies together and go to games and stuff." She says teenagers usually have "two or three close friends and fifteen to twenty casual friends."

Is Allison typical? Research shows that most teenagers have reciprocal friends (80 to 90%), usually with one or two best friends and several good friends. Adolescent friends exchange things (clothing or CDs), have shared activities, like watching movies together, and talk frequently on the phone or through texting. In fact, adolescents spend more time with friends than younger children do—roughly one-third of their waking hours (Hartup & Abecassis, 2002).

Homophily is stronger in adolescence than in middle childhood. Friends are especially similar to one another in achievement and in delinquency. An organized group of delinquent youth may become a "gang."

Table 11.1 Children's rules for contact with the opposite sex

Rule:	The contact is accidental.
Example:	You're not looking where you are going and you bump into someone.
Rule:	The contact is incidental.
Example:	You go to get some lemonade and wait while two children of the other gender get some. (There should be no conversation.)
Rule:	The contact is in the guise of some clear and necessary purpose.
Example:	You may say, "Pass the lemonade," to persons of the other gender at the next table. Do not express interest in them.
Rule:	An adult compels you to have contact.
Example:	"Go get that map from X and bring it to me."
Rule:	You are accompanied by someone of your own gender.
Example:	Two girls may talk to two boys though physical closeness with your own partner must be maintained and intimacy with the others is disallowed.
Rule:	The interaction or contact is accompanied by disavowal.
Example:	You say someone is ugly or hurl some other insult or (more commonly for boys) push or throw something at them as you pass by.

Source: From Sroufe, L. A., Bennett, C., Englund, M., Urban, J., & Shulman, S. (1993). The significance of gender boundaries in preadolescence: Contemporary correlates and antecedents of boundary violation and maintenance. *Child Development*, *64*, 455-466. Reprinted with permission from John Wiley & Sons.

Gangs

Tens of thousands of adolescents in the United States are involved in gangs. Many students report gang presence at their school—37% in one study (Howell & Lynch, 2000). Large cities and poor communities have more gangs, but gangs exist in all types of communities. Gang members are mostly male, between the ages of 15 and 24. Nationally, gang members are 44% Latino, 35% African American, 14% White, and 5% Asian, but this varies by region (Flannery, Hussey, Biebelhausen, & Wester, 2003).

Youth who join gangs tend to have low social status and reside in disorganized neighborhoods. The gang meets their need to belong, provides protection, and may replace dysfunctional families, but a gang also exerts negative peer pressure. Gang members tend to socialize each other not to care about academic achievement. Older gang members show disdain for schooling, and the youngsters imitate them. Youth who join gangs are more likely to use drugs, commit crimes, and be promiscuous (Howell & Lynch, 2000). Prominent gang members may be ex-prisoners who bring prison culture to the gang. As one Latino said, "I got more respect from the guys after I was *torcido* [twisted, i.e., arrested]" (Vigil, 2004, p. 98).

Gang membership can be temporary for some youth as they transition to high school—once comfortable in high school, they leave the gang. These temporary gang members wear gang colors or hang out with gang members, but are not as delinquent (Walker-Barnes & Mason, 2001). Many schools have gang-leaving programs to help.

Romance

Gender segregation continues into adolescence, meaning that adolescents' friends and peer networks are primarily members of the same gender. However, between 6th and 12th grades, adolescents begin crossing gender boundaries, forming cross-gender secondary friendships (Poulin & Pedersen, 2007). Girls who are antisocial or experience puberty early tend to have male friendships at an earlier age.

Some adolescents become romantically involved. About two-thirds of 12th-graders, but only one-third of 8th-graders, date once or twice a month or go steady (Bouchey & Furman, 2003; Henry et al., 2007). Generally, adolescents who date tend to select partners who are similar in popularity and attractiveness, but those who date more popular partners tend to become more popular over time (Simon, Aikins, & Prinstein, 2008).

Do youth benefit from romance? Romantic partners can be a source of social support to older adolescents, much like an attachment relationship. Romantic love can provide feelings of security, care, and comfort (Diamond, 2004). However, romance can also be a source of stress. Dating on a regular basis has been linked to lower GPA and test scores, lower academic motivation, and depression for 8th- through 12th-graders (Quatman, Sampson, Robinson, & Watson, 2001). Romance can be a risk factor for sexual victimization, substance use, and violence (Bouchey & Furman, 2003). In a national study of high school students, 10% had been

Maksim Toome, 2010/Used under license from Shutterstock.com

Some youth develop romantic relationships during adolescence.

Think About This Does the correlation between low achievement and dating mean that teens date because they are disengaged from school? Or, does dating cause teens to underachieve? Explain this based on the discussion of correlation in Chapter 1. What does your personal experience suggest?

physically assaulted on a date in the past year (Grunbaum et al., 2002). Bullies are likely to be aggressive in their romantic relationships.

Sexual behavior

Sexual attraction may begin as early as age 10 (Ruble, Martin, & Berenbaum, 2006). However, according to national studies, most high school students (55 to 75%) do not have sex. Another 5 to 20% may be promiscuous, having unprotected sex with multiple partners (Federal Interagency Forum on Child and Family Statistics, 2008; Henry et al., 2007). Boys are more likely to initiate sex early and to have more partners than girls. Girls are more likely to experience unwanted sex: 7% of adolescent girls reported being forced to have sex against their will, and another 24% said it was voluntary, but unwanted (Crockett, Raffaelli, & Moilanen, 2003).

Human Immunodeficiency Virus (HIV) a virus that undermines the immune system, contracted through extended contact with bodily fluids of infected persons.

Acquired Immunodeficiency Syndrome (AIDS) diagnosis given to HIV-positive individuals who develop severe symptoms indicating the immune system is activated.

Which teens are most likely to be sexually active? *Risk factors* for sexual activity among teens include early puberty, sexually active friends, early dating, and a permissive attitude about premarital sex. Risk factors also include being African American, living in a poor neighborhood, having behavior problems, having a single parent, having a mother who was young at her first birth, and experiencing too little or excessive parental monitoring (Dupere, Lacourse, Willms, Leventhal, & Tremblay, 2008; Raffaelli & Crockett, 2003; Zimmer-Gembeck & Helfand, 2008). Youth are more likely to have early sexual activity if they have multiple risk factors. Early sexual activity is associated with depression and substance use and is part of an overall pattern of delinquency (Meier, 2007). *Protective factors* include participation in extracurricular activities, religious affiliation, high educational aspirations, parental disapproval of premarital sex, and parent–child closeness (Crockett et al., 2003; Tinsley, Lees, & Sumartojo, 2004).

Sexual activity can result in pregnancy and sexually transmitted infections (STIs). About 5% of adolescents are involved in a pregnancy, or about 900,000 per year in the United States. Adolescent pregnancy rates vary by ethnicity; African American and Hispanic youth have four to five times the rate of Asian and White youth (Federal Interagency Forum on Child and Family Statistics, 2008). Because early relationships are short-lived, sexually active adolescents may have several partners, which increases the risk of STIs. As symptoms develop, infections can become sexually transmitted diseases (STDs). Among teen girls who have ever had sex, 40% have STDs (Hampton, 2008). See Box 11.1.

Lesbian, gay, and bisexual youth

Most youth will develop a heterosexual orientation. However, 1 to 8% identify as lesbian, gay, or bisexual (LGB), meaning they are attracted to either their own sex or to both sexes (Savin-Williams, 2006). The distinction between homosexuality and heterosexuality is not clear cut; roughly half of sexual-minority youth report sexual activity with someone of the opposite sex (Collins, Welsh, & Furman, 2009). Boys who experience same-sex attraction are likely to identify this attraction in high school, but girls often identify same-sex attraction in college and may change in sexual attraction for males versus females over time (Diamond, 2007).

Scientists do not yet know all the antecedents of LGB orientation. Hormone exposure during pregnancy may be linked to gender-atypical behavior in children and LGB orientation in adults (Mustanski, Chivers, & Bailey, 2002; Pasterski et al., 2005).

Challenges in Development Box 11.1

STIs and HIV/AIDS

Victorio's mother died of AIDS when he was 6. She was an intravenous drug user and had an AIDS-positive sexual partner before marrying Victorio's father. She was ashamed of the truth, so she said she got AIDS from a blood transfusion at Victorio's birth. Victorio lived with crushing guilt over this. After her death, her five children were adopted into three different families (their father was in prison). Victorio was aggressive, disruptive, and antagonistic with peers, but overly anxious to please adults. At age 12 he was deeply frightened by the possibility he might have AIDS, although tests were negative.

You may have children like Victorio in your classroom who are affected by HIV/AIDS in two ways: (1) a family member may be ill or die of AIDS and/or (2) the children may have HIV/AIDS themselves.

What are STIs and HIV/AIDS? Sexually transmitted infections (STIs) are infections spread through sexual contact. When symptoms develop, they are called sexually transmitted diseases (STDs) such as gonorrhea, chlamydia, syphilis, herpes simplex virus, and AIDS. They are among the most common diseases in the United States. STDs can cause inflammation in the reproductive tract, pain, infertility, premature birth, or fetal malformation (DiClemente & Crosby, 2003). They can also affect the nervous system, cardiovascular or liver functioning, and other biological functions. Some are fatal.

Human immunodeficiency virus (HIV) undermines the immune system, allowing other infections to overwhelm the body. People who are positive for the virus (HIV+) can vary from no symptoms, to mild flu-like symptoms, to severe symptoms like repeated episodes of pneumonia. A diagnosis of **acquired immunodeficiency syndrome (AIDS)** is made when symptoms become severe and the number of T cells in the body is high (T cells indicate that the immune system has been activated).

HIV/AIDS is spread through prolonged contact with bodily fluids, like blood or semen, of an infected person. This includes, but is not limited to, sexual contact. In the United States, AIDS was first reported among homosexual men and drug users, who continue to be primary risk groups. Currently about one-quarter of new cases are spread heterosexually (Centers for Disease Control and Prevention, 2009). A small number get it from blood transfusions. Most cases of HIV/AIDS in young children are transmitted mother-to-child at birth or during breastfeeding. Most cases of HIV/AIDS in adolescents are contracted through sex.

Prevalence of STDs and AIDS. STDs are epidemic among adolescents. Girls and African American youth are more likely to contract STDS than are other groups. In a national study, 48% of 14- to 19-year-old Black girls and 20% of White girls had at least one STD (Hampton, 2008). Youth most at risk for STDs have early sexual activity, multiple sex partners, frequent sex, and sex unprotected by a condom.

Co-morbidity. There are several behavior problems that are co-morbid, or go together, with HIV/AIDS. Like Victorio's mother, many HIV-infected parents are drug users (Forsyth, 2003). When children have HIV/AIDS themselves, they may have other problems such as depression, anxiety, ADHD, drug use, and sex while under the influence of drugs. They may also have delays in language, motor abilities, cognitive development, and attention regulation (Brown, Lescano, & Lourie, 2001; Mialky, Vagnoni, & Rutstein, 2001; Wachsler-Felder & Golden, 2002). For example, they may have lower IQ, an unusual walking gait, or difficulty holding a pencil and writing. However, the effects vary in severity. Some HIV+ children have normal cognitive development.

What can be done about HIV/AIDS? You are not likely to know if a student in your classroom is HIV+. In most cases, school personnel do not know. Many young children are not even told their own HIV status by parents (Mialky et al., 2001).

AIDS cannot be cured, but it is preventable. Prevention may need to start in elementary school because some youth, particularly African American males, report sexual activity as early as 5th grade (Schonfeld, 2000). Even preschoolers can be taught some aspects of prevention, such as not to touch other people's blood, and not to touch sharp objects like razors that have been used (Segal, Cole, & Fuld, 2002). Education may increase knowledge of AIDS, but it may not alter risky behavior (Gaskins, Beard, & Wang, 2002; Schonfeld, 2000). Adolescents typically underestimate their risk for contracting STIs and are more concerned about pregnancy than STIs (Brackis-Cott, Mellins, & Block, 2003). Thus, *prevention needs to focus on changing behavior, not just on informing children.*

Prevention programs aimed at changing behavior are either abstinence or safe-sex oriented. Abstinence programs ask youth to commit to not have sex before marriage or until

(continued)

Challenges in Development *(continued)*

adulthood. Safe-sex programs try to increase condom use. However, correct condom use may not prevent all STIs, and adolescents may not use condoms correctly (DiClemente & Crosby, 2003). Thus, a hierarchy of effective prevention messages would be: unprotected sex is unsafe, condom-protected sex is safer, and abstinence is safest.

Which programs are best? It depends on your goal. Safe-sex programs result in more condom use and do not increase, but sometimes reduce, sexual behavior (Johnson, Carey, Marsh, Levin, & Scott-Sheldon, 2003). Abstinence programs result in less sexual activity (DiClemente & Crosby, 2003). Successful programs focus on specific behaviors like abstaining from sex, using condoms, and avoiding problem situations, and they attempt to fit the youths' culture, age, and sexual experience (Kirby & Laris, 2009). Unfortunately, benefits of both types of programs are small and decay over time so that behavior may be back at preintervention levels just a few months later. Thus, it may be more effective to address the factors that lead to sexual behavior among youth, such as family functioning and attitudes toward sex (Tinsley et al., 2004). Factors that protect children from risky sex include feeling cared for, school bonding, parental monitoring, open parent–child communication, married parents, and parental disapproval of youth sex (DiClemente & Crosby, 2003).

Children's gender-atypical behavior, like a lack of interest in rough-and-tumble play for boys, may predict LGB orientation for some, but this does not mean that gender-atypical play *causes* same-sex attraction (Rieger, Linsenmeier, Gygax, & Bailey, 2008). Some LGB adults report gender-typical childhoods, and many gender-atypical children do not develop a LGB orientation. There may be moderate heritability to boys' sexual orientation, but the evidence is not conclusive and is even less so for girls' orientation (e.g., Mustanski et al., 2005). Thus, no single developmental path for LGB orientation has been identified. There are most likely multiple biological and environmental pathways.

Some LGB youth have a difficult time establishing healthy friendships. Their gender-atypical behavior can lead to peer rejection and feeling alienated at school—even before they have identified as LGB (Bos, Sandfort, de Bruyn, & Hakvoort, 2008). They may have difficulty dating because they do not know who else feels same-sex attraction. They may be victimized if they make overtures to the wrong person, or their orientation is known (Diamond & Savin-Williams, 2003; Rivers, 2002). They also are at higher risk for substance use, risky sex, violence, lower grades, and strained parent–child relationships (Busseri, Willoughby, Chalmers, & Bogaert, 2008). School personnel should prevent and address harassment problems, so that school is welcoming to all youth. Let's turn next to differences in friendships among children.

Individual Diversity in Friendship and Peer Networks

Did you have the same best friend from preschool to 12th grade? Many adults report having the same best friend across childhood, but this may be a false memory. Among preschoolers, less than 10% of friends are still friends the following school year, even when friends move into a new class together (Vaughn et al., 2001). Friendships in adolescence are more stable than in early childhood, but even in adolescence best friends change from year to year (Dishion & Owen, 2002).

The composition of cliques also changes. The most stable cliques retain only about 50% of members from one school year to the next, and other cliques completely dissolve. As children get older there is slightly more stability, so that 7th-grade cliques are more stable than those of 4th grade, which are more stable than 1st-grade cliques (Estell, Farmer, Cairns, & Cairns, 2002).

While the specific friends may change from year to year, students who have friends at one age are likely to have friends at a later age. That is, whether a child has friends or is friendless is fairly stable (Hartup & Abecassis, 2002). *Quality* of friendships is also stable. That is, children with high-quality friendships in preschool have high-quality friendships later (Howes & Tonyon, 2000). Children who have deviant friends earlier will tend to have deviant friends in adolescence (Dishion & Owen, 2002).

What Do Individual Differences in Friendship Predict?

Some students have more friends than others. Some students have higher-quality friends than do others. Friendships can contribute to healthy development, or they can be a source of risk. Let's discuss four outcomes linked to friendships.

Academic achievement

Friends promote academic achievement. In class, friends working together spend *more* time on task and work at a more cognitively advanced level than nonfriends do (Hartup & Abecassis, 2002). Friends exchange ideas; explore, remember, write, and help each other more; and have more positive emotions when working together. They work with less conflict and more constructive activity than do nonfriends (Strough, Berg, & Meegan, 2001). These short-term effects are likely to have long-term consequences if they occur frequently.

Clique membership may more strongly predict academic achievement than specific friendships or peer status. As you learned in Chapter 6, as students transition from elementary to middle school they decline in achievement and motivation. However, students who affiliate with high achievers decline less, and those who affiliate with low achievers decline more. From 1st to 12th grade, students tend to affiliate at the beginning of the year with other students who are academically similar to themselves, and then become more like their clique in achievement and motivation over the course of the school year (Estell et al., 2002; Kindermann, 2007).

Emotional well-being

Friends help each other manage, understand, and talk about emotions (Burgess, Wojslawowica, Rubin, Rose-Krasnor, & Booth-LaForce, 2006). Friends protect students from loneliness and depression (Asher & Paquette, 2003; Cheng & Furnham, 2002). Students with friends are happier and have higher self-esteem than friendless students. Friends share enjoyable activities, provide support during stress, and validate each other's worth. Youth with prosocial friends weather divorce better than students with deviant friends (Hetherington, 1999). Thus, good friendships promote emotional well-being.

Social well-being

Friends provide students with the opportunity to learn and practice social skills. For example, in one study, 6th-graders became more prosocial by 8th grade if they had a prosocial friend (Wentzel, Barry, & Caldwell, 2004). That is, a single friend's social behavior can predict a child's change in behavior two years later.

What happens when a student does not have friends? One friendless 6th-grade boy said, "I got no friends, but I don't care. When I am nice they still won't play with me. So I ignore them. Ain't no one gonna take care of you. You gotta take care of yourself. All I need is me. *They* need to change, not me." This boy has little social support for coping with emotions, nor opportunity to develop better social skills.

Delinquency

Thus far you have learned about the positive effects of friendship. Yet, you can probably think of a student who had a destructive friendship. Friends can victimize one another. Friends can plot and carry out crime together. Friends can serve as models of antisocial behavior. Students who choose antisocial friends become even more antisocial. In one longitudinal study, children's cliques at 5 to 10 years of age predicted their future dropping out of school and teenage parenthood (Cairns & Cairns, 1994). Students who hang out with friends who dislike school tend to come to like school less. Students with low-quality friendships tend to become less engaged in classroom activities and more disruptive (Berndt, 2002).

How does this "dark side" of friendship work? Antisocial students select each other as friends, and then train each other in deviancy. One study videotaped teenage boys interacting with their peers for twenty-five minutes (Dishion, McCord, & Poulin, 1999). When the boys talked about breaking rules, delinquent friends laughed, whereas nondelinquent friends paused or changed the subject. Thus, some friends reinforced delinquency through interest in misbehavior, which led to more substance use, delinquency, and violence two years later. This is particularly true of early-onset antisocial children. Youth whose antisocial behavior starts when they are older and is limited to the adolescent years are more likely to have typical friendships (Piehler & Dishion, 2007). Don't assume training in deviancy pertains only to teenagers—it occurs as young as kindergarten (Snyder et al., 2008).

> ***Think About This*** Imagine you have a friend whose 15-year-old has "gotten into the wrong crowd" and is using drugs. Your friend decides to move the child to a different school. Is this a good idea? What would you advise this friend, based on research?

What Predicts Quantity and Quality of Friendships?

Several factors predict whether students will have beneficial or destructive friendships. The student's social competence is a key predictor, as are parenting factors that contribute to students' social competence.

Social competence

Students who are prosocial, sociable, and skilled at entering groups are more likely to have a good friend. Prosocial students are especially likely to have reciprocated friendships (Gest, Graham-Bermann, & Hartup, 2001). Students want to be friends with other students who are more prosocial than they themselves are, which helps explain unilateral friendships.

Aggressive students tend to have fewer friends, but are not necessarily friendless (Ladd & Troop-Gordon, 2003). Bullies have friends. Gang members have friends. You learned earlier that tough/popular students are both aggressive and perceived as popular. However, aggressive students tend to have low-quality, conflict-ridden friendships with other aggressive students (Ladd, Buhs, & Troop, 2002). Prosocial Nadya, in the opening vignette, is not likely to be friends with aggressive Eleanor.

Parenting factors

Several parenting factors that are linked to children's social competence (see Chapter 10) are also linked to their friendships. First, parent–child attachment predicts friendship quality. Securely attached children tend to have high-quality friendships and a larger peer network. This effect is found for children of different ethnicities from preschool to young adulthood.[1] How does this happen? Children who are secure openly communicate about emotions, develop better language skills, and have less hostile attribution bias, which helps them develop higher-quality friendships (McElwain, Booth-LaForce, Lansford, Wu, & Dyer, 2008). Other parenting factors linked to friendships include:

1. *Authoritative parenting style.* Children whose parents are warm, communicate clearly with them, and monitor their activities are more likely to have positive friendships compared with children whose parents are authoritarian or permissive (Brody et al., 2001).
2. *Modeling.* Parents who have high-quality friendships tend to have children who have high-quality friendships (Simpkins & Parke, 2001).
3. *Coaching friendship skills.* Parents who talk to their children about how to repair relationships during conflicts between friends, rather than just stating rules like *"we always share!"* or simply ending the conflict, have children with more harmonious friendships (Putallaz, Costanzo, Grimes, & Sherman, 1998).
4. *Monitoring friendships.* Youth whose parents know their friends and guide them in choosing friends tend to have high-quality friendships. Guidance involves getting to know the friends' parents, telling the child to choose friends carefully, and helping the child recognize bad behavior in friends (Ladd & Pettit, 2002; Mounts, 2001).
5. *Supervision.* While friends are beneficial, youth who hang around too much with peers unsupervised have lower grades and more behavior problems than those who are supervised (Goldstein, Davis-Kean, & Eccles, 2005; Updegraff, Whiteman, McHale, Thayer, & Crouter, 2006).
6. *Abuse.* Children who have experienced abuse tend to have difficulty forming and maintaining friendships (Ladd & Pettit, 2002).

Low-quality parenting puts children on the track to antisocial behavior and deviant peers, and then peers may keep children on that track as they progress through school (Pettit, 2005). Unfortunately, schools contribute to delinquency when they group deviant students together through ability grouping, retaining low-achieving students, group counseling, alternative classrooms for unruly students, and in-school suspension (Dodge, Dishion, & Lansford, 2006). In Chapter 7 you met Paul, who is sent to in-school suspension (ISS) where his friends can often be found. The boys are given opportunity to strengthen deviant friendships in ISS. They are also being separated from other peers who model more-appropriate behavior.

Group Diversity in Friendship and Peer Networks

There are some gender, ethnic, and national differences in students' peer networks and their behavior within friendships.

[1]Many studies find this, just a few of which are listed here (Hartup & Abecassis, 2002; Howes & Tonyon, 2000; Ladd & Pettit, 2002; Schneider, Atkinson, & Tardif, 2001).

Alibi Productions/Alamy

Where are the boys sitting in this lunch room? Where are the girls sitting?

Gender

Girls tend to have more friends in the classroom than do boys, but cliques may be slightly smaller for girls from preschool through the primary grades (Estell et al., 2002; Hartup & Abecassis, 2002). Young boys tend to hang around with a larger group of friends. However, by middle school, boys' and girls' peer networks are similar in size, and by high school girls' networks are a little larger and less exclusive than boys' (Farmer et al., 2003; Lee, Howes, & Chamberlain, 2007).

Gender segregation results in boys and girls growing up in different peer cultures (Rose & Rudolph, 2006). Boys' friendships tend to be based on shared activities and interests like sports and video games. Girls' friendships tend to be based on emotional closeness and sharing feelings and personal information (Golombok & Hines, 2002). Girls expect and report greater affection, help, and intimacy from friendships than do boys. In spite of this greater intimacy, girl friends have just as much conflict and broken friendships, if not more so, than do boy friends from kindergarten through high school (Benenson & Christakos, 2003; Ladd, Kochenderfer, & Coleman, 1996).

Field Observation

Go to an elementary school lunchroom where seating is not assigned. Describe implicit rules for where boys and girls sit. What happens when someone violates gender boundaries? What kind of interactions are going on in the different gender groups? Compare your observation with the research.

Ethnicity

If you have been in a multiethnic school, you have probably observed homophily in action because same-ethnic youth tend to associate with each other. Homophily is stronger in high school than in elementary school. One study of 4th-graders found that White children were more likely to have cross-ethnic friendships than Black or Latino children. The students who managed to forge cross-ethnic friendships were usually prosocial leaders in the classroom (Kawabata & Crick, 2008). At the high school level, a large national study found that African American and White students are least likely to be friends (Quillian & Campbell, 2003).

Schools in which students are separated into academic tracks have the fewest cross-ethnic friendships (Stearns, 2004). Students whose ethnic group is small in number at the school are especially likely to choose same-ethnic friends, as though the small numbers drive them together. Still, students do not segregate by ethnicity as much as they do by gender (Lee et al., 2007).

How can you promote friendships for students whose ethnic group is small in number at your school? Some educators advocate clustering minority students in classrooms so that they can form same-ethnic friendships, rather than distributing them across classrooms or schools and forcing them into a lonely existence. However, others argue that this would resegregate schools and result in academic tracking because achievement varies by ethnicity. They advocate intentionally grouping students of different ethnicities together. This can increase cross-ethnic friendships, but also racial tension. Thus, educators have to weigh these considerations for the particular ethnic composition of their classroom and school.

Cross-National Comparisons

Across nations, one tends to find similar gender segregation and peer networks of similar size. For example, a study of 3rd-, 6th-, and 10th-graders in Shanghai found most groups were male or female, and clique size was remarkably similar to clique size of same-age U.S. students. However, one cultural difference was that, unlike U.S. students, members within a clique were not very similar to each other in social competence or delinquency (Chen et al., 2003). Instead, cliques in the Chinese schools were formed mainly on the basis of similar academic achievement, which is highly valued in China. Thus, the value system of a society may influence the basis on which peer groups form.

Classroom Implications of Friendship and Peer Networks

You have seen that friendships and peer networks influence academic achievement. Students with high-quality friendships in the classroom like school and actively participate, which promotes learning. In contrast, students who are friendless attend school less, are socially uncomfortable, and achieve less (Thorkildsen, Reese, & Corsino, 2002). Ideally each child has at least one good friend in your classroom. You can help your students form high-quality friendships by following these guidelines.

- *Help students develop prosocial behavior.* See Chapter 10 for how to do this.
- *Promote attachment at school.* Caring teacher–student relationships protect adolescents from the negative effect of delinquent friends (Crosnoe & Needham, 2004). See Chapter 6 for how to do this.
- *Keep friends together from year to year—if the friendships are not deviant.* Because students choose friends from among the pool of available classmates, when schools keep students together in classes from year to year, there is greater stability of friendships, even if the teacher changes. Students with good friends in their class make smoother transitions to kindergarten, middle school, and junior high (Berndt, Hawkins, & Jiao, 1999; Wentzel et al., 2004).
- *Place friends together* when forming cooperative learning groups in your classroom or constructing classroom placements for the next school year. Students without best friends *in their class* are lonelier than other students, regardless of their peer status or whether they have friends in other classes in the school (Parker & Asher, 1993). Some teachers mistakenly assume that students will be off-task if they work with friends, but research suggests the opposite in most situations (Pellegrini, Galda, Bartini, & Charak, 1998; Zajac & Hartup, 1997).
- *Promote opportunities to form friendships*, particularly early in the school year. Eliminate school policies that restrict students' peer interaction outside of class. For example, some schools require students to walk in a single-file line, without talking, to and from buses. Some schools punish students for talking with friends at lunch. Such policies promote friendlessness and undermine students' well-being.
- *Recruit the help of the school counselor to provide intervention for friendless students.* Friendship-building skills can be taught. For example, in one intervention, 5th-graders were taught to share, joke, smile, and talk to peers in 10 one-hour weekly sessions. Afterward, peers reported liking the intervention students better and feeling more liked by them (Murphy & Schneider, 1994).

One of the reasons friendlessness and peer rejection are detrimental is that they restrict students' opportunity to play. Playing together is a central feature of friendships, from early childhood to adolescence. Let's discuss play next.

Play

In a 9th-grade science class, the students were told how to do an experiment and then asked to put on their safety goggles. One boy put on three pairs of goggles so that he looked like a scuba diver. He shouted, "Heh, heh! Attack of the scuba monster!" and jabbed at his lab partners with his yardstick. His lab partners retaliated in a mock sword fight with their yardsticks. The teacher told the boys to "settle down and get to work." They did, completing their lab assignment with occasional playful jabs at one another and lots of laughter.

Play is almost inevitable when children are gathered together, even during science class when they should be working. Play is so much a part of being a child that it is often used to define childhood. Should you encourage play in your classroom? The answer depends on your understanding of play.

play behavior that has no immediate function and is pleasurable, spontaneous, flexible, and internally controlled.

Play is easy to recognize, yet difficult to define. Play is characterized by positive emotions (smiling or laughing), fantasy, spontaneity, and flexibility. It has no immediate function and does not involve competition. However, play may not always have all these features. For example, games-with-rules, like sports, may or may not be considered play because they are often competitive, lack spontaneity, and can involve negative emotion.

Types of Play

How children play helps you understand their development, so let's look at types of play. Play varies along two dimensions: (1) low to high cognitive involvement and (2) low to high social involvement. Table 11.2 displays different types of play. These types are hierarchical. In the cognitive domain, functional play is the least mature and games-with-rules the most mature form of play. However, even adolescents engage in functional play, like simply bouncing a ball. In the social domain, higher forms of play involve more social coordination. The most advanced forms of play are pretense and games-with-rules that involve coordination among multiple children. When pretense play involves cooperation with other children, it is called *sociodramatic play.*

rough-and-tumble play a form of social, pretense play that involves physically vigorous behavior and often resembles, but is not the same as, aggression.

physical play a type of play in which children move for the joy of movement, such as climbing, running, or chasing.

Another type of play, **rough-and-tumble** (R&T) **play**, or play fighting, combines pretense and **physical play**, like sword fighting in science class (Pellegrini, 2002). *It is not aggression.* This is an important distinction because R&T play is good for children, but aggression is not. R&T play is one way that boys express fondness for one another (Reed & Brown, 2001). Table 11.3 shows how R&T play is distinguished from aggression. R&T play is common on playgrounds, although it can occur in classrooms. Let's look next at how types of play change with age.

Age Trends in Play

Which age do you think is the most playful? The frequency of play peaks in early to middle childhood and generally follows an inverted U-shape. That is, play is less frequent in infancy/toddlerhood, becomes more frequent in middle childhood, and

Table 11.2 Cognitive and social dimensions of play from least to most mature

Least Mature →→→→→→→→→→→→→→→→→→→→→→→→→→ Most Mature				
Cognitive Dimensions of Play				
Functional Play	**Physical Play**	**Constructive Play**	**Pretense (or Dramatic) Play**	**Game-with-Rules**
Simple movement or a repetitive, practice-like behavior, such as shaking a rattle.	Large movement for the joy of movement, such as climbing, running, or chasing.	Creating, or building something, with a goal in mind, such as building with blocks or drawing with crayons.	Transforming objects and identities. Imaginary friends are a type of pretense.	Explicit prearranged rules where children must adapt their behavior to the rules, such as hopscotch or checkers.
Social Dimensions of Play				
Unoccupied and Onlooker	**Solitary Play**	**Parallel Play**	**Associative Play**	**Cooperative Play**
Following others around or watching their play, perhaps even talking to them, but not joining the play.	Playing alone when playmates are available, with no reference to what others are doing.	Playing near others with similar toys, but not seeking to interact; that is, children play beside rather than with others.	Borrowing toys or following each other, but the children do whatever each wants to.	Group is organized around a goal, or a formal game, and division of roles (e.g., "I'm the mommy and you're the doggie"). It is clear who belongs to the group and who does not.

Table 11.3 Characteristics of rough-and-tumble play compared with aggression

	Rough-and-Tumble Play	**Aggression**
Behavior	Soft, open-hand hitting, pushing, chasing, teasing, wrestling. Children help anyone who appears hurt.	Hard hits, shoving, kicking
Emotions	Smiling or laughing	Frowning or scowling
Results	Further shared activities, participants stay together afterward	Participants separate
Intent	Fun, expressing affection	Harm

then becomes less frequent again during adolescence (Pellegrini & Smith, 1998). Type of play also changes with age.

Early Childhood (Birth to 5 Years)

Infants primarily engage in functional play by themselves, like banging a pot over and over. This functional play diminishes and becomes rare by 4 to 5 years. Infants also engage in some rough-and-tumble play, but only if the play is scaffolded by the parent, like when Dad dandles the baby.

Toddlers engage in constructive play by themselves, like drawing, and this remains a common play activity throughout early childhood. At 15 to 24 months pretense play first emerges, and then dramatically increases from 2 to 5 years (Göncü, Patt,

Trista Weibell/iStockphoto

These children are playing side by side, but not together. What type of play is this?

& Kouba, 2002). The ability to cooperate with other children during pretense play emerges during this time. Three-year-olds can sustain play with an unfamiliar peer better than toddlers can, and 5-year-olds are even better. Preschoolers' pretense play involves longer sequences, greater complexity, and more fantasy than toddlers' play. For example, play might shift from toddlers simply feeding a doll to 5-year-olds making elaborate witch brew. There is also more agreement among children about the roles, rules, and themes in a play episode as they get older. These changes may be the result of improved perspective-taking ability (see Chapter 8) and theory of mind (see Chapter 9).

Middle Childhood (6 to 12 Years)

Each type of play found in early childhood continues into middle childhood; however, their prevalence shifts. Three kinds of play become more prevalent in middle childhood: constructive play, games-with-rules, and R&T play. Preschoolers seldom engage in games-with-rules, but elementary children often do, such as playing cards or foursquare at recess. R&T play accounts for about 5% of free play for preschoolers, about 10 to 17% for elementary children, and about 5% for middle school children (Pellegrini, 2002). In contrast, pretense play becomes less prevalent in middle childhood; it peaks at about 5 to 6 years of age, but is still observed among older children. For example, a group of 6th-grade boys formed a series of large circles in the snow at recess; they were UFO landing sites. Another group played "Jedi Knights." Thus, you will see pretense play in elementary school, but not to the same extent as in preschool.

Play takes on increased complexity with age. Constructive play becomes more complex, like building a Ferris wheel from an erector set. Simple motor activity gives way to complex physical activity like shooting baskets. Simple interactive chase games give way to more complex interactive games, like soccer, basketball, or jump rope (Pellegrini, Blatchford, Kato, & Baines, 2004). Let's visit an elementary playground for a classic example of how play changes over middle childhood.

Will, a kindergartener, spent recess running from place to place—swings, sandbox, and teeter-totter. He played with boys and girls. His teacher tried to keep a kickball game going among the kindergartners, but they had trouble understanding the rules, and the children came and went from the game. In contrast, the 5th-graders quickly organized three games (football, soccer, and foursquare). No adults helped with the games; they were child-run. Will's older brother, Ivan, stayed with the same game (football) the entire recess, as did most other 5th-graders. Ivan's game was boys only. Several girls played jump rope games with complicated rules, rhythms, and songs.

Adolescence (13 to 19 Years)

Teenagers are fun! They can rapidly turn work into play, as the 9th-graders in the opening vignette did. In high school classrooms you will see many forms of play, including the ask-questions-to-get-the-teacher-off-track game. In adolescence, play can be purely mental. Adolescents "play" with ideas much like younger children play with objects—combining them in new ways or substituting one for another. Using the mind as a playground fosters creativity and discovery.

Most types of play continue in adolescence. For example, constructive solitary play occurred when an adolescent built a remote-controlled car. Sociodramatic play occurred when a group of boys stumbled upon a high school storage room where they found two old chairs with wheels, and pretended to be NASCAR drivers in the hallway—until they were caught. Another group was assigned to write a skit for their German class that evolved into a complex pretend sword fight between nations—in German, of course.

R&T play continues, although with less frequency, in adolescence, where it serves at least two purposes:

1. Crossing gender boundaries. Because gender segregation is well-entrenched and crossing gender boundaries is socially risky, adolescents use R&T play to do so. A boy might playfully steal a girl's hat so that he can "save face" if the girl rejects his overture. This is known as "poke-and-push courtship."
2. Domination or disguised aggression. In early adolescence, boys who engage in R&T play also engage in more aggression (Pellegrini, 2003). This is not true of younger children.

Playing games-with-rules, like board games or freeze tag, diminishes in adolescence but does not disappear altogether. Adolescents are more likely to just hang out with friends than play structured games (Blatchford, 1998; Hughes, 1999).

Individual Diversity in Play

Do you know children who seem highly playful? Some children consistently play more, and in more advanced ways, than other children. Differences in play provide a window into a child's cognitive and social competence. Differences in play also affect opportunity for acquiring skills. Vygotsky believed that play promotes development because children play in their zone of proximal development. Older children, especially siblings, scaffold younger children's skills during play. Let's examine how youth differ in their play.

What Do Individual Differences in Play Predict?

Students who frequently play in age-appropriate ways have better cognitive abilities and academic achievement. They show higher intelligence, verbal ability, visual-spatial ability, problem solving, literacy skills, and math achievement.[2] They also demonstrate better divergent thinking, which refers to being able to come up with different ideas—like how many ways you can move across the room—and is a part of creativity (Lloyd & Howe, 2003).

[2] Many studies support this conclusion, just a few of which are listed here (Cheah, Nelson, & Rubin, 2001; Dunn & Hughes, 2001; Fantuzzo, Sekino, & Cohen, 2004; Robert & Heroux, 2004; Roskos, 2000; Wolfgang, Stannard, & Jones, 2003).

Students who frequently play in age-appropriate ways also have greater social and emotional competence. This includes self-control, theory of mind, prosocial behavior, emotional perspective-taking, emotion regulation, and happiness.[3] They also are less aggressive. These positive outcomes linked to play have been found for preschoolers to adolescents. These benefits are especially evident in low-SES students with poor impulse control.

Does play *cause* these good outcomes? It seems reasonable because play requires students to coordinate with others and to try to understand others' intentions. Play requires them to inhibit immediate impulses. It promotes peer acceptance because classmates seek out students who are playful. Play requires students to problem-solve and to use imagination, language skills, and symbolism where one thing stands for another. Thus, play should help students become socially skilled and intelligent. Still, it is also possible that play is the result, not the cause, of these abilities. That is, some students may engage in more-advanced play because they are already more socially skilled and intelligent. How might you answer the question of causation? One approach is an experiment. If students who have poor skills are trained to play more, and then their skills improve, you can conclude that play probably caused the improvement. Let's look at what experiments have revealed.

One stark example of a field experiment occurred at Mother Teresa's orphanage in India. Children's physical needs were met, but the overworked caregivers were reluctant to let children play because they believed it would increase their workload. The children had significant developmental delays, much like the children with hospitalism described in Chapter 6. Researchers convinced the caregivers to try a ninety-minute daily playtime. Within three months, the children's motor, cognitive, and social skills improved dramatically. Children who could not talk or feed themselves became able to. The children were more active, playful, responsive, and independent, which actually decreased the caregivers' workload (Taneja et al., 2002).

This is a dramatic example, but similar results are found when at-risk children in preschools or child care centers are trained in sociodramatic play, in the United States as well as in other countries (Roopnarine, Shin, Donovan, & Suppal, 2000). One review of forty-six intervention studies found that when play is enhanced, children increase in cognitive skills, language, social skills, and self-control—with a noteworthy effect size of 0.35 (Fisher, 1992).

How might you train children to play? One approach to training involves an adult who helps the children plan their play—like "Let's play grocery store"—and then backs away, only intervening if the children need help to sustain their play, followed by a debriefing session—like "What did you play? What did you say to . . . ?" (Craig-Unkefer & Kaiser, 2002). In another approach the adult might read fantasy books—like *The Three Little Pigs*—and then help the children enact the story (Saltz, Dixon, & Johnson, 1977). Interventions may be more powerful when children enact fantasy stories than when they enact realistic events such as grocery shopping. Let's look next at why some children need intervention but others are already highly playful.

---

[3]Many studies support this conclusion, just a few of which are listed here (Cheah et al., 2001; Dunn & Hughes, 2001; Elias & Berk, 2002; Fantuzzo et al., 2004; Lillard, 2002; Pellegrini et al., 2004).

What Predicts Individual Differences in Play?

Several *child factors* predict playfulness. Students who are humorous, imaginative, curious, expressive, social, verbal, active, and novelty-seeking play more than other students. In contrast, students who have poor emotion regulation, are immature, impulsive, aggressive, and rejected by peers play less. Students who have physical or mental limitations may be less playful. For example, visually impaired students tend to have less mature pretend play (Lewis, Norgate, Collis, & Reynolds, 2000). Their play may be limited because they cannot observe peer models at play and their attention is not visually drawn to play objects. Autistic students tend to have impoverished functional and pretense play. Play is so characteristic of children that atypical play is often used to diagnose developmental delays.

Several *parent factors* predict playfulness. Parents influence the quality and amount of their children's play by providing opportunities for play and through the type of relationship they have with their children. Children with power-assertive parents are more likely to withdraw from social play, whereas children with authoritative parents are more likely to play cooperatively. Children with secure parent–child attachment initiate more play and have richer, more creative, and more socially complex play. Children with avoidant attachment are more likely to play in ways that involve no people (Cassibba, Van IJzendoorn, & D'Odorico, 2000; Sroufe, 1996).

A Cautionary Note about Solitary Play

In Table 11.2 you learned that solitary play is a less-mature form of play. Solitary play can be a cause for concern, but it depends on the context and whether the play is active or passive. **Solitary-active play** involves either functional play or dramatic pretense play. It is a red flag for poor social skills, if a child plays *alone when others are available to play with.* For example, a child might play with a ball alone when there are several other children playing nearby with a ball. Solitary-*active* play could be a cause and/or consequence of social withdrawal and peer rejection.

solitary-active play a type of play involving functional or pretense play while alone.

In contrast, **solitary-passive play** is not necessarily a cause for concern. It involves constructive play—like doing puzzles, drawing, coloring, or building with blocks. These are activities that are typically done alone, even when playmates are abundant. Solitary-passive play is linked to high academic achievement and social competence for children under age 7 and sometimes for older children. However, older children who play in a solitary-passive way because of social anxiety may have low achievement and internalizing problems (Burgess, Rubin, Cheah, & Nelson, 2005). Thus, solitary-*passive* play warrants careful observation because children who miss the benefits of social play could lag in social and academic skills. However, solitary play is only a concern in the midst of a classroom of playmates, not when there is no one else to play with, such as at home.

solitary-passive play a type of play involving construction or exploring objects while alone.

Are Sports Like Play?

Whether sports constitute play is debatable because they are organized, competitive, and have rules. Yet they are like play in that youth often participate purely for fun. In fact, many youth say that sports are the most enjoyable aspect of their lives (Larson & Verma, 1999). Sports can occur during physical education (PE) classes or as an extracurricular school activity, but most are unrelated to school, like Little League Baseball or city soccer leagues (Danish, Taylor, & Fazio, 2003). Only 12% of sport participation across childhood involves sports between schools.

Participation in sports increases with age. Large national studies indicate that about 25% of kindergarten through 3rd-graders, 40% of 4th- through 8th-graders, and 60% of 10th-graders participate in sports (Broh, 2002; Federal Interagency Forum on Child and Family Statistics, 2008). Sports are the most common type of organized after-school activity, followed by religious activities. Males, high-SES children, and popular children are most likely to participate in sports.

Is participation in sports good for children? It can be. It provides opportunity for fun and the formation of friendships. It promotes psychological well-being and self-esteem as an athlete (but not global self-esteem, unless athleticism is highly valued by the child). It promotes better sleeping patterns. It promotes both immediate and long-term fitness because youth who participate in sports are more likely to continue fitness activities into adulthood (Perkins, Jacobs, Barber, & Eccles, 2004). Participation in interscholastic sports promotes school bonding. Teen athletes have higher grades, better attendance, and are less likely to drop out of school than nonathletes (Broh, 2002).

However, participation in sports can also promote injuries, overtraining, and burnout. It can preclude participation in other important activities; students who engage in a wider variety of extracurricular activities, not just sports, fare better (Linver, Roth, & Brooks-Gunn, 2009; Simpkins, Eccles, & Becnel, 2008). It can lead to drug use, because some sports have a culture of drug use (Fauth, Roth, & Brooks-Gunn, 2007; Gardner, Roth, & Brooks-Gunn, 2009). In addition, games played within a few hours of bedtime can disrupt sleep because sports activity raises cortisol levels, which keeps children awake (Kertes & Gunnar, 2004). Thus, whether sports are good for students depends on the situation.

Group Diversity in Play

Differences in play are linked to gender and socioeconomic status. Culture also influences differences in play, although some aspects of play may be universal. Let's look at these group differences next.

Gender

Gender segregation occurs during play throughout childhood. As boys play with boys and girls play with girls, different play cultures emerge. Preschool girls are more likely to play indoors, near adults. They play house and games that require verbal interaction. They typically play with only two or three others. Their play involves cooperation, discussion, support, and encouragement with themes oriented around domestic or romantic scripts and maintenance of order and safety (Maccoby, 2002). Boys' play involves dominance, competition, conflict, and risk-taking with themes of danger, destruction, and heroism. Boys' play is more active, with more rough-and-tumble play (Pellegrini, 2003). For example, a teacher of 2- to 3-year-olds described play among the students in her class:

> *The girls usually draw and play with dolls while the boys usually "drive" toy trucks. Both boys and girls play with the puzzles and books. When I bring out the puppets, the boys immediately begin making their puppets growl and try to gobble each other up. This is funny because the puppets are a turtle and a giraffe—neither of which are known for growling. The girls make their puppets meow, cry, and kiss each other.*

In early elementary school boys play more games with balls, like soccer, basketball, and football; and girls play more games that involve songs, chants, and rhymes—like jump rope—just as they did at Will and Ivan's school in the earlier vignette (Pellegrini et al., 2004). Boy–girl differences in play have been found during almost a century of research on play (Harper & Huie, 1998).

Where do these gender differences in play come from? Perhaps parents cause them by reinforcing gender-typed play and providing gender-typed toys, like footballs to baby boys (Lytton & Romney, 1991). Or, perhaps parents are simply responding to children's innate gender differences, rather than causing them. The peer group, rather than parents, may be more powerful in sustaining gender differences in play. Children who cross boundaries, especially boys who play in "girl" ways, tend to be rejected by their peer group (Rubin, Bukowski, & Parker, 1998).

I Love Images/SuperStock

Can you tell whether this is aggression or rough-and-tumble play? What clue(s) are you using?

Both *selection* and *socialization* are at work in the peer group. Children are exposed to both boy and girl play patterns at school, but they *select* playmates who have play patterns similar to their own. Gender differences become more pronounced over time as children *socialize* one another within their same-sex play groups (Martin & Fabes, 2001). This means that at the beginning of the school year, preschool and elementary teachers see fewer gender differences than they do at the end of the school year. Thus, gender segregation may be both a cause and a consequence of differences in play patterns.

Socioeconomic Status

SES affects the amount of space and the range of choices available for children's play. It is also linked to quality of play. Low-SES children tend to play in less elaborate ways than do middle-SES children. That is, during pretense play they have shorter episodes, fewer different roles, less imaginative use of props, more aggression, and less discussion. Their play involves less reading and writing, compared with higher-SES children (Roskos, 2000). These SES differences in play spawned the research on play intervention discussed previously. Scientists hypothesized that if low-SES children could be trained to play in more-advanced ways, they would develop better cognitive, language, and social skills. They appear to have been correct.

Culture

Cultures vary in the extent to which adults value and encourage play among children, whether children are given freedom to play, and whether play is realistic or fantasy oriented. For example, a study that was conducted across six countries—the United States, Japan, Mexico, the Philippines, Kenya, and India—found that children do less realistic role-play, such as pretending to tend a baby, in cultures where they are required to do more actual work, such as taking care of younger siblings (Edwards,

2000). Imaginative, fantasy play occurred more in cultures that were complex, stimulating, full of novelty, and provided opportunities to play without adult control. The study also found that children from the United States and Japan played more than children from Mexico or the Philippines, who in turn, played more than children from Kenya or India. However, there are important cultural similarities. Children in all six countries engaged in constructive play, such as drawing or building with mud and sticks. Children in all cultures engage in pretense play, and age trends in play are universal (Lillard, 2002).

Classroom Implications of Play

Play is important to your classroom in two ways. First, play promotes school success and achievement. It enhances cognitive development through exploration and problem solving. It fosters imagination and creativity. It also enhances social development, communication, and motor skills, such as handwriting. Students who play cooperatively are liked better by peers, which promotes liking of school and motivation in the classroom (Fantuzzo et al., 2004). Second, play is a legitimate classroom activity because students learn through play (McCune & Zanes, 2001).

Use Play to Support Learning

As a teacher, you face two difficult challenges:

1. Getting students to attend to your agenda.
2. Providing practice for skill development while sustaining interest.

Play helps meet both challenges. Play provides opportunity for practice, and mental freshening or physical wakening so that students can attend to school work with greater creativity and alertness. For example, in one study, 7-year-olds were randomly assigned to either free play with salt dough or to practice handwriting. After twenty-five minutes of these two activities, they were given an art task. The group that played was more productive and creative (Howard-Jones, Taylor, & Sutton, 2002). Play may promote creativity because students become more alert, more relaxed, more motivated, and more exploratory in their mindset. Thus, you may want to promote play in your classroom, particularly before an activity that calls for creativity. To promote play in your classroom, follow these guidelines:

- *Provide props, space, and time for pretense play.* This is primarily appropriate for preschools. Such play can facilitate literacy when preschoolers pretend to be a shopper buying items or a waitress taking orders (Roskos & Christie, 2001).
- *Use play centers.* Play centers can help students become more literate if they include props like books, paper, crayons, and letters. Play centers are common in preschools, but can be adapted to elementary classrooms. Play centers for math and science could include a fix-it shop, a grocery store, or a museum. Two examples follow:
    - In a unit on chemistry, 4th-, 5th-, and 6th-graders went to the classroom crime lab where they pretended to be detectives who had to analyze mysterious substances found on an envelope and in footprints in order to determine who was at the crime scene (Jarrett, 1997).

    - In a unit on early explorers (e.g., Columbus, Desoto) 5th-graders could go to a "time machine," created by enclosing an area with file cabinets. Inside the time machine they could play with a compass, goggles, protractor, map, journals, travel brochures, and reference books. The students enjoyed it more than covering the same content in lecture. Some chose to do worksheets in the time machine, but said it "doesn't feel like doing Social Studies" (Romeo & Young, 1999).

- *Incorporate mind-play into your lessons* (Barell, 1980). This is primarily appropriate in late elementary and secondary classrooms. Mind-play includes storytelling and imagining. For example, in history class you can role-play (e.g., dramatize a Salem witch trial) or play "what if" games, where a statement contrary to fact is held as true and students are asked to imagine the result (e.g., what if Napoleon had not sold Louisiana to the United States?). In language arts class, you can have students create stories or role-plays for their new vocabulary words, make up new combinations of words, or act out literature scenes. In science class, you can ask what would happen if the sun split in half or ask students to picture themselves in an atom and describe what they would see. Such mind-play promotes critical thinking and requires students to acquire and use knowledge, while being fun.

Think About This At an elementary school, many children arrive half an hour before school starts due to bus scheduling. The children must sit quietly in rows on the gym floor. Adults patrol the gym to quell any attempts at play. Is this a good policy? What do you think the school's rationale is? What would happen if children were encouraged to play? Defend your answer using the research discussed here.

Play is not just for preschoolers. Classroom activities that are play-like are more interesting and engaging even for adolescents. Too often adults view play as a break from adolescents' real work, instead of viewing play as useful. Play has a place in your classroom. Play also has a place in out-of-class time, such as lunch breaks, extracurricular activities, and recess. Let's discuss recess next.

Promote Recess

Recess is an opportunity to engage in physical activity, social interaction, and play—all of which are beneficial (Pellegrini & Bohn, 2005). Recess helps focus attention: when students have longer periods of time before recess, their attention wanes, but immediately following recess, they are significantly more attentive (Pellegrini & Bjorklund, 1997). Among older students, sports and PE may have the same effects as recess. Indeed, teens who participate in more sports and PE are likely to earn higher grades than those who do not (Robert Wood Johnson Foundation, 2009).

It is possible that the rising diagnosis of ADHD is partly a result of a growing intolerance for play at school. Students with ADHD may need more playtime in the school schedule. Even students without ADHD need a few hours of frolic each day. Students who are given ADHD medication increase their attention, but at the cost of playfulness. Attention-promoting drugs diminish desire to play (Panksepp, 1998).

Boys in particular may need more opportunity for rough-and-tumble play at school. R&T play is one of the few contexts in which boys experience physical contact among friends. It is an opportunity to demonstrate caring and friendship, as well has have fun. When educators prohibit R&T play at school, they deny boys the opportunity to express caring toward one another, which is important for their development (Reed & Brown, 2001).

There has been a trend in recent decades to devote less time to recess and physical education, although there is great variation across school districts in the United

States. Black students and low-SES students are less likely to have recess than are other students (Barros, Silver, & Stein, 2009). Countries with higher academic achievement than the United States provide more playtime during the school day. For example, Finland has one of the highest-achieving education systems in the world. Finnish students are given a fifteen-minute recess after every forty-five-minute lesson (Alvarez, 2004). Similarly, many Asian students are given ten to fifteen minutes of break with vigorous play after every forty- to forty-five-minute class. Asian students have twice as much recess time as U.S. students. Asian elementary students may have a longer school day, but this longer day has substantial playtime (Stevenson et al., 1990).

Unfortunately, the movement toward less playtime during school is coupled with less playtime outside of school. For example, students are more likely to be driven to school rather than walk with friends. They are more likely to replace neighborhood play with TV watching. Thus, fostering play at school is becoming more important, even as it is being increasingly neglected or actively prohibited (Ginsburg, 2007; Singer & Lythcott, 2002).

In summary, in this section on the social child, you have learned how important students' social competence is to success at school and what you can do as a teacher to promote their competence. In Chapter 9, you learned how to promote students' people-reading ability, moral character, and humor. In Chapter 10, you learned how to promote prosocial behavior, reduce aggression, and help students resolve conflicts. In this chapter, you learned how to promote their acceptance in the peer group, their friendships, and their play at school. In the next section, The Whole Child, you will learn how physical, cognitive, emotional, and social factors work together to influence your students.

Reflections on Practice: Checklist for Teachers

Important factors linked to students' peer status, friendships, and play have been discussed in other chapters. Review the "Reflections on Practice" sections from these other chapters. They include:

- Promote academic skills. Students with better skills are more accepted in the classroom (see Chapter 5).
- Develop a secure teacher–student relationship and promote school bonding. Secure relationships protect students from rejection and support play (see Chapter 6).
- Use effective discipline and an authoritative teaching style. Harsh, punitive discipline is linked to peer rejection. Authoritative teaching facilitates the acceptance of poorly behaved students and promotes mature play (see Chapter 7).
- Promote emotional competence. Emotionally competent students are more accepted by peers and have more-mature play (see Chapter 8).
- Promote social cognition. ToM ability promotes play and friendship formation. Humor is a form of playfulness linked to popularity (see Chapter 9).
- Promote social competence. Prosocial behavior enhances peer status and promotes high-quality friendships (see Chapter 10).

In addition, to ensure that you promote your students' peer status, friendships, and play, periodically ask the following:

1. Am I aware of the peer status of each student in my classroom? Do I know which are neglected and which are rejected?
2. Do I help rejected students develop social and academic competence? Do I coach friendship skills when needed? Can the counselor help me with rejected students?
3. Are my behaviors contributing negatively or positively to each student's reputation among classmates? Do I praise rejected students' positive behavior or special talents?
4. Do I use cooperative learning in my classroom? If so, do I hold both individuals and the group accountable? Do I teach students how to work cooperatively?
5. Am I aware of the friendships in my classroom? Could I draw a sociometric map of my students? Does each of my students have a close friend in class?
6. Does my school make an effort to keep friends together across school years? Do I encourage friends to work together? Do students have enough opportunity to socialize in the school day?
7. Is negative or positive peer pressure operating in my classroom? Does my school group delinquent students together unnecessarily?
8. Does my school have an effective STI or HIV/AIDS prevention program?
9. Do I facilitate play in my classroom? Do I use "mind-play" in the classroom?
10. Does our school provide enough recess or "break" time during the school day? Are students with ADHD in my class getting enough physical play time?

Summary of Age Trends in Peer Status, Friendship, and Play

	Peer Status	Friendship	Play
Early Childhood (Birth–5 Years)	Preschoolers can readily identify who they like and dislike in their classroom. Young children are not rejecting of withdrawn peers, unless their behavior is extreme.	Preschoolers can readily identify their friends. Gender segregation is apparent by age 3. However, it is normal for preschoolers to have male and female friends. Children use the word "*friend*" by age 3–4. The basis of friendship is primarily proximity. Anyone who plays with the child is a "friend."	Solitary functional play is the most common type of play in infancy. R&T play emerges but is not common in infancy. Sociodramatic play begins at about age 2, and increases dramatically, peaking at about age 5–6. Play becomes increasingly complex, social, and less realistic.
Middle Childhood (6–12 Years)	Social competence (especially aggression) is not strongly linked to peer status until 3rd grade, after which it becomes important. Between 1st and 4th grades, social withdrawal becomes more strongly linked to rejection. Peer status becomes more stable through elementary school.	Gender segregation peaks. Having both male and female friends is unusual. Children who cross gender boundaries have fewer friends. Girls' friendships are more intimate than are boys' by age 6. Most children have 3–8 friends, with peer networks averaging 5–13. Girls' networks are smaller and more exclusive than boys' initially, but then they become similar in size. Friendships become more stable. Homophily becomes stronger, particularly for aggression.	Frequency of play peaks in early to middle childhood. R&T play, constructive play, and games-with-rules all increase in frequency. Sports participation emerges. Pretend play diminishes, but is still present. Play becomes more complex and rule oriented.
Adolescence (13–19 Years)	Peer status tends to remain stable as children transition to high school. Adolescents who are vulnerable to negative peer pressure tend to be from authoritarian or permissive families. Teachers have less influence on students' reputation in adolescence than at younger ages.	Gender segregation still exists for friendships, but gender boundaries are crossed more frequently. Many adolescents have a romantic relationship by 12th grade. Most 9th- to 12th-graders are not sexually active, but more than half report having had intercourse by 12th grade. Some youth identify as lesbian, gay, or bisexual. STDS are among the most common diseases in adolescence. Adolescents spend more time with friends than do younger children. Girls' networks become larger than boys'. Delinquent youth may form a gang. Some children may temporarily join a gang as they transition to high school, but then leave it.	Adolescents often turn work into play. Adolescents often play "mind games." R&T play may be used to cross gender boundaries or to disguise aggression. Solitary constructive play and pretense play continue, but play of games-with-rules such as board games diminishes (but is still present). An exception is that participation in sports grows.

Chapter Summary

Peer Status

- Peer status refers to the student's level of acceptance in the group and is typically categorized as popular, neglected, rejected, controversial, or average.
- Peer status is fairly stable. Rejected status is the most stable.
- Prosocial behavior is linked to popularity. Aggression and withdrawal are linked to rejection. Tough/popular students are aggressive—they are not well liked, but have high status.
- Parenting factors associated with peer acceptance include authoritative parenting, sensitive parenting that fosters secure attachment, providing opportunities for peer interaction, and direct coaching.
- Rejection may lead to aggression, depression, school avoidance, and low academic achievement.
- There are generally no gender differences in peer status. Low-SES students are more likely to be rejected.
- Teachers can facilitate students' acceptance by improving their behavior, altering their reputation, and promoting cooperative learning.

Friendship and Peer Networks

- Most students, including rejected students, have friends. Friendships vary in quality. Small groups of friends are cliques.
- Students select friends who are similar to themselves, and then friends cause one another to become even more similar.
- Gender segregation grows through childhood, but in adolescence gender boundaries begin to be crossed. Romance can have positive or negative effects on adolescents.
- Most adolescents do not have sex; those who begin sexual activity early and have multiple partners are at risk for STIs. HIV/AIDS has become more prevalent among adolescents. It is associated with psychological, behavioral, cognitive, and motor problems in some students.
- Students who have high-quality friendships at one age are likely to have them at a later age, but they are not likely to be the same friends across time.
- Prosocial students are more likely to have high-quality friendships than are antisocial students, but antisocial students are not necessarily friendless. Low-quality friends are associated with increased delinquency.
- Students with friends in the classroom spend more time on-task, participate more, and like school more than do friendless students.

- Girls have more emotionally close, intimate friendships, but similar numbers of friends and just as much conflict among friends as boys.
- Teachers can help students develop friendships in the classroom in several ways: promote prosocial behavior, keep friends together within the class and across years, provide opportunities for socializing, promote school bonding, and recruit the help of the counselor for needy students.

Play

- Play is behavior that has no immediate function and is pleasurable, voluntary, spontaneous, and flexible. It promotes students' cognitive, social, physical, and language skills.
- Different types of play reflect different levels of social and cognitive maturity. Students with greater emotional and social competence play more maturely.
- Youth usually enjoy sports, which can facilitate development of social and physical skills, but can also lead to injuries and, in some cases, exposure to drug use or other misbehavior.
- Play in the classroom is motivating, and contributes to skill development. Recess benefits students by providing them with opportunity to play.

Accompanying Education CourseMate Website Resources

Visit the **Education CourseMate** website at **CengageBrain.com** to find resources and study aids for this chapter, including self-tests, a glossary, and additional print and website resources. The following videos illustrate concepts from this chapter:

- 2–5 Years: Play in Early Childhood
- 5–11 Years: Peer Acceptance in Middle Childhood
- 12–18 Years: Peers and Domain Influences in Adolescence
- 12–18 Year: Cliques, Crowds, and Conformity in Adolescence

section 5 The Whole Child

In previous sections you have learned how physical, cognitive, emotional, and social aspects of children each contribute to their success in classrooms. Having a separate section on each aspect helps you master the complexity of child development, but these aspects are not actually separate in real children; instead they are intertwined. For example, think about what causes young children to learn to talk; is it physical and cognitive growth, emotional well-being, or social interaction? If children do not develop normal verbal ability, is there more likely to be a cognitive, emotional, or social consequence? These are trick questions: the answers are "all of the above." Complex abilities, such as talking, draw on all aspects of the child. This final section on the whole child highlights the synergy in child development. In Chapter 12 (language and literacy) and Chapter 13 (self-system and motivation), you will learn that all four aspects of the child contribute to development in these domains. In addition, in Chapter 14 you will learn how the larger context children live in influences each aspect of their development. Let's begin our understanding of the whole child by considering Alex.

Alex Learns English in Chemistry Class

Nicolas Russell/Photodisc/Jupiter Images

Alex is in Mrs. Nair's high school chemistry class. He moved to the United States from China in 6th grade. His spoken English is adequate. For example, he can explain the difference between a gas and a vapor better than many U.S.-born classmates. However, like many English language learners, Alex writes as little as possible. On one assignment he simply writes, "Fish taste better when it freeze fast than slow." Mrs. Nair asks him to explain this to her verbally. Alex says, "When it freeze slow, the ice crystals get big damage the food so it not taste good later." Mrs. Nair knows that he wrote the shorter, incomplete explanation because Alex is less sure of his writing than of his speaking ability. She tells Alex to show his thinking rather than perfect the composition. So Alex begins writing more-complex answers on assignments, which Mrs. Nair helps him correct. When another student needs help, Alex explains the concept to her. Alex says,

Case 5 (continued)

"That was hard. Hard to explain. It's like not regular English to explain school work. Practice more."

Actually, most *native* English speakers in Alex's chemistry class struggle with advanced literacy. School English is different from regular English, so it can feel like a foreign language even to students who have spoken English all their lives. In fact, students' problems with subjects like chemistry are often literacy problems. For example, on a test Mrs. Nair asks what practical application research on phosphorous might have. Of her sixty-seven students, sixty-one do not know what "practical application" means. Some think it means physically applying something to a surface, like paint. Other words they do not know on the test are "suppressed" and "omit."

Mrs. Nair helps her students by having them memorize vocabulary. She also makes a point of using uncommon words in class. When she said "I'm nonplussed" in response to a student's comment, another student asked, "OK, that's a word you made up, right?" Yet another student used the dictionary to look up words Mrs. Nair used—*nonplussed, discombobulate,* and *gerfuffle*—reporting back to the class, "I think she made up gerfuffle."

Most of Mrs. Nair's students, not just Alex, resist writing. They write the shortest possible responses. Mrs. Nair tells them that all high-level jobs require writing thoughts, plans, or achievements. She requires them to write paragraph-length answers to questions, which she carefully models. She also uses writing to reveal student thinking. For example, she asks, "What did Thomson contribute to our understanding of the atom?" Some students write that Thomson thought the cathode ray was made of negatively charged particles and that the particles came from atoms. However, some incorrectly write that Thomson made the discovery using a plum pudding model, rather than using the model to describe his discovery, revealing they do not understand what a model is. Others incorrectly write that Thomson fired cathode rays at gold foil, which reveals co-mingling of the Thomson and Rutherford stories. Students' writing reveals misconceptions that Mrs. Nair could not imagine. It informs her teaching and helps students become more literate—a win–win situation.

Alex, like most children, wants to fit in with peers, so he resists speaking Chinese. When Mrs. Nair suggests he use a Chinese glossary to understand the textbook, he says, "I forgot a lot of Chinese." However, he admits, "My mother, she try to make me talk Chinese with her." Mrs. Nair worries about Alex forsaking his heritage culture. She knows he wants to be a doctor, so she tells Alex, "You need to speak and write both English and Chinese like a professional. You don't want to be a Chinese-American doctor whose Chinese is like a 6th-grader's." After this Alex says, "I told my mother to help me not forget Chinese. She was so happy." Alex becomes proud of his bilingualism. He brings Chinese newspapers and a Bible to show Mrs. Nair. Students cluster around him with excitement as they ask Alex to read Chinese characters to them. Yet, Alex's ethnic pride is mixed with reluctance to draw attention for being different. Mrs. Nair continues to be supportive and assigns Alex to work with a classmate who gently helps with his English.

How has Alex's bi-cultural heritage affected his language and literacy development? How might it affect his sense of self? Did Mrs. Nair use effective methods to motivate Alex and his classmates? This section on the whole child will address these important questions.

chapter 12

Language and Literacy

Richard Hutchings/PhotoEdit

HOW DO CHILDREN DEVELOP A GOOD COMMAND OF THE LANGUAGE AND LEARN TO READ AND WRITE WELL? Would it surprise you to learn that many teachers feel ill-prepared to teach these skills? Yet you will need to teach these skills *even if you are not an English teacher and have had no specialized training in literacy,* as did Mrs. Nair, a chemistry teacher. In this chapter, we will discuss how students acquire language and literacy skills. After you read this chapter, you will understand:

- How language and literacy skills develop with age.
- What factors might lead to individual and group differences in these skills.
- What you can do to foster these skills in your students.
- How the major theories of learning and cognition apply to teaching literacy.

Language Development

Mrs. Shafer finds out she will have Micah in her 4th-grade class. She is dismayed because she saw Micah being scolded in the hallway throughout 3rd grade; she doesn't want another problem student. Sure enough, as Micah begins 4th grade, he misbehaves constantly. He also arrives late every day. Mrs. Shafer wants to stop this immediately because entering class after activities are under way makes it hard for Micah to catch up. Mrs. Shafer buys Micah an alarm clock. Micah arrives at school on time. After a few weeks, Micah says to Mrs. Shafer, "Can I keep that... um... that... that time-keeper thing?" This simple question reveals that Micah does not know the word for clock. Intrigued, Mrs. Shafer begins noticing other signs of limited language. She arranges for Micah to work with a language specialist. As Micah's speech and vocabulary improve, so does his behavior. Today, Micah is in 9th grade, where his grades have improved substantially, to a B– GPA, and he is only occasionally misbehaving.

Micah's language problems undermined his success at school. Why did he have language problems? There could be several reasons, because all aspects of the child—physical, cognitive, emotional, and social—affect complex skills like language. Culture also affects language. We will discuss each of these topics, but let's begin by defining language. **Language** is a collection of words or signs used in a systematic way that allows people to communicate with each other. This can include speech, sign language, and gestures. Thus, language is both verbal and nonverbal.

language a collection of words or signs used in a systematic way that allows people to communicate with each other. Language can be verbal or nonverbal.

Types of Language: Nonverbal and Verbal

nonverbal language communication that does not include words, such as posture, gesture, and facial expression.

Nonverbal language is communication that does not include words, such as posture, gesture, and facial expression. Gesture may be innate language that forms the foundation of speech and thought. Speaking and gesture go hand-in-hand (pun intended). They are paired as early as 7 months (although infant babbling isn't exactly speaking) and on into adulthood (Iverson & Fagan, 2004). In fact, when you constrain adults' hands, their speech is less fluent.

Think About This Think about your experience reading "thin slices" of behavior. For example, have you tried speed-dating? Have you wanted to get to know someone better after just a few minutes of meeting? Have you decided to drop a class after just a few minutes of the professor's lecture? Describe the nonverbal messages you received.

You use nonverbal language to communicate emotions, assess others' motives, and establish rapport. Nonverbal messages can be conveyed very quickly from *thin slices* of behavior lasting just *seconds*. For example, from ten-second videos 4th-graders can tell whether a teacher likes a student, although the video shows only the teacher (Babad, Bernieri, & Rosenthal, 1991). Thus, as a teacher you convey important information nonverbally, which we will discuss later.

verbal language communication that involves words and speech, in contrast to nonverbal language.

Verbal language, on the other hand, does involve words and speech. It is typically divided into *receptive* and *expressive*. Receptive language refers to understanding others' speech, and expressive language refers to making one's thoughts known to others. Development of expressive language lags behind receptive language. For example, 1-year-olds may obey commands, like *"Get your shoes,"* before they are able to talk. Thus, language-impaired students in your classroom, like Micah, are more likely to have expressive than receptive problems.

There are five key components of verbal language: (1) phonemes, (2) morphemes, (3) semantics, (4) syntax, and (5) pragmatics. At the most basic level is a **phoneme**, or speech sound. The word *dog* has three phonemes: /d/ /o/ and /g/. The letter *g* expresses two phonemes: the hard (e.g., get) and soft (e.g., gin) pronunciations. There are a limited number of phonemes—roughly 50 in English and 100 to 800 in all the world's languages (Beatty, 2001; Gibbs, 2002). **Phonological awareness** is the ability to identify phonemes or the sounds of language. This is a critically important skill for learning to read. Students have phonological awareness if they can do tasks like say *plig* without the *l*, or tell which word doesn't rhyme among "bat, pad, had," or tap the number of sounds in mat: three taps for /m/ /ae/ /t/.

phoneme a sound in speech. The most basic unit of language.

phonological awareness the ability to identify phonemes or the sound structure of language.

At the next level, **morphemes** are the smallest language unit that contains meaning. Morphemes can be word roots, suffixes, and prefixes. The word "dogs" has two morphemes: /dog/ and /s/. If you change just one phoneme in "dog" to "fog" you get a different morpheme. Morphological awareness is also an important skill for learning to read. Students have morphological awareness when they know about the structure of words and how to manipulate them, like changing words from present tense (John feeds the fish) to past tense (John fed the fish).

morpheme the smallest unit of language that contains meaning. It can include word roots, suffixes, and prefixes.

Semantics refers to meaning-making, or the way you use words and word combinations to express ideas. When you teach vocabulary you build your students' semantic skills. **Syntax** refers to the way words are organized into phrases and sentences, such as a verb followed by a noun, or proceeded by an adjective. "He reads the book" is typical syntax in English, but "The book he reads" is typical in Turkish. **Pragmatics** refers to using language appropriately according to sociocultural rules. For example, you adjust your speech based on whether you are asking a favor or giving a command, and whether you are talking to a child or to your boss. To interpret a spoken sentence, you must identify phonemes, segment them into words, interpret their semantic meaning, analyze the syntax, and activate pragmatic rules (Trout, 2003). Your brain is able to process all these components almost instantly in your native language. Let's look at how this remarkable ability develops.

semantics the study of meaning in language.

syntax the way words are organized into phrases and sentences in a language.

pragmatics the study of how language is used in social context.

Age Trends in Language

Language develops dramatically in the first five years of life. By middle childhood, development is less dramatic, but important developments continue to adulthood.

Early Childhood (Birth to 5 Years)

Children first communicate nonverbally through emotional expression, tone of voice, and gesture. Pointing is important—infants will look where adults point, and infants point to direct adults' attention (Tomasello, Carpenter, & Liszkowski, 2007). Pointing to share interest in something is a uniquely human action (Tomasello, 2007). For example, a toddler might point at ducks because she wants her dad to look at them.

Provided by the author

Although this toddler cannot talk yet, she can command her parents' attention using the imperial toddler finger.

Toddlers then begin to combine gesture and words. When you talk with young children, gestures help them understand your speech. For example, you might say, "Hand me the book" while pointing at the book. If your speech and gesture are mismatched, like pointing at a crayon, young children will follow the gesture and hand you the crayon, whereas older children will follow the speech and hand you the book. Older children give primacy to speech (see Chapter 3).

Speech replaces gesture during the first three years (Iverson & Goldin-Meadow, 2005). The newborn is unable to speak, but the typical preschooler speaks almost fluently. The sequence of this dramatic development is outlined in Table 12.1. This sequence is universal, meaning it occurs across cultures and languages and even in

Table 12.1 Development of language abilities in the first 3 years

Age	Emergent Ability
Birth	Prefer human voices to other complex sounds. Prefer female voices over male voices. Prefer mother's voice over other females' voices. Cries have different sound properties, conveying different meanings.
1–4 months	Cooing begins, which means that infants produce sounds that resemble vowels such as "ooh" and "ahhh."
3–8 months	Babbling begins. Infants produce strings of consonant–vowel syllables (e.g., ma-ma-ma-ma). Babbling provides practice for making speech sounds. At 6 months, babbling includes phonemes that are not part of the native language. Deaf children also babble. Receptive language for family names begins. At 6 months, infants recognize their own name and know that "daddy" pertains to their own dad, not mom and not other men. Around 7–8 months, infants begin to segment individual words from the stream of fluent speech.
9–10 months	Receptive language for objects begins. If someone says "blankie," the infant will look at the object. Infants also understand "no." Infants may comprehend about fifty words, but say none. Deaf children stop babbling. *First gestures* emerge and are used to communicate, most often pointing.
10–15 months	Receptive language grows dramatically. *First words* emerge around 12 months. First words are highly social, such as "bye-bye," "hi," and the names of favorite people. Typically, a repeated phoneme is used to refer to an object (e.g., "baba" means bottle). Ability to generate all the phonemes in foreign languages is lost.
15–18 months	Toddlers can follow simple commands, such as "Get your shoes." Toddlers may produce sentence-long utterances with nonsense words that are expressed in meaningful tones, so that you cannot tell what the child is asking, but you can tell it is a question. Speech occurs in *holophrases*, or single-word utterances with multiple meanings (e.g., "cookie" may be used to mean "I want a cookie" or "Look, there is a cookie!") The fifty-word milestone is reached; the average expressive vocabulary is about fifty words. Word learning begins slowly at about two words per week. Sometime during this period a *vocabulary spurt* begins, when about nine words per day are learned.
18–24 months	*First sentences* emerge, where more than one word is combined in a meaningful way. This does not typically occur until toddlers know 50 to 200 words. The average length of utterances is only two words. This is the beginning of syntax and *telegraphic speech*, which refers to sentences that sound like a telegram because there are no function words (e.g., "Want Cookie" instead of "I want a cookie.") Common phrases (e.g., "thank you" or "stop it") are treated as a big word. Fast mapping (learning a new word from a single exposure) is evident.
24–30 months	Average vocabulary is about 500 to 600 words. Grammatical words (e.g., "of," "the") are now used as children begin to speak in full sentences.

Sources: Adapted from Conboy & Thal, 2006; Jusczyk, 2002; Snedeker et al., 2007.

deaf children who are exposed to sign language. This sequence is also followed by 2- to 6-year-olds learning a new language when they are adopted into another country, such as from China to the United States, although they go through the sequence more quickly than infants (Snedeker, Geren, & Shafto, 2007). The ages in Table 12.1 are approximations, because some variation is normal.

When you talk to young children, you probably use higher pitch, exaggerated ups and downs in pitch, slower tempo, and more rhythm than usual. This is known as **child-directed speech** (also called *motherese*). Adults across many cultures use child-directed speech. Even preschoolers use it toward younger children. Infants only a few days old prefer to hear child-directed speech compared with typical speech (Soderstrom, 2007).

child-directed speech a style of speech used with young children that involves higher pitch, exaggerated ups and downs in pitch, slower tempo, and more rhythm than other speech. Also called *motherese*.

Middle Childhood (6 to 12 Years)

Before 1st grade, children typically master phonemes, or the sound patterns, of their native language. They also master the basics of morphemes and syntax, or the grammatical rules for putting sentences together. Indeed, by 1st grade their use of language is so masterful that they begin to play with language, and much of their humor centers on language such as "knock knock" jokes (see Chapter 9). However, their semantic skills are still developing dramatically, particularly vocabulary.

Elementary students experience a vocabulary explosion, which is more dramatic than toddlers' vocabulary spurt. For example, in a study of Canadian children, the average 1st-graders' vocabulary was roughly 10,000 words, 3rd-graders' was 20,000, and 5th-graders' was 40,000 (Anglin, 1993). These estimates were calculated conservatively, yet they suggest a rate of twenty words learned per day in elementary school. Do you think you could learn that many now?

Direct instruction probably accounts for only a few hundred words learned in a year—not thousands. Instead, children figure out most words by reasoning. For example, one 10-year-old girl figured out what "treelet" meant by reasoning that if a piglet is a small pig, a treelet must be a small tree. While 1st-graders are capable of this kind of inference, they do not engage in it to the extent that 5th-graders do (Anglin, 1993).

Adolescence (13 to 19 Years)

Vocabulary continues to grow in adolescence. Adolescents, like younger children, learn vocabulary through reasoning, which is usually effective but sometimes leads to wrong conclusions. A 9th-grader assumed that *vocational* education meant "choir or voice training" because she reasoned that it must have to do with *vocal*. Days later she heard an adult praise the district's vocational computer programming class—"Oh, is *that* what vocational means?" she asked. Notice that she used memory and problem solving to correct herself.

Syntax also continues to develop into adolescence. Between kindergarten and 12th grade, sentences become longer and more complex. For example, 3rd-graders might say, "I got a book from the library," but 11th-graders are more likely to say, "When I went to the library, I got the book Linda recommended" (Nippold, Hesketh, Duthie, & Mansfield, 2005).

Pragmatics also continue to develop as adolescents learn to manipulate their listeners. They know that when they explain to the teacher why their homework is not done, they must use a different approach than when they gossip with their friends. Adolescents also process language more rapidly than do elementary students. All these skills combine together to produce humor that includes sophisticated wordplay, like double entendres, puns, and playing the dozens.

Language Learning Is Remarkable

To master language, young children must link words with objects or events; learn words that are abstract (e.g., *truth*) or are purely grammatical (e.g., *the, a, that*); segment words from the stream of speech; distinguish nouns, verbs, and prepositions; and put them in the correct order in a sentence. What a task! Add to this complexity the sheer volume of language—a 2-year-old typically listens to 20,000 to 40,000 words a day (Kuhl, 2000). Yet toddlers manage to learn their native language with remarkable ease from casual interaction, without formal training (Trout, 2003). How is this possible? Very young children already have several abilities that help them learn language:

1. *Ability to hear language in the womb.* At thirty weeks' gestation infants can tell the difference between male and female speakers, their mother's voice from those of other females, and different consonant-vowel sounds (Kisilevsky et al., 2003).
2. *Ability to distinguish grammatical from lexical words* (Shi & Werker, 2001). Lexical words are verbs and nouns like *chew, hide, chair*. Grammatical words provide skeletal structure to a sentence, like *the, a, and, you, that*.
3. *Ability to remember and learn* (see Chapters 3 & 4). Toddlers are capable of remembering a new word from a single exposure (Jaswal & Markman, 2001). This remarkable ability is known as **fast mapping**. In a famous experiment, adults asked preschoolers, "You see those two trays over there? Bring me the chromium one, not the red one, the chromium one." The preschoolers knew red, but had never heard the word *chromium* before. After this single indirect exposure to the word, when tested a week later, half the preschoolers could correctly identify the color chromium, which was olive green in the experiment (Carey & Bartlett, 1978).
4. *Ability to construct rules* without direct instruction (*see Chapter 3*). If told a bird is a "wug," preschoolers will tell you two birds are "wugs," showing they have constructed basic rules for syntax (Gleason, 1958). They also mistakenly apply syntax rules to irregular words. For example, they might say "goed" instead of "went." Goed is a logical application of the rule to add "ed" to make past tense. Such mistakes are called *overregularization*.
5. *Ability to reason* (see Chapter 4). Fast mapping is partly the result of reasoning. In the chromium study, the preschoolers reasoned that the nonred tray must be chromium. Toddlers also infer what a word means using the rules of syntax. For example, if you say, "She blicked the baby," they infer that "blick" is something you do to someone else (Yuan & Fisher, 2009). This ability to infer the meaning of words using syntax is called **syntactic bootstrapping**.

fast mapping The ability to learn a new word from a single, or very minimal, exposure without deliberate instruction or corrective feedback.

Field Observation

To understand the complexity of learning language, ask a speaker of a language you do not understand to make a request of you (without gestures) in that language. Can you tell where one word ends and another begins? Can you tell what each word means? Ask the person to make the request again using child-directed speech. Did it help?

syntactic bootstrapping a process where young children figure out the meaning of a new word, without explicit instruction, based on the syntax of the sentence in which the word is used.

Despite these abilities, some argue that language is simply too complex for children to learn at such a young age, suggesting language must be prewired into human brains. The question of how young children master language has been hotly debated (see Box 12.1). While all typical children will become language users, there are differences in ability among individual children. Let's turn to this topic next.

Theories & Theorists **Box 12.1**

Language as Core Knowledge—The Great Debate

How do children learn language in just a few short years? Historically, there have been two dramatically different views—the environmentalist (nurture) and the nativist (nature) views. B. F. Skinner was a champion of the environmentalist view. He believed language is learned. According to behaviorists, all behavior is responsive to the environment (see Chapter 3). Children's behavior results from a combination of their current and past history of reinforcement. Thousands of studies have shown that reinforcement shapes all kinds of behavior in humans and other animals. Why would verbal behavior be different? Children learn to speak when their infant babblings are reinforced. Children learn to speak like those around them. Children in Japan learn to speak Japanese, not Finnish. Skinner published a fascinating 1957 book on the topic, called *Verbal Behavior*.

Noam Chomsky is a champion of the nativist view. He believes that the rules of how words are put together to create meaning is innate, or biologically determined, not learned (Chomsky, 2006). Thus, syntax is core knowledge (see Chapter 5), which he calls the "universal grammar." Chomsky believes it is part of the human genotype that evolved through natural selection. Nevertheless, you learn the specific words in your native language. In 1959 he wrote a famous, scathing review of Skinner's book, which launched a debate that is still ongoing (Chomsky, 1959). Chomsky did acknowledge that behaviorism could adequately explain other domains of behavior, just not language.

What is the evidence for the nativist view? First, children do not merely imitate what they hear—given a limited vocabulary, using grammar, children can generate an infinite number of sentences that they have never heard before. Such sentences were not learned through conditioning. Second, typical children across the world proceed through the same sequence outlined in Table 12.1 at roughly the same time. Third, language is remarkably uniform across the human species. Vocabulary and phonetics vary from one language to another, but syntax does not vary much. Chomsky views all humans as having one language, with small variations. Fourth, lower animals have a biologically determined ability to communicate, so why not humans? Fifth, the most compelling evidence is that language is too big a task for young children to learn through operant conditioning. Chomsky wrote: "The great fact that all normal children acquire essentially comparable grammars of great complexity with remarkable rapidity suggests that human beings are somehow specially designed to do this ..." (Chomsky, 1959, p. 57).

Grammar is very complex, with abstract rules. No one deliberately teaches these rules to children. In fact, you probably cannot articulate the grammatical rules of your own language, but 3-year-olds can apply them. Why attribute language ability to a meager few years of learning rather than to millions of years of evolution (Chomsky, 2006)?

Skinner thought Chomsky's argument illogical. Anything that cannot be learned cannot be selected for through evolution, because anything that does not have consequences for the individual cannot confer a selective advantage. As one theorist put it, *"Both evolution and reinforcement theory provide that what survives behaviorally is what increases survival chances, or, roughly, what reinforces"* (MacCorquodale, 1970, p. 94). If grammar has consequences for the individual, then it can be learned.

What are contemporary views? Today, the behaviorist view that vocabulary depends on practice and modeling is widely accepted. However, the behaviorist view that children are passive learners is not. Instead, children are seen as active learners who figure out language using their information processing abilities. They *reason by analogy* (Ninio, 2006). For example, toddlers learn specific patterns of word combinations, like the verb–noun pattern "get blankie." They then apply the patterns to new combinations, like the verb–noun "want cookie" (Bannard & Matthews, 2008). They also *reason using statistics*. For example, if an infant hears "Whataprettybaby!" in the stream of speech, how does she know "pretty" and "baby" are words, but their intersection "tyba" is not? Because "pre" is the first syllable in words more often than "ty." "Tyba" is not likely to be a word, statistically speaking (Pelucchi, Hay, & Saffran, 2009). You may not think of them as statisticians, but 8-month-olds can find words in a stream of speech in a novel language based on frequency alone. An infant who hears "Mommylovesherlittlegirlareyoumommyslittlegirl?" would recognize that "mommy" was repeated.

Once infants have identified words in the stream of speech, they can begin to link words with meanings (Estes, Evans, Alibali, & Saffran, 2007). They do this using statistics as well. Although children can "fast map" a word to an object when they clearly go together, children usually hear so many words at once that it is not clear which word goes with the object. Infants assume the word that is paired with an object more often is the name of that object (Yu & Smith, 2007). Infants learn both vocabulary and syntax by actively pulling patterns from the speech they hear (Gentner & Namy, 2006).

The ability to learn through statistics and analogy, coupled with infants' other amazing learning abilities, supports a more environmentalist than nativist view. That is, much of language learning can be explained by the same general processes involved in all learning (Gentner & Namy, 2006). However, this does not rule out the possibility of biologically endowed abilities that combined with learning develop into full language ability (Spencer et al., 2009; Toro, Nespor, Mehler, & Bonatti, 2008).

Individual Diversity in Language Ability

You have just read about typical age trends in language. Some children have language delays, meaning their development falls *well outside of these age trends*. Language delays can have physical, cognitive, emotional, or social causes, such as hearing impairment, mental retardation, autism, disorganized attachment, and genetic predisposition (Bishop, 2006).

In addition, some children have lower verbal ability than others, even though they may not have delayed language. It is difficult to know whether to worry about a young child who talks "funny" or "late." Generally, as long as children clearly articulate words by 1st grade, talking a little funny in preschool is not a concern (Bishop & Snowling, 2004). Toddlers who begin talking a little late will typically develop normal language abilities by 5 or 6 years of age. Recall from Chapter 6 that shy Eric began to talk late but went on to be a high achiever. However, some children who do not begin talking until 24 to 30 months may have problems into adolescence, such as poor grammar, vocabulary, and reading comprehension (Rescorla, 2005). If you have concern about a particular child, seek the help of a language specialist. The federal Individuals with Disabilities Education Act (IDEA) mandates that screening services be available to all children.

What Do Individual Differences in Language Ability Predict?

Low verbal ability affects children's success in the classroom, as it did for Micah. He was difficult to understand in class and talked in a strange way. For example, when describing his dog, he might say, "A lot times he bark the kids. Sometimes he eat and drink." His inability to communicate clearly led to isolation from peers, so Micah often played alone at recess. He also struggled to read. His language problems had both academic and social consequences, until he received intervention.

Academic achievement

Nonverbal language ability predicts academic achievement. Students who don't read others' nonverbal cues tend to have lower standardized test scores (Nowicki & Duke, 1992). Similarly, poor *verbal* ability predicts academic problems and learning disabilities. Verbal ability is even linked to math ability, perhaps because the same areas of the brain are involved in both (Gelman & Butterworth, 2005).

One aspect of verbal ability, vocabulary size, may be particularly important because it influences reading. Students with large vocabularies learn to read more easily, enjoy reading, and read a lot, which increases their vocabulary even more. Vocabulary size also influences how fast students can process information, especially verbal information that is the basis for most classroom instruction (Fernald, Swingley, & Pinto, 2001). Imagine being Micah and trying to read 4th-grade books if you do not know words like "clock."

Social competence

Both nonverbal and verbal ability predict social competence. Students who don't read others' *nonverbal* cues tend to be friendless and rejected by peers. Similarly, children who have problems expressing themselves *verbally* tend to have behavior problems, like Micah (e.g., Dionne, Boivin, Tremblay, Laplante, & Perusse, 2003). You can see how this would work with 4-year-old Keegan:

Keegan was coloring with a pile of five crayons next to him. Another boy picked up the blue crayon. Keegan tried to tell him to put it back, but he began stuttering and couldn't get the words out. Frustrated, he slugged the boy and snatched the crayon back.

Keegan's speech impediment makes him more likely to communicate with aggression. Other students with language problems may withdraw from peers rather than aggress. In contrast, students with high verbal ability are likely to play cooperatively, resolve conflicts, and communicate effectively with peers (NICHD Early Child Care Research Network, 2001a).

What Predicts Individual Differences in Language Ability?

Let's look at aspects of the child—physical, cognitive, emotional, and social—that predict language development.

Physical factors

Genes influence verbal ability, which is partly heritable (see Chapter 1). Vocabulary and comprehension tend to be more heritable than grammar or articulation. Just as with intelligence, heritability may be stronger as students get older, while shared environment is largest in early childhood (Dionne, Dale, Boivin, & Plomin, 2003; Kovas et al., 2005).

Cognitive factors

By 5 months of age, some infants have learned that their babbling gets responses from others. How do we know this? When scientists ask parents to quit responding for a few minutes—to just look at their baby with a poker face—infants burst forth with vocalizations as they try to get their parents to respond again. Infants who learn that their babbling gets results develop better verbal ability (Goldstein, Schwade, & Bornstein, 2009). Ironically, adults only respond to 30 to 50% of infant vocalizations. This is a type of *intermittent reinforcement* that makes vocalizing resistant to extinction (see Chapter 3).

To learn language, children have to be able to perceive sounds, store language they hear, analyze it, recall it, and recombine it. This requires information processing (see Chapter 4). Students with slow processing, poor executive functions, and poor working memory are likely to have language impairments (Im-Bolter, Johnson, & Pascual-Leone, 2006). In contrast, students with better information processing skills, particularly *memorizing* and *problem solving*, tend to have high verbal ability (Rose, Feldman, & Jankowski, 2009).

Emotional factors

Students may develop language disorders in environments that are emotionally negative or unresponsive. Attachment is strongly associated with students' verbal ability. In Chapter 6 you learned that secure students tend to have greater verbal ability. In addition, in Chapter 7 you learned that parents who use induction tend to have children who are more competent communicators, presumably because they are allowed to negotiate during discipline. Also, when parents foster self-control in young children, the children develop better verbal ability (Lunkenheimer et al., 2009). In Chapter 8 you learned that students with good emotion regulation also have better verbal ability (Robinson & Acevedo, 2001).

Social factors

In Chapter 9 you learned that children with better social cognition, particularly *joint attention* and *theory of mind*, have better verbal ability. In fact, some scientists think joint attention is critical for language learning (Tomasello et al., 2007). This is because children's ability to figure out what others are looking at helps children learn new words. Imagine a toddler points at the ducks in a pond and one suddenly takes flight. Father watches the duck and says, "There he goes. Bye, bye duck." The child, seeing her father watch the duck, also watches the duck and imitates "Bye bye." Through joint attention, she links words with objects and actions. Infants who use more joint attention than other infants develop better language skills (Munday et al., 2007). Parents who talk with children during joint attention have children with better language skills than parents who talk a lot, but not in joint attention with their children (Tomasello et al., 2007).

Children's *theory of mind* allows them to go beyond joint attention to infer what an adult is talking about. If toddlers hear their mother use a new word while she is on the phone, they do not apply the word to whatever Mother is looking at. However, if toddlers hear their mother use a new word while she is touching, looking at, or using an object, toddlers will apply the new word to the object (Golinkoff & Hirsh-Pasek, 2006). They could not do this without ToM—that is, without knowing what their mother is thinking about.

In Chapter 11 you learned that students who engage in frequent, age-appropriate play also have better verbal ability. Intervention studies show that when young children with low verbal ability are trained to play more, they develop better verbal ability. Play provides motivation to use language with peers and opportunity to learn from them. Students learn language better when they attend preschool with peers who have high verbal ability (Mashburn, Justice, Downer, & Pianta, 2009).

Social interaction with adults is also important. Children with sensitive, responsive, nonintrusive parents acquire language faster (Pungello, Iruka, Dotterer, Mills-Koonce, & Reznick, 2009). Responsiveness includes saying, "OK, I'll put bubbles in your bath water" when a toddler says "Ba ba in wa wa." Toddlers with unresponsive, depressed mothers tend to have limited vocabularies (Pan, Rowe, Singer, & Snow, 2005). For example, Figure 12.1 shows that in one study almost all toddlers whose mothers were highly responsive said their first real word by 13 months, but only 20% of children with less-responsive mothers did.

In addition to responsiveness, parents who use uncommon words have children with higher verbal ability. The typical adult vocabulary is about 40,000 to 100,000 words, but only 3,000 of those words are used frequently. In one study, 99% of the talk between low-SES parents and their preschoolers involved only the 3,000 most common words (Weizman & Snow, 2001). Some children heard no uncommon words, but others heard dozens. Preschoolers whose parents tended to use

Field Observation

Visit two classrooms or public spaces (e.g., playground, mall) and listen to different adults talk with children of similar ages. Are there differences in responsiveness to the children's talk? Or variety of vocabulary used? Or responses to girls versus boys? Explain how these differences might affect children over time.

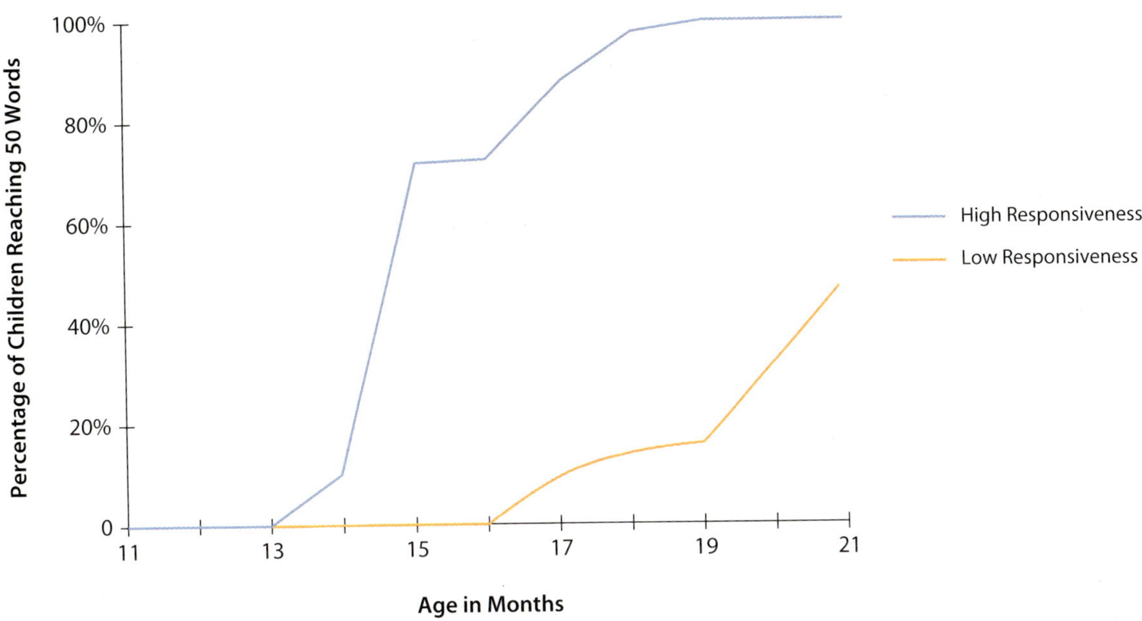

Figure 12.1 Maternal Responsiveness Predicts Toddlers' Verbal Ability.
Children whose mothers are highly responsive to their play and vocalizations reach the fifty-word vocabulary mark earlier than children with low-responsive mothers. The fifty-word vocabulary mark signals the vocabulary spurt and beginning of sentences. At what age did 40% of the children with highly responsive mothers reach the fifty-word mark? When did 40% of the children with low-responsive mothers reach this mark? *Source: Tamis-LeMonda, Cristofaro, Rodriguez, & Bornstein (2006).*

uncommon words had better vocabulary in 2nd grade. Mothers' general talkativeness does not predict children's vocabulary, but the variety of words mothers use does (Pan et al., 2005).

Another powerful predictor of verbal ability is joint reading. Children who are read to develop better vocabulary and cognitive ability than children who are not (Raikes et al., 2006). Book reading is not driven by the parent entirely. Children with higher verbal ability ask parents to read to them. There is probably a cascading effect, where parent book reading leads to children's larger vocabulary, which causes children to seek out book reading, which leads to improved vocabulary and knowledge. Each of these factors has been linked to group differences, our next topic.

Group Diversity in Language

There are group differences in nonverbal and verbal ability, but they tend to be smaller than individual differences within groups. For example, studies discussed earlier found substantial diversity within low-SES groups. Keep this *within*-group diversity in mind as you read about *between*-group diversity.

Gender

Girls may have a small advantage in language compared with boys. Girls tend to read nonverbal cues more accurately (Ambady, Bernieri, & Richeson, 2000). They also achieve language milestones a little earlier. For example, toddler girls in one study achieved a fifty-word speaking vocabulary on average about a month earlier than did boys (Tamis-LeMonda, Bornstein, & Baumwell, 2001). Such gender differences in language ability are not consistently found, but when found they favor girls (Halpern, 2000).

Socioeconomic Status

Low-SES students tend to have lower verbal ability than high-SES students. Students whose mothers did not graduate from high school are more likely to have a language delay (Campbell et al., 2003). By the age of 3, children in welfare-receiving homes have vocabularies that are half the size of those of their more affluent peers, and the gap persists through childhood (Pungello et al., 2009).

Why are there SES differences in verbal ability? One possibility is opportunity to learn at school and home (see Chapter 1). At school, low-SES students are segregated, beginning with preschool programs like Head Start, where they are exposed to peers with low verbal ability (Mashburn et al., 2009). At home, low-SES parents tend to speak less often and in less complex ways, use fewer uncommon words, and are less responsive to their children's talk (Evans, 2004; Pan et al., 2005). In contrast, educated parents are more likely to read to and talk with their children. For example, in one study Mexican American middle-class mothers discussed complex concepts (e.g., "Why do we need the flour?") and gave positive feedback (e.g., "Good job!) more than did working-class mothers while cooking with their children (Eisenberg, 2002). Researchers have estimated that by age 3, middle- and high-SES students have heard about 40 million words, low-SES students have heard 20 million, and students in poverty only 10 million (Hart & Risley, 1995).

African American Vernacular English

Standard English the form of English used in classroom instruction and textbooks, sometimes called School English.

African American Vernacular English (AAVE) a dialect of English spoken predominantly by African Americans, sometimes called Ebonics or Black English.

The predominant dialect used in classroom instruction and textbooks is **Standard English**, also called School English. *Most* students experience mismatch between the way language is used in the home compared with the more formal usage at school. However, the mismatch is larger for students who speak a dialect other than Standard English (SE). One such dialect is **African American Vernacular English** (AAVE), sometimes called Ebonics or Black English.

Linguists debate the origins of AAVE and whether it is currently converging with or diverging from Standard English (e.g., Wolfram & Thomas, 2002). AAVE is a full dialect that has its own rules. Many language forms that are incorrect in Standard English are accepted in AAVE. There are different versions of AAVE, but some commonalities include the following (Champion, 2003):

- Saying *ax*, *bidness*, and *posed to* for *ask*, *business*, and *supposed to*.
- Stressing the first syllable in words like *PO-lice* and *DE-troit*.
- Omitting possessive /s/ as in *That man hat is on the table*. (*That man's hat is on the table* in SE.)
- Omitting final /ed/ as in *They talk yesterday*. (*They talked yesterday* in SE.)
- Omitting contractions as in *She done well*. (*She's done well* in SE.)
- Omitting final consonants as in *las* for *last*.
- Unique use of *done* as in *I done did her hair* or *I done her hair*. (*I did her hair* in SE.)
- Unique use of *be* as in *He be happy*.
- Using *f* for *th* as in *toof* for *tooth*.

Thus, when AAVE-using students say, "My dog name Lady," they are not using incorrect Standard English, but rather are using the home dialect correctly.

Should you force students to use Standard English at school? You should respect students' right to maintain their heritage dialect. However, students also need to learn Standard English because it allows them to participate fully in school, commerce, and society (Baugh, 2002).

How should you teach Standard English? Simply correcting vernacular usage is not effective. Instead, compare the patterns of home speech to the patterns of SE, like teaching a second language. For example, point out that the possessive ("My dog name Lady") in AAVE is determined by proximity—the owner (dog) and the thing owned (name) are next to each other. In SE the possessive is determined by an apostrophe and an *s* ("My dog's name is Lady"). In addition to possessives, directly teach plurals, past tense, and subject–verb agreement. Research shows this helps AAVE-using students, but it can be applied to other dialects as well (Wheeler & Swords, 2006). This way SE becomes another language for the student. *Code switching* refers to the ability to use different language styles for different situations, such as SE at school and AAVE at home. Students benefit when they can code switch between the home and school language, depending on which is called for.

Immigrant Students and Bilingualism

According to the 2000 U.S. Census, about one in five children is an immigrant, meaning either the child or at least one parent was born outside the United States, like Alex in case 5 or Elena in case 1. This number is expected to increase in the next few decades—particularly for Mexican and Asian immigrants (Hernandez, Denton, & Macartney, 2008). Immigrant children are likely to speak a language other than English at home. Today, about half of such children speak Spanish. The next largest group speaks Chinese. However, immigrant children in the United States have many different heritage languages, such as Russian or Arabic.

bilingual the ability to speak two languages fluently.

English-Language Learner (ELL) a student whose first language is not English and who is less than proficient in English.

Most U.S. immigrant children are **bilingual**, meaning they speak both English and their heritage language fluently. Some children are **English-language learning (ELL)**, meaning they are not yet proficient in English. ELL students[1] constitute about 5 to 10% of the total U.S. school population (Abedi, 2004). California has roughly half of the ELL students in the nation. In some districts in California, 60 to 70% of students are ELL.

When first immersed in a second language, it is common for children to have a temporary silent period that lasts from weeks to months, as they focus on listening and comprehending. It is also common for children to be slightly delayed in language when mastering two languages simultaneously. Many ELL students exclusively speak their home language until age 3, when they enter preschool. Often their progress in the home language slows, but their growth in the new language is rapid. Do not be concerned about temporary delays—in the long term, bilingual students often have better language abilities than their monolingual peers.

Bilingualism may have cognitive benefits. Bilingual students are better at tests of executive functions, inhibitory control, and theory of mind than monolingual students. This has been found across several languages and as early as age 3

[1]Other terms you will hear are "language minority (LM) learners" and "English speakers of other languages (ESOL)." These are students who come from homes in which a language other than English is spoken, whether they are fluent in English or not. ELLs and "Limited English Proficients (LEPs)" are also students who come from homes in which a language other than English is spoken, but they are not yet fluent in English.

(e.g., Emmorey, Luk, Pyers, & Bialystok, 2009; Kovács, 2009). Perhaps experience switching between languages improves information processing skills.

Classroom Implications of Language Development

In a kindergarten classroom, the teacher asked Jared, the meteorologist for the day, to report on the weather. Jared said it was rather brisk. When an observer asked him why he chose such an unusual word to describe the weather, he replied, "Well, it's colder than cool, but it's a long way from frigid." (adapted from Lane & Allen, 2010, p. 363)

Many high school teachers wish their students had the vocabulary of this 5-year-old. How did he come to be so verbally precocious? His teacher, Ms. Barker, deliberately taught verbal ability in her class. She selected novel words that she scaffolded for her students, building on familiar class routines. Ms. Barker's students "distributed" rather than passed out paper, they lined up "adjacent" rather than next to the wall, and they "provided nutritional sustenance to our rodent friends" rather than fed the hamsters. Despite teaching in a high-poverty school, Ms. Barker demanded extraordinary vocabulary from her students and provided them with the support to use it competently. This is important because strong language skills are linked to academic achievement and appropriate classroom behavior for students of all ages (Forget-Dubois et al., 2009). To help your students develop better language ability, follow these guidelines:

- *Be responsive to students' talk.* If you teach infants, encourage them to make sounds. If you teach preschoolers, build on and expand what the child says. If a child says "sock on," you could say, "Do you want your sock on?" This is known as *elaboration*. Elaboration can also be used with adolescents who have limited proficiency in Standard English.
- *Encourage students to use Standard English*, while respecting their heritage language or dialect. Ask questions that require more than a yes/no response. Pause to let students contribute to classroom talk. To help students speak SE, one high-poverty high school that has narrowed the achievement gap requires students to give all answers in full sentences without slang. The teens initially resisted, but their ability to use SE has improved rapidly.
- *Use uncommon words in your talk.* Mrs. Nair did this in her high school chemistry class, and Ms. Barker did it in her kindergarten class.
- *Read to students, or encourage students to read to themselves.* Exposure to reading builds vocabulary (Connor, Morrison, & Slominski, 2006). Nonfiction information books are particularly useful for expanding vocabulary (Mol, Bus, & de Jong, 2009).
- *Require students to memorize vocabulary lists.* Help them use mnemonic strategies to do this, as discussed in Chapter 4. For example, to help 9th-graders remember "archaic" using the keyword method, have them visualize an *old* weathered arch.

- *Help students use new words in multiple ways.* Give the definition of a new word, use it in a context that makes its meaning clear, and then have students use it. Students need repeated exposure to words, and the opportunity to use them in context.

Direct instruction in vocabulary is not just for older students; it is effective in early childhood as well (Biemiller & Boote, 2006). In one study, teachers read low-SES kindergarteners trade books that had challenging vocabulary, like *miserable*, *evaded*, and *leisurely*, and then directly taught the vocabulary words. Their students developed larger vocabularies (Beck & McKeown, 2007). Promoting early vocabulary is particularly important because differences in vocabulary keep getting larger with age.

Nonverbal Language in the Classroom

Two aspects of nonverbal language are important in your classroom. First, gestures help students learn and teachers teach. Second, teachers' expectations for students can be unconsciously conveyed through nonverbal language.

Gestures and instruction

Gestures help students learn, understand, and problem-solve. For example, 3rd- and 4th-graders who are taught to gesture when solving math problems learn to solve more problems correctly (Goldin-Meadow, Cook, & Mitchell, 2009). See Figure 12.2. Similarly, adolescents who gesture when trying to explain science concepts that they learned during a lab experiment, such as what happens to electrons in static electricity, give deeper explanations (Roth & Welzel, 2001). Perhaps this is because gestures lighten the cognitive load as students talk about concepts they cannot fully articulate yet. Gestures serve as a bridge between concrete experiences and abstract concepts. As students become more expert, there is less need for gesture when they talk about abstract ideas.

Gestures can tell you about students' readiness for instruction. Students are particularly ready to learn when gestures suggest accurate thinking despite inaccurate spoken language. For example, a students explained his incorrect solution to the problem 7 + 6 + 5 = ___ + 5 as follows:

> *"I added 13 plus 10 equals 23" (an incorrect add-all-numbers strategy) while holding his whole hand under the 7 and the 6, pointing at the blank, and then pointing at the 7 and 6 (a correct grouping strategy).*

Verbally, this boy is communicating that he does not understand that the equal sign separates the two halves of the equation. However, his gestures communicate that at some level he does understand. He is ready for instruction because he is on the verge of change. His teacher built on his gestures, forcing him to notice that there was a 5 on each side:

> *"I am going to cover this up (while covering up the 7 and 6 with her hand). Now what do you see on both sides? Five and five, right?" (Goldin-Meadow & Singer, 2003, p. 516)*

Sage Publications

Figure 12.2 Gestures Promote Instruction. Gesture helps this child understand the equivalency concept in mathematics and reveals to her teacher what she does or does not understand. *Source: Goldin-Meadow et al. (2009).*

Teachers also convey information through gesture. Students are more likely to learn concepts when instruction includes *both* speech and gesture—from teaching preschoolers how to count to teaching high school students physics concepts (Ping & Goldin-Meadow, 2008). For example, in teaching the preceding equivalency problem, you might point at the 7 and 6, then flick away at the 5s.

Pygmalion in the classroom

When teachers hold high expectations for their students, their students tend to learn more. This was demonstrated in a 1966 classic experiment, known as "Pygmalion in the Classroom" (named after a Greek myth). Teachers were told that selected students would blossom with unusual intellectual growth over the school year, according to a special test. In reality, the students had been randomly chosen. Eight months later, the selected students did have greater intellectual gains than nonselected students, even though the only ability difference between the students was in the mind of the teachers. While there were flaws in the original experiment, the effect has been replicated in other studies (de Boer, Bosker, & van der Werf, 2010; Rosenthal, 2002).

How did this happen? One explanation is that teachers communicate their expectations to students nonverbally without being aware of it. Even when teachers try to hide low expectations and are good at emotional dissemblance, their real expectations leak out in body language and behavior (Porter & ten Brinke, 2008). Teachers tend to do the following at higher rates for students toward whom they have high expectations: express warmth, smile at, call on, teach, wait for answers, and give informative feedback (Rosenthal, 2003). Although these behaviors are subtle, observers can tell with some accuracy whether a teacher has low expectations of students from *ten-second* videos of the teacher interacting with students (Ambady et al., 2000).

Implications for your classroom from research on nonverbal language include:

- *Encourage students to use gestures* during explanations and problem-solving tasks. After activities, encourage students to describe their experience using gestures rather than just asking them to "write it up." This promotes deeper understanding and gives you a chance to clarify misunderstandings.

- *Use gestures in your instruction.* You can convey problem-solving strategies to students by combining speech and gestures as the teacher described earlier did.
- *Convey high expectations to every child.* Show warmth, demand strong answers, and provide plenty of feedback to all students, particularly low-SES and minority boys who may be most vulnerable to teacher expectations (Hinnant, O'Brien, & Ghazarian, 2009).

Each of the classroom implications discussed thus far pertains to all students, whether native English-speakers or not. However, teaching students who are ELL brings added considerations.

Bilingual Education

Imagine taking a chemistry class in Twi (a language in Ghana), or another language you do not speak well. You would not learn as much as if the class were in English. That is just what Alex faced in Mrs. Nair's class. Would Alex be better off in bilingual education? In the United States, **bilingual education** refers to the use of heritage language for instruction with ELL students. There are many different models of bilingual education. One model is to provide all instruction in the heritage language, and then transition to an all-English classroom. Another model is to teach academic content mainly in English, with occasional tutoring for that content in the heritage language. Yet another model is to teach academic content only in English and then teach English as a second language (ESL). Still another, nonbilingual, model is to simply immerse students abruptly in English-only classrooms. The first two models are not an option in small school districts, like Alex's, where few teachers are fluent in other languages, but they are feasible in large districts with high concentrations of a single heritage language, such as Spanish in Arizona.

bilingual education instruction that is provided in more than one language.

Revisiting Case 5

Alex's parents may have wanted him in an English immersion program so that he would learn to speak English well. Do you know parents with a different perspective? What is their rationale? How did immigrants in your own family learn English? Was this the ideal approach?

Which approach is best? The answer to this politically charged question is not completely clear. Some studies show an advantage for bilingual education over immersion, but some show no differences. Rarely do studies show an advantage for immersion. This suggests three key points:

1. Teaching in a student's heritage language does not impede English learning.
2. Students in bilingual classrooms can learn content as fast or faster than monolingual students.
3. Students may not fare better academically in bilingual classrooms, but are not likely to fare worse than in English-only classrooms.

These conclusions pertain from preschool through high school (Farver, Lonigan, & Eppe, 2009; Slavin & Cheung, 2003).

Although there is controversy about how best to educate ELL students, like Alex, there is one point scientists agree on: the *quality* of the program matters more than the language of instruction. Some "bilingual" programs are nothing more than dumping grounds with minimal expectations of students, and some immersion "programs" have no systematic design so that students are left floundering. In addition, research supports the following guidelines (Gersten & Baker,

2000), the first three of which are explicitly endorsed by the U.S. Department of Education:

- *Use cooperative learning* (see Chapter 11). This provides opportunity to practice speaking. Make sure students use full sentences in their responses, although they may resist. It may surprise you, but in many ELL classrooms students have little opportunity to speak English.
- *Directly teach vocabulary*. This includes everyday words and academic words in content areas like math, science, or history (Jansen, 2008). For example, students may struggle with comparative words like *probably*, *very likely*, and *almost certain*, or math words like *estimate*. Mrs. Nair has to directly teach words like *omit*.
- *Teach Standard English grammar and syntax explicitly*. Do not expect students to become proficient in English by chance as you teach math, social studies, or other content areas. Provide clear, frequent feedback on grammar and syntax, as Mrs. Nair does.
- *Teach these skills as early as possible*. Students who enter kindergarten with adequate English skills tend to do as well as native speakers, but students who do not may lag in achievement throughout elementary school (Kieffer, 2008).
- *Build strong skills in the heritage language among preschoolers*. Having a strong foundation in their first language helps young students develop skills in their second language, English, faster and transition to English-only classrooms faster (Proctor, August, Carlo, & Snow, 2006).
- *Encourage English use in informal settings at school*. Students who immigrate after the preschool years have extra challenges because they must learn complex content at school and become proficient in English quickly enough to pass gatekeeper tests that affect their future. Students who use English in the hallway, cafeteria, and with friends are more successful (Carhill, Suárez-Orozco, & Páez, 2008).
- *Remember Standard English lags behind conversational English*. Students who can converse in English with you and who seem English proficient, like Alex, may struggle to follow academic content and score poorly on standardized tests. When possible, test students in their dominant language. ELL students may know more math, science, and history than they can demonstrate in English (Abedi, 2004).
- *Support* **additive bilingualism**. This is where students maintain proficiency in their heritage language while becoming proficient in English. **Subtractive bilingualism** occurs when students learn a second, majority language in a context that does not value their heritage language, which they eventually lose. Students who are fluent in *both* English and their heritage language fare better academically and are less likely to drop out of school (Feliciano, 2001).

additive bilingualism acquiring a second language while still maintaining and valuing the heritage language.

subtractive bilingualism acquiring a second, majority language in a way that undermines ability in the heritage language.

After Alex crossed cultural borders, he was inclined to choose one culture over the other. Mrs. Nair encouraged him to be comfortable in English U.S. culture without losing his heritage culture; he learned to feel positive about both cultures. ELL students tend to participate more in classes where they feel welcome, like in Mrs. Nair's class, and where they share aspects of their heritage cultures, compared to classes where they feel like outsiders or invisible (Yoon, 2008).

These issues are clear for immigrant students, but they also apply to nonimmigrant students who have a mismatch between language at school and at home. You have already seen that dialects like AAVE are different from Standard English. In addition, many students, like Micah in the opening vignette, have limited opportunity to learn school vocabulary. Furthermore, students may use language in different ways at home compared to school (Hemphill & Snow, 1996). At home, family members scaffold, butt in, and clarify what a child is saying; children talk when they have something to say. In contrast, at school, the teacher controls who gets to talk and what the talk is about. Speaking in class often consists of one-word comments, with very little elaboration. Expository talk, rather than conversation, is used. **Expository talk** is formal, precise, and used to display information—like when a child is asked to summarize a text. You may need to help your students develop expository talk. This can be done through direct instruction and indirectly through exposure to reading and writing. Let's turn to the development of literacy next.

expository talk formal, precise talk that is used to display information, in contrast to conversational talk.

Literacy

The heart-warming note in the accompanying photo is from 6-year-old Nora, at the end of kindergarten. At this age Nora knows all her letters and can write some correctly. In this section, we will follow Nora's literacy progress from budding abilities in preschool to full literacy in 12th grade as we address how students become literate—but first let's clarify what literacy is.

Literacy can be defined broadly as communication or narrowly as communication in printed language. We will use the narrower definition in this chapter, focusing on reading and writing in school. However, this isn't the only kind of literacy. Children can have multiple literacies in contexts other than school. For example, some of your students may be more literate than you at decoding gangsta messages or at instant messaging emoticons and abbreviations, like :), -(, BBL, or L8R (for *smile, sad, be back later*, and *later*).

literacy narrowly defined, it is the ability to communicate in printed language through reading and writing, particularly in school settings.

Reading and writing ability are strongly correlated, meaning children who read well are likely to write well. Reading and writing share the same foundational skills: wide knowledge, large vocabulary, understanding how language works, and decoding ability. Students who correctly spell words while writing are better able to decode words they read (Conrad, 2008). Reading promotes writing by building vocabulary and storytelling ability.

Provided by the author

Nora's note reads: "I really, really like you and I hope you have a happy Mothers' Day."

However, instruction in reading cannot be substituted for instruction in writing, or vice versa.

decoding figuring out how to read or spell unknown words by applying phonetic rules.

phonetics rules regarding how written letters are linked to sounds and how a string of letters is correctly pronounced.

Reading skill has five components: (1) phonological awareness, (2) vocabulary, (3) decoding, (4) fluency, and (5) comprehension. Recall that *phonological awareness* is the ability to distinguish phonemes, or the sounds in language. *Vocabulary* is the number of words you know. **Decoding** is the ability to identify words you have never seen. You decode by applying **phonetic** skills, which include recognizing letters, knowing their sounds, and pronouncing a string of letters correctly. In English, irregular words, like *choir* or *yacht*, do not follow phonetic rules and must simply be memorized. *Fluency* is the rapid, automatic decoding of novel words or recognition of memorized words. It is typically measured in words accurately read per minute and abbreviated as *wpm*. *Comprehension* is the ability to understand text. Comprehension is the ultimate goal of reading. Next we examine how these components, as well as writing, develop with age.

Age Trends in Literacy

While dramatic development in verbal ability occurs early, the most dramatic development in literacy occurs in middle childhood and adolescence. Nevertheless, literacy development begins in infancy and continues across the lifespan.

Early Childhood (Birth to 5 Years)

emergent literacy abilities that are precursors to reading and writing, such as good verbal ability, knowing letter names, phonological awareness, and print concepts. These abilities are typically identifiable beginning about age 3.

print concepts basic concepts of how print symbolizes language, such as English books are read from left to right and spaces separate words. A key part of emergent literacy.

Toddlers' literacy is emerging as they develop skills that are precursors to reading and writing. By age 3, most children have several **emergent literacy** skills; they can say the alphabet, name a letter and tell what sound it makes, tell a story back to you, write their name, and recognize familiar words in the environment (such as a stop sign). They also have basic notions of how print stands for language, known as **print concepts**. Children have print concepts when they know that books are read from left to right, books begin with a title, there is space between words, pictures are different from print, and so forth. Emergent literacy skills prepare children to learn to read and write; they emerge before formal literacy instruction begins.

Literacy skills tend to emerge in predictable patterns. For example, young children first learn letters that are in their own names, "N! N is for Nora!" They discern the phonemes at the beginning or end of a word before the middle of the word. They learn letters whose names match their sounds (e.g., *v*, *k*) before letters whose names do not match their sounds (e.g., *h*, *w*). Some early childhood teachers mistakenly give equal time to learning all letter name-sound pairs, but more time should be given to difficult-to-learn letters (Treiman, 2000).

Before age 3 children typically write with scribbles or unrecognizable forms. At about age 3, their writing still may not include real letters, but it begins to look like letters and is written in left-to-right lines. Children believe they are writing, but no one else can read it (Levin & Bus, 2003). For example, Figure 12.3 displays a "shopping list" written by 4-year-old Nora. She has print concepts—that writing translates to speech, it occurs left to right in lines, with motions that are cursivelike—but her writing is not yet divided into words. The first real word children write is usually their own name.

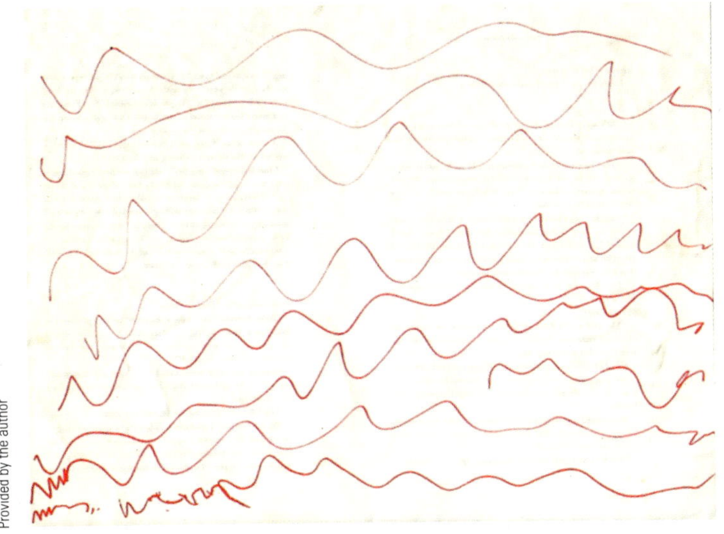

Provided by the author

Figure 12.3 Preschool Writing Sample. Nora's grocery shopping list at age 4. If her mother put something wrong in the cart, she said, "That's not on my list!" Notice that although there are no letters, she wrote from left to right in lines that resemble cursive. This demonstrates print concepts.

In kindergarten, most children learn how to form letters correctly and learn to pair letters with sounds. They begin to write with real letters, using invented phonetic spellings and pictures. A 5-year-old wrote, "THIS IS A HWS THE SUN WL SHIN ND MI GRDN WL GRO"—*This is a house. The sun will shine and my garden will grow* (Hemphill & Snow, 1996). Can you spot these features in Nora's kindergarten writing sample in Figure 12.4?

In early childhood, most children are not yet reading to themselves. Instead, a parent, sibling, or teacher reads to them. Nationally, about 55% of parents read daily with their young children (Forum on Child and Family Statistics, 2009). Joint storybook reading changes with age. For children under 18 months, parents do not "read," but label and comment on pictures instead. For children between 1 1/2 to 3 years old, parents tend to ask questions and converse about the story (Fletcher & Reese, 2005). For children older than 3, parents tend to read the text more and converse less, but they still may not strictly stick to the text. In addition, children increasingly control the reading experience by making demands and asking questions. Here 33-month-old Garrett "reads" a book with animals:

Garrett:	*What's that?*
Mom:	*A squirrel.*
Garrett:	*Squirrel. What is this? An animal?*
Mom:	*That's a lion.*
Garrett:	*I pick another animal. Here's a mommy one. A goat. What is this letter?*
Mom:	*"G," big goat. Little "g," little goat.*

Garrett uses the book as a platform for getting information from his mother, rather than as a narrative to read page-by-page.

Middle Childhood (6 to 12 Years)

As Garrett enters school, his "emergent" literacy will be replaced by "conventional" literacy. Joint storybook reading changes. As children begin to read in 1st grade, the child

Figure 12.4 Kindergarten Writing Sample. *"Dad. Mom. Sister. Brother. Baby"* At the beginning of kindergarten, age 5 1/2, Nora can write some letters and common words correctly. She reverses some letters and spells phonetically. "Brother" begins backwards on one line and proceeds forwards on the second line. Writing is brief and drawings dominate "stories."

Provided by the author

takes on responsibility for reading while parents watch for errors (Bergin, 2001). Joint storybook reading becomes rare after 3rd grade as children become independent readers.

The primary task of 1st grade is learning to read and write. Figures 12.5 and 12.6 show Nora's development of writing skills from the beginning to the end of 1st grade.

on

vocashwe

on vocoash we so boylling wodr

comming Our of the growd and we

wet topo 7 pecs 7 pecs is a wotr

prc ad cndit is FUN thr is atwisteslid

and thr is lase rivr the thr is

a crit that ccres you ulog that is the

end of My stry

Figure 12.5 Beginning 1st-Grade Writing Sample. *"On vacation. On vacation we saw boiling water coming out of the ground and we went to Seven Peaks. Seven Peaks is a water park and it is FUN. There is a twisty slide and there is a lazy river. There is a current that carries you along. That is the end of my story."* From kindergarten to 1st grade, there is tremendous improvement in Nora's writing. She now has a sense of audience (she clarifies for the reader what "7 pecs" is) and of conventional storytelling—there is a title and an ending. However, she does not use punctuation and continues to spell phonetically, with middle sounds left out.

Provided by the author

Dear Jary thaks for the potery I reille like it.
I in joid it.
My cllas is going for a felldtrip.
My tetres name this yire is miss bollin.
My cllas is starting the mad minit.
In the madminit you hav to do 30 math
poroblims the hiiste scor I got was 29.

Figure 12.6 End of 1st-Grade Writing Sample. First grade is a year of remarkable gains in literacy. You can now read most of Nora's writing without translation because of improved spelling. The last line reads *"In the Mad Minute you have to do 30 math problems. The highest score I got was 29."* Punctuation is beginning, with periods and new lines indicating sentences. Nora is in a Write-to-Read program, where children type using word processors to free them to concentrate on composing rather than forming letters.

Provided by the author

The task shifts around 4th grade to *using* reading and writing to learn other things. At first, children are asked to write mostly personal stories in order to practice writing, but by the end of elementary school, children are asked to write expository text, like reports, to show what they know. Expository text is more difficult to write than stories.

Children become better spellers across elementary school. As children begin to write, their misspellings make sense, such as "lik" in the opening vignette. They use letter names to spell words, such as "b" for *bee* or "yn" for *when* (McCutchen, 2006). At first, they leave out the internal phonemes of words, and may write "staps" for *stamps*. After 4th grade, they become more skilled at conventional spelling. Figure 12.7 shows that Nora is a conventional speller in 5th grade. Three other improvements in writing occur across elementary school:

1. Students write longer pieces (McCutchen, 2006). Initially their speech is longer and more complex than their writing; then they transition to writing that is more complex and elaborate than their speech. This transition occurs as early as 4th grade for advanced children, but not until 8th grade (or later) for others. Can you spot this transition in Nora's writing samples?
2. Students plan and revise more, which they seldom do in the primary grades. This is an important development because competent writing requires revision.
3. Students' writing is more reader-friendly. Before 4th grade, children have trouble taking the reader's perspective into account, probably because their working memory is overwhelmed by the other demands of writing. Nora's 5th-grade sample displays a keen sense of reader, including punctuation to influence the reader's rhythm. However, reader-friendly writing remains a challenge for some writers through adolescence, and into college as well.

Adolescence (13 to 19 Years)

Reading fluency improves during adolescence. In fact, reading becomes so automatic and rapid that it is difficult to turn it off on tasks like the Stroop test, where you must say the color a word is printed in rather than read the word (see Chapter

What is Pink?

dedicated to my baby sister

Pink is the color of something neat,
Or the color of a baby sweet.
Pink is the color of the Easter Bunny,
Or the color of your face when you think
some thing is funny.
Pink is the color of a rose,
Or-- if it's cold-- your nose.
It could even be the color of babies' t

Roses and noses and babies' sweet toeses,
Those are the color of pink

Provided by the author

Figure 12.7 Fifth-Grade Writing Sample.
At the end of elementary school, Nora is now secure enough in her writing skills to play with words by rhyming and playfully reversing conventional syntax for a musical quality (e.g., "a baby sweet"). She is able to use punctuation as a tool to control the reader's cadence. Her expository writing is now completely conventional.

Title: "High School Athletes and Enhancing Substances"

Abstract:
Athletes have been using enhancing substances for hundreds of years to improve their performance. Currently athletes still use substances to give them an edge over their competitors. With modern advances, there are many more products on the market. High school athletes have started taking advantage of such products. The hypothesis is that performance enhancing substances for student athletes are prevalent in high school. The rationale is that many students see professional athletes boosting their performance by taking such substances and the students assume that they would also improve. A survey will be administered to a sample population of students at a mid-west suburban high school. The survey will deal with sports, drugs, and performance enhancers.

Provided by the author

Figure 12.8 Twelfth-Grade Writing Sample.
This is an abstract written for a science-fair entry. Nora is not only fully literate for day-to-day writing needs, but she has also learned to write in a specialized, academic style for a scientific audience. She is ready for college and professional training. Look back at her earliest writings. What a change in twelve years!

4). Vocabulary and comprehension also improve during adolescence. Adolescents increasingly understand abstract vocabulary—such as *federalism* or *hypothesis*—that appears in school texts. For example, Figure 12.8 presents an abstract Nora wrote for a science fair in 12th grade. Notice the advances in vocabulary over earlier writing. Adolescents become able to use domain-specific vocabulary to read and write in domains like science, history, or art.

Quality of writing increases during adolescence in other ways as well. The writing of 2nd-graders reads like a stream of thought, as though they just wrote as ideas came to mind, but 8th-graders can produce an organized paper. Essays and sentences are longer. Adverb connectors (e.g., *however*, *finally*, *therefore*) and abstract nouns (e.g., *truth*, *liberty*, *deceit*) are used more. Adolescents use more-varied reasons to support their point (Nippold, Ward-Lonergan, & Fanning, 2005). They are also more likely to acknowledge conflicting views, showing flexibility of thought. Nevertheless, many adolescents cannot write a coherent persuasive essay. In one study, 52% of 11-year-olds and 35% of college students could not write a well-organized essay (Nippold et al., 2005). So there is still room for improvement.

Some people have been concerned that texting may undermine youth's literacy because texters use abbreviations, acronyms, and unusual punctuation, like the following:

Marta: *wat u doin?*
Liz: *nadda u?*
Marta: *i saw ur bf 2day*
Liz: *hes NOT my bf!!!!*
Marta: *hahahaha lol*

However, youth who are fluent at texting on cell phones may have higher literacy test scores. Thus, texting does not seem to interfere with conventional literacy, although excessive texting may (Plester, Wood, & Bell, 2008; Varnhagen et al., 2010).

Individual Diversity in Literacy

Some students write well while others do not. Some students struggle to read a book that their peers read with ease. Are these differences among students stable?

Stability of Individual Differences in Literacy

Reading ability is remarkably stable (Harlaar, Dale, & Plomin, 2007). This means that a child who is reading above grade level in the primary grades is likely to be reading above grade level in high school. Reading has a *Matthew effect*, a term taken from the Bible (Matthew 25:29), meaning the rich get richer and the poor get poorer (Stanovich, 1986). That is, children with better vocabulary comprehend what they read better, so they read more, so their vocabulary grows even more, so they comprehend even more, and so on. Struggling readers, on the other hand, tend to avoid reading and miss the growth that comes with reading.

Despite the stability of literacy skills, struggling readers can improve. In a study in which roughly two-thirds of low-SES children who were struggling in 1st grade remained struggling readers in 4th grade, one-third dramatically improved, becoming average readers by 4th grade (Spira, Bracken, & Fischel, 2005). Which struggling readers improved? Children with better phonological awareness, emergent literacy skills, and classroom behavior. Even if children lag a little in 1st grade, if they are proficient readers by 5th grade, they are likely to become lifetime readers (Cunningham & Stanovich, 1997).

What Do Individual Differences in Literacy Predict?

Literacy predicts academic achievement in other subjects. This effect begins with emergent literacy skills in kindergarten or earlier, and continues as conventional literacy develops (Duncan et al., 2007). This is not surprising, because literacy helps children learn. Reading allows children to take information from text. Writing improves thinking, helping children transform fuzzy thoughts into clear concepts. Literacy allows children to complete worksheets, take tests, and understand assignments. However, it might surprise you that literacy also predicts achievement in math—as early as 2nd grade before children are doing math word problems (Lee, Ng, & Ng, 2009; Swanson, Jerman, & Zheng, 2008). Perhaps this is because both literacy and math skills share the same causes, such as general intelligence, or a stimulating home (Hart, Petrill, Thompson, & Plomin, 2008).

Literacy predicts both emotional and social competence. Children who struggle to read feel angry, ashamed, anxious, and sad by 5th grade (Ackerman, Izard, Kobak, Brown, & Smith, 2007). These emotions reduce enjoyment of school and willingness to take on challenging tasks. This may explain why struggling readers also tend to misbehave more and are liked by fewer classmates over time. Unfortunately, misbehavior undermines their literacy development. In contrast, students who behave well become more literate over time (Miles & Stipek, 2006).

What Predicts Individual Differences in Literacy?

Learning to be literate takes a coming together of several skills. Thus, there can be a variety of reasons why some students become more literate than others. Students who have an unusually hard time learning to read may have dyslexia (see Box 12.2). Next we discuss the link between verbal ability and literacy and then each of the aspects of the child—physical, cognitive, emotional, and social—that contribute to literacy.

Verbal ability

Children with good verbal ability learn to read more easily than their peers. Good verbal ability includes a large vocabulary, ability to retell a story coherently, and both phonological and morphological awareness. Each of these verbal abilities helps children become better readers and spellers (Deacon, Wade-Woolley, & Kirby, 2007; Kendeou, Van den Broek, White, & Lynch, 2009). However, the most robust predictor of literacy may be phonological awareness. Children with poor phonological awareness tend to have reading problems.

Physical factors

Differences in brain structure are linked to literacy. For example, you learn in Box 12.2 that the neural system that connects speech to print is different for students with dyslexia. These brain differences may be genetic. Literacy is moderately heritable, with estimates ranging from 0.18 to 0.55 (Pennington et al., 2009). In fact, some scientists believe reading ability is stable across childhood because of its underlying genetic basis (Harlaar et al., 2007).

Genes may influence literacy through their effect on general cognitive abilities like processing speed, working memory, and attention control. Or, genes may influence literacy through how much children are read to, which is partly heritable and partly shared environment (Oliver, Dale, & Plomin, 2005). How do children inherit being read to? A genetic predisposition may lead some toddlers to respond more to books and show more interest, so their parents read more to them. Garrett, rather than his mother, initiated the reading episode in the earlier example.

Brain differences may also be due to experience. Experience alters brain circuitry (see Chapter 2). In Box 12.2 you also learn that intense instruction alters the brains of dyslexic children as they become more fluent readers. In addition, the areas of the brain that process sound are altered by music lessons, by hearing different languages like Mandarin versus English, and by phonetic instruction (Kraus & Banai, 2007). This is important because children whose brains are slow to process sound have difficulty learning to read.

Cognitive factors

Reading requires general cognitive abilities, like working memory, knowledge, reasoning, and processing speed. Students with good cognitive abilities become fluent readers earlier and with more ease. However, reading also requires language-specific cognitive abilities, like phonological awareness, print knowledge, vocabulary, and decoding ability (Swanson, Trainin, Necoechea, & Hammill, 2003).

Writing also requires general cognitive abilities like working memory. In preschool, the act of forming letters on the paper can tax working memory. As children get better at handwriting and spelling, they write with more fluency. Handwriting is largely automatic by 4th grade (McCutchen, 2006). Among older students, composing an essay can tax working memory. To write you must control attention, set goals, plan arguments, spell words, write sentences, and revise. Each sentence should

Challenges in Development | Box 12.2

Specific Reading Disability

In 3rd grade, Veronica is in the lowest reading group. Her classmates are reading "chapter books," but she is still struggling with beginning readers. At the school library, after children select a book, the librarian asks them to read a random page and hold up a finger for each word they can't read. If five fingers go up, the children are to choose an easier book. In 5th grade, Veronica is still using the five-finger method, but her classmates no longer need to. Veronica cannot read the social studies textbook, so an aide reads it to her. Her parents are both college educated and perplexed by the problem. In desperation, her mother buys a phonics program and drills Veronica in sounding out words. It works. In 10th grade, Veronica is in an Honors English class, but she still avoids reading when possible.

Veronica is not unusual. As many as 40% of children have reading problems. Reading problems can result from low IQ, neurological problems, low motivation, poor vocabulary, or inadequate instruction in phonics (Ferrer, Shaywitz, Holahan, Marchione, & Shaywitz, 2010). When these problems are ruled out, but a child still has difficulty learning to read, the child has **specific reading disability**, commonly called *dyslexia.* About 5 to 15% of children have dyslexia. Boys may have similar rates of dyslexia as girls, but boys are referred by teachers more often (Shaywitz, Morris, & Shaywitz, 2008). Veronica was never referred for reading intervention, although she needed it.

What is specific reading disability? It is the most common learning disability. It is primarily caused by poor phonological awareness (Pennington & Bishop, 2009). Dyslexic students have difficulty linking letters with sounds, blending sounds together, or judging whether two words rhyme. These phonological problems result in labored decoding, poor word recognition, and weak spelling (Ziegler & Goswami, 2005). Adolescents who are dyslexic, but manage to learn to read through great effort, can be identified by their slow, labored oral reading.

There is debate over the identification of dyslexia, just as there is with other learning disabilities. Recall that learning disability is sometimes defined by an IQ-achievement discrepancy (see Chapter 5). Some educators object to a discrepancy definition of dyslexia for three reasons:

1. Low-IQ or ELL students, and those who lack opportunity to learn, cannot qualify for intervention.
2. It suggests that either you have dyslexia or you do not, yet in reality difficulties fall along a continuum.
3. It results in diagnoses too late. An alternative way to identify dyslexia is to use test scores for reading or phonological awareness that are in the bottom 10th to 25th percentile.

Although dyslexic children have normal intelligence, they may have some information processing problems, particularly slow processing speed, poor executive functions, and limited working memory (Im-Bolter et al., 2006; Swanson & Jerman, 2006). Scientists believe this may explain why dyslexia co-occurs with other problems. About 40% of children with math disabilities, about 25 to 50% of children with ADHD, and about 50% of children with delayed language have reading difficulty, each of which may result from underlying information processing problems (Bishop & Snowling, 2004; Tallal, 2004). This means that your students with dyslexia may learn concepts adequately, but have difficulty with tasks that ask them to rapidly process multiple pieces of information at the same time.

Dyslexia and the brain. Some differences in the brains of dyslexic and nondyslexic children have been found. This might be heritable, especially for children with educated parents like Veronica (Friend, DeFries, & Olson, 2008; Pennington et al., 2009). That is, with less opportunity to learn, any child might have reading problems, but in a high-literacy home only children with a genetic marker are likely to be dyslexic. However, recall that:

1. The brain is modified by experience. After many hours of intervention, the brains of dyslexic children more closely resemble those of good readers (Shaywitz & Shaywitz, 2005).
2. Complex skills are rarely determined by biology alone. For example, in a study of 6th-graders, SES most strongly predicted reading problems, but brain differences also made a contribution (Eckert, Lombardino, & Leonard, 2001).

Why does it matter if children have dyslexia? Dyslexic students are frustrated in school because labored reading limits how rapidly they can learn from texts. They also tend to remain struggling readers across the lifespan (Shaywitz & Shaywitz, 2005). Nevertheless, dyslexic students can become proficient in reading in their career area. Many brilliant historical figures are believed to have been dyslexic—Thomas Edison, Albert Einstein, Niels Bohr, and Walt Disney, among others. We do not know if these claims are true, but dyslexic students can become professionally successful.

(continued)

Challenges in Development *(continued)* Box 12.2

What can be done about dyslexia? Intervention for dyslexia is the same high-quality reading instruction we hope all students get, but more of it. Interventions focus on letter knowledge, phonological awareness, decoding, and word recognition strategies. Word recognition strategies include simply memorizing common words and figuring out a new word by analogy ("like" is similar to "bike") or by taking off suffixes (change "looked" to "look"). Interventions also focus on guided oral reading with feedback. Experiments show that these interventions help dyslexic students become more fluent readers. Unfortunately, not all students readily respond to intervention. Struggling readers who become more fluent are likely to have received better instruction and be of higher SES with literate homes, like Veronica (Shaywitz, Mody, & Shaywitz, 2006). In addition to intervention, you can help dyslexic students by accommodating them in three ways: (1) provide extra time for tasks that involve reading, (2) use recorded books, and (3) allow oral test-taking (Shaywitz et al., 2008).

specific reading disability a learning disability in which a child with normal intelligence and exposure to print has difficulty learning to read. It is characterized by difficulty decoding and recognizing words accurately and/or fluently. It is also called dyslexia.

be grammatically correct, further an argument, and fit logically into a paragraph. Effective writers execute and monitor these multiple tasks at the same time. Poor writers do these tasks in sequence, step by step. As good writers write a sentence, they may think "That really belongs in this other section," so they revise as they write. This requires good working memory.

Emotional factors

Negative emotions, like anger or anxiety, can interfere with the information processing needed for reading and writing (see Chapter 8). Because negative emotions, low self-control, and ADHD-like symptoms are linked to parent–child attachment, it is not surprising that attachment predicts literacy. Secure children tend to develop better literacy skills and attitudes toward reading than do insecure children. Secure toddlers are more likely to stay in Mother's lap while reading. Garrett wants to read with his mother because he is securely attached to her. Secure kindergarteners are more likely to include print in their play, ask parents to read words to them, and later develop good reading comprehension (Pianta & Harbers, 1996). Secure children have pleasant encounters with print because their parents are sensitive, which makes them better literacy coaches (Clingenpeel & Pianta, 2007). Pleasant interaction during parent–child storybook reading predicts reading fluency and positive attitudes as children begin to read on their own (Bergin, 2001).

Social factors

Literacy is social; it is acquired through social interaction and is used to connect with others. Two aspects of the social environment—joint storybook reading and play—are important. Joint storybook reading is initially about using the book as a tool to converse; toddlers generally look at the pictures, not the print. Remember that Garrett was using the book to ask about animals: "What's that?" "A squirrel." So how does it help with literacy? It builds oral language, phonological awareness, and vocabulary. As early as 18 months, toddlers who are read to develop a larger vocabulary than other children, and they tend to have higher reading achievement as they grow older (Fletcher & Reese, 2005). As children begin to read on their own, parents promote their literacy by listening to them read and providing feedback (Sénéchal & Young, 2008).

Preschoolers who use literacy in their play—like reading to dolls, writing a shopping list, and putting letters in a mailbox—develop greater literacy. So do elementary children who make their own books, write a play for their puppets, write out rules for games they make up, or try to find letters in billboards during car trips. So do adolescents who play games like *Scrabble* and *Boggle* that involve literacy.

Play is beneficial because it provides practice and authentic reasons to read or write. **Authentic literacy activities** refer to reading for information one wants or writing to inform a reader (Duke, Purcell-Gates, Hall, & Tower, 2006). Nonauthentic literacy tasks are done for the purpose of learning to read or write, or just to complete an assignment. Besides play, authentic tasks may include text-messaging friends and reading the newspaper sports page to see how your team did.

authentic literacy activities reading for information one wants, or writing to inform a reader, as opposed to activities done for the purpose of learning to read or write or just to complete an assignment.

Think About This Do SES-related differences in verbal ability and literacy fit the "family investment" or "family stress" model of poverty you read about in Chapter 1? How do they fit the bioecological model?

Group Diversity in Literacy

On the average, students' literacy varies by gender, class, ethnicity, and nationality. Let's look at those differences next.

Gender

Recall from Chapter 5 that girls tend to have higher literacy achievement than boys. This gender difference begins in preschool, when girls have slightly higher emergent literacy abilities, and continues into high school. Gender differences are international; 4th-grade girls outperform boys in thirty-five countries (Baer, Baldi, Ayotte, & Green, 2007). However, in the United States, by high school the difference between boys' and girls' reading ability is small, although writing differences get larger. The reasons for early gender differences are not entirely clear, but for older children one explanation may be exposure. From 6th grade through adolescence, boys tend to spend less time reading for pleasure (Nippold, Duthie, & Larsen, 2005).

Socioeconomic Status

Low-SES students tend to have lower literacy than other students. Parents' education, a key component of SES, is particularly important. Parents with more years of school have children with better reading ability. Even among low-income children, those whose mothers have more education tend to have better literacy skills (Dickinson, McCabe, Anastasopoulos, Peisner-Feinberg, & Poe, 2003).

SES differences in literacy may be due to opportunity to learn, as with spoken language. Some families have dozens of children's books, and others have none at all. Some preschoolers are read to several times a day, culminating in thousands of hours before entering school, whereas others are not read to. College-educated parents are more likely to read to their children, to talk with them during storybook reading, and to take them to the public library (Aikens & Barbarin, 2008; Raikes et al., 2006). For example, a national report found that 74% of college-educated mothers read to their preschoolers daily compared to 40% of high-school educated mothers and mothers living in poverty (Federal Interagency Forum on Child and Family Statistics, 2009). Differences in opportunity to learn continue into adolescence, as high-SES students spend more non-school-time reading than low-SES students (Larson & Verma, 1999). Differences in opportunity to learn occur at school as well as home. Students in low-SES schools tend to spend less time-on-task and have more classmates who struggle with literacy (Aikens & Barbarin, 2008; Connor, Son, Hindman, & Morrison, 2005).

Like gender differences, SES differences in literacy occur internationally (IEA, 2001; OECD, 2004). However, across countries about 20% of low-SES children develop good literacy skills and like to read. In fact, being of low SES, but a keen reader, is an advantage over being of high SES, but not a keen reader. Thus, many of your low-SES students will become literate if they like to read and have good instruction.

Ethnicity

On the National Assessment of Educational Progress (NAEP), White and Asian students have consistently higher reading scores than Black or Latino students in 4th, 8th, and 12th grades. In Chapter 5, you learned about possible causes of this achievement gap. In addition, ethnic differences may be due to exposure to print at home. White children (64%) are more likely to be read to daily than Black (48%) or Latino (42%) children (Raikes et al., 2006).

Ethnic differences may also be due to language mismatch. For example, students who speak AAVE may hear different letter–sound pairs than Standard English (SE). To understand this, imagine that a student is reading the sentence "Their hands are cold." In AAVE this could sound like "Deir han' a' co'." The student has to learn that the letters *th* can spell the sound for *d* as in "their." The student also has to learn to spell the word "hand" with a *d*, even though there is no spoken sound for the d in the student's speech (Charity, Scarborough, & Griffin, 2004). Learning letter–sound pairs is simpler for SE-using students or for AAVE-using students who can readily imitate SE.

Another aspect of language mismatch is that some languages, like AAVE and Asian languages, do not indicate time with verb tense like Standard English does. For example, an AAVE speaker might say, "I be going to school and seen Devin." It is not clear whether this sentence means, in SE, "I went to school and saw Devin" or "I was going to school and saw Devin" or "I go to school everyday and see Devin." Some students need to be taught verb conjugation to master Standard English. For example, Hong is a U.S.-born 9th-grader with Vietnamese parents who lives in a neighborhood where Vietnamese and AAVE are spoken:

Hong cannot speak or write fluently in Standard English. She has low achievement, but gets passing grades on papers because she has friends edit them. When it becomes clear she will not pass the high school exit exam, she is referred to a language intervention teacher. Ms. Cole identifies a key problem: Hong does not distinguish different forms of verbs, like walk, walks, walked, and walking. Ms. Cole helps Hong learn to conjugate verbs by asking Hong to hold up a card with the correct ending (ed, ing, s) as Ms. Cole says a variety of verbs.

After just four training sessions, Hong conjugates verbs correctly in both her speech and her writing. Ms. Cole is a master teacher noted for her success in helping remedial students become literate in Standard English. Although all students experience some language mismatch between spoken English and written, formal English, students whose spoken language displays a greater mismatch may have more difficulty with school literacy.

Ethnic differences may also be due to cultural mismatch. As you learned in Chapter 1, cultural mismatch can lead students of color to resist school. Students who struggle

Brat-
Waz ↑ nothin Much here
just kicken it
do you like Tina?
She says you dont act
like it.
your HOMEGirl
Gina

Figure 12.9 Writing Sample from a Gang Member. Adolescents can have well developed out-of-school literacies. *Source*: Moje (2000).

with school literacy can be highly literate in out-of-school peer culture, such as in graffiti and tagging. For example, girls of color who were in gangs in Salt Lake City wrote notes that followed elaborate rules, such as crossing out the letter *O* because a rival gang's name began with *O* (see Figure 12.9). Some of these girls were indifferent to in-school writing but were meticulous in their out-of-school writing (Moje, 2000). Other youth cross cultural borders, becoming skilled in both in-school and out-of-school literacy. For example, Maria, a Mexican American, was a tagger (i.e., graffiti writer) and was in AP classes; she said that *The Old Man and the Sea* was a favorite book (MacGillivray & Curwen, 2007). The challenge for teachers is to channel the abilities of these talented youth.

Cross-National Comparisons

It is easier to acquire literacy in some languages than in others. Children acquire literacy quickly in languages where spelling is regular or rule-bound (Anthony & Francis, 2005). For example, German and Spanish are easier to learn than English because English is so irregular. Chinese is even more difficult than English because it is not an alphabetic language, meaning sounds and letters are not related. Chinese children have to memorize 3,000 different characters to become literate, which takes several years. Dyslexia can occur in any of these languages, in that a small percentage of students in all languages have difficulty learning to read (Ziegler & Goswami, 2005).

Classroom Implications of Literacy Development

You learned earlier that literacy affects achievement in other subjects. Because of this, literacy skills are emphasized in the early grades in the United States. However, some schools are more successful in promoting literacy than others (see Figure 12.10). What makes them more effective? The same general practices you read about in previous chapters—more time-on-task, positive teacher–student relationships, opportunity to engage in rich discussions rather than working alone, and so forth. In addition, literacy-specific practices make some schools more effective. Let's look at how those practices improve the five components of reading—phonological skills, decoding,

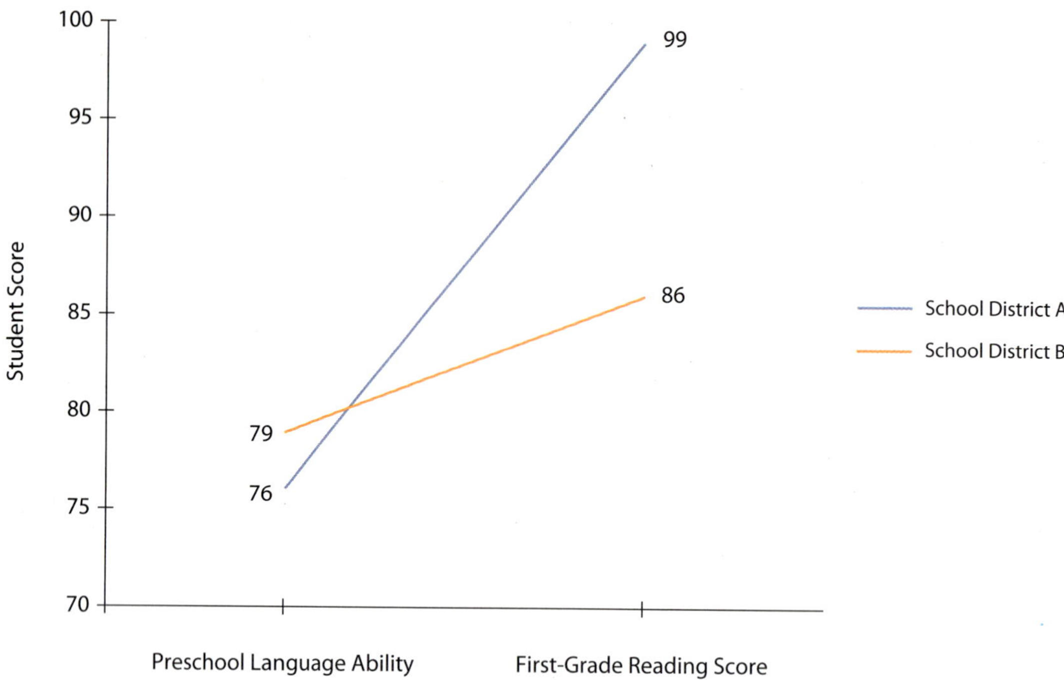

Figure 12.10 Schools Make a Difference in Literacy Development.
This chart shows two groups of students from the same Head Start preschool program. Those who went on to school district A developed better reading ability in 1st grade than students who went on to school district B. District A students were at grade level, and a whole standard deviation above their peers in district B. *Source: Adapted from Whitehurst & Lonigan (1998).*

fluency, vocabulary, and comprehension—and writing for all students. Then, we will discuss students who cross cultural and language boundaries.

Typically, in preschool through 2nd grade, schools emphasize phonological awareness, decoding, and beginning writing. From 3rd grade through high school, the emphasis shifts to fluency, comprehension, and advanced writing. Thus, the importance of the following guidelines will vary depending on the ages you teach.

Promoting Phonological Awareness and Decoding Skills

Phonological awareness is the foundation of reading ability (Dickinson et al., 2003). You promote your students' phonological awareness when you:

- *Directly teach students the names of letters and their corresponding sounds.* Remember to give more time to letters whose names do not match their sounds.
- *Sensitize students to phonemes through games and nursery rhymes.* For example, in one game, students take turns saying a word that begins with the same sound that the previous child's word ended in: Apple—Lion—Nap—Pepper. Learning nursery rhymes is linked to phonological awareness, probably because nursery rhymes play with sounds (Snowling, Gallagher, & Frith, 2003; Williams & Rask, 2003).
- *Give students spelling lists.* Young students who learn to spell words correctly learn to decode words better (Conrad, 2008).
- *Read to students.* Reading may be most effective if you read in small groups (three to four students), you read rather than tell the story, and you read about

four to five times a week (Adams, Treiman, & Pressley, 1998). Other aspects of reading are important as well:

- *Talk about the book.* Simple yes/no questions and pointing to pictures are appropriate with toddlers. Ask older students to predict events or analyze characters before and after reading, but not during the story, such as, "How do you think he feels?" Talk about new vocabulary words.
- *Read a balance of familiar and unfamiliar books.* When you read the same story a few times (there are diminishing effects after the second time), students comment more on the story, particularly low-ability students. However, new books expose students to new vocabulary.
- *Read information books*, like books on weather or animals. Expository books tend to elicit more child talk than storybooks (Fletcher & Reese, 2005).

Promoting Fluency

Even if students can decode words, they may not read fluently. Yet, teachers may not give enough attention to fluency. You may help your students become fluent readers when you:

- *Provide guided oral reading.* Providing immediate feedback as students read out loud improves literacy at all ages (Rasinski et al., 2005). It is ideally done one-on-one. To make this practical, some schools have senior citizens tutor struggling readers.
- *Provide frequent practice reading.* You can provide regular time in the school day for reading, or ask students to read when they finish assignments early, or ask students to read at home each day.

Some educators advocate independent silent reading, sometimes known as SSR (sustained silent reading) or DEAR (drop everything and read). However, just having students read more does not necessarily lead to better reading because students may not be comprehending (Kim, 2007). A major shortcoming of independent silent reading is that there is no feedback.

Promoting Vocabulary and Comprehension

The ultimate goal of reading is comprehension. Good vocabulary is critical to comprehension. When students know the words they read, they comprehend more. In the preceding section on language, you learned how to build students' vocabulary. To quickly review, this includes exposing students to literature, using unusual words in the classroom, and directly teaching vocabulary. When you build your students' vocabulary, you promote their comprehension. In addition, you promote your students' comprehension when you:

> **Field Observation**
>
> As you read this text, what strategies are you using to ensure you comprehend? Observe a child reading a text. Ask what strategies he or she is using. Are they the same as yours? Is the child using more than one strategy? Try interviewing students of different ages. Is there an age trend?

- *Directly teach comprehension strategies* (Edmonds et al., 2009), including overviewing before reading, encouraging students to make predictions, asking what the author is trying to communicate and why, asking what the more important ideas are, stopping periodically to clear up confusion (e.g., by going backward in the reading), summarizing, and applying the KWL approach (see Chapter 4). Students who summarize are better at judging whether they comprehend the text and are ready for a test—an ability called "metacomprehension" (Dunlosky & Lipko, 2007).

- *Discuss texts.* Students comprehend more and develop better reasoning ability when they critique and question texts in group discussion (Murphy, Wilkinson, Soter, Hennessey, & Alexander, 2009). However, you need to facilitate the discussion to be productive; mere student talk doesn't necessarily lead to deep thinking.

Marmaduke St. John/Alamy

When you build your students' vocabulary, you promote both their verbal ability and literacy.

Some evidence suggests that comprehension strategies are best taught embedded in content areas such as science and social studies (Kamil et al., 2008). For example, high school students who study history using multiple, conflicting texts, and who are taught to think about who, why, and when their texts were written, learn more content and learn to think more like historians (Nokes, Dole, & Hacker, 2007). That is, these *guidelines are not just for language arts teachers.*

Promoting Writing Skills

To become competent writers, students need many of the skills discussed earlier—good verbal ability, phonological awareness, spelling ability, adequate vocabulary, and exposure to print. Thus, as you follow the preceding guidelines, you will help your students become better writers. However, you will also need to provide writing instruction. You will help your students become better writers when you:

- *Provide instruction in writing strategies,* like how to generate and organize ideas before starting a draft and how to provide supporting arguments for a persuasive essay.
- *Teach specific steps of writing, give feedback, and guide revision.* Weak writers benefit from instruction in step-by-step writing. However, writers who are already capable of monitoring their own writing process may not (Pritchard & Honeycutt, 2006).
- *Provide opportunity to write, especially using authentic activities.* For example, after a lesson on volcanoes, 3rd-graders had many questions about where lava comes from and how hot it is, so their teacher assigned small groups to report the answers in writing to the class. In another class, students wrote about pond life in a brochure to be used at a nature center. Students given such authentic literacy assignments develop better writing skills (Purcell-Gates, Duke, & Martineau, 2007).

In addition, you can apply principles from other chapters that research has shown are linked to writing ability (Cutler & Graham, 2008; Rogers & Graham, 2008).

Reinforce students by praising them or posting their writing (see Chapter 3). Help students *set specific goals* for writing productivity, like writing three paragraphs each day (see Chapter 13). Spend more *time-on-task* actually writing in class (see Chapter 5). Even if you are not a writing teacher, adhering to these guidelines is helpful, as Mrs. Nair found in her chemistry class.

Research suggests that if you adhere to these guidelines, your students' literacy should improve. Programs that adhere to several guidelines at once help all students become more literate, while narrowing the gap for low-SES students (Borman et al., 2007; Correnti & Rowan, 2007). Still, some students will struggle. Seek the help of language intervention specialists for such students. There are effective literacy interventions for struggling students from 1st to 12th grade (D'Agostino & Murphy, 2004; Ehri, Dreyer, Flugman, & Gross, 2007; Kamil et al., 2008). One successful California high school assigns students to one of four literacy levels as they enter high school. Each level receives different instruction. For example, level 3 students, who read at the 6th-grade level, are helped to write in full sentences and to read fluently. In contrast, level 1 students are trained in phonological awareness. Many of the level 1 students are crossing cultural borders and are English language learners. Let's take a look at classroom implications for these students next.

Crossing Cultural Borders

Students may embrace literacy if they see it as personally relevant or resist literacy if it does not speak to them (Moller & Allen, 2000). One way to bridge cultural borders is to use multicultural literature. For example, one Black 4th-grade girl read a collection of poems written by African American authors, and then announced, "When I grow up ... I want to be a Black poetess" (McGinley & Kamberellis, 1996). Another 5th-grade boy tried to avoid literacy assignments until he discovered the biography of Fannie Lou Hamer, an African American voting advocate. Suddenly he couldn't read enough African American biographies (Smith, 1995). A Chinese-American high school student wrote that reading *The Joy Luck Club* made her proud of her culture (Athanases, 1998). At the same time, students should be encouraged to identify with people of other genders, ethnicities, and times. For example, one Black child read *Encyclopedia Brown,* about a White child detective, and said, "It seems like I'm in the story when I read it" (McGinley & Kamberellis, 1996). Similarly, a White adolescent read *House of Dies Drear* and said that when a runaway slave named Thomas dropped his light in a cave, she imagined that she was with him. Literature helps students understand others who are different (Mar & Oatley, 2008). Thus, students should be exposed to diverse literature, but also to literature that is personally relevant.

Teachers may also bridge cultural borders by engaging students' ethnic culture during instruction. For example, Ms. Lee, a teacher, used signifying to teach literary analysis to African American seniors. Recall from Chapter 9 that signifying is teasing using witty plays on words. Signifying is evident in rap and hip hop music. It is interpreted figuratively, not literally. Ms. Lee asked students to interpret samples of signifying and defend their interpretation. She then asked them to do the same with a short story and two novels set in a Black community that used AAVE (*Their Eyes Were Watching God* and *The Color Purple*). The students learned about irony and figurative language. They performed better on a literary test than students from the same school who had traditional instruction (Lee, 1995).

Teaching Bilingual and Biliterate Students

For some students, crossing cultural borders involves learning to use a completely different language. Students who speak English fluently as well as another language, like Vietnamese or Arabic, often have better literacy skills than monolingual students. Thus, being bilingual is not an impediment to becoming literate. Immigrant kindergartners who are not yet bilingual, but who are ELL, may struggle initially, but most will successfully learn to read in English by 4th grade (Lesaux, Lipka, & Siegel, 2006). Indeed, many immigrant students have higher reading and math achievement than native-born students—particularly if they attend schools with high-achieving peers (Han, 2008). What can you do to help your ELL students become biliterate? Research suggests the following:

- *Help ELL students develop literacy in their heritage language.* Some skills—phonological awareness, print concepts, and composition—transfer across languages (Deacon et al., 2007; Fitzgerald, 2006). Good literacy skills in a first language help students acquire a second language and achieve in school (Guglielmi, 2008; Sparks, Patton, Ganschow, Humbach, & Javorsky, 2008).
- *When possible, teach ELL students to read and write in a bilingual setting* (Farver et al., 2009). Students can simultaneously learn both literacies—it does not necessarily confuse them. However, do not wait for them to become literate in their heritage language. The U.S. Department of Education recommends that kindergarten through 5th-grade ELL students be taught to read English from their first day of school, regardless of whether they are also being taught to read in their native language.

advanced literacy reading and writing that involves a formal, academic style in particular content areas, such as science lab reports. It includes analyzing text; evaluating arguments; and writing extended, reasoned text.

After ELL students have acquired basic literacy skills in the primary grades, they may still struggle with advanced literacy in the upper grades, just as Alex did (Merino & Hammond, 2002). **Advanced literacy** includes being able to summarize texts, evaluate arguments, and write a reasoned essay. It is used in tasks like science lab reports or literary analysis. For example, one college-bound Spanish-speaking student wrote a science lab report that began, "The diffusivity of different solvents at different temperatures are determine by using the SDT experiment" (Schleppegrell, 2002). She is a good science student who speaks English well, but she is still struggling with advanced writing. To help ELL students develop advanced literacy, follow these guidelines:

- *Recognize that capable ELL students who understand everyday use of Standard English will sometimes falter with advanced school-related reading and writing.*
  - *Provide explicit instruction in grammar and the specialized writing used in your class.* Provide needed corrective feedback.
  - *Require ELL students to write as much as other students.* Even if they understand the topic, ELL students may write as little as possible in order to avoid getting points deducted for poor writing. Unfortunately, this hampers their ability to become more literate. Instead, encourage longer writing, but with sufficient scaffolding to be successful, as Mrs. Nair did.

Think About This Imagine that you teach science to an ELL student who writes a grammatically incorrect report. Should you deduct points for low-quality writing, even if the student does the experiment correctly and understands the concepts? What would be your best solution for assigning grades in this situation?

All of these guidelines for teaching ELL students may apply to other students placed at risk for low achievement in school. Indeed, the majority of students in Alex's chemistry class struggle with advanced literacy to some degree. Can you identify several of the guidelines from this chapter that Mrs. Nair implemented in case 5? Mrs. Nair has come to realize that as a high school science teacher, she needs to teach literacy. Thus, the lessons in this chapter are not just for preschool or primary teachers, nor are they just for English teachers.

When these guidelines are combined into a comprehensive program across the school, achievement in all subjects can rise. For example, in one California high school, all teachers in the school (i.e., not just English teachers) work on a school-wide academic vocabulary of words such as *discuss*, *evaluate*, *excerpt*, and *analyze*. Every class in the school engages in independent reading when students finish their work early. The entire faculty requires every student to answer questions in a full sentence. While these are only some approaches to intervention, this school district has won awards for narrowing the achievement gap for minority, ELL, and low-SES students.

Research suggests that if you follow these guidelines, you will help your students become more literate. But which guidelines should get priority? This is an important question because about 40% of students do not learn to read fluently by 4th grade, suggesting literacy instruction is not widely effective (Adams et al., 1998). Let's see what different theories suggest.

Putting the Theories to Work: The Case of Literacy

While basic language skills are typically mastered early, universally, and without formal instruction, literacy must be formally taught. But how? This is an important question because NAEP results suggest that only one-third of 8th-graders comprehend text proficiently and only one-fourth of 12th-graders write at or above the proficient level (NCES, 2010). How should you teach literacy?

Implications for Teachers from Different Theories

As with math (Chapter 4), your view of how literacy should be taught would vary depending on your theory about how students develop. Let's look at the implications for literacy from some major theories (key concepts from past chapters are italicized).

Behaviorism and Literacy

Behaviorists believe that learning (or conditioning) results from a pairing of behavior and its consequence. As a behaviorist teacher you would emphasize *direct instruction*, teaching each skill explicitly with no reliance on discovery learning. You would set goals for your students, watch their *observable behaviors* (such as using correct punctuation in writing), and then *reinforce* behavior toward the goals. You would use much *drill-and-practice*, giving frequent and immediate *feedback*.

As a behaviorist teacher you would teach skills in a *hierarchical sequence*. Students would first master *prerequisite low-level skills* and then move to more complex, advanced skills. For example, you would first teach young children letter names and sounds. Once children mastered these basic skills, they would progress to blending the sounds to read and spell small words and later move on to reading and writing sentences. Similarly, you would intervene with adolescent struggling readers by building basic skills first.

phonics an approach to teaching literacy that emphasizes training in phonological awareness and decoding words.

Behaviorists favor a phonics approach to literacy instruction. The **phonics** approach involves directly teaching students phonological awareness, pairing sounds with spelling, blending sounds together to decode words, and breaking words apart to spell them. Phonics instruction can include a variety of techniques such as learning nursery rhymes, playing games, and using worksheets.

Research supports the behaviorist approach. Students with good phonological awareness and decoding skills become better at reading and writing than students with weak basic skills (Adams et al., 1998; Graham, 2000). Research also shows that direct instruction may be the most effective approach for teaching decoding, vocabulary, reading comprehension strategies, writing strategies, and sentence construction (Graham & Perin, 2007). However, many educators do not like the behaviorist approach because it treats students as passive learners. They prefer a constructivist view—either Piagetian or Vygotskyan, or a combination.

Piaget's Theory of Cognitive Development and Literacy

In contrast to behaviorists, Piaget believed students are active thinkers who *construct their own knowledge*. Young students *assimilate* new experience with what they already know, creating unique language such as invented spellings (e.g., *lik* for *like*) and grammar (e.g., *footses* instead of *feet*). As a Piagetian teacher, you would teach literacy by providing students with a print-rich environment. You might encourage students to initiate their own literacy activities, such as writing a note to Daddy or letter to the editor. You might help students read a new word by asking them to use what they already know to figure it out, rather than telling them what it is. With young children, you would also use *hands-on activities* with concrete objects that allow them to reinvent literacy for themselves, rather than by directly teaching basic skills. For example, you could encourage young children to play with magnetic letters, crayons, paper, and books. However, research challenges the effectiveness of *unguided* hands-on play with concrete objects for literacy learning. Play with concrete objects can cause students to focus more on the object than on what it stands for (Uttal, Liu, & DeLoache, 2006).

Students cannot by themselves reinvent the print system. Some students will learn to read without formal schooling, but they are not reinventing literacy. Instead, they are internalizing the literacy experiences they have had during social interaction. This is a key point of difference between Vygotsky's and Piaget's constructivism. Sociocultural constructivists give greater emphasis to social interaction and cultural transmission.

Vygotsky's Sociocultural Theory and Literacy

Socioculturalists believe that literacy is learned through *social interaction* in *culturally organized activities*. To become literate, students' skills must move from interpsychological (between people) to intrapsychological (within the person). This happens through *apprenticeship*. In an apprenticeship, the expert, or teacher, *scaffolds* the child's literacy by gradually giving more responsibility to the child. The expert first performs the cognitive work and the child participates as a spectator. As the lessons progress, the child becomes more involved in the cognitive work, and eventually takes over while the expert becomes the supportive spectator. The degree of scaffolding depends on the child's *zone of proximal development*.

As a sociocultural teacher, you may scaffold toddlers' word learning during storybook reading by asking easy questions (e.g., "Point to the lynx") and moving to harder questions (e.g., "Why did the lynx growl?") as the child is ready (Blewitt, Rump, Shealy, & Cook, 2009). With older students, you may gradually move from reading all of the text, to reading difficult words, to merely supporting the students' reading of the text. Effective teachers provide different types of instruction to the same child across the school year as the zone of proximal development shifts (Connor et al., 2009).

Scaffolding can be done between students during *cooperative learning*. For example, students can do paired reading, edit each other's writing, memorize vocabulary together, or discuss the meaning of texts. Cooperative learning is an effective method for helping secondary students develop reading ability (Slavin, Cheung, Groff, & Lake, 2008). *Reciprocal teaching* (see Chapter 3) is effective for developing comprehension strategies. Let's take a look at how Ms. Cole scaffolds struggling high school students' writing ability:

> *First, we outline in detail. My students aren't yet skilled enough to think about WHAT to write as well as HOW to write, so the WHAT has to be completely thought out before the first draft is attempted. Second, we write one paragraph at a time. I remind students what the basic components of each paragraph should be. For example, an introduction paragraph should begin with a catchy opening followed by the name of the author, title of the work, and a short plot synopsis. The paragraph should be finished with a thesis sentence that lists the main points of the essay in the correct order. This approach may seem overly prescriptive, but my students learn to write. Third, we do peer editing, also one paragraph at a time as I walk them through it. Two peers go through the same paragraph—the first student for content, the second for grammar errors. We pass the papers on for the next paragraph; eventually students' papers are read by ten different editors. No student is "stuck" with a weak editor for more than one paragraph, and students see ten different samples of writing. This is eye-opening for the struggling writer. Then students go on to the next draft. We peer edit again to really polish the piece. I take serious time guiding students through peer editing because it has great benefits, but if not STRICTLY guided, it does not.*

Research supports the effectiveness of providing models of writing, and having students work together to plan, edit, and revise their writing—two tenets of sociocultural theory used by Ms. Cole (Graham & Perin, 2007).

The Information Processing Model and Literacy

The information processing model is concerned with how information is processed, regardless of whether the information was obtained through direct instruction, constructive thinking, or social interaction. Students tend to be better readers and writers if they have:

1. Faster *processing speed*, particularly speed in naming letters and identifying words.
2. Greater *executive functions*, or the ability to suppress irrelevant information and control attention, from kindergarteners to older students (Blair & Razza, 2007; McClelland et al., 2007). For example, during writing, greater executive functions help students shift between spelling a word, keeping in mind the overall plan for the sentence, and fitting the sentence into the total essay.

3. Greater *metacognition*, or the ability to monitor their reading or writing process as they are doing it.
4. Greater *long-term memory*, or prior knowledge. Students who know more in general, and more vocabulary in particular, comprehend more of what they read (Bast & Reitsma, 1998).
5. Greater *working memory*. This helps students juggle all the tasks involved in reading or writing, and also helps them learn new vocabulary as they read (Carretti, Borella, Cornoldi, & De Beni, 2009).

Students also tend to be better readers and writers if they have strategies for *memorizing* and *problem solving*, because literacy requires strategy use, like memorizing vocabulary words or figuring out how to spell a word. According to the *overlapping waves* model, students know and use multiple strategies, but gradually shift from less efficient to more efficient strategies. For example, the same child might use several strategies to spell a word—sound it out, try different spellings to see if they look right, apply rules like "*i* before *e* except after *c*," use an analogy to a familiar word like replacing the *d* in dish with an *f* to get "fish," or simple retrieval if they've memorized the word (Kwong & Varnhagen, 2005). Just as with math, *retrieval* is the most efficient strategy. Students who are better spellers use more retrieval and use backup strategies more effectively.

There are three key implications from the information processing model for your role as a teacher. First, help students acquire greater knowledge—both literacy-specific knowledge such as letter–sound pairs and vocabulary, as well as general knowledge. Students comprehend what they read and they write better when they know more about the topic (Graham & Perin, 2007; McCutchen, 2006). Second, help students make basic literacy skills, such as decoding, so automatic that they do not tax working memory. When struggling readers use all their working memory to decode words, they cannot comprehend what they are reading. Writing especially taxes working memory. You can help poor writers by scaffolding the steps of the writing process, as Ms. Cole did. Third, help students acquire efficient strategies for literacy tasks, from decoding *bat* to writing a scientific abstract. One way to help students shift from less-efficient to more-efficient strategies is to have students *explain their strategy*, which facilitates metacognition. Strategies can also be taught through modeling, direct instruction, *spaced practice*, and *frequent testing* with *feedback*.

Comparing the Theories

As you learned in Chapter 1, the different theories of child development are not so much contradictory as they are unrelated because they explain different pieces of development. But sometimes they conflict. Historically, two approaches to literacy instruction have been at odds. Behaviorists favor a phonics approach. Constructivists favor a whole-language approach in which reading and writing for meaning are emphasized and drilling students in mechanics, such as phonics and grammar, is deemphasized. Constructivists encourage writing for authentic reasons and ignore invented spelling and nonstandard punctuation in order to focus on the child's meaning.

Which approach is best? Many studies converge on the notion that teaching phonics is critically important, particularly for low-SES students and secondary students who are struggling readers (National Reading Panel, 2000; Slavin, Lake, Chambers,

Cheung, & Davis, 2009). Students with weak emergent literacy or phonological skills may need more phonics instruction than average readers (Connor et al., 2009). Students with strong emergent literacy skills can succeed with either a whole-language or phonics approach (Xue & Meisels, 2004). However, while phonetic skills are necessary, they are not sufficient for a child to become a fluent, skilled reader. Whole-language techniques such as focusing on meaning and using authentic literacy tasks are important. Ideally, teachers would use a combination of approaches (Connor et al., 2009; Steubing, Barth, Cirino, Francis, & Fletcher, 2008).

Each theory is true to some extent and can be applied in your classroom. For example, you can teach comprehension strategies effectively through direct instruction (behaviorism), modeling of more skilled others (social cognitive theory), and scaffolding in the child's zone of proximal development, with guided practice (sociocultural constructivism). Effective instruction draws on the best of each theory.

Reflections on Practice: Checklist for Teachers

There are several things from previous chapters that you can do to increase language and literacy skills in your students. Review the "Reflections on Practice" sections from these other chapters. They include:

- Scaffold children in their zone of proximal development during literacy tasks. Use guided practice and feedback to teach strategies. Promote general knowledge so that children write with knowledge and comprehend what they read. Help children overlearn basic skills so their working memory is freed for more-complex skills (see Chapters 3, 4, and 5).
- Develop secure relationships with students. Help children develop self-control and good emotion regulation so they benefit from literacy instruction (see Chapters 6, 7, and 8).
- Encourage play with literacy among younger children. Use cooperative learning, such as peer editing, with older children (see Chapter 11).

In addition, periodically ask the following:

1. Do I have any students with poor verbal ability? When a child misbehaves or performs worse than I expect, do I look for language problems?
2. Do I use uncommon words when I talk to my students? Do I directly teach vocabulary? Do I read to my students or encourage them to read?
3. Do my students have opportunity to talk in the classroom? Do I insist on full-sentence answers?
4. Do my students have a mismatch between home and school language? How can I help them cross language borders? Do I support their heritage language, encouraging additive bilingualism?
5. Do I provide multicultural literature? Do I build on literacies my students have besides school-based literacy?
6. As a preschool teacher, do I promote play with literacy and sensitize children to phonemes? As an elementary teacher, do I provide effective literacy instruction? As a secondary teacher, do I help students learn advanced literacy for my subject area?
7. Am I aware of students who are struggling readers—girls as well as boys? Do I allow extra time for reading tasks or provide oral testing? What interventions are available in my school?

Summary of Age Trends in Language and Literacy

	Language	Literacy
Early Childhood (Birth–5 Years)	Infants communicate nonverbally. Toddlers first learn the sounds of their language, then use single-word utterances, then multiword utterances without function words (e.g., *of, the*), and then use complete sentences. For more detail see Table 12.1. Adults use child-directed speech toward infants and preschoolers.	Emergent literacy skills and pseudo writing are evident by age 3. Children's first real written word is usually their name. "Reading" begins as pointing and talking about books, gradually becoming more written-word oriented. Gender differences in literacy emerge. Most kindergarteners can form letters and write words phonetically, but are not yet reading independently.
Middle Childhood (6–12 Years)	Basic syntax is mastered by 1st grade. Children now play with language and use it for humor. Vocabulary explodes between 1st and 5th grades. Vocabulary is often learned through reasoning, but should be directly taught as well.	Children develop conventional literacy. They first misspell words phonetically, but most become conventional spellers by 4th grade. By 4th grade, learning-to-read shifts to reading-to-learn. Children begin to write longer, more-complex pieces that are reader-friendly. They plan and revise their writing more. Children who lag in literacy, but catch up by 3rd to 5th grade, may fare well as readers; otherwise, poor literacy remains stable.
Adolescence (13–19 Years)	Language is processed more rapidly. Sentences become longer and more complex. Vocabulary continues to grow. Skill at manipulating listeners increases. Humor includes sophisticated wordplay.	Reading fluency increases. Abstract and specialized vocabulary is acquired, which increases comprehension. Writing is better organized, longer, and more persuasive. More-complex sentence constructions are used. Yet, few students have advanced writing ability. Gender differences diminish in reading, particularly among college-bound students. ELL students may struggle with advanced literacy, even if they know Standard English.

Chapter Summary

Language Development

- Nonverbal language develops before verbal language and continues to be used throughout childhood. Expressive language lags behind receptive.
- Some psychologists believe language is innate, core knowledge. Yet research suggests that general cognitive abilities such as reasoning and memory are used to learn language.
- Some children have low verbal ability, which is linked to misbehavior and low achievement.
- Verbal ability is predicted by genes, information processing ability, emotional regulation, theory of mind, sociodramatic play, joint attention, secure attachment, and parents' behaviors (such as induction, responsiveness to children's talk, and reading to children).
- Girls tend to have better verbal ability than boys. Higher-SES children tend to have better verbal ability than low-SES children.
- Most children's home language is different from school language. Greater mismatches occur for children who speak a dialect other than Standard English, such as AAVE, or a non-English language. Such children benefit from direct instruction in Standard English.
- Teachers can promote children's language ability by elaborating on their talk, using uncommon words, encouraging language use in the classroom, reading to children, and teaching vocabulary.

Literacy

- Reading and writing ability are correlated, although writing may be more complex. Both depend on vocabulary, phonological awareness, and decoding skills. Reading also depends on fluency and comprehension.
- Early struggling readers tend to remain struggling readers, but some children improve. Poor reading is linked to emotional distress, misbehavior, and low academic achievement.
- Dyslexia is a learning disability for reading. Interventions focus on phonological awareness and fluency. It often co-occurs with other information processing difficulties.
- Literacy is predicted by verbal ability, brain structure (which could be due to genes or experience), information processing abilities, emotional well-being, and social experiences with print such as play and joint storybook reading.
- Girls tend to be more literate than boys, high-SES children more than low-SES, and White and Asian children more than Black or Latino children. Reasons for

these group differences include opportunity to learn inside and outside of school and culture mismatch.

- Teachers can help young children become literate by promoting verbal ability, teaching letters, using nursery rhymes and phoneme-based games, and reading to children. Teachers can help older children by providing frequent practice with authentic literacy activities, giving feedback, and teaching reading and writing strategies.
- Children can learn multiple literacies, even if they are not yet literate in their heritage language. Biliterate students who have basic English ability may struggle with advanced literacy.

Putting the Theories to Work: The Case of Literacy

- Behaviorists emphasize direct instruction, with drill-and-practice of basic literacy skills. Behaviorist theory supports the phonics approach.
- Piagetian constructivists emphasize children as active learners who construct their own literacy from a print-rich environment with hands-on activities. Sociocultural constructivists emphasize scaffolding in the ZPD, modeling, guided practice, and cooperative learning. Constructivist perspectives support the whole-language approach.
- The information processing model emphasizes the role of knowledge, working memory, metacognition, strategy use, and processing speed in literacy development.
- Each theory contributes to effective classroom practices. Phonics is a necessary, but not sufficient, component of effective literacy instruction. Direct instruction, guided practice, and authentic literacy activities are particularly important.

Accompanying Education CourseMate Website Resources

Visit the **Education CourseMate** website at **CengageBrain.com** to find resources and study aids for this chapter, including self-tests, additional print and website resources, and glossary flashcards. In addition to the TeachSource Video Cases, the following videos illustrate concepts discussed in the chapter:

- 0–2 Years: Language Development in Infants and Toddlers
- 2–5 Years: Language Development for Early Childhood

TEACHSOURCE VIDEO CASE

Watch the video cases *Language Development: Oral and Literacy Related Activities in an Early Childhood Setting* and/or *Teaching English Language Learners: A Middle School Teacher's Story* and/or *Elementary Reading Instruction: A Balanced Literacy Program*. As you view the videos and artifacts think about the following:

1. Identify specific guidelines from the "Classroom Implications" section on both language and literacy development that the teacher is using.
2. Can you identify additional guidelines that the teacher could implement?

13 *chapter*

The Self-System and Motivation

Jamie Grill/Iconica/Getty Images

IN PREVIOUS CHAPTERS, YOU LEARNED THAT CHILDREN CAN DO POORLY IN SCHOOL FOR MANY REASONS BESIDES LOW INTELLIGENCE, SUCH AS LACK OF SELF-CONTROL OR EXCESSIVE AGGRESSION. In this chapter we will discuss two other factors that affect school success—self-concept, including gender and racial identity, and motivation. After you read this chapter, you will understand:

- Components of the self-system such as self-esteem, self-concept, and self-efficacy.
- How gender and ethnic identity affect school success.
- How self-concepts affect motivation, and what you can do to increase your students' motivation.

The Self-System

Sadie is an active 3rd-grader. Her teacher, Ms. Heck hands out a worksheet that contains several sentences about the Pilgrims. The instructions are to put the sentences in order to make an accurate paragraph. Sadie raises her hand: "Ms. Heck, I don't understand. I don't have them in order."

"Well, you need to pay attention, young lady." Ms. Heck did not answer Sadie's question, so Sadie tries again: "Ms. Heck, do we write the sentences or just the numbers?" Ms. Heck looks at Sadie, and then looks away without answering her. Sadie writes one sentence and then blurts out: "What comes second?"

"If you were to read carefully, maybe you would understand."

"Is it this one? The colony was the second after Jamestown?" Ms. Heck starts clapping and has the rest of the class join her, as she sarcastically says, "Very good! It's about time! Maybe you'll be able to figure out the next one, too." Then Sadie asks if they are supposed to use pen or pencil. Ms. Heck says, "Do we use pen for worksheets? No!" A few minutes later, Sadie asks to sharpen her pencil. When she returns to her seat, Sadie raises her hand a few more times. Ms. Heck looks at Sadie, but does not call on her. Sadie asks a peer for help.

Ms. Heck has recommended that Sadie be retained next year because she is not capable of doing 4th-grade work, is not a good student, and is unable to pay attention. However, she does not want Sadie in her class again next year.

Ms. Heck is remarkably negative with Sadie, but she is not negative with other students. Sadie is not doing well in school, but she is not doing poorly enough to justify retention (see Chapter 1). How do you think Ms. Heck influences Sadie's self-concept? Your answer depends on what self-concept is and what causes it. The **self** is a group of related thoughts that you hold about yourself (Harter, 2006). The thoughts include self-assessments like "Am I worthy of love?" and "What am I good at?" How might Sadie answer these questions in Ms. Heck's classroom?

self a group of related thoughts that people hold about themselves.

Psychologists use the term self-*system* because there are multiple aspects of the self. Part of the self is one's personal identity. The theorist who most popularized the notion of personal identity was Erik Erikson. Box 13.1 discusses his contributions. The aspect of the self that you probably hear about most is self-esteem. Other important aspects of the self-system in your classroom include self-concept and self-efficacy.

Self-Esteem, Self-Concept, and Self-Efficacy

self-esteem one's feelings of worth.

self-concept the differentiated conception of self that includes categories such as academic self-concept, social self-concept, and athletic self-concept. The term *global self-concept* is sometimes used synonymously with *self-esteem*.

Self-esteem refers to your general feelings of worth; it is a broad concept. **Self-concept** refers to both your general evaluation of yourself and evaluations of yourself in specific domains. You can have different self-concepts in domains like academics, social skills, sports, appearance, peer relations, romantic appeal, verbal skills, and mathematical skills (Cole et al., 2001; Marsh, Ellis, & Craven, 2002). *Global* self-concept and self-esteem are often considered to be the same.

Theories & Theorists **Box 13.1**

Erikson's Psychosocial Theory

Erik Erikson was born in Germany in 1902. During his childhood, he thought his father was the man he grew up with. However, as an adolescent he discovered that his birth was the result of an extramarital affair when his mother was in a previous marriage (Hopkins, 1995). Erikson did not publicly reveal this until he was 68. As you read on, think about how his history may have influenced his ideas.

Erikson developed a psycho*social* theory of development that paralleled Freud's psycho*sexual theory*. Their theories were similar in many ways, including outlining stages of development, but different in that (1) Erickson emphasized a crisis at each stage, (2) his theory covered the lifespan instead of only birth to adolescence, and (3) he emphasized the influence of culture and society. The accompanying table outlines Erikson's stages (Erikson, 1959, 1963).

In each stage, the individual experiences internal conflict. Some of these conflicts center on sexuality, bowel movements, and breastfeeding. For example, in the second stage—autonomy versus shame—Erikson believed toddlers fear adults who "attack one's power of autonomy and who would designate as evil those products of the bowels which were felt to be all right when they were being passed" (1963, p. 254). The resolution of each conflict, whether positive or negative, sets the stage for the next conflict.

The concept for which Erikson may be most famous is the *identity crisis*. This refers to a person's difficulty in deciding who to be and in finding meaning in life and work. For Erikson, adolescence was the onset of the identity crisis—and a period of storm. If the crisis "Who am I?" is resolved, then adolescents are ready to take on the challenges of the next stage.

Erikson may have been interested in the identity crisis because of his own struggles with identity. His stepfather was Jewish, but his parents were Danish and he was blond and blue-eyed. Was he Jewish or Nordic? His last name officially changed three times, from Salmonsen to Homburger to Erikson. He also had considerable difficulty choosing a career. He studied art, tried teaching school, and studied psychoanalysis. In his career as a psychologist, he did fieldwork among the Sioux and Yurok Native American groups, engaged in casework in Pittsburgh with poor immigrant families, and wrote books about Gandhi and Martin Luther.

Psychosocial Stage	Age Period	Description of Erikson's Stage	Freud's Parallel Stage
Basic trust versus mistrust	Birth to 1 year	Infants come to understand the world as trustworthy and safe or threatening and unsafe based on how they are treated. Trust comes from being cared for.	Oral
Autonomy versus shame and doubt	1 to 3 years	Toddlers want to feel that they have some autonomy or control over their environment and their choices. At the same time, they need to experience firm and reasonable control. Children need to feel a sense of self-control, or else they will feel shame and a desire to get away with misbehavior.	Anal
Initiative versus guilt	3 to 6 years	The child attempts to gain the mother's affection and is eager for cooperation with age mates. If parents demand excessive self-control, children become overcontrolled and lose their identity.	Phallic
Industry versus inferiority	6 to 11 years	The child begins to work and win recognition by producing things. This is linked with systematic instruction, which may occur in schools. If unsuccessful, the child feels inferiority and inadequacy. The stage is a lull before the storm of adolescence.	Latency
Identity versus identity confusion	Adolescence	The child seeks an identity and a profession or occupation. The child may experience role confusion, including sexual identity, and may become clannish and cliquish.	Genital
Intimacy versus isolation	Emerging adulthood	The young adult seeks intimacy and close friendships and, in their absence, feels isolation and self-absorption.	
Generativity versus stagnation	Adulthood	Adults need to be needed. They wish to guide the next generation, usually their own children. Otherwise, they may feel a need for pseudo-intimacy and may fall into stagnation and personal impoverishment.	
Integrity versus despair	Old age	Elderly adults feel that their lives were worthwhile, or they fear death and that it is too late to start another life.	

Ted Streshinsky/Historical/Corbis

Self-efficacy (see Chapter 3) is even more specific than self-concept, though the two concepts do overlap. Self-efficacy refers to your confidence that you can accomplish a specific behavior. You could have a positive social self-concept but still feel low self-efficacy for meeting new people in strange settings, like shy Eric from Chapter 6. Keep in mind that all three self terms (esteem, concepts, and efficacy) have to do with your *perceptions* of worthiness and competence, not your actual worthiness or competence. In this section, we will focus on self-concept and self-esteem. We will focus on self-efficacy later in this chapter.

Age Trends in the Self

A father saw his daughter splattered with mud. He said, "My, you're pretty dirty!" The girl replied, "Yes, but I'm even prettier clean." Could you guess that this child with a robust physical self-concept was 4 years old? Research suggests that self-concepts are high in early childhood, then decline through adolescence, bottom out, and then increase through adulthood, peaking in the late 60s (Marsh et al., 2002; Robins & Trzesniewski, 2005). Let's look at other age trends.

Early Childhood (Birth to 5 Years)

Some infants learn that they can affect the environment; for example, they learn that kicking causes the crib to bounce, and crying brings father. This fosters high self-esteem because they feel capable of influencing others and events. In Chapter 6, you learned that when parents are responsive, their children develop secure attachment and internal working models that "I am worthy of love" and "I am capable of getting important people (my parents) to respond to me." This becomes the bedrock of high self-esteem.

Self-esteem requires a sense of self, but just when do children have a sense of self? In a classic study, Amsterdam (1972) placed a spot on the noses of infants and toddlers. They were then shown their image in a mirror. She found that 6- to 12-month-olds behaved like the mirror image was a playmate, not an image of themselves. In contrast, older toddlers touched the spot, used the mirror to examine their noses, or acted embarrassed. Others admired themselves, looking coy, strutting, and clowning around. Few 15-month-olds but about half of 18-month-olds and most 24-month-olds clearly recognize the self, with some even saying their own name and pointing at their image (Nielsen, Suddendorf, & Slaughter, 2006).

Amsterdam inferred that older toddlers understand it is their own image in the mirror and that they have developed a sense of self. The fact that toddlers begin using words like "me," "mine," "I do it," and begin to feel self-conscious emotions like embarrassment and pride at this same age suggests that Amsterdam may be correct (Lewis & Ramsay, 2004). This development has been linked to maturation of the brain (Lewis & Carmody, 2008).

As young children develop a sense of self, they tend to be overly optimistic about their abilities. Every preschooler on a soccer team may think that he or she is the best player, and every student in a classroom may think that he or she is the smartest.

This inflated self-assessment is good because it prevents preschoolers from giving up, which they might do if they knew how incompetent they really are.

One reason young children have inflated self-assessment is that they are not good at social comparison yet. They have difficulty comparing their own competence to others'. They also are unlikely to understand that if others do something with *less* effort, it means that they are *more* skilled (Nicholls, 1989). For example, they do not understand that if a boy can read only after extensive practice, he is less skilled than another boy who easily reads with little practice.

Middle Childhood (6 to 12 Years)

During middle childhood, children's optimistic self-assessment is replaced with more realistic self-concepts. This occurs as children gain skill at social comparison (Harter, 2006). Ask children in middle childhood to tell you about themselves, and they might say something like, "I'm good at math. I like to play soccer, but I'm not very good at it." They now integrate their experiences in different activities into broad self-concepts like "I am good at school" or "I am good at sports."

Adolescence (13 to 19 Years)

Adolescents are better at self-assessment than very young children, but they still tend to have a positive bias. Garrison Keillor says that all children in Lake Wobegon are above average. While statistically impossible, this may be true outside Lake Wobegon also—according to self-report that is. In one study, almost all (98%) high school seniors said they had above-average leadership skills (Dunning, Heath, & Subs, 2004). Accuracy of self-assessment depends on the domain; social skill is the least accurate, while athletic skill is the most accurate, perhaps because of clear feedback.

> **Field Observation**
>
> Interview children of different ages. Ask them what sports they do, which they are best at, and who is the best person on the team. Ask them what subjects they are good in at school and who is best and worst in their class. What age trends in self-concept and social comparison did you find?

During adolescence there may be a proliferation of selves, such as the self in relation to parents, friends, and romantic partners, and also the self in different roles such as student, employee, and athlete (Harter, 1999). The proliferation occurs because, unlike younger children, adolescents are capable of viewing the self as mean *and* nice, klutzy *and* coordinated, smart *and* dumb, depending on the context.

Youth tend to show a downward trend in their perceptions of competence across the school years (see Figure 13.1). This may occur because their assessment of their competence becomes more accurate. It may also occur because youth increasingly are compared with others, in grading at school and in competitive extracurricular activities.

Individual Differences in the Self

Some children have higher self-esteem than others. These differences are fairly stable, meaning children with higher self-esteem are likely to stay that way over time (Robins & Trzesniewski, 2005). To remedy such inequality, in 1987 California created a task force charged with producing high self-esteem in *all* children. Why? High self-esteem was viewed as a "social vaccine" capable of curing social ills like teen pregnancy and poverty. (*The New York Times* had fun with this, calling it legislation conceived in a hot tub.) Let's look at whether this is a reasonable view.

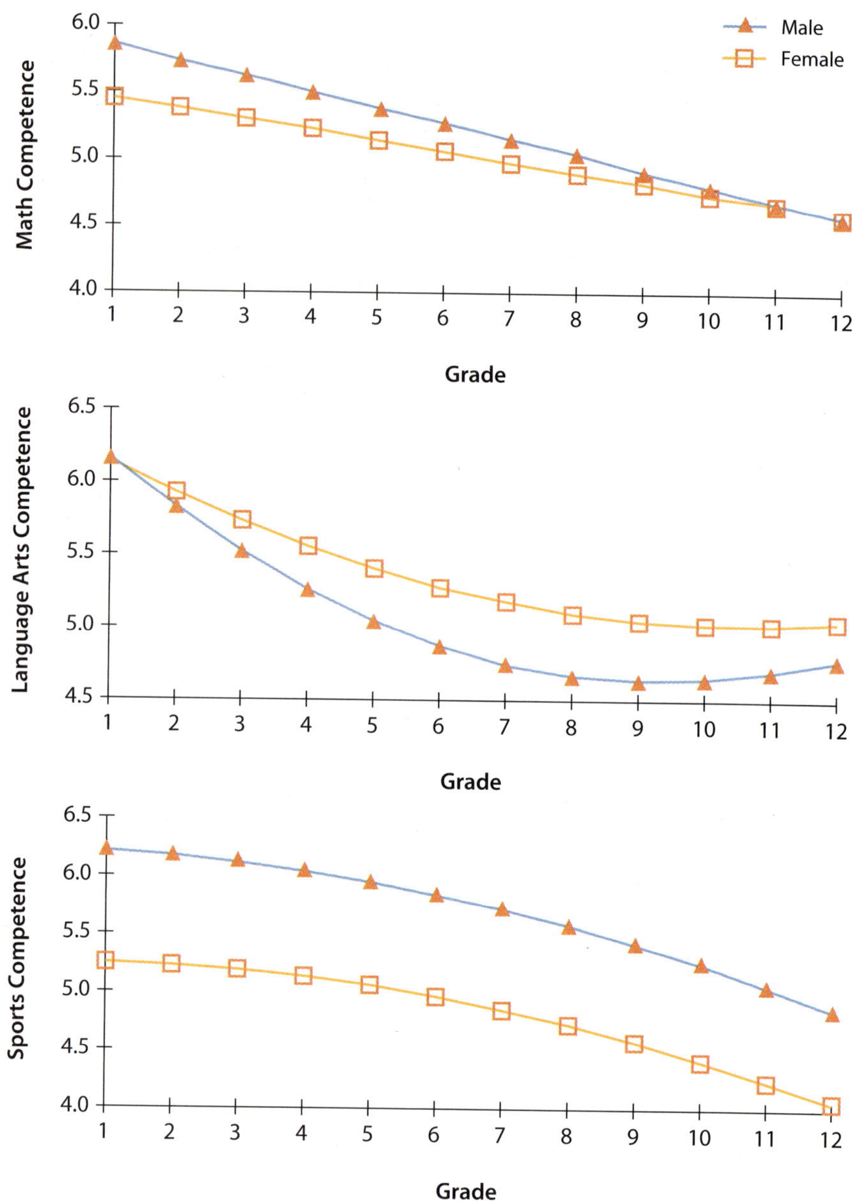

Figure 13.1 Perceptions of Competence from Grade 1 to Grade 12.
What do these graphs tell you about age trends in self-concept overall, boys versus girls, and specific domains? *Source: Jacobs et al. (2002).*

What Do Views of the Self Predict?

Students with higher self-esteem tend to have higher grades; this effect is small but consistent (Baumeister, Campbell, Krueger, & Vohs, 2003; Marsh & Hau, 2003). The link becomes stronger if you consider *domain-specific* self-concept and academic achievement *in that domain*. For example, students' *mathematical* self-concept correlates strongly with mathematics grades and test scores, but *global* self-concept correlates weakly with mathematics performance (Swann, Chang-Schneider, & McClarty, 2007).

Students with high self-esteem tend to fare better emotionally and socially. High self-esteem is linked to greater happiness, less delinquency, higher probability of graduating from college, and more stable employment (Baumeister et al., 2003; Cheng & Furnham, 2002; Gerard & Buehler, 2004). In contrast, students with low self-esteem tend to have more depression and anxiety (Orth, Robins, & Meier, 2009).

Low self-esteem is not generally linked to teen pregnancy despite the common belief that it is (Dogan-Ates & Carrion-Basham, 2007).

Students with high social self-concept, a *domain-specific* self-concept, tend to be better liked by peers (Berndt & Burgy, 1996). However, while people with high self-esteem tend to believe they are more popular than others, they are not actually liked any more than people with low self-esteem (Baumeister et al., 2003). Recall from Chapter 10 that for some youth, high self-esteem predicts aggression because some students with high self-esteem are bullies who are aggressive when their self-esteem is threatened (Baumeister, Bushman, & Campbell, 2000).

What Predicts Views of the Self?

Figure 13.2 shows a 2nd grader's essay about what makes her feel important. Does her self-reflection match the research? Self-esteem is influenced by attachment, students' perceptions of what important others think of them, and how their competence compares with others.

Attachment

Attachment figures are particularly powerful in shaping children's self-concepts. *Secure* children tend to have positive self-concepts, with a working model of the self as valued and capable (Verschueren, Marcoen, & Schoefs, 1996). *Ambivalent* children (whose parents may be inconsistently available or critical) tend to have low self-concept. They try to please the parent but seldom succeed (Mayseless, 1996). In contrast, both avoidant

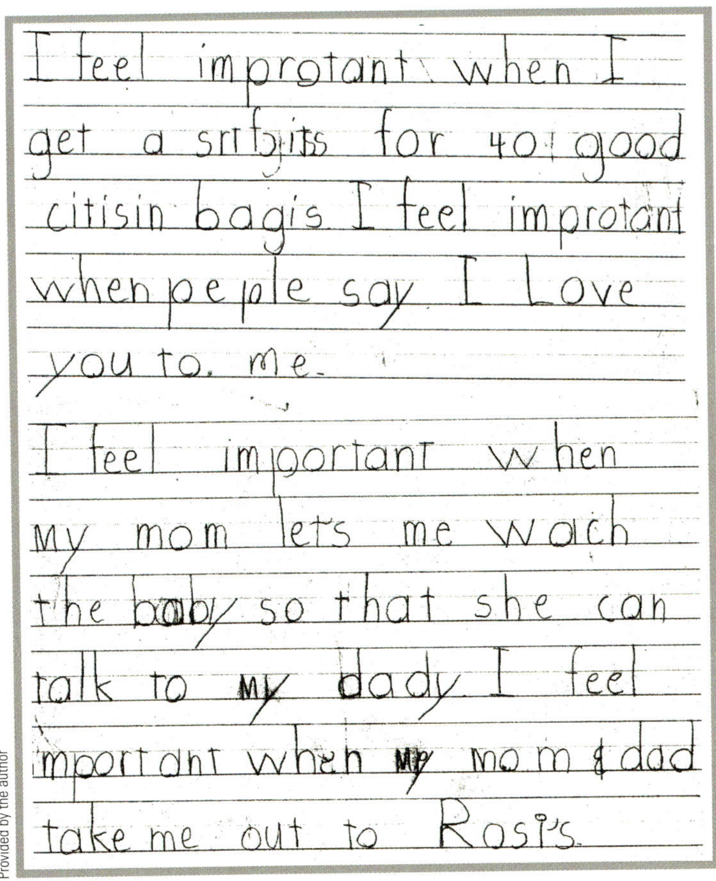

I feel improtant when I
get a srtbjits for 40 good
citisin bagis I feel improtant
when peple say I Love
you to. me.
I feel important when
My mom let's me wach
the baby so that she can
talk to my dady I feel
mportant when my mom & dad
take me out to Rosi's.

Provided by the author

Figure 13.2 Essay on Feeling Important. Does this child's views of what leads to self-esteem agree with the research? Translation: *I feel important when I get a certificate for 40 good citizen badges. I feel important when people say* I Love You *to me. I feel important when my Mom lets me watch the baby so that she can talk to my Daddy. I feel important when my Mom & Dad take me out to Rosie's* (restaurant).

and disorganized children can have moderate to high self-concepts. *Avoidant* children may express self-sufficiency, believing they do not need others. They think that they can earn parental regard through high achievement in a valued domain (academics, athletics, wealth), but not unconditional regard, so they defend their self-esteem by becoming workaholics, perfectionists, or materialists. *Disorganized* children may defend their self-esteem by being overly anxious to please others.

Other people's views

Students' sense of self is largely based on how they believe *other people* assess them: "Does my teacher think that I am competent at this activity?" "Do my parents believe that I am worthy of love?" "What do my friends think that I am good at?" When students are accepted and valued by others, they tend to feel high self-esteem.

Students' self-concept—particularly academic self-concept—is responsive to both peers' and teachers' views of them from about 3rd grade on. Students with positive school reputations have higher academic self-concept, better grades, and put forth more effort (Gest, Domitrovich, & Welsh, 2005). In Chapter 12, you learned about the Pygmalion effect—that teachers' beliefs about students' competence can alter students' performance. Sadie is likely to develop low self-esteem in her class because Ms. Heck communicates that Sadie is neither competent nor valued.

In Chapter 11, you learned that peer acceptance and friendship help students feel good about themselves. As long as they have a few good friends, emotionally healthy students outgrow the need for widespread peer approval sometime in childhood. Yet, some students continue to be overly vulnerable to peer approval. That is, if a few classmates do not like them, some students can shrug it off, but others feel shame and worthlessness. Such students feel more anxiety and depression (Rudolph, Caldwell, & Conley, 2005). Attachment plays a role in this process by influencing the peers with whom students choose to spend time. Students with secure attachment tend to seek others who provide positive feedback. Students with insecure attachment or depression may select peers who confirm their negative self-concepts (Cassidy, Aikins, & Chernoff, 2003; Cassidy, Ziv, Mehta, & Feeney, 2003).

Competence

Students' actual accomplishments also influence their self-concept. If experience suggests they are good at particular activities, they tend to have high self-concept for those activities (Guay, Marsh, & Boivin, 2003).

Counselor: Wow! You got a 30 on the ACT. That's great!
Student: No it's not. Everyone in my class got about the same.

big-fish-little-pond effect the tendency to experience higher academic self-concept when surrounded by peers whose academic achievement is lower.

As this brief conversation points out, self-concepts depend on the range of competence students observe around them. This student was "average" in a high-achieving school. What if this student were the best in a mediocre school?

Field Observation

Find a few friends who have been a big fish in a little pond or an average fish in a big pond. Ask how the experience influenced their self-concept. Do their answers vary by domain, like attractiveness, math, social skills, or sports?

There is a **big-fish-little-pond effect** in that students with the same ability tend to have higher academic self-concept in schools with low average achievement than in high-achieving schools (Marsh, Köller, & Baumert, 2001). Thus, attending a school where most students have high standardized test scores and go on to elite universities lowers students' academic self-concept. This pattern has been found in dozens of countries around the world and extends beyond the high school years, although it affects high achievers less than low achievers (Seaton, Marsh, & Craven, 2009; Trautwein, Lüdtke, Marsh, & Nagy, 2009). In addition, the academic self-concept of students in gifted classes declines at a greater rate than it does for students in other classes. This pattern also applies to the physical domain, with students in high-physical-ability classes feeling lower physical self-concept than if they had been in a different class. This is important because students with lower physical self-concept pursue less free-time physical activity.

Group Diversity in the Self

As a result of increased emphasis on self-esteem, are youth today more narcissistic and self-aggrandizing than in past generations? Do they have higher self-esteem? Some research supports this notion, although there is controversy on the topic. Research done in California, the center of the self-esteem movement, found that incoming college freshmen did not appear to be any more narcissistic than students from previous years (Trzesniewski, Donnellan, & Robins, 2008), but other research tends to show a substantial increase in self-esteem and narcissism (Twenge & Campbell, 2010). What about gender and ethnic differences in self-esteem?

Think About This Do you think the timing of the gender difference in self-esteem might be related to puberty? Review Chapter 2 to justify your answer. What other factors might contribute? Do they reflect real gender differences in competence in each domain? Base your answer on a review of gender differences in previous chapters.

Gender

Boys and girls have similar self-esteem in early childhood, but as they enter adolescence boys develop higher self-esteem, which persists through adulthood (Robins & Trzesniewski, 2005). Overall these gender differences are small. The effect size is about 0.21 (see Chapter 1). However, in some domains, gender differences are larger. After 3rd grade, boys tend to have higher appearance, mathematics, and physical/sports self-concept (see Figure 13.3). Girls tend to have higher verbal and social self-concept (Cole et al., 2001; Marsh, Trautwein, Lüdtke, Koller, & Baumert, 2005).

Ethnicity

A consistent finding is that African Americans have slightly higher self-esteem than do Whites (Gray-Little & Hafdahl, 2000). There is also evidence that African

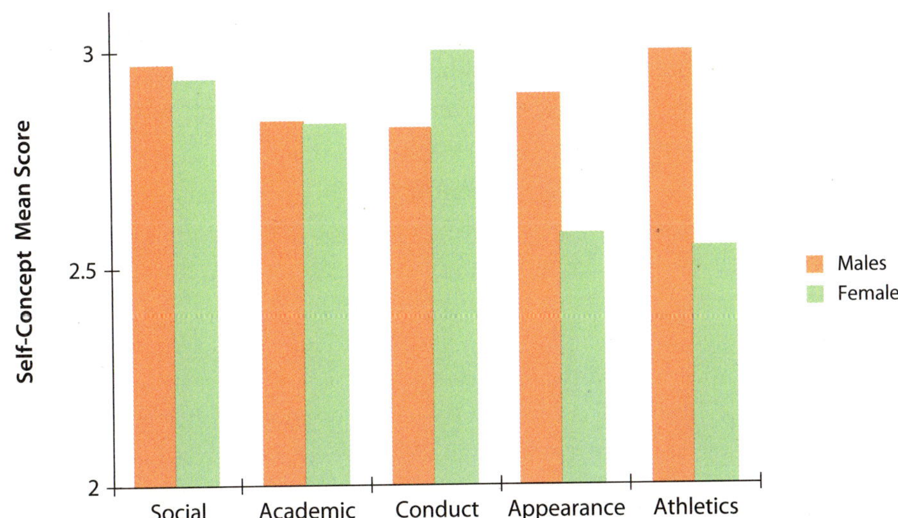

Figure 13.3 Gender Differences in Self-Concept for Five Domains. Which domain has the smallest gender difference, and which has the largest?

American's self-esteem is more impervious to risk factors in their lives; high-risk African American youth tend to have higher self-esteem than high-risk White youth (Gerard & Buehler, 2004). Physical self-concept also varies by ethnicity, with Black children averaging the highest and Asian American children the lowest (Crain, 1996).

Classroom Implications of the Self

One of my students, 3-year-old Miguel, requires more energy to control than all the other children. He never cooperates with classroom activities or with other children. He screams and cries if another child simply takes a crayon he wants. One day his mother, who knows he has behavior problems, asks me how he is doing. He is standing there listening, so I lie. I turn to Miguel and say, "Miguel is learning to share his crayons nicely with other children. He is learning to wait for his turn. He is learning to be quiet and sit in his chair during sharing time. You are a good boy, aren't you Miguel?" Miguel looks totally confused at first (he is probably wondering who I am talking about), but then beams proudly. I guess he thought about this because over the next week he is transformed. He actually does share, wait his turn, and sit (sometimes) quietly. One afternoon he hands a crayon to another child, and says out loud to himself, "I good. I share. Uh huh."

Miguel is constructing a positive social self-concept, thanks to his teacher's help. This is important because high self-concept is correlated with classroom success. But which causes which? In Chapter 1, you learned that correlation does not prove causation. Does high self-concept *cause* peer acceptance and high grades, perhaps by motivating students to try harder in the face of challenge? Or does being accepted, gaining skills, and earning high grades *cause* high self-concept? The answer appears to be both; research suggests the effect is bi-directional (Guay et al., 2003; Marsh & Craven, 2006). Research also suggests you can promote higher self-esteem in your students by following these guidelines:

- *Improve students' competence* in areas such as athletics, academics, or social skills. Focus on skills that are valued in the student's culture. For methods of promoting physical, cognitive, emotional, and social skills, review previous chapters.
- *Improve students' relationships* with others and yourself. Students with secure attachment to teachers and acceptance from classmates tend to feel worthy. Review Chapters 6 and 11 for how to do this.
- *Recognize that self-concept is multifaceted.* Building competence in a specific domain is more likely to influence self-concept for that domain than to influence global self-esteem. The more specific the self-concept, the stronger the link. For example, mathematics performance is more strongly linked to mathematics self-concept than verbal self-concept. Students who are good at math often have good verbal ability as well, yet they may have lower verbal self-concept because of "internal" comparisons—"I'm not good at English because it takes more effort, and I don't get as high test scores in English as I get in math" (Marsh & Craven, 2006). Yet, as you build each component of self-concept, you will contribute to global self-concept.

- *Be honest about academic achievement.* Do not attempt to protect students' self-esteem by telling them that they are doing well when they are not. Instead, point out how they have improved and give them supportive feedback about how to improve even more.

Can you talk students into having high self-esteem? *Explicit* self-esteem may be affected by persuasion, but probably not *implicit* self-esteem. In fact, it is possible that talking students into higher self-esteem, without building real skills or making them feel emotionally secure, could result in narcissism, not healthy self-esteem. Instead, implicit self-esteem comes from feeling accepted. Imagine how destructive an impatient and critical teacher could be. Let's look in a trigonometry class:

> *Ms. Kilroy is often impatient with her students. One day she is trying to get a girl to say that the tangent of X is equal to 1 over the cotangent of X. Instead, the girl keeps saying that the tangent of X is equal to 1 over the tangent. Ms. Kilroy raises her voice, grabs a piece of paper roughly off the girl's desk, tells her it is not true, and proceeds to do the problem for the girl. When a boy gives a correct answer, but with more detail than was required, Ms. Kilroy says, "You don't need to tell us all of that extra stuff—we already know it."*

You could see Ms. Kilroy's students deflate when she spoke to them, much like Sadie did in Ms. Heck's class in the opening vignette. Contrast this with how well Le'Raun did in Ms. Loeb's class in case 3 and Alex did in Ms. Nair's class in case 5. As a teacher, you can influence your students' self-concept both by building their competence and by communicating that you value them.

Social Identity: Gender and Ethnicity

Part of students' sense of self derives from membership in a group. Each student is a member of multiple social groups based on gender, SES, ethnicity, neighborhood, and religion. Let's next discuss two aspects of this **social identity**: gender and ethnic identity.

social identity the part of students' self-concept that derives from their membership in a group, such as gender, ethnic, religious, national, or other groups.

Gender Identity

Among the first questions asked at birth is, "Girl or boy?" Boys and girls often differ in hairstyle, clothes, voice, style of walk, and body shape, so that gender is one of the first things you notice about others. Gender follows you across your lifespan, influencing your name, play, friendships, and activities.

At the simplest level, **gender identity** refers to the ability to accurately label your own sex—are you a boy or a girl? Gender identity also includes more complex concepts—how typical of your gender you feel, how content you are with your gender, how much pressure you feel for gender conformity, and whether you feel that your gender is best (Corby, Hodges, & Perry, 2007). These concepts change with age.

gender identity the ability to accurately label your sex and your feelings about your gender.

Early Childhood (Birth to 5 Years)

In Chapter 5, you learned that infants spontaneously form categories. Gender is one such category. Infants just a few months old can distinguish male from female faces

Photodisc/Jupiter images

Children become gender detectives, seeking out same-gender activities and friends.

(Ramsey-Rennels & Langlois, 2006). By age 2, children begin to label people as boys and girls. Girls develop this ability earlier than boys (Zosuls et al., 2009). They are now capable of *gender labeling*. However, they base labels on appearance—if a boy wears a barrette in his hair and a skirt, he is a girl. They may not understand *gender constancy*, or that gender does not change just because a boy puts on a skirt. Gender constancy ("I am a boy and will always be a boy") emerges between 3 to 4 years of age, but may not be fully developed until age 7 or later (Golombok & Hines, 2002). We showed our 3-year-old daughter a picture of David when he had long, frizzy hair in the 1970s. A few days later she asked to see "the picture of when Daddy was a girl."

Once children figure out their gender, they become "gender detectives" who actively try to figure out how boys and girls differ and what are boy versus girl activities (Martin & Ruble, 2004). They then pay more attention to objects and activities that they think are for their own sex rather than for the other sex.

One cost to this detective work is the development of *gender stereotypes*. As early as 18 months, children judge which toys are for boys or girls. Boys play more with trucks and girls more with dolls by 21 months (Zosuls et al., 2009). If you tell young children that a toy is for girls, then girls are more likely to approach the toy. By kindergarten, children have full-blown knowledge of gender stereotypes, such as which occupations and attributes are more male or female (Miller, Trautner, & Ruble, 2006). At this age, they tend to be quite rigid about their stereotypes, such as saying, "*Only* girls can play with dolls," and they become biased toward seeing their own sex as best. It is normal for children to be rigid in applying knowledge they are just solidifying.

Middle Childhood (6 to 12 Years)

By the early school years, children understand gender constancy, that gender is a fundamental part of someone's identity and is constant across time and situations (Golombok & Hines, 2002). Children understand that even if someone wants to be the other sex, cross-dresses, and behaves like someone of the other sex, he or she does not become the other sex.

Children become more sexist in some ways in early elementary school as gender stereotypes are consolidated. Children begin to understand stereotypes about abilities, not just toys and activities, such as "boys are better at math" (Miller et al., 2006). They also understand whether their own behavior is typical for their sex (Egan & Perry, 2001).

In addition, as you learned in Chapter 11, gender segregation peaks in middle childhood as children seek clear gender boundaries and punish those who cross them. For example, in a class of kindergartners at the school library, a boy chose a book based on *Beauty and the Beast*. As they lined up to leave:

> *The boy standing behind him spotted the book in his friend's hands and began making gagging noises. Other boys soon joined in with, "Oooh, you're going to read a girls' book?" and taunting, "Ha ha, he's a girl, he's a girl." The accused quickly slipped out of line, ran to a nearby shelf, and exchanged his book.* (Dutro, 2002, p. 376)

Such gender boundaries are often more rigid for boys than for girls. If boys do "girl things," they get more criticism than if girls do "boy things." Over time, girls tend to focus less on "girl" activities, while boys continue to prefer "boy" activities. For example, a teacher set out a limited number of books to choose from (Dutro, 2002). No boys voluntarily chose babysitting books, though some girls chose basketball books—to the dismay of boys who then had to take the leftover babysitting books.

Toward the end of elementary school, despite continued preference for their own sex and strong gender segregation, children become less rigid in their stereotypes. Their interest in stereotypically feminine and masculine activities also declines (Crouter, Whiteman, McHale, & Osgood, 2007; McHale, Kim, Dotterer, Crouter, & Booth, 2009).

Adolescence (13 to 19 Years)

In adolescence, gender stereotypes may become stronger, which is called *gender intensification*. However, there is controversy about how strong or pervasive this is and what causes it (Crouter et al., 2007; Priess, Lindberg, & Hyde, 2009). It may result from puberty, which magnifies gender differences and can lead to differences in activities (see Chapter 2). It may also result from a desire to attract the opposite sex that develops in most youth (see Chapter 11).

Feeling typical and content with one's gender are both linked to better adjustment (Corby et al., 2007). For example, a study found that 4th- through 8th-graders who preferred activities stereotypical for their gender tended to be well adjusted, unless they felt excessive pressure to conform to stereotypes (Egan & Perry, 2001). However, well-adjusted youth also felt that they could try out activities typical of the other gender if they wanted to.

Ethnic Identity

Your **ethnic identity** is a part of your self-concept that includes a sense of membership in an ethnic group and your attitudes and feelings about that membership (Phinney, 1996). Ethnicity and race are not the same thing. *Ethnic group* refers to a group of people who share ancestry, language, and culture. *Racial group* refers to a group of people who share biological characteristics such as skin color. However, these terms are controversial (Markus, 2008). Many social scientists believe race is not biological; instead it is a label placed upon groups by society. In contrast, many medical scientists believe race is biological, pointing to differences across races in genetically based diseases and children's physical development. In Chapter 1, you were introduced to the largest ethnic minority groups recognized by the U.S. Census, referred to as ALANA (African, Latin, Asian, and Native American). Note that Latin, or Hispanic, is not a race. Latinos can be Black, White, Asian, or Native American.

ethnic identity a part of self-concept that includes a sense of membership in an ethnic group and attitudes and feelings about that membership.

In the United States, White youth tend to feel that their ethnic identity is less important than do ALANA youth. In fact, many White youth cannot even conceive of having ethnic identity unless they focus on their family's country of origin, like Ireland or Italy (Phinney, 1989). For some ALANA youth, ethnic identity may be magnified by physical features that set them apart. This helps children immediately recognize others of their ethnic group and feel the fictive kinship discussed in Chapter 1, even with strangers. It can also make them potential targets of discrimination.

Ethnic identity can be complex. In the United States, increasing numbers of children are of mixed heritage, like Barack Obama and actress Cameron Diaz. The identity that multiracial children develop may depend on skin color, parentage, social norms, and personal choice. Youth who are Black/White biracial tend to self-identify as Black (Doyle & Kao, 2007). Some multiracial youth change their self-identification over time—for example, from White to Native American. Multiracial children sometimes feel they are a minority within a minority, but they may also benefit from having multiple worldviews and support from multiple ethnic communities (Shih & Sanchez, 2005). Developing an ethnic identity can be challenging for multiracial children, but most will develop a positive identity (Herman, 2004).

Age Trends in Ethnic Identity

By 6 months of age, infants distinguish faces from their own race better than those from other races, and prefer and pay more attention to same-race faces (Kelly et al., 2007). Most preschoolers are able to correctly label their racial group, but they may not understand the label, and their understanding can be a little muddled (Bernal, Knight, Garza, Ocampo, & Cota, 1990). Listen to multiracial 4-year-old Corrine talk about the class's baby bunnies:

> *"How many babies are there?" Sarah asks Corinne.*
> *"Six!" Corinne announces, "Three boys and three girls."*
> *"How can you tell if they're boys or girls?" Sarah questions.*
> *"Well," Corinne begins, "my daddy is White, so the white ones are boys. My mommy is Black, so the black ones are girls."*
> *Sarah counts: "That's only five." (The remaining bunny is black and white.)*
> *"Well, that one is like me, so it's a girl," Corinne explains gently. She picks up the bunny and says, "See, this one is both, like me!"* (Van Ausdale & Feagin, 1996, p. 784)

Around age 6 children show a clear preference for their own ethnic or racial group, although this can begin as young as age 3 or 4 (Aboud, 2003). These positive feelings about their own ethnic group tend to grow across childhood. In one study, all groups increased in group-esteem as they transitioned from elementary, to middle, to high school, but European American students started high and increased only a little, while African American students started low and increased dramatically; Latino American youth also increased (French, Seidman, Allen, & Aber, 2006). High schools are often more diverse than elementary schools, which can make ethnic identity more salient to high school students, and also provide more opportunities for racism.

Around age 6, most children begin to understand racism at a superficial level. For example, Mexican American children may believe that some people do not like Mexican Americans because they do not like Mexico. Around age 10, they have a more sophisticated understanding—for example, that some people may not like Mexican Americans because of racial stereotypes. Around age 10 to 11, about 80 to 90% of children recognize broadly held racial stereotypes (McKown & Strambler, 2009; McKown & Weinstein, 2003; Quintana & Vera, 1999).

Once children understand that some groups are stigmatized, they can understand that they themselves could be stigmatized. **Stigma** refers to feeling different and less valued in the community. Perceptions of stigma due to race are uncommon in elementary school. For example, a study of Puerto Rican children in Boston found that only 12% of 1st-, 2nd-, and 3rd-graders perceived discrimination (Szalacha et al., 2003). However, perceptions of stigma increase through the end of high school (Brody et al., 2006; Seaton, Caldwell, Sellers, & Jackson, 2008).

stigma feeling different and of little value in a community.

Individual Differences in Ethnic Identity

Do members of the same ethnic group have similar ethnic identities? Not necessarily. For example, one study found that some African American high school students felt that being African American was central to their identity and were proud to be African American. Others did not strongly identify as African Americans and felt negatively about their racial group (Chavous et al., 2003). Such differences in ethnic identity influence students' well-being.

For ALANA youth, positive ethnic identity is linked to academic success (Caldwell, Zimmerman, Bernat, Sellers, & Notaro, 2002; Smith & Lalonde, 2003). Adolescents with a positive ethnic identity tend to like school, find it interesting and valuable, and feel bonded to school (Fuligni, Witkow, & Garcia, 2005). They are also more likely to complete high school and attend college than those with weak or negative ethnic identities, and may have higher GPAs (Altschul, Oyserman, & Bybee, 2006; Chavous et al., 2003). The specific ethnic group a student identifies with does not predict academic achievement or motivation, but a strong, positive identity does. Students have a positive ethnic identity when they feel good about the people in their ethnic group, see their group as having made major accomplishments, and feel like they derive personal strengths from being part of their group.

Ethnic identity is also linked to emotional well-being. ALANA youth who have a strong and positive ethnic identity are more likely to have high self-esteem, be happier, experience less depression, and be less anxious. They are also less likely to use drugs and are less accepting of drug use than peers with weak or negative ethnic identities (Kiang, Yip, Gonzales-Backen, Witkow, & Fuligni, 2006; Mandara, Gaylord-Harden, Richards, & Ragsdale, 2009; Marsiglia, Kulis, & Hecht, 2001). It is not psychologically healthy to be ashamed or ambivalent about who you are, and a major component of self-concept for youth of color is ethnic group.

Sexism and Racism

One potential cost of strongly identifying with any group is the development of prejudice toward other groups. It is human nature to categorize others into in-groups ("similar to me") and out-groups ("not like me"), to prefer your in-group, and to exaggerate the similarity of the out-group members. Your in-group may be based on gender, ethnicity, religion, or other factors. To see your in-group in a positive light enhances your self-concept. It does not necessarily lead to prejudice, but it may.

Prejudice occurs when people dislike and attach negative stereotypes to the out-group. Sexism and racism refer to judgments based on sex and race that the in-group is inherently superior to the out-group. Racism also refers to assuming that physical differences like skin color, hair texture, or facial features cause differences in behavior, personality, or intelligence. Preston, in case 4, was sexist when he said "dumb girls like you shouldn't be driving in the first place." In the following vignette, Riley expresses racial prejudice:

> *Riley is in the office for the third time this year for using racial slurs in class. He is not punished, but is told to never do it again and sent back to class. He was also accused of writing racial slurs in books in the library, but there was no proof and he denied it. Riley is not popular, but he is an exceptional two-sport athlete, which gives him some social status. Riley enjoys flaunting his racism. When his English teacher begins reading* Huckleberry Finn, *Riley and his buddies snicker each time they hear the "n-word." They enjoy the idea that the word is used in class. Riley says his parents use the word on a regular basis and that jokes aimed at other ethnic groups are common at his family dinner table. He says racism is appropriate, because that is what his parents believe.*

Prejudice like Riley's tends to develop when it is accepted in the in-group, the group is threatened by the out-group (whether the threat is real or imagined), competition with the out-group is emphasized, and the student strongly identifies with the in-group (Nesdale, Maass, Durkin, & Griffiths, 2005).

In North America, discrimination is socially and legally unacceptable. High-status groups do not want to be perceived as prejudiced, and low-status groups do not want to be victims of prejudice. This helps explain why children may become less prejudiced with age. Preschoolers as young as 3 categorize people into in- and out-groups, and attach stereotypes to the groups, but their prejudice begins to decline by age 7. By age 10, some carefully avoid talking about race (Aboud, 2008; Apfelbaum, Pauer, Ambady, Sommers, & Norton, 2008). Few adolescents and adults espouse *explicit* prejudice like Riley. However, some adults retain *implicit* prejudice, or negative feelings about the out-group that are not necessarily conscious or are conscious and hidden (Baron & Banaji, 2006).

Children can be victims of prejudice. Experiencing discrimination can affect children's motivation, peer relationships, and achievement at school. When children experience racism and discrimination, they are at greater risk for depression, low self-esteem, anxiety, behavior problems, illness, low grades, and health risks such as smoking (Benner & Kim, 2009; Brody et al., 2006; Seaton et al., 2008; Szalacha et al., 2003).

Whether children perceive discrimination depends on at least three factors:

1. Their *social-cognitive abilities*, like theory of mind, perspective-taking, hierarchical classification ability (i.e., people can belong to multiple groups), and moral judgment (Brown & Bigler, 2005). By age 6 or 7, children's social cognition is usually adequate to perceive discrimination, but as you learned earlier, older children tend to perceive more discrimination.

2. The *obviousness of the discrimination*. Young children recognize name calling, racial slurs, or direct comments such as "Girls aren't good at computer games" as discrimination. Older adolescents perceive more subtle forms of discrimination, such as unfair grading, harsher discipline, or specific groups being discouraged from taking higher-level classes.
3. Their *personal vigilance* toward discrimination. People who anticipate being the target of prejudice, and believe that society is prejudiced, tend to be more vigilant about subtle signs of prejudice (Kaiser, Vick, & Major, 2006). People who are part of stigmatized groups are more vigilant. For example, White youth are less likely to perceive subtle discrimination than are youth of color.

Think About This Throughout this text, we have advocated respecting children's heritage culture. What is your role as a teacher when your students' heritage culture espouses values contrary to your own—such as racism, sexism, violence, alcohol abuse, child abuse, religious intolerance, or promiscuity? What if cultural mismatches involve moral issues rather than social conventions?

Parents can help their children avoid internalizing negative perceptions about their race and ethnic group. A study of rural African American youth found that "Youths whose mothers conveyed messages about the realities of racial oppression, ways to succeed despite these obstacles, and pride in their families' African American heritage were more likely to report positive racial identity and elevated self-esteem than were youths whose mothers did not communicate these messages" (Murry, Berkel, Brody, Miller, & Chen, 2009, p. 6).

Teachers can help, too. However, teachers often feel uncomfortable about discussing ethnic issues because such discussions might lead to prejudice and stereotypes (Markus, 2008). Nevertheless, discussions can be positive if they lead to greater understanding and empathy for the out-group and help rectify inequities. Throughout this text, you have learned about potential ethnic differences among your students. In the next section, we will focus on how you can promote positive social identities among diverse students.

Classroom Implications of Gender and Ethnic Identity

Riley is White and attends a rural high school with little racial diversity. Prejudice can also be found in urban schools with lots of diversity and among ALANA students. As a teacher, you want to eliminate prejudice, while also encouraging your students to develop a strong, positive social identity. Let's discuss how to promote healthy social identity without promoting out-group bias, but first let's look at two issues that may affect your students in stigmatized groups—stereotype threat and fear of acting White.

Stereotype Threat

Widely known stereotypes can cause members of stigmatized groups to worry that they will be judged according to stereotypes and that their performance will confirm a negative stereotype. This is called **stereotype threat**. In school settings, African Americans and Latinos may feel stereotype threat when taking standardized tests because the achievement gap is widely known. Girls may feel stereotype threat on mathematics and science tests.

stereotype threat concern that one's performance will confirm negative stereotypes about one's group.

Scientists study stereotype threat by randomly assigning students to a condition of threat or no threat. In the threat condition, students may be told that the test they are about to take distinguishes high and low ability in a stereotype-relevant domain. For example, 6th- and 7th-graders were given a test that required them to remember a simple line drawing. Half the students were told it was a test of geometry ability, and the other half were told it was a test of memory ability. Girls got lower scores when they thought the test measured mathematical (geometry) ability (Huguet & Regner, 2007). Stereotype threat may help explain why girls get higher grades but lower test scores in "masculine" fields such as mathematics (Kenney-Benson, Pomerantz, Ryan, & Patrick, 2006).

Research also shows that when Asian girls are given a mathematics test and their *ethnicity* is emphasized, they score better than when their *gender* is emphasized (Ambady, Shih, Kim, & Pittinsky, 2001). Furthermore, Black students score lower when told a test assesses verbal ability than when told the test has other purposes (Steele & Aronson, 1995). In these studies, the only difference between whether students do better or worse on the test is whether a stereotype is activated before testing.

How does stereotype threat work? It may be akin to test anxiety, which impairs information processing and interferes with working memory. As students worry about confirming a stereotype, thoughts like "These math problems are too hard for me" and "I am not good at math" begin to consume working memory space and undermine test performance (Schmader, Johns, & Forbes, 2008). In an interesting experiment, Black college students who were waiting to take an intelligence test—which activates stereotype threat—performed worse on the Stroop test than similar students who were not about to take an intelligence test (Inzlicht, McKay, & Aronson, 2006). That is, dealing with stereotype threat apparently reduced executive functions. Research on stereotype threat suggests you may help your students by following these guidelines:

- *Consider testing in a same-sex environment for subjects that are sex-typed.* When girls and female college students take mathematics tests in the presence of boys, they perform worse (Huguet & Regner, 2007; Inzlicht & Ben-Zeev, 2000). See Figure 13.4.

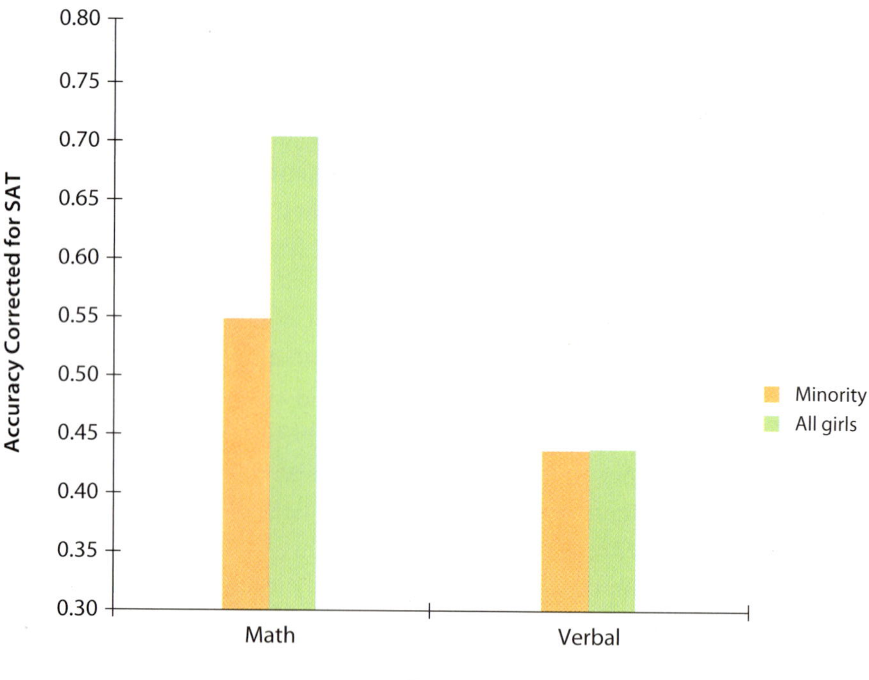

Figure 13.4 Girls' Test Performance and Stereotype Threat.
"Minority" means girls are outnumbered by boys in the testing situation. When girls take a math test in an all-girl setting, they perform better than when they are outnumbered by boys. Setting makes no difference for verbal ability tests. Why might this be?

- *Teach students that intelligence is changeable* and that they can increase their intelligence through effort. For example, in one study 7th-grade girls scored higher on mathematics tests, and low-SES and minority students scored higher on reading tests, after being encouraged to view intelligence as changeable (Good, Aronson, & Inzlicht, 2003). We discuss views of intelligence in the next section.
- *Teach older students about stereotype threat.* Studies with college students find that a brief lesson on stereotype threat, and a warning that if they feel anxious during the test it may be due to negative stereotypes that have nothing to do with their actual ability, reduces the effect of stereotype threat (Johns, Schmader, & Martens, 2005). It is likely that the same effect would occur for adolescents.

Stereotype threat not only affects test performance, but can also affect classroom engagement. One way to cope with stereotype threat is to disengage from academic activity, which is the next topic.

Fear of Acting White

Some students want to feel solidarity with their ethnic group and may fear that academic success could lead to rejection from their group. Some youth of color fear being accused of **acting White**. This might happen if they listen to White music, work hard for grades, dress preppy, date Whites, speak Standard English, and put on "airs" (Bergin & Cooks, 2002; Fordham & Ogbu, 1986). Listen to one high-achieving Black male student:

acting White the behavior of a student of color that is interpreted as engaging in activities that are marked as White, which might include listening to White music, studying hard, or speaking Standard English.

> *Interviewer: Were you ever accused of acting White?*
> *Student: Yeah. Plenty of times.*
> *Interviewer: Who accused you?*
> *Student: Black students. Usually other Black students who in fact weren't doing as well. I was accused of acting White simply because I got good grades. And I would say, "Is it wrong for Black people to do well?" I would go back and say, "Did W.E.B. DuBois act White his whole life?"*
> *Interviewer: Did they know who he was?*
> *Student: No. Often I would have to explain to them. They say, "Well that's different," and if I say, "Well, was Martin Luther King acting White?" they'll say, "No, that's different."* (Bergin & Cooks, 2002, p. 125)

In this study, high-achieving Black and Latino high school students said they had been accused of acting White, but that they also rejected the rejection, though it hurt their feelings. Thus, while accusations of acting White do occur, they may be exaggerated and do not affect all students of color. In fact, many Black and Latino students report competing for high grades (Bergin & Cooks, 2000). As you learned in Chapter 1, some ALANA youth resist the dominant culture by proving that they can excel in it. They use their awareness of racism to increase their motivation, not decrease it.

Despite the fact that many Western countries have a long history of free schooling for all children, in the past schools contributed to discrimination (see Box 13.2). Today, there are legal protections against inequities and discrimination at school, but there is still room for progress. Now let's turn to how you can strengthen your students' social identity.

Theories & Theorists **Box 13.2**

Theories and Theorists: Kenneth and Mamie Clark

"I can remember as a child wishing sometimes that I was White because it seemed like everything that was 'good' was white and things that were dark were evil or bad. In Star Wars Darth Vader was Black and Luke Skywalker was White, who just happened to be the super hero who saves the day. No child wants to be associated with bad things. Children's racial identity depends on whether adults show them positive examples who look like them, so they can be proud of who they are, no matter their color."

This comment was made by a Black man. Is his experience typical? Psychologists Kenneth Clark (1914–2005) and Mamie Phipps Clark (1917–1983), who were husband and wife, believed it might be. In a series of studies, the Clarks presented children with brown and white dolls and asked questions like, "Give me the doll that you like best" or "Give me the doll that looks bad" (Clark, 1963, p. 23). They found that the majority of the Black children preferred the white dolls and rejected the brown dolls. Kenneth Clark believed that this and other evidence suggested that African Americans experience self-hatred that is caused by a discriminatory system that communicates that they are racially inferior. He wrote: "As minority-group children learn the inferior status to which they are assigned and observe that they are usually segregated and isolated from the more privileged members of their society, they react with deep feelings of inferiority and with a sense of personal humiliation" (p. 63).

Clark argued that children who experience discrimination may develop aggression directed at themselves, their own group, or the dominant group, which results in delinquency, which in turn provides justification for further discrimination, creating a vicious cycle (Clark, Chein, & Cook, 2004). The children may feel defeated and lower their aspirations. More-privileged minority children may react with rigid conformity to middle-class standards or with an aggressive determination to succeed. A child can cope with a prejudiced individual by viewing the person as misguided, but cannot easily cope with a prejudiced authoritative institution such as a school.

The Clarks' research helped change American education (Keppel, 2002). In 1896, the Supreme Court had ruled in *Plessy v. Ferguson* that the government could require that Blacks and Whites have "separate but equal" facilities such as schools. In the South, this resulted in substandard schools for Black students. Sixty years later, this ruling was challenged in *Brown v. Board of Education*. The case was actually a compilation of four cases that were sponsored by the NAACP (National Association for the Advancement of Colored People). One of the cases, from Virginia, originated when 16-year-old Barbara Johns tricked the principal of her all-Black high school into leaving campus while she and other students organized a student strike against unequal Black and White school conditions. On May 17, 1954, *Brown v. Board of Education* repudiated the doctrine of "separate but equal." The Clarks' research was critically influential in the decision. It was used to attack the notion of schools that are separate "but equal" and to demonstrate that segregation was psychologically damaging to children.

The Clarks continued to use psychology to create a vision of racial equality in the United States. Mamie Clark worked tirelessly for New York City's minority children, establishing a center for child development in Harlem in 1946. Mamie's goal for the center was to provide emotional security and acceptance to poor children (Lal, 2002). She also served on the National Head Start Planning Committee. Kenneth Clark was the first African American to earn a PhD in psychology at Columbia University, the first to become a tenured professor in New York's City College system, and the first to become president of the American Psychological Association (APA).

Today, the Clarks' notion of Black self-hatred has been rejected (Jackson, 2000; Spencer, 2008). Contemporary scientists find children of color tend to experience positive ethnic identity. However, the Clarks' research and activism laid an important foundation that helped improve schools. They have been among the most influential twentieth-century psychologists.

Columbia University Archives

Kenneth and Mamie Clark

Promote Positive Social Identity

You can help your students develop a strong, positive social identity by valuing their group. In contrast, if you refrain from valuing your students' social group, this may be sufficient to foster alienation from school; you do not have to be racist or overtly hostile to create a negative environment. Claude Steele (1992), a Black researcher, wrote, "For too many black students school is simply the place where, more concertedly, persistently, and authoritatively than anywhere else in society, they learn how little valued they are" (p. 78). To prevent this perception, follow these guidelines:

- *Use a multicultural curriculum.* Select books, software, posters, and samples of work that portray different groups. Comment on the contributions of diverse people to the topic at hand. Depict each group in a positive way across the school year, not only during isolated celebrations like Black History Month and Cinco de Mayo. Clearly communicate appreciation for all cultures. Appreciate their language, music, history, and current events. In case 5, Mrs. Nair encouraged Alex, who was Chinese American, to develop his Chinese language skills.
- *Help each student feel valued in your classroom.* When students feel devalued, or stigmatized, they feel stress, frustration, and anxiety about whether they are being judged. As students expend mental effort to control these feelings, they have less available for self-control of other behaviors, such as paying attention (Salvatore & Shelton, 2007). Recall that self-control, like a muscle, can fatigue. In contrast, when students feel emotionally safe, they participate more in class activities.
- *Hold all students to high, but reasonable, standards.* When giving feedback to students of stigmatized groups, provide detailed feedback that makes it clear you have high standards and believe the students can reach those standards (Cohen, Steele, & Ross, 1999). Avoid stereotypes that might lead you to hold low expectations, recommend less challenging classes, or overlook talent, such as mathematical ability in girls. Because it is impossible to use group membership to accurately infer students' abilities, treat students as though they might be talented at anything, without regard to group. Provide equal opportunities for success to all students.
- *Be self-reflective.* Examine your view of the ideal student, and how that might affect students who don't fit the ideal. For example, a study in the western United States found that some teachers thought that ideal female students are sociable and good at sports; this disadvantaged Latinas who were more likely to be shy and not play sports (Meador, 2005). Such prejudices leak out. In one survey, one-quarter of Black youth felt their teachers treated them with less respect or thought they were not as smart as other students (Seaton et al., 2008). In another survey, girls reported that some teachers made negative comments about their mathematical, science, or computer abilities (Leaper & Brown, 2008).

Reduce Prejudice

In the years since *Brown v. Board of Education*, it has become clear that merely desegregating schools is not enough to reduce prejudice. What can you do to help students like Riley become less prejudiced? You can reduce prejudice when you build skills that were discussed in previous chapters, such as empathy (see Chapter 8) and moral judgment (see Chapter 9). In addition, using a multicultural curriculum tends to promote a spirit of mutual respect for diverse classmates. A multicultural curriculum does not consistently reduce prejudice, but it may make a small contribution (Pfeifer, Brown, & Juvonen, 2007). Three other interventions you can use to reduce prejudice include the following:

- *Use anti-bias training.* There are specific curricula designed to help you discuss prejudice, such as "More Than Meets the Eye," in which students learn to identify differences within their in-group and similarities between them and out-group members. Such curricula can be effective from kindergarten through high school (Pfeifer et al., 2007). In addition, make it clear that you do not tolerate sexual harassment, racial slurs, or other forms of derogatory speech. Reasoned argument during anti-bias training may reduce explicit, conscious prejudice, but it is more difficult to change implicit prejudice.
- *Teach about the history of race relations and discrimination.* White elementary students who learned about famous African Americans and the discrimination that they endured had more positive views of African Americans than students who learned about the famous people but not the discrimination (Hughes, Bigler, & Levy, 2007).
- *Use cooperative learning.* How to do this is discussed in Chapter 11. Research shows that contact between groups can reduce prejudice to a modest degree. However, just because students are in the same classroom or school does not mean they have contact, and mere contact is not enough (Pettigrew & Tropp, 2006). Being in a classroom with Black students is not going to make Riley less prejudiced. Even friendship with out-group others does not necessarily reduce implicit prejudice (Henry & Hardin, 2006). To reduce prejudice, contact should occur in a setting in which the different groups:

  ✓ Have equal status within the setting.

  ✓ Share goals, which helps create a "super-group" identity.

  ✓ Cooperate to pursue those goals.

  ✓ Feel support from authority figures. (Fiske, 2002; Pettigrew & Tropp, 2006)

When organized well, cooperative learning can result in greater reduction in prejudice than using a multicultural curriculum (Pfeifer et al., 2007; Slavin & Cooper, 1999). Athletics and extracurricular activities often meet these conditions in addition to classroom activities.

As an authority figure in your classroom, your students are likely to believe what you tell them about the value of social groups. For example, in one experiment, elementary school students were placed on academic teams. An adult told some teams to like students on both teams, but told others to "stick with their own team." The latter group had greater dislike for the other teams, or out-group (Nesdale et al., 2005). You can use your power to help students feel good about their own in-group identity and also the out-group.

You have learned that self-concept and social identity can influence success in the classroom. Self-concepts are important for understanding motivation. Self-concepts affect what tasks students are willing to do and the effort they put into tasks. Let's turn to the issue of motivation next.

Think About This Examine your own gender biases. Do you assign certain tasks to only girls, like taking notes during cooperative learning activities? When handing out jump ropes, footballs, and basketballs, do you give certain items to only boys? Are there other ways that you might convey gender stereotypes?

Motivation

Vinnie, a sophomore, is required to write an essay on Hawthorne's The Scarlet Letter *in his History/English class. He does not share his teacher's enthusiasm for Hawthorne. He thinks the book is a waste of time and the assignment is "interfering with his life." He is in the middle of building a computer and spends as little time as possible with* The Scarlet Letter. *Later, in the same class, he writes an essay about Alexander the Great, who was "way cool." His grades, a C and an A, reflect his opinion of each assignment.*

Vinnie's grades measure his motivation more than his ability. Some students always do their best on assignments, like the compulsive class valedictorian, and others never let school assignments interfere with their lives. Most, like Vinnie, are in the middle—working hard on assignments they view as interesting or important. Your challenge in teaching is to manipulate those views so that your students are motivated to learn.

In an ideal world, your students would engage in class learning activities because each activity itself is rewarding. This is called **intrinsic motivation**. In contrast, **extrinsic motivation** refers to engaging in an activity because of a result outside the activity itself—like getting a scholarship, earning money, avoiding punishment, getting a high grade, pleasing parents, and impressing friends. As you have noticed, this is not an ideal world; promoting intrinsic motivation in each of your students at all times is probably impossible. Your students are likely to feel a mix of intrinsic and extrinsic motivation.

intrinsic motivation the desire to pursue an activity for its own sake, not for external reasons.

extrinsic motivation the desire to pursue an activity for reasons external to the activity such as getting a reward, avoiding punishment, or earning a grade.

Motivation refers to internal states that affect the energy, direction, vigor, and persistence of behavior toward a goal (Pintrich, 2003). Based on this definition, nearly every topic discussed in this textbook—reinforcement, background knowledge, stereotype threat, emotion regulation, and so forth—affects motivation because it also affects the energy, direction, vigor, and persistence of behavior at school. However, in this chapter we will focus our discussion of motivation on two key questions: "Can I do this task?" and "Do I want to do this task?" But first, let's look at age trends in academic motivation.

motivation internal states that affect the energy level, direction, vigor, and persistence of behavior toward a goal.

Age Trends in Motivation

Preschoolers are motivated to explore the world, learn language, and become competent in their environment. Secondary teachers have a greater challenge motivating students than early childhood teachers because, on average, students' motivation for school declines across years of schooling. Motivation also declines within a single school year, from fall to spring (Gentry, Gable, & Rizza, 2002; Ryan, 2001; Skinner, Furrer, Marchand, & Kindermann, 2008). See Figure 13.5. One explanation for the decline is that across school years, there is an increase in extrinsic incentives and external control of students. This fits with the explanation you learned about in Chapter 6: that motivation declines when students transition from elementary school to junior high/middle school because school becomes more controlling. Motivation also declines when students transition from junior high to high school, but not as consistently (Barber & Olsen, 2004; Cole et al., 2001). The transition to high school

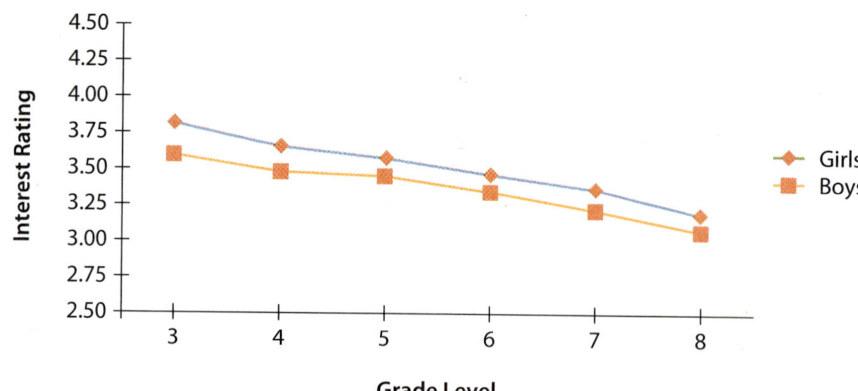

Figure 13.5 Classroom Interest by Gender. What happens to children's interest in the classroom across time based on this graph? Are boys or girls more interested at school? *Source: Gentry et al (2002).*

is especially difficult for youth of color who transition to a school with fewer same-ethnicity peers (Benner & Graham, 2009). The decline in motivation across childhood may partly result from older students' more negative responses to the questions "Can I do this?" and "Do I want to do this?"

Can I Do This?

In classrooms, students' answer to this question depends on their self-efficacy, their view of intelligence, and their attributions for academic success.

Self-Efficacy

Self-efficacy refers to your confidence that you can accomplish some behavior. It is a judgment about your competence. Self-efficacy is domain specific. Domains can be broad, such as self-efficacy for schoolwork in general, or narrow, such as self-efficacy to do long division. Students with high academic self-efficacy believe they can master school topics, can regulate their own learning, and can get peers and teachers to help them when needed. Self-efficacy is a key component of social cognitive theory, discussed previously in Box 3.2 (see Chapter 3).

Why does self-efficacy matter? Many studies have shown that when you feel high self-efficacy, you are more likely to (Bandura, 1997):

- ✓ Feel interest.
- ✓ Work hard.
- ✓ Perform well.
- ✓ Persist in the face of difficulty.
- ✓ Develop strategies for improvement.

Think About This Parents who have higher self-efficacy about parenting, and who believe that the way their child turns out depends on how well they parent, have children who are more compliant and self-regulated (Feldman & Klein, 2003). Why might this be? Do you think this applies to teachers as well?

For example, a girl with *high* self-efficacy for mathematics might choose to take calculus in high school, begin the class with low anxiety, work hard, and redouble her efforts when her first test comes back with a low score. Another girl with *low* self-efficacy might avoid taking the class to begin with. If forced to take it, she might enter with high anxiety and give up when the first low test score comes back. These two girls could have similar skill level, but their self-efficacy influences what they do with those skills. You might think self-efficacy pertains only to older students, but even 3-year-olds' behavior is affected by self-efficacy (Williamson, Meltzoff, & Markman, 2008).

Where do feelings of self-efficacy come from? There are four main sources (Bandura, 1997; Usher & Pajares, 2008):

1. *Previous experience.* If you have a history of success, you tend to expect success in the future, and if you have a history of failure, you tend to expect failure. This may be the most powerful influence on self-efficacy.
2. *Vicarious experience*, or experience that you have through observing someone else. If you observe someone else succeeding or failing, it affects your own self-efficacy. For example, our 6-year-old son quit trying to ride a bicycle because he kept falling over. Then he saw a *younger* neighbor riding a bicycle. He seemed to think, "If that little kid can, I can." Our son got back on his bicycle and quickly learned to ride. His level of skill did not change, but his belief that he could learn to ride did. An important point is that similar-aged models, or *peer models*, are particularly effective. Our son's self-efficacy did not increase from seeing adults riding bicycles. Nevertheless, children are sometimes influenced by adult models. This may partly explain why parents with high academic self-efficacy tend to have children with high academic self-efficacy.
3. *Verbal persuasion.* Other people can persuade you to feel more confident about your abilities. The persuader might remind you of previous successes, or point out your strengths and how they apply to the current situation. Respected experts tend to have greater persuasive power.
4. *Physiological reactions.* Emotional arousal, like a racing pulse, can convey information about the probability of success. For example, if you get sweaty palms during an exam, you might attribute the sweaty palms to being incompetent, which would undermine self-efficacy.

Self-efficacy is a powerful component of motivation, but when you ask yourself, "Can I do this?" you are also influenced by your view of ability.

Views of Ability

Ability refers to intelligence as well as other forms of aptitude such as artistic talent and athletic skill. You have an *entity* view if you believe ability is unchangeable, or a fixed entity. You have an *incremental* view if you believe ability is changeable and can be developed. Which view would lead you to improve your skills? Holding an incremental view of academic ability leads to higher achievement, persistence in the face of obstacles, and intrinsic motivation (Grant & Dweck, 2003). Failure undermines efficacy more if students hold an incremental view than if they hold an entity view.

Why might this be? Views of ability influence how you think about why you succeeded or failed. Which of the following thoughts is better for learning? "I failed my chemistry exam because I'm not smart enough and never will be" (entity view) or "I'll study chemistry more so I can become smarter" (incremental view). Which of the following thoughts is likely to lead to improved athletic ability? "I am just not coordinated" (entity view) or "If I practice, I can improve" (incremental view). You have a natural tendency to search for the causes of successes and failures, which is the basis of the next topic: attribution theory.

Attributions

attributions the causes that people perceive for their own and other people's behavior.

Attributions are the causes that you perceive for your own and your students' behaviors, successes, and failures. Attributions that you make for past behavior motivate your future behavior (Weiner, 1985). For example, Vinnie will behave differently if he attributes his poor performance on his *Scarlet Letter* essay to low ability, rather than low effort. He will have different motivation if he thinks, "I'm just not good at writing. I might as well not even try" compared to if he thinks, "I did poorly because I didn't try hard." Notice how views of ability discussed earlier are linked with attributions.

Think About This Imagine that some teachers attribute student failure to stable, external, uncontrollable (by the teacher) causes such as bad parenting, too much television, and low intelligence. How might this affect their motivation to improve their teaching?

For most academic situations, attributions to effort are ideal. When you attribute your successes and failures to effort, it means that the cause is under your control; thus, you are likely to increase effort in the face of failure rather than giving up. In contrast, when you attribute successes to ability, you may feel proud of your ability, but if you begin to fail, you might doubt your ability and give up. When students attribute their school failures to internal, stable shortcomings in themselves, they are more likely to have low grades and to be depressed (Foersterling & Binser, 2002). They are likely to avoid difficult courses or challenging tasks because they do not expect to succeed; they are likely to put in little effort because they do not believe that effort pays off. This effect begins to set in as early as age 5 and is fully developed by age 11 or 12 (Heyman, Gee, & Giles, 2003; Normandeau & Gobeil, 1998).

learned helplessness the perception developed through experience that no matter what you do, you will not be competent in a domain.

Some students learn to feel helpless, believing they cannot do something no matter how hard they try. **Learned helplessness** can be the result of an unresponsive environment—that is, the perception that no matter what they do, they cannot get things to change or improve. When students cannot get the environment to respond, they may attribute it to their own inadequacies, believing that other people could have been successful, but not them. This undermines motivation and self-esteem, which perpetuates a cycle of failure. In a study of children in Florida, helplessness was moderately stable as early as kindergarten, and such feelings in kindergarten predicted helplessness later in 5th grade (Ziegert, Kistner, Castro, & Robertson, 2001). Low-SES students are more vulnerable to helplessness at school than are high-SES children (Evans, Gonnella, Marcynyszyn, Gentile, & Salpekar, 2005).

Can you see how self-efficacy, views of intelligence, and attributions are linked? Students who feel high self-efficacy are likely to attribute failure to something other than a lack of ability. For example, if Vinnie has high self-efficacy for writing essays, he may attribute his C grade to bad luck, an off day, low effort, or an unfair teacher. He expects to do better next time. On the other hand, if Vinnie feels low self-efficacy, he is likely to attribute failure to something that fits with his self-image as lacking ability. He may attribute the C to being a mediocre writer who cannot improve. If Vinnie holds an incremental view of ability, he is likely to attribute his failures to something changeable and believe that he can improve through effort.

Classroom Implications of "Can I Do This?"

Your students' answer to the question "Can I do this?" will influence their persistence and willingness to take on challenges, which will then influence their success in your classroom. You can help your students feel more capable by following these guidelines:

- *Provide models of success.* Models can be live, on video, in books and magazines, or described verbally. You can be a model yourself by demonstrating effective strategies for an activity. You can even model thinking by thinking aloud. Academic activities such as solving mathematical problems and motor activities such as playing tennis have thinking aspects that can be modeled by thinking aloud. Some models are more effective than others:
    - *Peer models* tend to be particularly effective in promoting self-efficacy. Recall from case 2 that no child was willing to try three-digit addition at the board until Monica modeled success, with the teacher's scaffolding. Then when the teacher called for volunteers, most hands shot up. However, if the teacher had chosen the "smartest" student, the other students might not have felt greater self-efficacy.
    - *Multiple models* are more effective than a single model. Multiple models increase the likelihood that a student will see at least one with whom he or she identifies and think, "If they can do it, I can do it."
    - *Coping models* are more effective than watching an expert easily and flawlessly accomplish a task (Zimmerman & Kitsantas, 2002). Watching a renowned mathematician easily prove a theorem may not make you feel efficacious about doing the same. In contrast, when a model copes with difficulty and shows how to overcome failure, you are more likely to believe you might be successful also.
- *Promote an incremental view of ability.* In an experiment, when 7th-graders were taught that the brain is like a muscle that gets stronger with use and that the brain forms new connections every time learning occurs, their motivation and grades improved compared to those of a control group (Blackwell, Trzesniewski, & Dweck, 2007).
- *Attribute children's success to effort rather than ability.* Your attributions influence students' beliefs about themselves. If students do poorly and you say, "It's OK, math isn't my thing either," you are attributing their failure to low ability, and each student may think, "If the teacher thinks I'm no good at math, maybe I'm not." When you attribute their success to effort, your students are more likely to develop a view that ability is changeable (incremental view), but only if it is true they worked hard (Dweck, 2008). Be sure to praise for specific effort, not general ability. For example, you might say, "Your hard work paid off. You seem to really understand the material" rather than "You are so smart. You were born to do this." When students are praised for ability, they tend to prefer nonchallenging tasks and to lie in order to avoid exposing their failures (Dweck, 2006).
- *Change students' attribution style.* You can "retrain" students to make helpful, rather than harmful, attributions. One intervention, called "Best Foot Forward," helped African American and Latino elementary students attribute failure to lack of effort rather than to inability or poor teaching. After the intervention, students were more motivated and persistent in their schoolwork

(Hudley, Graham, & Taylor, 2007). You can improve students' attributions when you:

- Tell students that they are sufficiently able; that is, use your position as a knowledgeable person in authority to persuade them (but don't lie).
- Tell students that they need to try harder, unless of course they are already trying very hard and know it.
- Help them use better strategies and model the strategies.
- Draw attention to a model who fails, attributes the failure to lack of effort or bad strategies, and then succeeds through effort or good strategies. Encourage students to imitate the model.

Even students who are confident that they are *capable* of learning a skill or topic may wonder if they *want* to learn the skill or topic. This is the other half of motivation.

Do I Want to Do This?

Vinnie was able to write a good essay on "Alexander the Cool" (his title), but he did not want to write a good essay on *The Scarlet Letter*. What makes a student want to put effort into a learning task at school? Let's focus on three major factors: goals, self-determination, and emotions like interest.

Goals

Many studies show that goal setting improves motivation and performance (Locke & Latham, 2002). Why do goals improve motivation and performance? There are several reasons:

1. *Goals direct attention and action.* They help students focus on what they want to accomplish, which reduces distraction.
2. *Goals mobilize energy.* When students are tired or feel attention wandering, they are more likely to generate energy to refocus when they are committed to a goal.
3. *Goals prolong effort and persistence.* When students hold a specific goal for a learning task, they are more likely to persist in the face of distractions than when they have no specific goal in mind.
4. *Goals motivate problem solving.* When students start on mathematical problems, for example, and encounter difficulty, they are more likely to try to figure out strategies to solve the problems if they are committed to a goal of mathematical competence, or if they want to become an engineer. They may devise new study strategies like working multiple problems, attending tutoring, and studying with competent friends.

Goal setting applies to activities that range from sports to chemistry to painting a picture. Let's apply it to writing essays. In one study, when learning-disabled 7th- and 8th-graders set goals of providing a *specific* number of supporting reasons for their argument and of anticipating and refuting a *specific* number of counterarguments, their essays were longer, more convincing, and of higher quality (Page-Voth & Graham, 1999). Similarly, when learning-disabled 4th-, 5th-, and 6th-graders set a goal of adding at least three things to their papers to make them better, their papers were in fact better than papers of students who were merely told to revise and improve their papers (Graham, MacArthur, & Schwartz, 1995).

Not all goal-setting situations are equally effective. Goals are most effective if they are (Locke & Latham, 2002):

✓ Specific—not just "do my best" or "try hard."

✓ Challenging, but within a student's ability.

✓ Accompanied by feedback that helps the student improve.

✓ Committed to—if students are not truly committed to a goal, it tends to fall by the wayside.

✓ Divided into subgoals that mark progress toward a long-term goal.

In addition to goal *setting*, or whether students hold explicit goals or not, goal *content* is also important in your classroom. When students enter an achievement-oriented situation like a classroom or a sports setting, they tend to orient toward one of two types of broad achievement goals: **mastery goals** and **performance goals**. If you hold *mastery* goals, your broad goal is to *develop* your ability; this makes you prefer challenge, want to learn new things even if they are difficult, and focus on comparison with yourself rather than with other people—such as "Am I doing better than I used to?" If you hold *performance* goals, your broad goal is to *demonstrate* your ability and *do better than others*. Performance goals can be separated into performance-*approach* and performance-*avoid* goals. A performance-approach goal is the desire to perform better than others, or be the best in a group; a performance-avoid goal is the desire to avoid doing worse than others and to avoid looking dumb or incompetent. Thus, students might think, "I do my history assignment because I want to improve my skills" (mastery) or "because I want to get a higher grade than the other students" (performance-approach), or "because I want to avoid looking dumb" (performance-avoid).

Learning Laffs

mastery goal a goal to master a skill or topic.

performance goal a goal to demonstrate ability by performing better than others.

Mastery goals tend to be more adaptive than performance-avoid goals, particularly for learning concepts as opposed to rote learning. When students have mastery goals, they are more likely to use effective learning strategies, process deeply, have increased intrinsic motivation and self-efficacy, seek appropriate help, be less disruptive, and feel optimism, with less fear of mistakes—each of which can lead to greater learning.[1] *Performance-approach goals* can also be adaptive, especially if combined with mastery goals (Hulleman, Durik, Schweigert, & Harackiewicz, 2008); however, performance-approach goals that focus on doing better than others (competitive goal) can also undermine performance, especially for low-ability students. In contrast, *performance-avoid goals* are consistently linked to less-positive attitudes and lower achievement.

Students may have a mastery or performance orientation before they enter your classroom, but you can influence their goals in your classroom. For example, teachers who compare students to each other and criticize mistakes foster performance goals. Teachers who show students their improvement and recognize mistakes as part of

[1]Many studies have demonstrated this, a few of which are listed here (Friedel, Cortina, Turner, & Midgley, 2010; Kaplan, Gheen, & Midgley, 2002; Pintrich & Schunk, 2002; Shim, Ryan, & Anderson, 2008; Turner et al., 2002).

learning foster mastery goals. Mastery-oriented teachers also support students' need for self-determination, our next topic.

Self-Determination

You and your students have an innate need for self-determination—that is, a need to feel that you have some control over what you do (Deci & Ryan, 2000). When you feel that you chose to do a task and it was not imposed on you, you are more likely to feel intrinsic motivation for that task. In Chapter 6, you learned that one reason for the drop in achievement as students transition from elementary to junior high/middle school is that they have less autonomy. Recall that children tend to be given greater autonomy in the later elementary grades than in middle/junior high school, even though they want more autonomy as they grow older (Eccles et al., 1993). Also, students view teachers as more caring if they provide students with choice and autonomy whenever possible (Wentzel, 1997). In Chapter 7, you learned that one of the problems with power-assertive discipline is that children feel externally controlled.

Imagine Sally and Korin are both doing algebra problems. Sally enjoys mathematical problem solving and does extra problems. In contrast, Korin does only the required problems—and only because she wants a good grade. Sally is intrinsically motivated, while Korin is extrinsically motivated. Korin did not choose to do the math problems of her own free will, so she is likely to engage in mathematics at a superficial level. In real classrooms, students often feel extrinsic motivation. We will discuss later how you can maximize student's feelings of self-determination. Next, we discuss emotions in the classroom, especially interest.

Emotions—Interest

In Chapter 8, you learned that negative emotions can interfere with learning, while positive emotions can promote creativity and learning. In Chapter 6, you learned that children who like school are more likely to participate in the classroom and have higher achievement than other students. A key part of liking school is feeling cared for by the teacher. Warm, supportive teacher–student relationships promote academic motivation such as positive attitudes toward school, valuing class content, and classroom engagement and effort (Bergin & Bergin, 2009). Thus, positive emotions, like happiness and affection, are part of motivation. Another important classroom emotion is interest.

When your students are interested in something, they work harder at it, persist through challenges, remember it better, process it more deeply, and get better grades (Silvia, 2008). Interest also influences course selection in high school and later career selection. There are two types of interest (Krapp, Hidi, & Renninger, 1992). **Situational interest** refers to interest generated in a situation, like a classroom. It is sparked by the environment. In contrast, **personal interest** refers to enduring preferences that students have for certain activities or domains of knowledge. They bring personal interests with them to your classroom. Let's listen to a teacher describe toddlers in her class:

situational interest short-lived attention or curiosity that is generated by the conditions in a specific situation.

personal interest an individual's enduring interest in an activity or domain of knowledge.

When I play classical music in class, I set the CD player on the floor. Stuart, our most rambunctious toddler, immediately gets down on the floor with his nose against the CD player and listens intently. In contrast, when I get out books, Stuart is not interested, but Rowan literally drops whatever he is doing and clambers into my lap for reading.

These 2-year-olds have distinct personal interests. Both personal and situational interest are relevant to your classroom, but you have more control over situational interest.

What causes interest? Interest can come from encountering something that is novel, complex (simple or familiar things are not too interesting), and within your efficacy to understand (Silvia, 2008). Interest leads to knowledge, which then leads to more things being interesting. Interest also comes partly from your social identity. You are interested in things that are valued by your in-group. Interest could be based on your religion, gender, or SES group (Bergin, 1999). It could also be based on your geography, like deer hunting in rural areas or surfing in coastal areas. Interest could be due to family values; Stuart's mother is a music teacher who values music. It could be due to friends; you might become interested in car mechanics if your friends are. It could also be due to idiosyncratic experiences; you might develop a lifetime interest in minerals if you find a spectacular geode.

Interest is linked to mastery goals. Students who have initial interest in a topic tend to adopt mastery goals, and then develop increasing interest during a course (Harackiewicz, Durik, Barron, Linnenbrink-Garcia, & Tauer, 2008). Interest is also linked to self-determination. When students are free of external pressures, they tend to become more interested. For example, in one study some 6th-graders were allowed to choose from four options what they wanted to study, but others were assigned to study their second choice (McPhail, Pierson, Freeman, Goodman, & Ayappa, 2000). Students who studied their first choice were more positive about their learning than students who studied their second choice. However, too much choice can be overwhelming. Students may perform better when given a handful of choices, rather than dozens of choices (Iyengar & Lepper, 2000).

Field Observation

Observe a learning situation, like a classroom, sports team, or music lesson. Watch children's ebb and flow of interest. What triggers greater interest? Does interest vary by group (e.g., gender, ethnicity, or other factors)?

Interest influences how much students comprehend and learn from textbooks. Students feel more interest in topics for which they have personal interest, that they see as valuable, that meet their learning goal, and that connect to prior knowledge (and that they are told they will be quizzed on). They do not feel interest in texts that have excessively difficult vocabulary (which leads to frustration), do not seem credible, or that they do not understand due to lack of background knowledge (Fox, 2009).

Classroom Implications of "Do I Want to Do This?"

Your students' responses to the question "Do I want to do this?" depend on their goals, feelings of self-determination, and interest. You can influence these, to some extent, by following these guidelines:

- *Promote mastery rather than performance goals*, particularly among your students with low self-efficacy. You promote mastery goals when you emphasize learning new skills and working hard. You also promote mastery goals by showing individual students how they have improved over time, rather than showing them how they compare to others. In contrast, you promote performance goals when you emphasize comparing students with each other and demonstrating (rather than developing) their ability.
- *Break long-term goals down into short-term goals.* Help your students keep track of short-term goals—daily, weekly, or monthly. Mastery of each short-term goal fosters motivation for the next goal and increases efficacy for achieving

the long-term goal—"I may not be able to master this Beethoven sonata, but I can master these three measures of the piece." In one experiment, elementary students with weak arithmetic skills who used a series of short-term goals improved in arithmetic skills, self-efficacy, and interest in arithmetic. They even chose to do more arithmetic problems outside of the classroom, not for grades, compared to students who had only a long-term goal or no goal (Bandura & Schunk, 1981). Another example is to break writing a research paper into a series of short-term goals, like choosing a topic, finding references, writing summaries of the references, and writing an introduction.

- *Help students feel self-determination* (Jang, 2008; Skinner et al., 2008). If you support your students' sense of autonomy in the following ways, they are more likely to feel that they want to do assignments.
    - *Avoid practices that undermine perceptions of autonomy*, such as deadlines, rewards, surveillance, and messages that emphasize "should" and "ought."
    - *Provide a meaningful rationale* as to why the lesson, task, or activity is important.
    - *Give students freedom* to pursue their own agendas if possible, such as opportunity to choose, make decisions, and form their own goals when appropriate.
- *Put your students' personal interests to work.* Students will put more effort into activities they find interesting. For example, Vinnie's teacher might get him to read more history and write better essays by focusing on historical warriors. Similarly, Stuart's teacher might get him to learn the alphabet through song but get Rowan to learn it through picture books.

Unbelievable as it seems, some students will not have *personal* interest in the topic you are teaching. Vinnie's teacher was quite disappointed that he disliked *The Scarlet Letter*. As a teacher, you have much more influence on *situational* interest. Let's look in a freshman English class. They are studying the parts of speech, which is arguably not everyone's most interesting topic:

Several students moaned, "This is BORING!" Ms. Gray, their teacher, said, "I suppose you guys could teach it in an interesting way?" The students responded, "Yes!" Ms. Gray said, "OK, you can teach the figurative language unit." Ms. Gray divided the class into groups of five or six students and gave each group specific concepts to cover and a study guide. They were given one week to come up with the lesson. She said they would have a quiz on the material and would get both a group grade for their presentation and an individual grade based on the quiz and the peer evaluations of their contribution to the presentation.

The presentations included skits and pop-music examples of key concepts. Each group devised acronyms or songs to help their classmates remember the concepts. Students were attentive and engaged. The class average on the quiz was 94%, higher than on any other quiz during the year.

Ms. Gray is a master/mentor teacher who does many things to promote interest among her students. She is not unique. A study of 3rd-grade classrooms found that one effective teacher used forty-three different motivational practices (e.g., choosing interesting topics, using games, using praise), and did nothing to undermine student motivation (e.g., using criticism or public punishment). A less effective teacher used only four different motivational practices and a whopping eleven that tended to undermine student motivation (Dolezal, Welsh, Pressley, & Vincent, 2003). You can guess whose class was more engaged in learning. These guidelines will help you promote situational interest in your students:

- *Help children answer "yes" to "Can I do this?"* as discussed earlier. Students feel more interest for domains in which they feel able—whether English, mathematics, science, sports, or music (Denissen, Zarrett, & Eccles, 2007; Marsh & Craven, 2006). High achievement may lead to high self-concept, which leads to high interest, which leads to more effort, which leads to high achievement, and so forth.
- *Use hands-on activities* (Middleton, 1995). Youth (and adults) like to build, pour, cut, glue, and hammer. Hands-on activities often include an element of problem solving that engages attention. However, make sure the activity is relevant to learning. In one study, one-third of hands-on activities were not relevant to a learning goal (Zahorik, 1996). Impersonating Elvis does not really help students understand the 1950s better. Hands-on activities need to also be minds-on, focusing student thinking on the topic to be learned.
- *Use rewards, but sparingly.* Rewards can attract interest to a task for which students have no prior interest. Sometimes, as students engage in a task for a reward, they develop competence and intrinsic interest. However, rewards can also undermine *intrinsic* interest if students are already interested in a topic (Lepper, Keavney, & Drake, 1996).
- *Present students with a discrepancy.* For example, you can ask what themes the Romantic poets wrote about (*not* romance). Students are curious when something they believe to be true is false. They are motivated to resolve the discrepancy. A popular biology teacher begins his class with a picture of an animal that looks like a tree branch. He asks, "Is it an animal or plant?" Students become curious about the definition of animal as they debate what it is. Brain-scan research shows that when learners are curious, they are more likely to pay attention and to remember what they learn (Kang et al., 2009).
- *Exploit students' social goals.* Most children enjoy social interaction. They tend to be more interested, and learn more, during activities with friends (Zajac & Hartup, 1997). This is one of the reasons cooperative learning is often successful, as it was in Ms. Gray's class.
- *Tell a good story.* Narratives and stories are more interesting than analytic, expository discourse (Hidi & Anderson, 1992). Use stories to illustrate key points whenever possible. Mystery stories are especially engaging, perhaps because they also involve discrepancy. For example, you might show students amazing pictures of the rings of Saturn and ask what they are made of. Tell stories of how scientists argued and tried to determine if they are made of gas,

dust particles, or ice crystals (Cialdini, 2005). How did scientists finally resolve the disagreement? They discovered the rings are mostly dust but ice covered. However, do not use irrelevant stories that distract students from learning.

- *Help students find a purpose for the learning task.* One way to create purpose is to have students make a product they care about. This could be something abstract, like a solution to a problem, or something concrete, like a motor (Ainley, Pratt, & Hansen, 2006). Another way is to create a product or perform for another audience, such publishing a class newsletter.
- *Explain the value or relevance of the activity.* Describe how the students could benefit from their new knowledge, perhaps by seeing things in a new way, or developing a new skill, but not just because it will be on the test. A talented math student complained that teachers teach the material, but without showing why or when you use it. They tell her not to worry about how to use it, but she finds this unsatisfactory. "Once you have the theorem down, it would help to know how you could use it, instead of just strictly what it is. I think it makes it more interesting, and easier to learn" (Csikszentmihalyi, Rathunde, & Whalen, 1993, p. 183). Mrs. Nair encouraged Alex's Chinese language development by pointing out that he should develop Chinese skill so he could become a bilingual professional. She encouraged all the students' writing development by pointing out that high-level jobs they might pursue require writing skill.
- *Build on background knowledge.* Students tend to be interested in things that they already know about, and the more they know about something, the more interested they tend to become (Alexander, Jetton, & Kulikowich, 1995). For example, students who know a lot about physics, radiation, and energy are more likely to be interested in a magazine article about the Chernobyl accident than are other students. Thus, you may want to:
    - Find out about your students' background knowledge in order to link it with course content.
    - Activate your students' background knowledge so they realize what they already know about a topic. For example, they may think that they know nothing about World War II until you point out that films they might have seen such as *Atonement*, *Pearl Harbor*, *Saving Private Ryan*, *Band of Brothers*, *Flags of Our Fathers*, *Empire of the Sun*, and *Defiance* are set during the war.
    - Provide background knowledge to which students can attach new experiences and new factual knowledge. This could include showing films, taking field trips, telling stories, or sponsoring guest speakers.

Let's end this chapter with the inspiring story of Juliet Girard, a high school student. With her classmate Roshan Prabhu, Juliet won the Siemens Westinghouse Competition in Math, Science, and Technology—one of the most prestigious academic competitions in the world. She was the first African American to win. She and Roshan helped identify the gene in rice that controls its flowering time. This discovery could help feed more people in poverty-stricken areas.

Winning this competition typically involves 200 to 800 hours of extracurricular work. Juliet would go to school at 7 a.m.—90 minutes early every morning—to work on their project before school. What might lead to such intense motivation? Juliet's parents are not scientists; they are a UPS driver and a cashier. Juliet was a high-achieving, motivated student involved in other extracurricular activities as well, like most students who compete in science fairs. She edited the school newspaper and was in the Drama Club. Yet, Juliet credits Mr. Corcoran's science research class for her intense motivation.

© Siemens Foundation

Juliet Girard and Roshan Prabhu, high school seniors, stand in front of a poster of their winning entry at the Siemens Westinghouse competition.

What did Mr. Corcoran's class involve? Many of the guidelines you have just read about. In his class, students develop *explicit, specific goals* for research projects. They see *multiple, coping peers model success* in conducting research. They also have *self-determination*; they choose their own research projects based on *personal interest*. They see a *purpose* for their learning and engage in *hands-on activities*, which increase their interest even further. Mr. Corcoran is described as allowing students "to dance to the beat of your own drummer" and as "a glimmer of hope in a sometimes gloomy" urban school district. In addition, the school recognized Juliet and Roshan with a "letter" jacket, like other schools give athletes. Further, Juliet and Roshan both participated in the National Aeronautics and Space Administration's (NASA's) summer research program for ALANA students. The program helps build *self-concept*, *social support for achievement*, and *competence* in science. When so many factors work together, students are more likely to be highly motivated. Juliet also credits watching *Bill Nye the Science Guy* on TV for her early interest in science. We will discuss the power of media in the next chapter.

Reflections on Practice: Checklist for Teachers

Students who have a positive self-concept and social identity fare better and have greater motivation than those who do not. Teachers can influence students' self-concept and motivation through guidelines discussed in previous chapters. They include:

- Promote cognitive abilities and expertise through operant conditioning, scaffolding, and other approaches. How to do this is described in Chapters 3, 4, and 5.
- Promote emotional well-being through a secure teacher–student relationship, coping skills, and self-control. How to do this is described in Chapters 6, 7, and 8.
- Promote social cognition, prosocial behavior, and peer acceptance. How to do this is described in Chapters 9, 10, and 11.

In addition, periodically ask yourself the following:

1. Do I communicate that I value each individual? Do I point out students' accomplishments or strengths, but without overdoing it in a patronizing way?
2. How does my own social identity (such as gender and ethnicity) influence the way I evaluate my students? How do my students' social identities influence how they experience the school and my classroom?
3. Do I avoid pushing sex-typed behavior? Do I avoid making disparaging comments about girls' abilities in mathematics, science, computers, or athletics?
4. Do I avoid stereotyping based on ethnicity? Do I use materials and examples that include people from varied racial, ethnic, and income groups?
5. Do I avoid giving more attention to one group than to others? Do I avoid asking harder, more complex questions of one group than of others? Do I go out of my way to counter the stereotypes that exist about the groups that I teach?
6. Have I put effort into learning about and talking about my students' social group? For example, can I discuss prominent current and historical members of minority groups in my community (e.g., Art Tatum in Toledo, Cesar Chavez in Yuma)?
7. Do I create a classroom atmosphere where all students feel emotionally safe? Am I comfortable talking about race and ethnicity in my classroom?
8. Do I use models and persuasion to enhance my students' self-efficacy?
9. Do I foster mastery goals and stay away from performance-avoid goals? Do I avoid performance-goal-oriented individual competition in the classroom—such as offering a reward to whoever reads the most books?
10. Do I help students attribute their successes and failures to effort and good/bad strategies rather than innate ability? Do I teach that ability can change?
11. Do I use interesting activities as much as possible? Do I try to make most lessons spark situational interest? Am I promoting students' personal interest?

Summary of Age Trends in the Self-System and Motivation

	Self-Concept	Gender Identity	Ethnic Identity	Motivation
Early Childhood (Birth–5 Years)	Infants develop self-concept based on ability to affect the environment. Around 18 months, a sense of self develops. Children are overly positive about their own ability partly due to weak social comparison skills.	Infants categorize people into male or female. By age 3, children know if they are boys or girls. Understanding of gender constancy emerges. Understanding of gender stereotypes emerges—certain objects and activities are for girls and others are for boys.	About age 2 to 3, children become aware of their race or ethnicity, but their understanding is not well developed.	Preschoolers are naturally motivated to explore their world. They may not think about what causes success and failure, and may not notice what others think about their performance. They do not generally distinguish effort from ability.
Middle Childhood (6–12 Years)	More-realistic perceptions of self and of competence develop. Children develop a self-concept that is global (e.g., I am smart) as well as more differentiated. Perceptions of competence decline.	Understanding of gender constancy is fully developed. Gender segregation intensifies. Interest in the opposite sex begins in most children. Same-sex attraction begins in some children.	About age 6, children are able to label their ethnic group, and begin to show a preference for their own ethnic group. By age 7, most children do not express overt prejudice; by age 10, they may avoid talking about race. Most children can recognize broadly held racial stereotypes. Stereotype threat can affect achievement.	Academic intrinsic motivation declines. Distinction between mastery and performance goals becomes possible. By age 11 to 12, the tendency for students who attribute success to ability, rather than effort, and to give up in the face of failure, is developed, although it may appear in preschool.
Adolescence (13–19 Years)	Self-concept differentiates into different domains, such as academic, athletic, and social. At about 6th or 7th grade, the transition from elementary to junior high negatively affects self-concept. In particular, self-concept for academics declines during this transition. Erikson believed this is an age of identity crisis.	Interest in the opposite sex increases in most children, as does same-sex attraction for some children. Gender stereotypes and identity can intensify.	Adolescents show a preference for their own ethnic group. Understanding of prejudice is fully developed. Some youth may try to avoid acting White. Stereotype threat continues to affect achievement.	Academic intrinsic motivation continues to decline. Transition from elementary to junior high negatively affects motivation. Teens develop an orientation that tends to be mastery or performance oriented.

Chapter Summary

The Self-System

- The self-system includes self-esteem, self-concept, and self-efficacy, which are related but not identical.
- Self-esteem is relatively stable over time. Academic achievement is only weakly predicted by self-esteem but strongly predicted by domain-specific self-concept in that domain. Self-esteem generally predicts social and emotional competence, but some bullies have high self-esteem.
- Secure attachment, or being valued by important others, and competence in valued skills predict high self-esteem in students.
- Beyond early childhood, girls tend to have slightly lower self-esteem than boys. This varies by domain. There are few ethnic differences in self-esteem, but African Americans tend to have slightly higher self-esteem than The Self-System do European Americans.
- Teachers can promote students' self-esteem by improving students' social and academic competence, pointing out their accomplishments, building positive relationships, and conveying that they value students.

Gender and Ethnic Identity

- Students' self-concept is linked to the social group to which they belong, including their gender and ethnic group.
- Understanding of gender constancy and stereotyping change with age. Students seek out activities that match their gender. Students who are content with their gender tend to be better adjusted. Boys may be pressured more than girls to conform to stereotypes.
- Ethnic identity is more important to groups that are a minority. Students with positive ethnic identity fare better academically and socially.
- It is common to categorize people into "in-group" and "out-group." Students who feel discriminated against are more likely to have social, emotional, and academic problems.
- Stereotype threat can lower test scores. Teachers can reduce it by teaching students about stereotype threat and that intelligence is changeable.
- Teachers can help reduce discrimination and promote positive social identities in all students by valuing each student, holding all to a high standard, using a multicultural curriculum, and using well-structured cooperative learning.

Motivation

- Students' motivation is influenced by their answer to the question "Can I do this?" The answer depends on self-efficacy, views of intelligence, and attributions.
- Self-efficacy is a key component of social cognitive theory. Self-efficacy predicts goals, persistence, strategy development, achievement, and interest. There are four major influences on self-efficacy: previous experience, vicarious experience (models), verbal persuasion, and physiological experience.
- Students who have an incremental, rather than entity, view of intelligence have greater persistence and intrinsic motivation and are less hurt by failure. Their view

of intelligence influences their attributions for success or failure. When students attribute success to effort, they fare better emotionally and academically and are less likely to give up in the face of failure.

- Teachers can increase their students' motivation by fostering attachment in the classroom, providing models of success, encouraging an incremental view of intelligence, attributing success to effort rather than ability, and training students to do the same.
- Students' motivation is also influenced by their answer to the question "Do I want do this?" The answer depends on their goals, self-determination, and interest.
- Goal setting can improve performance and should involve goals that are specific, are challenging, are broken down into subgoals, are within ability, are adopted with full commitment, and receive feedback.
- Mastery goals reflect a goal to learn new things and a preference for challenge. Performance goals reflect a goal to demonstrate ability and to perform better than other people. Mastery goals are more adaptive in most situations. Performance goals can be divided into performance-approach, which are sometime adaptive, and performance-avoid goals, which are maladaptive.
- Students have an innate need for self-determination. They feel greater intrinsic motivation and interest for tasks for which they have some choice.
- Interest predicts achievement in school. Interest can be personal or situational. Interest is linked to holding mastery goals.
- Teachers can increase their students' motivation by promoting mastery goals, breaking down long-term goals into subgoals, fostering feelings of self-determination, and exploiting personal interests. Teachers can create situational interest by using hands-on activities, rewards, discrepant information, novel objects or tasks, social interaction, stories, and by pointing out the purpose and value of the topic. They can use personal interest by connecting lessons to students' goals and background knowledge.

Accompanying Education CourseMate Website Resources

Visit the **Education CourseMate** website at **CengageBrain.com** to find resources and study aids for this chapter, including self-tests, additional print and website resources, and glossary flashcards. In addition to the TeachSource Video Cases, the following videos illustrate concepts discussed in the chapter:

- 0–2 Years: Gender in Infants and Toddlers
- 2–5 Years: Gender in Early Childhood
- 5–11 Years: Gender in Middle Childhood
- 5–11 Years: Self-Concept in Middle Childhood

TEACHSOURCE VIDEO CASES

Watch the video cases *Motivating Adolescent Learners: Curriculum Based on Real Life, Modeling: Social Cognitive Theory in a High School Chemistry Lesson,* and/or *Gender Equity in the Classroom: Girls and Science.* As you view the videos and artifacts think about the following:

1. Identify specific guidelines from the "Classroom Implications" sections that the teacher is using.
2. Can you identify additional guidelines that the teacher could implement?

14 chapter

The Child in Context: Family Structure, Child Care, and Media

Todd Wright/Blend Images/Jupiter Images

WHAT WERE THE MOST POWERFUL INFLUENCES ON HOW YOU DEVELOPED AS A CHILD? According to the bioecological model, your answer should be "interactions with my family." In every chapter of this text, you have learned how family interactions affect children (e.g., attachment, parenting style, and talking to children). Yet, there were other layers of influence on your childhood. You have learned about some of these in every chapter as well (e.g., genes, culture, and school). In this chapter we will discuss three additional aspects of the context children live in—family structure, child care, and media. Why these three factors? Because they are pervasive, significant influences on children. After you read this chapter, you will understand:

- The variety of family structure, child care, and media contexts of your students.
- How these contexts influence development.
- How you can maximize strengths and mitigate risks from these contexts for your students.

Family Structure

Reagan is a challenge in preschool. He pokes and annoys other children. He does not stay focused in play. Instead of building with blocks, he kicks and throws them until the floor is littered, then runs on to activity after activity. His teachers have to hover over him and repeat directions to get him to clean up. In contrast, his classmate K'Shawn is obedient, concentrates intently on tasks like puzzles, and is kind.

Reagan rarely sees his father since his mother "threw him out" for beating her. Reagan's mother works full-time and attends school part-time. She is proud that she supports herself and her son. However, she says that she so seldom sees Reagan that she doesn't understand him. In contrast, K'Shawn lives with his married parents and 1st-grade sister.

K'Shawn and Reagan's teacher assumes their differences in behavior are caused by their family structure. Is this a reasonable assumption? Let's see what the research says, but first we will discuss how typical their families are.

family structure the composition of a child's household.

nuclear family a family composed of a father and mother who are in their original marriage, and their biological children. Sometimes called a "traditional" family.

Family structure refers to the composition of a child's household. According to the last U.S. Census, about 37 percent of households have children under age 18 (see Figure 14-1). Among households with children, more children (69%) live in married, two-parent households than in all other family structures combined. Some children in married, two-parent households are stepchildren, but 90% are not. Instead, they live in what is commonly called a **nuclear family** with only their biological siblings and parents who are in a first marriage (FIFCFS, 2009).

The second most common family structure is single-mother households. Some single mothers are divorced. More than half of first marriages remain intact, but about 40% of children born to married parents will experience divorce sometime in childhood (Bramlett & Mosher, 2002). Other single mothers were never married, like

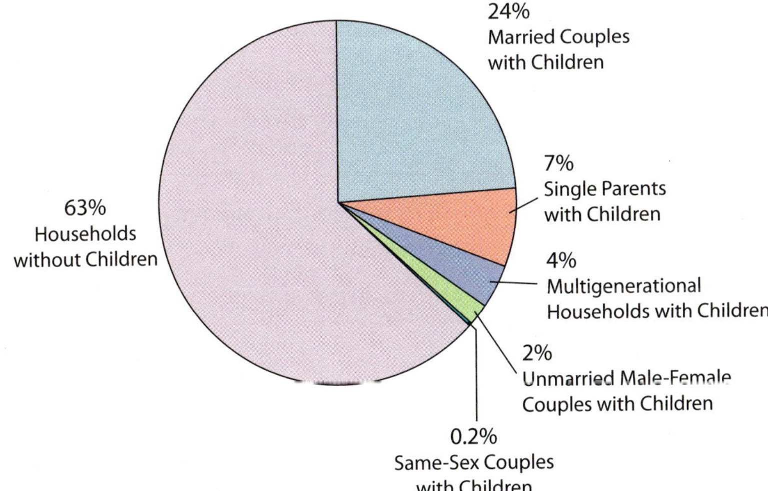

Figure 14.1 Household Types in the U.S.
This chart shows the percentage of different types of households according to the U.S. 2000 census. Where does your family structure fit on this chart?

Reagan's mother. In the past, unmarried mothers tended to be teenagers. Today they are more likely to be in their 20s. This may be partly because marriage occurs later. In the 1950s, the median age of marriage was 20 for women and 23 for men. Now it is 25 and 27, respectively.[1]

Unwed teen pregnancies are currently at record lows, particularly among African American teens.[2] Fewer teens are having sex, and those who do are more likely to use contraception (Miller, Bayley, Christensen, Leavitt, & Coyl, 2003). Still, teen birthrates in the United States are among the highest in Western industrialized countries.

Other less common family structures in the United States include multigenerational, meaning grandparents live in the home, and cohabiting, meaning parents are unmarried.

Most cohabiting parents are opposite-sex couples but a small number are same-sex. Children of gay and lesbian parents are typically the result of past heterosexual marriages, often before the parent identified as homosexual or bisexual (Patterson, 1996). However, some children enter homosexual families through adoption, sperm donation, or surrogate pregnancy. These children may be biologically related to only one parent, or to neither parent. In the United States and Britain same-sex families comprise less than 1% of households (Golombok et al., 2003).

What Does Family Structure Predict?

Although about two out of three children in the United States live in nuclear families, many children do not. Scientists typically compare child outcomes in other family structures with nuclear families because optimal outcomes are linked to living with both biological parents who are married. Let's discuss this research, beginning with divorce.

Divorce

Divorce is not a single event, but rather is a legal marker for a series of events. The series may begin with parents fighting, then a parent moves out, perhaps moves back in and out again, then families visit counselors and lawyers as they cope with anger or grief and argue about custody, housing, and money. The series may continue after the divorce with renewed arguing about custody and money as children's needs evolve. Divorce brings transitions, and children do not fare well if they experience many transitions. Divorce is linked to several child outcomes:[3]

- Externalizing disorders such as aggression, impulsivity, drug use, sexual promiscuity, and teenage parenthood.
- Internalizing disorders such as depression, anxiety, and low self-esteem.
- Medical problems and illnesses.
- Insecure attachment.

[1] These statistics come from the Centers for Disease Control and Prevention's National Center for Health Statistics in 2009. You can find updated statistics on the CDC's website at www.cdc.gov/nchs.
[2] Ibid.
[3] There are many studies that support these conclusions, just a few of which are listed here (Amato, 2001; Burt, Barnes, McGue, & Iacono, 2008; Joussemet et al., 2008; Kelly, 2000; Lansford, 2009; Macmillan, McMorris, & Kruttschnitt, 2004).

- Academic problems such as low test scores, low attendance, and dropping out.
- Relationship problems in adulthood such as divorce and distant relationships with parents.

Think About This You probably know someone who has emerged from childhood divorce fairly well and someone who has not. Compare their risk and protective factors (see Chapter 1). Analyze which factors might explain their different outcomes.

Does the age of the child matter? These problems occur for children of all ages, though problems may be more pronounced for misbehavior in preschoolers and low achievement in adolescents (Lansford, 2009; Lewis, Feiring, & Rosenthal, 2000; Woodward, Fergusson, & Belsky, 2000).

Does divorce always lead to problems? The link between divorce and these problems is robust, or consistently found in many studies with diverse children. However, *the effect is small*, meaning that many children adjust adequately following divorce (Amato, 2001). An exception to the small effect size is externalizing disorders. There may be a 300% increase in antisocial behavior among boys from divorced families compared with boys from nuclear families (Pagani, Boulerice, Vitaro, & Tremblay, 1999). Children are more likely to adjust adequately following divorce if their parents (1) are authoritative, (2) minimize conflict, and (3) provide financial security (Emery, Otto, & O'Donohue, 2005; Lansford, 2009).

Single-Parent and Stepfamilies

Children in single-parent and stepfamilies tend to have profiles similar to children in divorced families. They tend to have lower test scores, lower rates of graduation, and lower rates of college attendance (Sun & Li, 2001). They also tend to be more aggressive and have more emotional problems like anxiety or depression (Ackerman, Brown, & Izard, 2003; Boyle et al., 2004; Ho, Bluestein, & Jenkins, 2008). However, children in stepfamilies may only have these problems if they have other risk factors as well, like a depressed mother or negative family (Dunn et al., 1998). Children in stepfamilies may do just fine if the parents and the family are functioning well.

Teenage Mothers

Children of teenage mothers are more likely than other children to have behavior problems, use alcohol or other drugs, be placed in special education, be retained a grade, drop out, have inadequate employment, go to prison (especially boys), and become teen parents themselves (Miller et al., 2003). However, these are group trends. Some children of teenage mothers fare well. One study found that most children of young mothers did well either socially or academically, and 20% did well in both domains (Rhule, McMahon, Spieker, & Munson, 2006).

Why do many children of teen mothers struggle? Perhaps because their mothers tend to have low levels of education; early childbearing tends to curtail education. Perhaps because of mothers' circumstances before the children are born. Teen mothers tend to come from poor, single-mother, unstable families that move a lot. Teen mothers tend to be delinquent and have difficulty with employment, which can cause their children to have academic and social problems like truancy, fighting at school, and early sex (Levine, Pollack, & Comfort, 2001; Turley, 2003).

Teen mothers also have more premature, medically fragile infants with low birth weight, which can cause later problems (see Chapter 2). Older mothers—up to age 30—have healthier babies. However, mothers over age 30 and teen mothers have infants with similar medical risks. Does older mothers' maturity compensate for these medical risks? Perhaps not. Two large studies of mothers aged 15 to 45 found the older the mother, the better the parenting, up to age 27 to 30, but no improvement in parenting after age 30 (Bornstein & Putnick, 2007; Bornstein, Putnick, Suwalsky, & Gini, 2006). Thus, childbearing in the 20s may be ideal for both healthy birth and high-quality parenting. In the United States, childbearing from ages 20 to 24 is at record lows and from ages 30 to 34 at record highs.[4]

Gay and Lesbian Families

Research suggests that children with same-sex parents are similar to other children in their peer relationships, gender-typed play, self-esteem, depression, behavior problems at school, delinquency, victimization, and GPA (Patterson, 2009; Rivers, Poteat, & Noret, 2008; Wainright & Patterson, 2008). As adolescents, they have similar rates of romantic or sexual relationships (Wainright, Russell, & Patterson, 2004). They may be more tolerant of and experiment with homosexuality, but they do not have higher rates of identification as gay or lesbian (Golombok, Tasker, & Murray, 1997; Patterson, 1992). Same-sex parents tend to provide similar-quality parenting as heterosexual parents of the same SES, with parents in marriage-like relationships providing higher-quality parenting than single parents (Golombok et al., 2003; Wainright et al., 2004). However, unlike most other research discussed in this text, this research is based on small samples because so few children live with same-sex parents. For example, in a national study of 12,000 adolescents, only forty-four lived with lesbian mothers and six with gay fathers (Wainright & Patterson, 2008).

Cohabiting Families

Cohabitation, where parents live together but are not married, tends to be an unstable family structure. Cohabiting couples are more likely to separate than married couples (Raley & Wildsmith, 2004). Married couples who cohabited before their marriage are also more likely to break up. Thus, children tend to experience high rates of parental loss akin to divorce if their parents cohabit (Seltzer, 2000).

Children in cohabiting families may have typical development as preschoolers. However, by school age they tend to have lower cognitive skills, social competence, and academic achievement and later are more likely to use drugs. If their mothers have a series of cohabiting partners, they tend to be more aggressive (Cabrera, Shannon, West, & Brooks-Gunn, 2006; Hamilton, 2000).

In summary, family structure is linked to physical, cognitive, emotional, and social outcomes in children. Children can fare well in any family structure. However, having divorced, unmarried, remarried, or cohabiting parents are risk factors; happily married parents are a protective factor. Next, let's explore why this might be.

How Might Family Structure Influence Children?

Family structure may influence children through several paths. Compared to other family structures, nuclear families tend to have (1) higher parent education; (2) less financial strain; (3) fewer moves; (4) greater parent–child closeness, particularly for adolescents; and (5) less abuse (FIFCFS, 2009; Gruman, Harachi, Abbott, Catalano,

[4]Ibid. National Center for Health Statistics in 2009.

& Fleming, 2008; Hay & Nash, 2002; Hetherington, Bridges, & Insabella, 1998; Miller et al., 2003). Living with a stepparent or cohabiting adult is one of the largest risk factors for severe child maltreatment, which is dubbed the "Cinderella effect" (Daly & Wilson, 2005). However, most stepparents are not abusive; they are more likely to be distant. Let's discuss three other potent paths of influence: father presence, marital conflict, and quality of parenting.

Father Presence

Family structure affects father presence. In nuclear families, like K'Shawn's, children live with their father and mother. In single-parent homes, children typically live with their mothers. Only about 4% of children live with a single father (FIFCFS, 2009). Many divorced fathers intend to stay involved, but their contact drops off over time. Roughly 40% of nonresidential fathers have no contact with their children in a year's time (Emery et al., 2005). Never-married fathers, like Reagan's, are the least likely to see their children.

Think About This There is an old adage that "The best thing a father can do for his children is love their mother." Does research on family structure support this adage? How might you alter the adage, using research to support your alteration?

When fathers are absent, their children lose economic resources and a father's discipline, supervision, and nurturing. Their children are more likely to feel distressed, use drugs, not finish high school, and have employment problems (King, Harris, & Heard, 2004). Children with absent fathers are at risk for early sex and teen pregnancy (Mendle et al., 2009).

What if nonresidential fathers stay involved? Fathers who merely take their children to the movies may not contribute to their well-being, but nonresidential fathers who are authoritative, monitor their children, set limits, talk about problems, and help with homework do contribute to their children's well-being. Children do better academically after divorce if their fathers stay involved in their schoolwork (Kelly, 2000).

Other adults can sometimes fill a father's role. Children with father substitutes fare well, particularly African American children, if the substitutes are warm and discipline the children (Coley, 1998). However, stepfathers and cohabiting partners tend to spend less time with children than do biological fathers (Smolensky & Gootman, 2003).

Sometimes children benefit from father absence. Children may be relieved when an abusive father moves out. If fathers are abusive, drug addicts, or criminals, their children may fare better without them. Children are more likely to have conduct disorder if they have an antisocial father who lives with them than if he does not live with them (Jaffee, Moffitt, Caspi, & Taylor, 2003).

Goodshoot/Jupiter Images

Children's depression, hostility, and antisocial behavior increase when parents' conflict increases.

Parents' Conflict

Conflict is hard on children. In fact, the child problems linked to divorce may actually result from parents' conflict *before the divorce* (Lansford, 2009). Whether parents divorce or not, their conflict is linked to children's social, emotional, and academic problems (Sturge-Apple, Davies, & Cummings, 2006). Adolescents' delinquency, hostility, and depression increase when parents' conflict increases and decrease when the conflict decreases (Cui, Conger, & Lorenz, 2005). These problems in the child may lead to more parents' conflict, creating a vicious cycle (Cui, Donnellan, & Conger, 2007). Parents' conflict over childrearing may be particularly hard on children. Unfortunately, parents' most hostile fights are often over childrearing.

Are families better off divorcing if there is conflict? Children in high-conflict homes may fare better after divorce *if the conflict stops*, but children in moderate-conflict homes do not fare better after divorce. In addition, divorce does not necessarily end conflict, particularly if parents share custody (Emery et al., 2005). Conflict can escalate after divorce if parents argue over money, custody, and visitation. Children fare worse if parents' conflict continues to be intense and frequent after divorce (Kelly, 2000).

Is marital conflict a "shared environment" for siblings (see Chapter 1)? Some children bear more of the brunt of parent conflict than their siblings. Fighting parents tend to treat their children differently (Jenkins, Simpson, Dunn, Rasbash, & O'Connor, 2005). An angry parent might snap at and criticize one child, while affectionately comforting another child. Thus, parent conflict is often a "nonshared environment."

Why is parent conflict hard on children? For several reasons. Conflict may undermine emotional security, or arouse fear, sadness, and anger that children cannot regulate. It may lead to self-blame or feeling helpless. It may alter children's physiological response to stress. It may lead to poor sleep or attention deficits. It may undermine the quality of parenting.[5] When parents are angry with each other, they tend to be less responsive, affectionate, and supportive of their children. Each of these factors could lead to emotional disorders and behavior problems (Rhoades, 2008).

Quality of Parenting

Parents in any family structure can be sensitive and authoritative. However, many studies find that never-married, divorced, step, and teen parents tend to provide lower quality parenting than parents in nuclear families (e.g., Hay & Nash, 2002; Ho et al., 2008; Jenkins, Rasbash, & O'Connor, 2003). One large national study found that even when both biological parents live together, but are not married, mothers tend to be more negative toward their children (Gibson-Davis & Gassman-Pines, 2010). How might family structure influence parenting quality? Parents who feel distress due to financial strain, marital conflict, lack of emotional support, or other challenges are less likely to use effective discipline, be warm, parent authoritatively, and monitor or set limits for children.

Regardless of family structure, children will fare better if parents can maintain high-quality parenting (Rhule et al., 2006). For example, in one study, children of teenage mothers developed good cognitive ability if their mothers were responsive, warm, talked to them, set limits, and read to them (Luster, Bates, Fitzgerald, Vandenbelt,

---

[5] There are many studies that support these conclusions, just a few of which are listed here (Buehler, Lange, & Franck, 2007; Davies, Sturge-Apple, Cicchetti, & Cummings, 2007, 2008; El-Sheikh et al., 2009; Sturge-Apple et al., 2006).

& Key, 2000). When families divorce, if parents use an authoritative parenting style, children fare better (Hay & Nash, 2002). If they continue supervising the children and enforcing household rules, like being home for dinner or limiting TV, then their children are less likely to develop behavior problems (Pagani et al., 1999). Interventions that help divorced parents stay positive and use effective discipline result in children with better behavior and higher achievement at school (Forgatch & DeGarmo, 2002). The key lesson is that *quality of parenting is more important than family structure, but family structure influences quality of parenting.*

Revisiting Risk and Resilience

Some factors discussed earlier, such as father absence and parental conflict, contribute to the risk of problems for children in nonnuclear families. However, in Chapter 1 you learned that protective factors can mitigate risk, leading to resilient children. For example, Collin, just like Reagan in the opening vignette, had significant risk factors by age 3—when his mother divorced his abusive father. He is now in 7th grade. Let's see how he is doing:

> *Collin's mother became a nurse and was able to financially support the two of them. When he was 8, his mother married a man with two younger daughters. They have since had two more children. Collin's mother is now a homemaker, and the large family barely makes ends meet. However, the home is orderly, and the parents are loving. They set clear limits, like only one hour of videogames on school days. Collin's stepfather takes him fishing and camping, which Collin loves.*

Collin has several protective factors: an educated mother, adequate (but not plentiful) finances, and limited exposure to violent TV. The marital conflict ended with the divorce. Collin rarely sees his antisocial father, but he has an involved stepfather. Most importantly, his mother and stepfather are authoritative. So how is Collin faring? He earns above-average grades at school, excels in athletics, and is prosocial, but is a little prone to depression. Overall, he is a resilient child.

Group Diversity in Family Structure

There are gender differences in how children respond to family structure. There are also SES and ethnic differences in how common different family structures are.

Gender

Both boys and girls have higher achievement and fewer externalizing or internalizing problems in nuclear families than in single-parent, divorced, and stepfamilies (Sun & Li, 2001). However, boys in nonnuclear families may be at greater risk than girls for externalizing problems, like aggression and delinquency (Dunn et al., 1998).

In contrast, girls may be more at risk than boys for internalizing problems, like depression, anxiety, and low self-esteem, after divorce. In addition, girls may develop more problems over time, perhaps because nonresident fathers are more involved with boys. However, a subset of girls develop remarkable competence after divorce as they take over parenting responsibility. This may come at a price because they tend to feel anxiety and low self-esteem despite their competence (Hetherington & Stanely-Hagan, 1999).

Socioeconomic Status

SES is linked to family structure. Single motherhood leads to lower income, and mothers who grew up in low-SES homes are more likely to become teen, never-married, or divorced mothers (Bramlett & Mosher, 2002). High-SES teens who do become pregnant are more likely to relinquish the child for adoption, particularly if they aspire to college (Miller et al., 2003; see Box 14.1 for a discussion of adoption and related topics). Thus, SES influences the family structure that children enter into (see Figure 14.2).

Challenges in Development **Box 14.1**

Orphanages, Foster Care, and Adoption

Sometimes parents cannot care for children. In the past, children could be put in orphanages due to parents' death, incarceration, abandonment, or poverty. Orphanages were large institutions where caregivers were rotated so that children would not get "too attached." The idea was to spare children the trauma of separation (Rutter, 1995). We now know that never attaching is worse than losing an attachment figure. As Tennyson wrote, *"Tis better to have loved and lost, than never to have loved at all."* Orphanages are still common in some countries, but in the United States they have been largely replaced by foster care and adoption.

Foster care. Children are typically placed in foster care against the parents' will, often due to criminal neglect or parents' drug use. Many foster parents are loving. However, quality of care in 15 to 20% of foster homes may be as bad as in the child's original home (Orme & Buehler, 2001). Foster homes tend to be in low-SES, high-risk neighborhoods with single caregivers (Dozier, Stovall, Albus, & Bates, 2001). Foster children are often moved from one home to another, which is distressing to them. One child who had lived in five different homes by age 6, was told, *"You are a wonderful and special girl."* She responded: *"Then why does everybody leave me?"* (Adam, 2004, p. 211).

Does removing children from their homes lead to more behavior problems, even if it keeps them safer? One national study found no evidence of an increase or decrease in behavior problems (Berger, Bruch, Johnson, James, & Rubin, 2009). Still, decisions about removing children from potentially harmful parents are extremely difficult to make. Attachment needs may conflict with physical safety needs. For example, a toddler in foster care for less than a month was observed at a clinic:

He was playing in a listless way, ignoring his foster mother's attempts to interest him in toys. She signaled to him to come to her, but he turned away. When she left the room, he screamed. When she returned, he walked toward her, but stopped four feet away. When she tried to engage him with toys, he turned away and played several feet away. When his natural mother entered the room, he immediately went to her to be picked up. They hugged and he began playing actively and confidently, occasionally smiling. However, later he ignored his mother's overture to pick him up. (adapted from Gaensbauer, Mrazek, & Harmon, 1981)

This toddler is depressed. Separation from his mother is distressing, but he was not safe at home. Will he eventually become attached? Toddlers can securely attach to foster caregivers if they stay together for several months. However, there are high rates of disorganized attachment among foster children, and children tend to fare better if they are adopted, rather than in foster care (Brand & Brinich, 1999).

Adoption. Children adopted as infants tend to be as securely attached as nonadoptees. Most develop normal IQ and do as well in school as their nonadopted peers. However, a small percentage (12%) of adopted children have substantial behavior problems, such as aggression, delinquency, and mental health issues (Brand & Brinich, 1999; Deater-Deckard & Plomin, 1999). Some also have minor delays in language and a slightly higher rate of special education placement, particularly if adopted after 12 months of age or if they experience early abuse, neglect, or malnutrition—such as the children in the horrendous Romanian orphanages (Van IJzendoorn, Juffer, & Poelhuis, 2005).

(continued)

Challenges in Development *(continued)*

Romanian orphans. When the Ceausescu regime in Romania collapsed in 1989, the world found that tens of thousands of children had been placed in orphanages because their parents were too poor to feed them. The orphans were neglected and malnourished. Moved by their plight, many families in America and Europe adopted them.

How have they fared? It depends on how long the children were deprived. Children adopted before 6 months of age developed normal attachment. They were physically, socially, and mentally delayed at adoption, but by school entry they were only slightly underweight, had average social skills, and only 18% were still mentally delayed. Children adopted after 6 months of age also made substantial gains, but some problems lingered through age 11. Most developed attachment to their parents, but about one-third did not. They also had more behavior problems, including autism-like behavior. Their average IQ was 15 points lower than average, but most were still within normal ranges for cognitive development and weight (Beckett et al., 2006; Kreppner et al., 2007).

These lingering problems, despite many years in adoptive homes, suggest deprivation in the first few years of life can cause enduring changes in the brain. How does this happen? Children in unstimulating orphanages have less brain activity, which may cause too much pruning following synaptogenesis (Nelson, 2007).

An important lesson for teachers is that even severely deprived children can catch up, if not completely recover, in good homes. Adoption is a natural experiment of the power of environment. Adoptive families are typically better educated than average and take good care of children. In these families, adopted children tend to show remarkable gains compared with children who are left behind in an orphanage or their birth home. However, they need time for recovery. Within two to four years, most Romanian orphans (60 to 80%) no longer had problems. Even children who had still not caught up by age 6 continued to make gains through age 11. There was no age when it was too late for recovery.

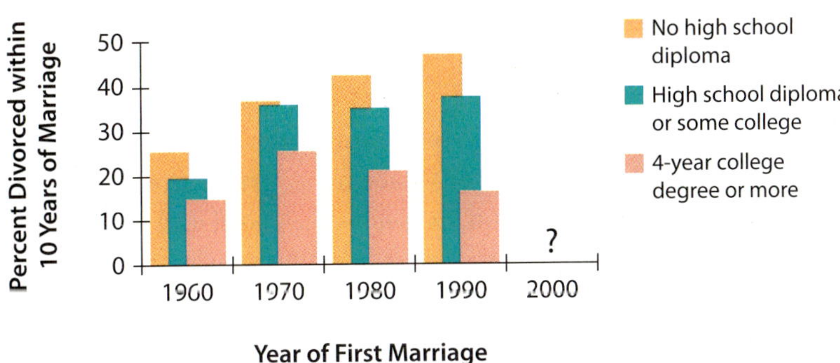

Figure 14.2 Maternal Education and Divorce.
Marriages are becoming less stable for women with less education and more stable for highly educated women. Interestingly, college-educated women are *less* likely to divorce if they marry before they finish their degree. Since the 1970s, low-SES women are marrying later and have more premarital births. Women first married in 2000 are just past their ten-year anniversary. Based on trends, what do you think their divorce rate will be? *Source: Martin (2006).*

Ethnicity

Family structure varies by ethnic group. Asian children are the most likely to live in a nuclear family (Bramlett & Mosher, 2002). Most White children (60%) grow up in nuclear families, even if they are poor, and another 12% live in a two-parent stepfamily. Among White children, 27% are born to unmarried women (Martin et al., 2009). Most Latino children (65%) also live with two parents, but they are less likely to be married than White parents (FIFCFS, 2009).

Most African American children (71%) are born to unmarried women. African American children tend to spend more years in a single-parent household than other children (FIFCFS, 2009). Their household structure tends to be less stable as their parents' relationships evolve (Bramlett & Mosher, 2002; Raley & Wildsmith, 2004). Grandparents and aunts are likely to be actively involved in childrearing, providing extended family stability.

These ethnic differences in family structure are linked to cultural differences in college aspirations and acceptance of teen parenthood and cohabitation (Miller et al., 2003). Four times as many Latino and African American teens are parents than are Asian teens. Despite their acceptance, teen parenthood and cohabitation remain risk factors for Latino and African American children. Children whose mothers change cohabiting relationships multiple times are particularly at risk for social and emotional problems (Ackerman, Brown, D'Eramo, & Izard, 2002).

Classroom Implications of Family Structure and Parent Involvement

I used to get A's and B's because I wanted to make my parents proud. I was happy and my family was happy. Then, when I was 13, I came home from school one day and my mom was crying. My little brother said my parents were fighting and my dad left. I was sad because my dad and I did everything together. I missed him so much. I didn't feel like doing anything; I didn't care no more about my schoolwork. I got D's for like the rest of that year and the next. Now I'm trying to get it together to prove to my dad that I can get on without him.

This poignant story told by a high school student shows how family structure affected her schoolwork. Research confirms her story; family structure is linked to test scores, attendance, retention, special education placement, graduation rates, educational aspirations, and homework completion, as well as the social and emotional problems you read about earlier. While family structure can affect children through any of the factors previously discussed, parents' conflict is particularly potent. Teachers view children as less prosocial, less academically competent, and less engaged in class when there is marital conflict at home (Sturge-Apple et al., 2006).

Living in divorced, single-parent, or cohabiting families is a risk factor for students—but the effect is small. This means many students in nonnuclear families, like Collin, are successful in school. This is important to realize because if you expect your students to underachieve or misbehave, they may fulfill your expectations through the Pygmalion effect (see Chapter 12). For your students who are struggling, there are several things you can do to help:

- Serve as an alternate attachment figure. Review Chapter 6 for how to do this.
- Teach students how to cope with their negative emotions and stress. Review Chapter 8 for how to do this.
- Advocate for students to continue attending your school even when the family moves out of the attendance area so that their school setting remains stable. Moving is stressful because it disrupts students' academic development and social ties (Adam, 2004; Gruman et al., 2008).

- Help students develop strong academic skills so that they experience success in your classroom. Review Chapters 4, 5, and 12 for how to do this.
- Help students replace aggression with prosocial behavior so that their peers will accept them. Friends help buffer students from the negative effects of divorce. Review Chapters 10 and 11 for how to do this.
- Use an authoritative style of classroom management rather than power assertion. Review Chapter 7 for how to do this. Encourage parents to be authoritative as well.

You can also seek the help of the school counselor, who may provide intervention. School-based interventions designed to help students of divorce focus on improving social support, coping skills for negative emotions, and parent–child relations. Typically, students meet in a small group at school for several sessions. Such interventions have had some success helping students with some skills—such as being more sociable, less frustrated, higher achievers, and less promiscuous and delinquent—but they have not been as successful in reducing anxiety and depression (Pedro-Carroll, 2005; Wolchik et al., 2002). Students benefit from high-quality intervention programs even if their families divorced several years earlier, because the stress of divorce tends to be ongoing.

Students weather family disruptions if their parents are authoritative, financially stable, and minimize their conflict and if nonresidential fathers remain involved in their children's schooling. Let's focus on this last factor—parental involvement—next.

Involving Parents in Education

While you cannot influence family structure, you can influence parent involvement in school. Parents can be involved in their children's education at school or at home. *School involvement* includes attending parent–teacher conferences, which about 60 to 70% of parents do, or volunteering at school, which about 20 to 50% of parents do (Pomerantz, Moorman, & Litwack, 2007). *Home involvement* includes supervising homework, taking children to the library, reading to children, and providing study space. Parents who are not visible at school may value their children's education and be involved at home. For example, one undocumented immigrant Latino father never went to his sons' school during the day because of his construction job and his fear of deportation. Yet he sat all four sons at the kitchen table after dinner and watched over their homework. He could not help his sons with their homework, but he felt that being present conveyed the importance of education (Carreón, Drake, & Barton, 2005).

Michael Newman/PhotoEdit

Parents who feel welcomed are more involved in their children's education at home and at school.

High-SES, White, and Asian parents are more likely to be visible at school than other groups. They tend to actively manage their children's education, like selecting classes. They tend to see themselves as collaborators in their children's education and entitled to school involvement.

Think About This Teachers tend to believe that parents who are present at the school value their children's education more—which in turn is linked to teachers viewing those students as more academically capable (Hill & Taylor, 2004). How does this relate to the Pygmalion effect described in Chapter 12?

In contrast, teachers are often unaware of the involvement of low-SES parents because it tends to occur at home, where parents may monitor their children's academic progress (Green, Walker, Hoover-Dempsey, & Sandler, 2007; Hill et al., 2004).

When parents are involved *at school* their children tend to be socially successful, well behaved, and relatively high achieving (Fan & Chen, 2001; Hill & Tyson, 2009; Pomerantz et al., 2007). This effect may be stronger for low-SES and African American children (Hill et al., 2004). This research is correlational, so it is not clear if parents of children who are successful and well behaved in school are more motivated to get involved or if their children are more successful because they are involved.

When parents are involved *at home*, child outcomes are not as consistently rosy. This is because *parents can be involved in positive or negative ways*. For example, parents might "help" with homework in ways that cause confusion or tension (Patall, Cooper, & Robinson, 2008). Let's quickly revisit 1st-grader Elena in case 1:

> *When they read storybooks, Elena's father insists she sound out every word. Instead of enjoying reading together, her father views it as a time to "practice" reading. When Elena looks at the pictures to figure out hard words—as 1st graders typically do—her father covers the picture and says she is cheating. Elena does not enjoy reading.*

When parents are overly controlling or negative, like Elena's father, their children have lower achievement. Children who are struggling academically are especially vulnerable to negative parent involvement. In contrast, when parents allow children to take initiative and solve their own problems, help only when needed, and focus on the pleasure of learning, their children have higher achievement (Pomerantz et al., 2007). A national study of 8th-graders found that parents who discussed school issues at home with their children—such as school activities, classroom topics, or which courses to take—had children who scored the equivalent of a full year's worth of schooling higher than parents who did not do this, regardless of SES (Ream & Palardy, 2008).

How does parent involvement help children? Probably through improved skills and motivation. Children with positively involved parents are more engaged in school and do more homework. They may also develop a self-identity as a good student (Oyserman, Brickman, & Rhodes, 2007). If their parents encourage intrinsic motivation, such as emphasizing the fun of learning and the importance of persistence, students feel more motivated than if their parents encourage extrinsic motivation, such as cash for good grades and grounding for poor grades (Gottfried, Marcoulides, Gottfried, & Oliver, 2009). In addition, involved parents develop cultural capital (see Chapter 1); they learn how to negotiate their children's path through school. Parents learn from teachers and teachers learn from parents what their expectations are. This promotes a cultural match so that children get the same message from home and school.

Why are some parents not involved? There may be barriers, like transportation problems, inflexible work schedules, their own history of school failure, fear of being viewed as incompetent by teachers, and language differences. Their beliefs may also be a barrier. Some believe the parents' job is to send the child to school fed and clothed, with proper manners such as saying "Yes sir" or "Yes ma'am," and to leave the teaching to the teachers. The biggest barrier may be lack of self-confidence about whether they can help their children succeed in school (Green et al., 2007). When teachers make an effort to engage them, parents are more involved at home and at school (Seitsinger, Felner, Brand, & Burns, 2008). Follow these guidelines to increase parent involvement at your school:

- *Personally invite parents to be involved.* This is a powerful tactic (Green et al., 2007). Whether this is best done through notes, e-mail, or phone depends on the age of your students, the literacy of their parents, and whether the family has a phone or Internet connection. Adolescents do not take notes home as reliably as younger children do.
- *Establish a regular forum for communication.* Preschools and elementary schools may use Parent Folders. Secondary schools may have a hotline or website and listserv.
- *Develop welcoming activities.* For example, host "Muffins for Mom" or "Doughnuts for Dad" before-school breakfasts. Invite parents with preschoolers to visit kindergarten, or invite 8th-graders to visit high school with their parents.
- *Avoid coercion.* Contracts or policies that require parent involvement are coercive. They are not linked to students' increased achievement. Instead, develop a strong parent–teacher relationship characterized by trust, support, and mutual respect.
- *When involving parents, help them remain positive.* Emphasize mastery, not performance goals (see Chapter 13) so that parents do not become overly controlling as they feel pressure to make their children perform. Make sure that they have the skills to help their children. When asking parents to do specific things, such as tutor their child in reading, you may need to directly train parents on how to do it successfully (Sénéchal & Young, 2008).

Generally, preschools and elementary schools are better than secondary schools at involving parents, but parental involvement remains important for adolescents (Hill & Taylor, 2004). Parents' involvement may drop off in secondary schools because schools are bigger, less personal, and more bureaucratic. When schools make parents feel welcomed, and provide opportunities for involvement, students' achievement increases, particularly for low-SES students. Unfortunately, schools serving low-SES students are less likely to reach out to parents (Schulting, Malone, & Dodge, 2005). Thus, if you teach in a secondary or low-SES school, you may need to prod your school to involve parents.

Family structure influences other contexts for children, such as whether mother works and children are in child care. Reagan's family structure meant that he spent long hours with a babysitter, but K'Shawn did not. Collin's family structure changed from married to divorced to remarried. Each change brought changes in his mother's employment and his child care. Let's discuss this next.

Maternal Employment and Child Care

Eleanor's mother works full-time, as an executive, and her father is a physician, with a family income of $500,000 a year. Although they work long hours, both parents take time off to attend their children's activities. Eleanor and her sister have had the same nanny since infancy. Eleanor has personal tutors and coaches whenever she wants them.

Cassie's mother has finally found a job, after months of looking, as an "assisted living" aide who dresses and feeds disabled adults. She makes $8 per hour with no benefits. She works irregular hours and sometimes weekends. They occasionally eat at soup kitchens when money runs out. Cassie's parents are divorced; her father neither visits nor sends child support. Cassie sometimes accompanies her mother to work, but mostly stays home alone watching TV. Cassie has had many cheap child care arrangements over the years as her mother has found, lost, and regained employment. Cassie's dream is to take piano lessons, but her mother can't afford them.

Jenna's mother has not worked outside the home since Jenna was born. Her mother plans to return to being a schoolteacher when Jenna graduates from high school. Her father is a store manager. Money is often tight, especially now that two brothers are in college, but Jenna has plenty of food and clothing. Her mother takes her to voice lessons and soccer after school. Jenna is seldom home alone.

Eleanor, Cassie, and Jenna are all in the same 9th-grade class, but they have very different experiences with maternal employment and child care. Jenna's experience is becoming less common in the United States because more mothers are in the workforce. More than half of women with children work: 54% who have infants, 64% who have children under age 6, and 77% who have children 6 to 17 years of age (U.S. Bureau of Labor Statistics, 2009). Most working mothers prefer to work part-time; only 20% feel that working full-time is ideal (Pew Research Center, 2007). Women at all income levels work full-time, or part-time, or stay home with their children. For example, in case 1, Elena's parents opted to have their mobile home foreclosed on, and moved in with the grandparents, rather than have Elena's mother work outside the home. Thus, these issues are deeply significant to many families. What does the research say about how maternal employment and child care may influence children like Eleanor, Cassie, and Jenna?

Maternal Employment

Research on maternal employment shows that child outcomes depend on the situation. Maternal employment has been linked to positive outcomes, such as good language ability, and negative outcomes, such as behavior problems. Why do outcomes vary by the situation? In Chapter 1, you learned about two models used to explain poverty's effects. These same models are used to explain maternal employment's effects. According to the *family investment model*, maternal employment would be positive if it leads to greater income to invest in the child or negative if it leads to less time to invest in the child. According to the *family stress model*, maternal employment would be positive if it enhances the mother's well-being or negative if it leads to stress that diminishes parenting quality. Research supports each possibility, but for different family situations.

Child outcomes tend to be negative when:

1. Mothers must work evenings or irregular schedules, like Cassie's. Nonstandard work hours are linked to parents' depression, sleepiness, divorce, health problems, and fewer family routines like eating dinner together. Mothers who work nonstandard hours tend to be less sensitive with their children (Han, 2005; Hsueh & Yoshikawa, 2007).
2. Mothers have a lengthy commute, or a low-pay, no-benefit job. Mothers' low-quality, unstable employment is linked to children's anxiety, depression, grade retention, dropping out of school, and low self-esteem (Dunifon, Kalil, & Bajracharya, 2005; Kalil & Ziol-Guest, 2005).
3. Mothers begin work during the child's infancy. Maternal employment during the child's first year is linked to later academic and behavior problems (Brooks-Gunn, Han, & Waldfogel, 2002; Han, Waldfogel, & Brooks-Gunn, 2001).
4. Mothers work more than thirty hours per week. (Goldberg, Prause, Lucas-Thompson, & Himsel, 2008; Hill, Waldfogel, Brooks-Gunn, & Han, 2005; Weiss et al., 2003). However, note that most working mothers work part-time rather than full-time, often entering and exiting the workforce. Part-time employment tends to be linked to positive child outcomes. (Bradley & Corwyn, 2006; Smolensky & Gootman, 2003).

Child outcomes tend to be positive when:

1. Mother's pay helps the family leave welfare, like Cassie's family (Hill et al., 2005). Welfare-leaving mothers feel greater self-esteem and more a part of the community (London, Scott, Edin, & Hunter, 2004). They tend to become less authoritarian, less depressed, and more satisfied with their lives (Raver, 2003).
2. Mothers are single. Single mothers who work are more likely to have children with better vocabularies than are single mothers who do not work (Brooks-Gunn et al., 2002; Goldberg et al., 2008).
3. Mothers enjoy their work, and believe their employment is good for their children, as compared to mothers who either work but do not feel good about it or do not work but wish they did (Harrison & Ungerer, 2002).
4. Mothers make sure that they spend time with their children after work hours. Working mothers spend less time with their children than nonworking mothers, but the differences are not as large as you might expect (Huston & Aronson, 2005).

In summary, there are costs and benefits to maternal employment. In general, among low-income families, the balance tips in the positive direction, particularly if Mom's job has standard hours, some prestige, and is stimulating to her. Maternal employment and child care go hand in hand, although not all children in child care have working mothers and not all employed mothers use child care. Let's discuss child care next.

Think About This Can you apply each of these findings to the family investment and family stress models to explain outcomes linked to maternal employment?

Comstock/Jupiter Images

The number of hours and quality of child care vary enormously for children.

Child Care

What are the effects of child care? Like maternal employment, it depends. To understand the research, you need to see how child care varies by (1) type, (2) amount, and (3) quality. First, child care can take place in a center, or the child's home, or the provider's home. Child care can occur in a group or one-on-one with a nanny. Child care can be provided by relatives for no fee or by strangers for profit. More than half of preschoolers in child care are in unpaid relative care, especially if the mother works part-time. Another 22% are in nonrelative home-based care. Even though people tend to think of centers when they think of child care, only 10 to 22% of preschoolers are in center-based care (NICHD Early Child Care Research Network, 2006a; Smolensky & Gootman, 2003). Children may be in more than one type of care, perhaps going to preschool for a few hours and then to Grandma's for a few hours.

Second, child care varies by amount. Some children spend sixty hours per week in child care, whereas others might spend only four hours. National studies have found that preschoolers spend an average of twenty hours per week, and kindergarteners and 1st-graders spend an average of eight to nine hours per week in child care (McCartney et al., 2010; NICHD Early Child Care Research Network, 2004).

Third, child care quality varies from excellent to harmful. One report of some child care centers in Texas described them as clean, attractive, and orderly (Lewin, 1998). Toddlers' misbehavior or distress was responded to promptly. However, adult speech was limited to short commands, like *"don't grab"* or *"time to clean up."* Infants spent most of the day in their cribs. They were seldom talked to, yet the infants seemed content. Does this constitute high-quality care?

Child care is high quality when caregivers (1) are sensitive and warm, (2) use rich language, (3) directly instruct children in emergent literacy and informal math in ways that are not overly structured, and (4) are stable so that attachment can form (Burchinal et al., 2008; Howes & James, 2002). This is more likely if child–caregiver ratios are low and caregivers are educated about child development (de Schipper, Riksen-Walraven, & Geurts, 2006; Marshall, 2004). In the United States, recommended ratios are 3:1 for infants and 8:1 for 4-year-olds.

Why do parents put their children in low-quality care? They may need low-cost care. They also may not know better. For example, in a classic study, parents were equally satisfied with the worst and the best child care programs; they did not seem to be aware of differences in quality (Miller, 1990). In addition, *there is a shortage of high-quality care* in the United States; research shows that as few as 10% of settings are high quality (Burchinal et al., 2000; NICHD Early Child Care Research Network, 2006a; Phillips, Mekos, Scarr, McCartney, & Abbott-Shim, 2000). It is especially difficult to maintain high-quality but affordable care for forty hours per week. Children in full-time care tend to be in lower-quality care (NICHD Early Child Care Research Network, 2000b).

There is selection bias in child care. That is, parents who place their children in low-quality care tend to be less educated, more stressed, and less involved with their children. Parents who place their children in high-quality care tend to be educated, psychologically healthy, married, sensitive, authoritative, and have good verbal ability (NICHD Early Child Care Research Network, 1998a, 2006a). Thus, children in high-quality care already have preexisting advantages. Research has to sort out the effects of child care quality from these preexisting differences. Many studies try to control for selection bias, but you should keep this bias in mind whenever you read about child care.

selection bias children and parents select into or choose certain kinds of experiences based on their preexisting characteristics. This makes it difficult to determine the effect of the experience.

Age Trends in Child Care

Type, amount, and quality of child care vary by age, as do outcomes linked to child care. You have already learned that child care in the first year of life is a risk factor. How common is early child care?

Early Childhood (Birth to 5 Years)

Of the children who will ever be in child care, about a quarter enter by 5 months of age. About 50% will have entered child care by age 2 1/2. These infants and toddlers are more likely to be in part-time, rather than full-time care. They are also more likely to be in home-based care. However, when children reach age 3, they are more likely to be placed in center-based care (FIFCFS, 2009; NICHD Early Child Care Research Network, 2003a). In the year prior to kindergarten entry, 83% of children are in some kind of group arrangement, but this varies from full-time child care to preschool for just a few hours per week (Flanagan, McPhee, & Mulligan, 2010).

Middle Childhood and Adolescence (6 to 19 Years)

School is the primary source of child care after age 6. School is enough for many families because the mother only works part-time or because the father is home for out-of-school hours. However, about half of school-aged children need child care before and/or after school (FIFCFS, 2009). Only 20% of child care center slots go to school-age children (Halpern, 2000). This means many school-age children are in after-school programs or self-sibling care, which are discussed next.

After-school programs

After-school programs are diverse; they may be run by schools, churches, organizations such as Boys & Girls Club, or city recreation offices. They have different motives, such as merely keeping kids off the streets or providing academic support. In a study in Boston, Chicago, and Seattle, most after-school programs were poor in quality (Halpern, 2000). They had problems such as staff with little education and high turnover. However, some were high-quality. A high-quality program has warm, supportive staff; multiple activities for children; and opportunity for positive socializing. As many as 15% of school-age children may be in after-school programs (After School Alliance, 2009). More children are in self-sibling care.

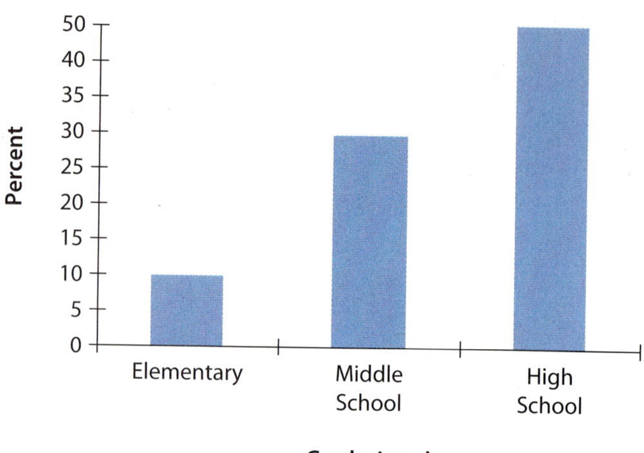

Figure 14.3 Percent of Children in Self-Sibling Care.

Self-sibling care

self-sibling care a prevalent form of nonmaternal care for school-age children, in which children are home alone or with a sibling under age 18.

Self-sibling care refers to children who are home alone or with a sibling under age 18. Self-sibling care typically occurs for two hours or less daily—just to fill in the after-school hours. At what age are children old enough to take care of themselves? In some states, it is illegal to leave children under age 13 home alone, but there is a rise in self-sibling care around 9 to 11 years of age, suggesting that some parents believe children can care for themselves and their siblings at this age.

After parental care, self-sibling care is the second most common form of care for school-age children, involving millions of children. National surveys indicate that slightly less than 10% of elementary age, 30% of middle school, and 50% of high school students are in some degree of self-care while their parents work. See Figure 14.3. Self-sibling care is more likely in suburban or rural high-SES, low-risk neighborhoods. However, *long hours* of self-care are more likely for youth living in poverty (Mahoney & Parente, 2009).

Safety is a concern with self-sibling care. Parents teach children not to talk to strangers or let them in the house when children are home alone. However, in a classic study, researchers pretended to be strangers phoning elementary students and delivering a package. All but two children readily gave their name during the phone conversation and said they were home alone—and let the stranger deliver the package (Kraizer, Witte, Fryer, & Miyoshi, 1990). *Every* parent predicted beforehand that their child would *not* do either because they had trained their child. Yet, the children were unable to carry out safety instructions when left alone. Let's turn next to what child outcomes are predicted by child care.

What Does Child Care Predict?

Did you notice in Chapter 1 that "long hours in child care" was listed as a risk factor, but "educational child care" was listed as a protective factor? Is this contradictory? Let's see.

Language and Cognitive Development

Type of care is linked to language and cognitive development. Children tend to have better language and cognitive skills in center-based care than in home-based care and in after-school programs than in self-sibling care, but only if the program has an academic emphasis and well-educated staff (Belsky, Bakermans-Kranenburg, & VanIJzendoorn, 2007; Bergin, Hudson, Chryst, & Resetar, 1992; Laurer et al., 2006; Mahoney, Lord, & Carryl, 2005).

Quality of care is also linked to language and cognitive development. Children in high-quality care and high-quality after-school programs have better language skills, greater school readiness, and higher grades and test scores than children in low-quality care (Burchinal et al., 2000; Granger, 2008; NICHD Early Child Care Research Network, 2006a). Perhaps this is because care is defined as high-quality if caregivers ask children questions, respond to vocalizations, and talk with children, which you learned in Chapter 12 are linked to children's language ability.

Attachment

Children in all societies are cared for by multiple attachment figures. Typically, attachment figures are stable and readily available. What if the primary attachment figure is not available most of the day or the caregiver changes periodically? Ainsworth said it is "hard to be a sensitively responsive mother if you're away from children ten hours a day" (Karen, 1994, p. 69). However, some psychologists believe children flexibly adjust to child care with no attachment problems. Which view does research support?

Type of child care does not appear to matter, but amount and quality of child care are linked to attachment. Children are more likely to be insecure in low-quality, unstable care and when they are in care for more than ten hours per week. However, insecure attachment occurs primarily when mothers are insensitive; *children in child care do become secure if their mothers are sensitive*. Perhaps less-sensitive mothers cannot buffer their children from the stress of child care or need more time to establish secure attachment. In addition, when secure toddlers enter child care, they may become insecure, particularly if their mother does not sensitively help them adjust (Ahnert, Gunnar, Lamb, & Barthel, 2004; Erel, Obermran, & Yirmiya, 2000; NICHD Early Child Care Research Network, 2000b).

Child care may be linked to insecure attachment for three reasons:

1. Many toddlers plead not to be left at child care, yet the mother leaves anyway. This may feel like rejection.
2. Mothers tend to be more responsive than caregivers; mothers soothe, stay near, communicate with, and share emotions more with their children. Mothers are more responsive than caregivers even in countries, like Germany, where child care is higher quality than in the United States (Ahnert, Rickert, & Lamb, 2000).
3. Mothers may fail to develop sensitivity. Long daily separations can interfere with mothers' development of mothering skills (Furman, 1989). Mothers who work full-time in the child's first year tend to be less sensitive (Brooks-Gunn et al., 2002; NICHD Early Child Care Research Network, 1997).

Stress

Bowlby believed that infants separated from their mother would feel stress no matter how well they were cared for. Research confirms that young children in child care have high levels of cortisol, a stress hormone (see Chapter 8). Typically, children's cortisol levels peak around wake-up and then decline slowly over the day, to reach a low at

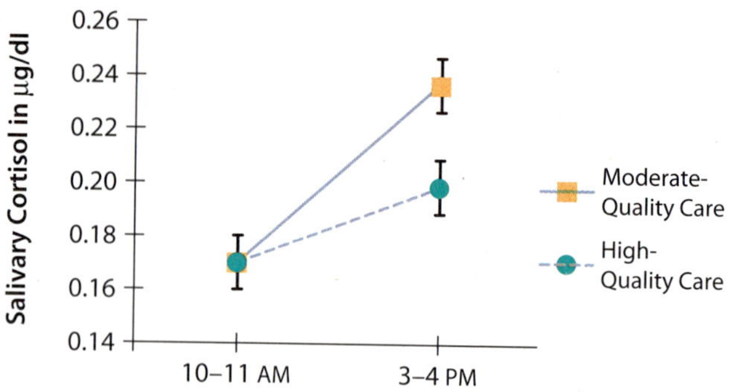

Figure 14.4 Cortisol Levels in Child Care.
Children in high-quality care have a smaller daytime rise in cortisol than children in moderate-quality care. Cortisol levels indicate stress. Children who are not in child care have a decrease, rather than rise, in cortisol over the day (Gunnar, 2000). *Source: Tout, de Haan, Kipp-Campbell, & Gunnar (1998).*

bedtime. But for children in full-day, center-based care, cortisol levels *rise* over the day—even in high-quality care (Watamura, Donzella, Alwin, & Gunnar, 2003). See Figure 14.4. In addition, cortisol levels are higher when children have a conflicted relationship with their teacher and they are in larger groups (Lisonbee, Mize, Payne, & Granger, 2008; Rappolt-Schlictmann et al., 2009). Children who live in poverty may be an exception; their cortisol levels may be lower in child care than at home (Rappolt-Schlictmann et al., 2009).

Does stress diminish after children get used to child care? Even after several months, child care remains stressful (Ahnert et al., 2004). Cortisol level is linked to being in child care as early as infancy; the link is strongest during toddlerhood, declines at 3 to 5 years, and disappears after age 7 (Watamura et al., 2003). Thus, older children feel less stress while at child care than younger children.

What does this mean for children? Scientists have found that youth who were in child care as infants and toddlers may continue to have abnormal cortisol levels at age 15 (Roisman et al., 2009). Recall from Chapter 8 that cortisol levels affect executive functioning and working memory capacity (Blair, Granger, & Razza, 2005). Furthermore, abnormal cortisol levels are linked to anxious and withdrawn behavior and aggression among children in child care, our next topic (Tout, de Haan, Campbell, & Gunnar, 1998).

Social Competence

Do young children in center-based care become more socially competent because they have opportunity to play with peers? A large, national study found the opposite. After age 3, and perhaps as early as age 2, children in child care tend to have more behavior problems such as teacher–student conflict, hyperactivity, aggression, impulsivity, and attention deficits; they tend to have less ability to work independently, use time wisely, or complete work promptly (NICHD Early Child Care Research Network, 2006a). Both center-based and nonrelative care were linked to more behavior problems in young children.

Amount of care is linked to behavior problems. Young children in full-time care tend to have more behavior problems than children in child care less than ten hours per week. Long hours in child care early in life continue to be linked to behavior problems through 6th grade (Belsky et al., 2007). Children tend to develop behavior problems even in high-quality care or after-school programs, but the effect is smaller (Howes & James, 2002; McCartney et al., 2010). The effect is also smaller when the child care occurs in smaller groups of less than four for 2-year-olds and less than eight for 4-year-olds.

Do older youth in self-sibling care become more responsible and self-reliant? Research suggests self-sibling care is linked to anxiety and behavior problems (Mahoney & Parente, 2009). Adolescents in self-sibling care are more likely to commit crime, use drugs, be sexually active, and have STDs. Adolescent crime peaks at 3 to 4 p.m., just after school, during parents' typical working hours. Just as with younger children, the effects depend on the amount of self-sibling care. Risk is greater when youth spend more than ten hours per week in self-care, and if self-care starts early in elementary school and continues for years (Mahoney & Parente, 2009). Adolescent sexual activity increases proportional to the amount of time spent alone after school, and is higher in the summer when youth are in self-care eight to ten hours per day (Cohen, Farley, Taylor, Martin, & Schuster, 2002). Thus, extended self-sibling care is a risk factor for delinquency. Effects are smaller when parents are authoritative (rather than permissive), monitor the child, and live in a safe neighborhood and when the child does not have preexisting behavior problems (Mahoney & Parente, 2009).

Field Observation

Ask a few adults what they believe are the effects of child care and why. What are the biggest issues for them? Compare their responses with the research. Did they miss any issues that scientists have investigated?

Play

Type and quality of care are linked to play. Children in high-quality care are more likely to play in advanced ways than children in low-quality care (Raspa, McWilliam, & Maher-Ridley, 2001). Children in center-based care with peers are more likely to play in advanced ways than children in home-based care (NICHD Early Child Care Research Network, 2001a). This is important because advanced play promotes social, cognitive, and language skills (see Chapter 11). Children in child care may have a play advantage over home-reared preschoolers at kindergarten entry, but home-reared preschoolers readily catch up once they have abundant classmates (NICHD Early Child Care Research Network, 2005a).

In summary, whether child care is a risk or protective factor depends on the type, amount, and quality of child care and whether you consider cognitive, emotional, or social outcomes. Table 14.1 provides a framework for organizing these factors. What can be done to mitigate the risk linked to child care? You have probably noticed a recurring theme in this research; children fare better when child care is high quality than low quality and when they spend less time in child care. Other conditions also mitigate the risk, such as stable staff, smaller groups, and better teacher–student relationships. Here are three important additional points:

1. Negative outcomes are strongest when child care begins during infancy.
2. Effects of early child care can be long term. Child care during infancy and the preschool years has been linked to behavior and academic problems through elementary school and into high school (Campbell, Lamb, & Hwant, 2000; NICHD Early Child Care Research Network, 2003a, 2005a, 2005b, 2006a).
3. Effects depend on socioeconomic status; child care can be a protective factor for low-SES children. We will discuss this more later.

Table 14.1 Summary of research on child care

Child Outcomes	Child Care Attributes		
	Quality	**Amount**	**Type**
Language and Cognitive Ability	High-quality care is linked to better abilities than low-quality. Effect is strongest for low-SES children.		Center care after age 3 is linked to better abilities than home-based child care. Extracurricular activities and high-quality after-school programs are linked to better abilities at school age. Effect is strongest for low-SES children.
Attachment	Low-quality and unstable care are linked to insecure attachment, especially if mother is less sensitive.	More than ten hours per week is linked to insecure attachment, especially if mother is less sensitive.	There is no effect of type of care, assuming comparable quality. Home care may be higher quality for infants.
Stress	Cortisol levels are high even in high-quality care.		Cortisol levels are higher in larger-group care
Behavior problems	Low-quality care is linked to more problems. Children in high-quality care have better social skills than children in low-quality care.	More than ten hours per week is linked to poor social skills and more behavior problems, especially if care began in infancy.	Center-based care is linked to behavior problems. Self-sibling care is linked to antisocial behavior if it is more than ten hours per week.
Play	Children in high-quality care have more-complex peer play than children in low-quality care.		Children in center-based care have more-complex peer play than children in home-based child care.

Does Parenting or Child Care Have a Larger Effect?

You might assume that parenting matters more than child care. To test this, scientists compare the effect size for quality of parenting with the effect size for quality of child care. What does the research show? For *language and cognitive abilities,* parenting quality may be more powerful than child care—the effect size of quality of child care is only about 20 to 75% the size of parenting. In contrast, for *behavior problems,* parenting quality may be less powerful than child care—the effect size of quality of child care is more than twice the size of parenting. Thus, child care makes a modest-to-large contribution to behavior problems and a small-to-modest contribution to language and cognitive abilities compared to parenting (NICHD Early Child Care Research Network, 2006a; Peisner-Feinberg et al., 2001).

Child care may reduce the effect of parenting. That is, parenting quality more strongly predicts outcomes for children in less child care than those in more child care (Adi-Japha & Klein, 2009; Howes, 1990; NICHD Early Child Care Research Network, 1998b). Whether this shift of influence from parent to child care is positive or negative depends on the quality of the home. On the negative side, children do not benefit as much from having two parents or sensitive, authoritative parents if they are in full-time child care. On the positive side, child care helps children from challenging homes. In fact, government programs designed to improve achievement for low-SES children often promote child care. The reason for this will become apparent in the next section.

Group Diversity in Child Care

The effects of maternal employment and child care may be different for boys and girls and for children from different SES and cultural backgrounds. Let's discuss these differences next.

Gender

Most studies find that maternal employment predicts similar outcomes for boys and girls, but when gender differences are found, they favor girls (Goldberg et al., 2008). For example, some studies find daughters of employed mothers tend to have higher aspirations, while sons tend to have lower achievement (Brooks-Gunn et al., 2002; Smolensky & Gootman, 2003).

Child care seems to be a greater risk factor for boys (Bornstein, Hahn, Gist, & Haynes, 2006). Insecure attachment and behavior problems are more strongly linked to child care for boys. On the other hand, high-quality care may be *more protective* for low-SES boys than girls (Votruba-Drzal, Coley, & Chase-Lansdale, 2004). Scientists don't know why boys may be more vulnerable than girls to their child care experience, whether positive or negative. One exception to this pattern is that adolescent girls may be at greater risk of delinquency in self-sibling care than boys (Mahoney & Parente, 2009).

Think About This A mother moved to a state with free pre-kindergarten. Her second child is turning 4. She has planned to keep the child home until kindergarten. The mother is an architect who quit to be a full-time mother. Her husband is a graduate student. Family income is very low. The mother asks you whether she should place the child in the pre-K program. Based on research, what would you advise? What additional information would you want to have, and why?

Socioeconomic Status

Socioeconomic status is linked to child care in two ways. First, child care tends to be economically segregated. Children of the lowest- and highest-income families are more likely to be in high-quality care. This is because poor families qualify for government-supported care and high-income families can pay for high-quality care and enriching after-school activities. Families in between tend to be unable to afford high-quality care (NICHD Early Child Care Research Network, 2006a; Smolensky & Gootman, 2003).

Second, child care is more beneficial to low-SES than high-SES children. Low-SES children in high-quality, center-based care tend to have better language ability, school readiness, and academic achievement than low-SES home-reared children (Loeb, Fuller, Kagan, & Carrol, 2004; NICHD Early Child Care Research Network & Duncan, 2003). That is, children from homes with little parental education, few books, little library use, high rates of TV watching, and low rates of reading benefit from being in child care, whereas children with well-educated mothers may not (Bornstein et al., 2006; Cote, Borge, Geoffroy, Rutter, & Tremblay, 2008; Peisner-Feinberg et al., 2001). Thus, Cassie is more likely to benefit from attending child care than Jenna. Jenna has the undivided attention of her teacher-mother, an advantage even high-quality child care cannot compete with.

Many school-readiness programs offer child care as an intervention for children who are at risk due to poverty or low birth weight. Low-SES children who spend more time in high-quality child care before age 4 1/2 have higher math and reading scores in 3rd and 5th grade than children in low-quality child care—and may score almost as well as higher-SES classmates (Dearing, McCartney, & Taylor, 2009).

Cross-National Comparisons

In the United States, child care is often provided by unqualified caregivers with minimal education. In countries where child care providers have higher education, and where care is subsidized by government, effects of child care tend to be more positive. For example, in Sweden, toddlers in high-quality care tend to have better language and math skills than home-reared toddlers (Broberg, Wessels, Lamb, & Hwang, 1997). Research in Australia finds that children in high-quality care do not have attachment or behavior problems; still, long hours of care are linked to distractible, off-task behavior in school (Love et al., 2003). On the other hand, in countries with lower standards, such as Israel, effects of child care tend to be more negative than in the United States (Love et al., 2003; Scharf, 2001).

Classroom Implications of Maternal Employment and Child Care

Maternal employment and child care can have positive and negative effects in your classroom. Low-SES students who have been in high-quality care may have better language and cognitive skills. However, they may also have more teacher–student conflict and behavior problems. Child care during infancy has been linked to these outcomes through high school. The more students in a classroom who have been in child care, the more aggression for the whole classroom, because home-reared students are influenced by classmates who have been in child care (Dmitrieva, Steinberg, & Belsky, 2007). Most effects of child care are small in size, but the effect on behavior problems is large. This could alter how much time you spend on discipline. Even small effects are important when many students are involved. As a teacher, if your students are benefiting from high-quality child care, build on their strengths. If they are experiencing academic and behavior problems linked to child care, mitigate these problems by following the guidelines outlined in Chapters 6 through 10.

Maternal employment can also influence parents' involvement in your classroom. Mothers who work part-time tend to be more involved in their children's school than mothers who work full-time or not at all. Part-time working mothers may be more likely to talk about school, check homework, restrict TV, promote after-school lessons, be involved in PTA or booster club, and serve as volunteers at school (Muller, 1995). You can help your students by following these guidelines:

- Help working parents stay involved in their children's education with creative, flexible solutions. You might suggest that grandparents meet with teachers, or that parents take the child to the workplace where they can supervise homework, or take "lunch hour" in the late afternoon to check on their children after school (Weiss et al., 2003).
- Advocate for policies that promote part-time work for mothers who desire it and maternal leave during infancy. A creative group of teachers in California did this for themselves; they arranged to have two teachers share one teaching position so that each worked half-time and could be with their children more.
- Advocate for higher-quality child care. This is important for school-age as well as early children care.

If you are a teacher in a child care program, the quality of relationship you have with children may be more important than the quality of instructional practices you use. Teacher–student relationships predict both social and academic competence, but instructional practices predict only academic competence for preschoolers (NICHD Early Child Care Research Network, 2000a; Peisner-Feinberg et al., 2001). Emotionally positive interaction and secure attachment to teachers are particularly important in center-based care. Perhaps this is because students with secure attachment to a teacher are more likely to play maturely with peers, which promotes their development.

How common is secure attachment with child care providers? Generally, fewer children develop secure attachments to caregivers than to parents. Many studies across varied cultures show that about 40% of children are securely attached to their caregivers, while about 60% are securely attached to a parent (Ahnert, Pinquart, & Lamb, 2006). Yet, children who are insecure with both parents can become secure with a caregiver. In the earlier vignette, Eleanor is more attached to her nanny than to her parents, sharing successes more eagerly with the nanny and seeking her out when tired or sick.

What influences whether a secure relationship develops? In Chapter 6, you learned that sensitive, responsive teachers develop secure relationships with children. In addition, the structure of child care can make a difference. Children are more likely to develop attachment to a caregiver if they stay with the same person throughout their preschool years and if they are in home-based rather than center-based care (Ahnert et al., 2006). Perhaps this is because caregivers converse and play with children more when they have fewer to care for and when they care for children longer (Elicker, Fortner-Wood, & Noppe, 1999).

In summary, the effects of child care depend on the type, amount, and quality of care, as well as children's gender and SES. High-quality care can promote cognitive abilities in low-SES children, but low-quality care can lead to aggression. Effects are small, but consequences for society could be large because so many children are involved. Prominent psychologists have called for improved child care quality and for policies that allow more parents to stay home or work part-time (Greenspan, 2003; Maccoby & Lewis, 2003). The panel of scientists conducting the largest national child care study concluded, "[O]ur results provide support for policies that reduce the amount of time children spend in child care" (NICHD Early Child Care Research Network, 2006a, p. 114). Let's turn next to media exposure, another powerful context of childhood.

Television and Other Media

Collin, the resilient 7th-grader you met earlier, has a Wii and a computer, which he plays for an hour a day (a limit set by his parents). He has only sports, fitness, and "tame" electronic games like Mario Brothers. He has no cell phone or iPod and does not watch TV on school days.

His classmate, Ricky, takes his iPod to school even though it is against the rules. The songs on his iPod contain profane lyrics about murder, domestic violence, rape, drugs, and sex. He says his favorite song is "The one where he strangles his wife, then throws her in the trunk and drives her into a lake." At home he routinely plays videogames like Mortal Kombat, and watches unlimited TV.

Most students, like Ricky and Collin, are exposed to a variety of media. Although students use newer technologies, TV still dominates their media use. Television entered U.S. homes in the 1950s and flooded the market by 1960. Today, 98% of homes have at least one TV. Most families also have a DVD player, videogames, and a computer. Half of U.S. teenagers go online daily (Lenhart, Madden, & Hitlin, 2005).

Do other students use as much violent media as Ricky, or are they more like Collin? Ricky's classmates say he is mean. He doesn't have any friends at school. He sits by himself on the bus and makes fun of others. Would Ricky be equally rejected if he used less violent media? These questions reflect two concerns about media use—time and content. Let's look at these concerns.

Field Observation

Watch two hours of a popular TV show during prime family-viewing time. Count the incidents of violence, sexual behavior, or innuendo. If children are also watching, describe their reaction to this content.

The Issue of Time

Preschoolers spend more time on entertainment media than on reading, being read to, and playing outside combined (Anderson et al., 2003). Five- to 18-year-olds spend an average of fifteen hours per week watching TV—more than is spent on homework, chores, or organized after-school activities (Mahoney, Harris, & Eccles, 2006; McHale, Crouter, & Tucker, 2001). When you add other media—cell phones, iPods, computers—youth consume an average of seven-and-a-half hours of media per day (Roberts, Foehr, & Rideout, 2005).

The Issue of Content

Some TV and computer programs are educational or prosocial. Shows like *Sesame Street*, *Cyberchase*, and *Zoboomafoo* are designed to build academic skills. Shows like *Arthur*, *Sagwa*, and *Clifford* are designed to teach social skills, like conflict resolution and kindness to others. Unfortunately, children spend substantially more time with antisocial media.

Antisocial media contains violence. The average child watches tens of thousands of violent acts on TV (Anderson et al., 2003). The violence is often depicted as glamorous or without traumatic consequences. Aggressors are often heroes with no remorse who go unpunished, and victims often miraculously recover. Videogames are even more violent than TV. Some people argue that violent media simply mirror society. This is a myth. Your students will seldom personally witness a murder, even in violent neighborhoods, but they will watch thousands in media. One movie critic estimated that if the level of violence on TV were realistic, within fifty days every U.S. citizen would have been murdered, and the last one could turn off the TV (Medved, 1995).

Antisocial media contains sexual content. About 84% of sitcoms have sexual content (Lorch, 2007). TV shows average five sex-related scenes per hour, including shows watched by children during prime time. Sexual content on TV has increased tenfold since the 1970s, and nearly doubled just since 1998 (Kunkel, Eyal, Finnerty, Biely, & Donnerstein, 2005). The average student may be exposed to 10,000 to 15,000 media references to sex each year. Women are often portrayed as sex objects. Sex is portrayed as superficial and risk free. It is portrayed outside marriage, and without emotional or physical consequences such as STIs or pregnancy (Ward, 2003).

Age Trends in Media Use

How much and which media children use changes with age. Across cultures, TV viewing increases into childhood, peaks around age 13, and then declines (Huston, Bickham, Lee, & Wright, 2007). Videogaming also peaks at ages 12 and13 (Gentile, 2009).

Early Childhood (Birth to 5 Years)

Young children tend to watch a lot of TV. About 40% live in homes where the TV is on most of the day as "background." On average, toddlers watch about two hours per day, and 3-year-olds watch about four hours per day (Courage & Setliff, 2009; Huston et al., 2007). They mostly watch shows designed for adults. However, young children are more likely to watch child-oriented educational or prosocial TV and play educational videogames than are older youth (Wartella, Caplovitz, & Lee, 2004).

Some shows such as *Teletubbies* are specifically designed for children under age 2. Do they even understand TV at this age? Infants can learn from the emotions of TV actors through social referencing. For example, if infants watch a video showing an adult acting frightened of a benign object, like a hose adapter, they will later get upset when they see the object and avoid touching it (Mummer & Fernald, 2003). However, they do not respond to video as readily as live interaction. For example, if a videotaped adult tells 2-year-olds that she hid a Piglet doll under the couch, they will not go look for Piglet. If the adult tells them face-to-face, they will find Piglet (Troseth, Saylor, & Archer, 2006). In response to this research, programs for young children try to mimic live interaction—with the actor looking directly into the camera, posing questions, and pausing for responses—as is done in *Blues Clues.*

Middle Childhood (6 to 12 Years)

Media use increases during elementary school and may peak among so-called tweens, or children ages 11 to 14 (Roberts et al., 2005). At this age, youth use a variety of media such as iPods/MP3 players, cell phones, the Internet, and videogames. In addition, TV viewing peaks during elementary school. They watch less educational and more entertainment TV than preschoolers (Huston et al., 2007). Entertainment TV tends to be violent. Elementary students are more aggressive after watching violent media compared to adolescents (Anderson et al., 2003).

Monkey Business Images, 2C10 Used under license from Shutterstock.com
Tweens use a variety of media for an average of several hours per day.

Adolescence (13 to 19 Years)

Adolescents spend an average of one to two-and-a-half hours per day watching TV (Larson, 2001). They spend as many hours *per week* watching TV as they do *per month* reading books not assigned in school. Still, they spend less time watching TV than younger children. Some TV time is replaced with computer use such as social networking (e.g., Facebook), YouTube, movie previews, or other uses. They are more likely to have Internet access at home than are younger children. Many 6th-graders (60%) use the Internet, but 94% of high school students do. Thus, computer use climbs with age, peaking in high school when youth average one to two hours per day on the Internet (Rosen, Cheever, & Carrier, 2008; Willoughby, 2008). These trends occur across industrialized nations (Valkenburg & Peter, 2007). Thus, if you teach high school, your students are likely to use the computer more than you do, but not if you teach early childhood or elementary school.

Individual Diversity in Media Use

These age trends mask huge individual differences, like Collin compared with Ricky. More than one-third of high school students play videogames less than one hour per week and others play twenty hours per week (Gentile, Lynch, Linder, & Walsh, 2004). About 11% of high school students seldom watch TV while 40% watch three or more hours per school day (Grunbaum et al., 2002). Children tend to maintain the viewing habits they start as toddlers—that is, heavy viewers remain heavy viewers (Huston et al., 2007).

What Do Differences in Media Use Predict?

How much media children use and the content of those media are linked to all domains of the child—physical, cognitive, emotional, and social. For example, the American Psychological Association (2007) concluded that the rampant sexualization of girls in the media is linked to impaired cognitive functioning, increased depression, eating disorders, and unhealthy sexual development. Let's look more closely at outcomes linked to media next.

Physical development

Media use can undermine physical well-being in four ways:

1. Media use replaces physical activity. Heavy media users tend to be overweight (pun unintended), particularly girls (Lorch, 2007). Do "exergaming" videogames help? Not really, although they may be better than no exercise at all (Daley, 2009).
2. Media use promotes bad eating habits. TV ads sell high-calorie foods, youth eat more high-calorie foods while watching TV, and metabolism during TV watching is lower than during sleep (Kaiser Family Foundation, 2004).
3. Media use disrupts sleep. Many youth use TV, movies on electronic devices, or music to help them drift off to sleep, but this is linked to sleeping fewer hours and feeling more tired (Eggermont & Van den Buick, 2006).
4. Media use glamorizes drug use, portraying smoking and alcohol use as normal, humorous, and risk free. Mel Gibson alone has 21 episodes of smoking in movies that have been watched 90 million times by U.S. teens. Heavy viewers use more alcohol and tobacco, even if they do not have other risk factors for drug use (Heatherton & Sargent, 2009; Lorch, 2007).

On the positive side, videogame players tend to develop good hand-eye coordination, better visual processing, and enhanced mental rotation skills (Dye, Green, & Bavelier, 2009). In experiments where nongamers practice playing action videogames, their visual processing improves (Green & Bavelier, 2007). Perhaps in the future, videogames will be used to improve visual processing in old age—hopefully before you get there!

Cognitive development

Media use may undermine cognitive ability. Amanda's mother told her teacher, *"Amanda don't read no newspapers. She get her news from the TV, and that's a good thing 'cause I pay 65 dollar a month for cable!"* Heavy TV viewers, like Amanda, read less and talk less with their parents. They have lower verbal and reading ability, lower grades, and spend less time studying. These effects occur from preschool through high school (Ennemoser & Schneider, 2007; Fuligni & Stevenson, 1995; Wright et al., 2001). A little TV watching is not a risk factor; less than two hours per day at age 9 and a half-hour per day at age 17 are not linked to low achievement. Every hour beyond these amounts has been linked to substantial drops in test scores (Razel, 2001).

On the positive side, students who use *educational* media read more and have better reading, math, and vocabulary test scores than those who use *entertainment* media (Schmidt & Anderson, 2007). Watching *Sesame Street* and using educational videogames helps low-SES 3-year-olds develop school-readiness skills (Huston et al., 2007; Li & Atkins, 2004). In one study, low-SES students were given a home computer with free Internet, and they developed better reading ability and grades (Jackson et al., 2006).

Think About This The American Academy of Pediatrics stated that at no age should children spend more than two hours a day in front of any screen, and under age 2, they should watch no TV. Their concern centers on the brain. Explain why they might have this concern based on brain and ADHD research from Chapters 2 and 4.

These positive effects of educational media are strongest for preschoolers. They are less consistent for older students (Ennemoser & Schneider, 2007; Schmidt & Anderson, 2007). The positive effects may be long term. Students who watch educational TV as preschoolers tend to become adolescents who earn high grades, read leisure books, take hard classes, and participate in extracurricular activities (Anderson, Huston, Schmitt, Linebarger, & Wright, 2001; Fisch & Truglio, 2001).

Does this mean "more is better" for educational media? Even educational programs could lead to short attention span, limited imagination, and passive children. Television is fast paced with many interruptions. Some research suggests the more TV toddlers watch, the more likely they will have ADHD-like problems later; however, this line of research is still developing (Christakis, Zimmerman, DiGiuseppe, & McCarty, 2004; Courage & Setliff, 2009).

Computer use is different from watching TV or videogaming. Computer use is linked to higher achievement, but only up to a point. Among adolescents, both little use and excessive use are linked to lower grades, but moderate use (perhaps one to two hours per day) is linked to higher grades (Willoughby, 2008).

Emotional development

Media violence desensitizes children so that they respond less to others' distress and are more tolerant of aggression (Bushman & Anderson, 2009). We got our first TV when our daughter was a toddler. The first few times that actors fought and shot guns, she raced up the stairs as fast as her short legs would go, clambered into the dry bathtub, and cowered behind the shower curtain until we coaxed her out (trying not to laugh). Now, two decades of TV later, she can watch highly violent shows with little arousal. She is desensitized, just as you probably are.

Media violence is also linked to anxiety and fear. Heavy users develop a "mean world" belief that the world is violent and that they are more likely to be victims than is really the case. Media violence activates areas of the brain that process emotions (Murray, 2007). As children repeatedly experience fear while using media, a rapid fear response becomes ingrained in their brains (see Chapter 2). Of course, prosocial media might have the opposite effect, ingraining feelings of well-being.

Scott Dunlap/iStockphoto

Computer use tends to foster social interaction, rather than isolate children.

Social development

Does adolescents' computer use replace live interaction, causing isolated, lonely children? Quite the opposite—much of adolescents' online time is used to connect with friends that they see during the day, making friendships closer. However, these social benefits may not apply to solitary use, or chatting with strangers, or excessive use—that is, more than two hours daily (Rosen et al., 2008; Valkenburg & Peter, 2009). Computers and texting have not replaced phone calls; teens still prefer to talk with their friends (Lenhart et al., 2005).

Prosocial behavior

One of our students had a difficult childhood with an absent father and a drug-addicted mother who was often incarcerated and disappeared for days at a time with boyfriends. Today, he is a tender father and husband, which he credits to watching *Father Knows Best* in childhood. He set a goal that when he grew up, he would imitate the father in the show, rather than his mother. Research supports his life story. Children who watch prosocial TV and play prosocial videogames (yes, they do exist) are more likely to share, help, and comfort others than other children (Gentile et al., 2009; Rosenkoetter, 1999). This effect is not just correlational. In experimental studies, participants are randomly assigned to play either a prosocial, neutral, or antisocial videogame. Those who play prosocial games are more likely to help others following the game (Greitemeyer & Osswald, 2010).

Aggression

Unfortunately, much of the media children are exposed to is antisocial. The Surgeon General of the United States issued a report that violent media lead to aggression in children (Anderson et al., 2003; Wartella et al., 2004). Key points of the report are:

1. A variety of types of studies—experimental, laboratory, and correlational—demonstrate that watching violent TV increases children's aggression and acceptance of violence. For example, when young children watch a violent film before playing together, they are more likely to be aggressive during play.
2. Similar effects of violence are found for viewing videos, listening to songs, and playing videogames. Some, but not all, studies find that videogames are more harmful than TV because gamers actually pull the trigger to shoot others and are rewarded for it.
3. Most children are affected by TV violence to at least a small degree, but some vulnerable children are affected to a large degree. Similar effects are found across countries such as Holland, Finland, Germany, Japan, England, the United States, and Canada. Thus, violent media is a compelling risk factor for aggression.

Sexual attitudes

Youth report feeling pressure from TV and music to be sexually active. Many report that their attitudes about sex come from media. Children who use more media tend to have callous attitudes toward sex and believe that everyone is doing it. They are also more likely to be promiscuous (Lorch, 2007; Polacek, Rojas, Levitt, & Mika, 2006; Ward, 2003). Today youth have easy access to pornography on the Internet. About 34% of teens stumble across unwanted pornography (Wolak, Mitchell, & Finkelhor, 2007). The effects of this exposure are not yet known. However, youth who repeatedly *seek* pornography develop reduced concern about rape and child abuse, cynical attitudes about love, less hope for monogamy, a disconnect between love and sex, and a view of marriage as sexually confining (Zillmann, 2001). Children are less likely to experience Internet pornography if they have authoritative parents and computers are kept in family areas (Wolak et al., 2007).

In summary, both media content and amount of use are linked to children's physical, cognitive, emotional, and social well-being. Nevertheless, some psychologists claim that violent media are simply entertainment, neither helping nor harming children (Ferguson, 2007). They argue that the scientific evidence discussed herein is not compelling because (1) effect sizes are small and (2) most of the research is correlational.

Thinking Like a Scientist

These same criticisms apply to most research on child development. In Chapter 1, you learned that today's teachers are expected to be skilled at interpreting research. Let's take a few minutes to hone your scientific skills by examining these criticisms.

Effect sizes

Not every child who uses violent media will behave aggressively. Just as with child care, the effect of violent media on aggression (0.16 to 0.32) is small-to-moderate in size (Anderson et al., 2003; Wartella et al., 2004). In Chapter 1, you learned that no single risk factor is likely to have a large effect because so many factors affect children. An effect size of 0.30 for any single factor may be as high as you will see for complex behavior that has multiple causes, which scientists call the "0.30 barrier." The same is true in medical sciences as well (Meyer et al., 2001).

So why pay attention to small effects? Small effects can have practical significance; over large populations they can alter society. Furthermore, although violent media have a small effect on most children, they have a large effect on vulnerable children. If just 25% of U.S. children are affected by violent media, then more than 10 million would be more violent. To put media effects in perspective, research suggests TV violence has a stronger effect on children's aggression than low IQ, divorce, child abuse, or antisocial friends (Bushman & Anderson, 2007). The effect size is larger than the effect for smoking or asbestos exposure on cancer. The government has taken action on these other issues, but has not protected children from violent media.

Correlational versus experimental research

In Chapter 1, you learned that only carefully controlled, randomized experiments can convincingly demonstrate that violent media *causes* aggression. Most parents object to scientists randomly assigning their children to use violent media for years to see if it makes them aggressive. So scientists resort to short-term, artificial experiments. For example, children are randomly assigned to watch a violent or a nonviolent film, then given the opportunity to play with peers, and their aggressive acts like shoving or name-calling are counted. Such studies cannot tell you whether a steady diet of violent media causes long-term aggression in real life. Correlational studies, on the other hand, can tell you whether TV viewing is linked to children's real-life aggression, but they cannot demonstrate causation. Children who are already aggressive may choose to watch more violent TV. Which causes which? Longitudinal research shows that current TV watching is correlated with aggression years later, but the reverse is not true—current aggression is not correlated with TV watching years later. This helps make a case for causation.

Think About This Laws have been proposed to restrict selling violent or sexually explicit videogames to minors. Some courts have ruled that protecting First Amendment rights of producers is more important than protecting children and that there is no causal connection between media use and children's antisocial behavior. If you prepared a brief for the court, how would you argue this issue? Is there a parallel with protecting children from purchasing alcohol? Should educational or prosocial TV be mandated?

Each form of research has shortcomings, but when many studies using different approaches all converge on the same conclusion, you can have some confidence in that conclusion. You can have further confidence when the conclusion is supported by evidence-based theories, such as social cognitive theory (see Chapter 13). This is the case for research on media and aggression.

What Predicts Individual Differences in Media Use?

Javall's mother has three rules for TV: No more than one hour a day, no TV in the summer, and TV is off at 8:30 pm for bedtime. Javall is popular in his 4th-grade classroom. He is a good sport, is kind, is already a track star, and is an avid reader of novels and Boys' Life *magazine.*

Javall's mother's rules about TV are part of her authoritative parenting style. How much and what media children use depends on parents. Children usually watch what their parents watch. Parents set limits, model media use, and provide alternative activities. If parents encourage playing, reading, or extracurricular activities, their children have less time for TV. If parents limit TV or videogaming, children tend to be less aggressive, like Javall (Gentile et al., 2004). As Javall becomes a teenager, he is less likely to use the Internet in risky ways, such as disclosing personal information on websites, if his mother remains authoritative (Rosen et al., 2008). Parents' authoritativeness and monitoring of media use depend on contexts described earlier: family structure and child care. Let's look at other group differences in media use.

Group Diversity in Media Use

Across the United States, Europe, and Asia, young children may watch similar amounts of TV (Larson & Verma, 1999). Yet, within countries there are gender, SES, and ethnic differences in TV and other media use.

Gender

Research does not always find gender differences in the amount of TV watching in the United States, but when differences are found, boys watch more TV than girls (Grunbaum et al., 2002; Huston et al., 2007). On the other hand, girls are more likely to use the Internet. As early as 6th grade, more girls are online than boys (Gross, 2004; Lenhart et al., 2005).

Boys and girls tend to use computers for somewhat different purposes. More boys than girls use a computer for games (Willoughby, 2008). Videogames tend to be dominated by sports, racing, and violence, which appeal more to boys. As many as 12% of boys ages 8 to 18 are heavy users who feel addicted to videogames, but only 3% of girls are heavy users (Gentile, 2009). More girls use a computer for word processing, communication (social networking or e-mail), and seeking information for school assignments. However, both boys' and girls' primary Internet activity is communicating with friends (Gross, 2004; Valkenburg & Peter, 2007). Their second most common Internet activity is downloading music. They typically multitask—while they look for information for homework, they might also be downloading music and communicating with friends.

Socioeconomic Status

Low-SES students watch more TV and play more videogames, whereas students with well-educated mothers and moderate-to-high income spend more time in sports, hobbies, and reading (see Figure 14.5). Low-SES students are more likely to watch violent TV than educational TV, have a TV in their bedroom, and own a videogame system (Barr-Anderson, van den Berg, Neumark-Sztainer, & Story, 2008; Ennemoser & Schneider, 2007; Willoughby, 2008). SES differences are not large in early childhood, but appear by middle childhood, and are quite large by adolescence (Larson, 2001; McHale et al., 2001). However, most students use substantial amounts of media regardless of SES, and there is great variation within SES. Some low-SES children, like Javall, watch very little TV.

Educators have been concerned about the *digital divide*, meaning that high-SES students are more likely to have access to technology, like the Internet, at home, which enhances their cultural capital. However, the Internet has flooded the market much in the way TV did, so the divide has narrowed. By 2004, 87% of U.S. adolescents had Internet access at home (Lenhart et al., 2005). Students who are not wired are more likely to be African American, have a single mother, and have low household income. They have Internet access at school or the public library, but are not likely to use it. Also, just as with cars, low-SES families have computers and Internet access that are slower and more prone to problems. You will need to be aware of your students' resources when you make Internet-based assignments.

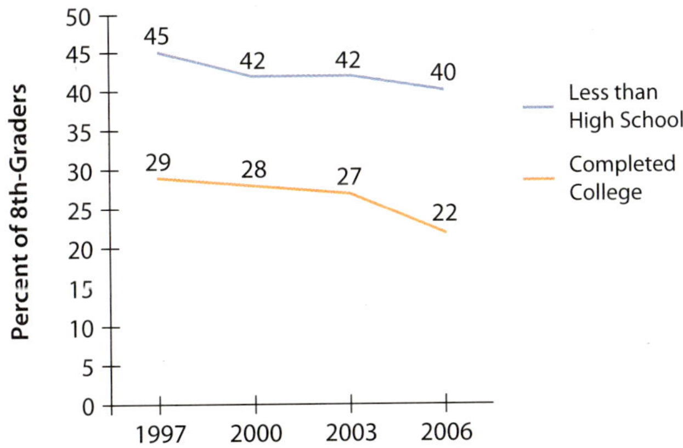

Figure 14.5 Amount of TV Watching by Parent Education Level.
Percent of 8th-graders who watch four or more hours of TV on school days for two levels of parent education. How would you describe the data here? *Source: Child Trends DataBank.*

Ethnicity

Large, national studies have found that African American and Latino children, particularly adolescents, spend more time watching TV and playing videogames than do Asian or White children (Mahoney et al., 2006; Roberts et al., 2005). These effects hold even when SES is controlled (Huston et al., 2007).

TV can promote racism by portraying certain groups in stereotyped ways that influence children's ideas of their own and other ethnic groups. TV often portrays tired or offensive stereotypes like "buxom Black mama," "Mexican bandit," "helpless female," or "inscrutable Asian." There have been significant improvements in the portrayal of some ethnic groups, but there are still problems. For example, middle-class Latinos are rarely depicted on TV, although Latinos are a growing minority in the United States and are significant consumers of TV (Berry, 2007).

Classroom Implications of Media Use

Media use is linked to students' behavior at school. Students with limited media use, like Javall and Collin, are likely to behave well in your classroom. In contrast, students who use violent media, like Ricky, are likely to argue with their teachers, get in physical fights, and earn lower grades (Gentile et al., 2004). Let's look next at how you can mitigate these effects.

Reducing the Negative Effects of Media

Researchers have developed classroom interventions that reduce the negative effects of media. For example, in a clever experiment, 3rd-graders who watched violent TV were randomly assigned to an intervention or control group (Huesmann, Eron, Klein, Brice, & Fischer, 1983). The intervention group had three lessons about how TV is not real—such as real men cannot fight four other men at the same time and not get hurt—and how real people solve conflicts in nonaggressive ways. The children then made a video to explain this to other kids who had been "fooled by TV." Children in the intervention group became less aggressive. In another school, 3rd- and 4th-graders were challenged to turn off TV for ten days and to limit themselves to seven hours per week of media afterward. Over time, the students became less obese and less aggressive (Robinson, Wilde, Navracruz, Haydel, & Varady, 2001). You could support similar interventions in your school. In addition, you can help your students avoid the negative effects of violent media by following these guidelines:

- Help students learn nonaggressive forms of conflict resolution, and promote prosocial behavior. Review Chapter 10 for how to do this.
- Set a good example. Do not model use of violent media. Tell students about positive media. If students discuss antisocial media, tell them why you do not use such media.
- Educate parents about the effects of media. We once watched several kindergarteners drawing a man with very long fingernails, Freddy Krueger, from a slasher film. Nearly all the children had seen several of these horror films—their mothers took them to the theater. Tell parents that when they watch violent shows without criticizing the violence, their children learn to accept aggression (Anderson et al., 2003). Notify parents when violent, media-related themes emerge in students' play.

- Educate students about the effects of media. Even an approach as simple as having them count the number of antisocial acts in a show is eye-opening.

Media can be prosocial and educational. Publicly available shows, like *Cyberchase*, a math show for 8- to 12-year-olds, have websites designed to help students learn at home and facilitate discussions at school. Educational videos can help students learn, particularly if you provide activities that complement the video (Singer, 1999). However, when you show educational videos in class, the content needs to be reinforced. For example, in one study students were shown a science film once, or once in combination with a classroom lesson discussing the film. They remembered more of the content later if they had both seen the film and had a lesson, compared to viewing the film just once (Beuscher & Roebers, 2005). This fits with the principle of repeated exposure you learned in Chapter 5. Computers can also facilitate learning in your classroom.

Computers in the Classroom

Almost all U.S. classrooms have computers and Internet access (Gray, Lewis, & Tice, 2009). The national ratio of students to computers is 3.8:1. Computers are used for many purposes in classrooms—for assessment and feedback to students, to post grades and assignments, to access information, to replace textbooks with e-lessons, and so on. In some ways, computers are simply another tool in the classroom, much like a pencil or paper. However, computers can contribute uniquely to student success if you follow these guidelines:

- Help your students develop fluency taking tests on computers. Computer-based testing is becoming more common. Computer-savvy students tend to score higher on tests administered on computers than students who are not fluent with computers (MacArthur, 2006).
- Encourage your students to use a computer to write. Writing tends to be higher quality when children use computers, particularly for struggling writers (Rogers & Graham, 2008). It is easier to brainstorm, write, revise, and spell correctly using a word processor.
- Use computer-assisted instruction (CAI) that tailors instruction to a student's ability. Just a few half-hour CAI sessions per week help most children learn, particularly in math. Your students who have high computer self-efficacy will learn the most from CAI (Slavin, Cheung, Groff, & Lake, 2008; Slavin & Lake, 2008). The What Works Clearinghouse provides summaries of research on many CAI programs to help you decide whether to adopt specific programs.
- Use computers in collaborative learning. When computers were new, people worried they would reduce interaction and lead to social deficits. The opposite is true; computers can promote social interaction from kindergarten to high school. For example, at one inner-city high school in St. Louis, students sit in clusters of three at a computer table. In a horticulture class, they collaborate to design landscapes, and in a biology class, they prepare presentations on the effects of smoking. However, in Chapter 11, you learned that cooperative learning groups must be carefully constructed, so keep in mind that boys often dominate computer use in mixed-gender groups (Light & Littleton, 1999).
- Attend workshops designed to help you effectively use technology in your classroom. Almost all (95%) school districts report providing such professional development (Gray et al., 2009).

Theories & Theorists — Box 14.2

The Bioecological Model Revisited

In Chapter 1 you were introduced to the bioecological model. Let's briefly review the model now that you have learned so much about children's development. According to the model, development is influenced by a hierarchy of systems. At the core are biologically endowed characteristics of the child. Children bring these characteristics to every interaction with others in the environment, particularly the family. These interactions may develop into relationships that become part of the child and part of a system of relationships that are embedded in the larger culture. Let's look at aggression to get a sense of how the model works.

Biological core. Biologically endowed characteristics include gender and temperament. Girls tend to be less aggressive than boys. Children with an emotionally positive temperament tend to be less aggressive.

Microsystem. This level refers to settings in which the child is physically present, such as families, classrooms, and child care. Family structure is linked to aggression; children in nuclear families, with parents who are authoritative and seldom fight, are less likely to be aggressive.

Mesosystem. This level refers to linkages between microsystems, such as the link between families, schools, and child care. Family structure influences whether parents are involved in school and whether children are in child care. Children are less aggressive if their parents are involved. Children are less aggressive if they are in higher-quality and fewer hours of child care.

Exosystem. This level refers to linkages between mesosystems that don't physically include the child. Exosystems include parent's workplace, media companies, institutions that train child care providers, and government agencies that regulate child care or enforce welfare policies that require mothers to work. Good work conditions—such as stable, well-paying jobs with standard, but flexible, hours—may promote parents' involvement at school and placement of their children in high-quality child care for fewer hours. Each of these factors is linked to less aggression.

Macrosystem. This level refers to the larger culture. Culture influences the following: acceptability of unwed teenage parenting, preference for violent and sexualized media, father involvement following divorce, whether schools invite parent involvement, whether a parent pays child support, and generosity of maternal leave policies. Each of these aspects of culture, in turn, influences family structure, placement in child care, quality of parenting, and media use, which are linked to children's aggression.

Chronosystem. "Chrono" refers to time, or changes over a child's life course. Family structure changes across time for many children, like it did for Collin. For example, Collin's married parents divorced, he lived with a single mother, and then his mother remarried. He experienced less and less contact with his father over time. Even without divorce, changes might have included new siblings, parents losing or gaining employment, and so on.

The chronosystem also refers to historical and societal changes. Today, parents are increasingly disconnecting childbearing with marriage. Television is becoming increasingly violent. Women have increasingly entered the workforce. Welfare-receiving mothers are increasingly required to work. These are huge social changes. Each of these changes influences children's aggression.

The key lesson of the bioecological model is that children's development is influenced by many layers of the context they live in. However, proximal factors—meaning family interaction—are more powerful than the more distant macrosystem (Bronfenbrenner & Ceci, 1994). Family interaction has a powerful effect because it takes place regularly over an extended period of time. However, distant factors can influence quality of parent–child interaction.

Farewell

We now come to the end of the section on the whole child. In the previous four sections of the book, you learned how students develop in the physical, cognitive, emotional, and social domains. In this section, you learned how all these domains work together to influence literacy, self-concepts, and motivation, as well as how contexts such as family structure, child care, and media influence child development. Box 14.2 takes you back through the bioecological model, which you were first introduced to in Chapter 1, to help you understand how there are multiple layers of influence on each student's development at any point in time. You have learned a great deal in this text—more than can reasonably be mastered in a single class. Refer back to this text in the future in order to improve your teaching, or to solve problems that will arise among your students (and they will). You will become a better teacher if you periodically refer back to the "Reflections on Practice" sections of each chapter over the years to come.

Reflections on Practice: Checklist for Teachers

The contexts children live in affect them at school. Children in positive contexts are likely to be successful in your classroom. Unfortunately, some children spend many hours in low-quality child care; use violent media; or live in unstable, conflict-ridden families. To help these students:

- Develop secure teacher–student attachments, which can help compensate for disrupted parent–child relationships. How to do this is described in Chapter 6.
- Help children develop good emotion regulation so that they are able to cope with stress from family disruption, child care, or violent media. How to do this is described in Chapter 8.
- Build children's friendships and conflict resolution skills to counter negative examples at home or on TV. How to do this is described in Chapters 10 and 11.

In addition, periodically ask yourself the following:

1. Am I aware of my students' family structure? (Be aware that while this can help you understand your students, it can also lead to stereotyped expectations.) Are any of my students acting out, anxious, or depressed because of family problems? Is my classroom a safe haven for them?
2. Do I know how involved parents are at home? What barriers to school involvement do parents face? Do I actively invite parents to be involved? Do I give homework assignments that a child could successfully complete without support at home?
3. If I teach in a child care program, are we providing high-quality care with stable staff and a low child–caregiver ratio? Are we educated about child development? Do we have warm relationships and talk with children?
4. If my school has an after-school program, are there opportunities for positive socializing with adults and peers? Can our school provide more before- and after-school care?
5. Am I aware of how much media and which kinds my students use? Do I convey disapproval of negative media and explain their harmful effects?
6. Do I model good media consumption? Do I suggest good TV shows or Internet sites that complement class activities?
7. Do I use media effectively to reinforce learning in my classroom? Do I encourage computer use for writing and for cooperative learning? Am I helping my students feel self-efficacy for computer use?

Summary of Age Trends of the Child in Context

	Family Structure	Maternal Employment and Child Care	TV and Media Use
Early Childhood (Birth–5 Years)	On average, children fare best in nuclear families. Divorce has similar effects across ages, but they may be stronger for preschoolers. Preschool girls with absent fathers are more likely to later become promiscuous. Children adopted by 6 months fare better than later adoptees, but all fare better if adopted rather than left behind in bad situations.	About half of mothers with young children work at least part time. Negative effects of maternal employment are greater before age 3 and greatest before age 1. Most children in child care are in part-time care. Home-based care may be higher quality for infants, but center-based care may be higher for preschoolers. Toddlers have high cortisol levels during child care. This starts to decline at 3–5 years. By age 3, children in child care tend to have more behavior problems.	Toddlers can learn from TV, but not as well as from real life. Preschoolers watch a higher proportion of educational shows than older children. Educational TV is linked to emergent literacy and later school achievement. Excessive TV is linked to later ADHD-like symptoms. Toddlers watch an average of one to two hours, and 3-year-olds watch four hours per day of TV. Videogame playing rises.
Middle Childhood (6–12 Years)	Children in cohabiting families have social and academic problems that were not apparent as preschoolers. Divorced fathers' involvement wanes over time. Parents are more involved with schooling during the elementary school years than later.	About two-thirds of mothers with elementary-age children work at least part time. Elementary children in child care tend to be there about ten nonschool hours per week. By school age, children no longer have high cortisol levels during child care. Half of children in child care are in self-sibling care.	Elementary children watch more violent TV than preschoolers. They are more likely to be aggressive after watching TV than older children. Children who watch more TV have lower literacy by 1st grade and fall further behind with age. Educational TV is linked to achievement, but less strongly than for preschoolers. TV viewing and videogame playing rise, peaking at age 13. About 60% of 6th-graders use a computer regularly.
Adolescence (13–19 Years)	Children continue to fare better, on average, in nuclear families. Relationships with parents are more distant in divorced than in nuclear families. Parent involvement in school drops off but is still important.	About three-fourths of mothers of teenagers work outside of the home. Adolescents in many hours of self-sibling care have higher rates of delinquency.	TV viewing wanes. Teens watch one to two hours daily on average. Teens who watch more have lower achievement and do less homework. SES and ethnic differences in TV viewing are pronounced. Most teens (94%) use a computer regularly. Half go online daily. School and homework depend more on computers than for younger children.

Chapter Summary

Family Structure

- Children grow up in a variety of family structures, but two-thirds live in nuclear families. The next most common family structure is a single mother and her children.
- Divorce, a process rather than an event, is strongly linked to externalizing problems, particularly for boys. It is also linked to medical, attachment, internalizing, and academic problems for children of all ages. Similar problems are linked to single-parent, teen mother, cohabiting, and stepfamilies. Children fare better if parenting quality remains high and nonresident fathers stay involved in an authoritative way.
- Family structure may affect child outcomes through several factors—parent education, financial stress, parent–child closeness, abuse, rate of moving, father presence, marital conflict, and quality of parenting. Quality of parenting is more important than family structure but is influenced by structure.
- Family structure varies by SES and ethnicity. Higher-SES and Asian families are most likely to have a nuclear structure.
- Teachers can help students with distressed families by forming a secure relationship and by teaching academic, emotional, and social skills. Teachers can enhance parent involvement through regular communication and by welcoming parents at school.
- Adopted children fare better than if they had not been adopted out of difficult situations. Adopted children tend to develop similar attachment security and cognitive abilities as nonadoptees. Children from horrendous early conditions may catch up somewhat following adoption.

Maternal Employment and Child Care

- Maternal employment has mixed effects on children. Effects are more positive if families leave welfare, mothers are single, mothers believe it is good for children, and they spend more of their nonwork hours with their children. Effects are more negative if mothers are middle class, work long hours, work before children are age 3, find work unrewarding, or have low-quality jobs.
- Child care varies by type, amount, and quality. About half of preschoolers are in unpaid relative care. Self-sibling care is the most common nonmaternal care for school-age children.
- Time spent in low-quality child care, or care for more than ten hours per week, is linked to insecure attachment and aggression. Long hours in self-sibling care are linked to delinquency. Most child care is low quality in the United States. In countries where care is of high quality, child outcomes tend to be more positive than in the United States.

- Child care is linked to elevated stress hormones. This effect may be long term.
- Low-SES students have better school-readiness skills after being in high-quality child care. Students have better language and cognitive abilities if they are in high- versus low-quality care, and center-based versus family care (for preschoolers) or after-school programs versus self-sibling care (for school-age students).
- Children can become more attached to care providers than to parents.
- Boys are more vulnerable to negative effects of child care and maternal employment than are girls.

Television and Media

- Media, particularly TV, dominate children's free time. Media content emphasizes violence and sex, although there are prosocial and educational media.
- Heavy TV use is linked to excessive weight, sleep problems, lower academic achievement, desensitization to violence, sexual activity, and a fearful view of the world. Many types of studies show that watching TV violence causes aggression. This effect is small for most children, but large for vulnerable children. Similar effects occur for other media, such as music and videogames.
- There are also positive effects of media use. Educational TV is linked to school readiness and achievement, particularly for preschoolers. Prosocial TV is linked to prosocial behavior. Computer use (in moderation) promotes friendships. Videogaming is linked to better visual processing.
- Parenting style and parents' media use influence how much and what type of media children use. Low-SES children are exposed to more entertainment media than are middle- and high-SES children. Boys tend to watch more TV, and girls tend to use the computer more. Boys use the computer for gaming, while girls use it for communication and information.
- Teachers can protect children from the effects of negative media by educating them about its effects, modeling positive media use, communicating disapproval of negative media, and challenging children to use it less.
- Media can reinforce content learned in the classroom. Computers can be used for cooperative learning groups, writing, and computer-assisted instruction.

Accompanying Education CourseMate Website Resources

Visit the **Education CourseMate** website at **CengageBrain.com** to find resources and study aids for this chapter, including self-tests, additional print and website resources, and glossary flashcards. In addition, the following videos illustrate how schools can involve parents, and how to use technology in the classroom:

- Communicating with Parents: Tips and Strategies for Future Teachers
- Parental Involvement in School Culture: A Literacy Project
- Technology Is Making Teaching and Learning More Fun

TEACHSOURCE VIDEO CASE

Watch the following video cases: *Expanding the Definition of Literacy: Meaningful Ways to Use Technology,* and/or *Using Technology to Promote Discovery Learning: A High School Geometry Lesson,* and/or *Integrating Technology to Improve Student Learning: A High School Science Simulation.* Think about the following:

1. What do computers allow these teachers to do that they could not do without the technology?
2. Which guidelines for good classroom practice discussed in previous chapters are these teachers enacting? Does use of computers fundamentally change what practices constitute effective teaching?

Glossary

A-not-B error Children observe an object being moved from hiding place A to hiding place B, but they search in hiding place A. Typical of the sensorimotor stage.

Academic achievement A measure of knowledge based on grades or standardized tests.

Accommodation The process by which children modify existing mental structures or schemes in order to adapt to new experience, according to Piaget.

Acculturation The long-term process of adapting to a new culture.

Acquired immunodeficiency syndrome (AIDS) Diagnosis given to HIV-positive individuals who develop severe symptoms indicating the immune system is activated.

Acronym A mnemonic technique that takes the first letters of words to be remembered and combines them into a word or phrase.

Acting White The behavior of a student of color that is interpreted as engaging in activities that are marked as White, which might include listening to White music, studying hard, or speaking Standard English.

Additive bilingualism Acquiring a second language while still maintaining and valuing the heritage language.

Adult Attachment Interview A lengthy interview designed to determine adolescents' or adults' "state of mind" regarding the quality of attachment to each parent.

Advanced literacy Reading and writing that involves a formal, academic style in particular content areas, such as science-lab reports. It includes analyzing text; evaluating arguments; and writing extended, reasoned text.

Affective perspective-taking Perceiving the emotions of another person.

African American Vernacular English (AAVE) A dialect of English spoken predominantly by African Americans, sometimes called Ebonics or Black English.

Aggression Behavior that harms others, or is intended to dominate others. It is a subset of antisocial behavior.

Agreeableness A personality trait contrasted with antagonism. It includes thoughtfulness, warmth, kindness, cooperation, and getting along with and pleasing others.

ALANA An acronym that stands for the most populous non-White ethnic groups in the United States: African, Latino, Asian, and Native American.

Allele A version of a gene that contributes to a specific type of attribute. For example, a gene that influences dopamine in the brain may have different alleles, one that leads to high levels of dopamine and another that leads to low levels.

Altruism Behavior that benefits others at the expense of the self. It is a subset of prosocial behavior.

Animism Attribution of lifelike qualities, like intention, to nonliving, inanimate objects.

Antisocial behavior Behavior that disrupts the functioning of society, such as aggression and delinquency.

Anxiety disorder A common internalizing disorder in which the child feels worried about future threats, or threats to the sense of self.

Apnea A sleep disturbance that consists of repeated periods without breathing, and snoring or gasping for breath.

Applied behavior analysis Controlled application of behaviorist principles to experimentally alter behavior. Overlaps with behavior modification.

Appraisal The meaning given to an event.

Apprenticeship A learner actively observes and participates with an expert in order to improve competence.

Arousal A person's physiological readiness for action.

Asperger's disorder A disorder characterized by impaired social interaction and restricted, repetitive behavior patterns, similar to autism, but with normal language and cognitive abilities.

Assimilation The process by which children incorporate experience into existing mental structures or schemes, according to Piaget.

Attachment A deep and enduring affectionate bond that connects one person to another across time and space.

Attachment hierarchy The vertical organization of primary and secondary attachment figures for a specific child, with a preferred attachment figure at the top.

Attention-deficit/hyperactivity disorder A neurobehavioral disorder characterized by hyperactivity, low impulse control, and inattention.

Attributions The causes that people perceive for their own and other people's behavior.

Authentic literacy activities Reading for information one wants, or writing to inform a reader, as opposed to activities done for the purpose of learning to read or write or just to complete an assignment.

Authoritarian parenting style Parents are high on control but low on acceptance. They discourage verbal give-and-take, value their authority, and tend to be power assertive.

Authoritative parenting style Parents are high on control, acceptance, and autonomy support. They maintain authority and enforce rules, but are responsive to their children.

Autism A disorder characterized by markedly abnormal social interaction; poor language ability; restricted, repetitive behavior patterns; and poor emotional perspective-taking. It commonly occurs with mental retardation.

Autonomous morality A reciprocity-oriented morality in which cooperation is internally motivated.

Avoidant (defended, dismissing) attachment A form of insecure attachment characterized by anxiety, emotional distancing, rejection, and anger.

Basic emotions Universal, innate emotions appearing in the first months of life (joy, sadness, anger, interest, disgust, and fear).

Behavior modification Operant conditioning used to change human behavior, frequently applied in psychotherapy and special education classrooms. Token economies may be used for reinforcement.

Behavioral genetics The study of how genes and the environment contribute to individual differences in behavior.

Behavioral inhibition The tendency to be wary and restrict one's approach to new people, events, or objects.

Behaviorism The scientific study of overt, observable behavior.

Bi-directional Variable A influences variable B, while B also influences A.

Big-fish-little-pond effect The tendency to experience higher academic self-concept when surrounded by peers whose academic achievement is lower.

Bilingual The ability to speak two languages fluently.

Bilingual education Instruction that is provided in more than one language.

Brain plasticity The brain's ability to change structure and function as a result of experience.

Bullying A type of proactive aggression in which the goal is intimidation or dominance over another person that occurs repeatedly over time and involves someone of greater power victimizing someone of lower status or power.

Canalization Genetically based restriction or channeling of development to a limited range of outcomes despite differences in environment.

Center (or centration) The child focuses on one aspect of a task to the exclusion of other aspects.

Child-directed speech A style of speech used with young children that involves higher pitch, exaggerated ups and downs in pitch, slower tempo, and more rhythm than other speech. Also called *motherese*.

Childhood amnesia The inability to recall things that occurred during infancy, typically from birth to about 3.5 years of age. Also called "infantile amnesia."

Classical conditioning A form of conditioning in which a neutral stimulus is paired with a stimulus that causes an involuntary response until the neutral stimulus becomes a conditioned stimulus and also causes the response.

Classroom management All aspects of managing the classroom, including physical arrangements of furniture, daily scheduling, and discipline.

Clique A tightly knit group of about two to ten friends, usually of the same sex and same age.

Coercive family cycle A cycle of negative reinforcement in hostile families in which negative parenting leads to child aggression, which leads to more parental hostility, which leads to more child aggression, and so on.

Cognition Mental processes like planning, reasoning, and remembering.

Cohort effect An effect upon development whose cause is specific to the particular time period in which the cohort grew up.

Collective monologues Children appear to be conversing with each other, but are really not addressing thoughts or adapting speech to their conversation partners.

Committed compliance Children accept the authority figure's agenda as their own.

Concrete operational stage Children are able to decenter and think logically about concrete objects and experience. Roughly ages 7 to 11.

Conditioning Learning, or creating conditions conducive to learning.

Conduct disorder A clinical diagnosis given to children, age 10 or older, who are excessively delinquent or aggressive for at least six months.

Conflict The behavior of one person interferes with the goals of another person who resists or protests the behavior. It is not the same as aggression.

Conscientiousness A personality trait contrasted with lack of direction. It includes getting things done, not giving up easily, being dependable, planning ahead, and orderliness.

Conservation Understanding that the properties of objects like mass, volume, and number do not change just because the objects' appearance changes.

Constructivist One who believes that knowledge acquisition is a process of construction rather than duplication (creating a mental copy of what is observed).

Constructivist teaching An approach to instruction in which teachers provide students with experiences that facilitate their personal construction of knowledge.

Continuous reinforcement Reinforcement occurs after every correct response.

Control group In an experiment, the group that does not receive the special treatment in order to provide a comparison group.

Controversial children Children who are liked by many and also disliked by many peers. They have high social impact.

Cooperative learning Collaboration among students in small groups, where the group has a shared learning goal, and interdependence is required to achieve the goal.

Coping strategies Deliberate attempts to change thoughts or behavior to try to manage strong emotions. They are usually divided into problem-focused or emotion-focused types.

Core knowledge Innate, skeletal conceptual structures that develop early and easily, without instruction, and are universal, but may require experience to fine-tune.

Corporal punishment Power-assertive discipline that involves bodily harm to the child, ranging in severity from light spanking to abuse.

Correlation coefficient A statistic that measures the relationship between two variables.

Cortisol A hormone that the body generates as a response to stress.

Cross-sectional research design Data are collected at one point in time from two or more age groups to investigate age trends.

Cultural capital Knowledge and social relationships that allow people to reap benefits within their culture.

Cultural mismatch A pattern of incompatibilities between home and school.

Cultural tools Concrete objects and symbolic tools that allow members of a culture to think, build, record, problem solve, and communicate.

Cyberbullying Bullying that occurs through interactive technologies.

Decenter (or decentration) Ability to think about multiple aspects of a task simultaneously.

Decoding Figuring out how to read or spell unknown words by applying phonetic rules.

Deferred imitation Ability to mentally represent and then imitate an action that was observed in the past.

Delay of gratification A test of self-control in which children are timed to see how long they can resist a tempting object, or delay their gratification.

Deliberate practice Activities specifically designed to increase competence that are effortful, use specialized facilities or materials, and require expert feedback.

Depression A common internalizing disorder in which feelings of sadness are severe for at least two weeks, or milder but chronic.

Differential susceptibility Children differ in the extent to which they are susceptible to a good or bad environment based on their genotype.

Direct instruction A didactic form of instruction largely based on operant conditioning.

Dishabituation Attention that has become habituated is renewed after a change in the stimulus.

Disorganized (disoriented, controlling, unresolved) attachment A form of insecure attachment characterized by no coherent pattern of response to the parent.

Effect size A measure of the strength of the relationship between two variables, or the size of the difference between the treatment and control group.

Egocentric The tendency to see the world from your own point of view while failing to see other people's point of view.

Elaboration A method of enhancing memory that involves creating visual or verbal links or representations to associate two or more items.

Emergent literacy Abilities that are precursors to reading and writing, such as good verbal ability, knowing letter names, phonological awareness, and print concepts. These abilities are typically identifiable beginning about age 3.

Emotion A subjective reaction to an important event, involving physiological or observable behavioral change.

Emotion contagion The emotions of one person through facial, vocal, or gestural cues generate a similar emotion in the other.

Emotion regulation The capacity to control the intensity and duration of emotions.

Emotion-focused coping strategies Strategies that involve trying to change emotions, such as changing one's thoughts about the situation or seeking comfort from others.

Emotional competence The ability to regulate your own emotions, and read others' emotions, so that you emerge from an emotional event having accomplished your goals.

Emotional dissemblance Altering the expression of felt emotion by expressing no emotion or expressing a different emotion.

Emotional intelligence The ability to think intelligently about emotions and use emotions to make thinking more intelligent. Sometimes defined more broadly to mean emotional competence.

Empathy An emotional state similar to what another person is feeling that results from perceiving the other's emotions.

Encoding The process of forming mental representations of information for storage.

Encoding specificity Aspects of the context are encoded with the target information so that retrieval is enhanced when retrieval context is similar to the original context.

English-language learner (ELL) A student whose first language is not English and who is less than proficient in English.

Epigenetic A process where phenotype, or gene expression, is altered through social experience, or other mechanisms, rather than change in DNA.

Equilibrium A state of cognitive balance or cognitive comfort.

Ethnic identity A part of self-concept that includes a sense of membership in an ethnic group and attitudes and feelings about that membership.

Ethology A subdiscipline of biology that seeks to understand the cause and function of animal (including human) behavior.

Executive functions The brain's control of its own information processing.

Experiment A controlled study comparing outcomes between people randomly assigned to a treatment group and a control group.

Expository talk Formal, precise talk that is used to display information, in contrast to conversational talk.

Externalizing disorders Emotional disorders based on anger, characterized by aggression and other antisocial behaviors.

Extinction (classical conditioning) The conditioned stimulus and unconditioned stimulus are repeatedly not paired until the conditioned stimulus no longer elicits the conditioned response.

Extinction (operant conditioning) The elimination or decline in response caused by stopping reinforcement.

Extraversion A personality trait contrasted with social inhibition. It includes high energy; talkativeness; emotional expressiveness; and being fast-paced, reactive, and full of life.

Extrinsic motivation The desire to pursue an activity for reasons external to the activity such as getting a reward, avoiding punishment, or earning a grade.

Family structure The composition of a child's household.

Fast mapping The ability to learn a new word from a single, or very minimal, exposure without deliberate instruction or corrective feedback.

Flynn effect The worldwide pattern of rising intelligence scores.

Formal operational stage Children are able to think abstractly about hypothetical events and systematically test hypotheses; roughly ages 11 to adulthood.

Fuzzy traces A distilled gist of an experience rather than an exact memory.

g General intelligence.

Gender identity The ability to accurately label your sex and your feelings about your gender.

Gender segregation When given a choice, boys affiliate with other boys and girls with other girls.

Gene–environment correlation Both genes and social contexts interact to contribute to children's development.

Genotype The set of genes that is directly inherited and transmitted to descendents.

Glucose rate The rate of consumption of glucose, an indicator of energy use in the brain.

Goodness of fit The degree of match between temperament and environmental demands, values, or expectations.

Guided participation A novice learns through an expert's scaffolding.

Habituation A reduction in attention to a continuously available or repeated stimulus.

Heritability estimate The amount of variation in a trait in a population (not individuals) that is attributable to genetic influences. Notated as h^2.

Heteronymous morality An authority-oriented morality in which rules are rigidly followed in order to avoid punishment, but not for internal reasons.

Hierarchical classification The ability to classify or place objects into superordinate and subordinate categories.

High-stakes tests Tests used to make decisions that have educational or financial impact.

Homophily The tendency to prefer and bond with similar others.

Hostile aggression A type of reactive or proactive aggression in which the primary aim is to harm another person.

Hostile attribution bias The tendency to assume hostile intent on the part of others in situations where it is not clear if there is hostile intent or not.

Human immunodeficiency virus (HIV) A virus that undermines the immune system, contracted through extended contact with bodily fluids of infected persons.

Inattentional blindness The tendency of children to not perceive obvious objects or events if they are concentrating on something else.

Indifferent parenting style Parents are low on both control and acceptance. They are not affectionate or responsive and have few rules. They are self- rather than child-centered. Also called neglectful or uninvolved.

Induction (discipline) A form of discipline in which the adult gives the child a reason for why behavior must change or a rule must be complied with.

Induction (reasoning) A form of reasoning in which a child detects generalizations, rules, or regularities, often, but not always, through comparison and contrast.

Indulgent parenting style Parents are low on control, but high on acceptance. They have few rules and avoid controlling their children. Also called permissive.

Information processing model A model of cognition that focuses on how children acquire, store, and use knowledge.

Inhibitory control The ability to inhibit processing irrelevant information or to suppress a response.

Instrumental aggression A type of proactive aggression in which the primary aim is to obtain an object, territory, or privilege, but not to hurt the victim.

Intelligence A general mental capability including the ability to reason, plan, solve problems, think abstractly, comprehend complex ideas, adapt, and learn quickly.

Interference Existing information in long-term memory prevents accurate retrieval of new information, or information learned recently prevents accurate retrieval of older information.

Intermittent reinforcement Reinforcement occurs after some, but not all, responses.

Internal working models Memories and expectations of the self and others that influence whether children approach or avoid others, with either positive or hostile emotions.

Internalization The child adopts the adult's values and rules as his or her own guide for behavior. The child complies or behaves appropriately without being monitored.

Internalizing disorders Emotional disorders based on sadness or anxiety, characterized by withdrawal.

Intrinsic motivation The desire to pursue an activity for its own sake, not for external reasons.

Involuntary minorities Nonimmigrant peoples who have been conquered, colonized, or enslaved.

IQ Intelligence quotient. An index of general cognitive ability that is no longer used, but the term is still common.

Joint attention Both the child and another person visually explore an object together.

Keyword method A mnemonic in which a keyword that *sounds* like the target word is chosen and then an *image* is linked with it.

Language A collection of words or signs used in a systematic way that allows people to communicate with each other. Language can be verbal or nonverbal.

Learned helplessness The perception developed through experience that no matter what you do, you will not be competent in a domain.

Learning According to behaviorists, a relatively permanent change in observable behavior that is the result of experience, not maturation or some other cause.

Learning disability defined as a discrepancy between a student's achievement and intelligence or as lack of response to instruction that is effective for most other students.

Literacy Narrowly defined, it is the ability to communicate in printed language through reading and writing, particularly in school settings.

Long-term memory The relatively permanent storage of information. Duration is long and capacity is very large, perhaps unlimited.

Longitudinal research design Data are collected from the same or different individuals two or more times separated by some period of time (e.g., months or years).

Love-withdrawal A form of discipline in which the adult manipulates the love relationship with the child. This can include withdrawing affection or attention, isolating the child, and expressing disapproval of the child.

Mandated reporters People who must by law report suspicion of child abuse and neglect. Laws vary by state, but in most states, teachers are mandated reporters.

Mastery goal A goal to master a skill or topic.

Mediation A neutral, impartial third person facilitates negotiation between two children in conflict.

Memory span A common measure of working memory that tests the number of items, usually presented rapidly, that a person can recall in exact order.

Metacognition Cognition that reflects on, monitors, or regulates other cognition.

Mnemonics Techniques for improving memory.

Moral judgment Reasoning about moral dilemmas that involve justice in a context where rules, laws, formal obligations, and authority are emphasized.

Moral transgression Behavior that is inherently wrong, independent of culture and regardless of rules.

Morpheme The smallest unit of language that contains meaning. It can include word roots, suffixes, and prefixes.

Motivation Internal states that affect the energy level, direction, vigor, and persistence of behavior toward a goal.

Multiple intelligences Gardner's theory of intelligence that proposes that there are various independent intelligences rather than just a dominant *g* factor.

Myelin A fatty substance that forms an insulating coating, called a myelin sheath, around axons that allows them to function efficiently.

Myelination The development of myelin.

Nativists Those who believe that competence in core domains is largely innate and little influenced by the environment.

Negative reinforcement Removal of an aversive stimulus. This increases the probability of a response. This is *not* punishment.

Neglected children Children who are neither liked nor disliked by many peers. They have low social impact.

Neuroticism A personality trait contrasted with emotional stability. It includes nervousness, worry, perseverating or falling apart under stress, insecurity, and needing reassurance.

Neurotransmitter A chemical that allows neurons to communicate across synapses.

Nonorganic failure to thrive Failure to grow adequately without any apparent medical reason.

Nonshared environment (NSE) Factors that make individuals in the same family different from each other.

Nonverbal language Communication that does not include words, such as posture, gestures, and facial expressions.

Nuclear family A family composed of a married father and mother and their children. Sometimes called a "traditional" family.

Object permanence The knowledge that objects that are out of view continue to exist.

Openness to experience A personality trait that includes curiosity, exploration, imaginative dreaming, creativeness, good self-expression, and being smart.

Operant conditioning Voluntary behavior is conditioned through its consequences.

Operation According to Piaget, mental actions or manipulations that follow rules.

Oppositional defiant disorder A clinical diagnosis given to children under age 8 who are excessively antisocial for at least six months.

Overcontrolled A nonresilient personality type characterized by high agreeableness and neuroticism, and particularly low extraversion.

Peer pressure Friends exert pressure on each other to conform to group norms. It is typically positive, but can be negative.

Peer status A measure of how accepted children are in a peer group.

Performance goal A goal to demonstrate ability by performing better than others.

Persistent persuasion An approach to discipline that uses induction repeatedly until the child complies, but without escalating the power level.

Personal distress A self-focused, aversive emotional reaction to someone else's negative emotion.

Personal interest An individual's enduring interest in an activity or domain of knowledge.

Personality A constellation of traits that distinguishes one person from another.

Personality traits The tendency to behave, think, and feel in certain consistent ways. Five traits that account for much of the variation in personality are openness, conscientiousness, extraversion, agreeableness, and neuroticism (OCEAN).

Personality types Clusters of personality traits that tend to occur together. The most commonly identified in children are resilient, overcontrolled, and undercontrolled types.

Phenotype Observable characteristics of a person.

Phoneme A sound in speech. The most basic unit of language.

Phonetics Rules regarding how written letters are linked to sounds and how a string of letters is correctly pronounced.

Phonics An approach to teaching literacy that emphasizes training in phonological awareness and decoding words.

Phonological awareness The ability to identify phonemes or the sound structure of language.

Physical aggression Behavior that harms others through physical means such as hitting, pushing, or kicking.

Physical play A type of play in which children move for the joy of movement, such as climbing, running, or chasing.

Play Behavior that has no immediate function and is pleasurable, spontaneous, flexible, and internally controlled.

Popular children Children who are liked by many and disliked by few peers.

Positive reinforcement The provision or introduction of a consequence that increases the probability of a response.

Power assertion A coercive form of discipline in which the adult controls the child's behavior by virtue of greater power or resources. It often includes an "or else" clause.

Pragmatics The study of how language is used in social context.

Preoperational stage Children are able to use symbolic thought, but unable to think logically, particularly to conserve or decenter. Roughly ages 2 to 7.

Pretense play A type of play in which children transform objects and identities as they act out imaginary scenarios.

Print concepts Basic concepts of how print symbolizes language, such as English books are read from left to right and spaces separate words. A key part of emergent literacy.

Private speech Talking to oneself out loud, partially out loud, or silently in one's mind to help regulate one's own behavior or solve problems.

Proactive aggression Aggression that is directed at achieving personal objectives, but that is not clearly provoked.

Problem-focused coping strategies Action-oriented strategies that involve trying to change the situation.

Prosocial behavior Voluntary behavior that benefits others or promotes harmonious relations with others.

Prosocial reasoning Reasoning about moral dilemmas in which one person's needs or desires conflict with another's, but in a context where laws, rules, or formal obligations are minimal.

Protective factor A factor that decreases the likelihood of poor outcomes in children at risk.

Puberty Physical changes that occur as children move into adulthood, including development of primary and secondary sex characteristics and capacity for reproduction.

Punishment Consequences that reduce the probability of a response.

Qualitative research Nonquantitative research characterized by the researcher being the instrument of data collection (rather than a test or questionnaire). May involve observations and interviews as data.

Random assignment Each research participant has an equal chance of being assigned to the treatment or control group.

Reactive aggression Aggression that is aimed at retaliation for a provocation, usually involving anger or frustration.

Reciprocal teaching Students take turns in the teacher role. A student-teacher summarizes, asks questions, clarifies, and predicts the content of a passage of text in a small group of other students.

Reciprocated friendship Both children nominate each other as a friend.

Rehearsal Mentally repeating information over and over in working memory.

Reinforcer A consequence that increases the probability of a response.

Rejected-aggressive children Children who are actively disliked by many peers and are highly aggressive; about 40 to 50% of rejected children.

Rejected-withdrawn children Children who are actively disliked by many peers, are not aggressive, but tend to avoid social interaction; about 10 to 20% of rejected children.

Reliability Consistency of a test or measurement.

Resilience Positive development despite adversity or risk.

Resilient A personality type characterized by very high levels of openness and conscientiousness, above-average levels of extraversion and agreeableness, and very low levels of neuroticism.

Resistant (coercive, preoccupied) attachment A form of insecure attachment characterized by exaggerated emotions, clinginess, and intense attachment behaviors.

Retrieval Finding items in long-term memory and placing them into working memory.

Reverse operations Ability to mentally reverse or negate an operation.

Risk factor A variable associated with negative child outcomes.

Rough-and-tumble play A form of social, pretense play that involves physically vigorous behavior and often resembles, but is not the same as, aggression.

Scaffolding A more competent person helps a child master new skills by breaking the tasks or subskills into small units and guiding performance to a higher level.

Schema An organized network of information.

Scheme A cognitive structure or piece of understanding constructed through experience.

School bonding A sense of belonging at school and having a network of relationships with peers and teachers.

Script A schema for how to do something or for an event.

Secure (balanced, autonomous) attachment A form of attachment characterized by feelings of security, open communication, and mutual delight.

Secure base An attachment figure who engenders a child's confidence and security, because of willingness to be available when needed, while the child explores novel environments.

Segregating genes Genes that are free to vary and that dictate individual differences.

Selection bias Children and parents select into or choose certain kinds of experiences based on their preexisting characteristics. This makes it difficult to determine the effect of the experience.

Selective attention Attending to task-relevant input while suppressing irrelevant input.

Self A group of related thoughts that people hold about themselves.

Self-actualization The process of fulfilling one's potential in a way that shows concern for society.

Self-concept The differentiated conception of self that includes categories such as academic self-concept, social self-concept, and athletic self-concept. The term *global self-concept* is sometimes used synonymously with *self-esteem*.

Self-control The ability to control one's own behavior and emotions, obey rules, inhibit inappropriate action, and focus attention.

Self-efficacy Belief that you have the capability to perform a specific task.

Self-esteem One's feelings of worth.

Self-sibling care A prevalent form of nonmaternal care for school-age children, in which children are home alone or with a sibling under age 18.

Semantics The study of meaning in language.

Sensitive period A biologically determined time period, typically early in life, in which a child readily develops specific abilities. Change is less likely before or after the sensitive period.

Sensitive responsiveness A style of interaction in which an adult responds promptly and appropriately to a child's signals, with accurate understanding of the child's perspective.

Sensorimotor stage Children rely on senses and behavioral schemes to acquire knowledge. Roughly birth to 2 years.

Sensory register The component of the information processing model where initial stimuli from the environment are briefly held.

Sexually transmitted diseases (STDs) Diseases that are contracted through sexual contact.

Sexually transmitted infections (STIs) Infections that are contracted through sexual contact. Children can be infected without showing symptoms of disease.

Shaping Reinforcement of successive approximations to a target behavior.

Shared environment (SE) Factors that make individuals residing in the same family similar to each other.

Sibling rivalry Conflict between siblings due to jealousy over parental love and attention. The concept was emphasized by Freud.

Sibling-contrast bias The tendency of family members to report greater difference among siblings than actually exists by evaluating them relative to each other.

Situational compliance Children comply with demands, but lack sincere commitment and require sustained control by the authority figure.

Situational interest Short-lived attention or curiosity that is generated by the conditions in a specific situation.

Social aggression Behavior that harms others through manipulating their relationships or peer-group status, such as spreading rumors or excluding the victim from a social clique. It is sometimes called relational aggression.

Social cognition Thought processes applied to the social domain.

Social constructivism The view that knowledge is not poured into learners' brains, but that knowledge is constructed through social interaction.

Social conventions Standards of behavior dictated by culture.

Social emotions Complex emotions that emerge later than basic emotions (shame, embarrassment, guilt, pride, and envy). Also called "self-conscious" or "moral" emotions.

Social identity The part of students' self-concept that derives from their membership in a group, such as gender, ethnic, religious, national, or other groups.

Social referencing Children read another's emotional expression to determine how they should respond in an ambiguous situation.

Sociocultural theory A theory of how children learn, largely based on Vygotsky's writings, that emphasizes social interaction, historical context, and culture.

Socioeconomic status (SES) Categorization based on parental education, income, and occupational status; often simplified as low, middle, and upper class.

Solitary-active play A type of play involving functional or pretense play while alone.

Solitary-passive play A type of play involving construction or exploring objects while alone.

Source monitoring Memory of the source or origin of information.

Spaced practice Multiple periods of practicing or studying over a period of time rather than in a single massed episode. Also referred to as distributed practice.

Specific reading disability A learning disability in which a child with normal intelligence and exposure to print has difficulty learning to read. It is characterized by difficulty decoding and recognizing words accurately and/or fluently. It is also called dyslexia.

Stability A term child psychologists use to refer to whether children's rank-ordering on a trait remains the same across time.

Standard English The form of English used in classroom instruction and textbooks, sometimes called School English.

Stereotype threat Concern that one's performance will confirm negative stereotypes about one's group.

Stigma Feeling different and of little value in a community.

Strange Situation Procedure A twenty-two-minute laboratory task designed to test quality of attachment in which children under age 6 are stressed by maternal separation and stranger presence.

Subtractive bilingualism Acquiring a second, majority language in a way that undermines ability in the heritage language.

Sudden infant death syndrome (SIDS) The sudden death of an infant for whom a cause of death cannot be determined.

Symbolic thought The cognitive ability to have one thing stand for, or represent, another.

Sympathy An emotional response that consists of feeling concern for a distressed other.

Synapse A junction where neurons communicate with each other, or with other kinds of cells.

Synaptogenesis A spurt in synaptic connections of the brain that occurs from the third trimester of gestation until about 2 years of age.

Syntactic bootstrapping A process where young children figure out the meaning of a new word, without explicit instruction, based on the syntax of the sentence in which the word is used.

Syntax The way words are organized into phrases and sentences in a language.

Temperament An individual characteristic pertaining to differences in the intensity and pattern of emotions and arousal.

Teratogen An agent that harms the developing fetus.

Test anxiety A dispositional proneness toward anxiety in test situations that interferes with performance.

Test bias A test has less validity for one group than another group. Predictive bias means members of two groups who have the same score are not predicted to have the same outcome.

Theory An organized group of concepts or principles used to explain a particular aspect of human development.

Theory of mind The ability to infer mental states in others, such as beliefs, desires, knowledge, and intentions. It is sometimes called people reading.

Theory theory A theory that asserts that children form naïve theories to explain and predict their world. These theories are tested and changed based on experience.

Toddler A child between 1 and 3 years of age; so-called because of their recent mastery of walking, often with a wobbly gait.

Underachievement Earning grades that are substantially below those of other students with similar cognitive ability as measured by standardized tests.

Undercontrolled A nonresilient personality type characterized by particularly low agreeableness and conscientiousness, but also low-average neuroticism and openness.

Unilateral friendships One child nominates another as a friend, but the other does not.

Validity The extent to which a measurement assesses what it is supposed to measure for a specific purpose.

Verbal aggression Behavior that harms others through verbal means such as threatening or name calling.

Verbal language Communication that involves words and speech, in contrast to nonverbal language.

Victim-centered induction A form of inductive discipline in which the adult points out how the child's behavior made the victim feel.

Voluntary minorities People of minority status who immigrated voluntarily.

Working memory The component of the information processing model where items of information are temporarily held for encoding or processing.

Zone of proximal development (ZPD) The distance between what students can do independently and what they can do with the assistance of a competent other.

References

Aarnoudse-Moens, C. S. H., Weisglas-Kuperus, N., van Goudoever, J. B., & Oosterlaan, J. (2009). Meta-analysis of neurobehavioral outcomes in very preterm and/or very low birth weight children. *Pediatrics, 124*, 717–728.

Abedi, J. (2004). The No Child Left Behind Act and English language learners: Assessment and accountability issues. *Educational Researcher, 33*(1), 4–14.

Aber, L., Brown, J., & Jones, S. (2003). Developmental trajectories toward violence in middle childhood: Course, demographic differences, and response to school-based intervention. *Developmental Psychology, 39*, 324–348.

Aboud, F. E. (2003). The formation of in-group favoritism and outgroup prejudice in young children: Are they distinct attitudes? *Developmental Psychology, 39*, 48–60.

Aboud, F. E. (2008). A social-cognitive developmental theory of prejudice. In S. M. Quintana & C. McKown (Eds.), *Handbook of race, racism and the developing child* (pp. 55–71). Hoboken, NJ: Wiley.

Achenbach, T. M., Dumenci, L., & Rescorla, L. A. (2002). Is American student behavior getting worse? Teacher ratings over an 18-year period. *School Psychology Review, 31*, 428–442.

Achenbach, T. M., Dumenci, L., & Rescorla, L. A. (2003). Are American children's problems still getting worse? A 23-year comparison. *Journal of Abnormal Child Psychology, 31*, 1–11.

Achenbach, T. M., & Howell, C. T. (1993). Are American children's problems getting worse? A 13-year comparison. *Journal of the American Academy of Child and Adolescent Psychiatry, 32*, 1145–1154.

Ackerman, B., Brown, E., & Izard, C. E. (2003). Continuity and change in levels of externalizing behavior in school of children from economically disadvantaged families. *Child Development, 74*, 694–709.

Ackerman, B., Brown, E., & Izard, C. E. (2004a). The relations between contextual risk, earned income, and the school adjustment of children from economically disadvantaged families. *Developmental Psychology, 40*, 204–216.

Ackerman, B., Brown, E., & Izard, C. E. (2004b). The relations between persistent poverty and contextual risk and children's behavior in elementary school. *Developmental Psychology, 40*, 367–377.

Ackerman, B., Izard, C. E., Schoff, K., Youngstrom, E., & Kogos, J. (1999). Contextual risk, caregiver emotionality, and the problem behaviors of six-and seven-year-old children from economically disadvantaged families. *Child Development, 70*, 1415–1427.

Ackerman, B. P., Brown, E. D., D'Eramo, K. S., & Izard, C. E. (2002). Maternal relationship instability and the school behavior of children from disadvantaged families. *Developmental Psychology, 38*, 694–704.

Ackerman, B. P., Izard, C. E., Kobak, R., Brown, E. D., & Smith, C. (2007). Relation between reading problems and internalizing behavior in school for preadolescent children from economically disadvantaged families. *Child Development, 78*, 581–596.

Ackerman, P. L., Beier, M. E., & Boyle, M. O. (2005). Working memory and intelligence: The same or different constructs? *Psychological Bulletin, 131*, 30–60.

Adam, E. (2004). Beyond quality: Parental and residential stability and children's adjustment. *Current Directions in Psychological Science, 13*, 210–213.

Adams, G. L., & Engelmann, S. (1996). *Research on direct instruction: 25 years beyond DISTAR*. Seattle, WA: Educational Achievement Systems.

Adams, M. J. (1990). *Beginning to read: Thinking and learning about print. A summary.* Urbana-Champaign: University of Illinois.

Adams, M. J., Treiman, R., & Pressley, M. (1998). Reading, writing, and literacy. In I. Sigel & K. A. Renninger (Eds.), *Handbook of child psychology: Child psychology in practice* (5th ed., Vol. 4, pp. 275–355). New York: Wiley.

Adi-Japha, E., & Klein, P. (2009). Relations between parenting quality and cognitive performance of children experiencing varying amounts of childcare. *Child Development, 80*, 893–906.

Administration for Children & Families. (2007). Head Start Program Fact Sheet. Washington, DC: U.S. Department of Health and Human Services. Accessed April 19, 2007 at http://www.acf.hhs.gov/programs/ohs/about/fy2007.html

After School Alliance. (2009). America After 3PM Key Findings. Retrieved 5/22/2010 from http://www.afterschoolalliance.org

Aguilar, B., Sroufe, A., Egeland, B., & Carlson, E. (2000). Distinguishing the early-onset/persistent and adolescence-onset antisocial behavior types: From birth to 16 years. *Development and Psychopathology, 12*, 109–152.

Ahamed, Y., MacDonald, H., Reed, K., Naylor, P.-J., Liu-Ambrose, T., & McKay, H. (2007). School-based physical activity does not compromise children's academic performance. *Medicine and Science in Sports and Exercise, 39*, 371–376.

Ahnert, L., Gunnar, M. R., Lamb, M. E., & Barthel, M. (2004). Transition to child care: Associations with infant-mother attachment, infant negative emotion, and cortisol elevations. *Child Development, 75*, 639–650.

Ahnert, L., Pinquart, M., & Lamb, M. E. (2006). Security of children's relationships with nonparental care providers: A meta-analysis. *Child Development, 77*, 664–679.

Ahnert, L., Rickert, H., & Lamb, M. (2000). Shared caregiving: Comparisons between home and child-care settings. *Developmental Psychology, 36*, 339–351.

Aikens, N. L., & Barbarin, O. A. (2008). Socioeconomic differences in reading trajectories: The contribution of family, neighborhood, and school contexts. *Journal of Educational Psychology, 100*, 235–251.

Ainley, J., Pratt, D., & Hansen, A. (2006). Connecting engagement and focus in pedagogic task design. *British Educational Research Journal, 32*, 23–38.

Ainsworth, M. D. S. (1973). The development of infant-mother attachment. In B. Caldwell & H. Ricciuti (Eds.), *Review of child development research* (Vol. 3, pp. 1–94). Chicago: University of Chicago Press.

Ainsworth, M. D. S. (1979). Infant-mother attachment. *American Psychologist, 34*, 932–937.

Ainsworth, M. D. S., Blehar, M., Waters, E., & Wall, S. (1978). *Patterns of attachment.* Hillsdale, NJ: Erlbaum.

Akiba, M., LeTendre, G. K., & Scribner, J. P. (2007). Teacher quality, opportunity gap, and national achievement in 46 countries. *Educational Researcher, 36*(7), 369–387.

Alaimo, K., Olson, C., Frongillo, E., & Briefel, R. (2001). Food insufficiency, family income, and health in U.S. preschool and school-aged children. *American Journal of Public Health, 91*, 781–786.

Alexander, K. L., Entwisle, D. R., & Kabbani, N. (2001). The dropout process in life course perspective: Early risk factors at home and school. *Teachers College Record, 103*, 760–822.

Alexander, P. A., Jetton, T. L., & Kulikowich, J. M. (1995). Interrelationship of knowledge, interest, and recall: Assessing a model of domain learning. *Journal of Educational Psychology, 87*, 559–575.

Alink, L. R. A., Mesman, J., van Zeijl, J., Stolk, M., Juffer, F., Koot, H. M., et al. (2006). The early childhood aggression curve: Development of physical aggression in 10- to 50-month-old children. *Child Development, 77*, 954–966.

Allen, J., & Land, D. (1999). Attachment in adolescence. In J. Cassidy & P. Shaver (Eds.), *Handbook of attachment: Theory, research, and clinical applications.* (pp. 319–335). New York: Guilford.

Allen, J., Porter, M., McFarland, C., McElhaney, K. B., & Marsh, P. (2007). The relation of attachment security to adolescents' paternal and peer relationships, depression, and externalizing behavior. *Child Development, 78*, 1222–1239.

Alloway, T. P., Gathercole, S. E., Kirkwood, H., & Elliott, J. (2009a). The cognitive and behavioral characteristics of children with low working memory. *Child Development, 80*, 606–621.

Alloway, T. P., Gathercole, S. E., Kirkwood, H., & Elliott, J. (2009b). The working memory rating scale: A classroom-based behavioral assessment of working memory. *Learning and Individual Differences, 19*, 242–245.

Altschul, I., Oyserman, D., & Bybee, D. (2006). Racial-ethnic identity in mid-adolescence: Content and change as predictors of academic achievement. *Child Development, 77*, 1155–1169.

Alvarez, G., & Cavanagh, P. (2004). The capacity of visual short-term memory is set both by visual information load and by number of objects. *Psychological Science, 15*, 106–111.

Alvarez, L. (2004, April 9). Educators flocking to Finland, land of literate children. *New York Times*, p. A4.

Amato, P. R. (2001). Children of divorce in the 1990s: An update of the Amato and Keith (1991) meta-analysis. *Journal of Family Psychology, 15*, 355–370.

Ambady, N., Bernieri, F. J., & Richeson, J. A. (2000). Toward a histology of social behavior: Judgmental accuracy from thin slices of the behavioral stream. *Advances in Experimental Social Psychology, 32*, 201–271.

Ambady, N., Shih, M., Kim, A., & Pittinsky, T. L. (2001). Stereotype susceptibility in children: Effects of identity activation on quantitative performance. *Psychological Science, 12*, 385–390.

Amedi, A., Merabet, L. B., Bermpohl, F., & Pascual-Leone, J. (2005). The occipital cortex in the blind: Lessons about plasticity and vision. *Current Directions in Psychological Science, 14*, 306–311.

American Academy of Pediatrics. (1999). Early brain development and child care. *Healthy Child Care America, 3*, 1–6.

American Academy of Pediatrics. (2000). Clinical practice guideline: Diagnosis and evaluation of the child with Attention-Deficit/Hyperactivity Disorder. *Pediatrics, 105*, 1158–1170.

American Academy of Pediatrics. (2001). The transfer of drugs and other chemicals into human milk. *Pediatrics, 108*, 776–789.

American Psychiatric Association. (2000). Diagnostic and statistical manual of mental disorders (4th ed.). Washington, DC: Author.

American Psychological Association. (2007). *Report of the task force on the sexualization of girls.* Washington, DC: APA.

Amsterdam, B. (1972). Mirror self-image reactions before age two. *Developmental Psychobiology, 5*, 297–305.

Amsterlaw, J. (2006). Children's beliefs about everyday reasoning. *Child Development, 77*, 443–464.

Anderman, E., Griesinger, T., & Westerfield, G. (1998). Motivation and cheating during early adolescence. *Journal of Educational Psychology, 90*, 84–93.

Anderson, C. A. (2001). Heat and violence. *Current Directions in Psychological Science, 10*, 33–38.

Anderson, C. A., Berkowitz, L., Donnerstein, E., Huesmann, L. R., Johnson, J. D., Linz, D., et al. (2003). The influence of media violence on youth. *Psychological Science in the Public Interest, 4,* 81–110.

Anderson, D. R., Huston, A. C., Schmitt, K. L., Linebarger, D. L., & Wright, J. C. (2001). Early childhood television viewing and adolescent behavior. *Monographs of the Society for Research in Child Development, 66* (1, Serial No. 264).

Anglin, J. (1993). Vocabulary development: A morphological analysis. *Monographs of the Society for Research in Child Development, 58* (10, Serial No. 238).

Anisfeld, E., Casper, V., Nozyce, M., & Cunningham, N. (1990). Does infant carrying promote attachment? An experimental study of the effects of increased physical contact on the development of attachment. *Child Development, 61,* 1617–1627.

Ansari, D., & Coch, D. (2006). Bridges over troubled waters: Education and cognitive neuroscience. *Trends in Cognitive Sciences, 10,* 146–161.

Anthony, J. L., & Francis, D. J. (2005). Development of phonological awareness. *Current Directions in Psychological Sciences, 14,* 255–259.

Apfelbaum, E. P., Pauer, K., Ambady, N., Sommers, S. R., & Norton, M. I. (2008). Learning (not) to talk about race: When older children underperform in social categorization. *Developmental Psychology, 44,* 1513–1518.

Apperly, I. A., Samson, D., & Humphreys, G. W. (2009). Studies of adults can inform accounts of Theory of Mind development. *Developmental Psychology, 45,* 190–201.

Archer, J. (2006). Testosterone and human aggression: An evaluation of the challenge hypothesis. *Neuroscience & Biobehavioral Reviews, 30,* 319–345.

Archer, J., & Coyne, S. M. (2005). An integrated review of indirect, relational, and social aggression. *Personality and Social Psychology Review, 9,* 212–230.

Archibald, A., Graber, J., & Brooks-Gunn, J. (2003). Pubertal processes and physiological growth in adolescence. In G. Adams & M. Berzonsky (Eds.), *Blackwell handbook of adolescence* (pp. 24–47). Malden, MA: Blackwell.

Armstrong, C. (1999, March). The Dog Ate My . . .; When a teacher gets rid of deadlines, students run out of excuses and do their work. *Teacher Magazine, 10,* 50–51.

Arsenio, W. F., Adams, E., & Gold, J. (2009). Social information processing, moral reasoning, and emotion attributions: Relations with adolescents' reactive and proactive aggression. *Child Development, 80,* 1739–1755.

Arsenio, W. F., Cooperman, S., & Lover, A. (2000). Affective predictors of preschoolers' aggression and peer acceptance: Direct and indirect effects. *Developmental Psychology, 36,* 438–448.

Asendorpf, J., & Van Aken, M. (1999). Resilient, overcontrolled, and undercontrolled personality prototypes in childhood: Replicability, predictive power, and the trait-type issue. *Journal of Personality and Social Psychology, 77,* 815–832.

Ashby, F. G., Isen, A. M., & Turken, A. U. (1999). A neuropsychological theory of positive affect and its influence on cognition. *Psychological Review, 106,* 529–550.

Asher, S. R., & Hopmeyer, A. (1997). Children's responses to peer conflicts involving a rights infraction. *Merrill-Palmer Quarterly, 43,* 235–254.

Asher, S. R., & Paquette, J. (2003). Loneliness and peer relations in childhood. *Current Directions in Psychological Science, 12,* 75–78.

Astor, R. A., Benbenishty, R., & Estrada, J. N. (2009). School violence and theoretically atypical schools: The principal's centrality in orchestrating safe schools. *American Educational Research Journal, 46,* 423–461.

Athanases, S. Z. (1998). Diverse learners, diverse texts: Exploring identity and difference through literary encounters. *Journal of Literacy Research, 30,* 273–296.

Atlas, R., & Pepler, D. (1998). Observations of bullying in the classroom. *Journal of Educational Research, 92,* 86–99.

Aunola, K., & Nurmi, J.-E. (2005). The role of parenting styles in children's problem behavior. *Child Development, 76,* 1144–1159.

Austin, J. L., & Soeda, J. M. (2008). Fixed-time teacher attention to decrease off-task behaviors of typically developing third graders. *Journal of Applied Behavior Analysis, 41,* 279–283.

Aviezer, O., Sagi, A., Resnick, G., & Gini, M. (2002). School competence in young adolescence: Links to early attachment relationships beyond concurrent self-perceived competence and representations of relationships. *International Journal of Behavioral Development, 26,* 387–409.

Ayduk, O., Mendoza-Denton, R., Mischel, W., Downey, G., Peake, P., & Rodriguez, M. (2000). Regulating the interpersonal self: Strategic self-regulation for coping with rejection sensitivity. *Journal of Personality and Social Psychology, 79,* 776–792.

Babad, E., Bernieri, F., & Rosenthal, R. (1991). Students as judges of teachers' verbal and nonverbal behavior. *American Educational Research Journal, 28,* 211–234.

Baer, J., Baldi, S., Ayotte, K., & Green, P. (2007). *The reading literacy of U.S. fourth-grade students in an international context: Results from the 2001 and 2006 Progress in International Reading Literacy Study (PIRLS)* (NCES 2008–017). National Center for Education Statistics, U.S. Department of Education. Washington, DC.

Bagwell, C., Coie, J., Terry, R., & Lochman, J. (2000). Peer clique participation and social status in preadolescence. *Merrill-Palmer Quarterly, 46,* 280–305.

Baillargeon, R. (1987). Object permanence in 3 1/2- and 4 1/2-month-old infants. *Developmental Psychology, 23,* 655–664.

Baillargeon, R. (2008). Innate ideas revisited: For a principle of persistence in infants' physical reasoning. *Perspectives on Psychological Science, 3,* 2–13.

Baillargeon, R., Kotovsky, L., & Needham, A. (1995). The acquisition of physical knowledge in infancy. In D. Sperber, D. Premack & A. J. Premack (Eds.), *Causal cognition: A multidisciplinary debate.* Oxford: Clarendon Press.

Baillargeon, R. H., Zoccolillo, M., Keenan, K., Cote, S., Perusse, D., Wu, H.-Z., et al. (2007). Gender differences in physical aggression: A prospective population-based survey of children before and after 2 years of age. *Developmental Psychology, 43,* 13–26.

Bakermans-Kranenburg, M. J., van IJzendoorn, M., & Juffer, F. (2003). Less is more: Meta-analyses of sensitivity and attachment interventions in early childhood. *Psychological Bulletin, 129,* 195–215.

Bakermans-Kranenburg, M. J., Van IJzendoorn, M. H., Pijlman, F. T. A., Mesman, J., & Juffer, F. (2008). Experimental evidence for differential susceptibility: Dopamine D4 receptor polymorphism (DRD4 VNTR) moderates intervention effects on toddlers' externalizing behavior in a randomized controlled trial. *Developmental Psychology, 44,* 293–300.

Baldwin, D. (2000). Interpersonal understanding fuels knowledge acquisition. *Current Directions in Psychological Science, 9*, 40–45.

Balfanz, R., Herzog, L., & MacIver, D. J. (2007). Preventing student disengagement and keeping students on the graduation path in urban middle-grades schools: Early identification and effective interventions. *Educational Psychologist, 42*, 223–235.

Ball, D. L., & Wilson, S. M. (1996). Integrity in teaching: Recognizing the fusion of the moral and intellectual. *American Educational Research Journal, 33*, 155–192.

Bandura, A. (1965). Influence of models' reinforcement contingencies on the acquisition of imitative responses. *Journal of Personality and Social Psychology, 1*, 589–595.

Bandura, A. (1997). *Self-efficacy: The exercise of control.* New York: Freeman.

Bandura, A. (2007). Albert Bandura. In G. Lindzey & W. M. Runyan (Eds.), *A history of psychology in autobiography* (Vol. IX, pp. 42–75). Washington, DC: American Psychological Association.

Bandura, A., Barbaranelli, C., Caprara, G., & Pastorelli, C. (1996). Multifaceted impact of self-efficacy beliefs on academic functioning. *Child Development, 67*, 1206–1222.

Bandura, A., Ross, D., & Ross, S. A. (1961). Transmission of aggression through imitation of aggressive models. *Journal of Abnormal and Social Psychology, 63*, 575–583.

Bandura, A., Ross, D., & Ross, S. A. (1963). Imitation of film-mediated aggressive models. *Journal of Abnormal and Social Psychology, 66*, 3–11.

Bandura, A., & Schunk, D. H. (1981). Cultivating competence, self-efficacy, and intrinsic interest through proximal self-motivation. *Journal of Personality and Social Psychology, 41*, 586–598.

Banich, M. (2009). Executive function: The search for an integrated account. *Current Directions in Psychological Science, 18*, 89–94.

Bannard, C., & Matthews, D. (2008). Stored word sequences in language learning: The effect of familiarity on children's repetition of four-word combinations. *Psychological Science, 19*, 241–248.

Barber, B., Stolz, H., & Olsen, J. (2005). Parental support, psychological control, and behavioral control: Assessing relevance across time, culture, and method. In *Monographs of the Society for Research in Child Development, 70* (No. 4, Serial No. 282).

Barber, B. K., & Olsen, J. A. (2004). Assessing the transitions to middle and high school. *Journal of Adolescent Research, 19*, 3–30.

Barell, J. (1980). *Playgrounds of our minds.* New York: Teachers College Press.

Bariaud, F. (1989). Age differences in children's humor. In P. McGhee (Ed.), *Humor and children's development: A guide to practical applications* (pp. 15–45). New York: Haworth.

Barkley, R. A. (2006). *Attention-deficit hyperactivity disorder: A handbook for diagnosis and treatment* (3rd ed.). New York: Guilford.

Barnett, D., Kidwell, S., & Leung, K. H. (1998). Parenting and preschooler attachment among low-income urban African American families. *Child Development, 69*, 1657–1671.

Barnett, S. (1995). Long-term effects of early childhood programs on cognitive and school outcomes. *The Future of Children, 5*, 25–50.

Baron, A. S., & Banaji, M. R. (2006). The development of implicit attitudes: Evidence of race evaluations from ages 6 and 10 and adulthood. *Psychological Science, 17*, 53–58.

Barr-Anderson, D. J., van den Berg, P., Neumark-Sztainer, D., & Story, M. (2008). Characteristics associated with older adolescents who have a television in their bedrooms. *Pediatrics, 121*, 718–724.

Barrett, L. F. (2006). Are emotions natural kinds? *Perspectives on Psychological Science, 1*, 28–58.

Barros, R. M., Silver, E. J., & Stein, R. E. (2009). School recess and group classroom behavior. *Pediatrics, 123*, 431–536.

Barrouillet, P., Gavens, N., Vergauwe, E., Gaillard, V., & Camos, V. (2009). Working memory span development: A time-based resource-sharing model account. *Developmental Psychology, 45*, 477–490.

Barth, H., Beckmann, L., & Spelke, E. S. (2008). Nonsymbolic, approximate arithmetic in children: Abstract addition prior to instruction. *Developmental Psychology, 44*, 1466–1477.

Bartlett, M. Y., & DeSteno, D. (2006). Gratitude and prosocial behavior: Helping when it costs you. *Psychological Science, 17*, 319–325.

Bartsch, K., & London, K. (2000). Children's use of mental state information in selecting persuasive arguments. *Developmental Psychology, 36*, 352–365.

Bast, J., & Reitsma, P. (1998). Analyzing the development of individual differences in terms of Matthew effects in reading: Results from a Dutch longitudinal study. *Developmental Psychology, 34*, 1373–1399.

Bates, J., Viken, R., Alexander, D., Beyers, J., & Stockton, L. (2002). Sleep and adjustment in preschool children: Sleep diary reports by mothers related to behavior reports by teachers. *Child Development, 73*, 62–74.

Batson, C. D., & Thompson, E. (2001). Why don't moral people act morally? Motivational considerations. *Current Directions in Psychological Science, 10*, 54–57.

Bauer, P. J. (2002). Long-term recall memory: Behavioral and neuro-developmental changes in the first 2 years of life. *Current Directions in Psychological Science, 11*, 137–141.

Bauer, P. J., Wiebe, S., Carver, L., Waters, J., & Nelson, C. (2003). Developments in long-term explicit memory late in the first year of life: Behavioral and electrophysiological indices. *Psychological Science, 14*, 629–635.

Baugh, J. (2002). African American language and literacy. In M. J. Schleppegrell & M. C. Colombi (Eds.), *Developing advanced literacy in first and second languages* (pp. 177–185). Mahwah, NJ: Erlbaum.

Baumeister, R. F., Bushman, B. J., & Campbell, W. K. (2000). Self-esteem, narcissism, and aggression: Does violence result from threatened egotism? *Current Directions in Psychological Science, 9*, 26–29.

Baumeister, R. F., Campbell, J. D., Krueger, J. I., & Vohs, K. D. (2003). Does high self-esteem cause better performance, interpersonal success, happiness, or healthier lifestyles? *Psychological Science in the Public Interest, 4*, 1–44.

Baumeister, R. F., Vohs, K. D., & Tice, D. (2007). The strength model of self-control. *Current Directions in Psychological Science, 16*, 351–355.

Bauminger, N. (2002). The facilitation of social-emotional understanding and social interaction in high-functioning children with autism: Intervention outcomes. *Journal of Autism and Developmental Disorders, 32*, 283–298.

Baumrind, D. (1991). The influence of parenting style on adolescent competence and substance use. *Journal of Early Adolescence, 11*, 56–95.

Baydar, N., Reid, J., & Webster-Stratton, C. (2003). The role of mental health factors and program engagement in the effectiveness of a preventive parenting program for Head Start mothers. *Child Development, 74*, 1433–1453.

Bayliss, D., Jarrold, C., Baddeley, A., Gunn, D., & Leigh, E. (2005). Mapping the developmental constraints on working memory span performance. *Developmental Psychology, 41*, 579–597.

Beatty, J. (2001). *The human brain: Essentials of behavioral neuroscience*. Thousand Oaks, CA: Sage.

Beck, I. L., & McKeown, M. (2007). Increasing young low-income children's oral vocabulary repertoires through rich and focused instruction. *The Elementary School Journal, 3*, 251–271.

Beckett, C., Maughan, B., Rutter, M., Castle, J., Colvert, E., Groothues, C., et al. (2006). Do the effects of early severe deprivation on cognition persist into early adolescence? Findings from the English and Romanian adoptees study. *Child Development, 77*, 696–711.

Behrens, K. Y., Hesse, E., & Main, M. (2007). Mothers' attachment status as determined by the adult attachment interview predicts their 6-year-olds' reunion responses: A study conducted in Japan. *Developmental Psychology, 43*, 1553–1567.

Beijersbergen, M. D., Bakermans-Kranenburg, M. J., Van IJzendoorn, M. H., & Juffer, F. (2008). Stress regulation in adolescents: Physiological reactivity during the adult attachment interview and conflict interaction. *Child Development, 79*, 1707–1720.

Beilock, S., & Carr, T. (2005). When high-powered people fail: Working memory and "choking under pressure" in math. *Psychological Science, 16*, 101–105.

Beishuizen, J., Hof, E., van Putten, C., Bouwmeester, S., & Asscher, J. (2001). Students' and teachers' cognitions about good teachers. *British Journal of Educational Psychology, 71*, 185–201.

Bell, S. K., & Morgan, S. B. (2000). Children's attitudes and behavioral intentions toward a peer presented as obese: Does a medical explanation for the obesity make a difference? *Journal of Pediatric Psychology, 25*, 137–145.

Belsky, J., Bakermans-Kranenburg, M. J., & Van IJzendoorn, M. H. (2007). For better and for worse: Differential susceptibility to environmental influences. *Current Directions in Psychological Science, 16*, 300–304.

Belsky, J., Steinberg, L., Houts, R. M., & Halpern-Felsher, B. L. (2010). The development of reproductive strategy in females: Early maternal harshness → earlier menarche → increased sexual risk taking. *Developmental Psychology, 46*, 120–128.

Belsky, J., Vandell, D. L., Burchinal, M., Clarke-Stewart, K. A., McCartney, K., Owen, M. T., et al. (2007). Are there long-term effects of early child care? *Child Development, 78*, 681–701.

BeLue, R., Francis, L. A., & Colaco, B. (2009). Mental health problems and overweight in a nationally representative sample of adolescents: Effects of race and ethnicity. *Pediatrics, 123*, 697–702.

Benbow, C., Lubinski, D., Shea, D., & Eftekhari-Sanjani, H. (2000). Sex differences in mathematical reasoning ability at age 13: Their status 20 years later. *Psychological Science, 11*, 474–480.

Bender, H. L., Allen, J. P., McElhaney, K. B., Antonishak, J., Moore, C. M., Kelly, H. O., et al. (2007). Use of harsh physical discipline and developmental outcomes in adolescence. *Development and Psychopathology, 19*, 227–242.

Benenson, J., & Christakos, A. (2003). The greater fragility of females' versus males' closest same-sex friendships. *Child Development, 74*, 1123–1129.

Benner, A. D., & Graham, S. (2009). The transition to high school as a developmental process among multiethnic urban youth. *Child Development, 80*, 356–376.

Benner, A. D., & Kim, S. Y. (2009). Experiences of discrimination among Chinese American adolescents and the consequences for socioemotional and academic development. *Developmental Psychology, 45*, 1682–1694.

Benninga, J., & Wynne, E. (1998). Keeping in character: A time-tested solution. *Phi Delta Kappan, 79*, 439–445, 448.

Beran, M., & Beran, M. (2004). Chimpanzees remember the results of one-by-one addition of food items to sets over extended time periods. *Psychological Science, 15*, 94–99.

Berger, K. S. (2007). Update on bullying at school: Science forgotten? *Developmental Review, 27*, 90–126.

Berger, L. M., Bruch, S. K., Johnson, E., James, S., & Rubin, D. (2009). Estimating the "impact" of out-of-home placement on child well-being: Approaching the problem of selection bias. *Child Development, 80*, 1856–1876.

Bergin, C. C. (1987). Prosocial development in toddlers: The patterning of mother-infant interactions. In M. E. Ford & D. H. Ford (Eds.), *Humans as self-constructing living systems: Putting the framework to work* (pp. 121–143). Hillsdale, NJ: Erlbaum.

Bergin, C. C. (2001). The parent–child relationship during beginning reading. *Journal of Literacy Research, 33*, 681–706.

Bergin, C. C., & Bergin, D. A. (1999). Classroom discipline that promotes self-control. *Journal of Applied Developmental Psychology, 20*, 189–206.

Bergin, C. C., & Bergin, D. A. (2009). Attachment in the classroom. *Educational Psychology Review, 21*, 141–170.

Bergin, C. C., & McCullough, P. (2009). Attachment in substance-exposed toddlers: The role of caregiving and exposure. *Infant Mental Health Journal, 30*, 407–423.

Bergin, C. C., Bergin, D. A., & French, E. (1995). Preschoolers' prosocial repertoires: Parents' perspectives. *Early Childhood Research Quarterly, 10*, 81–103.

Bergin, C. C., Talley, S., & Hamer, L. (2003). Prosocial behaviours of young adolescents: A focus group study. *Journal of Adolescence, 26*, 13–32.

Bergin, D. A. (1999). Influences on classroom interest. *Educational Psychologist, 34*, 87–98.

Bergin, D. A., & Cizek, G. J. (2001). Alfred Binet. In J. A. Palmer, L. Bresler & D. E. Cooper (Eds.), *Fifty major thinkers on education: From Confucius to Dewey* (pp. 160–164). London: Routledge.

Bergin, D. A., & Cooks, H. C. (2000). Academic competition among students of color: An interview study. *Urban Education, 35*, 442–472.

Bergin, D. A., & Cooks, H. C. (2002). High school students of color talk about accusations of "acting white." *The Urban Review, 34*, 113–134.

Bergin, D. A., Hudson, L. M., Chryst, C. F., & Resetar, M. (1992). An afterschool intervention program for educationally disadvantaged young children. *The Urban Review, 24*, 203–217.

Berk, R. A. (2002). *Humor as an instructional defibrillator*. Sterling, VA: Stylus Publishing.

Berkowitz, M., & Grych, J. (2000). Early character development and education. *Early Education and Development, 11*, 55–72.

Berlin, L., Ispa, J. M., Fine, M. A., Malone, P. S., Brooks-Gunn, J., Brady-Smith, C., et al. (2009). Correlates and consequences of spanking and verbal punishment for low-income White, African American, and Mexican American toddlers. *Child Development, 80*, 1403–1420.

Bernal, M. E., Knight, G. P., Garza, C. A., Ocampo, K. A., & Cota, M. K. (1990). The development of ethnic identity in Mexican-American children. *Hispanic Journal of Behavioral Sciences, 12*, 3–24.

Berndt, T. J. (2002). Friendship quality and social development. *Current Directions in Psychological Science, 11*, 7–10.

Berndt, T. J., & Burgy, L. (1996). Social self-concept. In B. A. Bracken (Ed.), *Handbook of self-concept: Developmental, social, and clinical considerations* (pp. 171–209). New York: Wiley.

Berndt, T. J., Hawkins, J., & Jiao, Z. (1999). Influences of friends and friendships on adjustment to junior high school. *Merrill-Palmer Quarterly, 45*, 13–41.

Bernier, A., & Meins, E. (2008). A threshold approach to understanding the origins of attachment disorganization. *Developmental Psychology, 44*, 969–982.

Bernstein, D., & Loftus, E. F. (2009). How to tell if a particular memory is true or false. *Perspectives on Psychological Science, 4*, 370–374.

Berry, G. L. (2007). Television, social roles, and marginality: Portrayals of the past and images for the future. In N. Pecora, J. P. Murray & E. Wartella (Eds.), *Children and television: Fifty years of research* (pp. 85–107). Mahwah, NJ: Erlbaum.

Bert, S. C., Guner, B. M., & Lanzi, R. G. (2009). The influence of maternal history of abuse on parenting knowledge and behavior. *Family Relations, 58*, 176–187.

Bessant, J. (2008). Hard wired for risk: Neurological science, "the adolescent brain" and developmental theory. *Journal of Youth Studies, 11*, 347–360.

Beunen, G., & Malina, R. (1988). Growth and physical performance relative to the timing of the adolescent spurt. *Exercise and Sport Sciences Reviews, 16*, 503–540.

Beuscher, E., & Roebers, C. M. (2005). *Enhancing knowledge acquisition from educational television*. Paper presented at the Society for Research in Child Devleopment, Atlanta, GA.

Biederman, J. (2005). Attention-deficit/hyperactivity disorder: A selective overview. *Biological Psychiatry, 57*, 1215–1220.

Biemiller, A., & Boote, C. (2006). An effective method for building meaning vocabulary in primary grades. *Journal of Educational Psychology, 98*, 44–62.

Bigler, R. S., Brown, C., & Markell, M. (2001). When groups are not created equal: Effects of group status on the formation of intergroup attitudes in children. *Child Development, 72*, 1151–1162.

Birch, L. L. (1999). Development of food preferences. *Annual Review of Nutrition, 19*, 41–62.

Birch, S., & Bloom, P. (2007). The curse of knowledge in reasoning about false beliefs. *Psychological Science, 18*, 382–578.

Bishop, D. V. (2006). What causes specific language impairment in children? *Current Directions in Psychological Science, 15*, 217–221.

Bishop, D. V., & Snowling, M. J. (2004). Developmental dyslexia and specific language impairment: Same or different? *Psychological Bulletin, 130*, 858–888.

Bishop, G., Spence, S., & McDonald, C. (2003). Can parents and teachers provide a reliable and valid report of behavioral inhibition? *Child Development, 74*, 1899–1917.

Bjorklund, D. F., & Pellegrini, A. (2000). Child development and evolutionary psychology. *Child Development, 71*, 1687–1708.

Bjorkqvist, K. (2001). Different names, same issue. *Social Development, 10*, 272–274.

Black, M., & Matula, K. (2000). *Essentials of Bayley Scales of Infant Development-II assessment*. New York: Wiley.

Blackwell, L. S., Trzesniewski, K. H., & Dweck, C. S. (2007). Implicit theories of intelligence predict achievement across an adolescent transition: A longitudinal study and an intervention. *Child Development, 78*, 246–263.

Blair, C. (2001). The early identification of risk for grade retention among African American children at risk for school difficulty. *Applied Developmental Science, 5*, 37–50.

Blair, C. (2002). School readiness: Integrating cognition and emotion in a neurobiological conceptualization of children's functioning at school entry. *American Psychologist, 57*, 111–127.

Blair, C., Granger, D., & Razza, R. (2005). Cortisol reactivity is positively related to executive function in preschool children attending Head Start. *Child Development, 76*, 554–567.

Blair, C., Granger, D. A., Kivlighan, K. T., Mills-Koonce, W. R., Willoughby, M., Greenberg, M. T., et al. (2008). Maternal and child contributions to cortisol response to emotional arousal in young children from low-income, rural communities. *Developmental Psychology, 44*, 1095–1109.

Blair, C., & Razza, R. P. (2007). Relating effortful control, executive function, and false belief understanding to emerging math and literacy ability in kindergarten. *Child Development, 78*, 647–663.

Blandon, A., Calkins, S. D., Keane, S. P., & O'Brien, M. (2008). Individual differences in trajectories of emotion regulation processes: The effects of maternal depressive symptomatology and children's physiological regulation. *Developmental Psychology, 44*, 1110–1123.

Blatchford, P. (1998). The state of play in schools. *Child Psychology & Psychiatry Review, 3*, 58–67.

Blatt-Eisengart, I., Drabick, D. A., Monahan, K. C., & Steinberg, L. (2009). Sex differences in the longitudinal relations among family risk factors and childhood externalizing symptoms. *Developmental Psychology, 45*, 491–502.

Bleske-Rechek, A., Lubinski, D., & Benbow, C. (2004). Meeting the educational needs of special populations: Advanced Placement's role in developing exceptional human capital. *Psychological Science, 15*, 217–224.

Blewitt, P., Rump, K. M., Shealy, S. E., & Cook, S. A. (2009). Shared book reading: When and how questions affect young children's word learning. *Journal of Educational Psychology, 101*, 291–304.

Bliss, L. S., & McCabe, A. (2008). Personal narratives: Cultural differences and clinical implications. *Topics in Language Disorders, 28*, 162–177.

Blum, R., Beuhring, T., Shew, M., Bearinger, L., Sieving, R., & Resnick, M. (2000). The effects of race/ethnicity, income, and family structure on adolescent risk behaviors. *American Journal of Public Health, 90*, 1879–1885.

Boddy, J., Skuse, D., & Andrews, B. (2000). The developmental sequelae of nonorganic failure to thrive. *Journal of Child Psychology & Psychiatry & Allied Disciplines, 41*, 1003–1014.

Bodenhausen, G. V., Gabriel, S., & Lineberger, M. (2000). Sadness and susceptiblity to judgmental bias: The case of anchoring. *Psychological Science, 11*, 320–323.

Boehnke, K. (2008). Peer pressure: A cause of scholastic underachievement? A cross-cultural study of mathematical achievement among German, Canadian, and Israeli middle school students. *Social Psychology of Education, 11*, 149–160.

Bogard, K., & Takanishi, R. (2005). PK-3: An aligned and coordinated approach to education for children 3 to 8 years old. *Social Policy Report, 19*, 3–23.

Bohlin, G., Hagekull, B., & Rydell, A. (2000). Attachment and social functioning: A longitudinal study from infancy to middle childhood. *Social Development, 9*, 24–39.

Bokhorst, C., Bakermans-Kranenburg, M., Fearon, P., van IJzendoorn, M., Fonagy, P., & Schuengel, C. (2003). The importance of shared environment in mother-infant attachment security: A behavioral genetic study. *Child Development, 74*, 1769–1782.

Bolger, K. E., & Patterson, C. J. (2001). Developmental pathways from child maltreatment to peer rejection. *Child Development, 72*, 549–568.

Bonanno, G., Papa, A., Lalande, K., Westphal, M., & Coifman, K. (2004). The importance of being flexible: The ability to both enhance and suppress emotional expression predicts long-term adjustment. *Psychological Science, 15*, 482–487.

Booth, J. L., & Siegler, R. S. (2008). Numerical magnitude representations influence arithmetic learning. *Child Development, 79*, 1016–1031.

Borman, G., Slavin, R. E., Cheung, A., Chamberlain, A. M., Madden, N., & Chambers, B. (2007). Final reading outcomes of the national randomized field trial of Success for All. *American Educational Research Journal, 44*, 701–731.

Bornstein, M. H., Hahn, C.-S., Bell, C., Haynes, O. M., Slater, A., Golding, J., et al. (2006). Stability in cognition across early childhood: A developmental cascade. *Psychological Science, 17*, 151–158.

Bornstein, M. H., Hahn, C.-S., Gist, N. F., & Haynes, O. M. (2006). Long-term cumulative effects of childcare on children's mental development and socioemotional adjustment in a non-risk sample: The moderating effects of gender. *Early Child Development and Care, 176*, 129–156.

Bornstein, M. H., & Putnick, D. L. (2007). Chronological age, cognitions, and practices in European American mothers: A multivariate study of parenting. *Developmental Psychology, 4*, 850–864.

Bornstein, M. H., Putnick, D. L., Suwalsky, J. T. D., & Gini, M. (2006). Maternal chronological age, prenatal and perinatal history, social support, and parenting of infants. *Child Development, 77*, 875–892.

Bos, H. M. W., Sandfort, T. G. M., de Bruyn, E. H., & Hakvoort, E. M. (2008). Same-sex attraction, social relationships, psychosocial functioning, and school performance in early adolescence. *Developmental Psychology, 44*, 59–68.

Bosacki, S., & Astington, J. (1999). Theory of mind in preadolescence: Relations between social understanding and social competence. *Social Development, 8*, 237–255.

Bost, K., Vaughn, B., Washington, W., Cielinski, K., & Bradbard, M. (1998). Social competence, social support, and attachment: Demarcation of construct domains, measurement, and paths of influence for preschool children attending Head Start. *Child Development, 69*, 192–218.

Bouchard, T. (2004). Genetic influence on human psychological traits. *Current Directions in Psychological Science, 13*, 148–151.

Bouchard, T. J., Lykken, D. T., McGue, M., Segal, N. L., & Tellegen, A. (1990). Sources of human psychological differences: The Minnesota study of twins reared apart. *Science, 150*, 223–228.

Bouchey, H., & Furman, W. (2003). Dating and romantic experiences in adolescence. In G. Adams & M. Berzonsky (Eds.), *Blackwell handbook of adolescence* (pp. 313–329). Malden, MA: Blackwell.

Bowes, L., Arseneault, L., Maughn, B., Taylor, A., Caspi, A., & Moffitt, T. (2009). School, neighborhood, and family factors are associated with children's bullying involvement: A nationally representative longitudinal study. *Journal of the American Academy of Child and Adolescent Psychiatry, 48*, 545–553.

Bowlby, J. (1940). The influence of early environment in the development of neurosis and neurotic character. *The International Journal of Psycho-analysis, 21*, 154–178.

Bowlby, J. (1952). *Maternal care and mental health.* Geneva: World Health Organization.

Bowlby, J. (1969). *Attachment* (Vol. I). New York: Basic Books.

Boyle, M., Jenkins, J., Georgiades, K., Cairney, J., Duku, E., & Racine, Y. (2004). Differential maternal parenting behavior: Estimating within- and between-family effects on children. *Child Development, 75*, 1457–1476.

Boyle, R. (2002). Effects of certain prenatal drugs on the fetus and newborn. *Pediatrics in Review, 23*, 17–23.

Brackis-Cott, E., Mellins, C., & Block, M. (2003). Current life concerns of early adolescents and their mothers: Influence of maternal HIV. *Journal of Early Adolescence, 23*, 51–77.

Bradley, R., & Corwyn, R. (2002). Socioeconomic status and child development. *Annual Review of Psychology, 53*, 371–399.

Bradley, R., Corwyn, R., Burchinal, M., McAdoo, H., & Garcia Coll, C. (2001). The home environments of children in the United States. Part II: Relations with behavioral development through age thirteen. *Child Development, 72*, 1868–1886.

Bradley, R. H., Caldwell, B. M., Rock, S. L., Barnard, K. E., Gray, C., Hammond, M. A., et al. (1989). Home environment and cognitive development in the first 3 years of life: A collaborative study involving six sites and three ethnic groups in North America. *Developmental Psychology, 25*, 217–235.

Bradley, R. H., & Corwyn, R. F. (2006). The family environment. In L. Balter & C. Tamis-LeMonda (Eds.), *Child psychology: A handbook of contemporary issues* (pp. 493–520). New York: Psychology Press.

Brainerd, C. J., Holliday, R., & Reyna, V. F. (2004). Behavioral measurement of remembering phenomenologies: So simple a child can do it. *Child Development, 75*, 505–522.

Bramlett, M., & Mosher, W. (2002). *Cohabitation, marriage, divorce, and remarriage in the United States*. Hyattsville, MD: National Center for Health Statistics.

Brand, A. E., & Brinich, P. M. (1999). Behavior problems and mental health contacts in adopted, foster, and nonadopted children. *Journal of Child Psychology & Psychiatry & Allied Disciplines, 40*, 1221–1229.

Branstetter, S. A., Furman, W., & Cottrell, L. (2009). The influence of representations of attachment, maternal-adolescent relationship quality, and maternal monitoring on adolescent substance use: A 2-year longitudinal examination. *Child Development, 80*, 1448–1462.

Braungart-Reiker, J. M., Garwood, M. M., Powers, B. P., & Wang, X. (2001). Parental sensitivity, infant affect, and affect regulation: Predictors of later attachment. *Child Development, 72*, 252–270.

Brendgen, M., Boivin, M., Vitaro, F., Bukowski, W. M., Dionne, G., Tremblay, R. E., et al. (2008). Linkages between children's and their friends' social and physical aggression: Evidence for a gene–environment interaction? *Child Development, 79*, 13–29.

Brendgen, M., Little, T., & Krappman, L. (2000). Rejected children and their friends: A shared evaluation of friendship quality? *Merrill-Palmer Quarterly, 46*, 45–70.

Brennan, P., Hall, J., Bor, W., Najman, J., & Williams, G. (2003). Integrating biological and social processes in relation to early-onset persistent aggression in boys and girls. *Developmental Psychology, 39*, 309–323.

Brenner, E. M., & Salovey, P. (1997). Emotion regulation during childhood: Developmental, interpersonal, and individual considerations. In P. Salovey & D. J. Sluyter (Eds.), *Emotional development and emotional intelligence: Educational implications* (pp. 168–192). New York: Basic Books.

Breslau, N., Johnson, E., & Lucia, V. (2001). Academic achievement of low birthweight children at age 11: The role of cognitive abilities at school entry. *Journal of Abnormal Child Psychology, 29*, 273–279.

Bretherton, I., & Munholland, K. (1999). Internal working models in attachment relationships: A construct revisited. In J. Cassidy & P. Shaver (Eds.), *Handbook of attachment: Theory, research, and clinical applications*. (pp. 89–111). New York: Guilford.

Breunlin, D., Bryant-Edwards, T., Hetherington, J., & Cimmarusti, R. (2002). Conflict resolution training as an alternative to suspension for violent behavior. *Journal of Educational Research, 95*, 349–357.

Broberg, A., Wessels, H., Lamb, M., & Hwang, P. (1997). Effects of day care on the development of cognitive abilities in 8-year-olds: A longitudinal study. *Developmental Psychology, 33*, 62–69.

Brody, G., Ge, X., Conger, R., Gibbons, F., Murry, V., Gerrard, M., et al. (2001). The influence of neighborhood disadvantage, collective socialization, and parenting on African American children's affiliation with deviant peers. *Child Development, 72*, 1231–1246.

Brody, G. H., Beach, S. R. H., Philibert, R. A., Chen, Y.-F., & Murry, V. M. (2009). Prevention effects moderate the association of 5-HTTLPR and youth risk behavior initiation: Gene-environment hypotheses tested via a randomized prevention design. *Child Development, 80*, 645–661.

Brody, G. H., Chen, Y.-F., Murry, V. M., Ge, X., Simons, R. L., Gibbons, F. X., et al. (2006). Perceived discrimination and the adjustment of African American youths: A five-year longitudinal analysis with contextual moderation effects. *Child Development, 77*, 1170–1189.

Brody, N. (1992). *Intelligence* (2nd ed.). New York: Academic Press.

Broh, B. (2002). Linking extracurricular programming to academic achievement: Who benefits and why? *Sociology of Education, 75*, 69–95.

Broidy, L., Tremblay, R., Brame, B., Fergusson, D., Horwood, J., Laird, R., et al. (2003). Developmental trajectories of childhood disruptive behaviors and adolescent delinquency: A six-site, cross-national study. *Developmental Psychology, 39*, 222–245.

Bronfenbrenner, U., & Ceci, S. J. (1994). Nature-nurture reconceptualized in developmental perspective: A bioecological model. *Psychological Review, 101*, 568–586.

Bronfenbrenner, U., & Morris, P. (1998). The ecology of developmental processes. In W. Damon & R. Lerner (Eds.), *Handbook of child psychology: Theoretical models of human development* (5th ed., Vol. 1, pp. 993–1028). New York: Wiley.

Bronfenbrenner, U., & Morris, P. A. (2006). The bioecological model of human development. In R. M. Lerner & W. Damon (Eds.), *Handbook of child psychology: Theoretical models of human development* (6th ed., Vol. 1, pp. 793–828). New York: Wiley.

Brooks-Gunn, J. (2003). Do you believe in magic? What we can expect from early childhood intervention programs. *Social Policy Report, 17*, 3–14.

Brooks-Gunn, J., Han, W.-J., & Waldfogel, J. (2002). Maternal employment and child cognitive outcomes in the first three years of life: The NICHD Study of Early Child Care. *Child Development, 73*, 1052–1072.

Brown, C. S., & Bigler, R. S. (2005). Children's perceptions of discrimination: A developmental model. *Child Development, 76*, 533–553.

Brown, J. S., Meadows, S. O., & Elder, G. H. (2007). Race-ethnic inequality and psychological distress: Depressive symptoms from adolescence to young adulthood. *Developmental Psychology, 43*, 1295–1311.

Brown, L., Lescano, C., & Lourie, K. (2001). Children and adolescents with HIV infection. *Psychiatric Annals, 31*, 63–68.

Brown, R. P., Osterman, L. L., & Barnes, C. D. (2009). School violence and the culture of honor. *Psychological Science, 20*, 1400–1405.

Brown, S., Tapert, S., Granholm, E., & Delis, D. (2000). Neurocognitive functioning of adolescents: Effects of protracted alcohol use. *Alcoholism: Clinical & Experimental Research, 24*, 164–171.

Brown, S. C., & Craik, F. I. M. (2000). Encoding and retrieval of information. In E. Tulving & F. I. M. Craik (Eds.), *The Oxford handbook of memory*. Oxford: Oxford University Press.

Brown, W. H., Pfeiffer, K. A., McIver, K. L., Dowda, M., Addy, C. L., & Pate, R. R. (2009). Social and environmental factors associated with preschoolers' nonsedentary physical activity. *Child Development, 80*, 45–58.

Brownell, M., & Walther-Thomas, C. (2001). Interview with Steven Shore: Understanding the autism spectrum—What teachers need to know. *Intervention in School and Clinic, 36*, 293–299.

Bruck, M., Ceci, S., & Principe, G. (2006). The child and the law. In K. A. Renninger & R. Lerner (Eds.), *Handbook of child psychology* (6th ed., Vol. 4, pp. 776–816). New York: Wiley.

Bryant, J., & Zillmann, D. (1989). Using humor to promote learning in the classroom. In P. McGhee (Ed.), *Humor and children's development: A guide to practical applications* (pp. 49–78). New York: Haworth.

Bub, K., McCartney, K., & Willett, J. B. (2007). Behavior problem trajectories and first-grade cognitive ability and achievement skills: A latent growth curve analysis. *Journal of Educational Psychology, 99,* 653–670.

Buckhalt, J. A., El-Sheikh, M., & Keller, P. (2007). Children's sleep and cognitive functioning: Race and socioeconomic status as moderators of effects. *Child Development, 78,* 213–231.

Buckhalt, J. A., El-Sheikh, M., Keller, P., & Kelly, R. J. (2009). Concurrent and longitudinal relations between children's sleep and cognitive functioning: The moderating role of parent education. *Child Development, 80,* 875–892.

Buehler, C., Lange, G., & Franck, K. L. (2007). Adolescents' cognitive and emotional responses to marital hostility. *Child Development, 78,* 775–789.

Bugental, D., & Happaney, K. (2004). Predicting infant maltreatment in low-income families: The interactive effects of maternal attributions and child status at birth. *Developmental Psychology, 40,* 234–243.

Buhs, E., & Ladd, G. W. (2001). Peer rejection as an antecedent of young children's school adjustment: An examination of mediating processes. *Developmental Psychology, 37,* 550–560.

Bukowski, W., Sippola, L., & Newcomb, A. (2000). Variations in patterns of attraction to same- and other-sex peers during early adolescence. *Developmental Psychology, 36,* 147–154.

Bunge, S. A., & Zelazo, P. D. (2006). A brain-based account of the development of rule use in childhood. *Current Directions in Psychological Science, 15,* 118–121.

Burchinal, M. R., Howes, C., Pianta, R. C., Bryant, D., Early, D. M., Clifford, R., et al. (2008). Predicting child outcomes at the end of kindergarten from the quality of pre-kindergarten teacher–child interactions and instruction. *Applied Developmental Psychology, 12,* 140–153.

Burchinal, M. R., Roberts, J., Riggins, R., Zeisel, S., Neebe, E., & Bryant, D. (2000). Relating quality of center-based child care to early cognitive and language development longitudinally. *Child Development, 71,* 339–357.

Burchinal, M. R., Roberts, J. E., Zeisel, S. A., & Rowley, S. (2008). Social risk and protective factors for African American children's academic achievement and adjustment during the transition to middle school. *Developmental Psychology, 44,* 286–292.

Burgess, K. B., Rubin, K. H., Cheah, C. S. L., & Nelson, L. J. (2005). Behavioral inhibition, social withdrawal, and parenting. In W. R. Crozier & L. E. Alden (Eds.), *The essential handbook of social anxiety for clinicians* (pp. 99–120). New York: Wiley.

Burgess, K. B., Wojslawowica, J. C., Rubin, K. H., Rose-Krasnor, L., & Booth-LaForce, C. (2006). Social information processing and coping strategies of shy/withdrawn and aggressive children: Does friendship matter? *Child Development, 77,* 371–383.

Burkam, D. T., Ready, D. D., Lee, V. E., & LoGerfo, L. F. (2004). Social class differences in summer learning between kindergarten and first grade: Model specification and estimation. *Sociology of Education, 77,* 1–31.

Burkett, E. (2001). *Another planet: A year in the life of a suburban high school.* New York: HarperCollins.

Burks, V., Laird, R. D., Dodge, K. A., Petit, G., & Bates, J. E. (1999). Knowledge structures, social information processing, and children's aggressive behavior. *Social Development, 8,* 220–236.

Burt, K. B., Obradovic, J., Long, J. D., & Masten, A. S. (2008). The interplay of social competence and psychopathology over 20 years: Testing transactional and cascade models. *Child Development, 79,* 359–374.

Burt, S. A., Barnes, A. R., McGue, M., & Iacono, W. G. (2008). Parental divorce and adolescent delinquency: Ruling out the impact of common genes. *Developmental Psychology, 44,* 1668–1677.

Burt, S. A., McGue, M., & Iacono, W. G. (2009). Nonshared environmental mediation of the association between deviant peer affiliation and adolescent externalizing behaviors over time: Results from a cross-lagged monozygotic twin differences design. *Developmental Psychology, 45,* 1752–1760.

Burt, S. A., & Neiderhiser, J. M. (2009). Aggressive versus nonaggressive antisocial behavior: Distinctive etiological moderation by age. *Developmental Psychology, 45,* 1164–1176.

Burton, S., & Mitchell, P. (2003). Judging who knows best about yourself: Developmental change in citing the self across middle childhood. *Child Development, 74,* 426–443.

Bus, A. G., & Van IJzendoorn, M. H. (1997). Affective dimension of mother-infant picturebook reading. *Journal of School Psychology, 35,* 47–60.

Bushman, B. J., & Anderson, C. A. (2007). Measuring the strength of the effect of violent media on aggression. *American Psychologist, 62,* 253–254.

Bushman, B. J., & Anderson, C. A. (2009). Comfortably numb: Desensitizing effects of violent media on helping others. *Psychological Science, 20,* 273–277.

Busseri, M. A., Willoughby, T., Chalmers, H., & Bogaert, A. F. (2008). On the association between sexual attraction and adolescent risk behavior involvement: Examining mediation and moderation. *Developmental Psychology, 44,* 69–80.

Bussey, K. (1999). Children's categorization and evaluation of different types of lies and truths. *Child Development, 70,* 1338–1347.

Byrnes, J., & Fox, N. (1998). The educational relevance of research in cognitive neuroscience. *Educational Psychology Review, 10,* 297–342.

Cabrera, N. J., Shannon, J., West, J., & Brooks-Gunn, J. (2006). Parental interactions with Latino infants: Variation by country of origin and English proficiency. *Child Development, 77,* 1190–1207.

Cairns, R. B., & Cairns, B. D. (1994). *Lifelines and risks: Pathways of youth in our time.* New York: Cambridge University Press.

Caldarella, P., & Merrell, K. W. (1997). Common dimensions of social skills of children and adolescents: A taxonomy of positive behaviors. *School Psychology Review, 26,* 264–278.

Caldwell, C. H., Zimmerman, M. A., Bernat, D. H., Sellers, R. M., & Notaro, P. C. (2002). Racial identity, maternal support, and psychological distress among African American adolescents. *Child Development, 73,* 1322–1336.

Calkins, S. (1994). Origins and outcomes of individual differences in emotion regulation. *The development of emotion regulation. Monographs of the Society for Research in Child Development* (Serial No. 240 Vol. 59, pp. 53–72).

Call, K. T., Mortimer, J. T., & Shanahan, M. J. (1995). Helpfulness and the development of competence in adolescence. *Child Development, 66*, 129–138.

Callaghan, T., Rocha, P., Lillard, A., Claux, M. L., Odden, H., Itakura, S., et al. (2005). Synchrony in the onset of mental-state reasoning. *Psychological Science, 16*, 378–384.

Campbell, F. A., Wasik, B. H., Pungello, E., Burchinal, M., Barbarin, O. A., Kainz, K., et al. (2008). Young adult outcomes of the Abecedarian and CARE early childhood educational interventions. *Early Childhood Research Quarterly, 23*, 452–466.

Campbell, J., Lamb, M., & Hwant, P. (2000). Early child-care experiences and children's social competence between 1 1/2 and 15 years of age. *Applied Developmental Science, 4*, 166–175.

Campbell, T. F., Dollaghan, C., Rockette, H. E., Paradise, J. L., Feldman, H. M., Shriberg, L. D., et al. (2003). Risk factors for speech delay of unknown origin in 3-year-old children. *Child Development, 74*, 346–357.

Caplan, M., & Hay, D. F. (1989). Preschoolers' responses to peers' distress and beliefs about bystander intervention. *Journal of Child Psychology & Psychiatry & Allied Disciplines, 30*, 231–242.

Caplan, M., Vespo, J., Pederson, J., & Hay, D. (1991). Conflict and its resolution in small groups of one- and two-year-olds. *Child Development, 62*, 1513–1524.

Cappuccio, F. P., Taggart, F. M., Kandala, N.-B., Currie, N., Peile, E., Stranges, S., et al. (2008). Meta-analysis of short sleep duration and obesity in children and adults. *Sleep, 31*, 619–626.

Caprara, G., Barbaranelli, C., & Pastorelli, C. (2001). Prosocial behavior and aggression in childhood and pre-adolescence. In A. Bohart & D. Stipek (Eds.), *Constructive and destructive behavior: Implications for family, school, and society* (pp. 187–203). Washington, DC: APA.

Card, N. A., Stucky, B. D., Sawalani, G. M., & Little, T. D. (2008). Direct and indirect aggression during childhood and adolescence: A meta-analytic review of gender differences, intercorrelations, and relations to maladjustment. *Child Development, 79*, 1185–1229.

Carey, S., & Bartlett, E. (1978). Acquiring a single new word. *Papers and Reports on Child Language Development, 15*, 17–29.

Carhill, A., Suárez-Orozco, C., & Paez, M. (2008). Explaining English language proficiency among adolescent immigrant students. *American Educational Research Journal, 45*, 1155–1179.

Carlo, G., Koller, S., Eisenberg, N., Da Silva, M., & Frohlich, C. (1996). A cross-national study on the relations among prosocial moral reasoning, gender role orientations, and prosocial behaviors. *Developmental Psychology, 32*, 231–240.

Carlson, C., Uppal, S., & Prosser, E. C. (2000). Ethnic differences in processes contributing to the self-esteem of early adolescent girls. *Journal of Early Adolescence, 20*, 44–67.

Carlson, S., & Moses, L. (2001). Individual differences in inhibitory control and children's theory of mind. *Child Development, 72*, 1032–1053.

Carlson, S., Moses, L., & Hix, H. (1998). The role of inhibitory processes in young children's difficulties with deception and false belief. *Child Development, 69*, 672–691.

Carpendale, J. (2000). Kohlberg and Piaget on stages and moral reasoning. *Developmental Review, 20*, 181–205.

Carr, E., & Ogle, D. (1987). K-W-L Plus: A strategy for comprehension and summarization. *Journal of Reading, 30*, 626–631.

Carresn, G. P., Drake, C., & Barton, A. C. (2005). The importance of presence: Immigrant parents' school engagement experiences. *American Educational Research Journal, 42*, 465–498.

Carretti, B., Borella, E., Cornoldi, C., & De Beni, R. (2009). Role of working memory in explaining the performance of individuals with specific reading comprehension difficulties: A meta-analysis. *Learning and Individual Differences, 19*, 246–251.

Carskadon, M., & Dement, W. (2000). Normal human sleep. In M. Kryger, T. Roth & W. Dement (Eds.), *Principles and practice of sleep medicine* (3rd ed., pp. 15-25). Philadelphia: W. B. Saunders.

Carta, J. J., Atwater, J. B., Greenwood, C. R., McConnell, S. R., McEvoy, M. A., & Williams, R. (2001). Effects of cumulative prenatal substance exposure and environmental risks on children's developmental trajectories. *Journal of Clinical Child Psychology, 30*, 327–337.

Case, R., Griffin, S., & Kelly, W. (2001). Socioeconomic differences in children's early cognitive development and their readiness for schooling. In S. Golbeck (Ed.), *Psychological perspectives on early childhood education: Reframing dilemmas in research and practice* (pp. 37–63). Mahwah, NJ: Erlbaum.

Caspi, A. (1998). Personality development across the life course. In N. Eisenberg (Ed.), *Handbook of child psychology: Social, emotional, and personality development* (5th ed., Vol. 3, pp. 311–388). New York: Wiley.

Caspi, A., Taylor, A., Moffitt, T., & Plomin, R. (2000). Neighborhood deprivation affects children's mental health: Enivronmental risks identified in a genetic design. *Psychological Science, 11*, 338–342.

Cassibba, R., Van IJzendoorn, M., & D'Odorico, L. (2000). Attachment and play in child care centres: Reliability and validity of the attachment Q-sort for mothers and professional caregivers in Italy. *International Journal of Behavioral Development, 24*, 241–255.

Cassidy, J. (1994). Emotion regulation: Influences of attachment relationships. In N. A. Fox (Ed.), *Emotion regulation: Behavioral and biological considerations. Monographs for the Society for Research in Child Development* (Vol. 59, pp. 228–249).

Cassidy, J., Aikins, J., & Chernoff, J. (2003). Children's peer selection: Experimental examination of the role of self-perceptions. *Developmental Psychology, 39*, 495–508.

Cassidy, J., Parke, R., Butovsky, L., & Braungart, J. (1992). Family–peer connections: The roles of emotional expressiveness within the family and children's understanding of emotions. *Child Development, 63*, 603–618.

Cassidy, J., Ziv, Y., Mehta, T., & Feeney, B. (2003). Feedback seeking in children and adolescents: Associations with self-perceptions, attachment representations, and depression. *Child Development, 74*, 612–628.

Cassidy, K., Fineberg, D., Brown, K., & Perkins, A. (2005). Theory of Mind may be contagious, but you don't catch it from your twin. *Child Development, 76*, 97–106.

Castellanos, F. X., Sonuga-Barke, E., Milham, M. P., & Tannock, R. (2006). Characterizing cognition in ADHD: Beyond executive dysfunction. *Trends in Cognitive Sciences, 10*, 117–123.

Castelli, D. M., Hillman, C. H., Buck, S. M., & Erwin, H. E. (2007). Physical fitness and academic achievement in third- and fifth-grade students. *Journal of Sport & Exercise Psychology, 29*, 239–252.

CDC. (2009). *Prevalence of the autism spectrum disorders (ASDs) in multiple areas of the United States*. Retrieved from http://www.cdc.gov/ncbddd/autism/index.html

Ceci, S. J. (1991). How much does schooling influence general intelligence and its cognitive components? A reassessment of the evidence. *Developmental Psychology, 27*, 703–722.

Ceci, S. J. (2003). Cast in six ponds and you'll reel in something: Looking back on 25 years of research. *American Psychologist, 58*, 855–864.

Centers for Disease Control and Prevention. (2009a). Availability of less nutritious snack foods and beverages in secondary schools—selected states, 2002–2008. *Morbidity and Mortality Weekly Report, 58*, 1102–1104.

Centers for Disease Control and Prevention. (2009b). HIV prevalence estimates - United States, 2006. *JAMA, 301*, 27–29.

Cepeda, N. J., Vul, E., Rohrer, D., Wixted, J. T., & Pashler, H. (2008). Spacing effects in learning: A temporal ridgeline of optimal retention. *Psychological Science, 19*, 1095–1102.

Chambliss, D. F. (1988). *Champions: The making of Olympic swimmers*. New York: William Morrow.

Champagne, F. A. (2009). Beyond nature vs. nurture: Philosophical insights from molecular biology. *APS Observer, 22*, 3–4, 27.

Champagne, F. A., & Curley, J. P. (2009). Epigenetic mechanisms mediating the long-term effects of maternal care on development. *Neuroscience and Biobehavioral Reviews, 33*, 593–600.

Champagne, F. A., & Mashoodh, R. (2009). Genes in context: Gene–environment interplay and the origins of individual differences in behavior. *Current Directions in Psychological Science, 18*, 127–131.

Champion, T. B. (2003). *Understanding storytelling among African American children: A journey from Africa to America*. Mahwah, NJ: Erlbaum.

Chandler, M., Fritz, A., & Hala, S. (1989). Small-scale deceit: Deception as a marker of two-, three-, and four-year-olds' early theories of mind. *Child Development, 60*, 1263–1277.

Chandler, M., Sokol, B., & Wainryb, C. (2000). Beliefs about truth and beliefs about rightness. *Child Development, 71*, 91–97.

Chang, L. (2004). The role of classroom norms in contextualizing the relations of children's social behaviors to peer acceptance. *Developmental Psychology, 40*, 691–702.

Chao, R. K. (1994). Beyond parental control and authoritarian parenting style: Understanding Chinese parenting through the cultural notion of training. *Child Development, 65*, 1111–1119.

Charity, A., Scarborough, H. S., & Griffin, D. (2004). Familiarity with school English in African American children and its relation to early reading achievement. *Child Development, 75*, 1340–1356.

Charness, N., Krampe, R., & Mayr, U. (1996). The role of practice and coaching in entrepreneurial skill domains: An international comparison of life-span chess skill acquisition. In K. A. Ericsson (Ed.), *The road to excellence: The acquisition of expert performance in the arts and sciences, sports, and games* (pp. 51–80). Mahwah, NJ: Erlbaum.

Chavajay, P., & Rogoff, B. (2002). Schooling and traditional collaborative social organization of problem solving by Mayan mothers and children. *Developmental Psychobiology, 38*, 55–66.

Chavous, T. M., Bernat, D. H., Schmeelk-Cone, K., Caldwell, C. H., Kohn-Wood, L., & Zimmerman, M. A. (2003). Racial identity and academic attainment among African American adolescents. *Child Development, 74*, 1076–1090.

Cheah, C., Nelson, L., & Rubin, K. (2001). Nonsocial play as a risk factor in social and emotional development. In A. Göncü & E. Klein (Eds.), *Children in play, story, and school* (pp. 39–71). New York: Guilford.

Checkley, K., & Gardner, H. (1997). The first seven ... and the eighth: A conversation with Howard Gardner. *Educational Leadership, 55*, 8–13.

Chen, D., Fein, G., Killen, M., & Tam, H.-P. (2001). Peer conflicts of preschool children: Issues, resolution, incidence, and age-related patterns. *Early Education and Development, 12*, 523–544.

Chen, E., Langer, D., Raphaelson, Y., & Matthews, K. (2005). Socioeconomic status and health in adolescents: The role of stress interpretations. *Child Development, 75*, 1039–1052.

Chen, X., Chang, L., & He, Y. (2003). The peer group as a context: Mediating and moderating effects on relations between academic achievement and social functioning in Chinese children. *Child Development, 74*, 710–727.

Chen, X., Chen, H., Li, D., & Wang, L. (2009). Early childhood behavioral inhibition and social and school adjustment in Chinese children: A 5-year longitudinal study. *Child Development, 80*, 1692–1704.

Chen, X., Dong, Q., & Zhou, H. (1997). Authoritative and authoritarian parenting practices and social and school performance in Chinese children. *International Journal of Behavioral Development, 21*, 855–873.

Chen, X., Gen, G., Li, D., & He, Y. (2005). Social functioning and adjustment in Chinese children: The imprint of historical time. *Child Development, 76*, 182–195.

Chen, X., Rubin, K., & Li, D. (1997). Relation between academic achievement and social adjustment: Evidence from Chinese children. *Developmental Psychology, 33*, 518–525.

Chen, Z., & Tse, H. C.-H. (2008). Social functioning and adjustment in Canadian-born children with Chinese and European backgrounds. *Developmental Psychology, 44*, 1184–1189.

Cheng, H., & Furnham, A. (2002). Personality, peer relations, and self-confidence as predictors of happiness and loneliness. *Journal of Adolescence, 25*, 327–339.

Choi, H., Meininger, J. C., & Roberts, R. E. (2006). Ethnic differences in adolescents' mental distress, social stress, and resources. *Adolescence, 41*, 263–283.

Chomsky, N. (1959). Reviews: Verbal Behavior by B. F. Skinner. *Language, 35*, 26–58.

Chomsky, N. (2006). *Language and mind* (3rd ed.). New York: Cambridge University Press.

Christakis, D., Zimmerman, F. J., DiGiuseppe, D. L., & McCarty, C. A. (2004). Early television exposure and subsequent attentional problems in children. *Pediatrics, 113*, 708–713.

Christian, K., Morrison, F., & Bryant, F. (1998). Predicting kindergarten academic skills: Interactions among child care, maternal education, and family literacy environments. *Early Childhood Research Quarterly, 13*, 501–521.

Chugani, H. (1998). A critical period of brain development: Studies of cerebral glucose utilization with PET. *Preventive Medicine, 27*, 184–188.

Chumlea, W. C., Schubert, C., Roche, A., Kulin, H., Lee, P., Himes, J., et al. (2003). Age at menarche and racial comparisons in US girls. *Pediatrics, 111*, 110–113.

Chung, E. K., Mathew, L., Rothkopf, A. C., Elo, I. T., Coyne, J. C., & Culhane, J. F. (2009). Parenting attitudes and infant spanking: The influence of childhood experiences. *Pediatrics, 124*, 278–285.

Cialdini, R. B. (2005). What's the best secret device for engaging student interest? The answer is in the title. *Journal of Social and Clinical Psychology, 24*, 22–29.

Cillessen, A., & Bellmore, A. (2002). Social skills and interpersonal perception in early and middle childhood. In P. Smith & C. Hart (Eds.), *Blackwell handbook of childhood social development* (pp. 355–374). Oxford: Blackwell.

Cillessen, A., & Mayeux, L. (2004). From censure to reinforcement: Developmental changes in the association between aggression and social status. *Child Development, 75*, 147–163.

Cizek, G. J. (1999). *Cheating on tests: How to do it, detect it, and prevent it*. Mahwah, NJ: Erlbaum.

Clark, C. A. A., Woodward, L. J., Horwood, L. J., & Moor, S. (2008). Development of emotional and behavioral regulation in children born extremely preterm and very preterm: Biological and social influences. *Child Development, 79*, 1444–1462.

Clark, D., & Linn, M. C. (2003). Designing for knowledge integration: The impact of instructional time. *Journal of the Learning Sciences, 12*, 451–493.

Clark, K., Chein, I., & Cook, S. (2004). The effects of segregation and the consequences of desegregation: A (September 1952) social science statement in the *Brown v. Board of Education* of Topeka Supreme Court case. *American Psychologist, 59*, 495–501.

Clark, K. B. (1963). *Prejudice and your child* (2nd ed.). Boston: Beacon Press.

Clarke, L., Ungerer, J., Chahoud, K., Johnson, S., & Stiefel, I. (2002). Attention deficit hyperactivity disorder is associated with attachment insecurity. *Clinical Child Psychology and Psychiatry, 7*, 1359–1045.

Clayton, M. C., & Helms, B. P. (2009). Increasing seat belt use on a college campus: An evaluation of two prompting procedures. *Journal of Applied Behavior Analysis, 42*, 161–164.

Clements, D. H., & Sarama, J. (2008). Experimental evaluation of the effects of a research-based preschool mathematics curriculum. *American Educational Research Journal, 45*, 443–494.

Clements, M., Aber, J. L., & Seidman, E. (2008). The dynamics of life stressors and depressive symptoms in early adolescence: A test of six theoretical models. *Child Development, 79*, 1168–1182.

Cleveland, M., Gibbons, F., Gerrard, M., Pomery, E., & Brody, G. (2005). The impact of parenting on risk cognitions and risk behavior: A study of mediation and moderation in a panel of African American adolescents. *Child Development, 76*, 900–916.

Clingenpeel, B. T., & Pianta, R. C. (2007). Mothers' sensitivity and book-reading interactions with first graders. *Early education and development, 18*, 1–22.

Coate, D., & Grossman, M. (1985). Effects of alcoholic beverage prices and legal drinking ages on youth alcohol use: Results from the Second National Health and Nutrition Examination Survey. [Unpublished manuscript.]

Coffman, J. L., Ornstein, P. A., McCall, L. E., & Curran, P. J. (2008). Linking teachers' memory-relevant language and the development of children's memory skills. *Developmental Psychology, 44*, 1640–1654.

Cohen, A. B. (2009). Many forms of culture. *American Psychologist, 64*, 194–204.

Cohen, D. A., Farley, T. A., Taylor, S. N., Martin, D. H., & Schuster, M. A. (2002). When and where do youths have sex? The potential role of adult supervision. *Pediatrics, 110*, e66.

Cohen, E., Lotan, R., Scarloss, B., & Arellano, A. (1999). Complex instruction: Equity in cooperative learning classrooms. *Theory into Practice, 38*, 80–86.

Cohen, G. L., Garcia, J., Purdie-Vaughns, V., Apfel, N., & Brzustoski, P. (2009). Recursive processes in self-affirmation: Intervening to close the minority achievement gap. *Science, 324*, 400–403.

Cohen, G. L., & Prinstein, M. J. (2006). Peer contagion of aggression and health risk behavior among adolescent males: An experimental investigation of effects on public conduct and private attitudes. *Child Development, 77*, 967–983.

Cohen, G. L., Steele, C. M., & Ross, L. D. (1999). The mentor's dilemma: Providing critical feedback across the racial divide. *Personality and Social Psychology Bulletin, 25*, 1302–1318.

Cohen, L., Rundell, L., Spellman, B., & Cashon, C. (1999). Infants' perception of causal chains. *Psychological Science, 10*, 412–418.

Coie, J. D., & Dodge, K. A. (1998). Aggression and antisocial behavior. In N. Eisenberg (Ed.), *Handbook of child psychology: Social, emotional, and personality development* (5th ed., Vol. 3, pp. 779–862). New York: Wiley.

Colarusso, R. P., Keel, M. C., & Dangel, H. L. (2001). A comparison of eligibility criteria and their impact on minority representation in LD programs. *Learning Disabilities Research, 16*, 1–7.

Colby, A., Kohlberg, L., Gibbs, J., & Lieberman, M. (1983). A longitudinal study of moral judgment. *Monographs of the Society for Research in Child Development, 48* (Nos. 1–2, Serial No. 200).

Cole, D. A., Martin, J. M., Peeke, L. A., Seroczynski, A. D., & Fier, J. (1999). Children's over- and underestimation of academic competence: A longitudinal study of gender differences, depression, and anxiety. *Child Development, 70*, 459–473.

Cole, D. A., Maxwell, S. E., Martin, J. M., Peeke, L. G., Seroczynski, A. D., Tram, J. M., et al. (2001). The development of multiple domains of child and adolescent self-concept: A cohort sequential longitudinal design. *Child Development, 72*, 1723–1746.

Cole, M. (1975). An ethnographic psychology of cognition. In R. W. Brislin, S. Bochner, & W. Lonner (Eds.), *Cross-cultural perspectives on learning*. New York: Wiley.

Cole, P. M. (1986). Children's spontaneous control of facial expression. *Child Development, 57*, 1309–1321.

Cole, P. M., Luby, J., & Sullivan, M. W. (2008). Emotions and the development of childhood depression: Bridging the gap. *Child Development Perspectives, 2*, 141–148.

Cole, P. M., Martin, S., & Dennis, T. (2004). Emotion regulation as a scientific construct: Methodological challenges and directions for child development research. *Child Development, 75*, 317–333.

Cole, P. M., Michel, M. K., & Teti, L. O. (1994). The development of emotion regulation and dysregulation: A clinical perspective. *Monographs of the Society for Research in Child Development* (Serial No. 240 ed., Vol. 59).

Coles, R. (1986). *The moral life of children*. Boston: Atlantic Monthly Press.

Coley, R. L. (1998). Children's socialization experiences and functioning in single-mother households: The importance of fathers and other men. *Child Development, 69*, 219–230.

Coley, R. L., Votruba-Drzal, E., & Schindler, H. S. (2009). Fathers' and mothers' parenting predicting and responding to adolescent sexual risk behaviors. *Child Development, 80*, 808–827.

Collins, A. (2002). Historical perspectives on contemporary research in social development. In P. Smith & C. Hart (Eds.), *Blackwell handbook of childhood social development* (pp. 3–23). Oxford: Blackwell.

Collins, W. A., Welsh, D. P., & Furman, W. (2009). Adolescent romantic relationships. *Annual Review of Psychology, 60*, 631–652.

Colom, R., Juan-Espinosa, M., Abad, F., & Garcia, L. F. (2000). Negligible sex differences in general intelligence. *Intelligence, 28*, 57–68.

Colom, R., Lluis-Font, J. M., & Andres-Pueyo, A. (2005). The generational intelligence gains are caused by decreasing variance in the lower half of the distribution: Supporting evidence for the nutrition hypothesis. *Intelligence, 33*, 83–91.

Colwell, M., Mize, J., Petit, G., & Laird, R. D. (2002). Contextual determinants of mothers' interventions in young children's peer interactions. *Developmental Psychology, 38*, 492–502.

Compton, R. J., Robinson, M. D., Ode, S., Quandt, L., Fineman, S. L., & Carp, J. (2008). Error monitoring ability predicts daily stress regulation. *Psychological Science, 19*, 702–708.

Conboy, B., & Thal, D. (2006). Ties between the lexicon and grammar: Cross-sectional and longitudinal studies of bilingual toddlers. *Child Development, 77*, 712–735.

Connell, A. M., Dishion, T. J., Yasui, M., & Kavanagh, K. (2007). An adaptive approach to family intervention: Linking engagement in family-centered intervention to reductions in adolescent problem behavior. *Journal of Consulting and Clinical Psychology, 75*, 568–579.

Connor, C. M., Morrison, F. J., & Slominski, L. (2006). Preschool instruction and children's emergent literacy growth. *Journal of Educational Psychology, 98*, 665–689.

Connor, C. M., Piasta, S. B., Fishman, B., Glasney, S., Schatschneider, C., Crowe, E., et al. (2009). Individualizing student instruction precisely: Effects of child X instruction interactions on first graders' literacy development. *Child Development, 80*, 77–100.

Connor, C. M., Son, S.-H., Hindman, A. H., & Morrison, F. J. (2005). Teacher qualifications, classroom practices, family characteristics, and preschool experience: Complex effects on first graders' vocabulary and early reading outcomes. *Journal of School Psychology, 43*, 343–375.

Conrad, N. J. (2008). From reading to spelling and spelling to reading: Transfer goes both ways. *Journal of Educational Psychology, 100*, 869–878.

Constantino, J. N., Lavesser, P., Zhang, Y., Abbacchi, A., Gray, T., & Todd, R. D. (2007). Rapid quantitative assessment of autistic social impairment by classroom teachers. *Journal of the American Academy of Child and Adolescent Psychiatry, 46*, 1668–1676.

Coon, K., Goldberg, J., Rogers, B., & Tucker, K. (2001). Relationships between use of television during meals and children's food consumption patterns. *Pediatrics, 107*, e7.

Cooper, H. (2008). The search for meaningful ways to express the effects of interventions. *Child Development Perspectives, 2*, 181–186.

Cooper, H., & Valentine, J. C. (2001). Using research to answer practical questions about homework. *Educational Psychologist, 36*, 143–153.

Cooper, L., Shaver, P., & Collins, N. (1998). Attachment styles, emotion regulation, and adjustment in adolescence. *Journal of Personality and Social Psychology, 74*, 1380–1397.

Coplan, R. J., & Armer, M. (2007). A "multitude" of solitude: A closer look at social withdrawal and nonsocial play in early childhood. *Child Development Perspectives, 1*, 26–32.

Corby, B. C., Hodges, E. V. E., & Perry, D. G. (2007). Gender identity and adjustment in black, Hispanic, and white preadolescents. *Developmental Psychology, 43*, 261–266.

Cordeiro, P. A., & Carspecken, P. F. (1993). How a minority of the minority succeed: A case study of twenty Hispanic achievers. *Qualitative Studies in Education, 6*, 277–290.

Cornelius-White, J. (2007). Learner-centered teacher–student relationships are effective: A meta-analysis. *Review of Educational Research, 77*, 113-143.

Correnti, R., & Rowan, B. (2007). Opening up the black box: Literacy instruction in schools participating in three comprehensive school reform programs. *American Educational Research Journal, 44*, 298-338.

Corsaro, W. A. (1997). *The sociology of childhood*. Thousand Oaks, CA: Pine Forge Press.

Corsello, C. M. (2005). Early intervention in autism. *Infants & Young Children, 18*, 74–85.

Cote, S., Borge, A. I. H., Geoffroy, M.-C., Rutter, M., & Tremblay, R. E. (2008). Nonmaternal care in infancy and emotional/behavioral difficulties at 4 years old: Moderation by family risk characteristics. *Developmental Psychology, 44*, 155–168.

Courage, M. L., & Setliff, A. E. (2009). Debating the impact of television and video material on very young children: Attention, learning, and the developing brain. *Child Development Perspectives, 3*, 72–78.

Craig, S. D., Chi, M. T., & VanLehn, K. (2009). Improving classroom learning by collaboratively observing human tutoring videos while problem solving. *Journal of Educational Psychology, 101*, 779–789.

Craig-Unkefer, L., & Kaiser, A. (2002). Improving the social communication skills of at-risk preschool children in a play context. *Topics in Early Childhood Special Education, 22*, 3–13.

Crain, R. M. (1996). The influence of age, race, and gender on child and adolescent multidimensional self-concept. In B. A. Bracken (Ed.), *Handbook of self-concept: Developmental, social, and clinical considerations* (pp. 395–420). New York: Wiley.

Crick, N. R., & Dodge, K. A. (1994). A review and reformulation of social information-processing mechanisms in children's social adjustment. *Psychological Bulletin, 115*, 74–101.

Criss, M., Pettit, G., Bates, J., Dodge, K., & Lapp, A. (2002). Family adversity, positive peer relationships, and children's externalizing behavior: A longitudinal perspective on risk and resilience. *Child Development, 73*, 1220–1237.

Crittenden, P. M. (1992). Quality of attachment in the preschool years. *Development and Psychopathology, 4*, 209–241.

Crockenberg, S., & Litman, C. (1990). Autonomy as competence in 2-year-olds: Maternal correlates of child defiance, compliance, and self-assertion. *Developmental Psychology, 26*, 961–971.

Crockett, L., Raffaelli, M., & Moilanen, K. (2003). Adolescent sexuality: Behavior and meaning. In G. Adams & M. Berzonsky (Eds.), *Blackwell handbook of adolescence* (pp. 371–392). Malden, MA: Blackwell.

Crosnoe, R. (2007). Gender, obesity, and education. *Sociology of Education, 80*, 241–260.

Crosnoe, R., & Needham, B. (2004). Holism, contexual variability, and the study of friendships in adolescent development. *Child Development, 75*, 264–279.

Crosnoe, R., Riegle-Crumb, C., Field, S., Frank, K., & Muller, C. (2008). Peer group contexts of girls' and boys' academic experiences. *Child Development, 79*, 139–155.

Crouter, A. C., Bumpus, M. F., Davis, K. D., & McHale, S. M. (2005). How do parents learn about adolescents' experiences? Implications for parental knowledge and adolescent risky behavior. *Child Development, 76*, 869–882.

Crouter, A. C., Whiteman, S. D., McHale, S. M., & Osgood, D. W. (2007). Development of gender attitude traditionality across middle childhood and adolescence. *Child Development, 78*, 911–926.

Crowell, J., Treboux, D., & Waters, E. (2002). Stability of attachment representations: The transition to marriage. *Developmental Psychology, 38*, 467–479.

Csikszentmihalyi, M., Rathunde, K., & Whalen, S. (1993). *Talented teenagers: The roots of success and failure*. Cambridge, UK: Cambridge University Press.

Cui, M., Conger, R. D., & Lorenz, F. O. (2005). Predicting change in adolescent adjustment from change in marital problems. *Developmental Psychology, 41*, 812–823.

Cui, M., Donnellan, M. B., & Conger, R. D. (2007). Reciprocal influences between parents' marital problems and adolescent internalizing and externalizing behavior. *Developmental Psychology, 43*, 1544–1552.

Cullerton-Sen, C., Cassidy, A. R., Murray-Close, D., Cicchetti, D., Crick, N. R., & Rogosch, F. A. (2009). Childhood maltreatment and the development of relational and physical aggression: The importance of a gender-informed approach. *Child Development, 79*, 1736–1751.

Cummings, E. M., Zahn-Waxler, C., & Radke-Yarrow, M. (1981). Young children's responses to expressions of anger and affection by others in the family. *Child Development, 52*, 1274–1282.

Cunningham, A. E., & Stanovich, K. E. (1997). Early reading acquisition and its relation to reading experience and ability 10 years later. *Developmental Psychology, 33*, 934–945.

Curby, T. W., Rimm-Kaufman, S. E., & Ponitz, C. C. (2009). Teacher–child interactions and children's achievement trajectories across kindergarten and first grade. *Journal of Educational Psychology, 101*, 912–925.

Cutler, L., & Graham, S. (2008). Primary grade writing instruction: A national survey. *Journal of Educational Psychology, 100*, 907–919.

Cutrona, C., Wallace, G., & Wesner, K. A. (2006). Neighborhood characteristics and depression: An examination of stress processes. *Current Directions in Psychological Science, 15*, 188–192.

Cutting, A., & Dunn, J. (1999). Theory of mind, emotion understanding, language, and family background: Individual differences and interrelations. *Child Development, 70*, 853–865.

Czeschlik, T., & Rost, D. (1995). Sociometric types and children's intelligence. *British Journal of Developmental Psychology, 13*, 177–189.

D'Agostino, J. V., & Murphy, J. A. (2004). A meta-analysis of Reading Recovery in the United States schools. *Educational Evaluation and Policy Analysis, 26*, 23–38.

Dahl, R., & Lewin, D. (2002). Pathways to adolescent health: Sleep regulation and behavior. *Journal of Adolescent Health, 31*, 175–184.

Daley, A. J. (2009). Can exergaming contribute to improving physical activity levels and health outcomes in children? *Pediatrics, 124*, 763–771.

Daly, M., & Wilson, M. (2005). The "Cinderella effect" is no fairy tale: Comment. *Trends in Cognitive Sciences, 9*, 507–508.

Damon, W., & Killen, M. (1982). Peer interaction and the process of change in children's moral reasoning. *Merrill-Palmer Quarterly, 28*, 347–367.

Danish, S., Taylor, T., & Fazio, R. (2003). Enhancing adolescent development through sports and leisure. In G. Adams & M. Berzonsky (Eds.), *Blackwell handbook of adolescence* (pp. 92–108). Malden, MA: Blackwell.

Danner, F., & Phillips, B. (2008). Adolescent sleep, school start times, and teen motor vehicle crashes. *Journal of Clinical Sleep Medicine, 4*, 533–535.

Darling, N., Cumsille, P., & Martinez, L. M. (2008). Individual differences in adolescents' beliefs about the legitimacy of parental authority and their own obligation to obey: A longitudinal investigation. *Child Development, 79*, 1103–1118.

Darling-Hammond, L. (2007). The flat earth and education: How America's commitment to equity will determine our future. *Educational Researcher, 36*(6), 318–334.

Darwin, C. (1965/1872). *The expression of the emotions in man and animals*. Chicago: University of Chicago Press.

Davidov, M., & Grusec, J. (2006). Untangling the links of parental responsiveness to distress and warmth to child outcomes. *Child Development, 77*, 444–458.

Davidson, R. J. (2000). Affective style, psychopathology, and resilience: Brain mechanisms and plasticity. *American Psychologist, 55*, 1196–1214.

Davies, P. T., Sturge-Apple, M. L., Cicchetti, D., & Cummings, E. M. (2007). The role of child adrenocortical functioning in pathways between interparental conflict and child maladjustment. *Developmental Psychology, 43*, 918–930.

Davies, P. T., Sturge-Apple, M. L., Cicchetti, D., & Cummings, E. M. (2008). Adrenocortical underpinnings of children's pyschological reactivity to interparental conflict. *Child Development, 79*, 1693–1706.

Davison, D., Susman, E., & Birch, L. (2003). Percent body fat at age 5 predicts earlier pubertal development among girls at age 9. *Pediatrics, 111*, 815–821.

Dawson, G., & Ashman, S. (2000). On the origins of a vulnerability to depression: The influence of the early social environment on the development of psychobiological systems related to risk for affective disorder. In C. Nelson (Ed.), *The effects of early adversity on neurobehavioral development* (pp. 245-279). Mahwah, NJ: Erlbaum.

Dawson, G., Ashman, S., Panagiotides, H., Hessl, D., Self, J., Yamada, E., et al. (2003). Preschool outcomes of children of depressed mothers: Role of maternal behavior, contextual risk, and children's brain activity. *Child Development, 74*, 1158–1175.

Dawson, G., Frey, K., Panagiotides, H., Yamada, E., Hessl, D., & Osterling, J. (1999). Infants of depressed mothers exhibit atypical frontal elecrical brain activity during interactions with mother and with a familiar, nondepressed adult. *Child Development, 70*, 1058–1066.

Dawson, M., Soulihres, I., Gernsbacher, M. A., & Mottron, L. (2007). The level and nature of autistic intelligence. *Psychological Science, 18*, 657–662.

De Boer, H., Bosker, R., & van der Werf, M. (2010). Sustainability of teacher expectation bias effects on long-term student performance. *Journal of Educational Psychology, 102*, 168–179.

De Brauwer, J., & Fias, W. (2009). A longitudinal study of children's performance on simple multiplication and division problems. *Developmental Psychology, 45*, 1480–1496.

De Clercq, B., Van Leeuwen, K., De Fruyt, F., Van Hiel, A., & Mervielde, I. (2008). Maladaptive personality traits and psychopathology in childhood and adolescence: The moderating effect of parenting. *Journal of Personality, 76*, 357–383.

De Rosnay, M., & Harris, P. (2002). Individual differences in children's understanding of emotion: The roles of attachment and language. *Attachment & Human Development, 4*, 39–54.

de Schipper, E. J., Riksen-Walraven, M., & Geurts, S. A. E. (2006). Effects of child–caregiver ratio on the interactions between caregivers and children in child-care centers: An experimental study. *Child Development, 77*, 861–874.

Deacon, S. H., Wade-Woolley, L., & Kirby, J. (2007). Crossover: The role of morphological awareness in French immersion children's reading. *Developmental Psychology, 43*, 732–746.

Dean, D., & Kuhn, D. (2006). Direct instruction vs. discovery: The long view. *Science Education, 91*, 384–397.

Dearing, E. (2004). The developmental implications of restrictive and supportive parenting across neighborhoods and ethnicities: Exceptions are the rule. *Journal of Applied Developmental Psychology, 25*, 555–575.

Dearing, E., McCartney, K., & Taylor, B. (2001). Change in family income-to-needs matters more for children with less. *Child Development, 72*, 1779–1793.

Dearing, E., McCartney, K., & Taylor, B. A. (2009). Does higher quality early child care promote low-income children's math and reading achievement in middle childhood? *Child Development, 80*, 1329–1349.

Deary, I. J., Whiteman, M. C., Starr, J. M., Whalley, L. J., & Fox, H. C. (2004). The impact of childhood intelligence on later life: Following up the Scottish mental surveys of 1932 and 1947. *Journal of Personality and Social Psychology, 86*, 130–147.

Deater-Deckard, K. (2000). Parenting and child behavioral adjustment in early childhood: A quantitative genetic approach to studying family processes. *Child Development, 71*, 468–484.

Deater-Deckard, K., Lansford, J. E., Dodge, K. A., Pettit, G. S., & Bates, J. E. (2003). The development of attitudes about physical punishment: An 8-year longitudinal study. *Journal of Family Psychology, 17*, 351–360.

Deater-Deckard, K., & Plomin, R. (1999). An adoption study of the etiology of teacher and parent reports of externalizing behavior problems in middle childhood. *Child Development, 70*, 144–154.

Deci, E. L., & Ryan, R. M. (2000). The "what" and "why" of goal pursuits: Human needs and the self-determination of behavior. *Psychological Inquiry, 11*, 227–268.

Degnan, K. A., Calkins, S. D., Keane, S. P., & Hill-Soderlund, A. L. (2008). Profiles of disruptive behavior across early childhood: Contributions of frustration reactivity, physiological regulation, and maternal behavior. *Child Development, 79*, 1357–1376.

Deloache, J., Miller, K., & Pierroutsakos, S. (1998). Reasoning and problem solving. In D. Kuhn & R. Siegler (Eds.), *Handbook of child psychology: Cognition, perception and language* (5th ed., Vol. 2, pp. 801–850). New York: Wiley.

Delpit, L. D. (1988). The silenced dialogue: Power and pedagogy in educating other people's children. *Harvard Educational Review, 58*, 280–298.

Dempster, F. N. (1981). Memory span: Sources of individual and developmental differences. *Psychological Bulletin, 89*, 63–100.

DeMulder, E., Denham, S., Schmidt, M., & Mitchell, J. (2000). Q-sort assessment of attachment security during the preschool years: Links from home to school. *Developmental Psychology, 36*, 274–282.

Denham, S. A., Blair, K., DeMulder, E., Levitas, J., Sawyer, K., Auerbach-Major, S., et al. (2003). Preschool emotional competence: Pathway to social competence? *Child Development, 74*, 238–256.

Denham, S. A., Mason, & Couchoud. (1995). Scaffolding young children's prosocial responsiveness: Preschooler's responses to adult sadness, anger, and pain. *International Journal of Behavioral Development, 18*, 489–504.

Denham, S. A., McKinley, M., Couchoud, E. A., & Holt, R. (1990). Emotional and behavioral predictors of preschool peer ratings. *Child Development, 61*, 1145–1152.

Denham, S. A., Mitchell-Copeland, J., Strandberg, K., Auerbach, S., & Blair, K. (1997). Parental contributions to preschoolers' emotional competence: Direct and indirect effects. *Motivation and Emotion, 21*, 65–86.

Denham, S. A., Zoller, D., & Couchoud, E. A. (1994). Socialization of preschoolers' emotion understanding. *Developmental Psychology, 30*, 928–936.

Denissen, J. J. A., Zarrett, N. R., & Eccles, J. S. (2007). I like to do it, I'm able, and I know I am: Longitudinal couplings between domain-specific achievement, self-concept, and interest. *Child Development, 78*, 430–447.

DePaulo, B. (1991). Nonverbal behavior and self-presentation: A developmental perspective. In R. S. Feldman & B. Rime (Eds.), *Fundamentals of nonverbal behavior* (pp. 351–397). New York: Cambridge University Press.

Der, G., Batty, G. D., & Deary, I. J. (2009). The association between IQ in adolescence and a range of health outcomes at 40 in the 1979 US National Longitudinal Study of Youth. *Intelligence, 37*, 573–580.

DeRosier, M., & Thomas, J. (2003). Strengthening sociometric prediction: Scientific advances in the assessment of children's peer relations. *Child Development, 75*, 1379–1392.

Derr, A. M. (1986). How learning disabled adolescent boys make moral judgments. *Journal of Learning Disabilities, 19*, 160–164.

Desmond, M., & Turley, R. N. L. (2009). The role of familism in explaining the Hispanic-White college application gap. *Social Problems, 56*, 311–334.

Desrochers, S. (2008). From Piaget to specific Genevan developmental models. *Child Development Perspectives, 2*, 7–12.

DeVries, R., Hildebrandt, C., & Betty, Z. (2000). Constructivist early education for moral development. *Early Education and Development, 11*, 9–35.

Diamond, A., & Kirkham, N. (2005). Not quite as grown-up as we like to think. *Psychological Science, 16*, 291–297.

Diamond, A., Barnett, W. S., Thomas, J., & Munro, S. (2007). Preschool program improves cognitive control. *Science, 318*, 1387–1388.

Diamond, L. (2004). Emerging perspectives on distinctions between romantic love and sexual desire. *Current Directions in Psychological Science, 13*, 116–119.

Diamond, L. (2007). A dynamical systems approach to the development and expression of female same-sex sexuality. *Perspectives on Psychological Science, 2*, 142–161.

Diamond, L., & Savin-Williams, R. (2003). The intimate relationships of sexual-minority youths. In G. Adams & M. Berzonsky (Eds.), *Blackwell handbook of adolescence* (pp. 393–412). Malden, MA: Blackwell.

Dick, D., & Rose, R. (2002). Behavior genetics: What's new? What's next? *Current Directions in Psychological Science, 11*, 70–74.

Dick, D., Rose, R., Viken, R., & Kaprio, J. (2000). Pubertal timing and substance use: Associations between and within families across later adolescence. *Developmental Psychology, 36*, 180–189.

Dickens, W. T., & Flynn, J. R. (2001). Heritability estimates versus large environmental effects: The IQ paradox resolved. *Psychological Review, 108*, 346–369.

Dickens, W. T., & Flynn, J. R. (2006). Black Americans reduce the racial IQ gap. *Psychological Science, 17*, 913–920.

Dickinson, D. K., McCabe, A., Anastasopoulos, L., Peisner-Feinberg, E. S., & Poe, M. D. (2003). The comprehensive language approach to early literacy: The interrelationships among vocabulary, phonological sensitivity, and print knowledge among preschool-aged children. *Journal of Educational Psychology, 95*, 465–481.

DiClemente, R., & Crosby, R. (2003). Sexually transmitted diseases among adolescents: Risk factors, antecedents, and prevention strategies. In G. Adams & M. Berzonsky (Eds.), *Blackwell handbook of adolescence* (pp. 573–605). Malden, MA: Blackwell.

Diener, M. L., Isabella, R. A., Behunin, M., & Wong, M. S. (2007). Attachment to mothers and fathers during middle childhood: Association with child gender, grade, and competence. *Social Development, 17*, 84–101.

DiLalla, L. F. (2000). Behavior genetics of aggression in children: Review and future directions. *Developmental Review, 22*, 593–622.

Dilworth-Bart, J. E., & Moore, C. F. (2006). Mercy mercy me: Social injustice and the prevention of environmental pollutant exposure among ethnic minority and poor children. *Child Development, 77*, 247–265.

Dimant, R. J., & Bearison, D. J. (1991). Development of formal reasoning during successive peer interactions. *Developmental Psychology, 27*, 277–284.

Dinkes, R., Kemp, J., & Baum, K. (2009). *Indicators of school crime and safety: 2009*. Washington, DC: U.S. Department of Education and U.S. Department of Justice. Retrieved from http://nces.ed.gov/pubs2010/2010012_1.pdf

Dionne, G., Boivin, M., Tremblay, R., Laplante, D., & Perusse, D. (2003). Physical aggression and expressive vocabulary in 19-month-old twins. *Developmental Psychology, 39*, 261–273.

Dionne, G., Dale, P. S., Boivin, M., & Plomin, R. (2003). Genetic evidence for bidirectional effects of early lexical and grammatical development. *Child Development, 74*, 394–412.

DiPietro, J. (2004). The role of prenatal maternal stress in child development. *Current Directions in Psychological Science, 13*, 71–74.

Dirix, C. E. H., Nijhuis, J. G., Jongsma, H. W., & Hornstra, G. (2009). Aspects of fetal learning and memory. *Child Development, 80*, 1251–1258.

DiScala, C., Lescohier, I., Barthel, M., & Li, G. (1998). Injuries to children with attention deficit hyperactivity disorder. *Pediatrics, 102*, 1415–1421.

Dishion, T. J., Connell, A., Weaver, C., Shaw, D., Gardner, F., & Wilson, M. (2008). The Family Check-Up with high-risk indigent families: Preventing problem behavior by increasing parents' positive behavior support in early childhood. *Child Development, 79*, 1395–1414.

Dishion, T. J., & Kavanagh, K. (2002). The Adolescent Transitions Program: A family-centered prevention strategy for schools. In J. Reid, G. Patterson & J. Snyder (Eds.), *Antisocial behavior in children and adolescents: A developmental analysis and model for intervention* (pp. 257–272). Washington, DC: APA.

Dishion, T. J., McCord, J., & Poulin, F. (1999). When interventions harm. *American Psychologist, 54*, 755–764.

Dishion, T. J., & Owen, L. (2002). A longitudinal analysis of friendships and substance use: Bidirectional influence from adolescence to adulthood. *Developmental Psychology, 38*, 480–491.

Dix, T., & Meunier, L. N. (2009). Depressive symptoms and parenting competence: An analysis of 13 regulatory processes. *Developmental Review, 29*, 45–68.

Dix, T., Stewart, A. D., Gershoff, E. T., & Day, W. H. (2007). Autonomy and children's reactions to being controlled: Evidence that both compliance and defiance may be positve markers in early development. *Child Development, 78*, 1204–1221.

Dmitrieva, J., Steinberg, L., & Belsky, J. (2007). Child-care history, classroom composition, and children's functioning in kindergarten. *Psychological Science, 18*, 1032–1039.

Dodge, K. A. (2008). Framing public policy and prevention of chronic violence in American youths. *American Psychologist, 63*, 573–590.

Dodge, K. A. (2009). Mechanisms of gene-environment interaction effects in the development of conduct disorder. *Perspectives on Psychological Science, 4*, 408–414.

Dodge, K. A., Coie, J. D., Pettit, G., & Price, J. (1990). Peer status and aggression in boys' groups: Developmental and contextual analysis. *Child Development, 61*, 1289–1309.

Dodge, K. A., Dishion, T. J., & Lansford, J. E. (2006). Deviant peer influences in intervention and public policy for youth. *Social Policy Report, 20*, 3–20.

Dodge, K. A., Greenberg, M. T., Malone, P. S., & Conduct Problems Prevention Research Group. (2008). Testing an idealized dynamic cascade model of the development of serious violence in adolescence. *Child Development, 79*, 1907–1927.

Dodge, K. A., Lansford, J., Burks, V., Bates, J. E., Pettit, G. S., Fontaine, R., et al. (2003). Peer rejection and social information-processing factors in the development of aggressive behavior problems in children. *Child Development, 74*, 374–393.

Dodge, K. A., Malone, P. S., Lansford, J. E., Miller, S., Pettit, G. S., & Bates, J. E. (2009). A dynamic cascade model of the development of substance-use onset. *Monographs of the Society for Research in Child Development, 74* (Serial No. 294).

Dodge, K. A., McLoyd, V. C., & Lansford, J. E. (2005). The cultural context of physically disciplining children. In V. C. McLoyd, N. E. Hill & K. A. Dodge (Eds.), *African American Family Life* (pp. 245–263). New York: Guilford.

Dodge, K. A., Pettit, G. S., Bates, J. E., & Valente, E. (1995). Social information-processing patterns partially mediate the effect of early physical abuse on later conduct problems. *Journal of Abnormal Psychology, 104*, 632–643.

Dogan-Ates, A., & Carrion-Basham, C. Y. (2007). Teenage pregnancy among Latinas: Examining risk and protective factors. *Hispanic Journal of Behavioral Sciences, 29*, 554–569.

Dolezal, S. E., Welsh, L. M., Pressley, M., & Vincent, M. M. (2003). How nine third-grade teachers motivate student academic engagement. *The Elementary School Journal, 103*, 239–267.

Donaldson, M. (1978). *Children's minds*. New York: Norton.

Dong, M., Anda, R. F., Dube, S. R., Giles, W. H., & Felitti, V. J. (2003). The relationship of exposure to childhood sexual abuse to others forms of abuse, neglect, and household dysfunction during childhood. *Child Abuse & Neglect, 27*, 625–639.

Donnellan, B., Trzeniewski, K., Robins, R., Moffitt, T., & Caspi, A. (2005). Low self-esteem is related to aggression, antisocial behavior, and delinquency. *Psychological Science, 16*, 328–335.

Douglas, E. M. (2006). Familial violence socialization in childhood and later life approval of corporal punishment: A cross-cultural perspective. *American Journal of Orthopsychiatry, 76*, 23–30.

Downey, D. B., von Hippel, P. T., & Broh, B. A. (2004). Are schools the great equalizers? Cognitive inequality during the summer months and the school year. *American Sociological Review, 69*, 613–635.

Downing, P. (2000). Interactions between visual working memory and selective attention. *Psychological Science, 11*, 467–473.

Doyle, J. M., & Kao, G. (2007). Are racial identities of multiracials stable? Changing self-identification among single and multiple race individuals. *Social Psychology Quarterly, 70*, 405–423.

Dozier, M., Stovall, K. C., Albus, K., & Bates, B. (2001). Attachment for infants in foster care: The role of caregiver state of mind. *Child Development, 72*, 1467–1477.

Drover, J., Hoffman, D. R., Castaqeda, Y. S., Morale, S. E., & Birch, E. E. (2009). Three randomized controlled trials of early long-chain polyunsaturated fatty acid supplementation on means-end problem solving in 9-month-olds. *Child Development, 80*, 1376–1384.

Drucker, R., Hammer, L., Agras, W. S., & Bryson, S. (1999). Can mothers influence their child's eating behavior? *Journal of Developmental and Behavioral Pediatrics, 20*, 88–92.

Duckworth, A., & Seligman, M. (2005). Self-discipline outdoes IQ in predicting academic performance of adolescents. *Psychological Science, 16*, 939–944.

Duke, N. K., Purcell-Gates, V., Hall, L. A., & Tower, C. (2006). Authentic literacy activities for developing comprehension and writing. *The Reading Teacher, 60*, 344–355.

Duncan, G., & Brooks-Gunn, J. (2000). Family poverty, welfare reform, and child development. *Child Development, 71*, 188–196.

Duncan, G., Dowsett, C. J., Claessens, A., Magnuson, K., Huston, A. C., Klebanov, P., et al. (2007). School readiness and later achievement. *Developmental Psychology, 43*, 1428–1446.

Duncan, G., & Magnuson, K. (2007). Penny wise and effect size foolish. *Child Development Perspectives, 1*, 46–51.

Dunifon, R., Kalil, A., & Bajracharya, A. (2005). Maternal working conditions and child well-being in welfare-leaving families. *Developmental Psychology, 41*, 851–859.

Dunlosky, J., & Lipko, A. R. (2007). Metacomprehension: A brief history and how to improve its accuracy. *Current Directions in Psychological Science, 16*, 228–232.

Dunn, J., Brown, J., & Beardsall, L. (1991). Family talk about feeling states and children's later understanding of others' emotions. *Developmental Psychology, 27*, 448–455.

Dunn, J., Brown, J. R., & Maguire, M. (1995). The development of children's moral sensibility: Individual differences and emotion understanding. *Developmental Psychology, 31*, 649–659.

Dunn, J., Deater-Deckard, K., Pickering, K., O'Connor, T., Golding, J., & ALSPAC Study Team. (1998). Children's adjustment and prosocial behavior in step-, single-parent, and non-stepfamily settings: Findings from a community study. *Journal of Child Psychology & Psychiatry & Allied Disciplines, 39*, 1083–1095.

Dunn, J., & Hughes, C. (2001). "I got some swords and you're dead!": Violent fantasy, antisocial behavior, friendship, and moral sensibility in young children. *Child Development, 72*, 491–505.

Dunning, D., Heath, C., & Subs, J. M. (2004). Flawed self-assessment: Implications for health, education, and the workplace. *Psychological Science in the Public Interest, 5*, 69–106.

Dunning, D., Johnson, K., Ehrlinger, J., & Kruger, J. (2003). Why people fail to recognize their own incompetence. *Current Directions in Psychological Science, 12*, 83–87.

Dupere, V., Lacourse, E., Willms, J. D., Leventhal, T., & Tremblay, R. E. (2008). Neighborhood poverty and early transition to sexual activity in young adolescents: A developmental ecological approach. *Child Development, 79*, 1463–1476.

Durbin, D. L., Darling, N., Steinberg, L., & Brown, B. B. (1993). Parenting style and peer group membership among European-American adolescents. *Journal of Research on Adolescence, 3*, 87–100.

Dutro, E. (2002). "But that's a girls' book!" Exploring gender boundaries in children's reading practices. *The Reading Teacher, 55*, 376–384.

Dweck, C. S. (2006). *Mindset: The new psychology of success*. New York: Random House.

Dweck, C. S. (2008). Can personality be changed? The role of beliefs in personality and change. *Current Directions in Psychological Science, 17,* 391–394.

Dye, M. W. G., Green, C. S., & Bavelier, D. (2009). Increasing speed of processing with action video games. *Current Directions in Psychological Science, 18,* 321–326.

Eaton, W., McKeen, N., & Campbell, D. (2001). The waxing and waning of movement: Implications for psychological development. *Developmental Review, 21,* 205–223.

Eberly, M. B., & Montemayor, R. (1998). Doing good deeds: An examination of adolescent prosocial behavior in the context of parent-adolescent relationships. *Journal of Adolescent Research, 13,* 403–432.

Eccles, J. S., Midgley, C., Wigfield, A., Buchanan, C., Reuman, M., Flanagan, C., et al. (1993). Development during adolescence: The impact of stage-environment fit on young adolescents' experiences in schools and in families. *American Psychologist, 48,* 90–101.

Eckert, M. A., Lombardino, L. J., & Leonard, C. M. (2001). Planar asymmetry tips the phonological playground and environment raises the bar. *Child Development, 72,* 988–1002.

Eder, D. (1991). The role of teasing in adolescent peer group culture. *Sociological Studies of Child Development, 4,* 181–197.

Edmonds, M. S., Vaughn, S., Wexler, J., Reutebuch, C., Cable, A., Tackett, K. K., et al. (2009). A synthesis of reading interventions and effects on reading comprehension outcomes for older struggling readers. *Review of Educational Research, 79,* 262–300.

Edwards, C. (2000). Children's play in cross-cultural perspective: A new look at the Six Cultures Study. *Cross-Cultural Research: The Journal of Comparative Social Science, 34,* 318–338.

Egan, S. K., & Perry, D. G. (2001). Gender identity: A multidimensional analysis with implications for psychosocial adjustment. *Developmental Psychology, 37,* 451–463.

Eggermont, S., & Van den Buick, J. (2006). Nodding off or switching off? The use of popular media as a sleep aid in secondary-school children. *Journal of Paediatrics and Child Health, 42,* 428–433.

Ehrenberg, R., Brewer, D., Gamoran, A., & Willms, D. (2001). Class size and student achievement. *Psychological Science in the Public Interest, 2,* 1–30.

Ehri, L. C., Dreyer, L. G., Flugman, B., & Gross, A. (2007). Reading Rescue: An effective tutoring intervention model for language-minority students who are struggling readers in first grade. *American Educational Research Journal, 44,* 414–448.

Eiden, R. D., Yvette, V., & Granger, D. A. (2009). Prenatal cocaine exposure and infant cortisol reactivity. *Child Development, 80,* 528–543.

Eigsti, I.-M., Zayas, V., Mischel, W., Shoda, Y., Ayduk, O., Dadlani, M. B., et al. (2006). Predicting cognitive control from preschool to late adolescence and young adulthood. *Psychological Science, 17,* 478–484.

Eikeseth, S. (2009). Outcome of comprehensive psycho-educational interventions for young children with autism. *Research in Developmental Disabilities, 30,* 158–178.

Eisenberg, A. R. (2002). Maternal teaching talk within families of Mexican descent: Influences of talk and socioeconomic status. *Hispanic Journal of Behavioral Sciences, 24,* 206–224.

Eisenberg, N., Carlo, G., Murphy, B., & Van Court, P. (1995). Prosocial development in late adolescence: A longitudinal study. *Child Development, 66,* 1179–1197.

Eisenberg, N., Fabes, R. A., Bernzweig, J., Karbon, M., Poulin, R., & Hanish, L. (1993). The relations of emotionality and regulation to preschoolers' social skills and sociometric status. *Child Development, 64,* 1418–1438.

Eisenberg, N., Fabes, R. A., Schaller, M., Carlo, G., & Miller, P. A. (1991). The relations of parental characteristics and practices to children's vicarious emotional responding. *Child Development, 62,* 1393–1408.

Eisenberg, N., Fabes, R. A., Shepard, S. A., Murphy, B. C., Guthrie, I. K., Jones, S., et al. (1997). Contemporaneous and longitudinal prediction of children's social functioning from regulation and emotionality. *Child Development, 68,* 642–664.

Eisenberg, N., Fabes, R. A., & Spinrad, T. L. (2006). Prosocial development. In N. Eisenberg (Ed.), *Handbook of child psychology: Social, emotional, and personality development* (6th ed., Vol. 3, pp. 646–718). New York: Wiley.

Eisenberg, N., Guthrie, I. K., Murphy, B., Shepard, S. A., Cumberland, A., & Carlo, G. (1999). Consistency and development of prosocial dispositions: A longitudinal study. *Child Development, 70,* 1360–1372.

Eisenberg, N., Spinrad, T. L., Fabes, R. A., Reiser, M., Cumberland, A., Shepard, S. A., et al. (2004). The relations of effortful control and impulsivity to children's resiliency and adjustment. *Child Development, 75,* 25–46.

Eisenberg, N., Valiente, C., Spinrad, T. L., Cumberland, A., Liew, J., Reiser, M., et al. (2009). Longitudinal relations of children's effortful control, impulsivity, and negative emotionality to their externalizing, internalizing, and co-occuring behavior problems. *Developmental Psychology, 45,* 988–1008.

Eisenberg, N., Wolchik, S., Goldberg, L., & Engle, I. (1992). Parental values, reinforcement, and young children's prosocial behavior: A longitudinal study. *Journal of Genetic Psychology, 153,* 19–36.

Eisenberg, N., Zhou, Q., & Koller, S. (2001). Brazilian adolescents' prosocial moral judgment and behavior: Relations to sympathy, perspective taking, gener-role orientation, and demographic characteristics. *Child Development, 72,* 518–534.

Eisenberg, N., Zhou, Q., Losoya, S. H., Fabes, R. A., Shepard, S. A., Murphy, B. C., et al. (2003). The relations of parenting, effortful control, and ego control to children's emotional expressivity. *Child Development, 74,* 875–895.

Eitle, T. M., & Eitle, D. J. (2002). Race, cultural capital, and the educational effects of participation in sports. *Sociology of Education, 75,* 123–146.

Ekman, P. (1973). *Darwin and facial expression: A century of research in review*. New York: Academic Press.

Ekman, P. (2009). Darwin's contributions to our understanding of emotion and expression. *APS Observer, 22,* 15–17.

Ekman, P., O'Sullivan, M., & Frank, M. (1999). A few can catch a liar. *Psychological Science, 10,* 263–266.

El-Sheikh, M., Kouros, C. d., Erath, S. A., Cummings, E. M., Keller, P., & Staton, L. (2009). Marital conflict and children's externalizing behavior: Interactions between parasympathetic and sympathetic nervous system activity, *Monographs of the Society for Research in Child Development, 74* (1, Serial No 292).

Elfenbein, H., & Ambady, N. (2003). Universals and cultural differences in recognizing emotions. *Current Directions in Psychological Science, 12*, 159–164.

Elicker, J., Fortner-Wood, C., & Noppe, I. (1999). The context of infant attachment in family child care. *Journal of Applied Developmental Psychology, 20*, 219–336.

Elliott, D. S. (1994). Serious violent offenders: Onset, developmental course, and termination. *Criminology, 32*, 1–21.

Ellis, B. J., & Boyce, W. T. (2008). Biological sensitivity to context. *Current Directions in Psychological Science, 17*, 183–187.

Ellis, B. J., & Essex, M. J. (2007). Family environments, adrenarche, and sexual maturation: A longitudinal test of a life history model. *Child Development, 78*, 1799–1817.

Ellis, S., Rogoff, B., & Cromer, C. (1981). Age segregation in children's social interactions. *Developmental Psychology, 17*, 399–407.

Ellis, W. E., & Zarbatany, L. (2007). Peer group status as a moderator of group influence on children's deviant, aggressive, and prosocial behavior. *Child Development, 78*, 1240–1254.

Else-Quest, N. M., Hyde, J. S., Goldsmith, H. H., & Van Hulle, C. A. (2006). Gender differences in temperament: A meta-analysis. *Psychological Bulletin, 132*, 33–72.

Emde, R. (1998). Early emotional development: New modes of thinking for research and intervention. *Pediatrics, 102*, 1236–1243.

Emde, R., Biringen, Z., Clyman, R., & Oppenheim, D. (1991). The moral self of infancy: Affective core and procedural knowledge. *Developmental Review, 11*, 251–279.

Emery, R. E., Otto, R. K., & O'Donohue, W. T. (2005). A critical assessment of child custody evaluations. *Psychological Science in the Public Interest, 6*, 1–29.

Emmer, E., & Gerwels, M. (2002). Cooperative learning in elementary classrooms: Teaching practices and lesson characteristics. *Elementary School Journal, 103*, 75–91.

Emmer, E. T., Evertson, C., & Worsham, M. E. (2000). *Classroom management for secondary teachers* (5th ed.). Boston: Allyn and Bacon.

Emmorey, K., Luk, G., Pyers, J. E., & Bialystok, E. (2009). The source of enhanced cognitive control in bilinguals: Evidence from bimodal bilinguals. *Psychological Science, 19*, 1201–1206.

Englund, M. M., Luckner, A. E., Whaley, G. J. L., & Egeland, B. (2004). Children's achievement in early elementary school: Longitudinal effects of parental involvement, expectations, and quality of assistance. *Journal of Educational Psychology 96*, 723–730.

Ennemoser, M., & Schneider, W. (2007). Relations of television viewing and reading: Findings from a 4-year longitudinal study. *Journal of Educational Psychology, 99*, 349–368.

Ennett, S. T., Foshee, V. A., Bauman, K. E., Hussong, A., Cai, L., Luz, H., et al. (2008). The social ecology of adolescent alcohol misuse. *Child Development, 79*, 1777–1791.

Ensor, R., & Hughes, C. (2008). Content or connectedness? Mother-child talk and early social understanding. *Child Development, 79*, 201–216.

Epstein, M., Atkins, M., Cullinan, D., Kutash, K., & Weaver, R. (2008). *Reducing behavior problems in the elementary school classroom.* Washington, DC: National Center for Education Evaluation and Regional Assistance, U.S. Department of Education. Retrieved from http://ies.ed.gov/ncee/wwc/publications/practiceguides.

Erath, S. A., El-Sheikh, M., & Cummings, E. M. (2009). Harsh parenting and child externalizing behavior: Skin conductance level reactivity as a moderator. *Child Development, 80*, 578–592.

Erel, O., Obermran, Y., & Yirmiya, N. (2000). Maternal versus non-maternal care and seven domains of children's development. *Psychological Bulletin, 126*, 727–747.

Ericsson, K. A., Krampe, R., & Tesch-Römer, C. (1993). The role of deliberate practice in the acquisition of expert performance. *Psychological Review, 100*, 363–406.

Ericsson, K. A., & Ward, P. (2007). Capturing the naturally occurring superior performance of experts in the laboratory: Toward a science of expert and exceptional performance. *Current Directions in Psychological Science, 16*, 346–350.

Erikson, E. H. (1959). Identity and the life cycle. *Psychological Issues, 1*, 18–171.

Erikson, E. H. (1963). *Childhood and society* (2nd ed.). New York: W. W. Norton.

Erkman, F., & Rohner, R. P. (2006). Youths' perceptions of corporal punishment, parental acceptance, and psychological adjustment in a Turkish metropolis. *Cross-Cultural Research, 40*, 250–267.

Eskritt, M., & Lee, K. (2002). "Remember where you last saw that card": Children's production of external symbols as a memory aid. *Developmental Psychology, 38*, 254–266.

Espelage, D., Holt, M., & Henkel, R. (2003). Examination of peer-group contextual effects on aggression during early adolescence. *Child Development, 74*, 205–220.

Espy, K., Molfese, V., & DiLalla, L. (2001). Effects of environmental measures on intelligence in young children: Growth curve modeling of longitudinal data. *Merrill-Palmer Quarterly, 47*, 42–73.

Estell, D., Farmer, T., Cairns, R., & Cairns, B. (2002). Social relations and academic achievement in inner-city early elementary classrooms. *International Journal of Behavioral Development, 26*, 518–528.

Estes, K. G., Evans, J. L., Alibali, M. W., & Saffran, J. R. (2007). Can infants map meaning to newly segmented words? Statistical segmentation and word learning. *Psychological Science, 18*, 254–260.

Evans, G. W. (2004). The environment of childhood poverty. *American Psychologist, 59*, 77–92.

Evans, G. W., Gonnella, C., Marcynyszyn, L., Gentile, L., & Salpekar, N. (2005). The role of chaos in poverty and children's socioemotional adjustment. *Psychological Science, 16*, 560–565.

Evans, G. W., & Rosenbaum, J. (2008). Self-regulation and the income-achievement gap. *Early Childhood Research Quarterly, 23*, 504–514.

Fabes, R. A., Eisenberg, N., Hanish, L., & Spinrad, T. L. (2001). Preschoolers' spontaneous emotion vocabulary: Relations to likability. *Early Education and Development, 12*, 11–27.

Fabes, R. A., Eisenberg, N., Jones, S., Smith, M., Guthrie, I., Poulin, R., et al. (1999). Regulation, emotionality, and preschoolers' socially competent peer interactions. *Child Development, 70*, 432–442.

Fabrizi, M., & Pollio, H. (1987). A naturalistic study of humorous activity in a third, seventh, and eleventh grade classroom. *Merrill-Palmer Quarterly, 33*, 107–128.

Fagan, J. F., & Holland, C. R. (2002). Equal opportunity and racial differences in IQ. *Intelligence, 30*, 361–387.

Fagan, J. F., Holland, C. R., & Wheeler, K. (2007). The prediction, from infancy, of adult IQ and achievement. *Intelligence, 35*, 225–231.

Fan, Z., & Chen, M. (2001). Parental involvement and students' academic achievement: A meta-analysis. *Educational Psychology Review, 13*, 1–22.

Fantuzzo, J., Sekino, Y., & Cohen, H. (2004). An examination of the contributions of interactive peer play to salient classroom competencies for urban Head Start children. *Psychology in the Schools, 41*, 323–336.

Farmer, T., Estell, D., Bishop, J., O'Neal, K., & Cairns, B. (2003). Rejected bullies or popular leaders? The social relations of aggressive subtypes of rural African American early adolescents. *Developmental Psychology, 39*, 992–1004.

Farrell, A., Meyer, A., & White, K. (2001). Evaluation of Responding in Peaceful and Positive Ways (RIPP): A school-based prevention program for reducing violence among urban adolescents. *Journal of Clinical Child Psychology, 30*, 451–463.

Farrington, D. P. (2009). Conduct disorder, aggression, and delinquency. In R. M. Lerner & L. Steinberg (Eds.), *Handbook of adolescent psychology* (pp. 683–722). Hoboken, NJ: Wiley.

Farver, J. A. M., Lonigan, C., & Eppe, S. (2009). Effective early literacy skill development for young Spanish-speaking English language learners: An experimental study of two methods. *Child Development, 80*, 703–719.

Fauth, R. C., Roth, J., & Brooks-Gunn, J. (2007). Does neighborhood context alter the link between youth's after-school time activities and developmental outcomes? A multilevel analysis. *Developmental Psychology, 43*, 760–777.

Federal Interagency Forum on Child and Family Statistics. (2002). *America's children: Key national indicators of well-being, 2002*. Washington, DC: U.S. Government Printing Office.

Federal Interagency Forum on Child and Family Statistics. (2008). *America's children: Key national indicators of well-being*. Washington, DC: U.S. Government Printing Office.

Feldman, R., & Klein, P. (2003). Toddlers' self-regulated compliance to mothers, caregivers, and fathers: Implications for theories of socialization. *Developmental Psychology, 39*, 680–692.

Feldman, R., Weller, A., Sirota, L., & Eidelman, A. (2002). Skin-to-skin contact (Kangaroo Care) promotes self-regulation in premature infants: Sleep-wake cyclicity, arousal modulation, and sustained exploration. *Developmental Psychology, 38*, 194–207.

Feliciano, C. (2001). The benefits of biculturalism: Exposure to immigrant culture and dropping out of school among Asian and Latino youths. *Social Science Quarterly, 82*, 865–879.

Felner, R. D., Seitsinger, A. M., Brand, S., Burns, A., & Bolton, N. (2007). Creating small learning communities: Lessons from the Project on High-Performing Learning Communities about "what works" in creating productive, developmentally enhancing, learning contexts. *Educational Psychologist, 42*, 209–221.

Feng, J., Spence, I., & Pratt, J. (2007). Playing an action video game reduces gender differences in spatial cognition. *Psychological Science, 18*, 850–855.

Feng, X., Keenan, K., Hipwell, A. E., Henneberger, A. K., Rischall, M. S., Butch, J., et al. (2009). Longitudinal associations between emotion regulation and depression in preadolescent girls: Moderation by the caregiving environment. *Developmental Psychology, 45*, 798–808.

Fenske, M. J., & Raymond, J. E. (2006). Affective influences of selective attention. *Current Directions in Psychological Science, 15*, 312–316.

Ferguson, C. J. (2007). Evidence for publication bias in video game violence effects literature: A meta-analytic review. *Aggression and Violent Behavior, 12*, 470–482.

Ferguson, T., Stegge, H., & Damhuis, I. (1991). Children's understanding of guilt and shame. *Child Development, 62*, 827–839.

Fernald, A., Swingley, D., & Pinto, J. P. (2001). When half a word is enough: Infants can recognize spoken words using partial phonetic information. *Child Development, 72*, 1003–1015.

Ferrando, P. J., Varea, M. D., & Lorenzo, U. (1998). A psychometric study of the test anxiety scale for children in a Spanish sample. *Personality and Individual Differences, 27*, 37–44.

Ferrer, E., Shaywitz, B. A., Holahan, J. M., Marchione, K., & Shaywitz, S. E. (2010). Uncoupling of reading and IQ over time: Empirical evidence for a definition of dyslexia. *Psychological Science, 21*, 93–101.

Field, A., Camargo, C., Taylor, B., Berkey, C., Frazier, L., Gillman, M., et al. (1999). Overweight, weight concerns, and bulimic behaviors among girls and boys. *Journal of the American Academy of Child and Adolescent Psychiatry, 38*, 754–760.

Field, T. M. (1998). Early interventions for infants of depressed mothers. *Pediatrics, 102*, 1305–1310.

Field, T. M., Healy, B., Goldstein, S., & Guthertz, M. (1988). Behavior-state matching and synchrony in mother–infant interactions of nondepressed versus depressed dyads. *Developmental Psychology, 26*, 7–14.

Field, T. M., Hernandez-Reif, M., & Freedman, J. (2004). Stimulation programs for preterm infants. *Social Policy Report, 18*, 3–19.

Field, T. M., Hossain, Z., & Malphurs, J. (1999). "Depressed" fathers' interaction with their infants. *Infant Mental Health Journal, 20*, 3322–3332.

FIFCFS. (2008). *America's children: Key national indicators of well-being*. Washington, DC: U.S. Government Printing Office.

Fincham, F. (2000). The kiss of the porcupines: From attributing responsibility to forgiving. *Personal Relationships, 7*, 1–23.

Finn, J. D., Gerber, S. B., Achilles, C. M., & Boyd-Zaharias, J. (2001). The enduring effects of small classes. *Teachers College Record, 103*, 145–183.

Fisch, S., & Truglio, R. T. (2001). *"G" is for "Growing": Thirty years of research on children and Sesame Street*. Mahwah, NJ: Erlbaum.

Fisher, A., Kramer, R., Hoven, C., King, R., Bird, H., Davies, M., et al. (2000). Risk behavior in a community sample of children and adolescents. *Journal of the American Academy of Child and Adolescent Behavior, 39*, 881–887.

Fisher, E. (1992). The impact of play on development: A meta-analysis. *Play and Culture, 5*, 159–181.

Fiske, S. T. (2002). What we know now about bias and intergroup conflict, the problem of the century. *Current Directions in Psychological Science, 11*, 123–128.

Fitzgerald, J. (2006). Multilingual writing in preschool through 12th grade: The last 15 years. In C. A. MacArthur, S. Graham & J. Fitzgerald (Eds.), *Handbook of writing research* (pp. 337–354). New York: Guilford.

Fitzsimmons, P., & McKenzie, B. (2003). Play on words: Humor as the means of developing authentic learning. In D. Lytle (Ed.), *Play and educational theory and practice* (Vol. 5, pp. 197–211). Westport, CT: Praeger.

Fivush, R., & Nelson, K. (2004). Culture and language in the emergence of autobiographical memory. *Psychological Science, 15*, 573–577.

Flanagan, K. D., McPhee, C., & Mulligan, G. (2010). *The Children Born in 2001 at Kindergarten Entry*. (NCES 2010-005). National Center for Education Statistics, U.S. Department of Education. Washington, DC.

Flannery, D., Hussey, D., Biebelhausen, A., & Wester, K. (2003). Crime, delinquency, and youth gangs. In G. Adams & M. Berzonsky (Eds.), *Blackwell handbook of adolescence* (pp. 502–522). Malden, MA: Blackwell.

Flavell, J. H. (1999). Cognitive development: Children's knowledge about the mind. *Annual Review of Psychology, 50*, 21–45.

Fletcher, A. C., Darling, N. E., Steinberg, L., & Dornbusch, S. M. (1995). The company they keep: Relations of adolescents' adjustment and behavior to their friends' perceptions of authoritative parenting in the social network. *Developmental Psychology, 31*, 300–310.

Fletcher, A. C., Walls, J. K., Cook, E. C., Madison, K. J., & Bridges, T. H. (2008). Parenting style as a moderator of associations between maternal disciplinary strategies and child well-being. *Journal of Family Issues, 29*, 1724–1744.

Fletcher, J. M., Shaywitz, S. E., Shankweiler, D. P., Katz, L., Liberman, I. Y., Stuebing, K. K., et al. (1994). Cognitive profiles of reading disability: Comparisons of discrepancy and low achievement definitions. *Journal of Educational Psychology, 86*, 6–23.

Fletcher, J. M., & Vaughn, S. (2009). Response to intervention: Preventing and remediating academic difficulties. *Child Development Perspectives, 3*, 30–37.

Fletcher, K., & Reese, E. (2005). Picture book reading with young children: A conceptual framework. *Developmental Review, 25*, 64–103.

Flook, L., & Fuligni, A. J. (2008). Family and school spillover in adolescents' daily lives. *Child Development, 79*, 776–787.

Flook, L., Repetti, R., & Ullman, J. (2005). Classroom social experiences as predictors of academic performance. *Developmental Psychology, 41*, 319–327.

Flynn, J. R. (2007). *What is intelligence? Beyond the Flynn effect*. New York: Cambridge University Press.

Foersterling, F., & Binser, M. (2002). Depression, school performance and the veridicality of perceived grades and causal attributions. *Personality and Social Psychology Bulletin, 28*, 1441–1449.

Fontaine, J. R., Scherer, K. R., Roesch, E. B., & Ellsworth, P. C. (2007). The world of emotions is not two-dimensional. *Psychological Science, 18*, 1050–1057.

Fontaine, R. G., Yang, C., Dodge, K. A., Pettit, G. S., & Bates, J. E. (2009). Development of response evaluation and decision (RED) and antisocial behavior in childhood and adolescence. *Developmental Psychology, 45*, 447–459.

Fordham, S., & Ogbu, J. U. (1986). Black students' school success: Coping with the "burden of 'acting white.'" *The Urban Review, 18*, 176–206.

Forgatch, M., & DeGarmo, D. (2002). Extending and testing the social interaction learning model with divorce samples. In J. Reid, G. Patterson & J. Snyder (Eds.), *Antisocial behavior in children and adolescents: A developmental analysis and model for intervention* (pp. 235–256). Washington, DC: American Psychological Association.

Forgays, D., & Forgays, J. (1952). The nature of the effect of free-environmental experience in the rat. *Journal of Comparative and Physiological Psychology, 45*, 322–328.

Forget-Dubois, N., Dionne, G., Lemelin, J.-P., Perusse, D., Tremblay, R. E., & Boivin, M. (2009). Early child language mediates the relation between home environment and school readiness. *Child Development, 80*, 736–749.

Forsyth, B. (2003). Psychological aspects of HIV infection in children. *Child and Adolescent Psychiatric Clinics, 12*, 423–437.

Forum on Child and Family Statistics. (2009). Family Reading to Young Children. *America's Children: Key National Indicators of Well-Being, 2009*. Retrieved February 20, 2010, from http://www.childstats.gov/americaschildren/edu1.asp

Foster, H. L. (1986). *Ribbin', jivin', and playin' the dozens*. Cambridge, MA: Ballinger.

Fox, E. (2009). The role of reader characteristics in processing and learning from informational text. *Review of Educational Research, 79*, 197–261.

Fraley, C., & Spieker, S. (2003). Are infant attachment patterns continuously or categorically distributed? A taxometric analysis of strange situation behavior. *Developmental Psychology, 39*, 387–404.

Frazier, J., & Morrison, F. (1998). The influence of extended-year schooling on growth of achievement and perceived competence in early elementary school. *Child Development, 69*, 495–517.

Fredrickson, B. L. (2001). The role of positive emotions in positive psychology: The broaden-and-build theory of positive emotions. *American Psychologist, 56*, 218–226.

Fredriksen, K., Rhodes, J., Reddy, R., & Way, N. (2004). Sleepless in Chicago: Tracking the effects of adolescent sleep loss during the middle school years. *Child Development, 75*, 84–95.

Freeman, H., & Brown, B. (2001). Primary attachment to parents and peers during adolescence: Differences by attachment style. *Journal of Youth and Adolescence, 30*, 653–674.

Freiberg, H. J. (1999). Consistency management and cooperative discipline. In H. J. Freiberg (Ed.), *Beyond behaviorism: Changing the classroom management paradigm* (pp. 75–97). Boston: Allyn and Bacon.

Freiberg, H. J., Huzinec, C. A., & Templeton, S. M. (2009). Classroom management—a pathway to student achievement: A study of fourteen inner-city elementary schools. *The Elementary School Journal, 110*, 63–80.

French, D., & Conrad, J. (2001). School dropout as predicted by peer rejection and antisocial behavior. *Journal of Research on Adolescence, 11*, 225–244.

French, S. E., Seidman, E., Allen, L., & Aber, J. L. (2006). The development of ethnic identity during adolescence. *Developmental Psychology, 42*, 1–10.

Freud, S. (1905/1960). *Jokes and their relation to the unconscious* (J. Strachey, Trans.). New York: Norton.

Freud, S. (1923/1961). The ego and the id (J. Strachey, A. Freud, A. Strachey & A. Tyson, Trans.). In J. Strachey (Ed.), *The standard edition of the complete psychological works of Sigmund Freud* (Vol. XlX). London: Hogarth.

Freud, S. (1933/1964). New introductory lectures on psycho-analysis. In J. Strachey, A. Freud, A. Strachey & A. Tyson (Eds.), *The standard edition of the complete psychological works of Sigmund Freud* (Vol. XXll). London: Howarth.

Frey, K. S., Hirschstein, M., Snell, J., Edstrom, L., MacKenzie, E., & Broderick, C. (2005). Reducing playground bullying and supporting beliefs: An experimental trial of the Steps to Respect program. *Developmental Psychology, 41*, 479–491.

Frey, M., & Detterman, D. (2004). Scholastic assessment or *g*? The relationship between the Scholastic Assessment Test and general cognitive ability. *Psychological Science, 15*, 373–378.

Friedel, J. M., Cortina, K. S., Turner, J. C., & Midgley, C. (2010). Changes in efficacy beliefs in mathematics across the transition to middle school: Examining the effects of perceived teacher and parent goal emphases. *Journal of Educational Psychology, 102*, 102–114.

Friedman, N. P., Haberstick, B. C., Willcutt, E. G., Miyake, A., Young, S. E., Corley, R. P., et al. (2007). Greater attention problems during childhood predict poorer executive functioning in late adolescence. *Psychological Science, 18*, 893–900.

Friedman, W. (2007). The development of temporal metamemory. *Child Development, 78*, 1472–1491.

Friend, A., DeFries, J. C., & Olson, R. K. (2008). Parental education moderates genetic influences on reading disability. *Psychological Science, 19*, 1124–1130.

Fuchs, L. S., Fuchs, D., Kazdan, S., Karns, K., Calhoon, M. B., Hamlett, C. L., et al. (2000). Effects of workgroup structure and size on student productivity during collaborative work on complex tasks. *Elementary School Journal, 100*, 183–212.

Fujiwara, T., Barber, C., Schaechter, J., & Hemenway, D. (2009). Characteristics of infant homicides: Findings from a U.S. multisite reporting system. *Pediatrics, 124*, 210–217.

Fuligni, A. J., & Stevenson, H. W. (1995). Time use and mathematics achievement among American, Chinese, and Japanese high school students. *Child Development, 66*, 830–842.

Fuligni, A. J., Witkow, M., & Garcia, C. (2005). Ethnic identity and the academic adjustment of adolescents from Mexican, Chinese, and European backgrounds. *Developmental Psychology, 41*, 799–811.

Furman, E. (1989). Mothers, toddlers, and care. In S. Greenspan & G. Pollock (Eds.), *The course of life* (Vol. 2, pp. 61–82). Madison, CT: International Universities Press.

Furman, W., Rahe, D., & Hartup, W. (1979). Rehabilitation of socially withdrawn preschool children through mixed-age and same-age socialization. *Child Development, 50*, 915–922.

Gable, P. A., & Harmon-Jones, E. (2008). Approach-motivated positive affect reduces breadth of attention. *Psychological Science, 19*, 476–482.

Gable, S., Krull, J. L., & Chang, Y. (2009). Implications of overweight onset and persistence for social and behavioral development between kindergarten entry and third grade. *Applied Developmental Science, 13*, 88–103.

Gaensbauer, T. J., Mrazek, D., & Harmon, R. (1981). Emotional expression in abused and/or neglected infants. In N. Frude (Ed.), *Psychological approaches to child abuse* (pp. 120–135). Totowa, NJ: Rowman & Littlefield.

Gailliot, M. T. (2008). Unlocking the energy dynamics of executive functioning: Linking executive functioning to brain glycogen. *Perspectives on Psychological Science, 3*, 245–263.

Galambos, N., Barker, E., & Almeida, D. (2003). Parents do matter: Trajectories of change in externalizing and internalizing problems in early adolescence. *Child Development, 74*, 578–594.

Galliger, C., Tisak, M. S., & Tisak, J. (2008). When the wheels on the bus go round: Social interactions on the school bus. *Social Psychology of Education, 12*, 43–62.

Ganiban, J. M., Saudino, K. J., Ulbricht, J., Neiderhiser, J. M., & Reiss, D. (2008). Stability and change in temperament during adolescence. *Journal of Personality and Social Psychology, 95*, 222–236.

Gao, F., Levine, S., & Huttenlocher, J. (2000). What do infants know about continuous quantity? *Journal of Experimental Child Psychology, 77*, 20–29.

Garcma, E., & Jensen, B. (2009). Early educational opportunities for children of Hispanic origins. *Social Policy Report, 23*, 3–19.

Gardner, A. W., Wacker, D. P., & Boelter, E. W. (2009). An evaluation of the interaction between quality of attention and negative reinforcement with children who display escape-maintained problem behavior. *Journal of Applied Behavior Analysis, 42*, 343–348.

Gardner, H. (1999). *Intelligence reframed: Multiple intelligences for the 21st century*. New York: Basic Books.

Gardner, H. (2006). *Multiple intelligences: New horizons*. New York: Basic Books.

Gardner, M., Roth, J., & Brooks-Gunn, J. (2009). Sports participation and juvenile delinquency: The role of the peer context among adolescent boys and girls with varied histories of problem behavior. *Developmental Psychology, 45*, 341–353.

Garrard, W., & Lipsey, M. W. (2007). Conflict resolution education and antisocial behavior in U.S. schools: A meta-analysis. *Conflict Resolution Quarterly, 25*, 9–38.

Garry, M., & Gerrie, M. P. (2005). When photographs create false memories. *Current Directions in Psychological Science, 14*, 321–325.

Gaskins, S., Beard, S., & Wang, M. (2002). An HIV/AIDS education program for children in grades K–5. *Journal of HIV/AIDS Prevention and Education for Adolescents and Children, 5*, 31–43.

Gates, H. L, Jr. (1988). *The signifying monkey: A theory of Afro-American literary criticism*. New York: Oxford University Press.

Gaultney, J. F., Bjorklund, D. F., & Schneider, W. (1992). The role of children's expertise in a strategic memory task. *Contemporary Educational Psychology, 17*, 244–257.

Gauvain, M., & Monroe, R. L. (2009). Contributions of societal modernity to cognitive development: A comparison of four cultures. *Child Development, 80*, 1628–1642.

Gazelle, H. (2006). Class climate moderates peer relations and emotional adjustment in children with an early history of anxious solitude: A child x environment model. *Developmental Psychology, 42*, 1179–1192.

Gazelle, H., & Druhen, M. J. (2009). Anxious solitude and peer exclusion predict social helplessness, upset affect, and vagal regulation in response to behavioral rejection by a friend. *Developmental Psychology, 45*, 1077–1096.

Gazelle, H., & Ladd, G. (2003). Anxious solitude and peer exclusion: A diathesis-stress model of internalizing trajectories in childhood. *Child Development, 74*, 257–278.

Ge, X., Brody, G., Conger, R., Simons, R., & Murry, V. (2002). Contextual amplification of pubertal transition effects on deviant peer affiliation and externalizing behavior among African American children. *Developmental Psychology, 38*, 42–54.

Ge, X., Kim, I., Brody, G., Conger, R., Simon, R., Gibbons, F., et al. (2003). It's about timing and change: Pubertal transition effects on symptoms of major depression among African American youth. *Developmental Psychology, 39*, 430–439.

Ge, X., & Natsuaki, M. N. (2009). In search of explanations for early pubertal timing effects on developmental psychopathology. *Current Directions in Psychological Science, 18*, 327–331.

Geary, D., & Bjorklund, D. F. (2000). Evolutionary developmental psychology. *Child Development, 71*, 57–65.

Geary, D. C., Hoard, M. K., Byrd-Craven, J., Nugent, L., & Numtee, C. (2007). Cognitive mechanisms underlying achievement deficits in children with mathematical learning disability. *Child Development, 78*, 1343–1359.

Gelman, R. (2006). Young natural-number arithmeticians. *Current Directions in Psychological Science, 15*, 193–197.

Gelman, R., & Baillargeon, R. (1983). A review of some Piagetian concepts. In J. H. Flavell & E. Markman (Eds.), *Handbook of child psychology: Cognitive development* (Vol. 3, pp. 167–230). New York: Wiley.

Gelman, R., & Butterworth, B. (2005). Number and language: How are they related? *Trends in Cognitive Sciences, 9*, 6–10.

Gelman, R., & Williams, E. (1998). Enabling constraints for cognitive development and learning: Domain specificity and epigenesis. In D. Kuhn & R. Siegler (Eds.), *Handbook of child psychology. Cognition, perception, and language* (5th ed., Vol. 2, pp. 575–630). New York: Wiley.

Gentile, D. A. (2009). Pathological video-game use among youth ages 8 to 18: A national study. *Psychological Science, 20*, 594–602.

Gentile, D. A., Anderson, C. A., Yukawa, S., Ihori, N., Saleem, M., Ming, L. K., et al. (2009). The effects of prosocial video games on prosocial behaviors: International evidence from correlational, longitudinal, and experimental studies. *Personality and Social Psychology Bulletin, 35*, 752–763.

Gentile, D. A., Lynch, P. J., Linder, J. R., & Walsh, D. (2004). The effects of violent video game habits on adolescent hostility, aggressive behaviors, and school performance. *Journal of Adolescence, 27*, 5–22.

Gentner, D., Loewenstein, J., & Hung, B. (2007). Comparison facilitates children's learning of names for parts. *Journal of Cognition and Development, 8*, 285–307.

Gentner, D., & Namy, L. L. (2006). Analogical processes in language learning. *Current Directions in Psychological Science, 15*, 297–301.

Gentry, M., Gable, R. K., & Rizza, M. G. (2002). Students' perceptions of classroom activities: Are there grade-level and gender differences? *Journal of Educational Psychology, 94*, 539–544.

Gerard, J., & Buehler, C. (2004). Cumulative environmental risk and youth maladjustment: The role of youth attributes. *Child Development, 75*, 1832–1849.

Gernsbacher, M. A., Stevenson, J. L., Khandakar, S., & Goldsmith, H. H. (2008). Why does joint attention look atypical in autism? *Child Development Perspectives, 2*, 38–45.

Gershoff, E. T. (2002). Corporal punishment by parents and associated child behaviors and experiences: A meta-analytic and theoretical review. *Psychological Bulletin, 128*, 539–579.

Gershoff, E. T., Aber, J. L., Raver, C. C., & Lennon, M. C. (2007). Income is not enough: Incorporating material hardship into models of income associations with parenting and child development. *Child Development, 78*, 70–95.

Gersten, R., & Baker, S. (2000). What we know about effective instructional practices for English-language learners. *Exceptional Children, 66*, 54–70.

Gervais, J., Tremblay, R., Desmarais-Gervais, L., & Vitaro, F. (2000). Children's persistent lying, gender differences, and disruptive behaviours: A longitudinal perspective. *International Journal of Behavioral Development, 24*, 213–221.

Gesell, A. (1933). Maturation and the patterning of behavior. In C. Murchison (Ed.), *A handbook of child psychology*. Worcester, MA: Clark University Press.

Gesell, A. (1940). *The first five years of life*. New York: Harper & Row.

Gest, S., Domitrovich, C. E., & Welsh, J. A. (2005). Peer academic reputation in elementary school: Associations with changes in self-concept and academic skills. *Journal of Educational Psychology, 97*, 337–346.

Gest, S., Graham-Bermann, S., & Hartup, W. (2001). Peer experience: Common and unique features of number of friendships, social network centrality, and sociometric status. *Social Development, 10*, 23–40.

Gibbs, J. T., Huang, L. N., & Associates. (2003). *Children of color: Psychological interventions with culturally diverse youth*. San Francisco: Jossey Bass.

Gibbs, W. W. (2002, August). From mouth to mind. *Scientific American, 287*, 26.

Gibson-Davis, C. M., & Gassman-Pines, A. (2010). Early childhood family structure and mother-child interactions: Variation by race and ethnicity. *Developmental Psychology, 46*, 151–164.

Giedd, J. N., LaLonde, F. M., Celano, M. J., White, S. L., Wallace, G. L., Less, N. R., et al. (2009). Anatomical brain magnetic resonance imaging of typically developing children and adolescents. *Journal of the American Academy of Child and Adolescent Psychiatry, 48*, 465-470.

Giles-Sims, J., & Lockhart, C. (2005). Culturally shaped patterns of disciplining children. *Journal of Family Issues, 26*, 196–218.

Gill, B. P., & Schlossman, S. L. (2003). A nation at rest: The American way of homework. *Educational Evaluation and Policy Analysis, 25*, 319–337.

Gilliam, W., & Zigler, E. (2000). A critical meta-analysis of all evaluations of state-funded preschool from 1977 to 1998: Implications for policy, service delivery and program evaluation. *Early Childhood Research Quarterly, 15*, 441–473.

Gillies, R. (2003). The behaviors, interactions, and perceptions of junior high students during small-group learning. *Journal of Educational Psychology, 95*, 137–147.

Gilligan, C. (1982). *In a different voice: Psychological theory and women's development*. Cambridge, MA: Harvard University Press.

Gilliom, M., Shaw, D., Beck, J., Schonberg, M., & Lukon, J. (2002). Anger regulation in disadvantaged preschool boys: Strategies, antecedents, and the development of self-control. *Developmental Psychology, 38*, 222–235.

Gilovich, T., & Savitsky, K. (1999). The spotlight effect and the illusion of transparency: Egocentric assessments of how we are seen by others. *Current Directions in Psychological Science, 8*, 165–168.

Ginsburg, A., Cooke, G., Leinwand, S., Noell, J., & Pollock, E. (2005). *Reassessing U.S. international mathematics performance.* Washington, DC: American Institutes for Research.

Ginsburg, H., Klein, A., & Starkey, P. (1998). The development of children's mathematical thinking: Connecting research with practice. In I. Sigel & K. A. Renninger (Eds.), *Handbook of child psychology: Child psychology in practice.* (5th ed., Vol. 4, pp. 401–476). New York: Wiley.

Ginsburg, H., Lee, J. S., & Boyd, J. S. (2008). Mathematics education for young children: What it is and how to promote it. *Social Policy Report, 22*, 3–22.

Ginsburg, K. R. (2007). The importance of play in promoting healthy child development and maintaining strong parent–child bonds. *Pediatrics, 119*, 182–191.

Gleason, J. B. (1958). The child's learning of English morphology. *Word, 14*, 150–177.

Gleason, T., Sebanc, A., & Hartup, W. (2000). Imaginary companions of preschool children. *Developmental Psychology, 36*, 419–428.

Gobet, F., & Campitelli, G. (2007). The role of domain-specific practice, handedness, and starting age in chess. *Developmental Psychology, 43*, 159–172.

Goldberg, W. A., Prause, J., Lucas-Thompson, R., & Himsel, A. (2008). Maternal employment and children's achievement in context: A meta-analysis of four decades of research. *Psychological Bulletin, 134*, 77–108.

Goldenberg, C. (1992). The limits of expectations: A case for case knowledge about teacher expectancy effects. *American Educational Research Journal, 29*, 517–544.

Goldfried, J., & Miner, M. (2002). Quest religion and the problem of limited compassion. *Journal for the Scientific Study of Religion, 41*, 685–695.

Goldin-Meadow, S., Cook, S. W., & Mitchell, Z. A. (2009). Gesturing gives children new ideas about math. *Psychological Science, 20*, 267–272.

Goldin-Meadow, S., & Singer, M. (2003). From children's hands to adult's ear: Gesturer's role in the learning process. *Developmental Psychology, 39*, 509–520.

Goldman, L., Genel, M., Bexman, R., & Slanetz, P. (1998). Diagnosis and treatment of attention-deficit/hyperactivity disorder in children and adolescents. *Journal of the American Medical Association, 279*, 1100–1107.

Goldsmith, H., Lemery, K., Buss, K., & Campos, J. (1999). Genetic analyses of focal aspects of infant temperament. *Developmental Psychology, 35*, 972–985.

Goldstein, M. H., Schwade, J. A., & Bornstein, M. H. (2009). The value of vocalizing: Five-month-old infants associate their own noncry vocalizations with responses from caregivers. *Child Development, 80*, 636–644.

Goldstein, S., Davis-Kean, P., & Eccles, J. S. (2005). Parents, peers, and problem behavior: A longitudinal investigation of the impact of relationship perceptions and characteristics on the development of adolescent problem behavior. *Developmental Psychology, 41*, 401–413.

Goldwyn, R., Stanley, C., Smith, V., & Green, J. (2000). The Manchester Child Attachment Story Task: Relationship with parental AAI, SAT and child behaviour. *Attachment & Human Development, 2*, 71–84.

Golinkoff, R. M., & Hirsh-Pasek, K. (2006). Baby wordsmith: From associationist to social sophisticate. *Current Directions in Psychological Science, 15*, 30–33.

Golombok, S., & Hines, M. (2002). Sex differences in social behavior. In P. Smith & C. Hart (Eds.), *Blackwell handbook of childhood social development* (pp. 117–136). Oxford: Blackwell.

Golombok, S., Perry, B., Burston, A., Murray, C., Mooney-Somers, J., Stevens, M., et al. (2003). Children with lesbian parents: A community study. *Developmental Psychology, 39*, 20–33.

Golombok, S., Tasker, F., & Murray, C. (1997). Children raised in fatherless families from infancy: Family relationships and the socioemotional development of children of lesbian and single heterosexual mothers. *Journal of Child Psychology & Psychiatry & Allied Disciplines, 28*, 783–791.

Göncü, A., Patt, M., & Kouba, E. (2002). Understanding young children's pretend play in context. In P. Smith & C. Hart (Eds.), *Blackwell handbook of childhood social development* (p. 418). Oxford: Blackwell.

Good, C., Aronson, J., & Inzlicht, M. (2003). Improving adolescents' standardized test performance: An intervention to reduce the effects of stereotype threat. *Applied Developmental Psychology, 24*, 645–662.

Goodman, G. S., Emery, R. E., & Haugaard, J. J. (1998). Developmental psychology and law: Divorce, child maltreatment, foster care, and adoption. In I. Sigel & K. A. Renninger (Eds.), *Handbook of child psychology: Child psychology in practice* (5th ed., Vol. 4, pp. 775–874). New York: Wiley.

Goodman, G. S., & Quas, J. A. (2008). Repeated interviews and children's memory. *Current Directions in Psychological Science, 17*, 386–390.

Goodman, J. (2000). Moral education in early childhood: The limits of constructivism. *Early Education and Development, 11*, 37–54.

Goodson, B., Layzer, J., St. Pierre, R., Bernstein, L., & Lopez, M. (2000). Effectiveness of a comprehensive, five-year family support program for low-income children and their families: Findings from the Comprehensive Child Development Program. *Early Childhood Research Quarterly, 15*, 5–39.

Goodwin, M. H. (1998). Games of stance: Conflict and footing in hopscotch. In S. M. Hoyle & C. T. Adger (Eds.), *Kids talk: Strategic language use in later childhood* (pp. 23–46). New York: Oxford University Press.

Goosby, B. J., & Cheadle, J. E. (2009). Birth weight, math and reading achievement growth: A multilevel between-sibling, between families approach. *Social Forces, 87*, 1291–1320.

Gordon-Larsen, P., McMurray, R., & Popkin, B. (2000). Determinants of adolescent physical activity and inactivity patterns. *Pediatrics, 105*, e83.

Gormley, W., Gayer, T., Phillips, D., & Dawson, B. (2005). The effects of universal pre-K on cognitive development. *Developmental Psychology, 41*, 872–884.

Gottfredson, L. S. (1997). Mainstream science on intelligence: An editorial with 52 signatories, history, and bibliography. *Intelligence, 24*, 13–23.

Gottfried, A. E., Marcoulides, G. A., Gottfried, A. W., & Oliver, P. H. (2009). A latent curve model of parental motivational practices and developmental decline in math and science academic intrinsic motivation. *Journal of Educational Psychology, 101*, 729–739.

Gozal, D. (1998). Sleep-disordered breathing and school performance in children. *Pediatrics, 102*, 616–620.

Grabill, C., & Kerns, K. (2000). Attachment style and intimacy in friendships. *Personal Relationships, 7*, 363–378.

Graham, S. (2000). Should the natural learning approach replace spelling instruction? *Journal of Educational Psychology, 92*, 235–247.

Graham, S., Kilbreath, C., & Welder, A. (2004). Thirteen-month-olds rely on shared labels and shape similarity for inductive inferences. *Child Development, 75*, 409–427.

Graham, S., MacArthur, C., & Schwartz, S. (1995). Effects of goal setting and procedural facilitation on the revising behavior and writing performance of students with writing and learning problems. *Journal of Educational Psychology, 87*, 230–240.

Graham, S., & Perin, D. (2007). A meta-analysis of writing instruction for adolescent students. *Journal of Educational Psychology, 99*, 445–476.

Granger, D. A., Weisz, J. R., McCracken, J. T., & Ikeda, S. C. (1996). Reciprocal influences among adrenocortical activation, psychosocial processes, and the behavioral adjustment of clinic-referred children. *Child Development, 67*, 3250–3262.

Granger, R. C. (2008). After-school programs and academics: Implications for policy, practice, and research. *Social Policy Report, 23*, 3–17.

Granot, D., & Mayseless, O. (2001). Attachment security and adjustment to school in middle childhood. *International Journal of Behavioral Development, 25*, 530–541.

Grant, H., & Dweck, C. S. (2003). Clarifying achievement goals and their impact. *Journal of Personality and Social Psychology, 85*, 541–553.

Grant, K., O'Koon, J., Davis, T., Roache, N., Poindexter, L., Armstrong, M., et al. (2000). Protective factors affecting low-income urban African American youth exposed to stress. *Journal of Early Adolescence, 20*, 388–417.

Graue, E., Hatch, K., Rao, K., & Oen, D. (2007). The wisdom of class-size reduction. *American Educational Research Journal, 44*, 670–700.

Gray, L., Lewis, L., & Tice, P. (2009). *Educational technology in public school districts: Fall 2008*. (NCES 2010–003). National Center for Education Statistics, U.S. Department of Education. Washington, DC.

Gray, W. M. (1976). *How is your logic?* (Experimental edition, Form A). Boulder, CO: Biological Sciences Curriculum Study.

Gray-Little, B., & Hafdahl, A. R. (2000). Factors influencing racial comparisons of self-esteem: A quantitative review. *Psychological Bulletin, 126*, 26–54.

Gredler, M. E. (2009). Hiding in plain sight: The stages of mastery/self-regulation in Vygotsky's cultural-historical theory. *Educational Psychologist, 44*, 1–19.

Green, C. L., Walker, J. M. T., Hoover-Dempsey, K. V., & Sandler, H. M. (2007). Parents' motivations for involvement in children's education: An empirical test of a theoretical model of parental involvement. *Journal of Educational Psychology, 99*, 532–544.

Green, C. S., & Bavelier, D. (2007). Action-video-game experience alters the spatial resolution of vision. *Psychological Science, 18*, 88–94.

Green, G., Rhodes, J., Hirsch, A. H., Suarez-Orozco, C., & Camic, P. M. (2008). Supportive adult relationships and the academic engagement of Latin American immigrant youth. *Journal of School Psychology, 46*, 393–412.

Greenberg, M. T., & Kusche, C. A. (2006). Building social and emotional competence: The PATHS curriculum. In S. R. Jimerson & M. Furlong (Eds.), *Handbook of school violence and school safety: From research to practice* (pp. 395–412). Mahwah, NJ: Erlbaum.

Greener, S. (2000). Peer assessment of children's prosocial behaviour. *Journal of Moral Education, 29*, 47–61.

Greener, S., & Crick, N. R. (1999). Normative beliefs about prosocial behavior in middle childhood: What does it mean to be nice? *Social Development, 8*, 349–363.

Greenfield, P. M. (1998). The cultural evolution of IQ. In U. Neisser (Ed.), *The rising curve: Long-term gains in IQ and related measures* (pp. 81–123). Washington, DC: American Psychological Association.

Greenspan, S. (2003). Child care research: A clinical perspective. *Child Development, 74*, 1064–1068.

Greenwood, C. (1991). Longitudinal analysis of time, engagement, and achievement in at-risk versus non-risk students. *Exceptional Children, 57*, 521–535.

Greenwood, C., Carta, J., Hart, B., Kamps, D., Terry, B., Arreaga-Mayer, C., et al. (1992). Out of the laboratory and into the community: 26 years of applied behavior analysis at the Juniper Gardens Children's Project. *American Psychologist, 47*, 1464–1474.

Gregory, A., & Ripski, M. B. (2008). Adolescent trust in teachers: Implications for behavior in the high school classroom. *School Psychology Review, 37*, 337–353.

Gregory, A., & Weinstein, R. S. (2008). The discipline gap and African Americans: Defiance or cooperation in the high school classroom. *Journal of School Psychology, 46*, 455–475.

Gregory, A. M., Light-Hdusermann, J. H., Rijsdijk, F., & Eley, T. C. (2009). Behavioral genetic analyses of prosocial bheavior in adolescents. *Developmental Psychology, 12*, 165–174.

Gregory, L. W. (1995). The "turnaround" process: Factors influencing the school success of urban youth. *Journal of Adolescent Research, 10*, 136–154.

Greitemeyer, T., & Osswald, S. (2010). Effects of prosocial video games on prosocial behavior. *Journal of Personality and Social Psychology, 98*, 211–221.

Grolnick, W. S. (2003). *The psychology of parental control: How well-meant parenting backfires*. Mahwah, NJ: Lawrence Erlbaum.

Grolnick, W. S., & Pomerantz, E. M. (2009). Issues and challenges in studying parental control: Toward a new conceptualization. *Child Development Perspectives, 3*, 165–170.

Gross, E. F. (2004). Adolescent internet use: What we expect, what teens report. *Journal of Applied Developmental Psychology, 25*, 633–649.

Grossman, D., Neckerman, H., Koepsell, T., Liu, P.-Y., Asher, K., Beland, K., et al. (1997). Effectiveness of a violence prevention curriculum among children in elementary school: A randomized controlled trial. *JAMA, 277*, 1605–1611.

Grossmann, K. E., & Grossmann, K. (1991). Attachment quality as an organizer of emotional and behavioral responses in a longitudinal perspective. In C. M. Parkes, J. Stevenson-Hinde & P. Marris (Eds.), *Attachment across the life cycle.* (pp. 93–114). London: Tavistock/Routledge.

Gruman, D., Harachi, T. W., Abbott, R. D., Catalano, R. F., & Fleming, C. B. (2008). Longitudinal effects of student mobility on three dimensions of elementary school engagement. *Child Development, 79*, 1833–1852.

Grunbaum, J. A., Kann, L., Kinchen, S., Williams, B., Ross, J., Lowry, R., et al. (2002). Youth risk behavior surveillance—United States, 2001. *Morbidity & Mortality Weekly Report, 51* (24, SS-4), 1–62.

Grusec, J., & Goodnow, J. J. (1994). The impact of parental discipline methods on the child's internalization of values: A reconceptualization of current points of view. *Developmental Psychology, 30*, 4–19.

Grusec, J., Goodnow, J. J., & Cohen, L. (1997). Household work and the development of concern for others. *Developmental Psychology, 32*, 999–1007.

Guay, F., Marsh, H. W., & Boivin, M. (2003). Academic self-concept and academic achievement: Developmental perspectives on their causal ordering. *Journal of Educational Psychology, 95*, 124–136.

Guerra, N., Huesmann, R., & Spindler, A. (2003). Community violence exposure, social cognition, and aggression among urban elementary school children. *Child Development, 74*, 1561–1576.

Guglielmi, R. S. (2008). Native language proficiency, English literacy, academic achievement and occupational attainment in limited-English-proficient students: A latent growth modeling perspective. *Journal of Educational Psychology, 100*, 322–342.

Gummerum, M., Keller, M., Takezawa, M., & Mata, J. (2008). To give or not to give: Children's and adolescents' sharing and moral negotiations in economic decision situations. *Child Development, 79*, 562–576.

Gunnar, M. R. (1996, Spring). Quality of care and neuroendocrine activity in children: The role of caregivers in buffering stress reactions. *APA Division Newsletter, 7*.

Gunnar, M. R. (2000). Early adversity and the development of stress reactivity and regulation. In C. Nelson (Ed.), *The effects of early adversity on neurobehavioral development* (pp. 163–200). Mahwah, NJ: Erlbaum.

Gunnoe, M. L., Hetherington, M., & Reiss, D. (1999). Parental religiosity, parenting style, and adolescent social responsibility. *Journal of Early Adolescence, 19*, 199–225.

Gurland, S. T., & Grolnick, W. S. (2005). Perceived threat, controlling parenting, and children's achievement orientations. *Motivation and Emotion, 29*, 103–121.

Gutman, L., Sameroff, A., & Eccles, J. S. (2002). The academic achievement of African American students during early adolescence: An examination of multiple risk, promotive, and protective factors. *American Journal of Community Psychology, 30*, 367–400.

Gutman, L. M., & Eccles, J. S. (2007). Stage-environment fit during adolescence: Trajectories of family relations and adolescent outcomes. *Developmental Psychology, 43*, 522–537.

Haden, C., Ornstein, P. A., Eckerman, C., & Didow, S. (2001). Mother-child conversational interactions as events unfold: Linkages to subsequent remembering. *Child Development, 72*, 1016–1031.

Haeffel, G. J., Getchell, M., Koposov, R. A., Yrigollen, C. M., DeYoung, C. G., af Klinteberg, B., et al. (2008). Association between polymorphisms in the dopamine transporter gene and depression: Evidence for a gene–environment interaction in a sample of juvenile detainees. *Psychological Science, 19*, 62–69.

Hagekull, B., & Bohlin, G. (2003). Early temperament and attachment as predictors of the Five Factor Model of personality. *Attachment & Human Development, 5*, 2–18.

Hagen, J. W. (2007). Closing remarks. *Developments: Newsletter of the Society for Research in Child Development, 50*, 1, 8.

Haith, M., & Benson, J. (1998). Infant cognition. In D. Kuhn & R. Siegler (Eds.), *Handbook of child psychology: Cognition, perception, and language* (5th ed., Vol. 2, pp. 199–254). New York: Wiley.

Hale, L., Berger, L. M., LeBourgeois, M., & Brooks-Gunn, J. (2009). Social and demographic predictors of preschoolers' bedtime routines. *Journal of Developmental and Behavioral Pediatrics, 30*, 394–402.

Halford, G., Baker, R., McGredden, J., & Bain, J. (2005). How many variables can humans process? *Psychological Science, 16*, 70–76.

Halgunseth, L. C., Ispa, J. M., & Rudy, D. (2006). Parental control in Latino famlies: An integrated review of the literature. *Child Development, 77*, 1282–1297.

Hallinan, M. T. (2008). Teacher influences on students' attachment to school. *Sociology of Education, 81*, 271–283.

Halpern, D. F. (2000). *Sex differences in cognitive abilities* (3rd ed.). Mahwah, NJ: Erlbaum.

Halpern, D. F., Benbow, C. P., Geary, D. C., Gur, R. C., Hyde, J. S., & Gernsbacher, M. A. (2007). The science of sex differences in science and mathematics. *Psychological Science in the Public Interest, 8*, 1–51.

Halpern, R. (2000). The promise of after-school programs for low-income children. *Early Childhood Research Quarterly, 15*, 185–214.

Hamilton, C. (2000). Continuity and discontinuity of attachment from infancy through adolescence. *Child Development, 71*, 690–694.

Hammen, C. (2009). Adolescent depression: Stressful interpersonal contexts and risk for recurrence. *Current Directions in Psychological Science, 18*, 200–204.

Hamond, N. R., & Fivush, R. (1991). Memories of Mickey Mouse: Young children recount their trip to Disneyworld. *Cognitive Development, 6*, 433–448.

Hampson, S. E. (2008). Mechanisms by which childhood personality traits influence adult well-being. *Current Directions in Psychological Science, 17*, 264–268.

Hampton, T. (2008). Researchers seek ways to stem STDs. *JAMA, 299*, 1888–1889.

Hamre, B. K., & Pianta, R. (2001). Early teacher–child relationships and the trajectory of children's school outcomes through eighth grade. *Child Development, 72*, 625–638.

Hamre, B. K., Pianta, R. C., Downer, J. T., & Mashburn, A. J. (2007). Teachers' perceptions of conflict with young students: Looking beyond problem behaviors. *Social Development, 17*, 115–136.

Han, W.-J. (2005). Maternal nonstandard work schedules and child cognitive outcomes. *Child Development, 76*, 137–154.

Han, W.-J. (2008). The academic trajectories of children of immigrants and their school environments. *Developmental Psychology, 44*, 1572–1590.

Han, W.-J., Waldfogel, J., & Brooks-Gunn, J. (2001). The effects of early maternal employment on later cognitive and behavioral outcomes. *Journal of Marriage and Family, 63*, 336–354.

Hane, A. A., Fox, N. A., Henderson, H. A., & Marshall, P. J. (2008). Behavioral reactivity and approach-withdrawal bias in infancy. *Developmental Psychology, 44*, 1491–1496.

Hanes, A. A., & Fox, N. A. (2006). Ordinary variation in maternal caregiving influences human infants' stress reactivity. *Psychological Science, 17*, 550–556.

Hanish, L., & Guerra, N. (2000). Predictors of peer victimization among urban youth. *Social Development, 9*, 5221–5543.

Hansen, M., Janssen, I., Schiff, A., Zee, P., & Dubocovich, M. (2005). The impact of school daily schedule on adolescent sleep. *Pediatrics, 115*, 1555–1562.

Hanushek, E. A. (1999). Some findings from an independent investigation of the Tennessee STAR experiment and from other investigations of class size effects. *Educational Evaluation and Policy Analysis, 21*, 143–163.

Happe, F., Winner, E., & Brownell, H. (1998). The getting of wisdom: Theory of mind in old age. *Developmental Psychology, 34*, 358–362.

Harackiewicz, J. M., Durik, A. M., Barron, K. E., Linnenbrink-Garcia, L., & Tauer, J. M. (2008). The role of achievement goals in the development of interest: Reciprocal relations between achievement goals, interest , and performance. *Journal of Educational Psychology, 100*, 105–122.

Hardman, E. L., & Smith, S. W. (2003). An analysis of discipline-related content in elementary education journals. *Behavioral Disorders, 28*, 173–186.

Hardway, C., & Fuligni, A. J. (2006). Dimensions of family connectedness among adolescents with Mexican, Chinese, and European backgrounds. *Developmental Psychology, 42*, 1246–1258.

Harkness, S. (2002). Culture and social development: Explanations and evidence. In P. Smith & C. Hart (Eds.), *Blackwell handbook of childhood social development* (pp. 60–77). Oxford: Blackwell.

Harlaar, N., Dale, P. S., & Plomin, R. (2007). From learning to read to reading to learn: Substantial and stable genetic influence. *Child Development, 78*, 116–131.

Harper, L., & Huie, K. (1998). Free play use of space by preschoolers from diverse backgrounds: Factors influencing activity choices. *Merrill-Palmer Quarterly, 44*, 423–446.

Harrison, L., & Ungerer, J. (2002). Maternal employment and infant–mother attachment security at 12 months postpartum. *Developmental Psychology, 38*, 758–773.

Hart, B., & Risley, R. (1995). *Meaninfgul differences in the everyday experience of young American children*. Baltimore: Brookes.

Hart, C., Yang, C., Nelson, L., Robinson, C., Olsen, J., Nelson, D., et al. (2000). Peer acceptance in early childhood and subtypes of socially withdrawn behaviour in China, Russia, and the United States. *International Journal of Behavioral Development, 24*, 71–81.

Hart, D., Atkins, R., & Fegley, S. (2003). Personality and development in childhood: A person-centered approach. *Monographs of the Society for Research in Child Development, 68* (Serial No. 272).

Hart, D., Atkins, R., & Matsuba, M. K. (2008). The association of neighborhood poverty with personality change in childhood. *Journal of Personality and Social Psychology, 94*, 1048–1061.

Hart, D., Donnelly, T. M., Youniss, J., & Atkins, R. (2007). High school community service as a predictor of adult voting and volunteering. *American Educational Research Journal, 44*, 197–219.

Hart, D., Hofmann, V., Edelstein, W., & Keller, M. (1997). The relation of childhood personality types to adolescent behavior and development: A longitudinal study of Icelandic children. *Developmental Psychology, 33*, 195–205.

Hart, S. A., Petrill, S. A., Thompson, L. A., & Plomin, R. (2008). The ABCs of math: A genetic analysis of mathematics and its links with reading ability and general cognitive ability. *Journal of Educational Psychology, 101*, 388–402.

Harter, S. (1999). *The construction of the self: A developmental perspective*. New York: Guilford.

Harter, S. (2006). The self. In N. Eisenberg (Ed.), *Handbook of child psychology: Social, emotional, and personality development* (6th ed., Vol. 3, pp. 505–570). New York: Wiley.

Hartos, J. L., Eitel, P., Haynie, D. L., & Simons-Morton, B. G. (2000). Can I take the car? Relations among parenting practices and adolescent problem-driving practices. *Journal of Adolescent Research, 15*, 352–367.

Hartshorne, H., & May, M. (1928). *Studies in deceit*. New York: MacMillan.

Hartup, W. W. (1974). Aggression in childhood: Developmental perspectives. *American Psychologist, 29*, 336–341.

Hartup, W. W., & Abecassis, M. (2002). Friends and enemies. In P. Smith & C. Hart (Eds.), *Blackwell handbook of childhood social development* (pp. 285–306). Oxford: Blackwell.

Harwell, M., Post, T. R., Cutler, A., Maeda, Y., Anderson, E., Norman, K. W., et al. (2009). The preparation of students from National Science Foundation-funded and commercially developed high school mathematics curricula for their first university mathematics course. *American Educational Research Journal, 46*, 203–231.

Hastings, P., Zahn-Waxler, C., Robinson, J., Usher, B., & Bridges, D. (2000). The development of concern for others in children with behavior problems. *Developmental Psychology, 36*, 531–546.

Hattie, J. (2009). *Visible learning: A synthesis of over 800 meta-analyses relating to achievement*. London: Routledge.

Hattie, J., & Timperley, H. (2007). The power of feedback. *Review of Educational Research, 77*, 81–112.

Hauck, F., Herman, S., Donovan, M., Iyasu, S., Moore, C., Donoghue, E., et al. (2003). Sleep environment and the risk of sudden infant death syndrome in an urban population: The Chicago Infant Mortality Study. *Pediatrics, 111*, 1207–1214.

Hay, D. F. (1994). Prosocial development. *Journal of Child Psychology & Psychiatry & Allied Disciplines, 35*, 29–71.

Hay, D. F., Angold, A., Pawlby, S., Harold, G., & Sharp, D. (2003). Pathways to violence in the children of mothers who were depressed postpartum. *Developmental Psychology, 39*, 1083–1094.

Hay, D. F., Castle, J., & Davies, L. (2000). Toddlers' use of force against familiar peers: A precursor of serious aggression? *Child Development, 71*, 457–467.

Hay, D. F., Castle, J., Davies, L., Demetriou, H., & Stimson, C. A. (1999). Prosocial action in very early childhood. *Journal of Child Psychology & Psychiatry & Allied Disciplines, 40*, 905–916.

Hay, D. F., & Nash, A. (2002). Social development in different family arrangements. In P. Smith & C. Hart (Eds.), *Blackwell handbook of childhood social development* (pp. 238–261). Oxford: Blackwell.

Hay, D. F., & Pawlby, S. (2003). Prosocial development in relation to children's and mother's psychological problems. *Child Development, 74*, 1314–1327.

Haynie, D., Nansel, T., Eitel, P., Crump, A., Saylor, K., Yu, K., et al. (2001). Bullies, victims, and bully/victims: Distinct groups of at-risk youth. *Journal of Early Adolescence, 21*, 29–49.

Heatherton, T. F., & Sargent, J. D. (2009). Does watching smoking in movies promote teenage smoking? *Current Directions in Psychological Science, 18*, 63–67.

Hebb, D. O. (1949). *The organization of behavior*. New York: Wiley.

Hedges, L. V. (2008). What are effect sizes and why do we need them? *Child Development Perspectives, 2*, 167–171.

Heine, S. J., & Buchtel, E. E. (2009). Personality: The universal and the culturally specific. *Annual Review of Psychology, 60*, 369–394.

Heine, S. J., Buchtel, E. E., & Norenzayan, A. (2008). What do cross-national comparisons of personality trait tell us? The case of conscientiousness. *Psychological Science, 19*, 309–313.

Helms, J. E. (2006). Fairness is not validity or cultural bias in racial-group assessment: A quantitative perspective. *American Psychologist, 61*, 845–857.

Helwig, C., & Jasiobedzka, U. (2001). The relation between law and morality: Children's reasoning about socially beneficial and unjust laws. *Child Development, 72*, 1382–1393.

Helwig, C., & Turiel, E. (2002). Children's social and moral reasoning. In P. Smith & C. Hart (Eds.), *Blackwell handbook of childhood social development* (pp. 475–490). Oxford: Blackwell.

Helwig, C., Zelazo, P., & Wilson, M. (2001). Children's judgments of psychological harm in normal and noncanonical situations. *Child Development, 72*, 66–81.

Hembree, R. (1988). Correlates, causes, effects, and treatment of test anxiety. *Review of Educational Research, 58*, 47–77.

Hemphill, J. (2003). Interpreting the magnitudes of correlation coefficients. *American Psychologist, 58*, 78–80.

Hemphill, L., & Snow, C. E. (1996). Language and literacy development: Discontinuities and differences. In D. R. Olson & N. Torrance (Eds.), *The handbook of education and human development* (pp. 173–201). Oxford: Blackwell.

Henry, D. B., Schoeny, M. E., Deptula, D., & Slavick, J. T. (2007). Peer selection and socialization effects on adolescent intercourse without a condom and attitudes about the costs of sex. *Child Development, 78*, 825–838.

Henry, P. J., & Hardin, C. (2006). The contact hypothesis revisited: Status bias in the reduction of implicit prejudice in the United States and Lebanon. *Psychological Science, 17*, 862–868.

Herman, M. (2004). Forced to choose: Some determinants of racial identification in multiracial adolescents. *Child Development, 75*, 730–748.

Herman, M. R. (2009). The Black-White-Other achievement gap: Testing theories of academic performance among multiracial and monoracial adolescents. *Sociology of Education, 82*, 20–46.

Hernandez, D. J., Denton, N. A., & Macartney, S. E. (2008). Child in immigrant families: Looking to America's future. *Social Policy Report, 22*, 3–22.

Hespos, S. J., Ferry, A. L., & Rips, L. J. (2009). Five-month-old infants have different expectations for solids and liquids. *Psychological Science, 20*, 603–611.

Hess, U., & Thibault, P. (2009). Darwin and emotion expression. *American Psychologist, 64*, 120–128.

Hesse, E. (1999). The adult attachment interview: Historical and current perspectives. In J. Cassidy & P. Shaver (Eds.), *Handbook of attachment: Theory, research, and clinical applications* (pp. 395–433). New York: Guilford.

Hestenes, L., Kontos, S., & Bryan, Y. (1993). Children's emotional expressions in childcare centers varying in quality. *Early Childhood Research Quarterly, 8*, 295–307.

Hetherington, E. M. (1999). Social capital and the development of youth from nondivorced, divorced, and remarried families. In W. Collins & B. Laursen (Eds.), *Minnesota symposia on child psychology* (Vol. 30, pp. 177–209). Mahwah, NJ: Erlbaum.

Hetherington, E. M., Bridges, M., & Insabella, G. M. (1998). What matters? What does not? Five perspectives on the association between marital transitions and children's adjustment. *American Psychologist, 53*, 167–184.

Hetherington, E. M., & Stanely-Hagan, M. (1999). The adjustment of children with divorced parents: A risk and reisliency perspective. *Journal of Child Psychology & Psychiatry & Allied Disciplines, 40*, 129–140.

Heyman, G., Gee, C., & Giles, J. (2003). Preschool children's reasoning about ability. *Child Development, 74*, 516–534.

Hidi, S., & Anderson, V. (1992). Situational interest and its impact on reading and expository writing. In K. A. Renninger, S. Hidi & A. Krapp (Eds.), *The role of interest in learning and development* (pp. 215–238). Hillsdale, NJ: Lawrence Erlbaum.

Hill, J. L., Waldfogel, J., Brooks-Gunn, J., & Han, W.-J. (2005). Maternal employment and child development: A fresh look using newer methods. *Developmental Psychology, 41*, 833–850.

Hill, N. E., Castellino, D. R., Lansford, J. E., Nowlin, P., Dodge, K. A., Bates, J. E., et al. (2004). Parent academic involvement as related to school behavior, achievement, and aspirations: Demographic variations across adolescence. *Child Development, 75*, 1491–1509.

Hill, N., Bush, K., & Roosa, M. (2003). Parenting and family socialization strategies and children's mental health: Low-income Mexican-American and Euro-American mothers and children. *Child Development, 74*, 189–204.

Hill, N. E., & Taylor, L. C. (2004). Parental school involvement and children's academic achievement. *Current Directions in Psychological Science, 13*, 161–164.

Hill, N. E., & Tyson, D. F. (2009). Parental involvement in middle school: A meta-analytic assessment of the strategies that promote achievement. *Developmental Psychology, 45*, 740–763.

Hillman, C. H., Buck, S. M., Themanson, J. R., Pontifex, M. B., & Castelli, D. M. (2009). Aerobic fitness and cognitive development: Event-related brain potential and task performance indices of executive control in preadolescent children. *Developmental Psychology, 45*, 114–129.

Hinde, E., & Perry, N. (2007). Elementary teachers' application of Jean Piaget's theories of cognitive development during social studies curriculum debates in Arizona. *The Elementary School Journal, 108*, 63–79.

Hinnant, J. B., O'Brien, M., & Ghazarian, S. R. (2009). The longitudinal relations of teacher expectations to achievement in the early school years. *Journal of Educational Psychology, 101*, 662–670.

Hirt, E. R., Melton, R. J., McDonald, H. E., & Harackiewicz, J. M. (1996). Processing goals, task interest, and the mood-performance relationship: A mediational analysis. *Journal of Personality and Social Psychology, 71*, 245–261.

Ho, C., Bluestein, D. N., & Jenkins, J. M. (2008). Cultural differences in the relationship between parenting and children's behavior. *Developmental Psychology, 44*, 507–522.

Hodges, E., Finnegan, R., & Perry, D. (1999). Skewed autonomy-relatedness in preadolescents' conceptions of their relationships with mother, father, and best friend. *Developmental Psychology, 35*, 737–748.

Hofer, M. A. (2006). Psychobiological roots of early attachment. *Current Directions in Psychological Science, 15*, 84–88.

Hoffman, D. M. (2009). Reflecting on social emotional learning: A critical perspective on trends in the United States. *Review of Educational Research, 79*, 533–556.

Hoffman, M. L. (1975). Altruistic behavior and the parent–child relationship. *Journal of Personality and Social Psychology, 31*, 937-943.

Hogan, K., & Corey, C. (2001). Viewing classrooms as cultural contexts for fostering scientific literacy. *Anthropology & Education Quarterly, 32*, 214-243.

Hoglund, W., & Leadbeater, B. (2004). The effects of family, school, and classroom ecologies on changes in children's social competence and emotional and behavioral problems in first grade. *Developmental Psychology, 40*, 533-544.

Holden, G. W., & Miller, P. C. (1999). Enduring and different: A meta-analysis of the similarity in parents' child rearing. *Psychological Bulletin, 125*, 223–254.

Hollon, S., Thase, M., & Markowitz, J. (2002). Treatment and prevention of depression. *Psychological Science in the Public Interest, 3*, 39–77.

Holtz, B. A., & Lehman, E. B. (1995). Development of children's knowledge and use of strategies for self-control in a resistance-to-distraction task. *Merrill-Palmer Quarterly, 41*, 361–380.

Hong, G., & Yu, B. (2008a). Early-grade retention and children's reading and math learning in elementary years. *Educational Evaluation and Policy Analysis, 29*, 239–261.

Hong, G., & Yu, B. (2008b). Effects of kindergarten retention on children's social-emotional development: An application of propensisty score method to multivariate, multilevel data. *Developmental Psychology, 44*, 407–421.

Hopkins, J. R. (1995). Erik Homburger Erikson (1902-1994). *American Psychologist, 50*, 796–797.

Hopkins, W. D., & Cantalupo, C. (2008). Theoretical speculations on the evolutionary origins of hemispheric specialization. *Current Directions in Psychological Science, 17*, 233–237.

Horowitz, T., Cade, B., Wolfe, J., & Czeisler, C. (2003). Searching night and day: A dissociation of effects of circadian phase and time awake on visual selective attention and vigilance. *Psychological Science, 14*, 549–557.

Horvat, E. M., Weininger, E. B., & Lareau, A. (2003). From social ties to social capital: Class differences in the relations between schools and parent networks. *American Educational Research Journal, 40*, 319–351.

Howard-Jones, P., Taylor, J., & Sutton, L. (2002). The effect of play on the creativity of young children during subsequent activity. *Early Child Development and Care, 172*, 323–328.

Howe, M. L. (2003). Memories from the cradle. *Current Directions in Psychological Science, 12*, 62–65.

Howell, J., & Lynch, J. (2000). *Youth gangs in schools.* Retrieved January 9, 2010, from http://www.ncjrs.gov/pdffiles1/ojjdp/183015.pdf

Howes, C. (1990). Can the age of entry into child care and the quality of child care predict adjustment in kindergarten? *Developmental Psychology, 26*, 292–303.

Howes, C., & James, J. (2002). Children's social development within the socialization context of childcare and early childhood education. In P. Smith & C. Hart (Eds.), *Blackwell handbook of childhood social development* (pp. 137–155). Oxford: Blackwell.

Howes, C., & Ritchie, S. (1999). Attachment organizations in children with difficult life circumstances. *Development and Psychopathology, 11*, 251–268.

Howes, C., & Tonyon, H. (2000). Links between adult and peer relations across four developmental periods. In K. Kerns, J. Contreras & A. Neal-Barnett (Eds.), *Family and peers: Linking two social worlds* (pp. 85–113). Westport, CT: Praeger.

Hsueh, J., & Yoshikawa, H. (2007). Working nonstandard schedules and variable shifts in low-income families: Associations with parental psychological well-being, family functioning, and child well-being. *Developmental Psychology, 43*, 620–632.

Hubbs-Tait, L., Nation, J. R., Krebs, N. F., & Bellinger, D. C. (2006). Neurotoxicants, micronutrients, and social environments: Individual and combined effects on children's development. *Psychological Science in the Public Interest, 6*, 57–121.

Hudley, C., & Graham, S. (1993). An attributional intervention to reduce peer-directed aggression among African-American boys. *Child Development, 64*, 124–138.

Hudley, C., Graham, S., & Taylor, A. (2007). Reducing aggressive behavior and increasing motivation in school: The evolution of an intervention to strengthen school adjustment. *Educational Psychologist, 42*, 251–260.

Hudziak, J., Rudiger, L., Neale, M., Heath, A., & Todd, R. (2000). A twin study of inattentive, aggressive, and anxious/depressed behaviors. *Journal of the American Academy of Child and Adolescent Psychiatry, 39*, 469–476.

Huesmann, L. R., Eron, L. D., Klein, R., Brice, P., & Fischer, P. (1983). Mitigating the imitation of aggressive behaviors by children's attitudes about media violence. *Journal of Personality and Social Psychology, 44*, 899–910.

Huey, E. D., Krueger, F., & Grafman, J. (2006). Representations in the human prefrontal cortex. *Current Directions in Psychological Science, 15*, 167–171.

Hughes, C., & Ensor, R. (2007). Executive function and theory of mind: Predictive relations from ages 2 to 4. *Developmental Psychology, 43*, 1447–1459.

Hughes, C., & Leekam, S. (2004). What are the links between theory of mind and social relations? Review, reflections and new directions for studies of typical and atypical development. *Social Development, 13*, 590–619.

Hughes, F. (1999). *Children, play, and development* (3rd ed.). Boston: Allyn & Bacon.

Hughes, J. M., Bigler, R. S., & Levy, S. R. (2007). Consequences of learning about historical racism among European American and African American children. *Child Development, 78*, 1689–1705.

Hughes, J. N., Luo, W., Kwok, O.-M., & Loyd, L. K. (2008). Teacher-student support, effortful engagement, and achievement: A 3-year longitudinal study. *Journal of Educational Psychology, 100*, 1–14.

Huguet, P., & Regner, I. (2007). Stereotype threat among schoolgirls in quasi-ordinary classroom circumstances. *Journal of Educational Psychology, 99*, 545–560.

Hulleman, C. S., Durik, A. M., Schweigert, S. A., & Harackiewicz, J. M. (2008). Task values, achievement goals, and interest: An integrative analysis. *Journal of Educational Psychology, 100*, 398–416.

Hunt, E., & Carlson, J. (2007). Considerations relating to the study of group differences in intelligence. *Perspectives on Psychological Science, 2*, 194–213.

Hunt, E., Streissguth, A. P., Kerr, B., & Olson, H. C. (1995). Mothers' alcohol consumption during pregnancy: Effect on spatial-visual reasoning in 14-year-old children. *Psychological Science, 6*, 339–342.

Huntley-Fenner, G., & Cannon, E. (2000). Preschoolers' magnitude comparisons are mediated by a preverbal analog mechanism. *Psychological Science, 11*, 147–152.

Huntsinger, C. S., & Jose, P. E. (2006). A longitudinal investigation of personality and social adjustment among Chinese American and European American adolescents. *Child Development, 77*, 1309–1324.

Huston, A. C., & Aronson, S. R. (2005). Mothers' time with infant and time in employment as predictors of mother–child relationships and children's early development. *Child Development, 76*, 467–482.

Huston, A. C., Bickham, D. S., Lee, J. H., & Wright, J. C. (2007). From attention to comprehension: How children watch and learn from television. In N. Pecora, J. P. Murray & E. A. Wartella (Eds.), *Children and television: Fifty years of research* (pp. 41–63). Mahwah, NJ: Erlbaum.

Huttenlocher, J., Levine, S., & Vevea, J. (1998). Environmental input and cognitive growth: A study using time-period comparisons. *Child Development, 69*, 1012–1029.

Hyde, J. S., Lindberg, S. M., Linn, M. C., Ellis, A. B., & Williams, C. C. (2008). Gender similarities characterize math performance. *Science, 321*, 494–495.

Hygge, S., Evans, G., & Bullinger, M. (2002). A prospective study of some effects of aircraft noise on cognitive performance in schoolchildren. *Psychological Science, 13*, 469–474.

Hymel, S., Vaillancourt, T., McDougall, P., & Renshaw, P. (2002). Peer acceptance and rejection in childhood. In P. Smith & C. Hart (Eds.), *Blackwell handbook of childhood social development* (pp. 265–284). Oxford: Blackwell.

Iacoboni, M. (2009). Imitation, empathy, and mirror neurons. *Annual Review of Psychology, 60*, 653–670.

Ialongo, N., Edelsohn, G., & Kellam, S. (2001). A further look at the prognostic power of young children's reports of depressed mood and feelings. *Child Development, 72*, 736–747.

Ialongo, N., Edelsohn, G., Werthamer-Larsson, L., Crockett, L., & Kellam, S. (1994). The significance of self-reported anxious symptoms in first-grade children. *Journal of Abnormal Child Psychology, 22*, 441–445.

Iglowstein, I., Jenni, O. G., Molinari, L., & Largo, R. H. (2003). Sleep duration from infancy to adolescence: Reference values and generational trends. *Pediatrics, 111*, 302–307.

Ikonomidou, C., Bittigau, P., Ishimaru, M. J., Wozniak, D. F., Koch, C., Genz, K., et al. (2000). Ethanol-induced apoptotic neurodegeneration and Fetal Alcohol Syndrome. *Science, 287*, 1056–1060.

Im-Bolter, N., Johnson, J., & Pascual-Leone, J. (2006). Processing limitations in children with specific language impairment: The role of executive function. *Child Development, 77*, 1822–1841.

Inhelder, B., & Piaget, J. (1958). *The growth of logical thinking from childhood to adolescence* (A. Parsons & S. Milgram, Trans.). New York: Basic Books.

International Human Genome Sequencing Consortium. (2004). Finishing the euchromatic sequencing of the human genome. *Nature, 431*, 931–945.

Inzlicht, M., & Ben-Zeev, T. (2000). A threatening intellectual environment: Why females are susceptible to experiencing problem-solving deficits in the presence of males. *Psychological Science, 11*, 365–371.

Inzlicht, M., & Gutsell, J. N. (2007). Running on empty: Neural signals for self-control failure. *Psychological Science, 18*, 933–937.

Inzlicht, M., McKay, L., & Aronson, J. (2006). Stigma as ego depletion: How being the target of prejudice affects self-control. *Psychological Science, 17*, 262–269.

Isbister, J. (1985). *Freud: An introduction to his life and work.* Cambridge, UK: Polity Press.

Iverson, J. M., & Fagan, M. K. (2004). Infant vocal-motor coordination: Precursor to the gesture-speech system? *Child Development, 75*, 1053–1066.

Iverson, J. M., & Goldin-Meadow, S. (2005). Gesture paves the way for language development. *Psychological Science, 16*, 367–371.

Iyengar, S. S., & Lepper, M. R. (1999). Rethinking the value of choice: A cultural perspective on intrinsic motivation. *Journal of Personality and Social Psychology, 76*, 349–366.

Iyengar, S. S., & Lepper, M. R. (2000). When choice is demotivating: Can one desire too much of a good thing? *Journal of Personality and Social Psychology, 79*, 995–1006.

Izard, C. E. (2007). Basic emotions, natural kinds, emotion schemas, and a new paradigm. *Perspectives on Psychological Science, 2*, 260–280.

Izard, C. E. (2009). Emotion theory and research: Highlights, unanswered questions, and emerging issues. *Annual Review of Psychology, 60*, 1–25.

Izard, C. E., Fine, S., Schultz, D., Mostow, A., Ackerman, B., & Youngstrom, E. (2001). Emotion knowledge as a predictor of social behavior and academic competence in children at risk. *Psychological Science, 12*, 18–23.

Izard, C. E., & Harris, P. (1995). Emotional development and developmental psychopathology. In D. Cicchetti & D. J. Cohen (Eds.), *Developmental psychopathology: Theory and methods* (Vol. 1, pp. 467–503). New York: Wiley.

Jabusch, H.-C., Alpers, H., Kopiez, R., Vauth, H., & Altenmüller, E. (2009). The influence of practice on the development of motor skills in pianists: A longitudinal study in a selected motor task. *Human Movement Science, 28*, 74–84.

Jaccard, J., Blanton, H., & Dodge, T. (2005). Peer influences on risk behavior: An analysis of the effects of a close friend. *Developmental Psychology, 41*, 135–147.

Jack, F., MacDonald, S., Reese, E., & Hayne, H. (2009). Maternal reminiscing style during early childhood predicts the age of adolescents' earliest memories. *Child Development, 80*, 496–505.

Jackson, C., & Foshee, V. A. (1998). Violence-related behaviors of adolescents: Relations with responsive and demanding parenting. *Journal of Adolescent Research, 13*, 343–359.

Jackson, J. P. (2000). The triumph of the segregationists? A historiographical inquiry into psychology and *Brown* litigation. *History of Psychology, 3*, 239–261.

Jackson, L. A., von Eye, A., Biocca, F. A., Barbatsis, G., Zhao, Y., & Fitzgerald, H. E. (2006). Does home internet use influence the academic performance of low-income children? *Developmental Psychology, 42*, 429–435.

Jacobs, J. E., Lanza, S., Osgood, D. W., Eccles, J. S., & Wigfield, A. (2002). Changes in children's self-competence and values: Gender and domain differences across grades one through twelve. *Child Development, 73*, 509–527.

Jacobson, S. W., Chiodo, L. M., Sokol, R. J., & Jacobson, J. L. (2002). Validity of maternal report of prenatal alcohol, cocaine, and smoking in relation to neurobehavioral outcome. *Pediatrics, 109*, 815–825.

Jaffee, S., & Hyde, J. (2000). Gender differences in moral orientation: A meta-analysis. *Psychological Bulletin, 126*, 703–726.

Jaffee, S. R., Moffitt, T. E., Caspi, A., & Taylor, A. (2003). Life with (or without) father: The benefits of living with two biological parents depend on the father's antisocial behavior. *Child Development, 74*, 109–126.

Jang, H. (2008). Supporting students' motivation, engagement, and learning during an uninteresting activity. *Journal of Educational Psychology, 100*, 798–811.

Jansen, J. (2008). Teaching English language learners in the content areas. *Review of Educational Research, 78*, 1010–1038.

Jansen, J., de Weerth, C., & Riksen-Walraven, J. M. (2008). Breastfeeding and the mother-infant relationship: A review. *Developmental Review, 28*, 503–521.

Janssens, J., & Dekovic, M. (1997). Child rearing, prosocial moral reasoning, and prosocial behaviour. *International Journal of Behavioral Development, 20*, 509–527.

Jarrett, O. (1997). Science and math through role-play centers in the elementary school classroom. *Science Activities, 34*, 13–19.

Jaswal, V., & Dodson, C. S. (2009). Metamemory development: Understanding the role of similarity in false memories. *Child Development, 80*, 629–635.

Jaswal, V., & Markman, E. (2001). Learning proper and common names in inferential versus ostensive contexts. *Child Development, 72*, 768–786.

Jenkins, J., & Astington, J. (2000). Theory of mind and social behavior: Causal models tested in a longitudinal study. *Merrill-Palmer Quarterly, 46*, 203–220.

Jenkins, J., Turrell, S., Kogushi, Y., Lollis, S., & Ross, H. (2003). A longitudinal investigation of the dynamics of mental state talk in families. *Child Development, 74*, 905–920.

Jenkins, J. M., Rasbash, J., & O'Connor, T. G. (2003). The role of the shared family context in differential parenting. *Developmental Psychology, 39*, 99–113.

Jenkins, J. M., Simpson, A., Dunn, J., Rasbash, J., & O'Connor, T. G. (2005). Mutual influence of marital conflict and children's behavior problems: Shared and nonshared family risks. *Child Development, 76*, 24–39.

Jenkins, S., Ritblatt, S., & McDonald, J. (2008). Conflict resolution among early childhood educators. *Conflict Resolution Quarterly, 25*, 429–450.

Jennings, P. A., & Greenberg, M. T. (2009). The prosocial classroom: Teacher social and emotional competence in relation to student and classroom outcomes. *Review of Educational Research, 79*, 491–525.

Jensen, L., Arnett, J., Feldman, S., & Cauffman, E. (2002). It's wrong, but everybody does it: Academic dishonesty among high school and college students. *Contemporary Educational Psychology, 27*, 209–238.

Jeynes, W. (2002). The relationship between the consumption of various drugs by adolescents and their academic achievement. *American Journal of Drug and Alcohol Abuse, 28*, 15–35.

Jia, Y., Way, N., Ling, G., Yoskihawa, H., Chen, X., Hughes, D., et al. (2009). The influence of student perceptions of school climate on socioemotional and academic adjustment: A comparison of Chinese and American adolescents. *Child Development, 80*, 1514–1530.

Jimerson, S. R., & Ferguson, P. (2007). A longitudinal study of grade retention: Academic and behavioral outcomes of retained students through adolescence. *School Psychology Quarterly, 22*, 314–339.

John, O., Caspi, A., Robins, R., Moffitt, T., & Stouthamer-Loeber, M. (1994). The "little five": Exploring the nomological network of the five-factor model of personality in adolescent boys. *Child Development, 65*, 160–178.

Johns, M., Schmader, T., & Martens, A. (2005). Knowing is half the battle: Teaching stereotype threat as a means of improving women's math performance. *Psychological Science, 16*, 175–179.

Johnson, B., Carey, M., Marsh, K., Levin, K., & Scott-Sheldon, L. (2003). Interventions to reduce sexual risk for the Human Immunodeficiency Virus in adolescents, 1985–2000: A research synthesis. *Archives of Pediatrics and Adolescent Medicine, 157*, 381–388.

Johnson, C., & Blasco, P. (1997). Infant growth and development. *Pediatrics in Review, 18*, 224–242.

Johnson, C. I., & Mayer, R. E. (2009). A testing effect with multimedia learning. *Journal of Educational Psychology 101*, 621–629.

Johnson, D. W., & Johnson, R. T. (2006). Conflict resolution, peer mediation, and peace making. In C. M. Evertson & C. S. Weinstein (Eds.), *Handbook of classroom management: Research, practice, and contemporary issues* (pp. 803–832). Mahwah, NJ: Erlbaum.

Johnson, J., Im-Bolter, N., & Pascual-Leone, J. (2003). Development of mental attention in gifted and mainstream children: The role of mental capacity, inhibition, and speed of processing. *Child Development, 74*, 1594–1614.

Johnson, M. H., Grossmann, T., & Kadosh, K. C. (2009). Mapping functional brain development: Building a social brain through interactive specialization. *Developmental Psychology, 45*, 151–159.

Johnson, M. K., Crosnoe, R., & Elder, G. H. (2001). Students' attachment and academic engagement: The role of race and ethnicity. *Sociology of Education, 74*, 318–340.

Johnson, S. C., Dweck, C. S., & Chen, F. S. (2007). Evidence for infants' internal working models of attachment. *Psychological Science, 18*, 501–502.

Jones, E., Parker, B., Joyner, H., & Ulku-Steiner, B. (1999). The influences of behavior valence and actor race on Black and White children's moral and liking judgments. *Journal of Psychology, 133*, 194–204.

Jones, S. B. (2007). Imitation in infancy: The development of mimicry. *Psychological Science, 18*, 592–599.

Jordan, N. C., Kaplan, D., Olah, L. N., & Locuniak, M. N. (2006). Number sense growth in kindergarten: A longitudinal investigation of children at risk for mathematics difficulties. *Child Development, 77*, 153–175.

Jordan, N. C., Kaplan, D., Ramineni, C., & Locuniak, M. N. (2009). Early math matters: Kindergarten number competence and later mathematics outcomes. *Developmental Psychology, 45*, 850–867.

Joseph, R. (2000). Fetal brain behavior and cognitive development. *Developmental Review, 20*, 81–98.

Jostad, C. M., Miltenberger, R. G., Kelso, P., & Knudson, P. (2008). Peer tutoring to prevent firearm play: Acquisition, generalization, and long-term maintenance of safety skills. *Journal of Applied Behavior Analysis, 41*, 117–123.

Joussemet, M., Vitaro, F., Barker, E. D., Cote, S., Nagin, D. S., Zoccolillo, M., et al. (2008). Controlling parenting and physical aggression during elementary school. *Child Development, 79*, 411–425.

Jusczyk, P. (2002). How infants adapt speech-processing capacities to native-language structure. *Current Directions in Psychological Sciences, 11*, 15–18.

Juvonen, J. (2007). Reforming middle schools: Focus on continuity, social connectedness, and engagement. *Educational Psychologist, 42*, 197–208.

Kagan, J. (2008). In defense of qualitative changes in development. *Child Development, 79*, 1606–1624.

Kagan, J., Snidman, N., Kahn, V., & Towsley, S. (2007). The preservation of two infant temperaments into adolescence. *Monographs of the Society for Research in Child Development, 72* (Serial No. 287).

Kagitcibasi, C. (1996). *Family and human development across cultures.* Mahwah, NJ: Erlbaum.

Kail, R. V., & Ferrer, E. (2007). Processing speed in childhood and adolescence: Longitudinal models for examining developmental change. *Child Development, 78*, 1760–1770.

Kaiser Family Foundation. (2004). *The role of media in childhood obesity.* Menlo Park, CA: Kaiser Family Foundation.

Kaiser, C. R., Vick, S. B., & Major, B. (2006). Prejudice expectations moderate preconscious attention to cues that are threatening to social identity. *Psychological Science, 17*, 332–338.

Kalil, A., & Ziol-Guest, K. M. (2005). Single mothers' employment dynamics and adolescent well-being. *Child Development, 76*, 196–211.

Kamberelis, G., & Bovino, T. D. (1999). Cultural artifacts as scaffolds for genre development. *Reading Research Quarterly, 34*, 138–170.

Kamii, C., Pritchett, M., & Nelson, K. (1997). 52 × 8: The importance of children's initiative. *The Constructivist, 12*, 5–11.

Kamil, M. L., Borman, G. D., Dole, J. A., Kral, C. C., Salinger, T., & Torgesen, J. K. (2008). *Improving adolescent literacy: Effective classroom and intervention practices: A Practice Guide (NCEE #2008-4027).* Washington, DC: Institute of Education Sciences, U.S. Department of Education. Retrieved from http://ies.ed.gov/ncee/wwc.

Kang, M. J., Hsu, M., Krajbich, I. M., Loewenstein, G., McClure, S. M., Wang, J. T., et al. (2009). The wick in the candle of learning: Epistemic curiosity activates reward circuitry and enhances memory. *Psychological Science, 20*, 963–973.

Kaplan, A., Gheen, M., & Midgley, C. (2002). Classroom goal structure and student disruptive behaviour. *British Journal of Educational Psychology, 72*, 191–211.

Kaplow, J. B., Curran, P. J., Dodge, K. A., & Conduct Problems Prevention Research Group. (2002). Child, parent, and peer predictors of early-onset substance use: A multisite longitudinal study. *Journal of Abnormal Child Psychology, 30*, 199–216.

Karavasilis, L., Doyle, A. B., & Markiewicz, D. (2003). Associations between parenting style and attachment to mother in middle childhood and adolescence. *International Journal of Behavioral Development, 17*, 153–164.

Karen, R. (1994). *Becoming Attached.* New York: Warner.

Karevold, E., Rxysamb, E., Ystrom, E., & Mathiesen, K. S. (2009). Predictors and pathways from infancy to symptoms of anxiety and depression in early adolescence. *Developmental Psychology, 45*, 1051–1060.

Karpicke, J. D., & Roediger, H. L. (2008). The critical importance of retrieval for learning. *Science, 319*, 966–968.

Katz, L. (1999). International perspectives on early childhood education: Lessons from my travels. *Early Childhood Research & Practice, 1.*

Katz, L. F., & Hunter, E. C. (2007). Maternal meta-emotion philosophy and adolescent depressive symptomatology. *Social Development, 16*, 343–360.

Kaufman, A. S. (2000). Tests of intelligence. In R. J. Sternberg (Ed.), *Handbook of intelligence* (pp. 445–476). Cambridge, UK: Cambridge University Press.

Kawabata, Y., & Crick, N. R. (2008). The role of cross-racial/ethnic friendships in social adjustment. *Developmental Psychology, 44*, 1177–1183.

Kelly, D. J., Quinn, P. C., Slater, A. M., Lee, K., Ge, L., & Pascalis, O. (2007). The other-race effect develops during infancy: Evidence of perceptual narrowing. *Psychological Science, 18*, 1084–1089.

Kelly, J. B. (2000). Children's adjustment in conflicted marriage and divorce: A decade's review of research. *Journal of the American Academy of Child and Adolescent Psychiatry, 39*, 963–973.

Keltner, D., Capps, L., Kring, A. M., Young, R. C., & Heerey, E. A. (2001). Just teasing: A conceptual analysis and empirical review. *Psychological Bulletin, 83*, 229–248.

Kemps, E., De Rammelaere, S., & Desmet, T. (2000). The development of working memory: Exploring the complementarity of two models. *Journal of Experimental Child Psychology, 77*, 89–109.

Kendeou, P., Van den Broek, P., White, M. J., & Lynch, J. S. (2009). Predicting reading comprehension in early elementary school: The independent contributions of oral language and decoding skills. *Journal of Educational Psychology, 101*, 765–778.

Kennedy, D. (2000). The roots of child study: Philosophy, history, and religion. *Teachers College Record, 102*, 514–538.

Kenney-Benson, G. A., Pomerantz, E. M., Ryan, A. M., & Patrick, H. (2006). Sex differences in math performance: The role of children's approach to schoolwork. *Developmental Psychology, 42*, 11–26.

Kensinger, E. A. (2007). Negative emotion enhances memory accuracy: Behavioral and neuroimaging evidence. *Current Directions in Psychological Science, 16*, 213–218.

Keppel, B. (2002). Kenneth B. Clark in the patterns of American culture. *American Psychologist, 57*, 29–37.

Kerr, D. C., Lopez, N. L., Olson, S. L., & Sameroff, A. J. (2004). Parental discipline and externalizing behavior problems in early childhood. The roles of moral regulation and child gender. *Journal of Abnormal Child Psychology, 32*, 369–383.

Kertes, D., & Gunnar, M. (2004). Evening activities as a potential confound in research on the adrenocortical system in children. *Child Development, 75*, 193–204.

Kiang, L., Yip, T., Gonzales-Backen, M., Witkow, M., & Fuligni, A. J. (2006). Ethnic identity and the daily psychological well-being of adolescents from Mexican and Chinese backgrounds. *Child Development, 77*, 1338–1350.

Kidder, T. (1989). *Among schoolchildren*. Boston: Houghton Mifflin.

Kiefer, S. M., & Ryan, A. M. (2008). Striving for social dominance over peers: The implications for academic adjustment during early adolescence. *Journal of Educational Psychology, 100*, 417–428.

Kieffer, M. J. (2008). Catching up or falling behind? Initial English proficiency, concentrated poverty, and the reading growth of language minority learners in the United States. *Journal of Educational Psychology, 100*, 851–868.

Killen, M., & de Waal, F. (2000). The evolution and development of morality. In A. Filippo & F. de Waal (Eds.), *Natural conflict resolution* (pp. 352–372). Berkeley: University of California Press.

Killen, M., & Smetana, J. (1999). Social interactions in preschool classrooms and the development of young children's conceptions of the personal. *Child Development, 70*, 486–501.

Killen, M., & Sueyoski, L. (1995). Conflict resolution in Japanese social interactions. *Early Education and Development, 6*, 317–334.

Kim, J., & Cicchetti, D. (2006). Longitudinal trajectories of self-system processes and depressive symptoms among maltreated and nonmaltreated children. *Child Development, 77*, 624–639.

Kim, J., & Sunderman, G. (2005). Measuring academic proficiency under the No Child Left Behind Act: Implications for educational equity. *Educational Researcher, 34*, 3–13.

Kim, J. S. (2007). The effects of a voluntary summer reading intervention on reading activities and reading achievement. *Journal of Educational Psychology, 99*, 505–515.

Kim-Cohen, J., & Gold, A. L. (2009). Measured gene-environment interactions and mechanisms promoting resilient development. *Current Directions in Psychological Science, 18*, 138–142.

Kim-Cohen, J., Moffitt, T., Caspi, A., & Taylor, A. (2004). Genetic and environmental processes in young children's resilience and vulnerability to socioeconomic deprivation. *Child Development, 75*, 651–668.

Kindermann, T. A. (2007). Effects of naturally existing peer groups on changes in academic engagement in a cohort of sixth graders. *Child Development, 78*, 1186–1203.

King, P. E., & Furrow, J. L. (2004). Religion as a resource for positive youth development: Religion, social capital, and moral outcomes. *Developmental Psychology, 40*, 703–713.

King, V., Harris, K. M., & Heard, H. E. (2004). Racial and ethnic diversity in nonresident father involvement. *Journal of Marriage and Family, 66*, 1–21.

Kirby, D., & Laris, B. A. (2009). Effective curriculum-based sex and STD/HIV education programs for adolescents. *Child Development Perspectives, 3*, 21–29.

Kirschner, P. A., Sweller, J., & Clark, R. E. (2006). Why minimal guidance during instruction does not work: An analysis of the failure of constructivist, discovery, problem-based, experiential and inquiry-based teaching. *Educational Psychologist, 41*, 75–86.

Kisilevsky, B., Hains, S., Lee, K., Xie, X., Huang, H., Ye, H. H., et al. (2003). Effects of experience on fetal voice recognition. *Psychological Science, 14*, 220–224.

Kitzman, K., Dalton, W. T., & Buscemi, J. (2008). Beyond parenting practices: Family context and the treatment of pediatric obesity. *Family Relations, 57*, 13–23.

Klahr, D., & Chen, Z. (2003). Overcoming the positive-capture strategy in young children: Learning about indeterminacy. *Child Development, 74*, 1275–1296.

Klahr, D., & Nigam, M. (2004). The equivalence of learning paths in early science instruction: Effects of direct instruction and discovery learning. *Psychological Science, 15*, 661–667.

Klauer, K. J., & Phye, G. D. (2008). Inductive reasoning: A training approach. *Review of Educational Research, 78*, 85–123.

Klibanoff, R. S., Levine, S. C., Huttenlocher, J., Vasilyeva, M., & Hedges, L. V. (2006). Preschool children's mathematical knowledge: The effect of teacher "math talk." *Developmental Psychology, 42*, 59–69.

Kliewer, W. (1991). Coping in middle childhood: Relations to competence, Type A behavior, monitoring, blunting, and locus of control. *Developmental Psychology, 27*, 689–697.

Klimes-Dougan, B., & Kistner, J. (1990). Physically abused preschoolers' responses to peers' distress. *Developmental Psychology, 26*, 599–602.

Kline, P. (2001). Ability and temperament. In J. Collis & S. Messick (Eds.), *Intelligence and personality: Bridging the gap in theory and measurement* (pp. 113–117). Mahwah, New Jersey: Erlbaum.

Klingberg, T., Fernell, E., Olesen, P. J., Johnson, M., Gustafsson, P., Dahlstreom, K., et al. (2005). Computerized training of working memory in children with ADHD—A randomized, controlled trial. *Journal of the American Academy of Child and Adolescent Psychiatry, 44*, 177–186.

Knez, I., & Hygge, S. (2002). Irrelevant speech and indoor lighting: Cognitive performance and self-reported affect. *Applied Cognitive Psychology, 16*, 709–718.

Kochanska, G. (2002). Mutually responsive orientation between mothers and their young children: A context for the early development of conscience. *Current Directions in Psychological Science, 11*, 191–195.

Kochanska, G., Aksan, N., & Carlson, J. (2005). Temperament, relationships, and young children's receptive cooperation with their parents. *Developmental Psychology, 41*, 648–660.

Kochanska, G., Aksan, N., & Joy, M. E. (2007). Children's fearfulness as a moderator of parenting in early socialization: Two longitudinal studies. *Developmental Psychology, 43*, 222–237.

Kochanska, G., Barry, R. A., Stellern, S. A., & O'Bleness, J. J. (2009). Early attachment organization moderates the parent-child mutually coercive pathway to children's antisocial conduct. *Child Development, 80*, 1288–1300.

Kochenderfer-Ladd, B., & Wardrop, J. (2001). Chronicity and instability of children's peer victimization experiences as predictors of loneliness and social satisfaction trajectories. *Child Development, 72*, 134–151.

Kodak, T., Northrup, J., & Kelley, M. E. (2007). An evaluation of the types of attention that maintain problem behavior. *Journal of Applied Behavior Analysis, 40*, 167–171.

Kohlberg, L. (1981). *The philosophy of moral development. Volume 1. Moral stages and the idea of justice*. San Francisco: Harper & Row.

Kokko, K., & Pulkkinen, L. (2000). Aggression in childhood and long-term unemployment in adulthood: A cycle of maladaptation and some protective factors. *Developmental Psychology, 36*, 463–472.

Kolb, B., & Whishaw, I. (1998). Brain plasticity and behavior. *Annual Review of Psychology, 49*, 43–64.

Konstantopoulos, S. (2008). Do small classes reduce the achievement gap between low and high achievers? Evidence from Project STAR. *The Elementary School Journal, 108*, 275–291.

Koren-Karie, N., Oppenheim, D., Dolev, S., Sher, E., & Etzion-Carasso, A. (2002). Mothers' insightfulness regarding their infants' internal experience: Relations with maternal sensitivity and infant attachment. *Developmental Psychology, 38*, 534-542.

Kornell, N., & Bjork, R. A. (2008). Learning concepts and categories: Is spacing the "enemy of induction"? *Psychological Science, 19*, 585–592.

Kovács, A. M. (2009). Early bilingualism enhances mechanisms of false-belief reasoning. *Developmental Science, 12*, 48–54.

Kovas, Y., Hayiou-Thomas, M., Oliver, B. R., Dale, P. S., Bishop, D., & Plomin, R. (2005). Genetic influences in different aspects of language development: The etiology of language skills in 4.5-year-old twins. *Child Development, 76*, 632–651.

Kowalski, R. M. (2000). "I was only kidding!": Victims' and perpetrators' perceptions of teasing. *Personality and Social Psychology Bulletin, 26*, 231–241.

Kraizer, S., Witte, S., Fryer, G., & Miyoshi, T. (1990). Children in self-care: A new perspective. *Child Welfare, 69*, 571–581.

Krajcik, J., Czerniak, C., & Berger, C. (1999). *Teaching children science: A project-based approach*. Boston: McGraw-Hill.

Kramarski, B., & Mevarech, Z. (2003). Enhancing mathematical reasoning in the classroom: The effects of cooperative learning and metacognitive training. *American Educational Research Journal, 40*, 281–310.

Kramer, M., & Kakuma, R. (2004). The optimal duration of exclusive breastfeeding: A systematic review. *Advances in Experimental Medicine & Biology, 554*, 63–77.

Krapp, A., Hidi, S., & Renninger, K. A. (1992). Interest, learning, and development. In K. A. Renninger, S. Hidi & A. Krapp (Eds.), *The role of interest in learning and development* (pp. 3–25). Hillsdale, NJ: Lawrence Erlbaum.

Kraus, N., & Banai, K. (2007). Auditory-processing malleability: Focus on language and music. *Current Directions in Psychological Science, 16*, 105–110.

Krebs, D. L. (2008). Morality: An evolutionary account. *Perspectives on Psychological Science, 3*, 149–172.

Kreppner, J. M., Rutter, M., Beckett, C., Castle, J., Colvert, E., Groothues, C., et al. (2007). Normality and impariment following profound early institutional deprivation: A longitudinal follow-up in early adolescence. *Developmental Psychology, 43*, 931–946.

Krevans, J., & Gibbs, J. C. (1996). Parents' use of inductive discipline: Relations to children's empathy and prosocial behavior. *Child Development, 67*, 3263–3277.

Krishnamoorthy, J. S., Hart, C., & Jelalian, E. (2006). The epidemic of childhood obesity: Review of research and implications for public policy. *Social Policy Report, 19*, 3–17.

Krumboltz, J. D., & Krumboltz, H. B. (1972). *Changing children's behavior*. Englewood Cliffs, NJ: Prentice-Hall.

Kubiszyn, T., & Borich, G. (2003). *Educational testing and measurement* (7th ed.). New York: Wiley.

Kuczynski, L., & Kochanska, G. (1990). Development of children's noncompliance strategies from toddlerhood to age 5. *Developmental Psychology, 26*, 398–408.

Kuhl, P. (2000). Language, mind, and brain: Experience alters perception. In M. Gazzaniga (Ed.), *The new cognitive neurosciences* (2nd ed., pp. 99–115). Cambridge, MA: MIT Press.

Kuhn, D. (2000). Metacognitive development. *Current Directions in Psychological Science, 9*, 178–181.

Kuhn, D. (2006). Do cognitive changes accompany developments in the adolescent brain? *Perspectives on Psychological Science, 1*, 59–67.

Kuhn, D., Black, J., Keselman, A., & Kaplan, D. (2000). The development of cognitive skills to support inquiry learning. *Cognition and Instruction, 18*, 495–523.

Kuhn, D., & Udell, W. (2003). The development of argument skills. *Child Development, 74*, 1245–1260.

Kunkel, D., Eyal, K., Finnerty, K., Biely, E., & Donnerstein, E. (2005). *Sex on TV*. Menlo Park, CA: Kaiser Family Foundation.

Kuppens, S., Grietens, H., Onghena, P., Michiels, D., & Subramanian, S. V. (2008). Individual and classroom variables associated with relational aggression in elementary-school aged children: A multilevel analysis. *Journal of School Psychology, 46*, 639–660.

Kurdek, L. A., & Sinclair, R. J. (2001). Predicting reading and mathematics achievement in fourth-grade children from kindergarten reading readiness scores. *Journal of Educational Psychology, 93*, 451–455.

Kuther, T., & Higgins-D'Alessandro, A. (2000). Bridging the gap between moral reasoning and adolescent engagement in risky behavior. *Journal of Adolescence, 23*, 409–422.

Kwong, T. E., & Varnhagen, C. K. (2005). Strategy development and learning to spell new words: Generalization of a process. *Developmental Psychology, 41*, 148–159.

La Paro, K., & Pianta, R. (2000). Predicting children's competence in the early school years: A meta-analytic review. *Review of Educational Research, 70*, 443–484.

Laboratory of Comparative Human Cognition. (1998). Culture and cognitive development. In R. M. Lerner (Ed.), *Handbook of child psychology: Theoretical models of human development* (5th ed., Vol. 1, pp. 295–356). New York: Wiley.

Lac, A., & Crano, W. D. (2009). Monitoring matters: Meta-analytic review reveals the reliable linkage of parental monitoring with adolescent marijuana use. *Perspectives on Psychological Science, 4*, 578–586.

Ladd, G. W. (2006). Peer rejection, aggressive or withdrawn behavior, and psychological maladjustment from ages 5 to 12: An examination of four predictive models. *Child Development, 77*, 822–846.

Ladd, G. W., Buhs, E., & Troop, W. (2002). Children's interpersonal skills and relationships in school settings: Adaptive significance and implications for school-based prevention and intervention programs. In P. Smith & C. Hart (Eds.), *Blackwell handbook of childhood social development* (pp. 394–415). Oxford: Blackwell.

Ladd, G. W., & Burgess, K. (2001). Do relational risks and protective factors moderate the linkages between childhood aggression and early psychological and school adjustment? *Child Development, 72*, 1579–1601.

Ladd, G. W., & Dinella, L. M. (2009). Continuity and change in early school engagement: Predictive of children's achievement trajectories from first to eighth grade? *Journal of Educational Psychology, 101*, 190–206.

Ladd, G. W., Herald-Brown, S. L., & Reiser, M. (2008). Does chronic classroom peer rejection predict the development of children's classroom participation during the grade school years? *Child Development, 79*, 1001–1015.

Ladd, G. W., Kochenderfer, B. J., & Coleman, C. C. (1996). Friendship quality as a predictor of young children's early school adjustment. *Child Development, 67*, 1103–1118.

Ladd, G. W., & Pettit, G. S. (2002). Parenting and the development of children's peer relationships. In M. Bornstein (Ed.), *Handbook of parenting* (2nd ed., Vol. 5, pp. 269–309). Hillsdale, NJ: Erlbaum.

Ladd, G. W., & Troop-Gordon, W. (2003). The role of chronic peer difficulties in the development of children's psychological adjustment problems. *Child Development, 74*, 1344–1367.

LaFontana, K., & Cillessen, A. (2002). Children's perceptions of popular and unpopular peers: A multimethod assessment. *Developmental Psychology, 38*, 635–647.

Lagattuta, K. H., & Wellman, H. (2002). Differences in early parent–child conversations about negative versus positive emotions: Implications for the development of psychological understanding. *Developmental Psychology, 38*, 564–580.

Lahey, B. B. (2009). Public health significance of neuroticism. *American Psychologist, 64*, 241–256.

Laible, D., Panfile, T., & Makariev, D. (2008). The quality and frequency of mother–toddler conflict: Links with attachment and temperament. *Child Development, 79*, 426–443.

Laible, D., & Thompson, R. (2000). Mother-child discourse, attachment security, shared positive affect, and early conscience development. *Child Development, 71*, 1424-1440.

Laird, R. D., Pettit, G. S., Bates, J. E., & Dodge, K. A. (2003). Parents' monitoring-relevant knowledge and adolescents' delinquent behavior: Evidence of correlated developmental changes and reciprocal influences. *Child Development, 74*, 752–768.

Lal, S. (2002). Giving children security: Mamie Phipps Clark and the racialization of child psychology. *American Psychologist, 57*, 20–28.

Lamb, M. (1998). Nonparental child care: Context, quality, correlates, and consequences. In I. Sigel & K. A. Renninger (Eds.), *Handbook of child psychology. Child psychology in practice* (5th ed., Vol. 4, pp. 73–133). New York: Wiley.

Lamborn, S. D., Mounts, N. S., Steinberg, L., & Dornbusch, S. M. (1991). Patterns of competence and adjustment among adolescents from authoritative, authoritarian, indulgent, and neglectful families. *Child Development, 62*, 1049–1065.

Lampert, M., Rittenhouse, P., & Crumbaugh, C. (1996). Agreeing to disagree: Developing sociable mathematical discourse. In D. R. Olson & N. Torrance (Eds.), *The handbook of education and human development* (pp. 731–764). Oxford: Blackwell.

Landry, S., Smith, K., Miller-Loncar, C., & Swank, P. (1997). Predicting cognitive-language and social growth curves from early maternal behaviors in children at varying degreees of biological risk. *Developmental Psychology, 33*, 1040–1053.

Lane, H. B., & Allen, S. A. (2010). The vocabulary-rich classroom: Modeling sophisticated word use to promote word consciousness and vocabulary growth. *The Reading Teacher, 63*, 362–370.

Lansford, J. E. (2004). Ethnic differences in the link between physical discipline and later adolescent externalizing behaviors. *Journal of Child Psychology & Psychiatry & Allied Disciplines, 45*, 801–812.

Lansford, J. E. (2009). Parental divorce and children's adjustment. *Perspectives on Psychological Science, 4*, 140–152.

Lansford, J. E., Chang, L., Dodge, K., Malone, P., Oburur, P., Palmerus, K., et al. (2005). Physical discipline and children's adjustment: Cultural normativeness as a moderator. *Child Development, 76*, 1234–1246.

Lansford, J. E., Criss, M. M., Dodge, K. A., Shaw, D. S., Pettit, G. S., & Bates, J. E. (2009). Trajectories of physical discipline: Early childhood antecedents and developmental outcomes. *Child Development, 80*, 1385–1402.

Lareau, A. (1989). *Home advantage: Social class and parental intervention in elementary education*. London: Falmer Press.

Lareau, A. (2003). *Unequal childhoods: Class, race, and family life*. Berkeley: University of California Press.

Lareau, A., & Horvat, E. M. (1999). Moments of social inclusion and exclusion: Race, class, and cultural capital in family–school relationships. *Sociology of Education, 72*, 37–53.

Larivee, S., Normandau, S., & Parent, S. (2000). The French connection: Some contributions of French-language research in the post-Piagetian era. *Child Development, 71*, 823–839.

Larsen, J. T., To, Y. M., & Fireman, G. (2007). Children's understanding and experience of mixed emotions. *Psychological Science, 18,* 186–191.

Larson, R. (2001). How U.S. children and adolescents spend time: What it does (and doesn't) tell us about their development. *Current Directions in Psychological Science, 10,* 160–164.

Larson, R., & Richards, M. H. (1994). *Divergent realities: The emotional lives of mothers, fathers, and adolescents.* New York: BasicBooks.

Larson, R., & Verma, S. (1999). How children and adolescents spend time around the world: Work, play, and developmental opportunities. *Psychological Bulletin, 125,* 701–736.

Laurer, P. A., Akiba, M., Wilkerson, S. B., Apthorp, H. S., Snow, D., & Martin-Glenn, M. L. (2006). Out-of-school-time programs: A meta-analysis of effects for at-risk students. *Review of Educational Research, 76,* 275–313.

Laursen, B., Bukowski, W. M., Aunola, K., & Nurmi, J.-E. (2007). Friendship moderates prospective associations between social isolation and adjustment problems in young children. *Child Development, 78,* 1395–1404.

Laursen, B., Finkelstein, B., & Betts, N. (2001). A developmental meta-analysis of peer conflict resolution. *Developmental Review, 21,* 423–449.

Laursen, B., Pulkkinen, L., & Adams, R. (2002). The antecedents and correlates of agreeableness in adulthood. *Developmental Psychology, 38,* 591–603.

Leadbeater, B. J., & Hoglund, W. L. G. (2009). The effects of peer victimization and physical aggression on changes in internalizing from first to third grade. *Child Development, 80,* 843–859.

Leaper, C., & Brown, C. S. (2008). Perceived experiences with sexism among adolescent girls. *Child Development, 79,* 685–704.

Lear, J. (2003). School-based health centers: A long road to travel. *Archives of Pediatrics and Adolescent Medicine, 157,* 118–119.

Lee, C. D. (1995). A culturally based cognitive apprenticeship: Teaching African American high school students skills in literary interpretation. *Reading Research Quarterly, 30,* 608–630.

Lee, D. L. (2005). Increasing compliance: A quantitative synthesis of applied research on high-probability request sequences. *Exceptionality, 13,* 141–154.

Lee, J. (2008). Is test-driven external accountability effective? Synthesizing the evidence from cross-state causal-comparative and correlational studies. *Review of Educational Research, 78,* 608–644.

Lee, K., Cameron, C. A., Xu, F., Fu, G., & Board, J. (1997). Chinese and Canadian children's evaluations of lying and truth telling: Similarities and differences in the context of pro- and antisocial behaviors. *Child Development, 68,* 924–934.

Lee, K., Ng, E. L., & Ng, S. F. (2009). The contributions of working memory and executive functioning to problem representation and solution generation in algebraic word problems. *Journal of Educational Psychology, 101,* 373–387.

Lee, L., Howes, C., & Chamberlain, B. (2007). Ethnic heterogeneity of social networks and cross-ethnic friendships of elementary school boys and girls. *Merrill-Palmer Quarterly, 53,* 325–346.

Lee, P. W. (1999). In their own voices: An ethnographic study of low-achieving students within the context of school reform. *Urban Education, 34,* 212–244.

Lee, V., Brooks-Gunn, J., Schnur, E., & Liaw, F.-R. (1990). Are Head Start effects sustained? A longitudinal follow-up comparison of disadvantaged children attending Head Start, no preschool, and other preschool programs. *Child Development, 61,* 495–507.

Lee, V., Loeb, S., & Lubeck, S. (1998). Contextual effects of prekindergarten classrooms for disadvantaged children on cognitive development: The case of Chapter 1. *Child Development, 69,* 479–494.

Lee, V., & Smith, J. B. (1999). Social support and achievement for young adolescents in Chicago: The role of school academic press. *American Educational Research Journal, 36,* 907–945.

Leerkes, E. M., Blankson, N., & O'Brien, M. (2009). Differential effects of maternal sensitivity to infant distress and nondistress on social-emotional functioning. *Child Development, 80,* 762–775.

Lefcourt, H. M. (2002). Humor. In C. Snyder & S. Lopez (Eds.), *Handbook of positive psychology* (pp. 619–631). London: Oxford University Press.

Lehmann, M., & Hasselhorn, M. (2007). Variable memory strategy use in children's adaptive intratask learning behavior: Developmental changes and working memory influences in free recall. *Child Development, 78,* 1068–1082.

Lei, J. L. (2003). (Un)Necessary toughness?: Those "loud black girls" and those "quiet Asian boys." *Anthropology & Education Quarterly, 34,* 158–181.

Lemelin, J.-P., Boivin, M., Forget-Dubois, N., Dionne, G., Seguin, J. R., Brendgen, M., et al. (2007). The genetic-environmental etiology of cognitive school readiness and later academic achievement in early childhood. *Child Development, 78,* 1855–1869.

Lemerise, E. A., & Arsenio, W. F. (2000). An integrated model of emotion processes and cognition in social information processing. *Child Development, 71,* 107–118.

Lenhart, A., Madden, M., & Hitlin, P. (2005). *Teens and technology.* Washington, DC: Pew Internet & American Life Project.

Leon, D. A., Lawlor, D. A., Clark, H., Batty, G. D., & Macintyre, S. (2009). The association of childhood intelligence with mortality risk from adolescence to middle age: Findings from the Aberdeen Children of the 1950s cohort study. *Intelligence, 37,* 520–528.

Leppanen, J. M., Moulson, M. C., Vogel-Farley, V. K., & Nelson, C. A. (2007). An ERP study of emotional face processing in the adult and infant brain. *Child Development, 78,* 232–245.

Lepper, M. R. (1983). Social-control processes and the internalization of social values: An attributional perspective. In E. T. Higgins, D. Ruble & W. Hartup (Eds.), *Social cognition and social development: A sociocultural perspective* (pp. 294–330). Cambridge, UK: Cambridge University Press.

Lepper, M. R., Greene, D., & Nisbett, R. E. (1973). Undermining children's intrinsic interest with extrinsic reward: A test of the "overjustification" hypothesis. *Journal of Personality and Social Psychology, 28,* 129–137.

Lepper, M. R., Keavney, M., & Drake, M. (1996). Intrinsic motivation and extrinsic rewards: A commentary on Cameron and Pierce's meta-analysis. *Review of Educational Research, 66,* 5–32.

Lerner, J. V. (1983). The role of temperament in psychosocial adaptation in early adolescents: A test of a "goodness of fit" model. *Journal of Genetic Psychology, 143,* 149–157.

Lerner, J. V., Lerner, R., & Zabski, S. (1985). Temperament and elementary school children's actual and rated academic performance:

A test of a "goodness of fit" model. *Journal of Child Psychology & Psychiatry & Allied Disciplines, 26*, 125–136.

Lesaux, N. K., Lipka, O., & Siegel, L. S. (2006). Investigating cognitive and linguistic abilities that influence the reading comprehension skills of children from diverse linguistic backgrounds. *Reading and Writing, 19*, 99–131.

Lesesne, C., Visser, S., & White, C. (2003). Attention-deficit/hyperactivity disorder in school-aged children: Association with maternal mental health and use of health care resources. *Pediatrics, 111*, 1232–1237.

Leslie, A. M., Knobe, J., & Cohen, A. (2006). Acting intentionally and the side-effect effect: Theory of mind and moral judgment. *Psychological Science, 17*, 421–427.

Leventhal, T., & Brooks-Gunn, J. (2003). Child and youth in neighborhood contexts. *Current Directions in Psychological Science, 12*, 27–31.

Levin, I., & Bus, A. G. (2003). How is emergent writing based on drawing? Analyses of children's products and their sorting by children and mothers. *Developmental Psychology, 39*, 891–905.

Levine, J., Pollack, H., & Comfort, M. E. (2001). Academic and behavioral outcomes among the children of young mothers. *Journal of Marriage and Family, 63*, 355–369.

Lewin, T. (1998, April 27). Struggling for personal attention in day care. *New York Times*, pp. A1, A13.

Lewinsohn, P. M., Hops, H., Roberts, R., Seeley, J., & Andrews, J. (1993). Adolescent psychopathology: I. Prevalence and incidence of depression and other DSM-III-R disorders in high school students. *Journal of Abnormal Psychology, 102*, 133–144.

Lewis, B., Singer, L. T., Short, E., Minnes, S., Arendt, R., Weishampel, P., et al. (2004). Four-year language outcomes of children exposed to cocaine in utero. *Neurotoxicology and Teratology, 26*, 617–627.

Lewis, C., & Carpendale, J. (2002). Social cognition. In P. Smith & C. Hart (Eds.), *Blackwell handbook of childhood social development* (pp. 375–393). Oxford: Blackwell.

Lewis, E. E., Dozier, M., Ackerman, J., & Sepulveda-Kozakowski, S. (2007). The effect of placement instability on adopted children's inhibitory control abilities and oppositional behavior. *Developmental Psychology, 43*, 1415–1427.

Lewis, M., & Carmody, D. P. (2008). Self-representation and brain development. *Developmental Psychology, 44*, 1329–1334.

Lewis, M., Feiring, C., & Rosenthal, S. (2000). Attachment over time. *Child Development, 71*, 707–720.

Lewis, M., & Ramsay, D. (2004). Development of self-recognition, personal pronoun use, and pretend play during the 2nd year. *Child Development, 75*, 1821–1831.

Lewis, M., Ramsay, D., & Kawakami, K. (1993). Differences between Japanese infants and Caucasian American infants in behavioral and cortisol response to inoculation. *Child Development, 64*, 1722–1731.

Lewis, V., Norgate, S., Collis, G., & Reynolds, R. (2000). The consequences of visual impairment for children's symbolic and functional play. *British Journal of Developmental Psychology, 18*, 449–464.

Li, X., & Atkins, M. S. (2004). Early childhood computer experience and cognitive and motor development. *Pediatrics, 113*, 1715–1722.

Li-Grining, C. P. (2007). Effortful control among low-income preschoolers in three cities: Stability, change, and individual differences. *Developmental Psychology, 43*, 208–221.

Light, P., & Littleton, K. (1999). *Social processes in children's learning*. Cambridge, UK: Cambridge University Press.

Lightner, R., Bollmer, J., Harris, M., Milich, R., & Scambler, D. (2000). What do you say to teasers? Parent and child evluations of responses to teasing. *Journal of Applied Developmental Psychology, 21*, 403–427.

Lillard, A. (2002). Pretend play and cognitive development. In U. Goswami (Ed.), *Blackwell handbook of childhood cognitive development* (pp. 189–205). Malden, MA: Blackwell.

Linver, M., Brooks-Gunn, J., & Kohen, D. (2002). Family processes as pathways from income to young children's development. *Developmental Psychology, 38*, 719–734.

Linver, M. R., Roth, J., & Brooks-Gunn, J. (2009). Patterns of adolescents' participation in organized activities: Are sports best when combined with other activities? *Developmental Psychology, 45*, 354–367.

Lipsey, M., & Wilson, D. (1993). The efficacy of psychological, educational, and behavioral treatment. *American Psychologist, 48*, 1181–1209.

Lisonbee, J. A., Mize, J., Payne, A. L., & Granger, D. A. (2008). Children's cortisol and the quality of teacher-child relationships in child care. *Child Development, 79*, 1818–1832.

Liu, D., Wellman, H. M., Tardif, T., & Sabbagh, M. A. (2008). Theory of mind development in Chinese Children: A meta-analysis of false-belief understanding across cultures and languages. *Developmental Psychology, 44*, 523–531.

Lloyd, B., & Howe, N. (2003). Solitary play and convergent and divergent thinking skills in preschool children. *Early Childhood Research Quarterly, 18*, 22–41.

Lloyd, M. E., Doydum, A. O., & Newcombe, N. S. (2009). Memory binding in early childhood: Evidence for a retrieval deficit. *Child Development, 80*, 1321–1328.

Locke, E. A., & Latham, G. P. (2002). Building a practically useful theory of goal setting and task motivation. *American Psychologist, 57*, 705–717.

Loe, I. M., Balestrino, M. D., Phelps, R. A., Kurs-Lasky, M., Chaves-Gnecco, D., Paradise, J. L., et al. (2008). Early histories of school-aged children with attention-deficit/hyperactivity disorder. *Child Development, 79*, 1853–1868.

Loeb, S., Fuller, B., Kagan, S., & Carrol, B. (2004). Child care in poor communities: Early learning effects of type, quality, and stability. *Child Development, 75*, 47–65.

Lohmann, H., & Tomasello, M. (2003). The role of language in the development of false belief understanding: A training study. *Child Development, 74*, 1130–1144.

London, A., Scott, E., Edin, K., & Hunter, V. (2004). Welfare reform, work-family tradeoffs, and child well-being. *Family Relations, 53* (2), 148–158.

Lopez, V., Katsulis, Y., & Robillard, A. (2009). Drug use with parents as a relational strategy for incarcerated female adolescents. *Family Relations, 58*, 135–147.

Lorber, M. F., & Egeland, B. (2009). Infancy parenting and externalizing psychopathology from childhood through adulthood: Developmental trends. *Developmental Psychology, 45*, 909–912.

Lorch, E. P. (2007). Health, drugs, and values. In N. Pecora, J. P. Murray & E. A. Wartella (Eds.), *Children and television: Fifty years of research* (pp. 205–231). Mahwah, NJ: Erlbaum.

Losoya, S. H., & Eisenberg, N. (2000). Affective empathy. In J. Hall & F. J. Bernieri (Eds.), *Interpersonal sensitivity: Theory and measurement* (pp. 21–44). Mahwah, NJ: Erlbaum.

Loury, L. D. (2004). Does church attendance really increase schooling? *Journal for the Scientific Study of Religion, 43*, 119–127.

Love, J., Kisker, E., Ross, C., Raikes, H., Constantine, J., Boller, K., et al. (2005). The effectiveness of Early Head Start for 3-year-old children and their parents: Lessons for policy and programs. *Developmental Psychology, 41*, 885–901.

Love, J. M., Harrison, L., Sagi-Schwartz, A., Van IJzendoorn, M. H., Ross, C., Ungerer, J. A., et al. (2003). Child care quality matters: How conclusions may vary with context. *Child Development, 74*, 1021–1033.

Lubinski, D., Benbow, C. P., Webb, R. M., & Bleske-Rechek, A. (2006). Tracking exceptional human capital over two decades. *Psychological Science, 17*, 194–199.

Lubman, D., Yucei, M., & Hall, W. D. (2007). Substance use and the adolescent brain: A toxic combination? *Journal of Psychopharmacology, 21*, 792–794.

Luciana, M., Conklin, H., Hooper, C., & Yarger, R. (2005). The development of nonverbal working memory and executive control processes in adolescents. *Child Development, 76*, 697–712.

Ludwig, D., Peterson, K., & Gortmaker, S. (2001). Relation between consumption of sugar-sweetened drinks and childhood obesity: A prospective, observational analysis. *Lancet, 357*, 505–508.

Ludwig, J., & Phillips, D. (2007). The benefits and costs of Head Start. *Social Policy Report, 21*, 3–18.

Luginbuehl, M., Bradley-Klug, K., Ferron, J., Anderson, W. M., & Benbadis, S. R. (2008). Pediatric sleep disorders: Validation of the Sleep Disorders Inventory for Students. *School Psychology Quarterly, 37*, 409–431.

Lugo-Gil, J., & Tamis-LeMonda, C. (2008). Family resources and parenting quality: Links to children's cognitive development across the first 3 years. *Child Development, 79*, 1065–1085.

Luna, B. (2004). Algebra and the adolescent brain. *Trends in Cognitive Sciences, 8*, 437–439.

Luna, B., Garver, K., Urban, T., Lazar, N., & Sweeney, J. (2004). Maturation of cognitive processes from late childhood to adulthood. *Child Development, 75*, 1357–1372.

Lunkenheimer, E. S., Dishion, T. J., Shaw, D., Connell, A., Gardner, F., Wilson, M. N., et al. (2009). Collateral benefits of the Family Check-up on early childhood school readiness: Indirect effects of parents' positive behavior support. *Developmental Psychology, 44*, 1737–1752.

Lunkenheimer, E. S., Shields, A. M., & Cortina, K. S. (2007). Parental emotion coaching and dismissing in family interactions. *Social Development, 16*, 232–248.

Luster, T., Bates, L., Fitzgerald, H., Vandenbelt, M., & Key, J. P. (2000). Factors related to successful outcomes among preschool children born to low-income adolescent mothers. *Journal of Marriage and the Family, 62*, 133–146.

Lustig, D. F. (1997). Of Kwanzaa, Cinco de Mayo, and whispering: The need for intercultural education. *Anthropology & Education Quarterly, 28*, 574–592.

Luthar, S. (2003). The culture of affluence: Psychological costs of material wealth. *Child Development, 74*, 1581–1593.

Luthar, S. S. (2006). Resilience in development: A synthesis of research across five decades. In D. Cicchetti & D. J. Cohen (Eds.), *Developmental Psychopathology: Volume Three: Risk, Disorder, and Adaptation* (2nd ed.). New York: Wiley.

Luthar, S. S., & Latendresse, S. J. (2008). Children of the affluent: Challenges to well-being. *Current Directions in Psychological Science, 14*, 49–53.

Lynch, S. K., Turkheimer, E., D'Onofrio, B. M., Mendle, J., Emery, R. E., Slutske, W. S., et al. (2006). A genetically informed study of the association between harsh punishment and offspring behavioral problems. *Journal of Family Psychology, 20*, 190–198.

Lyon, T., Malloy, L., Quas, J., & Talwar, V. (2008). Coaching, truth induction, and young maltreated children's false allegation and false denials. *Child Development, 79*, 914–929.

Lytton, H. (2000). Toward a model of family-environmental and child-biological influences on development. *Developmental Review, 20*, 150–179.

Lytton, H., & Romney, D. M. (1991). Parents' differential socialization of boys and girls: A meta-analysis. *Psychological Bulletin, 109*, 267–296.

MacArthur, C. A. (2006). The effects of new technologies on writing and writing processes. In C. A. MacArthur, S. Graham & J. Fitzgerald (Eds.), *Handbook of writing research* (pp. 248–262). New York: Guilford.

Maccoby, E. (2002). Gender and group process: A developmental perspective. *Current Directions in Psychological Science, 11*, 54–58.

Maccoby, E. E. (1992). The role of parents in the socialization of children: An historical overview. *Developmental Psychology, 28*, 1006–1017.

Maccoby, E. E., & Lewis, C. C. (2003). Less day care or different day care? *Child Development, 74*, 1069–1075.

Maccoby, E. E., & Martin, J. A. (1983). Socialization in the context of the family: Parent–child interaction. In P. H. Mussen (Ed.), *Handbook of child psychology: Vol. 4. Socialization, personality, and social development.* In E. M. Hetherington (Series Ed.) (4th ed., pp. 1–101). New York: Wiley.

MacCorquodale, K. (1970). On Chomsky's review of Skinner's *Verbal Behavior. Journal of the Experimental Analysis of Behavior, 13*, 83–99.

MacGillivray, L., & Curwen, M. S. (2007). Tagging as a social literacy practice. *Journal of Adolescent & Adult Literacy, 50*, 354–369.

Macmillan, R., McMorris, B., & Kruttschnitt, C. (2004). Linked lives: Stability and change in maternal circumstances and trajectories of antisocial behavior in children. *Child Development, 75*, 205–220.

Madhavi, M., Tobin, D. D., Corby, B. C., Menon, M., Hodges, E. V. E., & Perry, D. G. (2007). The developmental costs of high self-esteem for antisocial children. *Child Development, 78*, 1627–1639.

Magnuson, K., Meyers, M., Ruhm, C., & Waldfogel, J. (2004). Inequality in preschool education and school readiness. *American Educational Research Journal, 41*, 115–157.

Mahoney, J. L., Harris, A. L., & Eccles, J. S. (2006). Organized activity participation, positive youth development, and the over-scheduling hypothesis. *Social Policy Report, 20*, 3–30.

Mahoney, J. L., Lord, H., & Carryl, E. (2005). An ecological analysis of after-school program participation and the development of academic performance and motivational attributes for disadvantaged children. *Child Development, 76* (4), 811–825.

Mahoney, J. L., & Parente, M. E. (2009). Should we care about adolescents who care for themselves? What we have learned and what we need to know about youth in self-care. *Child Development Perspectives, 3,* 189–195.

Maier, S. F., & Watkins, L. R. (2000). The immune system as a sensory system: Implications for psychology. *Current Directions in Psychological Science, 9,* 98–102.

Malatesta, C. Z., Culver, C., Tesman, J. R., & Shepard, B. (1989). The development of emotion expression during the first two years of life. *Monographs of the Society for Research in Child Development* (Vol. 54).

Malecki, C., & Elliot, S. (2002). Children's social behaviors as predictors of academic achievement: A longitudinal analysis. *School Psychology Quarterly, 17,* 1–23.

Males, M. (2009). Does the adolescent brain make risk taking inevitable? A skeptical appraisal. *Journal of Adolescent Research, 24,* 3–20.

Malina, R. (1996). Tracking of physical activity and physical fitness across the lifespan. *Research Quarterly for Exercise and Sport, 67,* S48–S57.

Malina, R., Bouchard, C., & Bar-Or, O. (2004). *Growth, maturation, and physical activity* (2nd ed.). Champaign, IL: Human Kinetics.

Malti, T., Gummerum, M., Keller, M., & Buchmann, M. (2009). Children's moral motivation, sympathy, and prosocial behavior. *Child Development, 80,* 442–460.

Malti, T., Schwartz, S. E. O., Liu, C. H., & Noam, G. G. (2008). Program evaluation: Relationships as key to student development. *New Directions in Youth Development, 31,* 151–177.

Mandara, J., Gaylord-Harden, N. K., Richards, M. H., & Ragsdale, B. L. (2009). The effects of changes in racial identity and self-esteem on changes in African American adolescents' mental health. *Child Development, 80,* 1660–1675.

Mannuzza, S., Klein, R. G., & Moulton, J. L. (2002). Young adult outcome of children with "situational" hyperactivity: A prospective, controlled follow-up study. *Journal of Abnormal Child Psychology, 30,* 191–198.

Mar, R. A., & Oatley, K. (2008). The function of fiction is the abstraction and simulation of social experience. *Perspectives on Psychological Science, 3,* 173–192.

Markovits, H., Fleury, M.-L., Quinn, S., & Venet, M. (1998). The development of conditional reasoning and the structure of semantic memory. *Child Development, 69,* 742–755.

Markus, H. R. (2008). Pride, prejudice, and ambivalence: Toward a unified theory of race and ethnicity. *American Psychologist, 63,* 651–670.

Marsh, H. W., & Craven, R. G. (2006). Reciprocal effects of self-concept and performance from a multidimensional perspective: Beyond seductive pleasure and unidimensional perspectives. *Perspectives on Psychological Science, 1,* 133–163.

Marsh, H. W., Ellis, L. A., & Craven, R. G. (2002). How do preschool children feel about themselves? Unraveling measurement and multidimensional self-concept structure. *Developmental Psychology, 38,* 376–393.

Marsh, H. W., & Hau, K.-T. (2003). Big-fish-little-pond effect on academic self-concept. *American Psychologist, 58,* 364–376.

Marsh, H. W., Hau, K.-T., & Kong, C.-K. (2002). Multilevel causal ordering of academic self-concept and achievement: Influence of language of instruction (English compared with Chinese) for Hong Kong students. *American Educational Research Journal, 39,* 727–763.

Marsh, H. W., Koller, O., & Baumert, J. (2001). Reunification of East and West German school systems: Longitudinal multilevel modeling study of the big-fish-little-pond effect on academic self-concept. *American Educational Research Journal, 38,* 321–350.

Marsh, H. W., Trautwein, U., Lüdtke, O., Koller, O., & Baumert, J. (2005). Academic self-concept, interest, grades, and standardized test scores: Reciprocal effects models of causal ordering. *Child Development, 76,* 397–416.

Marshall, N. (2004). The quality of early child care and children's development. *Current Directions in Psychological Science, 13,* 165–168.

Marsiglia, F. F., Kulis, S., & Hecht, M. L. (2001). Ethnic labels and ethnic identity as predictors of drug use among middle school students in the Southwest. *Journal of Research on Adolescence, 11,* 21–48.

Martin, A. J. (2009). Age appropriateness and motivation, engagement, and performance in high school: Effects of age within cohort, grade retention, and delayed school entry. *Journal of Educational Psychology, 101,* 101–114.

Martin, C. L., & Fabes, R. (2001). The stability and consequences of young children's same-sex peer interactions. *Developmental Psychology, 37,* 431–446.

Martin, C. L., & Ruble, D. N. (2004). Children's search for gender cues: Cognitive perspectives on gender development. *Current Directions in Psychological Science, 13,* 67–70.

Martin, D. M., Preiss, R. W., Gayle, B. M., & Allen, M. (2006). A meta-analytic assessment of the effect of humorous lectures on learning. In B. M. Gayle, R. W. Preiss, N. Burrell, & M. Allen (Eds.), *Classroom communication and instructional processes.* Mahwah, NJ: Erlbaum.

Martin, G., & Pear, J. (2003). *Behavior modification: What it is and how to do it* (7th ed.). Upper Saddle River, NJ: Prentice Hall.

Martin, J. A., Hamilton, B. E., Sutton, P. D., Ventura, S. J., Menacker, F., Kirmeyer, S., et al. (2009). *Births: Final data for 2006.* Hyattsville, MD: National Center for Health Statistics.

Martin, R. (2002). Is laughter the best medicine? Humor, laughter, and physical health. *Current Directions in Psychological Science, 11,* 216–220.

Martin, S. P. (2006). Trends in marital dissolution by women's education in the United States. *Demographic Research, 15,* 537–560.

Mashburn, A. J., Justice, L. M., Downer, J. T., & Pianta, R. C. (2009). Peer effects on children's language achievement during pre-kindergarten. *Child Development, 80,* 686–702.

Mashburn, A. J., Pianta, R. C., Hamre, B., Downer, J. T., Barbarin, O. A., Bryant, D., et al. (2008). Measures of classroom quality in prekindergarten and children's development of academic, language, and social skills. *Child Development, 79,* 732–749.

Maslow, A. (1970). *Motivation and personality* (2nd ed.). New York: Harper & Row.

Masten, A., & Reed, M.-G. (2002). Resilience in development. In C. Snyder & S. Lopez (Eds.), *Handbook of positive psychology* (pp. 74–88). London: Oxford University Press.

Masten, A., Roisman, G., Long, J., Burt, K., Obradovic, J., Riley, J., et al. (2005). Developmental cascades: Linking academic achievement and externalizing and internalizing symptoms over 20 years. *Developmental Psychology, 41*, 733–746.

Mather, M. (2007). Emotional arousal and memory binding: An object-based framework. *Perspectives on Psychological Science, 2*, 33–52.

Mathews, J. (1988). *Escalante: The best teacher in America*. New York: Henry Holt.

Matsumoto, D. (1987). The role of facial response in the experience of emotion: More methodological problems and a meta-analysis. *Journal of Personality and Social Psychology, 52*, 769–774.

Maunder, R. G., & Hunter, J. J. (2001). Attachment and psychosomatic medicine: Developmental contributions to stress and disease. *Psychosomatic Medicine, 63*, 556–567.

Mauro, C., & Harris, Y. (2000). The influence of maternal childrearing attitudes and teaching behaviors on preschoolers' delay of gratification. *The Journal of Genetic Psychology, 161*, 292–306.

Mayer, J., & Salovey, P. (1997). What is emotional intelligence? In P. Salovey & D. J. Sluyter (Eds.), *Emotional development and emotional intelligence: Educational implications* (pp. 3–34). New York: Basic Books.

Mayer, J. D., Roberts, R. D., & Barsade, S. G. (2008). Human abilities: Emotional intelligence. *Annual Review of Psychology, 59*, 507–536.

Mayes, L. C. (2002). A behavioral teratogenic model of the impact of prenatal cocaine exposure on arousal regulatory systems. *Neurotoxicology and Teratology, 24*, 385–395.

Mayseless, O. (1996). Attachment patterns and their outcomes. *Human Development, 39*, 206–233.

McCabe, D. (1999). Academic dishonesty among high school students. *Adolescence, 34*, 681–687.

McCaffrey, D. F., Hamilton, L. S., Stecher, B. M., Klein, S. P., Bugliari, D., & Robyn, A. (2001). Interactions among instructional practices, curriculum, and student achievement: The case of standards-based high school mathematics. *Journal for Research in Mathematics Education, 32*, 493–517.

McCall, R., Evahn, C., & Kratzer, L. (1992). *High school underachievers*. Newbury Park, CA: Sage.

McCartney, K., Burchinal, M. R., Clarke-Stewart, K. A., Bub, K. L., Owen, M. T., & Belsky, J. (2010). Testing a series of causal propositions relating time in child care to children's externalizing behavior. *Developmental Psychology, 46*, 1–17.

McClelland, M., & Morrison, F. (2003). The emergence of learning-related social skills in preschool children. *Early Childhood Research Quarterly, 18*, 206–224.

McClelland, M. M., Cameron, C. E., Connor, C. M., Farris, C. L., Jewkes, A. M., & Morrison, F. J. (2007). Links between behavioral regulation and preschoolers' literacy, vocabulary, and math skills. *Developmental Psychology, 43*, 947–959.

McCormick, M., Brooks-Gunn, J., Buka, S. L., Goldman, J., Yu, J., Saiganik, M., et al. (2006). Early intervention in low birth weight premature infants: Results at 18 years of age for the Infant Health and Development Program. *Pediatrics, 117*, 771–780.

McCrae, R. R., & Terracciano, A. (2006). National character and personality. *Current Directions in Psychological Science, 15*, 156–162.

McCrae, R. R., Terracciano, A., & 79 Members of the Personality Profiles of Cultures Project. (2005). Personality profiles of cultures: Aggregate personality traits. *Journal of Personality and Social Psychology, 89*, 407–425.

McCullough, M. E., Kimeldorf, M. B., & Cohen, A. D. (2008). An adaptation for altruism? The social causes, social effects, and social evolution of gratitude. *Current Directions in Psychological Science, 17*, 281–285.

McCullough, M. E., & Willoughby, B. L. B. (2009). Religion, self-regulation, and self-control: Associations, explanations, and implications. *Psychological Bulletin, 135*, 69–93.

McCune, L., & Zanes, M. (2001). Learning, attention, and play. In S. Golbeck (Ed.), *Psychological perspectives on early childhood education: Reframing dilemmas in research and practice* (pp. 92–106). Mahwah, NJ: Lawrence Erlbaum.

McCutchen, D. (2006). Cognitive factors in the development of children's writing. In C. A. MacArthur, S. Graham & J. Fitzgerald (Eds.), *Handbook of writing research* (pp. 115–130). New York: Guilford.

McDaniel, M. A., Howard, D. C., & Einstein, G. O. (2009). The read-recite-review study strategy: Effective and portable. *Psychological Science, 20*, 516–522.

McDowell, D., O'Neil, R., & Parke, R. D. (2000). Display rule application in a disappointing situation and children's emotional reactivity: Relations with social competence. *Merrill-Palmer Quarterly, 46*, 306–324.

McElhaney, K. B., Antonishak, J., & Allen, J. P. (2008). "They like me, they like me not": Popularity and adolescents' perceptions of acceptance predicting social functioning over time. *Child Development, 79*, 720–731.

McElwain, N., Olson, S. L., & Volling, B. (2002). Concurrent and longitudinal associations among preschool boys' conflict management, disruptive behavior, and peer rejection. *Early Education and Development, 13*, 245–263.

McElwain, N. L., Booth-LaForce, C., Lansford, J. E., Wu, X., & Dyer, W. J. (2008). A process model of attachment-friend linkages: Hostile attribution biases, language ability, and mother-child affective mutuality as intervening mechanisms. *Child Development, 79*, 1891–1906.

McEvoy, A., & Welker, R. (2000). Antisocial behavior, academic failure, and school climate: A critical review. *Journal of Emotional and Behavioral Disorders, 8*, 130–140.

McGinley, W., & Kamberellis, G. (1996). Maniac Magee and Ragtime Tumpie: Children negotiating self and world through reading and writing. *Research in the Teaching of English, 30*, 75–113.

McGraw, M. (1935). *Growth: A study of Johnny and Jimmy*. New York: Appleton-Century.

McGuigan, N., & Doherty, M. (2002). The relation between hiding skill and judgment of eye direction in preschool children. *Developmental Psychology, 38*, 418–427.

McGuire, S., Manke, B., Eftekhari, A., & Dunn, J. (2000). Children's perceptions of sibling conflict during middle childhood: Issues and sibling (dis)similarity. *Social Development, 9*, 173–190.

McHale, K., & Cermak, S. (1992). Fine motor activities in elementary school: Preliminary findings and provisional implication for children with fine motor problems. *American Journal of Occupational Therapy, 46*, 898–903.

McHale, S. M., Crouter, A. C., & Tucker, C. J. (2001). Free-time activities in middle childhood: Links with adjustment in early adolescence. *Child Development, 72*, 1764–1778.

McHale, S. M., Kim, J.-Y., Dotterer, A. M., Crouter, A. C., & Booth, A. (2009). The development of gendered interests and personality qualities from middle childhood through adolescence: A biosocial analysis. *Child Development, 80*, 482–495.

McKown, C., & Strambler, M. J. (2009). Developmental antecedents and social and academic consequences of stereotype-consciousness in middle childhood. *Child Development, 80*, 1643–1659.

McKown, C., & Weinstein, R. S. (2003). The development and consequences of stereotype consciousness in middle childhood. *Child Development, 74*, 498–515.

McKown, C., & Weinstein, R. S. (2008). Teacher expectations, classroom context, and the achievement gap. *Journal of School Psychology, 46*, 235–261.

McLaughlin, A., Campbell, F., Pungello, E., & Skinner, M. (2007). Depressive symptoms in young adults: The influences of the early home environment and early educational child care. *Child Development, 78*, 746–756.

McMillen, B. (2001). A statewide evaluation of academic achievement in year-round schools. *Journal of Educational Research, 95*, 67–74.

McNeely, C., Nonnemaker, J., & Blum, R. (2002). Promoting school connectedness: Evidence from the National Longitudinal Study of Adolescent Health. *Journal of School Health, 72*, 138–146.

McNeil, N., & Alibali, M. (2005). Why won't you change your mind? Knowledge of operational patterns hinders learning and performance on equations. *Child Development, 76*, 883–899.

McPhail, J. C., Pierson, J. M., Freeman, J. G., Goodman, J., & Ayappa, A. (2000). The role of interest in fostering sixth grade students' identities as competent learners. *Curriculum Inquiry, 30*, 43–70.

Meador, E. (2005). The making of marginality: Schooling for Mexican immigrant girls in the rural Southwest. *Anthropology and Education Quarterly, 36*, 149–164.

Medved, M. (1995, October). Hollywood's three big lies. *Readers' Digest*, 156–157.

Meehan, B., Hughes, J., & Cavell, T. (2003). Teacher–student relationships as compensatory resources for aggressive children. *Child Development, 74*, 1145–1157.

Meier, A. M. (2007). Adolescent first sex and subsequent mental health. *American Journal of Sociology, 112*, 1811–1847.

Meins, E., Fernyhough, C., Wainwright, R., Clark-Carter, D., Das Gupta, M., Fradley, E., et al. (2003). Pathways to understanding mind: Construct validity and predictive validity of maternal mind-mindedness. *Child Development, 74*, 1194–1211.

Melnick, M., Miller, K., Sabo, D., Farrell, M., & Barnes, G. (2001). Tobacco use among high school athletes and nonathletes: Results of the 1997 Youth Risk Behavior Survey. *Adolescence, 36*, e8.

Mendle, J., Harden, K. P., Turkheimer, E., Van Hulle, C. A., D'Onofrio, B. M., Brooks-Gunn, J., et al. (2009). Associations between father absence and age of first sexual intercourse. *Child Development, 80*, 1463–1480.

Merino, B. J., & Hammond, L. (2002). Writing to learn: Science in the upper-elementary bilingual classroom. In M. J. Schleppegrell & M. C. Colombi (Eds.), *Developing advanced literacy in first and second languages* (pp. 227–243). Mahwah, NJ: Erlbaum.

Meyer, G. J., Finn, S. E., Eyde, L. D., Kay, G. G., Moreland, K. L., Dies, R. R., et al. (2001). Psychological testing and psychological assessment. *American Psychologist, 56*, 128–165.

Meyers, A., Sampson, A., Weitzman, M., Rogers, B., & Kayne, H. (1989). School breakfast program and school performance. *American Journal of Diseases of Children, 143*, 1234–1239.

Mialky, E., Vagnoni, J., & Rutstein, R. (2001). School-age children with perinatally acquired HIV infection: Medical and psychosocial issues in a Philadelphia cohort. *AIDS Patient Care and STDs, 15*, 575–579.

Michalik, N. M., Eisenberg, N., Spinrad, T. L., Ladd, B., Thompson, M., & Valiente, C. (2007). Longitudinal relations among parental emotional expressivity and sympathy and prosocial behavior in adolescence. *Social Development, 16*, 286–309.

Michiels, D., Grietens, H., Onghena, P., & Kuppens, S. (2008). Parent-child interactions and relational aggression in peer relationships. *Developmental Review, 28*, 522–540.

Middleton, J. A. (1995). A study of intrinsic motivation in the mathematics classroom: A personal constructs approach. *Journal for Research in Mathematics Education, 26*, 254–279.

Mikulineer, M., & Shaver, P. (2005). Attachment security, compassion, and altruism. *Current Directions in Psychological Science, 14*, 34–38.

Milan, S., Snow, S., & Belay, S. (2009). Depressive symptoms in mothers and children: Preschool attachment as a moderator of risk. *Developmental Psychology, 45*, 1019–1033.

Miles, S., & Stipek, D. (2006). Contemporaneous and longitudinal associations between social behavior and literacy achievement in a sample of low-income elementary school children. *Child Development, 77*, 103–117.

Miller, A. (1990). *The day care dilemma: Critical concerns for American families.* New York: Plenum.

Miller, B., Bayley, B., Christensen, M., Leavitt, S., & Coyl, D. (2003). Adolescent pregnancy and childbearing. In G. Adams & M. Berzonsky (Eds.), *Blackwell handbook on adolescence* (pp. 415–449). Malden, MA: Blackwell.

Miller, C. F., Trautner, H. M., & Ruble, D. N. (2006). The role of gender stereotypes in children's preferences and behavior. In L. Balter & C. Tamis-LeMonda (Eds.), *Child psychology: A handbook of contemporary issues* (2nd ed., pp. 293–323). New York: Psychology Press.

Miller, G. A. (1956). The magical number seven, plus or minus two: Some limits on our capacity for processing information. *Psychological Review, 63*, 81–97.

Miller, P., Danaher, D., & Forbes, D. (1986). Sex-related strategies for coping with interpersonal conflict in children aged five and seven. *Developmental Psychology, 22*, 543–548.

Milligan, K., Astington, J. W., & Dack, L. A. (2007). Language and theory of mind: Meta-analysis of the relation between language ability and false-belief understanding. *Child Development, 78*, 622–646.

Mills, R. S. L., & Grusec, J. E. (1989). Cognitive, affective, and behavioral consequences of praising altruism. *Merrill-Palmer Quarterly, 35*, 299–326.

Minde, K. (2002). Sleep disorder in infants and young children. In M. Maldonado-Duran (Ed.), *Infant and toddler mental health* (pp. 269–307). Washington DC: American Psychiatric Publishing.

Mischel, W. (1996). From good intentions to willpower. In P. M. Gollwitzer & J. A. Bargh (Eds.), *The psychology of action: linking cognition and motivation to behavior* (pp. 197–218). New York: Guilford.

Mischel, W., Shoda, Y., & Mendoza-Denton, R. (2002). Situation-behavior profiles as a locus of consistency in personality. *Current Directions in Psychological Science, 11*, 50–54.

Mischel, W., Shoda, Y., & Rodriguez, M. L. (1989). Delay of gratification in children. *Science, 244*, 933–938.

Mitchell-Copeland, J., Denham, S., & DeMulder, E. (1997). Q-sort assessment of child–teacher attachment relationships and social competence in the preschool. *Early Education and Development, 8*, 27–39.

Moely, B. E., Hart, S. S., Leal, L., Santulli, K. A., Rao, N., Johnson, T., et al. (1992). The teacher's role in facilitating memory and study strategy development in the elementary school classroom. *Child Development, 63*, 653–672.

Moffitt, T. (2005). The new look of behavioral genetics in developmental psychopathology: Gene–environment interplay in antisocial behaviors. *Psychological Bulletin, 131*, 533–554.

Moje, E. B. (1996). "I teach students, not subjects": Teacher-student relationships as contexts for secondary literacy. *Reading Research Quarterly, 31*, 172–195.

Moje, E. B. (2000). "To be part of the story": The literacy practices of gangsta adolescents. *Teachers College Record, 102*, 651–690.

Mokdad, A., Marks, J., Stroup, D., & Gerberding, J. (2004). Actual causes of death in the United States, 2000. *JAMA, 291*, 1238–1245.

Mol, S. E., Bus, A. G., & de Jong, M. T. (2009). Interactive book reading in early education: A tool to stimulate print knowledge as well as oral language. *Review of Educational Research, 79*, 979–1007.

Molina, B. S., Hinshaw, S. P., Swanson, J. M., Arnold, L. E., Vitiello, B., Jensen, P. S., et al. (2009). The MTA at 8 years: Prospective follow-up of children treated for combined-type ADHD in a multisite study. *The Journal of the American Academy of Child and Adolescent Psychiatry, 48*, 484–500.

Moller, K. J., & Allen, J. (2000). Connecting, resisting, and searching for safer places: Students respond to Mildred Taylor's *The Friendship*. *Journal of Literacy Research, 32*, 145–186.

Mondloch, C., Lewis, T., Budreau, R., Maurer, D., Dannemiller, J., Stephens, B., et al. (1999) Face perception during early infancy. *Psychological Science, 10*, 419–422.

Monroe, S. M., & Reid, M. W. (2008). Gene–environment interactions in depression research: Genetic polymorphisms and life-stress polyprocedures. *Psychological Science, 19*, 947–956.

Monzó, L. D., & Rueda, R. (2009). Passing for English fluent: Latino immigrant children masking language proficiency. *Anthropology & Education Quarterly, 40*, 20–40.

Mooij, T. (1999). Promoting prosocial pupil behavior: 2. Secondary school intervention and pupil effects. *British Journal of Educational Psychology, 69*, 479–504.

Moon, R. Y., Patel, K. M., & McDermott Shaefer, S. J. (2000). Sudden Infant Death Syndrome in child care settings. *Pediatrics, 106*, 295–300.

Moore, C. (2008). The development of gaze following. *Child Development Perspectives, 2*, 66–70.

Moore, D. S., & Johnson, S. P. (2008). Mental rotation in human infants: A sex difference. *Psychological Science, 19*, 1063–1070.

Morgan, B., Maybery, M., & Durkin, K. (2003). Weak central coherence, poor joint attention, and low verbal ability: Independent deficits in early autism. *Developmental Psychology, 39*, 646–656.

Morland, K., Wing, S., Diez Roux, A., & Poole, C. (2002). Neighborhood characteristics associated with the location of food stores and food service places. *American Journal of Preventive Medicine, 22*, 23–29.

Morrell, J., & Murray, L. (2003). Parenting and the development of conduct disorder and hyperactive symptoms in childhood: A prospective longitudinal study from 2 months to 8 years. *Journal of Child Psychology & Psychiatry & Allied Disciplines, 44*, 489–508.

Morris, A. S., Silk, J. S., Steinberg, L., Myers, S. S., & Robinson, L. R. (2007). The role of the family context in the development of emotion regulation. *Social Development, 16*, 361–388.

Morrison, F., Griffith, E., & Alberts, D. (1997). Nature-nurture in the classroom: Entrance age, school readiness, and learning in children. *Developmental Psychology, 33*, 254–262.

Morrow, J., Jackson, A., & Payne, G. (1999). Physical activity promotion and school physical education. *Research Digest: President's Council on Physical Fitness and Sports*. Retrieved January 8, 2010, from http://fitness.gov/digest_sep1999.htm

Mortensen, E., Michaelsen, K., Sanders, S., & Reinisch, J. (2002). The association between duration of breastfeeding and adult intelligence. *JAMA, 287*, 2365–2371.

Mortimore, P., Sammons, P., Stoll, L., Lewis, D., & Ecob, R. (1988). *School matters*. Berkeley: University of California Press.

Moshman, D. (1998). Cognitive development beyond childhood. In D. Kuhn & R. Siegler (Eds.), *Handbook of child psychology: Cognition, perception, and language* (5th ed., Vol. 2, pp. 947–978). New York: Wiley.

Moss, E., & St-Laurent, D. (2001). Attachment at school age and academic performance. *Developmental Psychology, 37*, 863–874.

Mounts, N. (2001). Young adolescents' perceptions of parental management of peer relationships. *Journal of Early Adolescence, 21*, 92–122.

Mouton, S., Hawkins, J., McPherson, R., & Copley, J. (1996). School attachment: Perspectives of low-attached high school students. *Educational Psychology, 16*, 297–304.

Muller, C. (1995). Maternal employment, parent involvement, and mathematics achievement among adolescents. *Journal of Marriage and the Family, 57*, 85–100.

Mulvaney, M. K., & Mebert, C. J. (2007). Parental corporal punishment predicts behavior problems in early childhood. *Journal of Family Psychology, 21*, 389–397.

Mummer, D. L., & Fernald, A. (2003). The infant as onlooker: Learning from emotional reactions observed in a television scenario. *Child Development, 74*, 221–237.

Munday, P., Block, J., Delgado, C., Pomares, Y., Van Hecke, A. V., & Parlade, M. V. (2007). Individual differences and the development of joint attention in infancy. *Child Development, 78*, 938–954.

Murdock, T., Hale, N., & Weber, M. J. (2001). Predictors of cheating among early adolescents: Academic and social motivations. *Contemporary Educational Psychology, 26*, 96–115.

Murphy, K., & Schneider, B. (1994). Coaching socially rejected early adolescents regarding behaviors used by peers to infer liking: A dyad-specific intervention. *Journal of Early Adolescence, 14*, 83–95.

Murphy, P. K., Wilkinson, I. A. G., Soter, A. O., Hennessey, M. N., & Alexander, J. F. (2009). Examining the effects of classroom discussion on students' comprehension of text: A meta-analysis. *Journal of Educational Psychology, 101*, 740–764.

Murray, J. P. (2007). TV violence: Research and controversy. In N. Pecora, J. P. Murray & E. A. Wartella (Eds.), *Children and television: Fifty years of research*. Mahwah, NJ: Erlbaum.

Murray, L., de Rosnay, M., Pearson, J., Bergeron, C., Schofield, E., Royal-Lawson, M., et al. (2008). Intergenerational transmission of social anxiety: The role of social referencing processes in infancy. *Child Development, 79*, 1049–1064.

Murray-Close, D., Crick, N. R., & Galotti, K. (2006). Children's moral reasoning regarding physical and relational aggression. *Social Development, 15*, 345–372.

Murry, V. M., Berkel, C., Brody, G. H., Miller, S. J., & Chen, Y.-F. (2009). Linking parental socialization to interpersonal protective processes, academic self-presentation, and expectations among rural African American youth. *Cultural Diversity and Ethnic Minority Psychology, 15*, 1–10.

Mussen, P., & Eisenberg, N. (2001). Prosocial development in context. In A. Bohart & D. Stipek (Eds.), *Constructive and destructive behavior: Implications for family, school, and society* (pp. 103–126). Washington, DC: APA.

Mustanski, B., Chivers, M., & Bailey, M. (2002). A critical review of recent biological research on human sexual orientation. *Annual Review of Sex Research, 13*, 89–140.

Mustanski, B., DuPree, M., Nievergelt, C., Bocklandt, S., Schork, N., & Hamer, D. (2005). A genomewide scan of male sexual orientation. *Human Genetics, 116*, 272–278.

Nachmias, M., Gunnar, M., Mangelsdorf, S., Parritz, R. H., & Buss, K. (1996). Behavioral inhibition and stress reactivity: The moderating role of attachment security. *Child Development, 67*, 508–522.

NAEYC. (2009). Position statement: Developmentally appropriate practice in early childhood programs serving children from birth through age 8. Retrieved October 15, 2009, from NAEYC.org

Nansel, T., Overpeck, M., Pilla, R., Ruan, J., Simons-Morton, B., & Scheidt, P. (2001). Bullying behaviors among US youth: Prevalence and association with psychosocial adjustment. *JAMA, 285*, 2094–2100.

Narusyte, J., Neiderhiser, J. M., D'Onofrio, B. M., Reiss, D., Spotts, E. L., Ganiban, J. M., et al. (2008). Testing different types of genotype–environment correlation: An extended children-of-twins model. *Developmental Psychology, 44*, 1591–1603.

Narvaez, D. (2002). Does reading moral stories build character? *Educational Psychology Review, 14*, 155–171.

National Institute of Mental Health. (2008). *Attention Deficit Hyperactivity Disorder NIH Publication No. 08-3572*. Washington, DC.

National Mathematics Advisory Panel. (2008). *Foundations for success: The final report of the National Mathematics Advisory Panel*. Washington, DC: U. S. Department of Education.

National Reading Panel. (2000). *Teaching children to read: An evidence-based assessment of the scientific research literature on reading and its implications for reading instruction*. Washington, DC: U.S. Government Printing Office.

Natsuaki, M. N., Ge, X., Reiss, D., & Neiderhiser, J. M. (2009). Aggressive behavior between siblings and the development of externalizing problems: Evidence from a genetically sensitive study. *Developmental Psychology, 45*, 1009–1018.

Naylor, A., Gardner, D., & Zaichkowsky, L. (2001). Drug use patterns among high school athletes and nonathletes. *Adolescence, 36*, e1.

NCES. (2010). *National Assessment of Educational Progress*, from http://nationsreportcard.gov/

Neisser, U., Boodoo, G., Bouchard, T. J. J., Boykin, A. W., Brody, N., Ceci, S. J., et al. (1996). Intelligence: Knowns and unknowns. *American Psychologist, 51*, 77–101.

Neisser, U., & Marian, V. (2000). Language-dependent recall of autobiographical memories. *Journal of Experimental Psychology: General, 129*, 361–368.

Nelson, C. A. (1999). Neural plasticity and human development. *Current Directions in Psychological Science, 8*, 42–45.

Nelson, C. A. (2007). A neurobiological perspective on early human deprivation. *Child Development Perspectives, 1*, 13–18.

Nelson, C. A., Monk, C., Lin, J., Carver, L., Thomas, K., & Truwit, C. (2000). Functional neuroanatomy of spatial working memory in children. *Developmental Psychology, 36*, 100–116.

Nelson, D. A., Hart, C. H., Yang, C., Olsen, J. A., & Jin, S. (2006). Aversive parenting in China: Association with child physical and relational aggression. *Child Development, 77*, 554–572.

Nesdale, D., Maass, A., Durkin, K., & Griffiths, J. (2005). Group norms, threat, and children's racial prejudice. *Child Development, 76*, 652–663.

Newcombe, N. (2002). The nativist-empiricist controversy in the context of recent research on spatial and quantitative development. *Psychological Science, 13*, 395–401.

Newman, R., Murray, B., & Lussier, C. (2001). Confrontation with aggressive peers at school: Students' reluctance to seek help from the teacher. *Journal of Educational Psychology, 93*, 398–410.

Newman, R. S. (2008). Adaptive and nonadaptive help seeking with peer harassment: An integrative perspective of coping and self-regulation. *Educational Psychologist, 43*, 1–15.

Newton, P., Vasudevi, R., & Bull, R. (2000). Children's everyday deception and performance of false-belief tasks. *British Journal of Developmental Psychology, 18*, 297–317.

NICHD Early Child Care Research Network. (1997). The effects of infant child care on infant-mother attachment security: Results of the NICHD study of early child care. *Child Development, 68*, 860–879.

NICHD Early Child Care Research Network. (1998a). Early child care and self-control, compliance, and problem behavior at twenty-four and thirty-six months. *Child Development, 69*, 1145–1170.

NICHD Early Child Care Research Network. (1998b). Relations between family predictors and child outcomes: Are they weaker for children in child care? *Child Development, 34*, 1119–1128.

NICHD Early Child Care Research Network. (1999). Chronicity of maternal depressive symptoms, maternal sensitivity, and child functioning at 36 months. *Developmental Psychology, 35*, 1297–1310.

NICHD Early Child Care Research Network. (2000a). Does quality of child care affect child outcomes at age 4 1/2? *Child Development, 39*, 451–469.

NICHD Early Child Care Research Network. (2000b). The relation of child care to cognitive and language development. *Child Development, 71*, 960–980.

NICHD Early Child Care Research Network. (2001a). Child care and children's peer interaction at 24 and 36 months: The NICHD study of early child care. *Child Development, 72*, 1478–1500.

NICHD Early Child Care Research Network. (2001b). Child-care and family predictors of preschool attachment and stability from infancy. *Developmental Psychology, 37*, 847–862.

NICHD Early Child Care Research Network. (2002). The relation of global first-grade environment to structural classroom features and teacher and student behaviors. *Elementary School Journal, 102*, 367–387.

NICHD Early Child Care Research Network. (2003a). Does amount of time spent in child care predict socioemotional adjustment during the transiiton to kindergarten? *Child Development, 74*, 976–1005.

NICHD Early Child Care Research Network. (2003b). Frequency and intensity of activity in third-grade children in physical education. *Archives of Pediatrics & Adolescent Medicine, 157*, 185–190.

NICHD Early Child Care Research Network. (2004). Are child developmental outcomes related to before- and after-school care arrangements? Results from the NICHD Study of Early Child Care. *Child Development, 75*, 280–295.

NICHD Early Child Care Research Network. (2005a). Early child care and children's development in the primary grades: Follow-up results from the NICHD Study of Early Child Care. *American Educational Research Journal, 42*, 537–570.

NICHD Early Child Care Research Network. (2005b). Predicting individual differences in attention, memory, and planning in first graders from experiences at home, child care, and school. *Developmental Psychology, 41*, 99–114.

NICHD Early Child Care Research Network. (2006a). Child-care effect sizes for the NICHD study of early child care and youth development. *American Psychologist, 61*, 99–116.

NICHD Early Child Care Research Network. (2006b). Infant–mother attachment classification: Risk and protection in relation to changing maternal caregiving quality. *Developmental Psychology, 42*, 38–58.

NICHD Early Child Care Research Network, & Duncan, G. (2003). Modeling the impacts of child care quality on children's preschool cognitive development. *Child Development, 74*, 1454–1475.

Nicholls, J. G. (1989). *The competitive ethos and democratic education*. Cambridge, MA: Harvard University Press.

Nickerson, A., Mele, D., & Princiotta, D. (2008). Attachment and empathy as predictors of roles as defenders or outsiders in bullying interactions. *Journal of School Psychology, 46*, 687–703.

Nielsen, M., Suddendorf, T., & Slaughter, V. (2006). Mirror self-recognition beyond the face. *Child Development, 77*, 176–185.

Nielsen, S., & Popkin, B. (2003). Patterns and trends in food portion sizes, 1977–1998. *JAMA, 289*, 450–453.

Nieto, S. (2000). *Affirming diversity: The sociopolitical context of multicultural education* (3rd ed.). White Plains, NY: Longman.

Nievar, M. A., & Becker, B. J. (2007). Sensitivity as a privileged predictor of attachment: A second perspective on De Wolff and van IJzendoorn's meta-analysis. *Social Development, 17*, 102–114.

Ninio, A. (2006). *Language and the learning curve: A new theory of syntactic development*. Oxford: Oxford University Press.

Nippold, M. A., Duthie, J. K., & Larsen, J. T. (2005). Literacy as a leisure activity: Free-time preferences of older children and young adolescents. *Language, Speech, and Hearing Services in Schools, 36*, 93–102.

Nippold, M. A., Hesketh, L. J., Duthie, J. K., & Mansfield, T. C. (2005). Conversational versus expository discourse: A study of syntactic development in children, adolescents, and adults. *Journal of Speech, Language and Hearing Research, 48*, 1048–1064.

Nippold, M. A., Ward-Lonergan, J. M., & Fanning, J. L. (2005). Persuasive writing in children, adolescents, and adults: A study of syntactic, semantic, and pragmatic development. *Language, Speech, and Hearing Services in Schools, 36*, 125–138.

Nisbett, R. E. (2003). *The geography of thought: How Asians and Westerners think differently, and why*. New York: Free Press.

Nishina, A., & Juvonen, J. (2005). Daily reports of witnessing and experiencing peer harassment in middle school. *Child Development, 76*, 435–450.

Noddings, N. (1992). *The challenge to care in schools: An alternative approach to education*. New York: Teachers College Press.

Noël, M.-P. (2009). Counting on working memory when learning to count and to add: A preschool study. *Developmental Psychology, 45*, 1630–1643.

Noftle, E. E., & Robins, R. W. (2007). Personality predictors of academic outcomes: Big Five correlates of GPA and SAT scores. *Journal of Personality and Social Psychology, 93*, 116–130.

Nokes, J. D., Dole, J. A., & Hacker, D. J. (2007). Teaching high school students to use heuristics while reading historical texts. *Journal of Educational Psychology, 99*, 492–504.

Nolen-Hoeksema, S., Wisco, B., & Lyubomirsky, S. (2008). Rethinking rumination. *Perspectives on Psychological Science, 3*, 400–424.

Normandeau, S., & Gobeil, A. (1998). A developmental perspective on children's understanding of causal attributions in achievement-related situations. *International Journal of Behavioral Development, 22*, 611–632.

Northcutt, W. (2000). *The Darwin Awards*. New York: Dutton.

Nowakowski, R. S., & Hayes, N. L. (2002). General principles of CNS development. In M. H. Johnson, Y. Munakata & R. O. Gilmore (Eds.), *Brain development and cognition: A reader* (2nd ed., pp. 57–82). Malden, MA: Blackwell.

Nowicki, S., & Duke, M. P. (1992). The association of children's nonverbal decoding abilities with their popularity, locus of control, and academic achievement. *Journal of Genetic Psychology, 153*, 385–393.

Nuthall, G. (2000). The anatomy of memory in the classroom: Understanding how students acquire memory processes from classroom activities in science and social studies units. *American Educational Research Journal, 37*, 247–304.

Nye, B., Hedges, L. V., & Konstantopoulos, S. (2001). Are effects of small classes cumulative? Evidence from a Tennessee experiment. *Journal of Educational Research, 94*, 336–345.

Nylund, K., Bellmore, A., Nishina, a., & Graham, S. (2007). Subtypes, severity, and structural stability of peer victimization: What does latent class analysis say? *Child Development, 78*, 1706–1722.

O'Connor, C., & Fernandez, S. D. (2006). Race, class, and disproportionality: Reevaluating the relationship between poverty and special education placement. *Educational Researcher, 35*, 6–11.

O'Connor, E., & McCartney, K. (2007). Examining teacher–child relationships and achievement as part of an ecological model of development. *American Educational Research Journal, 44*, 340–369.

O'Connor, T., Rutter, M., Beckett, C., Keaveney, L., Kreppner, J., & English and Romanian Adoptees Study Team. (2000). The effects of global severe privation on cognitive competence: Extension and longitudinal follow-up. *Child Development, 71*, 376–390.

O'Neil, J. (2004, December 29). Slow-motion miracle: One boy's journey out of autism's grasp, *The New York Times*.

Oakland, T., Mogaji, A., & Dempsey, J. (2006). Temperament styles of Nigerian and U.S. children. *Journal of Psychology in Africa, 1*, 27–34.

Odegard, T. N., Cooper, C. M., Lampinen, J. M., Reyna, V. F., & Brainerd, C. J. (2009). Children's eyewitness memory for multiple real-life events. *Child Development, 80*, 1877–1890.

Odgers, C. L., Caspi, A., Nagin, D. S., Piquero, A. R., Slutske, W. S., Milne, B. J., et al. (2008). Is it important to prevent early exposure to drugs and alcohol among adolescents? *Psychological Science, 19*, 1035–1044.

Odgers, C. L., Moffitt, T. E., Tach, L. M., Sampson, R. J., Taylor, A., Matthews, C. L., et al. (2009). The protective effects of neighborhood collective efficacy on British children growing up in deprivation: A developmental analysis. *Developmental Psychology, 45*, 942–957.

OECD. (2004). Learning for tomorrow's world: First results from PISA 2003. Retrieved January 10, 2010, from http://www.pisa.oecd.org.

Offord, D. R., Boyle, M. H., & Racine, Y. A. (1991). The epidemiology of antisocial behavior in childhood and adolescence. In D. J. Pepler & K. H. Rubin (Eds.), *The development and treatment of childhood aggression* (pp. 31–54). Hillsdale, NJ: Erlbaum.

Ogbu, J. U., & Simons, H. D. (1998). Voluntary and involuntary minorities: A cultural-ecological theory of school performance with some implications for education. *Anthropology & Education Quarterly, 29*, 155–188.

Ogden, C. L., Carroll, M. D., Curtin, L. R., McDowell, M. A., Tabak, C. J., & Flegal, K. M. (2006). Prevalence of overweight and obesity in the United States, 1999–2004. *JAMA, 295*, 1549–1555.

Ogden, D. C., & Hilt, M. L. (2003). Collective identity and basketball: An explanation for the decreasing number of African-Americans on America's baseball diamonds. *Journal of Leisure Research, 35*, 213–227.

Ohayon, M., Carskadon, M. A., Guilleminault, C., & Vitiello, M. V. (2004). Meta-analysis of quantitative sleep parameters from childhood to old age in healthy individuals: Developing normative sleep values across the human lifespan. *Sleep Medicine Reviews, 27*, 1255–1273.

Ojanen, T., Gronroos, M., & Salmivallie, C. (2005). An interpersonal circumplex model of children's social goals: Links with peer-reported behavior and sociometric status. *Developmental Psychology, 41*, 699–710.

Okagaki, L., & Sternberg, R. J. (1993). Parental beliefs and children's school performance. *Child Development, 64*, 36–56.

Oliver, B. R., Dale, P. S., & Plomin, R. (2005). Predicting literacy at age 7 from preliteracy at age 4: A longitudinal genetic analysis. *Psychological Science, 16*, 861–865.

Ollendick, T., & Schroeder, C. (2003). *Encyclopedia of clinical child and pediatric psychology*. New York: Kluwer Academic.

Olweus, D. (1994). Bullying at school: Basic facts and effects of a school-based intervention program. *Journal of Child Psychology & Psychiatry & Allied Disciplines, 35*, 1171–1190.

Orfield, G., Losen, D., Wald, J., & Swanson, C. B. (2004). *Losing our future: How minority youth are being left behind by the graduation rate crisis*. Cambridge, MA: Civil Rights Project at Harvard. Available at http://www.urban.org/publications/410936.html

Orme, J., & Buehler, C. (2001). Foster family characteristics and behavioral and emotional problems of foster children: A narrative review. *Family Relations, 50*, 3–15.

Orth, U., Robins, R. W., & Meier, L. L. (2009). Disentangling the effects of low self-esteem and stressful events on depression: Findings from three longitudinal studies. *Journal of Personality and Social Psychology, 97*, 307–321.

Osterman, K. (2000). Students' need for belonging in the school community. *Review of Educational Research, 70*, 323–367.

Oswald, D. P., Best, A. M., Coutinho, M. J., & Nagle, H. A. L. (2003). Trends in the special education identification rates of boys and girls: A call for research and change. *Exceptionality, 11*, 223–237.

Overskeid, G. (2007). Looking for Skinner and finding Freud. *American Psychologist, 62*, 590–595.

Owens, J., Maxim, R., McGuinn, M., Nobile, C., Msall, M., & Alario, A. (1999). Television-viewing habits and sleep disturbance in school children. *Pediatrics, 104*, 1–8.

Oyserman, D., Brickman, D., & Rhodes, M. (2007). School success, possible selves, and parent school involvement. *Family Relations, 56*, 479–489.

Paciello, N., Fida, R., Tramontano, C., Lupinetti, C., & Caprara, G. V. (2008). Stability and change of moral disengagement and its impact on aggression and violence in late adolescence. *Child Development, 79*, 1288–1309.

Pagani, L., Boulerice, B., Vitaro, F., & Tremblay, R. E. (1999). Effects of poverty on academic failure and delinquency in boys: A change and process approach. *Journal of Child Psychology & Psychiatry & Allied Disciplines, 40*, 1209–1219.

Pagani, L., Tremblay, R. E., Vitaro, F., Boulerice, B., & McDuff, P. (2001). Effects of grade retention on academic performance and behavioral development. *Development and Psychopathology, 13*, 297–315.

Page-Voth, V., & Graham, S. (1999). Effects of goal setting and strategy use on the writing performance and self-efficacy of students with writing and learning problems. *Journal of Educational Psychology, 91*, 230–240.

Palacios, N., Guttmannova, K., & Chase-Lansdale, P. L. (2008). Early reading achievement of children in immigrant families: Is there an immigrant paradox? *Developmental Psychology, 44*, 1381–1395.

Palincsar, A. S. (1998). Social constructivist perspectives on teaching and learning. *Annual Review of Psychology, 49*, 345–375.

Palincsar, A. S., & Brown, A. L. (1984). Reciprocal teaching of comprehension-fostering and comprehension-monitoring activities. *Cognition and Instruction, 1,* 117–175.

Pan, B. A., Rowe, M. L., Singer, J. D., & Snow, C. E. (2005). Maternal correlates of growth in toddler vocabulary production in low-income families. *Child Development, 76,* 763–782.

Panksepp, J. (1998). Attention deficit hyperactivity disorders, psychostimulants, and intolerance of childhood playfulness: A tragedy in the making? *Current Directions in Psychological Science, 7,* 91–98.

Panksepp, J. (2000). The riddle of laughter: Neural and psychoevolutionary underpinnings of joy. *Current Directions in Psychological Science, 9,* 183–186.

Pape, L., & Ryba, K. (2004). *Practical considerations for school-based occupational therapists.* Bethesda, MD: AOTA Press.

Park, G., Lubinski, D., & Benbow, C. P. (2007). Contrasting intellectual patterns predict creativity in the arts and sciences. *Psychological Science, 18,* 948–952.

Park, G., Lubinski, D., & Benbow, C. P. (2008). Ability differences among people who have commensurate degrees matter for scientific creativity. *Psychological Science, 19,* 957–961.

Parker, J. G., & Asher, S. R. (1993). Friendship and friendship quality in middle childhood: Links with peer group acceptance and feelings of loneliness and social dissatisfaction. *Developmental Psychology, 29,* 611–621.

Pasterski, V., Geffner, M., Brain, C., Hindmarsh, P., Brook, C., & Hines, M. (2005). Prenatal hormones and postnatal socialization by parents as determinants of male-typical toy play in girls with congenital adrenal hyperplasia. *Child Development, 76,* 264–278.

Patall, E. A., Cooper, H., & Robinson, J. C. (2008). Parent involvement in homework: A research synthesis. *Review of Educational Research, 78,* 1039–1101.

Patrick, E., & Abravanel, E. (2000). The self-regulatory nature of preschool children's private speech in a naturalistic setting. *Applied Psycholinguistics, 21,* 45–61.

Patterson, C. J. (1992). Children of lesbian and gay parents. *Child Development, 63,* 1025–1042.

Patterson, C. J. (1996). Lesbian and gay parents and their children. In R. Savin-Williams & K. Cohen (Eds.), *The lives of lesbians, gays, and bisexuals: Children to adults* (pp. 274–304). Ft. Worth, TX: Harcourt Brace.

Patterson, C. J. (2009). Children of lesbian and gay parents: Psychology, law, and policy. *American Psychologist, 54,* 727–736.

Patterson, C. J., Vaden, N., & Kupersmidt, J. B. (1991). Family background, recent life events and peer rejection during childhood. *Journal of Social and Personal Relationships, 8,* 347–361.

Patterson, G. R., & Bank, C. L. (1989). Some amplifying mechanisms for pathologic processes in families. In M. Gunnar & E. Thelen (Eds.), *Systems and development: Symposia on child psychology* (pp. 167–210). Hillsdale, NJ: Erlbaum.

Patterson, G. R., DeBaryshe, B., & Ramsey, E. (1989). A developmental perspective on antisocial behavior. *American Psychologist, 44,* 329–355.

Pauli-Pott, U., Haverkock, A., Pott, W., & Beckmann, D. (2007). Negative emotionality, attachment quality, and behavior problems in early childhood. *Infant Mental Health Journal, 28,* 39–53.

Paulussen-Hoogeboom, M. C., Stams, G. J., Hermanns, J. M., & Peetsma, T. T. (2007). Child negative emotionality and parenting from infancy to preschool: A meta-analytic review. *Developmental Psychology, 43,* 438–453.

Paus, T. (2005). Mapping brain maturation and cognitive development during adolescence. *Trends in Cognitive Sciences, 9,* 60–68.

Payne, V., & Issacs, L. (1994). *Human motor development: A life-span approach* (2nd ed.). Mountain View, CA: Mayfield.

Pearce, M., Jones, S., Schwab-Stone, M., & Ruchkin, V. (2003). The protective effects of religiousness and parent involvement on the development of conduct problems among youth exposed to violence. *Child Development, 74,* 1682–1696.

Pedersen, S., Vitaro, F., Barker, E. D., & Borge, A. I. H. (2007). The timing of middle-childhood peer rejection and friendship: Linking early behavior to early-adolescent adjustment. *Child Development, 78,* 1037–1051.

Pedro-Carroll, J. L. (2005). Fostering resilience in the aftermath of divorce: The role of evidence-based programs for children. *Family Court Review, 52,* 52–64.

Peisner-Feinberg, E., Burchinal, M., Clifford, R., Culkin, M., Howes, C., Kagan, S., et al. (2001). The relation of preschool child-care quality to children's cognitive and social developmental trajectories through second grade. *Child Development, 72,* 1534–1553.

Pellegrini, A. D. (2002). Rough-and-tumble play from childhood through adolescence: Development and possible functions. In P. Smith & C. Hart (Eds.), *Blackwell handbook of childhood social development* (pp. 438–453). Oxford: Blackwell.

Pellegrini, A. D. (2003). Perceptions and functions of play and real fighting in early adolescence. *Child Development, 74,* 1522–1533.

Pellegrini, A. D., & Bartini, M. (2000). An empirical comparison of methods of sampling aggression and victimization in school settings. *Educational Psychology, 92,* 360–366.

Pellegrini, A. D., & Bjorklund, D. F. (1997). The role of recess in children's cognitive performance. *Educational Psychologist, 32,* 35–40.

Pellegrini, A. D., Blatchford, P., Kato, K., & Baines, E. (2004). A short-term longitudinal study of children's playground games in primary school: Implications for adjustment to school and social adjustment in the USA and the UK. *Social Development, 13,* 107–123.

Pellegrini, A. D., & Bohn, C. (2005). The role of recess in children's cognitive performance and school adjustment, *Educational Researcher, 34*(1), 13–19.

Pellegrini, A. D., Galda, L., Bartini, M., & Charak, D. (1998). Oral language and literacy learning in context: The role of social relationships. *Merrill-Palmer Quarterly, 44,* 38–54.

Pellegrini, A. D., & Smith, P. (1998). Physical activity play: The nature and function of a neglected aspect of play. *Child Development, 69,* 577–598.

Pellicano, E. (2007). Links between theory of mind and executive function in young children with autism: Clues to developmental primacy. *Developmental Psychology, 43,* 974–990.

Pelucchi, B., Hay, J. F., & Saffran, J. R. (2009). Statistical learning in a natural language by 8-month-old infants. *Child Development, 80,* 674–685.

Pennington, B. F., & Bishop, D. (2009). Relations among speech, language, and reading disorders. *Annual Review of Psychology, 60,* 283–306.

Pennington, B. F., McGrath, L. M., Rosenberg, J., Barnard, H., Smith, S. D., Willcutt, E. G., et al. (2009). Gene X Environment interactions in reading disability and attention-deficit/hyperactivity disorder. *Developmental Psychology, 45,* 77–89.

Penrod, B., Wallace, M. D., & Dyer, E. J. (2008). Assessing potency of high- and low-preference reinforcers with respect to response rate and response patterns. *Journal of Applied Behavior Analysis, 41,* 177–188.

Pepler, D., Jiang, D., Craig, W., & Connolly, J. (2008). Developmental trajectories of bullying and associated factors. *Child Development, 79,* 325–338.

Perkins, D., Jacobs, J., Barber, B., & Eccles, J. (2004). Childhood and adolescent sports participation as predictors of participation in sports and physical fitness activities during young adulthood. *Youth & Society, 35,* 495–520.

Perry, B. (1997). Incubated in terror: Neurodevelopmental factors in the "cycle of violence." In J. Osofsky (Ed.), *Children in a violent society.* New York: Guilford.

Perry, C. L., Komro, K., Veblen-Mortensen, S., Bosma, L., Farbakhsh, K., Munson, K., et al. (2003). A randomized controlled trial of the middle and junior high school D.A.R.E. and D.A.R.E. Plus programs. *Archives of Pediatrics & Adolescent Medicine, 157,* 178–184.

Perry, C. L., Sellers, D. E., Johnson, C., Pedersen, S., Bachman, K. J., Parcel, G. S., et al. (1997). The child and adolescent trial for cardiovascular health (CATCH): Intervention, implementation, and feasibility for elementary schools in the United States. *Health Education & Behavior, 24,* 716–735.

Peterson, C., Peterson, J., & Seeto, D. (1983). Developmental changes in ideas about lying. *Child Development, 54,* 1529–1535.

Peterson, C., Peterson, J., & Webb, J. (2000). Factors influencing the development of a theory of mind in blind children. *British Journal of Developmental Psychology, 18,* 431–447.

Petterson, S., & Albers, A. (2001). Effects of poverty and maternal depression on early child development. *Child Development, 72,* 1794–1813.

Pettigrew, T. F., & Tropp, L. R. (2006). A meta-analytic test of intergroup contact theory. *Journal of Personality and Social Psychology, 90,* 751–783.

Pettit, G. S. (2005). Violent children in developmental perspective: Risk and protective factors and the mechanisms through which they (may) operate. *Current Directions in Psychological Science, 13,* 194–197.

Pettit, G. S., Laird, R., Bates, J., & Dodge, K. (1997). Patterns of after-school care in middle childhood: Risk factors and developmental outcomes. *Merrill-Palmer Quarterly, 43,* 515–538.

Pettit, G. S., Laird, R. D., Dodge, K. A., Bates, J. E., & Criss, M. M. (2001). Antecedents and behavior-problem outcomes of parental monitoring and psychological control in early adolescence. *Child Development, 72,* 583–598.

Petts, R. J. (2009). Family and religious characteristics' influence on delinquency trajectories from adolescence to young adulthood. *American Sociological Review, 74,* 465–483.

Pew Research Center. (2007). From 1997 to 2007: Fewer mothers prefer full-time work. *A Social & Demographic Trends Report.* Retrieved 5/22/2010 from http://pewresearch.org/assets/social/pdf/WomenWorking.pdf

Pezdek, K., Berry, T., & Renno, P. A. (2002). Children's mathematics achievement: The role of parents' perceptions and their involvement in homework. *Journal of Educational Psychology, 94,* 771–777.

Pfeifer, J. H., Brown, C. S., & Juvonen, J. (2007). Prejudice reduction in schools: Teaching tolerance in schools: Lessons learned since *Brown v. Board of Education* about the development and reduction of children's prejudice. *Social Policy Report, 21,* 3–23.

Phelan, P., Davidson, A. L., & Cao, H. T. (1991). Students' multiple worlds: Negotiating the boundaries of family, peer, and school cultures. *Anthropology & Education Quarterly, 22,* 224–250.

Phillips, D., Mekos, D., Scarr, S., McCartney, K., & Abbott-Shim, M. (2000). Within and beyond the classroom door: Assessing quality in childcare centers. *Early Childhood Research Quarterly, 15,* 475–496.

Phillips, L. M., Norris, S. P., Osmond, W. C., & Maynard, A. M. (2002). Relative reading achievement: A longitudinal study of 187 children from first through sixth grades. *Journal of Educational Psychology, 94,* 3–13.

Phinney, J. S. (1989). Stages of ethnic identity development in minority group adolescents. *Journal of Early Adolescence, 9,* 34–49.

Phinney, J. S. (1996). When we talk about American ethnic groups, what do we mean? *American Psychologist, 51,* 918–927.

Piaget, J. (1926/1959). *The language and thought of the child* (M. Gabain & R. Gabain, Trans. 3rd ed.). London: Routledge & Kegan Paul.

Piaget, J. (1929/1963). *The child's conception of the world* (J. Tomlinson & A. Tomlinson, Trans.). Paterson, NJ: Littlefield, Adams & Company.

Piaget, J. (1932). *The moral judgment of the child.* Glencoe, IL: Free Press.

Piaget, J. (1954). *The construction of reality in the child* (M. Cook, Trans.). New York: Basic Books.

Piaget, J. (1965). *The moral judgment of the child* (M. Gabain, Trans.). New York: The Free Press.

Piaget, J. (1970). Piaget's theory (G. Gellerier & J. Langer, Trans.). In P. H. Mussen (Ed.), *Carmichael's manual of child psychology* (3rd ed., Vol. 1, pp. 703–732). New York: Wiley.

Piaget, J., & Inhelder, B. (1956). *The child's conception of space* (F. J. Langdon & J. L. Lunzer, Trans.). London: Routledge & Kegan Paul.

Piaget, J., & Inhelder, B. (1964). *The early growth of logic in the child. Classification and seriation* (E. A. Lunzer & D. Papert, Trans.). London: Routledge & Kegan Paul.

Pianta, R. C. (1999). *Enhancing relationships between children and teachers.* Washington, DC: American Psychological Association.

Pianta, R. C., Belsky, J., Vandergrift, N., Houts, R. M., & Morrison, F. J. (2008). Classroom effects on children's achievement trajectories in elementary school. *American Educational Research Journal, 45,* 365–397.

Pianta, R. C., & Harbers, K. (1996). Observing mother and child behavior in a problem-solving situation at school entry: Relations with academic achievement. *Journal of School Psychology, 67,* 307–322.

Pianta, R. C., Nimetz, S., & Bennett, E. (1997). Mother–child relationships, teacher–child relationships, and school outcomes in preschool and kindergarten. *Early Childhood Research Quarterly, 12,* 263–280.

Piehler, T. F., & Dishion, T. J. (2007). Interpersonal dynamics within adolescent friendships: Dyadic mutuality, deviant talk, and patterns of antisocial behavior. *Child Development, 78*, 1611–1624.

Pierce, S., & Lange, G. (2000). Relationships among metamemory, motivation and memory performance in young school-age children. *British Journal of Developmental Psychology, 18*, 121–135.

Pike, A. (2002). Behavioral genetics, shared and nonshared environment. In P. Smith & C. Hart (Eds.), *Blackwell handbook of childhood social development* (pp. 27–43). Oxford: Blackwell.

Pillow, B., Hill, V., Boyce, A., & Stein, C. (2000). Understanding inference as a source of knowledge: Children's ability to evaluate the certainty of deduction, perception, and guessing. *Developmental Psychology, 36*, 169–179.

Ping, R. M., & Goldin-Meadow, S. (2008). Hands in the air: Using ungrounded iconic gestures to teach children conservation of quantity. *Developmental Psychology, 44*, 1277–1287.

Pintrich, P. R. (2003). A motivational science perspective on the role of student motivation in learning and teaching contexts. *Journal of Educational Psychology, 95*, 667–686.

Pintrich, P. R., & Schunk, D. H. (2002). *Motivation in education: Theory, research, and applications* (2nd ed.). Upper Saddle River, NJ: Pearson.

Pittman, L. D., & Chase-Lansdale, P. L. (2001). African American adolescent girls in impoverished communities: Parenting style and adolescent outcomes. *Journal of Research on Adolescence, 11*, 199–224.

Planty, M., Hussar, W., Snyder, T., Kena, G., KewalRamani, A., Kemp, J., et al. (2009). *The condition of education 2009 (NCES 2009-081)*. Washington, DC: National Center for Education Statistics, Institute of Education Sciences, U.S. Department of Education.

Plester, B., Wood, C., & Bell, V. (2010). Txt msg n school literacy: Does texting and knowledge of text abbreviations adversely affect children's literacy attainment? *Literacy, 23*, 719–733.

Plomin, R., DeFries, J., McClearn, G. E., & McGuffin, P. (2001). *Behavioral genetics* (4th ed.). New York: Worth.

Polacek, G. J., Rojas, V., Levitt, S., & Mika, V. S. (2006). Media and sex: Perspectives from Hispanic teens. *American Journal of Sexuality Education, 1*, 51–69.

Polaha, J., Larzelere, R. E., Shapiro, S. K., & Pettit, G. S. (2004). Physical discipline and child behavior problems: A study of ethnic group differences. *Parenting: Science and Practice, 4*, 339–360.

Polivy, J., Herman, P., Mills, J., & Wheller, H. (2003). Eating disorders in adolescence. In G. Adams & M. Berzonsky (Eds.), *Blackwell handbook on adolescence* (pp. 523–549). Malden, MA: Blackwell.

Pollak, S. D. (2008). Mechanisms linking early experience and the emergence of emotions: Illustrations from the study of maltreated children. *Current Directions in Psychological Science, 17*, 370–375.

Pollak, S. D., Cicchetti, D., Hornung, K., & Reed, A. (2000). Recognizing emotion in faces: Developmental effects of child abuse and neglect. *Developmental Psychology, 36*, 679–688.

Pollak, S. D., & Sinha, P. (2002). Effects of early experience on children's recognition of facial displays of emotion. *Developmental Psychology, 38*, 784–791.

Pomerantz, E. M., Moorman, E. A., & Litwack, S. D. (2007). The how, whom, and why of parents' involvement in children's academic lives: More is not always better. *Review of Educational Research, 77*, 373–410.

Pomerantz, E. M., & Rudolph, K. (2003). What ensues from emotional distress? Implications for competence estimation. *Child Development, 74*, 329–345.

Ponitz, C. C., McClelland, M. M., Matthews, J. S., & Morrison, F. J. (2009). A structured observation of behavioral self-regulation and its contribution to kindergarten outcomes. *Developmental Psychology, 45*, 605–619.

Poropat, A. E. (2009). A meta-analysis of the five-factor model of personality and academic performance. *Psychological Bulletin, 135*, 322–338.

Porter, A. C., & Polikoff, M. S. (2007). NCLB: State interpretations, early effects, and suggestions for reauthorization. *Social Policy Report, 21*, 3–14.

Porter, S., & ten Brinke, L. (2008). Reading between the lies: Identifying concealed and falsified emotions in universal facial expressions. *Psychological Science, 19*, 508–514.

Poulin, F., & Boivin, M. (2000). The role of proactive and reactive aggression in the formation and development of boys' friendships. *Developmental Psychology, 36*, 223–240.

Poulin, F., & Pedersen, S. (2007). Developmental changes in gender composition of friendship networks in adolescent girls and boys. *Developmental Psychology, 43*, 1484–1496.

Powell, G. F., Brasel, J. A., & Blizzard, R. M. (1967). Emotional deprivation and growth retardation simulating idiopathic hypopituitarism: 1. Clinical evaluation of the syndrome. *New England Journal of Medicine, 276*, 1271–1278.

Powell, J. P., & Andresen, L. W. (1985). Humour and teaching in higher education. *Studies in Higher Education, 10*, 79–90.

Pratt, M., Arnold, M. L., Pratt, A., & Diessner, R. (1999). Predicting adolescent moral reasoning from family climate. *Journal of Early Adolescence, 19*, 148–175.

Pratt, S. B. (1998). Razzing: Ritualized uses of humor as a form of identification among American Indians. In D. V. Tanno & A. Gonzalez (Eds.), *Communication and identity across cultures* (pp. 56–79). Thousand Oaks, CA: Sage.

Price, T., & Jaffee, S. R. (2008). Effects of the family environment: Gene–environment interaction and passive gene–environment correlation. *Developmental Psychology, 44*, 305–315.

Priel, B., & Besser, A. (2000). Adult attachment styles, early relationships, antenatal attachment, and perceptions of infant temperament: A study of first-time mothers. *Personal Relationships, 7*, 291–310.

Priess, H. A., Lindberg, S. M., & Hyde, J. S. (2009). Adolescent gender-role identity and mental health: Gender intensification revisited. *Child Development, 80*, 1531–1544.

Principe, G., Kanaya, T., Ceci, S., & Singh, M. (2006). Believeing is seeing: How rumors can engender false memories in preschoolers. *Psychological Science, 17*, 243–248.

Prior, M., Smart, D., Sanson, A., & Oberklaid, F. (2000). Does shy-inhibited temperament in childhood lead to anxiety problems in adolescence? *Journal of the American Academy of Child and Adolescent Psychiatry, 39*, 461–468.

Pritchard, R. J., & Honeycutt, R. (2006). The process approach to writing instruction: Examining its effectiveness. In C. A. MacArthur, S. Graham & J. Fitzgerald (Eds.), *Handbook of writing research* (pp. 275–290). New York: Guilford.

Proctor, C. P., August, D., Carlo, M. S., & Snow, C. E. (2006). The intriguing role of Spanish language vocabulary knowledge in predicting English reading comprehension. *Journal of Educational Psychology, 98*, 159–169.

Pronin, E., & Jacobs, E. (2008). Thought speed, mood, and the experience of mental motion. *Perspectives on Psychological Science, 3*, 461–485.

Propper, C., Moore, G. A., Mills-Koonce, W. R., Halpern, C. T., Hill-Soderlund, A. L., Calkins, S. D., et al. (2008). Gene–environment contributions to the development of infant vagal reactivity: The interaction of dopamine and maternal sensitivity. *Child Development, 79*, 1377–1394.

Provine, R. R. (2000). *Laughter*. New York: Viking.

Pulkkinen, L. (2001). Reveller or striver? How childhood self-control predicts adult behavior. In A. Bothart & D. Stipek (Eds.), *Constructive and destructive behavior: Implications for family, school, and society* (pp. 167–185). Washington, DC: APA.

Puma, M., Bell, S., Cook, R., Heid, C., & Lopez, M. (2005). *Head Start impact study: First year findings*. Washington, DC.: U.S. Department of Health and Human Services.

Pungello, E. P., Iruka, I. U., Dotterer, A. M., Mills-Koonce, R., & Reznick, J. S. (2009). The effects of socioeconomic status, race, and parenting on language development in early childhood. *Developmental Psychology, 45*, 544–557.

Purcell-Gates, V., Duke, N. K., & Martineau, J. A. (2007). Learning to read and write genre-specific text: Roles of authentic experience and explicit teaching. *Reading Research Quarterly, 42*, 8–45.

Putallaz, M., Costanzo, P., Grimes, C., & Sherman, D. (1998). Intergenerational continuities and their influences on children s social development. *Social Development, 7*, 389–427.

Putallaz, M., Grimes, C. L., Foster, K. J., Kupersmidt, J. B., Coie, J. D., & Dearing, K. (2007). Overt and relational aggression and victimization: Multiple perspectives within the school setting. *Journal of School Psychology, 45*, 523–547.

Putallaz, M., & Wasserman, A. (1990). Children's entry behavior. In S. Asher & J. Coie (Eds.), *Peer rejection in childhood* (pp. 60–89). New York: Cambridge University Press.

Qin, L., Pomerantz, E. M., & Wang, Q. (2009). Are gains in decision-making autonomy during early adolescence beneficial for emotional functioning? The case of the United States and China. *Child Development, 80*, 1705–1721.

Quartz, S., & Sejnowski, T. (2002). *Liars, lovers, and heroes: What the new brain science reveals about how we become who we are*. New York: Morrow.

Quatman, T., Sampson, K., Robinson, C., & Watson, C. (2001). Academic, motivational, and emotional correlates of adolescent dating. *Genetic, Social & General Psychology Monographs, 127*, 211–235.

Quay, H. C. (1993). The psychobiology of undersocialized aggressive conduct disorder. A theoretical perspective. *Development and Psychopathology, 5*, 165–180.

Quillian, L., & Campbell, M. E. (2003). Beyond black and white: The present and future of multiracial friendship segregation. *American Sociological Review, 68*, 540–566.

Quintana, S. M., & Vera, E. M. (1999). Mexican American children's ethnic identity, understanding of ethnic prejudice, and parental ethnic socialization. *Hispanic Journal of Behavioral Sciences, 21*, 387–404.

Radke-Yarrow, M., Cummings, M., Kuczynski, L., & Chapman, M. (1985). Patterns of attachment in two- and three-year-olds in normal families and families with parental depression. *Child Development, 56*, 884–893.

Radke-Yarrow, M., Zahn-Waxler, C., Richardson, D., Susman, A., & Martinez, P. (1994). Caring behavior in children of clinically depressed and well mothers. *Child Development, 65*, 1405–1414.

Raffaelli, M., & Crockett, L. (2003). Sexual risk taking in adolescence: The role of self-regulation and attraction to risk. *Developmental Psychology, 39*, 1036–1046.

Raikes, H., Pan, B. A., Luze, G., Tamis-LeMonda, C., Brooks-Gunn, J., Constantine, J., et al. (2006). Mother–child bookreading in low-income families: Correlates and outcomes during the first three years. *Child Development, 77*, 924–953.

Raley, R. K., & Wildsmith, E. (2004). Cohabitation and children's family instability. *Journal of Marriage and Family, 66*, 210–219.

Ramani, G. B., & Siegler, R. S. (2008). Promoting broad and stable improvements in low-income children's numerical knowledge through playing number board games. *Child Development, 79*, 375–394.

Ramaswamy, V., & Bergin, C. C. (2009). Do reinforcement and induction increase prosocial behavior? Results of a teacher-based intervention in preschools. *Journal of Research in Childhood Education, 23*, 525–536.

Ramos-Marcuse, F., & Arsenio, W. (2001). Young children's emotionally-charged moral narratives: Relations with attachment and behavior problems. *Early Education and Development, 12*, 165–184.

Rampey, B. D., Dion, G. S., & Donahue, P. L. (2009). *NAEP 2008: Trends in academic progress (NCES 2009–479)*. Washington, DC: U.S. Department of Education.

Ramsey-Rennels, J. L., & Langlois, J. H. (2006). Infants' differential processing of female and male faces. *Current Directions in Psychological Science, 15*, 59–62.

Rank, M., & Hirschl, T. (1999). The economic risk of childhood in America: Estimating the probability of poverty across the formative years. *Journal of Marriage and the Family, 61*, 1058–1067.

Rao, R., & Georgieff, M. (2000). Early nutrition and brain development. In C. Nelson (Ed.), *The effects of early adversity on neurobehavioral development* (pp. 1–30). Mahwah, NJ: Erlbaum.

Rappolt-Schlictmann, G., Willett, J. B., Ayoub, C., Lindsley, R., Hulette, A., & Fischer, K. (2009). Poverty, relationship conflict, and the regulation of cortisol in small and large group contexts at child care. *Mind, Brain, and Education, 3*, 131–142.

Rasch, B., & Born, J. (2008). Reactivation and consolidation of memory during sleep. *Current Directions in Psychological Science, 17*, 188–192.

Rasinski, T. V., Padak, N. D., McKeon, C. A., Wilfong, L. G., Friedauer, J. A., & Heim, P. (2005). Is reading fluency a key for successful high school reading? *Journal of Adolescent & Adult Literacy, 49*, 22–27.

Raskauskas, J., & Stoltz, A. D. (2007). Involvement in traditional and electronic bullying among adolescents. *Developmental Psychology, 43*, 564–573.

Raspa, M., McWilliam, R., & Maher-Ridley, S. (2001). Child care quality and children's engagement. *Early Education and Development, 12*, 209–224.

Raudenbush, S. W. (2009). The Brown legacy and the O'Connor challenge: Transforming schools in the images of children's potential. *Educational Researcher, 38*(3), 169–180.

Rauscher, F. H., & Hinton, S. C. (2006). The Mozart Effect: Music listening is not music instruction. *Educational Psychologist, 41,* 233–238.

Raver, C. (2003). Does work pay psychologically as well as economically? The role of employment in predicting depressive symptoms and parenting among low-income families. *Child Development, 74,* 1720–1736.

Raver, C. C. (2004). Placing emotional self-regulation in sociocultural and socioeconomic contexts. *Child Development, 75,* 346–353.

Raver, C. C., Gershoff, E. T., & Aber, J. L. (2007). Testing equivalence of mediating models of income, parenting, and school readiness for White, Black, and Hispanic children in a national sample. *Child Development, 78,* 96–115.

Raymond, J., Fenskey, M., & Tavassoli, N. (2003). Selective attention determines emotional resonses to novel visual stimuli. *Psychological Science, 14,* 537–542.

Razel, M. (2001). The complex model of television viewing and educational achievement. *Journal of Educational Psychology, 94,* 371–379.

Ream, R. K., & Palardy, G. J. (2008). Reexamining social class differences in the availability and the educational utility of parental social capital. *American Educational Research Journal, 45,* 238–273.

Recchia, H. E., & Howe, N. (2009). Associations between social understanding, sibling relationship quality, and siblings' conflict strategies and outcomes. *Child Development, 80,* 1564–1578.

Reed, T., & Brown, M. (2001). The expression of care in the rough and tumble play of boys. *Journal of Research in Childhood Education, 15,* 104–116.

Reese, E., & Newcombe, R. (2007). Training mothers in elaborative reminiscing enhances children's autobiographical memory and narrative. *Child Development, 78,* 1153–1170.

Reingold, E. M., Charness, N., Pomplun, M., & Stampe, D. M. (2001). Visual span in expert chess players. *Psychological Science, 12,* 48–55.

Reiss, D. (2005). The interplay between genotypes and family relationships: Reframing concepts of development and prevention. *Current Directions in Psychological Science, 14,* 139–143.

Repacholi, B. M., & Meltzoff, A. N. (2007). Emotional eavesdropping: Infants selectively respond to indirect emotional signals. *Child Development, 78,* 503–521.

Repetti, R. L., Wang, S.-w., & Saxbe, D. (2009). Bringing it all back home: How outside stressors shape families' everyday lives. *Current Directions in Psychological Science, 18,* 106–111.

Reschly, D. J., & Hosp, J. L. (2004). State SLD identification policies and practices. *Learning Disability Quarterly, 27,* 197–213.

Rescorla, L. (2005). Age 13 language and reading outcomes in late-talking toddlers. *Journal of Speech, Language and Hearing Research, 48,* 459–472.

Resetar, J. L., & Noell, G. H. (2008). Evaluating preference assessments for use in the general education population. *Journal of Applied Behavior Analysis, 41,* 447–451.

Resnick, M., Bearman, P., Blum, R., Bauman, K., Harris, K., Jones, J., et al. (1997). Protecting adolescents from harm: Findings from the National Longitudinal Study on Adolescent Health. *JAMA, 278,* 823–832.

Reynolds, A., Ou, S.-R., & Topitzes, J. (2004). Path of effects of early childhood intervention on educational attainment and delinquency: A confirmatory analysis of the Chicago Child–Parent Centers. *Child Development, 75,* 1299–1328.

Reynolds, C. R., & Shaywitz, S. E. (2009). Response to intervention: Prevention and remediation, perhaps. Diagnosis, no. *Child Development Perspectives, 3,* 44–47.

Rhoades, K. A. (2008). Children's responses to interparental conflict: A meta-analysis of their associations with child adjustment. *Child Development, 79,* 1942–1956.

Rhule, D. M., McMahon, R. J., Spieker, S. J., & Munson, J. A. (2006). Positive adjustment and associated protective factors in children of adolescent mothers. *Journal of Child and Family Studies, 15,* 231–251.

Richardson, G. A., Ryan, C., Willford, J., Day, N. L., & Goldschmidt, L. (2002). Prenatal alcohol and marijuana exposure: Effects on neuropsychological outcomes at 10 years. *Neurotoxicology and Teratology, 24,* 309–320.

Richardson, R., & Hayne, H. (2007). You can't take it with you: The translation of memory across development. *Current Directions in Psychological Science, 16,* 223–227.

Rickards, A., Kelly, E., Doyle, L., & Callanan, C. (2001). Cognition, academic progress, behavior and self-concept at 14 years of very low birth weight children. *Journal of Developmental and Behavioral Pediatrics, 22,* e11.

Rieger, G., Linsenmeier, J. A. W., Gygax, L., & Bailey, J. M. (2008). Sexual orientation and childhood gender nonconformity: Evidence from home videos. *Developmental Psychology, 44,* 46–58.

Rigby, K. (2002). Bullying in childhood. In P. Smith & C. Hart (Eds.), *Blackwell handbook of childhood social development* (pp. 549–568). Oxford: Blackwell.

Rimm-Kaufman, S., Pianta, R., & Cox, M. (2000). Teacher's judgments of problems in the transition to kindergarten. *Early Childhood Research Quarterly, 15,* 147–166.

Rimm-Kaufman, S. E., Curby, T. W., Grimm, K. J., Nathanson, L., & Brock, L. (2009). The contribution of children's self-regulation and classroom quality to children's adaptive behaviors in the kindergarten classroom. *Developmental Psychology, 45,* 958–972.

Rittle-Johnson, B. (2007). Promoting transfer: Effects of self-explanation and direct instruction. *Child Development, 77,* 1–15.

Rittle-Johnson, B., & Star, J. (2009). Compared with what? The effects of different comparisons on conceptual knowledge and procedural flexibility for equation solving. *Journal of Educational Psychology, 101,* 529–544.

Rittle-Johnson, B., Star, J., & Durkin, K. (2009). The importance of prior knowledge when comparing examples: Influences on conceptual and procedural knowledge of equation solving. *Journal of Educational Psychology, 101,* 836–852.

Rivers, I. (2002). Developmental issues for lesbian and gay youth. In A. Coyle & C. Kitzinger (Eds.), *Lesbian and gay psychology* (pp. 30–44). Oxford: Blackwell.

Rivers, I., Poteat, V. P., & Noret, N. (2008). Victimization, social support, and psychosocial functioning among children of same-sex and opposite-sex couples in the United Kingdom. *Developmental Psychology, 44*, 127–134.

Robert Wood Johnson Foundation. (2009). Active education: Physical education, physical activity and academic performance [Electronic Version]. *Research Brief, Summer 2009*. Retrieved from activelivingresearch.org

Robert, M., & Heroux, G. (2004). Visuo-spatial play experience: Forerunner of visuo-spatial achievement in preadolescent and adolescent boys and girls? *Infant and Child Development, 13*, 49–78.

Roberts, B. W., & Mroczek, D. (2008). Personality trait change in adulthood. *Current Directions in Psychological Science, 17*, 31–35.

Roberts, D. F., Foehr, U. G., & Rideout, V. (2005). *Generation M: Media in the lives of 8–18 year-olds*. Kaiser Family Foundation (#7251). Retrieved 5/22/2010 from http://www.kff.org

Roberts, K. P., & Blades, M. (2000). Children's memory and source monitoring of real-life and televised events. *Journal of Applied Developmental Psychology, 20*, 575–596.

Robins, R., John, O., Caspi, A., Moffitt, T., & Stouthamer-Loeber, M. (1996). Resilient, overcontrolled and undercontrolled boys: Three replicable personality types. *Journal of Personality and Social Psychology, 70*, 157–171.

Robins, R. W., & Trzesniewski, K. (2005). Self-esteem development across the lifespan. *Current Directions in Psychological Science, 14*, 158–162.

Robinson, J. L., & Acevedo, M. C. (2001). Infant reactivity and reliance on mother during emotion challenges: Prediction of cognition and language skills in a low-income sample. *Child Development, 72*, 402–415.

Robinson, P. W., Newby, T. J., & Hill, R. D. (1981). *Manipulating parents: Tactics used by children of all ages and ways parents can turn the tables*. Englewood Cliffs, NJ: Prentice-Hall.

Robinson, T. N., Wilde, M. L., Navracruz, L., Haydel, F., & Varady, A. (2001). Effects of reducing children's television and video game use on aggressive behavior: A randomized controlled trial. *Archives of Pediatric & Adolescent Medicine, 155*, 17–23.

Roderick, M., & Camburn, E. (1999). Risk and recovery from course failure in the early years of high school. *American Educational Research Journal, 36*, 303–343.

Roebers, C. M., & Kauer, M. (2009). Motor and cognitive control in a normative sample of 7-year-olds. *Developmental Science, 12*, 175–181.

Roediger, H. L. (2008). Relativity of remembering: Why the laws of memory vanished. *Annual Review of Psychology, 59*, 225–254.

Roehrs, T., & Roth, T. (2008). Caffeine: Sleep and daytime sleepiness. *Sleep Medicine Reviews, 12*, 153–162.

Rogers, L. A., & Graham, S. (2008). A meta-analysis of single subject design writing intervention research. *Journal of Educational Psychology, 100*, 879–906.

Rogoff, B. (1990). *Apprenticeship in thinking: Cognitive development in social context*. Oxford: Oxford University Press.

Rogoff, B., Mosier, C., Mistry, J., & Göncü, A. (1993). Toddlers' guided participation with their caregivers in cultural activity. In E. A. Forman, N. Minick, & C. A. Stone (Eds.), *Contexts for learning: Sociocultural dynamics in children's development* (pp. 230–253). Oxford: Oxford University Press.

Rogol, A., Roemmich, J., & Clark, P. (2002). Growth at puberty. *Journal of Adolescent Health, 31*, 192–200.

Rohrer, D., & Pashler, H. (2007). Increasing retention without increasing study time. *Current Directions in Psychological Science, 16*, 183–186.

Roisman, G., Susman, E., Barnett-Walker, K., Booth-LaForce, C., Owen, M. T., Belsky, J., et al. (2009). Early family and child-care antecedents of awakening cortisol levels in adolescence. *Child Development, 80*, 907–920.

Roisman, G. I., & Fraley, R. C. (2006). The limits of genetic influence: A behavior–genetic analysis of infant–caregiver relationship quality and temperament. *Child Development, 77*, 1656–1667.

Rome, E., Ammerman, S., Rosen, D., Keller, R., Lock, J., Mammel, K., et al. (2003). Children and adolescents with eating disorders: The state of the art. *Pediatrics, 111*, e98–e108.

Romeo, L., & Young, S. (1999). Using literacy play centers to engage middle grade students in content area learning. In J. A. Dugan, P. Linder, W. Linek, & E. Sturtevant (Eds.), *Advancing the world of literacy: Moving into the 21st century: The twenty-first yearbook of the College Reading Association* (pp. 122–136). Readyville, TN: College Reading Association.

Romero, A. J., & Roberts, R. E. (2003). Stress within a bicultural context for adolescents of Mexican descent. *Cultural Diversity and Ethnic Minority Psychology, 9*, 171–184.

Roopnarine, J. L., Shin, M., Donovan, B., & Suppal, P. (2000). Sociocultural contexts of dramatic play: Implications for early education. In K. A. Roskos & J. F. Christie (Eds.), *Play and literacy in early childhood* (pp. 205–230). Mahwah, NJ: Erlbaum.

Rose, A. J., & Rudolph, K. D. (2006). A review of sex differences in peer relationship processes: Potential trade-offs for the emotional and behavioral development of girls and boys. *Psychological Bulletin, 132*, 1–34.

Rose, R., Viken, R., Dick, D., Bates, J. E., Pulkkinen, L., & Kaprio, J. (2003). It does take a village: Nonfamilial environments and children's behavior. *Psychological Science, 14*, 272–277.

Rose, S., & Feldman, J. (2000). The relation of very low birthweight to basic cognitive skills in infancy and childhood. In C. Nelson (Ed.), *The effects of early adversity on neurobehavioral development* (pp. 31–59). Mahwah, NJ: Erlbaum.

Rose, S. A., Feldman, J. F., & Jankowski, J. J. (2009). A cognitive approach to the development of early language. *Child Development, 80*, 134–150.

Rose, S. A., Futterweit, L. R., & Jankowski, J. J. (1999). The relation of affect to attention and learning in infancy. *Child Development, 70*, 549–559.

Rosen, L. D., Cheever, N. A., & Carrier, L. M. (2008). The association of parenting style and child age with parental limit setting and adolescent MySpace behavior. *Journal of Applied Developmental Psychology, 29*, 459–471.

Rosenberg, N., Pritchard, J., Weber, J., Cann, H., Kidd, K., Zhivotovsky, L., et al. (2002). Genetic structure of human populations. *Science, 298*, e2381.

Rosenkoetter, L. I. (1999). The television situation comedy and children's prosocial behavior. *Journal of Applied Social Psychology, 29*, 979–993.

Rosenshine, B. (1987). Explicit teaching and teacher training. *Journal of Teacher Education, 38*, 34–36.

Rosenthal, R. (2002). Covert communication in classrooms, clinics, courtrooms, and cubicles. *American Psychologist, 57*, 839–849.

Rosenthal, R. (2003). Covert communication in laboratories, classrooms, and the truly real world. *Current Directions in Psychological Science, 12*, 151–154.

Roseth, C. J., Johnson, D. W., & Johnson, R. T. (2008). Promoting early adolescents' achievement and peer relationships: The effects of cooperative, competitive, and individualistic goal structures. *Psychological Bulletin, 134*, 223–246.

Roskos, K. (2000). Through the bioecological lens: Some observations of literacy in play as a proximal process. In K. Roskos & J. Christie (Eds.), *Play and literacy in early childhood: Research from multiple perspectives* (pp. 125–137). Mahwah, NJ: Lawrence Erlbaum.

Roskos, K., & Christie, J. (2001). Examining the play-literacy interface: A critical review and future directions. *Journal of Early Childhood Literacy, 1*, 59–89.

Ross, H., Ross, M., Stein, N., & Trabasso, T. (2006). How siblings resolve their conflicts: The importance of first offers, planning, and limited opposition. *Child Development, 77*, 1730–1745.

Rostosky, S. S., Wilcox, B. L., Wright, M. L., & Randall, B. A. (2004). The impact of religiosity on adolescent sexual behavior: A review of the evidence. *Journal of Adolescent Research, 19*.

Roth, P., BeVier, C., Switzer, F., & Schippmann, J. (1996). Meta-analyzing the relationship between grades and job performance. *Journal of Applied Psychology, 81*, 548–556.

Roth, W. M., & Welzel, M. (2001). From activity to gestures and scientific language. *Journal of Research in Science Teaching, 38*, 103–136.

Rothbart, M. K. (2007). Temperament, development, and personality. *Current Directions in Psychological Science, 16*, 207–212.

Rothbart, M. K., & Bates, J. E. (1998). Temperament. In N. Eisenberg (Ed.), *Handbook of child psychology: Social, emotional, and personality development* (5th ed., Vol. 3, pp. 105–176). New York: Wiley.

Rubin, K. H., Bukowski, W., & Parker, J. G. (1998). Peer interactions, relationships, and groups. In N. Eisenberg (Ed.), *Handbook of child psychology: Social, emotional, and personality development* (5th ed., Vol. 3, pp. 619–700). New York: Wiley.

Rubin, K. H., Burgess, K., & Coplan, R. (2002). Social withdrawal and shyness. In P. Smith & C. Hart (Eds.), *Blackwell handbook of childhood social development* (pp. 329–352). Oxford: Blackwell.

Rubin, K. H., Burgess, K., Dwyer, K., & Hastings, P. (2003). Predicting preschoolers' externalizing behaviors from toddler temperament, conflict, and maternal negativity. *Developmental Psychology, 39*, 164–176.

Rubin, K. H., Coplan, R. J., & Bowker, J. C. (2009). Social withdrawal in childhood. *Annual Review of Psychology, 60*, 141–171.

Ruble, D. N., Martin, C. L., & Berenbaum, S. A. (2006). Gender development. In N. Eisenberg (Ed.), *Handbook of child psychology: Social, emotional, and personality development* (6th ed., Vol. 3, pp. 858–932). New York: Wiley.

Rudasill, K. M., & Rimm-Kaufman, S. E. (2009). Teacher–child relationship quality: The roles of child temperament and teacher–child interactions. *Early Childhood Research Quarterly, 24*, 107–120.

Rudolph, K. D., Caldwell, M. S., & Conley, C. S. (2005). Need for approval and children's well-being. *Child Development, 76*, 309–323.

Rudy, D., & Grusec, J. (2006). Authoritarian parenting in individualist and collectivist groups: Associations with maternal emotion and cognition and children's self-esteem. *Journal of Family Psychology, 20*, 68–78.

Ruowei, L., Zhao, Z., Mikdad, A., Barker, L., & Grummer-Strawn, L. (2003). Prevalence of breastfeeding in the United States: The 2001 National Immunization Survey. *Pediatrics, 111*, 1198–1200.

Rutter, M. (1995). Clinical implications of attachment concepts: Retrospect and prospect. *Journal of Child Psychology & Psychiatry & Allied Disciplines, 36*, 549–571.

Rutter, M. (2000). Resilience reconsidered: Conceptual considerations, empirical findings, and policy implications. In J. P. Shonkoff & S. Meisels (Eds.), *Handbook of early childhood intervention* (2nd ed., pp. 651–682). New York: Cambridge University Press.

Ryan, A. M. (2001). The peer group as a context for the development of young adolescent motivation and achievement. *Child Development, 72*, 1135–1150.

Ryan, R. M., & Deci, E. L. (1996). Intrinsic motivation and extrinsic rewards: A commentary on Cameron and Pierce's meta-analysis. *Review of Educational Research, 66*, 33–38.

Rydell, A. M., Berlin, L., & Bohlin, G. (2003). Emotionality, emotion regulation, and adaptation among 5- to 8-year-old children. *Emotion, 3*, 30–47.

Ryder, A., Alden, L. E., & Paulhus, D. (2000). Is acculturation unidimensional or bidimensional? A head-to-head comparison in the prediction of personality, self-identity, and adjustment. *Journal of Personality and Social Psychology, 79*, 49–65.

Saarni, C. (1997). Coping with aversive feelings. *Motivation and Emotion, 21*, 45–63.

Saarni, C. (1999). *The development of emotional competence*. New York: Guilford.

Saarni, C., Mumme, D., & Campos, J. (1998). Emotional development: Action, communication, and understanding. In N. Eisenberg (Ed.), *Handbook of child psychology: Social, emotional, and personality development* (5th ed., Vol. 3, pp. 237–309). New York: Wiley.

Sabbagh, M. A., Xu, F., Carlson, S. M., Moses, L. J., & Lee, K. (2006). The development of executive functioning and theory of mind. *Psychological Science, 17*, 74–81.

Sackett, P. R., Borneman, M. J., & Connelly, B. S. (2008). High-stakes testing in higher education and employment: Appraising the evidence for validity and fairness. *American Psychologist, 63*, 215–227.

Sadeh, A., Gruber, R., & Raviv, A. (2003). The effects of sleep restriction and extension on school-age children: What a difference an hour makes. *Child Development, 74*, 444–455.

Salmivalli, C., Ojanen, T., Haanpaa, J., & Peets, K. (2005). "I'm OK but you're not" and other peer-relational schemas: Explaining individual differences in children's social goals. *Developmental Psychology, 41*, 363–375.

Salomon, G. (Ed.). (1993). *Distributed cognitions: Psychological and educational considerations*. Cambridge, UK: Cambridge University Press.

Saltz, E., Dixon, D., & Johnson, J. (1977). Training disadvantaged preschoolers on various fantasy activities: Effects on cognitive functioning and impulse control. *Child Development, 48*, 367–380.

Salvatore, J., & Shelton, J. N. (2007). Cognitive costs of exposure to racial prejudice. *Psychological Science, 18*, 810–815.

Sameroff, A. J. (1998). Environmental risk factors in infancy. *Pediatrics, 102*, 1287–1292.

Sameroff, A. J., Seifer, R., Baldwin, A., & Baldwin, C. (1993). Stability of intelligence from preschool to adolescence: The influence of social and family risk factors. *Child Development, 64*, 80–97.

SAMHSA. (2008a). *The NSDUH Report: Underage Alcohol Use.* Rockville, MD.: Office of Applied Studies.

SAMHSA. (2008b). *Results from the 2007 National Survey on Drug Use and Health: National Findings (NSDUH Series H-34, DHHS Publication No. SMA 08-4343)*. Rockville, MD.

Sanson, A., Hemphill, S., & Smart, D. (2004). Connections between temperament and social development: A review. *Social Development, 13*, 142–170.

Saroglou, V., Pichon, E., Trompette, L., Verschueren, M., & Dernelle, R. (2005). Prosocial behavior and religion: New evidence based on projective measures and peer ratings. *Journal for the Scientific Study of Religion, 44*, 323–348.

Saudino, K. J., & Zapfe, J. A. (2008). Genetic influences on activity level in early childhood: Do situations matter? *Child Development, 79*, 930–943.

Savin-Williams, R. (2006). Who's gay? Does it matter? *Current Directions in Psychological Science, 15*, 40–44.

Saxe, R., Tenenbaum, J. B., & Carey, S. (2005). Secret agents: Inferences about hidden causes by 10- and 12-month-old infants. *12, 16*, 995–1001.

Schab, F. (1991). Schooling without learning: Thirty years of cheating in high school. *Adolescence, 26*, 839–847.

Schaeffer, C., Petras, H., Ialongo, N., Poduska, J., & Kellam, S. (2003). Modeling growth in boys' aggressive behavior across elementary school: Links to later criminal involvement, conduct disorder, and antisocial personality disorder. *Developmental Psychology, 39*, 1020–1035.

Scharf, M. (2001). A "natural experiment" in childrearing ecologies and adolescents' attachment and separation representations. *Child Development, 72*, 236–251.

Schellenberg, E. G. (2004). Music lessons enhance IQ. *Psychological Science, 15*, 511–514.

Schellenberg, E. G. (2005). Music and cognitive abilities. *Current Directions in Psychological Science, 14*, 317–325.

Schellenberg, E. G. (2006). Long-term positive associations between music lessons and IQ. *Journal of Educational Psychology, 98*, 457–468.

Scher, A., & Mayseless, O. (2000). Mothers of anxious/ambivalent infants: Maternal characteristics and child-care context. *Child Development, 71*, 1629–1639.

Schick, B., de Villers, P., de Villers, J., & Hoffmeister, R. (2007). Language and theory of mind: A study of deaf children. *Child Development, 78*, 376–396.

Schlaefli, A., Rest, J., & Thomas, S. (1985). Does moral education improve moral judgment? A meta-analysis of intervention studies using the Defining Issues Test. *Review of Educational Research, 55*, 319–352.

Schleppegrell, M. J. (2002). Challenges of the science register for ESL students: Errors and meaning-making. In M. J. Schleppegrell & M. C. Colombi (Eds.), *Developing advanced literacy in first and second languages* (pp. 119–142). Mahwah, NJ: Erlbaum.

Schliemann, A., & Carraher, D. (2002). The evolution of mathematical reasoning: Everyday versus idealized understandings. *Developmental Review, 22*, 242–266.

Schlievert, S. (2001, April). *Academic dishonesty: Everybody cheats?* Paper presented at the American Educational Research Association, Seattle, Washington.

Schmader, T., Johns, M., & Forbes, C. (2008). An integrated process model of stereotype threat effects on performance. *Psychological Review, 115*, 336–356.

Schmidt, L., & Fox, N. (2002). Individual differences in childhood shyness: Origins, malleability, and developmental course. In D. Cervone & W. Mischel (Eds.), *Advances in personality science* (pp. 83–105). New York: Guilford Press.

Schmidt, M. E., & Anderson, D. R. (2007). The impact of television on cognitive development and educational achievement. In N. Pecora, J. P. Murray & E. Wartella (Eds.), *Children and television: Fifty years of research* (pp. 65–84). Mahwah, NJ: Erlbaum.

Schmitz, S., Fulker, D., Plomin, R., Zahn-Waxler, C., Emde, R., & DeFries, J. (1999). Temperament and problem behavior during early childhood. *International Journal of Behavioral Development, 23*, 333–355.

Schneider, B., Atkinson, L., & Tardif, C. (2001). Child–parent attachment and children's peer relations: A quantitative review. *Developmental Psychology, 37*, 86–100.

Schneider, M., Grabner, R. H., & Paetsch, J. (2009). Mental number line, number line estimation, and mathematical achievement: Their interrelations in grades 5 and 6. *Journal of Educational Psychology, 101*, 359–372.

Schneider, M., & Moore, C. (2000). Effect of prenatal stress on development: A nonhuman primate model. In C. Nelson (Ed.), *The effects of early adversity on neurobehavioral development* (pp. 201–244). Mahwah, NJ: Erlbaum.

Schneider, W. (2000). Research on memory development: Historical trends and current themes. *International Journal of Behavioral Development, 24*, 407–420.

Schneider, W., & Bjorklund, D. F. (1998). Memory. In D. Kuhn & R. S. Siegler (Eds.), *Handbook of child psychology: Cognition, perception, and language* (5th ed., Vol. 2, pp. 467–521). New York: Wiley.

Schneider, W., Gruber, H., Gold, A., & Opwis, K. (1993). Chess expertise and memory for chess positions in children and adults. *Journal of Experimental Child Psychology, 56*, 328–349.

Schoenfeld, A. H. (1991). On mathematics as sense-making: An informal attack on the unfortunate divorce of formal and informal mathematics. In J. F. Voss, D. N. Perkins & J. W. Segal (Eds.), *Informal reasoning and education* (pp. 311–343). Hillsdale, NJ: Erlbaum.

Schoenthaler, S., Dorax, W., & Wakefield, J. (1987). The testing of various hypotheses as explanations for the gains in national standardized academic test scores in the 1978–1983 New York City Nutrition Policy Modification Project. *International Journal of Biosocial Research, 8*, 196–203.

Scholl, B., & Leslie, A. (2001). Minds, modules, and meta-analysis. *Child Development, 72*, 696–701.

Schonberg, K. (1997). Marijuana. *Pediatrics in Review, 18*, 26–27.

Schonfeld, D. (2000). Teaching young children about HIV and AIDS. *Children Affected by HIV/AIDS, 9*, 375–387.

Schore, A. (2000). Attachment and the regulation of the right brain. *Attachment and Human Development, 2*, 23–47.

Schulting, A. B., Malone, P. S., & Dodge, K. (2005). The effect of school-based kindergarten transition policies and practices on child academic outcomes. *Developmental Psychology, 41*, 860–871.

Schwebel, D., & Plummert, J. (1999). Longitudinal and concurrent relations among temperament, ability estimation, and injury proneness. *Child Development, 70*, 700–712.

Schwenck, C., Bjorklund, D. F., & Schneider, W. (2007). Factors influencing the incidence of utilization deficiencies and other patterns of recall/strategy-use relations in a strategic memory task. *Child Development, 78*, 1771–1787.

Sciutto, M. J., Terjesen, M. D., & Frank, A. S. B. (2000). Teachers' knowledge and misperceptions of Attention-Deficit/Hyperactivity Disorder. *Psychology in the Schools, 37*, 115–122.

Seaton, E. K., Caldwell, C. H., Sellers, R. M., & Jackson, J. S. (2008). The prevalence of perceived discrimination among African American and Caribbean Black youth. *Developmental Psychology, 44*, 1288–1297.

Seaton, M., Marsh, H. W., & Craven, R. G. (2009). Earning its place as a pan-human theory: Universality of the big-fish-little-pond effect across 41 culturally and economically diverse countries. *Journal of Educational Psychology, 101*, 403–419.

Segal, L., Cole, C., & Fuld, J. (2002). Developing an HIV/AIDS education curriculum for Takalani Sesame, South Africa's Sesame Street. *Early Education & Development, 13*, 363–378.

Seiffge-Krenke, I., Aunola, K., & Nurmi, J.-E. (2009). Changes in stress perception and coping during adolescence: The role of situational and personal factors. *Child Development, 80*, 259–279.

Seitsinger, A. M., Felner, R. D., Brand, S., & Burns, A. (2008). A large-scale examination of the nature and efficacy of teachers' practices to engage parents: Assessment, parental contact, and student-level impact. *Journal of School Psychology, 46*, 477–505.

Seltzer, J. (2000). Families formed outside of marriage. *Journal of Marriage and the Family, 62*, 1247–1268.

Sénéchal, M., & Young, L. (2008). The effect of family literacy intervention on children's acquisition of reading from kindergarten to Grade 3: A meta-analytic review. *Review of Educational Research, 78*, 880–907.

Serbin, L. A., & Karp, J. (2003). Intergenerational studies of parenting and the transfer of risk from parent to child. *Current Directions in Psychological Science, 12*, 138–142.

Shammi, P., & Stuss, D. T. (1999). Humour appreciation: A role of the right frontal lobe. *Brain, 122*, 657–666.

Shamosh, N. A., DeYoung, C. G., Green, A. E., Reis, D. L., Johnson, M. R., Conway, A., et al. (2008). Individual differences in delay discounting: Relation to intelligence, working memory, and anterior prefrontal cortex. *Psychological Science, 19*, 904–911.

Shantz, C. (1987). Conflicts between children. *Child Development, 58*, 283–305.

Shatz, M., Diesendruck, G., Martinez-Beck, I., & Akar, D. (2003). The influence of language and socieconomic status on children's understanding of false belief. *Developmental Psychology, 39*, 717–729.

Shaw, D., Gilliom, M., Ingoldsby, E., & Nagin, D. (2003). Trajectories leading to school-age conduct problems. *Developmental Psychology, 39*, 189–200.

Shaywitz, S. E., Mody, M., & Shaywitz, B. A. (2006). Neural mechanisms in dyslexia. *Current Directions in Psychological Science, 15*, 278–281.

Shaywitz, S. E., Morris, R., & Shaywitz, B. A. (2008). The education of dyslexic children from childhood to adulthood. *Annual Review of Psychology, 59*, 451–475.

Shaywitz, S. E., & Shaywitz, B. A. (2005). Dyslexia (Specific Reading Disability). *Biological Psychiatry, 57*, 1301–1309.

Shepard, L. (1997). Children not ready to learn? The invalidity of school readiness testing. *Psychology in the Schools, 34*, 85–97.

Shi, R., & Werker, J. (2001). Six-month-old infants' preference for lexical words. *Psychological Science, 12*, 70–75.

Shih, M., & Sanchez, D. T. (2005). Perspectives and research on the positive and negative implications of having multiple racial identities. *Psychological Bulletin, 131*, 569–591.

Shim, S. S., Ryan, A. M., & Anderson, C. J. (2008). Achievement goals and achievement during early adolescence: Examining time-varying predictor and outcome variables in growth-curve analysis. *Journal of Educational Psychology, 100*, 655–671.

Shiner, R. (1998). How shall we speak of children's personalities in middle childhood? A preliminary taxonomy. *Psychological Bulletin, 124*, 308–332.

Shipman, K. L., Schneider, R., Fitzgerald, M. M., Sims, C., Swisher, L., & Edwards, A. (2007). Maternal emotion socialization in maltreating and non-maltreating families: Implications for children's emotion regulation. *Social Development, 16*, 268–285.

Shirtcliff, E. A., Dahl, R. E., & Pollak, S. D. (2009). Pubertal development: Correspondence between hormonal and physical development. *Child Development, 80*, 327–337.

Shonk, S. M., & Cicchetti, D. (2001). Maltreatment, competency deficits, and risk for academic and behavioral maladjustment. *Developmental Psychology, 37*, 3–17.

Short, E. J., Basili, L. A., & Schatschneider, C. W. (1993). Analysis of humor skills among elementary school students: Comparisons of children with and without intellectual handicaps. *American Journal on Mental Retardation, 98*, 63–73.

Shure, M. (2001). How to think, not what to think: A problem-solving approach to prevention of early high-risk behaviors. In A. Bohart & D. Stipek (Eds.), *Constructive and destructive behavior: Implications for family, school, and society* (pp. 271–290). Washington, DC: APA.

Sidebotham, P., Heron, J., & The ALSPAC Study Team. (2003). Child maltreatment in the "children of the nineties": The role of the child. *Child Abuse & Neglect, 27*, 337–352.

Siegler, R. S. (1995). How does change occur: A microgenetic study of number conservation. *Cognitive Psychology, 28*, 225–273.

Siegler, R. S. (2000). The rebirth of children's learning. *Child Development, 71*, 26–35.

Siegler, R. S., & Booth, J. (2004). Development of numerical estimation in young children. *Child Development, 75*, 428–444.

Siegler, R. S., & Mu, Y. (2008). Chinese children excel on novel mathematics problems even before elementary school. *Psychological Science, 19*, 759–763.

Siegler, R. S., & Ramani, G. B. (2009). Playing linear number board games—but not circular ones—improves low-income preschoolers' numerical understanding. *Journal of Educational Psychology, 101*, 545–560.

Sigman, M., Cohen, S., & Beckwith, L. (1997). Why does infant attention predict adolescent intelligence? *Infant Behavior and Development, 20*, 133–140.

Silk, J., Steinberg, L., & Morris, A. (2003). Adolescents' emotion regulation in daily life: Links to depressive symptoms and problems behavior. *Child Development, 74*, 1869–1880.

Silver, E. A., Mesa, V. M., Morris, K. A., Star, J. R., & Benken, B. M. (2009). Teaching mathematics for understanding: An analysis of lessons submitted by teachers seeking NBPTS certification. *American Educational Research Journal, 46*, 501–531.

Silvia, P. J. (2008). Interest—The curious emotion. *Current Directions in Psychological Science, 17*, 57–60.

Simon, V. A., Aikins, J. W., & Prinstein, M. J. (2008). Romantic partner selection and socialization during early adolescence. *Child Development, 79*, 1676–1692.

Simpkins, S., & Parke, R. (2001). The relations between parental friendships and children's friendships: Self-report and observational analysis. *Child Development, 72*, 569–582.

Simpkins, S. D., Eccles, J. S., & Becnel, J. N. (2008). The mediational role of adolescents' friends in relations between activity breadth and adjustment. *Developmental Psychology, 44*, 1081–1094.

Simpson, R. (2004). Finding effective intervention and personnel preparation practices for students with autism spectrum disorders. *Exceptional Children, 70*, 135–144.

Singer, D. (1999). Imaginative play and television: Factors in a child's development. In J. Singer & P. Salovey (Eds.), *At play in the fields of consciousness: Essays in honor of Jerome L. Singer* (pp. 303–326). Mahwah, NJ: Lawrence Erlbaum.

Singer, J., & Lythcott, M. (2002). Fostering school achievement and creativity through sociodramatic play in the classroom. *Research in the Schools, 9*, 43–52.

Singer, M. (1999). The role of concern for others and moral intensity in adolescents' ethicality judgments. *The Journal of Genetic Psychology, 160*, 155–166.

Singh, H., & O'Boyle, M. (2004). Interhemispheric interaction during global-local processing in mathematically gifted adolescents, average-ability youth, and college students. *Neuropsychology, 18*, 371–377.

Sirin, S. R. (2005). Socioeconomic status and academic achievement: A meta-analytic review of research. *Review of Educational Research, 75*, 417–453.

Skinner, B. F. (1948). *Walden two*. New York: Macmillan.

Skinner, B. F. (1971). *Beyond freedom and dignity*. New York: Bantam.

Skinner, B. F. (1972). *Cumulative record: A selection of papers* (3rd ed.). New York: Appleton-Century-Crofts.

Skinner, E. A., Furrer, C., Marchand, G., & Kindermann, T. A. (2008). Engagement and disaffection in the classroom: Part of a larger motivational dynamic? *Journal of Educational Psychology, 100*, 765–781.

Slaughter, V., Peterson, C. C., & Mackintosh, E. (2007). Mind what mother says: Narrative input and theory of mind in typical children and those on the autism specturm. *Child Development, 78*, 839–858.

Slavin, R. E. (1996). Research on cooperative learning and achievement: What we know, what we need to know. *Contemporary Educational Psychology, 21*, 43–69.

Slavin, R. E., & Cheung, A. (2003). *Effective reading programs for English language learners: A best-evidence synthesis*. Center for Research on the Education of Students Placed At Risk. Retrieved from http://www.csos.jhu.edu/crespar/techReports/Report66.pdf

Slavin, R. E., Cheung, A., Groff, C., & Lake, C. (2008). Effective reading programs for middle and high schools: A best-evidence synthesis. *Reading Research Quarterly, 43*, 290–322.

Slavin, R. E., & Cooper, R. (1999). Improving intergroup relations: Lessons learned from cooperative learning programs. *Journal of Social Issues, 55*, 647–663.

Slavin, R. E., & Lake, C. (2008). Effective programs in elementary mathematics: A best-evidence synthesis. *Review of Educational Research, 78*, 427–515.

Slavin, R. E., Lake, C., Chambers, B., Cheung, A., & Davis, S. (2009). Effective reading programs for the elementary grades: A best-evidence synthesis. *Review of Educational Research, 79*, 1391–1466.

Sletta, O., Sobstad, F., & Valas, H. (1995). Humour, peer acceptance and perceived social competence in preschool and school-aged children. *British Journal of Educational Psychology, 65*, 179–195.

Smith, A., & Lalonde, R. N. (2003). "Racelessness" in a Canadian context? Exploring the link between black students' identity, achievement, and mental health. *Journal of Black Psychology, 29*, 142–164.

Smith, C., & Denton, M. L. (2005). *Soul searching: The religious and spiritual lives of American teenagers*. New York: Oxford University Press.

Smith, E. B. (1995). Anchored in our literature: Students responding to African American literature. *Language Arts, 72*, 571–574.

Smith, J., & Ross, H. (2007). Training parents to mediate sibling disputes affects children's negotiation and conflict understanding. *Child Development, 78*, 790–805.

Smith, J. D., Schneider, B., Smith, P., & Ananiadou, K. (2004). The effectiveness of whole-school antibullying programs: A synthesis of evaluation research. *School Psychology Review, 33*, 547–560.

Smith, M. S. (2000). Balancing old and new: An experienced middle school teacher's learning in the context of mathematics instructional reform. *The Elementary School Journal, 100*, 351–375.

Smith, P., & Myron-Wilson, R. (1998). Parenting and school bullying. *Clinical Child Psychology and Psychiatry, 3*, 1359–1045.

Smith, R. E., Bayen, U. J., & Martin, C. (2010). The cognitive processes underlying event-based prospective memory in school-age children and young adults: A formal model-based study. *Developmental Psychology, 46*, 230–244.

Smith, S., Daunic, A., Miller, D., & Robinson, R. (2002). Conflict resolution and peer mediation in middle schools: Extending the process and outcome knowledge base. *Journal of Social Psychology, 142*, 567–586.

Smitherman, G. (2000). *Black talk: Words and phrases from the hood to the amen corner* (Revised ed.). Boston: Houghton Mifflin.

Smolak, L., & Thompson, J. K. (Eds.). (2009). *Body image, eating disorders, and obesity in youth: Assessment, prevention, and treatment* (2nd ed.). Washington, DC: American Psychological Association.

Smolensky, E., & Gootman, J. (Eds.). (2003). *Working families and growing kids: Caring for children and adolescents*. Washington, DC: National Academies Press.

Smyke, A. (1997). Theories of spoiling and fear of spoiling: Historical and contemporary perspectives. *The Signal, 5*, 1–9.

Snedeker, J., Geren, J., & Shafto, C. L. (2007). Starting over: International adoption as a natural experiment in language development. *Psychological Science, 18*, 79–87.

Snell, E. K., Adam, E. K., & Duncan, G. (2007). Sleep and the body mass index and overweight status of children and adolescents. *Child Development, 78*, 309–323.

Snowling, M. J., Gallagher, A., & Frith, U. (2003). Family risk of dyslexia is continuous: Individual differences in the precursors of reading skill. *Child Development, 74*, 358–373.

Snyder, H. N. (2000). Sexual assault of young children as reported to law enforcement: Victim, incident, and offender characteristics. Washington, DC: U.S. Department of Justice. Retrieved January 12, 2009 from http://www.ojp.usdoj.gov/bjs/pub/pdf/saycrle.pdf

Snyder, J., Cramer, A., Afrank, J., & Patterson, G. (2005). The contributions of ineffective discipline and parental hostile attributions of child misbehavior to the development of conduct problems at home and school. *Developmental Psychology, 41*, 30–41.

Snyder, J., Schrepferman, L., McEachern, A., Barner, S., Johnson, K., & Provines, J. (2008). Peer deviancy training and peer coercion: Dual processes associated with early-onset conduct problems. *Child Development, 79*, 252–268.

Snyder, J. J., & Patterson, G. R. (1995). Individual differences in social aggression: A test of a reinforcement model of socialization in the natural environment. *Behavior Therapy, 26*, 371–391.

Socha, T. J., & Kelly, B. (1994). Children making "fun": Humorous communication, impression managment, and moral development. *Child Study Journal, 24*, 237–252.

Soderstrom, M. (2007). Beyond babytalk: Re-evaluating the nature and content of speech input to preverbal infants. *Developmental Review, 27*, 501–532.

Soken, N. H., & Pick, A. D. (1999). Infants' perception of dynamic affective expressions: Do infants distinguish specific expressions? *Child Development, 70*, 1275–1282.

Soliday, E. (2007). Infant feeding and cognition: Integrating a developmental perspective. *Child Development Perspectives, 1*, 19–25.

Solomon, D., Battistich, V., Watson, M., Schaps, E., & Lewis, C. (2000). A six-district study of educational change: Direct and mediated effects of the Child Development Project. *Social Psychology of Education, 41*, 3–51.

Sophian, C., & Madrid, S. (2003). Young children's reasoning about many-to-one correspondences. *Child Development, 74*, 1418–1432.

Sorce, J. F., Emde, R. M., Campos, J. J., & Klinnert, M. D. (1985). Maternal emotional signaling: Its effect on the visual cliff behavior of 1-year-olds. *Developmental Psychology, 21*, 195–200.

Sourander, A., Jensen, P., Davies, M., Niemela, S., Elonheimo, H., Ristkari, T., et al. (2007). Who is at greatest risk of adverse long-term outcomes? The Finnish From a Boy to a Man Study. *Journal of the American Academy of Child and Adolescent Psychiatry, 46*, 1148–1161.

Southgate, D. E., & Roscigno, V. J. (2009). The impact of music on childhood and adolescent achievement. *Social Science Quarterly, 90*, 4–22.

Sparks, R. L., Patton, J., Ganschow, L., Humbach, N., & Javorsky, J. (2008). Early first-language reading and spelling skills predict later second-language reading and spelling skills. *Journal of Educational Psychology, 100*, 162–174.

Spear, L. (2000). Neurobehavioral changes in adolescence. *Current Directions in Psychological Science, 9*, 111–114.

Spearman, C. (1904). General intelligence, objectively determined and measured. *American Journal of Psychology, 15*, 201–293.

Spelke, E. (2005). Sex differences in intrinsic aptitude for mathematics and science? A critical review. *American Psychologist, 60*, 950–958.

Spence, I., Yu, J. J., Feng, J., & Marshman, J. (2009). Women match men when learning a spatial skill. *Journal of Experimental Psychology: Learning, Memory, and Cognition, 35*, 1097–1103.

Spencer, J. P., Blumberg, M. S., McMurray, B., Robinson, S. R., Samuelson, L. K., & Tomblin, J. B. (2009). Short arms and talking eggs: Why we should no longer abide the nativist-empiricist debate. *Child Development Perspectives, 3*, 79–87.

Spencer, M. B. (2008). Lessons learned and opportunities ignored since *Brown v. Board of Education:* Youth development and the myth of a color-blind society. *Educational Researcher, 37*, 253–266.

Spera, C. (2005). A review of the relationship among parenting practices, parenting styles, and adolescent school achievement. *Educational Psychology Review, 17*, 125–146.

Spira, E. G., Bracken, S. S., & Fischel, J. E. (2005). Predicting improvement after first-grade reading difficulties: The effects of oral language, emergent literacy, and behavior skills. *Developmental Psychology, 41*, 225–234.

Spitz, R. (1945). Hospitalism. *The Psychoanalytic Study of the Child, 1*, 53–74.

Spörer, N., Brunstein, J. C., & Kieschke, U. (2009). Improving students' reading comprehension skills: Effects of strategy instruction and reciprocal teaching. *Learning and Instruction, 19*, 272–286.

Spotts, E. L., Neiderhiser, J. M., Hetherington, E. M., & Reiss, D. (2001). The relation between observational measures of social problem solving and familial antisocial behavior: Genetic and environmental influences. *Journal of Research on Adolescence, 11*, 351–374.

Sroufe, L. A. (1996). *Emotional development: The organization of emotional life in the early years.* Cambridge, UK: Cambridge University Press.

Sroufe, L. A., Bennett, C., Englund, M., Urban, J., & Shulman, S. (1993). The significance of gender boundaries in preadolescence: Contemporary correlates and antecedents of boundary violation and maintenance. *Child Development, 64*, 455–466.

Sroufe, L. A., Fox, N., & Pancake, V. (1983). Attachment and dependency in developmental perspective. *Child Development, 54*, 1615–1627.

St. Petersburg-USA Orphanage Research Team. (2008). The effects of early social-emotional and relationship experience on the development of young orphanage children. *Monographs of the Society for Research in Child Development, 73* (Serial No. 291).

Stams, G.-J., Juffer, F., & van IJzendoorn, M. (2002). Maternal sensitivity, infant attachment, and temperament in early childhood predict adjustment in middle childhood: The case of adopted children and their biologically unrelated parents. *Developmental Psychology, 38*, 806–821.

Stanovich, K. E. (1986). Matthew effects in reading: Some consequences of individual differences in the acquisition of literacy. *Reading Research Quarterly, 21*, 360–406.

Stanovich, K. E. (1992). *How to think straight about psychology* (3rd ed.). New York: HarperCollins.

Stanovich, K. E., & Siegel, L. S. (1994). Phenotypic performance profile of children with reading disabilities: A regression-based test of the phonological-core variable-difference model. *Journal of Educational Psychology, 86*, 24–53.

Stanton-Salazar, R. D., & Spina, S. U. (2003). Informal mentors and role models in the lives of urban Mexican-origin adolescents. *Anthropology & Education Quarterly, 34*, 231–254.

Starkes, J. L., Deakin, J. M., Allard, F., Hodges, N. J., & Hayes, A. (1996). Deliberate practice in sports: What is it anyway? In K. A. Ericsson (Ed.), *The road to excellence: The acquisition of expert performance in the arts and sciences, sports, and games* (pp. 81–106). Mahwah, NJ: Erlbaum.

Stasz, C., & Stecher, B. M. (2000). Teaching mathematics and language arts in reduced size and non-reduced size classrooms. *Educational Evaluation and Policy Analysis, 22*, 313–329.

Stattin, H., & Kerr, M. (2000). Parental monitoring: A reinterpretation. *Child Development, 71*, 1072–1085.

Stearns, E. (2004). Interracial friendliness and the social organization of schools. *Youth & Society, 35*, 395–419.

Stearns, E., Moller, S., Blau, J., & Potochnick, S. (2007). Staying back and dropping out: The relationship between grade retention and school drop out. *Sociology of Education, 80*, 210–240.

Stedman, L. (1997). International achievement differences: An assessment of a new perspective. *Educational Researcher, 26*(3), 4–15.

Steele, C. M. (1992, April). Race and the schooling of black Americans. *The Atlantic Monthly*, 68–78.

Steele, C. M., & Aronson, J. (1995). Stereotype threat and the intellectual test performance of African Americans. *Journal of Personality and Social Psychology, 69*, 797–811.

Stein, N., & Trabasso, T. (1989). Children's understanding of changing emotional states. In C. Saarni & P. Harris (Eds.), *Children's understanding of emotion* (pp. 50–80). Cambridge, UK: Cambridge University Press.

Steinberg, L. (1999). *Adolescence* (5th ed.). Boston: McGraw-Hill.

Steinberg, L. (2009). Should the science of adolescent brain development inform public policy? *American Psychologist, 64*, 739–750.

Steinberg, L., Albert, D., Cauffman, E., Banich, M., Graham, S., & Woolard, J. (2008). Age differences in sensation seeking and impulsivity as indexed by behavior and self-report: Evidence for a dual systems model. *Developmental Psychology, 44*, 1764–1778.

Steinberg, L., Blatt-Eisengart, I., & Cauffman, E. (2006). Patterns of competence and adjustment among adolescents from authoritative, authoritarian, indulgent, and neglectful homes: A replication in a sample of serious juvenile offenders. *Journal of Research on Adolescence, 16*, 47–58.

Steinberg, L., Graham, S., O'Brien, L., Woolard, J., Cauffman, E., & Banich, M. (2009). Age differences in future orientation and delay discounting. *Child Development, 80*, 28–44.

Steinberg, L., & Silk, J. S. (2002). Parenting adolescents. In M. H. Bornstein (Ed.), *Handbook of parenting* (2nd ed., Vol. 1, pp. 103–133). Mahwah, NJ: Erlbaum.

Stemler, S. E., Grigorenko, E. L., Jarvin, L., & Sternberg, R. J. (2006). Using the theory of successful intelligence as a basis for augmenting AP exams in psychology and statistics. *Intelligence, 31*, 344–376.

Stern, B., & Peterson, L. (1999). Linking wrongdoing and consequence: A developmental analysis of children's punishment orientation. *The Journal of Genetic Psychology, 160*, 205–224.

Sternberg, R. J. (1988). *The triarchic mind: A new theory of human intelligence*. New York: Viking.

Sternberg, R. J. (1996). *Successful intelligence: How practical and creative intelligence determine success in life*. New York: Simon & Schuster.

Sternberg, R. J., & Berg, C. A. (1986). Quantitative integration: Definitions of intelligence: A comparison of the 1921 and 1986 symposia. In D. K. Detterman (Ed.), *What is intelligence? Contemporary viewpoints on its nature and definition* (pp. 155–162). Norwood, NJ: Ablex.

Sternberg, R. J., Grigorenko, E., & Bundy, D. (2001). The predictive value of IQ. *Merrill-Palmer Quarterly, 47*, 1–41.

Sternberg, R. J., Grigorenko, E., & Kidd, K. (2005). Intelligence, race, and genetics. *American Psychologist, 60*, 46–59.

Sternberg, R. J., & Grigorenko, E. L. (2004). Successful intelligence in the classroom. *Theory into Practice, 43*, 274–280.

Sternberg, R. J., Grigorenko, E. L., & Zhang, L.-f. (2008). Styles of learning and thinking matter in instruction and assessment. *Perpsectives on Psychological Science, 3*, 486–506.

Sternberg, R. J., & Kaufman, J. (1998). Human abilities. *Annual Review of Psychology, 49*, 479–502.

Steubing, K. K., Barth, A. E., Cirino, P. T., Francis, D. J., & Fletcher, J. M. (2008). A response to recent reanalyses of the National Reading Panel report: Effects of systematic phonics instruction are practically significant. *Journal of Educational Psychology, 100*, 123–134.

Stevens, V., Van Oost, P., & de Bourdeaudhuij, I. (2000). The effects of an anti-bullying intervention programme on peers' attitudes and behaviour. *Journal of Adolescence, 23*, 21–34.

Stevenson, H. W., Lee, S.-Y., Chen, C., Stigler, J., Hsu, C.-C., & Kitamura, S. (1990). Contexts of achievement: A study of American, Chinese, and Japanese children. *Monographs of the Society for Research in Child Development, 55* (Serial No. 221).

Stevenson, H. W., & Stigler, J. (1992). *The learning gap: Why our schools are failing and what we can learn from Japanese and Chinese education*. New York: Summit.

Stevenson-Hinde, J., & Verschueren, K. (2002). Attachment in childhood. In P. Smith & C. Hart (Eds.), *Blackwell handbook of childhood social development* (pp. 182–204). Oxford: Blackwell.

Stice, E., & Shaw, H. (2004). Eating disorder prevention programs: A meta-analytic review. *Psychological Bulletin, 130*, 206–227.

Stiles, J. (2009). On genes, brains, and behavior: Why should developmental psychologists care about brain development? *Child Development Perspectives, 3*, 196–202.

Stinson, D. (2006). African American male adolescents, schooling (and mathematics): Deficiency, rejection, and achievement. *Review of Educational Research, 76*, 477–506.

Stinson, D. W. (2008). Negotiating sociocultural discourses: The counter-storytelling of academically (and mathematically) successful African American male students. *American Educational Research Journal, 45*, 975–1010.

Stipek, D. (2001). Pathways to constructive lives: The importance of early school success. In A. Bohart & D. Stipek (Eds.), *Constructive and destructive behavior: Implications for family, school, and society* (pp. 291–315). Washington, DC: APA.

Stipek, D., & Miles, S. (2008). Effects of aggression on achievement: Does conflict with the teacher make it worse? *Child Development, 79*, 1721–1735.

Stocker, C. M., Richmond, M. K., Rhoades, G. K., & Kuang, L. (2007). Family emotional proesses and adolescents' adjustment. *Social Development, 16*, 310–325.

Stormshak, E., Bierman, K., Bruschi, C., Dodge, K. A., Coie, J., & Conduct Problems Prevention Research Group. (1999). The relation between behavior problems and peer preference in different classroom contexts. *Child Development, 70* (1), 169–182.

Straus, M. A., & Savage, S. A. (2005). Neglectful behavior by parents in the life history of university students in 17 countries and its relation to violence against dating partners. *Child Maltreatment, 10*, 124–135.

Straus, M. A., Sugarman, D. B., & Giles-Sims, J. (1997). Spanking by parents and subsequent antisocial behavior of children. *Archives of Pediatric and Adolescent Medicine, 151*, 761-767.

Strauss, R. S. (2000). Childhood obesity and self-esteem. *Pediatrics, 105*, e15.

Strauss, R. S., & Knight, J. (1999). Influence of the home environment on the development of obesity in children. *Pediatrics, 103*, e85.

Strayer, J., & Roberts, W. (1997). Children's personal distance and their empathy: Indices of interpersonal closeness. *International Journal of Behavioral Development, 20*, 385–403.

Strenze, T. (2007). Intelligence and socioeconomic success: A meta-analytic review of longitudinal research. *Intelligence, 35*, 401–426.

Strickgold, R., & Walker, M. (2004). To sleep, perchance to gain creative insight? *Trends in Cognitive Sciences, 8*, 191–192.

Striegel-Moore, R. H., & Bulik, C. (2007). Risk factors for eating disorders. *American Psychologist, 62*, 181–198.

Strough, J., Berg, C., & Meegan, S. (2001). Friendship and gender differences in task and social interpretations of peer collaborative problem solving. *Social Development, 10*, 1–22.

Stukas, A., Clary, G., & Snyder, M. (1999). Service learning: Who benefits and why. *SRCD Social Policy Report, 13*, 1–19.

Stumpf, H., & Stanley, J. C. (1996). Gender-related differences on the College Board's Advanced Placement and achievement tests, 1982–1992. *Journal of Educational Psychology, 88*, 353–364.

Sturge-Apple, M. L., Davies, P. T., & Cummings, E. M. (2006). Impact of hostility and withdrawal in interparental conflict on parental emotional unavailability and children's adjustment difficulties. *Child Development, 77*, 1623–1641.

Sullivan, M., & Lewis, M. (2003). Contextual determinants of anger and other negative expressions in young infants. *Developmental Psychology, 39*, 693–705.

Summer, L. (2003). *Learning joy from dogs without collars*. New York: Simon & Schuster.

Sun, Y., & Li, Y. (2001). Marital disruption, parental investment, and children's academic achievement: A prospective analysis. *Journal of Family Issues, 22*, 27–62.

Sundet, J. M., Eriksen, W., & Tambs, K. (2008). Intelligence correlations between brothers decrease with increasing age difference: Evidence of shared environmental effects in young adults. *Psychological Science, 19*, 843–847.

Supple, A. J., & Small, S. A. (2006). The influence of parental support, knowledge, authoritative parenting on Hmong and European American adolescent development. *Journal of Family Issues, 27*, 1214–1232.

Susman, E. J., Dorn, L. D., Inoff-Germain, G., Nottelman, E. D., & Chrousos, G. P. (1997). Cortisol reactivity, distress behavior, and behavioral and psychological problems in young adolescents: A longitudinal perspective. *Journal of Research on Adolescence, 7*, 81–105.

Swann, W. B., Chang-Schneider, C., & McClarty, K. L. (2007). Do people's self-views matter: Self-concept and self-esteem in everyday life. *American Psychologist, 62*, 84–94.

Swanson, H. L. (2008). Working memory and intelligence in children: What develops? *Journal of Educational Psychology, 100*, 581–602.

Swanson, H. L., & Jerman, O. (2006). Math disabilities: A selective meta-analysis of the literature. *Review of Educational Research, 76*, 249–274.

Swanson, H. L., Jerman, O., & Zheng, X. (2008). Growth in working memory and mathematical problem solving in children at risk and not at risk for serious math difficulties. *Journal of Educational Psychology, 100*, 343–379.

Swanson, H. L., Trainin, G., Necoechea, D. M., & Hammill, D. D. (2003). Rapid naming, phonological awareness, and reading: A meta-analysis of the correlation evidence. *Review of Educational Research, 73*, 407–440.

Swearer, S. M., Espelage, D. L., Vaillancourt, T., & Hymel, S. (2010). What can be done about school bullying? Linking research to educational practice. *Educational Researcher, 39*(1), 38–47.

Swinford, S. P., DeMaris, A., Cernkovich, S. A., & Giordano, P. C. (2000). Harsh physical discipline in childhood and violence in later romantic involvements: The mediating role of problem behaviors. *Journal of Marriage and the Family, 62*, 508–519.

Syer, C., & Shore, B. (2001). Science fairs: What are the sources of help for students and how prevalent is cheating? *School Science and Mathematics, 101*, 206–220.

Szalacha, L. A., Erkut, S., Coll, C. G., Alarcsn, O., Fields, J. P., & Ceder, I. (2003). Discrimination and Puerto Rican children's and adolescents' mental health. *Cultural Diversity and Ethnic Minority Psychology, 9*, 141–155.

Szynal-Brown, C., & Morgan, R. (1983). The effects of reward on tutor's behavior in a cross-age tutoring context. *Journal of Experimental Child Psychology, 36*, 196–208.

Taing, V. (2009). Boy lifts book; librarian changes boy's life [NPR Morning Edition, interview from StoryCorps]. Retrieved October 2, 2009, from http://www.npr.org/templates/story/story.php?storyId=113357239

Tallal, P. (2004). Improving language and literacy is a matter of time. *Nature Reviews: Neuroscience, 5*, 721–728.

Talwar, V., Gordon, H. M., & Lee, K. (2007). Lying in the elementary school years: Verbal deception and its relation to second-order belief understanding. *Developmental Psychology, 43*, 804–810.

Talwar, V., & Lee, K. (2002). Emergence of white-lie telling in children between 3 and 7 years of age. *Merrill-Palmer Quarterly, 48,* 160–181.

Talwar, V., & Lee, K. (2008). Social and cognitive correlates of children's lying behavior. *Child Development, 79,* 866–881.

Tamis-LeMonda, C., Bornstein, M. H., & Baumwell, L. (2001). Maternal responsiveness and children's achievement of language milestones. *Child Development, 72,* 748–767.

Tamis-LeMonda, C., Cristofaro, T. N., Rodriguez, E. T., & Bornstein, M. H. (2006). Early language development: Social influences in the first years of life. In L. Balter & C. Tamis-LeMonda (Eds.), *Child psychology: A handbook of contemporary issues* (2nd ed., pp. 79–108). New York: Hove.

Tamis-LeMonda, C., Way, N., Hughes, D., Yoshikawa, H., Kalman, R. K., & Niwa, E. Y. (2008). Parents' goals for children: The dynamic coexistence of individualism and collectivism in cultures and individuals. *Social Development, 17,* 183–209.

Taneja, V., Sriram, S., Beri, R., Sreenivas, V., Aggarwal, R., Kaur, R., et al. (2002). "Not by bread alone": Impact of a structured 90-minute play session on development of children in an orphanage. *Child: Care, Health, & Development, 28,* 95–100.

Tang, C. (2006). Corporal punishment and physical maltreatment against children: A community study on Chinese parents in Hong Kong. *Child Abuse & Neglect, 30,* 893–907.

Tangney, J. P., Stuewig, J., & Mashek, D. J. (2007). Moral emotions and moral behavior. *Annual Review of Psychology, 58,* 345–372.

Tanner, J. M. (1973). Growing up. *Scientific American, 229,* 34–43.

Tanner, J. M. (1985). Growth regulation and the genetics of growth. *Progress in Clinical & Biological Research, 200,* 19–32.

Tarabulsy, G. M., Bernier, A., Provost, M. A., Maranda, J., Larose, S., Moss, E., et al. (2005). Another look inside the gap: Ecological contributions to the transmission of attachment in a sample of adolescent mother-infant dyads. *Developmental Psychology, 41,* 212–234.

Taumoepeau, M., & Ruffman, T. (2008). Stepping stones to others' minds: Maternal talk relates to child mental state language and emotion undertanding at 15, 24, and 33 months. *Child Development, 79,* 284–302.

Taylor, G., Klein, N., & Hack, M. (2000). School-age consequences of birth weight less than 750g: A review and update. *Developmental Neuropsychology, 17,* 289–321.

Taylor, G., Klein, N., Minich, N., & Hack, M. (2000). Middle-school-age outcomes in children with very low birthweight. *Child Development, 71,* 1495–1511.

Taylor, M., Carlson, S., Maring, B., Gerow, L., & Charley, C. (2004). The characteristics and correlates of fantasy in school-age children: Imaginary companions, impersonation, and social understanding. *Developmental Psychology, 40,* 1173–1187.

Teisl, M., & Cicchetti, D. (2008). Physical abuse, cognitive and emotional processes, and aggressive/disruptive behavior problems. *Social Development, 17,* 1–23.

Telzer, E. H., & Fuligni, A. J. (2009). Daily family assistance and the psychological well-being of adolescents from Latin American, Asian, and European backgrounds. *Developmental Psychology, 45,* 1177–1189.

Terwogt, M. M., & Olthof, T. (1989). Awareness and self-regulation of emotion in young children. In C. Saarni & P. Harris (Eds.), *Children's understanding of emotion* (pp. 209–237). New York: Cambridge University Press.

Tessier, R., Cristo, M., Velez, S., Giron, M., Figueroa de Calume, Z., Ruiz-Palaez, J., et al. (1998). Kangaroo mother care and the bonding hypothesis. *Pediatrics, 102,* 1–8.

Thelen, E. (1995). Motor development: A new synthesis. *American Pyschologist, 50,* 79–103.

Thijs, J., & Verkuyten, M. (2008). Peer victimization and academic achievement in a multiethnic sample: The role of perceived academic self-efficacy. *Journal of Educational Psychology, 100,* 754–764.

Thoma, S. (2000). Models of moral behavior. *Journal of Mind and Behavior, 21,* 129–136.

Thomaes, S., Bushman, B. J., Orobio de Castro, B., Cohen, G. L., & Denissen, J. J. A. (2009). Reducing narcissistic aggression by buttressing self-esteem: An experimental field study. *Psychological Science, 20,* 1536–1542.

Thomas, A., & Chess, S. (1984). Genesis and evolution of behavioral disorders: From infancy to early adult life. *American Journal of Psychiatry, 141,* 1–9.

Thomas, A., Chess, S., & Birch, H. (1970). The origin of personality. *Scientific American, 223,* 102–109.

Thomas, A., Chess, S., & Korn, S. (1982). The reality of difficult temperament. *Merrill-Palmer Quarterly, 28,* 1–40.

Thomas, M. S. C., & Johnson, M. H. (2008). New advances in understanding sensitive periods in brain development. *Current Directions in Psychological Science, 17,* 1–5.

Thompson, R. A. (1991). Emotional regulation and emotional development. *Educational Psychology Review, 3,* 269–307.

Thompson, R. A. (1994). Emotion regulation: A theme in search of definition. *Monographs of the Society for Research in Child Development* (Vol. 59, pp. 25–52).

Thompson, R. A., & Nelson, C. (2001). Developmental science and the media: Early brain development. *American Psychologist, 56,* 5–15.

Thompson, W. F., Schellenberg, E. G., & Husain, G. (2001). Arousal, mood, and the Mozart effect. *Psychological Science, 12,* 248–251.

Thorell, L. B., Lindqvist, S., Nutley, S. B., Bohlin, G., & Klingberg, T. (2009). Training and transfer effects of executive functions in preschool children. *Developmental Science, 12,* 106–113.

Thorkildsen, T., Reese, D., & Corsino, A. (2002). School ecologies and attitudes about exclusionary behavior among adolescents and young adults. *Merrill-Palmer Quarterly, 48,* 25–51.

Thornton, S. (1999). Creating the conditions for cognitive change: The interaction between task structures and specific strategies. *Child Development, 70,* 588–603.

Tinsley, B., Lees, N., & Sumartojo, E. (2004). Child and adolescent HIV risk: Familial and cultural perspectives. *Journal of Family Psychology, 18,* 208–224.

Tobin, J. J. (Writer). (1989). A video companion to "Preschool in three cultures: Japan, China, and the United States" [VHS]. In Fourth Wave Productions (Producer). USA: Yale University Press.

Tomasello, M. (2007). Cooperation and communication in the 2nd year of life. *Child Development Perspectives, 1,* 8–12.

Tomasello, M., Carpenter, M., & Liszkowski, U. (2007). A new look at infant pointing. *Child Development, 78,* 705–722.

Toner, I. J., Moore, L. P., & Emmons, B. A. (1980). The effect of being labeled on subsequent self-control in children. *Child Development, 51*, 618–621.

Topping, K. J., & Barron, I. G. (2009). School-based child sexual abuse prevention programs: A review of effectiveness. *Review of Educational Research, 79*, 431–463.

Torff, B., & Gardner, H. (1999). The vertical mind—The case for multiple intelligences. In M. Anderson (Ed.), *The development of intelligence* (pp. 139–159). East Sussex, UK: Psychology Press.

Torgesen, J. K. (2009). The response to intervention instructional model: Some outcomes from a large-scale implementation in Reading First schools. *Child Development Perspectives, 3*, 38–40.

Toro, J. M., Nespor, M., Mehler, J., & Bonatti, L. L. (2008). Finding words and rules in a speech stream: Functional differences betwen vowels and consonants. *Psychological Science, 19*, 137–144.

Tout, K., de Haan, M., Campbell, E., & Gunnar, M. (1998). Social behavior correlates of cortisol activity in child care: Gender differences and time-of-day effects. *Child Development, 69*, 1247–1262.

Towers, H., Spotts, E. L., Neiderhiser, J. M., Hetherington, E., Plomin, R., & Reiss, D. (2000). Genetic and environmental influences on teacher ratings of the Child Behavior Checklist. *International Journal of Behavioral Development, 24*, 373-381.

Trautwein, U., Lüdtke, O., Marsh, H. W., & Nagy, G. (2009). Within-school social comparison: How students perceive the standing of their class predicts academic self-concept. *Journal of Educational Psychology, 101*, 853–866.

Treboux, D., Crowell, J., & Waters, E. (2004). When "new" meets "old": Configurations of adult attachment representations and their implications for marital functioning. *Developmental Psychology, 40*, 295–314.

Treiman, R. (2000). The foundations of literacy. *Current Directions in Psychological Science, 9*, 89–92.

Tremblay, R. (2000). The development of aggressive behavior during childhood: What have we learned in the past century? *International Journal of Behavioral Development, 24*, 129–141.

Trionfi, G., & Reese, E. (2009). A good story: Children with imaginary companions create richer narratives. *Child Development, 80*, 1301–1313.

Tronick, E. Z. (1989). Emotions and emotional communication in infants. *American Psychologist, 44*, 112–119.

Troseth, G., Saylor, M. M., & Archer, A. (2006). Young children's use of video as a source of socially relevant information. *Child Development, 77*, 786–799.

Trout, J. (2003). Biological specializations for speech: What can the animals tell us? *Current Directions in Psychological Science, 12*, 155–159.

True, M. M., Pisani, L., & Oumar, F. (2001). Infant–mother attachment among the Dogon of Mali. *Child Development, 72*, 1451–1466.

Trzesniewski, K., Moffitt, T., Caspi, A., Taylor, A., & Maughan, B. (2006). Revisiting the association between reading achievement and antisocial behavior: New evidence of an environmental explanation from a twin study. *Child Development, 77*, 72–88.

Trzesniewski, K. H., Donnellan, M. B., & Robins, R. W. (2008). Do today's young people really think they are so extraordinary? An examination of secular trends in narcissism and self-enhancement. *Psychological Science, 19*, 181–188.

Tsai, J. L. (2007). Ideal affect: Cultural causes and behavioral consequences. *Perspectives on Psychological Science, 2*, 242–259.

Tuerk, P. (2005). Research in the high-stakes era: Achievement, resources, and No Child Left Behind. *Psychological Science, 16*, 419–425.

Tuncay, E. (2003). Effective interventions on test anxiety reduction: A meta-analysis. *School Psychology International, 24*, 313–328.

Turkheimer, E. (2000). Three laws of behavior genetics and what they mean. *Current Directions in Psychological Science, 9*, 160–164.

Turley, R. N. L. (2003). Are children of young mothers disadvantaged because of their mother's age or family background? *Child Development, 74*, 465–474.

Turner, J. C., Meyer, D. K., Midgley, C., & Patrick, H. (2003). Teacher discourse and sixth graders' reported affect and achievement behavior in two high-mastery/high-performance mathematics classrooms. *The Elementary School Journal, 103*, 357–382.

Turner, J. C., Midgley, C., Meyer, D., Gheen, M., Anderman, E., Kang, Y., et al. (2002). The classroom environment and students' reports of avoidance strategies in mathematics: A multimethod study. *Journal of Educational Psychology, 94*, 88–106.

Tversky, B. (2000). Remembering spaces. In E. Tulving & F. I. M. Craik (Eds.), *The Oxford handbook of memory* (pp. 363–378). Oxford: Oxford University Press.

Twenge, J. (2000). The age of anxiety? Birth cohort change in anxiety and neuroticism, 1952–1993. *Journal of Personality and Social Psychology, 79*, 1007–1021.

Twenge, J. M., & Campbell, W. K. (2010). Birth cohort differences in the Monitoring the Future dataset and elsewhere: Further evidence for Generation Me—Commentary on Trzesniewski & Donnellan (2010). *Perspectives on Psychological Science, 5*, 81–88.

Underwood, M. (2002). Sticks and stones and social exclusion: Aggression among girls and boys. In P. Smith & C. Hart (Eds.), *Blackwell handbook of childhood social development* (pp. 533–548). Oxford: Blackwell.

Underwood, M., Galen, B., & Paquette, J. (2001). Top ten challenges for understanding gender and aggression in children: Why can't we all just get along? *Social Development, 10*, 248–266.

U.S. Bureau of Labor Statistics. (2009). Employment characteristics of families in 2008. Retrieved 5/22/2010, from http://www.bls.gov/news.release/pdf/famee.pdf

U.S. Census Bureau. (2008). Table 3: Annual Estimates of the Resident Population by Sex, Race, and Hispanic Origin for the United States: April 1, 2000 to July 1, 2008. Retrieved January 14, 2010, from http://www.census.gov/popest/national/asrh/NC-EST2008-srh.html

U.S. Department of Health and Human Services. (2009). *Child maltreatment 2007*: Administration on Children, Youth, and Families. Washington, DC: Government Printing Office. Retrieved from http://www.acf.hhs.gov/

Updegraff, K. A., Whiteman, S. D., McHale, S. M., Thayer, S. M., & Crouter, A. C. (2006). The nature and correlates of Mexican-American adolescents' time with parents and peers. *Child Development, 77*, 1470–1486.

Urdan, T. (2004). Predictors of academic self-handicapping and achievement: Examining achievement goals, classroom goal structures, and culture. *Journal of Educational Psychology, 96*, 251–264.

Usher, E. L., & Pajares, F. (2008). Sources of self-efficacy in school: Critical review of the literature and future directions. *Review of Educational Research, 78*, 751–796.

Uttal, D. H., Liu, L. L., & DeLoache, J. (2006). Concreteness and symbolic development. In L. Balter & C. Tamis-LeMonda (Eds.), *Child psychology: A handbook of contemporary issues* (2nd ed., pp. 167–184). New York: Hove.

Vaish, A., Carpenter, M., & Tomasello, M. (2009). Sympathy through affective perspective taking and its relation to prosocial behavior in toddlers. *Developmental Psychology, 45*, 534–543.

Valenzuela, M. (1990). Attachment in chronically underweight young children. *Child Development, 61*, 1984–1996.

Valiente, C., Lemery-Chalfant, K., & Reiser, M. (2007). Pathways to problem behaviors: Chaotic homes, parent and child effortful control, and parenting. *Social Development, 16*, 249–267.

Valiente, C., Lemery-Chalfant, K., Swanson, J., & Reiser, M. (2008). Prediction of children's academic competence from their effortful control, relationships, and classroom participation. *Journal of Educational Psychology, 100*, 67–77.

Valkenburg, P. M., & Peter, J. (2007). Preadolescents' and adolescents' online communication and their closeness to friends. *Developmental Psychology, 43*, 267–277.

Valkenburg, P. M., & Peter, J. (2009). Social consequences of the internet for adolescents: A decade of research. *Current Directions in Psychological Science, 18*, 1–5.

Van Ausdale, D., & Feagin, J. R. (1996). Using racial and ethnic concepts: The critical case of very young children. *American Sociological Review, 61*, 779–793.

van den Bergh, B., & Marcoen, A. (2004). High antenatal maternal anxiety is related to ADHD symptoms, externalizing problems, and anxiety in 8- and 9-year-olds. *Child Development, 75*, 1085–1097.

van Goozen, S., Fairchild, G., & Harold, G. T. (2008). The role of neurobiological deficits in childhood antisocial behavior. *Current Directions in Psychological Science, 17*, 224–228.

Van Horn, M. L., Karlin, E. O., Ramey, S. L., Aldridge, J., & Snyder, S. W. (2005). Effects of developmentally appropriate practices on children's development: A review of research and discussion of methodological and analytic issues. *The Elementary School Journal, 105*, 325–351.

Van Horn, M. L., & Ramey, S. (2003). The effects of developmentally appropriate practices on academic outcomes among former Head Start students and classmates, Grades 1–3. *American Educational Research Journal, 40*, 961–990.

Van IJzendoorn, M. H., Juffer, F., & Poelhuis, C. W. K. (2005). Adoption and cognitive development: A meta-analytic comparison of adopted and nonadopted children's IQ and school performance. *Psychological Bulletin, 131*, 301–316.

van Lieshout, C. (2000). Lifespan personality development: Self-organizing goal-oriented agents and developmental outcome. *International Journal of Behavioral Development, 24*, 276–288.

Varma, S., McCandliss, B. D., & Schwartz, D. L. (2008). Scientific and pragmatic challenges for bridging education and neuroscience. *Educational Researcher, 37*(3), 140–152.

Varnhagen, C., McFall, G. P., Pugh, N. P., Routledge, L., Sumida-MacDonald, H., & Kwong, T. E. (in press). lol: new language and spelling in instant messaging. *Reading and Writing.*

Vasterling, J. J., Duke, L. M., Brailey, K., Constans, J. I., Allain, A. N., & Sutker, P. B. (2002). Attention, learning, and memory performances and intellectual resources in Vietnam veterans: PTSD and no disorder comparisons. *Neuropsychology, 16*, 5–14.

Vaughn, B. E., Colvin, T., Azria, M., Caya, L., & Krzysik, L. (2001). Dyadic analyses of friendship in a sample of preschool-age children attending Head Start: Correspondence between measures and implications for social competence. *Child Development, 72*, 862–878.

Vazquez Garcma, H. A., García Coll, C., Erkut, S., Alarcsn, O., & Tropp, L. R. (1999). Family values of Latino adolescents. In M. Montero-Sieburth & F. Villarruel (Eds.), *Making invisible Latino adolescents visible*. New York: Falmer.

Vazsonyi, A. T., & Huang, L. (2010). Where self-control comes from: On the development of self-control and its relationship to deviance over time. *Developmental Psychology, 46*, 245–257.

Vecchiotti, S. (2003). Kindergarten: An overlooked educational policy priority. *Social Policy Report, 17*, 3–19.

Veenstra, R., Lindenberg, S., Oldehinkel, A., De Winter, A., Verhulst, F., & Ormel, J. (2005). Bullying and victimization in elementary schools: A comparison of bullies, victims, bully/victims, and uninvolved preadolescents. *Developmental Psychology, 41*, 672–682.

Verschueren, K., Marcoen, A., & Schoefs, V. (1996). The internal working model of the self, attachment, and competence in five-year-olds. *Child Development, 67*, 2493–2511.

Vigil, J. D. (2004). Gangs and group membership: Implications for schooling. In M. A. Gibson, P. Gandara & J. P. Koyama (Eds.), *School connections: U.S. Mexican youth, peers, and school achievement*. New York: Teachers College Press.

Voss, L. (1997). Teasing, disputing, and playing: Cross-gender interactions and space utilization among first and third graders. *Gender & Society, 11*, 238–256.

Votruba-Drzal, E., Coley, R., & Chase-Lansdale, L. (2004). Child care and low-income children's development: Direct and moderated effects. *Child Development, 75*, 296–312.

Votruba-Drzal, E., Li-Grining, C. P., & Maldonado-Carreno, C. (2008). A developmental perspective on full- versus part-day kindergarten and children's academic trajectories through fifth grade. *Child Development, 79*, 957–978.

Vygotsky, L. S. (1978). *Mind in society: The development of higher psychological processes*. Cambridge, MA: Harvard University Press.

Wachs, T. (2000). Nutritional deficits and behavioral development. *International Journal of Behavioral Development, 24*, 435–441.

Wachs, T. D. (2006). The nature, etiology, and consequences of individual differences in temperament. In L. Balter & C. Tamis-LeMonda (Eds.), *Child psychology: A handbook of contemporary issues* (2nd ed., pp. 27–52). New York: Hove.

Wachs, T. D., Black, M. M., & Engle, P. L. (2009). Maternal depression: A global threat to children's health, development, and behavior and to human rights. *Child Development Perspectives, 3*, 51–59.

Wachsler-Felder, J., & Golden, C. (2002). Neuropsychological consequences of HIV in children: A review of current literature. *Clinical Psychology Review, 22*, 441–462.

Wahlstrom, K., Davison, M., Choi, J., & Ross, J. (2001). *Minneapolis Public Schools Start Time Study*. University of Minnesota: Center for Applied Research and Educational Improvement.

Wainright, J. L., & Patterson, C. J. (2008). Peer relations among adolescents with female same-sex parents. *Developmental Psychology, 44*, 117–126.

Wainright, J. L., Russell, S. T., & Patterson, C. J. (2004). Psychosocial adjustment, school outcomes, and romantic relationships of adolescents with same-sex parents *Child Development, 75*, 1886–1898.

Wainryb, C., Brehl, B., & Matwin, S. (2005). Being hurt and hurting others: Children's narrative accounts and moral judgments of their own interpersonal conflicts. *Monographs of the Society for Research in Child Development, 70*.

Wakschlag, L. S., Leventhal, B., Pine, D., Pickett, K. E., & Carter, A. S. (2006). Elucidating early mechanisms of developmental psychopathology: The case of prenatal smoking and disruptive behavior. *Child Development, 77*, 893–906.

Walker, E. N. (2006). Urban high school students' academic communities and their effects on mathematics success. *American Educational Research Journal, 43*, 43–73.

Walker, L. J., Hennig, K., & Krettenauer, T. (2000). Parent and peer contexts for children's moral reasoning development. *Child Development, 71*, 1033–1048.

Walker, L. J., & Pitts, R. (1998). Naturalistic conceptions of moral maturity. *Developmental Psychology, 34*, 403–419.

Walker-Barnes, C., & Mason, C. (2001). Ethnic differences in the effect of parenting on gang involvement and gang delinquency: A longitudinal, hierarchical linear modeling perspective. *Child Development, 72*, 1814–1831.

Wang, Q., Pomerantz, E. M., & Chen, H. (2007). The role of parents' control in early adolescents' psychological functioning: A longitudinal investigation in the United States and China. *Child Development, 78*, 1592–1610.

Ward, L. M. (2003). Understanding the role of entertainment media in the sexual socialization of American youth: A review of empirical research. *Developmental Review, 23*, 347–388.

Warneken, F., & Tomasello, M. (2008). Extrinsic rewards undermine altruistic tendencies in 20-month-olds. *Developmental Psychology, 44*, 1785–1788.

Wartella, E., Caplovitz, A. G., & Lee, J. H. (2004). From Baby Einstein to Leapfrog, from Doom to the Sims, from instant messaging to internet chat rooms: Public interest in the role of interactive media in children's lives. *Social Policy Report, 18*, 3–19.

Watamura, S. E., Donzella, B., Alwin, J., & Gunnar, M. R. (2003). Morning-to-afternoon increases in cortisol concentrations for infants and toddlers at child care: Age differences and behavioral correlates. *Child Development, 74*, 1006–1020.

Waters, E., & Cummings, M. (2000). A secure base from which to explore close relationships. *Child Development, 71*, 164–172.

Waters, E., Matas, L., & Sroufe, L. A. (1975). Infants' reactions to an approaching stranger: Description, validation and functional significance of wariness. *Child Development, 46*, 348–365.

Waters, H. (2000). Memory strategy development: Do we need yet another deficiency? *Child Development, 71*, 1004–1012.

Watkins, D. E., & Wentzel, K. R. (2008). Training boys with ADHD to work collaboratively: Social and learning outcomes. *Contemporary Educational Psychology, 33*, 625–646.

Watson, J. B. (1924). *Psychology from the standpoint of a behaviorist* (2nd ed.). Philadelphia, PA: Lippincott.

Watson, M., Battistich, V., & Solomon, D. (1997). Enhancing students' social and ethical development in school: An intervention program and its effects. *International Journal of Educational Research, 27*, 571–586.

Webber, M., Carpiniello, K., Oruwariye, T., Lo, Y., Burton, W., & Appel, D. (2003). Burden of asthma in inner-city elementary schoolchildren: Do school-based health centers make a difference? *Archives of Pediatrics & Adolescent Medicine, 157*, 125–129.

Webster-Stratton, C., & Herman, K. C. (2008). The impact of parent behavior-management training on child depressive symptoms. *Journal of Counseling Psychology, 55*, 473–484.

Weinberg, K., & Tronick, E. Z. (1998). Emotional characteristics of infants associated with maternal depression and anxiety. *Pediatrics, 102*, 1298–1304.

Weinberg, M. K., Tronick, E. Z., Cohn, J. F., & Olson, K. L. (1999). Gender differences in emotional expressivity and self-regulation during early infancy. *Developmental Psychology, 33*, 175–188.

Weiner, B. (1985). An attributional theory of achievement motivation and emotion. *Psychological Review, 92*, 548–573.

Weinfield, N. S., Sroufe, A., & Egeland, B. (2000). Attachment from infancy to early adulthood in a high-risk sample: Continuity, discontinuity, and their correlates. *Child Development, 71*, 695–702.

Weinfield, N. S., Sroufe, A., Egeland, B., & Carlson, E. (1999). The nature of individual differences in infant-caregiver attachment. In J. Cassidy & P. Shaver (Eds.), *Handbook of attachment: Theory, research, and clinical applications* (pp. 68–88). New York: Guilford.

Weinstein, C. S., Tomlinson-Clarke, S., & Curran, M. (2004). Toward a conception of culturally responsive classroom management. *Journal of Teacher Education, 55*, 25–38.

Weisberg, D. S., Keil, F. C., Goodstein, J., Rawson, E., & Gray, J. R. (2008). The seductive allure of neuroscience explanations. *Journal of Cognitive Neuroscience, 20*, 470–477.

Weiss, H., Mayer, E., Kreider, H., Vaughan, M., Dearing, E., Hencke, R., et al. (2003). Making it work: Low-income working mothers' involvement in their children's education. *American Educational Research Journal, 40*, 879–901.

Weissberg, R. P. (2000). Improving the lives of millions of school children. *American Psychologist, 55*, 1360-1372.

Weisz, J. R., Rothbaum, F. M., & Blackburn, T. C. (1984). Standing out and standing in: The psychology of control in America and Japan. *American Psychologist, 39*, 955–969.

Weizman, Z. O., & Snow, C. E. (2001). Lexical input as related to children's vocabulary acquisition: Effects of sophisticated exposure and support for meaning. *Developmental Psychology, 37*, 265–279.

Wellman, H., Cross, D., & Watson, J. (2001). Meta-analysis of theory-of-mind development: The truth about false belief. *Child Development, 72*, 655–684.

Wellman, H., & Liu, D. (2004). Scaling of theory-of-mind tasks. *Child Development, 75*, 523–541.

Wellman, H., Lopez-Duran, S., LaBounty, J., & Hamilton, B. (2008). Infant attention to intentional action predicts preschool theory of mind. *Developmental Psychology, 44*, 618–623.

Wentzel, K. R. (1991). Relations between social competence and academic achievement in early adolescence. *Child Development, 62*, 1066–1078.

Wentzel, K. R. (1993). Does being good make the grade? Social behavior and academic competence in middle school. *Journal of Educational Psychology, 85*, 357–364.

Wentzel, K. R. (1997). Student motivation in middle school: The role of perceived pedagogical caring. *Journal of Educational Psychology, 89*, 411–419.

Wentzel, K. R. (2002). Are effective teachers like good parents? Teaching styles and student adjustment in early adolescence. *Child Development, 73*, 287–301.

Wentzel, K. R., & Asher, S. R. (1995). The academic lives of neglected, rejected, popular, and controversial children. *Child Development, 66*, 754–763.

Wentzel, K. R., Barry, C., & Caldwell, K. (2004). Friendships in middle school: Influences on motivation and school adjustment. *Journal of Educational Psychology, 96*, 195–203.

Wentzel, K. R., Filisetti, L., & Looney, L. (2007). Adolescent prosocial behavior: The role of self-processes and contextual cues. *Child Development, 78*, 895–910.

Werner, E. (1994). Overcoming the odds. *Journal of Developmental and Behavioral Pediatrics, 15*, 131–136.

Wheeler, R. S., & Swords, R. (2006). *Code-switching: Teaching standard English in urban classrooms.* Urbana, IL: National Council of Teachers of English.

Whitbeck, L., Hoyt, D., & Wa-Ning, B. (2000). Depressive symptoms and co-occurring depressive symptoms, substance abuse, and conduct problems among runaway and homeless adolescents. *Child Development, 71*, 721–732.

White, B., & Watts, J. (1973). *Experience and environment: Major influences on the development of the young child.* Englewood Cliffs, NJ: Prentice-Hall.

White, K., & Jones, K. (2000). Effects of teacher feedback on the reputations and peer perceptions of children with behavior problems. *Journal of Experimental Child Psychology, 76*, 302–326.

Whitehurst, G. J., & Lonigan, C. J. (1998). Child development and emergent literacy. *Child Development, 69*, 848–872.

Whiting, B., & Edwards, C. (1988). *Children of different worlds: The formation of social behavior.* Cambridge, MA: Harvard University Press.

Whiting, B. B. (1983). The genesis of prosocial behavior. In D. Bridgeman (Ed.), *The nature of prosocial development: Interdisciplinary theories and strategies* (pp. 221–242). London: Academic Press.

Whitney, I., & Smith, P. (1993). A survey of the nature and extent of bullying in junior/middle and secondary schools. *Educational Research, 35*, 3–25.

Widdowson, E. (1951). Mental contentment and physical growth. *Lancet, 1*, 1316–1318.

Widen, S., & Russell, J. A. (2003). A closer look at preschoolers' freely produced labels for facial expressions. *Developmental Psychology, 39*, 114–128.

Wiebe, S. A., Espy, K. A., Stopp, C., Respass, J., Stewart, P., Jameson, T., et al. (2009). Gene–environment interactions across development: Exploring DRD2 genotype and prenatal smoking effects on self-regulation. *Developmental Psychology, 45*, 31–44.

Wiggan, G. (2007). Race, school achievement, and educational inequality: Toward a student-based inquiry perspective. *Review of Educational Research, 77*, 310–333.

Wilkins, J., & Ma, X. (2002). Predicting student growth in mathematical content knowledge. *Journal of Educational Research, 95*, 288–298.

Williams, C. A., & Forehand, R. (1984). An examination of predictor variables for child compliance and noncompliance. *Journal of Abnormal Child Psychology, 12*, 491–503.

Williams, M., & Rask, H. (2003). Lieracy through play: How families with able children support their literacy development. *Early Child Development and Care, 173*, 527–533.

Williams, S. T., Conger, K. J., & Blozis, S. A. (2007). The development of interpersonal aggression during adolescence: The importance of parents, siblings, and family economics. *Child Development, 78*, 1526–1542.

Williams, W., Blythe, T., White, N., Li, J., Gardner, H., & Sternberg, R. (2002). Practical intelligence for school: Developing metacognitive sources of achievement in adolescence. *Developmental Review, 22*, 162–210.

Williamson, R. A., Meltzoff, A. N., & Markman, E. M. (2008). Prior experiences and perceived efficacy influence 3-year-olds' imitation. *Developmental Psychology, 44*, 275–285.

Willoughby, T. (2008). A short-term longitudinal study of internet and computer game use by adolescent boys and girls: Prevalence, frequency of use, and psychosocial predictors. *Developmental Psychology, 44*, 195–204.

Wills, T. A., & Stoolmiller, M. (2002). The role of self-control in early escalation of substance use: A time-varying analysis. *Journal of Consulting and Clinical Psychology, 70*, 986–997.

Wills, T. A., & Yaeger, A. (2003). Family factors and adolescent substance use: Models and mechanisms. *Current Directions in Psychological Science, 12*, 222–226.

Wilson, S., Lipsey, M., & Derzon, J. (2003). The effects of school-based intervention programs on aggressive behavior: A meta-analysis. *Journal of Consulting and Clinical Psychology, 71*, 136–149.

Wilson, S. J., & Lipsey, M. W. (2007). School-based interventions for aggressive and disruptive behavior: Update of a meta-analysis. *American Journal of Preventive Medicine, 33*, 130–143.

Windle, M., & Windle, R. (2003). Alcohol and other substance use and abuse. In G. Adams & M. Berzonsky (Eds.), *Blackwell handbook on adolescence* (pp. 450–469). Malden, MA: Blackwell.

Winner, E. (1996). The rage to master: The decisive role of talent in the visual arts. In K. A. Ericsson (Ed.), *The road to excellence: The acquisition of expert performance in the arts and sciences, sports, and games* (pp. 271–301). Mahwah, NJ: Erlbaum.

Winner, E. (2000). Giftedness: Current theory and research. *Current Directions in Psychological Science, 9*, 153–156.

Winsler, A., Carlton, M. P., & Barry, M. J. (2000). Age-related changes in preschool children's systematic use of private speech in a natural setting. *Journal of Child Language, 27*, 665–687.

Winsler, A., Diaz, R. M., Atencio, D. J., McCarthy, E. M., & Chabay, L. A. (2000). Verbal self-regulation over time in preschool children at risk for attention and behavior problems. *Journal of Child Psychology & Psychiatry & Allied Disciplines, 41*, 875–886.

Wispe, L. (1972). Positive forms of social behavior: An overview. *Journal of Social Issues, 28*, 1–20.

Wissow, L. S. (2001). Ethnicity, income, and parenting contexts of physical punishment in a national sample of families with young children. *Child Maltreatment, 6*,118–129.

Wixted, J. (2005). A theory about why we forget what we once knew. *Current Directions in Psychological Science, 14*, 6–9.

Wolak, J., Mitchell, K., & Finkelhor, D. (2007). Unwanted and wanted exposure to online pornography in a national sample of youth internet users. *Pediatrics, 119*, 247–257.

Wolchik, S., Sandler, I. N., Millsap, R. E., Plummer, B. A., Greene, S. M., Anderson, E. R., et al. (2002). Six-year follow-up of preventive interventions for children of divorce: A randomized controlled trial. *JAMA, 288*, 1874–1881.

Wolfgang, C., Stannard, L., & Jones, I. (2003). Advanced construction play with LEGOs among preschoolers as a predictor of later school achievement in mathematics. *Early Child Development and Care, 17*, 467–475.

Wolfram, W., & Thomas, E. R. (2002). *The development of African American English*. Oxford: Blackwell.

Wood, D., Bruner, J. S., & Ross, G. (1976). The role of tutoring in problem solving. *Journal of Child Psychology and Psychiatry, 17*, 89–100.

Woodlee, M. T., & Schallert, T. (2006). The impact of motor activity and inactivity on the brain: Implications for the prevention and treatment of nervous-system disorders. *Current Directions in Psychological Science, 15*, 203–206.

Woodward, L., Fergusson, D., & Belsky, J. (2000). Timing of parental separation and attachment to parents in adolescence: Results of a prospective study from birth to age 16. *Journal of Marriage and the Family, 62*, 162–174.

Wright, J. C., Huston, A. C., Murphy, K. C., St. Peters, M., Piqon, M., Scantlin, R., et al. (2001). The relations of early television viewing to school readiness and vocabulary of children from low-income families: The Early Window Project. *Child Development, 72*, 1347–1366.

Wu, W., West, S. G., & Hughes, J. N. (2008). Effect of retention in first grade on children's achievement trajectories over 4 years: A piecewise growth analysis using propensity score matching. *Journal of Educational Psychology, 100*, 727–740.

Wulfert, E., Block, J. A., Santa Ana, E., Rodriguez, M. L., & Colsman, M. (2002). Delay of gratification: Impulsive choices and problem behaviors in early and late adolescence. *Journal of Personality, 70*, 533–552.

Wyer, R., & Collins, J. (1992). A theory of humor elicitation. *Psychological Review, 99*, 663–688.

Wynn, K. (1992). Addition and subtraction by human infants. *Nature, 358*, 749–750.

Wyshak, G. (2000). Teenaged girls, carbonated beverage consumption and bone fractures. *Archives of Pediatrics & Adolescent Medicine, 154*, 610–613.

Xie, H., Farmer, T. W., & Cairns, B. (2003). Different forms of aggression among inner-city African-American children: Gender, configurations, and school social networks. *Journal of School Psychology, 41*, 355–375.

Xue, Y., & Meisels, S. (2004). Early literacy instruction and learning in kindergarten: Evidence from the Early Childhood Longitudinal Study—Kindergarten class of 1998-1999. *American Educational Research Journal, 41*, 191–229.

Yang, N., Huang, T.-A., Schaller, J., Wang, M., & Tsai, S.-F. (2003). Enhancing appropriate social behaviors for children with autism in general education classrooms: An analysis of six cases. *Education and Training in Developmental Disabilities, 38*, 405–416.

Yap, M. B. H., Allen, N. B., & Ladouceur, C. D. (2008). Maternal socialization of positive affect: The impact of invalidation on adolescent emotion regulation and depressive symptomatology. *Child Development, 79*, 1415–1431.

Yarrow, M., Scott, P., & Waxler, C. (1973). Learning concern for others. *Developmental Psychology, 8*, 240–260.

Yeargin-Allsopp, M., Rice, C., Karapurkar, T., Doernberg, N., Boyle, C., & Murphy, C. (2003). Prevalence of autism in a US metropolitan area. *JAMA, 289*, 49–55.

Yirmiya, N., Erel, O., Shaked, M., & Solomonica-Levi, D. (1998). Meta-analyses comparing theory of mind abilities of individuals with autism, individuals with mental retardation, and normally developing individuals. *Psychological Bulletin, 124*, 283–307.

Yoon, B. (2008). Uninvited guests: The influence of teachers' roles and pedagogies on the positioning of English language learners in the regular classroom. *American Educational Research Journal, 45*, 495–422.

Yoshikawa, H., & Hsueh, J. (2001). Child development and public policy: Toward a dynamc systems perspective. *Child Development, 72*, 1887–1903.

Youniss, J., McLellan, J. A., Su, Y., & Yates, M. (1999). The role of community service in identity development: Normative, unconventional, and deviant orientations. *Journal of Adolescent Research, 14*, 248–261.

Yu, C., & Smith, L. B. (2007). Rapid word learning under uncertainty via cross-situational statistics. *Psychological Science, 18*, 414–420.

Yuan, S., & Fisher, C. (2009). "Really? She blicked the baby?" Two-year-olds learn combinatorial facts about verbs by listening. *Psychological Science, 20*, 619–626.

Yumoto, C., Jacobson, S. W., & Jacobson, J. L. (2008). Fetal substance exposure and cumulative environmental risk in an African American cohort. *Child Development, 79*, 1761–1776.

Zahn-Waxler, C., Friedman, R. J., Cole, P. M., Mizuta, I., & Hiruma, N. (1996). Japanese and United States preschool children's responses to conflict and distress. *Child Development, 67*, 2462–2477.

Zahn-Waxler, C., Kochanska, G., Krupnick, J., & McKnew, D. (1990). Patterns of guilt in children of depressed and well mothers. *Developmental Psychology, 26*, 51–59.

Zahn-Waxler, C., & Robinson, J. (1995). Empathy and guilt: Early origins of feelings of responsibility. In J. P. Tangney & K. W. Fischer (Eds.), *Self-conscious emotions: The psychology of shame, guilt, embarrassment, and pride* (pp. 143–173). New York: Guilford Press.

Zahorik, J. A. (1996). Elementary and secondary teachers' reports of how they make learning interesting. *Elementary School Journal, 96*, 551–564.

Zajac, R. J., & Hartup, W. W. (1997). Friends as coworkers: Research review and classroom implications. *Elementary School Journal, 98*, 3–13.

Zaki, J., Bolger, N., & Ochsner, K. (2008). It takes two: The interpersonal nature of empathic accuracy. *Psychological Science, 19*, 399–404.

Zanobini, M., & Usai, C. (2002). Domain-specific self-concept and achievement motivation in the transition from primary to low middle school. *Educational Psychology, 22*, 203–217.

Zeidner, M. (1998). *Test anxiety: The state of the art*. New York: Plenum.

Zelazo, P., M|ller, U., Frye, D., & Marcovitch, S. (2003). The development of executive function in early childhood. *Monographs of the Society for Research in Child Development, 68* (Serial No. 274).

Zeller, M., Vannatta, K., Schafer, J., & Noll, R. (2003). Behavioral reputation: A cross-age perspective. *Developmental Psychology, 39*, 129–139.

Zettergren, P. (2003). School adjustment in adolescence for previously rejected, average and popular children. *British Journal of Educational Psychology, 73*, 207–221.

Zheng, B., & Horgan, D. (2001, April). *Cultural values and character education: A comparative study of Chinese and American fourth grade reading textbooks*. Paper presented at the American Educational Research Association, Seattle, WA.

Zhou, Q., Eisenberg, N., Wang, Y., & Reiser, M. (2004). Chinese children's effortful control and dispositional anger/frustration: Relations to parenting styles and children's social functioning. *Developmental Psychology, 40*, 352–366.

Zhou, Q., Hofer, C., Eisenberg, N., Reiser, M., Spinrad, T. L., & Fabes, R. A. (2007). The developmental trajectories of attention focusing, attentional and behavioral persistence, and externalizing problems during school-age years. *Developmental Psychology, 43*, 369–385.

Zhou, Q., Lengua, L., & Wang, Y. (2009). The relations of temperament reactivity and effortful control to children's adjustment problems in China and the United States. *Developmental Psychology, 45*, 724–739.

Ziegert, D., Kistner, J., Castro, R., & Robertson, B. (2001). Longitudinal study of young children's responses to challenging achievement situations. *Child Development, 72*, 609–624.

Ziegler, J. C., & Goswami, U. (2005). Reading acquisition, developmental dyslexia and skilled reading across languages. *Psychological Bulletin, 131*, 3–29.

Zillmann, D. (2001). Influence of unrestrained access to erotica on adoelscents' and young adults' dispositions toward sexuality. *Journal of Adolescent Health, 27* (2-supplement), 41–44.

Zillmann, D., Williams, B. R., Bryant, J., Boynton, K. R., & Wolf, M. A. (1980). Acquisition of information from educational television programs as a function of differently paced humorous inserts. *Journal of Educational Psychology, 72*, 170–180.

Zimmer-Gembeck, M. J., & Helfand, M. (2008). Ten years of longitudinal research on U.S. adolescent sexual behavior: Developmental correlates of sexual intercourse, and the importance of age, gender and ethnic background. *Developmental Review, 28*, 153–224.

Zimmer-Gembeck, M. J., & Skinner, E. A. (2008). Adolescents coping with stress: Development and diversity. *The Prevention Researcher, 15*, 3–7.

Zimmerman, B. J., & Kitsantas, A. (2002). Acquiring writing revision and self-regulatory skill through observation and emulation. *Journal of Educational Psychology, 94*, 660–668.

Ziv, A. (1989). Using humor to develop creative thinking. In P. McGhee (Ed.), *Humor and children's development: A guide to practical applications* (pp. 99–116). New York: Haworth.

Zosuls, K. M., Ruble, D. N., Tamis-LeMonda, C., Shrout, P. E., Bornstein, M. H., & Greulich, F. K. (2009). The acquisition of gender labels in infancy: Implications for gender-typed play. *Developmental Psychology, 45*, 688–701.

Zsolnai, A. (2002). Relationship between children's social competence, learning motivation and school achievement. *Educational Psychology, 22*, 317–329.

Name Index

Subject Index

Introduction: Getting Started

The 10 W's of Week by Week

EXERCISE **Observe (or imagine):**

- a clock
- the inside of a refrigerator
- a traffic light

Exactly what do you see? What are your observations telling you? What will you do as a result of what you see? Write down what decisions you might make based on those observations.

The word *observe* brings to mind the action of looking, seeing, not participating but viewing the action as an outsider. In any context, observing is just the first step in determining action. The first stage, taking in information, occurs simultaneously with evaluation and selection of a course of action. The clock is observed, usually not to admire the design but to determine the time. Looking inside a refrigerator may indicate that a trip to the store is needed or that the source of a foul odor should be investigated. The traffic light is a lovely shade of green, but its meaning is more important. That observation produces action: Go!

Everything we see is not just observed but also immediately interpreted for meaning. A decision is made either to do nothing or to act. The observation may be so insignificant that it is sensed but not acted on. Later it might prove to be important, like that traffic light that was green but the car in the cross street came through the intersection anyway.

IN THIS INTRODUCTION

When filling out the accident report, those details are important.

Why Observe?

When a teacher observes a child, information is collected and could be measured against a whole body of knowledge about child development in general and that child in particular (Figure I–1). Information is then used to make decisions about the next actions. Someone has estimated that a teacher makes thousands of decisions in a day. And each decision is based on observations evaluated for meaning and most appropriate responses. This *observe-decide-act* sequence is repeated over and over again throughout the day.

Let's observe a child painting at the easel and see what we can see in Figure I–2.

Safety. The most important reason for watching children is to keep them safe. Seeing a potentially dangerous situation and rushing to prevent an injury is the most basic example of observe-decide-act. A child waiting to paint may be observed trying to wrestle the brush away from the painter. With angry looks and harsh words, she is trying to gain control of the painting area. The teacher rushes over and intervenes before the painter is knocked aside or a brush is poked into someone's eye.

Physical Health. Recognizing the signs of sickness or disease is another reason to observe, decide, and act. This also can protect the physical health of others. The teacher may notice a few small red spots

Figure I–2 Common activities yield knowledge of the child.

Figure I–1 Why observe?

behind the painter's ear. She casually pats the child's arm and feels bumps beneath the skin. These observations, along with the knowledge that the child's brother had chicken pox two weeks ago, prompts the teacher's decision to isolate the child and call the child's family to take the child home. For chicken pox, of course, it's already too late. Everyone's been exposed! Figure I–3 shows artwork that the child painted on her return to school after having chicken pox.

Assistance. Observation may indicate that help is needed. A child is observed preparing to paint at the easel. The teacher sees that the paper supply is gone. He gets more from the cupboard and shows the child how to attach the sheets with the big clips and where to hang the painting to dry.

Discover Interests. The adult observes the child choose a play area and talks with the child about the play. This observing, remembering, and affirming is a friendly thing to do. It also is another way of building bridges from interests to planning, from home to

Figure I–3 Observing a child's work, as well as the child as she works, gives valuable information.

school, and of making the curriculum relevant. The theme of animals (in the beginning stages of drawing recognizable objects!) emerges in the painting. The observer remembers the home visit where this child showed a menagerie of pets, who might be potential classroom visitors!

Learning Styles and Teaching Strategies. Watching a child reveals personality and learning styles and could give clues to teaching strategies. By observing the painter, learning styles are indicated that will work better for her, maybe verbal directions, or being shown, or trial and error. Reflective observation of the student's learning process leads the teacher to adapt teaching strategies to the child's styles and needs.

Curriculum Planning. Teaching is building bridges, making connections between new information and old. The teacher plans related experiences and activities. The group has enjoyed and mastered easel painting, so the teacher plans that next week he will introduce watercolors, demonstrating the technique of washing the brush between colors.

Extend Children's Learning. Through observations, teachers can see that teachable moment, that budding interest, and that blossoming skill. Providing materials, activities, and opportunities to build on that observed development will capitalize on it. From observing the painting filled with alphabet letters, the teacher decides this is a good time to bring out the alphabet magnets and invite the painter to play with them.

Communication with the Child. Teachers should talk with every child, and what better subject to discuss with them than the child's activities? Every child deserves the individual attention of the teacher. By discussing what the teacher observes with the child, the child can give the reason or explanation in a way that makes sense only if the teacher asks the child. That is the basis for Piaget's cognitive questioning method (Piaget & Inhelder, 1969), to delve more deeply into children's "wrong" answers. In that way, thinking processes are explored. Results or answers are not simply considered incorrect, but teachers reflect on possible reasons for the answers to explain how the answer was derived. This may involve more conversation with the child, or the family, to get a better understanding of the background knowledge leading to the answer.

The teacher says to the painter, "You worked hard on that painting. You used red, blue, and yellow, and you made straight lines and curved lines. Would you like to tell me how you did it? What did you do first?"

Guidance. Prevention is always better than remedy. Redirection is better than discipline or punishment. From observations, potential problems can be averted. The painter's brush is approaching the wall. The teacher reminds the child, "Paint on paper," guiding the brush back to the paper on the easel.

Measure Progress. Children change so quickly. Based on knowledge of child development, certain changes are expected and anticipated. Comparisons over time can measure that development. The teacher observes that the painter moved from experimentation with line and color to painting recognizable objects. She proclaims that the smiling face with dots is a picture of her brother who is just getting over the chicken pox. The teacher can see her control of small muscles and the frustration when the paint does not flow in the way the painter thinks it should. The child's social world is portrayed in the pictures she paints. Many areas of development can be observed in this one activity and in changes from paintings done a few weeks ago.

Assessment. Teachers watch children to gather information. That is **assessment**, the process of documenting a child's knowledge, skills, and attitudes in measurable terms. Assessment may take many forms, but the premise here is that observation is the best method. Information is gathered to measure the child's development against accepted stages or a set of developmental norms. Assessment measures where the child is at this point in time. It may alert the observer to unusually delayed or accelerated development.

Evaluation. **Evaluation** is the decision-making step of assessment, probably the most precarious because it is the step that considers the information gathered through assessment upon which judgements are drawn and decisions made about future directions.

The observer of the painter has collected paintings over several weeks and judges that this child is in the stage when children are beginning to represent thought, not just experimenting with the materials. A sticky note as to the importance of this example may be placed on the back of the painting, noting "She has moved from making circles and controlled straight lines to painting faces, and was smiling and singing while painting." The teacher may decide to bring out a plastic skeleton for the Science Area or read a story about sick children to give the painter ideas about anatomy. A copy of this drawing is filed in the child's Portfolio to make later comparisons.

For all of these good reasons, teachers observe children. That informed observation, measuring what is seen against what is known, is assessment and evaluation of the child's development and behavior.

Referral. Sometimes questions or even red flags arise when a teacher observes a child. Certain behaviors, actions, and skills, or lack of them, will send an alert calling for a closer look at a developmental area.

From the child's paintings, the teacher observes some alarming messages. The teacher may ask a probing question such as, "Would you like to tell me about your painting?" and the child's answers may lead only to more questions.

Further reflection and closer observation of behavior over time may warrant the discussion of a concern first with the family or other professionals within the agency, and then perhaps a suggested referral to the family. The **referral** may be for further evaluation in a specific area such as hearing, speech, physical, or cognitive development. Family involvement and decision making in the referral process are the pivotal factors. Families are recognized and deferred to as the authority on the child.

There may be situations where it is necessary to report suspicions of neglect or abuse. Knowledge, careful judgment, empathy, and consideration are important skills for the teacher in all of these circumstances, both referrals and reporting.

Communication with the Family. Talking with the **family** about the child's daily activities communicates the following to them:

- Their child is under a watchful eye.
- This teacher observes and relates important development in their child's actions rather than giving the family a test score they might not understand how to evaluate.
- The family is included in the world that the teacher and their child share.

Unfortunately, many children and families have come to expect to receive only bad reports, phone calls, and notes from school, bringing a sense of dread. Too often, the only communications they receive about their child relate misbehaviors, failure to perform to expectations, or commands to the child or family to take remedial action. In contrast, discussing the observations from the day's observed activities or documentation from the Portfolio with the child's family gives positive, substantive information about the child's progress, compared only to her previous work, not anyone else's. Observation gives descriptive accounts of the child's behavior and skills from the point of view of achievement rather than deficit, what she can or has done rather than cannot or will not. Observations are shared with families in formal and informal ways.

The paintings in the child's Portfolio previously were scribbles, then become pages filled with lines and deliberate designs. The teacher and child show her family the collection in the Portfolio. The family realizes that the teacher *knows and observes* their child's work from a different point of view.

Self-Reflection of Teaching Methods. Observing is not just looking at a child but also thinking about our influence on the child and the child's effect on us. The teacher notices that no one is painting anymore and wonders what the cause could be. By observing and recording, questions can be answered and the teacher's own effectiveness can be measured. The interest a child has in the planned activities will indicate to the teacher if the activities are appropriate. Activities that are not challenging or are too difficult will be avoided or abandoned by the child. By closely observing what keeps a child involved, the observer can learn what skills the child is working on and then modify activities to meet those needs.

This type of observation is active research, constantly accumulating data to analyze for its meaning. Yetta Goodman (2002) says "kid watching" involves "teachers who interact with students and who monitor class activities in order to understand more about teaching and learning, mostly learning (p13)."

Accountability. Programs for children before they enter school are funded through special governmental funding at the state and federal level, with private funds through foundations and organizations and by the parents of the children themselves. Initiatives with the expected outcomes of school readiness by enhancing social, language, and cognitive skills, especially for children from economically disadvantaged homes and for children of special needs, are under scrutiny to demonstrate their effectiveness. Is the teacher, curriculum, program, or school doing what it says it will do? Proof is needed to show that children are learning and meeting the standards and expected outcomes. This area of child assessment is the focus of close examination to prove their worth.

Accountability takes on many forms. The program or school is accountable to the funding or sponsoring agency. Assessment for funders calls for statistical data, gathered by research-based methods, showing demonstrable outcomes of groups of children. Policy makers also use this kind of assessment to measure the benefits of one type of program or initiative over another. The purpose is to maximize the investment for the greatest gain.

The type of accountability that is mostly addressed in this text is that of the teacher to the child and the family. By systematically using observation, along with other types of assessment tools, the classroom teacher and caregiver can gather information to show each child's progress, raise an awareness of potential difficulties, and to plan curriculum that will help the child develop and learn. A teacher might observe the following:

"This child's painting shows increases in small muscle control, attention span, interest in alphabet, and is increasingly detailed." The teacher's notes on the back of the painting relate the significance of this work in light of developmental progress. It shows the child is learning. Documentation of all types can

- provide evidence of children's learning in all domains.
- provide insight into learning experiences.
- provide a framework for recording each child's interests and developmental progress.
- emphasize learning as an interactive process.
- show advantages of concrete activities and materials as opposed to group testing situations.
- enable teachers to assess knowledge and abilities in order to increase the challenge to match the child's level. (Helm, Beneke, & Steinheimer, 2007)

Why Write It Down?

EXERCISE Using a separate sheet of paper, list the kinds of writing you do in a day. Jot down the reason for each.

"I'll remember this and write it down later." Everyone has said this and then did not write it down. It is lost with all the other details of life that intercede and blur the image, blotting out specifics and erasing the exact words. **Recording** is used here to refer to a written account or notation of what has been observed. What are the reasons for writing down what has been seen? See Figure I–4.

To Remember. The grocery list (Figure I–5), even if it is left home on the refrigerator door, sticks in the memory longer because it was written down. Many students copy their notes over or condense them as a study technique. There is a connection between writing and memory. The words that are written form a visual and kinetic

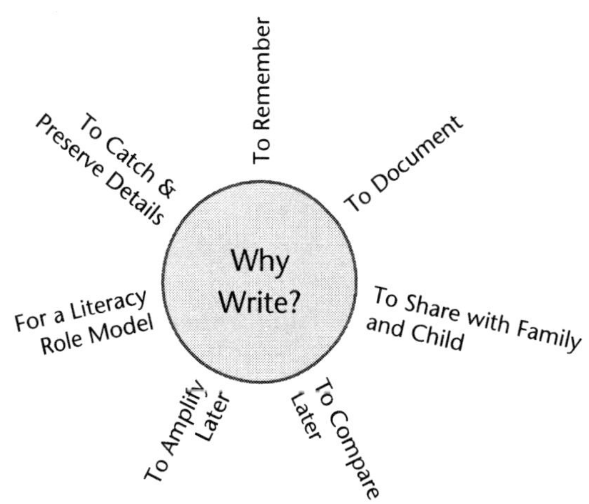

Figure I–4 Why Write?

Figure I–5 Write to Remember.

or physical connection in the brain, assisting memory and recall even when the visual cues are not present.

To Compare. A child's height is measured with a line on the wall, and it is surprising a few months later how much she has grown without anyone realizing it. If that mark had not been made, the change would not have been noticed. Children are expected to change, so a mark of comparison is needed. Relying on the memory of the child one, three, or six months ago is inaccurate and unreliable. By writing observations down, teachers have tangible comparison points. Portfolios, collections of the child's work and written observations, are becoming an accepted method of documenting a child's progress. Written observations that are thorough, objective, regular, and done during daily routines and child-initiated play are accurate measures of the child's progress.

To Amplify Later. Sometimes there is no time to write the whole incident, so a few strategic notes written and dated at the time can be just enough to jog the memory for a longer, more complete narrative written later.

The teacher shows a new song chart and has just said, "Look up here, all eyes on the chart." Andrew asks, "What's sixteen plus sixteen?" A puzzled look comes over the teacher's face, followed immediately by one of irritation for the interruption. Andrew repeats his question louder. "Thirty-two, now let's look at this new song chart." Andrew replies, "Oh, you want all thirty-two eyes looking at the chart." This tells us about Andrew's thinking, his beginning understanding of math concepts, and causes the teacher to vow to listen more closely to children's questions. This is a wonderful incident to relay to Andrew's family to demonstrate his thinking and his humor. The teacher just had time to write "eyes, 16, 32" with the ever-present pad and pen. That was enough to enable the teacher to fully write about the incident later.

To Catch and Preserve Details. Details are quickly forgotten. Insurance companies want auto accident reports written at the scene because of the frailty of human memory. Fine details that seem so clear or seem so unimportant now can best be preserved by writing them down. These details can give clues to trends or correlations that are not seen at the time. On closer examination and comparison later, they gain significance. For example, keeping some data on which areas of the classroom the child spends their free time in and how long they stay there gives much information about the child. Without some method of tracking, there is no way to recall details like this that can yield important information.

To Serve as a Literacy Role Model. Children need to see adults writing. Literacy is an important concept to teach young children. The importance of the written word is emphasized when children see its usefulness and practical application by their role models, the adults in their lives. When an adult writes something down, a child often asks, "What are you doing?" A reply such as "I'm writing this down so I won't forget" is laying literacy foundations for the child (Figure I–6). It shows that writing is a way to help memory, that what is written is constant, and it stirs the child's desire to want to write himself. Accessible writing materials encourage him to do just that (Figure I–7).

To Document. Reliable research demands hard data. It is necessary to preserve in writing—to **document**—what has been observed to substantiate it. Recording methods that include facts rather than inferences along with date and time of the recording are essential to meaningful documentation. The

Figure I–6 Busy teachers jot short notes to amplify later.

details must be preserved to see progress, trends, and correlations.

It is especially critical if a child discloses an incident of abuse. The reports must be accurate and show that the child was not led or influenced in order for the disclosure to be supportable evidence. One would like never to deal with this, but for the protection of the child it is important not to jeopardize the testimony by failure to document or inaccurate records. You will read more about this in Chapter 12.

Dramatic Play Area—paper and pencil next to the play phone, sheets cut for grocery lists attached to a pad on the play refrigerator, calendars on which children can write important events to remember

Block Area—paper, markers, tape for signs on buildings

Large Motor—paper, markers, tape for signs signifying what the climber is today (a rocket ship, a house on fire, Jenny's house)

Sand/Water—paper and pencil nearby to write down a mark to indicate what sinks or floats, draw pictures of what has been found hidden in the sand; paper to list who is waiting for a turn

Cubbies—paper and pencil to list what children say they want to do outside today, to decide which toys to load in the wagon

Group Area—chart paper, markers to take surveys of favorite things, lists of things to remember contributed by the group, safety rules

Figure I–7 A Literacy-Rich Environment.

What Are the Roles of the Observer?

You may have various roles or reasons or situations for observing:

Participant observer. If you are a teacher, then you observe children all the time, but *Week by Week* will guide you to use a different lens while you go about the various activities in leading and caring for the children in your group. You might be a student teacher who is learning about children by being in a classroom, assisting where you are needed and perhaps fulfilling assignments at the same time. Either way, you will need to have paper and pen handy at all times to be sure you jot down important notes (remember, writing aids the memory). If you are planning to observe a specific child or all the children with a specific type of recording tool, have the time and place planned so that you are prepared. Each chapter in *Week by Week* will give you some tips on How to Find the Time.

Non-Participant Observer. You may have the luxury of having no responsibility in a classroom other than observing and recording. You may be a teacher visiting someone else's classroom to learn, or you may be a student completing an assignment. Your place in the classroom should be out of the way but in a place where you can see and hear what is happening. The teacher of the classroom can assist you in finding the right spot to sit. Try to avoid letting any child "feel" watched by gazing around the room rather than staring. Avoid eye contact or conversations with the children yet appear friendly and nonthreatening. Answer the children's questions about what you are doing directly by saying you are writing down what is happening in the classroom and go back to your work.

Some schools (especially lab schools) have an observation booth where students, family members, or other professionals can observe children. This nonintrusive vantage point does not influence the children's behavior. Sometimes vision or clear sound may be hampered by the placement and technology available. Video recordings of classroom activity is another way of observing. This will be explored in Chapter 11.

Why Use Different Methods?

EXERCISE How many ways can you cook a chicken? Make a list. Here's a start:

- fry
- broil
- stew
- microwave

Why are there so many ways to cook a chicken? Because there are different end results from each method. The cook may be looking for a certain consistency, lowering calories, tenderizing, or working within a short period of time. Similarly, there are many different methods of recording observations because the end result from each method is different. Yes, they are all based on observing the child and measuring the observation against standards in order to make decisions about immediate and future actions, but they differ in technique, content, and approach. *Week by Week* presents many different methods, along with a review of a developmental area, but the method is not limited to recording only that particular area. In the cooking example above, once the technique of frying or stewing or microwaving is mastered, it can be applied to other foods and modified for a variety of desired results. Just like cooking, once the recording technique is mastered, it can be applied to other developmental areas and modified to fit the recorder's style and selected outcome. The recording methods can be classified using the web design (Figure I–8).

Each method is a technique to focus on a behavior, skill, or action of an individual child or the whole group. The **narrative** recordings, such as Anecdotal Recordings, Running Records, and Interviews, tell a story. They bring the reader along by providing the actual details of actions, words, and results. The **criterion-referenced** recordings, such as Class List Logs, Checklists, and Rating Scales, provide a predetermined skill or standard to look for and measure against. The **quantitative** recordings, such as Time Samples and Frequency Counts, provide a numerical count of individual or group actions that then can be interpreted in various ways. These methods lose most of the raw data, the actual details that narratives preserve, but are useful for certain purposes.

The **Work Samples**, such as drawings, writings, constructions, sculptures, and media-preserved work (audio or video recordings or photographs), give a visual account of the child's activities from which assessments are made. Each category and method within the category is distinctive and useful, with its own specific technique, advantages and disadvantages, and best applications. These methods will be presented, practiced, and recommended for specific purposes throughout this book.

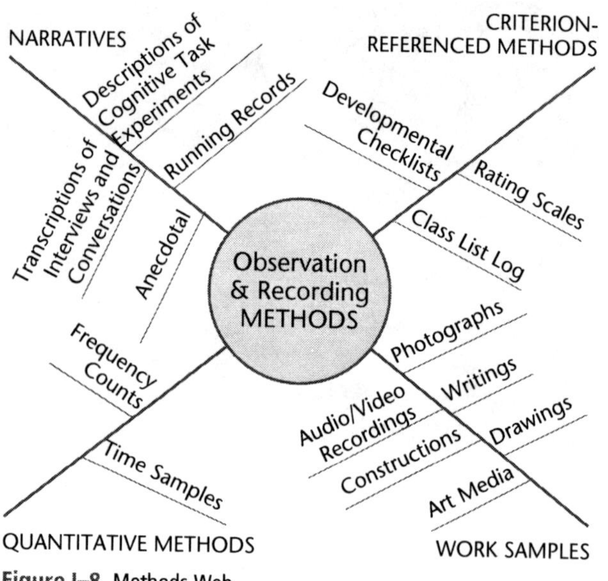

Figure I–8 Methods Web.

What Is a Portfolio and What's In it?

The systematic gathering of information about the child is **Portfolio** assessment. Portfolios are more than a scrapbook or folder full of unrelated pieces of paper. Gronlund (2003) states, "Simply collecting samples of students' work and putting it in a file does not constitute a Portfolio. Much greater care is required in the development of a Portfolio that will be useful in instruction and assessment" (p. 159). Portfolios provide information on each child as an individual, on child development in general, and on the diversity of children. Portfolios give the opportunity for family involvement through communication centered on the child's work, and they help the family become involved in the curriculum. From building Portfolios, teachers learn to assess and plan a curriculum for each child individually, see progress over time, and reflect on teaching practices (Shores & Grace, 2005).

Danielson and Abrutyn (1997) describe three types of Portfolios. *Display* Portfolios are scrapbooks of photographs of children's activities and learning experiences in the classroom without teacher comment or showing progress over time. *Showcase* Portfolios are the best pieces of the child's work, either self- or teacher-selected and without evaluation or information about progress or affecting the curriculum. *Working* Portfolios include selected but typical Work Samples along with teacher documentation to show the child's progress as well as the teacher's observations. It is on these Portfolios that curriculum is based and future actions planned for the child, with input from the child, the family, and other professionals if needed. *Week by Week* guides the teacher in the collection of documents for this last type, the **Working Portfolio.**

Portfolios draw from multiple information sources and are gathered in the child's natural surroundings by persons familiar with the child and the environment. They are collected over time, so they clearly show the child's progress.

A Portfolio is an individual folder for each child in the class, gathering information from multiple sources (Figure I–9). Eventually it may hold many pieces of the child's work, teachers' observations, photos, and video or audio recordings, so it should be expandable. All Portfolios should be stored in a locked file cabinet or file box to assure that they are accessible only to authorized people, including the staff working with the children and the director. The Portfolio is available to the family upon request and to the child.

Child. The child contributes Work Samples such as drawings, artwork, and samples of writing and language. Media, such as audio and video recordings and photographs, also can be included. The Portfolio is a book about the child, so from a very early age, the child has a voice in the included works.

Families. Families, the true authority on the child since they know the child better than anyone—submit information to the Portfolio on forms and written comments.

Teachers. Teachers who see the child regularly submit formal observations using a variety of methods to best record different kinds of data in the most objective styles. Informal observations are included as important events worthy of remembering for a variety of reasons. Copies of periodic progress reports prepared for the family are also included.

Staff. Staff in the program who have contact with the child may write a submission for the Portfolio. The cook, the bus driver, and the nurse all see the child from a different perspective in different settings and have information to contribute.

Previous Teachers. Previous teachers' records may be passed on in the Portfolio or may remain in the

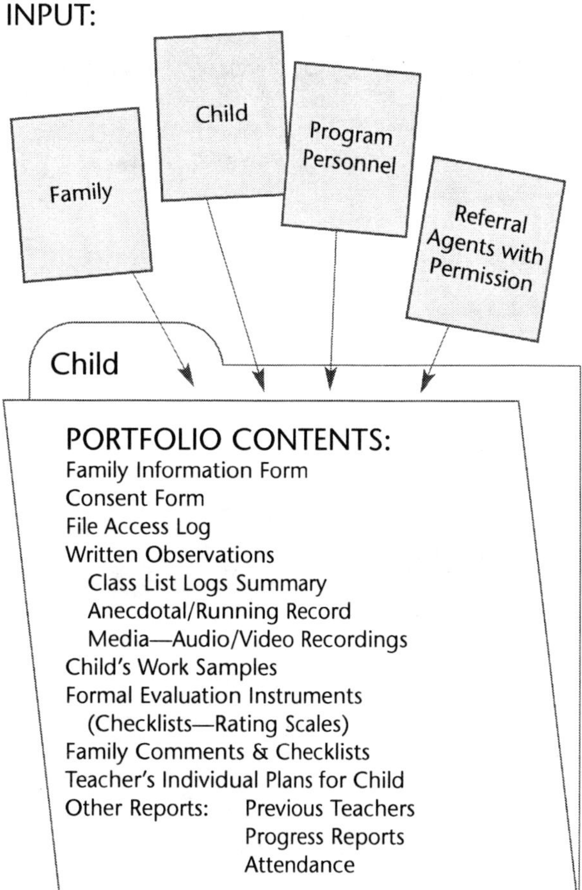

PURPOSES:
Hold information about the child
Document child's development
Periodically review progress
Plan individually for child
Hold examples of child's work
Share with family, child, teaching team

Figure I–9 Portfolios contain information from multiple sources.

Administrator's file, depending on the program or school policy.

Referral Agents. With consent forms, the program and referral agencies can exchange information. A release form must be used before information is shared. See Figure I–10. Referral agencies may include reports or suggestions for working with the child in the Portfolio.

What Is Not in the Portfolio?

There is another file accessible to the parents or legal guardian, the teachers, and licensing authority on request. Those files are kept in an administrative filing cabinet, separate from the child's Working

INFORMATION RELEASE FORM

I understand the confidentiality of any personally identifiable information concerning my child shall be maintained in accordance with the Family Education Rights and Privacy Act (P.L.93-380), federal and state regulations, and used only for the educational benefit of my child. Personally identifiable information about my child will be released only with my written consent. With this information, I hereby grant the

____
(Name of program, agency, or person)

permission to release the following types of information:

Medical information ________________
Assessment reports ________________
Child histories ________________
Progress reports ________________
Clinical reports ________________
(Other) ________________

to: ____
(Name of agency or person to whom information is to be sent)

regarding________________________ ____________ ________
Child's Name Birthdate Gender

____
Signature of Parent or Guardian

____
Relationship of Representative

____
Date

Figure I–10 Information Release Form (From Marotz, *Health, Safety, and Nutrition for the Young Child,* 7th edition by Marotz, 2009 Wadsworth, a part of Cengage Learning, Inc. Reproduced by permission. www.cengage.com/permissions.

Portfolio that is accumulated by week-by-week records. The contents of the administrative file include extensive medical information and any other confidential information that is not appropriate for the child's Working Portfolio. If there are any suspected, but as yet unsubstantiated, concerns about possible child abuse, those records should be kept in a separate confidential file, separate from the child's health records and Working Portfolio. Any Anecdotal Recordings that document a possible disclosure of child abuse should be placed in this confidential file. A copy of the filed Child Abuse Reporting Form and notations tracking the action should also be retained there. The teacher's Reflective Journal is the writer's private property, not to be kept with children's records (preferably kept at home).

Who Can Read the Portfolio?

The Portfolio includes documentation of all developmental areas for helping, measuring, and reporting the child's progress. Documentation is arranged chronologically and by developmental areas, logged in on an Overview Sheet so that contents are noted. Because of the completeness and intimacy of a Portfolio, its contents must be protected from unauthorized viewers. The National Association for the Education of Young Children's *Code of Ethical Conduct* (NAEYC, 2005) under the section on Ethical Responsibilities to Families reads:

P-2.7—We shall inform families about the nature and purpose of the program's child assessments and how data about their child will be used.

P-2.8—We shall treat child assessment information confidentially and share this information only when there is a legitimate need for it.

Families. Families can read the portfolio contents to receive feedback about their child, to learn about the curriculum and approaches the teachers are using, and to provide them with glimpses into the child's day to share and discuss with the child. Custodial parents or legal guardians have a right to see and control school records under the Family Educational Rights and Privacy Act (Buckley Amendment) passed by Congress in 1974. In the basic belief that early childhood programs are in partnership with families, the records are subject to their inspection. The systematic plan of gathering information has nothing to hide, for it seeks to provide objective, descriptive documentation.

As a part of the enrollment process or on the necessity to make a referral, the family should complete an Information Release Form (see Figure I–10). Permission must be obtained before releasing certain information to outside agencies. The family has the right to know and give permission. This form is kept on file with the child's medical history and records in the administrative office.

Program handbooks should inform families that their child's Portfolio is open to them any time. At the end of the year, the family usually determines whether it will go to the next teacher, next center, the public school, or home. The school will obtain written permission before releasing any Portfolio document to others. The exceptions are school officials with a legitimate educational interest and officials for use in audit or accreditation associations (with names deleted). In emergencies, the information is used to protect the health of the individual (Berger, 2008).

Practitioners. Other teachers and program personnel who interact with the child may look at the portfolio contents to get to know the child, to collaborate and share ideas about how to plan curriculum that will fit the child's expanding development. These discussions are a form of professional development as teachers reflect and interpret documented observations.

Community Agencies. Occasionally, people who have a need or a right to know may see the contents of the Portfolio. Those people may include a program evaluator who is gathering developmental level data, not on individual children but on an aggregate of all the children, or an accreditation validator looking at how the program records developmental information or seeking proof of a systematic authentic assessment plan. An ethical way to inform the families and the program of who has seen the contents of the file is to include a **file access log** (Figure I–11) in each file. Each person who views the file, other than the teacher(s), signs the log, providing the date, identity, agency represented, and reason for looking at the file.

The Child. Children above the toddler age can be involved in seeing, contributing to, and talking about the contents of the portfolio. They can participate in self-assessment and feel satisfaction in their work samples and the written observations as they see it collected in the Portfolio. *Week by Week* will address this in each chapter in the What to Do with It section.

Why Use Portfolio Assessment Rather Than Testing?

Chapter 8 will discuss standardized testing and its use and misuse; this book will guide you in using Portfolios as an authentic, reliable way to assess children's development. Much has been written to promote Portfolio assessments (Gronlund, 2009; Martin, 2007; NAEYC, 2003; Neisworth & Bagnato, 2004; Pack & Knight, 2000; Wiener & Cohen, 2002). A review of the benefits of Portfolio assessment includes its ongoing purposeful assessment done during authentic

The record of ______________________ was reviewed by the following:
(child's name)

DATE	NAME/TITLE	AGENCY	REASON	SIGNATURE

Figure I–11 File Access Log.

activities (play) in a naturalistic setting without diverting children from natural learning processes.

Portfolios can be a valid, reliable replacement or augmentation for standardized testing. Organizations such as the NAEYC and National Association of Early Childhood Specialists in State Departments of Education (NAECS/SDE) take this position on assessment: "To assess young children's strengths, progress and needs, use assessment methods that are developmentally appropriate, culturally and linguistically responsive, tied to children's daily activities, supported by professional development, inclusive of families and connected to specific, beneficial purposes" (NAEYC, 2003, p. 2). They call for more authentic assessment methods that provide documentation gathered from multiple sources over a period of time in the child's natural environment (Figure I–12).

Here are eight principles for guiding the decision on how to assess children (Neisworth & Bognato, 2004, pp. 204–208):

- *Utility*—Can the assessment be used to guide the individualized curriculum?
- *Acceptability*—Is the assessment socially and culturally relevant?
- *Authenticity*—Does it yield information about the child's typical behavior in natural settings?
- *Equity*—Does the assessment collect and interpret findings fairly?
- *Sensitivity*—Does the assessment provide for the measurement of a full range of abilities?
- *Convergence*—Does the assessment look at all the domains of development?
- *Collaboration*—Does the assessment gather information from several sources with the family as the authority on the child?
- *Congruence*—Does the assessment make allowances for differing abilities, evidence based?

Figure I–12 Close observation of routine events helps the teacher evaluate and make decisions.

The *Week by Week* systematic plan for Portfolio building will enable the user to gather data to meet the need of authentic assessment as outlined in the eight principles above in a manageable way. It meets the guidelines for appropriate assessment for planning instruction and communicating with families, identifying children with special needs, and for program evaluation and accountability. (See the Book Companion Website at www.cengage.com/education/Nilsen for the full NAEYC position statement.)

Many kinds of scientists—sociologists, anthropologists, archeologists, biologists—gather field data of their subjects, carefully describing and cataloguing to make meaning of their specimens later. Teachers are just such kind of scientists, taking the **ecological view** by studying children in their naturalistic settings, not a controlled laboratory but an environment that is just a part of the child's world that centers around the family and the community.

When to Observe?

From what you have read so far, you see that seeing children in the natural setting of the classroom, while they are actively participating, gives us the best indicators of their capabilities. This means that while children are engaged in play they gain knowledge, organize their world, and develop their bodies, minds, emotions, social skills, and language. In play, children can be themselves with their behavior speaking the language of who they are and what they think and feel. While observing play, every domain of development can be assessed by documenting behavior and analyzing it for indicators of development. In the chapters that follow, documentation methods are presented along with a review of child development so that the observer will look at children's play as opportunities to measure attainment, support the forward progress, and plan the environment and curriculum to help achieve it. *Week by Week* is a play-based assessment system.

What Is the Week by Week Plan?

EXERCISE How long do these big projects take? What steps lead to completion of the project?

- Conception to birth
- Earn a college degree

- Lose 25 pounds
- Crochet a bedspread

Some of those projects take months, some take years, some take a lifetime. Each one begins with a plan with small steps along the way, leading to the completion of the project. None can happen overnight. Some may even seem impossible, but when broken down into manageable steps, planned and worked on over a period of time, they can be accomplished. Eventually the desired goal will be reached.

Teachers of young children *know* they should be keeping written records on each child's behavior for many good reasons, but there is one seemingly insurmountable obstacle: *time*. This book begins with the premise that writing down observations of children's activities is the preferred method of assessing and documenting children's development.

"But I don't have time!" Every busy adult working with children has said it. The teacher's priority is to applaud the climb to the top of the ladder, redirect that arm ready to throw a block, or give a thoughtful response to a family member as she hurriedly says on her way out, "He's running a little fever and had a touch of diarrhea this morning, but he says he feels fine." The role of the teacher is to provide physical and psychological safety and intellectual challenge to each child. The teacher also strives to maximize the teachable moment and expand on the child's interests and conversations.

Those two responsibilities, accurate record keeping and responsiveness to the needs of each child, seem incompatible. Time and attention for record keeping is minimal. Teachers who know they should be making written records are caught in a bind. They recognize the importance of keeping accurate records on which to base evaluations or plan individualized curricula. The difficulty, and for some the impossibility, is doing this while interacting with the children.

Major accomplishments require time and planning. A meaningful Portfolio of a child's development and work is not gathered in a few days. Authentic assessment is achieved when each child's development is observed and documented objectively and periodically. The results are strategies to facilitate the child's progress to the next developmental level by individualizing the curriculum. When the teacher knows that one or more children in the class have reached a certain level of development, plans can be specified for them to advance. There is a pattern of observe, assess, plan, implement, evaluate, and record. This is repeated in each developmental area for each child, but only when an authentic performance-based assessment system is in place that allows this to happen efficiently.

To accomplish this desirable goal, the task must be broken down into manageable segments, planned, and executed in a systematic manner. "A responsive play-based curiculum has always required educarers to be systematic and careful observers of individual children's ability to develop skills, integrate experiences, and construct knowledge"(Bergen, Reid, & Torelli, 2009, p. 5). Programs need a system for gathering and using developmental information through observations and note-taking. The teacher can place materials for recording observations in strategic places around the room, thus preplanning and organizing for successful recording of observations. Skills, tools, materials, help, and dedication to the plan are needed to systematically build a Portfolio demonstrating a child's development.

I was teaching a college course in observation techniques but struggling to apply the methods in my own classroom. There were mounds of checklists—one for each child—index cards, and notepads all over the room. When I tried to write a daily journal or mark a checklist, I could not remember children like Johnny who floated all over the room, never doing anything "noteworthy." This plagued me until I realized *I had to have a plan*. I went looking for one but had no success. After calculating the weeks in the school year, what I wanted to know, and the appropriate method to record it, I had a systematic plan. That plan, refined through many years of teaching and research, is presented in this book.

In *Week by Week*, when the word *teacher* is used, it refers to the recorder who is documenting the child's behavior. It may be the early childhood student in a practicum experience, a teacher in a child-care setting, or a teacher in a classroom setting. The recorder may have the minimum required hours of in-service training, a CDA (Child Development Associate), associate degree to advanced degrees, or teacher certification. Whatever the qualifications on paper, the children call this person "teacher" because she is in the teacher role, and she will be called by that worthy name in this text.

How to Use This Book

Every chapter has two main parts, instruction on a method or tool to use in observing and recording young children's development, and a section on an area (domain) of child development. This does not mean that the method is the *only* way to gather information on the child but is an effective, efficient tool. In addition to the textbook, there is the Book Companion Website (www.cengage.com/education/Nilsen). In each of the next 14 chapters, a recording method is presented and practiced.

Using the . . . Observation and Recording Method

Each chapter presents a different method of writing down or documenting what the observer sees and hears in the classroom or on the playground, during the regular activities and routines of the day, as they are happening.

Throughout the book are Exercises, interactive sections inviting the reader to answer a question or formulate a list. Readers should write their "answers" in pencil, to be erased for privacy, or on a separate sheet of paper. These exercises are designed to introduce a concept that is applied in the following portion of the text. These are called exercises because they serve to strengthen the reader's understanding.

EXERCISE A house builder uses many tools. Next to each of the following, write its purpose:

- Hammer:
- Screwdriver:
- Saw:
- Tape measurer:
- Sandpaper:

Just as a builder has many tools, each with a distinctive purpose, so should the teacher have many recording tools and observation methods to use for specific purposes. There are several different kinds for different occasions or situations. Some are better than others at capturing certain kinds of behaviors, skills, and activities. If it were physical development we were observing and recording, then a developmental checklist would be more efficient than a narrative describing every action of the child's movements. Speech and language are best captured on an audio recording but can also be recorded efficiently on a checklist, but then we lose the exact words, inflections, and context of the situation. Each chapter will present a method or technique along with a description and examples of that method linked to one of the developmental areas in which it can be used. That is not the *only* method for that development area, nor is that method only to be used in that developmental area.

Advantages and Disadvantages. A hammer is not adequate to turn a screw; likewise, a screwdriver does not efficiently drive in a nail (although some of us have attempted to do so). We present an observation in each chapter, described and illustrated with examples. Some are methods that will be familiar, some will be new. Some will be simple to grasp and use, while others will take more practice. Some are used often, whereas others are used periodically or only in special circumstances.

Pitfalls to Avoid. With every one of the builder's tools, incorrect use may result in a dangerous situation or an outcome that is less than desirable. Using a stiff paintbrush leaves unwanted streaks in the paint or varnish, for example. The description of the observation method will also include some cautions about the method or its use. These are not necessarily disadvantages, but they are presented to raise awareness of misuse or common mistakes and are included to maximize the usefulness of the method.

Using Technology. New products and electronic devices can be used to more efficiently manage documenting children's development. This section in each chapter will suggest some products or applications that could be used to collect, organize, store, and report the documentation. Some are inexpensive and handy, while others may require financial investment and a change in practice. Teachers are change agents, seeking to facilitate change in others, so we, of all people, should be open to change ourselves.

How to Find the Time. In this section, there will be some suggestions on how to find the few minutes that it takes to accomplish the documenting of children's behavior while managing the classroom at the same time. It can be done!

Time? When is there time to write? A developmentally appropriate classroom for young children dedicates blocks of time to children's choice of activities. These are self-initiated, with materials and equipment available on shelves the children can reach themselves. Whole-group activities are limited to very short periods, if at all. That leaves the teacher with time, once the environment is prepared, to observe, make notes, and even closely follow and document a child's play. If there is no time for this, the teacher should look at the environment, the schedule, the ratio of children to adults, the curriculum, and the teaching practices. Program and school administrators who support time given to observation value it with resources that empower the teacher. Perhaps there is work to be done in those areas before observation techniques can be implemented.

If you are a student using the recording method to complete an assignment, you have the advantage of time. You can concentrate on children's movements and listen and write down their exact words without interruption. Now imagine yourself as the teacher trying to capture the same information using the same method while supervising the whole room for safety, reading a book, wiping a nose, washing your hands, and keeping track of the time to transition to the next part of the daily routine. It is tough, but it can be done. However, it takes time-management skills, flexibility, concentration, classroom organization, and cooperation from the other adults in the classroom (Figure I–13).

Figure I–13 Planning to observe is the secret to meaningful, useful, and authentic assessment.

Review Box. At the end of each recording method section is a short definition of the method and other areas of development or behavior on which it can be used now that you have a working knowledge of the method's procedure, advantages, and disadvantages.

At the end of each child development section, other recording methods are suggested for documenting the progress in that area. This demonstrates that the methods and areas of development are linked in *Week by Week* and are not exclusive of each other. Using some kind of reliable, regular documentation system is the goal.

Looking at . . . Child Development

The other half of each chapter is a discussion of one area of child development. That is what you are recording, each child's development, so you need to know what to look for. When the radiologist shows the X-ray of a broken bone to the parents of the crying child, they look at it but may not *see it as she does.* Without her specialized knowledge, they look at the same visual image but understand it at a different level. The teacher needs the specialized knowledge base of child development in order to understand the recorded events.

Child Development. Without a foundation knowledge of child development, behavior is observed, seen, but not recognized for its importance. For that reason, each chapter includes an overview of a developmental area discussing influences, milestones, terminology, and key theories. There is an emphasis on the child's observable skills and behaviors that demonstrate progress. This is not a comprehensive child development text but does present and review each developmental domain as it relates to that chapter.

The word *development* is an important one to understand. It is more than just change. Some important developmental principles include the following:

1. Development in one area influences and is influenced by what takes place in other developmental areas.
2. Development is sequential with later abilities, skills, and knowledge building on those already acquired.
3. Development occurs at varying rates from child to child and at uneven rates across different areas in the same child.

4. Development results from biological maturation and experiences.
5. Early experiences, positive or negative, have later effects and there are optimal periods for certain types of development to occur.
6. Development progresses from simple to complex.
7. Development occurs best when children have secure relationships with responsive adults and peers.
8. Development is influenced by social, emotional, and cultural contexts.
9. Children learn in multiple ways, seeking meaning of the world around them, so a range of teaching strategies are effective in supporting learning.
10. Play is an important vehicle for all areas of development.
11. Development advances when children are challenged with opportunities to practice new skills just beyond their level of mastery.
12. Child's experiences shape their motivation and approaches to learning.

(adapted from Copple & Bredekamp, 2009)

The inverted triangle, illustrating the expanding nature of development, is used throughout the book to represent the expansion of skills and knowledge that begins in a limited, crude way but broadens and builds upon prior experiences.

Figure I–14 Observing infants and toddlers requires flexibility but discipline.

Observing Infants and Toddlers. Observing infants and toddlers takes patience and perseverance. The changes in infants are very subtle so that a trained eye must be an alert observer as well as knowledgeable in developmental milestones that occur with frequency during the first two years. Young infants have long periods of seeming inaction while they sleep, gaze around the room when awake, or perform repeated motions such as opening and closing their mouth as their hand comes into view. Some kinds of recording methods just are not helpful in capturing young infant behavior. As the infant develops into an active mover, it is more challenging for the recorder to write rapidly enough to describe the actions. An even bigger challenge is to step back and process what is observed and recorded into meaningful, significant developmental events (Figure I–14).

Each chapter will include insight about infant and toddler development and suggest efficient ways that careful observing and meaningful recording can be accomplished. Usually the best times for recording infant and toddler behavior is during routines such as arrivals and departures and routines such as eating, toileting, napping, and interaction with children and adults including language exchanges (beginning with sounds and responses). Baby-watching is fascinating, but even more important is applying what we know about development to make meaning of those movements and sounds.

Helping all Children. An important part of each chapter's discussion of child developent is a section that discusses differences that may be observed in a child's behavior and development because of other factors such as special needs or diverse cultures.

Children with Special Needs. Whether or not a child has been diagnosed with developmental delays or learning difficulties, often the early childhood teacher is one of the first people outside the home to interact with the child and begin to notice differences beyond the range of normal expectations.

This section of each chapter will discuss that particular developmental domain, such as physical or language, and how those special needs may manifest themselves and what the teacher could do to help the child and the family.

Diverse Cultures. The word *culture* may have many meanings, but we are using this one: "Culture is a shared system of meaning, which includes values, beliefs, and assumptions expressed in daily interactions of individuals within a group through a definite pattern of language, behavior, customs, attitudes and practices" (Mashinot, 2008, p. 6). This expands the traditional list of physical appearance and personality traits, foods, dress, and language to ways of understanding an individual's attitudes, intentions, and motivations that guide their behavior. The goal is to better understand one another's culture so that the focus on the child we are sharing is not placed in an environment that is in conflict.

One of the biggest difference between individualistic and interdependent cultures is the view of the indivdual. Considering these basic values can guide an awareness of other cultures toward a better understanding of "where they are coming from." In individualistic cultures, such as mainstream America, children's autonomy, independence, and ability to make choices and problem solve is valued. This undergirds the practices of promoting early self-help skills, applauding assertiveness, and leadership. In interdependent cultures, the values are of obedience, "fitting in," and sacrificing personal goals for the good of the group. Each chapter will include a section to guide your thinking of how cultural differences may affect behavior and development and what the teacher can do to understand and negotiate on behalf of the child.

Helping Professionals. When working with children and families, teachers are often the resource or intermediary between people who need specialized advice and services and the professionals and agencies. This section is included in each chapter to acquaint the reader with the terminology of specialists to whom the teacher may refer the family. Each program should have a list of specific referral agences and professionals from which the family can choose, with guidance from the people they trust.

Other Methods. The recording methods and developmental areas are linked in this book to familiarize you with both. However, once you have learned about the methods, you will see that development may be assessed using several different methods. At the conclusion of each chapter, there is a feature that suggests which other methods would be suitable for documenting the developmental area featured in the chapter.

Standards. Almost every profession has established standards for itself and its constituents to describe the guiding principles and practices: the Association for Childhood Education International (ACEI), the National Association for the Education of Young Children (NAEYC), National Association for Family Child Care (NAFCC), Division for Early Childhood—Special Education (DEC), along with many others with standards for particular segments such as teacher preparation, curriculum areas, and federal, state, and local standards. The United States Department of Health and Human Services has developed Head Start Program Standards as well as Child Outcomes Standards. Included in Week by Week are selected examples of relevant standards that apply to the chapter topics (see Figure I–15).

Week by Week seeks to assist in meeting these standards, whether for accreditation, preparation program improvement, or for more qualified early childhood professionals. (Rubrics for each of the types of observation methods, as well as the child study where all elements of the standards can be measured, are included in the Book Companion website at www.cengage.com/education/Nilsen.) Students can use them as self-checks, and instructors can use them as grading rubrics and for data collection for accountability and program improvement.

Child performance standards that guide early childhood program administrators, teachers, and curriculum planners in areas such as physical, social, emotional, language, literacy, and creativity will be introduced in each chapter. These standards are often available on the Internet and in publications from the organizations that will be referenced in the Resource Area of each chapter. (The Book Companion website at www.cengage.com/education/Nilsen also has links to them.)

Chapter Features

Exercises. You have already seen the Exercise feature that occurs periodically within the book, designed to personalize the concepts, involve the reader, and focus attention on what follows. The reader is invited to think and write the answers to these exercises to build connections with the content.

Selected Examples of STANDARDS/ACCREDITATION CRITERIA featured in each chapter

Chapter	NAEYC Early Childhood Program Standards and Accreditation Criteria	Child Development Associate—Council for Early Childhood Professional Recognition	Head Start Program Performance Standards	Head Start Child Outcomes	Division of Early Childhood Recommended Practices	National Association of Family Child Care Accreditation	NAEYC Professional Early Childhood Preparation Standards	Content Associations and Others
Intro							Section 3 Observation and Documentation	NAEYC Code of Ethical Conduct
1		Functional Area: Physical						American Academy of Pediatrics, Caring for our Children 2.004
2					Self-Assessment: Child-Focused Interventions			American Academy of Pediatrics, Caring for our Children 4.024
3								American Academy of Pediatrics, Caring for our Children 2.009; National Associations of Sports and Physical Education
4								National Council for Social Studies, Association of Childhood International
5			1304.24 Work with families for emotional health			1.21 Understanding Feelings		

6				Language: Speak & Comm Standard Area 1				Teachers of English as a Second Language TESOL #1 Communication for social and learning
7	2B03 Emotional Development				Practice 2 Environment design for physical & emotional health			
8							4.b Teachers' approaches	National Council of Teachers of Mathematics Counting
9				Domain 2 Literacy—phonological awareness				International Reading Association 4.3 Model reading
10		Functional Area 7: Creative		Creative Arts Area 5				
11					Technology applications			McREL Compendium of Standards and Benchmarks—Theater
12	Code of Ethics P1:8-11							
13			Management 1304.51 Program Assessment			5.14 Business and Professional Practices		
14		Functional Area 11 Relationships with families						NAEYC Code of Ethical Conduct—Sharing information with families

Figure I–15 Standards Chart.

[**Professional Preparation Standards** In professional preparation, whether in the initial licensure of early childhood teachers or in associate degree programs, observation and assessment of children's development is an integral part. We are guided by the National Association for the Education of Young Children's *Preparing Early Childhood Professionals: Standards for Initial Licensure, Advanced, and Associate Degree Programs* (Hyson, 2003).]

Key elements of Standard 3

3a.—Understanding the goals and benefits, and uses of assessment.

Week by Week—explains the reasons why observation of all developmental domains is important in assessing and planning for the young child.

3b.—Knowing about and using observation, documentation and other appropriate assessment tools and approaches.

Week by Week—introduces and leads practice of several methods of documenting observations, pointing out the benefits and disadvantages of each. It presents information on standardized assessments and their proper use.

3c.—Understanding and practice responsible assessment.

Week by Week—stresses the ethics of equitable, factual, and confidential documentation.

3d.—Knowing about assessment partnerships with families and other professionals.

Week by Week—provides guidance in sharing documentation with the child, the family, and specific helping professionals in each weekly plan.

It Happened to Me. Vignettes of my classroom experiences are scattered throughout the book. These anecdotes illustrate points about child development from children I have known and mistakes I have made that taught me what not to do. Some are observations my college students have written. Others are humorous stories related to me. All are stories, incredible yet true. There are millions that *got away* because I never wrote them down! Many of these are remembered because after reflection on the real meaning of the incident, they taught me a lesson. Why is it that we often learn best from our mistakes? Many events became more important than I thought they were at the time. I hope you will begin to collect your own stories that have taught you lessons about teaching and life.

Do you have an IT HAPPENED TO ME story? I'm gathering them and would love to read yours and possibly use it in future editions. Please send it to me at Weekbyweek@ymail.com.

Topics in Observation. Within each chapter there is a separate section that gives insight into a related topic to child development or observation. This is to stimulate the reader's thinking about an issue or a concept to deepen knowledge.

Key Terms. Every profession has terms that are common to people who work in that field. Throughout the chapter, important words appear in red, bold type to draw your attention. They are listed at the end of each chapter; you can use this list as a self-check to be sure you understand their meaning. Each term is listed and defined in the Glossary at the end of the book.

Resources. Resources listing helpful books and articles on selected topics are included at the end of the chapters.

References. At the back of the book is a complete alphabetical bibliography of all the references used to substantiate the content of the book and give credit to ideas and concepts. Every effort has been made to include the most current research and to cite them accurately so that you can seek them out for further information.

In the Companion Website

Week by Week Plans. In the Preface, and earlier in this chapter, I explained the dual purpose of this book. It is primarily a textbook to introduce early

it happened to me

Why Doesn't Johnny Paint?

Early in my preschool teaching career, a mother asked me after class, "Why doesn't my Johnny ever paint? He never has any paintings to bring home." I thought, "Of course he paints! Everyone paints at the easel. There are always children on both sides for more than an hour every day. We use gallons of paint and reams of paper every year. Of course, he paints!" I started watching Johnny closely. Sure enough, he never chose easel painting. Even more revealing from my closer observation was how little I knew about what Johnny ever did. He was one of those children who did not draw attention to himself by negative behavior. He played and followed the rules of the classroom. At the end of the day, I had no idea what Johnny, and many others like him, had done. This is why we need to plan observations to include all children, not just those who demand our attention.

Do you recall an incident about a child or yourself regarding record keeping, assessment, referrals, your attempts at systematically gathering child data, or slip-ups in confidentiality? Send it to me at Weekbyweek@ymail.com.

childhood students to the importance of documenting children's development and building individual child Portfolios for authentic assessment and curriculum planning, all within the context of child development milestones. In the Book Companion Website is a student assignment to complete during that week of field experience. Alternatively, several chapter assignments could be combined and completed in three or four lengthy visits over a semester.

For the Student. You will practice this recording method by following the assignment in the Book Companion Website (www.cengage.com/education/Nilsen). You or your instructor may need to modify this depending on your field placement situation.

For the Practitioner. To achieve the goal of gathering a fairly equal amount of documentation on each child, use various methods and revisit developmental areas three times over a school year. An organizational system can be used to ensure that you are gathering an approximately equal distribution of Portfolio documentation on all children.

The monumental task of documenting every child in the class will become a series of small weekly plans, using the methods learned in each chapter to observe the developmental area that has been reviewed. *Week by Week* is a systematic plan to gather documentation on each child, in every developmental area, over a period of time, using a variety of recording methods. Some methods record small specific bits of information on all the children in the class. Other methods focus on one child, gathering detailed information. The *Week by Week* plan usually gathers both kinds of information each week, rotating developmental areas and individual children. The children are arbitrarily divided evenly into four observation groups (A, B, C, D) so that selection of children for individual focus is by predesigned plan (Figure I–16). This gives every child a fair representation rather than depending on attention-getting behavior as the documentation cue, resulting in large folders on some children and thin ones on others.

You will notice that new methods are introduced each week and preceding ones are used again, perhaps in a different developmental area and on a different group of children. This shows the versatility of various methods while assuring that all children are recorded equally and in all developmental areas. The Book Companion Website includes an extended chart so that the teacher can continue to plan past the first 14 weeks, following them to build a meaningful progressive Portfolio on which to base curriculum decisions and to chart achievement.

What to Do with It. This phrase will become familiar to the reader. At the end of each chapter presenting a recording method, a filing place is suggested along with a Portfolio Overview Sheet (Figure I–17) on which to note its presence, similar to a table of contents. These recordings are the teacher's contributions to the Portfolio being built on each child. The child, the family, and other program personnel also may contribute meaningful data to the Portfolio. Again, the goal is not just a collection of papers but a working, growing body of knowledge about the child for the purposes of

- documenting progress
- documenting typical and atypical behavior for intervention
- planning curriculum and classroom environment changes

TOPICS IN OBSERVATION

Ethics of Documentation

Ethics should guide documentation in the following ways.

Accuracy

With every method of observation, there is a responsibility to record the raw data (facts) as accurately as possible. This is done by making notes as completely and promptly after observing as possible.

As time passes, our memory dims and details slip away. The best recording is done *as the behavior is observed.* Some methods you will learn about are strictly factual, while others do have elements of judgment inherent in them. Carefully choose those methods and use them wisely.

Objectivity

Methods that preserve the raw data (just record the facts) are more **objective** (without bias or opinion) than others. That does not mean that one method is better than another or that biases and opinions can't enter into any recording. It is the responsibility of the recorder to capture what is seen and heard without interpretation. Again, the methods will contribute to the recording of data or interpretation. Be aware of that possibility.

Another aspect of objectivity is selecting children to document. By leaving it solely to the observer, it is possible to end up with thick files on children who have challenging behavior, resist classroom routines, or have social difficulties with other children or teachers. Such children are interesting to write about, for we are drawn to negative examples. However, there are children who follow the rules, flow with the routines, and get along with other children and adults. These children seldom are chosen for specimen recordings, but all children deserve an equal representation in observing practices. The *Week by Week* plan seeks to make that selection of subjects more arbitrary, thus equalizing the number and topic of the documentation added to each child's Portfolio.

Labeling

We all sort and categorize the information we take in. That is how we attempt to make sense of the world. It is important not to draw premature conclusions or diagnoses about a child based on limited information or to label a child or behavior. Our observation methods are designed to document the facts and to try to avoid categorizing a child as "bold," "hyperactive," or "shy." Our role as observers is to describe, document, and measure progress, not to draw conclusions about the isolated behavior we observe at any one time.

Intended Purposes

Students are writing about children for the purpose of observing and interpreting milestones in child development, to see theories in action, and to practice recording methods. The actual files should be destroyed once the course is completed since their purpose has been served. The child's work within the student's practice Portfolio could be given to parents, but the observations and child study should

(Continued)

TOPICS IN OBSERVATION (Continued)

be cleared with the instructor and classroom teacher before it is given to the family. Unintentional breaches of confidentiality or inferential and biased statements could be made by the practicing student.

Practitioners' purpose in recording is to document a child's behavior, assess, and plan for that child accordingly. Documenting should not be used to build a case against a child for any reason or to threaten or humiliate a child or family.

Sharing with the Family

For students, sharing with the family is only done under the direction of and with the approval of the teacher. For practitioners, observations should be related to parents using tact and much deliberation about how they will be received. Occasionally, what the teacher thinks is a triumph is seen in a different light by the family because of a different perspective or value. The teacher shows the painting to the family member and relates, "She stayed there a long time and painted over the whole page." The family member looks at it and says, "But it doesn't look like anything."

Talking to the child in front of the family should also be done with consideration. Sometimes children want privacy and a sense of being a person apart from the family. The teacher could ask the child, "May I tell your family about how long you painted today as we show them the painting?" Sometimes the child needs to hear their accomplishments related to their family. Discussing misdeeds or concerns, however, should be done in private, away from the child and other families.

CONFIDENTIALITY

Students will mask the identity of the children they observe by using only initials or some other neutral identifier. No last names should ever appear on any student's recording. Permission from a family member may be required by the school or program. It is the student's responsibility to inquire about the policy and abide by it. The file must keep the documentation private from anyone other than the instructor, the child, the child's family, and those who have a legal "right to know."

Writing enhances memory. This point has been strongly emphasized as the reason for writing observations. It is also true that what is remembered is discussed. As one becomes a better observer and recorder, it will also be only natural that conversations will be full of anecdotes. Cute stories, interesting quotes, and even concerns and *inside* information are on the observer's mind and sometimes lips.

Discussions outside the classroom with friends, or one's own family, require discretion. Sometimes stories are related for illustration, but they should never include children's names or details that could identify the child or their family. Complaining, satirizing, or criticizing children or families is unprofessional.

Professional behavior is guided by wisdom, kindness, and most of all, respect for an individual's privacy. Let's make a commitment to uphold NAEYC'S *Code of Ethical Conduct* (NAEYC, 2005).

WEEK	METHOD	AREA	ON WHOM
1	Class List Log Work Samples Reflective Journal	Separation and Adjustment Art	All All Self
2	Anecdotal Record Class List Log Reflective Journal	Self-Care Self-Care	Group A All Self
3	Checklist Anecdotal Record Reflective Journal	Physical Development Physical Development	All Group B Self
4	Running Record Class List Log Reflective Journal	Social Development Social Play Stage	Group C All Self
5	Frequency Count Anecdotal Record Reflective Journal	Emotional Development Emotional Development	All Group D Self
6	Interview and Checklist Class List Log Reflective Journal	Speech and Language Speech and Language	Group A All Self
7	Time Sample Interview and Checklist Reflective Journal	Attention Span Speech and Language	All Group B Self
8	Developmental Checklist Checklist Interview and Checklist Reflective Journal	Cognitive Math and Science Speech Language	Choice All Group C Self
9	Rating Scale Interview and Checklist Reflective Journal	Literacy Speech and Language	All Group D Self
10	Work Samples Anecdotal Record Progress Reports* Reflective Journal	Creative Creative Process	All Group A Group A Self

(continued)

Figure I–16 *Week by Week* Plan.

WEEK	METHOD	AREA	ON WHOM
11	Media	Dramatic Play and Blocks	All
	Running Record	Dramatic Play	Group B
	Progress Reports*		Group B
	Reflective Journal		Self
12	Class List Log	Self-Esteem	All
	Anecdotal Record	Self-Identity	Group C
	Progress Reports*		Group C
	Reflective Journal		Self
13	Setting Observation	Environment	Visit
	Class List Log	Group Interactions	All
	Anecdotal Record	Group Interactions	Group D
	Progress Reports*		Group D
	Reflective Journal		Self
14	Class List Log	Interactions with Adults	All
	Checklist	Physical Development	All
	Progress Reports		Group D
	Reflective Journal		Self
	*See Week 14, Assignment C		

Figure I–16 (continued).

Much has been written in the last 10 years concerning Portfolio building. The lack of a systematic plan for gathering that information, using a variety of methods, has led to this book. The purpose of the methods, rationale, instruction, and child development is to come to *know the whole child.* By knowing, then reflecting on this knowing, the teacher can truly plan and assess learning and progress.

Sharing with the Child and the Family. At the end of the day or session, what the teacher observes can be related to the child. What a wonderful send-off when the teacher says, "You painted a long time at the easel today" or "Today was a good day of sharing toys for you." The teacher shows by specific positive reference that the child's activities of the day were noticed and important. This is not the time for reminders of misdeeds or warnings about tomorrow. This is also an opportune time to share that same kind of positive information with the family member picking the child up. If the routine does not provide that face-to-face contact, a note (even in the form of a quick email message, perhaps with a digital photo attached) or a phone call (even to an answering machine) communicates to the family that the teacher has been carefully watching their child and saw something important. It builds relationships between child, family, and school, and the self-esteem of all. Examples of this type of communication are included in each of the weekly observation plans.

As a student, most likely it will not be your role to communicate with the family, although it depends on your field experience situation. Examples are included for those who do have this responsibility and as a model for those who will someday have direct communication with families. Communication with the child and family members about what we observe is an important part of our job, yet one for which teachers receive little preparation. Reading this section will help you begin to formulate your own family communication attitudes and practices.

By now you have probably noticed the shift in language from *parent* to *family* as explained in the Preface. This term includes the parents and close family members who provide primary care for the child. Chapter 14 contains a further discussion of this

PORTFOLIO OVERVIEW SHEET

NAME ______________________________ BIRTH DATE ______________

SEPARATIONS AND ADJUSTMENT			
Documentation Type	Filed in: Child's Portfolio Class File Other	Observer/ Writer	Date

SELF-CARE			
Documentation Type	Filed in: Child's Portfolio Class File Other	Observer/ Writer	Date

PHYSICAL DEVELOPMENT			
Documentation Type	Filed in: Child's Portfolio Class File Other	Observer/ Writer	Date

SOCIAL DEVELOPMENT			
Documentation Type	Filed in: Child's Portfolio Class File Other	Observer/ Writer	Date

EMOTIONAL DEVELOPMENT			
Documentation Type	Filed in: Child's Portfolio Class File Other	Observer/ Writer	Date

SPEECH AND LANGUAGE			
Documentation Type	Filed in: Child's Portfolio Class File Other	Observer/ Writer	Date

MEMORY AND ATTENTION SPAN			
Documentation Type	Filed in: Child's Portfolio Class File Other	Observer/ Writer	Date

COGNITIVE DEVELOPMENT			
Documentation Type	Filed in: Child's Portfolio Class File Other	Observer/ Writer	Date

LITERACY DEVELOPMENT			
Documentation	Filed in:	Observer/	Date
Documentation Type	Filed in: Child's Portfolio Class File Other	Observer/ Writer	Date

CREATIVITY— ART AND BLOCKS			
Documentation	Filed in:	Observer/	Date
Documentation Type	Filed in: Child's Portfolio Class File Other	Observer/ Writer	Date

CREATIVE—DRAMATIC PLAY			
Documentation Type	Filed in: Child's Portfolio Class File Other	Observer/ Writer	Date

SELF-IDENTITY			
Documentation Type	Filed in: Child's Portfolio Class File Other	Observer/ Writer	Date

GROUP INTERACTIONS			
Documentation Type	Filed in: Child's Portfolio Class File Other	Observer/ Writer	Date

INTERACTIONS WITH ADULTS			
Documentation Type	Filed in: Child's Portfolio Class File Other	Observer/ Writer	Date

OTHER DOCUMENTATION

____

____

REPRODUCED WITH THE PERMISSION OF AUTHOR: Nilsen, B. (2008). *Week by Week: Plans for Documenting the Development of Young Children, 3E.* Clifton Park, NY: Thomson Delmar Learning.

Figure I–17 Portfolio Overview Sheet.

rationale when it addresses sharing the Portfolio in family conferences (formerly Parent Conferences).

Actions. Because observations are meant to stimulate a decision, a section called *Actions* is included with *Read a Book* suggestions of a few books to read with children about the area of development. The *In the Environment* section suggests small changes or additions to the environment to help stimulate this area of development. *In the Curriculum* gives a few ideas about curriculum projects based on children's interests. Read *Engaging Children's Minds: The Project Approach* (Katz & Chard, 2000) for a full description of this topic. This section also includes ways to individualize the curriculum. The section *In the Newsletter* suggests topics for newsletter articles or ways of sharing anecdotes or children's work.

The Reflective Journal. For each week, a group of open-ended questions are provided to guide the teacher in looking inward. These are for the writer's own consideration of the events of the week, personal attitudes, self-analysis, and promises for the future. These are private journal entries, not a part of the child's records. These will be discussed again in Chapter 1. These are found on the Book Companion Website, usually in Part C of each week's plan. Please keep them in a safe place because they should be your honest self-reflection and a log that you keep week by week.

The Week by Week Plan

The *Week by Week* plan guides the student so that all developmental areas are observed at least once. In real life, the areas must be revisited repeatedly to accomplish the objective of seeing change over time, so the plans are extended to 40 weeks in the total plan. Care has been taken to observe each child equally in all developmental areas using a variety of methods. (See the Book Companion Website for an overview of that plan.) The weekly plans for the rest of the year are included on the Book Companion Website, so it can be a manual for use in an early childhood program throughout the year. Adaptations for class size and situation are explained.

That is how this book is arranged. It is meant to be a weekly plan for recording observations of each child's development and used as a basis for planning curriculum. The outcome of the plan is a meaningful, comprehensive Portfolio.

You will need a new file folder for each child in your class, plus a few extras for new children through the year. Write names on tabs, last name first, and place the folders in alphabetical order. Place in the file any information supplied by the parents.

A Portfolio Overview Sheet is a summary of all the recordings in the Portfolio so that the reader can see at a glance what is contained there, a type of table of contents. You will duplicate the one supplied at the end of Chapter 1 to place in each Portfolio.

This introduction sets the stage, gives you the background, and acquaints you with the format of the book. The next steps are yours. Complete the exercises and adapt the plans for your particular group of children. At the end of 14 weeks, you will have accumulated sizable Portfolios on each child, with documentation in each developmental area. If you continue the plans throughout the year (see Section C of the Book Companion Website), you will see the progress the children make and will become a better observer, recorder, and teacher.

Key Terms

- **assessment**
- **confidentiality**
- **criterion-referenced**
- **document**
- **ecological view**
- **ethics**
- **evaluation**
- **family**
- **file access log**
- **narrative**
- **objective**
- **Portfolio**
- **quantitative**
- **recording**
- **referral**
- **Work Samples**
- **Working Portfolio**

Plans

Go to the Book Companion Website (www.cengage.com/education/Nilsen) for the following:

- The week's plan (Parts A and B) for observing and recording individual children and the whole group on a specific developmental domain. This includes the forms you will need. You can print them off or fill them out on the computer or handheld device.
- What to Do with It—where to file the week's documentation.
- Sharing with the Child and Family—suggestions on the way to discuss your observations.
- Actions—curriculum suggestions for reading specific titles of children's books to enhance that developmental area, changes or additions to the learning environment, curriculum activities, and suggestions for your newsletter for family activities to reinforce the learning.

Part C is the Reflective Journal for you to fill in and keep private.

References

Week by Week is based on research in the fields of assessment, child development, and professional practice. Each chapter will include references used in the chapter. I invite you to explore the subject more thoroughly by reading the sources listed in the References at the end of the book for a fuller explanation of a topic.

Resources

Copple, C., & Bredekamp, S. (eds.) 2009. *Developmentally appropriate practice in early childhood programs.* Washington, DC: National Association for the Education of Young Children.

Helm, J. H., Beneke, S., & Steinheimer, K. (2007). *Windows on learning: Documenting young children's work* (2nd ed.). New York: Teachers College Press.

Hyson, M. (Ed.). (2003). *Preparing early childhood professionals: NAEYC standards for programs.* Washington, DC: National Association for the Education of Young Children.

Shores, E. F., & Grace, C. (2005). *The Portfolio book: A step-by-step guide for teachers.* Upper Saddle River, NJ: Pearson Education.

Snow, C. E., & VanHemel, S. B (Eds.). (2008). *Early childhood assessment: Why, what, and how.* Washington, DC: National Academies Press.

CHAPTER 4

Using Running Records to Look at Social Development

IN THIS CHAPTER

Using Running Records

EXERCISE Read the Running Record that focuses on Larry (Figure 4–1). Cover the right-hand column with a sheet of paper; make comments or inferences about Larry as indicated from this incident.

From the exercise, you see that a **Running Record** uses the same technique as the Anecdotal Recording. It is a factual, detailed, written account over a span of time. Actions are described and quotes are recorded as precisely as possible. Commentary or interpretation about the recording is written separately from the actual account. The recorder decides to observe and write for a period of time, focusing on one child or one play area. A nonselective narrative documents a specimen of that child's or that area's action.

The Running Record is written as the events are happening, while the Anecdotal Recording usually is written shortly after a significant event. The Anecdotal Recording is a little story with a beginning, the action, and an ending. Running Records are indiscriminate, giving a more objective glimpse into a normal (or what may turn out to be an abnormal) segment of time. That is not known, however, before the recorder begins to write. Everything that happens in that time segment is recorded: the mundane, the boring, the unexplained. At the end of a time period, the recording stops. This may not necessarily be at the end of the event. A Running Record is like turning on a video camera and just letting it run for a certain amount of time, recording whatever occurs. A Running Record is the most useful in giving a naturalistic view of a short time in the life of a child.

When a learning center or area of the classroom is the focus of a Running Record, the Record can evaluate the usefulness of the area and if the area needs any modifications. Particular learning centers or classroom areas are more suitable for viewing specific skills. A Running Record in the large muscle area obviously gives information on children's climbing, running, or jumping skills but also can yield valuable information on social, emotional, and verbal development. Imaginative play, social interactions, and self-concept are illustrated vividly in the dramatic play area as well as the block area. Small muscle skills, literacy development, and social and verbal skills are observed easily in the art area or during play at the sand or water table. Running Records of 10 minutes at any one of these areas can be extremely informative.

The Running Record requires intense concentration and focused attention. Other staff are needed in the room to be sure all children are supervised adequately; any recording in progress is secondary to a child in need. Any time, recording must be interrupted, a line is drawn and the ending and return times are noted. Recording may be resumed if the situation is now under control.

EXERCISE **On a separate sheet of paper, describe how you might feel if someone were watching you for 10 minutes and writing notes.**

One caution in using the Running Record, or any other recording technique, is the possible effect it may have on the child's behavior (Figure 4–2). It may make the child feel uncomfortable or act in an artificial way. The recorder must be sensitive to that self-consciousness. When such behavior is observed, the writing would then stop and efforts be made to be less obvious in the future. In a classroom where observation and recording go on all the time as a natural part of everyday life, children often cease to notice. If they are shown the notes, even if they are not yet able to read, they feel more comfortable about the writing. Talking with them about what was observed helps them understand the purpose behind the writing. When they hear the teacher talk with their family

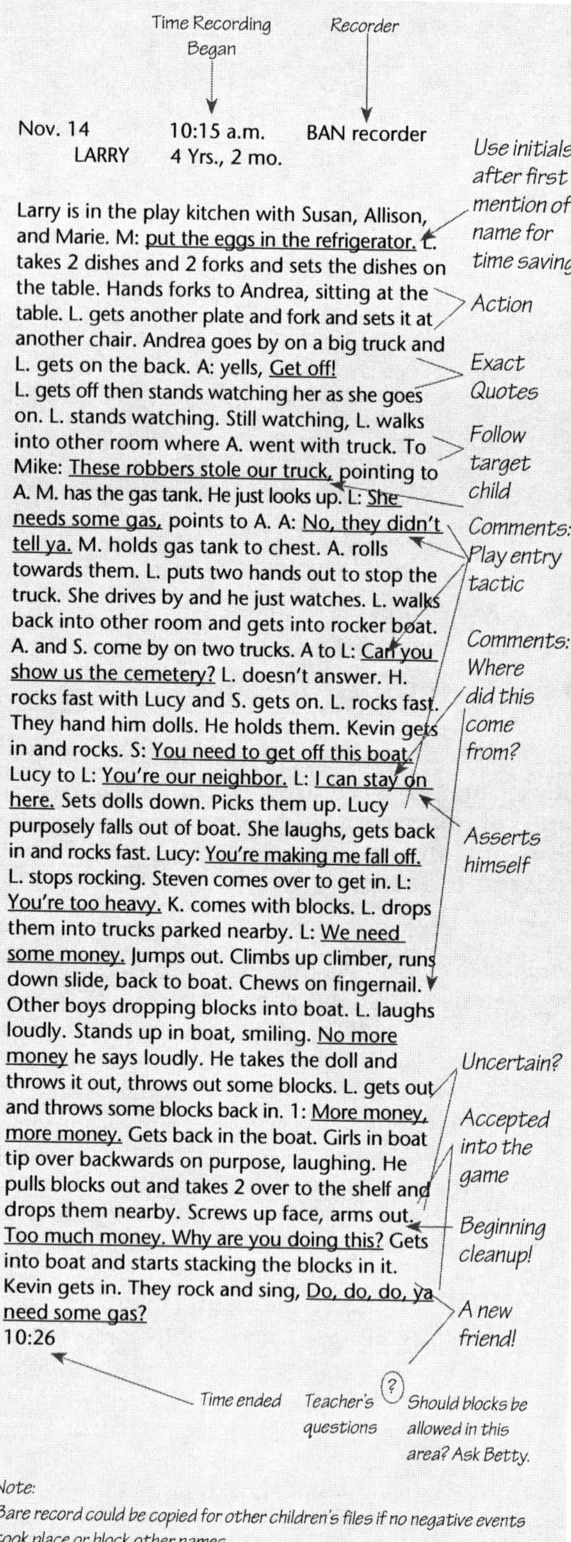

Figure 4–1 Running Record Example.

Figure 4–2 Observation may change behavior, so the observer attempts to be unobtrusive.

it happened to me

Artist's Model?

I was sightseeing on a bus in a foreign country, feeling very special, looking all around at the scenery, when I felt someone watching me. A young man toward the rear of the bus was sketching on a pad. "Oh," I thought, "he's an artist. This country's full of artists. He must be sketching me." So I turned my best side toward him, sat up straighter in the seat, and sat still with a facial expression I wanted captured on his pad. As he was leaving the bus I craned my neck to see the pad. It was a forest scene, apparently from memory, he was working on. Because I thought he was watching me, I changed my behavior.

Do you have an IT HAPPENED TO ME story about how observation changed behavior? I'd love to read it. Please send it to Weekbyweek@ymail.com.

about the episodes from the notes, they realize that their actions are important and meaningful. Warning: Any negative occurrences or difficulties observed should not be discussed with the family in the presence of the child.

Uses

The Running Record

- records detailed segments of behavior occurring in a certain time block.
- focuses on an individual child to show a naturalistic view of a part of the day.
- can be analyzed for evaluation of many developmental areas: physical, social, emotional, language, self-concept, attention span, problem solving, memory, learning style.
- documents evaluation of developmental areas for child study.
- can focus on a particular learning center or classroom area to see what typically occurs there.

Advantages

The Running Record is helpful because it

- is written at the time the behavior occurs, so it is less likely to be affected by bias and more likely to include lots of detail.
- can be used for a variety of purposes—developmental assessment, deeper understanding of the child, information for other professionals for further analysis
- details a normal segment of time in the day, giving a more natural view.
- reveals many areas of development in one recording.
- can evaluate the effectiveness of a learning center or area.

Disadvantages

The Running Record may

- make the subject feel watched, become uncomfortable, and change behavior, destroying the nature of the recording.

- not show normally occuring behavior in the time segment.
- make the adult unavailable to facilitate or observe what is happening in the rest of the room because attention is focused on the recording.
- tire and drain the recorder because of its intensity.

EXERCISE Figure 4–3 contains a Running Record on which to practice. Find the recorder's mistakes, then return to this point and check yourself.

The term *plays* is too generic.

Ann is standing at the sand table, filling tiny containers with a scoop, tongue between teeth. Q and T are also filling cups.

"Talks" is not recording exact quotes.

To Q: "I can get these all fuller than you."

"As usual" can be in the right column as a note by the recorder to indicate knowledge about Ann's play partner preference

This was an example of good action description. The reader can "see" the action.

Oops. Not the exact quote.

"Snow"

How does the observer know what Ann thinks? Exact quotes were not written down.

A grabs the shovel away from Q

It is helpful to know what other children joined the group.

B, K, and S come over.

This is a summary.

A watches them fill empty containers. To B, K, S: These are mine and they're filled with snow. What's in yours?

But where did she go?

A skips over to the Dramatic Play area where C and D are putting on dress-up clothes.

Recorder wrote the quote with the pronunciation as it was heard. Good.

	ABC Center Ann Wade 4 yr. old class BAN recorder Sep. 28
9:30	Ann plays with other children at the sand table. She talks with Q most of the time.
	She picks up a shovel and scoops sand into a sifter, watching it sprinkle and calling it snow.
	When Q picks up the shovel, Ann thinks she should have it back so she grabs it away. Q gets another one. As children come over, Ann gives them attention and asks them questions.
	After a while, Ann skips over to another group of children she wants to play with. She says, "Hey, watcha doin?"

Figure 4–3 Find the record's errors in this Running Record.

Not much detail here

A puts on a skirt, gloves (works to get every finger in), and then wraps herself in a shawl. "There, now I'm ready to go to the dance!" She twirls away.

Recorder did not include the end time.

9:39

EXERCISE Practice writing a Running Record. Take a separate sheet of paper right now, fold it in half, select a person to watch, and write down everything that person does and says for 10 minutes.

Rate your Running Record.

- Did you mention the setting so the reader knows where it took place?
- Did you write the date and time you started?
- Did you write your name on it as the recorder?

Look over the words you used and make sure they described actions, not summarized them or gave reasons for them. The words should form mental pictures.

- If you used any of the following words, perhaps you fell in the trap of summarizing: *because, wanted to, tried, saw, played, looked (emotion), noticed, pretended.*
- If more than one person was involved, did you write down the conversation word for word?
- Now go back and in the right column write what judgments you would make about this person's physical, cognitive, social, and emotional development.
- What did this segment of action show about that person? What questions did it raise about why the person acted that way?

Running and Anecdotal Records are like written movie scripts, exactly describing actions, facial expressions, and exact words of the players.

Pitfalls to Avoid

Running Records are time and energy intensive, so the recorder must be sure that the children are safely involved and under the supervision of at least one other adult for interaction; only then should a Running Record be started. Because of the objective technique, it probably is not a method that a volunteer could be asked to do, but the supervision could be assigned. Attention to safety and the interactive needs of children always takes precedence over recording.

Another pitfall is that close observation tends to make the target child feel observed, which can alter behavior. The recorder must be careful to observe from far enough away so as to not interfere with the child's actions but close enough to hear conversations. Sometimes, the location of a chair on the other side of a piece of equipment, behind the child's line of vision but within hearing distance, can be effective.

Often other children enter into the Running Record in interactions with the target child. Because this will be filed in one child's Portfolio, other children's names should be blotted from this particular recording for anonymity.

A Running Record can yield a great deal of insight into a child's usual activities, but it can be so mundane as to seem unimportant. It is not. As a true measure of a child's development and behavior, naturalistic observation like a Running Record is invaluable.

Using Technology

A video camera is a wonderful tool for capturing live action. There is no way a written Anecdotal or Running Record can compare, but using a video camera does take time, patience, and the knack for being in the right place at the right time. Using a video camera can also be intrusive. Whenever anyone but the most experienced model sees a camera aimed their way, they change their behavior. It is difficult to capture spontaneous, meaningful video footage.

Handheld computers can accommodate a portable keyboard that unfolds, which can be helpful because many people can type faster than they can write. Using a keyboard also makes it easier to add the Running Record to an electronic file on each child. Electronic files, mentioned in Chapter 3, are easy to manipulate, do not take up classroom storage space, are easier to keep confidential, and can also store artwork and photographs.

How to Find the Time

Running Records are one of the most time-intensive recording methods. To concentrate fully on one child and write accurately and descriptively about the child's every action and conversation takes undivided attention. That means that this recording method, in its purest sense, done as the action is taking place, is not practical for the person who is also responsible for the classroom. A modification can be to jot notes and amplify them later; however, time dulls the accuracy of the memory, so it is never as

TOPICS IN OBSERVATION

"The Stew"

Once upon a time, a chef set out to make a stew by preparing the ingredients and placing them on the stove to cook. After a period of time, the chef took a deep ladle and sampled a bit of each of the ingredients to judge the progress of the stew. Some needed more time to cook, so the chef extended the cooking time. The broth was lacking in flavor, so the chef added some spices. It was too salty, so the chef added a potato to take away some saltiness. The chef still was unsatisfied with the taste, so a master chef, a stew expert, was called in to give an opinion. More modifications were made to the stew.

The stew was then served to the first diner, the chef's mother, who declared the stew "Marvelous!" The Board of Health inspector closely examined each part of the stew, looking for irregularities, without actually caring about the whole stew. The vegetarian, repulsed by the meat in the stew, stopped eating, vowing to make comments to the cook. One diner thought it needed more salt, while another thought it was too salty. The unserved portions of the stew were refrigerated and reheated the next day with flavors mellowed and texture softer. The smart chef wrote down the recipe so that future stews could be as flavorful, but the chef knew it all depended on the ingredients available. But alas, some of the diners had moved on to other restaurants, so they never got the full, aged taste of the stew. Ah, if they could only taste the stew now.

Meaning

The stew is the child made up of many areas of development. The family brings the child to the teacher with knowledge, skills, and abilities. The teacher works with those to bring them to a certain expected level. A sample of the child's development is made to determine progress in development and further actions. In some areas, nothing is needed but time. In other areas, additions are made in the curriculum to assist in development. Sometimes, behaviors that are getting in the way of learning are modified. Expert advice is sometimes needed, so the family and teachers seek the referral and advice of helping professionals.

Hopefully, the family is pleased with the progress of the child, overlooking some areas still developing. Some observers look at specific areas while not seeing the whole child, such as a speech pathologist, dentist, or physical therapist. The child's progress may not be acceptable to some who have special interests or biases. Over time, the child grows, develops, and changes, but past teachers and resource people do not have the opportunity to observe the progress. The family and teachers who have a record of the changes know what worked for that child. Each child is unique, however, and the teacher realizes the necessity for adapting environment and curriculum for each child and group. It is sad that not everyone gets the opportunity to appreciate the transformation.

rich as what really happened. We are therefore faced with the dilemma of how to make time to complete Running Records.

The student teacher or student visitor may have the luxury of doing Running Records and having no other classroom responsibility. This is a wonderful learning experience and one that should be practiced. Not only can it be a great help to the teacher, but it can be a learning experience for the student by sharing the Running Record with the teacher and then discussing the interpretation. Another option is for the program administrator to arrange for coverage of the teacher's classroom for a brief period each day so that the teacher can sit and watch children's play. Or, a classroom volunteer could be trained in this method under the direction of the teacher. However it is arranged, Running Records are valuable pieces of documentation, and a 10-minute observation in every developmental area usually provides enough detail or depth to enable the observer and the reader to draw some conclusions about the child's level.

What to Do with It

Following the actual recording, the teacher can make notes in the right-hand column in the same categories as the Anecdotal Record:

- explanations
- comments about development
- questions for further investigation
- plans for the child based on the observation

The Running Record is filed in the target child's Portfolio after noting its presence on the Portfolio Overview Sheet. It may be read to the child at a later date for the basis of a conversation about the child's activities. The teacher can ask questions such as "When you were piling the blocks up and ran out of blocks, you stopped building. Is there something else you could have used to continue playing there?" or "When you were at the Writing Center, I heard you say something about writing a letter and an elephant but I couldn't hear what you said. Do you remember?"

The Running Record that includes other children who interacted with the target child can be copied, with the teacher then making notations in the right-hand column about the second child. When the record is filed in a child's Portfolio, the names of the other children should be blotted out.

Go to the Book Companion website (www.cengage.com/education/Nilsen) for Running Record forms, plans, and resources.

REVIEW

Running Record

Detailed account of a segment of the child's day, written as observed. Includes settings, descriptions of actions and interactions, and exact quotes.

TYPES OF INFORMATION TO RECORD USING RUNNING RECORDS

Any segment of the child's day, usual or unusual. It can yield information on the following:

separation and adjustment
self-care skills
physical development
social development
emotional development
language and speech
attention span and interests
cognitive development
literacy
creativity
socio-dramatic play
self-esteem

Looking at Social Development

Two children are pulling on the same toy. "It's mine!" "No, I want it!" An adult comes over, takes it away from one and gives it to the other. "You've got to share! Don't be so selfish."

That is not sharing. That is robbery. That is reinforcing the concept that bigger people can take things away from smaller people. True sharing is the willing relinquishing of one's rightful possession to another person. Social competence is the ability to get along with others. It is the ability to express, understand, and control emotions, and display social problem-solving skills. "OK, Jasmine, you can have it as soon as I finish playing with it and I'm almost done." But how do children learn not to be selfish? How do they develop an awareness that other people have wants and needs? How are they able to express their own needs in a nonaggressive yet assertive way and control their own emotions? Social competence, just as all other developmental domains, is affected by three realms: biology (temperament and genetic influences), relationships (responsive adults), and environmental (exposures to threats such as extreme poverty, violence, substance abuse, abuse, and neglect).

During the early years, children learn how to establish and maintain relationships with others, to enter into groups and get along, and to adapt their own wants and needs to meet society's expectations. Through this process, children are integrated into their society. They enter this learning process with their own particular dispositions and relationship history. When children are in child care, the quality of the relationship with the caregivers and the peer groups as well as the social and emotional climate all have a reciprocal effect on the socialization process (Howes & James, 2002). Observation of a child's play gives indicators of social behavior, cognitive, language, and motor skills. A careful recording and assessment of social play can give specific information about the level of the child's functioning in each domain.

The Importance of Play to Social Development

Think About It . . .

How do you play? Play is a part of life, not just for children but for adults as well. Looking at play can be interpreted from many different perspectives: psychological, educational, cultural, and anthropological.

- Individual and team sports?
- Arts?
- Computer games?
- Hobbies?

Some early childhood programs are criticized for emphasizing or even allowing play. "They're not learning anything there. All they ever do is just play." The word *play* is used repeatedly in discussing social development and many other areas as well. An understanding of play and its importance is necessary to child observers because it is a vehicle for learning. In fact, play equals learning, learning *to* play and learning *from* play (Singer, 2006). The tendency to play is natural and emerges sequentially in most children. It can be negatively impacted by brain disorders such as autism, social neglect, and trauma. For play to thrive, motivate, and enhance all areas of development, it requires scaffolding support of an adult, not to dictate or restrict the play but to set the stage and supply the necessary ingredients of time, materials, approval, and modeling.

The phrase "Play is the child's work," or variations of it, has been the theme or motto for defending play. The Concept Map in Figure 4–4 illustrates the developmental areas involved in play, the kinds of play, its connection with language arts, and the necessary provisions for play. The opposite word from *play* is *work*. The constructivist theory (DeVries & Kohlberg, 1987) contends it is through play and interaction with the environment that children construct mental images and processes. This is *work* in the sense that it has purpose and a definite goal. When an attempt is made to differentiate play from work, the dividing line becomes blurred. Play has been described and researched by many people.

Rubin, Fein, and Vandenberg (1983) formed this description of play:

- Play is intrinsically motivated.
- Play is relatively free of externally imposed rules.
- Play is carried out as if the activity were real.
- Play focuses on the process rather than any product.
- Play is dominated by the players.
- Play requires the active involvement of the players.

The International Association for the Child's Right to Play (IPA) has in its declaration that play, along with the basic needs of nutrition, health, shelter, and education, is vital to develop the potential of all children. Play is instinctive, voluntary, and spontaneous. Play helps children develop physically, mentally, emotionally, and socially. Play is a means of learning to live, not merely a way to pass time.

It is obvious that play can take place without other people, so solitary play is not just a stage but a type of play. Play with other people involved is democratic, without rules. Each player has some authority over the play. By observing, it is evident that not every player has equal power or as much power as they may want. Conflict in play erupts when the social development of the players is uneven. All the other developmental areas—cognitive, language, physical, and emotional—contribute to play's success.

Social Competence and School Readiness. Successful interaction with age-mates is a crucial predictor of not only academic success but also mental health and well-being. Social-emotional skills that support school readiness enable children to learn. They include confidence, curiosity, intentionality,

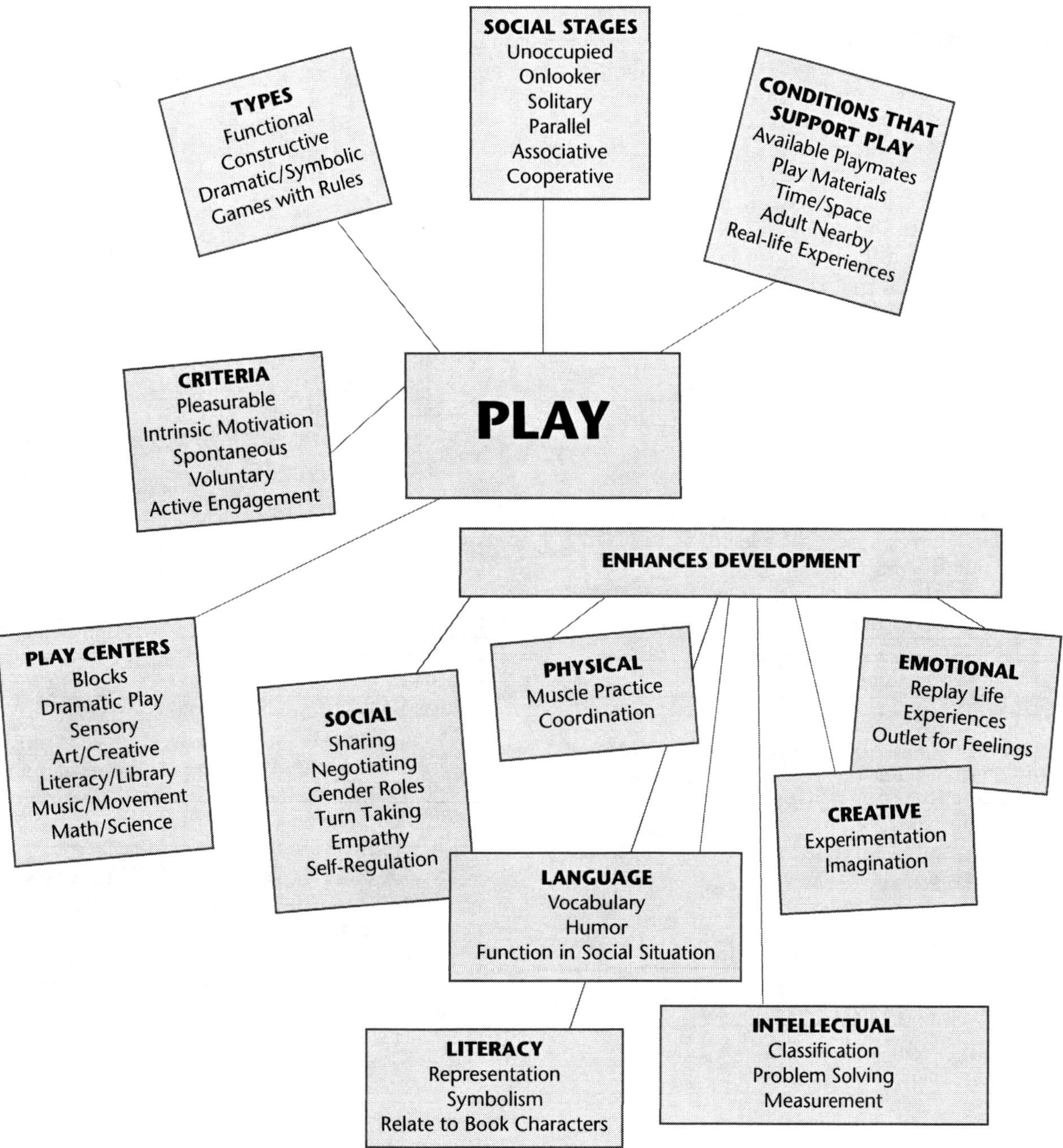

Figure 4–4 Concept Map of Play.

self-control, relatedness, capacity to communicate, and cooperativeness (Cohen et al., 2005). Barriers to the development of these skills place the child at risk of difficulty adjusting to school routines and later problems such as potential academic difficulties, delinquency, and drug abuse. During the preschool years, young children without emotional and social competencies are less accepted by classmates and teachers, receiving less instruction and positive feedback. They dislike school and learn less. In classrooms where there is a positive social climate, children are more enthused about learning (LaParo et al., 2004). The large NICHD Early Child Care Research study indicated that when young children have quality academic and social preschool experiences, the effects can persist into later elementary years and in antisocial behavior (NICHD, 2002; Raver & Knitzer, 2002).

Young Children and Social Studies. When children begin to move out from beyond the family into their own social groups in child care or preschool, their world broadens to include children from other families and, other cultures. They learn the rules about the rights of others and about the rule of the majority. They learn about the community, careers, transportation, how goods and services are made and distributed, concepts of time, and historical perspective. These are common themes in the curriculum of the young child as their world expands. In the same way that they learn anything, they learn from their experiences (both planned and spontaneous), from watching others, from books, and from direct instruction. Seefeldt (2006) lists the early childhood content topics based on the National Council for the Social Studies:

culture
time, continuity, and change
people, places, and environment
individual development and identity
individuals, groups, and institutions
power, authority, and governance
production, distribution, and consumption
science, technology, and society
global connections
civic ideals and practices

Looking at the list, common early childhood themes lend themselves to these categories: All About Me, Celebrations in My Family, See How I Grow, People in My Family, Inside/Outside, Transportation, Community Helpers, Playing Store, My Friends and How We Play, We Share, and All Around the World. Wallace (2006) says, "Among the most important elements of the social studies curriculum are the strategies and skills that teach students how to learn, how to make decisions, and how to work effectively with others"(p. 8).

Theories of Social Development

Many in the past have pondered the origins of how people relate to one another.

Freud (1953) attributes social behavior to the sexual nature of humans hidden in the subconscious. He saw a strong parental role in developing the superego, or conscience, to balance the id, the unconscious part of the psyche that demands the satisfaction of desires. The parental influences on the child's knowledge and feelings of right and wrong are deeply ingrained and differ from one family to another. It is important for the teacher to know and work cooperatively with parents to reduce the dissonance of differing messages and to cope with them when they do occur. Freudian theory also reminds teachers that the child also has a sexual nature. Although they are very young, basic sex roles and attitudes are forming through experiences in early childhood.

Erikson's psychosocial developmental theory (1950/1963) looks at not just biology but also at the changing mind and emotions and the effects of society in forming behavior patterns. His "Eight Stages of Man" illustrate the observable, predictable stages through which humans move. The first four stages are explained here, with the last four included to complete the concept.

Stage 1—Infancy: the challenge of trust (versus mistrust). Between birth and about 18 months, infants face the first of life's challenges: to gain a sense of trust that their world is a safe place. Family members play a key role in how any infant meets this challenge.

Stage 2—Toddlerhood: the challenge of autonomy (versus doubt and shame). The next challenge, up to age 3, is to learn skills to cope with the world in a confident way. Failure to gain self-control leads children to doubt their abilities.

Stage 3—Preschool: the challenge of initiative (versus guilt). Four- and five-year-olds must learn to engage their surroundings—including people outside the family—or experience guilt at having failed to meet the expectations of parents and others.

Stage 4—Preadolescence: the challenge of industriousness (versus inferiority). Between ages 6 and 13, children enter school, make friends, and strike out on their own more and more. They feel proud of their accomplishments or, at times, fear that they do not measure up.

Stage 5—Adolescence: the challenge of gaining identity (versus confusion).

Stage 6—Young adulthood: the challenge of intimacy (versus isolation).

Stage 7—Middle adulthood: the challenge of making a difference (versus self-absorption).

Stage 8—Old age: the challenge of integrity (versus despair).

These stages include the developing social role in each stage. Unlike Freud, who looked into the past to find reasons for pathological behavior, Erikson looked to the future, not giving up hope that the past can be overcome. Erikson's theory also stresses the importance of the adults in understanding and meeting children's needs in each stage. This affects how the child feels about himself and interacts with others.

Piaget's work in cognitive theory (Flavell, 1977) has significance for children's social development. Children's thinking governs their actions. As the child takes in new information, the child interprets it differently at different stages. Before infants reach **object permanence**, that is, until they acquire the awareness that objects continue to exist outside their sight, infants will not "miss" their mother. Once infants have cognitively reached that stage, other people's faces are compared to the mental image of the mother, and that mismatch results in separation anxiety. The young child is described in Piaget's theory as **egocentric**, only able to see things from his own point of view. The child thinks, "I want this ball so I should have it," and takes the ball from another child. When the adult says, "How would you like it if he did that to you?" it has no meaning. The child cannot mentally picture himself with the ball in his hands with another child taking the ball away. This is just too much abstract cognitive processing for his ability at this stage. This is the underlying factor of social actions in the preschool years: the conflict between what one child wants (and thinks he should have) and that of another. Recognizing this, the adults take many actions to account for this, such as having enough duplicate toys so that the need for possession is met. Once the child becomes verbal, the adult repeats phrases children can use. Phrases such as "You could say, 'I want to play with that ball when you're done'" or "Tell her 'I don't like it when you take that away from me'" help the child function socially.

Behaviorists' social learning theory (Skinner, 1953; Watson, 1950) describes how learning takes place when it is reinforced either negatively or positively. This behaviorism is the reason that spanking or punishment works (for a while) and that praise or reward encourages behavior to occur again. This is external reinforcement of behavior. Parents and teachers, however, want the child to be *intrinsically motivated,* that is, to do the right thing even when no one is there to say, "Good job," or "No." When appropriate recognition for *right* and *wrong* deeds is given, the child sees the results from those actions and forms a thinking process for making choices about right and wrong for next time. Hopefully, the adult does not have to be present for reinforcement for the child to make the *right choice.*

Maslow's work (1970) investigating the causes of behavior also was based on met or unmet needs. His "Hierarchy of Human Needs" chart is familiar to students of psychology (Figure 4–5). It has the

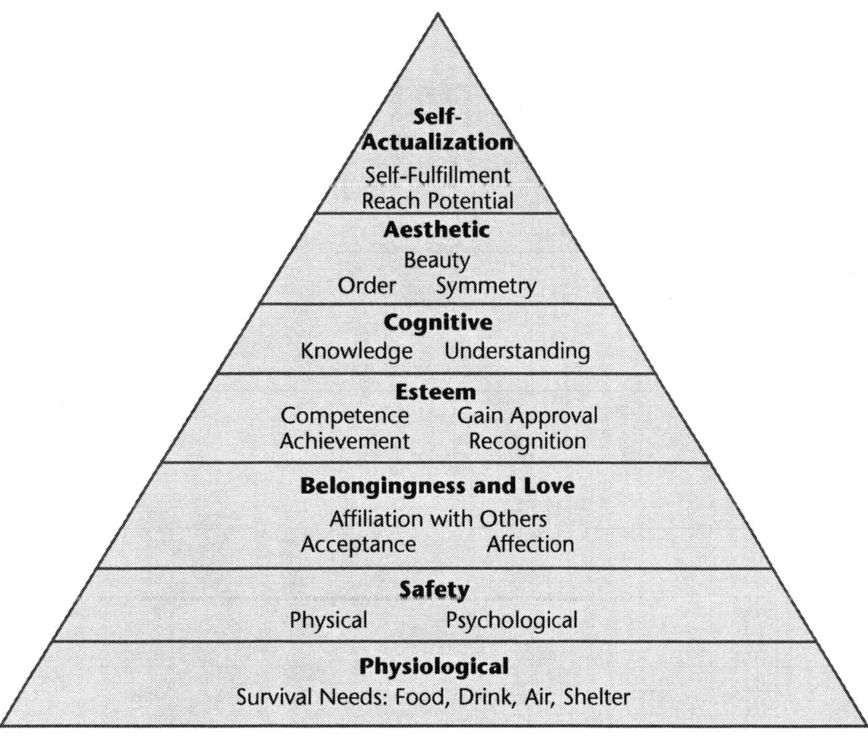

Figure 4–5 Maslow's Hierarchy of Needs (Adapted from Maslow, A. H., 1970, *Motivation and Personality*, 2nd ed., New York: Harper & Row).

most basic survival needs at the bottom of the pyramid, moving up to social needs, and eventually to self-actualization. This is where satisfaction comes from—from serving others rather than self.

From Maslow's work, it is clear that physical and psychological safety are necessary for children to develop. Schools have learned that a hungry child cannot learn, so national programs provide nutritious breakfasts and lunches. Similarly, the physical and aesthetic environment influences behavior, so millions of dollars are spent in homes, schools, restaurants, arcades, and businesses on color, furnishings, lighting, and aesthetics to influence human behavior. The classroom environment is an important factor in learning, since it attends to both the physical and psychological needs of the children and adults. The affective needs of acceptance, recognition, affection, belonging, and love are the work of the curriculum of the social development area. From names on the cubbies to hugs at the end of the day, children thrive socially in the environment that meets their emotional needs.

> Vygotsky (1978) heavily emphasized the role that culture and play have on children's development, providing the foundation of skills in preparation for later learning and functioning. He saw play pretending "Let's pretend we're driving to the store" as representations in practice for literacy. In pretend play "I'll be the baby," children explore social roles. Through language, the child explains his mental context, "I'm the husband." Social play especially with an older child or adult stretches the child's play to a level beyond the present, providing a **scaffold** (Bodrova & Leong, 2006). This word is appropriate by thinking of a scaffold making the painter tall enough to reach when in reality she cannot reach the highest spot. It is the assistance that provides success. This **zone of proximal development (ZPD)** is the level where a child can function through a support system of more mature thinkers. Think of it as a child riding a two-wheeled bicycle yelling "I'm riding the bike!" as her dad runs alongside holding onto the seat. She feels what successful riding is like though she has not yet attained that level.

Implications of Social Learning Theory on Early Childhood Practices. In recent years, there has been an increased interest in identifying social factors such as the ability to have friends, maintain interactions, and cultivate **social competence**. Children who are able to control their physiological, emotional, and behavioral responses are socially competent, which enables them to function in a social atmosphere as well as in a learning environment. It is during the preschool years that this regulatory control system is formed. Five major clusters of social skill behaviors, with the acronym CARES, have been identified (Elliott, McKevitt, & DiPerna, 2002, p. 1042):

1. *cooperation*—behaviors such as helping others, sharing materials with a peer, and complying with rules
2. *assertion*—initiating behaviors such as asking others for information, and behaviors that are responses to others' actions, such as responding to peer pressure
3. *responsibility*—behaviors that demonstrate the ability to communicate with adults and show concern about one's property
4. *empathy*—behaviors that reflect concern for peers' or significant adults' feelings
5. *self-control*—behaviors that often emerge in conflict situations, such as responding appropriately to teasing or to corrective feedback from an adult

Stages of Social Development. The word *development* indicates that the change that takes place in the way the child interacts with other people is qualitative. It is a change that can be measured not in numbers but in refinement. It moves from simple to more complex, in a predictable sequence, but at different rates for individual people (Figure 4–6).

Stages of Play. Parten's Stages of Social Play have long been referred to when classifying the development of social play (Figure 4–7). Although we will speak of them as stages, they have been found not to

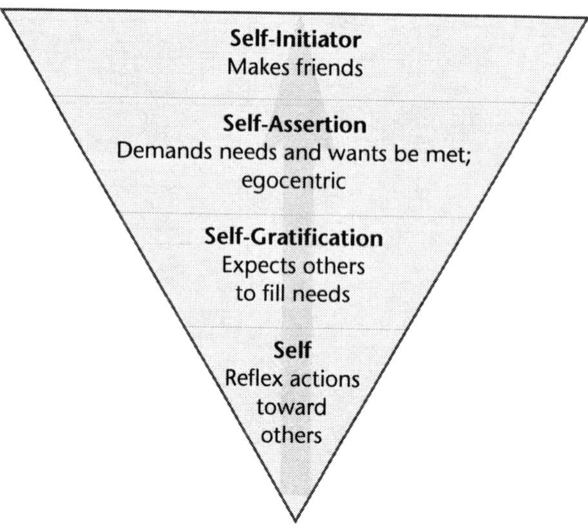

Figure 4–6 Stages of Social Development.

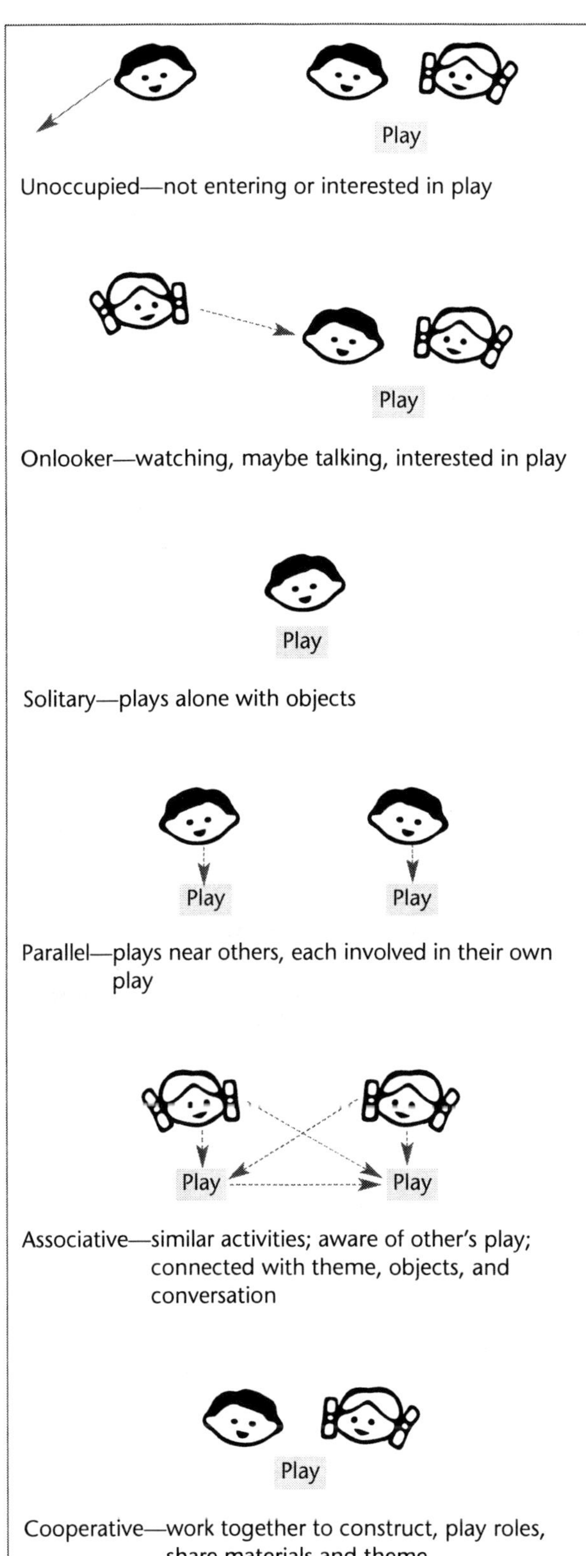

Figure 4–7 The Stages of Social Play.

be stages with an ascending level of involvement but rather more like forms of social play seen at all ages at varying times. Parten's stages have been modified (Hampton & Fantuzzo, 2003).

***Negative play or nonplay** (unoccupied play):* The child does not focus on any toy or activity: He follows the adult but does not engage in any sustained way.

Onlooker play: The child watches other children play but does not get involved. This is used frequently by children in new situations. They scope out the territory. It is also the style of children who are shy, emotionally depressed, or just not feeling like getting involved. The teacher attends to both behaviors, assesses possible causes, and decides if action is indicated. The adult may decide to issue an invitation to play. In this way, she can role-model how to join in the play. The decision may be to allow the child to have control over joining or not.

Solitary play: The child plays independently, totally focused on one's own play without looking or talking to other children. This type of play is often used for manipulation and practice, stress release, or by choice. It is the way of gaining familiarity with a new toy, game, or sports equipment. It is the repetitive motion that makes a skill become natural. Many find this relaxing and rewarding.

***Social attention play** (parallel play):* The child plays independently but is aware of other children. There is minimal social contact. It is not solitary play, but it is not involved either. It entails companionship but not cooperation, affiliation but not association.

***Associate play** (associative play):* The child talks to others, smiles, and exchanges toys but does not adjust behavior to match or complement the other child's.

***Collaborative play** (cooperative play):* The child engages in mutual, reciprocal roles, and adjusts behavior to the actions of the other child.

Types of Play. Besides the stages of play, another dynamic enters play. Children's play can be also observed and coded using Rubin's play matrix (Rubin, Maioni, & Hornung, 1976). It is the how of play. Four categories of play are seen in the social stages of play (Figure 4–8).

Functional play: Actions are repeated for practice and exploration. A child paints all over the paper, his hands, and the legs of the easel. Clay is squeezed, patted, rolled, poked, and cut. Blocks are piled and knocked down, containers filled with them, then dumped. No end product is in mind; it is manipulation of materials. People do this all the time in sporting goods stores as they take practice swings with golf clubs or baseball bats.

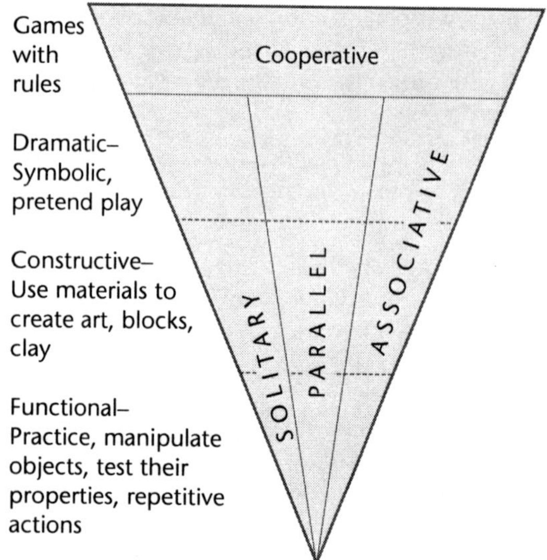

Figure 4–8 Types of Play.

Constructive play: This play produces a product. The manipulation of the paintbrush turns into a recognizable flower. Clay balls are piled on one another and named a "snowman." Blocks are piled, and the builder calls it "The Umpire (sic) State Building."

Dramatic play: This play takes the player into the world of pretend. The paintbrush becomes a bee buzzing toward the flower, gathering nectar. The snowman is moved along the table, talking to other clay creations and wondering what will happen when the sun comes out. The builder takes a monkey from the jungle set and has King Kong climbing up the building. Participation, with or without props, in the world of fantasy is classified as this type of play. It is in dramatic play in that children exercise power, power over a world that they now can control, over objects and over others (including dolls and action figures).

Games with rules become part of the play repertoire as children move toward the fifth and sixth years. This coincides with mathematical reasoning and the social-emotional stage of industry, of putting things in order. By this age, children are bringing themselves into control, passing the egocentric stage, so now they can see from another's point of view. This stage also appears at a time when children's language skills are more developed, and they are able to play in a more cooperative way.

EXERCISE **Observers of social development should be able to recognize and label social play using Parten's stages (forms) of play (unoccupied, onlooker, solitary, parallel, associative, cooperative) and Smilansky's and Piaget's play categories (functional, constructive, dramatic, games with rules).**

Using Parten and Hampton's, Smilansky's, and Piaget's terms, classify the following players.

1. Jake and Donald are sitting across from each other, building with separate Lego sets. Jake and Donald are in the ______________ stage, demonstrating the ______________ type of play.
2. Heather, Greg, and Lisa are putting on a puppet play in a cardboard stage. Louise has been watching for several minutes. Louise is in the ______________ stage, while Heather, Greg, and Lisa are in the ______________ stage, demonstrating ______________ type of play.
3. Piku is at the art table making balls of clay and poking them with a pencil. He is in the ______________ stage of play, demonstrating ______________ type of play.

it happened to me

"Bad Dolly"

As I observed children in dramatic play episodes, I frequently saw the child who I knew had never been spanked viciously spanking the dolls for "bad" deeds. While we had a "no guns" rule, children were very creative in forming Legos, Tinkertoys, and even artistically chewed pieces of bread into guns. We later gave up on that rule after reading *The War Play Dilemma* (Carlsson-Paige & Levin, 1987). But what was the motivating factor for violent dramatic play? Power!

Do you have an IT HAPPENED TO ME story about a child exercising power? I'd love to read it. Send it to Weekbyweek@ymail.com.

4. Barry is laying parallel rows of blocks and Birdie is riding a truck back and forth between them. Barry and Birdie are in the ____________ stage of play, Barry demonstrating ____________ type of play. Birdie is demonstrating ____________. She says, "I'm delivering bread to the store." Now her play is ____________.

In checking your understanding of the play stages and types, you should have recognized the following: (1) parallel, constructive; (2) onlooker, cooperative, dramatic; (3) solitary, functional; (4) associative, constructive, functional, dramatic.

The Need for a Selfless Society

Moving from selfish to selfless takes more than changing a few alphabet letters. It is a total transformation from self-centered, immediate gratification to other-centered, altruistic generosity. The goal of maturity in a moral society is to become less concerned with one's own needs and desires by giving priority to others'. A person, group, or society that only lives for itself is constantly in conflict (Figure 4–9). Often, more than one person wants a particular object or for their own opinion to prevail, and everyone cannot be satisfied. From that conflict came the rules of the tribe, then laws. Now laws are so numerous and complex that entire buildings are needed to hold the books that list and interpret them all. People devote their lives to interpreting, enforcing, changing, and even breaking them. There are also some people in a society who cannot fill their own needs, so others are needed to generously help if they are to survive. The task of raising the young to be selfless is necessary for the survival of the society. What a responsibility! This is a long struggle that begins with small steps.

Figure 4–9 Attaining social development is not without its struggles.

Think About It . . .

Think about how the following laws or rules restrict your freedom for the good of society.

- Only licensed physicians can practice medicine.
- Drive on the right side of the road.
- Items in a store must be exchanged for payment.
- Use utensils, not hands, for serving items from the salad bar.
- Buckle up your seat belt in the car.

In caring for, teaching, or working with young children, the development of the social domain is a high priority. It does not develop separately from physical, cognitive, or emotional areas but simultaneously moves forward, influenced by many of the same factors of genetics, environment, culture, and society. Helping a child to learn the rules of the tribe will help him function in that group. It is a necessary skill for both physical and psychological well-being.

The infant is only concerned with fulfillment of needs, totally dependent on reflexes and signals calling for responses to those signals. The hungry baby never considers the mother's dinner getting cold. The baby crying in the middle of the night pays no heed to parents' early work schedules. The crawler pulls the cat's tail, or the toddler takes a truck from another. The needs and wants of the other person are not deliberated or weighed or even considered at all. Years and much growing and developing must take place before the child sees the point of view of the other person. It takes even longer before she can place the other person's needs ahead of her own with generosity and empathy. She has much growing up to do before living up to society's expectations and taking on the responsibility for others. Along that path there are observable stages—developmental milestones—which are aided in their arrival by interactions with adults.

EXERCISE List some social rules, not developed naturally, that children must be taught.

Self. The newborn infant (neonate) is governed by reflexes:

Rooting reflex—When stroked on the cheek, the neonate turns toward that side. (It is not to see his mother better.)

Babkin reflex—When the palms are stimulated, the neonate's fingers curl around it and grasp it. (It is not to play with daddy's finger.)

Walking and stepping reflex—When held so that feet or toes touch the floor, the neonate makes a walking, stepping motion. (It is not to dance with her sister.)

Moro reflex—When a loud noise, bright light, or loss of support is experienced, the neonate startles and flings out his arms. (It is not reaching out to be held because he was scared.)

But what is the neonate doing socially? The infant can see very well close up, looking at close faces and registering information about what is seen and heard. The baby's kinesthetic sense (body movement and position) is present so the baby senses she is held, rocked, or touched. Babies are usually soothed by motion, crying less when rocked. The baby imitates and matches facial expressions. As early as one month, infants are aware of what is going on around them, and by four months, they try to change their parent's facial expressions to be happier. Some babies right from the start are more gregarious, responsive to others, and open to friendly overtures (Figure 4–10). Others are much more serious and reserved, limiting social contacts to just a few people. This personality type affects social interactions, and it may be evident throughout the child's life. All areas of development—physical, cognitive, and emotional—are being affected by and are affecting social development.

The implications for social development seem clear. The adult role is to meet the baby's needs, first of all in physical care but also in the social and emotional realm. The infant who has attention and is prompted to respond to coos and words is being prepared for verbal conversations. The environment stimulates cognitive development. Psychological needs are met by being close and by handling the baby gently and responsively. Interactions are initiated and provide an interesting environment that responds to what the baby indicates she likes. These met needs give the infant a secure base from which to emerge into the social realm with the abilities to function in it.

Figure 4–10 Social development begins with the infant's needs being met.

Self-Gratification. During the first year, the infant is focused on receiving what he needs to survive and be happy, whatever that takes. This is the stage of his attachment to his parents, as well as the beginning of his independence from them. During the first months of life, the baby increases imitative behavior with smiles and laughs as the adult feeds, dresses, and cares for him. In the second half of the first year, the baby shows separation anxiety, trying to recapture the presence of the ones who meet his needs. He also begins some social exchanges by reaching out his hands and arms to be held, kicking or making noises to gain attention. He is becoming mobile, so he now can crawl to his mother and pull on her leg. He is beginning to learn that he is no longer allowed to cry, sleep, play, eat, or act strictly by his own desires. He may be put down for a nap when he is not "ready" or be told "No" when he reaches for his grandpa's glasses. He cries and uses whatever social skills he has learned to get what he wants. He also is beginning to exert social control by turning away from the spoon, withdrawing a plaything, or by withdrawing from a smiling auntie, pulling back his social self.

The play that infants engage in during the first year is mainly manipulation. They experience the object in every way possible: touching, squeezing, biting, smelling, shaking to listen, and throwing to see the reaction. A favorite game is peekaboo, which builds the cognitive structure of what goes away is not gone forever but returns. This game prepares the infant for separation. Another favorite game is to throw the toy away and have someone return it. It is a social give-and-take, action and response. It also reinforces not only object permanence but also that power over other people to get them to do what he wants them to do. It is the precursor for taking turns, sharing, and playing baseball.

This process over the first two years is moving from being solely focused on the self to the consideration of others. It is dependent on the infant's capabilities and the supportive adult behaviors. Figure 4–11 graphically portrays the stages involved, the roles of child and adult, as well as the desired outcomes (Kostelnik et al., 2009).

Self-Assertion. In the second year, the child generalizes all other social relationships. She expects that everyone, especially other children, will treat her in the same way as her parents: accepting, acquiescent, providing what she needs and wants. When this does not happen, she cannot understand it.

Language is developing at this time also, so vocabulary and verbal expression come into the social realm. Words and phrases such as "No!" "Mine!" and "Gimme" are repeatedly used in social gatherings. "Please" is expected to yield miraculous results, with objects or toys being the lure of toddler friendships.

Self-Initiator. Three-, four-, and five-year-olds are blossoming social beings. At this age, they have the verbal, physical, and cognitive skills to begin to interact more with each other. They engage in **associative play**—doing a similar type of activity, involving the same play theme or with similar types of toys—but in this stage they still are "doing their own thing." They are not working together toward a common goal; they just happen to be near each other, talking about what each of them is doing.

Some children begin collaborative or cooperative play as four-year-olds, producing a common product such as a block building, a road in the sand connecting areas, or dinner in the dramatic area. All players are working out a common plan. They are still in the Preoperational Stage, still egocentric, but they are beginning to engage in this kind of play. The teacher prepares an environment that will enhance social development by providing enough materials so that solitary and parallel play are not thwarted by having to "steal" from others. Cooperation and sharing are planned into the routines and curriculum by such things as helper charts, joint projects, songs, stories, and puppet plays. Competition during this period is not understood, so it is not an appropriate method of group interaction. Games with winners and losers—who can be the best, the fastest, or the neatest—reinforce selfish attitudes. Cooperation and concern for others are the major social tasks of this age. Children who have had experiences in rule-making for the classroom and in their enforcement in an acceptable way get along better. They know and understand the reasons why rules exist. They are careful observers of others who are breaking the rules. This is the beginning of moral development, recognizing right from wrong.

Difficulties between children are best handled not by the teacher as the judge. The teacher's role is as a facilitator for negotiation, helping those involved to tell each other their point of view. The children decide in a democratic manner. This kind of facilitation assists children in cognitive development (problem solving) and moral development (beginning to see someone else's point of view). Because bullying, victimizing another child by exclusion, teasing, or even physical aggression are seen in three- and four-year-old children, the teacher's role is more active than that of a facilitator alone; the teacher must first of all be a protector, then an active encourager of friendship formation through curriculum and intervention (Dunn, 2004).

Excluded children, those who have difficulty being accepted by peers, have some common characteristics. Disliked children often ignore other children's overtures to play, misunderstand peers' emotions, and are aggressive (Kemple, 2004). A strategy to help excluded or disliked children is to pair them with a younger child with whom they can feel more socially confident. Likewise, they may be paired with those who are socially competent as a model. Alternatives to aggressiveness through role

PHASE	AGE OF ONSET IN MONTHS	INFANT CAPABILITIES	SOCIAL OUTCOME	ROLE IN INDIVIDUATION PROCESS	ADULT BEHAVIORS THAT SUPPORT INDIVIDUATION
I	0–1	Sucking; visual tracking; grasping; cuddling; vocalizes; social attunement	Reflexes; shared gazing; orienting toward caregiver	Proximity to caregiver	Observation of states; prompt basic care
II	1–2	More time quietly alert; sensory learning about people and objects; molding to caregiver's body; continues interesting activities; coos and goos	Beginning social responsiveness; mutual cueing	Begins differentiation between self and objects; more ways of maintaining proximity	Provide objects; engage in turn-taking play; give prompt basic care; respond sensitively to different states
III	4–8	Sits, grasps; creeps; increased interest in objects; sensory learning: mouthing, manipulating, examining, banging; laughs, yells, and squeals; babbling	Recognizes familiar people; shows clear preferences among people; intentionality limited to previously learned actions; playful; social smile, laughter	Beginnings of social expectations; stranger fear; maintains proximity by following, checking back on caregiver after short excursions	Provide a safe environment for floor exploration; establish limits for child; respond predictably
IV	9–14	Walking, climbing, running; joyful exploration; curious; excited; beginning use of language and gesture; person and object permanence becoming clearer; trial-and-error problem solving; intentions conveyed by language, gesture, and action; makes requests; comprehends words; complex babbling	Strong desire for approval, inclined to comply; self-willed; increased self-control; variety of emotions; social play with adults; interest in events	Maintains proximity by following and calling caregiver; strong preferences for particular people; protests separation; uses caregiver as a "base of operations" and moves outward; recognizes that others act; beginning to cooperate	Protect from hazards (child has mobility without judgment); respond promptly to communicative acts; set and maintain routines and limits; provide opportunity for independence; use language to comfort; explain leaving child with familiar adults; have patience
V	15–24	Increase of all motor tasks; skillful exploration; rapid increase in language and nonverbal communication skills; offers objects to preferred adults; self-recognition and person permanence; pointing, says words, then word combinations	Is likely to cling, then run away; plays "mother chase me!"; self-willed: "No" before compliance; considerable amount of self-control; self-comforting; may show sudden fear after departure from caregiver; may cry from relief at caregiver's return	Realizes caregiver's goals are not own goals; may be ambivalent about dependence/independence; can play happily in absence of preferred person; uses "gifts" of toys in seeking proximity, more language	Verbalize about departures, reassure; tolerate rapid changes in approach and withdrawal; use language to discuss events, relationships, objects, etc.; allow child to control some holding on, letting go; make social expectations clear over and over; have patience
VI	24–30	Good understanding of ordinary language; intentionality well developed; mental problem solving; ability to ask for help based on need; goal-directed behavior; self-definition of gender and age	Increasing interest in other children; peer play and communication stronger; mutually regulated social interactions; pretend play	Realistic sense of self and others; uses a wide array of techniques to maintain proximity (helping, conversation, play stories); can cope well with separations	Continue to reassure, support, and provide affection; praise efforts at self-control and independent behavior; provide experience with another toddler

Figure 4–11 The Individuation Process and Appropriate Adult Responses from Kostelnik, Phipps-Whiren, Soderman/Gregory. *Guiding Children's Social Development & Learning 6E.* © Wadsworth, a part of Cengage Learning, Inc. Reproduced by Permission. Hyperlink "http://www.cengage.com/permissions"

it happened to me

"The Overheard Parent Conference"

I was in a conference with the parent of probably the brightest child I ever had in my preschool class. We were talking about his development when he appeared at the door, obviously listening. We invited him in, and we discussed his progress in the various areas of development. In talking about social development, I remarked that I had not seen him playing with any other children. Indeed, he could make elaborate block structures, read books on his own, draw and paint recognizable objects, but he had no friends. He was just a shadow player. He asked, "Am I supposed to play with other children?" His mother explained that he could do all these other things at home, which he did, but at school he had other children to play with and that is why he was here. "Oh, OK." And from that day forward, he moved into play groups, talked with them, interacted, and became a welcome play partner. It was his intellectual ability that helped him be a friend. It taught me a lesson that it helps if children know adults' expectations of them (and to be sure that conferences are private, although this one was all positive and turned out successfully).

Do you have an IT HAPPENED TO ME story about a child learning to make friends? I'd love to read it. Send it to Weekbyweek@ymail.com.

plays, books, and puppet plays may give such children problem-solving ideas to be remembered when conflicts arise. Asking provocative questions when children are engaged in good guy/bad guy play is a strategy to divert possible antisocial activities: "How does Spiderman weave the web?"(Jones & Cooper, 2006).

Observing Social Development in Play

The observation of children interacting with each other—or "kidwatching," as Goodman (2002) calls it—can be extremely amusing. They reveal so much of themselves and all areas of development as they play. Information on physical, cognitive, language, emotional, and social development can be gathered as children interact with the environment and other people.

Anecdotal and Running Records. Social play observations are caught vividly with Anecdotal and Running Recordings that capture both the actions and the words. Such a narrative gives a lasting memory of an event that can be fraught with meaning to every reader. One of the foremost kidwatchers is Vivian Paley. Her books of Anecdotal Recordings, many about boys and girls in dramatic play, are not only entertaining but also full of meaning. In Boys and Girls: Superheroes in the Doll Corner (1984), she relates a discussion with the children about where the real work of school is happening in the classroom.

Paley is skillful in asking open-ended questions such as, "How can you tell if you're working or playing?" She accurately records children's conversations as well as her questions that explore their thinking. Reeny, an African American child in *The Girl with the Brown Crayon* (Paley, 1997), joins her classmates in a study of the books of Leo Lionni as well as leads them to learn about self-identity. These books are wonderful examples of Anecdotal Recording and thoughtful teaching.

Children with Challenging Behavior. One of the biggest challenges in group settings is disruptive behavior. An alarming Yale study found that preschoolers in state-funded programs were being expelled for behavior at more than three times the rate of children K–12, with a higher rate for African American boys (Gilliam, 2005). When young children are together, conflicts are inevitable and they often challenge teachers, families, and administrators. Through behavior, the child is communicating what may not be able to be put into words. Sometimes, children's behavior is a normal part of a developmental stage, but misunderstanding or lack of understanding on the part of adults misinterprets the behavior as defiance, "naughty," or obstinate. All behavior should be viewed within the context of biology, interactions, and environment. There is a tremendous cost when a child has extreme, challenging behavior. They suffer peer rejection, mostly punitive contacts with teachers, family interactions are unpleasant, and they even face potential school failure (Center for Evidence-Based Practice, 2003). Programs that focus on social skills such as getting along with others, following directions, identifying and regulating one's behavior, and engaging in social conversation and cooperative play have been shown to improve outcomes in school (Zins et al., 2004). Documentation of children's behavior through anecdotal and running records can show what happens right before and exactly describes the behavior and what happens after each outburst. This can give clues to the teacher and consultants for supportive suggestions to help meet the child's needs.

Checklists. Most developmental checklists have a section for social play, usually using the stages and types previously mentioned. One that has been developed to help teachers and parents monitor a child's social behavior is shown in Figure 4–12. It comes with the admonition from the authors, Katz and McClellan, that the intent is not to prescribe "correct social behavior" (1997). Rather, it is to uncover children who may be doing poorly on many items on the list. Those children may have personality and temperament differences that are completely normal for them. Children from diverse cultural and family backgrounds may not *usually* do many of these things. When this checklist shows children are having social difficulties, the teacher assesses the cause and plans for a classroom that is supportive and accepting.

The Penn Interactive Peer Play Scale (Hampton & Fantuzzi, 2003) lists social behaviors such as play disruption (physical and verbal aggression, grabbing, demanding, destroying, tattling, whining), play disconnection (ignored, withdraws, unable to enter or sustain play), and play interaction (helps, makes up play activities, problem solves, invites others to join).

I. Individual Attributes

The child:

1. Is **usually** in a positive mood
2. Is not **excessively** dependent on the teacher, assistant, or other adults
3. **Usually** comes to the program or setting willingly
4. **Usually** copes with rebuffs and reverses adequately
5. Shows the capacity to empathize
6. Has a positive relationship with one or two peers; shows capacity to really care about them, miss them if absent, etc.
7. Displays the capacity for humor
8. Does not seem to be acutely or chronically lonely

II. Social Skill Attributes

The child **usually**

1. Approaches others positively
2. Expresses wishes and preferences clearly; gives reasons for actions and positions
3. Asserts own rights and needs appropriately
4. Is not easily intimidated by bullies
5. Expresses frustrations and anger effectively and without harming others or property
6. Gains access to ongoing groups at play and work
7. Enters ongoing discussion on the subject; makes relevant contributions to ongoing activities
8. Takes turns fairly easily
9. Shows interest in others; exchanges information with and requests information from others appropriately
10. Negotiates and compromises with others appropriately
11. Does not draw inappropriate attention to self
12. Accepts and enjoys peers and adults of ethnic groups other than his or her own
13. Gains access to ongoing groups at play and work
14. Interacts nonverbally with other children with smiles, waves, nods, etc.

III. Peer Relationship Attributes

The child is

1. **Usually** accepted, versus neglected or rejected, by other children
2. **Sometimes** invited by other children to join them in play, friendship, and work.

Figure 4–12 Social Competence Checklist Adapted from L. B. Katz & D. E. McClellan, *Fostering Children's Social Competence: The Teacher's Role* (Washington, DC: NAEYC, 1997, p. 106. Reprinted with permission from the National Association for the Education of Young Children.

Observing Infants and Toddlers in Social Play

The infant is not developmentally able to sustain a higher level of play because of limited language and still-developing cognitive, social, and emotional skills. That does not keep the child from seeking out those social contacts. In the second year, walking widens the social world considerably. Now the child can walk over to other children and initiate interactions. Because of social immaturity, however, those overtures to play may be in the form of grabbing a toy, biting, or screaming. The responses may be less than friendly.

By the end of the second year, children have begun to make friends. They recognize other children with whom they have frequent contact. They imitate and initiate overtures of affection such as hugging, kissing, and giving objects to others. Occasionally, they make eye contact, engaging in little conversation. Mostly they are involved in their own play and play objects. Still possessing immature cognitive, social, and emotional structures, sharing and turn-taking are limited, if present at all. Some very young children have been observed in friendships. In *The Friendship Factor* (2002), Rubin discusses some factors that contributed to these early friendships:

- secure relationships with their mothers
- relationships with older siblings or children
- their mothers were friends
- the children were at similar developmental levels, had similar temperaments and behavioral Styles

Helping all Children with Social Development

Children with disabilities can function quite well in classrooms where the staff understands the capabilities as well as the disabilities and modifies the environment so that each child can succeed to the highest level possible.

Disabilities and the Social Environment

Free play in smaller spaces for close proximity play, with teachers providing low structure with minimal rules but a wide variety of toys, provides the best environment for social interactions for children with or without disabilities. While meeting the learning needs of children with disabilities, inclusive settings have been shown to contribute to emotional understanding and acceptance in typically developing children (Diamond, 2001). There seems to be little difference between the number or quality of friendships for children with disabilities and typically developing children in inclusive settings (Goldman & Buysse, 2007). This environment promotes imitation of peers by younger children and those with developmental delays. Some modifications to the environment are made specific to the child's need.

Social interactions depend heavily on communication. For the child with a hearing loss, this is a barrier. Early involvement with hearing children as social role models and alternative communication techniques are helpful in promoting social development. For the teacher, this also means learning some way to communicate with the child to facilitate social interactions with the child's peers and to interpret the classroom environment.

Vision impairment does not necessarily cause social problems, but more likely it is society's reaction to the impairment that has a negative effect. Curiously, the more severe the impairment, the less negative the reaction, possibly because of the sympathy effect. Children with thick corrective lenses may be rejected as a playmate by other children just from appearances. The teacher can inform children of the nature of the child's vision and how it may affect the child in the classroom, inviting other children's assistance and acceptance. The teacher as a role model provides an environment that is safe but allows all the freedom and challenge other children receive.

Children with physical limitations are now included in regular classrooms, advertisements, and television shows. Familiarity with prostheses, walkers, and wheelchairs is helping to bring about more social peer acceptance in group settings. Children have a desire to be helpful, yet the danger exists for them to do too much, reinforcing learned helplessness. It is important for every child to be included in every classroom activity to the fullest of her ability. This will go a long way in facilitating peer acceptance as well.

Children with Autism

More and more children have been diagnosed with **autism**, a pervasive developmental disorder that affects verbal and nonverbal communication and social interaction. Autism's onset and recognition of symptoms occur between 18 months and 4 years of age. It is a spectrum disorder that ranges from mild to severe and sometimes is displayed in repetitive motions such as hand flapping or word repititions, rocking, sniffing, resistance to change in routines, and unusual responses to sensory experiences. About 40% of children in autism are nonverbal, so sign language, computer tools, and picture boards are often helpful. Because the early childhood classroom is a highly stimulating place, with many social learners, as well as sensory experiences, children with autism have difficulty that may be seen as behavior problems, sometimes before diagnosis. The classroom staff need to be aware of the child's diagnosis and particular behavioral characteristics in order to help the child adjust to the group environment and to make modifications for the transition. A screening tool recommended for children aged 6–24 months by the American Academy of Pediatrics and widely used is the CSBS-DP (Weatherby & Prizant, 2003). It asks families to answer 24 multiple-choice items on emotion and eye gaze, communication, gestures, sounds, words, understanding, and object use. The results determine if a full evaluation is needed.

When there is a child with autism in the classroom, the adult's reactions and interactions will be models for the group. Dr. Stanley Greenspan, well known for his floortime techniques, has many sugestions of how to help children with autism to relate, communicate, and think (see Resources, Greenspan, 2006).

Culture and Social Interactions

Children from other cultures may have different social styles, depending on their cultural values and practices. The teacher familiarizes himself with the cultures of the children in the group and transfers that awareness to assist the child to feel comfortable socially in the classroom. If a child does not speak English, the teacher, even though he may not speak the child's language, can act as a body language translator and an advocate for the child with the other children. The family, through an interpreter, can supply the teacher with a list of common words and their meanings.

Some cultures hold a belief in collectivism, the view that the good of the group is more important than that of the individual (Bornstein & Cote, 2001; Tyler et al., 2005). This can impact the child's social relationships to others such as sharing, giving up toys to younger children, the right to privacy, and being unique and distinct from each other; these are concepts that are learned from family attitudes very early in life (Gonzales-Mena, 2008). Sensitivity to these attitudes may explain children's and family's reactions to emphasis placed on the importance of the individual.

The social climate of acceptance for all children will be extended to any child with differences. Having a friend is one of the most important motivators in learning and feeling successful and happy. The teacher must do all in his power to make that happen.

Helping Professionals for Social Development Concerns

If all the efforts of the staff and observations documented by Anecdotal and Running Records or social checklists indicate a child is having a problem in social development, some action must be taken. In a talk with the family, the teacher can discuss his concerns. This is a sensitive area since no family wants to hear that their child is rejected and friendless. Family dynamics and values are closely woven with social development, so the utmost care should be taken. The family probably already has clues that the child is having difficulty. The child may be reluctant to come to school, with crying and tantrums every morning. The child may be getting into fights, hurting and being hurt. Together, some of the possible causes are explored and some plans agreed on.

If the problem is prolonged or appears so severe that it is determined inadvisable to delay advising the family and seeking professional help, then helping professionals may be consulted. After the medical personnel have ruled out any possible physical cause, then the psychological causes could be examined. Some of those professionals might include one or more of the following:

social worker—counsels individuals and families, serves as advocate or consultant to agencies or schools

family therapist—psychologist specializing in working with families in the treatment of an individual or family group

play therapist—psychologist or psychiatrist using play for diagnosis, dialogue, and treatment of childhood social-emotional disorders

child psychologist—evaluates, diagnoses, and treats children for emotional, social, cognitive, and behavioral disorders

Other Methods

Other Methods to Record Social Development

Class List Log—who plays with whom
Notation of level of social play stage:
Anecdotal Recording
Checklists and Rating Scales

Frequency Counts—How many play encounters occur with another child during one day? How frequently does a child lead/follow another child during one day?
Interviews or discussions about friends
Time Samples—who the child is with during free choice time
Work Samples—child's friends depicted in artwork, collaborative work such as murals, joint buildings
Photographs, audio, or video recordings capturing child's interactions with others

Standards

Here are selected examples of standards related to social development:

National Council for the Social Studies (1994). Expectations of Excellence: Curriculum Standards for Social Studies. IV. Individual Development and Identity:

The teacher will

assist learners as they work independently and cooperatively within groups and institutions to accomplish goals.

The Association for Childhood Education International has developed *Global Guidelines for the Education and Care of Young Children in the 21st Century* (2006) in an effort to assess the status of early childhood education globally. The guidelines consider the following areas:

environment and physical space and settings for children
curriculum content and pedagogy
early childhood educators and caregivers
partnership with families and communities
acountability, supervision, and management of programs for children

In the "Early Childhood Educators and Caregivers" section is a standard directly related to social studies:

#48 Educators/Caregivers respect children, their culture, and family practice.

Key Terms

associative play
autism
constructive play
cooperative play
parallel play
Running Record
scaffold
social competence
dramatic play
egocentric
functional play
games with rules
object permanence
onlooker play
solitary play
unoccupied play
Zone of proximal development (ZPD)

Plans

Go to the Book Companion website (www.cengage.com/education/Nilsen) for the following:

Anecdotal/Running Record form
Plan Week 4, Part A, Directions for Running Records of Social Development for Group C, including What to Do with It, Portfolio Overview Example, Sharing with Child and Family, Actions—Read a Book, In the Environment, In the Curriculum, and In the Newsletter
Plan Week 4, Part B, Class List Log of Social Development for All, including What to Do with It and Sharing with Child and Family
Plan Week 4, Part C, Reflective Journal

Resources

Association for Childhood Education International. (2006). *Global guidelines for the education and care of young children in the 21st century.* http://www.acei.org.

Greenspan, S., & Wieder, S. (2006) Engaging autism: *Using the floortime approach to help children relate, communicate and think.* Cambridge, MA: DaCapo Lifelong Books.

Kostelnik, M. J., Whiren, A. P., Soderman, A. K., Stein, L. C., & Gregory, K. (2009). *Guiding children's social development and learning* (6th ed.). Clifton Park, NY: T Delmar Cengage Learning.

Levin, D. E. (2003). *Teaching young children in violent times: Building a peaceable classroom.* Cambridge, MA: Educators for Social Responsibility.

Miller, K. (2000). Caring for the little ones: Friendships in the baby room. *Child Care Information Exchange* (133, 62), May/June 2000.

NAEYC Early Childhood Program Standards and Accreditation Criteria (2005). Washington, DC: National Association for the Education of Young Children.

National Council for the Social Studies (1994). *Expectations of excellence: Curriculum standards for social studies.* Waldorf, MD: Author. www.socialstudies.org

Palmer, D., & Neugebauer, B. (2006). *Connecting: Friendships in the lives of young children and their teachers.* Redmond, WA: Exchange Press.

Sluss, D. J. (2005). *Supporting play: Birth through age eight.* Clifton Park, NY: Thomson Delmar Learning.

Stephens, K. (2006). *Social skills children need to make and keep friends.* Redmond, WA: Exchange Press.

Willis, C. (2009, January). Young children with autism spectrum disorder: Strategies that work. *Young Children,* 64 (1): 81–89.